FUNDAMENTALS OF INVESTING

The Addison-Wesley Series in Finance

FUNDAMENTALS *of* INVESTING

Tenth Edition

LAWRENCE J. GITMAN, CFP®

San Diego State University

MICHAEL D. JOEHNK, CFA

Arizona State University

PEARSON
Addison
Wesley

Boston San Francisco New York
London Toronto Sydney Tokyo Singapore Madrid
Mexico City Munich Paris Cape Town Hong Kong Montreal

Dedicated to
Robin F. Gitman
and to the twins,
Grace Hesketh Joehnk and
Rhett Weaver Joehnk

Publisher: Greg Tobin
Editor in Chief: Denise Clinton
Senior Acquisitions Editor: Donna Battista
Director of Development: Kay Ueno
Development Editor: Ann Torbert
Assistant Editor: Allison Stendardi
Managing Editor: Nancy Fenton
Supplements Editor: Heather McNally
Media Producers: Bethany Tidd and Bridget Page
Senior Marketing Manager: Roxanne Hoch
Rights and Permissions Advisor: Shannon Barbe
Senior Manufacturing Buyer: Carol Melville
Cover Design: MADA Design
Production Coordination, Text Design, Art Studio, and Composition: Thompson Steele Inc.

ISBN: 978-0-321-46851-2
ISBN: 0-321-46851-1

If you purchased this book within the United States or Canada you should be aware that it has been wrongfully imported without the approval of the Publisher or the Author.

2 3 4 5 6 7 8 9 10—QWT—10 09 08 07

Brief Contents

Contents

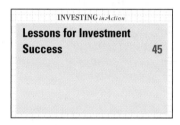

The images:

INVESTING in Action
Lessons for Investment Success   45

ETHICS in INVESTING
The Price for Behaving Badly   50

INVESTING in Action
Stock Around the Clock   81

Chapter 11

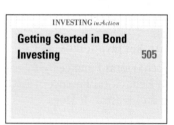

INVESTING *in Action*

**Getting Started in Bond
Investing**   **505**

Bond Valuation 475

ETHICS *in* INVESTING
When Mutual Funds Behaved Badly 523

INVESTING *in Action*
Adding ETFs to Your Investment Portfolio 528

INVESTING *in Action*
Keep Your Balance 573

ETHICS *in* INVESTING
The Virtues of Ethical Investing: The Remarkable Life of John Templeton 589

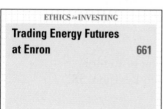

Preface

"**Great firms aren't great investments unless the price is right.**" Those words of wisdom come from none other than Warren Buffett, who is, without question, one of the greatest investors ever. The words of Mr. Buffett sum up very nicely the essence of this book—namely, to help students learn to make *informed investment decisions*, not only when buying stocks, but also when investing in bonds, mutual funds, or any other type of investment vehicle.

The fact is, investing may sound simple, but it's not. Many decisions and challenges are involved in the process of investing in today's changing financial marketplace. For example, students want to know, what are the best investments for me? Should I buy individual securities or mutual funds? What's the market outlook in the next few years? What about risk? Do I need professional help with my investments, and can I afford it? Clearly, investors need answers to questions like these in order to make informed investment decisions.

The language, concepts, vehicles, and strategies of investing are foreign to many. In order to become informed investors, students must first become conversant with the many aspects of investing. Building on that foundation, they can learn how to make informed decisions in the highly dynamic investment environment. This tenth edition of *Fundamentals of Investing* provides the information and guidance needed by individual investors to make such informed decisions and to achieve their investment goals.

This book meets the needs of professors and students in the first investments course offered at colleges and universities, junior and community colleges, professional certification programs, and continuing education courses. Focusing on both individual securities and portfolios, *Fundamentals of Investing* explains how to develop, implement, and monitor investment goals after considering the risk and return of both markets and investment vehicles. A conversational tone and liberal use of examples guide students through the material and demonstrate important points.

Hallmarks of *Fundamentals of Investing*

Using information gathered from both academicians and practicing investment professionals, plus feedback from adopters, the tenth edition reflects the realities of today's investment environment. At the same time, the following characteristics provide a structured framework for successful teaching and learning.

▮ Clear Focus on the Individual Investor

Today, about half of all U.S. households own stock either directly or indirectly through mutual funds or participation in 401(k)s, and with new rules that encourage participation of young workers in 401(k)s, that percentage should grow in the coming years. The focus of *Fundamentals of Investing* has always been on the individual investor. This focus gives students the information they need to develop, implement, and monitor a successful investment program. It also provides students with a solid foundation of basic concepts, tools, and techniques. Subsequent courses can build on that foundation by presenting the advanced concepts, tool, and techniques used by institutional investors and money managers.

▮ Comprehensive Yet Flexible Organization

The text provides a firm foundation for learning by first describing the overall investment environment, including the various investment markets, information, and transactions. Next, it presents conceptual tools needed by investors—the concepts of return and risk and the basic approaches to portfolio management. It then examines the most popular investment vehicles—common stocks, bonds, and mutual funds. Following this series of chapters on investment vehicles is a chapter on how to construct and administer one's own portfolio. The final section of the book focuses on derivative securities—options and futures—which require more expertise. Although the first two parts of the textbook are best covered at the start of the course, instructors can cover particular investment vehicles in just about any sequence. The comprehensive yet flexible nature of the book enables instructors to customize it to their own course structure and teaching objectives.

We have organized each chapter according to a decision-making perspective, and we have been careful always to point out the pros and cons of the various vehicles and strategies we present. With this information, individual investors can select the investment actions that are most consistent with their objectives. In addition, we have presented the various investment vehicles and strategies in such a way that students learn the decision-making implications and consequences of each investment action they contemplate.

▮ Timely Topics

Various issues and developments constantly reshape financial markets and investment vehicles. Virtually all topics in this book take into account changes in the investment environment. For example, various corporate and accounting misdeeds and scandals are covered in the tenth edition via the eight *Ethics in Investing* boxes scattered throughout the text. The growing role of exchange-traded funds, the post-9/11 investment environment, online investing, and a host of other timely topics also embellish this new edition.

▮ Globalization

One issue that is reshaping the world of investing is the growing globalization of securities markets. As a result, *Fundamentals of Investing* continues to stress the global aspects of investing. We initially look at the growing importance of international markets, investing in foreign securities (directly or indirectly), international investment performance, and the risks of international investing. In later chapters, we describe popular international investment opportunities and strategies as part of the coverage of each specific type of investment vehicle. This integration of international topics helps students understand the importance of maintaining a global focus when planning, building, and managing an investment portfolio. Global topics are highlighted by a globe icon in the margin.

■ Comprehensive, Integrated Learning System

Another feature of the tenth edition is its comprehensive and integrated learning system, which makes clear to students what they need to learn in the chapter and helps them focus their study efforts as they progress through the chapter. For more detailed discussion of the learning system, see the feature walkthrough later in the preface (beginning on page xxiii).

■ Online Trading and Investment Simulator—OTIS

A component of our teaching and learning system is OTIS, a powerful trading and investment simulator, developed at the Alfred P. West, Jr., Learning Lab at the Wharton School of the University of Pennsylvania. This Web-based simulator makes the student a virtual fund manager. The simulator enables students to make trades, view holdings, assess performance, and evaluate performance against that of classmates. Through activities in OTIS, students can experience the mechanics, risks, and requirements of margin trading; appreciate the benefits of short selling; grasp the concept of liquidity as it applies to meeting short- and long-term needs; and learn how to construct and manage portfolios. OTIS will quickly propel students into a hands-on, interactive learning environment.

New for the Tenth Edition

Our many adopters are interested in how we have changed the content from the ninth to the tenth edition. We hope that that this same information will also interest potential adopters, because it indicates our mandate to stay current in the field of investments and to continue to craft a book that will truly meet the needs of students and professors.

The table on pages 20–22 outlines in detail the chapter-by-chapter revisions we have made to the tenth edition and the benefits that we think accrue as a result of these changes. Some of the major changes made in the tenth edition are the following:

- Updated all real-world data through 2005 or early 2006, including text, tables, and figures.

- Increased the number of *HotLinks*, and checked and updated all *HotLinks* URLs.

- Adapted select end-of-chapter exercises in MyFinanceLab for added practice.

- Shortened all *Investing in Action* and *Ethics in Investing* boxes, for a crisper presentation that is more inviting to students.

- Increased the number of *Ethics in Investing* boxes.

- Updated the discussion of the post-9/11 investment environment, both in the stock and bond markets, and the long recovery from the 2000–2002 bear market.

- Updated the boxed discussions of corporate ethics scandals and efforts to prevent them in the future.

- Restructured the discussion of secondary markets, dividing them into broker markets, and placing greater emphasis on how the Nasdaq market differs from both broker markets and the OTC market (Chapter 2).

- Moved the time value of money material to a chapter-end appendix to Chapter 4.

- Tightened up the material on convertible securities and moved that material into Chapter 10 ("Fixed-Income Securities"), and moved the material on preferred stocks to new online Chapter 16, "Investing in Preferred Stocks."

- Increased the coverage of mutual funds, with more coverage devoted to exchange-traded funds, REITs, and hedge funds (Chapter 12).

- Moved the discussion of constructing a portfolio using asset allocation from Chapter 5 to Chapter 13.

- Added a list of key terms at the end of each chapter, to help students focus on vocabulary to master.

REVISIONS	BENEFITS

PART ONE: Preparing to Invest

Chapter 1 The Investment Environment	Added new chapter opener about access to investment information. Streamlined the section on steps in investing. Updated tax rates. Revised section on conditions of the economy. Added new *Ethics in Investing* box on "The Price for Behaving Badly"—Sarbanes-Oxley. Added new *Investor Fact* boxes on mutual funds, and on recent increases in dividend payouts. Moved box on investment IQ to book's Web site.	Sets the scene for the course, with up-to-date information and greater clarity.
Chapter 2 Markets and Transactions	Added new chapter-opener about the New York Stock Exchange. Updated IPO data. Revised coverage of secondary markets; added a new figure on the makeup of the secondary markets. Expanded coverage of broker and dealer markets. Updated coverage of mergers and cooperative arrangements among foreign stock exchanges. Revised and updated discussion of ADRs. Added new *Investor Fact* box on a Paris bar modeled after the London stock exchange. Added new *Investing in Action* box at the Web site on the powerful role of market specialists.	Focuses on the structure, operation, and regulation of the securities markets.
Chapter 3 Investment Information and Securities Transactions	Revised chapter opener. Added new information on some of the best free information sites and other popular investment sites. Updated data in discussions of market averages and indexes. Updated *Ethics in Investing* box about Martha Stewart and ImClone trading. Deleted table on features of discount brokers. Added new *Investing in Action* box on performance returns of day traders. Updated/added *Investor Facts* boxes on election returns; online brokerage trading, and the incorrect return claimed by the Beardstown Ladies.	Provides a clear and up-to-date description of the primary traditional and online sources of investment information. Outlines services available to individual investors.

PART TWO: Important Conceptual Tools

Chapter 4 Return and Risk	Added new chapter opener on Apple Computer. Moved section on time value of money into a chapter-end appendix, and revised learning goals to reflect this content change. Revised and moved to Web site *Investing in Action* box on investing when the market is bad. Separated homework materials for time value of money appendix from the regular chapter-end homework.	Revised chapter better highlights the core concepts of return and risk. Separate appendix on time value of money allows those who do not want to cover this topic to isolate it.
Chapter 5 Modern Portfolio Concepts	Updated chapter opener about use of formula screens to pick stocks. Clarified coverage of correlation coefficient and its ranges. Added discussion of herding. Moved section on constructing a portfolio using an asset allocation scheme to Chapter 13, and revised learning goals to reflect this content change. Streamlined *Investing in Action* box on student-managed portfolios. Added new *Investor Facts* box on costs of mutual funds that invest globally.	Increases reader understanding of the key concepts underlying modern portfolio theory.

PART THREE: Investing in Common Stocks

Chapter 6 Common Stocks	Updated chapter opener, now about Microsoft. Streamlined the discussion of stock market quotes to concentrate on the NYSE and Nasdaq. Updated stocks cited as examples of the various types of common stock. Updated discussion of international investing, including comparative returns of U.S. stocks vs. those from other major markets. Clarified discussion of how ADRs are traded in the market. Added a new *Investing in Action* box on how to stay safe in a bear market. Added new *Investor Facts* boxes on price performance of stocks that pay dividends; dividends being back in fashion; and the Nikkei. Moved to the Web site some discussion on how foreign exchange rates can impact returns, and the *Investing in Action* boxes on the market meltdown in the late 1990s-2003 and effect of currencies in international investing.	Presents clear view of the current investment environment and of the impact that the market and issues like dividends can have on investor returns.

	REVISIONS	BENEFITS
Chapter 7 Analyzing Common Stocks	Added *Investing in Action* box on EBITDA. Added *Investor Facts* box on indicators that show a company may be in poor financial health. Tightened up the chapter to provide more clarity and focus on the overall concept of financial statement analysis. Moved *Investing in Action* box on financial statement analysis to Web site. Put several elements on *MyFinanceLab*, including one that links to an interactive Web site covering industry leaders and laggards, and another where users can obtain a brief description of any accounting entry in financial statements.	Maintains a clear and well-defined focus on the role that the economy, the industry, and the company play in security analysis and stock valuation.
Chapter 8 Stock Valuation	Updated chapter opener to focus on valuation of NIKE's stock. Added discussion on preparation and use of common-size income statements. Expanded discussion of assumptions underlying the dividend valuation model. Added considerable discussion linking the DVM to other stock valuation procedures, showing that in many cases these models are simply variations of one another. Added *Investing in Action* box on predictive power of the price-to-sales ratio. Added *Investor Facts* boxes on using earnings yield to spot an under- or overvalued market; information content in stock rating upgrades or downgrades; and free cash flow.	Provides a concise discussion of fundamental analysis and valuation, from the generation of the variables used in the valuation process to the various stock valuation models.
Chapter 9 Technical Analysis, Market Efficiency, and Behavioral Finance	Changed the chapter title. Expanded the discussion of the confidence index, to show its calculation and use. Tightened discussion of some technical measures, to cut out redundancy. Added *Investor Facts* boxes on returns of buy-and-hold investors, and on evidence that women tend to make fewer investment mistakes. Moved *Investing in Action* box on EMH to Web site.	Focuses on market behavior, the principles and procedures used to assess the market, and the major theories that describe how prices are set in the market and how investors select securities.

PART FOUR: Investing in Fixed-Income Securities

	REVISIONS	BENEFITS
Chapter 10 Fixed-Income Securities	New chapter opener on GE's bond offerings. Shifted chapter focus from how bonds are quoted to how they're priced in the marketplace. Restructured discussion of essential bond features to cover bond ratings as a key issue characteristic. Updated discussion of the effects of 2006 federal tax rates on the taxable equivalent yields of municipal bonds. To consolidate the coverage of alternative fixed-income investment vehicles, we added a section on the basic features and valuation of convertible bonds. Added *Investor Facts* boxes on junk bonds of some big-name companies; returns of long-term vs. intermediate-term bonds; and "busted convertibles." Moved the material on preferred stocks to online Chapter 16 at book's Web site.	Explains the practical side of the bond market and emphasizes the variables that drive bond price behavior and the wide array of securities available in the bond market.
Chapter 11 Bond Valuation	New chapter opener on FedEx's bonds. Updated data and discussion of Treasury yield curve. Added new section on basic bond valuation model, including discussion of variables that drive bond value. Clarified discussion of bond duration by linking impact of variables to the duration measure and price volatility. Added *Investor Facts* box on forecasting bond prices. Tightened up discussion of the role of duration in bond valuation and portfolio management.	Increases readers' understanding of the principles and properties of bond valuation, as well as the uses and limitations of the popular yield and price volatility measures.

REVISIONS	BENEFITS

PART FIVE: Portfolio Management

Chapter 12 Mutual Funds: Professionally Managed Portfolios

Revised chapter opener on Vanguard 500 Index fund. Updated all mutual fund performance data and market statistics through 2005 or early 2006. Streamlined material on open- and closed-end investment company quotes. Expanded discussion of exchange-traded funds to emphasize organizational structure and different kinds of ETFs. Expanded discussion of real estate investment trusts. Added *Investing in Action* box on the use of EFTs in a portfolio. Added *Investor Facts* boxes on mutual funds and taxes, and on comparing returns of index funds to those of actively managed funds. Moved material on unit investment trusts to book's Web site.

Maintains the strong focus on mutual funds as investment vehicles, the roles that these securities can play in an investment program, and the mutual fund selection process.

Chapter 13 Managing Your Own Portfolio

Updated chapter opener on Warren Buffett. Added section (formerly in Chapter 5) on constructing a portfolio using asset allocation; section includes *Investing in Action* box on keeping a portfolio in balance. Added *Ethics in Investing* box on the virtues of ethical investing, as demonstrated by John Templeton. Moved section on portfolio planning in action to book's Web site.

Gives readers insight into asset allocation and how to evaluate, monitor, and assess the performance of both individual investments and portfolios.

PART SIX: Derivative Securites

Chapter 14 Options: Puts and Calls

Moved the material on warrants to book's Web site. Added new options products and deleted inactive products, as appropriate. Updated the list of options exchanges and added new players, including ISE and NYSE Arca. Enhanced discussion of the various ways investors can use puts and calls as trading and hedging vehicles. Added *Investor Facts* box on settlement of options on indexes and ETFs. Moved *Investing in Action* box on using index options to protect a portfolio to book's Web site.

Clearly presents how options are valued and how the options market works. Increases understanding of the uses of various types of options as investment vehicles.

Chapter 15 Commodities and Financial Futures

New chapter opener on trading of ethanol futures on the CME. Streamlined discussion of ways that investors can use commodities and financial futures, with emphasis on speculating and hedging. Added new products and deleted inactive ones, along with update of all futures market data. Expanded discussion of the CME Globex market and its electronic trading platform. Added new *Investing in Action* box on direct exchange of foreign currencies. Added new *Investor Facts* box on single stock futures (SSFs). Added, at book's Web site, new *Investing in Action* box on pork bellies.

Focuses on the basic properties and uses of commodities and financial futures.

Web Chapters

Chapter 16 Investing in Preferred Stocks

New Web chapter. Includes full array of end-of-chapter homework material.

Describes the basic features of preferred stock. Addresses valuation and investment strategies for preferred stock.

Chapter 17 Tax-Advantaged Investments

Revised chapter opener focuses on Google. Chapter updated to include tax rates for 2006. Retains two *Investing in Action* boxes—on 401(k) plans and Roth IRAs. Includes end-of-chapter homework material.

Presents tax fundamentals and basic strategies for tax avoidance, tax deferral, and how to earn tax-favored income.

Chapter 18 Real Estate and Other Tangible Investments

Revised chapter opener focuses on equity REITs. Retains two *Investing in Action* boxes—on REITs and on investing in collectibles. Includes end-of-chapter homework material.

Describes and demonstrates valuation techniques for real estate. Discusses the appeal of REITs. Presents tangible investments such as precious metals.

The Gitman & Joehnk

PROVEN TEACHING/LEARNING/MOTIVATIONAL SYSTEM

Users of *Fundamentals of Investing* have praised the effectiveness of the Gitman/Joehnk teaching and learning system, which has been hailed as one of its hallmarks. In the tenth edition we have retained and polished the system, which is driven by a set of carefully developed learning goals. Users have also praised the rich motivational framework that underpins each chapter. Key elements of the pedagogical and motivational features are illustrated and described below.

THE LEARNING GOAL SYSTEM

The Learning Goal system begins each chapter with **six Learning Goals**, labeled with numbered icons. These goals anchor the most important concepts and techniques to be learned. The Learning Goal icons are then tied to key points in the chapter's structure, including

- First-level headings
- Summary
- Discussion Questions
- Problems
- Cases

This tightly knit structure provides a clear roadmap for students—they know what they need to learn, where they can find it, and whether they've mastered it by the end of the chapter.

An **opening story** sets the stage for the content that follows by focusing on an investment situation involving a real company or real event, which is in turn linked to the chapter topics. Students see the relevance of the vignette to the world of investments.

Chapter 4

Return and Risk

LEARNING GOALS

After studying this chapter, you should be able to:

LG 1 Review the concept of return, its components, the forces that affect the level of return, and historical returns.

LG 2 Discuss the role of time value of money in measuring return and defining a satisfactory investment.

LG 3 Describe real, risk-free, and required returns and the calculation and application of holding period return.

LG 4 Explain the concept and the calculation of yield, and how to find growth rates.

LG 5 Discuss the key sources of risk that might affect potential investment vehicles.

LG 6 Understand the risk of a single asset, risk assessment, and the steps that combine return and risk.

Apple Computer has sold over 42 million iPods. Since October 2004, the iPod has dominated digital music player sales in the United States, with over 90% of the market for hard-drive-based players and 70% of the market for all types of players. Several generations of iPods have fueled a dramatic rise in Apple's stock price. Shares soared 122% in 2005, far exceeding the 4.9% return for the broader Standard & Poor's 500 stock index. News that Apple's revenue jumped 65%, and that the company's net income during its fiscal quarter ended December 31, 2005, jumped 91% from the year earlier, was music to investors' ears.

This promising picture might increase your desire to buy the stock. But before you place that buy order, you should investigate the risks associated with the stock. Apple Computer itself disclosed in its most recent K-10 annual report a host of potential risks facing the company, ranging from current economic and political uncertainty to substantial inventory risks and dependency upon manufacturing and logistics services provided by third parties, many of whom are located outside the United States. Apple has higher research and development and higher selling, general, and administrative costs, as a percentage of revenue, than many of its competitors. Apple also faces risk in its transition from PowerPC microprocessors used by the Macintosh computers to those built by Intel. Any of these risks could have a material adverse effect on the company's operating results and financial position.

In this chapter we will discuss the concept of return and risk. You will learn how to calculate an investment's return and also become aware of the many types of risk faced by a public company. Many of the risks that Apple faces are the same types of risks faced by any other public company. The key factor in making an investment decision is to weigh those risks in relation to the potential return of the stock.

Sources: Matt Krantz, "Take a Bite of Apple?," *USA Today*, downloaded from www.usatoday.com/money/perfi/columnist/krants/2006-01-31-apple_x.htm (accessed July 2006); Apple Computer K-10 annual report, http://ccbn.tenkwizard.com (accessed July 2006).

ETHICS in INVESTING

The Price for Behaving Badly

In recent years, business headlines were full allegations of massive financial fraud committed by prominent business leaders. These allegations shocked the investment community and resulted in spectacular bankruptcies of some of the largest U.S. corporations. High-profile indictments and court convictions soon followed. Among the list of convicted felons were Jeff Skilling and Ken Lay of Enron, Bernard Ebbers of WorldCom, Dennis Kozlowski of Tyco International, Martha Stewart of Martha Stewart Omnimedia, and John Rigas of Adelphia Communications.

In many cases, the primary weapon of fraudulent CEOs was the use of corporate accounting to report huge, fictitious profits. When the fraud was discovered, a catastrophic crash of the stock price followed. This is what happened at Enron, WorldCom, and Global Crossing. In some cases, accounting firms and Wall Street

bankers aided in the schemes. Phony profits helped dishonest CEOs reap fantastic benefits in the form of huge performance bonuses and cash stock options. Many corporate crooks also used their companies as personal piggy banks, as was the case at Tyco International and Adelphia. These executives were able to defeat or completely dismantle internal and external supervision mechanisms and to manipulate their boards of directors to their advantage.

Fraudulent CEOs showed the ability to fool investors, securities analysts, and government regulators for years. In 2002, the U.S. Congress passed the Sarbanes-Oxley Act in the hope of preventing future corporate financial frauds.

CRITICAL THINKING QUESTION Why did accounting "irregularities" become such a widespread problem plaguing public companies in recent years?

Ethics boxes—short, boxed discussions of real-life scenarios in the investments world that focus on ethics—appear in eight selected chapters and on the book's Web site. Each ethics box contains a Critical Thinking Question for class discussion, with guideline answers given in the Instructor's Manual.

Each chapter features a short boxed essay, called *Investing in Action*, which describe real-life investing situations or events. These high-interest boxes, which have been written specifically for this textbook, demonstrate the book's concepts at work in the world of investing. Some of the new topics explored are performance returns of day traders, how to invest in a bear market, companies' use of EBITDA, the predictive power of the price-to-sales ratio, use of exchange-traded funds, and direct exchange of foreign currencies. These boxes contain Critical Thinking Questions for class discussion, with suggested answers given in the Instructor's Manual.

INVESTING in Action

Are You Ready To Quit Your Day Job? Perhaps Not Just Yet

Day trading refers to the practice of buying and selling stocks or other securities during the trading day; positions are not usually held overnight. Day traders spend most hours when the market is open glued to computers, tracking movements of stocks and trading them back and forth. Since commissions for online trading often amount to only a fraction of a penny per share, even a small price movement between bid and ask spread may be profitable.

How well do day traders perform? A recent study by the North American Securities Administrators Association suggests that only about 11.5% trade profitably. Those profits range from a few hundred to several thousand dollars a month. The best day traders make annual profits in the low $100,000s. According to managers of day-trading firms cited in a *Washington Post Magazine* article, about 90% of day traders "are washed up within three months." David Shellenberger of the

Massachusetts Securities Division noted, "Most traders will lose all of their money." Former SEC Chairman Arthur Levitt recommends that people day trade only with "money they can afford to lose."

The people who appear to be making the biggest return from day trading are those running day-trading firms. These firms provide day traders with computer terminals connected to exchanges and all necessary trading software in exchange for a commission per trade. With each customer making trades all day long, their coffers fill very quickly.

CRITICAL THINKING QUESTIONS What are the major risks associated with day trading of stocks? Why have so few people been able to make a living by day trading?

Source: Selena Maranjian, "The Perils of Day Trading," September 24, 2002, *The Motley Fool*, www.fool.com.

Each chapter contains a handful of **Investor Facts**—brief sidebar items that give an interesting statistic or cite an unusual investment experience. These facts add a bit of seasoning to the concepts under review and capture a real-world flavor. Among the many snapshots provided by the Investor Facts are recent increases in dividend payouts, costs of mutual funds that trade globally, indicators of poor financial health, and free cash flow.

INVESTOR FACTS

A VOTRE SANTÉ—In a creative application of the principles of broker market supply and demand, a bar in Paris has modeled its drink pricing on the London Stock Exchange. Drink prices start at a set amount each night and then rise and fall based on customer demand. A run on Heineken beer, for example, will send its price up, while other less-ordered drinks fall in price. Screens above the bar, which refresh every 4 minutes, show price changes. Periodically each evening, "market crashes" reset prices, and everything starts over again.

WITHIN THE CHAPTER

Key Equations are screened in blue throughout the text to help readers identify the most important mathematical relationships.

Equation 4A.4 ➤ $\quad x = \dfrac{\$1,000}{(1 + 0.08)} = \underline{\$925.93}$

Calculator Keystrokes   At appropriate spots in the text the student will find sections on the use of financial calculators, with marginal calculator graphics that show the inputs and functions to be used.

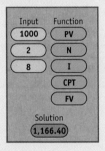

Input	Function
1000	PV
2	N
8	I
	CPT
	FV

Solution
1,166.40

For help in study and review, **Key Terms** and their definitions appear in the margin when they are first introduced.

discount rate
the annual rate of return that could be earned currently on a similar investment; used when finding present value; also called *opportunity cost*.

Hot Links refer students to Web sites related to topics under discussion in the text and help to reinforce the use of the Internet in the investments world.

HOTLINKS
If you want to review everything you need for portfolio planning, go to:
www.sec.gov/investor/pubs/ assetallocation.htm

Web Extension callouts refer students to content extensions and enhancements at the book's Companion Website. Extended content includes additional boxes, readings, and online chapters. In this edition, the Web Extensions are differentiated from HotLinks, which refer to independent sites not specifically linked to the textbook.

WEBEXTENSION
For discussion of that intriguing commodity *pork bellies*, see the *Investing in Action* box at our Web site:
www.myfinancelab.com

Concepts in Review questions appear at the end of each section of the chapter. These review questions allow students to test their understanding of each section before moving on to the next section of the chapter. Answers for these questions are available at the book's Web site, and by review of the preceding text.

CONCEPTS IN REVIEW
Answers available at: www.myfinancelab.com

4.1   Explain what is meant by the *return* on an investment. Differentiate between the two components of return—current income and capital gains (or losses).

4.2   What role do historical performance data play in estimating the expected return from a given investment? Discuss the key factors affecting investment returns—internal characteristics and external forces.

4.3   What is a *satisfactory investment?* When the present value of benefits exceeds the cost of an investment, what is true of the rate of return earned by the investor relative to the discount rate?

STILL MORE LEARNING TOOLS

Each **Summary** lists the chapter's key concepts and ideas, which correspond directly to the numbered Learning Goals at the begining of the chapter.

Learning Goal icons precede each summary item, which begins with a bold-faced restatement of the learning goal.

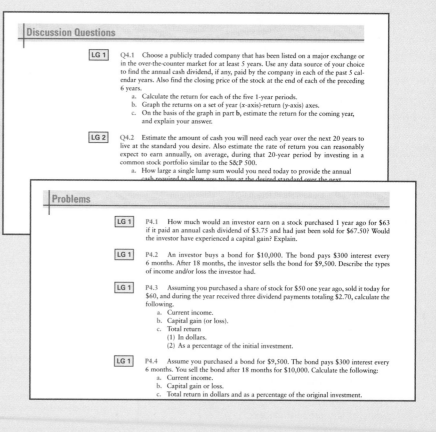

Summary

LG 1 **Review the concept of return, its components, the forces that affect the level of return, and historical returns.** Return is the reward for investing. The total return provided by an investment includes current income and capital gains (or losses). Return is commonly calculated on a historical basis and then used to project expected returns. The level of return depends on internal characteristics and external forces, which include the general level of price changes. Significant differences exist between the average annual rates of return realized over time on various types of security investments.

LG 2 **Discuss the role of time value of money in measuring return and defining a satisfactory investment.** Because investors have opportunities to earn interest on their funds, money has a time value. Time value concepts should be considered when making investment decisions. Financial tables, financial calculators, and electronic spreadsheets can be used to streamline time-value calculations. A satisfactory investment is one for which the present value of its benefits equals or exceeds the present value of its costs.

LG 3 **Describe real, risk-free, and required returns and the calculation and application of holding period return.** The required return is the rate of return an investor must earn to be fully compensated for an investment's risk. It represents the sum of the real rate of return and the expected inflation premium (which together represent the risk-free rate), plus the risk premium. The risk premium varies depending on issue and issuer characteristics. The holding period return (HPR) is the return earned over a specified period of time. It is frequently used to compare returns earned in periods of one year or less.

Discussion Questions, keyed to Learning Goals, guide students to integrate, investigate, and analyze the key concepts presented in the chapter. Many questions require that students apply the tools and techniques of the chapter to investment information they have obtained, and then make a recommendation with regard to a specific investment strategy or vehicle. These project-type questions are far broader than the Concepts in Review questions within the chapter. Answers to odd-numbered questions are available to students at the book's Web site.

Expanded Problem Sets—offer additional review and homework opportunities and are keyed to Learning Goals. Answers to odd-numbered Problems are available to students at the book's Web site, while all answers/solutions are available for instructors in the Instructor's Manual.

Discussion Questions

LG 1 Q4.1 Choose a publicly traded company that has been listed on a major exchange or in the over-the-counter market for at least 5 years. Use any data source of your choice to find the annual cash dividend, if any, paid by the company in each of the past 5 calendar years. Also find the closing price of the stock at the end of each of the preceding 6 years.
  a. Calculate the return for each of the five 1-year periods.
  b. Graph the returns on a set of year (*x*-axis)-return (*y*-axis) axes.
  c. On the basis of the graph in part **b**, estimate the return for the coming year, and explain your answer.

LG 2 Q4.2 Estimate the amount of cash you will need each year over the next 20 years to live at the standard you desire. Also estimate the rate of return you can reasonably expect to earn annually, on average, during that 20-year period by investing in a common stock portfolio similar to the S&P 500.
  a. How large a single lump sum would you need today to provide the annual cash required to allow you to live at the desired standard over the next

Problems

LG 1 P4.1 How much would an investor earn on a stock purchased 1 year ago for $63 if it paid an annual cash dividend of $3.75 and had just been sold for $67.50? Would the investor have experienced a capital gain? Explain.

LG 1 P4.2 An investor buys a bond for $10,000. The bond pays $300 interest every 6 months. After 18 months, the investor sells the bond for $9,500. Describe the types of income and/or loss the investor had.

LG 1 P4.3 Assuming you purchased a share of stock for $50 one year ago, sold it today for $60, and during the year received three dividend payments totaling $2.70, calculate the following:
  a. Current income.
  b. Capital gain (or loss).
  c. Total return
    (1) In dollars.
    (2) As a percentage of the initial investment.

LG 1 P4.4 Assume you purchased a bond for $9,500. The bond pays $300 interest every 6 months. You sell the bond after 18 months for $10,000. Calculate the following:
  a. Current income.
  b. Capital gain or loss.
  c. Total return in dollars and as a percentage of the original investment.

AT CHAPTER END

Case Problem 4.1   *Solomon's Decision*

LG 2   **LG 4**

Dave Solomon, a 23-year-old mathematics teacher at Xavier High School, recently received a tax refund of $1,100. Because Dave didn't need this money for his current living expenses, he decided to make a long-term investment. After surveying a number of alternative investments costing no more than $1,100, Dave isolated 2 that seemed most suitable to his needs.

Each of the investments cost $1,050 and was expected to provide income over a 10-year period. Investment A provided a relatively certain stream of income. Dave was a little less certain of the income provided by investment B. From his search for suitable alternatives, Dave found that the appropriate discount rate for a relatively certain investment was 12%. Because he felt a bit uncomfortable with an investment like B, he

Case Problem 4.2   *The Risk-Return Tradeoff: Molly O'Rourke's Stock Purchase Decision*

LG 3   **LG 6**

Over the past 10 years, Molly O'Rourke has slowly built a diversified portfolio of common stock. Currently her portfolio includes 20 different common stock issues and has a total market value of $82,500.

Molly is at present considering the addition of 50 shares of one of two common stock issues—X or Y. To assess the return and risk of each of these issues, she has gathered dividend income and share price data for both over each of the last 10 years (1999 through 2008). Molly's investigation of the outlook for these issues suggests that each will, on average, tend to behave in the future just as it has in the past. She therefore believes that the expected return can be estimated by finding the average holding period return (HPR) over the past 10 years for each of the stocks. The historical dividend income and stock price data collected by Molly are given in the accompanying table.

| | | Stock X | | | Stock Y | |
| | | Share Price | | | Share Price | |
Year	Dividend Income	Beginning	Ending	Dividend Income	Beginning	Ending
1999	$1.00	$20.00	$22.00	$1.50	$20.00	$20.00

Two **Case Problems**, keyed to the Learning Goals, encourage students to use higher-level critical thinking skills: to apply techniques presented in the chapter, to evaluate alternatives, and to recommend how an investor might solve a specific problem. Again, Learning Goals show the student the chapter topics on which the case problems focus.

Excel with Spreadsheets problems, appearing at the end of all chapters, challenge students to solve financial problems and make decisions through the creation of spreadsheets. In Chapter 1 students are directed to the Web site, **www.myfinancelab.com**, where they can complete a spreadsheet tutorial, if needed. In addition, selected tables within the text carrying a spreadsheet icon are available in spreadsheet form on the text Web site. Solutions to the end-of-chapter Excel with Spreadsheets exercises are also on the Instructor's Resource Disk.

Excel with Spreadsheets

While most people believe that it is not possible to consistently time the market, there are several plans that allow investors to time purchases and sales of securities. These are referred to as formula plans—mechanical methods of managing a portfolio that attempt to take advantage of cyclical price movements. The objective is to mitigate the level of risk facing the investor.

One such formula plan is dollar-cost averaging. Here, a fixed dollar amount is invested in a security at fixed intervals. One objective is to increase the value of the security of interest over time. If prices decline, more shares are purchased; when market prices increase, fewer shares are purchased per period. The essence is that an investor is more likely not to buy overvalued securities.

Over the past 12 months, March 2008 through February 2009, Mrs. Paddock has used the dollar-cost averaging formula to purchase $1,000 worth of Neo common stock each month. The monthly price per share paid over the 12-month period is given below. Assume that Mrs. Paddock paid no brokerage commissions on these transactions.

Create a spreadsheet model similar to the spreadsheet for Table 13.9, which you can view at www.myfinancelab.com, to analyze the following investment situation for Neo common stock through dollar-cost averaging.

2008	March	$14.30
	April	16.18
	May	18.37
	June	16.25
	July	14.33
	August	15.14
	September	15.93
	October	19.36
	November	23.25
	December	18.86
2009	January	22.08
	February	22.01

Questions

a. What is the total investment over the period from March 2008 through February 2009?

b. What is the total number of Neo shares purchased over the 12-month period?

c. What is the average cost per share?

d. What is the year-end (February 2009) portfolio value?

e. What is the profit or loss as of the end of February 2009?

f. What is the return on the portfolio after the 12-month period?

Trading Online with OTIS. The world of electronic investing comes alive with the addition of OTIS—the Online Trading and Investment Simulator, developed at the Alfred West, Jr. Learning Lab at the Wharton School of the University of Pennsylvania. OTIS enables students to become "fund managers" and to buy and sell equities using real data from today's markets. By doing the OTIS activities, students learn such key concepts as portfolio management, benchmarking, liquidity, and pricing in a hands-on environment.

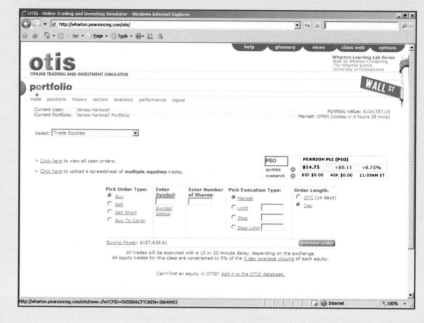

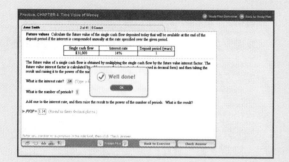

MyFinanceLab, a fully integrated homework and tutorial system, solves one of the biggest teaching problems in finance courses: students learn better when they practice by doing homework problems, but grading complex multipart problems is time-consuming. Students can work the end-of-chapter problems with algorithmically-generated values in MyFinanceLab for unlimited practice. Instructors can also create assignments in MyFinanceLab that will be automatically graded and recorded in the online Gradebook. MyFinanceLab: hands-on practice, hands-off grading.

Supplemental Materials

We recognize the key role of a complete and creative package of materials to supplement a basic textbook. We believe that the following materials, offered with the tenth edition, will enrich the investments course for both students and instructors.

▮ *Fundamentals of Investing* Companion Website

The book's Companion Website offers students and professors a rich, dynamic, and up-to-date source of supplemental materials. This resource is located at www.aw-bc.com/gitman_joehnk. Visitors will find links to the sites mentioned in the Hot Links boxes in each chapter; information on more investors' resources; a calculator keystrokes manual; Web exercises, enhanced for pedagogical value, to accompany each chapter of the book; additional *Investing in Action* and *Ethics in Investing* boxes on various topics; answers to odd-numbered Discussion Questions and Problems; and other readings and material that are beyond the normal scope of the first-level investments course (e.g., the Black-Scholes options pricing model, rights and warrants, and unit investment trusts).

Also at the book's Web site are three complete chapters that appeared in the book in earlier editions: "Investing in Preferred Stocks," "Tax-Advantaged Investments," and "Real Estate and Other Tangible Investments." These highly informative chapters have been substantively updated and moved to the Web site in response to user, reviewer, and our own preference that the text focus solely on securities investing. In addition to its improved focus, moving these chapters to the Web site allows us both to tighten and improve a number of text discussions and to shorten the text's overall length. We feel this change improves the text's effectiveness in terms of both content and length.

▮ Study Guide

The Study Guide to accompany *Fundamentals of Investing,* Tenth Edition, prepared by Karin B. Bonding, CFA, lecturer at the McIntire School at University of Virginia and President of Capital Markets Institute, Inc., Ivy, Virginia, has been completely revised. Each chapter of the *Study Guide* contains a chapter summary, a chapter outline, and a self-test that consists of true-false and multiple-choice questions with answers. Also contained in the self-test are problems with detailed solutions and, where appropriate, calculator key strokes and/or Excel input to solve certain problems. All elements are similar in form and content to those found in the book.

▮ Instructor's Manual

Revised by Thomas Krueger of the University of Wisconsin-La Crosse, the *Instructor's Manual* contains chapter outlines; lists of key concepts discussed in each chapter; detailed chapter overviews; answers/suggested answers to all Concepts in Review and Discussion Questions, Problems, and Critical Thinking Questions to *Investing in Action* and *Ethics in Investing* boxes; solutions to the Case Problems; and ideas for outside projects. The Instructor's Manual is error-free thanks to accuracy checker Michael Woodworth of Purdue University.

▮ Test Bank

Revised for the tenth edition by Robert J. Hartwig of Worcester State College, the *Test Bank* includes a substantial number of new questions. Each chapter features true-false and multiple-choice questions, as well as several problems and short-essay questions. The *Test Bank* is also available in Test Generator Software (TestGen with QuizMaster). Fully networkable, this software is available for Windows and Macintosh. TestGen's graphical interface enables instructors to easily view, edit, and add questions; export questions to create tests; and print tests in a variety of fonts and forms. Search and sort features let the instructor quickly locate questions and arrange them in a preferred order. QuizMaster, working with your school's computer network, automatically grades the exams, stores results on disk, and allows the instructor to view or print a variety of reports. The Test Bank is error-free thanks to accuracy checker, Thomas Krueger of the University of Wisconsin-La Crosse.

▮ PowerPoint Lecture Slides

To facilitate classroom presentations, PowerPoint slides of all text images and classroom lecture notes are available for Windows and Macintosh. A PowerPoint viewer is provided for use by those who do not have the full software program. The slides were developed by Robert Maxwell, College of the Canyons.

▮ Instructor's Resource Disk

The Instructor's Resource Disk contains every Instructor Resource for this book on one convenient CD-ROM. It is fully compatible with Windows and Macintosh systems, and includes: Word and PDF files of the Instructor's Manual and Test Bank; PowerPoint Lecture Slides; and the Computerized TestGen Test Bank. To order, contact your sales representative or go to http://www.aw-bc.com/irc to download any instructor resources at any time.

Acknowledgments

Many people gave their generous assistance during the initial development and revisions of *Fundamentals of Investing*. The expertise, classroom experience, and general advice of both colleagues and practitioners have been invaluable. Reactions and suggestions from students throughout the country—comments we especially enjoy receiving—sustained our belief in the need for a fresh, informative, and teachable investments text.

A few individuals provided significant subject matter expertise in the initial development of the book. They are Terry S. Maness of Baylor University, Arthur L. Schwartz, Jr., of the University of South Florida at St. Petersburg, and Gary W. Eldred. Their contributions are greatly appreciated. In addition, Addison-Wesley obtained the advice of a large group of experienced reviewers. We appreciate their many suggestions and criticisms, which have had a strong influence on various aspects of this volume. Our special thanks go to the following people, who reviewed all or part of the manuscript for the previous nine editions of the book.

M. Fall Ainina
Joan Anderssen
Gary Baker
Harisha Batra
Richard B. Bellinfante
Cecil C. Bigelow
Paul Bolster
A. David Brummett
Gary P. Cain
Gary Carman
Daniel J. Cartell
P. R. Chandy
Steven P. Clark
David M. Cordell
Timothy Cowling
Robert M. Crowe
Richard F. DeMong
Clifford A. Diebold
James Dunn
Betty Marie Dyatt
Steven J. Elbert
Thomas Eyssell
Frank J. Fabozzi
Robert A. Ford
Albert J. Fredman
John Gerlach

Chaim Ginsberg
Joel Gold
Frank Griggs
Brian Grinder
Harry P. Guenther
Mahboubul Hassan
Gay Hatfield
Robert D. Hollinger
Sue Beck Howard
Roland Hudson, Jr.
Ping Hsiao
Donald W. Johnson
Samuel Kyle Jones
Ravindra R. Kamath
Bill Kane
Daniel J. Kaufmann, Jr.
Nancy Kegelman
Phillip T. Kolbe
Sheri Kole
Christopher M. Korth
Marie A. Kratochvil
Thomas M. Krueger
George Kutner
Robert T. LeClair
Chun I. Lee
James Lock

Larry A. Lynch
Weston A. McCormac
David J. McLaughlin
Anne Macy
James Mallett
Keith Manko
Timothy Manuel
Kathy Milligan
Warren E. Moeller
Homer Mohr
Majed R. Muhtaseb
Joseph Newhouse
Michael Nugent
Joseph F. Ollivier
Michael Palermo
John Palffy
John Park
Thomas Patrick
Michael Polakoff
Barbara Poole
Ronald S. Pretekin
Stephen W. Pruitt
S. P. Umamaheswar Rao
William A. Richard
Linda R. Richardson
William A. Rini

Roy A. Roberson
Edward Rozalewicz
William J. Ruckstuhl
David Russo
Arthur L. Schwartz, Jr.
William Scroggins
Daniel Singer
Keith V. Smith
Pat R. Stout
Nancy E. Strickler
Glenn T. Sweeney
Amir Tavakkol
Phillip D. Taylor
Wenyuh Tsay
Robert C. Tueting
Howard E. Van Auken
P. V. Viswanath
John R. Weigel
Peter M. Wichert
John C. Woods
Richard H. Yanow
Ali E. Zadeh
Edward Zajicek

The following people provided extremely useful reviews and input to the tenth edition:

Kevin Ahlgrim, Illinois State University
Felix O. Ayadi, Texas Southern University
Imad Elhaj, University of Louisville
Tom Geurts, New York University Real Estate Institute
Robert J. Boldin, Indiana University of Pennsylvania
William Lepley, University of Wisconsin
Mahboubul Hassan, Southern New Hampshire University
Blake LeBaron, Brandeis University
Larry Lynch, Roanoke College
Ralph Lim, Sacred Heart University
Sally Wells, Columbia College
Rathin Rathinasamy, Ball State University
Robert Hartwig, Worcester State College

Because of the wide variety of topics covered in the book, we called upon many experts for advice. We thank them and their firms for allowing us to draw on their insights and awareness of recent developments, to ensure that the text is as current as possible. In particular, we want to mention Aaron Kohn, CFM, Merrill Lynch Global Private Client Group, Lake Oswego, OR; Jeff Buetow, CFA, BFRC Services, Charlottesville, VA; Bill Bachrach, Bachrach & Associates, San Diego, CA; John Markese, President, American Association of Individual Investors, Chicago, IL; Frank Hatheway, CFA, Chief Economist, Nasdaq, New York, NY; George Ebenhack, Oppenheimer & Co., Los Angeles, CA; Mark D. Erwin, ChFC, Commonwealth Financial Network, San Diego, CA; Andrew Temte, CFA, Schweser Study Program, La Crosse, WI; Martin P. Klitzner, Sunrise Capital Management, Del Mar, CA; David M. Love, C.P. Eaton and Associates, La Jolla, CA; David H. McLaughlin, Chase Investment Counsel Corp., Charlottesville, VA; Michael R. Murphy, Sceptre Investment Counsel, Toronto, Ontario, Canada; Mark S. Nussbaum, CFP®, UBS Financial Services, Inc., La Jolla, CA; John Richardson, Northern Trust Bank of Arizona, Phoenix, AZ; Richard Russell, Dow Theory Letters, La Jolla, CA; Mike Smith, Economic Analysis Corporation, Los Angeles, CA; Michael J. Steelman, Bank of America, San Diego, CA; Fred Weaver, Washington Mutual, Phoenix, AZ; and Lynn Yturri, BancOne Arizona, Phoenix, AZ.

Special thanks to attorney Robert J. Wright of Wright & Wrights, CPAs, San Diego, for his help in revising and updating the many tax discussions, and to Professor Terry Grieb of the University of Idaho for his help in revising and updating the two chapters on derivative securities. We also thank Michael D. Woodworth of Purdue University for writing and revising the chapter-opening vignettes; Tom Guerts of New York University for revising and preparing Hot Links and new Investor Facts; Edward Zajicek of Winston-Salem State University for his writing and revising of the *Investing in Action* and *Ethics in Investing* boxes; Steven Lifland of High Point University for his authoring of the Excel with Spreadsheet exercises; Karin Bonding of the University of Virginia for her useful feedback and for revising the *Study Guide;* Robert Hartwig of Worchester State College for revising and updating the *Test Bank;* and Thomas Krueger of the University of Wisconsin, La Crosse, for revising and updating the *Instructor's Manual.*

The staff at Addison-Wesley, particularly Donna Battista and Denise Clinton, contributed their creativity, enthusiasm, and commitment to this textbook. Addison-Wesley Assistant Editor of Finance Allison Stendardi and development editor Ann Torbert managed and pulled together the various strands of the project. Nancy Freihofer of Thompson Steele, Inc., and other dedicated Addison-Wesley staff, including managing editor Nancy Fenton, senior designer Charles Spaulding, director of media Michelle Neil, media producers Bethany Tidd and Bridget Page, senior marketing manager Roxanne Hoch, and supplements editor Heather McNally warrant special thanks for shepherding the project through the development, production, marketing, and Web site construction stages. Without their care and concern, this text would not have evolved into the teachable and interesting text and package we believe it to be.

Finally, our wives, Robin and Charlene, and our children, Jessica, Zachary, and Caren, and Chris, Terry, and Sara, played important roles by providing support and understanding during the book's development, revision, and production. We are forever grateful to them, and we hope that this edition will justify the sacrifices required during the many hours we were away from them working on this book.

LAWRENCE J. GITMAN

MICHAEL D. JOEHNK

Part One

Preparing to Invest

Chapter 1

The Investment Environment

Chapter 2

Markets and Transactions

Chapter 3

Investment Information and Securities Transactions

Chapter 1

The Investment Environment

Y ou have worked hard for your money. Now it is time to make your money work for you. Welcome to the world of investments. There are literally thousands of investments, from all around the world, from which to choose. How much should you invest, when should you invest, and which investments are right for you? The answers depend upon the knowledge and financial circumstances of each individual investor.

There is plenty of financial news available, and finding that information has become easier than ever. At one time, the only exposure most people had to investment news was a 10-second announcement on the evening news about the change in the Dow Jones Industrial Average that day. Today Americans are bombarded with financial news: Cable TV stations like CNBC specialize in business and financial news, and network newscasters feature business news more prominently. In print, besides the *Wall Street Journal,* you can subscribe to *Investor's Business Daily, Barron's, Kiplinger's Personal Finance Magazine, Money, Smart Money,* and many other publications that focus on investing.

Today, almost half of all Americans own stocks or stock mutual funds, and many of them are new investors. The Internet has played a major role in opening the world of investing to them. It makes enormous amounts of information readily available and puts a way to trade securities just a few clicks away. In short, technology makes investing much easier. Access to tools formerly restricted to investment professionals helps create a more level playing field—yet at the same time, such easy access can increase the risks for inexperienced investors.

Regardless of whether you conduct transactions online or use a traditional broker, the same investment fundamentals presented in this textbook apply. Chapter 1 introduces the various types of investments, the investment process, key investment vehicles, the role of investment plans, and the importance of meeting liquidity needs. Becoming familiar with investment alternatives and developing realistic investment plans should greatly increase your chance of achieving financial success.

Investments and the Investment Process

LG 1   LG 2

Note: The Learning Goals shown at the beginning of the chapter are keyed to text discussions using these icons.

investment
any vehicle into which funds can be placed with the expectation that it will generate positive income and/or preserve or increase its value.

returns
the rewards from investing, received as current income and/or increased value.

You are probably already an investor. If you have money in a savings account, you already have at least one investment to your name. An **investment** is simply any vehicle into which funds can be placed with the expectation that it will generate positive income and/or preserve or increase its value.

The rewards, or **returns**, from investing are received in two basic forms: current income and increased value. Money invested in a savings account provides *current income* in the form of periodic interest payments. A share of common stock purchased as an investment is expected to offer *increased value* from the time it is purchased to the time it is sold. Since 1926 the average annual return on a savings account has been about 3%. The average annual return on the common stock of large companies has been about 12.3%. Of course, during major market downturns (such as that which started in 2000 and ran until late 2002), the returns on nearly all investment vehicles were well below these long-term historical averages. (We'll look more carefully at historical returns in Chapter 4.)

Is cash placed in a simple (no-interest) checking account an investment? No, because it fails both tests of the definition: It does not provide added income, nor does its value increase. (In fact, if the money kept in a checking account is in excess of the amount needed to pay bills or if the interest rate is high, its value is likely to decrease, because it is eroded over time by inflation.)

We begin our study of investments by looking at types of investments and at the structure of the investment process.

▌ Types of Investments

Note: Web Extensions provide additional interesting content at the book's companion Web site.

WEBEXTENSION

You might want to establish a baseline on your investing "know-how" by testing your Investment IQ using the questions given in the *Investing in Action* box at the book's companion Web site. Click on Chapter 1, "Test Your Investment IQ."

www.myfinancelab.com

When you invest, the organization in which you invest—whether it is a company or a government entity—offers you an expected future benefit in exchange for the current use of your funds. Organizations compete for the use of your funds. The one that will get your investment dollars is the one that offers a benefit you judge to be better than any competitor offers. Different investors judge benefits differently. As a result, investments of every type are available, from "sure things" such as earning 1% interest on your bank savings account, to the possibility of tripling your money fast by investing in a newly issued biotech stock. The investments you choose will depend on your resources, your goals, and your personality. We can differentiate types of investments on the basis of a number of factors.

securities
investments that represent debt or ownership or the legal right to acquire or sell an ownership interest.

property
investments in real property or tangible personal property.

Securities or Property Investments that represent debt or ownership or the legal right to acquire or sell an ownership interest are called **securities**. The most common types of securities are stocks, bonds, and options. The focus of this book is primarily on securities, particularly common stocks.

Property, on the other hand, consists of investments in real property or tangible personal property. *Real property* is land, buildings, and that which is permanently affixed to the land. *Tangible personal property* includes items such as gold, artwork, antiques, and other collectibles.

direct investment
investment in which an investor directly acquires a claim on a security or property.

indirect investment
investment made in a collection of securities or properties.

debt
funds lent in exchange for interest income and the promised repayment of the loan at a given future date.

equity
ongoing ownership in a business or property.

derivative securities
securities that are structured to exhibit characteristics similar to those of an underlying security or asset and that derive their value from the underlying security or asset.

risk
the chance that actual investment returns will differ from those expected.

speculation
the purchase of high-risk investment vehicles that offer highly uncertain returns and future value.

short-term investments
investments that typically mature within one year

long-term investments
investments with maturities of longer than a year or with no maturity at all.

domestic investments
debt, equity, and derivative securities of U.S.-based companies.

foreign investments
debt, equity, and derivative securities of foreign-based companies.

Direct or Indirect A **direct investment** is one in which an investor directly acquires a claim on a security or property. If you buy a stock or bond in order to earn income or preserve value, you have made a direct investment.

An **indirect investment** is an investment made in a collection of securities or properties, typically constructed to meet one or more investment goals. Rather than invest directly in a given security or property, you invest in it indirectly by purchasing an interest in a professionally managed collection of securities or properties.

Debt, Equity, or Derivative Securities Usually, an investment represents either a debt or an equity interest. **Debt** represents funds lent in exchange for interest income and the promised repayment of the loan at a given future date. When you buy a debt instrument like a *bond*, in effect you lend money to the issuer. The issuer agrees to pay you a stated rate of interest over a specified period of time, at the end of which the issuer will return the original sum.

Equity represents ongoing ownership in a business or property. An equity investment may be held as a security or by title to a specific property. The most popular type of equity security is *common stock*.

Derivative securities are neither debt nor equity. They derive their value from, and have characteristics similar to those of, an underlying security or asset. *Options* are an example: An investor essentially buys the opportunity to sell or buy another security at a specified price during a given period of time.

Low- or High-Risk Investments are sometimes differentiated on the basis of risk. As used in finance, **risk** is the chance that actual investment returns will differ from those expected. The broader the range of possible values or returns associated with an investment, the greater its risk.

Investors are confronted with a continuum of investments that range from low risk to high risk. Each type of investment vehicle has a basic risk characteristic, although the actual level of risk depends on the specific vehicle. For example, stocks are generally considered more risky than bonds. However, it is not difficult to find high-risk bonds that are more risky than the stock of a financially sound firm such as IBM or McDonald's.

Low-risk investments are those considered safe with regard to a positive return. *High-risk investments* are considered speculative; their levels of return are highly uncertain. **Speculation** offers highly uncertain returns and future value. Because of this greater risk, the returns associated with speculation are expected to be greater. In this book we will use the term *investment* for both investment and speculation.

Short- or Long-Term The life of an investment can be described as either short- or long-term. **Short-term investments** typically mature within one year. **Long-term investments** are those with longer maturities or, like common stock, with no maturity at all.

Domestic or Foreign As recently as 20 years ago, U.S. investors invested almost exclusively in purely **domestic investments**: the debt, equity, and derivative securities of U.S.-based companies. Today, investors routinely also look for **foreign investments** (both direct and indirect) that might offer more attractive returns than purely domestic investments. Information on foreign compa-

Note: Discussions of international investing are highlighted by this icon.

financial institutions
organizations that channel the savings of governments, businesses, and individuals into loans or investments.

financial markets
forums in which suppliers and demanders of funds make financial transactions, often through intermediaries.

nies is now readily available, and it is now relatively easy to make foreign investments. We therefore routinely consider all aspects of foreign investing throughout this book.

■ The Structure of the Investment Process

The investment process brings together *suppliers* who have extra funds with *demanders* who need funds. Suppliers and demanders of funds most often come together by means of a financial institution or a financial market. (Occasionally, especially in property transactions, buyers and sellers deal directly with one another.) **Financial institutions** are organizations that channel the savings of governments, businesses, and individuals into loans or investments. Banks and insurance companies are financial institutions. **Financial markets** are forums in which suppliers and demanders of funds make financial transactions, often through intermediaries. They include securities, commodities, and foreign exchange markets.

The dominant financial market in the United States is the *securities market*. It includes stock markets, bond markets, and options markets. Similar markets exist in most major economies throughout the world. Their common feature is that the price of an investment vehicle at any point in time results from an equilibrium between the forces of supply and demand. As new information about returns and risk becomes available, the changes in supply and demand may result in a new equilibrium or *market price*. Financial markets streamline the process of bringing together suppliers and demanders of funds, and they allow transactions to be made quickly and at a fair price. They also publicize security prices.

Figure 1.1 diagrams the investment process. Note that the suppliers of funds may transfer their resources to the demanders through financial institutions, through financial markets, or in direct transactions. As the broken lines show, financial institutions can participate in financial markets as either suppliers or demanders of funds.

FIGURE 1.1

The Investment Process

Financial institutions participate in the financial markets as well as transfer funds between suppliers and demanders. Although the arrows go only from suppliers to demanders, for some transactions (e.g., the sale of a bond or a college loan), the principal amount borrowed by the demander from the supplier (the lender) is eventually returned.

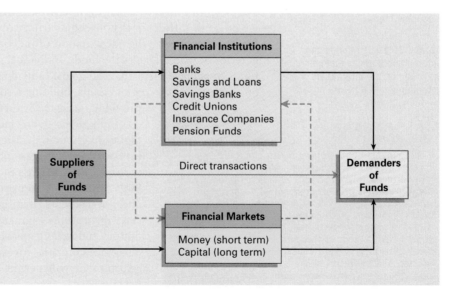

Note: Investor Facts offer interesting or entertaining tidbits of information.

INVESTOR FACTS

AMERICANS LOVE STOCKS— A recent survey showed that 52% of Americans now own stocks or stock mutual funds, compared to just 19% in 1983. Financial assets represent 42% of total assets. Stocks and mutual funds now account for about 34% of total household financial assets, up from 28% in 1995—and this figure does not include investments held in retirement accounts, which represent another 28% of financial assets.

Source: Ana M. Azicorbe, Arther B. Kennickell, and Kevin B. Moore, "Recent Changes in U.S. Family Finances: Results from the 1998 and 2001 Survey of Consumer Finances," *Federal Reserve Bulletin,* Board of Governors of the Federal Reserve System, Washington, D.C., January 2003, pp. 9, 15.

individual investors
investors who manage their own funds.

institutional investors
investment professionals who are paid to manage other people's money.

Note: Addresses of additional information sources that can be found on the Internet are interspersed in HotLinks boxes throughout the chapters.

HOTLINKS

Getting investment information is now only a few "clicks" away. Everything from stock quotations, to news articles, to Wall Street research is on the Web. Many Web sites provide financial information tutorials.

InvestorGuide.com contains links to many of the Web's resources, and free investing guides. Check out [University] and follow some of the links to the educational information available for free. Also follow the [Links Directory] link to the list of other sites that you can access from there.

www.investorguide.com

Suppliers and Demanders of Funds Government, business, and individuals are the key participants in the investment process. Each may act as a supplier or a demander of funds. For the economy to grow and prosper, funds must be available to qualified individuals and to government and business. If individuals began suddenly hiding their excess funds under floorboards rather than putting them in financial institutions or investing them in the financial markets, then government, business, and individuals in need of funds would have difficulty obtaining them. As a result, government spending, business expansion, and consumer purchases would decline, and economic activity would slow.

Government All levels of government—federal, state, and local—require vast sums of money to finance long-term projects related to the construction of public facilities and to keep the government running. Occasionally, governments supply funds by making short-term investments to earn a positive return on temporarily idle funds. In general, though, government is a *net demander of funds*—it demands more funds than it supplies. The financial activities of governments significantly affect the behavior of financial institutions and financial markets.

Business Most business firms require large sums of money to support operations. Like government, business has both long- and short-term financial needs. Businesses issue a wide variety of debt and equity securities to finance these needs. They also supply funds when they have excess cash. But like government, business firms in general are *net demanders of funds.*

Individuals You might be surprised to learn that the individual's role in the investment process is significant. Individuals frequently demand funds in the form of loans to finance the acquisition of property—typically automobiles and houses—and education. Although the individual demand for funds seems great, individuals as a group are *net suppliers of funds:* They put more funds into the financial system than they take out.

Types of Investors When we refer to individuals in the investment process, we do so to differentiate households from government and business. We can further characterize the participation of individuals in the investment process in terms of who manages the funds. **Individual investors** manage their personal funds to achieve their financial goals. Individual investors usually concentrate on earning a return on idle funds, building a source of retirement income, and providing security for their families.

Individuals who lack the time or expertise to make investment decisions often employ **institutional investors**—investment professionals who are paid to manage other people's money. These professionals trade large volumes of securities for individuals, businesses, and governments. Institutional investors include financial institutions—banks, life insurance companies, mutual funds, and pension funds. For example, a life insurance company invests its premium receipts to earn returns that will permit payments to policyholders or beneficiaries.

Both individual and institutional investors apply similar fundamental principles. However, institutional investors generally invest larger sums of money on behalf of others and therefore are often more sophisticated in investment knowledge and methods. *The information presented in this textbook is aimed primarily at individual investors.* It represents only the first step toward developing the expertise needed to qualify as an institutional investor.

Note: The Concepts in Review questions at the end of each text section encourage you, before you move on, to test your understanding of the material you've just read.

CONCEPTS IN REVIEW

Answers available at: www.myfinancelab.com

1.1 Define the term *investment*, and explain why individuals invest.

1.2 Differentiate among the following types of investments, and cite an example of each: (a) securities and property investments; (b) direct and indirect investments; (c) debt, equity, and derivative securities; and (d) short-term and long-term investments.

1.3 Define the term *risk,* and explain how risk is used to differentiate among investments.

1.4 What are *foreign investments*, and what role do they play today for the individual investor?

1.5 Describe the structure of the overall investment process. Explain the role played by *financial institutions* and *financial markets*.

1.6 Classify the role of (a) government, (b) business, and (c) individuals as net suppliers or net demanders of funds.

1.7 Differentiate between *individual investors* and *institutional investors*.

Investment Vehicles

LG 3

A wide variety of investment vehicles are available to individual investors. Vehicles differ in terms of maturities (lives), costs, return and risk characteristics, and tax considerations. We devote the bulk of this book—Chapters 6 through 15—to describing the characteristics, special features, returns and risks, and possible investment strategies of the vehicles available to individual investors. Here we will introduce these investment vehicles. Table 1.1 (on page 40) summarizes the information presented in this section.

■ Short-Term Vehicles

short-term vehicles
savings instruments that usually have lives of 1 year or less.

Short-term vehicles include savings instruments that usually have lives of one year or less. Short-term vehicles generally carry little or no risk. Often such instruments are used to "warehouse" idle funds and earn a return until those funds are invested in long-term vehicles. They are also popular among conservative investors, who may use short-term vehicles as a primary investment outlet.

liquidity
the ability of an investment to be converted into cash quickly and with little or no loss in value.

Short-term vehicles also provide **liquidity**. That is, they can be converted into cash quickly and with little or no loss in value. Provision for liquidity is an important part of any financial plan. We discuss the role of short-term vehicles in financial planning and the key features of the most popular short-term vehicles later in this chapter.

TABLE 1.1   Overview of Investment Vehicles

Type	Description	Examples	Where Covered in This Book
Short-term vehicles	Savings instruments with lives of 1 year or less. Used to warehouse idle funds and to provide liquidity.	Deposit accounts Series EE savings bonds U.S. Treasury bills (T-bills) Certificates of deposit (CDs) Commercial paper Banker's acceptances Money market mutual funds	Ch. 1
Common stock	Equity investment vehicles that represent ownership in a corporation.		Chs. 6–9
Fixed-income securities	Investment vehicles that offer a fixed periodic return.	Bonds Convertible securities Preferred stock	Chs. 10, 11 Ch. 10 Web Ch. 16
Mutual funds	Companies that raise money from sale of shares and invest in and professionally manage a diversified group of securities.		Ch. 12
Derivative securities	Securities that are neither debt nor equity but are structured to exhibit the characteristics of the underlying securities or assets from which they derive their value.	Options Futures	Ch. 14 Ch. 15
Other popular investment vehicles	Various other investment vehicles that are widely used by investors.	Tax-advantaged investments Real estate Tangibles	Web Ch. 17 Web Ch. 18 Web Ch. 18

common stock
equity investment that represents ownership in a corporation; each share represents a fractional ownership interest in the firm.

dividends
periodic payments made by firms to their shareholders.

capital gains
the amount by which the sale price of an asset *exceeds* its original purchase price.

▌Common Stock

Common stock is an equity investment that represents ownership in a corporation. Each share of common stock represents a fractional ownership interest in the firm. For example, one share of common stock in a corporation that has 10,000 shares outstanding would represent 1/10,000 ownership interest. Next to short-term vehicles and home ownership, common stock is the most popular form of investment vehicle. Today more than half of all U.S. families own some common stock, either directly or indirectly.

The return on investment in common stock comes from either of two sources: dividends or capital gains. **Dividends** are periodic payments the corporation makes to its shareholders from its current and past earnings. **Capital gains** result from selling the stock (or any asset) at a price that *exceeds* its original purchase price.

For example, say you purchased a single share of One Tech Industries common stock for $40 per share. During the first year you owned it, you received $2.50 per share in cash dividends. At the end of the year, you sold the stock for $44 per share. If we ignore the costs associated with buying and selling the stock, you earned $2.50 in dividends and $4 in capital gains ($44 sale price—$40 purchase price).

As mentioned earlier, since 1926, the average annual rate of return on common stocks of large firms has been about

fixed-income securities
investment vehicles that offer a fixed periodic return.

bonds
long-term debt instruments (IOUs), issued by corporations and governments, that offer a known interest return plus return of the bond's *face value* at maturity.

convertible security
a fixed-income obligation with a feature permitting the investor to convert it into a specified number of shares of common stock.

preferred stock
ownership interest in a corporation; has a stated dividend rate, payment of which is given preference over common stock dividends of the same firm.

mutual fund
a company that raises money from sale of its shares and invests in and professionally manages a diversified portfolio of securities.

money market mutual funds
mutual funds that invest solely in short-term investment vehicles.

12.3%. The more risky common stocks of smaller firms have earned an average annual return of about 17.4%.

▌Fixed-Income Securities

Fixed-income securities are investment vehicles that offer a fixed periodic return. Some offer contractually guaranteed returns. Others have specified, but not guaranteed, returns. Because of their fixed returns, fixed-income securities tend to be popular during periods of high interest rates, when investors seek to "lock in" high returns. The key forms of fixed-income securities are bonds, convertible securities, and preferred stock.

Bonds **Bonds** are long-term debt instruments (IOUs) issued by corporations and governments. A bondholder has a contractual right to receive a known interest return, plus return of the bond's *face value* (the stated value given on the certificate) at maturity (typically 20 to 40 years).

If you purchased a $1,000 bond paying 9% interest in semiannual installments, you would expect to be paid $45 (9% × ½ year × $1,000) every six months. At maturity you would receive the $1,000 face value of the bond. Depending on the bond, you may be able to buy or sell a bond prior to maturity.

Since 1926, the average annual rate of return on long-term corporate bonds has been about 6.2%. The average annual return on less risky long-term government bonds has been about 5.8%.

Convertible Securities A **convertible security** is a special type of fixed-income obligation. It has a feature permitting the investor to convert it into a specified number of shares of common stock. Convertibles provide the fixed-income benefit of a bond (interest) while offering the price-appreciation (capital gain) potential of common stock.

Preferred Stock Like common stock, **preferred stock** represents an ownership interest in a corporation. Unlike common stock, preferred stock has a stated dividend rate. Payment of this dividend is given preference over common stock dividends of the same firm. Preferred stock has no maturity date. Investors typically purchase it for the dividends it pays, but it may also provide capital gains.

▌Mutual Funds

A company that raises money from sale of its shares and invests in and professionally manages a diversified group of securities is called a **mutual fund**. Investors in the fund own an interest in the fund's collection of securities. All mutual funds issue and repurchase shares of the fund at a price that reflects the value of the portfolio at the time the transaction is made. **Money market mutual funds** are mutual funds that invest solely in short-term investment vehicles.

▌Derivative Securities

As noted earlier, *derivative securities* derive their value from an underlying security or asset. They typically possess high levels of risk, because they usually have uncertain returns or unstable market values. But, because of their above-average risk, these vehicles also have high levels of expected return. The key derivative securities are options and futures.

options
securities that give the investor an opportunity to sell or buy another security at a specified price over a given period of time.

Options Options are securities that give the investor an opportunity to sell or buy another security at a specified price over a given period of time. Most often, investors purchase options to take advantage of an anticipated change in the price of common stock. However, the purchaser of an option is not guaranteed a return and could even lose the entire amount invested if the option does not become attractive enough to use. Two common types of options are *puts* and *calls*.

futures
legally binding obligations stipulating that the seller of the contract will make delivery and the buyer of the contract will take delivery of an asset at some specific date, at a price agreed on at the time the contract is sold.

Futures Futures are legally binding obligations stipulating that the seller of the futures contract will make delivery and the buyer of the contract will take delivery of an asset at some specific date, at a price agreed on at the time the contract is sold. Examples of commodities sold by contract include soybeans, pork bellies, platinum, and cocoa. Examples of financial futures are contracts for Japanese yen, U.S. Treasury securities, interest rates, and stock indexes. Trading in commodity and financial futures is generally a highly specialized, high-risk proposition.

■ Other Popular Investment Vehicles

Investors also use various other investment vehicles. The most common are tax-advantaged investments, real estate, and tangibles.

tax-advantaged investments
investment vehicles and strategies for legally reducing one's tax liability.

Because the federal income tax rate for an individual can be as high as 35%, many investors look for **tax-advantaged investments**. These are investment vehicles and strategies for legally reducing one's tax liability. With them, investors find that their after-tax rates of return can be far higher than with conventional investments.

real estate
entities such as residential homes, raw land, and income property.

Real estate consists of entities such as residential homes, raw land, and a variety of forms of income property, including warehouses, office and apartment buildings, and condominiums. The appeal of real estate investment is the potential returns in the form of rental income, tax write-offs, and capital gains.

tangibles
investment assets, other than real estate, that can be seen or touched.

Tangibles are investment assets, other than real estate, that can be seen or touched. They include gold and other precious metals, gemstones, and collectibles such as coins, stamps, artwork, and antiques. People purchase these assets as investments in anticipation of price increases.

CONCEPTS IN REVIEW
Answers available at: www.myfinancelab.com

1.8 What are *short-term vehicles?* How do they provide *liquidity?*

1.9 What is *common stock,* and what are its two sources of potential return?

1.10 Briefly define and differentiate among the following investment vehicles. Which offer fixed returns? Which are derivative securities? Which offer professional investment management?
a. Bonds   b. Convertible securities
c. Preferred stock   d. Mutual funds
e. Options   f. Futures

Making Investment Plans

LG 4   LG 5

Investing can be carried out in a logical progression of steps. Here, we outline those steps and then consider three other key aspects of making investment plans—the impact of taxes, your stage in the life cycle, and the changing economic environment.

▮ Steps in Investing

Investing can be conducted on a strictly intuitive basis or on the basis of plans carefully developed to achieve specific goals. Evidence favors the planned approach. It begins with establishing a set of overall financial goals and then developing and executing an investment program consistent with those goals. The following overview of the steps in investing provides a framework for the concepts, tools, and techniques presented throughout the book.

Step 1: Meeting Investment Prerequisites Before investing, you must make certain that you have adequately provided for the *necessities of life*. This includes funds for housing, food, transportation, taxes, and clothing. In addition, you should have a pool of easily accessible funds for meeting emergency cash needs.

Another prerequisite is adequate protection against various "common" risks. Protection against such risks can be acquired through life, health, property, and liability insurance.

Step 2: Establishing Investment Goals Once you have satisfied the prerequisites, the next step is to establish *investment goals*. **Investment goals** are the financial objectives you wish to achieve by investing. Clearly, your investment goals will determine the types of investments you will make. Common investment goals include:

investment goals
the financial objectives that one wishes to achieve by investing.

1. *Accumulating retirement funds.* Accumulating funds for retirement is the *single most important reason for investing.* The earlier in life you assess your retirement needs, the greater your chance of accumulating sufficient funds to meet them.

2. *Enhancing current income.* Investments enhance current income by earning dividends or interest. Retirees frequently choose investments offering *high current income at low risk*.

3. *Saving for major expenditures.* Families often put aside money over the years to accumulate the funds needed for major expenditures. The most common of these are the down payment on a home, education, vacation travel, and capital to start a business. The appropriate types of investment vehicles depend on the purpose and the amount of money needed.

4. *Sheltering income from taxes.* Federal income tax law allows taxpayers to deduct certain noncash charges from specified sources of income. Such deductions allow an investor to avoid

(or defer) paying taxes on the income from an investment, thereby leaving more funds for reinvestment.

Step 3: Adopting an Investment Plan Once you have established your general goals, you should adopt an **investment plan**—a written document describing how you will invest funds. You can develop a series of supporting investment goals for each long-term goal. For each goal, specify the target date for achieving it and the amount of tolerable risk. The more specific you can be in your statement of investment goals, the easier it will be to establish an investment plan consistent with your goals.

Step 4: Evaluating Investment Vehicles Next you will want to evaluate investment vehicles by assessing each vehicle's potential return and risk. (Chapter 4 offers a general discussion of the procedures for measuring these key dimensions of potential investments.)

Step 5: Selecting Suitable Investments You now gather additional information and use it to select specific investment vehicles consistent with your goals. You must assess factors such as expected return, risk, and tax considerations. Careful selection of investment vehicles is essential to successful investing.

Step 6: Constructing a Diversified Portfolio To achieve your investment goals, you will assemble an investment **portfolio** of suitable investments. You will use **diversification**, the inclusion of a number of different investment vehicles in a portfolio, to earn higher returns or be exposed to less risk than if you limited your investments to just one or two vehicles. Diversification is the financial term for the age-old advice, "Don't put all your eggs in one basket." (Chapter 5 includes discussions of diversification and other modern portfolio concepts.)

Many individual investors buy mutual funds to achieve diversification and receive the benefit of professional management (see Chapter 12); others will construct and manage their own portfolios (see Chapter 13).

Step 7: Managing the Portfolio Once you have constructed your portfolio, you should measure its actual behavior in relation to expected performance. If the investment results are not consistent with your objectives, you may need to take corrective action.

The *Investing in Action* box on page 45 summarizes some general tips for successful investing.

■ Considering Personal Taxes

A knowledge of the tax laws can help you reduce taxes and increase the amount of after-tax dollars available for investing. Because tax laws are complicated and subject to frequent revision, we present only the key concepts and how they apply to popular investment transactions.

Basic Sources of Taxation The two major types of taxes are those levied by the federal government and those levied by state and local governments. The federal *income tax* is the major form

INVESTING *in Action*

Lessons for Investment Success

Becoming a successful investor takes time and discipline; there are no sure ways to beat the market. Here are some tips to start you on the road to financial security.

- **Harness the power of compounding.** With compounding, time is your biggest ally. The longer you invest your money, the faster it will grow. If you earn a 12% annual return on your investment and reinvest your yearly earnings, you will be able to double your money every six years, or so. Start now.

- **Don't wait for the "right" time to invest.** You can always find a reason to put off taking the plunge. The "best" time to start is always *now*. Studies show it's more important to start investing than to pick the right time.

- **Diversify your portfolio.** Spreading your money among different types of investments is less risky than putting all your eggs in one investment basket. If some of your holdings go down, others go up, and vice versa. Invest in several types of securities and over various time horizons. No one knows which sector will be hot tomorrow.

- **Monitor your investments.** Review your portfolio regularly to check your progress against your goals. Weed out poor performers. Don't be too quick to unload an investment, though, or to chase hot tips. Be sure you have a good reason to buy or sell.

- **Use tax-advantaged accounts.** To minimize the impact of taxes on your investment savings and to maximize the power of compounding, use tax-free or tax-deferred accounts such as traditional IRA, Roth IRA, and 401(k) plans.

CRITICAL THINKING QUESTIONS Why is it important to start investing now? Why is it a good idea to diversify?

---

of personal taxation. Federal rates currently range from 10% to 35% of taxable income.

State and local taxes vary from area to area. Some states have income taxes that range as high as 15% or more of income. Some cities, especially large East Coast cities, also have local income taxes that typically range between 1% and 5% of income. In addition to income taxes, state and local governments rely heavily on sales and property taxes as a source of revenue.

Income taxes at the federal, state, and local levels have the greatest impact on security investments, whose returns are in the form of dividends, interest, and increases in value. Property taxes can have a sizable impact on real estate and other forms of property investment.

Types of Income The income of individuals is classified into one of *three basic categories:*

1. *Active income* consists of everything from wages and salaries to bonuses, tips, pension income, and alimony. Active income is made up of income earned on the job as well as most other forms of *noninvestment* income.
2. *Portfolio income* is earnings generated from various types of investments. This category covers most (but not all) types of investments, from savings accounts, stocks, bonds, and mutual funds to options and futures. For the most part, portfolio income consists of interest, dividends, and capital gains (the profit on the sale of an investment).

3. *Passive income* is a special category of income, composed chiefly of income derived from real estate, limited partnerships, and other forms of tax-advantaged investments.

Tax laws limit the amount of deductions (write-offs) that can be taken for each category, particularly for portfolio and passive income. The amount of allowable deductions for portfolio and passive income is *limited to the amount of income derived from these two sources.* For example, if you had a total of $380 in portfolio income for the year, you could deduct no more than $380 in investment-related interest expense. For deduction purposes, the portfolio and passive income categories cannot be mixed or combined with each other or with active income. *Investment-related expenses can be used only to offset portfolio income,* and (with a few exceptions) *passive investment expenses can be used only to offset the income from passive investments.*

Ordinary Income Regardless of whether it's classified as active, portfolio, or passive, ordinary income is taxed at one of six rates: 10%, 15%, 25%, 28%, 33%, or 35%. There is one structure of tax rates for taxpayers who file *individual* returns and another for those who file *joint* returns with a spouse. Table 1.2 shows the 2006 tax rates and income brackets for these two categories. Note that the rates are *progressive.* That is, taxpayers with taxable income above a specified amount are taxed at a higher rate.

An example will demonstrate how ordinary income is taxed. Consider the Ellis sisters, Joni and Cara. Both are single. Joni's taxable income is $25,000. Cara's is $50,000. Using Table 1.2, we can calculate their taxes as follows:

Joni:
$(0.10 \times \$7,550) + [0.15 \times (\$25,000 - \$7,550)] = \$755 + \$2,618 = \underline{\$3,373}$

Cara:
$(0.10 \times \$7,550) + [0.15 \times (\$30,650 - \$7,550)]$
$\quad + [0.25 \times (\$50,000 - \$30,650)] = \$755 + \$3,465 + \$4,838 = \underline{\$9,058}$

The progressive nature of the federal income tax structure can be seen by the fact that although Cara's taxable income is twice Joni's, her income tax is about 2.7 times Joni's.

Capital Gains and Losses A *capital asset* is property owned and used by the taxpayer for personal reasons, pleasure, or investment. The most common types are securities and real estate, including one's home. A *capital gain* represents the amount by which the proceeds from the sale of a capital asset *exceed*

TABLE 1.2   **Tax Rates and Income Brackets for Individual and Joint Returns (2006)**

Tax Rates	Taxable Income	
	Individual Returns	Joint Returns
10%	$0 to $7,550	$0 to $15,100
15%	$7,551 to $30,650	$15,101 to $61,300
25%	$30,651 to $74,200	$61,301 to $123,700
28%	$74,201 to $154,800	$123,701 to $188,450
33%	$154,801 to $336,550	$188,451 to $336,550
35%	Over $336,551	Over $336,551

its original purchase price. Capital gains are taxed at two different rates depending on the holding period.

The capital gains tax rate is 15% if the asset is held for more than 12 months. This 15% capital gains tax rate assumes that you're in the 25%, 28%, 33%, or 35% tax bracket. If you're in the 10% or 15% tax bracket, then the capital gains tax rate on an asset held for more than 12 months is just 5%. *Note that under current tax law, dividends received on stock in domestic corporations are taxed as long-term capital gains rather than ordinary income.* If the asset is held for less than 12 months, then the amount of any capital gain realized is added to other sources of income, and the total is taxed at the rates given in Table 1.2.

For example, imagine that James McFail, a single person who has other taxable income totaling $75,000, sold 500 shares of stock at $12 per share. He originally purchased this stock at $10 per share. The total capital gain on this transaction was $1,000 [500 shares × ($12/share − $10/share)]. Thus James's taxable income would total $76,000, which puts him in the 28% tax bracket (see Table 1.2).

If the $1,000 capital gain resulted from an asset that was held for more than 12 months, and because James is in the 28% tax bracket, the capital gain would be taxed at the maximum rate of 15%. His total tax would be calculated as follows:

Ordinary income ($75,000)
$(0.10 \times \$7,550) + [0.15 \times (\$30,650 - \$7,550)]$
$+ [0.25 \times (\$74,200 - \$30,650)] + [0.28 \times (\$75,000 - \$74,200)]$
$= \$755 + \$3,465 + \$10,888 + \$224 = \$15,332$

Capital gain ($1,000)
$(0.15 \times \$1,000) =$ $\underline{\hspace{2cm} 150}$

Total tax $\underline{\underline{\$15,482}}$

James's total tax would be $15,482. Had his other taxable income been below $30,651 (i.e., in the 15% bracket), the $1,000 capital gain would have been taxed at 5% rather than 15%. Had James held the asset for less than 12 months, his $1,000 capital gain would have been taxed as ordinary income, which in James's case would result in a 28% rate.

Capital gains are appealing because they are not taxed until actually realized. For example, if you own a stock originally purchased for $50 per share that at the end of the tax year has a market price of $60 per share, you have a "paper gain" of $10 per share. This *paper (unrealized) gain* is not taxable, because you still own the stock. *Only realized gains are taxed.* If you sold the stock for $60 per share during the tax year, you would have a realized—and therefore taxable—gain of $10 per share.

A **capital loss** results when a capital asset is sold for *less than* its original purchase price. Before taxes are calculated, all gains and losses must be netted out. Taxpayers can apply up to $3,000 of **net losses** against ordinary income in any year. Losses that cannot be applied in the current year may be carried forward and used to offset future income, subject to certain conditions.

capital loss
the amount by which the proceeds from the sale of a capital asset are *less than* its original purchase price.

net losses
the amount by which capital losses exceed capital gains; up to $3,000 of net losses can be applied against ordinary income in any year.

tax planning
the development of strategies that will defer and minimize an individual's level of taxes over the long run.

Investments and Taxes The opportunities created by the tax laws make tax planning important in the investment process. **Tax planning** involves looking at your earnings, both current and projected, and developing strategies that will defer and minimize the level of taxes. The tax plan should guide your investment activities so that over the long run you will achieve maximum after-tax returns for an acceptable level of risk.

For example, the fact that capital gains are not taxed until actually realized allows you to defer tax payments on them as well as control the timing of these payments. However, investments that are likely to lead to capital gains income generally have higher risk than those that provide only current investment income. Therefore, the choice of investment vehicles cannot be made solely on the basis of the possible reduction of tax payments. The levels of both return and risk need to be viewed in light of their tax effects. *It is the after-tax return and associated risk that matter.*

Tax-Advantaged Retirement Vehicles The federal government over the years has established a number of types of retirement vehicles. Employer-sponsored plans include profit-sharing plans, thrift and savings plans, and 401(k) plans. These plans are often *voluntary* and allow employees to both increase the amount of money held for retirement and enjoy attractive tax-deferral benefits. Individuals can also set up their own tax-sheltered retirement programs—for example, Keogh plans and SEP-IRAs for self-employed people. Individual retirement arrangements (IRAs), both deductible and nondeductible, and Roth IRAs, can be set up by just about anybody, subject to certain qualifications. In general, these plans allow individuals to defer taxes, typically on both the contributions and the earnings on them, until retirement. Clearly, the individual investor should take advantage of these vehicles when they are available and appropriate to achieving his or her investment goals.

▮ Investing Over the Life Cycle

Investors tend to follow different investment philosophies as they move through different stages of the life cycle. Generally speaking, most investors tend to be more aggressive when they're young and more conservative as they grow older. Typically, investors move through these investment stages:

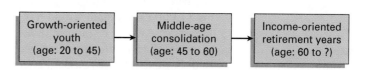

Most young investors, in their twenties and thirties, tend to prefer growth-oriented investments that stress *capital gains* rather than current income. Often young investors don't have much in the way of investable funds, so capital gains are viewed as the quickest (if not necessarily the surest) way to build capital. Young investors tend to favor growth-oriented and speculative vehicles, particularly high-risk common stocks, options, and futures.

As investors approach the middle-age consolidation stage of life (the mid-forties), family demands and responsibilities such as educational expenses and retirement contributions become more important. The whole portfolio goes through a transition to *higher-quality securities*. Low-risk growth and income stocks, high-grade bonds, preferred stocks, convertibles, and mutual funds are all widely used at this stage.

Finally, when investors approach their retirement years, preservation of capital and current income become the principal concerns. A secure, high level

INVESTOR FACTS

TAX BITE—If you invest just $4,000 per year in tax-deferred accounts and investments for the next 30 years, make no withdrawals, and earn an 8% average compounded annual rate of return, you'll accumulate about $453,000—until you pay Uncle Sam his share. Then you will have only $359,760, assuming that an average federal income tax rate of 28% is applied to your earnings above the total investment of $120,000 ($4,000 × 30 years). Taxes will reduce your earnings from the investment by slightly more than one-fourth!

of income is paramount. Capital gains are viewed as merely a pleasant, occasional by-product of investing. The investment portfolio now becomes *highly conservative*. It consists of low-risk income stocks and mutual funds, high-yielding government bonds, quality corporate bonds, bank certificates of deposit (CDs), and other short-term vehicles. At this stage, investors reap the rewards of a lifetime of saving and investing.

▉ Investing in Different Economic Environments

Despite the government's arsenal of weapons for moderating economic swings, numerous changes are sure to occur in the economy during your lifetime of investing. At all stages of the life cycle, your investment program must be flexible enough to allow you to recognize and react to changing economic conditions. The first rule of investing is to know *where* to put your money. The second is to know *when* to make your moves.

The first question is easier to deal with, because it involves matching the risk and return objectives of your investment plan with the available investment alternatives. For example, if you're a seasoned investor who can tolerate the risk, then speculative stocks may be right for you. If you're a novice who wants a fair return on your capital, perhaps you should consider a good growth-oriented mutual fund. Unfortunately, although stocks and growth funds may do well when the economy is expanding, they can turn out to be disasters at other times. This leads to the second, and more difficult, question: What effect do economic and market conditions have on investment returns?

The question of when to invest is difficult because it deals with *market timing*. The fact is that most economists and most professional money managers—not to mention most investors—cannot consistently predict the economy and market movements. It's a lot easier to get a handle on the *current state* of the economy/market. That is, knowing whether the economy/market is in a state of expansion or decline is considerably easier than being able to pinpoint when it's about to change course. Thus, for our purposes, we can define **market timing** as the process of identifying the current state of the economy/market and assessing the likelihood of its continuing on its present course.

The economy/market can exhibit three distinct conditions: (1) a state of *recovery* or *expansion*, (2) a state of *decline* or *recession*, or (3) *a change in the general direction* of its movement. Figure 1.2 illustrates these different stages. It's easy to see when things are moving up (recovery/expansion) and when they

market timing
the process of identifying the current state of the economy/market and assessing the likelihood of its continuing on its present course.

FIGURE 1.2

Different Stages of an Economic/Market Cycle

The economic/market cycle shows three different conditions: (1) a state of recovery/expansion, (2) a state of decline/recession, and (3) a change in the general direction in which the economy/market moves (shown by the shaded areas).

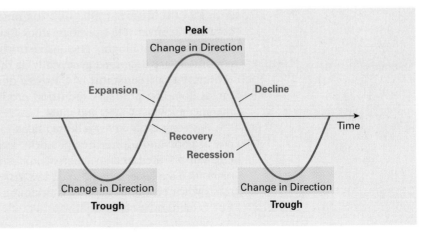

ETHICS *in* INVESTING

The Price for Behaving Badly

In recent years, business headlines were full allegations of massive financial fraud committed by prominent business leaders. These allegations shocked the investment community and resulted in spectacular bankruptcies of some of the largest U.S. corporations. High-profile indictments and court convictions soon followed. Among the list of convicted felons were Jeff Skilling and Ken Lay of Enron, Bernard Ebbers of WorldCom, Dennis Kozlowski of Tyco International, Martha Stewart of Martha Stewart Omnimedia, and John Rigas of Adelphia Communications.

In many cases, the primary weapon of fraudulent CEOs was the use of corporate accounting to report huge, fictitious profits. When the fraud was discovered, a catastrophic crash of the stock price followed. This is what happened at Enron, WorldCom, and Global Crossing. In some cases, accounting firms and Wall Street bankers aided in the schemes. Phony profits helped dishonest CEOs reap fantastic benefits in the form of huge performance bonuses and cash stock options. Many corporate crooks also used their companies as personal piggy banks, as was the case at Tyco International and Adelphia. These executives were able to defeat or completely dismantle internal and external supervision mechanisms and to manipulate their boards of directors to their advantage.

Fraudulent CEOs showed the ability to fool investors, securities analysts, and government regulators for years. In 2002, the U.S. Congress passed the Sarbanes-Oxley Act in the hope of preventing future corporate financial frauds.

CRITICAL THINKING QUESTION Why did accounting "irregularities" become such a widespread problem plaguing public companies in recent years?

Note: Ethics boxes, which appear in many chapters, focus on the ethical dimensions of particular situations and issues in the investments world. Each box includes a Critical Thinking Question for discussion.

are moving down (decline/recession). It is more difficult to know whether the existing state of the economy will continue or change direction. In the figure, these turning points are shaded. How you will respond to these market conditions depends on the types of investment vehicles you hold (for example, stocks or bonds).

Whatever the state of the economy, the willingness of investors to enter the capital market, and to buy stocks in particular, depends on a basic trust in fair and accurate financial reporting. That trust was shaken by corporate scandals in recent years, as the *Ethics* box above discusses.

Stocks and the Business Cycle Common stocks and other equity-related securities (convertible securities, stock mutual funds, stock options, and stock index futures) are highly responsive to conditions in the economy. Economic conditions are described generically as the *business cycle*. The business cycle reflects the current status of a variety of economic variables, including GDP (gross domestic product), industrial production, personal disposable income, the unemployment rate, and more.

A strong economy is reflected in an expanding business cycle. When business is good and profits are up, stocks react by increasing in value and return. Growth-oriented and speculative stocks tend to do especially well in strong markets. To a lesser extent, so do low-risk and income-oriented stocks. In contrast, when economic activity is declining, the values and returns on common stocks tend to be off as well.

Bonds and Interest Rates Bonds and other forms of fixed-income securities (bond funds and preferred stocks) are highly sensitive to movements in interest rates. In fact, interest rates are the single most important variable in determining bond price behavior and returns to investors. Interest rates and bond prices move in opposite directions (as will be explained in Chapters 10 and 11). Therefore, rising interest rates are unfavorable for bonds already held in an investor's portfolio. Of course, high interest rates enhance the attractiveness of new bonds because these bonds must offer high returns to attract investors.

CONCEPTS IN REVIEW
Answers available at: www.myfinancelab.com

1.11 What should an investor first establish before developing and executing an investment program? Briefly describe each of the seven steps involved in investing.

1.12 What are four common investment goals?

1.13 Define and differentiate among the following. Explain how each is related to federal income taxes.

    a. Active income
    b. Portfolio and passive income
    c. Capital gain
    d. Capital loss
    e. Tax planning
    f. Tax-advantaged retirement vehicles

1.14 Describe the differing investment philosophies typically applied during each of the following stages of an investor's life cycle.

    a. Youth (ages 20 to 45)
    b. Middle age (ages 45 to 60)
    c. Retirement years (age 60 on)

1.15 Describe the four stages of the economic/market cycle, and discuss the impact of this cycle on stock and bond investments.

Meeting Liquidity Needs: Investing in Short-Term Vehicles

LG 6

As discussed earlier, you should ensure that you have adequate liquidity. This provision is a prerequisite to implementing long-term investment goals. *Liquidity* is the ability to convert an investment into cash quickly and with little or no loss in value. A checking account is highly liquid. Stocks and bonds are not liquid, because there is no definite assurance that you will be able to quickly sell them at a price equal to or greater than their purchase price.

■ The Role of Short-Term Vehicles

Short-term vehicles are an important part of most savings and investment programs. They generate income—which can be quite high during periods of high interest rates. However, their primary function is to provide a pool of reserves that can be used for emergencies or simply to accumulate funds for some specific purpose. As a rule of thumb, financial planners often suggest that you hold anywhere from three to six months' worth of after-tax income in short-term vehicles. These funds enable you to meet unexpected needs or to take advantage of attractive opportunities.

Investors usually hold short-term vehicles in their investment portfolios as a *temporary,* highly liquid investment until something better comes along. Some individuals choose to hold short-term vehicles because they simply are more comfortable with them. In fact, this approach has considerable merit during periods of economic and investment instability. Regardless of your motives for holding short-term vehicles, you should evaluate them in terms of their risk and return, just as you would longer-term investments.

Interest on Short-Term Investments Short-term investments earn interest in one of two ways. Some investments, such as savings accounts, pay a *stated rate of interest*. In this case, you can easily find the interest rate—it's the stated rate on the account.

Alternatively, some short-term investments earn interest on a **discount basis**. This means that the security is purchased at a price below its redemption value, and the difference is the interest the investment will earn. U.S. Treasury bills (T-bills), for example, are issued on a discount basis.

Risk Characteristics Short-term investments are generally considered low in risk. Their primary risk results from *inflation risk*—the loss of potential purchasing power that occurs when the rate of return on these investments falls short of the inflation rate. This has often been the case with such vehicles as passbook savings accounts, the traditional bank savings accounts that generally pay a low rate of interest and have no minimum balance. Over long periods of time most other short-term investments have rates of return that are about equal to, or maybe slightly higher than, the average inflation rate.

The *risk of default*—nonpayment—is virtually nonexistent with short-term investment vehicles. The principal reason is that the primary issuers of most short-term vehicles are highly reputable institutions, such as the U.S. Treasury, large banks, and major corporations. In addition, government agencies insure deposits in commercial banks, savings and loans, savings banks, and credit unions for up to $100,000 per account. Finally, because the value of short-term investments does not change much in response to changing interest rates, exposure to capital loss is correspondingly low.

Advantages and Disadvantages of Short-Term Investments As noted, the major advantages of short-term investments are their high liquidity and low risk. Most are available from local financial institutions and can be readily converted to cash with minimal inconvenience. Finally, because the returns on most short-term investments vary with inflation and market interest rates, investors can readily capture higher returns as rates move up. On the negative side, when interest rates go down, returns drop as well.

Although a decline in market rates has undesirable effects on most short-term vehicles, perhaps their biggest disadvantage is their relatively low return. Because these securities are generally so low in risk, you can expect the returns on short-term investments to average less than the returns on long-term investments.

---

discount basis
a method of earning interest on a security by purchasing it at a price below its redemption value; the difference is the interest earned.

WEB EXTENSION

A relatively simple formula can be applied when interest is earned on a discount basis in order to compare returns with vehicles earning a stated rate of interest. See this text's Web site for discussion of the formula.

www.myfinancelab.com

▮ Popular Short-Term Investment Vehicles

A variety of short-term investment vehicles are available to the individual investor. Some are deposit-type accounts in which investors can place money, earn a relatively low rate of interest, and conveniently withdraw funds at their discretion. Part A of Table 1.3 on page 54 summarizes the popular deposit-type accounts. Another group of short-term investment vehicles are those issued by the federal government. The more popular of those vehicles are summarized in Part B of Table 1.3. The final group of short-term vehicles are non-government issues, typically issued by a financial institution, a corporation, or a professional money manager. Part C of Table 1.3 summarizes some of the more popular nongovernment issues.

▮ Investment Suitability

Individual investors use short-term vehicles for both savings and investment. They use short-term vehicles to maintain a desired level of savings that will be readily available if the need arises—in essence, to provide *safety and security.* For this purpose, high yield is less important than safety, liquidity, and convenience. Passbook savings accounts, NOW accounts, and Series EE savings bonds are the most popular savings vehicles.

When investors use short-term vehicles for *investment purposes*, yield is often just as important as liquidity. However, because the objective is different, the short-term vehicles tend to be used much more aggressively. Most investors will hold at least a part of their portfolio in short-term, highly liquid securities, if for no other reason than to be able to act on unanticipated investment opportunities. Some investors, in fact, devote all or most of their portfolios to such securities.

One of the most common uses of short-term securities as investment vehicles is as temporary outlets. For example, if you have just sold some stock but do not have a suitable long-term investment alternative, you might place the proceeds in a money fund until you find a longer-term use for them. Or if you feel that interest rates are about to rise sharply, you might sell your long-term bonds and use the proceeds to buy T-bills. The higher-yielding securities—like MMDAs, CDs, commercial paper, banker's acceptances, and money funds—are generally preferred for this warehousing function, as are asset management accounts at major brokerage firms.

To decide which securities are most appropriate for a particular situation, you need to consider such characteristics as availability, safety, liquidity, and yield. Though all the investments we have discussed satisfy the basic liquidity demand, they do so to varying degrees. A NOW account is unquestionably the most liquid of all. You can write as many checks on the account as you wish and for any amount. A certificate of deposit, on the other hand, is not so liquid, because early redemption involves an interest penalty. Table 1.4 (on page 55) summarizes the key characteristics of the short-term investments described in Table 1.3. The letter grade assigned for each characteristic reflects an estimate of the investment's quality in that area. For example, MMMFs rate only a B+ on liquidity, because withdrawals must usually be made in a minimum amount of $250 to $500. NOW accounts are somewhat better in this respect, because a withdrawal can be

TABLE 1.3   Popular Short-Term Investment Vehicles

Part A. Deposit-Type Accounts

Type of Account	Description	Minimum Balance	Interest Rate	Federal Insurance
Passbook savings account	Savings accounts offered by banks.* Used primarily for convenience or if investors lack sufficient funds to purchase other short-term vehicles.	Typically none	0.5%–4% depending on economy	Yes, up to $100,000 per deposit.
NOW (negotiated order of withdrawal) account	Bank checking account that pays interest on balances.	No legal minimum, but often set at $500 to $1,000	At or near passbook rates	Yes, up to $100,000 per deposit.
Money market deposit account (MMDA)	Bank deposit account with limited check-writing privileges.	No legal minimum, but often set at about $2,500	Typically slightly above passbook rate	Yes, up to $100,000 per deposit.
Asset management account	Deposit account at bank, brokerage house, mutual fund, or insurance company that combines checking, investing, and borrowing. Automatically "sweeps" excess balances into short-term investments and borrows to meet shortages.	Typically $5,000 to $20,000	Similar to MMDAs	Yes, up to $100,000 per deposit in banks. Varies in other institutions.

Part B. Federal Government Issues

Security	Issuer	Description	Initial Maturity	Risk and Return
Series EE savings bonds	U.S. Treasury	Savings bonds issued by the U.S. Treasury in varying denominations, at 50% of face value; earn a fixed rate of interest (set every 6 months in May and December) compounded semianually for 30 years from issue date.	None	Lowest, virtually risk-free
Treasury bills	U.S. Treasury	Issued weekly at auction; sold at a discount; strong secondary market; exempt from local and state income taxes.	91 and 182 days	Lowest, virtually risk-free

Part C. Nongovernment Issues

Security	Issuer	Description	Initial Maturity	Risk and Return
Certificates of deposit (CDs)	Commercial banks	Represent specific cash deposits in commercial banks; amounts and maturities tailored to investor needs.	1 month to 3 years or more	Higher than U.S. Treasury issues and comparable to commercial paper.
Commercial paper	Corporation with a high credit standing	Unsecured note of issuer; large denominations.	3 to 270 days	Higher than U.S. Treasury issues and comparable to negotiable CDs.
Banker's acceptances	Banks	Results from a bank guarantee of a business transaction; sold at a discount from maturity value.	30 to 180 days	About the same as negotiable CDs and commercial paper but higher than U.S. Treasury issues.
Money market mutual funds	Professional portfolio management companies	Professionally managed portfolios of marketable securities; provide instant liquidity.	None—depends on wishes of investor	Vary, but generally higher than U.S. Treasury issues and comparable to negotiable CDs and commercial paper.

*The term *bank* refers to commercial banks, savings and loans (S&Ls), savings banks, and credit unions.

TABLE 1.4 A Scorecard for Short-Term Investment Vehicles

Savings or Investment Vehicle	Availability	Safety	Liquidity	Average Rate*	
Passbook savings account	A+	A+	A	D	(0.6%)
NOW account	A–	A+	A+	F	(0.5%)
Money market deposit account (MMDA)	B	A+	A	B–	(0.7%)
Asset management account	B–	A	A+	B	(1.0%)
Series EE savings bond	A+	A++	C–	B+	(3.7%)
U.S. Treasury bill (91-day)	B–	A++	A–	A–	(5.0%)
Certificate of deposit (3-month, large denomination)	B	A+	C	A	(5.4%)
Commercial paper (90-day)	B–	A–	C	A–	(5.3%)
Banker's acceptance (90-day)	B–	A	B	A–	(5.3%)
Money market mutual fund (MMMF)	B	A/A+	B+	A–	(4.7%)

*The average rates reflect representative or typical rates that existed in late October 2006.

for any amount. Average rates are self-explanatory. You should note, though, that if an investment scores lower on availability, safety, or liquidity, it will generally offer a higher rate.

CONCEPTS IN REVIEW

Answers available at: www.myfinancelab.com

1.16 What makes an asset *liquid?* Why hold liquid assets? Would 100 shares of IBM stock be considered a liquid investment? Explain.

1.17 Explain the characteristics of short-term investments with respect to purchasing power and default risk.

1.18 Briefly describe the key features and differences among the following deposit accounts.
   a. Passbook savings account
   b. NOW account
   c. Money market deposit account
   d. Asset management account

1.19 Define, compare, and contrast the following short-term investments.
   a. Series EE savings bonds
   b. U.S. Treasury bills
   c. Certificates of deposit
   d. Commercial paper
   e. Banker's acceptances
   f. Money market mutual funds

Summary

Note: The end-of-chapter Summaries restate the chapter's Learning Goals and review the key points of information related to each goal.

LG 1   **Understand the meaning of the term *investment* and the factors used to differentiate types of investments.** An investment is any vehicle into which investors can place funds with the expectation of generating positive income and/or of preserving or increasing their value. The returns from investing are received either as current income or as increased value.

Types of investments are securities or property; direct or indirect; debt, equity, or derivatives; low risk or high risk; short-term or long-term; domestic or foreign.

LG 2   **Describe the investment process and types of investors.** Financial institutions and financial markets bring together suppliers and demanders of funds. The dominant U.S. financial market is the securities markets for stocks, bonds, and options. The participants in the investment process are government, business, and individuals. Only individuals are net suppliers of funds. Investors can be either individual investors or institutional investors.

LG 3   **Discuss the principal types of investment vehicles.** Short-term investment vehicles have low risk. They are used to earn a return on temporarily idle funds, to serve as a primary vehicle for conservative investors, and to provide liquidity. Common stocks offer dividends and capital gains. Fixed-income securities—bonds, convertible securities, and preferred stock—offer fixed periodic returns with some potential for gain in value. Mutual funds allow investors to buy or sell interests in a professionally managed, diversified group of securities.

Derivative securities such as options and futures are high-risk, high-expected-return vehicles. Options offer an opportunity to buy or sell another security at a specified price over a given period of time. Futures are contracts between a seller and a buyer for delivery of a specified commodity or financial instrument, at a specified future date, at an agreed-on price. Other popular investment vehicles include tax-advantaged investments, real estate, and tangibles.

LG 4   **Describe the steps in investing and review fundamental personal tax considerations.** Investing should be driven by well-developed plans established to achieve specific goals. It involves a set of steps: meeting investment prerequisites, establishing investment goals, adopting an investment plan, evaluating investment vehicles, selecting suitable investments, constructing a diversified portfolio, and managing the portfolio.

Investors must also consider the tax consequences associated with various investment vehicles and strategies. The key dimensions are ordinary income, capital gains and losses, tax planning, and the use of tax-advantaged retirement vehicles.

LG 5   **Discuss investing over the life cycle and in different economic environments.** The investment vehicles selected are affected by the investor's stage in the life cycle and by economic cycles. Younger investors tend to prefer growth-oriented investments that stress capital gains. As they age, investors move to higher-quality securities. As they approach retirement they become even more conservative. The current and predicted stages of the economy/market—(1) recovery or expansion, (2) decline or recession, or (3) a change in the general direction of its movement—affect investment choice.

LG 6   **Understand the popular types of short-term investment vehicles.** Liquidity needs can be met by investing in various short-term vehicles, which can earn interest at a stated rate or on a discount basis. They typically have low risk. Banks, the government, and brokerage firms offer numerous short-term vehicles. Their suitability depends on the investor's attitude toward availability, safety, liquidity, and rate of return.

Key Terms

Note: A list of Key Terms gathers in one place the new vocabulary presented in each chapter.

bonds, *p. 41*
capital gains, *p. 40*
capital loss, *p. 47*
common stock, *p. 40*
convertible security, *p. 41*
debt, *p.36*
derivative securities, *p. 36*
direct investment, *p. 36*
discount basis, *p. 52*
diversification, *p. 44*
dividends, *p. 40*
domestic investments, *p. 36*
equity, *p. 36*
financial institutions, *p. 37*
financial markets, *p. 37*
fixed-income securities, *p. 41*
foreign investments, *p. 36*
futures, *p. 42*
indirect investment, *p. 36*
individual investors, *p. 37*
institutional investors, *p. 37*
investment, *p. 35*

investment goals, *p. 43*
investment plan, *p. 44*
liquidity, *p. 39*
long-term investments, *p. 36*
market timing, *p. 49*
money market mutual funds, *p. 41*
mutual fund, *p. 41*
net losses, *p. 47*
options, *p. 42*
portfolio, *p. 44*
preferred stock, *p. 41*
property, *p. 35*
real estate, *p. 42*
returns, *p. 35*
risk, *p. 36*
securities, *p. 35*
short-term investments, *p. 36*
short-term vehicles, *p. 39*
speculation, *p. 36*
tangibles, *p. 42*
tax-advantaged investments, *p. 42*
tax planning, *p. 47*

Discussion Questions

LG 4 LG 5

Note: The Discussion Questions at the end of the chapter ask you to analyze and synthesize information presented in the chapter. These questions, like all other end-of-chapter assignment materials, are keyed to the chapter's learning goals.

LG 6

Q1.1. Assume that you are 35 years old, are married with two young children, are renting a condo, and have an annual income of $90,000. Use the following questions to guide your preparation of a rough investment plan consistent with these facts.
   a. What are your key investment goals?
   b. How might personal taxes affect your investment plans? Use current tax rates to assess their impact.
   c. How might your stage in the life cycle affect the types of risk you might take?

Q1.2. What role, if any, will short-term vehicles play in your portfolio? Why? Complete the following table for the short-term investments listed. Find their yields in a current issue of the *Wall Street Journal*, and explain which, if any, you would include in your investment portfolio.

Savings or Investment Vehicle	Minimum Balance	Interest Rate	Federal Insurance	Method and Ease of Withdrawing Funds
a. Passbook savings account	None		Yes	In person or through teller machines; very easy
b. NOW account				Unlimited check-writing privileges
c. Money market deposit account (MMDA)				
d. Asset management account				
e. Series EE savings bond	Virtually none			
f. U.S. Treasury bill				
g. Certificate of deposit (CD)				
h. Commercial paper				
i. Banker's acceptance				
j. Money market mutual fund (MMMF)				

Problems

LG 4   **LG 5**

Note: The Problems at the end of the chapter offer opportunities to perform calculations using the tools and techniques learned in the chapter. Visit www.myfinancelab.com to find select end-of-chapter problems online and additional practice opportunities.

P1.1 Sonia Gomez, a 45-year-old widow, wishes to accumulate $250,000 over the next 15 years to supplement the retirement programs that are being funded by the federal government and her employer. She expects to earn an average annual return of about 8% by investing in a low-risk portfolio containing about 20% short-term securities, 30% common stock, and 50% bonds.

Sonia currently has $31,500 that at an 8% annual rate of return will grow to about $100,000 at the end of 15 years (found using time-value techniques that will be described in Chapter 4 Appendix). Her financial adviser indicated that for every $1,000 Sonia wishes to accumulate at the end of 15 years, she will have to make an annual investment of $36.83. (This amount is also calculated on the basis of an 8% annual rate of return using the time-value techniques that are described in the Chapter 4 Appendix.) Sonia plans to accumulate needed funds by making equal, annual, end-of-year investments over the next 15 years.

a. How much money does Sonia need to accumulate by making equal, annual, end-of-year investments to reach her goal of $250,000?

b. How much must Sonia deposit annually to accumulate at the end of year 15 the sum calculated in part **a**?

LG 4

P1.2 During 2006, the Allens and the Zells both filed joint tax returns. The Allens' taxable income was $130,000, and the Zells had total taxable income of $65,000 for the tax year ended December 31, 2006.

a. Using the federal tax rates given in Table 1.2, calculate the taxes for both the Allens and the Zells.

b. Calculate and compare the ratio of the Allens' to the Zells' taxable income and the ratio of the Allens' to the Zells' taxes. What does this demonstrate about the federal income tax structure?

LG 4   P1.3   Robert Pang, a 53-year-old software engineer, and his wife, Jean, have $50,000 to invest. They will need the money at retirement in 10 years. They are considering 2 investments. The first is a utility company common stock that costs $50 per share and pays dividends of $2 per share per year (a 4% dividend yield). Note that these dividends will be taxed at the same rates that apply to long-term capital gains. The Pangs do not expect the value of this stock to increase. The other investment under consideration is a highly rated corporate bond that currently sells at par in $1,000 increments, and pays annual interest at a rate of 5%, or $50 per $1,000 invested. After 10 years, these bonds will be repaid at par, or $1,000 per $1,000 invested. Assume that the Pangs keep the income from their investments, but do not reinvest it (they keep the cash under a mattress). They will, however, need to pay income taxes on their investment income. They will sell the stock after 10 years if they buy it. If they buy the bonds, in 10 years they will get back the amount they invested. The Pangs are in the 33% tax bracket.

- a. How many shares of the stock can the Pangs buy?
- b. How much will they receive each year in dividend income if they buy the stock, after taxes?
- c. What is the total amount they would have from their original $50,000 if they purchased the stock and it all went as planned?
- d. How much will they receive each year in interest if they purchase the bonds, after taxes?
- e. What is the total amount they would have from their original $50,000 if they purchased the bonds and all went as planned?
- f. Based only on your calculations and ignoring other risk factors, should they buy the stock or the bonds?

LG 4   P1.4   Mike and Linda Smith are a working couple. They will file a joint income tax return. This year, they have the following taxable income:

1. $125,000 from salary and wages (ordinary income).
2. $1,000 in interest income.
3. $3,000 in dividend income.
4. $2,000 in profit from sale of a stock they purchased 2 years ago.
5. $2,000 in profit from a stock they purchased this year and sold this year.

Use the federal income tax rates given in Table 1.2 to work this problem.

- a. How much will Mike and Linda pay in federal income taxes on **2** above?
- b. How much will Mike and Linda pay in federal income taxes on **3** above? (*Note:* Remember that dividend income is taxed differently than ordinary income.)
- c. How much will Mike and Linda pay in federal income taxes on **4** above?
- d. How much will Mike and Linda pay in federal income taxes on **5** above?

See www.myfinancelab.com **for Web Exercises, Spreadsheets, and other online resources.**

Case Problem 1.1   *Investments or Golf?*

LG 1   LG 2   LG 3

Note: Two Case Problems appear at the end of every chapter. They ask you to apply what you have learned in the chapter to a hypothetical investment situation.

Judd Read and Judi Todd, senior accounting majors at a large midwestern university, have been good friends since high school. Each has already found a job that will begin after graduation. Judd has accepted a position as an internal auditor in a medium-sized manufacturing firm. Judi will be working for one of the major public accounting firms. Each is looking forward to the challenge of a new career and to the prospect of achieving success both professionally and financially.

Judd and Judi are preparing to register for their final semester. Each has one free elective to select. Judd is considering taking a golf course offered by the physical education department, which he says will help him socialize in his business career. Judi is planning to take a basic investments course. Judi has been trying to convince Judd to take investments instead of golf. Judd believes he doesn't need to take investments, because he already knows what common stock is. He believes that whenever he has accumulated excess funds, he can invest in the stock of a company that is doing well. Judi argues that there is much more to it than simply choosing common stock. She feels that exposure to the field of investments would be more beneficial than learning how to play golf.

Questions

a. Explain to Judd the structure of the investment process and the economic importance of investing.

b. List and discuss the other types of investment vehicles with which Judd is apparently unfamiliar.

c. Assuming that Judd already gets plenty of exercise, what arguments would you give to convince Judd to take investments rather than golf?

Case Problem 1.2   *Preparing Carolyn Bowen's Investment Plan*

LG 4   LG 5   LG 6

Carolyn Bowen, who just turned 55, is a widow currently employed as a receptionist for the Xcon Corporation, where she has worked for the past 20 years. She is in good health, lives alone, and has 2 grown children. A few months ago, her husband died. Carolyn's husband left her with only their home and the proceeds from a $75,000 life insurance policy. After she paid medical and funeral expenses, $60,000 of the life insurance proceeds remained. In addition to the life insurance proceeds, Carolyn has $37,500 in a savings account, which she had secretly built over the past 10 years. Recognizing that she is within 10 years of retirement, Carolyn wishes to use her limited resources to develop an investment program that will allow her to live comfortably once she retires.

Carolyn is quite superstitious. After consulting with a number of psychics and studying her family tree, she feels certain she will not live past 80. She plans to retire at either 62 or 65, whichever will better allow her to meet her long-run financial goals. After talking with a number of knowledgeable individuals—including, of course, the psychics—Carolyn estimates that to live comfortably, she will need $45,000 per year, before taxes, once she retires. This amount will be required annually for each of 18 years if she retires at 62 or for each of 15 years if she retires at 65. As part of her financial plans, Carolyn intends to sell her home at retirement and rent an apartment. She has estimated that she will net $112,500 if she sells the house at 62 and $127,500 if she sells it at 65. Carolyn has no financial dependents and is not concerned about leaving a sizable estate to her heirs.

If Carolyn retires at age 62, she will receive from Social Security and an employer-sponsored pension plan a total of $1,359 per month ($16,308 annually); if she waits until age 65 to retire, her total retirement income will be $1,688 per month ($20,256 annually). For convenience, Carolyn has already decided that to convert all her assets at the time of retirement into a stream of annual income, she will at that time purchase an annuity by paying a single premium. The annuity will have a life just equal to the number of years remaining until her 80th birthday. Because Carolyn is uncertain as to the actual age at which she will retire, she obtained the following interest factors from her insurance agent to estimate the annual annuity benefit provided for a given purchase price.

Life of Annuity	Interest Factor
15 years	11.118
18 years	12.659

The yearly annuity benefit can be calculated by dividing the factors into the purchase price. Carolyn plans to place any funds currently available into a savings account paying 6% compounded annually until retirement. She does not expect to be able to save or invest any additional funds between now and retirement. To calculate the future value of her savings, she will need to multiply the amount of money currently available to her by one of the following factors, depending on the retirement age being considered.

Retirement Age	Time to Retirement	Future-Value Interest Factor
62	7 years	1.504
65	10 years	1.791

Questions

a. Assume that Carolyn places currently available funds in the savings account. Determine the amount of money Carolyn will have available at retirement once she sells her house if she retires at (1) age 62 and (2) age 65.

b. Using the results from question (a) and the interest factors given above, determine the level of annual income that will be provided to Carolyn through purchase of an annuity at (1) age 62 and (2) age 65.

c. With the results found in the preceding questions, determine the total annual retirement income Carolyn will have if she retires at (1) age 62 and (2) age 65.

d. From your findings, do you think Carolyn will be able to achieve her long-run financial goal by retiring at (1) age 62 or (2) age 65? Explain.

e. Evaluate Carolyn's investment plan in terms of her use of a savings account and an annuity rather than some other investment vehicles. Comment on the risk and return characteristics of her plan. What recommendations might you offer Carolyn? Be specific.

Excel with Spreadsheets

Note: Excel spreadsheet exercises at the end of each chapter will assist you in learning some useful applications of this tool in the personal investing process.

In the following chapters of this text, you will be asked to solve spreadsheet problems using Microsoft Excel®. While each person's skill and experience with Excel will vary, we assume that you understand the basics of Excel. This includes the entering of text and numbers, copying or moving a cell, moving and copying using "drag and drop," inserting and deleting rows and columns, and checking your spelling. The review in this chapter focuses on entering and editing data in the worksheet.

To complete the spreadsheet review, go to www.myfinancelab.com and go to "Student Resources." Click on "Spreadsheet Review." There you will be asked to create a spreadsheet and perform the following tasks.

Questions

a. Add and subtract data with a formula.
b. Multiply and divide data with a formula.
c. Total cells using the sum function and calculate an average.
d. Use the average function.
e. Copy a formula using the "drag and drop" method.

Chapter 2

Markets and Transactions

LEARNING GOALS

After studying this chapter, you should be able to:

LG 1 Identify the basic types of securities markets and describe the IPO process.

LG 2 Explain the characteristics of broker markets.

LG 3 Understand dealer markets, alternative trading systems, and the general conditions of securities markets.

LG 4 Review the key aspects of global securities markets, including the risks associated with foreign investments.

LG 5 Discuss trading hours and the regulation of securities markets.

LG 6 Explain long purchases, margin transactions, and short sales.

"Wall Street" is synonymous with investing and capital markets. From its beginning in 1792, when only three government bonds and two bank stocks were traded, the securities industry has grown to the point where tens of billions of dollars in securities are traded daily. Wall Street gets its name from the original street that ran parallel to the 12-foot-high wooden stockade erected in 1653 across lower Manhattan to protect the Dutch settlers from attacks by the British and Indians.

Through a series of acquisitions and mergers, the NYSE Group, Inc. has become the largest-ever securities exchange. Formed in April 2006, it combines into one publicly-owned exchange the New York Stock Exchange, the Pacific Stock Exchange, and the Archipelago Exchange. In mid-2006, the NYSE Group agreed to a merger with Euronext, a consortium of Paris, Brussels, Lisbon, and Amsterdam stock exchanges and the London-based electronic derivatives market Euronext.liffe.

The NYSE had been criticized for its adherence to a traditional people-centered trading system. Institutional investors had been moving more of their trades from the exchange floor to electronic communications networks (ECNs) such as Archipelago and Instinet. The NYSE–Archipelago merger will help the NYSE address the electronic trading issue.

The NYSE is not the only exchange pursuing mergers. A few years ago Nasdaq, the pioneer of an electronic trading system that eliminates intermediaries, was grabbing market share from the NYSE. Its less stringent listing requirements and state-of-the-art technology made Nasdaq the preferred route for entrepreneurial companies to raise capital. Today, Nasdaq owns Instinet and remains popular with many investors.

The increasing competition among exchanges should benefit investors. It will promote better governance, encourage more innovation, and result in technological advances that improve the quality, fairness, and accuracy of securities transactions.

In this chapter, we will study the capital markets, the exchanges, the regulations, and the transactions that enable companies to raise money in capital markets and institutions, and individuals to invest in these companies.

Sources: "Timeline," downloaded from http://www.nyse.com (accessed July 14, 2006); Chris Rice, "Market Mergers Good News for Investors," downloaded from http://www.ssga.com (accessed July 14, 2006); and "NYSE Group and Euronext N.V. Agree to a Merger of Equals," NYSE press release, dated June 2, 2006, downloaded from http://www.nyse.com (accessed July 14, 2006).

Securities Markets

LG 1 LG 2 LG 3

securities markets
forums that allow suppliers
and demanders of *securities*
to make financial transactions;
they include both the *money
market* and the *capital market*.

money market
market where *short-term*
securities (with maturities
less than one year) are bought
and sold.

capital market
market in which *long-term*
securities (with maturities
greater than one year) such as
stocks and bonds are bought
and sold.

primary market
the market in which *new issues*
of securities are sold to the
public.

initial public offering (IPO)
the first public sale of a
company's stock.

**Securities and Exchange
Commission (SEC)**
federal agency that regulates
securities offerings and markets.

public offering
the sale of a firm's securities to
the general public.

rights offering
an offer of new shares of stock
to existing stockholders on a pro
rata basis.

private placement
the sale of new securities
directly, without SEC
registration, to selected
groups of investors.

Securities markets are forums that allow suppliers and demanders of *securities* to make financial transactions. They permit such transactions to be made quickly and at a fair price. In this section we will look at the various types of markets, their organization, and their general behavior.

▮ Types of Securities Markets

Securities markets may be classified as either money markets or capital markets. The **money market** is the market where *short-term* securities (with maturities less than one year) are bought and sold. Investors turn to the **capital market** to make transactions involving *long-term* securities (with maturities greater than one year), such as stocks and bonds. In this book we will devote most of our attention to the capital market. There, investors can make transactions in stocks, bonds, mutual funds, options, and futures. Capital markets can be classified as either *primary* or *secondary*, depending on whether securities are being sold initially by the issuing company or are resold by intervening owners.

The Primary Market The market in which *new issues* of securities are sold to the public is the **primary market**. In the primary market, the issuer of the equity or debt securities receives the proceeds of sales. In 2005, only 162 companies offered their stock for sale in the primary market. This number compared unfavorably with the 457 companies that went public six years earlier. The main vehicle in the primary market is the **initial public offering (IPO)**, the first public sale of a company's stock. The primary markets also provide a forum for the sale of new securities, called s*easoned new issues*, by companies that are already public.

Before offering its securities for public sale, the issuer must register them with and obtain approval from the **Securities and Exchange Commission (SEC)**. This federal regulatory agency must confirm both the adequacy and the accuracy of the information provided to potential investors before a security is publicly offered for sale. In addition, the SEC regulates the securities markets.

To market its securities in the primary market, a firm has three choices. It may make (1) a **public offering**, in which the firm offers its securities for sale to the general public; (2) a **rights offering**, in which the firm offers new shares to existing stockholders on a pro rata basis; or (3) a **private placement**, in which the firm sells new securities directly, without SEC registration, to selected groups of investors such as insurance companies and pension funds.

Going Public: The IPO Process Most companies that go public are small, fast-growing companies that require additional capital to continue expanding. For example, FortuNet, Inc., a manufacturer of multi-player, computer-based casino gaming software, raised about $22.5 million when it went public in January 2006 at $9 per share. In addition, large companies may decide to spin off a unit into a separate public corporation. McDonald's did this when it spun off its Chipotle Mexican Grill, a 489-location, Mexican-food restaurant chain, in January 2006, raising about $174 million at $22 per share.

HOTLINKS
The SEC site, in addition to providing access
to corporate filings and documents offers
a wealth of investor information.
www.sec.gov

prospectus
a portion of a security registration statement that describes the key aspects of the issue, the issuer, and its management and financial position.

red herring
a preliminary *prospectus* made available to prospective investors during the waiting period between the registration statement's filing with the SEC and its approval.

investment banker
financial intermediary that specializes in selling new security issues and advising firms with regard to major financial transactions.

When a company decides to go public, it first must obtain the approval of its current shareholders, the investors who own its privately issued stock. Next, the company's auditors and lawyers must certify that all documents for the company are legitimate. The company then finds an investment bank willing to *underwrite* the offering. This underwriter is responsible for promoting the stock and facilitating the sale of the company's IPO shares. The underwriter often brings in other investment banking firms as participants. We'll discuss the role of the investment banker in more detail in the next section.

The company files a registration statement with the SEC. One portion of this statement is called the **prospectus**. It describes the key aspects of the issue, the issuer, and its management and financial position. During the waiting period between the statement's filing and its approval, prospective investors can receive a preliminary prospectus. This preliminary version is called a **red herring**, because a notice printed in red on the front cover indicates the tentative nature of the offer. The cover of the preliminary prospectus describing the 2006 stock issue of J. Crew, a nationally recognized apparel and accessories brand with a multi-channel distribution system, is shown in Figure 2.1. Note the red herring printed vertically on its left edge.

After the SEC approves the registration statement, the investment community can begin analyzing the company's prospects. However, from the time it files until at least one month after the IPO is complete, the company must observe a *quiet period*, during which there are restrictions on what company officials may say about the company. The purpose of the quiet period is to make sure that all potential investors have access to the same information about the company—that which is presented in the preliminary prospectus—and not to any unpublished data that might give them an unfair advantage.

The investment bankers and company executives promote the company's stock offering through a *road show*, a series of presentations to potential investors—typically institutional investors—around the country and sometimes overseas. In addition to providing investors with information about the new issue, road show sessions help the investment bankers gauge the demand for the offering and set an expected pricing range. After the underwriter sets terms and prices the issue, the SEC must approve the offering.

Table 2.1 (on page 68) shows, for each year between 1996 and 2005, the number of offerings, the average first-day return, and the gross proceeds of the given years' IPOs. Note the exceptionally high first-day returns and large number of offerings during 1999 and 2000 caused by the technology-stock-driven bull market that ended in late 2000. Since then, the number of offerings and the first-day returns have declined dramatically, consistent with the precipitous market decline that occurred in 2001 and 2002.

The IPO markets have become more active in recent years. Their improvement has been a direct result of a strengthening of the public equity markets. Investing in IPOs is risky business, particularly for individual investors who can't easily acquire shares at the offering price. Most of those shares go to institutional investors and brokerage firms' best clients. Although news stories may chronicle huge first-day gains, the stocks may not be good long-term investments.

The Investment Banker's Role Most public offerings are made with the assistance of an **investment banker**. The investment banker is a financial inter-

FIGURE 2.1

Cover of a Preliminary Prospectus for a Stock Issue

Some of the key factors related to the 2006 common stock issue by J. Crew are summarized on the cover of the prospectus. The type printed vertically on the left edge is normally red, which explains its name "red herring." (*Source:* J. Crew Group, Inc., June 13, 2006, p. 1.)

The information in this preliminary prospectus is not complete and may be changed. These securities may not be sold until the registration statement filed with the Securities and Exchange Commission is effective. This preliminary prospectus is not an offer to sell nor does it seek an offer to buy these securities in any jurisdiction where the offer or sale is not permitted.

Subject to Completion. Dated June 13, 2006.

18,800,000 Shares

J.CREW

Common Stock

This is the initial public offering of shares of common stock of J.Crew Group, Inc.

J.Crew® is offering all of the shares to be sold in the offering.

Prior to this offering, there has been no public market for the common stock. It is currently estimated that the initial public offering price per share will be between $15.00 and $17.00. The common stock has been approved for listing on the New York Stock Exchange under the symbol "JCG."

See "Risk Factors" beginning on page 9 to read about factors you should consider before buying shares of the common stock.

Neither the Securities and Exchange Commission nor any other regulatory body has approved or disapproved of these securities or passed upon the accuracy or adequacy of this prospectus. Any representation to the contrary is a criminal offense.

	Per Share	Total
Initial public offering price	$	$
Underwriting discount	$	$
Proceeds, before expenses, to J.Crew	$	$

To the extent that the underwriters sell more than 18,800,000 shares of common stock, the underwriters have the option to purchase up to an additional 2,820,000 shares from J.Crew at the initial public offering price less the underwriting discount.

The underwriters expect to deliver the shares against payment in New York, New York on   , 2006.

Goldman, Sachs & Co.   **Bear, Stearns & Co. Inc.**

Banc of America Securities LLC   **Citigroup**   **Credit Suisse**

JPMorgan   **Lehman Brothers**   **Wachovia Securities**

Prospectus dated   , 2006.

underwriting
the role of the *investment banker* in bearing the risk of reselling, at a profit, the securities purchased from an issuing corporation at an agreed-on price.

underwriting syndicate
a group formed by an investment banker to share the financial risk associated with *underwriting* new securities.

mediary (such as Goldman, Sachs & Co. or Citigroup) that specializes in selling new security issues and advising firms with regard to major financial transactions. The main activity of the investment banker is **underwriting**. This process involves purchasing the security issue from the issuing corporation at an agreed-on price and bearing the risk of reselling it to the public at a profit. The investment banker also provides the issuer with advice about pricing and other important aspects of the issue.

In the case of very large security issues, the investment banker brings in other bankers as partners to form an **underwriting syndicate**. The syndicate shares the financial risk associated with buying the entire issue from the issuer and reselling the new securities to the public. The originating investment

TABLE 2.1   Annual IPO Data, 1996–2005

Year	Number of Offerings	Average First-Day Return (%)	Gross Proceeds ($ billion)
1996	621	16.7	40.65
1997	432	13.9	28.97
1998	269	22.3	32.20
1999	457	71.7	62.69
2000	346	56.1	60.54
2001	76	14.4	33.97
2002	67	8.9	22.11
2003	62	12.1	9.58
2004	179	12.1	32.04
2005	162	10.0	28.37

Source: Jay R. Ritter, "Some Factoids About the 2005 IPO Market," downloaded from Web site (http://bearcba.ufl.edu/ritter/work_papers/SomeFactoidsAboutthe2005IPOMarket.pdf), June 27, 2006, Table 1.

selling group
a large number of brokerage firms that join the originating investment banker(s); each accepts responsibility for selling a certain portion of a new security issue.

banker and the syndicate members put together a **selling group**, normally made up of themselves and a large number of brokerage firms. Each member of the selling group accepts the responsibility for selling a certain portion of the issue and is paid a commission on the securities it sells. The selling process for a large security issue is depicted in Figure 2.2.

The relationships among the participants in this process can also be seen on the cover of the June 13, 2006, preliminary prospectus for the common stock offering for J. Crew in Figure 2.1 on page 67. The layout of the prospectus cover indicates the roles of the various participating firms. Isolated firm names or a larger typeface differentiates the underwriter or underwriting syndicate

FIGURE 2.2

The Selling Process for a Large Security Issue

The investment banker hired by the issuing corporation may form an underwriting syndicate. The underwriting syndicate buys the entire security issue from the issuing corporation at an agreed-on price. The underwriter then has the opportunity (and bears the risk) of reselling the issue to the public at a profit. Both the originating investment banker and the other syndicate members put together a selling group to sell the issue on a commission basis to investors.

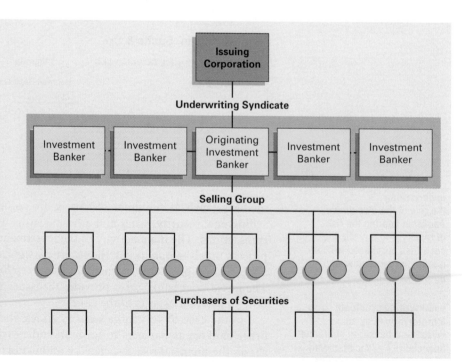

(Goldman, Sachs & Co. and Bear, Stearns & Co. Inc.) from the selling group (names in smaller font below).

Compensation for underwriting and selling services typically comes in the form of a discount on the sale price of the securities. For example, an investment banker may pay the issuing firm $24 per share for stock that will be sold for $26 per share. The investment banker may then sell the shares to members of the selling group for $25.25 per share. In this case, the original investment banker earns $1.25 per share ($25.25 sale price − $24 purchase price). The members of the selling group earn 75 cents for each share they sell ($26 sale price − $25.25 purchase price). Although some primary security offerings are directly placed by the issuer, the majority of new issues are sold through public offering via the mechanism just described.

secondary market
the market in which securities are traded *after they have been issued;* an *aftermarket.*

Nasdaq market
a major segment of the *secondary market* that employs an all-electronic trading platform to execute trades.

over-the-counter (OTC) market
a segment of the *secondary market* that involves trading in smaller, unlisted securities.

Secondary Markets The **secondary market**, or the *aftermarket*, is the market in which securities are traded *after they have been issued*. It permits an investor to easily sell his or her holdings to someone else. Unlike the primary market, secondary-market transactions do not involve the corporation that issued the securities. The secondary market gives securities purchasers *liquidity*. It also provides a mechanism for continuous pricing of securities to reflect their value at each point in time, on the basis of the best information then available.

One major segment of the secondary markets consists of the various *securities exchanges*, which are forums where the buyers and sellers of securities are brought together to execute trades. Another major segment of the market is made up of those securities that are listed and traded on the **Nasdaq market**, which employs an all-electronic trading platform to execute trades. Finally, there is the **over-the-counter (OTC) market**, which involves trading in smaller, unlisted securities. Each of these markets is covered in more detail below.

▌Broker Markets and Dealer Markets

By far, the vast majority of trades made by individual investors take place in the secondary market, and as a result, we'll primarily focus on it throughout the rest of this section. When you look at the secondary market *on the basis of how securities are traded*, you'll find you can essentially divide the market into two segments: broker markets and dealer markets. Figure 2.3 (on page 70) depicts the makeup of the secondary market in terms of broker or dealer markets. As you can see, the *broker market* consists of national and regional "securities exchanges," whereas the *dealer market* is made up of both the Nasdaq market and the OTC market.

broker market
the *securities exchanges* on which the two sides of a transaction, the buyer and seller, are brought together to trade securities.

dealer market
the market in which the buyer and seller are not brought together directly but instead have their orders executed by *dealers* that make markets in the given security.

Before we look at these markets in more detail, it's important to understand that probably *the biggest difference in the two markets is a technical point dealing with the way trades are executed*. That is, when a trade occurs in a **broker market** (on one of the so-called "securities exchanges"), the two sides to the transaction, the buyer and the seller, are brought together and the trade takes place at that point: Party A sells his or her securities directly to the buyer, Party B. In a sense, with the help of a *broker*, the securities effectively change hands on the floor of the exchange.

In contrast, when trades are made in a **dealer market**, the buyer and the seller are never brought together directly. Instead, their buy/sell orders are

FIGURE 2.3

Broker and Dealer Markets

On a typical trading day, the secondary market is a beehive of activity, where literally billions of shares change hands. The market consists of two distinct parts—the *broker market* and the *dealer market*. As shown, each of these markets is made up of various exchanges and trading venues.

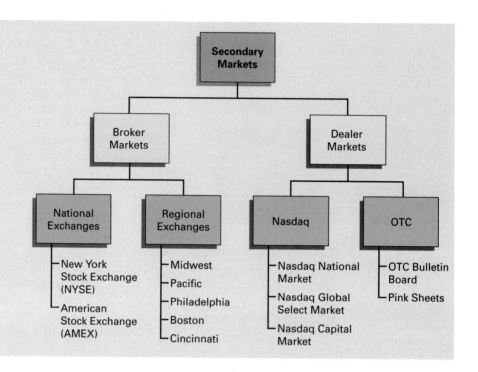

market makers
securities dealers that "make markets" by offering to buy or sell certain securities at stated prices.

executed by **market makers**, who are *securities dealers* that "make markets" by offering to buy or sell certain securities at stated prices. Essentially, two separate trades are made: Party A sells his or her securities (in, say, the XYZ Corp.) to a dealer, and Party B buys his or her securities (in the same XYZ Corp.) from another, or possibly even the same, dealer. Thus, there is always a dealer (*market maker*) on one side of a dealer-market transaction.

Broker Markets If you're like most individual investors, when you think of the "stock market" the first name to come to mind is the New York Stock Exchange (NYSE). Actually, the NYSE is the dominant broker market. Also included in this market are the American Stock Exchange (AMEX), another *national exchange*, as well as several so-called *regional exchanges*. One of the things that these exchanges have in common is that all the trading takes place on centralized trading floors. These exchanges account for about 60% of the *total dollar volume* of all shares traded in the U.S. stock market.

The *New York Stock Exchange (NYSE)* is one of two national exchanges in the United States, and is, in fact, the biggest securities exchange in the world. Known as "the Big Board," it accounts for over 350 billion shares of stock that, at year-end 2005, had a market value of some $13.3 trillion. It has very stringent listing requirements, and in 2006, there were more than 2,700 firms from around the world that listed their shares on the NYSE.

The *American Stock Exchange (AMEX)* is the second largest stock exchange in terms of the number of listed companies. However, when it comes to the dollar volume of trading, the AMEX is actually smaller than the largest regional exchange (the Midwest, in Chicago). It is home to about 700 listed stocks and handles about 4% of the total annual dollar volume of shares traded on all U.S. securities exchanges. In contrast, the NYSE handles around 90% of all common shares traded on organized exchanges, so the AMEX is far smaller than the New York Stock Exchange in terms of size or stature. Even so, the AMEX has created a strong market niche for itself through the listing and trading of the very popular exchange-traded funds (ETFs), a type of index-based mutual fund that we will discuss in Chapter 12.

In addition to the NYSE and AMEX, there are also a handful of so-called *regional exchanges* that are part of the broker market. The number of securities listed on each of these exchanges is typically in the range of 100 to 500 companies. As a group they handle around 6% of all shares traded on organized exchanges. The best known of these are the Midwest, Pacific, Philadelphia, Boston, and Cincinnati exchanges. These exchanges deal primarily in securities with local and regional appeal. Most are modeled after the NYSE, but their membership and listing requirements are considerably more lenient. To enhance their trading activity, regional exchanges will often list securities that are also listed on the NYSE or AMEX.

Other broker markets include foreign stock exchanges that list and trade shares of firms in their own foreign markets. Also, separate domestic exchanges exist for options trading and for trading in futures. Here we will consider the basic structure, rules, and operations of each of the major exchanges in the broker markets. (We'll discuss foreign exchanges later.)

The New York Stock Exchange Most securities exchanges are modeled after the New York Stock Exchange (NYSE). It is the dominant organized exchange. To be a member, an individual or firm must own or lease one of the 1,366 "seats" on the exchange. The word "seat" is used only figuratively, because its members trade securities standing up. The majority of seat holders are brokerage firms, and each typically owns more than one seat.

Firms such as Merrill Lynch designate officers to occupy seats. Only such designated individuals can make transactions on the floor of the exchange. There are two main types of floor brokers—commission brokers and independent brokers. *Commission brokers* execute orders for their firm's customers. An *independent broker* works for himself or herself and handles orders on a fee basis, typically for smaller brokerage firms or large firms that are too busy to handle their own orders.

Trading Activity The floor of the NYSE is an area about the size of a football field. Its operation is typical of the various exchanges (though details vary). The NYSE floor has 20 trading posts. Certain stocks trade at each post. (Bonds and less active stocks are traded in an annex.) Around the perimeter are telephones and electronic equipment that transmit buy and sell orders from brokers' offices to the exchange floor and back again after members execute the orders.

All transactions on the floor of the exchange occur through an auction process. The goal is to fill all buy orders at the lowest price and to fill all sell orders at the highest price, with supply and demand determining the price. The actual auction takes place at the post where the particular security trades. Members interested in purchasing a given security publicly negotiate a transaction with members interested in selling that security. The job of the **specialist**—an exchange member who specializes in making transactions in one or more stocks—is to manage the auction process. The specialist buys or sells (at specified prices) to provide a continuous, fair, and orderly market in those securities assigned to her or him.

HOT LINKS
What are the stock markets doing today? Get the latest market summary and other statistics at the New York Stock Exchange site.
http://www.nyse.com/home.html

INVESTOR FACTS
A VOTRE SANTÉ—In a creative application of the principles of broker market supply and demand, a bar in Paris has modeled its drink pricing on the London Stock Exchange. Drink prices start at a set amount each night and then rise and fall based on customer demand. A run on Heineken beer, for example, will send its price up, while other less-ordered drinks fall in price. Screens above the bar, which refresh every 4 minutes, show price changes. Periodically each evening, "market crashes" reset prices, and everything starts over again.

WEB EXTENSION
An *Ethics in Investing* box at the book's Web site discusses the powerful role of specialists, and its possible abuse.
www.myfinancelab.com

specialist
stock exchange member who specializes in making transactions in one or more stocks and manages the auction process.

Listing Policies To list its shares on a stock exchange, a firm must file an application and meet certain listing requirements. As noted earlier, some firms have **dual listing**, or listings on more than one exchange.

The New York Stock Exchange has the strictest listing requirements. To be listed on the NYSE, a U.S. firm must have at least 2,200 stockholders owning 100 or more shares and a minimum of 1.1 million shares of publicly held stock outstanding; aggregate pretax earnings of at least $10 million over the previous three years, with no loss in the previous two years; and a minimum market value of public shares of $100 million. Foreign companies are subject to slightly higher listing requirements. The firm also must pay a listing fee of between $150,000 and $250,000. Once the NYSE accepts a firm's securities for listing, the company must continue to meet SEC requirements for exchange-listed securities. Listed firms that fail to meet specified requirements may be *de-listed* from the exchange.

The American Stock Exchange The American Stock Exchange (AMEX) has organization and procedures similar to those of the NYSE. Because its listing requirements are less stringent, many smaller and younger firms choose to list on the AMEX. The AMEX has approximately 850 seats and about 800 listed stocks.

In recent years the AMEX has reinvented itself to focus on more specialized market instruments. Today about two-thirds of its daily volume comes from *exchange-traded funds (ETFs)*, a security pioneered by AMEX more than 10 years ago. These funds are baskets of securities that are designed to generally track an index of the broad stock or bond market, a stock industry sector, or an international stock, but that trade like a single stock. Trading in stock options accounts for another large segment of the AMEX's business.

Regional Stock Exchanges Most regional exchanges are modeled after the NYSE, but their membership and listing requirements are considerably more lenient. Trading costs are also lower. The majority of securities listed on regional exchanges are also listed on the NYSE or the AMEX. About 100 million NYSE shares pass through one of the regional exchanges on a typical trading day. This dual listing may enhance a security's trading activity. In addition, the *Intermarket Trading System (ITS)* links nine markets—five regional exchanges, the NYSE, the AMEX, the Nasdaq National Market, and the Chicago Board Options Exchange—through an electronic communications network that allows brokers and other traders to make transactions at the best prices.

Options Exchanges *Options* allow their holders to sell or to buy another security at a specified price over a given period of time. The dominant options exchange is the Chicago Board Options Exchange (CBOE). Options are also traded on the AMEX, on the Boston, Pacific, Philadelphia exchanges, and on the International Securities Exchange (ISE). Usually, an option to sell or buy a given security is listed on all five options exchanges. Options exchanges deal only in security options. Other types of options (not discussed in this text) result from private transactions made directly between sellers and buyers.

Futures Exchanges *Futures* are contracts that guarantee the delivery of a specified commodity or financial instrument at a specific future date at an agreed-on price. The dominant exchange for trading commodity and financial futures is the Chicago Board of Trade (CBT). There are a number of other futures exchanges, some of which specialize in certain commodities and financial instruments rather than handling the broad spectrum listed on the CBT. The largest of these exchanges are the New York Mercantile Exchange, the Chicago Mercantile Exchange, the Deutsche Terminboerse, the London International Financial Futures and Options Exchange, the New York Coffee, Sugar & Cocoa Exchange, the New York Cotton Exchange, the Kansas City Board of Trade, and the Minneapolis Grain Exchange.

Dealer Markets One of the key features of the *dealer market* is that it has no centralized trading floors. Instead, it is made up of a large number of "market makers" who are linked together via a mass telecommunications network. Each market maker is actually a securities dealer who makes a market in one or more securities by offering to buy or sell them at stated bid/ask prices. (The **bid price** and **ask price** represent, respectively, the highest price offered to purchase a given security and the lowest price at which the security is offered for sale. In effect, an investor pays the ask price when *buying* securities and receives the bid price when *selling* them.) The dealer market is made up of both the Nasdaq and the OTC markets, which account for about 40% of all shares traded in the U.S. market—with the Nasdaq accounting for the overwhelming majority of those trades. (As an aside, the *primary market* is also a dealer market, because all new issues—*IPOs* and **secondary distributions**, which involve the public sale of large blocks of previously issued securities held by large investors—are sold to the investing public by securities dealers, acting on behalf of the investment banker.)

The largest dealer market is made up of a select list of stocks that are listed and traded on the *National Association of Securities Dealers Automated Quotation System*, typically referred to as *Nasdaq*. Founded in 1971, Nasdaq had its origins in the OTC market, but is today considered *a totally separate entity that's no longer a part of the OTC market*. In fact, in 2006 the Nasdaq was formally recognized by the SEC as a "listed exchange," giving it pretty much the same stature and prestige as the NYSE.

To be traded on the Nasdaq, all stocks must have at least two market makers, though the bigger, more actively traded stocks, like Cisco Systems, will have many more than that. These dealers electronically post all their bid/ask prices, so that when investors place market orders, they are immediately filled at the best available price.

The Nasdaq sets various listing standards, the most comprehensive of which are for the 2,000 or so stocks traded on the *Nasdaq National Market (NNM)*, and the roughly 1,000 stocks traded on the *Nasdaq Global Select Market*. (Created in 2006, the Global Select Market is reserved for the biggest and the "bluest"—highest quality—of the Nasdaq stocks.) Stocks included on these two markets are all widely quoted, actively traded, and, in general, have a *national following*. The trades, all executed electronically, are every bit as efficient as they are on the floor of the NYSE. Indeed, the big-name stocks traded on the Nasdaq Global Select Market, and to some extent, on the NNM, receive as much national visibility and are as liquid as those traded on the NYSE. As a result, just as the NYSE has its list of big-name players (like ExxonMobil, GE, Citigroup, Wal-Mart, Pfizer, IBM, Procter & Gamble, Coca-Cola, Home Depot, and UPS), so too does Nasdaq. Its list includes companies

bid price
the highest price offered to purchase a security.

ask price
the lowest price at which a security is offered for sale.

secondary distributions
the public sales of large blocks of previously issued securities held by large investors.

like Microsoft, Intel, Cisco Systems, Dell, eBay, Google, Yahoo!, Apple, Starbucks, and Staples. The *Nasdaq Capital Market* is still another Nasdaq market; it makes a market in about 600 or 700 stocks that, for one reason or another, are not eligible for the NNM.

The other part of the dealer market is made up of securities that trade in the *over-the-counter (OTC) market*. These non-Nasdaq issues include mostly small companies that either cannot or do not wish to comply with Nasdaq's listing requirements. They trade on either the *OTC Bulletin Board (OTCBB)* or in the so-called *"Pink Sheets."* The OTCBB is an electronic quotation system that links the market makers who trade the shares of small companies. The Bulletin Board is regulated by the SEC, which among other things, requires all companies traded on this market to file audited financial statements and comply with federal securities law.

In sharp contrast, the OTC Pink Sheets is the *unregulated* segment of the market, where the companies are not even required to file with the SEC. This market is broken into two tiers. The biggest is populated by many small and often questionable companies that provide little or no information about their operations. The top, albeit smaller tier is reserved for those companies that choose to provide audited financial statements and other required information. While the name comes from the color of paper these quotes used to be printed on, the "pinks" today use an electronic quotation system. Even so, liquidity is often minimal, or almost non-existent, and the market, especially the bottom tier, is littered with scores of nearly worthless stocks. It is definitely not a market for the prudent individual investor.

▊ Alternative Trading Systems

Some individual and institutional traders now make direct transactions, outside of the broker and dealer markets, in the *third* and *fourth markets*. The **third market** consists of over-the-counter transactions made in securities listed on the NYSE, the AMEX, or one of the other exchanges. These transactions are typically handled by market makers that are not members of a securities exchange. They charge lower commissions than the exchanges and bring together large buyers and sellers. Institutional investors, such as mutual funds, pension funds, and life insurance companies, are thus often able to realize sizable savings in brokerage commissions and to have minimal impact on the price of the transaction.

The **fourth market** consists of transactions made through a computer network, rather than on an exchange, directly between large institutional buyers and sellers of securities. Unlike third-market transactions, fourth-market transactions bypass the market maker. **Electronic communications networks (ECNs)** are at the heart of the fourth market. Archipelago (part of the NYSE Group), Bloomberg Tradebook, Island, Instinet, and MarketXT are some of the many ECNs that handle these trades.

ECNs are most effective for high-volume, actively traded securities, and they play a key role in after-hours trading, discussed later in this chapter. They automatically match buy and sell orders that customers place electronically. If there is no immediate match, the ECN, acting like a broker, posts its request under its own name or an exchange or with a market maker. The trade will be executed if another trader is willing to make the transaction at the posted price.

third market
over-the-counter transactions typically handled by market makers and made in securities listed on the NYSE, the AMEX, or one of the other exchanges.

fourth market
transactions made directly between large institutional buyers and sellers of securities.

electronic communications networks (ECNs)
electronic trading networks that automatically match buy and sell orders that customers place electronically.

ECNs can save customers money because they take only a transaction fee, either per share or based on order size. For this reason, money managers and institutions such as pension funds and mutual funds with large amounts of money to invest favor ECNs. Many also use ECNs or trade directly with each other to find the best prices for their clients.

▮ General Market Conditions: Bull or Bear

bull markets
favorable markets normally associated with rising prices, investor optimism, economic recovery, and government stimulus.

bear markets
unfavorable markets normally associated with falling prices, investor pessimism, economic slowdown, and government restraint.

Conditions in the securities markets are commonly classified as "bull" or "bear," depending on whether securities prices are rising or falling over time. Changing market conditions generally stem from changes in investor attitudes, changes in economic activity, and government actions aimed at stimulating or slowing down economic activity. **Bull markets** are favorable markets normally associated with rising prices, investor optimism, economic recovery, and government stimulus. **Bear markets** are unfavorable markets normally associated with falling prices, investor pessimism, economic slowdown, and government restraint. Since 2003, the stock market has been generally bullish.

In general, investors experience higher (or positive) returns on common stock investments during a bull market. However, some securities are bullish in a bear market or bearish in a bull market. During bear markets, many investors choose vehicles other than securities to obtain higher and less risky returns. Market conditions are difficult to predict and usually can be identified only after they exist. In Chapter 3, we describe sources of information that can be used to assess market conditions. Chapters 7 through 9 show how to apply such information to the analysis and valuation of common stock price behavior.

CONCEPTS IN REVIEW
Answers available at: www.myfinancelab.com

2.1 Differentiate between each of the following pairs of terms:
- a. *Money market* and *capital market*
- b. *Primary market* and *secondary market*
- c. *Broker market* and *dealer market*

2.2 Briefly describe the *IPO* process and the role of the *investment banker* in underwriting a public offering. Differentiate among the terms *public offering, rights offering,* and *private placement*.

2.3 For each of the items in the left-hand column, select the most appropriate item in the right-hand column. Explain the relationship between the items matched.

a.	AMEX	1.	Trades unlisted securities
b.	CBT	2.	Futures exchange
c.	NYSE	3.	Options exchange
d.	Boston Stock Exchange	4.	Regional stock exchange
e.	CBOE	5.	Second largest organized U.S. exchange
f.	OTC	6.	Has the most stringent listing requirements

2.4 Explain how the *dealer market* works. Be sure to mention *market makers, bid and ask prices,* the *Nasdaq market,* and the *OTC market*. What role does this market play in initial public offerings (IPOs) and *secondary distributions?*

2.5 What are the *third* and *fourth markets?* Differentiate between a *bull market* and a *bear market*.

Globalization of Securities Markets

LG 4

diversification
the inclusion of a number of different investment vehicles in a portfolio to increase returns or reduce risk.

Today investors, issuers of securities, and securities firms look beyond the markets of their home countries to find the best returns, lowest costs, and best international business opportunities. The basic goal of most investors is to earn the highest return with the lowest risk. This outcome is achieved through **diversification**—the inclusion of a number of different investment vehicles in a portfolio to increase returns or reduce risk. The investor who includes foreign investments in a portfolio can greatly increase the potential for diversification by holding (1) a wider range of industries and securities, (2) securities traded in a larger number of markets, and (3) securities denominated in different currencies. The smaller and less diversified an investor's home market is, the greater the potential benefit from prudent international diversification. However, even investors from the United States and other highly developed markets can benefit from global diversification.

In short, globalization of the securities markets enables investors to seek out opportunities to profit from rapidly expanding economies throughout the world. Here we consider the growing importance of international markets, international investment performance, ways to invest in foreign securities, and the risks of investing internationally.

■ Growing Importance of International Markets

Securities exchanges now operate in over 100 countries worldwide. Both large (Tokyo) and small (Fiji), they are located not only in the major industrialized nations such as Japan, Great Britain, Canada, and Germany but also in emerging economies such as Brazil, Chile, India, South Korea, Malaysia, Mexico, Poland, Russia, and Thailand. The top four securities markets worldwide (based on dollar volume) are the New York, Nasdaq, London, and Tokyo stock exchanges. Other important foreign exchanges include Paris, Osaka, Toronto, Montreal, Sydney, Hong Kong, Zurich, and Taiwan.

HOTLINKS

International markets are growing, especially due to the fact that investors can use the Internet to access other markets. See the following site for a listing of international markets.

www.wall-street.com/foreign.html

The economic integration of the European Monetary Union (EMU), along with pressure from financial institutions that want an efficient process for trading shares across borders, is changing the European securities market environment. Instead of many small national exchanges, countries are banding together to create cross-border markets and to compete more effectively in the pan-European equity-trading markets. The Paris, Amsterdam, Brussels, and Lisbon exchange, plus a derivatives exchange in London, merged to form Euronext, and the Scandinavian markets formed Norex. In mid-2006, Euronext and the NYSE Group—the NYSE parent—signed an agreement to combine their businesses in a merger of equals. Some stock exchanges are forming cooperative agreements—for example, Tokyo and Australia. Others are discussing forming a 24-hour global market alliance, trading the stocks of selected large international companies via an electronic order-matching system. Nasdaq, with joint ventures in Japan, Hong Kong, Canada, and Australia, plans to expand into Latin America and the Middle East. The increasing number of mergers and cooperative arrangements represent steps toward a worldwide stock exchange.

INVESTOR FACTS

U.S. MARKET SHARE—Even though the U.S. securities markets lead the world in terms of market share, the U.S. accounts for about 47% of the market value of companies in the worldwide equity markets.

Bond markets, too, have become global, and more investors than ever before regularly purchase government and corporate fixed-income securities in foreign markets. The United States dominates the international government bond market, followed by Japan, Germany, and Great Britain.

▮ International Investment Performance

A primary motive for investing overseas is the lure of high returns. In fact, only once since 1980 did the United States finish first among the major stock markets of the world in the rate of increase in its stock price index. For example, in 2005, an overall good year, investors would have earned higher returns in many foreign markets. During that year the Dow Jones Global Index in U.S. dollars for South Korea increased 58%; for Mexico increased 40%; for Japan increased 25%; for Finland increased 14%; for France increased 9%; for Germany increased 8%; and for Thailand increased 5%. By comparison, the U.S. stock price index increased about 4%. Of course, foreign securities markets tend to be more risky than U.S. markets. A market with high returns in one year may not do so well in the next.

Investors can compare activity on U.S. and foreign exchanges by following market indexes that track the performance of those exchanges. For instance,

the Dow Jones averages and the Standard & Poor's indexes are popular measures of the U.S. markets, and indexes for more than 20 different stock markets are available. (We'll discuss indexes in more detail in Chapter 3.) The *Wall Street Journal* publishes daily reports on most major indexes, trading activity in selected stocks on major foreign exchanges, and currency exchange rates. Other financial publications also include regular reports. Also, the *Wall Street Journal*'s "World Stock Markets" in Section C frequently compares the performance of the U.S. exchanges with that of selected foreign markets.

▮ Ways to Invest in Foreign Securities

Investors can make foreign security transactions either indirectly or directly. One form of *indirect* investment is to purchase shares of a U.S.-based multinational with substantial foreign operations. Many U.S.-based multinational firms, such as ExxonMobil, IBM, Citigroup, Dow Chemical, Coca-Cola, Colgate-Palmolive, and Hewlett-Packard, receive more than 50% of their revenues from overseas operations. By investing in the securities of such firms, an investor can achieve a degree of international diversification. Purchasing shares in a mutual fund that invests primarily in foreign securities is another way to invest indirectly. Investors can make both of these indirect foreign securities investment transactions through a stockbroker, as explained in Chapter 3 and in Chapter 12 (on mutual funds).

To make *direct* investments in foreign companies, investors have three options: They can purchase securities on foreign exchanges, buy securities of foreign companies that trade on U.S. exchanges, or buy *American depositary receipts (ADRs)*.

The first way—purchasing securities on foreign exchanges—involves additional risks because the securities do not trade in U.S. dollars. This approach is not for the timid or inexperienced investor. Because each country's exchange has its own regulations and procedures, investors must cope with currency exchange (dollars to pesos, for example). They also must cope with different securities exchange rules, transaction procedures, accounting standards, tax laws, and language barriers. Direct transactions are best handled either through brokers at major Wall Street firms with large international operations or through major banks, such as JPMorgan Chase and Citibank, that have special units to handle foreign securities transactions. Alternatively, investors can deal with foreign broker-dealers, but such an approach is more complicated and more risky.

The second form of direct investment is to buy the securities of foreign companies that trade on both organized and over-the-counter U.S. exchanges. Transactions in foreign securities that trade on U.S. exchanges are handled in the same way as exchange-traded domestic securities. These securities are issued by large, well-known foreign companies. Stocks of companies such as Alcan (Canada), DaimlerChrysler (Germany), France Telecom (France), Head (Netherlands), Sony (Japan), and Unilever (U.K.) trade directly on U.S. exchanges. In addition, **Yankee bonds**, dollar-denominated debt securities issued by foreign governments or corporations and traded in U.S. securities markets, trade in both broker and dealer markets in the United States.

Finally, foreign stocks also trade on U.S. exchanges in the form of **American depositary shares (ADSs)**. These securities have been created to permit U.S. investors to hold shares of non-U.S. companies and trade them on U.S. stock exchanges. They are backed by **American depositary receipts (ADRs)**, which are dollar-denominated receipts for the stocks of foreign companies that are held in the vaults of banks in the companies' home countries. Today, more than 2,000 ADRs representing more than 50 different home countries are traded (as ADSs) on U.S. exchanges. About one-fourth of them are actively traded. Included are ADSs of well-known companies such as Cadbury Schweppes, Hitachi, Nippon, LG Philips, Pearson, Reed Elsivier, and Siemans. ADSs, which trade in the same way as standard domestic securities, are further discussed in Chapter 6.

▮ Risks of Investing Internationally

Investing abroad is not without pitfalls. In addition to the usual risks involved in any security transaction, investors must consider the risks of doing business in a particular foreign country. Changes in trade policies, labor laws, and taxation may affect operating conditions for the country's firms. The government itself may not be stable. You must track similar environmental factors in each foreign market in which you invest. This is clearly more difficult than following your home market.

U.S. securities markets are generally viewed as highly regulated and reliable. Foreign markets, on the other hand, may lag substantially behind the United States in both operations and regulation. Some countries place various restrictions on foreign investment. In Korea and Taiwan, for example, mutual funds are the only way for foreigners to invest. Mexico has a two-tier market, with certain securities restricted to foreigners. Some countries make it difficult for foreigners to get their funds out, and many impose taxes on dividends. For example, Swiss taxes are about 20% on dividends paid to foreigners. Other difficulties include illiquid markets and an

Yankee bonds
dollar-denominated debt securities issued by foreign governments or corporations and traded in U.S. securities markets.

American depositary receipts (ADRs)
dollar-denominated receipts for the stocks of foreign companies that are held in the vaults of banks in the companies' home countries. Serve as backing for *American depositary shares (ADSs).*

American depositary shares (ADSs)
securities created to permit U.S. investors to hold shares of non-U.S. companies and trade them on U.S. stock exchanges. They are backed by *American depositary receipts.*

HOTLINKS

There are many risks associated with investing abroad. The following site provides information on country credit ratings.

www.countryrisk.com/guide/

inability to obtain reliable investment information because of a lack of reporting requirements.

In addition, accounting standards vary from country to country. Differences in accounting practices can affect a company's apparent profitability, conceal other assets (such as the hidden reserves and undervalued assets that are permitted in many countries), and fail to disclose other risks. As a result, it is difficult to compare the financial performances and positions of firms operating in different foreign countries. Although the accounting profession is working on a set of international standards, it will be years until they are complete and even longer until companies apply them.

Furthermore, international investing involves securities denominated in foreign currencies. Trading profits and losses are affected not only by a security's price changes but also by changes in currency exchange rates. The values of the world's major currencies fluctuate with respect to each other on a daily basis. The relationship between two currencies at a specified date is called the **currency exchange rate**. On February 27, 2006, the currency exchange rate for the European Monetary Union euro (€) and the U.S. dollar (US$) was expressed as follows:

currency exchange rate
the relationship between two currencies on a specified date.

$$US\$ = € 0.8432 \qquad € = US\$ 1.1860$$

On that day, you would have received 0.8432 euros for every $1. Conversely, each euro was worth $1.1860.

Changes in the value of a particular foreign currency with respect to the U.S. dollar—or any other currency—are called *appreciation* and *depreciation*. For example, on June 30, 2006, the euro/US$ exchange rate was 0.7817. In the 3 months since February 27, 2006, the European Monetary Union euro had *appreciated* relative to the dollar (and the dollar had *depreciated* relative to the euro). On June 30 it took less euros to buy $1 (0.7817 versus 0.8432), so each euro was worth more in dollar terms ($1.2792 versus $1.1860). Had the European Monetary Union euro instead *depreciated* (and the dollar *appreciated* relative to the euro), each euro would have been worth less in dollar terms.

currency exchange risk
the risk caused by the varying exchange rates between the currencies of two countries.

Currency exchange risk is the risk caused by the varying exchange rates between the currencies of two countries. For example, assume that on February 27, 2006, you bought 100 shares of a French stock at 100 euros per share, held it for about 3 months, and then sold it for its original purchase price of 100 euros. The following table summarizes these transactions:

Date	Transaction	Number of Shares	Price in Euros	Value of Transaction Euros	Exchange Rate Euros/US$	Value in US$
2/27/06	Purchase	100	100	10,000	0.8432	$11,860.00
6/30/06	Sell	100	100	10,000	0.7817	$12,792.00

Although you realized the original purchase price in euros, in dollar terms the transaction resulted in a gain of $932.00 ($12,792.00 − $11,860.00). The value of the stock in dollars increased because the European Monetary Union euro was worth more—had appreciated—relative to the dollar. Investors in foreign securities must be aware that the value of the foreign currency in relation to the dollar can have a profound effect on returns from foreign security transactions.

CONCEPTS IN REVIEW

Answers available at: www.myfinancelab.com

2.6   Why is globalization of securities markets an important issue today? How have international investments performed in recent years?

2.7   Describe how foreign security investments can be made, both indirectly and directly.

2.8   Describe the risks of investing internationally, particularly *currency exchange risk*.

Trading Hours and Regulation of Securities Markets

LG 5

Understanding the structure of domestic and international securities markets is an important foundation for developing a sound investment program. Now let's look at market trading hours and the regulation of U.S. securities markets.

■ Trading Hours of Securities Markets

crossing markets
after-hours trading in stocks that involve filling buy and sell orders by matching identical sell and buy orders at the desired price.

The regular trading session for organized U.S. exchanges runs from 9:30 A.M. to 4:00 P.M. eastern time. However, trading is no longer limited to these hours. The exchanges, Nasdaq, and ECNs offer extended trading sessions before and after regular hours. Most of the after-hours markets are **crossing markets** in which orders are filled only if they can be matched. That is, buy and sell orders are filled only if they can be matched with identical opposing sell and buy orders at the desired price. These allow U.S. securities markets to compete more effectively with foreign securities markets, in which investors can execute trades when U.S. markets are closed.

The NYSE has two short electronic-trading sessions that begin after the 4:00 P.M. closing bell. One session, from 4:15 to 5:00 P.M., trades stocks at that day's closing prices via a computer matching system. Transactions occur only if a match can be made and are handled on a first-come, first-served basis. The other session lasts from 4:00 to 5:15 P.M. and allows institutional investors to trade large blocks of stock valued at $1 million or more. Since their inception, the NYSE has experienced increased volume in both sessions.

Nasdaq has its own extended-hours electronic-trading sessions from 4:00 to 6:30 P.M. eastern time, as well as two SelectNet trading sessions, from 8:00 to 9:30 A.M. eastern time and from 4:00 to 5:15 P.M. eastern time. Regional exchanges have also moved to after-hours trading sessions. Now individual investors can participate in after-hours trading activity. Many large brokerage firms, both traditional and online, offer after-hours trading services for their individual clients.

It appears that after-hours trading will continue to expand and will approximate a 24-hour market in the not too distant future. Yet, it is important to recognize that the term "after-hours trading" is becoming obsolete because of the ability to trade major stocks on a variety of exchanges around the globe. For example, the stock of DaimlerChrysler, a major global automobile manufacturer, is traded in identical form on worldwide exchanges in Asia, Europe, and the Americas. Clearly, by working through these exchanges you can effectively trade DaimlerChrysler on a 24-hour basis. The *Investing in Action* box on page 81 further discusses extended trading hours.

INVESTING *in Action*

Stock Around the Clock

Trading 24/7—the idea sounds great. Pick up the phone or go to your computer at any hour to buy or sell stocks and mutual funds. While such round-the-clock trading is not yet a reality, individual investors can trade securities before and after the close of regular trading sessions. Most after-hours trading now takes place from 8:00 A.M. to 9:30 A.M., before the NYSE and Nasdaq open at 9:30, and from 4:00 P.M. to 6:30 P.M. after these markets close at 4:00.

What's the appeal of extended trading hours? Some investors don't have time to reflect on market news during the day. Investors in the Pacific time zone (3 hours behind New York) want a longer trading day; their regular trading day ends at 1 P.M. Pacific time. Others want to act on company news that is released after the markets close, or during the business day of companies outside the United States. After-hours traffic represents only about 2% of the NYSE and Nasdaq combined daily trading volume, but investors who understand how to use extended hours can profit, or at least reduce losses.

While still risky, after-hours trading has become less so since its introduction in 2000 and with the advent of higher volume. If you want to benefit from extended-day trading, here are some basics to prepare you to enter this new arena:

- Understand how your brokerage firm handles after-hour trades. Different firms have different rules.
- Learn how stock prices react to different types of company news, economic announcements, and changes to major indexes.
- Most extended-day trading is in Nasdaq and NYSE stocks, so follow the after-hours trading patterns of those exchanges' most active lists.
- Understand limit orders (discussed in Chapter 3), which most brokerages require for after-hours trades, so that investors can set their highest buy/lowest sell price.

CRITICAL THINKING QUESTION What risks should individual investors consider before engaging in after-hours trading?

Sources: Jonathan Birchall "Shipping Costs Dent Amazon Earnings," *Financial Times Online*, February 2, 2006, us.ft.com; Gregg Greenberg "Ask the Street: Late Trading" *TheStreet.com*, February 5, 2006, www.thestreet.com.

▮ Regulation of Securities Markets

Securities laws protect investors and participants in the financial marketplace. A number of state and federal laws require that investors receive adequate and accurate disclosure of information. Such laws also regulate the activities of participants in the securities markets. State laws that control the sale of securities within state borders are commonly called *blue sky laws* because they are intended to prevent investors from being sold nothing but "blue sky." These laws typically establish procedures for regulating both security issues and sellers of securities doing business within the state. Most states have a regulatory body, such as a state securities commission, that is charged with enforcing the related state statutes. Table 2.2 (on page 82) summarizes the most important securities laws enacted by the federal government (listed in chronological order).

The intent of these federal securities laws is to protect investors. Most of these laws were passed in response to observed damaging abuses by certain market participants. Congress passed two laws recently in response to public concern over corporate financial scandals: The *Insider Trading and Fraud Act of 1988* aims at stopping **insider trading**, the use of *nonpublic* information

insider trading
the use of *nonpublic* information about a company to make profitable securities transactions.

TABLE 2.2 Important Federal Securities Laws

Act	Brief Description
Securities Act of 1933	Passed to ensure full disclosure of information about new security issues. Requires the issuer of a new security to file with the Securities and Exchange Commission (SEC) a registration statement containing information about the new issue. The firm cannot sell the security until the SEC approves the registration statement, which usually takes about 20 days. Approval of the registration statement by the SEC merely indicates that the facts presented in the statement appear to reflect the firm's true position.
Securities Exchange Act of 1934	Formally established the SEC as the agency in charge of administering federal securities laws. The act gave the SEC the power to regulate the organized exchanges and the OTC market; their members, brokers, and dealers; and the securities traded in these markets. Each of these participants must file reports with the SEC and periodically update them. The 1934 act has been amended several times over the years.
Maloney Act of 1938	An amendment to the Securities Exchange Act of 1934, it provided for the establishment of trade associations to self-regulate the securities industry. Only one such trade association, the National Association of Securities Dealers (NASD), has been formed. NASD members include nearly all of the nation's securities firms that do business with the public. The NASD, operating under SEC supervision, establishes standardized procedures for securities trading and ethical behavior, monitors and enforces compliance with these procedures, and serves as the industry spokesperson. Today, any securities firms that are not members of the NASD must agree to direct SEC supervision.
Investment Company Act of 1940	Established rules and regulations for investment companies and formally authorized the SEC to regulate their practices and procedures. It required investment companies to register with the SEC and to fulfill certain disclosure requirements. An *investment company* obtains funds by selling its shares to investors and uses the proceeds to purchase securities. The dominant type of investment company is the *mutual fund*. A 1970 amendment prohibits investment companies from paying excessive fees to to advisers and from charging excessive commissions to purchasers of company shares.
Investment Advisers Act of 1940	Requires *investment advisers*, persons hired by investors to advise them about security investments, to disclose all relevant information about their backgrounds, conflicts of interest, and any investments they recommend. Advisers must register and file periodic reports with the SEC. A 1960 amendment extended the SEC's powers to permit inspection of the records of investment advisers and to revoke the registration of advisers who violate the act's provisions.
Securities Acts Amendments of 1975	Requires the SEC and the securities industry to develop a competitive national system for trading securities. First, the SEC abolished fixed-commission schedules, thereby providing for negotiated commissions. Second, it established the *Intermarket Trading System (ITS),* an electronic communications network linking nine markets and trading over 4,000 eligible issues, that allows trades to be made across these markets wherever the network shows a better price for a given issue.
Insider Trading and Fraud Act of 1988	Established penalties for *insider trading,* using *nonpublic* information to make profitable securities transactions. Insiders include anyone who obtains nonpublic information, typically a company's directors, officers, major shareholders, bankers, investment bankers, accountants, or attorneys. The SEC requires corporate insiders to file monthly reports detailing all transactions made in the company's stock. Recent legislation substantially increased the penalties for insider trading and gave the SEC greater power to investigate and prosecute claims of illegal insider-trading activity.
Sarbanes-Oxley Act of 2002	Passed to protect investors against corporate fraud, particularly accounting fraud. It created an oversight board to monitor the accounting industry, tightened audit regulations and controls, toughened penalties against executives who commit corporate fraud, strengthened accounting disclosure requirements and ethical guidelines for financial officers, established corporate board structure and membership guidelines, established guidelines for analyst conflicts of interest, and increased the SEC's authority and budgets for auditors and investigators. The act also mandated instant disclosure of stock sales by corporate executives.

ethics
standards of conduct or moral judgment.

about a company to make profitable securities transactions. The *Sarbanes-Oxley Act of 2002* focuses on eliminating corporate fraud related to accounting and other information releases. Both of these acts heightened the public's awareness of **ethics**—standards of conduct or moral judgment—in business. The government and the financial community are continuing to develop and enforce ethical standards that will motivate market participants to adhere to laws and regulations. Although it is difficult to enforce ethical standards, it appears that opportunities for abuses in the financial markets are being reduced, thereby providing a more level playing field for all investors.

CONCEPTS IN REVIEW

Answers available at: www.myfinancelab.com

2.9 How are after-hours trades typically handled? What is the outlook for after-hours trading?

2.10 Briefly describe the key requirements of the following federal securities laws:
   a. Securities Act of 1933.
   b. Securities Exchange Act of 1934.
   c. Maloney Act of 1938.
   d. Investment Company Act of 1940.
   e. Investment Advisers Act of 1940.
   f. Securities Acts Amendments of 1975.
   g. Insider Trading and Fraud Act of 1988.
   h. Sarbanes-Oxley Act of 2002.

Basic Types of Securities Transactions

LG 6

An investor can make a number of basic types of security transactions. Each type is available to those who meet certain requirements established by government agencies as well as by brokerage firms. Although investors can use the various types of transactions in a number of ways to meet investment objectives, we describe only the most popular use of each transaction here, as we consider the long purchase, margin trading, and short selling.

▮ Long Purchase

long purchase
a transaction in which investors buy securities in the hope that they will increase in value and can be sold at a later date for profit.

The **long purchase** is a transaction in which investors buy securities in the hope that they will increase in value and can be sold at a later date for profit. The object, then, is to *buy low and sell high*. A long purchase is the most common type of transaction. Because investors generally expect the price of a security to rise over the period of time they plan to hold it, their return comes from any dividends or interest received during the ownership period, *plus* the difference (capital gain or loss) between the purchase and selling prices. Transaction costs, of course, reduce this return.

Ignoring any dividends and transaction costs, we can illustrate the long purchase by a simple example. After studying Varner Industries, you are convinced that its common stock, which currently sells for $20 per share, will increase in value over the next few years. You expect the stock price to rise to

$30 per share within 2 years. You place an order and buy 100 shares of Varner for $20 per share. If the stock price rises to, say, $40 per share, you will profit from your long purchase. If it drops below $20 per share, you will experience a loss on the transaction. Obviously, one of the major motivating factors in making a long purchase is an expected rise in the price of the security.

▌ Margin Trading

margin trading
the use of borrowed funds to purchase securities; magnifies returns by reducing the amount of equity that the investor must put up.

Security purchases do not have to be made on a cash basis; investors can use borrowed funds instead. This activity is referred to as **margin trading**. It is used for one basic reason: to magnify returns. As peculiar as it may sound, the term *margin* refers to the amount of equity (stated as a percentage) in an investment, or the amount that is *not* borrowed. If an investor uses 75% margin, for example, it means that 75% of the investment position is being financed with the person's own funds and the balance (25%) with borrowed money. Brokers must approve margin purchases. The brokerage firm then lends the purchaser the needed funds and retains the purchased securities as collateral. It is important to recognize that margin purchasers must pay a specified rate of interest on the amount they borrow.

margin requirement
the minimum amount of equity that must be a margin investor's own funds; set by the Federal Reserve Board (the "Fed").

The Federal Reserve Board (the "Fed") sets the **margin requirement**, specifying the minimum amount of equity that must be the margin investor's own funds. The margin requirement for stocks has been at 50% for some time. By raising and lowering the margin requirement, the Fed can depress or stimulate activity in the securities markets.

A simple example will help to clarify the basic margin transaction. Assume that you wish to purchase 70 shares of common stock, which is currently selling for $63.50 per share. With the prevailing margin requirement of 50%, you need put up only $2,222.50 in cash ($63.50 per share × 70 shares × 0.50). Your brokerage firm will lend you the remaining $2,222.50. You will, of course, have to pay interest on the amount you borrow, plus the applicable brokerage fees. With the use of margin, you can purchase more securities than you could afford on a strictly cash basis. In this way, you can magnify your returns (as demonstrated in the next section).

Although margin trading can lead to increased returns, it also presents substantial risks. One of the biggest is that the issue may not perform as expected. If this occurs, no amount of margin trading can correct matters. Margin trading can only magnify returns, not produce them. And if the security's return is negative, margin trading magnifies the loss. Because the security being margined is always the ultimate source of return, choosing the right securities is critical to this trading strategy.

Essentials of Margin Trading Investors can use margin trading with most kinds of securities. They regularly use it, for example, to buy common and preferred stocks, most types of bonds, mutual funds, options, warrants, and futures. It is not normally used with tax-exempt municipal bonds, because the interest paid on such margin loans is not deductible for income tax purposes. It is also possible to use margin on certain foreign stocks and bonds that meet prescribed criteria and appear on the Fed's "List of Foreign Margin Stocks," which is published semiannually. For simplicity, we will use common stock as the vehicle in our discussion of margin trading.

financial leverage
the use of debt financing to
magnify investment returns.

HOTLINKS

Read about margin trading at:

www.sec.gov/investor/pubs/margin.htm

Magnified Profits and Losses With an investor's equity serving as a base, the idea of margin trading is to employ **financial leverage**—the use of debt financing to magnify investment returns.

Here is how it works: Suppose you have $5,000 to invest and are considering the purchase of 100 shares of stock at $50 per share. If you do not margin, you can buy outright 100 shares of the stock (ignoring brokerage commissions). If you margin the transaction—for example, at 50%—you can acquire the same $5,000 position with only $2,500 of your own money. This leaves you with $2,500 to use for other investments or to buy on margin another 100 shares of the same stock. Either way, by margining you will reap greater benefits from the stock's price appreciation.

Table 2.3 more fully illustrates the concept of margin trading. It shows an unmargined (100% equity) transaction, along with the same transaction using various margins. Remember that the margin rates (e.g., 65%) indicate the investor's equity in the investment. When the investment is unmargined and the price of the stock goes up by $30 per share (see Table 2.3, part A), the investor enjoys a very respectable 60% rate of return. However, observe what happens when margin is used: The rate of return shoots up as high as 120%, depending on the amount of equity in the investment. This occurs because the gain is the same ($3,000) *regardless of how the investor finances the transaction*. Clearly, as the investor's equity in the investment *declines* (with lower margins), the rate of return *increases* accordingly.

EXCEL with SPREADSHEETS

TABLE 2.3 The Effect of Margin Trading on Security Returns

	Without Margin (100% Equity)	With Margins of		
		80%	65%	50%
Number of $50 shares purchased	100	100	100	100
Cost of investment	$5,000	$5,000	$5,000	$5,000
Less: Borrowed money	0	1,000	1,750	2,500
Equity in investment	$5,000	$4,000	$3,250	$2,500
A. Investor's position if price rises by $30 to $80/share				
Value of stock	$8,000	$8,000	$8,000	$8,000
Less: Cost of investment	5,000	5,000	5,000	5,000
Capital gain	$3,000	$3,000	$3,000	$3,000
Return on investor's equity (capital gain/ equity in investment)	60%	75%	92.3%	120%
B. Investor's position if price falls by $30 to $20/share				
Value of stock	$2,000	$2,000	$2,000	$2,000
Less: Cost of investment	5,000	5,000	5,000	5,000
Capital loss*	($3,000)	($3,000)	($3,000)	($3,000)
Return on investor's equity (capital loss/ equity in investment)*	(60%)	(75%)	(92.3%)	(120%)

*Both the capital loss and the return on investor's equity are *negative* as noted by the parentheses.

Three facets of margin trading become obvious from the table:

1. The price of the stock will move in whatever way it is going to, regardless of how the position is financed.
2. The lower the amount of the investor's equity in the position, the *greater the rate of return* the investor will enjoy when the price of the security rises.
3. The *loss is also magnified* (by the same rate) when the price of the security falls (see Table 2.3, part B).

Note that Table 2.3 has an "Excel with Spreadsheets" icon. Throughout the text, tables with this icon indicate that they are available as spreadsheets on this book's Web site, www.myfinancelab.com. The use of electronic spreadsheets in finance and investments, as well as in all functional areas of business, is pervasive. We use spreadsheets from time to time throughout the text to demonstrate how the content has been constructed or calculated. As you know from Chapter 1, we include Excel spreadsheet exercises at the end of most chapters, to give you practice with spreadsheets and help you develop the ability to clearly set out the logic needed to solve investment problems.

Advantages and Disadvantages of Margin Trading A magnified return is the major advantage of margin trading. The size of the magnified return depends on both the price behavior of the security and the amount of margin used. Another, more modest benefit of margin trading is that it allows for greater diversification of security holdings, because investors can spread their limited capital over a larger number of investments.

The major disadvantage of margin trading, of course, is the potential for magnified losses if the price of the security falls. Another disadvantage is the cost of the margin loans themselves. A **margin loan** is the official vehicle through which the borrowed funds are made available in a margin transaction. All margin loans are made at a stated interest rate, which depends on prevailing market rates and the amount of money being borrowed. This rate is usually 1% to 3% above the **prime rate**—the lowest interest rate charged the best business borrowers. For large accounts, it may be at the prime rate. The loan cost, which investors pay, will increase daily, reducing the level of profits (or increasing losses) accordingly.

Making Margin Transactions To execute a margin transaction, an investor must establish a **margin account** with a minimum of $2,000 in equity or 100% of the purchase price, whichever is less, in the form of either cash or securities. The broker will retain any securities purchased on margin as collateral for the loan.

The margin requirement established by the Federal Reserve Board sets the minimum amount of equity for margin transactions. Investors need not execute all margin transactions by using exactly the minimum amount of margin; they can use more than the minimum if they wish. Moreover, it is not unusual for brokerage firms and the major exchanges to establish their own margin requirements, which are more restrictive than those of the Federal Reserve. Brokerage firms also may have their own lists of especially volatile stocks for which the margin requirements are higher. There are basically two types of margin requirements: initial margin and maintenance margin.

margin loan
vehicle through which borrowed funds are made available, at a stated interest rate, in a margin transaction.

prime rate
the lowest interest rate charged the best business borrowers.

margin account
a brokerage account for which margin trading is authorized.

TABLE 2.4 Initial Margin Requirements for Various Types of Securities

Security	Minimum Initial Margin (Equity) Required
Listed common and preferred stock	50%
OTC stocks traded on Nasdaq	50%
Convertible bonds	50%
Corporate bonds	30%
U.S. government bills, notes, and bonds	10% of principal
U.S. government agencies	24% of principal
Options	Option premium plus 20% of market value of underlying stock
Futures	2% to 10% of the value of the contract

initial margin
the minimum amount of equity that must be provided by a margin investor *at the time of purchase.*

Initial Margin The minimum amount of equity that must be provided by the investor *at the time of purchase* is the **initial margin**. It prevents overtrading and excessive speculation. Generally, this is the margin requirement to which investors refer when discussing margin trading. All securities that can be margined have specific initial requirements, which the governing authorities can change at their discretion. Table 2.4 shows initial margin requirements for various types of securities. The more stable investment vehicles, such as U.S. government issues, generally have substantially lower margin requirements and thus offer greater opportunities to magnify returns. Stocks traded on the Nasdaq National Market can be margined like listed securities; OTC stocks are considered to have no collateral value and therefore cannot be margined.

restricted account
a margin account whose equity is less than the initial margin requirement; the investor may not make further margin purchases and must bring the margin back to the initial level when securities are sold.

As long as the margin in an account remains at a level equal to or greater than prevailing initial requirements, the investor may use the account in any way he or she wants. However, if the value of the investor's holdings declines, the margin in his or her account will also drop. In this case, the investor will have what is known as a **restricted account**, one whose equity is less than the initial margin requirement. It does not mean that the investor must put up additional cash or equity. But as long as the account is restricted, the investor may not make further margin purchases and must bring the margin back to the initial level when securities are sold.

maintenance margin
the absolute minimum amount of margin (equity) that an investor must maintain in the margin account at all times.

Maintenance Margin The absolute minimum amount of margin (equity) that an investor must maintain in the margin account at all times is the **maintenance margin**. When an insufficient amount of maintenance margin exists, an investor will receive a **margin call**. This call gives the investor a short period of time (perhaps 72 hours) to bring the equity up above the maintenance margin. If this doesn't happen, the broker is authorized to sell enough of the investor's margined holdings to bring the equity in the account up to this standard.

margin call
notification of the need to bring the equity of an account whose margin is below the maintenance level up above the maintenance margin level or to have enough margined holdings sold to reach this standard.

Margin investors can be in for a surprise if markets are volatile. When the Nasdaq stock market fell 14% in one day in early April 2000, brokerages made many more margin calls than usual. Investors rushed to sell shares, often at a loss, to cover their margin calls—only to watch the market bounce back a few days later.

The maintenance margin protects both the brokerage house and investors: Brokers avoid having to absorb excessive investor losses, and investors avoid being wiped out. The maintenance margin on equity securities is currently 25%. It rarely changes, although it is often set slightly higher by brokerage firms for the added protection of brokers and customers. For straight debt securities such as government bonds, there is no official maintenance margin except that set by the brokerage firms themselves.

The Basic Margin Formula The amount of margin is always measured in terms of its relative amount of equity, which is considered the investor's collateral. A simple formula can be used with all types of long purchases to determine the amount of margin in the transaction at any given time. Basically, only two pieces of information are required: (1) the prevailing market value of the securities being margined, and (2) the **debit balance**, which is the amount of money being borrowed in the margin loan. Given this information, we can compute margin according to Equation 2.1.

debit balance
the amount of money being borrowed in a margin loan.

Equation 2.1 ➤

$$\text{Margin} = \frac{\text{Value of securities} - \text{Debit balance}}{\text{Value of securities}}$$

Equation 2.1a ➤

$$= \frac{V - D}{V}$$

To illustrate, consider the following example. Assume you want to purchase 100 shares of stock at $40 per share at a time when the initial margin requirement is 70%. Because 70% of the transaction must be financed with equity, you can finance the (30%) balance with a margin loan. Therefore, you will borrow $0.30 \times \$4,000$, or $1,200. This amount, of course, is the *debit balance*. The remainder ($4,000 − $1,200 = $2,800) represents your equity in the transaction. In other words, equity is represented by the numerator ($V − D$) in the margin formula.

What happens to the margin as the value of the security changes? If over time the price of the stock moves to $65, the margin is then

$$\text{Margin} = \frac{V - D}{V} = \frac{\$6,500 - \$1,200}{\$6,500} = 0.815 = \underline{81.5\%}$$

Note that the margin (equity) in this investment position has risen from 70% to 81.5%. *When the price of the security goes up, your margin also increases.*

On the other hand, *when the price of the security goes down, so does the amount of margin.* For instance, if the price of the stock in our illustration drops to $30 per share, the new margin is only 60% [($3,000 − $1,200) ÷ $3,000]. In that case, we would be dealing with a *restricted account*, because the margin level would have dropped below the prevailing initial margin of 70%.

Finally, note that although our discussion has been couched largely in terms of individual transactions, the same margin formula applies to margin accounts. The only difference is that we would be dealing with input that applies to the account *as a whole*—the value of all securities held in the account and the total amount of margin loans.

Return on Invested Capital When assessing the return on margin transactions, you must take into account the fact that you put up only part of the funds. Therefore, you are concerned with the *rate of return* earned on only the portion of the funds that you provided. Using both current income received from dividends or interest and total interest paid on the margin loan, we can apply Equation 2.2 to determine the return on invested capital from a margin transaction.

Equation 2.2 ➤

$$\begin{array}{c}\text{Return on} \\ \text{invested capital} \\ \text{from a margin} \\ \text{transaction}\end{array} = \dfrac{\begin{array}{c}\text{Total} \\ \text{current} \\ \text{income} \\ \text{received}\end{array} - \begin{array}{c}\text{Total} \\ \text{interest} \\ \text{paid on} \\ \text{margin loan}\end{array} + \begin{array}{c}\text{Market} \\ \text{value of} \\ \text{securities} \\ \text{at sale}\end{array} - \begin{array}{c}\text{Market} \\ \text{value of} \\ \text{securities} \\ \text{at purchase}\end{array}}{\text{Amount of equity at purchase}}$$

We can use this equation to compute either the expected or the actual return from a margin transaction. To illustrate: Assume you want to buy 100 shares of stock at $50 per share because you feel it will rise to $75 within six months. The stock pays $2 per share in annual dividends, and during your six-month holding period you will receive half of that amount, or $1 per share. You are going to buy the stock with 50% margin and will pay 10% interest on the margin loan. Therefore, you are going to put up $2,500 equity to buy $5,000 worth of stock that you hope will increase to $7,500 in six months. Because you will have a $2,500 margin loan outstanding at 10% for six months, you will pay $125 in total interest costs ($2,500 × 0.10 × 6/12 = $125). We can substitute this information into Equation 2.2 to find the expected return on invested capital from this margin transaction:

$$\begin{array}{c}\text{Return on} \\ \text{invested capital} \\ \text{from a margin} \\ \text{transaction}\end{array} = \dfrac{\$100 - \$125 + \$7,500 - \$5,000}{\$2,500} = \dfrac{\$2,475}{\$2,500} = 0.99 = \underline{\underline{99\%}}$$

Keep in mind that the 99% figure represents the rate of return earned over a six-month holding period. If you wanted to compare this rate of return to other investment opportunities, you could determine the transaction's annualized rate of return by multiplying by 2 (the number of six-month periods in a year). This would amount to an annual rate of return of 198% (99% × 2 = 198%).

pyramiding
the technique of using paper profits in margin accounts to partly or fully finance the acquisition of additional securities.

excess margin
more equity than is required in a margin account.

Uses of Margin Trading Investors most often use margin trading in one of two ways. As we have seen, one of its uses is to magnify transaction returns. The other major margin tactic is called pyramiding, which takes the concept of magnified returns to its limits. **Pyramiding** uses the paper profits in margin accounts to partly or fully finance the acquisition of additional securities. This allows investors to make such transactions at margins below prevailing initial margin levels, and sometimes substantially so. In fact, with this technique it is even possible to buy securities with no new cash at all. Rather, they can all be financed entirely with margin loans. The reason is that the paper profits in the account lead to **excess margin**—more equity in the account than required. For instance, if a margin account holds $60,000 worth of securities and has a debit balance of $20,000, it is at a margin level of 66⅔% [($60,000 − $20,000) ÷ $60,000]. This account would hold a substantial amount of excess margin if the prevailing initial margin requirement were only 50%.

The principle of pyramiding is to use the excess margin in the account to purchase additional securities. The only constraint—and the key to pyramiding—is that when the additional securities are purchased, your margin account must be at or above the prevailing required initial margin level. Remember that it is the *account,* not the individual transactions, that must meet the minimum standards. If the account has excess margin, you can use it to build up security holdings. Pyramiding can continue as long as there are additional paper profits in the margin account and as long as the margin level exceeds the initial requirement that prevails when purchases are made. The tactic is somewhat complex but is also profitable, especially because it minimizes the amount of new capital required in the investor's account.

In general, margin trading is simple, but it is also risky. Risk is primarily associated with potential price declines in the margined securities. A decline in prices can result in a *restricted account.* If prices fall enough to cause the actual margin to drop below the maintenance margin, the resulting margin call will force you to deposit additional equity into the account almost immediately. In addition, losses (resulting from the price decline) are magnified in a fashion similar to that demonstrated in Table 2.3, part B. Clearly, the chance of a margin call and the magnification of losses make margin trading more risky than nonmargined transactions. Margin should be used only by investors who fully understand its operation and appreciate its pitfalls. The *Ethics* box on page 91 discusses the perilous side of margin trading in the story of margin trading that went spectacularly wrong.

▊ Short Selling

In most cases, investors buy stock hoping that the price will rise. What if you expect the price of a particular security to fall? By using short selling, you may be able to profit from falling security prices. Almost any type of security can be "shorted": common and preferred stocks, all types of bonds, convertible securities, listed mutual funds, options, and warrants. In practice, though, the short-selling activities of most investors are limited almost exclusively to common stocks and to options. (However, investors are prohibited from using short selling to *protect* themselves from falling security prices, a strategy called *shorting-against-the-box.*)

short selling
the sale of borrowed securities, their eventual repurchase by the short seller, and their return to the lender.

Essentials of Short Selling **Short selling** is generally defined as the practice of selling borrowed securities. Unusual as it may sound, selling borrowed securities is (in most cases) legal and quite common. Short sales start when an investor borrows securities from a broker and sells these securities in the marketplace. Later, when the price of the issue has declined, the short seller buys back the securities, and then returns them to the lender. A short seller must make an initial equity deposit with the broker, subject to rules similar to those for margin trading. The deposit plus the proceeds from sale of the borrowed shares assure the broker that sufficient funds are available to buy back the shorted securities at a later date, even if their price increases. Short sales, like margin transactions, require investors to work through a broker.

sell certain securities at stated bid/ask prices. Dealer markets also serve as primary markets for both IPOs and secondary distributions. Over-the-counter transactions in listed securities take place in the third market. Direct transactions between buyers and sellers are made in the fourth market. Market conditions are commonly classified as "bull" or "bear," depending on whether securities prices are generally rising or falling.

LG 4   **Review the key aspects of global securities markets, including the risks associated with foreign investments.** Securities exchanges operate in over 100 countries—both large and small. Foreign security investments can be made indirectly by buying shares of a U.S.-based multinational with substantial foreign operations or by purchasing shares of a mutual fund that invests primarily in foreign securities. Direct foreign investment can be achieved by purchasing securities on foreign exchanges, by buying securities of foreign companies that are traded on U.S. exchanges, or by buying American depositary shares (ADSs). International investments can enhance returns, but they entail added risk, particularly currency exchange risk.

LG 5   **Discuss trading hours and the regulation of securities markets.** Investors now can trade securities outside of regular market hours (9:30 A.M. to 4:00 P.M., eastern time). Most after-hours markets are crossing markets, in which orders are filled only if they can be matched. Trading activity during these sessions can be quite risky. The securities markets are regulated by the federal Securities and Exchange Commission (SEC) and by state commissions. The key federal laws regulating the securities industry are the Securities Act of 1933, the Securities Exchange Act of 1934, the Maloney Act of 1938, the Investment Company Act of 1940, the Investment Advisers Act of 1940, the Securities Acts Amendments of 1975, the Insider Trading and Fraud Act of 1988, and the Sarbanes-Oxley Act of 2002.

LG 6   **Explain long purchases, margin transactions, and short sales.** Most investors make long purchases—buy low, sell high—in expectation of price increases. Many investors establish margin accounts to use borrowed funds to enhance their buying power. The Federal Reserve Board establishes the margin requirement—the minimum investor equity in a margin transaction. The return on capital in a margin transaction is magnified, for both positive returns *and* negative returns. Paper profits can be used to pyramid a margin account by investing its excess margin. The risks of margin trading are the chance of a restricted account or margin call and the consequences of magnified losses due to price declines.

Short selling is used when a decline in security prices is anticipated. It involves selling securities, typically borrowed from the broker, to earn a profit by repurchasing them at a lower price in the future. The short seller makes an initial equity deposit with the broker. If the price of a shorted stock rises, the investor may receive a margin call, and must then either increase the deposit with the broker or buy back the stock to cover the short position. The major advantage of selling short is the chance to profit from a price decline. The disadvantages of selling short are the unlimited potential for loss, and the fact that short sellers never earn dividend (or interest) income. Short selling is used primarily to seek speculative profits.

Key Terms

American depositary receipts
    (ADRs), *p. 78*
American depositary shares
    (ADSs), *p. 78*

ask price, *p. 73*
bear markets, *p. 75*
bid price, *p. 73*
broker market, *p. 69*

bull markets, *p. 75*
capital market, *p. 65*
crossing markets, *p. 80*
currency exchange rate, *p. 79*
currency exchange risk, *p. 79*
dealer market, *p. 69*
debit balance, *p. 88*
diversification, *p. 76*
dual listing, *p. 72*
electronic communications network
    (ECN), *p. 74*
ethics, *p. 83*
excess margin, *p. 89*
financial leverage, *p. 85*
fourth market, *p. 74*
initial margin, *p. 87*
initial public offering (IPO), *p. 65*
insider trading, *p. 81*
investment banker, *p. 66*
long purchase, *p. 83*
maintenance margin, *p. 87*
margin account, *p. 86*
margin call, *p. 87*
margin loan, *p. 86*
margin requirement, *p. 84*
margin trading, *p. 84*

market makers, *p. 70*
money market, *p. 65*
Nasdaq market, *p. 69*
over-the-counter (OTC) market, *p. 69*
primary market, *p. 65*
prime rate, *p. 86*
private placement, *p. 65*
prospectus, *p. 66*
public offering, *p. 65*
pyramiding, *p. 89*
red herring, *p. 66*
restricted account, *p. 87*
rights offering, *p. 65*
secondary distributions, *p. 73*
secondary market, *p. 69*
Securities and Exchange Commission
    (SEC), *p. 65*
securities markets, *p. 65*
selling group, *p. 68*
short selling, *p. 90*
specialist, *p. 71*
third market, *p. 74*
underwriting, *p. 67*
underwriting syndicate, *p. 67*
Yankee bonds, *p. 78*

Discussion Questions

LG 1   **Q2.1** From 1990 to 2005, the average IPO rose by more than 20% in its first day of trading. In 1999, 117 deals doubled in price on the first day, compared to only 39 in the previous 24 years combined. Since 2000, no deals doubled on the first day. What factors might contribute to the huge first-day returns on IPOs? Some critics of the current IPO system claim that underwriters may knowingly underprice an issue. Why might they do this? Why might issuing companies accept lower IPO prices? What impact do institutional investors have on IPO pricing?

LG 2 **LG 3**   **Q2.2** Why do you think some large, well-known companies such as Cisco Systems, Intel, and Microsoft prefer to trade on the Nasdaq National Market rather than on a major securities exchange such as the NYSE (for which they easily meet the listing requirements)? Discuss the pros and cons of listing on a major securities exchange.

LG 2 **LG 3** **LG 4**   **Q2.3** On the basis of the current structure of the world's financial markets and your knowledge of the NYSE and Nasdaq markets, describe the key features, functions, and problems that would be faced by a single global market (exchange) on which transactions can be made in all securities of all of the world's major companies. Discuss the likelihood of such a market developing.

LG 5   **Q2.4** Critics of longer trading hours believe that expanded trading sessions turn the stock market into a casino and place the emphasis more on short-term gains than on long-term investment. Do you agree? Why or why not? Is it important to have a "breathing period" to reflect on the day's market activity? Why are smaller brokerages and ECNs, more than the NYSE and Nasdaq, pushing for longer trading hours?

LG 6   Q2.5   Describe how, if at all, conservative and aggressive investors might use each of the following types of transactions as part of their investment programs. Contrast these two types of investors in view of these preferences.
   a. Long purchase
   b. Margin trading
   c. Short selling

Problems

LG 4   P2.1   The current exchange rate between the U.S. dollar and the Japanese yen is 116.915 (Yen/$). How many dollars would you get for 1,000 Japanese yen?

LG 4   P2.2   An investor recently sold some stock that was a Eurodollar investment for 20,000 euros. The U.S.$/euro exchange rate is currently 1.100. How many U.S. dollars will the investor receive?

 LG 4   P2.3   In each of the following cases, calculate the price of one share of the foreign stock measured in United States dollars (US$).
   a. A Belgian stock priced at 103.2 euros (€) when the exchange rate is .8595 €/US$.
   b. A Swiss stock priced at 93.3 Swiss francs (Sf) when the exchange rate is 1.333 Sf/US$.
   c. A Japanese stock priced at 1,350 yen (¥) when the exchange rate is 110 ¥/US$.

LG 4   P2.4   Lola Paretti purchased 50 shares of BMW, a German stock traded on the Frankfurt Exchange, for 64.5 euros (€) per share exactly 1 year ago, when the exchange rate was .78 €/US$. Today the stock is trading at 68.4 € per share, and the exchange rate is .86 €/US$.
   a. Did the € *depreciate* or *appreciate* relative to the US$ during the past year? Explain.
   b. How much in US$ did Lola pay for her 50 shares of BMW when she purchased them a year ago?
   c. For how much in US$ can Lola sell her BMW shares today?
   d. Ignoring brokerage fees and taxes, how much profit (or loss) in US$ will Lola realize on her BMW stock if she sells it today?

LG 4   P2.5   An investor believes that the U.S. dollar will rise in value relative to the Japanese yen. The same investor is considering two investments with identical risk and return characteristics: One is a Japanese yen investment and the other is a U.S. dollar investment. Should the investor purchase the Japanese yen investment?

LG 6   P2.6   Elmo Inc.'s stock is currently selling at $60 per share. For each of the following situations (ignoring brokerage commissions), calculate the gain or loss that Maureen Katz realizes if she makes a 100-share transaction.
   a. She sells short and repurchases the borrowed shares at $70 per share.
   b. She takes a long position and sells the stock at $75 per share.
   c. She sells short and repurchases the borrowed shares at $45 per share.
   d. She takes a long position and sells the stock at $60 per share.

LG 6   **P2.7**   Assume that an investor buys 100 shares of stock at $50 per share, putting up a 60% margin.
    a. What is the *debit balance* in this transaction?
    b. How much equity capital must the investor provide to make this margin transaction?

LG 6   **P2.8**   Assume that an investor buys 100 shares of stock at $50 per share, putting up a 60% margin. If the stock rises to $60 per share, what is the investor's new margin position?

LG 6   **P2.9**   Assume that an investor buys 100 shares of stock at $50 per share, putting up a 70% margin.
    a. What is the *debit balance* in this transaction?
    b. How much equity funds must the investor provide to make this margin transaction?
    c. If the stock rises to $80 per share, what is the investor's new margin position?

LG 6   **P2.10**   Doug purchased 100 shares of Can'tWin.com for $50 per share, using as little of his own money as he could. His broker has a 50% *initial margin* requirement and a 30% *maintenance margin* requirement. The price of the stock falls to $30 per share. What does Doug need to do?

LG 6   **P2.11**   Jerri Kingston bought 100 shares of stock at $80 per share, using an *initial margin* of 60%. Given a *maintenance margin* of 25%, how far does the stock have to drop before Ms. Kingston faces a *margin call*? (Assume that there are no other securities in the margin account.)

LG 6   **P2.12**   An investor buys 200 shares of stock selling at $80 per share, using a margin of 60%. The stock pays annual dividends of $1 per share. A margin loan can be obtained at an annual interest cost of 8%. Determine what return on invested capital the investor will realize if the price of the stock increases to $104 within 6 months. What is the *annualized* rate of return on this transaction?

LG 6   **P2.13**   Marlene Bellamy purchased 300 shares of Writeline Communications stock at $55 per share, using the prevailing minimum *initial margin* requirement of 50%. She held the stock for exactly 4 months and sold it without any brokerage costs at the end of that period. During the 4-month holding period, the stock paid $1.50 per share in cash dividends. Marlene was charged 9% annual interest on the margin loan. The minimum *maintenance margin* was 25%.
    a. Calculate the initial value of the transaction, the *debit balance,* and the equity position on Marlene's transaction.
    b. For each of the following share prices, calculate the actual margin percentage, and indicate whether Marlene's margin account would have excess equity, would be restricted, or would be subject to a margin call.
        (1) $45
        (2) $70
        (3) $35
    c. Calculate the dollar amount of (1) dividends received and (2) interest paid on the margin loan during the 4-month holding period.
    d. Use each of the following sale prices at the end of the 4-month holding period to calculate Marlene's *annualized* rate of return on the Writeline Communications stock transaction.
        (1) $50
        (2) $60
        (3) $70

LG 6   **P2.14** Not long ago, Dave Edwards bought 200 shares of Almost Anything Inc. at $45 per share; he bought the stock on margin of 60%. The stock is now trading at $60 per share, and the Federal Reserve has recently lowered *initial margin* requirements to 50%. Dave now wants to do a little *pyramiding* and buy another 300 shares of the stock. What is the minimum amount of equity that he'll have to put up in this transaction?

LG 6   **P2.15** An investor short sells 100 shares of a stock for $20 per share. The initial margin is 50%. How much equity will be required in the account to complete this transaction?

LG 6   **P2.16** An investor short sells 100 shares of a stock for $20 per share. The initial margin is 50%. Ignoring transaction costs, how much will be in the investor's account after this transaction if this is the only transaction the investor has undertaken and the investor has deposited only the required amount?

LG 6   **P2.17** An investor short sells 100 shares of a stock for $20 per share. The *initial margin* is 50%, and the *maintenance margin* is 30%. The price of the stock falls to $12 per share. What is the margin, and will there be a *margin call*?

LG 6   **P2.18** An investor short sells 100 shares of a stock for $20 per share. The *initial margin* is 50%, and the *maintenance margin* is 30%. The price of the stock rises to $28 per share. What is the margin, and will there be a *margin call*?

LG 6   **P2.19** Calculate the profit or loss per share realized on each of the following short-sale transactions.

Transaction	Stock Sold Short at Price/Share	Stock Purchased to Cover Short at Price/Share
A	$75	$83
B	30	24
C	18	15
D	27	32
E	53	45

LG 6   **P2.20** Charlene Hickman expected the price of Bio International shares to drop in the near future in response to the expected failure of its new drug to pass FDA tests. As a result, she sold short 200 shares of Bio International at $27.50. How much would Charlene earn or lose on this transaction if she repurchased the 200 shares 4 months later at each of the following prices per share?
    a. $24.75
    b. $25.13
    c. $31.25
    d. $27.00

See www.myfinancelab.com **for Web Exercises,**
Spreadsheets, and other online resources.

Case Problem 2.1   *Dara's Dilemma: What to Buy?*

LG 6   Dara Simmons, a 40-year-old financial analyst and divorced mother of two teenage children, considers herself a savvy investor. She has increased her investment portfolio considerably over the past 5 years. Although she has been fairly conservative with her investments, she now feels more confident in her investment knowledge and would like to branch out into some new areas that could bring higher returns. She has between $20,000 and $25,000 to invest.

Attracted to the hot market for technology stocks, Dara was interested in purchasing a tech IPO stock and identified "NewestHighTech.com," a company that makes sophisticated computer chips for wireless Internet connections, as a likely prospect. The 1-year-old company had received some favorable press when it got early-stage financing and again when its chip was accepted by a major cell phone manufacturer.

Dara also was considering an investment in 400 shares of Casinos International common stock, currently selling for $54 per share. After a discussion with a friend who is an economist with a major commercial bank, Dara believes that the long-running bull market is due to cool off and that economic activity will slow down. With the aid of her stockbroker, Dara researches Casinos International's current financial situation and finds that the future success of the company may hinge on the outcome of pending court proceedings on the firm's application to open a new floating casino on a nearby river. If the permit is granted, it seems likely that the firm's stock will experience a rapid increase in value, regardless of economic conditions. On the other hand, if the company fails to get the permit, the falling stock price will make it a good candidate for a short sale.

Dara felt that the following alternatives were open to her:

Alternative 1: Invest $20,000 in NewestHighTech.com when it goes public.

Alternative 2: Buy Casinos International now at $54 per share and follow the company closely.

Alternative 3: Sell Casinos short at $54 in anticipation that the company's fortunes will change for the worse.

Alternative 4: Wait to see what happens with the casino permit and then decide whether to buy or short the Casinos International stock.

Questions

a. Evaluate each of these alternatives. On the basis of the limited information presented, recommend the one you feel is best.

b. If Casinos International's stock price rises to $60, what will happen under alternatives 2 and 3? Evaluate the pros and cons of these outcomes.

c. If the stock price drops to $45, what will happen under alternatives 2 and 3? Evaluate the pros and cons of these outcomes.

Case Problem 2.2   *Ravi Dumar's High-Flying Margin Account*

LG 6   Ravi Dumar is a stockbroker who lives with his wife, Sasha, and their 5 children in Milwaukee, Wisconsin. Ravi firmly believes that the only way to make money in the market is to follow an aggressive investment posture—for example, to use margin trading. In fact, Ravi himself has built a substantial margin account over the years. He currently holds $75,000 worth of stock in his margin account, though the *debit balance* in the account amounts to only $30,000. Recently, Ravi uncovered a stock that, on the basis of extensive analysis, he feels is about to take off. The stock, Running Shoes (RS), currently trades at $20 per share. Ravi feels it should soar to at least $50 within a year. RS pays no dividends, the prevailing *initial margin* requirement is 50%, and margin loans are now carrying an annual interest charge of 10%. Because Ravi feels so strongly about RS, he wants to do some *pyramiding* by using his margin account to purchase 1,000 shares of the stock.

Questions

a. Discuss the concept of pyramiding as it applies to this investment situation.

b. What is the present margin position (in percent) of Ravi's account?

c. Ravi buys the 1,000 shares of RS through his margin account (bear in mind that this is a $20,000 transaction).
1. What will the margin position of the account be after the RS transaction if Ravi follows the prevailing initial margin (50%) and uses $10,000 of his money to buy the stock?
2. What if he uses only $2,500 equity and obtains a margin loan for the balance ($17,500)?
3. How do you explain the fact that the stock can be purchased with only 12.5% margin when the prevailing initial margin requirement is 50%?

d. Assume that Ravi buys 1,000 shares of RS stock at $20 per share with a minimum cash investment of $2,500 and that the stock does take off and its price rises to $40 per share in 1 year.
1. What is the *return on invested capital* for this transaction?
2. What return would Ravi have earned if he had bought the stock without margin—that is, if he had used all his own money?

e. What do you think of Ravi's idea to pyramid? What are the risks and rewards of this strategy?

Excel with Spreadsheets

You have just learned about the mechanics of margin trading and want to take advantage of the potential benefits of financial leverage. You have decided to open a margin account with your broker and to secure a margin loan. The specifics of the account are as follows:

- Initial margin requirement is 70%.
- Maintenance margin is 30%.
- You are informed that if the value of your account falls below the maintenance margin, your account will be subject to a margin call.

You have been following the price movements of a stock over the past year and believe that it is currently undervalued and that the price will rise in the near future. You feel that the opening of a margin account is a good investment strategy. You have decided to purchase three round lots (i.e., 100 shares per round lot) of the stock at its current price of $25 per share.

Create a spreadsheet similar to the spreadsheet for Table 2.3, which can be viewed at www.myfinancelab.com, to model and analyze the following market transactions.

Questions

a.   Calculate the value of the investment in the stock as if you did not make use of margin trading. In other words, what is the value of the investment if it is funded by 100% cash equity?

b.   Calculate the debit balance and the cash equity in the investment at the time of opening a margin account, adhering to the initial margin requirement.

c.   If you use margin and the price of the stock rises by $15 to $40/share, calculate the capital gain earned and the return on investor's equity.

d.   What is the current margin percentage based on question **b**?

e.   If you use margin and the price of the stock falls by $15 to $10/share, calculate the capital loss and the respective return on investor's equity.

f.   What is the new margin percentage based on question **e**, and what is the implication for you, the investor?

Chapter 3

Investment Information and Securities Transactions

Millions of Web pages devoted to stocks and investment strategies put everything at your fingertips—literally—and most of it is free. Here are some basic steps to follow in finding and using that information.

First, determine your investment objectives and do some initial research to identify your risk tolerance and investment time horizon. Online risk tolerance surveys at www.fizone.com/Investing/RiskTolerance.asp and at www.wellsfargo.com/retirement_tools/risk_tolerance, among others, can help you determine your investing style. Next, visit financial portal sites such as those offered by Yahoo! (http://finance.yahoo.com), Morningstar (www.morningstar.com), and CNN/Money (http://money.cnn.com). These sites can help you familiarize yourself with stocks and what's happening currently in the markets.

With the recent high fuel prices, you might be interested in investing in oil company stocks. Stock screening tools at sites like Quicken (www.quicken.com) and Morningstar will help narrow the field. For example, you can define search criteria such as energy stocks with a price/earnings (P/E) ratio of less than 15, return on equity (ROE) greater than 20%, and a 5-year total return that exceeds the S&P 500. (In subsequent chapters you'll learn what these measures mean.) Within a few seconds, you'll have a list of stocks that meet your parameters, including Chevron, ExxonMobil, Marathon Oil, and Valero Energy.

Then, head to each company's Web site to find the latest annual report and press releases. More detailed Securities and Exchange Commission (SEC) filings are available online as well at www.sec.gov and at www.freeedgar.com. Find out what the securities analysts say: You can buy individual stock research reports at Yahoo! or Reuters Investor (go to www.investor.reuters.com, then click on [Analyst Research]). Armed with this information, you can evaluate your finalists and make your selection.

In reality, picking stocks may not be quite that easy. Nevertheless, the power of the Internet enables you to access in minutes information that in the past was either unavailable to the average investor or would take weeks to accumulate. In Chapter 3, you'll learn more about the many sources of investment information, both online and offline, as well as how to make transactions.

Sources: http://screen.morningstar.com/StockSelector.html?tsection=toolsssel (accessed July 2006); http://finance.yahoo.com/ (accessed July 2006); and http://search.yahoo.com/search?ei=utf-8&fr=slvl-&p=risk+tolerance+survey (accessed July 2006).

Online Investing

LG 1

Today the Internet is a major force in the investing environment. It has opened the world of investing to individual investors, providing access to tools formerly restricted to professionals. You can trade many types of securities online and also find a wealth of information. This information ranges from real-time stock price quotes to securities analysts' research reports and tools for investment analysis. The time and money savings from online investing are huge. Instead of wading through mounds of paper, you can quickly sort through vast databases to find appropriate investments, monitor your current investments, and make securities transactions—all without leaving your computer.

Because new Web sites appear every day and existing ones change constantly, it's impossible to describe all the good ones. Our intent is to give you a sampling of Web sites that will introduce you to the wealth of investing information available on the Internet. You'll find plenty of good sources to help you stay current.

▌Getting Started in Online Investing

Online investing's popularity continues to grow at a rapid pace. Why? Because the Internet makes buying and selling securities convenient, relatively simple, inexpensive, and fast. It provides the most current information, updated continuously. Even if you prefer to use a human broker, the Internet provides an abundance of resources to help you become a more informed investor.

To successfully navigate the cyberinvesting universe, open your Web browser and explore the multitude of investing sites. These sites typically include a combination of resources for novice and sophisticated investors alike. For example, look at brokerage firm TD Ameritrade's homepage (www.tdameritrade.com), shown in Figure 3.1 (on page 106). With a few mouse clicks you can learn about TD Ameritrade's services, open an account, and begin trading. In addition, you will find the day's and week's market activity, price quotes, news, analysts' research reports, and more. You can learn about various aspects of investing, including products, and plan to achieve your financial goals through Ameritrade.

All this information can be overwhelming and intimidating. It takes time and effort to use the Internet wisely. But the Internet itself helps you sort through the maze. Educational sites are a good place to start. Then you can check out the many investment tools. In the following section, we'll discuss how to use the Internet wisely to become a smarter investor.

Investment Education Sites The Internet offers many tutorials, online classes, and articles to educate the novice investor. Even experienced investors will find sites that expand their investing knowledge. Although most investing-oriented Web sites and financial portals (described later) include many educational resources, here are a few good sites that feature investing fundamentals.

- *Investing Online Resource Center* (www.investingonline.org) is an educational site that provides a wealth of information for those getting started online as well as those already investing online. It includes an

| FIGURE 3.1 | Investment Resources at the TD Ameritrade Web Site |

TD Ameritrade's Web site presents a wealth of investment resources. You can open an account, assess market activity, obtain news, access analysts' research, and more. (*Source:* TD Ameritrade Investor Services, Inc., New York, www.tdameritrade.com. ©2006 TD Ameritrade IP Company, Inc. All Rights Reserved. Used with permission.)

investment simulator that creates an online interactive learning experience that allows the user to "test drive" online trading.

- *InvestorGuide.com* (www.investorguide.com) is a free educational site offering InvestorGuide University, which is a collection of educational articles about investing and personal finance. In addition, the site provides access to quotes and charts, portfolio tracking software, research, news and commentary, and a glossary through InvestorWords.com (www.investorwords.com).

- *The Motley Fool* (www.fool.com) has sections on investing basics, mutual fund investing, choosing a broker, and investment strategies and styles, as well as lively discussion boards and more.

- Investopedia (www.investopedia.com) is an educational site featuring tutorials on numerous basic and advanced investing and personal finance topics, a dictionary of investing terms, and other useful investment aids.

- *WSJ.com* (www.wsj.com), a free site from the *Wall Street Journal*, is an excellent starting place to learn what the Internet can offer investors.

- Nasdaq (www.nasdaq.com) has a Personal Finance section that provides links to a number of investment education resources.

Other good educational sites include leading personal finance magazines such as *Money* (money.cnn.com), *Kiplinger's Personal Finance Magazine* (www .kiplinger.com), and *Smart Money* (www.smartmoney.com).

Investment Tools Once you are familiar with investing basics, you can use the Internet to develop financial plans and set investment goals, find securities that meet your objectives, analyze potential investments, and organize your portfolio. Many of these tools, once used only by professional investment advisers, are free online. You'll find financial calculators and worksheets, screening and charting tools, and stock quotes and portfolio trackers at general financial sites (described in the later section on financial portals) and at the Web sites of larger brokerage firms. You can even set up a personal calendar that notifies you of forthcoming earnings announcements and can receive alerts when one of your stocks has hit a predetermined price target.

Planning Online calculators and worksheets help you find answers to your financial planning and investing questions. With them you can figure out how much to save each month for a particular goal, such as the down payment for your first home, a college education for your children, or retiring when you are 60. For example, the brokerage firm Fidelity (www.fidelity.com) has a number of planning tools: college planning, retirement planning, and research tools. One of the best sites for financial calculators is Kiplinger's Personal Finance (kiplinger.com/personalfinance/tools/?). It includes numerous calculators for financial planning, insurance, auto and home buying, and investing. Figure 3.2 (on page 108) lists, in question form, a series of calculators specifically concerned with stocks. Other investment-related calculators focus on bonds and mutual funds. (Because not all calculators give the same answer, you may want to try out those at several sites.)

Screening With screening tools, you can quickly sort through huge databases of stocks, bonds, and mutual funds to find those that have specific characteristics. For stocks, you can specify low or high price/earnings ratios, small market value, high dividend return, specific revenue growth, and/or a low debt-to-equity ratio. For bonds, you can specify a given industry, maturity date, or yield. For mutual funds, you might specify low minimum investment, a particular industry or geographical sector, and low fees. Each screening tool uses a different method to sort. You answer a series of questions to specify the type of stock or fund, performance criteria, cost parameters, and so on. Then you can do more research on the stocks, bonds, or mutual funds that meet your requirements.

FIGURE 3.2   **Financial Calculators Concerned with Stocks**

At sites like Kiplinger's Personal Finance, you'll find many calculators that you can use to solve specific problems. Below is the screen listing, in question form, of a series of investment-related stock calculators available at Kiplinger's site. Input the variables for your situation, and the calculator will show you the selling price at which you will earn the desired return on your stock investment. (*Source:* Kiplinger's Personal Finance, **www.kiplingers.com/personalfinance/tools/investing**. Screenshot courtesy of Kiplinger's Personal Finance. ©2006 The Kiplinger Washington Editors.)

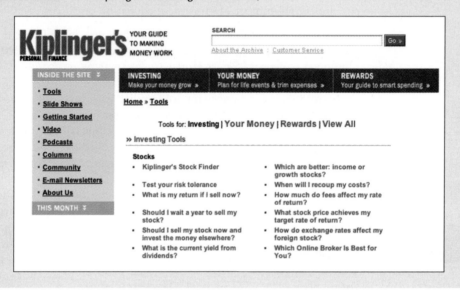

Zacks.com (www.zacks.com/research/screening/index.php) provides some of the best free tools. Figure 3.3 shows the opening page for Zacks "Predefined Screener" that lists searches based on the most popular investment strategies. The "Custom Screener" includes 96 items from the proprietary Zacks database. MSN Money (moneycentral.msn.com/investor/finder/customstocksdl.asp) also offers some excellent free tools, both "Power Searches" that offer a number of preset searches and "Custom Searches" that allow you to create your own stock search. Yahoo!Finance (screen.yahoo.com/stocks.html) offers some of the best screening tools. You can check out the site's prebuilt screens—for example, "Stocks with Greatest Sales Revenue" and "Stocks with Strong Forecasted Growth." Morningstar (www.morningstar.com) also offers some free tools but charges $14.95 a month or $135 per year for its premium tools.

Charting Charting is a technique that plots the performance of stocks over a specified time period, from months to decades and beyond. Looking at the 1-year stock chart for Qualcomm (QCOM) in Figure 3.4 (on page 110), it's obvious that charting can be tedious and therefore expensive. But by going online, you can see the chart for a selected stock in just seconds. With another click you can compare one company's price performance to that of other stocks, industries, sectors, or market indexes, choosing the type of chart, time frame, and indicators. Several good sites are Barchart (www.barchart.com), BigCharts (bigcharts.marketwatch.com), and StockCharts.com (www.stockcharts.com). All have free charting features; Barchart charges a monthly fee for advanced capabilities.

FIGURE 3.3   **Zacks Predefined Screener**

Search for stocks based on popular investment strategies. The predefined searches allow selection from a list of predefined criteria such as "Top EPS Growth," "Highest Dividend Yields," and "Top (%) Price Movers 4 Weeks." Zacks stock screening tool will give you a list of stocks that meet your specifications. (*Source:* Zacks, www.zacks.com/research/screening/index.php. Screenshot courtesy of Zacks. Reprinted with permission from Zacks Investment Research. ©2006 Zacks Investment Research, Inc.)

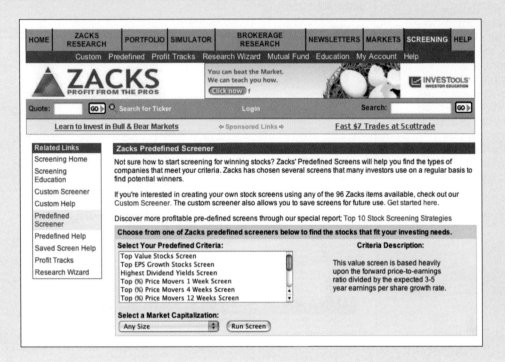

Stock Quotes and Portfolio Tracking Almost every investment-oriented Web site includes stock quotation and portfolio tracking tools. Simply enter the stock symbol to get the price, either in real time or delayed several minutes. Once you create a portfolio of stocks in a portfolio tracker, the tracker automatically updates your portfolio's value every time you check. You can usually link to more detailed information about each stock. Many sites let you set up multiple portfolios. The features, quality, and ease of use of stock and portfolio trackers varies, so check several to find the one that best meets your needs. Yahoo! Finance (edit.finance.yahoo.com/e3?.scr=quote.intl.=us), MSN.Money (moneycentral.msn.com/investor), and Morningstar (portfolio.morningstar.com/portasp/allview.asp?pgid=hetabport) have portfolio trackers that are easy to set up and customize.

▮ Pros and Cons of Using the Internet as an Investment Tool

The power of the Internet as an investing tool is alluring. "Do-it-yourself" investing is readily available to the average investor, even to novices who have never before bought stock. However, online investing also carries risks. Trading on the Internet requires that investors exercise the same—and possibly more—caution than they would if they were getting information from and

FIGURE 3.4

Stock Chart for Qualcomm
Specify the company's time frame and frequency (e.g., daily, weekly), and BigCharts will in seconds perform the tedious process of charting the selected stock's price (in this case, the price of Qualcomm) over the specified time frame (in this case, the year ended July 10, 2006). (*Source:* BigCharts Inc. is a service of MarketWatch, Inc., 201 California Street, San Francisco, CA 94111. bigcharts.marketwatch .com.)

placing orders with a human broker. You don't have the safety net of a live broker suggesting that you rethink your trade. The ease of point-and-click investing can be the financial downfall of inexperienced investors. Drawn by stories of others who have made lots of money, many novice investors take the plunge before they acquire the necessary skills and knowledge—often with disastrous results.

Online or off, the basic rules for smart investing are the same. Know what you are buying, from whom, and at what level of risk. Be skeptical. If it sounds too good to be true, it probably is! Always do your own research; don't accept someone else's word that a security is a good buy. Perform your own analysis before you buy, using the skills you will develop in later chapters of this book.

Here is some additional advice:

- Don't let the speed and ease of making transactions blind you to the realities of online trading. More frequent trades mean high total transaction costs. Although some brokers advertise per-trade costs as low as $3, the average online transaction fee is higher (generally about $10 to $15). If you trade often, it will take longer to recoup your costs. Studies reveal that the more often you trade, the harder it is to beat the market. In addition, on short-term trades of less than one year, you'll pay taxes on profits at the higher, ordinary income tax rates, not the lower capital gains rate.

- Don't believe everything you read on the Internet. It's easy to be impressed with a screen full of data touting a stock's prospects or to act on a hot tip you find on a discussion board or in an online chat (more on this later). But what do you know about the person who posts the information? He or she could be a shill for a dealer, posing as an enthusiastic investor to push a stock. Stick to the sites of major brokerage firms, mutual funds, academic institutions, and well-known business and finance publications.

- If you get bitten by the online buying bug, don't be tempted to use margin debt to increase your stock holdings. As noted in Chapter 2, you may instead be magnifying your losses.

We will return to the subject of online investment fraud and scams and will discuss guidelines for online transactions in subsequent sections of this chapter.

CONCEPTS IN REVIEW

Answers available at: www.myfinancelab.com

3.1 Discuss the impact of the Internet on the individual investor, and summarize the types of resources it provides.

3.2 Identify the four main types of online investment tools. How can they help you become a better investor?

3.3 What are some of the pros and cons of using the Internet to choose and manage your investments?

Types and Sources of Investment Information

LG 2

As you learned in Chapter 1, becoming a successful investor starts with developing investment plans and meeting your liquidity needs. Once you have done that, you can search for the right investments to implement your investment plan and monitor your progress toward achieving your goals. Whether you use the Internet or print sources, you should examine various kinds of investment information to formulate expectations of the risk–return behaviors of potential investments and to monitor them once they are acquired. This section describes the key types and sources of investment information; the following section focuses on market averages and indexes.

descriptive information
factual data on the past behavior of the economy, the market, the industry, the company, or a given investment vehicle.

Investment information can be either descriptive or analytical. **Descriptive information** presents factual data on the past behavior of the economy, the market, the industry, the company, or a given investment vehicle. **Analytical information** presents available current data in conjunction with projections and recommendations about potential investments. The sample page from *Value Line* included in Figure 3.5 (on page 112) provides both descriptive and analytical information on Wal-Mart Stores. We have marked items that are primarily descriptive with a D, and analytical items with an A. The key below the Value Line page explains the marked items. Examples of descriptive information are the company's capital structure (7D) and monthly stock price ranges for the past 13 years (13D). Examples of analytical information are

analytical information
available current data in conjunction with projections and recommendations about potential investments.

FIGURE 3.5   A Report Containing Descriptive and Analytical Information

Value Line's full-page report on Wal-Mart Stores from May 12, 2006, contains both descriptive (marked D) and analytical (marked A) information. (*Source:* Adapted from *The Value Line Investment Survey*, Ratings and Reports, May 12, 2006. ©Value Line Publishing, Inc., www.valueline.com. ©2006 Reproduced with the permission of Value Line Publishing, Inc.)

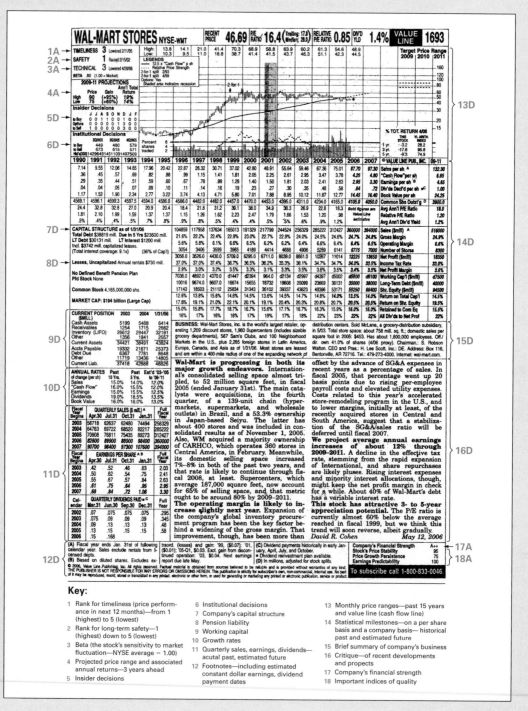

Key:

1. Rank for timeliness (price performance in next 12 months)—from 1 (highest) to 5 (lowest)
2. Rank for long-term safety—1 (highest) down to 5 (lowest)
3. Beta (the stock's sensitivity to market fluctuation—NYSE average = 1.00)
4. Projected price range and associated annual returns—3 years ahead
5. Insider decisions

6. Institutional decisions
7. Company's capital structure
8. Pension liability
9. Working capital
10. Growth rates
11. Quarterly sales, earnings, dividends—acutal past, estimated future
12. Footnotes—including estimated constant dollar earnings, dividend payment dates

13. Monthly price ranges—past 15 years and value line (cash flow line)
14. Statistical milestones—on a per share basis and a company basis— historical past and estimated future
15. Brief summary of company's business
16. Critique—of recent developments and propects
17. Company's financial strength
18. Important indices of quality

rank for timeliness (1A) and projected price range and associated annual total returns for the next 3 years (4A).

Some forms of investment information are free; others must be purchased individually or by annual subscription. You'll find free information on the Internet; in newspapers, in magazines, and at brokerage firms; and at public, university, and brokerage firm libraries. Alternatively, you can subscribe to free and paid services that provide periodic reports summarizing the investment outlook and recommending certain actions. Many Internet sites now offer free e-mail newsletters and alerts. You can even set up your own personalized home page at many financial Web sites so that stock quotes, portfolio tracking, current business news, and other information on stocks of interest to you appear whenever you visit the site. Other sites charge for premium content, such as brokerage research reports, whether in print or online form.

Although the Internet has increased the amount of free information, it may still make sense to pay for services that save you time and money by gathering material you need. But first consider the value of potential information: For example, paying $40 for information that increases your return by $27 would not be economically sound. The larger your investment portfolio, the easier it is to justify information purchases, because they are usually applicable to a number of investments.

■ Types of Information

Investment information can be divided into five types, each concerned with an important aspect of the investment process.

1. *Economic and current event information:* Includes background as well as forecast data related to economic, political, and social trends on a domestic as well as a global scale. Such information provides a basis for assessing the environment in which decisions are made.
2. *Industry and company information:* Includes background as well as forecast data on specific industries and companies. Investors use such information to assess the outlook in a given industry or a specific company. Because of its company orientation, it is most relevant to stock, bond, or options investments.
3. *Information on alternative investment vehicles:* Includes background and predictive data for securities other than stocks, bonds, and options, such as mutual funds and futures.
4. *Price information:* Includes current price quotations on certain investment vehicles, particularly securities. These quotations are commonly accompanied by statistics on the recent price behavior of the vehicle.
5. *Information on personal investment strategies:* Includes recommendations on investment strategies or specific purchase or sale actions. In general, this information tends to be educational or analytical rather than descriptive.

■ Sources of Information

A complete listing of the sources of each type of investment information is beyond the scope of this book. Our discussion focuses on the most common online and traditional sources of information on economic and current events, industries and companies, and prices, as well as other online sources.

Economic and Current Event Information Investors who are aware of current economic, political, and business events tend to make better investment decisions. Popular sources of economic and current event information include financial journals, general newspapers, institutional news, business periodicals, government publications, and special subscription services. These are available in print and online versions; often the online versions are free but may have limited content. Most offer free searchable article archives and charge a nominal fee for each article downloaded.

Financial Journals The *Wall Street Journal* is the most popular source of financial news. Published daily Monday through Saturday in regional, European, and Asian editions, the *Journal* also has an online version called the *WSJ Online* (www.wsj.com), which is updated frequently throughout the day and on the weekends. In addition to giving daily price quotations on thousands of investment vehicles, the *Journal* reports world, national, regional, and corporate news. The first page of its third section usually contains a column called "Heard on the Street" that focuses on specific market and company events. In addition, a fourth section containing articles that address personal finance issues and topics is included in the Tuesday, Wednesday, and Thursday editions, and an expanded version of that section, called "Weekend Journal," is included in Friday's edition. A full-price print subscription to the *Wall Street Journal* costs $215 annually, compared to $99 per year for the online version; print subscribers pay $49 to add the online edition. *WSJ Online* includes features such as quotes and news that provide stock and mutual fund charting, company profiles, financials, and analyst ratings; article searches; special online-only articles; and access to the Dow Jones article archives.

A second popular source of financial news is *Barron's*, which is published weekly. *Barron's* generally offers lengthier articles on a variety of topics of interest to individual investors. Probably the most popular column in *Barron's* is "Up & Down Wall Street," which provides a critical, and often humorous, assessment of major developments affecting the stock market and business. *Barron's* also includes current price quotations and a summary of statistics on a range of investment vehicles. Subscribers to *WSJ Online* also have access to *Barron's* online edition (www.barrons.com) because both are published by Dow Jones & Company.

Investor's Business Daily is a third national business newspaper published Monday through Friday. It is similar to the *Wall Street Journal* but contains more detailed price and market data. Its Web site (www.investors.com) has limited free content. Another source of financial news is the *Financial Times* (www.ft.com), with U.S., U.K., European, and Asian editions.

General Newspapers Major metropolitan newspapers such as the *New York Times, Washington Post, Los Angeles Times,* and *Chicago Tribune* provide investors with a wealth of financial information in their print and online editions. Most major newspapers contain stock price quotations for major exchanges, price quotations on stocks of local interest, and a summary of the major stock market averages and indexes. Local newspapers are another convenient source of financial news. In most large cities, the daily newspaper devotes at least a few pages to financial and business news.

Wall Street Journal
a daily business newspaper, published regionally; the most popular source of financial news.

HOTLINKS

Federal Reserve Economic Data (FRED) has a historical database of economic and financial statistics.

www.research.stlouisfed.org/fred2/

Barron's
a weekly business newspaper; a popular source of financial news.

Another popular source of financial news is *USA Today,* the national newspaper published daily Monday through Friday. It is available in print and online versions (usatoday.com). Each issue contains a "Money" section (Section B) devoted to business and personal financial news and to current security price quotations and summary statistics.

Institutional News The monthly economic letters of the nation's leading banks, such as Bank of America (based in Charlotte, North Carolina), Northern Trust (Chicago), and Wells Fargo (San Francisco), provide useful economic information. Wire services such as Dow Jones, Bloomberg Financial Services, AP (Associated Press), and UPI (United Press International) provide economic and business news feeds to brokerages, other financial institutions, and Web sites that subscribe to them. Bloomberg has its own comprehensive site (www.bloomberg.com). Business.com (www.business.com) offers industry-by-industry news, targeted business searches, and employment resources by industry. Web sites specializing in financial news include CNNMoney (money.cnn.com) and MarketWatch (www.marketwatch.com).

Business Periodicals Business periodicals vary in scope. Some present general business and economic articles, others cover securities markets and related topics, and still others focus solely on specific industries. Regardless of the subject matter, most business periodicals present descriptive information, and some also include analytical information. They rarely offer recommendations.

The business sections of general-interest periodicals such as *Newsweek, Time,* and *U.S. News & World Report* cover business and economic news. Strictly business- and finance-oriented periodicals, including *Business Week, Fortune,* and *The Economist,* provide more in-depth articles. These magazines also have investing and personal finance articles.

Some financial periodicals specialize in securities and marketplace articles. The most basic, commonsense articles appear in *Forbes, Kiplinger's Personal Finance, Money, SmartMoney,* and *Worth.* Published every two weeks, *Forbes* is the most investment-oriented. *Kiplinger's Personal Finance, Money, Smart-Money,* and *Worth* are published monthly and contain articles on managing personal finances and on investments.

All these business and personal finance magazines have Web sites with free access to recent, if not all, content. Most include a number of other features. For example, *SmartMoney* has interactive investment tools, including a color-coded "Market Map 1000" that gives an aerial view of 1,000 U.S. and international stocks so that you can see which sectors and stocks are hot.

Government Publications A number of government agencies publish economic data and reports useful to investors. The annual *Economic Report of the President* (www.access.gpo.gov/eop/) provides a broad view of the current and expected state of the economy. This document reviews and summarizes economic policy and conditions and includes data on important aspects of the economy.

The *Federal Reserve Bulletin,* published monthly by the Board of Governors of the Federal Reserve System, and periodic reports published by each of the 12 Federal Reserve District Banks provide articles and data on various aspects of economic and business activity. (Visit www.federalreserve.gov to read many of these publications.)

A useful Department of Commerce publication is the *Survey of Current Business* (www.bea.gov/bea/pubs.htm). Published monthly, it includes indicators and data related to economic and business conditions. A good source of financial statement information on all manufacturers, broken down by industry and asset size, is the *Quarterly Financial Report for U.S. Manufacturing, Mining, and Wholesale Trade Corporations* (www.census.gov/csd/qfr/view/qfr_mg.html), published by the Department of Commerce.

Special Subscription Services Investors who want additional insights into business and economic conditions can subscribe to special services. These reports include business and economic forecasts and give notice of new government policies, union plans and tactics, taxes, prices, wages, and so on. One popular service is the *Kiplinger Washington Letter*, a weekly publication that provides a wealth of economic information and analyses.

Industry and Company Information Of special interest to investors is information on particular industries and companies. Often, after choosing an industry in which to invest, an investor will want to analyze specific companies. A recent change in disclosure rules, discussed below, gives individual investors access to more company information than before. General business periodicals such as *Business Week, Forbes*, the *Wall Street Journal*, and *Fortune* carry articles on the activities of specific industries and individual companies. Trade publications such as *Chemical Week, American Banker, Computerworld, Industry Week, Oil and Gas Journal*, and *Public Utilities Fortnightly* provide more focused industry and company information. *Red Herring, PC Magazine, Business 2.0*, and *Fast Company* are magazines that can help you keep up with the high-tech world; all have good Web sites.

The Internet makes it easy to research specific industries and companies at the company's Web site, a publication's archive search, or database services such as the Dow Jones Publications Library. Company Web sites typically offer a wealth of information about the company—investor information, annual reports, filings, and financial releases, press releases, and more. Table 3.1 presents several free and subscription resources that emphasize industry and company information.

TABLE 3.1   **Online Sources for Industry and Company Information**

Web Site	Description	Cost
Hoover's Online (www.hoovers.com)	Reports and news on public and private companies with in-depth coverage of 43,000 of the world's top firms.	$599 per year for individual accounts.
CNET (news.com.com)	One of the best sites for high-tech news, analysis, breaking news, great search capabilities, links.	Free.
Yahoo! Finance (finance.yahoo.com)	Provides information on companies from around the Web: stock quotes, news, investment ideas, research, financials, analyst ratings, insider trades, and more.	Free.
Market Watch (www.marketwatch.com)	Latest news from various wire services. Searchable by market or industry. Good for earnings announcements and company news.	Free.

fair disclosure rule (Regulation FD)
rule requiring senior executives to disclose critical information simultaneously to investment professionals and the public via press releases or SEC filings.

Fair Disclosure Rules In August 2000, the SEC passed the **fair disclosure rule**, known as **Regulation FD**, a rule requiring senior executives to disclose critical information such as earnings forecasts and news of mergers and new products simultaneously to investment professionals and the public via press releases or SEC filings. Companies may limit contact with analysts if they are unsure whether the information requires a press release. However, Regulation FD does not apply to communications with journalists and securities ratings firms like Moody's Investors Service and Standard & Poor's. Violations of the rule carry injunctions and fines but are not considered fraud.

stockholders' (annual) report
a report published yearly by a publicly held corporation; contains a wide range of information, including financial statements for the most recent period of operation.

Stockholders' Reports An excellent source of data on an individual firm is the **stockholders' report**, or **annual report**, published yearly by publicly held corporations. These reports contain a wide range of information, including financial statements for the most recent period of operation, along with summarized statements for several prior years. These reports are free and may be obtained from the companies themselves, from brokers, or downloaded from the company's Web site. The cover and a sample page from Wal-Mart Stores, Inc. 2005 stockholders' report are shown in Figure 3.6 (on page 118). Most companies now place their annual reports on their Web sites. Report Gallery (www.annualreports.com) provides links to more than 2,000 company reports.

In addition to the stockholders' report, many serious investors review a company's **Form 10-K**. This is a statement that firms with securities listed on a securities exchange or traded in the OTC market must file annually with the SEC. Finding 10-K and other SEC filings is now a simple task, thanks to SEC/Edgar (Electronic Data Gathering and Analysis Retrieval), which has reports filed by all companies traded on a major exchange. You can read them free either at the SEC's Web site (www.sec.gov/edgar.shtml) or at EDGAR Online's FreeEdgar site (www.freeedgar.com).

Form 10-K
a statement that must be filed annually with the SEC by all firms having securities listed on a securities exchange or traded in the OTC market.

Comparative Data Sources Sources of comparative data, typically broken down by industry and firm size, are a good tool for analyzing the financial condition of companies. Among these sources are Dun & Bradstreet's *Key Business Ratios*, RMA's *Annual Statement Studies*, the *Quarterly Financial Report for U.S. Manufacturing, Mining, and Wholesale Trade Corporations* (cited above), and the *Almanac of Business & Industrial Financial Ratios*. These sources, which are typically available in public and university libraries, are a useful benchmark for evaluating a company's financial condition.

Subscription Services A variety of subscription services provide data on specific industries and companies. Today, many of these services are available on the Internet. Generally, a subscriber pays a basic fee to access the service's information and can purchase premium services for greater depth or range. The major subscription services provide both descriptive and analytical information, but they generally do not make recommendations. Most investors, rather than subscribing to these services, access them through their stockbrokers or a large public or university library. The Web sites for most services offer some free information and charge for the rest.

Standard & Poor's Corporation (S&P)
publisher of a large number of financial reports and services, including *Corporation Records* and *Stock Reports*.

The dominant subscription services are those offered by Standard & Poor's, Mergent, and Value Line. Table 3.2 (on page 119) summarizes the most popular services of these companies. **Standard & Poor's Corporation (S&P)**

FIGURE 3.6 Pages from a Stockholders' Report

The "Financial Highlights" on the right-hand page from the 2005 Annual Report of Wal-Mart Stores, Inc., quickly acquaints the investor with some key information on the firm's operations over the past year. The cover of the Annual Report is shown on the left-hand page. The actual Annual Report is available at Wal-Mart's Web site www.walmartfacts.com/articles/2231.aspx. (*Source:* Wal-Mart Stores, Inc. 2005 Annual Report; Wal-Mart Stores, Inc., Investor Relations, 479-273-8446, Wal-Mart Stores, Inc., Bentonville, AR 72716-8611.)

Financial Highlights

Fiscal Years Ended January 31, (In Millions Except Per Share Data)	2005	2004	2003	2002	2001
Net Sales	$285,222	$256,329	$229,616	$204,011	$180,787
Cost of Sales	$219,793	$198,747	$178,299	$159,097	$140,720
Net Income	$ 10,267	$ 9,054	$ 7,955	$ 6,592	$ 6,235
Diluted Earnings Per Share	$ 2.41	$ 2.07	$ 1.79	$ 1.47	$ 1.39
Long-term Debt	$ 20,087	$ 17,102	$ 16,597	$ 15,676	$ 12,489
Return on Assets[1]	9.3%	9.2%	9.2%	8.4%	8.6%
Return on Shareholders' Equity[2]	22.1%	21.3%	20.9%	19.4%	21.3%

(1) Income from continuing operations before minority interest divided by average assets.
(2) Income from continuing operations divided by average shareholders' equity.

Wal-Mart also returned to our shareholders more than $6.7 billion, in the form of more than $2.2 billion in dividends and more than $4.5 billion in share repurchase.

Outstanding Growth Prospects
In the coming year, we plan to open as many as 530 new stores. This includes adding up to 250 more Supercenters, 45 new Discount Stores, 40 new SAM'S CLUBS® and 30 new Neighborhood Markets in the United States. Internationally, our plan is to open as many as 165 new locations. Combined, these new stores will represent more than an eight percent square footage growth or, put another way, the addition of approximately 55 million square feet of new retail space, and this does not include the square footage of our distribution centers.

Our ability to add successfully this many stores to our business, year after year, is one of Wal-Mart's most significant achievements and core strengths. Yet, even internally, we sometimes take this accomplishment for granted since we do it with such apparent ease. In fact, this is not as easy as it looks, but we hope it is a unique and special capability that you take pride in as a Wal-Mart shareholder.

"As we look back on last year and reflect on the overall performance of our company, we hope one thing is crystal clear to you as a shareholder: Wal-Mart's health and future growth prospects have never been stronger."

As part of this growth, we are making a concerted effort to work more collaboratively with our communities. This includes being more flexible with city leaders on our individual store designs, and making sure we are a good local citizen as we open new stores. Last year in the U.S., for example, Wal-Mart donated more than $170 million to local community organizations and causes, making us the largest cash contributor to charity in corporate America.

However, if we can put all the big numbers aside for a moment, one of the most exciting aspects about Wal-Mart today is how much room we have yet to grow, both in the U.S. and around the world, and how much career opportunity we are creating for our associates as we grow.

For example, even with the size and success we have achieved, today Wal-Mart has earned less than three percent of the global retail market share. In other words, about 97 percent of the retail business around the world is not being done at Wal-Mart today.

In the U.S. alone, we estimate there is room for almost 4,000 more Supercenters. In some areas, we locate new stores close to existing stores, a fact some have questioned. We take this approach in growing markets for several reasons. First, as the market continues to grow, we are

12 WAL-MART 2005 ANNUAL REPORT

Mergent
publisher of a variety of financial material, including *Mergent's Manuals.*

Value Line Investment Survey
one of the most popular subscription services used by individual investors; subscribers receive three basic reports weekly.

(www2.standardandpoors.com) offers a large number of different financial reports and services. Its Investing Web site, owned by *Business Week* (www.businessweek.com/investor), is geared toward individual investors. Although basic news and market commentary is free, *Business Week* subscribers obtain access to premium online services. **Mergent** (formerly Moody's Financial Information Services Division) (www.mergent.com) also publishes a variety of material, including its equity and bond portraits, corporate research, well-known reference manuals on eight industries, and numerous other products. The *Value Line Investment Survey* (www.valueline.com) is one of the most popular subscription services used by individual investors. It is available at most libraries and provides online access to additional services including data, graphing, portfolio tracking, and technical indicators.

TABLE 3.2 Popular Offerings of the Major Subscription Services

Subscription Service/Offerings	Coverage	Frequency of Publication
Standard & Poor's Corporation (www2.standardandpoors.com)		
Corporation Records	Detailed descriptions of publicly traded securities of over 12,000 public corporations.	Annually with updates throughout the year.
Stock Reports (sample shown in Figure 7.1, page 313)	Summary of financial history, current finances, and future prospects of about 5,000 companies.	Annually with updates throughout the year.
Stock Guide	Statistical data and analytical rankings of investment desirability for major stocks.	Monthly.
Bond Guide	Statistical data and analytical rankings of investment desirability of over 10,000 bonds.	Monthly.
The Outlook	Analytical articles with investment advice on the economy, market, and investments.	Weekly magazine.
Mergent (www.mergent.com)		
Mergent's Manuals	Eight reference manuals—*Bank and Finance, Industrial, International, Municipal and Government, OTC Industrial, OTC Unlisted, Public Utility,* and *Transportation*—with historical and current financial, organizational, and operational data on major firms.	Annually with monthly print updates (weekly online updates).
Handbook of Common Stocks	Common stock data on nearly 900 NYSE companies.	Quarterly.
Dividend Record	Recent dividend announcements and payments on more than 30,000 securities.	Twice weekly, with annual summary.
Bond Record	Price and interest rate behavior of over 68,000 issues.	Monthly.
Value Line Investment Survey (www.valueline.com)		
Includes three reports:		Weekly.
1. *Ratings and Reports* (sample shown in Figure 3.5)	Full-page report including financial data, descriptions, analysis, and ratings for each of about 130 stocks.	
2. *Selection and Opinion*	A 12- to 16-page report featuring a discussion of the U.S. economy and the stock market, sample portfolios for different types of investors, and an in-depth analysis of selected stocks.	
3. *Summary and Index*	A 40-page update listing about 1,700 of the most widely held stocks. Also includes a variety of stock screens.	

back-office research reports
a brokerage firm's analyses of and recommendations on investment prospects; available on request at no cost to existing and potential clients or for purchase at some Web sites.

Brokerage Reports Brokerage firms often make available to their clients reports from the various subscription services and research reports from their own securities analysts. They also provide clients with prospectuses for new security issues and *back-office research reports*. As noted in Chapter 2, a *prospectus* is a document that describes in detail the key aspects of the issue, the issuer, and its management and financial position. The cover of the preliminary prospectus describing the 2006 stock issue of J. Crew, was shown in Figure 2.1 (on page 67). **Back-office research reports** include the brokerage firm's analyses of and recommendations on prospects for the securities markets, specific industries, or specific securities. Usually a brokerage firm publishes lists of securities classified by its research staff as either "buy," "hold," or "sell." Brokerage research reports are available on request at no cost to existing and potential clients.

Securities analysts' reports are now available on the Web, either from brokerage sites or from sites that consolidate research from many brokerages. At Reuters Investing (www.investor.reuters.com), a leading research site, over 1.5 million reports on companies and industries from over 700 brokerage and research firms cost from zero to $150 each. Investors can use Zacks's (www.zacks.com) Research Digest Reports to find and purchase analyst reports on over 700 widely followed stocks for $10 to $150 per report or to read free brokerage report abstracts with earnings revisions and recommendations.

investment letters
newsletters that provide, on a subscription basis, the analyses, conclusions, and recommendations of experts in securities investment.

Investment Letters **Investment letters** are newsletters that provide, on a subscription basis, the analyses, conclusions, and recommendations of experts in securities investment. Some letters concentrate on specific types of securities; others are concerned solely with assessing the economy or securities markets. Among the more popular investment letters are *Blue Chip Advisor, Dick Davis Digest, The Dines Letter, Dow Theory Letters,* the *Growth Stock Outlook, Louis Rukeyser's Wall Street, The Prudent Speculator,* and *Zacks Advisor.* Most investment letters come out weekly or monthly and cost from $75 to $400 a year. Advertisements for many of these investment letters can be found in *Barron's* and in various business periodicals.

The Hulbert Financial Digest (www3.marketwatch.com/store/products/hfd_30_day.aspx?) monitors the performance of investment letters. It is an excellent source of objective information on investment letters and a good place to check out those that interest you. Many investment letters now offer online subscriptions. Use a general search engine or Newsletter Access (www.newsletteraccess.com), a searchable database of newsletters that lists about 1,000 investment newsletters!

quotations
price information about various types of securities, including current price data and statistics on recent price behavior.

Price Information Price information about various types of securities is contained in their **quotations**, which include current price data and statistics on recent price behavior. The Web makes it easy to find price quotes for actively traded securities, and many financially oriented sites include a stock price look-up feature or a stock ticker running across the screen, much like the ones that used to be found only in brokerage offices. The ticker consolidates and reports stock transactions made on the NYSE, AMEX, regional exchanges, and Nasdaq National Market as they occur. Cable TV subscribers in many areas can watch the ticker at the bottom of the screen on certain channels, including Bloomberg TV, CNBC, and CNN Headline News. Table 3.3 lists the ticker symbols for some well-known companies.

Investors can easily find the prior day's security price quotations in the published news media, both nonfinancial and financial. They also can find delayed or real-time quotations for free at numerous Web sites, including *financial portals* (described below), most business periodical Web sites, and brokerage sites. The Web site for CNBC TV has real-time stock quotes, as do sites that subscribe to their news feed.

The major published source of security price quotations is the *Wall Street Journal,* which presents quotations for each previous business day's activities in all major markets. (We'll explain how to read and interpret actual price quotations in later chapters.)

Other Online Investment Information Sources Many other excellent Web sites provide information of all sorts to increase your investment skills and knowledge. Let's now look at financial portals, sites for bonds and mutual

TABLE 3.3   Symbols for Some Well-Known Companies

Company	Symbol	Company	Symbol
Amazon.com	AMZN	McDonald's Corporation	MCD
Apple Computer	AAPL	Merrill Lynch	MER
AT&T	T	Microsoft	MSFT
Cisco	CSCO	Nike	NKE
The Coca-Cola Company	KO	Oracle	ORCL
Dell	DELL	PepsiCo, Inc.	PEP
Eastman Kodak	EK	Reebok	RBK
ExxonMobil	XOM	Sears Holdings	SHLD
Federal Express	FDX	Starbucks	SBUX
General Electric	GE	Sun Microsystems	SUNW
Google	GOOG	Texas Instruments	TXN
Hewlett-Packard	HP	Time Warner	TWX
Intel	INTC	United Parcel Service	UPS
Int'l. Business Machines	IBM	Wal-Mart Stores	WMT
Lucent Technologies	LU	Yahoo!	YHOO

funds, international sites, and investment discussion forums. Table 3.4 (on page 122) lists some of the most popular financial portals, bond sites, and mutual fund sites. We'll look at online brokerage and investment adviser sites later in the chapter, and you'll find more specialized Web links in all chapters.

financial portals
supersites on the Web that bring together a wide range of investing features, such as real-time quotes, stock and mutual fund screens, portfolio trackers, news, research, and transaction capabilities, along with other personal finance features.

Financial Portals **Financial portals** are supersites that bring together a wide range of investing features, such as real-time quotes, stock and mutual fund screens, portfolio trackers, news, research, and transaction capabilities, along with other personal finance features. These sites want to be your investing home page.

Some financial portals are general sites such as Yahoo! and Excite that offer a full range of investing features along with their other services, or they may be investing-oriented sites. You should check out several to see which best suits your needs, because their strengths and features vary greatly. Some portals, to motivate you to stay at their site, offer customization options so that your start page includes the data you want. Although finding one site where you can manage your investments is indeed appealing, you may not be able to find the best of what you need at one portal. You'll want to explore several sites to find the ones that meet your needs. Table 3.4 summarizes the features of several popular financial portals.

HOTLINKS

Superstar Investor provides descriptive summaries and about 20,000 links to the best investing sites on the Internet. The Wall Street DEX provides basic contact information for over 60,000 services and products of interest to investors and traders (including non-electronic resources).

www.superstarinvestor.com
www.wallstreetdex.com

Bond Sites Although many general investment sites include bond and mutual fund information, you can also visit sites that specialize in these investments. Because Internet bond-trading activity is fairly limited at the present time, there are fewer online resources for individuals. Some brokerage firms are starting to allow clients access to bond information that formerly was restricted to investment professionals. In addition to the sites listed in Table 3.4, other good sites for bond and interest rate information include Bloomberg.com's Market Data Rates & Bonds (bloomberg.com/markets/rates/index.html) and WSJ.com (wsj.com).

TABLE 3.4 Popular Investment Web Sites

The following Web sites are just a few of the thousands of sites that provide investing information. Unless otherwise mentioned, all are free.

Web Site	Description
Financial Portals	
America Online (proprietary portal) (money.aol.com)	Subscriber-only Money & Finance channel includes Investing and Personal Finance areas containing business news, market and stock quotes, stocks, mutual funds, investment research, retirement, saving and planning, credit and debt, banking and loans, and more. Each area offers education, tools, and message boards. Ease of use is a big plus.
Excite (www.excite.com)	Offers a money and investing channel that provides news, market data, and research capabilities along with a variety of links for tracking stocks, portfolios, screening stocks, participating in conference calls, and obtaining SEC filings.
MSN MoneyCentral Investor (www.moneycentral.msn.com)	More editorial content than many sites; good research and interactive tools like Research Wizard; can consolidate accounts in portfolio tracker. (Many tools don't run on Macintosh.)
Motley Fool (www.fool.com)	Comprehensive and entertaining site with educational features, research, news, and message boards. Model portfolios cover a variety of investment strategies. Free but offers premium services such as its *Stock Advisor* monthly newsletter for $149 per year.
Yahoo! Finance (http://finance.yahoo.com)	Simple design, content-rich; easy to find information quickly. Includes financial news, price quotes, portfolio trackers, bill paying, personalized home page, and a directory of other major sites.
Yodlee (www.yodlee.com)	Aggregation site that collects financial account data from banking, credit card, brokerage, mutual fund, mileage, and other sites. One-click access saves time and enables users to manage and interact with their accounts; offers e-mail accounts; easy to set up and track finances. Security issues concern potential users; few analytical tools.
Bond Sites	
Investing in Bonds (www.investinginbonds.com)	The Bond Market Association's Web site; good for novice investors. Bond education, research reports, historical data, and links to other sites. Searchable database.
BondsOnline (www.bondsonline.com)	Comprehensive site for news, education, free research, ratings, and other bond information. Searchable database. Some charges for newsletters and research.
CNNMoney.com Bonds (www.money.com/markets/ bondcenter)	Individual investors can search for bond-related news, market data, and bond offerings.
Bureau of the Public Debt Online (www.publicdebt.treas.gov)	Run by U.S. Treasury Department; information about U.S. savings bonds and Treasury securities; can also buy Treasury securities online through Treasury Direct program.
Mutual Fund Sites	
Morningstar (www.morningstar.com)	Profiles of over 3,000 funds with ratings; screening tools, portfolio analysis and management; fund manager interviews, e-mail newsletters; educational sections. Advanced screening and analysis tools are $14.95 a month or $135 per year.
Mutual Fund Investor's Center (www.mfea.com)	Not-for-profit, easy-to-navigate site from the Mutual Fund Education Alliance with investor education, search feature, and links to profiles of funds, calculators for retirement, asset allocation, and college planning.
Fund Alarm (www.fundalarm.com)	Takes a different approach and identifies underperforming funds to help investors decide when to sell; alerts investors to fund manager changes. Lively commentary from the site founder, a CPA.
MAXfunds (www.maxfunds.com)	Offers several custom metrics and data points to help find the best funds and give investors tools other than past performance to choose funds. Covers more funds than any other on- or offline publication. MAXadvisor Powerfund Portfolios, a premium advisory service, costs $24.95 per 90 days.
IndexFunds.com (www.indexfunds.com)	Comprehensive site covering only index funds.
Personal Fund (www.personalfund.com)	Especially popular for its Mutual Fund Cost Calculator that shows the true cost of ownership, after fees, brokerage commissions, and taxes. Suggests lower-cost alternatives with similar investment objectives.

The sites of the major bond ratings agencies—Moody's Investors Services (www.moodys.com), Standard & Poor's (www.standardandpoors.com), and Fitch (www.fitchibca.com)—provide ratings lists, recent ratings changes, and information about how they determine ratings.

Mutual Fund Sites With thousands of mutual funds, how do you find the ones that match your investment goals? The Internet makes this task much easier, offering many sites with screening tools and worksheets. Almost every major mutual fund family has its own Web site as well. Some allow visitors to hear interviews or participate in chats with fund managers. Fidelity (www.fidelity.com) is one of the most comprehensive sites, with educational articles, fund selection tools, fund profiles, and more. Portals and brokerage sites also offer these tools. Table 3.4 includes some independent mutual fund sites that are worth checking out.

HOTLINKS

FundAlarm is a great source of information on poorly performing funds. The site maintains a list of "3-alarm" funds that have under-performed their benchmarks for the past 12 months, 3 years, and 5 years.

www.fundalarm.com

International Sites The international reach of the Internet makes it a natural resource to help investors sort out the complexity of global investing, from country research to foreign currency exchange. Site-by-Site! International Investment Portal & Research Center (www.site-by-site.com) is a comprehensive portal just for international investing. Free daily market data, news, economic insights, research, and analysis and commentary covering numerous countries and investment vehicles are among this site's features. For more localized coverage, check out Euroland European Investor (www.europeaninvestor.com), UK-Invest (www.uk-invest.com), LatinFocus (www.latin-focus.com), and similar sites for other countries and regions. J.P. Morgan's ADR site (www.adr.com) is a good place to research American depositary receipts and learn about their financial positions. For global business news, the *Financial Times* site (www.ft.com) gets high marks. Dow Jones's MarketWatch (www.marketwatch.com/news) has good technology and telecommunications news, as well as coverage of global markets.

Investment Discussion Forums Investors can exchange opinions about their favorite stocks and investing strategies at the *online discussion forums* (message boards and chat rooms) found at most major financial Web sites. However, remember that the key word here is *opinion*. You don't really know much about the qualifications of the person posting the information. *Always do your own research before acting on any hot tips!* The Motley Fool's (www.fool.com) discussion boards are among the most popular, and Fool employees monitor the discussions. Message boards at Yahoo! Finance (http://messages.yahoo.com) are among the largest online, although many feel that the quality is not as good as at other sites. The Raging Bull (www.ragingbull.lycos.com) includes news and other links along with its discussion groups. Technology investors flock to Silicon Investor (www.siliconinvestor.com), a portal site whose high-tech boards are considered among the best.

Avoiding Online Scams Just as the Internet increases the amount of information available to all investors, it also makes it easier for scam artists and others to spread false news and manipulate information. Anyone can sound like an investment expert online, posting stock tips with no underlying substance. As mentioned earlier, you may not know the identity of the person touting or panning a stock on the message boards. The person panning a stock could be a disgruntled former employee or a short seller. For example, the ousted former chief executive of San Diego's Avanir Pharmaceuticals posted negative remarks on stock message boards, adversely affecting share price. The company sued and won a court order prohibiting him from ever posting derogatory statements about the company on any Internet message boards.

In the fast-paced online environment, two types of scams turn up frequently: "pump-and-dump" schemes, and get-rich-quick scams. In *pump-and-dump* schemes, promoters hype stocks, quickly send the prices sky-high, and then dump them at inflated prices. In *get-rich-quick* scams, promoters sell worthless investments to naïve buyers.

One well-publicized pump-and-dump scheme demonstrates how easy it is to use the Internet to promote stocks. In September 2000, the SEC caught a 15-year-old boy who had made over $270,000 by promoting small-company stocks. The self-taught young investor would buy a block of a company's shares and then send out a barrage of false and/or misleading e-mail messages and message board postings singing the praises of that stock and the company's prospects. Once this misinformation pushed up the stock price, he sold and moved on to a new target company. His postings were so articulate that others at Silicon Investor's message boards thought he was a 40-year-old.

To crack down on cyber-fraud, in 1998 the SEC formed the Office of Internet Enforcement. Its staff members quickly investigate reports of suspected hoaxes and prosecute the offenders. Former SEC Chairman Arthur Levitt cautions investors to remember that the Internet is basically another way to send and receive information, one that has no controls for accuracy or truthfulness. The SEC Web site (www.sec.gov/investor/pubs/scams.htm) includes tips to avoid investment scams. Three key questions that investors should ask are:

- *Is the investment registered?* Check the SEC's EDGAR database (www.sec.gov/edgar/quickedgar.htm) and with your state securities regulator (www.nasaa.org.QuickLinks/ContactYourRegulator.efm).

- *Is the person licensed and law-abiding?* Make sure the seller is licensed in your state. Check with the NASD for any record of complaints or fraud.

- *Does the investment sound too good to be true?* Then it probably is. Just being on the Web doesn't mean it's legitimate.

Another place to check on online frauds is the various state securities commissions which typically provide useful advice regarding online investment fraud and how to avoid it.

CONCEPTS IN REVIEW
Answers available at: www.myfinancelab.com

3.4 Differentiate between *descriptive information* and *analytical information*. How might one logically assess whether the acquisition of investment information or advice is economically justified?

3.5 What popular financial business periodicals would you use to follow the financial news? General news? Business news? Would you prefer to get your news from print sources or online, and why?

3.6 Briefly describe the types of information that the following resources provide.
   a. Stockholders' report. b. Comparative data sources.
   c. Standard & Poor's Corporation. d. Mergent.
   e. *Value Line Investment Survey.*

3.7 How would you access each of the following types of information, and how would the content help you make investment decisions?
   a. Prospectuses. b. Back-office research reports.
   c. Investment letters. d. Price quotations.

3.8 Briefly describe several types of information that are especially well suited to being made available on the Internet. What are the differences between the online and print versions, and when would you use each?

Understanding Market Averages and Indexes

LG 3

The investment information we have discussed in this chapter helps investors understand when the economy is moving up or down and how individual investments have performed. You can use this and other information to formulate expectations about future investment performance. It is also important to know whether market behavior is favorable or unfavorable. The ability to interpret various market measures should help you to select and time investment actions.

A widely used way to assess the behavior of securities markets is to study the performance of market averages and indexes. These measures allow you conveniently to (1) gauge general market conditions, (2) compare your portfolio's performance to that of a large, diversified (market) portfolio, and (3) study market cycles, trends, and behaviors in order to forecast future market behavior. Here we discuss key measures of stock and bond market activity. In later chapters, we will discuss averages and indexes associated with other investment vehicles. Like price quotations, these measures of market performance are available at many Web sites.

▮ Stock Market Averages and Indexes

averages
numbers used to measure the general behavior of stock prices by reflecting the arithmetic average price behavior of a representative group of stocks at a given point in time.

Stock market averages and indexes measure the general behavior of stock prices over time. Although the terms *average* and *index* tend to be used interchangeably when people discuss market behavior, technically they are different types of measures. **Averages** reflect the arithmetic average price behavior of a representative group of stocks at a given point in time. **Indexes** measure the current price behavior of a representative group of stocks in relation to a base value set at an earlier point in time.

indexes
numbers used to measure the general behavior of stock prices by measuring the current price behavior of a representative group of stocks in relation to a base value set at an earlier point in time.

Averages and indexes provide a convenient method of capturing the general mood of the market. Investors also can compare them at different points in time to assess the relative strength or weakness of the market. Current and recent values of the key averages and indexes are quoted daily in the financial news, in most local newspapers, and on many radio and television news programs. Figure 3.7 (on page 126), a version of which is published daily in the *Wall Street Journal*, provides a summary and statistics on the major stock market averages and indexes. Let's look at the key averages and indexes listed there.

Major Stock Market Averages and Indexes (July 12, 2006)

The "Major Stock Indexes" summarizes the key stock market averages and indexes. It includes statistics showing the change from the previous day, the 52-week change, and the year-to-date change. (*Source: Wall Street Journal*, July 13, 2006, p. C2. ©Dow Jones & Company, Inc. All rights reserved.)

Major Stock Indexes

Dow Jones Averages	DAILY HIGH	DAILY LOW	DAILY CLOSE	NET CHG	% CHG	52-WEEK HIGH	52-WEEK LOW	52-WEEK % CHG	YTD % CHG
30 Industrials	11149.96	10995.97	11013.18	−121.59	−1.09	11642.65	10215.22	+ 4.32	+ 2.76
20 Transportations	4871.16	4781.95	4788.29	− 70.65	−1.45	4998.95	3581.45	+32.65	+14.11
15 Utilities	422.49	417.96	418.30	− 3.23	−0.77	437.63	380.98	+ 5.40	+ 3.26
65 Composite	3930.68	3874.90	3878.82	− 45.15	−1.15	4018.04	3357.09	+13.13	+ 6.62
Dow Jones Indexes									
Wilshire 5000	12828.76	12667.59	12677.95	−144.82	−1.13	13457.28	11722.81	+ 3.69	+ 1.28
Wilshire 2500	3035.84	2997.34	3000.09	− 33.93	−1.12	3181.39	2778.88	+ 3.60	+ 1.18
Wilshire Lrg Gro	2593.95	2560.31	2563.03	− 29.77	−1.15	2751.14	2458.75	+ 1.57	− 2.81
Wilshire Lrg Val	3105.16	3067.91	3071.13	− 31.18	−1.01	3191.63	2773.35	+ 4.76	+ 4.10
Wilshire Sml Gro	3188.05	3130.94	3132.16	− 50.28	−1.58	3552.62	2787.68	+ 6.68	+ 2.42
Wilshire Sml Val	5335.97	5260.14	5263.49	− 69.64	−1.31	5646.85	4618.40	+ 5.99	+ 5.98
Wilshire Micro	7210.83	7118.62	7118.79	− 91.92	−1.27	7933.46	6455.14	+ 6.69	+ 3.42
Global Titans 50	205.60	203.02	203.11	− 2.02	−0.98	212.05	188.61	+ 4.12	+ 3.31
Asian Titans 50	153.98	151.45	151.58	− 2.23	−1.45	169.99	115.89	+30.80	+ 6.30
DJ STOXX 50	3414.06	3371.96	3380.50	+ 0.09	...	3595.30	3073.63	+ 9.18	+ 0.94
Nasdaq Stock Market									
Nasdaq Comp	2128.86	2090.23	2090.24	− 38.62	−1.81	2370.88	2037.47	− 2.51	− 5.22
Nasdaq 100	1533.06	1499.77	1501.46	− 31.60	−2.06	1758.24	1501.46	− 3.61	− 8.74
Biotech	741.80	730.09	730.57	− 4.61	−0.63	874.18	709.85	− 0.47	− 7.56
Computer	896.02	874.33	874.33	− 21.69	−2.42	1066.53	864.49	− 9.64	−11.84
Standard & Poor's Indexes									
500 Index	1273.31	1257.29	1258.60	− 13.92	−1.09	1325.76	1176.84	+ 2.89	+ 0.83
MidCap 400	755.82	744.65	745.87	− 9.09	−1.20	817.95	672.12	+ 5.40	+ 1.06
SmallCap 600	372.30	365.68	365.83	− 6.34	−1.70	404.89	326.84	+ 5.58	+ 4.32
SuperComp 1500	288.63	284.92	285.20	− 3.26	−1.13	302.01	265.32	+ 3.22	+ 1.00
New York Stock Exchange and Others									
NYSE Comp	8206.40	8104.82	8113.18	− 93.10	−1.13	8646.96	7234.09	+ 9.63	+ 4.63
NYSE Financial	8432.33	8315.84	8322.87	−108.75	−1.29	8910.79	7256.58	+12.57	+ 4.08
Russell 2000	714.67	700.93	701.17	− 13.22	−1.85	781.83	621.57	+ 5.02	+ 4.15
Value Line	418.02	411.75	411.86	− 6.10	−1.46	457.11	383.53	+ 0.66	− 0.16
Amex Comp	1939.15	1921.66	1922.11	− 14.74	−0.76	2044.78	1534.84	+23.03	+ 9.27

Source: Reuters

Dow Jones Industrial Average (DJIA)
a stock market average made up of 30 high-quality stocks selected for total market value and broad public ownership and believed to reflect overall market activity.

The Dow Jones Averages Dow Jones & Company, publisher of the *Wall Street Journal*, prepares four stock averages. The most popular is the **Dow Jones Industrial Average (DJIA)**. This average is made up of 30 stocks selected for total market value and broad public ownership. The group consists of high-quality stocks whose behaviors are believed to reflect overall market activity. The list at the bottom of Figure 3.8 includes the 30 stocks currently in the DJIA.

Occasionally, a merger, bankruptcy, or extreme lack of activity causes a change in the makeup of the average. For example, SBC Communications' 2005 merger with AT&T moved it (AT&T) to the DJIA. Changes to the 30 stocks also occur when Dow Jones believes that the average does not reflect the broader market. For example, in 2004 pharmaceutical company Pfizer and technology company Verizon replaced Eastman Kodak and International Paper. When a new stock is added, the average is readjusted so that it continues to behave in a manner consistent with the immediate past.

FIGURE 3.8

The DJIA from January 13, 2006, to July 12, 2006

During this 6-month period, the stock market remained mildly bullish beginning in mid-January and continuing through mid-May. (*Source:* From The *Wall Street Journal,* July 13, 2006, p. C2. ©Dow Jones & Company, Inc. Reproduced with permission from Dow Jones & Company, Inc. via Copyright Clearance Center.)

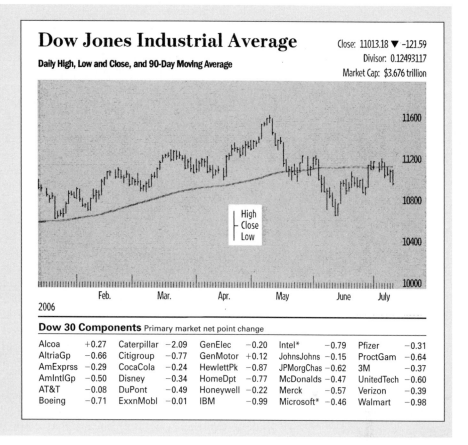

Dow Jones Industrial Average

Daily High, Low and Close, and 90-Day Moving Average

Close: 11013.18 ▼ –121.59
Divisor: 0.12493117
Market Cap: $3.676 trillion

Dow 30 Components Primary market net point change

Alcoa	+0.27	Caterpillar	–2.09	GenElec	–0.20	Intel*	–0.79	Pfizer	–0.31
AltriaGp	–0.66	Citigroup	–0.77	GenMotor	+0.12	JohnsJohns	–0.15	ProctGam	–0.64
AmExprss	–0.29	CocaCola	–0.24	HewlettPk	–0.87	JPMorgChas	–0.62	3M	–0.37
AmIntlGp	–0.50	Disney	–0.34	HomeDpt	–0.77	McDonalds	–0.47	UnitedTech	–0.60
AT&T	–0.08	DuPont	–0.49	Honeywell	–0.22	Merck	–0.57	Verizon	–0.39
Boeing	–0.71	ExxnMobl	–0.01	IBM	–0.99	Microsoft*	–0.46	Walmart	–0.98

The value of the DJIA is calculated each business day by substituting the *closing share prices* of each of the 30 stocks in the average into the following equation:

Equation 3.1 ➤

$$DJIA = \frac{\begin{array}{c}\text{Closing share price} \\ \text{of stock 1}\end{array} + \begin{array}{c}\text{Closing share price} \\ \text{of stock 2}\end{array} + \cdots + \begin{array}{c}\text{Closing share price} \\ \text{of stock 30}\end{array}}{\text{DJIA divisor}}$$

The value of the DJIA is merely the sum of the closing share prices of the 30 stocks included in it, divided by a "divisor." The purpose of the divisor is to adjust for any stock splits, company changes, or other events that have occurred over time. Without the divisor, whose calculation is very complex, the DJIA value would be totally distorted. The divisor makes it possible to use the DJIA to make time-series comparisons. On July 12, 2006, the sum of the closing prices of the 30 industrials was 1375.89, which, when divided by the divisor of 0.12493117, resulted in a DJIA value of 11013.18. The current divisor is included in the *Wall Street Journal* figure "Dow Jones Industrial Average" (printed in the upper-right corner, as seen in Figure 3.8).

Because the DJIA results from summing the prices of the 30 stocks, higher-priced stocks tend to affect the index more than do lower-priced stocks. For example, a 5% change in the price of a $50 stock (i.e., $2.50) has less impact on the index than a 5% change in a $100 stock (i.e., $5.00). In spite of this and other criticisms leveled at the DJIA, it remains the most widely cited stock market indicator.

The actual value of the DJIA is meaningful only when compared to earlier values. For example, the DJIA on July 12, 2006, closed at 11013.18. This value is meaningful only when compared to the previous day's closing value of 11134.77, a change of about −1.10%. Many people mistakenly believe that one DJIA "point" equals $1 in the value of an average share. Actually, one point currently translates into about 0.42 cents in average share value. Figure 3.8 shows the DJIA over the 6-month period January 13, 2006, to July 12, 2006. During this 6-month period, the stock market remained mildly bullish between mid-January and mid-May. It started at about 1100 and rose to about 11600 in mid-May. During the following 60 days, the market steadily declined to about 10800 and slowly rose to around 11200 by mid-July.

The three other Dow Jones averages are the transportation, utilities, and composite. The *Dow Jones Transportation Average* is based on 20 stocks, including railroads, airlines, freight forwarders, and mixed transportation companies. The *Dow Jones Utilities Average* is computed using 15 public-utility stocks. The *Dow Jones 65 Stocks Composite Average* is made up of the 30 industrials, the 20 transportations, and the 15 utilities. Like the DJIA, each of the other Dow Jones averages is calculated using a divisor to allow for continuity of the average over time. The transportation, utilities, and 65-stocks composite are often cited in the financial news along with the DJIA, as shown in Figure 3.7.

Dow Jones also publishes numerous indexes as seen in the second section of Figure 3.7. The first one listed, the **Wilshire 5000 Index**, is a market-weighted index. "Market-weighted" means that companies with large total market values have the most effect on the index's movement. The Dow Jones Wilshire 5000 tracks the returns of more than 6,000 companies—practically all publicly traded, U.S-headquartered stocks that trade on the major exchanges. It represents the dollar vaue (in billions of dollars) of the more than 6,000 actively traded stocks it incudes. The base value of the index is 100, which represents its value on June 30, 1997.

Wilshire 5000 index
measure of the total dollar value (in billions of dollars) of more than 6,000 actively traded stocks on the major exchanges.

Standard & Poor's Indexes
Standard & Poor's Corporation, another leading financial publisher, publishes six major common stock indexes. One oft-cited S&P index is the 500-stock composite index. Unlike the Dow Jones averages, **Standard & Poor's indexes** are true indexes. They are calculated each business day by substituting the *closing market value of each stock* (closing price × number of shares outstanding) into the following equation:

Standard & Poor's indexes
true indexes that measure the current price of a group of stocks relative to a base (set in the 1941–1943 period) having an index value of 10.

Equation 3.2 ▶

$$\text{S\&P Index} = \frac{\substack{\text{Current closing} \\ \text{market value} \\ \text{of stock 1}} + \substack{\text{Current closing} \\ \text{market value} \\ \text{of stock 2}} + \cdots + \substack{\text{Current closing} \\ \text{market value} \\ \text{of last stock}}}{\substack{\text{Base period} \\ \text{closing market} \\ \text{value of stock 1}} + \substack{\text{Base period} \\ \text{closing market} \\ \text{value of stock 2}} + \cdots + \substack{\text{Base period} \\ \text{closing market} \\ \text{value of last stock}}} \times 10$$

The value of the S&P index is found by dividing the sum of the market values of all stocks included in the index by the market value of the stocks in the base period and then multiplying the resulting quotient by 10, the base value of the S&P indexes. Most S&P indexes are calculated in a similar fashion. The main differences lie in the stocks included in the index, the base period, and the base value of the index. For example, on July 12, 2006, the ratio of the closing market values of the S&P 500 composite stocks to the 1941–1943 base-period closing market values was 125.860, which, when multiplied by the base value of the S&P index of 10, results in an index value of 1258.60 (as shown in Figure 3.7).

Certain of the S&P indexes contain many more shares than the Dow averages do, and all of them are based on *market values* rather than *share prices*. Therefore, many investors feel that the S&P indexes provide a more broad-based and representative measure of general market conditions than do the Dow averages. Although some technical computational problems exist with these indexes, they are widely used—frequently as a basis for estimating the "market return," an important concept that is introduced in Chapter 4.

Like the Dow averages, the S&P indexes are meaningful only when compared to values in other time periods or to the 1941–1943 base-period value of 10. For example, the July 12, 2006, value of the S&P 500 Stock Composite Index of 1258.60 means that the market values of the stocks in the index increased by a factor of 125.860 (1258.60 ÷ 10) since the 1941–1943 period. The July 12, 2006, market value of the stocks in the index was 1.07 times the lowest index value of 1176.84 in the preceding 52-week period (1258.60 ÷ 1176.84), and hence represented an increase of 7%.

The eight major common stock indexes published by Standard & Poor's are:

- The *industrials index*, made up of the common stock of 400 industrial firms.

- The *transportation index*, which includes the stock of 20 transportation companies.

- The *utilities index*, made up of 40 public utility stocks.

- The *financials index*, which contains 40 financial stocks.

- The *composite index* (described above), which consists of the total of 500 stocks that make up the industrials, transportation, utilities, and financials indexes.

- The *MidCap index*, made up of the stocks of 400 medium-sized companies.

- The *SmallCap index*, made up of 600 small-sized companies.

- The *1500 SuperComp index*, which includes all stocks in the composite, MidCap, and SmallCap indexes.

Like the Dow averages and indexes, many of the S&P indexes are frequently quoted in the financial news, as shown in Figure 3.7.

Although the Dow Jones averages and S&P indexes tend to behave in a similar fashion over time, their day-to-day magnitude and even direction (up or down) can differ significantly because the Dows are averages and the S&Ps are indexes.

INVESTOR FACTS

ELECTION RETURNS— Presidential elections seem to benefit the stock market, except in 2000. Look at the market returns for U.S. presidential elections since 1976: In every year until the election of George W. Bush, the market rose substantially more than the average annual increase. The 2000 election was unique in every way: it was the only time the market actually declined.

Year and Election Winner	S&P 500 Return for the Year
2004—George W. Bush	+8.99%
2000—George W. Bush	−10.1%
1996—Bill Clinton	+16.0%
1992—Bill Clinton	+17.7%
1988—George H. W. Bush	+12.4%
1984—Ronald Reagan	+25.8%
1980—Ronald Reagan	+19.1%
1976—Jimmy Carter	+15.6%

NYSE, AMEX, and Nasdaq Indexes   Three indexes measure the daily results of the New York Stock Exchange (NYSE), the American Stock Exchange (AMEX), and the National Association of Securities Dealers Automated Quotation (Nasdaq) system. Each reflects the movement of stocks listed on its exchange.

NYSE composite index
measure of the current price behavior of stocks listed on the NYSE, relative to a base of 5000 set at December 31, 2002.

The **NYSE composite index** includes about 2,100 or so stocks listed on the "Big Board." The index's base of 5000 reflects the December 31, 2002, value of stocks listed on the NYSE. In addition to the composite index, the NYSE publishes indexes for financial and other subgroups. The behavior of the NYSE composite index is normally similar to that of the DJIA and the S&P 500 indexes.

AMEX composite index
measure of the current price behavior of all shares traded on the AMEX, relative to a base of 550 set at December 29, 1995.

The **AMEX composite index** reflects the price of all shares traded on the American Stock Exchange, relative to a base of 550 set at December 29, 1995. Although it does not always closely follow the S&P and NYSE indexes, the AMEX index tends to move in the general direction they do.

Nasdaq Stock Market indexes
measures of current price behavior of securities traded in the Nasdaq stock market, relative to a base of 100 set at specified dates.

The **Nasdaq Stock Market indexes** reflect Nasdaq stock market activity. The most comprehensive of the Nasdaq indexes is the *composite index,* which is calculated using the more than 4,000 domestic common stocks traded on the Nasdaq stock market. It is based on a value of 100 set at February 5, 1971. Also important is the *Nasdaq 100,* which includes 100 of the largest domestic and international nonfinancial companies listed on Nasdaq. It is based on a value of 125, set on January 1, 1994. The other two commonly quoted Nasdaq indexes are the *biotech* and *computer indexes.* Although their degrees of responsiveness may vary, the Nasdaq indexes tend to move in the same direction at the same time as the other major indexes.

Value Line Indexes   Value Line publishes a number of stock indexes constructed by equally weighting the price of each stock included. This is accomplished by considering only the percentage changes in stock prices. This approach eliminates the effects of differing market price and total market value on the relative importance of each stock in the index. The **Value Line**

Value Line composite index
stock index that reflects the percentage changes in share price of about 1,700 stocks, relative to a base of 100 set at June 30, 1961.

composite index includes the about 1,700 stocks in the *Value Line Investment Survey* that are traded on the NYSE, AMEX, and OTC markets. The base of 100 reflects the stock prices on June 30, 1961. In addition to its composite index, Value Line publishes other specialized indexes.

Other Averages and Indexes   A number of other indexes are available. Frank Russell Company, a pension advisory firm, publishes three primary indexes. The *Russell 1000* includes the 1,000 largest companies, the most widely quoted *Russell 2000* includes 2,000 small- to medium-sized companies, and the *Russell 3000* includes all 3,000 companies in the Russell 1000 and 2000.

In addition, the *Wall Street Journal* publishes a number of global and foreign stock market indexes summarized in the "International Stocks & Indexes" section, normally in Section C. Included are Dow Jones indexes for countries in the Americas, Europe, Africa, Asia, and the Pacific region that are based on a value of 100 set at December 31, 1991. About 35 foreign stock market indexes are also given for major countries, including a *World Index* and the *Europe/Australia/Far East (EAFE MSCI) Index.* Like the purely domestic averages and indexes, these international averages and indexes measure the general price behavior of the stocks that are listed and traded in the given market. Useful comparisons of the market averages and indexes over time and across markets are often made to assess both trends and relative strengths of foreign markets throughout the world.

▮ Bond Market Indicators

A number of indicators are available for assessing the general behavior of the bond markets. A "Bond Market Data Bank" that includes a wealth of return and price index data for various types of bonds and various domestic and foreign markets is published daily in the *Wall Street Journal*. However, there are fewer indicators of overall bond market behavior than of stock market behavior. The key measures of overall U.S. bond market behavior are bond yields and bond indexes.

bond yield
summary measure of the total return an investor would receive on a bond if it were purchased at its current price and held to maturity; reported as an annual rate of return.

Bond Yields A **bond yield** is a summary measure of the total return an investor would receive on a bond if it were purchased at its current price and held to maturity. Bond yields are reported as annual rates of return. For example, a bond with a yield of 5.50% would provide its owner with a total return from periodic interest and capital gain (or loss) that would be equivalent to a 5.50% annual rate of earnings on the amount invested, if the bond were purchased at its current price and held to maturity.

Typically, bond yields are quoted for a group of bonds that are similar with respect to type and quality. For example, *Barron's* quotes the yields on the Dow Jones bond averages of 10 high-grade corporate bonds, 10 medium-grade corporate bonds, and a confidence index that is calculated as a ratio of the high-grade to medium-grade indexes. In addition, like the *Wall Street Journal*, it quotes numerous other bond indexes and yields, including those for Treasury and municipal bonds. Similar bond yield data are available from S&P, Moody's, and the Federal Reserve. Like stock market averages and indexes, bond yield data are especially useful when viewed over time.

Dow Jones Corporate Bond Index
mathematical averages of the *closing prices* for 96 bonds—32 industrial, 32 financial, and 32 utility/telecom.

Bond Indexes There are a variety of bond indexes. The **Dow Jones Corporate Bond Index** includes 96 bonds—32 industrial, 32 financial, and 32 utility/telecom bonds. It reflects the simple mathematical average of the *closing prices* for the bonds. It is based on a value of 100 set at December 31, 1996. The Index is published daily in the *Wall Street Journal* and summarized weekly in *Barron's*. Similar bond market indexes, prepared by investment bankers Merrill Lynch and Lehman Brothers, are also published daily in the *Wall Street Journal* and summarized weekly in *Barron's*.

CONCEPTS IN REVIEW
Answers available at: www.myfinancelab.com

3.9 Describe the basic philosophy and use of stock market averages and indexes. Explain how the behavior of an average or index can be used to classify general market conditions as bull or bear.

3.10 List each of the major averages or indexes prepared by (a) Dow Jones & Company and (b) Standard & Poor's Corporation. Indicate the number and source of the securities used in calculating each average or index.

3.11 Briefly describe the composition and general thrust of each of the following indexes.
  a. NYSE composite index.
  b. AMEX composite index.
  c. Nasdaq Stock Market indexes.
  d. Value Line composite index.

3.12 Discuss each of the following as they are related to assessing bond market behavior.
  a. Bond yields.
  b. Bond Indexes.

Making Securities Transactions

LG 4   LG 5

Now that you know how to find information to help you locate attractive security investments, you need to understand how to make securities transactions. Whether you decide to start a self-directed online investment program or to use a traditional stockbroker, you must first open an account with a stockbroker. In this section, we will look at the role stockbrokers play and how that role has changed with the growth in online investing. We will also explain the basic types of orders you can place, the procedures required to make regular and online securities transactions, the costs of investment transactions, and investor protection.

▮ The Role of Stockbrokers

stockbrokers
individuals licensed by both the SEC and the securities exchanges to facilitate transactions between buyers and sellers of securities.

Stockbrokers—also called *account executives, investment executives,* and *financial consultants*—act as intermediaries between buyers and sellers of securities. They typically charge a commission to facilitate these securities transactions. Stockbrokers must be licensed by both the SEC and the securities exchanges on which they place orders and must follow the ethical guidelines of those bodies.

Although the procedure for executing orders in broker markets may differ from that in dealer markets, it starts the same way: An investor places an order with his or her stockbroker. The broker works for a brokerage firm that owns seats on the securities exchanges, and members of the securities exchange execute orders that the brokers in the firm's various sales offices transmit to them. For example, the largest U.S. brokerage firm, Merrill Lynch, transmits orders for listed securities from its offices in most major cities throughout the country to the main office of Merrill Lynch and then to the floor of the broker market exchanges (NYSE and AMEX), where Merrill Lynch exchange members execute them. Confirmation of the order goes back to the broker placing the order, who relays it to the customer. This process can take a matter of seconds with the use of sophisticated telecommunications networks and Internet trading.

For a dealer market securities transaction (Nasdaq and OTC markets), brokerage firms transmit orders to *market makers,* who are dealers in the market that specializes in the given security. As we learned in Chapter 2, the Nasdaq and OTC systems, along with the available information on who makes markets in certain securities, enable brokers to execute orders in dealer markets. Normally, dealer market transactions are executed rapidly, because market makers maintain inventories of the securities in which they deal.

Brokerage Services The primary activity of stockbrokers is to execute clients' purchase and sale transactions at the best possible price. Brokerage firms will hold the client's security certificates for safekeeping; the securities kept by the firm in this manner are said to be held in **street name**. Because the brokerage house issues the securities in its own name and holds them in trust for the client (rather than issuing them in the client's name), the firm can transfer the securities at the time of sale without the client's signature. Street name is actually a common way of buying securities, because most investors do not want to be bothered with the handling and safekeeping of stock certificates. In such cases, the brokerage firm records the details of the client's transaction and keeps track of his or her investments through a series of bookkeeping entries. Dividends and notices received by the broker are forwarded to the client who owns the securities.

Stockbrokers also offer clients a variety of other services. For example, the brokerage firm normally provides free information about investments. Quite often, the firm has a research staff that periodically issues analyses of economic, market, industry, or company behavior and makes recommendations to buy, sell, or hold certain securities. As a client of a large brokerage firm, you can expect to receive regular bulletins on market activity and possibly a recommended investment list. You will also receive a statement describing your transactions for the month and showing commission and interest charges, dividends and interest received, and detailed listings of your current holdings.

Today, most brokerage firms will invest surplus cash left in a client's account in a money market mutual fund, allowing the client to earn a reasonable rate of interest on these balances. Such arrangements help the investor earn as much as possible on temporarily idle funds.

Types of Brokerage Firms Just a few years ago, there were three distinct types of brokerage firms: full-service, premium discount, and basic discount. No longer are the lines between these categories clear-cut. Most brokerage firms, even the most traditional ones, now offer online services. And many discount brokers now offer services, like research reports for clients, that were once available only from a full-service broker.

The traditional broker, or so-called **full-service broker**, in addition to executing clients' transactions, offers investors a full array of brokerage services: providing investment advice and information, holding securities in street name, offering online brokerage services, and extending margin loans.

Investors who wish merely to make transactions and are not interested in taking advantage of other services should consider either a premium or basic discount broker.

Premium discount brokers focus primarily on making transactions for customers. They charge low commissions and provide limited free research information and investment advice. The investor visits the broker's office, calls a toll-free number, or accesses the broker's Web site to initiate a transaction. The broker confirms the transaction in person or by phone, e-mail, or regular mail. Premium discount brokers like Charles Schwab, the first discount broker, now offer many of the same services that you'd find at a full-service broker. Other premium discounters are similar.

---

street name
security certificates issued in the brokerage firm's name but held in trust for its client, who actually owns them.

full-service broker
broker who, in addition to executing clients' transactions, provides them with a full array of brokerage services.

premium discount broker
broker who charges low commissions to make transactions for customers but provides limited free research information and investment advice.

basic discount broker
typically a deep-discount broker through which investors can execute trades electronically online via a commercial service, on the Internet, or by phone. (Also called *online brokers* or *electronic brokers*.)

Basic discount brokers, also called *online brokers* or *electronic brokers,* are typically deep-discount brokers through which investors can execute trades electronically online via a commercial service, on the Internet, or by phone. The investor accesses the basic discounter's Web site to open an account, review the commission schedule, or see a demonstration of the available transactional services and procedures. Confirmation of online trades can take as little as 10 seconds, and most trades occur within 1 minute. Most basic discount brokers operate primarily online, but also provide telephone and live broker backup in case there are problems with the Web site or the customer is away from his or her computer. In response to the rapid growth of online investors, particularly among young investors who enjoy surfing the Web, most brokerage firms now offer online trading. These firms usually charge higher commissions when live broker assistance is required.

The rapidly growing volume of business done by both premium and basic discount brokers attests to their success. Today, many full-service brokers, banks, and savings institutions are making discount and online brokerage services available to their customers and depositors who wish to buy stocks, bonds, mutual funds, and other investment vehicles. Some of the major full-service, premium discount, and basic discount brokers are listed in Table 3.5.

Selecting a Stockbroker If you decide to start your investing activities with the assistance of either a full-service or premium discount stockbroker, select the person you believe best understands your investment goals. Choosing a broker whose disposition toward investing is similar to yours is the best way to establish a solid working relationship. Your broker should also make you aware of investment possibilities that are consistent with your objectives and attitude toward risk.

You should also consider the cost and types of services available from the firm with which the broker is affiliated, to receive the best service at the lowest possible cost to you. The premium discount brokerage service is primarily transactional, and the basic discount brokerage service is *purely* transactional. Contact with a broker, advice, and research assistance generally are available only at a higher price. Investors must weigh the added commissions they pay a full-service broker against the value of the advice they receive, because the amount of available advice is the only major difference among the three types of brokers.

TABLE 3.5   **Major Full-Service, Premium Discount, and Basic Discount Brokers**

Type of Broker		
Full-Service	Premium Discount	Basic Discount
A.G. Edwards	Banc of America	Firstrade
Merrill Lynch	Charles Schwab	Scottrade
Morgan Stanley	E*Trade	Sieberg Net
Smith Barney	Fidelity.com	Thinkorswim
UBS Financial Services	Quick & Reilly	TradeKing
Wells Fargo	TD Ameritrade	Wall Street*E
	Wells Trade	

ETHICS *in* INVESTING

Did Martha Stewart Cross the Line?

On March 5, 2004, a jury returned a guilty verdict convicting homemaking queen Martha Stewart and her former stockbroker, Peter Bacanovic, of obstructing justice and lying about a well-timed stock sale. According to the prosecution, Martha Stewart committed illegal insider trading when she sold stock in biotech company ImClone Systems, and then made false statements to federal investigators. The government also accused Stewart and Bacanovic of creating an alibi for her ImClone sales and attempting to obstruct justice during investigations into her trades. Stewart found herself tarred by the scandal, during which she resigned as chair of the board and CEO of her company. In addition, the stock of her company dropped more that 20%, and her holdings took nearly a $200 million hit, wiping out more than a quarter of her net worth.

The government alleged that Bacanovic tipped off Stewart that two of his other clients, ImClone's CEO Samuel Waksal and Waksal's daughter, had just placed orders to sell their ImClone stock. Waksal, a long-time friend of Stewart, had obtained information that the U.S. Food and Drug Administration (FDA) was about to reject ImClone's new cancer product, Erbitux. Stewart promptly sold all 3,928 shares of her ImClone stock, thus avoiding about $50,000 in losses. The very next day, ImClone announced that the FDA had rejected its application for Erbitux. Quickly, the price of ImClone stock dropped 16%, to $46 per share. According to authorities, Stewart and Bacanovic fabricated an alibi for Stewart's trades—that she and her broker had decided earlier that she would sell if the price fell below $60 per share.

As a result of the conviction, Martha Stewart spent five months in jail and another five months under house arrest. Interestingly, she was not convicted on a more serious charge of insider trading—which the judge dismissed—but for obstructing the federal investigation. By an ironic twist of fate, in February 2004 the drug at the heart of the scandal received FDA approval to treat certain forms of cancer.

CRITICAL THINKING QUESTION In light of the *Insider Trading and Fraud Act of 1988,* does Martha Stewart, or any other investor, have the right to sell stock any time a broker advises them to?

Referrals from friends or business associates are a good way to begin your search for a stockbroker. (Don't forget to consider the investing style and goals of the person making the recommendation.) However, it is not important—and often not even advisable—to know your stockbroker personally. In this age of online brokers, you may never meet your broker face to face. A strictly business relationship eliminates the possibility that personal concerns will interfere with the achievement of your investment goals. For an example of a stockbroker-client business relationship that crossed the line, see the *Ethics* box above.

However, your broker's main interest should not be commissions. Responsible brokers do not engage in **churning**—that is, causing excessive trading of their clients' accounts to increase commissions. Churning is both illegal and unethical under SEC and exchange rules, though it is often difficult to prove.

churning
an illegal and unethical practice engaged in by a broker to increase commissions by causing excessive trading of clients' accounts.

Opening an Account To open an account, you will fill out various documents that establish a legal relationship between the customer and the brokerage firm. A signature card and a personal data card provide the information needed to identify your account. The stockbroker must also have a reasonable understanding of your personal financial situation to assess your investment goals—and to be sure that you can pay for the securities purchased. You also provide the broker with instructions regarding the transfer and custody of securities. Customers who wish to borrow money to make transactions must establish a margin account (described below). If you are acting as a custodian, trustee, executor, or corporation, the brokerage firm will require additional documents. Today, all of this can be done online at most brokerage firms.

Investors may have accounts with more than one stockbroker. Many investors establish accounts at different types of firms to obtain the benefit and opinions of a diverse group of brokers and to reduce their overall cost of making purchase and sale transactions.

Next you must select the type of account best suited to your needs. We will briefly consider several of the more popular types.

Single or Joint A brokerage account may be either single or joint. Joint accounts are most common between husband and wife or parent and child. The account of a minor (a person younger than 18 years of age) is a **custodial account**, in which a parent or guardian must be part of all transactions. Regardless of the form of the account, the name(s) of the account holder(s) and an account number are used to identify it.

custodial account
the brokerage account of a minor; requires a parent or guardian to be part of all transactions.

Cash or Margin A **cash account**, the more common type, is one in which the customer can make only cash transactions. Customers can initiate cash transactions via phone or online and are given 3 business days in which to transmit the cash to the brokerage firm. The firm is likewise given 3 business days in which to deposit the proceeds from the sale of securities in the customer's cash account.

cash account
a brokerage account in which a customer can make only cash transactions.

A **margin account** is an account in which the brokerage firm extends borrowing privileges to a creditworthy customer. By leaving securities with the firm as collateral, the customer can borrow a prespecified proportion of the securities' purchase price. The brokerage firm will, of course, charge the customer a stated rate of interest on borrowings. (The mechanics of margin trading are covered in Chapter 2.)

margin account
a brokerage account in which the customer has been extended borrowing privileges by the brokerage firm.

Wrap The **wrap account** (also called a *managed account*) allows brokerage customers with large portfolios (generally $100,000 or more) to shift stock selection decisions conveniently to a professional money manager, either in-house or independent. In return for a flat annual fee, commonly between 1% and 3% of the portfolio's total asset value, the brokerage firm helps the investor select a money manager, pays the manager's fee, and executes the money manager's trades. Initially the investor, broker, and/or manager discuss the client's overall goals.

wrap account
a brokerage account in which customers with large portfolios pay a flat annual fee that covers the cost of a money manager's services and the commissions on all trades. (Also called a *managed account*.)

Wrap accounts are appealing for a number of reasons other than convenience. The annual fee in most cases covers commissions on all trades, virtually eliminating the chance of the broker churning the account. In addition, the broker monitors the manager's performance and provides the investor with detailed reports, typically quarterly.

Odd-Lot or Round-Lot Transactions Investors can buy stock in either odd or round lots. An **odd lot** consists of less than 100 shares of a stock. A **round lot** is a 100-share unit or a multiple thereof. You would be dealing in an odd

odd lot
less than 100 shares of stock.

round lot
100-share units of stock or multiples thereof.

lot if you bought, say, 25 shares of stock, but in round lots if you bought 200 shares. A trade of 225 shares would be a combination of an odd lot and two round lots.

Transactions in odd lots require either additional processing by the brokerage firm or the assistance of a specialist. For odd lots, an added fee—known as an *odd-lot differential*—is tacked on to the normal commission charge, driving up the costs of these small trades. Small investors in the early stages of their investment programs are primarily responsible for odd-lot transactions.

■ Basic Types of Orders

Investors can use different types of orders to make security transactions. The type placed normally depends on the investor's goals and expectations. The three basic types of orders are the market order, the limit order, and the stop-loss order.

market order
an order to buy or sell stock at the best price available when the order is placed.

Market Order An order to buy or sell stock at the best price available when the investor places the order is a **market order**. It is generally the quickest way to fill orders, because market orders are usually executed as soon as they reach the exchange floor or are received by the market maker. Because of the speed with which market orders are executed, the buyer or seller of a security can be sure that the price at which the order is transacted will be very close to the market price prevailing at the time the order was placed.

limit order
an order to buy at or below a specified price or to sell at or above a specified price.

Limit Order A **limit order** is an order to buy at or below a specified price or to sell at or above a specified price. When the investor places a limit order, the broker transmits it to a specialist dealing in the security. The specialist notes the number of shares and price of the limit order in his or her book and executes the order as soon as the specified market price (or better) exists. The specialist must first satisfy all other orders with precedence—similar orders received earlier, buy orders at a higher specified price, or sell orders at a lower specified price. Investors can place the limit order in one of the following forms:

1. A *fill-or-kill order,* which is canceled if not immediately executed.
2. A *day order,* which if not executed is automatically canceled at the end of the day.
3. A *good-'til-canceled (GTC) order,* which generally remains in effect for 6 months unless executed, canceled, or renewed.

Assume, for example, that you place a limit order to buy, at a limit price of $30, 100 shares of a stock currently selling at $30.50. Once the specialist clears all similar orders received before yours, and once the market price of the stock falls to $30 or less, he or she executes your order. It is possible, of course, that your order might expire (if it is not a GTC order) before the stock price drops to $30.

Although a limit order can be quite effective, it can also keep you from making a transaction. If, for instance, you wish to buy at $30 or less and the stock price moves from its current $30.50 price to $42 while you are waiting, you have missed the opportunity to make a profit of $11.50 per share ($42 − $30.50). If you had placed a *market order* to buy at the best available price ($30.50), the profit of $11.50 would have been yours. Limit orders for the sale of a stock are also disadvantageous when the stock price closely approaches, but does not attain, the minimum sale price limit before dropping substantially. Generally speaking, limit orders are most effective when the price of a stock fluctuates greatly, because there is then a better chance that the order will be executed.

Stop-Loss Order When an investor places a **stop-loss order** or **stop order**, the broker tells the specialist to sell a stock when its market price reaches or drops below a specified level. Stop-loss orders are *suspended orders* placed on stocks; they are activated when and if the stock reaches a certain price. The stop-loss order is placed on the specialist's book and becomes active once the stock reaches the stop price. Like limit orders, stop-loss orders are typically day or GTC orders. When activated, the stop order becomes a *market order* to sell the security at the best price available. Thus it is possible for the actual price at which the sale is made to be well below the price at which the stop was initiated. Investors use these orders to protect themselves against the adverse effects of a rapid decline in share price.

For example, assume you own 100 shares of Ballard Industries, which is currently selling for $35 per share. Because you believe the stock price could decline rapidly at any time, you place a stop order to sell at $30. If the stock price does in fact drop to $30, the specialist will sell the 100 shares at the best price available at that time. If the market price declines to $28 by the time your stop-loss order comes up, you will receive less than $30 per share. Of course, if the market price stays above $30 per share, you will have lost nothing as a result of placing the order, because the stop order will never be initiated. Often investors raise the level of the stop as the price of the stock rises. Such action helps to lock in a higher profit when the price is increasing.

Investors can also place stop orders to *buy* a stock, although buy orders are far less common than sell orders. For example, you may place a stop order to buy 100 shares of MJ Enterprises, currently selling for $70 per share, once its price rises to, say, $75 (the stop price). These orders are commonly used either to limit losses on short sales (discussed in Chapter 2) or to buy a stock just as its price begins to rise.

To avoid the risk of the market moving against you when your stop order becomes a market order, you can place a *stop-limit order*, rather than a plain stop order. This is an order to buy or sell stock at a given price, or better, once a stipulated stop price has been met. For example, in the Ballard Industries example, had a stop-limit order been in effect, then when the market price of Ballard dropped to $30, the broker would have entered a limit order to sell your 100 shares at $30 a share or *better*. Thus you would have run no risk of getting less than $30 a share for your stock—unless the price of the stock kept right on falling. In that case, as is true for any limit order, you might miss the market altogether and end up with stock worth much less than $30. Even though the stop order to sell was triggered (at $30), the stock will not be sold, with a stop-limit order, if it keeps falling in price.

▪ Online Transactions

The competition for your online business increases daily as more players enter an already crowded arena. Brokerage firms are encouraging customers to trade online and offering a variety of incentives to get their business, including

stop-loss (stop) order
an order to sell a stock when its market price reaches or drops below a specified level; can also be used to buy stock when its market price reaches or rises above a specified level.

free trades! However, low cost is not the only reason to choose a brokerage firm. As with any financial decision, you must consider your needs and find the firm that best matches them. One investor may want timely information, research, and quick, reliable trades from a full-service broker like Merrill Lynch or Smith Barney or a premium discounter like Charles Schwab or TD Ameritrade. Another, who is an active trader, will focus on cost and fast trades rather than research and so will sign up with a basic discounter like Firstrade or Wall Street*E. Ease of site navigation is a major factor in finding a basic discount broker to use in executing online transactions. Some online brokers also offer online trading of bonds and mutual funds as well.

Day Trading For some investors, online stock trading is so compelling that they become day traders. The opposite of buy-and-hold investors with a long-term perspective, **day traders** buy and sell stocks quickly throughout the day. They hope that their stocks will continue to rise in value for the very short time they own them—sometimes just seconds or minutes—so they can make quick profits. Some also sell short, looking for small price decreases. True day traders do not own any stocks overnight—hence the term "day trader"—because they believe that the extreme risk of prices changing radically from day to day will lead to large losses.

Day trading is not illegal or unethical, but it *is* highly risky. To compound their risk, day traders usually buy on margin to use leverage to earn higher profits. But as we saw in Chapter 2, margin trading also increases the risk of large losses.

Because the Internet makes investment information and transactions accessible to the masses, day trading has grown in popularity. It's a very difficult task—essentially a very stressful, full-time job. Although sales pitches for day trading make it seem like an easy route to quick riches, quite the reverse is true. Day traders typically incur major financial losses when they start trading. In addition, they have high expenses for brokerage commissions, training, and computer equipment. They must earn sizable trading profits annually to break even on fees and commissions alone. Some never achieve profitability. The *Investing in Action* box on page 140 provides details on day traders' results.

Technical and Service Problems As the number of online investors increases, so do the problems that beset brokerage firms and their customers. During the past few years most brokerage firms have upgraded their systems to reduce the number of service outages. But the potential problems go beyond the brokerage sites. Once an investor places a trade at a firm's Web site, it goes through several other parties to be executed. Most online brokers don't have their own trading desks and have agreements with other trading firms to execute their orders on the *New York Stock Exchange* or *Nasdaq Stock Market*. Slowdowns at any point in the process can create problems confirming trades. Investors, thinking that their trades had not gone through, might place the order again—only to discover later that they have bought the same stock twice. Online investors who don't get immediate trade execution and confirmation use the telephone when they can't get through online or to solve other problems with their accounts, and they often face long waiting times on hold.

day trader
an investor who buys and sells stocks quickly throughout the day in hopes of making quick profits.

INVESTING *in Action*

Are You Ready To Quit Your Day Job? Perhaps Not Just Yet

Day trading refers to the practice of buying and selling stocks or other securities during the trading day; positions are not usually held overnight. Day traders spend most hours when the market is open glued to computers, tracking movements of stocks and trading them back and forth. Since commissions for online trading often amount to only a fraction of a penny per share, even a small price movement between bid and ask spread may be profitable.

How well do day traders perform? A recent study by the North American Securities Administrators Association suggests that only about 11.5% trade profitably. Those profits range from a few hundred to several thousand dollars a month. The best day traders make annual profits in the low $100,000s. According to managers of day-trading firms cited in a *Washington Post Magazine* article, about 90% of day traders "are washed up within three months." David Shellenberger of the

Massachusetts Securities Division noted, "Most traders will lose all of their money." Former SEC Chairman Arthur Levitt recommends that people day trade only with "money they can afford to lose."

The people who appear to be making the biggest return from day trading are those running day-trading firms. These firms provide day traders with computer terminals connected to exchanges and all necessary trading software in exchange for a commission per trade. With each customer making trades all day long, their coffers fill very quickly.

CRITICAL THINKING QUESTIONS What are the major risks associated with day trading of stocks? Why have so few people been able to make a living by day trading?

Source: Selena Maranjian, "The Perils of Day Trading," September 24, 2002, *The Motley Fool,* www.fool.com.

Tips for Successful Online Trades Successful online investors take additional precautions before submitting their orders. Here are some tips to protect yourself from common problems:

- *Know how to place and confirm your order before you begin trading.* This simple step can keep you from having problems later.

- *Verify the stock symbol of the security you wish to buy.* Two very different companies can have similar symbols. Some investors have bought the wrong stock because they didn't check before placing their order.

- *Use limit orders.* The order you see on your computer screen may not be the one you get. With a limit order, you avoid getting burned in fast-moving markets. Although limit orders cost more, they can save you thousands of dollars. For example, customers eager to get shares of a hot IPO stock placed market orders. Instead of buying the stock near the offering price of $9, some were shocked to find that their orders were filled at prices as high as $90 during the stock's first trading day. Investors who were aware of the price run-up tried to cancel orders but couldn't get through to brokers. Because of this, some brokers accept only limit orders for online IPO purchases on the first day of trading.

- *Don't ignore the online reminders that ask you to check and recheck.* It's easy to make a typo that adds an extra digit to a purchase amount.

INVESTOR FACTS

UP, UP, AND AWAY—Although online brokerage firms' share of trading volume on the NYSE and Nasdaq plummeted from 42% to about 12% during the 2000–2003 bear market, activity rose again as the market improved. Retail investors, who account for most of the online brokerages' customers, began buying stocks again fairly quickly. This rejuvenated the markets in general due to the inflow of funds. Furthermore, fierce competition among online brokers ensured that fees dropped rapidly, making trading cheaper, which attracted even more investing. This inflow of funds is considered by analysts a positive sign of investor confidence.

fixed-commission schedules
fixed brokerage commissions that typically apply to the small transactions usually made by individual investors.

negotiated commissions
brokerage commissions agreed to by the client and the broker as a result of their negotiations; typically apply on large institutional transactions and to individual investors who maintain large accounts.

- *Don't get carried away.* It's easy to churn your own account. In fact, new online investors trade about twice as much as they did before they went online. To control impulse trading, have a strategy and stick to it.

- *Open accounts with two brokers.* This protects you if your online brokerage's computer system crashes. It also gives you an alternative if one brokerage is blocked with heavy trading volume.

- *Double-check orders for accuracy.* Make sure each trade was completed according to your instructions. It's very easy to make typos or use the wrong stock symbol, so review the confirmation notice to verify that the right number of shares was bought or sold and that the price and commissions or fees are as quoted. Check your account for "unauthorized" trades.

▌Transaction Costs

Making transactions through brokers or market makers is considerably easier for investors than it would be to negotiate directly, trying to find someone who wants to buy that which you want to sell (or vice versa). To compensate the broker for executing the transaction, investors pay transaction costs, which are usually levied on both the purchase and the sale of securities. When making investment decisions, you must consider the structure and magnitude of transaction costs, because they affect returns.

Since the passage of the *Securities Acts Amendments of 1975*, brokers have been permitted to charge whatever brokerage commissions they deem appropriate. Most firms have established **fixed-commission schedules** that apply to small transactions, the ones most often made by individual investors. On large institutional transactions, the client and broker may arrange a **negotiated commission**—commissions to which both parties agree. Negotiated commissions are also available to individual investors who maintain large accounts, typically above $50,000. The commission structure varies with the type of security and the type of broker. In subsequent chapters we'll describe the basic commission structures for various types of securities.

Because of the way brokerage firms charge commissions on stock trades, it is difficult to compare prices precisely. Traditional brokers generally charge on the basis of number of shares and the price of the stock at the time of the transaction. Internet brokers usually charge flat rates, often for transactions up to 1,000 shares, with additional fees for larger or more complicated orders. However, many traditional brokerage firms have reduced their commissions on broker-assisted trades and have instituted annual flat fees (on wrap accounts) set as a specified percentage of the value of the assets in the account. Unless you are a very active trader, you will probably be better off paying commissions on a per-transaction basis.

Obviously, premium and basic discount brokers charge substantially less than full-service brokers for the same transaction. However, some discounters charge a minimum fee, to discourage small orders. The savings from the discounter are substantial: Depending on the size and type of transaction, premium and basic discount brokers can typically save investors between 30% and 80% of the commission charged by the full-service broker.

▊ Investor Protection: SIPC and Arbitration

Although most investment transactions take place safely, it is important for you to know what protection you have if things *don't* go smoothly. As a client, you are protected against the loss of the securities or cash held by your broker. The **Securities Investor Protection Corporation (SIPC)**, a nonprofit membership corporation, was authorized by the *Securities Investor Protection Act of 1970* to protect customer accounts against the consequences of financial failure of the brokerage firm. The SIPC currently insures each customer's account for up to $500,000, with claims for cash limited to $100,000 per customer. Note that SIPC insurance does not guarantee that the investor will recover the dollar value of the securities; it guarantees only that the securities themselves will be returned. Some brokerage firms also insure certain customer accounts for amounts in excess of $500,000. Certainly, in light of the diversity and quality of services available among brokerage firms, this may be an additional service you should consider when you select a firm and an individual broker.

Securities Investor Protection Corporation (SIPC)
a nonprofit membership corporation, authorized by the federal government, that insures each brokerage customer's account for up to $500,000, with claims for cash limited to $100,000 per customer.

The SIPC provides protection in case your brokerage firm fails. But what happens if your broker gave you bad advice and, as a result, you lost a lot of money on an investment? Or what if you feel your broker is *churning* your account? In either case, the SIPC won't help. It's not intended to insure you against bad investment advice or churning. Instead, if you have a dispute with your broker, the first thing you should do is discuss the situation with the managing officer at the branch where you do business. If that doesn't do any good, then contact the firm's compliance officer and the securities regulator in your home state.

HOTLINKS

The Securities Investor Protection Corporation (SIPC) protects customers of broker-dealers registered with the U.S. Securities and Exchange Commission.

www.sipc.org

If you still don't get any satisfaction, you can use litigation (judicial methods in the courts) to resolve the dispute. Alternative dispute-resolution processes that may avoid litigation include *mediation* and *arbitration*. **Mediation** is an informal, voluntary approach in which you and the broker agree to a mediator, who facilitates negotiations between the two of you to resolve the case. The mediator does not impose a solution on you and the broker. The NASD and securities-related organizations encourage investors to mediate disputes rather than arbitrate them, because mediation can reduce costs and time for both investors and brokers.

mediation
an informal, voluntary dispute-resolution process in which a client and a broker agree to a mediator, who facilitates negotiations between them to resolve the case.

If mediation is not pursued or if it fails, you may have no choice but to take the case to **arbitration**, a formal process whereby you and your broker present the two sides of the argument before an arbitration panel. The panel then decides the case. Many brokerage firms require you to resolve disputes by *binding arbitration;* in this case, you don't have the option to sue. You must accept the arbitrator's decision, and in most cases you cannot go to court to review your case. Before you open an account, check whether the brokerage agreement contains a binding-arbitration clause.

arbitration
a formal dispute-resolution process in which a client and a broker present their argument before a panel, which then decides the case.

Mediation and arbitration proceedings typically cost less and are resolved more quickly than litigation. Recent legislation has given many investors the option of using either securities industry panels or independent arbitration panels such as those sponsored by the American Arbitration Association (AAA). Independent panels are considered more sympathetic toward investors. In addition, only one of the three arbitrators on a panel can be connected with the securities industry. However, in 2005, in only about 43% of the arbitration cases did the claimant recover monetary damages or non-monetary relief.

Probably the best thing you can do to avoid the need to mediate, arbitrate, or litigate is to select your broker carefully, understand the financial risks involved in the broker's recommendations, thoroughly evaluate the advice he or she offers, and continuously monitor the volume of transactions that he or she recommends and executes. Clearly, it is much less costly to choose the right broker initially than to incur later the financial and emotional costs of having chosen a bad one.

If you have a problem with an online trade, immediately file a written—not e-mail—complaint with the broker. Cite dates, times, and amounts of trades, and include all supporting documentation. File a copy with the NASD regulatory arm Web site (www.nasdr.com) and with your state securities regulator. If you can't resolve the problems with the broker, you can try mediation and then resort to arbitration, litigation being the last resort.

CONCEPTS IN REVIEW

Answers available at: www.myfinancelab.com

3.13 Describe the types of services offered by brokerage firms, and discuss the criteria for selecting a suitable stockbroker.

3.14 Briefly differentiate among the following types of brokerage accounts:
a. Single or joint
b. Custodial
c. Cash
d. Margin
e. Wrap

3.15 Differentiate among *market orders, limit orders,* and *stop-loss orders.* What is the rationale for using a stop-loss order rather than a limit order?

3.16 Differentiate between the services and costs associated with *full-service, premium discount,* and *basic discount* brokers. Be sure to discuss online transactions.

3.17 What is *day trading,* and why is it risky? How can you avoid problems as an online trader?

3.18 In what two ways, based on the number of shares transacted, do brokers typically charge for executing transactions? How are online transaction fees structured relative to the degree of broker involvement?

3.19 What protection does the *Securities Investor Protection Corporation (SIPC)* provide securities investors? How are mediation and arbitration procedures used to settle disputes between investors and their brokers?

Investment Advisers and Investment Clubs

LG 6

investment advisers
individuals or firms that provide investment advice, typically for a fee.

Many investors feel that they have neither the time nor the expertise to analyze financial information and make decisions on their own. Instead, they turn to an **investment adviser**, an individual or firm that provides investment advice, typically for a fee. Alternatively, some small investors join investment clubs. Here we will discuss using an investment adviser and then briefly cover the key aspects of investment clubs.

▮ Using an Investment Adviser

The "product" provided by an investment adviser ranges from broad, general advice to detailed, specific analyses and recommendations. The most general form of advice is a newsletter published by the adviser. These letters comment on the economy, current events, market behavior, and specific securities. Investment advisers also provide complete individualized investment evaluation, recommendation, and management services.

Regulation of Advisers As we noted in Chapter 2, the *Investment Advisers Act of 1940* ensures that investment advisers make full disclosure of information about their backgrounds, conflicts of interest, and so on. The act requires professional advisers to register and file periodic reports with the SEC. A 1960 amendment permits the SEC to inspect the records of investment advisers and to revoke the registration of those who violate the act's provisions. However, financial planners, stockbrokers, bankers, lawyers, and accountants who provide investment advice in addition to their main professional activity are not regulated by the act. Many states have also passed similar legislation, requiring investment advisers to register and to abide by the guidelines established by the state law.

Be aware that the federal and state laws regulating the activities of professional investment advisers do not guarantee competence. Rather, they are intended to protect the investor against fraudulent and unethical practices. It is important to recognize that, at present, no law or regulatory body controls entrance into the field. Therefore, investment advisers range from highly informed professionals to totally incompetent amateurs. Advisers who possess a professional designation are usually preferred because they have completed academic courses in areas directly or peripherally related to the investment process. Such designations include CFA (Chartered Financial Analyst), CIMA (Certified Investment Management Analyst), CIC (Chartered Investment Counselor), CFP® (Certified Financial Planner), ChFC (Chartered Financial Consultant), CLU (Chartered Life Underwriter), and CPA (Certified Public Accountant).

Online Investment Advice You can also find financial advice online. Whether it's a retirement planning tool or advice on how to diversify your assets, automated financial advisers may be able to help you. If your needs are specific rather than comprehensive, you can find good advice at other sites. For example, T. Rowe Price has an excellent college planning section (www.troweprice.com/college). Financial Engines (www.financialengines .com), AdviceAmerica (www.adviceamerica.com), and DirectAdvice (www .directadvice.com) are among several independent advice sites that offer broader planning capabilities. Many mutual fund family Web sites have online financial advisers. For example, The Vanguard Group (www.vanguard.com) has a personal investors section that helps you choose funds for specific investment objectives, such as retirement or financing a college education.

The Cost and Use of Investment Advice Professional investment advice typically costs, annually, between 0.25% and 3% of the dollar amount of money being managed. For large portfolios, the fee is typically in the range of 0.25% to 0.75%. For small portfolios (less than $100,000), an annual fee ranging from 2% to 3% of the dollar amount of funds managed would not be unusual. These fees generally cover complete management of a client's money, excluding any purchase or sale commissions. The cost of periodic investment advice not provided as part of a subscription service could be based on a fixed-fee schedule or quoted as an hourly charge for consultation. Online advisers are much less expensive; they either are free or charge an annual fee.

Whether you choose a traditional investment advisory service or decide to try an online service, some are better than others. More expensive services do not necessarily provide better advice. It is best to study carefully the track record and overall reputation of an investment adviser before purchasing his or her services. Not only should the adviser have a good performance record, but he or she also should be responsive to your personal goals.

How good is the advice from online advisers? It's very hard to judge. Their suggested plans are only as good as the input. Beginning investors may not have sufficient knowledge to make wise assumptions on future savings, tax, or inflation rates or to analyze results thoroughly. A good face-to-face personal financial planner will ask lots of questions to assess your investing expertise and explain what you don't know. Automated tools for these early-stage questions may take too narrow a focus and not consider other parts of your investment portfolio. For many investors, online advisers lack what leads them to get help in the first place—the human touch. They want hand-holding, reassurance, and gentle nudging to follow through on their plans.

▌ Investment Clubs

Another way to obtain investment advice and experience is to join an investment club. This route can be especially useful for those of moderate means who do not want to incur the cost of an investment adviser. An **investment club** is a legal partnership binding a group of investors (partners) to a specified organizational structure, operating procedures, and purpose. The goal of most clubs is to earn favorable long-term returns by making investments in moderate-risk vehicles.

Individuals with similar goals usually form investment clubs to pool their knowledge and money in a jointly owned and managed portfolio. Certain members are responsible for obtaining and analyzing data on a specific investment vehicle or strategy. At periodic meetings, the members present their findings for discussion and further analysis by the members. The group decides whether to pursue the proposed vehicle or strategy. Most clubs require members to make scheduled contributions to the club's treasury, thereby regularly increasing the pool of investable funds. Although most clubs concentrate on investments in stocks and bonds, some may concentrate on specialized investments such as options or futures.

Membership in an investment club provides an excellent way for the novice investor to learn the key aspects of portfolio construction and investment management, while (one hopes) earning a favorable return on his or her funds. In fact, many investment clubs regularly earn returns above the market and even above professional money managers. The reason? Investment clubs typically buy stocks for the long term, rather than trying to make the quick buck.

As you might expect, investment clubs have also joined the online investing movement. By tapping into the Internet, clubs

investment club
a legal partnership through which a group of investors are bound to a specified organizational structure, operating procedures, and purpose, which is typically to earn favorable long-term returns from moderate-risk investments.

HOTLINKS

A good source of information about investment clubs can be found at fool.com. Go to:

www.fool.com/InvestmentClub/
InvestmentClubIntroduction.htm

are freed from geographical restrictions. Now investors around the world, many who have never met, can form a club and discuss investing strategies and stock picks just as easily as if they gathered in person. Finding a time or place to meet is no longer an issue. Some clubs are formed by friends; others are strangers who have similar investing philosophies and may have met online. Online clubs conduct business via e-mail or set up a private Web site. Members of the *Better Investing Community,* a not-for-profit organization, have access to educational materials, investment tools, and other investment features.

Better Investing, which has over 200,000 individual and club investors and over 16,000 investment clubs, publishes a variety of useful materials and also sponsors regional and national meetings. (To learn how to start an investment club, visit the Better Investing Web site at www.betterinvesting.org. Or order an information package by calling the toll-free number 877-275-6242 or writing Better Investing, P.O. Box 220, Royal Oak, MI 48068.)

CONCEPTS IN REVIEW
Answers available at: www.myfinancelab.com

3.20 Describe the services that professional investment advisers perform, how they are regulated, online investment advisers, and the cost of investment advice.

3.21 What benefits does an *investment club* offer the small investor? Why do investment clubs regularly outperform the market and the pros? Would you prefer to join a regular or an online club, and why?

Summary

LG 1 **Discuss the growth in online investing and the pros and cons of using the Internet as an investment tool.** The Internet has empowered individual investors by providing information and tools formerly available only to investing professionals and by simplifying the investing process. The time and money savings it provides are huge. Investors get the most current information, including real-time stock price quotes, market activity data, research reports, educational articles, and discussion forums. Tools such as financial planning calculators, stock-screening programs, charting, and stock quotes and portfolio tracking are free at many sites. Buying and selling securities online is convenient, relatively simple, inexpensive, and fast.

LG 2 **Identify the major types and sources of traditional and online investment information.** Investment information, descriptive or analytical, includes information about the economy and current events, industries and companies, and alternative investment vehicles, as well as price information and personal investment strategies. It can be obtained from financial journals, general newspapers, institutional news, business periodicals, government publications, special subscription services, stockholders' reports, comparative data sources, subscription services, brokerage reports, investment letters, price quotations, and electronic and online sources. Most print publications also have Web sites with access to all or part of their content. Financial portals bring together a variety of financial information online. Investors will also find specialized sites for bond, mutual fund, and international information, as well as discussion forums that discuss individual securities and investment strategies. Because it is hard to know the qualifications of those who make postings on message boards, participants must do their own homework before acting on an online tip.

LG 3 **Explain the key aspects of the commonly cited stock and bond market averages and indexes.** Investors commonly rely on stock market averages and indexes to stay abreast of market behavior. The most often cited are the Dow Jones averages, which include the Dow Jones Industrial Average (DJIA). Also widely followed are the Standard & Poor's indexes, the NYSE composite index, the AMEX composite index, the Nasdaq Stock Market indexes, and the Value Line indexes. Numerous other averages and indexes, including a number of global and foreign market indexes, are regularly reported in financial publications.

Bond market indicators are most often reported in terms of bond yields and bond indexes. The Dow Jones Corporate Bond Index is among the most popular. Yield and price index data are also available for various types of bonds and various domestic and foreign markets. Both stock and bond market statistics are published daily in the *Wall Street Journal* and summarized weekly in *Barron's*.

LG 4 **Review the role of stockbrokers, including the services they provide, selection of a stockbroker, opening an account, and transaction basics.** Stockbrokers facilitate buying and selling of securities, and provide other client services. An investor should select a stockbroker who has a compatible disposition toward investing and whose firm offers the desired services at competitive costs. Today the distinctions among full-service, premium discount, and basic discount (online) brokers are blurring. Most brokers now offer online trading capabilities, and many no-frills brokers are expanding their services to include research and advice. Investors can open a variety of types of brokerage accounts, such as single, joint, custodial, cash, margin, and wrap. Transactions take place in odd-lot (less than 100 shares) or round-lot (100 shares or multiples thereof). Odd-lot transactions usually incur an added fee.

LG 5 **Describe the basic types of orders, online transactions, transaction costs, and the legal aspects of investor protection.** A market order is an order to buy or sell stock at the best price available. A limit order is an order to buy at a specified price or below, or to sell at a specified price or above. Stop-loss orders become market orders as soon as the minimum sell price or the maximum buy price is hit. Limit and stop-loss orders can be placed as fill-or-kill orders, day orders, or good-'til-canceled (GTC) orders.

On small transactions, most brokers have fixed-commission schedules; on larger transactions, they will negotiate commissions. Commissions also vary by type of security and type of broker. The Securities Investor Protection Corporation (SIPC) insures customers' accounts against the brokerage firm's failure. Mediation and arbitration procedures are frequently employed to resolve disputes. These disputes typically concern the investor's belief that the broker either gave bad advice or churned the account.

LG 6 **Discuss the roles of investment advisers and investment clubs.** Investment advisers charge an annual fee ranging from 0.25% to 3% of the dollar amount being managed and are often regulated by federal and state law. Web sites that provide investment advice are now available as well. Investment clubs provide individual investors with investment advice and help them gain investing experience. Online clubs have members in various geographical areas and conduct business via e-mail or at a private Web site.

Key Terms

AMEX composite index, *p. 130*
analytical information, *p. 111*
arbitration, *p. 142*
averages, *p. 125*
back-office research reports, *p. 119*
Barron's, *p. 114*
basic discount broker, *p. 134*
bond yield, *p. 131*
cash account, *p. 136*
churning, *p. 135*
custodial account, *p. 136*
day trader, *p. 139*
descriptive information, *p. 111*
Dow Jones Corporate Bond Index,
    p. 131
Dow Jones Industrial Average (DJIA),
    p. 126
fair disclosure rule (Regulation FD),
    p. 117
financial portals, *p. 121*
fixed-commission schedules, *p. 141*
Form 10-K, *p. 117*
full-service broker, *p. 133*
indexes, *p. 125*
investment advisers, *p. 143*
investment club, *p. 145*
investment letters, *p. 120*

limit order, *p. 137*
margin account, *p. 136*
market order, *p. 137*
mediation, *p. 142*
Mergent, *p. 118*
Nasdaq Stock Market indexes, *p. 130*
negotiated commissions, *p. 141*
NYSE composite index, *p. 130*
odd lot, *p. 136*
premium discount broker, *p. 133*
quotations, *p. 120*
round lot, *p. 136*
Securities Investor Protection
    Corporation (SIPC), *p. 142*
Standard & Poor's Corporation (S&P),
    p. 117
Standard & Poor's indexes, *p. 128*
stockbrokers, *p. 132*
stockholders' (annual) report, *p. 117*
stop-loss (stop) order, *p. 138*
street name, *p. 133*
Value Line composite index, *p. 130*
Value Line Investment Survey, *p. 118*
Wall Street Journal, *p. 114*
Wilshire 5000 index, *p. 128*
wrap account, *p. 136*

Discussion Questions

LG 2   **Q3.1**   Thomas Weisel, chief executive of a securities firm that bears his name, believes that individual investors already have too much information. "Many lose money by trading excessively on stray data," he says. Other industry professionals oppose the SEC's fair disclosure rule (Regulation FD) for the same reason. The Securities Industry Association's general counsel expressed concern that the rule restricts rather than encourages the flow of information. Other securities professionals argue that individual investors aren't really capable of interpreting much of the information now available to them. Explain why you agree or disagree with these opinions.

LG 2   **Q3.2**   Innovative Internet-based bookseller Amazon.com has expanded into other retail categories. Gather appropriate information from relevant sources to assess the following with an eye toward investing in Amazon.com.
   a. Economic conditions and the key current events during the past 12 months.
   b. Information on the status and growth (past and future) of the bookselling industry and specific information on Amazon.com and its major competitors.
   c. Brokerage reports and analysts' recommendations with respect to Amazon.com.

d. A history of the past and recent dividends and price behavior of Amazon.com, which is traded on the Nasdaq National Market.

e. A recommendation with regard to the advisability of investing in Amazon.com.

LG 2 **LG 6** Q3.3 Visit four financial portals or other financial information Web sites listed in Table 3.4. Compare them in terms of ease of use, investment information, investment tools, advisory services, and links to other services. Also catalog the costs, if any, of obtaining these services. Which would you recommend, and why?

LG 3 Q3.4 Gather and evaluate relevant market averages and indexes over the past 6 months to assess recent stock and bond market conditions. Describe the conditions in each of these markets. Using recent history, coupled with relevant economic and current event data, forecast near-term market conditions. On the basis of your assessment of market conditions, would you recommend investing in stocks, in bonds, or in neither at this time? Explain the reasoning underlying your recommendation.

LG 4 Q3.5 Prepare a checklist of questions and issues you would use when shopping for a stockbroker. Describe both the ideal broker and the ideal brokerage firm, given your investment goals and disposition. Discuss the pros and cons of using a full-service rather than a premium discount or basic discount broker. If you plan to trade online, what additional questions would you ask?

LG 4 Q3.6 Find and visit the sites of two basic discount brokerages listed in Table 3.5 or any others you know. After exploring the sites, compare them for ease of use, quality of information, availability of investing tools, reliability, other services, and any other criteria important to you. Summarize your findings and explain which you would choose if you were to open an account, and why.

LG 5 Q3.7 Describe how, if at all, a conservative and an aggressive investor might use each of the following types of orders as part of their investment programs. Contrast these two types of investors in view of these preferences.
   a. Market.
   b. Limit.
   c. Stop-loss.

LG 5 Q3.8 Learn more about day trading at sites such as Edgetrade (www.edgetrade.com), Daytradingthemarkets.com (www.daytradingthemarkets.com), TrendVue (www.1day tradingstockadviceandpicks.com), and The Rookie DayTrader (www.rookiedaytrader .com). On the basis of your research, summarize the way in which day trading works, some strategies for day traders, the risks, and the rewards. What type of person would make a good day trader?

LG 6 Q3.9 Differentiate between the financial advice you would receive from a traditional investment adviser and one of the new online planning and advice sites. Which would you personally prefer to use, and why? How could membership in an investment club serve as an alternative to a paid investment adviser?

Problems

LG 2 P3.1 Bill Shaffer estimates that if he does 5 hours of research using data that will cost $75, there is a good chance that he can improve his expected return on a $10,000, 1-year investment from 8% to 10%. Bill feels that he must earn at least $20 per hour on the time he devotes to his research.

a. Find the cost of Bill's research.
b. By how much (in dollars) will Bill's return increase as a result of the research?
c. On a strict economic basis, should Bill perform the proposed research?

LG 3   **P3.2**   Imagine that the Mini-Dow Average (MDA) is based on the closing prices of five stocks. The divisor used in the calculation of the MDA is currently 0.765. The closing prices for each of the 5 stocks in the MDA today and exactly a year ago, when the divisor was 0.790, are given in the accompanying table.

Stock	Closing Stock Price	
	Today	One Year Ago
Ace Computers	$ 65	$74
Coburn Motor Company	37	34
National Soap & Cosmetics	110	96
Ronto Foods	73	72
Wings Aircraft	96	87

a. Calculate the MDA today and that of a year ago.
b. Compare the values of the MDA calculated in part (a) and describe the apparent market behavior over the last year. Was it a bull or a bear market?

LG 3   **P3.3**   The SP-6 index (a fictitious index) is used by many investors to monitor the general behavior of the stock market. It has a base value set equal to 100 at January 1, 1973. In the accompanying table, the closing market values for each of the 6 stocks included in the index are given for 3 dates.

Stock	Closing Market Value of Stock		
	June 30, 2008 (Thousands)	January 1, 2008 (Thousands)	January 1, 1973 (Thousands)
1	$ 430	$ 460	$240
2	1,150	1,120	630
3	980	990	450
4	360	420	150
5	650	700	320
6	290	320	80

a. Calculate the value of the SP-6 index on both January 1, 2008, and June 30, 2008, using the data presented here.
b. Compare the values of the SP-6 index calculated in part (a) and relate them to the base index value. Would you describe the general market condition during the 6-month period January 1 to June 30, 2008, as a bull or a bear market?

LG 3   **P3.4**   Carla Sanchez wishes to develop an average or index that can be used to measure the general behavior of stock prices over time. She has decided to include 6 closely followed, high-quality stocks in the average or index. She plans to use August 15, 1981, her birthday, as the base and is interested in measuring the value of the average or index on August 15, 2005, and August 15, 2008. She has found the closing prices for each of the 6 stocks, A through F, at each of the 3 dates and has calculated a divisor that can be used to adjust for any stock splits, company changes, and so on that have occurred since the base year, which has a divisor equal to 1.00.

	Closing Stock Price		
Stock	August 15, 2008	August 15, 2005	August 15, 1981
A	$46	$40	$50
B	37	36	10
C	20	23	7
D	59	61	26
E	82	70	45
F	32	30	32
Divisor	0.70	0.72	1.00

Note: The number of shares of each stock outstanding has remained unchanged at each of the 3 dates. Therefore, the closing stock prices will behave identically to the closing market values.

a. Using the data given in the table, calculate the market average, using the same methodology used to calculate the Dow averages, at each of the 3 dates—the 15th of August 1981, 2005, and 2008.

b. Using the data given in the table and assuming a base index value of 10 on August 15, 1981, calculate the market index, using the same methodology used to calculate the S&P indexes, at each of the 3 dates.

c. Use your findings in parts **a** and **b** to describe the general market condition— bull or bear—that existed between August 15, 2005, and August 15, 2008.

d. Calculate the percentage changes in the average and index values between August 15, 2005, and August 15, 2008. Why do they differ?

LG 5 P3.5   Al Cromwell places a *market order* to buy a round lot of Thomas, Inc., common stock, which is traded on the NYSE and is currently quoted at $50 per share. Ignoring brokerage commissions, how much money would Cromwell probably have to pay? If he had placed a market order to sell, how much money will he probably receive? Explain.

LG 5 P3.6   Imagine that you have placed a *limit order* to buy 100 shares of Sallisaw Tool at a price of $38, though the stock is currently selling for $41. Discuss the consequences, if any, of each of the following.

a. The stock price drops to $39 per share 2 months before cancellation of the limit order.

b. The stock price drops to $38 per share.

c. The minimum stock price achieved before cancellation of the limit order was $38.50. When the limit order was canceled, the stock was selling for $47.50 per share.

LG 5 P3.7   If you place a *stop-loss order* to sell at $23 on a stock currently selling for $26.50 per share, what is likely to be the minimum loss you will experience on 50 shares if the stock price rapidly declines to $20.50 per share? Explain. What if you had placed a *stop-limit order* to sell at $23, and the stock price tumbled to $20.50?

LG 5 P3.8   You sell 100 shares of a stock short for $40 per share. You want to limit your loss on this transaction to no more than $500. What order should you place?

LG 5 P3.9   You have been researching a stock that you like, which is currently trading at $50 per share. You would like to buy the stock if it were a little less expensive—say, $47 per share. You believe that the stock price will go to $70 by year-end, and then level off or decline. You decide to place a limit order to buy 100 shares of the stock at $47, and a limit order to sell it at $70. It turns out that you were right about the direction of the stock price, and it goes straight to $75. What is your current position?

LG 5   **P3.10** You own 500 shares of Ups&Downs, Inc., stock. It is currently priced at $50. You are going on vacation, and you realize that the company will be reporting earnings while you are away. To protect yourself against a rapid drop in the price, you place a limit order to sell 500 shares at $40. It turns out the earnings report was not so good, and the stock price fell to $30 right after the announcement. It did, however, bounce back, and by the end of the day it was back to $42. What happened in your account?

LG 5   **P3.11** You have $5,000 in a 50% margin account. You have been following a stock that you think you want to buy. The stock is priced at $52. You decide that if the stock falls to $50, you would like to buy it. You place a limit order to buy 300 shares at $50. The stock falls to $50. What happens?

See www.myfinancelab.com **for Web Exercises,**
Spreadsheets, and other online resources.

Case Problem 3.1   *The Perezes' Good Fortune*

LG 2   LG 4   LG 6   Angel and Marie Perez own a small pool hall located in southern New Jersey. They enjoy running the business, which they have owned for nearly 3 years. Angel, a retired professional pool shooter, saved for nearly 10 years to buy this business, which he and his wife own free and clear. The income from the pool hall is adequate to allow Angel, Marie, and their 2 children, Mary (age 10) and José (age 4), to live comfortably. Although he lacks formal education beyond the tenth grade, Angel has become an avid reader. He enjoys reading about current events and personal finance, particularly investing. He especially likes *Money* magazine, from which he has gained numerous ideas for better managing the family's finances. Because of the long hours required to run the business, Angel can devote 3 to 4 hours a day (on the job) to reading.

Recently, Angel and Marie were notified that Marie's uncle had died and left them a portfolio of stocks and bonds with a current market value of $300,000. They were elated to learn of their good fortune but decided it would be best not to change their lifestyle as a result of this inheritance. Instead, they want their newfound wealth to provide for their children's college education as well as their own retirement. They decided that, like their uncle, they would keep these funds invested in stocks and bonds.

Angel felt that in view of this plan, he needed to acquaint himself with the securities currently in the portfolio. He knew that to manage the portfolio himself, he would have to stay abreast of the securities markets as well as the economy in general. He also realized that he would need to follow each security in the portfolio and continuously evaluate possible alternative securities that could be substituted as conditions warranted. Because Angel had plenty of time in which to follow the market, he strongly believed that with proper information, he could manage the portfolio. Given the amount of money involved, Angel was not too concerned with the information costs; rather, he wanted the best information he could get at a reasonable price.

Questions

a. Explain what role the *Wall Street Journal* and/or *Barron's* might play in meeting Angel's needs. What other general sources of economic and current event information would you recommend to Angel? Explain.

b. How might Angel be able to use the services of Standard & Poor's Corporation, Mergent, and the *Value Line Investment Survey* to learn about the securities in the portfolio? Indicate which, if any, of these services you would recommend, and why.

c. Recommend some specific online investment information sources and tools to help Angel and Marie manage their investments.

d. Explain to Angel the need to find a good stockbroker and the role the stockbroker could play in providing information and advice. Should he consider hiring a financial adviser to manage the portfolio?

e. Give Angel a summary prescription for obtaining information and advice that will help to ensure the preservation and growth of the family's newfound wealth.

Case Problem 3.2   *Peter and Deborah's Choices of Brokers and Advisers*

LG 4   LG 5   LG 6   Peter Chang and Deborah Barry, friends who work for a large software company, decided to leave the relative security of their employer and join the staff of OnlineSpeed Inc., a 2-year-old company working on new broadband technology for fast Internet access. Peter will be a vice president for new-product development; Deborah will be treasurer. Although they are excited about the potential their new jobs offer, they recognize the need to consider the financial implications of the move. Of immediate concern are their 401(k) retirement plans. On leaving their current employer, each of them will receive a lump-sum settlement of about $75,000 that they must roll over into self-directed, tax-deferred retirement accounts. The friends met over lunch to discuss their options for investing these funds.

Peter is 30 years old and single, with a bachelor's degree in computer science. He rents an apartment and would like to buy a condominium fairly soon but is in no rush. For now, he is happy using his money on the luxuries of life. He considers himself a bit of a risk taker and has dabbled in the stock market from time to time, using his technology expertise to invest in software and Internet companies.

Deborah's undergraduate degree was in English, followed by an M.B.A. in finance. She is 32, is married, and hopes to start a family very soon. Her husband is a physician in private practice.

Peter is very computer-savvy and likes to pick stocks on the basis of his own Internet research. Although Deborah's finance background gives her a solid understanding of investing fundamentals, she is more conservative and has thus far stayed with blue-chip stocks and mutual funds. Among the topics that come up during their lunchtime conversation are stockbrokers and financial planners. Peter is leaning toward a bare-bones basic discount broker with low cost per online trade that is offering free trades for a limited time. Deborah is also cost-conscious but warns Peter that the low costs can be deceptive if you have to pay for other services or find yourself trading more often. She also thinks Peter is too focused on the technology sector and encourages him to seek financial advice to balance his portfolio. They agree to research a number of brokerage firms and investment advisers and meet again to compare notes.

Questions

a. Research at least 2 different full-service, premium discount, and basic discount stock brokerage firms, and compare the services and costs. What brokers would suit Peter's needs best, and why? What brokers would suit Deborah's needs best, and why? What are some key questions each should ask when interviewing potential brokers?

b. What factors should Peter and Deborah consider before deciding to use a particular broker? Compare the pros and cons of getting the personal attention of a full-service broker with the services provided by the discount brokers.

c. Do you think that a broker that assists in making transactions and focuses on personal attention would be a good choice for either Peter or Deborah?

d. Peter mentioned to Deborah that he had read an article about *day trading* and wanted to try it. What would you advise Peter about the risks and rewards of this strategy?

e. Prepare a brief overview of the traditional and online sources of investment advice that could help Peter and Deborah create suitable portfolios. Which type of adviser would you recommend for Peter? For Deborah? Explain your reasoning.

Excel with Spreadsheets

Peter Tanaka is interested in starting a stock portfolio. He has heard many financial reporters talk about the Dow Jones Industrial Average (DJIA) as being a proxy for the overall stock market. From visiting various online investment sites, Peter is able to track the variability in the Dow. Peter would like to develop an average or index that will measure the price performance of his selected portfolio over time. He has decided to create a price-weighted index, similar to the Dow, where the stocks are held in proportion to their share prices. He wishes to form an index based on the following 10 high-quality stocks and has designated October 13, 1974, as the base year. The number of shares outstanding has remained constant over the time period 1974 through 2008. The implication is that the closing stock prices will behave just like the closing market values. Given the data below, create a spreadsheet to model and analyze the use of an index.

	Prices		
Stocks	10/13/2008	10/13/2004	10/13/1974
A	45	50	55
B	12	9	15
C	37	37	37
D	65	66	67
E	36	42	48
F	26	35	43
G	75	68	59
H	35	38	30
I	67	74	81
J	84	88	92

Questions

a. The divisor is 1.00 on October 13, 1974, .75 on October 13, 2004, and .85 on October 13, 2008. Using this information and the data supplied above, calculate the market average, using the same methodology used to calculate the Dow averages, on each of the 3 dates—the 13th of October 1974, 2004, and 2008.

b. The DJIA is the most widely cited stock market indicator, yet there are criticisms of the model. One criticism is that the higher-priced securities in the portfolio will impact the Dow more than the relatively lower-priced stocks. Assume that Stock J increases by 10%. Recalculate the market averages on each of the 3 dates.

c. Next, assume Stock J is back to its original level and Stock B increases by 10%. Recalculate the market averages on each of the 3 dates. Compare your findings in all 3 scenarios. Do you find support for the criticism of the Dow? Explain.

Chapter 4

Return and Risk

After studying this chapter, you should be able to:

LG 1 Review the concept of return, its components, the forces that affect the level of return, and historical returns.

LG 2 Discuss the role of time value of money in measuring return and defining a satisfactory investment.

LG 3 Describe real, risk-free, and required returns and the calculation and application of holding period return.

LG 4 Explain the concept and the calculation of yield, and how to find growth rates.

LG 5 Discuss the key sources of risk that might affect potential investment vehicles.

LG 6 Understand the risk of a single asset, risk assessment, and the steps that combine return and risk.

Apple Computer has sold over 42 million iPods. Since October 2004, the iPod has dominated digital music player sales in the United States, with over 90% of the market for hard-drive–based players and 70% of the market for all types of players. Several generations of iPods have fueled a dramatic rise in Apple's stock price. Shares soared 122% in 2005, far exceeding the 4.9% return for the broader Standard & Poor's 500 stock index. News that Apple's revenue jumped 65%, and that the company's net income during its fiscal quarter ended December 31, 2005, jumped 91% from the year earlier, was music to investors' ears.

This promising picture might increase your desire to buy the stock. But before you place that buy order, you should investigate the risks associated with the stock. Apple Computer itself disclosed in its most recent K-10 annual report a host of potential risks facing the company, ranging from current economic and political uncertainty to substantial inventory risks and dependency upon manufacturing and logistics services provided by third parties, many of whom are located outside the United States. Apple has higher research and development and higher selling, general, and administrative costs, as a percentage of revenue, than many of its competitors. Apple also faces risk in its transition from PowerPC microprocessors used by the Macintosh computers to those built by Intel. Any of these risks could have a material adverse effect on the company's operating results and financial position.

In this chapter we will discuss the concept of return and risk. You will learn how to calculate an investment's return and also become aware of the many types of risk faced by a public company. Many of the risks that Apple faces are the same types of risks faced by any other public company. The key factor in making an investment decision is to weigh those risks in relation to the potential return of the stock.

Sources: Matt Krantz, "Take a Bite of Apple?," *USA Today*, downloaded from www.usatoday.com/money/perfi/columnist/krants/2006-01-31-apple_x.htm (accessed July 2006); Apple Computer K-10 annual report, http://ccbn.tenkwizard.com (accessed July 2006).

The Concept of Return

LG 1   LG 2

return
the level of profit from an investment—that is, the reward for investing.

Investors are motivated to invest in a given vehicle by its expected return. The **return** is the level of profit from an investment—that is, the reward for investing. Suppose you have $1,000 in an insured savings account paying 5% annual interest, and a business associate asks you to lend her that much money. If you lend her the money for one year, at the end of which she pays you back, your return will depend on the amount of interest you charge. If you make an interest-free loan, your return will be zero. If you charge 5% interest, your return will be $50 (0.05 × $1,000). Because you are already earning a safe 5% on the $1,000, it seems clear that to equal that return you should charge your associate a minimum of 5% interest.

Some investment vehicles guarantee a return; others do not. The return earned on $1,000 deposited in an insured savings account at a large bank can be viewed as certain. The return earned on a $1,000 loan to your business associate might be less certain. The size and the certainty of the expected return are important factors in choosing a suitable investment.

▮ Components of Return

The return on an investment may come from more than one source. The most common source is periodic payments, such as dividends or interest. The other source of return is appreciation in value, the gain from selling an investment vehicle for more than its original purchase price. We call these two sources of return *current income* and *capital gains* (or *capital losses*), respectively.

Current Income   Current income may take the form of dividends from stocks, interest received on bonds, or dividends received from mutual funds. To be considered income, it must be in the form of cash or be readily convertible into cash. For our purposes, **current income** is usually cash or near-cash that is periodically received as a result of owning an investment.

Using the data in Table 4.1 (on page 160), we can calculate the current income from investments A and B, both purchased for $1,000, over a one-year period of ownership. Investment A would provide current income of $80, investment B $120. Solely on the basis of the current income received over the 1-year period, investment B seems preferable.

Capital Gains (or Losses)   The second dimension of return is concerned with the change in the market value of an investment. As noted in Chapter 1, the amount by which the proceeds from the sale of an investment exceed its original purchase price is a *capital gain*. If an investment is sold for less than its original purchase price, a *capital loss* results.

We can calculate the capital gain or loss of the investments as shown in Table 4.1. For investment A, a capital gain of $100 ($1,100 sale price − $1,000 purchase price) is realized over the one-year period. For investment B, a $40 capital loss results ($960 sale price − $1,000 purchase price).

Combining the capital gain (or loss) with the current income (calculated in the preceding section) gives the **total return**. Table 4.2 (on page 160) shows the total return for investments A and B over the one-year ownership period. In terms of the total return earned on the $1,000 investment over the one-year period, investment A is superior to investment B.

current income
usually cash or near-cash that is periodically received as a result of owning an investment.

total return
the sum of the current income and the capital gain (or loss) earned on an investment over a specified period of time.

TABLE 4.1   Profiles of Two Investments

	Investment	
	A	B
Purchase price (beginning of year)	$1,000	$1,000
Cash received		
1st quarter	$ 10	$ 0
2nd quarter	20	0
3rd quarter	20	0
4th quarter	30	120
Total current income (for year)	$ 80	$ 120
Sale price (end of year)	$1,100	$ 960

TABLE 4.2   Total Returns of Two Investments

	Investment	
Return	A	B
Current income	$ 80	$120
Capital gain (loss)	100	(40)
Total return	$180	$ 80

It is generally preferable to use *percentage returns* rather than dollar returns. Percentages allow direct comparison of different sizes and types of investments. Investment A earned an 18% return ($180 ÷ $1,000); B yielded only an 8% return ($80 ÷ $1,000). At this point investment A appears preferable, but as we'll see, differences in risk might cause some investors to prefer B.

▮ Why Return Is Important

Return is a key variable in the investment decision: It allows us to compare the actual or expected gains of various investments with the levels of return we need. For example, you would be satisfied with an investment that earns 12% if you need it to earn only 10%. You would not be satisfied with a 10% return if you need a 14% return. Return can be measured historically, or it can be used to formulate future expectations.

Historical Performance   Most people recognize that future performance is not guaranteed by past performance, but past data often provide a meaningful basis for future expectations. A common practice in the investment world is to look closely at the historical performance of a given vehicle when formulating expectations about its future.

Interest rates and other measures of financial return are most often cited on an annual basis. Evaluation of past investment returns is typically done on the same basis. Consider the data for a hypothetical investment presented in Table 4.3. Two aspects of these data are important. First, we can determine the *average level of return* generated by this investment over the past 10 years. Second, we can analyze the *trend* in this return. As a percentage, the average

TABLE 4.3   Historical Investment Data for a Hypothetical Investment

		Market Value (Price)			Total Return	
Year	(1) Income	(2) Beginning of Year	(3) End of Year	(4) (3) − (2) Capital Gain	(5) (1) + (4) ($)	(6) (5) ÷ (2) (%)*
1999	$4.00	$100	$ 95	−$ 5.00	−$ 1.00	− 1.00%
2000	3.00	95	99	4.00	7.00	7.37
2001	4.00	99	105	6.00	10.00	10.10
2002	5.00	105	115	10.00	15.00	14.29
2003	5.00	115	125	10.00	15.00	13.04
2004	3.00	125	120	− 5.00	− 2.00	− 1.60
2005	3.00	120	122	2.00	5.00	4.17
2006	4.00	122	130	8.00	12.00	9.84
2007	5.00	130	140	10.00	15.00	11.54
2008	5.00	140	155	15.00	20.00	14.29
Average	$4.10			$ 5.50	$ 9.60	8.20%

*Percent return on beginning-of-year market value of investment.

total return (column 6) over the past 10 years was 8.20%. Looking at the yearly returns, we can see that after the negative return in 1999, four years of positive and generally increasing returns occurred before the negative return was repeated in 2004. From 2005 through 2008, positive and increasing returns were again realized.

Expected Return   In the final analysis, of course, it's the future that matters when we make investment decisions. Therefore, **expected return** is a vital measure of performance. It's what you think the investment will earn in the future that determines what you should be willing to pay for it.

To demonstrate, let's return to the data in Table 4.3. Looking at the historical return figures in the table, an investor would note the increasing trend in returns from 2005 through 2008. But to project future returns, we need insights into the investment's prospects. If the trend in returns seems likely to continue, an expected return in the range of 12% to 15% for 2009 or 2010 would seem reasonable. On the other hand, if future prospects seem poor, or if the investment is subject to cycles, an expected return of 8% to 9% may be a more reasonable estimate. Over the past ten years, the investment's returns have cycled from a poor year (1999 and 2004) to four years of increasing returns (2000–2003 and 2005–2008). We might therefore expect low returns in 2009 to be followed by increasing returns in the 2010–2013 period.

expected return
the return an investor thinks an investment will earn in the future.

▌Level of Return

The level of return achieved or expected from an investment will depend on a variety of factors. The key factors are internal characteristics and external forces.

Internal Characteristics   Certain characteristics of an investment affect its level of return. Examples include the type of investment vehicle, the quality of management, its financing, and the issuer's customer base. For example, the common stock of a large, well-managed, completely equity-financed plastics manufacturer whose major customer is Nokia would be expected to provide a level of return different from that of a small, poorly managed, largely debt-financed clothing manufacturer whose customers are small specialty stores. As we will see in later chapters, assessing internal factors and their impact on return is one important step in analyzing potential investments.

External Forces External forces such as Federal Reserve actions, shortages, war, price controls, and political events may also affect the level of return. None of these are under the control of the issuer of the investment vehicle. Investment vehicles are affected differently by these forces. The expected return from one vehicle may increase, while that of another decreases. Likewise, the economies of various countries respond to external forces in different ways.

Another external force is the *general level of price changes,* either up—**inflation**—or down—**deflation.** Inflation tends to have a positive impact on investment vehicles such as real estate, and a negative impact on vehicles such as stocks and fixed-income securities. Rising interest rates, which normally accompany increasing rates of inflation, can significantly affect returns. The actions, if any, the Federal Reserve takes to control inflation can also have significant effects on investments. Furthermore, the return on each type of investment vehicle exhibits its own unique response to inflation.

inflation
a period of generally rising prices.

deflation
a period of generally declining prices.

▮ Historical Returns

Investment returns vary both over time and between different types of investments. By averaging historical returns over a long period of time, it is possible to eliminate the impact of various types of risk. This enables the investor to focus on the differences in return that are attributable primarily to the types of investment. Table 4.4 shows the arithmetic average annual rates of return for a number of popular security investments (and inflation) over the 80-year period January 1, 1926, through December 31, 2005. Each rate represents the arithmetic average annual rate of return an investor would have realized had he or she purchased the investment on January 1, 1926, and sold it on December 31, 2005. You can see that significant differences exist between the average annual rates of return realized on various types of stocks, bonds, and bills. Later in this chapter, we will see how we can link these differences in return to differences in the risk of each of these investments.

TABLE 4.4   **Historical Returns for Popular Security Investments (1926–2005)**

Investment	Arithmetic Average Annual Return
Large-company stocks	12.3%
Small-company stocks	17.4
Long-term corporate bonds	6.2
Long-term government bonds	5.8
U.S. Treasury bills	3.8
Inflation	3.1%

Source: Stocks, Bonds, Bills, and Inflation, 2006 Yearbook (Chicago: Ibbotson Associates, Inc., 2006), p. 31.

We now turn our attention to the role that time value of money concepts play in determining investment returns.

▍Time Value of Money and Returns

As a general rule, *the sooner you receive a return on a given investment, the better.* For example, two investments each requiring a $1,000 outlay and each expected to return $100 interest over a two-year holding period are *not necessarily* equally desirable. If the first investment returns $100 at the end of the first year, and the second investment returns the $100 at the end of the second year, the first investment is preferable (assuming that the base value of each remains at $1,000). Investment 1 is preferable because the $100 it earns could be *reinvested to earn more interest* while the $100 in interest from investment 2 is still accruing at the end of the first year. You should not fail to consider time value concepts when making investment decisions.

We now review the key computational aids available for streamlining time value of money calculations, and then we demonstrate the application of time value of money techniques to determine an acceptable investment.

Computational Aids for Use in Time Value Calculations The often time-consuming calculations involved in applying time value of money techniques can be simplified with a number of computational aids. Throughout this book we will demonstrate the use of financial tables, hand-held financial calculators, and electronic spreadsheets. *Financial tables* contain various interest factors that can be indexed by the interest rate (in columns) and the number of periods (in rows). A full set of the four basic financial tables is included in Appendix A at the end of the book. *Financial calculators* include numerous preprogrammed financial routines. To demonstrate the calculator keystrokes for various financial computations, we show a keypad in the margin of the book, with the keys as defined at the left. *Electronic spreadsheet* use has become a prime skill for today's investors. Like financial calculators, electronic spreadsheets have built-in routines that simplify time value calculations. For most time value calculations in the book, we show spreadsheet solutions that identify cell entries.

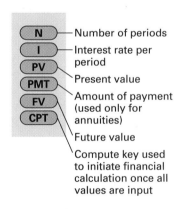

N —— Number of periods
I —— Interest rate per period
PV —— Present value
PMT —— Amount of payment (used only for annuities)
FV —— Future value
CPT —— Compute key used to initiate financial calculation once all values are input

satisfactory investment
an investment whose present value of benefits (discounted at the appropriate rate) *equals* or *exceeds* the present value of its costs.

Determining a Satisfactory Investment Time value of money techniques can be used to determine an acceptable investment. Ignoring risk at this point, a **satisfactory investment** would be one for which the present value of benefits (discounted at the appropriate rate) *equals* or *exceeds* the present value of its costs. Because the cost of the investment would be incurred initially (at time zero), the cost and its present value are viewed as one and the same. The three possible benefit–cost relationships and their interpretations follow:

1. If the present value of the benefits *just equals the cost,* you would earn a rate of return equal to the discount rate.
2. If the present value of benefits *exceeds the cost,* you would earn a rate of return greater than the discount rate.
3. If the present value of benefits is *less than the cost,* you would earn a rate of return less than the discount rate.

EXCEL with SPREADSHEETS

TABLE 4.5   Present Value Applied to an Investment

End of Year	(1) Return	(2) 8% Present-Value Interest Factor*	(3) (1) × (2) Present Value
2008	$ 90	.926	$ 83.34
2009	100	.857	85.70
2010	110	.794	87.34
2011	120	.735	88.20
2012	100	.681	68.10
2013	100	.630	63.00
2014	1,200	.583	699.60
		Present value of returns	$1,175.28

*Column 2 values are from Appendix A, Table A.3, for an 8% discount rate and 1 through 7 periods (years).

You would prefer only those investments for which the present value of benefits equals or exceeds its cost—situations 1 and 2. In these cases, the rate of return would be equal to or greater than the discount rate.

The information in Table 4.5 demonstrates the application of present value to investment decision making using a financial table. (*Note:* A financial calculator or an Excel spreadsheet could have been used to find the present value of this mixed-stream investment.) Assuming an 8% discount rate, we can see that the present value (at the beginning of 2008) of the returns (benefits) to be received over the assumed seven-year period (year-end 2008 through year-end 2014) is $1,175.28. If the cost of the investment (beginning of 2008) were any amount less than or equal to the $1,175.28 present value, it would be acceptable. At that cost, a rate of return equal to at least 8% would be earned. At a cost above the $1,175.28 present value, the investment would not be acceptable because the rate of return would be less than 8%. Clearly, in that case it would be preferable to find an alternative investment with a present value of benefits that equals or exceeds its cost.

For your convenience, **Appendix 4A provides a complete review of the key time value of money techniques.** Be sure to review it before reading ahead, to make sure you have adequate understanding of this important financial concept.

CONCEPTS IN REVIEW

Answers available at: www.myfinancelab.com

4.1   Explain what is meant by the *return* on an investment. Differentiate between the two components of return—current income and capital gains (or losses).

4.2   What role do historical performance data play in estimating the expected return from a given investment? Discuss the key factors affecting investment returns—internal characteristics and external forces.

4.3   What is a *satisfactory investment?* When the present value of benefits exceeds the cost of an investment, what is true of the rate of return earned by the investor relative to the discount rate?

Measuring Return

LG 3   LG 4

Thus far, we have discussed the concept of return in terms of its two components (current income and capital gains) and the key factors that affect the level of return (internal characteristics and external forces). These discussions intentionally oversimplified the computations involved in determining the historical or expected return. To compare returns from different investment vehicles, we need to incorporate time value of money concepts that explicitly consider differences in the timing of investment income and capital gains. We must also be able to place a current value on future benefits. Here we will look at several measures that enable us to compare alternative investment vehicles. First, we must define and consider the relationships among various rates of return.

▐ Real, Risk-Free, and Required Returns

Rational investors will choose investments that fully compensate them for the risk involved. The greater the risk, the greater the return required by investors. The rate of return that fully compensates for an investment's risk is called the **required return**.

required return
the rate of return an investor must earn on an investment to be fully compensated for its risk.

To better understand required returns, it is helpful to consider their makeup. The required return on any investment j consists of three basic components: the real rate of return, an expected inflation premium, and a risk premium, as noted in Equation 4.1.

Equation 4.1 ➤

$$\text{Required return on investment } j = \text{Real rate of return} + \text{Expected inflation premium} + \text{Risk premium for investment } j$$

Equation 4.1a ➤

$$r_j = r^* + IP + RP_j$$

real rate of return
the rate of return that could be earned in a perfect world where all outcomes are known and certain—where there is no risk.

The **real rate of return** is the rate of return that could be earned in a perfect world where all outcomes were known and certain—where there is no risk. In such a world, the real rate of return would create an equilibrium between the supply of savings and the demand for funds. The real rate of return changes with changing economic conditions, tastes, and preferences. Historically, it has been relatively stable and in the range of 0.5% to 2%. For convenience, we'll assume a real rate of return of 2%.

expected inflation premium
the average rate of inflation expected in the future.

The **expected inflation premium** represents the average rate of inflation expected in the future. Because expected inflation affects all returns, we add the expected inflation premium to the real rate of return to get the **risk-free rate**. This is the rate of return that can be earned on a risk-free investment, most commonly a three-month U.S. Treasury bill. The formula for this rate is shown in Equation 4.2.

risk-free rate
the rate of return that can be earned on a risk-free investment; the sum of the real rate of return and the expected inflation premium.

Equation 4.2 ➤

$$\text{Risk-free rate} = \text{Real rate of return} + \text{Expected inflation premium}$$

Equation 4.2a ➤

$$R_F = r^* + IP$$

To demonstrate, a real rate of return of 2% and an expected inflation premium of 4% would result in a risk-free rate of return of 6%.

risk premium
a return premium that reflects the issue and issuer characteristics associated with a given investment vehicle.

The required return can be found by adding to the risk-free rate a **risk premium**, which varies depending on specific issue and issuer characteristics. *Issue characteristics* are the type of vehicle (stock, bond, etc.), its maturity (two years, five years, infinity, etc.), and its features (voting/nonvoting, callable/noncallable, etc.). *Issuer characteristics* are industry and company factors such as the line of business and financial condition of the issuer. Together, the issue and issuer factors cause investors to require a risk premium above the risk-free rate.

Substituting the risk-free rate, R_F, from Equation 4.2a, into Equation 4.1a for the first two terms to the right of the equals signs ($r^* + IP$), we get Equation 4.3.

Equation 4.3 ➤

$$\text{Required return on investment } j = \text{Risk-free rate} + \text{Risk premium for investment } j$$

Equation 4.3a ➤

$$r_j = R_F + RP_j$$

For example, if the required return on Nike common stock is 11% when the risk-free rate is 6%, investors require a 5% risk premium (11% − 6%) as compensation for the risk associated with common stock (the issue) and Nike (the issuer). Later, in Chapter 5, we will explore further the relationship between the risk premium and required returns.

Next, we consider the specifics of return measurement. We look at two return measures—one used primarily for short-term investments and the other for longer-term vehicles.

▎ Holding Period Return

The return to a *saver* is the amount of interest earned on a given deposit. Of course, the amount "invested" in a savings account is not subject to change in value, as is the amount invested in stocks, bonds, and mutual funds. Because we are concerned with a broad range of investment vehicles, we need a measure of return that captures both periodic benefits and changes in value. One such measure is *holding period return.*

holding period
the period of time over which one wishes to measure the return on an investment vehicle.

The **holding period** is the period of time over which one wishes to measure the return on an investment vehicle. When comparing returns, be sure to use holding periods of the same length. For example, comparing the return on a stock over the six-month period ended December 31, 2007, with the return on a bond over the one-year period ended June 30, 2007, could result in a poor investment decision. To avoid this problem, be sure you define the holding period. It is often best to annualize the holding period and use that as a standard. And when comparing the returns from alternative investment vehicles, you should use similar periods in time.

realized return
current income actually received by an investor during a given period.

Understanding Return Components   Earlier in this chapter we identified the two components of investment return: current income and capital gains (or losses). The portion of current income received by the investor during the period is a **realized return**. Most but not all current income is realized. (Accrued interest on taxable zero-coupon bonds is treated as current income for tax purposes but is not a realized return until the bond is sold or matures.) Capital gains returns, on the other hand, are realized only when the investment vehicle is actually sold at the end of the holding period. Until the vehicle is sold, the capital gain is merely a **paper return**.

paper return
a return that has been achieved but not yet realized by an investor during a given period.

For example, the capital gain return on an investment that increases in market value from $50 to $70 during a year is $20. For that capital gain to be realized, you would have to have sold the investment for $70 at the end of that year. An investor who purchased the same investment but plans to hold it for another three years would also have experienced the $20 capital gain return during the year specified, but he or she *would not have realized the gain in terms of cash flow.* However, *even if the capital gains return is not realized during the period over which the total return is measured, it must be included in the return calculation.*

A second point to recognize about returns is that both the current income and the capital gains component can have a negative value. Occasionally, an investment may have negative current income. That is, you may be required to pay out cash to meet certain obligations. (This situation is most likely to occur in various types of property investments.) A capital loss can occur on *any* investment vehicle: Stocks, bonds, mutual funds, options, futures, real estate, and gold can all decline in market value over a given holding period.

holding period return (HPR)
the total return earned from holding an investment for a specified *holding period* (*usually one year or less*).

Computing the Holding Period Return (HPR) The **holding period return (HPR)** is the total return earned from holding an investment for a specified period of time (the holding period). *The HPR is customarily used with holding periods of one year or less.* (We'll explain why later.) It represents the sum of current income and capital gains (or losses) achieved over the holding period, divided by the beginning investment value (market price). The equation for HPR is

Equation 4.4 ➤ $$\text{Holding period return} = \frac{\begin{array}{c}\text{Current income} \\ \text{during period}\end{array} + \begin{array}{c}\text{Capital gain (or loss)} \\ \text{during period}\end{array}}{\text{Beginning investment value}}$$

Equation 4.4a ➤ $$\text{HPR} = \frac{C + CG}{V_0}$$

where

Equation 4.5 ➤ $$\begin{array}{c}\text{Capital gain (or loss)} \\ \text{during period}\end{array} = \begin{array}{c}\text{Ending} \\ \text{investment value}\end{array} - \begin{array}{c}\text{Beginning} \\ \text{investment value}\end{array}$$

Equation 4.5a ➤ $$CG = V_n - V_0$$

The HPR equation provides a convenient method for either measuring the total return realized or estimating the total return expected. For example, Table 4.6 (on page 168) summarizes the key financial variables for four investment vehicles over the past year. The total current income and capital

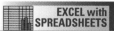

TABLE 4.6   Key Financial Variables for Four Investment Vehicles

	Investment Vehicle			
	Savings Account	Common Stock	Bond	Real Estate
Cash received				
1st quarter	$15	$10	$ 0	$0
2nd quarter	15	10	70	0
3rd quarter	15	10	0	0
4th quarter	15	15	70	0
(1) Total current income	$60	$45	$140	$0
Investment value				
End-of-year	$1,000	$2,200	$ 970	$3,300
(2) Beginning-of-year	1,000	2,000	1,000	3,000
(3) Capital gain (loss)	$ 0	$ 200	($ 30)	$ 300
(4) Total return [(1) + (3)]	$ 60	$ 245	$ 110	$ 300
(5) Holding period return [(4) ÷ (2)]	6.00%	12.25%	11.00%	10.00%

gain or loss during the holding period are given in the lines labeled (1) and (3), respectively. The total return over the year is calculated, as shown in line (4), by adding these two sources of return. Dividing the total return value [line (4)] by the beginning-of-year investment value [line (2)], we find the holding period return, given in line (5). Over the one-year holding period the common stock had the highest HPR (12.25%). The savings account had the lowest (6%).

As these calculations show, to find the HPR we need the beginning- and end-of-period investment values, along with the value of current income received during the period. Note that if the current income and capital gain (or loss) values in lines (1) and (3) of Table 4.6 had been drawn from a six-month rather than a one-year period, the HPR values calculated in line 5 would have been *the same*.

Holding period return can be negative or positive. HPRs can be calculated with Equation 4.4 using either historical data (as in the preceding example) or forecast data.

Using the HPR in Investment Decisions The holding period return is easy to use in making investment decisions. Because it considers both current income and capital gains relative to the beginning investment value, it tends to overcome any problems that might be associated with comparing investments of different size.

If we look only at the total returns calculated for each of the four investments in Table 4.6 [line (4)], the real estate investment appears best, because it has the highest total return. However, the real estate investment would require the largest dollar outlay ($3,000). The holding period return offers a *relative comparison,* by dividing the total return by the amount of the investment. Comparing HPRs [line (5)], we find the investment alternative with the *highest return per invested dollar* to be the common stock's HPR of 12.25%. Because the return per invested dollar reflects the efficiency of the investment, the HPR provides a logical method for evaluating and comparing investment returns, particularly for holding periods of one year or less.

▮ Yield: The Internal Rate of Return

An alternative way to define a satisfactory investment is in terms of the compound annual rate of return it earns. Why do we need an alternative to the HPR? Because *HPR fails to consider the time value of money.* Although the holding period return is useful with investments held for one year or less, it is generally inappropriate for longer holding periods. Sophisticated investors typically do not use HPR when the time period is greater than one year. Instead, they use a present-value-based measure, called **yield** (or **internal rate of return**), to determine the compound annual rate of return earned on investments held for longer than one year. Yield can also be defined as the discount rate that produces a present value of benefits just equal to its cost.

yield (internal rate of return) the compound annual rate of return earned by a long-term investment; the discount rate that produces a present value of the investment's benefits that just equals its cost.

Once you know the yield you can decide whether an investment is acceptable. If the yield on an investment *is equal to or greater than the required return,* then the investment is acceptable. An investment with a yield *below the required return* is unacceptable.

The yield on an investment providing a *single* future cash flow is relatively easy to calculate. The yield on an investment providing a *stream* of future cash flows generally involves more time-consuming calculations. Many hand-held financial calculators and Excel spreadsheets are available for simplifying these calculations.

Yield for a Single Cash Flow Some investments, such as U.S. savings bonds, stocks paying no dividends, zero-coupon bonds, and futures contracts, are purchased by paying a fixed amount up front. The investor expects them to provide *no periodic income,* but to provide a single—and, the investor hopes, a large—future cash flow at maturity or when the investment is sold. The yield on investments expected to provide a single future cash flow can be estimated using financial tables, a financial calculator, or an Excel spreadsheet.

TABLE USE Assume you wish to find the yield on an investment costing $1,000 today that you expect will be worth $1,400 at the end of a five-year holding period. We can find the yield on this investment by solving for the discount rate that causes the present value of the $1,400 to be received five years from now to equal the initial investment of $1,000.

The first step involves dividing the present value ($1,000) by the future value ($1,400), which results in a value of 0.714. The second step is to find in the table of present-value interest factors the five-year factor that is closest to 0.714. Referring to the present-value table (Appendix A, Table A.3), we find that for five years the factor closest to 0.714 is 0.713, which occurs at a 7% discount rate. Therefore, the yield on this investment is about 7%. If you require a 6% return, this investment is acceptable (7% expected return ≥ 6% required return).

Input	Function
1000	PV
-1400	FV
5	N
	CPT
	I
Solution	
6.96	

CALCULATOR USE Using a financial calculator to find the yield for the investment described above, we can treat the earliest value as a present value, **PV**, and the latest value as a future value, **FV**. (*Note:* Most calculators require you to key in *either* the **PV** or the **FV** value as a negative number to calculate an unknown yield.) Using the inputs shown at the left, we find the yield to be 6.96%. This is consistent with, but more precise than, the value found using Appendix A, Table A.3.

Spreadsheet Use The yield for the single cash flow also can be calculated as shown on the following Excel spreadsheet.

	A	B
1	**YIELD FOR A SINGLE CASH FLOW**	
2	Point in Time	Cash Flow
3	Future	$1,400
4	Present	$1,000
5	Number of Years	5
6	Yield	6.96%

Entry in Cell B6 is
= Rate((B5),0,–B4,B3,0),
The minus sign appears before B4
because the present investment
is treated as a cash outflow.

Yield for a Stream of Income Investment vehicles such as income-oriented stock and bonds typically provide the investor with a *stream of income*. The yield (or internal rate of return) for a stream of income (returns) is generally more difficult to estimate. The most accurate approach is based on searching for the discount rate that produces a present value of income just equal to the cost of the investment. We can do that using financial tables, a financial calculator, or an Excel spreadsheet.

Table Use If we use the investment in Table 4.5 and assume that its cost is $1,100, we find that the yield must be greater than 8%. At an 8% discount rate, the present value of income (calculated in column 3 of Table 4.5) is greater than the cost ($1,175.28 versus $1,100). The present values at 9% and 10% discount rates are calculated in Table 4.7. If we look at the present values of income calculated at the 9% and 10% rates, we see that the yield on the investment must be somewhere between 9% and 10%. At 9% the present value ($1,117.61) is too high. At 10% the present value ($1,063.08) is too

EXCEL with SPREADSHEETS

TABLE 4.7 Yield Calculation for an $1,100 Investment

Year	(1) Income	(2) 9% Present-Value Interest Factor	(3) (1) × (2) Present Value at 9%	(4) 10% Present-Value Interest Factor	(5) (1) × (4) Present Value at 10%
2008	$ 90	.917	$ 82.53	.909	$ 81.81
2009	100	.842	84.20	.826	82.60
2010	110	.772	84.92	.751	82.61
2011	120	.708	84.96	.683	81.96
2012	100	.650	65.00	.621	62.10
2013	100	.596	59.60	.564	56.40
2014	1,200	.547	656.40	.513	615.60
	Present value of income		$1,117.61		$1,063.08

low. The discount rate that causes the present value of income to be closer to the $1,100 cost is 9%, because it is only $17.61 away from $1,100. Thus, if you require an 8% return, the investment is clearly acceptable.

CALCULATOR USE We can use a financial calculator to find the yield (or *internal rate of return*) on an investment that will produce a stream of income. This procedure typically involves three steps: (1) Punch in the cost of the investment (typically referred to as the *cash outflow* at time zero). (2) Punch in all of the income expected each period (typically referred to as the *cash inflow* in year *x*). (3) Calculate the yield (typically referred to as the *internal rate of return, IRR*).

Because calculators provide solutions that are more precise than those based on rounded table factors, the yield of 9.32% found for the investment in Table 4.5 using a financial calculator (keystrokes not shown) is close to, but not equal to, the 9% value estimated above using Table 4.7.

SPREADSHEET USE We can also calculate the yield for a stream of income as shown on the following Excel spreadsheet.

	A	B
1	YIELD FOR A STREAM OF INCOME	
2	Year	Cash Flow
3	2014	$1,200
4	2013	$100
5	2012	$100
6	2011	$120
7	2010	$110
8	2009	$100
9	2008	$90
10	Yield	9.32%

Entry in Cell B10 is
=RATE((A3–A9),0,B9,–B3,0).
The expression A3–A9 in the entry
calculates the number of years of growth.
The minus sign appears before B3 because
the investment in 2014
is treated as a cash outflow.

Interest on Interest: The Critical Assumption The critical assumption underlying the use of yield as a return measure is an ability to earn a return equal to the yield on *all income* received during the holding period. This concept can best be illustrated with a simple example. Suppose you buy a $1,000 U.S. Treasury bond that pays 8% annual interest ($80) over its 20-year maturity. Each year you receive $80, and at maturity the $1,000 in principal is repaid. There is no loss of capital, no default; all payments are made right on time. But in order to earn 8% on this investment, you must be able to reinvest the $80 annual interest receipts.

Figure 4.1 (see page 172) shows the elements of return on this investment to demonstrate the point. If you don't *reinvest* the interest income of $80 per year, you'll end up on the 5% line. You'll have $2,600—the $1,000 principal plus $1,600 interest income ($80/year × 20 years)—at the end of 20 years.

FIGURE 4.1

Earning Interest on Interest

If you invested in a $1,000, 20-year bond with an 8% coupon, you would have only $2,600 at the end of 20 years if you did not reinvest the $80 annual interest receipts—only about a 5% rate of return.

If you reinvested the interest at the 8% interest rate, you would have $4,661 at the end of 20 years—an 8% rate of return. To achieve the calculated yield of 8%, you must therefore be able to earn interest on interest at that rate.

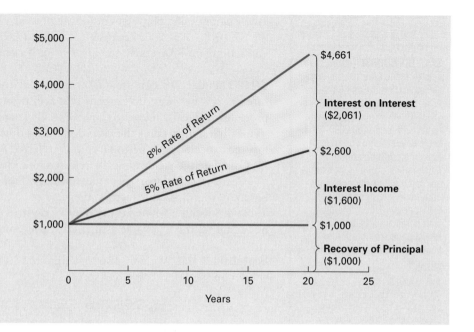

(The yield on a single cash flow of $1,000 today that will be worth $2,600 in 20 years is about 5%.) To move to the 8% line, you have to earn 8% on the annual interest receipts. If you do, at the end of 20 years you'll have $4,661— the $1,000 principal plus the $3,661 future value of the 20-year $80 annuity of interest receipts invested at 8% [$80/year × 45.762 (the 8%, 20-year factor from Appendix A, Table A.2)]. (The yield on a single cash flow of $1,000 today that will be worth $4,661 in 20 years is 8%.) The future value of the investment would be $2,061 greater ($4,661 − $2,600) with interest on interest than without reinvestment of the interest receipts. Even though we used a bond in this illustration, the same principle applies to any other type of investment vehicle.

It should be clear to you that if you start out with an 8% investment, *you have to earn that same rate of return when reinvesting your income.* The rate of return you start with is the required, or minimum, **reinvestment rate**. This is the rate of return earned on interest or other income received over the relevant investment horizon. By putting your current income to work at this rate, you'll earn the rate of return you set out to. If you fail to do so, your return will decline accordingly.

The earning of interest on interest is what the market refers to as a **fully compounded rate of return**. It's an important concept: You can't start reaping the full potential from your investments until you start earning a fully compounded rate of return on them.

Interest on interest is a particularly important element of return for investment programs that involve a lot of current income. You have to reinvest current income. (With capital gains, the investment vehicle itself is automatically doing the reinvesting.) It follows, therefore, that for investment programs that lean toward income-oriented securities, the continued reinvestment of income plays an important role in investment success.

reinvestment rate
the rate of return earned on interest or other income received from an investment over its investment horizon.

fully compounded rate of return
the rate of return that includes interest earned on interest.

TABLE 4.8 Dividends Per Share

Year	Year Number	Dividends per Share
1999	0	$2.45
2000	1	2.60
2001	2	2.80
2002	3	3.00
2003	4	3.20
2004	5	3.15
2005	6	3.20
2006	7	3.20
2007	8	3.40
2008	9	3.50

▌ Finding Growth Rates

rate of growth
the compound annual rate of change in the value of a stream of income.

In addition to finding compound annual rates of return, we frequently need to find the **rate of growth**. This is the compound annual *rate of change* in the value of a stream of income, particularly dividends or earnings. Here we use an example to demonstrate a simple technique for estimating growth rates using a financial table, a financial calculator, or an Excel spreadsheet.

TABLE USE Imagine that you wish to find the rate of growth for the dividends given in Table 4.8. The year numbers in the table show that 1999 is viewed as the base year (year 0); the subsequent years, 2000–2008, are considered years 1 through 9, respectively. Although ten years of data are presented in Table 4.8, they represent only nine years of growth, because the value for the earliest year must be viewed as the initial value at time zero.

To find the growth rate, we first divide the dividend for the earliest year (1999) by the dividend for the latest year (2008). The resulting quotient is 0.700 ($2.45 ÷ $3.50). It represents the value of the present-value interest factor for nine years. To estimate the compound annual dividend growth rate, we find the discount rate in Appendix A, Table A.3 associated with the factor closest to 0.700 for nine years. Looking across year 9 in Table A.3 shows that the factor for 4% is 0.703—very close to the 0.700 value. Therefore, the growth rate of the dividends in Table 4.8 is approximately 4%.

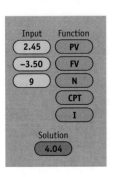

Input	Function
2.45	PV
−3.50	FV
9	N
	CPT
	I
Solution	
4.04	

CALCULATOR USE Using a financial calculator to find the growth rate for the dividend stream shown in Table 4.8, we treat the earliest (1999) value as a present value, **PV**, and the latest (2008) value as a future value, **FV**. (*Note:* Most calculators require you to key in *either* the **PV** or the **FV** value as a negative number to calculate an unknown growth rate.) As noted above, although ten years of dividends are shown in Table 4.8, there are only nine years of growth (**N** = 9) because the earliest year (1999) must be defined as the base year (year 0). Using the inputs shown at the left, we calculate the growth rate to be 4.04%. This rate is consistent with, but more precise than, the value found using the financial tables.

SPREADSHEET USE The growth rate for a dividend stream can also be calculated as shown on the Excel spreadsheet on page 174.

	A	B
1	**GROWTH RATE FOR A DIVIDEND STREAM**	
2	Year	Dividend/share
3	2008	$3.50
4	2007	$3.40
5	2006	$3.20
6	2005	$3.20
7	2004	$3.15
8	2003	$3.20
9	2002	$3.00
10	2001	$2.80
11	2000	$2.60
12	1999	$2.45
13	Annual growth rate	4.04%

Entry in Cell B13 is
=RATE((A3–A12),0,–B12,B3,0).
The expression A3–A12 in the entry
calculates the number of years of growth.
The minus sign appears before B12 because
the investment in 1999
is treated as a cash outflow.

In Chapter 8 we explore in greater detail the use of growth rates, which are often an important input to the common stock valuation process.

CONCEPTS IN REVIEW

Answers available at: www.myfinancelab.com

4.4 Define the following terms and explain how they are used to find the risk-free rate of return and the required rate of return for a given investment.
  a. *Real rate of return.*
  b. *Expected inflation premium.*
  c. *Risk premium* for a given investment.

4.5 What is meant by the *holding period,* and why it is advisable to use holding periods of equal length when comparing alternative investment vehicles? Define the *holding period return (HPR),* and explain for what length holding periods it is typically used.

4.6 Define *yield* (*internal rate of return*). When is it appropriate to use yield rather than the HPR to measure the return on an investment?

4.7 Explain why you must earn 10% on *all* income received from an investment during its holding period in order for its yield actually to equal the 10% value you've calculated.

4.8 Explain how either the present value (of benefits versus cost) or the yield measure can be used to find a *satisfactory investment.* Given the following data, indicate which, if any, of these investments is acceptable. Explain your findings.

	Investment		
	A	B	C
Cost	$200	$160	$500
Required return	7%	10%	9%
Present value of benefits	—	$150	—
Yield	8%	—	8%

Risk: The Other Side of the Coin

LG 5   LG 6

risk
the chance that the actual return from an investment may differ from what is expected.

Thus far, our primary concern in this chapter has been return. However, we cannot consider return without also looking at risk. Expanding a bit on its definition in Chapter 1, **risk** is the chance that the actual return from an investment may differ from what is expected.

The risk associated with a given investment is directly related to its expected return. In general, the broader the range of possible returns, the greater the investment's risk, and vice versa. Put another way, riskier investments should provide higher levels of return. Otherwise, what incentive is there for an investor to risk his or her capital? To get a feel for your own risk-taking orientation, read the *Investing in Action* box on page 176.

In general, investors attempt to minimize risk for a given level of return or to maximize return for a given level of risk. This relationship between risk and return is called the **risk-return tradeoff**. We introduce it here and will discuss it in greater detail in Chapter 5. Here we begin by examining the key sources of risk. We then consider the measurement and assessment of risk: the risk of a single asset, the assessment of risk associated with a potential investment, and the steps by which return and risk can be combined in the decision process.

risk-return tradeoff
the relationship between risk and return, in which investments with more risk should provide higher returns, and vice versa.

▮ Sources of Risk

The risk associated with a given investment vehicle may result from a combination of possible sources. A prudent investor considers how the major sources of risk might affect potential investment vehicles. The combined impact of the presence of any of the sources of risk, discussed below, in a given investment vehicle would be reflected in its *risk premium*. As discussed earlier in the chapter and shown in Equation 4.3, we can find the required return on an investment by adding its risk premium to the risk-free rate. This premium in a broad sense results from the sources of risk, which derive from characteristics of both the issue and the issuer. Of course, as discussed in Chapter 2, *currency exchange risk* is another source of risk that should also be considered when investing internationally.

business risk
the degree of uncertainty associated with an investment's earnings and the investment's ability to pay the returns owed investors.

Business Risk In general, **business risk** is the degree of uncertainty associated with an investment's earnings and the investment's ability to pay the returns (interest, principal, dividends) owed investors. For example, business owners may receive no return if the firm's earnings are not adequate to meet obligations. Debtholders, on the other hand, are likely to receive some (but not necessarily all) of the amount owed them, because of the preferential treatment legally accorded to debt.

Much of the business risk associated with a given investment vehicle is related to its kind of business. For example, the amount of business risk in a public utility common stock differs from the amount in the common stock of a high-fashion clothing manufacturer or an Internet start-up. Generally, investments in similar kinds of firms have similar business risk, although differences in management, costs, and location can cause varying levels of risk.

WEBEXTENSION
See an example where shareholders allegedly bore more risk than top executives, in the *Ethics* box for Chapter 4 on the book's Web site at
www.myfinancelab.com

INVESTING *in Action*

What's Your Risk Tolerance?

During the strong bull market of the 1990s and early 2000s, it seemed that investors couldn't lose. Even when the market took a nosedive, they rushed to buy at lower prices and assumed that their stocks would go up again. The lure of easy money pushed the idea of risk into the background for many investors.

The key to risk taking is to determine your personal level of *risk tolerance*—how comfortable you feel with the volatility of your investments. Understanding your risk tolerance will prevent you from taking on more risk than you can handle and will reduce the likelihood that you will panic and abandon your plan in midstream.

The following quiz can help you evaluate your personal capacity for risk. With this knowledge, you can build a portfolio that will let you sleep better at night.

What Is Your Investment Risk Tolerance?

1. Which best describes your feelings about investing?
   a. Better safe than sorry.
   b. Moderation in all things.
   c. Nothing ventured, nothing gained.

2. Which is the most important to you as an investor?
   a. Steady income
   b. Steady income and growth
   c. Rapid price appreciation

3. You won! Which prize would you select?
   a. $4,000 in cash
   b. A 50% chance to win $10,000
   c. A 20% chance to win $100,000

4. The stocks in your retirement account have dropped 20% since last quarter.

The market experts are optimistic. What would you do?
   a. Transfer out of stocks to avoid losing more.
   b. Stay in stocks and wait for them to come back.
   c. Shift more money into stocks. If they made sense before, they're a bargain now.

5. The stocks in your retirement account have suddenly gone up 20%. You have no more information. What would you do?
   a. Transfer out of stocks and lock in my gains.
   b. Stay in stocks, hoping for more gains.
   c. Transfer more money into stocks. They might go higher.

6. Would you borrow money to take advantage of a good investment opportunity?
   a. Never   b. Maybe   c. Yes

7. How would you characterize yourself as an investor?
   a. Conservative
   b. Moderate risk taker
   c. Aggressive

How to determine your score:

Each (a) answer is worth 1 point. Each (b) is worth 2 points. Each (c) is worth 3 points. Add them up to find your total score.

> 7-11 points: a conservative investor
> 12-16 points: a moderate risk taker
> 17-21 points: an aggressive investor

CRITICAL THINKING QUESTION   Judging by your quiz results, what is your personal tolerance for investment risk?

---

financial risk
the degree of uncertainty of payment resulting from a firm's mix of debt and equity; the larger the proportion of debt financing, the greater this risk.

Financial Risk   The degree of uncertainty of payment resulting from a firm's mix of debt and equity is **financial risk**. The larger the proportion of debt used to finance a firm, the greater its financial risk. Debt financing obligates the firm to make interest payments as well as to repay the debt, thus increasing risk. Inability to meet debt obligations could result in business failure and in losses for bondholders as well as stockholders and owners.

purchasing power risk
the chance that changing price levels (inflation or deflation) will adversely affect investment returns.

Purchasing Power Risk The chance that changing price levels (inflation or deflation) will adversely affect investment returns is **purchasing power risk**. Specifically, this risk is the chance that generally rising prices (inflation) will reduce *purchasing power* (the amount of a given commodity that can be purchased with a dollar). If last year a dollar would buy three candy bars and today it can buy only two because candy bars now cost 50 cents each, the purchasing power of your dollar has decreased. In periods of declining price levels (deflation), the purchasing power of the dollar increases. (More candy!)

In general, investments whose values move with general price levels have low purchasing power risk and are most profitable during periods of rising prices. Those that provide fixed returns have high purchasing power risk, and they are most profitable during periods of low inflation or declining price levels. The returns on stocks of durable-goods manufacturers, for example, tend to move with the general price level, whereas returns from deposit accounts and bonds do not.

interest rate risk
the chance that changes in interest rates will adversely affect a security's value.

Interest Rate Risk Securities are especially affected by interest rate risk. This is particularly true for those securities that offer purchasers a fixed periodic return. **Interest rate risk** is the chance that changes in interest rates will adversely affect a security's value. The interest rate changes themselves result from changes in the general relationship between the supply of and the demand for money.

As interest rates change, the prices of many securities fluctuate. As we will see in greater detail in Chapters 10, 11, and Online Chapter 16, the prices of fixed-income securities (bonds and preferred stock) typically drop when interest rates rise. They thus provide purchasers with the same rate of return that would be available at prevailing rates. The opposite occurs when interest rates fall: The return on a fixed-income security is adjusted downward to a competitive level by an upward adjustment in its market price.

A second, more subtle aspect of interest rate risk is associated with reinvestment of income. As noted earlier, only if you can earn the initial rate of return on income received from an investment can you achieve a *fully compounded rate of return* equal to the initial rate of return. In other words, if a bond pays 8% annual interest, you must be able to earn 8% on the interest received during the bond's holding period in order to earn a fully compounded 8% rate of return over that period. This same aspect of interest rate risk applies to reinvestment of the proceeds received from an investment at its maturity or sale.

A final aspect of interest rate risk is related to investing in short-term securities such as U.S. Treasury bills and certificates of deposit (discussed in Chapter 1). Investors face the risk that when short-term securities mature, they may have to invest those proceeds in lower-yielding, new short-term securities. By initially making a long-term investment, you can lock in a return for a period of years, rather than face the risk of declines in short-term interest rates. Clearly, when interest rates are declining, the returns from investing in short-term securities are adversely affected. (On the other hand, interest rate increases have a positive impact on such a strategy.) The chance that interest rates will decline is therefore the interest rate risk of a strategy of investing in short-term securities.

Most investment vehicles are subject to interest rate risk. Although interest rate movements most directly affect fixed-income securities, they also affect other long-term vehicles such as common stock and mutual funds. *Generally, the higher the interest rate, the lower the value of an investment vehicle, and vice versa.*

liquidity risk
the risk of not being able
to liquidate an investment
conveniently and at a
reasonable price.

Liquidity Risk   The risk of not being able to liquidate an investment conveniently and at a reasonable price is called **liquidity risk**. One can generally sell an investment vehicle merely by significantly cutting its price. However, to be liquid, an investment must be easily sold *at a reasonable price*. For example, a security recently purchased for $1,000 would not be viewed as highly liquid if it could be quickly sold only at a greatly reduced price, such as $500.

The liquidity of a given investment vehicle is an important consideration. In general, investment vehicles traded in *thin markets*, where demand and supply are small, tend to be less liquid than those traded in *broad markets*. Vehicles such as stocks and bonds of major companies listed on the New York Stock Exchange are generally highly liquid; others, such as the stock of a small company in a declining industry, are not.

tax risk
the chance that Congress will
make unfavorable changes in
tax laws, driving down the after-
tax returns and market values
of certain investments.

Tax Risk   The chance that Congress will make unfavorable changes in tax laws is known as **tax risk**. The greater the chance that such changes will drive down the after-tax returns and market values of certain investments, the greater the tax risk. Undesirable changes in tax laws include elimination of tax exemptions, limitation of deductions, and increases in tax rates.

In recent years, Congress has passed numerous changes in tax laws. One of the most significant, the *Tax Reform Act of 1986*, contained provisions that reduced the attractiveness of many investment vehicles, particularly real estate and other tax shelters. More recently, the *Jobs and Growth Tax Relief Reconciliation Act of 2003* reduced tax rates, taxes on dividends, and taxes on capital gains. Clearly, these changes benefit investors and do not represent the unfavorable consequences of tax risk.

Though virtually all investments are vulnerable to increases in tax rates, certain tax-advantaged investments, such as municipal and other bonds, real estate, and natural resources, generally have greater tax risk.

market risk
risk of decline in investment
returns because of market
factors independent of the
given investment.

Market Risk   **Market risk** is the risk that investment returns will decline because of market factors independent of the given investment. Examples include political, economic, and social events, as well as changes in investor tastes and preferences. Market risk actually embodies a number of different risks: purchasing power risk, interest rate risk, and tax risk.

The impact of market factors on investment returns is not uniform. Both the degree and the direction of change in return differ among investment vehicles. For example, legislation placing restrictive import quotas on Japanese goods may result in a significant increase in the value (and therefore the return) of domestic automobile and electronics stocks. Essentially, market risk is reflected in the *price volatility* of a security—the more volatile the price of a security, the greater its perceived market risk.

event risk
risk that comes from an
unexpected event that has
a significant and usually
immediate effect on the
underlying value of an
investment.

Event Risk   **Event risk** occurs when something happens to a company that has a sudden and substantial impact on its financial condition. Event risk goes beyond business and financial risk. It does not necessarily mean the company or market is doing poorly. Instead, it involves an unexpected event that has a significant and usually immediate effect on the underlying value of an investment. An example of event risk is the July 2005 voluntary recall of about 50,000 pacemakers by Guidant Corporation due to a faulty seal within the units that allowed moisture to affect their electronic circuits and possibly fail. The problem could occur without warning and lead to a loss of consciousness, and possibly heart failure and death. The stock of Guidant was quickly and negatively affected. One year after the announcement Guidant was acquired by Boston Scientific.

Event risk can take many forms and can affect all types of investment vehicles. Fortunately, its impact tends to be isolated in most cases.

▮ Risk of a Single Asset

Most people have at some time in their lives asked themselves how risky some anticipated course of action is. In such cases, the answer is usually a subjective judgment, such as "not very" or "quite." In finance, we are able to quantify the measurement of risk, which improves comparisons between investments and enhances decision making.

We can measure statistically the risk or variability of both single assets and portfolios of assets. Here we focus solely on the risk of single assets. We first consider standard deviation, which is an absolute measure of risk. Then we consider the coefficient of variation, a relative measure of risk. We will consider the risk and return of portfolios of assets in Chapter 5.

standard deviation, s
a statistic used to measure the dispersion (variation) of returns around an asset's average or expected return.

Standard Deviation: An Absolute Measure of Risk The most common single indicator of an asset's risk is the **standard deviation, s**. It measures the dispersion (variation) of returns around an asset's average or expected return. The formula is

Equation 4.6 ➤

$$\text{Standard deviation} = \sqrt{\frac{\sum_{j=1}^{n}\left(\begin{array}{c}\text{Return for} \\ \text{outcome } j\end{array} - \begin{array}{c}\text{Average or} \\ \text{expected return}\end{array}\right)^2}{\text{Total number} \atop \text{of outcomes}} - 1}$$

Equation 4.6a ➤

$$s = \sqrt{\frac{\sum_{j=1}^{n}(r_j - \bar{r})^2}{n - 1}}$$

Consider two competing investments—A and B—described in Table 4.9. Note that both investments earned an average return of 15% over the six-year period shown. Reviewing the returns shown for each investment in light of

TABLE 4.9   Returns on Investments A and B

	Rate of Return (r_j)	
Year (j)	Investment A	Investment B
2003	15.6%	8.4%
2004	12.7	12.9
2005	15.3	19.6
2006	16.2	17.5
2007	16.5	10.3
2008	13.7	21.3
Average ($\bar{r}$)	15.0%	15.0%

TABLE 4.10 Calculation of Standard Deviations of Returns for Investments A and B

		Investment A		
	(1)	(2) Average	(3) (1) − (2)	(4) (3)²
Year (j)	Return, r_j	Return, $\bar{r}$	$r_j - \bar{r}$	$(r_j - \bar{r})^2$
2003	15.6%	15.0%	.6%	0.36%
2004	12.7	15.0	−2.3	5.29
2005	15.3	15.0	.3	0.09
2006	16.2	15.0	1.2	1.44
2007	16.5	15.0	1.5	2.25
2008	13.7	15.0	−1.3	1.69

$$\sum_{j=1}^{6}(r_j - \bar{r})^2 = 11.12$$

$$s_A = \sqrt{\frac{\sum_{j=1}^{6}(r_j - \bar{r})^2}{n-1}} = \sqrt{\frac{11.12}{6-1}} = \sqrt{2.224} = \underline{1.49\%}$$

		Investment B		
	(1)	(2) Average	(3) (1) − (2)	(4) (3)²
Year (j)	Return, r_j	Return, $\bar{r}$	$r_j - \bar{r}$	$(r_j - \bar{r})^2$
2003	8.4%	15.0%	−6.6%	43.56%
2004	12.9	15.0	−2.1	4.41
2005	19.6	15.0	4.6	21.16
2006	17.5	15.0	2.5	6.25
2007	10.3	15.0	−4.7	22.09
2008	21.3	15.0	6.3	39.69

$$\sum_{j=1}^{6}(r_j - \bar{r})^2 = 137.16$$

$$s_B = \sqrt{\frac{\sum_{j=1}^{6}(r_j - \bar{r})^2}{n-1}} = \sqrt{\frac{137.16}{6-1}} = \sqrt{27.432} = \underline{5.24\%}$$

their 15% averages, we can see that the returns for investment B vary more from this average than do the returns for investment A.

The standard deviation provides a quantitative tool for comparing investment risk. Table 4.10 demonstrates the calculation of the standard deviations, s_A and s_B, for investments A and B, respectively. We can see that the standard deviation of 1.49% for the returns on investment A is, as expected, considerably below the standard deviation of 5.24% for investment B. The greater absolute dispersion of investment B's return, reflected in its larger standard deviation, indicates that B is the more risky investment. Of course, these values are absolute measures based on *historical* data. There is no assurance that the risks of these two investments will remain the same in the future.

coefficient of variation, CV
a statistic used to measure the *relative* dispersion of an asset's returns; it is useful in comparing the risk of assets with differing average or expected returns.

Coefficient of Variation: A Relative Measure of Risk

The **coefficient of variation, CV,** is a measure of the *relative* dispersion of an asset's returns. It is useful in comparing the risk of assets with differing average or expected returns. Equation 4.7 gives the formula for the coefficient of variation.

Equation 4.7 ➤

$$\text{Coefficient of variation} = \frac{\text{Standard deviation}}{\text{Average or expected return}}$$

Equation 4.7a ➤

$$CV = \frac{s}{r}$$

As was the case for the standard deviation, the higher the coefficient of variation, the greater the risk.

We can substitute into Equation 4.7a the standard deviation values (from Table 4.10) and the average returns (from Table 4.9) for investments A and B. We get a coefficient of variation for A of 0.099 (1.49% ÷ 15%) and for B of 0.349 (5.24% ÷ 15%). Investment B has the higher coefficient of variation and, as expected, has more relative risk than investment A. Because both investments have the same average return, the coefficient of variation in this case has not provided any more information than the standard deviation.

The real utility of the coefficient of variation is in comparing investments that have *different* expected returns. For example, assume you want to select the less risky of two alternative investments—X and Y. The average return, the standard deviation, and the coefficient of variation for each of these investments are as follows.

Statistics	Investment X	Investment Y
(1) Average return	12%	20%
(2) Standard deviation	9%*	10%
(3) Coefficient of variation [(2) ÷ (1)]	0.75	0.50*

*Preferred investment using the given risk measure.

If you compared the investments solely on the basis of their standard deviations, you would prefer investment X. It has a lower standard deviation than investment Y (9% versus 10%). But by comparing the coefficients of variation, you can see that you would be making a mistake in choosing X over Y. The *relative* dispersion, or risk, of the investments, as reflected in the coefficient of variation, is lower for Y than for X (0.50 versus 0.75). Clearly, the coefficient of variation considers the relative size, or average return, of each investment.

Historical Returns and Risk We can now use the standard deviation and coefficient of variation as a measure of risk to assess the historical (1926–2005) investment return data in Table 4.4. Table 4.11 (on page 182) repeats the historical returns and shows the standard deviations and coefficients of variation associated with each of them. A close relationship can be seen between the investment returns and the standard deviations and coefficients of variation: Investments with higher return have higher standard deviations and coefficients of variation. Because higher standard deviations and coefficients of variation are associated with greater risk, the historical data confirm the existence of a positive relationship between risk and return. That relationship reflects the fact that market participants require higher returns as compensation for greater risk. The historical data in Table 4.11 clearly show that during the 1926–2005 period investors were rewarded with higher returns on higher-risk investments.

TABLE 4.11 Historical Returns, Standard Deviations, and Coefficients of Variation for Popular Security Investments (1926–2005)

Investment	Arithmetic Average Annual Return	Standard Deviation	Coefficient of Variation*
Large-company stocks	12.3%	20.2%	1.64
Small-company stocks	17.4	32.9	1.89
Long-term corporate bonds	6.2	8.5	1.37
Long-term government bonds	5.8	9.2	1.59
U.S. Treasury bills	3.8	3.1	0.82
Inflation	3.1%	4.3%	1.39

*Calculated by dividing the standard deviation by the average annual return.

Source: Stocks, Bonds, Bills, and Inflation, 2006 Yearbook (Chicago: Ibbotson Associates, Inc., 2006), p. 31.

Assessing Risk

Techniques for quantifying the risk of a given investment vehicle are quite useful. However, they will be of little use if you are unaware of your feelings toward risk. Individual investors typically seek answers to these questions: "Is the amount of perceived risk worth taking to get the expected return?" "Can I get a higher return for the same level of risk or a lower risk for the same level of return?" A look at the general risk-return characteristics of alternative investment vehicles and at the question of an acceptable level of risk will help shed light on how to evaluate risk.

Risk-Return Characteristics of Alternative Investment Vehicles A wide variety of risk-return behaviors are associated with each type of investment vehicle. Some common stocks offer low returns and low risk. Others offer high returns and high risk. In general, ignoring differences in maturity, the risk-return characteristics of the major investment vehicles are as shown in Figure 4.2. Of course, a broad range of risk-return behaviors exists for specific investments of each type. In other words, once you have selected the appro-

FIGURE 4.2

Risk-Return Tradeoffs for Various Investment Vehicles

A risk-return tradeoff exists such that for a higher risk one expects a higher return, and vice versa. In general, ignoring differences in maturity, low-risk/low-return investment vehicles include U.S. government securities and deposit accounts. High-risk/high-return vehicles include real estate and other tangible investments, options, and futures.

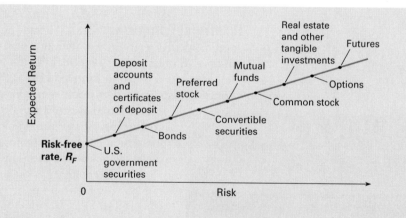

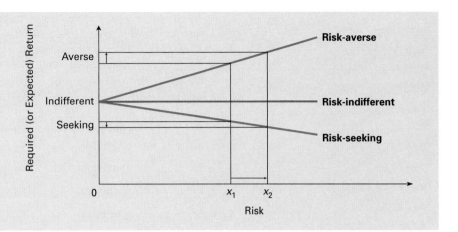

FIGURE 4.3

Risk Preferences

The risk-indifferent investor requires no change in return for a given increase in risk. The risk-averse investor requires an increase in return for a given risk increase. The risk-seeking investor gives up some return for more risk. The majority of investors are risk-averse.

priate type of vehicle, you must still decide which specific security to acquire. (*Note:* In Chapter 5 we will present a quantitative techniques for linking risk and return.)

An Acceptable Level of Risk The three basic risk preferences (risk-indifferent, risk-averse, and risk-seeking) are depicted graphically in Figure 4.3.

- For the **risk-indifferent** investor, the required return does not change as risk goes from x_1 to x_2. In essence, no change in return would be required for the increase in risk.

- For the **risk-averse** investor, the required return increases for an increase in risk. Because they shy away from risk, these investors require higher expected returns to compensate them for taking greater risk.

- For the **risk-seeking** investor, the required return decreases for an increase in risk. Theoretically, because they enjoy risk, these investors are willing to give up some return to take more risk.

Most investors are risk-averse: For a given increase in risk, they require an increase in return. This risk-averse behavior is also depicted in Figure 4.2.

Of course, the amount of return required by each investor for a given increase in risk differs depending on the investor's degree of risk aversion (reflected in the slope of the line). Investors generally tend to be conservative when accepting risk. The more aggressive an investor you are (the farther to the right you operate on the risk-averse line), the greater your tolerance for risk, and the greater your required return. Look back at the box about risk tolerance on page 176. Using the graph in Figure 4.2, determine what investment vehicles might be appropriate for your level of risk tolerance.

▮ Steps in the Decision Process: Combining Return and Risk

When you are deciding among alternative investments, you should take the following steps to combine return and risk.

1. Using historical or projected return data, estimate the expected return over a given holding period. Use yield (or present-value) techniques to make sure you give the time value of money adequate consideration.

risk-indifferent
describes an investor who does not require a change in return as compensation for greater risk.

risk-averse
describes an investor who requires greater return in exchange for greater risk.

risk-seeking
describes an investor who will accept a lower return in exchange for greater risk.

2. Using historical or projected return data, assess the risk associated with the investment. Subjective risk assessment, use of the standard deviation or coefficient of variation of returns, and use of more sophisticated measures, such as beta (developed in Chapter 5), are the primary approaches available to individual investors.

3. Evaluate the risk-return behavior of each alternative investment to make sure that the return expected is reasonable given the level of risk. If other vehicles with lower levels of risk provide equal or greater returns, the investment is not acceptable.

4. Select the investment vehicles that offer the highest returns associated with the level of risk you are willing to take. As long as you get the highest return for your acceptable level of risk, you have made a "good investment."

Probably the most difficult step in this process is assessing risk. Aside from return and risk considerations, other factors, such as portfolio considerations, taxes, and liquidity, affect the investment decision. We will develop portfolio concepts in Chapter 5 and, in later chapters, will look at all of these factors as they are related to specific investment vehicles.

CONCEPTS IN REVIEW
Answers available at: www.myfinancelab.com

4.9   Define *risk*. Explain what we mean by the *risk-return tradeoff*. What happens to the required return as risk increases? Explain.

4.10   Define and briefly discuss each of the following sources of risk.
    a.   Business risk
    b.   Financial risk
    c.   Purchasing power risk
    d.   Interest rate risk
    e.   Liquidity risk
    f.   Tax risk
    g.   Market risk
    h.   Event risk

4.11   Briefly describe each of the following measures of risk or variability, and explain their similarity. Under what circumstances is each preferred when comparing the risk of competing investments?
    a.   Standard deviation
    b.   Coefficient of variation

4.12   Differentiate among the three basic risk preferences: *risk-indifferent, risk-averse,* and *risk-seeking.* Which of these behaviors best describes most investors?

4.13   Describe the steps involved in the investment decision process. Be sure to mention how returns and risks can be evaluated together to determine acceptable investments.

Summary

LG 1 **Review the concept of return, its components, the forces that affect the level of return, and historical returns.** Return is the reward for investing. The total return provided by an investment includes current income and capital gains (or losses). Return is commonly calculated on a historical basis and then used to project expected returns. The level of return depends on internal characteristics and external forces, which include the general level of price changes. Significant differences exist between the average annual rates of return realized over time on various types of security investments.

LG 2 **Discuss the role of time value of money in measuring return and defining a satisfactory investment.** Because investors have opportunities to earn interest on their funds, money has a time value. Time value concepts should be considered when making investment decisions. Financial tables, financial calculators, and electronic spreadsheets can be used to streamline time-value calculations. A satisfactory investment is one for which the present value of its benefits equals or exceeds the present value of its costs.

LG 3 **Describe real, risk-free, and required returns and the calculation and application of holding period return.** The required return is the rate of return an investor must earn to be fully compensated for an investment's risk. It represents the sum of the real rate of return and the expected inflation premium (which together represent the risk-free rate), plus the risk premium. The risk premium varies depending on issue and issuer characteristics. The holding period return (HPR) is the return earned over a specified period of time. It is frequently used to compare returns earned in periods of one year or less.

LG 4 **Explain the concept and calulation of yield, and how to find growth rates.** Yield (or internal rate of return) is the compound annual rate of return earned on investments held for more than one year. If the yield is greater than or equal to the required return, the investment is acceptable. The concept of yield assumes that the investor will be able to earn interest at the calculated yield rate on all income from the investment. Present-value techniques can be used to find a rate of growth, which is the compound annual rate of change in the value of a stream of income, particularly dividends or earnings.

LG 5 **Discuss the key sources of risk that might affect potential investment vehicles.** Risk is the chance that the actual return from an investment will differ from what is expected. Total risk results from a combination of sources: business, financial, purchasing power, interest rate, liquidity, tax, market, and event risk. These risks have varying effects on different types of investments. The combined impact of any of the sources of risk in a given investment vehicle would be reflected in its risk premium.

LG 6 **Understand the risk of a single asset, risk assessment, and the steps that combine return and risk.** The standard deviation measures the absolute risk of both single assets and portfolios of assets. The coefficient of variation provides a relative measure of risk for both single assets and portfolios. Investors require higher returns as compensation for greater risk. Generally, each type of investment vehicle displays certain risk-return characteristics. Most investors are risk-averse: for a given increase in risk, they require an increase in return. Investors estimate the return and risk of each alternative and then select investments that offer the highest returns for the level of acceptable risk.

Key Terms

business risk, *p. 175*
coefficient of variation, CV, *p. 180*
current income, *p. 159*
deflation, *p. 162*
event risk, *p. 178*
expected inflation premium, *p. 165*
expected return, *p. 161*
financial risk, *p. 176*
fully compounded rate of return,
    p. 172
holding period, *p. 166*
holding period return (HPR), *p. 167*
inflation, *p. 162*
interest rate risk, *p. 177*
liquidity risk, *p. 178*
market risk, *p. 178*
paper return, *p. 167*
purchasing power risk, *p. 177*
rate of growth, *p. 173*

real rate of return, *p. 165*
realized return, *p. 166*
reinvestment rate, *p. 172*
required return, *p. 165*
return, *p. 159*
risk, *p. 175*
risk-averse, *p. 183*
risk-free rate, *p. 165*
risk-indifferent, *p. 183*
risk-return tradeoff, *p. 175*
risk-seeking, *p. 183*
risk premium, *p. 166*
satisfactory investment, *p. 163*
standard deviation, s, *p. 179*
tax risk, *p. 179*
total return, *p. 159*
yield (internal rate of return),
    p. 169

Discussion Questions

LG 1   Q4.1   Choose a publicly traded company that has been listed on a major exchange or in the over-the-counter market for at least 5 years. Use any data source of your choice to find the annual cash dividend, if any, paid by the company in each of the past 5 calendar years. Also find the closing price of the stock at the end of each of the preceding 6 years.
    a. Calculate the return for each of the five 1-year periods.
    b. Graph the returns on a set of year (*x*-axis)-return (*y*-axis) axes.
    c. On the basis of the graph in part **b**, estimate the return for the coming year, and explain your answer.

LG 2   Q4.2   Estimate the amount of cash you will need each year over the next 20 years to live at the standard you desire. Also estimate the rate of return you can reasonably expect to earn annually, on average, during that 20-year period by investing in a common stock portfolio similar to the S&P 500.
    a. How large a single lump sum would you need today to provide the annual cash required to allow you to live at the desired standard over the next 20 years? (*Hint:* Be sure to use the appropriate discount rate.)
    b. Would the lump sum calculated in part **a** be larger or smaller if you could earn a higher return during the 20-year period? Explain.
    c. If you had the lump sum calculated in part **a** but decided to delay your planned retirement in 20 years for another 3 years, how much extra cash would you have accumulated over the 3-year period if you could invest it to earn a 7% annual rate of return?

LG 3   Q4.3   Access appropriate estimates of the expected inflation rate over the next year, and the current yield on 1-year risk-free securities (the yield on these securities is referred to as the *nominal* rate of interest). Use the data to estimate the current risk-free *real* rate of interest.

LG 3 **LG 6** Q4.4 Choose 3 NYSE-listed stocks and maintain a record of their dividend payments, if any, and closing prices each week over the next 6 weeks.
- a. At the end of the 6-week period, calculate the 1-week holding period returns (HPRs) for each stock for each of the 6 weeks.
- b. For each stock, average the six weekly HPRs calculated in part **a** and compare them.
- c. Use the averages you computed in part **b** and compute the standard deviation of the six HPRs for each stock. Discuss the stocks' relative risk and return behavior. Did the stocks with the highest risk earn the greatest return?

Problems

LG 1 P4.1 How much would an investor earn on a stock purchased 1 year ago for $63 if it paid an annual cash dividend of $3.75 and had just been sold for $67.50? Would the investor have experienced a capital gain? Explain.

LG 1 P4.2 An investor buys a bond for $10,000. The bond pays $300 interest every 6 months. After 18 months, the investor sells the bond for $9,500. Describe the types of income and/or loss the investor had.

LG 1 P4.3 Assuming you purchased a share of stock for $50 one year ago, sold it today for $60, and during the year received three dividend payments totaling $2.70, calculate the following.
- a. Current income.
- b. Capital gain (or loss).
- c. Total return
  - (1) In dollars.
  - (2) As a percentage of the initial investment.

LG 1 P4.4 Assume you purchased a bond for $9,500. The bond pays $300 interest every 6 months. You sell the bond after 18 months for $10,000. Calculate the following:
- a. Current income.
- b. Capital gain or loss.
- c. Total return in dollars and as a percentage of the original investment.

LG 1 P4.5 Consider the historical data given in the accompanying table.
- a. Calculate the total return (in dollars) for each year.
- b. Indicate the level of return you would expect in 2009 and in 2010.
- c. Comment on your forecast.

Year	Income	Market Value (Price)	
		Beginning	Ending
2004	$1.00	$30.00	$32.50
2005	1.20	32.50	35.00
2006	1.30	35.00	33.00
2007	1.60	33.00	40.00
2008	1.75	40.00	45.00

LG 1   P4.6   Refer to the table in Problem 4.5. What is the total return in dollars and as a percentage of your original investment if you purchased 100 shares of the investment at the beginning of 2004 and sold it at the end of 2006?

LG 3   P4.7   Given a real rate of interest of 3%, an expected inflation premium of 5%, and risk premiums for investments A and B of 3% and 5% respectively, find the following.
   a. The risk-free rate of return R_F.
   b. The required returns for investments A and B.

LG 3   P4.8   The risk free rate is 7%, and expected inflation is 4.5%. If inflation expectations change such that future expected inflation rises to 5.5%, what will the new risk-free rate be?

LG 3   P4.9   Calculate the holding period return (HPR) for the following two investment alternatives. Which, if any, of the return components is likely not to be realized if you continue to hold each of the investments beyond 1 year? Which vehicle would you prefer, assuming they are of equal risk? Explain.

	Investment Vehicle	
	X	Y
Cash received		
1st quarter	$ 1.00	$ 0
2nd quarter	1.20	0
3rd quarter	0	0
4th quarter	2.30	2.00
Investment value		
End of year	$29.00	$56.00
Beginning of year	30.00	50.00

LG 3   P4.10   You are considering two investment alternatives. The first is a stock that pays quarterly dividends of $0.50 per share and is trading at $25 per share; you expect to sell the stock in 6 months for $27. The second is a stock that pays quarterly dividends of $0.60 per share and is trading at $27 per share; you expect to sell the stock in 1 year for $30. Which stock will provide the better annualized holding period return?

LG 3   P4.11   You are considering purchasing a bond that pays annual interest of $50 per $1,000 of par value. The bond matures in 1 year, when you will collect the par value and the interest payment. If you can purchase this bond for $950, what is the holding period return?

LG 4   P4.12   Assume you invest $5,000 today in an investment vehicle that promises to return $9,000 in exactly 10 years.
   a. Use the present-value technique to estimate the yield on this investment.
   b. If a minimum return of 9% is required, would you recommend this investment?

LG 4   P4.13   You invest $7,000 in stock and receive $65, $70, $70, and $65 in dividends over the following 4 years. At the end of the 4 years, you sell the stock for $7,900. What was the yield on this investment?

LG 4   P4.14   Your friend asks you to invest $10,000 in a business venture. Based on your estimates, you would receive nothing for 4 years, at the end of year 5 you would receive interest on the investment compounded annually at 8%, and at the end of year 6 you would receive $14,500. If your estimates are correct, what would be the yield on this investment?

LG 4   P4.15   Use the appropriate present-value interest factor table, a financial calculator, or an Excel spreadsheet to estimate the yield for each of the following investments.

Investment	Initial Investment	Future Value	End of Year
A	$ 1,000	$ 1,200	5
B	10,000	20,000	7
C	400	2,000	20
D	3,000	4,000	6
E	5,500	25,000	30

LG 4   P4.16   Rosemary Santos must earn a return of 10% on an investment that requires an initial outlay of $2,500 and promises to return $6,000 in 8 years.
   a. Use present-value techniques to estimate the yield on this investment.
   b. On the basis of your finding in part **a**, should Rosemary make the proposed investment? Explain.

LG 4   P4.17   Use the appropriate present-value interest factors, a financial calculator, or an Excel spreadsheet to estimate the yield for each of the following two investments.

	Investment	
	A	B
Initial Investment	$8,500	$9,500
End of Year	Income	
1	$2,500	$2,000
2	2,500	2,500
3	2,500	3,000
4	2,500	3,500
5	2,500	4,000

LG 4   P4.18   Elliott Dumack must earn a minimum rate of return of 11% to be adequately compensated for the risk of the following investment.

Initial Investment	$14,000
End of Year	Income
1	$ 6,000
2	3,000
3	5,000
4	2,000
5	1,000

   a. Use present-value techniques to estimate the yield on this investment.
   b. On the basis of your finding in part **a**, should Elliott make the proposed investment? Explain.

LG 4   P4.19   Assume that an investment generates the following income stream and can be purchased at the beginning of 2009 for $1,000 and sold at the end of 2015 for $1,200. Estimate the yield for this investment. If a minimum return of 9% is required, would you recommend this investment? Explain.

End of Year	Income Stream
2009	$140
2010	120
2011	100
2012	80
2013	60
2014	40
2015	20

LG 4

P4.20 For each of the following streams of dividends, estimate the compound annual rate of growth between the earliest year for which a value is given and 2008.

	Dividend Stream		
Year	A	B	C
1999		$1.50	
2000		1.55	
2001		1.61	
2002		1.68	$2.50
2003		1.76	2.60
2004	$5.00	1.85	2.65
2005	5.60	1.95	2.65
2006	6.40	2.06	2.80
2007	7.20	2.17	2.85
2008	8.00	2.28	2.90

LG 4

P4.21 A company paid dividends of $1.00 per share in 2000, and just announced that it will pay $2.21 in 2007. Estimate the compound annual growth rate of the dividends.

LG 4

P4.22 A company reported net income in 2003 of $350 million. In 2007, the company expects net income to be $441.7 million. Estimate the annual compound growth rate of net income.

LG 6

P4.23 The historical returns for two investments—A and B—are summarized in the table below for the period 2004 to 2008. Use the data to answer the questions that follow.

	Investment	
	A	B
Year	Rate of Return	
2004	19%	8%
2005	1	10
2006	10	12
2007	26	14
2008	4	16
Average	12%	12%

a. On the basis of a review of the return data, which investment appears to be more risky? Why?

b. Calculate the standard deviation and the coefficient of variation for each investment's returns.

c. On the basis of your calculations in part **b**, which investment is more risky? Compare this conclusion to your observation in part **a**.

d. Does the coefficient of variation provide better risk comparison than the standard deviation in the case? Why or why not?

LG 6   P4.24 Referring to Problem 4.23, if one investment's required return is 12% and the other is 14%, which one is 14%?

See www.myfinancelab.com **for Web Exercises,**
Spreadsheets, and other online resources.

Case Problem 4.1   *Solomon's Decision*

LG 2   LG 4   Dave Solomon, a 23-year-old mathematics teacher at Xavier High School, recently received a tax refund of $1,100. Because Dave didn't need this money for his current living expenses, he decided to make a long-term investment. After surveying a number of alternative investments costing no more than $1,100, Dave isolated 2 that seemed most suitable to his needs.

Each of the investments cost $1,050 and was expected to provide income over a 10-year period. Investment A provided a relatively certain stream of income. Dave was a little less certain of the income provided by investment B. From his search for suitable alternatives, Dave found that the appropriate discount rate for a relatively certain investment was 12%. Because he felt a bit uncomfortable with an investment like B, he estimated that such an investment would have to provide a return at least 4% *higher* than investment A. Although Dave planned to reinvest funds returned from the investments in other vehicles providing similar returns, he wished to keep the extra $50 ($1,100 − $1,050) invested for the full 10 years in a savings account paying 5% interest compounded annually.

As he makes his investment decision, Dave has asked for your help in answering the questions that follow the expected return data for these investments.

| | Expected Returns | |
Year	A	B
2009	$ 150	$100
2010	150	150
2011	150	200
2012	150	250
2013	150	300
2014	150	350
2015	150	300
2016	150	250
2017	150	200
2018	1,150	150

Questions

a. Assuming that investments A and B are equally risky and using the 12% discount rate, apply the present-value technique to assess the acceptability of each investment and to determine the preferred investment. Explain your findings.

b. Recognizing that investment B is more risky than investment A, reassess the 2 alternatives, adding the 4% risk premium to the 12% discount rate for investment A and therefore applying a 16% discount rate to investment B. Compare your findings relative to acceptability and preference to those found for question a.

c. From your findings in questions a and b, indicate whether the yield for investment A is above or below 12% and whether that for investment B is above or below 16%. Explain.

d. Use the present-value technique to estimate the yield on each investment. Compare your findings and contrast them with your response to question c.

e. From the information given, which, if either, of the two investments would you recommend that Dave make? Explain your answer.

f. Indicate to Dave how much money the extra $50 will have grown to by the end of 2018, assuming he makes no withdrawals from the savings account.

Case Problem 4.2   *The Risk-Return Tradeoff: Molly O'Rourke's Stock Purchase Decision*

LG 3   LG 6

Over the past 10 years, Molly O'Rourke has slowly built a diversified portfolio of common stock. Currently her portfolio includes 20 different common stock issues and has a total market value of $82,500.

Molly is at present considering the addition of 50 shares of 1 of 2 common stock issues—X or Y. To assess the return and risk of each of these issues, she has gathered dividend income and share price data for both over each of the last 10 years (1999 through 2008). Molly's investigation of the outlook for these issues suggests that each will, on average, tend to behave in the future just as it has in the past. She therefore believes that the expected return can be estimated by finding the average holding period return (HPR) over the past 10 years for each of the stocks. The historical dividend income and stock price data collected by Molly are given in the accompanying table.

	Stock X			Stock Y		
		Share Price			Share Price	
Year	Dividend Income	Beginning	Ending	Dividend Income	Beginning	Ending
1999	$1.00	$20.00	$22.00	$1.50	$20.00	$20.00
2000	1.50	22.00	21.00	1.60	20.00	20.00
2001	1.40	21.00	24.00	1.70	20.00	21.00
2002	1.70	24.00	22.00	1.80	21.00	21.00
2003	1.90	22.00	23.00	1.90	21.00	22.00
2004	1.60	23.00	26.00	2.00	22.00	23.00
2005	1.70	26.00	25.00	2.10	23.00	23.00
2006	2.00	25.00	24.00	2.20	23.00	24.00
2007	2.10	24.00	27.00	2.30	24.00	25.00
2008	2.20	27.00	30.00	2.40	25.00	25.00

Questions

a. Determine the holding period return (HPR) for each stock in each of the preceding 10 years. Find the expected return for each stock, using the approach specified by Molly.

b. Use the HPRs and expected return calculated in question **a** to find both the standard deviation and the coefficient of variation of the HPRs for each stock over the 10-year period 1999 to 2008.

c. Use your findings to evaluate and discuss the return and risk associated with stocks X and Y. Which stock seems preferable? Explain.

d. Ignoring her existing portfolio, what recommendations would you give Molly with regard to stocks X and Y?

Excel with Spreadsheets

From her Investment Analysis class, Laura has been given an assignment to evaluate several securities on a risk-return tradeoff basis. The specific securities to be researched are International Business Machines, Helmerich & Payne, Inc., and the S&P 500 Index. The respective ticker symbols for the stocks are IBM and HP. She finds the following (assumed) data on the securities in question. It is as follows:

Year	2003	2004	2005	2006	2007	2008
Price$_{IBM}$	$ 49.38	$ 91.63	$112.25	$112.00	$107.89	$ 92.68
Dividend$_{IBM}$	$ 0.40	$ 0.44	$ 0.48	$ 0.52	$ 0.56	$ 0.64
Price$_{HP}$	$ 25.56	$ 17.56	$ 23.50	$ 47.81	$ 30.40	$ 27.93
Dividend$_{HP}$	$ 0.28	$ 0.28	$ 0.28	$ 0.30	$ 0.30	$ 0.32
Value$_{S\&P}$	980.3	1,279.6	1,394.6	1,366.0	1,130.2	1,121.8

Note: The value of the S&P 500 Index includes dividends.

Questions

Part One

a. Use the given data that Laura has found on the three securities and create a spreadsheet to calculate the holding period return (HPR) for each year and the average return over a 5-year period. Specifically, the HPR will be based upon 5 unique periods of 1 year (i.e., 2003 to 2004, 2004 to 2005, 2005 to 2006, 2006 to 2007, 2007 to 2008). Use the following formula:

$$HPR = [C + (V_n - V_0)] / V_0$$

Where

C = current income during period
V_n = ending investment value
V_0 = beginning investment value

Part Two

Create a spreadsheet similar to the spreadsheet for Table 4.10, which can be viewed at www.myfinancelab.com, in order to evaluate the risk-return tradeoff.

b.   Calculate the standard deviations of the returns for IBM, HP, and the S&P 500 Index.

c.   Calculate the coefficients of variation for IBM, HP, and the S&P 500 Index.

d.   What industries are associated with IBM and HP?

e.   Based on your answer in part **d** and your results for the average return and the standard deviation and coefficient of variation, what conclusions can Laura make about investing in either IBM or HP?

The Time Value of Money

Imagine that at age 25 you begin making annual cash deposits of $1,000 into a savings account that pays 5% annual interest. After 40 years, at age 65, you will have made deposits totaling $40,000 (40 years × $1,000 per year). Assuming you made no withdrawals, what do you think your account balance will be—$50,000? $75,000? $100,000? The answer is none of the above. Your $40,000 will have grown to nearly $121,000! Why? Because the time value of money allows the deposits to earn interest, and that interest also earns interest over the 40 years. **Time value of money** refers to the fact that as long as an opportunity exists to earn interest, the value of money is affected by the point in time when the money is received.

time value of money
the fact that as long as an opportunity exists to earn interest, the value of money is affected by the point in time when the money is received.

Interest: The Basic Return to Savers

A savings account at a bank is one of the most basic forms of investment. The saver receives interest in exchange for placing idle funds in an account. **Interest** can be viewed as the "rent" paid by a borrower for use of the lender's money. The saver will experience neither a capital gain nor a capital loss, because the value of the investment (the initial deposit) will change only by the amount of interest earned. For the saver, the interest earned over a given time frame is that period's current income.

interest
the "rent" paid by a borrower for use of the lender's money.

■ Simple Interest

The income paid on investment vehicles that pay interest (such as CDs and bonds) is most often calculated using **simple interest**—interest paid only on the initial deposit for the amount of time it is held. For example, if you held a $100 initial deposit in an account paying 6% interest for 1½ years, you would earn $9 in interest (1½ × 0.06 × $100) over this period. Had you withdrawn $50 at the end of half a year, the total interest earned over the 1½ years would be $6. You would earn $3 interest on $100 for the first half-year (½ × 0.06 × $100) and $3 interest on $50 for the next full year (1 × 0.06 × $50).

When an investment earns simple interest, the stated rate of interest is the **true rate of interest (return)**. This is the actual rate of interest earned. In the foregoing example, the true rate of interest is 6%. Because the interest rate reflects the rate at which current income is earned regardless of the size of the deposit, it is a useful measure of current income.

simple interest
interest paid only on the initial deposit for the amount of time it is held.

true rate of interest (return)
the actual rate of interest earned.

■ Compound Interest

Compound interest is interest paid not only on the initial deposit but also on any interest accumulated from one period to the next. This is the method typically used by savings institutions. When interest is compounded annually over

compound interest
interest paid not only on the initial deposit but also on any interest accumulated from one period to the next.

TABLE 4A.1 Savings Account Balance Data
(5% interest compounded annually)

Date	(1) Deposit (Withdrawal)	(2) Beginning Account Balance	(3) 0.05 × (2) Interest for Year	(4) (2) + (3) Ending Account Balance
1/1/07	$1,000	$1,000.00	$50.00	$1,050.00
1/1/08	(300)	750.00	37.50	787.50
1/1/09	1,000	1,787.50	89.38	1,876.88

a single year, compound and simple interest calculations provide similar results. In such a case, the stated interest rate and the true interest rate are equal.

The data in Table 4A.1 illustrate compound interest. In this case, the interest earned each year is left on deposit rather than withdrawn. The $50 of interest earned on the $1,000 initial deposit during 2007 becomes part of the beginning (initial) balance on which interest is paid in 2008, and so on. *Note that simple interest is used in the compounding process;* that is, interest is paid only on the initial balance held during the given time period.

When an investment earns compound interest, the stated and true interest rates are equal only when interest is compounded annually. In general, *the more frequently interest is compounded at a stated rate, the higher the true rate of interest.*

The interest calculations for the deposit data in Table 4A.1, assuming that interest is compounded semiannually (twice a year), are shown in Table 4A.2 . The interest for each six-month period is found by multiplying the beginning (initial) balance for the six months by half of the stated 5% interest rate (see column 3 of Table 4A.2). You can see that larger returns are associated with more frequent compounding: Compare the end-of-2009 account balance at 5% compounded annually with the end-of-2009 account balance at 5% compounded semiannually. The semiannual compounding results in a higher balance ($1,879.19 versus $1,876.88). Clearly, with semiannual compounding, the true rate of interest is greater than the 5% annually compounded rate. Table 4A.3 (on page 198) shows the true rates of interest associated with a 5% stated rate and various compounding frequencies.

TABLE 4A.2 Savings Account Balance Data
(5% interest compounded semiannually)

Date	(1) Deposit (Withdrawal)	(2) Beginning Account Balance	(3) 0.05 × 1/2 × (2) Interest for 6 Months	(4) (2) + (3) Ending Account Balance
1/1/07	$1,000	$1,000.00	$25.00	$1,025.00
7/1/07		1,025.00	25.63	1,050.63
1/1/08	(300)	750.63	18.77	769.40
7/1/08		769.40	19.24	788.64
1/1/09	1,000	1,788.64	44.72	1,833.36
7/1/09		1,833.36	45.83	1,879.19

TABLE 4A.3 True Rate of Interest for Various Compounding Frequencies (5% stated rate of interest)

Compounding Frequency	True Rate of Interest	Compounding Frequency	True Rate of Interest
Annually	5.000%	Monthly	5.120%
Semiannually	5.063	Weekly	5.125
Quarterly	5.094	Continuously	5.127

continuous compounding
interest calculation in which interest is compounded over the smallest possible interval of time.

    Continuous compounding calculates interest by compounding over the smallest possible interval of time. It results in the maximum true rate of interest that can be achieved with a given stated rate of interest. Table 4A.3 shows that the more frequently interest is compounded, the higher the true rate of interest. Because of the impact that differences in compounding frequencies have on return, you should evaluate the true rate of interest associated with various alternatives before making a deposit.

Computational Aids for Use in Time Value Calculations

Time-consuming calculations are often involved in adjusting for the time value of money. Although you should understand the concepts and mathematics underlying these calculations, the application of time value techniques can be streamlined. We will demonstrate the use of financial tables, hand-held financial calculators, and computers and spreadsheets as computational aids.

▌Financial Tables

Financial tables include various interest factors that simplify time value calculations. The values in these tables are easily developed from formulas, with various degrees of rounding. The tables are typically indexed by the interest rate (in columns) and the number of periods (in rows). Figure 4A.1 shows this

FIGURE 4A.1

Financial Tables

Layout and use of a financial table

Period	1%	2%	⋯	10%	⋯	20%	⋯	50%
1			⋯		⋯	⋮	⋯	
2			⋯		⋯	⋮	⋯	
3			⋯		⋯	⋮	⋯	
⋮	⋮	⋮	⋯	⋮	⋯	⋮	⋯	⋮
→ 10	⋯	⋯	⋯	⋯	⋯	X.XXX	⋯	⋯
⋮	⋮	⋮	⋯	⋮	⋯	⋮	⋯	⋮
20			⋯		⋯		⋯	
⋮	⋮	⋮	⋯	⋮	⋯	⋮	⋯	⋮
50			⋯		⋯		⋯	

Interest Rate ↓

general layout. The interest factor at a 20% interest rate for 10 years would be found at the intersection of the 20% column and the 10-period row, as shown by the dark blue box. A full set of the four basic financial tables is included in Appendix A at the end of the book. These tables are described more fully later in this appendix.

■ Financial Calculators

We also can use financial calculators for time value computations. Generally, *financial calculators* include numerous preprogrammed financial routines. Throughout this book, we show the keystrokes for various financial computations.

We focus primarily on the keys pictured and defined in Figure 4A.2. We typically use four of the five keys in the left column, plus the compute (**CPT**) key. One of the four keys represents the unknown value being calculated. (Occasionally, all five of the keys are used, with one representing the unknown value.) The keystrokes on some of the more sophisticated calculators are menu-driven: After you select the appropriate routine, the calculator prompts you to input each value; on these calculators, a compute key is not needed to obtain a solution. Regardless, any calculator with the basic time value functions can be used in lieu of financial tables. The keystrokes for other financial calculators are explained in the reference guides that accompany them.

Once you understand the basic underlying concepts, you probably will want to use a calculator to streamline routine financial calculations. With a little practice, you can increase both the speed and the accuracy of your financial computations. Note that because of a calculator's greater precision, slight differences are likely to exist between values calculated by using financial tables and those found with a financial calculator. Remember that *conceptual understanding of the material is the objective.* An ability to solve problems with the aid of a calculator does not necessarily reflect such an understanding, so don't just settle for answers. Work with the material until you are sure you also understand the concepts.

■ Computers and Spreadsheets

Like financial calculators, computers and spreadsheets have built-in routines that simplify time value calculations. We provide in the text a number of spreadsheet solutions that identify the cell entries for calculating time values. The value for each variable is entered in a cell in the spreadsheet, and the

---

FIGURE 4A.2

Calculator Keys

Important financial keys on the typical calculator

N	—	Number of periods
I	—	Interest rate per period
PV	—	Present value
PMT	—	Amount of payment (used only for annuities)
FV	—	Future value
CPT	—	Compute key used to initiate financial calculation once all values are input

calculation is programmed using an equation that links the individual cells. If you change values of the variables, the solution automatically changes. In the spreadsheet solutions in this book, we show at the bottom of the spreadsheet the equation that determines the calculation.

The ability to use spreadsheets has become a prime skill for today's investors. As the saying goes, "Get aboard the bandwagon, or get run over." The spreadsheet solutions we present in this book will help you climb up onto that bandwagon!

We now turn to the key time value concepts, beginning with future value.

Future Value: An Extension of Compounding

future value
the amount to which a current deposit will grow over a period of time when it is placed in an account paying compound interest.

Future value is the amount to which a current deposit will grow over a period of time when it is placed in an account paying compound interest. Consider a deposit of $1,000 that is earning 8% (0.08 in decimal form) compounded annually. The following calculation yields the future value of this deposit at the end of one year.

Equation 4A.1 ▶

$$\text{Future value at end of year 1} = \$1,000 \times (1 + 0.08) = \underline{\$1,080}$$

If the money were left on deposit for another year, 8% interest would be paid on the account balance of $1,080. Thus, at the end of the second year, there would be $1,166.40 in the account. This amount would represent the beginning-of-year balance of $1,080 plus 8% of the $1,080 ($86.40) in interest. The future value at the end of the second year would be calculated as follows.

Equation 4A.2 ▶

$$\text{Future value at end of year 2} = \$1,080 \times (1 + 0.08) = \underline{\$1,166.40}$$

To find the future value of the $1,000 at the end of year n, the procedure illustrated above would be repeated n times. Future values can be determined either mathematically or by using a financial table, financial calculator, or a computer and spreadsheet. Here we demonstrate use of a table of future-value interest factors, use of a calculator, and use of an Excel spreadsheet.

TABLE USE The factors in Appendix A, Table A.1 represent the amount to which an initial $1 deposit would grow for various periods (typically years) and interest rates. For example, a dollar deposited in an account paying 8% interest and left there for two years would accumulate to $1.166. Using the future-value interest factor for 8% and 2 periods (in this case, years) (1.166), we can find the future value of an investment that can earn 8% over two years: We would *multiply* the amount invested by the appropriate interest factor. In the case of $1,000 left on deposit for two years at 8%, the resulting future value is $1,166 (1.166 × $1,000). This agrees (except for a slight rounding difference) with the value calculated in Equation 4A.2.

A few points with respect to Appendix A, Table A.1, Future-Value Interest Factors for One Dollar, should be emphasized:

1. The values in the table represent factors for determining the future value of one dollar at the *end* of the given period.
2. As the interest rate increases for any given period, the future-value interest factor also increases. The higher the interest rate, the greater the future value.
3. For a given interest rate, the future value of a dollar increases with the passage of time.
4. The future-value interest factor is always greater than 1. Only if the interest rate were zero would this factor equal 1, and the future value would therefore equal the initial deposit.

CALCULATOR USE* A financial calculator can be used to calculate the future value directly.** First punch in $1,000 and depress **PV**; next punch in 2 and depress **N**; then punch in 8 and depress **I**.[†] Finally, to calculate the future value, depress **CPT** and then **FV**. The future value of $1,166.40 should appear on the calculator display, as shown in the art at the left. On many calculators, this value will be preceded by a minus sign (−1,166.40). *If a minus sign appears on your calculator, ignore it here as well as in all other "Calculator Use" illustrations in this text.*[‡]

The calculator is more accurate than the future value factors, which have been rounded to the nearest 0.001. Therefore, a slight difference will frequently exist between the values found by these alternative methods. In this case, there is a $0.40 difference. Clearly, the improved accuracy and ease of calculation tend to favor the use of the calculator. (*Note:* In future examples of calculator use, we will use only a display similar to that shown on the previous page. If you need a reminder of the procedure involved, come back and review the preceding paragraph.)

---

* Many calculators allow the user to set the number of payments per year. Most of these calculators are preset for monthly payments—12 payments per year. Because we work primarily with annual payments—one payment per year—it is important *to be sure that your calculator is set for one payment per year.* And although most calculators are preset to recognize that all payments occur at the end of the period, it is important *to make sure that your calculator is correctly set on the END mode.* Consult the reference guide that accompanies your calculator for instructions for setting these values.

** To avoid including previous data in current calculations, *always clear all registers of your calculator before inputting values and making each computation.*

† The known values *can be punched into the calculator in any order.* The order specified in this as well as other demonstrations of calculator use included in this text merely reflects convenience and personal preference.

‡ The calculator differentiates inflows from outflows with a negative sign. For example, in the problem just demonstrated, the $1,000 present value (**PV**), because it was keyed as a positive number (1000), is considered an inflow or deposit. Therefore, the calculated future value (**FV**) of −1166.40 is preceded by a minus sign to show that it is the resulting outflow or withdrawal. Had the $1,000 present value been keyed in as a negative number (−1000), the future value of $1166.40 would have been displayed as a positive number (1166.40). Simply stated, *present value (**PV**) and future value (**FV**) cash flows will have opposite signs.*

SPREADSHEET USE The future value of the single amount also can be calculated as shown on the following Excel spreadsheet.

	A	B
1	**FUTURE VALUE OF A SINGLE AMOUNT**	
2	Present value	$1,000
3	Interest rate, pct per year compounded annually	8%
4	Number of years	2
5	Future value	$1,166.40

Entry in Cell B5 is =FV(B3,B4,0,–B2,0).
The minus sign appears before B2 because the present value
is an outflow (i.e., the initial deposit).

Future Value of an Annuity

annuity
a stream of equal cash flows that occur at equal intervals over time.

ordinary annuity
an annuity for which the cash flows occur at the *end* of each period.

An **annuity** is a stream of equal cash flows that occur at equal intervals over time. Receiving $1,000 per year at the end of each of the next eight years is an example of an annuity. The cash flows can be *inflows* of returns earned from an investment or *outflows* of funds invested (deposited) to earn future returns.

Investors are sometimes interested in finding the future value of an annuity. Their concern is typically with what's called an **ordinary annuity**—one for which the cash flows occur at the *end* of each period. Here we can simplify our calculations by using either tables of the factors for an annuity, a financial calculator, or an Excel spreadsheet. (A complete set of these tables appears in Appendix A, Table A.2.)

TABLE USE The factors in Appendix A, Table A.2 represent the amount to which annual end-of-period deposits of $1 would grow for various periods (years) and interest rates. For example, a dollar deposited at the end of each year for eight years into an account paying 6% interest would accumulate to $9.897. Using the future-value interest factor for an eight-year annuity earning 6% (9.897), we can find the future value of this cash flow: We would *multiply* the annual investment by the appropriate interest factor. In the case of $1,000 deposited at the end of each year for eight years at 6%, the resulting future value is $9,897 (9.897 × $1,000).

CALCULATOR USE When using a financial calculator to find the future value of an annuity, we key in the annual deposit using the **PMT** key (rather than the **PV** key, which we used to find the future value of a single deposit). Use of the **PMT** key tells the calculator that a stream of **N** (the number of years input) end-of-year deposits in the amount of **PMT** dollars represents the deposit stream.

Using the calculator inputs shown at the left, we find the future value of the $1,000, eight-year ordinary annuity earning a 6% annual rate of interest to be $9,897.47. This is a slightly more precise answer than that found by using the table.

SPREADSHEET USE We also can calculate the future value of the ordinary annuity as shown on the following Excel spreadsheet.

	A	B
1	**FUTURE VALUE OF AN ORDINARY ANNUITY**	
2	Annual payment	$1,000
3	Annual rate of interest, compounded annually	6%
4	Number of years	8
5	Future value of an ordinary annuity	$9,897.47

Entry in Cell B5 is =FV(B3,B4,–B2)
The minus sign appears before B2 because
the annual payment is a cash outflow.

Present Value: An Extension of Future Value

present value
the *value today* of a sum to be received at some future date; the inverse of future value.

Present value is the inverse of future value. That is, rather than measuring the value of a present amount at some future date, **present value** expresses the *current value of a future sum*. By applying present-value techniques, we can calculate the *value today* of a sum to be received at some future date.

When determining the present value of a future sum, we are answering the basic question, "How much would have to be deposited today into an account paying $i\%$ interest in order to equal a specified sum to be received so many years in the future?" The applicable interest rate when we are finding present value is commonly called the **discount rate** (or *opportunity cost*). It represents the annual rate of return that could be earned currently on a similar investment.

discount rate
the annual rate of return that could be earned currently on a similar investment; used when finding present value; also called *opportunity cost*.

The basic present-value calculation is best illustrated using a simple example. Imagine that you are offered an opportunity that will provide you, one year from today, with exactly $1,000. If you could earn 8% on similar types of investments, how much is the most you would pay for this opportunity? In other words, what is the present value of $1,000 to be received one year from now, discounted at 8%? Letting x equal the present value, we can use Equation 4A.3 to describe this situation.

Equation 4A.3 ➤

$$x \times (1 + 0.08) = \$1,000$$

Solving Equation 4A.3 for x, we get:

Equation 4A.4 ➤

$$x = \frac{\$1,000}{(1 + 0.08)} = \underline{\underline{\$925.93}}$$

Thus, the present value of $1,000 to be received one year from now, discounted at 8%, is $925.93. In other words, $925.93 deposited today into an account paying 8% interest will accumulate to $1,000 in one year. To check this conclusion, *multiply* the future-value interest factor for 8% and 1 period (in this case, a year), or 1.080 (from Appendix A, Table A.1), by $925.93. The result is a future value of $1,000 (1.080 × $925.93).

The calculations involved in finding the present value of sums to be received in the distant future are more complex than those for a one-year investment. Here we use either tables of present-value interest factors to simplify these calculations, a financial calculator, or an Excel spreadsheet. (A complete set of these tables appears in Appendix A, Table A.3.)

TABLE USE The factors in Appendix A, Table A.3 represent the present value of $1 associated with various combinations of periods (years) and discount (interest) rates. For example, the present value factor for $1 to be received one period from now discounted at 8% is 0.926. We can find the present value of $1,000 to be received one year from now at an 8% discount rate by *multiplying* this factor (0.926) by $1,000. The resulting present value of $926 (0.926 × $1,000) agrees (except for a slight rounding difference) with the value calculated in Equation 4A.4.

Another example may help clarify the use of present-value tables. The present value of $500 to be received seven years from now, discounted at 6%, is calculated as follows:

$$\text{Present value} = 0.665 \times \$500 = \underline{\$332.50}$$

The 0.665 represents the present-value interest factor from Appendix A, Table A.3 for seven years discounted at 6%.

A few points with respect to Appendix A, Table A.3, Present-Value Interest Factors for One Dollar, should be emphasized:

1. The present-value interest factor for a single sum is always less than 1. Only if the discount rate were zero would this factor equal 1.
2. The higher the discount rate for a given period, the smaller the present-value interest factor. In other words, the greater your opportunity cost, the less you have to invest today in order to have a given amount in the future.
3. The further in the future a sum is to be received, the less it is worth at present.
4. At a discount rate of 0%, the present-value interest factor always equals 1. Therefore, in such a case the future value of a sum equals its present value.

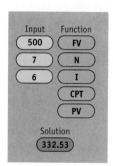

CALCULATOR USE Using the financial calculator inputs shown at the left, we find the present value of $500 to be received seven years from now, discounted at 6%, to be $332.53. This value is slightly more precise than that found using the table, but for our purposes the difference is insignificant.

SPREADSHEET USE The present value of the single future amount also can be calculated as shown on the following Excel spreadsheet.

	A	B
1	**PRESENT VALUE OF A SINGLE FUTURE AMOUNT**	
2	Future value	$500
3	Interest rate, pct per year compounded annually	6%
4	Number of years	7
5	Present value	$332.53
	Entry in Cell B5 is =−PV(B3,B4,0,B2). The minus sign appears before PV to change the present value to a positive amount.	

The Present Value of a Stream of Returns

In the preceding paragraphs we illustrated the technique for finding the present value of a single sum to be received at some future date. Because the returns from a given investment are likely to be received at *various* future dates rather than as a single lump sum, we also need to be able to find the present value of a *stream of returns*.

mixed stream
a stream of returns that, unlike an annuity, exhibits no special pattern.

A stream of returns can be viewed as a package of single-sum returns; it may be classified as a mixed stream or an annuity. A **mixed stream** of returns is one that exhibits no special pattern. As noted earlier, an *annuity* is a stream of equal periodic returns. Table 4A.4 shows the end-of-year returns illustrating each of these types of patterns. To find the present value of each of these streams (measured at the *beginning* of 2008), we must calculate the total of the present values of the individual annual returns. Because shortcuts can be used for an annuity, we will illustrate calculation of the present value of each type of return stream separately.

▮ Present Value of a Mixed Stream

To find the present value of the mixed stream of returns given in Table 4A.4, we must find and then total the present values of the individual returns. Assuming a 9% discount rate, we can streamline the calculation of the present value of the mixed stream using financial tables, a financial calculator, or an Excel spreadsheet.

TABLE USE Table A.3 in Appendix A can be used to find the appropriate present-value interest factors for each of the five years of the mixed stream's life at the 9% discount rate. Table 4A.5 (on page 206) demonstrates the use of these factors (shown in column 2), with the corresponding year's return (shown in column 1), to calculate the present value of each year's return (shown in column 3). The total of the present values of the returns for each of the five years is found by summing column 3. The resulting present value of $187.77 represents the amount today (*beginning* of 2008) that, invested at 9%, would provide the same returns as those shown in column 1 of Table 4A.5.

CALCULATOR USE You can use a financial calculator to find the present value of each individual return, as demonstrated on page 204. You then sum the present values to get the present value of the stream. However, most financial

EXCEL with SPREADSHEETS

TABLE 4A.4 Mixed and Annuity Return Streams

End of Year	Returns	
	Mixed Stream	Annuity
2008	$30	$50
2009	40	50
2010	50	50
2011	60	50
2012	70	50

EXCEL with SPREADSHEETS

TABLE 4A.5 Mixed-Stream Present-Value Calculation

End of Year	(1) Return	(2) 9% Present-Value Interest Factor	(3) (1) × (2) Present Value
2008	$30	.917	$ 27.51
2009	40	.842	33.68
2010	50	.772	38.60
2011	60	.708	42.48
2012	70	.650	45.50
		Present value of stream	$187.77

Note: Column 1 values are from Table 4A.4. Column 2 values are from Appendix A, Table A.3, for a 9% discount rate and 1 through 5 periods (years).

calculators have a function that allows you to punch in *all returns* (typically referred to as *cash flows*), specify the discount rate, and then directly calculate the present value of the entire return stream. Because calculators provide solutions more precise than those based on rounded table factors, the present value of the mixed stream of returns in Table 4A.4, found using a calculator, will be close to, but not precisely equal to, the $187.77 (see Table 4A.5).

SPREADSHEET USE The present value of the mixed stream of returns also can be calculated as shown on the following Excel spreadsheet.

	A	B
1	PRESENT VALUE OF A MIXED STREAM OF RETURNS	
2	Discount Rate, pct/year	9%
3	Year	Year-End Return
4	1	$30
5	2	$40
6	3	$50
7	4	$60
8	5	$70
9	Present value	$187.80

Entry in Cell B9 is =NPV(B2,B4:B8).

Investing about $188 would provide exactly a 9% return.

▪ Present Value of an Annuity

We can find the present value of an annuity in the same way as the present value of a mixed stream. Fortunately, however, there are simpler approaches. Here we simplify our calculations by using either tables of these factors for an annuity, a financial calculator, or an Excel spreadsheet. (A complete set of these tables appears in Appendix A, Table A.4.)

TABLE USE The factors in Appendix A, Table A.4 represent the present value of a $1 annuity for various periods (years) and discount (interest) rates. For example, the present value of $1 to be received at the end of each year for the next five years discounted at 9% is $3.890. Using the present-value interest factor for a five-year annuity discounted at 9% (3.890), we can find the present value of the $50, five-year annuity (given in Table 4A.4) at a 9% discount rate: We *multiply* the annual return by the appropriate interest factor. The resulting present value is $194.50 (3.890 × $50).

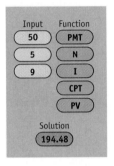

CALCULATOR USE Using the calculator inputs shown at the left, we find the present value of the $50, five-year ordinary annuity of returns, discounted at a 9% annual rate, to be $194.48. (*Note:* Because the return stream is an annuity, the annual return is input using the **PMT** key rather than the **FV** key, which we used for finding the present value of a single return.) The value obtained with the calculator is slightly more accurate than the answer found using the table.

SPREADSHEET USE The present value of the annuity of returns also can be calculated as shown on the following Excel spreadsheet.

	A	B
1	**PRESENT VALUE OF ANNUITY RETURNS**	
2	Annual return	$50
3	Annual discount rate, compounded annually	9%
4	Number of years	5
5	Present value of an ordinary annuity	$194.48

Entry in Cell B5 is =PV(B3,B4,–B2).
The minus sign appears before B2 because
the annual return is a cash outflow.

CONCEPTS IN REVIEW

Answers available at: www.myfinancelab.com

4A.1 What is the *time value of money?* Explain why an investor should be able to earn a positive return.

4A.2 Define, discuss, and contrast the following terms.
    a. Interest   b. Simple interest
    c. Compound interest   d. True rate of interest (or return)

4A.3 When interest is compounded more frequently than annually at a stated rate, what happens to the *true rate of interest?* Under what condition would the stated and true rates of interest be equal? What is *continuous compounding?*

4A.4 Describe, compare, and contrast the concepts of *future value* and *present value.* Explain the role of the *discount rate* in calculating present value.

4A.5 What is an *annuity?* How can calculation of the future value of an annuity be simplified? What about the present value of an annuity?

4A.6 What is a *mixed stream* of returns? Describe the procedure used to find the present value of such a stream.

Summary

Because investors have opportunities to earn interest on their funds, money has a time value. Interest can be applied using either simple interest or compound interest. The more frequently interest is compounded at a stated rate, the higher the true rate of interest. Financial tables, financial calculators, and computers and spreadsheets can be used to streamline time-value calculations. The future value of a present sum or an annuity can be found using compound interest concepts.

The present value of a future sum is the amount that would have to be deposited today, into an account earning interest at a given rate, to accumulate the specified future sum. The present value of streams of future returns can be found by adding the present values of the individual returns. When the stream is an annuity, its present value can be more simply calculated.

Key Terms

annuity, *p. 202*
compound interest, *p. 196*
continuous compounding, *p. 198*
discount rate, *p. 203*
future value, *p. 200*
interest, *p. 196*

mixed stream, *p. 205*
ordinary annuity, *p. 202*
present value, *p. 203*
simple interest, *p. 196*
time value of money, *p. 196*
true rate of interest (return), *p. 196*

Problems

P4A.1 For each of the savings account transactions in the accompanying table, calculate the following.
   a. End-of-year account balance. (Assume that the account balance at December 31, 2007, is zero.)
   b. Annual interest, using 6% simple interest and assuming all interest is withdrawn from the account as it is earned.
   c. True rate of interest, and compare it to the stated rate of interest. Discuss your finding.

Date	Deposit (Withdrawal)	Date	Deposit (Withdrawal)
1/1/08	$5,000	1/1/10	$2,000
1/1/09	(4,000)	1/1/11	3,000

P4A.2 Using the appropriate table of interest factors found in Appendix A or a financial calculator, calculate the following.
   a. The future value of a $300 deposit left in an account paying 7% annual interest for 12 years.
   b. The future value at the end of 6 years of an $800 *annual* end-of-year deposit into an account paying 7% annual interest.

P4A.3 For each of the following initial investment amounts, calculate the future value at the end of the given investment period if interest is compounded annually at the specified rate of return over the given investment period.

Investment	Investment Amount	Rate of Return	Investment Period
A	$ 200	5%	20 years
B	4,500	8	7
C	10,000	9	10
D	25,000	10	12
E	37,000	11	5

P4A.4 Using the appropriate table of interest factors found in Appendix A or a financial calculator, calculate the future value in 2 years of $10,000 invested today in an account that pays a stated annual interest rate of 12%, compounded monthly.

P4A.5 For each of the following annual deposits into an account paying the stated annual interest rate over the specified deposit period, calculate the future value of the *annuity* at the end of the given deposit period.

Deposit	Amount of Annual Deposit	Interest Rate	Deposit Period
A	$ 2,500	8%	10 years
B	500	12	6
C	1,000	20	5
D	12,000	6	8
E	4,000	14	30

P4A.6 If you deposit $1,000 into an account at the end of each of the next 5 years, and the account pays an annual interest rate of 6%, how much will be in the account after 5 years?

P4A.7 If you could earn 9% on similar-risk investments, what is the least you would accept at the end of a 6-year period, given the following amounts and timing of your investment?
  a. Invest $5,000 as a lump sum today.
  b. Invest $2,000 at the end of *each* of the next 5 years.
  c. Invest a lump sum of $3,000 today and $1,000 at the end of *each* of the next 5 years.
  d. Invest $900 at the end of years 1, 3, and 5.

P4A.8 For each of the following investments, calculate the present value of the future sum, using the specified discount rate and assuming the sum will be received at the end of the given year.

Investment	Future Sum	Discount Rate	End of Year
A	$ 7,000	12%	4
B	28,000	8	20
C	10,000	14	12
D	150,000	11	6
E	45,000	20	8

P4A.9 A Florida state savings bond can be converted to $1,000 at maturity 8 years from purchase. If the state bonds are to be competitive with U.S. savings bonds, which pay 6% interest compounded annually, at what price will the state's bonds sell, assuming they make no cash payments prior to maturity?

P4A.10 Referring to Problem 4A.9 above, at what price would the bond sell if U.S. savings bonds were paying 8% interest compounded annually? Compare your answer to your answer to the preceding problem.

P4A.11 How much should you be willing to pay for a lump sum of $10,000 5 years from now if you can earn 3% every 6 months on other similar investments?

P4A.12 Find the present value of each of the following streams of income, assuming a 12% discount rate.

A		B		C	
End of Year	Income	End of Year	Income	End of Year	Income
1	$2,200	1	$10,000	1-5	$10,000/yr
2	3,000	2-5	5,000/yr	6-10	8,000/yr
3	4,000	6	7,000		
4	6,000				
5	8,000				

P4A.13 Consider the streams of income given in the following table.
   a. Find the present value of each income stream, using a 15% discount rate.
   b. Compare the calculated present values and discuss them in light of the fact that the undiscounted total income amounts to $10,000 in each case.

	Income Stream	
End of Year	A	B
1	$ 4,000	$ 1,000
2	3,000	2,000
3	2,000	3,000
4	1,000	4,000
Total	$10,000	$10,000

P4A.14 For each of the investments below, calculate the present value of the *annual* end-of-year returns at the specified discount rate over the given period.

Investment	Annual Returns	Discount Rate	Period
A	$ 1,200	7%	3 years
B	5,500	12	15
C	700	20	9
D	14,000	5	7
E	2,200	10	5

P4A.15 Congratulations! You have won the lottery! Would you rather have $1 million at the end of each of the next 20 years or $15 million today? (Assume an 8% discount rate.)

P4A.16 Using the appropriate table of interest factors found in Appendix A, a financial calculator, or an Excel spreadsheet, calculate the following.
   a. The present value of $500 to be received 4 years from now, using an 11% discount rate.
   b. The present value of the following end-of-year income streams, using a 9% discount rate and assuming it is now the beginning of 2009.

End of Year	Income Stream A	Income Stream B
2009	$80	$140
2010	80	120
2011	80	100
2012	80	80
2013	80	60
2014	80	40
2015	80	20

P4A.17 Terri Allessandro has an opportunity to make any of the following investments. The purchase price, the amount of its lump-sum future value, and its year of receipt are given below for each investment. Terri can earn a 10% rate of return on investments similar to those currently under consideration. Evaluate each investment to determine whether it is satisfactory, and make an investment recommendation to Terri.

Investment	Purchase Price	Future Value	Year of Receipt
A	$18,000	$30,000	5
B	600	3,000	20
C	3,500	10,000	10
D	1,000	15,000	40

P4A.18 Kent Weitz wishes to assess whether the following two investments are satisfactory. Use his required return (discount rate) of 17% to evaluate each investment. Make an investment recommendation to Kent.

	Investment	
	A	B
Purchase price	$13,000	$8,500
End of Year	Income Stream	
1	$2,500	$4,000
2	3,500	3,500
3	4,500	3,000
4	5,000	1,000
5	5,500	500

P4A.19 You purchased a car using some cash and borrowing $15,000 (the present value) for 50 months at 12% per year. Calculate the monthly payment (annuity).

P4A.20 Referring to Problem 4A.19 above, assume you have made 10 payments. What is the balance (present value) of your loan?

Chapter 5

Modern Portfolio Concepts

After studying this chapter, you should be able to:

LG 1 Understand portfolio objectives and the procedures used to calculate portfolio return and standard deviation.

LG 2 Discuss the concepts of correlation and diversification, and the key aspects of international diversification.

LG 3 Describe the components of risk and the use of beta to measure risk.

LG 4 Explain the capital asset pricing model (CAPM)—conceptually, mathematically, and graphically.

LG 5 Review the traditional and modern approaches to portfolio management.

LG 6 Describe portfolio betas, the risk-return tradeoff, and reconciliation of the two approaches to portfolio management.

S ome would call it skilled stock picking. Others may say it's a way to ride cyclically hot sectors of the market. Whatever label one applies to the methodology, the returns generated by Neil Hennessy's quantitative approach to investing have recently trounced those of many actively managed funds that rely on more complex, fundamentals-driven techniques.

The 50-year-old president and portfolio manager of the Hennessy Funds avoids emotions, letting his quantitative screens do the stock picking. "The secret is really staying highly disciplined," he says. This method has helped make one of Hennessy's six funds a star. The $288 million Focus 30 fund (HFTFX) was the top-performing mid-cap growth fund for the one-year period through March 31, 2006, with a gain of 44.5%, double the return of its peers. The fund screens for stocks with market capitalization of $1 to $10 billion, price-to-sales ratio below 1.5, annual earnings up from the previous year, and the best relative strength over a 12-month period. Hennessey's other funds focus on different screening criteria, though they too follow strict formula-driven strategies.

Once a portfolio is allocated according to formula, the Hennessy Fund keeps the same stocks for approximately one year, then runs the screens again and constructs a new portfolio for each of the six funds. The approach, according to Hennessy, takes the hand-wringing and guesswork out of investing. He retools each portfolio once a year because "you need to give stocks at least a year to work out." He doesn't announce the exact rebalancing dates, which differ from fund to fund, because he doesn't want outside speculators to try to profit from changes to the portfolio.

Individuals who choose to build their own portfolios must answer some of the same questions as the professionals. How should I allocate my assets among fixed-income securities, equities, and cash? Is my portfolio diversified enough? What investment strategy or style should I follow? As we'll see in this chapter, understanding your investment objectives and developing appropriate strategies are the way to build your own portfolio.

Sources: Marla Brill, "This Guy Has a Hot Hand," *Financial Advisor Magazine,* February 2006; "The Importance of Staying Disciplined," April 26, 2006, downloaded from **http://www.businessweek.com/investor/content/apr2006/pi20060426_639078.htm?** (accessed July 2006).

Principles of Portfolio Planning

growth-oriented portfolio
a portfolio whose primary objective is long-term price appreciation.

income-oriented portfolio
a portfolio that stresses current dividend and interest returns.

efficient portfolio
a portfolio that provides the highest return for a given level of risk or that has the lowest risk for a given level of return.

Investors benefit from holding portfolios of investments rather than single investment vehicles. Without sacrificing returns, investors who hold portfolios can reduce risk, often to a level below that of any of the investments held in isolation. In other words, when it comes to portfolios and risk, $1 + 1 < 1$.

As defined in Chapter 1, a *portfolio* is a collection of investment vehicles assembled to meet one or more investment goals. Of course, different investors have different objectives for their portfolios. The primary goal of a **growth-oriented portfolio** is long-term price appreciation. An **income-oriented portfolio** stresses current dividend and interest returns.

■ Portfolio Objectives

Setting portfolio objectives involves definite tradeoffs: between risk and return, between potential price appreciation and current income, and between varying risk levels in the portfolio. These will depend on your tax bracket, current income needs, and ability to bear risk. The key point is that your portfolio objectives must be established *before* you begin to invest.

The ultimate goal of an investor is an **efficient portfolio**, one that provides the highest return for a given level of risk or that has the lowest risk for a given level of return. Efficient portfolios aren't necessarily obvious: You usually must search out investment alternatives to get the best combinations of risk and return.

■ Portfolio Return and Standard Deviation

The return on a portfolio is calculated as a weighted average of returns on the assets (investment vehicles) from which it is formed. The portfolio return, r_p, can be found by using Equation 5.1:

Equation 5.1 ➤

$$\text{Return on portfolio} = \begin{pmatrix} \text{Proportion of portfolio's total dollar value represented by asset 1} \times \text{Return on asset 1} \end{pmatrix} + \begin{pmatrix} \text{Proportion of portfolio's total dollar value represented by asset 2} \times \text{Return on asset 2} \end{pmatrix} + \cdots + \begin{pmatrix} \text{Proportion of portfolio's total dollar value represented by asset } n \times \text{Return on asset } n \end{pmatrix} = \sum_{j=1}^{n} \begin{pmatrix} \text{Proportion of portfolio's total dollar value represented by asset } j \times \text{Return on asset } j \end{pmatrix}$$

Equation 5.1a ➤

$$r_p = (w_1 \times r_1) + (w_2 \times r_2) + \cdots + (w_n \times r_n) = \sum_{j=1}^{n}(w_j \times r_j)$$

Of course, $\sum_{j=1}^{n} w_j = 1$, which means that 100% of the portfolio's assets must be included in this computation.

TABLE 5.1 Expected Return, Average Return, and Standard Deviation of Returns for Portfolio XY

A. Expected Portfolio Returns

	(1)	(2)	(3)	(4)
	Expected Return			Expected Portfolio Return, r_p
Year	Asset X	Asset Y	Portfolio Return Calculation*	
2009	8%	16%	$(.50 \times 8\%) + (.50 \times 16\%) =$	12%
2010	10	14	$(.50 \times 10) + (.50 \times 14) =$	12
2011	12	12	$(.50 \times 12) + (.50 \times 12) =$	12
2012	14	10	$(.50 \times 14) + (.50 \times 10) =$	12
2013	16	8	$(.50 \times 16) + (.50 \times 8) =$	12

B. Average Expected Portfolio Return, 2009–2013

$$\bar{r}_p = \frac{12\% + 12\% + 12\% + 12\% + 12\%}{5} = \frac{60\%}{5} = \underline{12\%}$$

C. Standard Deviation of Expected Portfolio Returns**

$$s_p = \sqrt{\frac{(12\% - 12\%)^2 + (12\% - 12\%)^2 + (12\% - 12\%)^2 + (12\% - 12\%)^2 + (12\% - 12\%)^2}{5 - 1}}$$

$$= \sqrt{\frac{0\% + 0\% + 0\% + 0\% + 0\%}{4}} = \sqrt{\frac{0\%}{4}} = \underline{\underline{0\%}}$$

*Using Equation 5.1.
**Using Equation 4.6 presented in Chapter 4.

The *standard deviation of a portfolio's returns* is found by applying Equation 4.6, the formula we used to find the standard deviation of a single asset. Assume that we wish to determine the return and standard deviation of returns for portfolio XY, created by combining equal portions (50%) of assets X and Y. The expected returns of assets X and Y for each of the next five years (2009–2013) are given in columns 1 and 2, in part A of Table 5.1. In columns 3 and 4, the weights of 50% for both assets X and Y, along with their respective returns from columns 1 and 2, are substituted into Equation 5.1 to get an expected portfolio return of 12% for each year, 2009 to 2013. As shown in part B of Table 5.1, the average expected portfolio return, $\bar{r}_p$, over the five-year period is also 12%. Substituting into Equation 4.6, we calculate Portfolio XY's standard deviation, s_p, of 0% in part C of Table 5.1. This value should not be surprising. Because the expected return each year is the same (12%), no variability is exhibited in the expected returns from year to year shown in column 4 of part A of the table.

■ Correlation and Diversification

As noted in Chapter 2, *diversification* involves the inclusion of a number of different investment vehicles in a portfolio. It is an important aspect of creating an efficient portfolio. Underlying the intuitive appeal of diversification is the statistical concept of *correlation*. For effective portfolio planning, you need to understand the concepts of correlation and diversification and their relationship to a portfolio's total risk and return.

FIGURE 5.1

The Correlation Between Series M, N, and P

The perfectly positively correlated series M and P in the graph on the left move exactly together. The perfectly negatively correlated series M and N in the graph on the right move in exactly opposite directions.

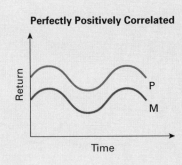

Perfectly Positively Correlated

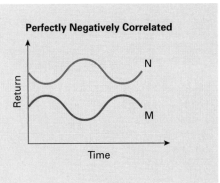

Perfectly Negatively Correlated

---

correlation
a statistical measure of the relationship, if any, between series of numbers representing data of any kind.

positively correlated
describes two series that move in the same direction.

negatively correlated
describes two series that move in opposite directions.

correlation coefficient
a measure of the degree of correlation between two series.

perfectly positively correlated
describes two positively correlated series that have a correlation coefficient of +1.

perfectly negatively correlated
describes two negatively correlated series that have a correlation coefficient of −1.

uncorrelated
describes two series that lack any relationship or interaction and therefore have a correlation coefficient close to zero.

Correlation Correlation is a statistical measure of the relationship, if any, between series of numbers representing data of any kind. If two series move in the same direction, they are **positively correlated**. If the series move in opposite directions, they are **negatively correlated**.

The degree of correlation—whether positive or negative—is measured by the **correlation coefficient**. Given adequate data points for each series, investors can use a financial calculator or Excel spreadsheet to do linear regression with very little effort, and the correlation coefficient is effectively a byproduct of that calculation. Because our focus is intuitive rather than quantitative, we do not demonstrate the calculation of the correlation coefficient here.

The correlation coefficient ranges from +1 for **perfectly positively correlated** series to −1 for **perfectly negatively correlated** series. These two extremes are depicted in Figure 5.1 for series M, N, and P. The perfectly positively correlated series (M and P) move exactly together. The perfectly negatively correlated series (M and N) move in exactly opposite directions. Although the following discussions give equal attention to both positively and negatively correlated series, *the correlations between most asset returns exhibit some degree (ranging from high to low) of positive correlation.* Negative correlation is the exception.

Diversification To reduce overall risk in a portfolio, it is best to combine assets that have a negative (or a low-positive) correlation. Combining negatively correlated assets can reduce the overall variability of returns, *s*, or risk. Figure 5.2 (on page 216) shows negatively correlated assets F and G, both having the same average expected return, $\bar{r}$. The portfolio that contains those negatively correlated assets also has the same return, $\bar{r}$, but has less risk (variability) than either of the individual assets. Even if assets are not negatively correlated, the lower the positive correlation between them, the lower the resulting risk.

Some assets are **uncorrelated**: They are completely unrelated, with no interaction between their returns. Combining uncorrelated assets can reduce risk—not as effectively as combining negatively correlated assets, but more effectively than combining positively correlated assets. The correlation coefficient for uncorrelated assets is close to zero and acts as the midpoint between perfect positive and perfect negative correlation.

Correlation is important to reducing risk, but it can do only so much. A portfolio of two assets that have perfectly positively correlated returns *cannot*

FIGURE 5.2

Combining Negatively Correlated Assets to Diversify Risk

The risk or variability of returns, resulting from combining negatively correlated assets F and G, both having the same expected return, $\bar{r}$, results in a portfolio (shown in the right-most graph) with the same level of expected return but less risk.

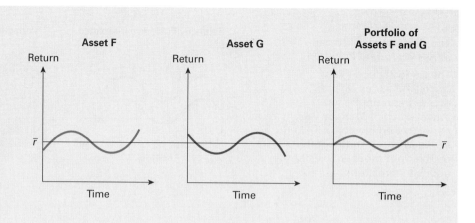

reduce the portfolio's overall risk below the risk of the less risky asset. However, a portfolio combining two assets with less than perfectly positive correlation *can* reduce total risk to a level below that of either of the components, which in certain situations may be zero.

For example, assume you own the stock of a machine tool manufacturer that is very *cyclical*. This company has high earnings when the economy is expanding and low earnings during a recession. If you bought stock in another machine tool company, which would have earnings positively correlated with those of the stock you already own, the combined earnings would continue to be cyclical. The risk would remain the same.

As an alternative, however, you could buy stock in a sewing machine manufacturer, which is *countercyclical*. It typically has low earnings during economic expansion and high earnings during recession. Combining the machine tool stock and the sewing machine stock should reduce risk: The low machine tool earnings during a recession would be balanced out by high sewing machine earnings, and vice versa.

A numeric example will provide an even better understanding. Table 5.2 presents the expected returns from three different assets—X, Y, and Z—over the next five years (2009–2013), along with their average returns and standard deviations. Each of the assets has an expected value of return of 12% and a standard deviation of 3.16%. The assets therefore have equal return and equal risk, although their return patterns are not identical. The returns of assets X and Y are perfectly negatively correlated—they move in exactly opposite directions over time. The returns of assets X and Z are perfectly positively correlated—they move in precisely the same direction. (The returns for X and Z are identical, although it is not necessary for return streams to be identical for them to be perfectly positively correlated.)

Portfolio XY (shown in Table 5.2) combines equal portions of assets X and Y—the perfectly negatively correlated assets. Calculation of portfolio XY's annual expected returns, average expected return, and the standard deviation of expected portfolio returns was demonstrated in Table 5.1. The risk of the portfolio created by this combination, as reflected in the standard deviation, is reduced to 0%, while its average return remains at 12%. Because both assets have the same average return, are combined in the optimal proportions (a 50–50 mix in this case), and are perfectly negatively correlated, the combination results in the complete elimination of risk. Whenever assets are perfectly nega-

TABLE 5.2 Expected Returns, Average Returns, and Standard Deviations for Assets X, Y, and Z and Portfolios XY and XZ

	Assets			Portfolios	
				XY*	XZ**
Year	X	Y	Z	(50%X + 50%Y)	(50%X + 50%Z)
2009	8%	16%	8%	12%	8%
2010	10	14	10	12	10
2011	12	12	12	12	12
2012	14	10	14	12	14
2013	16	8	16	12	16
Statistics:					
Average return[†]	12%	12%	12%	12%	12%
Standard deviation[‡]	3.16%	3.16%	3.16%	0%	3.16%

*Portfolio XY illustrates *perfect negative correlation,* because these two return streams behave in completely opposite fashion over the 5-year period. The return values shown here were calculated in part A of Table 5.1.

**Portfolio XZ illustrates *perfect positive correlation,* because these two return streams behave identically over the 5-year period. These return values were calculated using the same method demonstrated for portfolio XY in part A of Table 5.1.

[†]The average return for each asset is calculated as the arithmetic average found by dividing the sum of the returns for the years 2009–2013 by 5, the number of years considered.

[‡]Equation 4.6 was used to calculate the standard deviation. Calculation of the average return and standard deviation for portfolio XY is demonstrated in parts B and C, respectively, of Table 5.1. The portfolio standard deviation can be directly calculated from the standard deviation of the component assets using the following formula:

$$s_p = \sqrt{w_1^2 s_1^2 + w_2^2 s_2^2 + 2w_1 w_2 p_{1,2} s_1 s_2}$$

where w_1 and w_2 are the proportions of the component assets 1 and 2; s_1 and s_2 are the standard deviations of the component assets 1 and 2; and $p_{1,2}$ is the correlation coefficient between the returns of component assets 1 and 2.

tively correlated, an optimal combination (similar to this 50–50 mix of assets X and Y) exists for which the resulting standard deviation will equal 0.

Portfolio XZ (shown in Table 5.2) is created by combining equal portions of assets X and Z—the perfectly positively correlated assets. The risk of this portfolio, reflected by its standard deviation, which remains at 3.16%, is unaffected by this combination. Its average return remains at 12%. Whenever perfectly positively correlated assets (such as X and Z) are combined, the standard deviation of the resulting portfolio cannot be reduced below that of the least risky asset; the maximum portfolio standard deviation will be that of the riskiest asset. Because assets X and Z have the same standard deviation (3.16%), the minimum and maximum standard deviations are both 3.16%.

Impact on Risk and Return In general, the lower (less positive and more negative) the correlation between asset returns, the greater the potential diversification of risk. For each pair of assets, there is a combination that will result in the lowest risk (standard deviation) possible. *The amount of potential risk reduction for this combination depends on the degree of correlation of the two assets.* Many potential combinations could be made, given the expected return of the two assets, the standard deviation for each, and the correlation coefficient. However, *only one combination* of the infinite number of possibilities will minimize risk.

Three possible correlations—perfect positive, uncorrelated, and perfect negative—illustrate the effect of correlation on the diversification of risk and return. Table 5.3 (on page 218) summarizes the impact of correlation on the range of return and risk. The table shows that as you move from perfect positive correlation to perfect negative correlation, you reduce risk. Note that in

TABLE 5.3   **Correlation, Return, and Risk for Various Two-Asset Portfolio Combinations**

Correlation Coefficient	Range of Return	Range of Risk
+1 (perfect positive)	Between returns of two assets held in isolation.	Between risk of two assets held in isolation.
0 (uncorrelated)	Between returns of two assets held in isolation.	Between risk of most-risky asset and less than risk of least-risky asset, but greater than 0.
−1 (perfect negative)	Between returns of two assets held in isolation.	Between risk of most-risky asset and 0.

no case will a portfolio of assets have risk greater than that of the riskiest asset included in the portfolio.

To demonstrate, assume that a firm has carefully calculated the average return, $\bar{r}$, and risk, s, for each of two assets, A and B, as summarized below.

Asset	Average Return, $\bar{r}$	Risk (Standard Deviation), s
A	6%	3%
B	8%	8%

From these data, we can see that asset A is clearly a lower-risk, lower-return asset than asset B.

To evaluate possible combinations, let's consider three possible correlations: perfect positive, uncorrelated, and perfect negative. Figure 5.3 shows the results. The ranges of return and risk exhibited are consistent with those in

FIGURE 5.3

Range of Portfolio Return and Risk for Combinations of Assets A and B for Various Correlation Coefficients

The range of a portfolio's return (r_p) is between that of the lowest and highest component asset returns and is unaffected by the degree of asset correlation. Portfolio risk (s_p), on the other hand, can be reduced below the risk of the least-risky asset as the asset correlation moves from perfectly positive to uncorrelated to perfectly negative, where it can be reduced to zero by combining assets in the proper proportion.

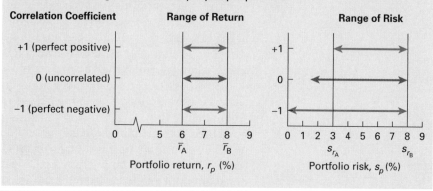

Risk and Return for All Combinations of Assets A and B for Various Correlation Coefficients

For each correlation coefficient there exist an infinite number of combinations of two assets A and B that result in many possible risk-return combinations, the ranges of which are consistent with those shown in Figure 5.3. The less positive and more negative the correlation, the greater the potential risk reduction.

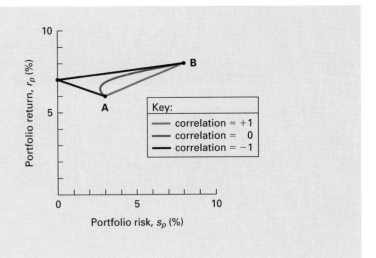

Table 5.3. In all cases, the return will range between the 6% return of A and the 8% return of B. The risk (standard deviation), on the other hand, has a wider variability. That variability depends on the degree of correlation: In the case of perfect positive correlation, the risk ranges between the individual risks of A and B (from 3% to 8%). In the uncorrelated case, the risk ranges from below 3% (the risk of A) but greater than 0%, to 8% (the risk of B). In the case of perfect negative correlation, the risk ranges between 0% and 8%.

Note that *only in the case of perfect negative correlation can the risk be reduced to 0%.* As the correlation becomes less positive and more negative (moving from the top of Figure 5.3 down), the ability to reduce risk improves. If we had numerous risk-return observations for each of the three correlations—perfect positive, uncorrelated, and perfect negative—we could plot all possible combinations of assets A and B for each correlation on a set of risk (s_p)-return (r_p) axes as shown in Figure 5.4. For each correlation coefficient, there exist an infinite number of combinations of the two assets A and B that result in numerous risk-return combinations, the range of which is consistent with that shown in Figure 5.3. The less positive and more negative the correlation, the greater the potential risk reduction. Again, it should be clear that for any two-asset portfolio, the ability to reduce risk depends on both the degree of correlation and the proportions of each asset in the portfolio.

Although determining the risk-minimizing combination is beyond the scope of this discussion, you should know that it is an important issue in developing portfolios of assets. The *Investing in Action* box on page 220 describes the success of student-managed portfolios. Later in this chapter we use modern portfolio theory to explain the risk-return combinations available from all possible portfolios.

▮ International Diversification

Diversification is clearly a primary consideration when constructing an investment portfolio. As noted earlier, many opportunities for international diversification are now available. Here we consider three aspects of international diversification: effectiveness, methods, and benefits.

INVESTING *in Action*

Student-Managed Portfolios Earn Top Grades

Imagine having $100,000 or more to invest while you are still in college—real money, not fantasy portfolios. According to the Association of Student-Managed Investment Programs at Florida's Stetson University, more than 110 colleges and universities allocate funds, often from endowment portfolios or alumni donations, to student portfolio managers.

Undergraduate students at the University of Dayton's Center for Portfolio Management, which was founded in 1999, manage a portfolio of more than $3 million, one of the country's largest student-managed portfolios. The Center offers a professional investment environment, complete with news feeds from cable financial and news channels, real-time stock quotes, opportunities to talk to securities analysts, and institutional-caliber portfolio management tools. As a result, explains David Sauer, associate professor of finance and founder of the Center, "[students get] the equivalent of two years or more of real work experience."

Dayton's students debate potential investment decisions; a two-thirds vote is required to take action. Portfolio assets are evenly divided between equities and fixed-income securities. The focus is typically mid-cap and large-cap companies, with each student following a particular industry.

In such programs, students learn first-hand about the realities of investment management,

including the considerable time and research needed to keep up with market trends, investigate new investment opportunities, and track portfolio holdings. "The added pressure makes people a lot more in tune with what's going on. You can't take a day off," Dayton's Rick Davis says.

How have student managers done? Dayton's teams have significantly outperformed the S&P 500, and other schools report similar results. Says Doug North, president of Alaska Pacific University, which has such a program, "When you thrust responsibility on students, they rise to the occasion."

CRITICAL THINKING QUESTION After reading the rest of this chapter, develop a brief proposal for a student-managed investment portfolio at your school.

Sources: Jim Bohman, "Executive to Donate $1M to UD," *Dayton Daily News*, May 13, 2003, p. D.1; Dee Klees, "Youthful Stocks and Bonds; Young Investors Study Market, Create Network," *The Post-Standard* (Syracuse), September 29, 2003, p. 5; Sarana Schell, "Analyze This: APU Students Master Global Finance by Investing Real Money," *Anchorage Daily News*, November 3, 2003, p. F1; and "Students Play the Market with Colleges' Money," *Houston Chronicle*, September 26, 2002, p. 2.

Effectiveness of International Diversification Investing internationally offers greater diversification than investing only domestically. That is true for U.S. investors. It is even truer for investors from countries with capital markets that offer much more limited diversification opportunities than are available in the United States.

However, does international diversification actually reduce risk, particularly the variability of rates of return? Two classic studies overwhelmingly support the argument that well-structured international diversification does indeed reduce the risk of a portfolio and increase the return on portfolios of comparable risk. One study looked at diversification across 12 European countries in seven different industries between 1978 and 1992. It found that an investor could actually reduce the risk of a portfolio much more by diversifying internationally *in the same industry* than by diversifying across industries within one country. If the investor diversified across both countries and industries, the opportunities for risk reduction were even greater.

Another study examined the risk-return performance between January 1984 and November 1994 of diversified stock portfolios: the S&P 500 in the United States and Morgan Stanley's Europe/Australia/Far East (EAFE) Index. It found that a 100% EAFE portfolio offered a much greater return than a 100% S&P 500 portfolio did—but at much greater risk. However, a portfolio composed of various combinations of the two indexes would have been better: It would have realized both lower risk and a higher return than did the 100% S&P 500 portfolio, and less risk and a moderately lower return than did the 100% EAFE portfolio. For the U.S. investor, a portfolio consisting of 70% S&P 500 coupled with 30% EAFE would have reduced risk by about 5% and increased return by about 7% (from around 14% to more than 15%). Or, for the same degree of risk, an investor could have increased return by about 18% (from around 14% to more than 16.5%).

Methods of International Diversification In later chapters we will examine a wide range of alternatives for international portfolio diversification. We will see that investors can make investments in bonds and other debt instruments in U.S. dollars or in foreign currencies—either directly or via foreign mutual funds. Foreign currency investment, however, brings currency exchange risk. This risk can be hedged with contracts such as currency forwards, futures, and options. Even if there is little or no currency exchange risk, investing abroad is generally less convenient, more expensive, and riskier than investing domestically. When making direct investments abroad, you must know what you're doing: You should have a clear idea of the benefits being sought and enough time to monitor foreign markets.

International diversification can also be achieved by U.S. domestic investments. Investors can buy stock of foreign companies listed on U.S. exchanges or over the counter. Many foreign issuers, both corporate and government, sell their bonds (called *Yankee bonds*) in the United States. The stocks of more than 2,000 foreign companies, from more than 50 different countries, trade in the United States in the form of American Depositary Shares (ADSs). Finally, international mutual funds (such as the Fidelity Japan Fund and the AIM Global Equity Fund) provide foreign investment opportunities.

It is important to realize that international diversification typically cannot be achieved by investing in U.S. multinationals. Although U.S.-based firms with major foreign operations may generate sizable revenues and profits abroad, most of their costs and expenses—particularly labor costs—are incurred in the United States. Thus, the firm's behavior tends to be more U.S.-driven than foreign-driven. The multinational firm's results tend to be positively correlated with those in the domestic market. The strategy of investing in domestic companies that have major foreign operations therefore is generally not as effective as investing in foreign companies in the given country.

Benefits of International Diversification Can you find greater returns overseas than in the United States? Yes! Can you reduce a portfolio's risk by including foreign investments? Yes! Is international diversification desirable for you? We don't know! A successful global investment strategy depends on many things, just as a purely domestic strategy does. Included are factors such as your resources, goals, sophistication, and psychology. What percentage of your portfolio you allocate to foreign investments depends on your overall investment goals and risk preferences. Commonly cited allocations to foreign investments are about 20% to 30%, with two-thirds of this allocation in established foreign markets and the other one-third in emerging markets.

In general, you should avoid investing directly in foreign-currency-denominated instruments. Unless the magnitude of each foreign investment is in hundreds of thousands of dollars, the transactions costs will tend to be high. A safer choice for international diversification would be international mutual funds, which offer diversified foreign investments and the professional expertise of fund managers. ADSs can be used by those who want to make foreign investments in individual stocks. With either mutual funds or ADSs, you can obtain international diversification along with low cost, convenience, transactions in U.S. dollars, protection under U.S. security laws, and (usually) attractive markets.

We should not leave this topic without saying that some of the benefits of international diversification are diminishing over time. Technological advances in communication have greatly improved the quality of information on foreign companies. Participation by a growing number of better-informed investors in the foreign markets continues to reduce the opportunities to earn "excess" returns on the additional risk embodied in foreign investments, thereby leveling the playing field. However, the relatively low correlation of returns in Asian and emerging markets with U.S. returns continues to make international investments appealing as a way to diversify your portfolio. Today, an important motive for international investment is portfolio diversification rather than realizing sizable excess returns.

CONCEPTS IN REVIEW
Answers available at: www.myfinancelab.com

5.1   What is an *efficient portfolio*, and what role should such a portfolio play in investing?

5.2   How can the return and standard deviation of a portfolio be determined? Compare the portfolio standard deviation calculation to that for a single asset.

5.3   What is *correlation*, and why is it important with respect to asset returns? Describe the characteristics of returns that are (a) positively correlated, (b) negatively correlated, and (c) uncorrelated. Differentiate between *perfect positive correlation* and *perfect negative correlation*.

5.4   What is *diversification?* How does the diversification of risk affect the risk of the portfolio compared to the risk of the individual assets it contains?

5.5   Discuss how the correlation between asset returns affects the risk and return behavior of the resulting portfolio. Describe the potential range of risk and return when the correlation between two assets is (a) perfectly positive, (b) uncorrelated, and (c) perfectly negative.

5.6   What benefit, if any, does international diversification offer the individual investor? Compare and contrast the methods of achieving international diversification by investing abroad versus investing domestically.

The Capital Asset Pricing Model (CAPM)

LG 3   LG 4

From an investor's perspective, the relevant risk is the *inescapable risk* of the firm. This risk significantly affects the returns earned and the value of the firm in the financial marketplace. As you'll learn in Chapter 8, the firm's value is directly determined by its risk and the associated return. The basic theory that links return and the relevant risk for all assets is the *capital asset pricing model (CAPM)*.

▮ Components of Risk

diversifiable (unsystematic) risk
the portion of an investment's risk that results from uncontrollable or random events that are firm-specific; can be eliminated through diversification.

nondiversifiable (systematic) risk
the inescapable portion of an investment's risk attributable to forces that affect all investments and therefore are not unique to a given vehicle.

The risk of an investment consists of two components: diversifiable and non-diversifiable risk. **Diversifiable risk**, sometimes called **unsystematic risk**, results from uncontrollable or random events that are firm-specific, such as labor strikes, lawsuits, and regulatory actions. It is the portion of an investment's risk that can be eliminated through diversification. **Nondiversifiable risk**, also called **systematic risk**, is the inescapable portion of an investment's risk. It is attributed to more general forces such as war, inflation, and political events that affect all investments and therefore are not unique to a given vehicle. The sum of nondiversifiable risk and diversifiable risk is called **total risk**.

Equation 5.2 ➤ | Total risk = Nondiversifiable risk + Diversifiable risk

total risk
the sum of an investment's *nondiversifiable risk* and *diversifiable risk*.

Any careful investor can reduce or virtually eliminate diversifiable risk by holding a diversified portfolio of securities. Studies have shown that investors can eliminate most diversifiable risk by carefully selecting a portfolio of 8 to 15 securities. Therefore, *the only relevant risk is nondiversifiable risk*, which is inescapable. Each security has its own unique level of nondiversifiable risk, which we can measure, as we'll show in the following section.

▮ Beta: A Popular Measure of Risk

During the past 40 years, the finance discipline has developed much theory on the measurement of risk and its use in assessing returns. The two key components of this theory are *beta*, which is a measure of risk, and the *capital asset pricing model (CAPM)*, which uses beta to estimate return.

beta
a measure of *nondiversifiable*, or *market*, *risk* that indicates how the price of a security responds to market forces.

First we will look at **beta**, a number that measures *nondiversifiable*, or *market*, *risk*. Beta indicates how the price of a security responds to market forces. The more responsive the price of a security is to changes in the market, the higher that security's beta. Beta is found by relating the historical returns for a security to the market return. **Market return** is the average return for all (or a large sample of) stocks. Analysts commonly use the average return on all stocks in the *Standard & Poor's 500-Stock Composite Index* or some other broad stock index to measure market return. You don't have to calculate betas yourself; you can easily obtain them for actively traded securities from a variety of published and online sources. But you should understand how betas are derived, how to interpret them, and how to apply them to portfolios.

market return
the average return for all (or a large sample of) stocks, such as those in the *Standard & Poor's 500-Stock Composite Index*.

FIGURE 5.5

Graphical Derivation of Beta for Securities C and D*

Betas can be derived graphically by plotting the coordinates for the market return and security return at various points in time and using statistical techniques to fit the "characteristic line" to the data points. The slope of the characteristic line is beta. For securities C and D, beta is found to be 0.80 and 1.30, respectively.

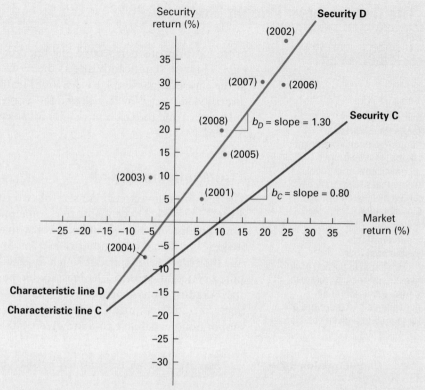

* All data points shown are associated with security D. No data points are shown for security C.

Deriving Beta We can demonstrate graphically the relationship between a security's return and the market return, and its use in deriving beta. Figure 5.5 plots the relationship between the returns of two securities, C and D, and the market return. Note that the horizontal (x) axis measures the historical market returns, and the vertical (y) axis measures the individual security's historical returns.

The first step in deriving beta is plotting the coordinates for the market return and the security return at various points in time. Figure 5.5 shows such annual market-return and security-return coordinates *for security D only* for the years 2001 through 2008 (the years are noted in parentheses). For example, in 2008, security D's return was 20% when the market return was 10%.

By use of statistical techniques, the "characteristic line" that best explains the relationship between security-return and market-return coordinates is fit to the data points. *The slope of this line is beta.* The beta for security C is about 0.80; for security D it is about 1.30. Security D's higher beta—steeper characteristic line slope—indicates that its return is more responsive to changing market returns. *Therefore security D is more risky than security C.*

Interpreting Beta The beta for the overall market is considered to be 1.00. All other betas are viewed in relation to this value. Table 5.4 shows some selected beta values and their associated interpretations. As you can see, betas can be positive or negative, though *nearly all betas are positive.* The positive or

TABLE 5.4   Selected Betas and Associated Interpretations

Beta	Comment	Interpretation
2.00 1.00 0.50	Move in same direction as the market	Twice as responsive as the market Same response as the market Only half as responsive as the market
0		Unaffected by market movement
−0.50 −1.00 −2.00	Move in opposite direction to the market	Only half as responsive as the market Same response as the market Twice as responsive as the market

negative sign preceding the beta number merely indicates whether the stock's return changes in the *same direction as the general market* (positive beta) or in the *opposite direction (*negative beta).

Most stocks have betas that fall between 0.50 and 1.75. The return of a stock that is half as responsive as the market ($b = 0.50$) is expected to change by ½ of 1% for each 1% change in the return of the market portfolio. A stock that is twice as responsive as the market ($b = 2.0$) is expected to experience a 2% change in its return for each 1% change in the return of the market port-folio. Listed here, for illustration purposes, are the actual betas for some pop-ular stocks, as reported by *Value Line Investment Survey* on July 21, 2006:

Stock	Beta	Stock	Beta
Amazon.com	1.35	Int'l Business Machines	1.05
Anheuser-Busch	0.65	Merrill Lynch & Co.	1.45
Bank of America Corp.	1.10	Microsoft	1.05
Colgate-Palmolive	0.55	Nike, Inc.	0.90
Disney	1.35	PepsiCo, Inc.	0.70
eBay	1.20	Qualcomm	1.10
ExxonMobil Corp.	0.90	Sempra Energy	1.05
Gap (The), Inc.	1.15	Wal-Mart Stores	0.80
General Motors Corp.	1.35	Xerox	1.40
Intel	1.25	Yahoo! Inc.	1.60

Many large brokerage firms, as well as subscription services like *Value Line,* publish betas for a broad range of securities. They also can be obtained online through sites such as finance.yahoo.com. The ready availability of secu-rity betas has enhanced their use in assessing investment risks. Later in this chapter we discuss the importance of beta in planning and building portfolios of securities.

Applying Beta   Individual investors will find beta useful. It can help in assess-ing market risk and in understanding the impact the market can have on the return expected from a share of stock. In short, beta reveals how a security responds to market forces. For example, if the market is expected to experience a 10% *increase* in its rate of return over the next period, we would expect a stock with a beta of 1.50 to experience an *increase* in return of about 15% ($1.50 \times 10\%$). Because its beta is greater than 1.00, this stock is more volatile than the market as a whole.

For stocks with positive betas, increases in market returns result in increases in security returns. Unfortunately, decreases in market returns are translated into decreasing security returns. In the preceding example, if the market is expected to experience a 10% *decrease* in its rate of return, then a stock with a beta of 1.50 should experience a 15% *decrease* in its return. Because the stock has a beta greater than 1.00, it is more responsive than the market, either up or down.

Stocks that have betas less than 1.00 are, of course, less responsive to changing returns in the market. They are therefore considered less risky. For example, a stock with a beta of 0.50 will increase or decrease its return by about half that of the market as a whole. Thus, if the market return went down by 8%, such a stock's return would probably experience only about a 4% ($0.50 \times 8\%$) decline.

Here are some important points to remember about beta:

- Beta measures the nondiversifiable (or market) risk of a security.
- The beta for the market is 1.00.
- Stocks may have positive or negative betas. Nearly all are positive.
- Stocks with betas greater than 1.00 are more responsive to changes in the market return and therefore are more risky than the market. Stocks with betas less than 1.00 are less risky than the market.
- Because of its greater risk, the higher a stock's beta, the greater its level of expected return.

■ The CAPM: Using Beta to Estimate Return

About 40 years ago, finance professors William F. Sharpe and John Lintner developed a model that uses beta to formally link the notions of risk and return. Called the **capital asset pricing model (CAPM)**, it explains the behavior of security prices. It also provides a mechanism whereby investors can assess the impact of a proposed security investment on their portfolio's risk and return.

capital asset pricing model (CAPM)
model that formally links the notions of risk and return; it uses beta, the risk-free rate, and the market return to help investors define the required return on an investment.

The CAPM can be viewed as an equation, in terms of historical risk premiums, and as a graph, as we show in the next sections.

The Equation With beta, *b*, as the measure of nondiversifiable risk, the capital asset pricing model defines the required return on an investment as follows.

Equation 5.3 ➤

$$\text{Required return on investment } j = \text{Risk-free rate} + \left[\text{Beta for investment } j \times \left(\text{Market return} - \text{Risk-free rate} \right) \right]$$

Equation 5.3a ➤

$$r_j = R_F + [b_j \times (r_m - R_F)]$$

where

r_j = the required return on investment j, given its risk as measured by beta

R_F = the risk-free rate of return; the return that can be earned on a risk-free investment

b_j = beta coefficient or index of nondiversifiable risk for investment j

r_m = the market return; the average return on all securities (typically measured by the average return on all securities in the Standard & Poor's 500-Stock Composite Index or some other broad stock market index)

The CAPM can be divided into two parts: (1) the risk-free rate of return, R_F, and (2) the *risk premium*, $b_j \times (r_m - R_F)$. The risk premium is the amount of return investors demand beyond the risk-free rate to compensate for the investment's nondiversifiable risk as measured by beta. The equation shows that *as beta increases, the risk premium increases, thereby causing the required return for the given investment to increase.*

We can demonstrate use of the CAPM with the following example. Assume you are considering security Z with a beta (b_Z) of 1.25. The risk-free rate (R_F) is 6% and the market return (r_m) is 10%. Substituting these data into the CAPM equation, Equation 5.3a, we get:

$$r_z = 6\% + [1.25 \times (10\% - 6\%)] = 6\% + [1.25 \times 4\%]$$

$$= 6\% + 5\% = \underline{11\%}$$

You should therefore expect—indeed, require—an 11% return on this investment as compensation for the risk you have to assume, given the security's beta of 1.25.

If the beta were lower, say 1.00, the required return would be lower:

$$r_z = 6\% + [1.00 \times (10\% - 6\%)] = 6\% + 4\% = \underline{10\%}$$

If the beta were higher, say 1.50, the required return would be higher:

$$r_z = 6\% + [1.50 \times (10\% - 6\%)] = 6\% + 6\% = \underline{12\%}$$

Clearly, the CAPM reflects the positive mathematical relationship between risk and return: The higher the risk (beta), the higher the risk premium, and therefore the higher the required return.

Historical Risk Premiums Using the historical return data for selected security investments for the 1926–2005 period shown in Chapter 4, Table 4.4 on page 162, we can calculate the risk premiums for each investment category. The calculation (consistent with Equation 5.3) involves merely subtracting the historical U.S. Treasury bill's average return (the assumed risk-free rate of return, R_F) from the historical average return for a given investment:

Investment	Risk Premium*
Large-company stocks	12.3% − 3.8% = 8.5%
Small-company stocks	17.4 − 3.8 = 13.6
Long-term corporate bonds	6.2 − 3.8 = 2.4
Long-term government bonds	5.8 − 3.8 = 2.0
U.S. Treasury bills	3.8 − 3.8 = 0.0

*Return values obtained from Chapter 4, Table 4.4 on page 162.

Reviewing the risk premiums calculated above, we can see that the risk premium is highest for small-company stocks, followed by large-company stocks, long-term corporate bonds, and long-term government bonds. This outcome makes sense intuitively because small-company stocks are riskier than large-company stocks, which are riskier than long-term corporate bonds (equity is riskier than debt investment). Long-term corporate bonds are riskier than long-term government bonds (because the government is less likely to renege on debt). And of course, U.S. Treasury bills, because of their lack of default risk and their very short maturity, are virtually risk-free, as indicated by their lack of any risk premium.

The Graph: The Security Market Line (SML)

security market line (SML)
the graphical depiction of the capital asset pricing model; reflects the investor's required return for each level of nondiversifiable risk, measured by beta.

When the capital asset pricing model is depicted graphically, it is called the **security market line (SML)**. Plotting the CAPM, we would find that the SML is, in fact, a straight line. For each level of nondiversifiable risk (beta), the SML reflects the required return the investor should earn in the marketplace.

We can plot the CAPM at a given point in time by simply calculating the required return for a variety of betas. For example, as we saw earlier, using a 6% risk-free rate and a 10% market return, the required return is 11% when the beta is 1.25. Increase the beta to 2.00, and the required return equals 14% ($6\% + [2.00 \times (10\% - 6\%)]$). Similarly, we can find the required return for a number of betas and end up with the following combinations of risk (beta) and required return.

Risk (beta)	Required Return
0.0	6%
0.5	8
1.0	10
1.5	12
2.0	14
2.5	16

Plotting these values on a graph (with beta on the horizontal axis and required returns on the vertical axis) would yield a straight line like the one in Figure 5.6. The shaded area shows the amount by which the required return exceeds the risk-free rate. It represents the risk premiums. It is clear from the SML that as risk (beta) increases, so do the risk premium and required return, and vice versa.

Some Closing Comments

The capital asset pricing model generally relies on historical data. The betas may or may not actually reflect the *future* variability of returns. Therefore, the required returns specified by the model can be viewed only as rough approximations. Analysts who use betas commonly make subjective adjustments to the historically determined betas to reflect their expectations of the future.

Is there a better model? Although CAPM has been widely accepted, a broader theory, **arbitrage pricing theory (APT)**, first described by Stephen A. Ross in 1976, has received a great deal of attention in the financial literature. APT suggests that the risk premium on securities may be better explained by a number of factors underlying and in some cases replacing the market return used in the CAPM. The CAPM, in effect, can be viewed as being derived from APT. As a result of APT's failure to identify other risk factors clearly, as well

arbitrage pricing theory (APT)
a theory that suggests that the market risk premium on securities may be better explained by a number of factors underlying and in some cases replacing the market return used in CAPM; the CAPM can be viewed as being derived from APT.

FIGURE 5.6

The Security Market Line (SML)

The security market line clearly depicts the tradeoff between risk and return. At a beta of 0, the required return is the risk-free rate of 6%. At a beta of 1.0, the required return is the market return of 10%. Given these data, the required return on an investment with a beta of 1.25 is 11% and its risk premium is 5% (11% − 6%).

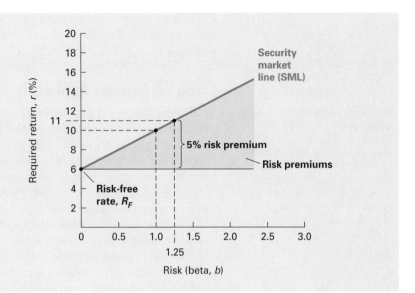

as APT's lack of practical acceptance and usage, attention remains focused on CAPM.

Despite its predictive limitations, the CAPM provides a useful conceptual framework for evaluating and linking risk and return. Its simplicity and practical appeal cause beta and CAPM to remain important tools for investors who seek to measure risk and link it to required returns in security markets.

CONCEPTS IN REVIEW

Answers available at: www.myfinancelab.com

5.7 Briefly define and give examples of each of the following components of total risk. Which is the relevant risk, and why?
a. Diversifiable risk   b. Nondiversifiable risk

5.8 Explain what is meant by *beta*. What is the relevant risk measured by beta? What is the *market return*? How is the interpretation of beta related to the market return?

5.9 What range of values does beta typically exhibit? Are positive or negative betas more common? Explain.

5.10 What is the *capital asset pricing model (CAPM)?* What role does beta play in it? What is the *risk premium?* How is the *security market line (SML)* related to the CAPM?

5.11 Is the CAPM a predictive model? How is the CAPM related to *arbitrage pricing theory (APT)?* Why do beta and the CAPM remain important to investors?

Traditional Versus Modern Portfolio Management

LG 5   LG 6

Individual and institutional investors currently use two approaches to plan and construct their portfolios. The *traditional approach* refers to the less-quantitative methods that investors have been using since the evolution of the public securities markets. *Modern portfolio theory (MPT)* is a more recent, more mathematical development that continues to grow in popularity and acceptance.

▮ The Traditional Approach

traditional portfolio management
an approach to portfolio management that emphasizes "balancing" the portfolio by assembling a wide variety of stocks and/or bonds of companies from a broad range of industries.

Traditional portfolio management emphasizes "balancing" the portfolio by assembling a wide variety of stocks and/or bonds. The typical emphasis is *interindustry diversification*. This produces a portfolio with securities of companies from a broad range of industries. Traditional portfolios are constructed using the security analysis techniques discussed in Chapters 7 and 8.

Table 5.5 presents the industry groupings and the percentages invested in them by a typical mutual fund that is managed by professionals using the traditional approach. This fund, The Growth Fund of America (GFA), is an open-end mutual fund. Its portfolio value at August 31, 2006, was approximately $147 billion. Its objective is to invest in a wide range of companies that appear to offer superior opportunities for growth of capital. The GFA holds shares of more than 250 different stocks from 11 broad industry groups, as well as short-term securities of around 50 different issuers.

Analyzing the stock position of The Growth Fund of America, which accounts for about 90% of the fund's total assets, we observe the traditional approach to portfolio management at work. This fund holds numerous stocks from a broad cross-section of the total universe of available stocks. The stocks are a mix of large and small companies. By far the largest industry group is information technology, representing 20.16% of the total portfolio. The fund's largest individual holding is Roche Holding, a leading healthcare company that discovers, develops, manufactures, and markets healthcare solutions, which accounts for 2.25% of the total portfolio. Google, one of the most frequently used Web site search engines in the world, ranks second at 2.12%. The third largest holding—1.74%—is Schlumberger, a large oilfield services company that operates in the United States and internationally. Although many of the fund's more than 250 stocks are those of large recognizable companies, its portfolio does include stocks of smaller, less-recognizable companies.

Those who manage traditional portfolios want to invest in well-known companies for three reasons. First, because these are known as successful enterprises, investing in them is perceived as less risky than investing in lesser-known firms. Second, the securities of large firms are more liquid and are available in large quantities. Third, institutional investors prefer successful well-known companies because it is easier to convince clients to invest in them. Called *window dressing,* this practice of loading up a portfolio with successful well-known stocks makes it easier for institutional investors to sell their services.

One tendency often attributed to institutional investors during recent years is that of "herding"—investing in securities similar to those held by their competitors. These institutional investors effectively mimic the actions of their competitors. In the case of The Growth Fund of America, for example, its managers would buy stocks in companies that are held by other large growth-oriented mutual funds. While we really don't know why The Growth Fund of America's managers bought specific stocks, it is clear that most funds with similar objectives hold many of the same well-known stocks.

TABLE 5.5   The Growth Fund of America, August 31, 2005

The Growth Fund of America (GFA) appears to adhere to the traditional approach to portfolio management. Its total portfolio value is about $147 billion, of which 90% ($131 billion) is common stock, including more than 250 different stocks in 11 broad industry groupings, plus about 11% ($16 billion) in short-term securities of about 50 different issuers. In addition, the fund has a very small position in fixed-income securities ($190 million).

The Growth Fund of America Investments by Broad Industry Group as of August 31, 2006	
Industry Group	Percentage
Equity Securities	**89.19%**
Information technology	20.16
Health care	13.65
Energy	13.36
Consumer discretionary	10.55
Financials	7.81
Industrials	7.78
Consumer staples	5.68
Materials	3.97
Telecommunication services	2.09
Utilities	0.14
Miscellaneous	4.00
Fixed-Income Securities	**0.31**
Preferred stocks	0.00
Convertible securities	0.00
Bonds and notes	0.13
Short-Term Securities	**10.58**
Other Assets Less Liabilities	**0.10**

Source: Data from The Growth Fund of America, *Annual Report, August 31, 2006*, pp. 11–15.

▊ Modern Portfolio Theory

During the 1950s, Harry Markowitz, a trained mathematician, first developed the theories that form the basis of modern portfolio theory. Many other scholars and investment experts have contributed to the theory in the intervening years. **Modern portfolio theory** (MPT) utilizes several basic statistical measures to develop a portfolio plan. Included are *expected returns* and *standard deviations of returns* for both securities and portfolios, and the *correlation between returns*. According to MPT, diversification is achieved by combining securities in a portfolio *in such a way that individual securities have negative (or low-positive) correlations between each other's rates of return*. Thus, the statistical diversification is the deciding factor in choosing securities for an MPT portfolio. Two important aspects of MPT are the *efficient frontier* and *portfolio betas*.

modern portfolio theory (MPT)
an approach to portfolio management that uses several basic statistical measures to develop a portfolio plan.

The Efficient Frontier   At any point in time, you are faced with virtually hundreds of investment vehicles from which to choose. You can form any number of possible portfolios. In fact, using only, say, 10 of the vehicles, you could create hundreds of portfolios by changing the proportion of each asset in the portfolio.

   If we were to create all possible portfolios, calculate the return and risk of each, and plot each risk-return combination on a set of risk-return axes, we would have the *feasible* or *attainable set* of all possible portfolios. This set is represented by the shaded area in Figure 5.7 (on page 232). It is the area bounded by ABYOZCDEF. As defined earlier, an *efficient portfolio* is a portfolio that provides the highest return for a given level of risk or provides

The Feasible or Attainable Set and the Efficient Frontier

The *feasible* or *attainable set* (shaded area) represents the risk-return combinations attainable with all possible portfolios; the *efficient frontier* is the locus of all efficient portfolios. The point O where the investor's highest possible indifference curve is tangent to the efficient frontier is the optimal portfolio. It represents the highest level of satisfaction the investor can achieve given the available set of portfolios.

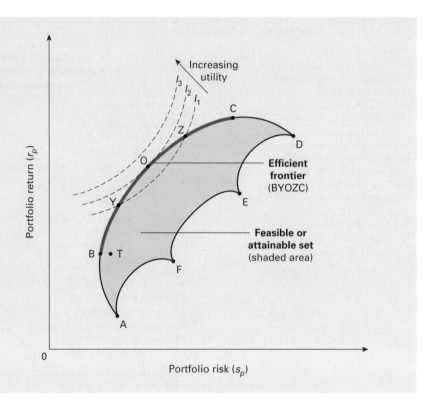

minimum risk for a given level of return. For example, let's compare portfolio T to portfolios B and Y shown in Figure 5.7. Portfolio Y appears preferable to portfolio T because it has a higher return for the same level of risk. Portfolio B also "dominates" portfolio T because it has lower risk for the same level of return.

The boundary BYOZC of the feasible set of portfolios represents *all efficient portfolios*—those portfolios that provide the best tradeoff between risk and return. This boundary is called the **efficient frontier**. *All portfolios on the efficient frontier are preferable to all other portfolios in the feasible set.* Any portfolios that would fall to the left of the efficient frontier are not available for investment, because they fall outside of the attainable set. Portfolios that fall to the right of the efficient frontier are *not desirable,* because their risk-return tradeoffs are inferior to those of portfolios on the efficient frontier.

We can, in theory, use the efficient frontier to find the highest level of satisfaction the investor can achieve given the available set of portfolios. To do this, we would plot on the risk-return axes an *investor's utility function,* or *risk-indifference curves.* These curves indicate, for a given level of utility (satisfaction), the set of risk-return combinations among which an investor would be indifferent. These curves, labeled I_1, I_2, and I_3 in Figure 5.7, reflect increasing satisfaction as we move from I_1 to I_2 to I_3. The optimal portfolio, O, is the point at which indifference curve I_2 meets the efficient frontier. The higher utility provided by I_3 cannot be achieved given the best available portfolios represented by the efficient frontier.

efficient frontier
the leftmost boundary of the *feasible (attainable) set* of portfolios that includes all *efficient portfolios*—those providing the best attainable tradeoff between risk (measured by the standard deviation) and return.

When coupled with a risk-free asset, the efficient frontier can be used to develop the *capital asset pricing model* (introduced earlier) in terms of portfolio risk (measured by the standard deviation, s_p) and return (r_p). Rather than focus further on theory, let's shift our attention to the more practical aspects of the efficient frontier and its extensions. To do so, we consider the use of *portfolio betas*.

Portfolio Betas As we have noted, investors strive to diversify their portfolios by including a variety of noncomplementary investment vehicles so as to reduce risk while meeting return objectives. Remember that investment vehicles embody two basic types of risk: (1) *diversifiable risk*, the risk unique to a particular investment vehicle, and (2) *nondiversifiable risk*, the risk possessed by every investment vehicle.

A great deal of research has been conducted on the topic of risk as it relates to security investments. The results show that in general, *to earn more return, you must bear more risk*. More startling, however, are research results showing that only with nondiversifiable risk is there a positive risk-return relationship. High levels of *diversifiable risk* do not result in correspondingly high levels of return. Because there is no reward for bearing diversifiable risk, investors should minimize this form of risk by diversifying the portfolio so that only nondiversifiable risk remains.

Risk Diversification As we've seen, diversification minimizes diversifiable risk by offsetting the poor return on one vehicle with the good return on another. Minimizing diversifiable risk through careful selection of investment vehicles requires that the vehicles chosen for the portfolio come from a wide range of industries.

To understand better the effect of diversification on the basic types of risk, let's consider what happens when we begin with a single asset (security) in a portfolio and then expand the portfolio by randomly selecting additional securities. Using the standard deviation, s_p, to measure the portfolio's *total risk*, we can depict the behavior of the total portfolio risk as more securities are added, as done in Figure 5.8 (see page 234). As securities are added (*x*-axis), the total portfolio risk (*y*-axis) declines because of the effects of diversification, and it tends to approach a limit.

On average, most of the risk-reduction benefits of diversification can be gained by forming portfolios containing 8 to 15 randomly selected securities. Unfortunately, because an investor holds but one of a large number of possible *x*-security portfolios, it is unlikely that he or she will experience the average outcome. As a consequence, some researchers suggest that the individual investor needs to hold about 40 different stocks to achieve efficient diversification. This suggestion tends to support the popularity of investment in mutual funds.

Because any investor can create a portfolio of assets that will eliminate virtually all diversifiable risk, the only **relevant risk** is that which is nondiversifiable. You must therefore be concerned solely with nondiversifiable risk. The measurement of nondiversifiable risk is thus of primary importance.

relevant risk
risk that is nondiversifiable.

Calculating Portfolio Betas As we saw earlier, *beta* measures the *nondiversifiable* or *relevant risk* of a security. The beta for the market is equal to 1.00. Securities with betas greater than 1.00 are more risky than the market, and

FIGURE 5.8

Portfolio Risk and Diversification

As randomly selected securities are combined to create a portfolio, the total risk of the portfolio (measured by its standard deviation, s_p) declines. The portion of the risk eliminated is the *diversifiable risk;* the remaining portion is the *nondiversifiable* or *relevant risk.* On average, most of the benefits of diversification result from forming portfolios that contain 8 to 15 randomly selected securities.

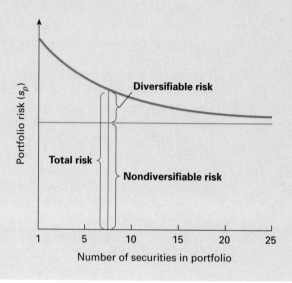

portfolio beta, b_p
the beta of a portfolio; calculated as the weighted average of the betas of the individual assets it includes.

those with betas less than 1.00 are less risky than the market. The beta for the risk-free asset is 0.

The **portfolio beta, b_p,** is merely the weighted average of the betas of the individual assets it includes. It can be easily estimated using the betas of the component assets. To find the portfolio beta, b_p, we can use Equation 5.4.

Equation 5.4 ➤

$$\text{Portfolio beta} = \begin{pmatrix} \text{Proportion of} \\ \text{portfolio's total} \\ \text{dollar value} \\ \text{represented by} \\ \text{asset 1} \end{pmatrix} \times \begin{matrix} \text{Beta} \\ \text{for} \\ \text{asset 1} \end{matrix} + \begin{pmatrix} \text{Proportion of} \\ \text{portfolio's total} \\ \text{dollar value} \\ \text{represented by} \\ \text{asset 2} \end{pmatrix} \times \begin{matrix} \text{Beta} \\ \text{for} \\ \text{asset 2} \end{matrix} + \cdots +$$

Equation 5.4a ➤

$$\begin{pmatrix} \text{Proportion of} \\ \text{portfolio's total} \\ \text{dollar value} \\ \text{represented by} \\ \text{asset } n \end{pmatrix} \times \begin{matrix} \text{Beta} \\ \text{for} \\ \text{asset } n \end{matrix} = \sum_{j=1}^{n} \begin{pmatrix} \text{Proportion of} \\ \text{portfolio's total} \\ \text{dollar value} \\ \text{represented by} \\ \text{asset } j \end{pmatrix} \times \begin{matrix} \text{Beta} \\ \text{for} \\ \text{asset } j \end{matrix}$$

$$b_p = (w_1 \times b_1) + (w_2 \times b_2) + \cdots + (w_n \times b_n) = \sum_{j=1}^{n} (w_j \times b_j)$$

TABLE 5.6	Austin Fund's Portfolios V and W			
	Portfolio V		Portfolio W	
Asset	Proportion	Beta	Proportion	Beta
1	0.10	1.65	0.10	0.80
2	0.30	1.00	0.10	1.00
3	0.20	1.30	0.20	0.65
4	0.20	1.10	0.10	0.75
5	0.20	1.25	0.50	1.05
Total	1.00		1.00	

Of course, $\sum_{j=1}^{n} w_j = 1$, which means that 100% of the portfolio's assets must be included in this computation.

Portfolio betas are interpreted in exactly the same way as individual asset betas. They indicate the degree of responsiveness of the *portfolio's* return to changes in the market return. For example, when the market return increases by 10%, a portfolio with a beta of 0.75 will experience a 7.5% increase in its return $(0.75 \times 10\%)$. A portfolio with a beta of 1.25 will experience a 12.5% increase in its return $(1.25 \times 10\%)$. Low-beta portfolios are less responsive, and therefore less risky, than high-beta portfolios. Clearly, a portfolio containing mostly low-beta assets will have a low beta, and vice versa.

To demonstrate, consider the Austin Fund, a large investment company that wishes to assess the risk of two portfolios, V and W. Both portfolios contain five assets, with the proportions and betas shown in Table 5.6. We can calculate the betas for portfolios V and W, b_v and b_w, by substituting the appropriate data from the table into Equation 5.4, as follows.

$$b_v = (0.10 \times 1.65) + (0.30 \times 1.00) + (0.20 \times 1.30) + (0.20 \times 1.10) + (0.20 \times 1.25)$$

$$= 0.165 + 0.300 + 0.260 + 0.220 + 0.250 = 1.195 \approx \underline{1.20}$$

$$b_w = (0.10 \times 0.80) + (0.10 \times 1.00) + (0.20 \times 0.65) + (0.10 \times 0.75) + (0.50 \times 1.05)$$

$$= 0.080 + 0.100 + 0.130 + 0.075 + 0.525 = \underline{0.91}$$

Portfolio V's beta is 1.20, and portfolio W's is 0.91. These values make sense because portfolio V contains relatively high-beta assets and portfolio W contains relatively low-beta assets. Clearly, portfolio V's returns are more responsive to changes in market returns—and therefore more risky—than portfolio W's.

Using Portfolio Betas The usefulness of beta depends on how well it explains return fluctuations. We can use *the coefficient of determination* (R^2) to evaluate a beta coefficient statistically. This coefficient indicates the percentage of the change in an individual security's return that is explained by its relationship with the market return. R^2 can range from 0 to 1.0. If a regression equation has an R^2 of 0, then none (0%) of the variation in the security's return is explained by its relationship with the market. An R^2 of 1.0 indicates the existence of perfect correlation (100%) between a security and the market.

TABLE 5.7 Portfolio Betas and Associated Changes in Returns

Portfolio Beta	Change in Market Return	Change in Expected Portfolio Return
+2.00	+10.0%	+20.0%
	−10.0	−20.0
+0.50	+10.0	+ 5.0
	−10.0	− 5.0
−1.00	+10.0	−10.0
	−10.0	+10.0

Beta is much more useful in explaining a portfolio's return fluctuations than a security's return fluctuations. A well-diversified stock portfolio will have a beta equation R^2 of around 0.90. This means that 90% of the stock portfolio's fluctuations are related to changes in the stock market as a whole. Individual security betas have a wide range of R^2s but tend to be in the 0.20 to 0.50 range. Other factors (diversifiable risk, in particular) also cause individual security prices to fluctuate. When securities are combined in a well-diversified portfolio, most of the fluctuation in that portfolio's return is caused by the movement of the entire stock market.

Interpreting Portfolio Betas If a portfolio has a beta of +1.00, the portfolio experiences changes in its rate of return equal to changes in the market's rate of return. The +1.00 beta portfolio would tend to experience a 10% increase in return if the stock market as a whole experienced a 10% increase in return. Conversely, if the market return fell by 6%, the return on the +1.00 beta portfolio would also fall by 6%.

Table 5.7 lists the expected returns for three portfolio betas in two situations: an increase in market return of 10% and a decrease in market return of 10%. The 2.00 beta portfolio is twice as volatile as the market. When the market return increases by 10%, the portfolio return increases by 20%. When the market return declines by 10%, the portfolio's return will fall by 20%. This portfolio would be considered a high-risk, high-return portfolio.

The middle, 0.50 beta portfolio is considered a low-risk, low-return portfolio. This would be a conservative portfolio for investors who wish to maintain a low-risk investment posture. The 0.50 beta portfolio is half as volatile as the market.

A portfolio with a beta of −1.00 moves in the opposite direction from the market. A bearish investor would probably want to own a negative-beta portfolio, because this type of investment tends to rise in value when the stock market declines, and vice versa. Finding securities with negative betas is difficult, however. Most securities have positive betas, because they tend to experience return movements in the same direction as changes in the stock market.

The Risk-Return Tradeoff: Some Closing Comments Another valuable outgrowth of modern portfolio theory is the specific link between nondiversifiable risk and investment return. The basic premise is that an investor must have a portfolio of relatively risky investments to earn a relatively high rate of return. That relationship is illustrated in Figure 5.9. The upward-sloping line

FIGURE 5.9

The Portfolio Risk-Return Tradeoff

As the risk of an investment portfolio increases from zero, the return provided should increase above the risk-free rate, R_F. Portfolios A and B offer returns commensurate with their risk, portfolio C provides a high return at a low-risk level, and portfolio D provides a low return for high risk. Portfolio C is highly desirable; portfolio D should be avoided.

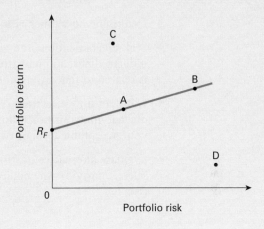

risk-return tradeoff
the positive relationship between the risk associated with a given investment and its expected return.

risk-free rate, R_F
the return an investor can earn on a risk-free investment such as a U.S. Treasury bill or an insured money market deposit account.

shows the **risk-return tradeoff.** The point where the risk-return line crosses the return axis is called the **risk-free rate, R_F.** This is the return an investor can earn on a risk-free investment such as a U.S. Treasury bill or an insured money market deposit account.

As we proceed upward along the risk-return tradeoff line, portfolios of risky investments appear, as depicted by four investment portfolios, A through D. Portfolios A and B are investment opportunities that provide a level of return commensurate with their respective risk levels. Portfolio C provides a high return at a relatively low risk level—and therefore would be an excellent investment. Portfolio D, in contrast, offers high risk but low return—an investment to avoid.

■ Reconciling the Traditional Approach and MPT

We have reviewed two fairly different approaches to portfolio management: the traditional approach and MPT. The question that naturally arises is which technique should you use? There is no definite answer; the question must be resolved by the judgment of each investor. However, we can offer a few useful ideas.

The average individual investor does not have the resources, computers, and mathematical acumen to implement a total MPT portfolio strategy. But most individual investors can extract and use ideas from *both* the traditional and MPT approaches. The traditional approach stresses security selection, which is discussed in Chapters 7 and 8. It also emphasizes diversification of the portfolio across industry lines. MPT stresses negative correlations between

HOTLINKS

A variety of articles on diversification and risk can be found at the following sites:

www.russell.com/ca/Education_centre/
Article_Library/Diversification_and_Risk.asp
www.moneychimp.com/articles/
risk/portfolio.htm

rates of return for the securities within the portfolio. This approach calls for diversification, to minimize diversifiable risk. Thus, diversification must be accomplished to ensure satisfactory performance with either strategy. Also, beta is a useful tool for determining the level of a portfolio's nondiversifiable risk and should be part of the decision-making process.

We recommend the following portfolio management policy, which uses aspects of both approaches:

- Determine how much risk you are willing to bear.

- Seek diversification among different types of securities and across industry lines, and pay attention to how the return from one security is related to that from another.

- Consider how a security responds to the market, and use beta in diversifying your portfolio as a way to keep the portfolio in line with your acceptable level of risk.

- Evaluate alternative portfolios to make sure that the portfolio selected provides the highest return for the given level of acceptable risk.

CONCEPTS IN REVIEW

Answers available at: www.myfinancelab.com

5.12 Describe *traditional portfolio management*. Give three reasons why traditional portfolio managers like to invest in well-established companies.

5.13 What is *modern portfolio theory (MPT)?* What is the *feasible* or *attainable set* of all possible portfolios? How is it derived for a given group of investment vehicles?

5.14 What is the *efficient frontier?* How is it related to the attainable set of all possible portfolios? How can it be used with an investor's utility function to find the optimal portfolio?

5.15 Define and differentiate among the diversifiable, nondiversifiable, and total risk of a portfolio. Which is considered the *relevant risk?* How is it measured?

5.16 Define *beta*. How can you find the beta of a portfolio when you know the beta for each of the assets included within it?

5.17 What does the *coefficient of determination (R^2)* for the regression equation used to derive a beta coefficient indicate? Would this statistic indicate that beta is more useful in explaining the return fluctuations of individual assets than of portfolios?

5.18 Explain how you can reconcile the traditional and modern portfolio approaches.

Summary

LG 1 **Understand portfolio objectives and the procedures used to calculate portfolio return and standard deviation.** A portfolio is a collection of investment vehicles assembled to achieve one or more investment goals. It involves a tradeoff between risk and return, potential price appreciation and current income, and varying risk levels. The return on a portfolio is calculated as a weighted average of the returns of the assets from which it is formed. The standard deviation of a portfolio's returns is found by applying the same formula that is used to find the standard deviation of a single asset.

LG 2 **Discuss the concepts of correlation and diversification, and the key aspects of international diversification.** Correlation is a statistic used to measure the relationship, if any, between the returns on assets. To diversify, it is best to add assets with negatively correlated returns. In general, the less positive and more negative the correlation between asset returns, the more effectively a portfolio can be diversified to reduce its risk. Diversification can reduce the risk (standard deviation) of a portfolio below the risk of the least risky asset (sometimes to zero). The return of the resulting portfolio will be no lower than the smallest return of its component assets. For any two-asset portfolio, the ability to reduce risk depends on both the degree of correlation and proportion of each asset in the portfolio.

International diversification may allow an investor to reduce portfolio risk without a corresponding reduction in return. It can be achieved by investing abroad or through domestic investment in foreign companies or funds, but it typically cannot be achieved by investing in U.S. multinationals. The preferred method of international diversification for individual investors is the use of ADSs or international mutual funds available in the United States. Although opportunities to earn "excess" returns in international investments are diminishing over time, they continue to be effective diversification vehicles.

LG 3 **Describe the components of risk and the use of beta to measure risk.** The two basic components of total risk are diversifiable (unsystematic) and nondiversifiable (systematic) risk. Nondiversifiable risk is the relevant risk. Beta measures the nondiversifiable, or market, risk associated with a security investment. It is derived from the historical relationship between a security's return and the market return.

LG 4 **Explain the capital asset pricing model (CAPM)—conceptually, mathematically, and graphically.** The capital asset pricing model (CAPM) relates risk (as measured by beta) to return. It can be divided into two parts: (1) the risk-free rate of return, R_F, and (2) the risk premium, $b \times (r_m - R_F)$. The graphic depiction of the CAPM is the security market line (SML). The CAPM reflects increasing required returns for increasing risk. The CAPM relies on historical data, can be viewed as being derived from arbitrage pricing theory (APT), and provides a useful conceptual framework for linking risk and return.

LG 5 **Review traditional and modern approaches to portfolio management.** The traditional approach constructs portfolios by combining a large number of securities issued by companies from a broad cross-section of industries. Modern portfolio theory (MPT) uses statistical diversification to develop efficient portfolios. To determine the optimal portfolio, MPT finds the efficient frontier and couples it with an investor's risk-indifference curves.

LG 6 Describe portfolio betas, the risk-return tradeoff, and reconciliation of the two approaches to portfolio management. In practice, portfolio betas can be used to develop efficient portfolios consistent with the investor's risk-return preferences. Portfolio betas are merely a weighted average of the betas of the individual assets included in the portfolio. Generally, investors use elements of both the traditional approach and MPT to create portfolios. This approach involves determining how much risk you are willing to bear, seeking diversification, using beta to diversify your portfolio, and evaluating alternative portfolios to select the one that offers the highest return for an acceptable level of risk.

Key Terms

arbitrage pricing theory (APT), *p. 228*
beta, *p. 223*
capital asset pricing model (CAPM),
    p. 226
correlation, *p. 215*
correlation coefficient, *p. 215*
diversifiable (unsystematic) risk,
    p. 223
efficient frontier, *p. 232*
efficient portfolio, *p. 213*
growth-oriented portfolio, *p. 213*
income-oriented portfolio, *p. 213*
market return, *p. 123*
modern portfolio theory (MPT), *p. 231*
negatively correlated, *p. 215*

nondiversifiable (systematic) risk,
    p. 223
perfectly negatively correlated, *p. 215*
perfectly positively correlated, *p. 215*
portfolio beta, b_p, *p. 234*
positively correlated, *p. 215*
relevant risk, *p. 233*
risk-free rate, R_F, *p. 236*
risk-return tradeoff, *p. 236*
security market line (SML), *p. 228*
total risk, *p. 223*
traditional portfolio management,
    p. 130
uncorrelated, *p. 215*

Discussion Questions

LG 1 **Q5.1** State your portfolio objectives. Then construct a 10-stock portfolio that you feel is consistent with your objectives. (Use companies that have been public for at least 5 years.) Obtain annual dividend and price data for each of the past 5 years.

  a. Calculate the historical return for each stock for each year.
  b. Calculate the historical portfolio return for each of the 5 years, using your findings in part **a**.
  c. Use your findings in part **b** to calculate the average portfolio return over the 5 years.
  d. Use your findings in parts **b** and **c** to find the standard deviation of the portfolio's returns over the 5-year period.
  e. Use the historical average return from part **c** and the standard deviation from part **d** to evaluate the portfolio's return and risk in light of your stated portfolio objectives.

LG 2 Q5.2 Using the following guidelines, choose the stocks—A, B, and C—of 3 firms that have been public for at least 10 years. Stock A should be one you are interested in buying. Stock B should be a stock, possibly in the same line of business or industry, that you feel will have high positive return correlation with stock A. Stock C should be one you feel will have high negative return correlation with stock A.

    a. Calculate the annual rates of return for each of the past 10 years for each stock.

    b. Plot the 10 annual return values for each stock on the same set of axes, where the *x*-axis is the year and the *y*-axis is the annual return in percentage terms.

    c. Join the points for the returns for each stock on the graph. Evaluate and describe the returns of stocks A and B in the graph. Do they exhibit the expected positive correlation? Why or why not?

    d. Evaluate and describe the relationship between the returns of stocks A and C in the graph. Do they exhibit the expected negative correlation? Why or why not?

    e. Compare and contrast your findings in parts **c** and **d** to the expected relationships among stocks A, B, and C. Discuss your findings.

LG 3 Q5.3 From the *Wall Street Journal*, a Web site such as Yahoo! Finance (finance .yahoo.com), or some other source, obtain a current estimate of the risk-free rate (use a 10-year Treasury bond). Use the *Value Line Investment Survey* or Yahoo! Finance to obtain the beta for each of the following stocks:

    General Motors (autos)
    Dell (computers)
    Sempra Energy (utilities)
    Kroger (groceries)
    Merrill Lynch (financial services)

Use the information you gathered, along with the market risk premium on large stocks given in the chapter, to find the required return for each stock with the capital asset pricing model (CAPM).

LG 3 **LG 4** Q5.4 From the *Wall Street Journal*, a Web site such as Yahoo! Finance (finance .yahoo.com), or some other source, obtain a current estimate of the risk-free rate (use a 10-year Treasury bond). Use the *Value Line Investment Survey* or Yahoo! Finance to obtain the beta for each of the companies listed on page 225.

    a. Compare the current betas to the July 21, 2006, betas given in the chapter for each of the companies.

    b. What might cause betas to change over time, even in a stable economic environment?

    c. Use the current betas, along with the market risk premium on large stocks given in the chapter, to find the required return for each stock with the capital asset pricing model (CAPM).

    d. Compare and discuss your findings in part **c** with regard to the specific business that each company is in.

LG 2 **LG 5** **LG 6** Q5.5 Obtain a prospectus and an annual report for a major mutual fund that includes some international securities. Carefully read the prospectus and annual report and study the portfolio's composition in light of the fund's stated objectives.

    a. Evaluate the amount of diversification and the types of industries and companies held. Is the portfolio well-diversified?

    b. Discuss the additional risks faced by an investor in this fund compared to an investor in a domestic stock portfolio such as the S&P 500.

LG 6   Q5.6   Use *Value Line Investment Survey* or some other source to select 4 stocks with betas ranging from about 0.50 to 1.50. Record the current market prices of each of these stocks. Assume you wish to create a portfolio that combines all 4 stocks in such a way that the resulting portfolio beta is about 1.10.

  a. Through trial and error, use all 4 stocks to create a portfolio with the target beta of 1.10.
  b. If you have $100,000 to invest in this portfolio, on the basis of the weightings determined in part **a**, what dollar amounts would you invest in each stock?
  c. Approximately how many shares of each of the 4 stocks would you buy, given the dollar amounts calculated in part **b**?
  d. Repeat parts **a**, **b**, and **c** with a different set of weightings that still result in a portfolio beta of 1.10. Can only 1 unique portfolio with a given beta be created from a given set of stocks?

Problems

LG 1   P5.1   Your portfolio had the values in the following table for the 4-year period listed. Calculate your average return over the 4-year period.

	Beginning Value	Ending Value
2005	$50,000.00	$55,000.00
2006	$55,000.00	$58,000.00
2007	$58,000.00	$65,000.00
2008	$65,000.00	$70,000.00

LG 1   P5.2   Using your data from Problem 5.1 above, calculate the portfolio standard deviation.

LG 1 LG 2   P5.3   Assume you are considering a portfolio containing two assets, L and M. Asset L will represent 40% of the dollar value of the portfolio, and asset M will account for the other 60%. The expected returns over the next 6 years, 2009–2014, for each of these assets are summarized in the following table.

	Expected Return (%)	
Year	Asset L	Asset M
2009	14	20
2010	14	18
2011	16	16
2012	17	14
2013	17	12
2014	19	10

  a. Calculate the expected portfolio return, $\bar{r}_p$, for each of the 6 years.
  b. Calculate the average expected portfolio return, $\bar{r}_p$, over the 6-year period.
  c. Calculate the standard deviation of expected portfolio returns, s_p, over the 6-year period.
  d. How would you characterize the correlation of returns of the two assets L and M?

e. Discuss any benefits of diversification achieved through creation of the portfolio.

LG 1 LG 2 **P5.4** Refer to Problem 5.3 above. Assume that asset L represents 60% of the portfolio and asset M 40%. Calculate the average expected return and standard deviation of expected portfolio returns over the 6-year period. Compare your answers to the answers from Problem 5.3.

LG 1 LG 2 **P5.5** You have been given the following return data on 3 assets—F, G, and H—over the period 2009–2012.

| | Expected Return (%) | | |
Year	Asset F	Asset G	Asset H
2009	16	17	14
2010	17	16	15
2011	18	15	16
2012	19	14	17

Using these assets, you have isolated 3 investment alternatives:

Alternative	Investment
1	100% of asset F
2	50% of asset F and 50% of asset G
3	50% of asset F and 50% of asset H

a. Calculate the portfolio return over the 4-year period for each of the 3 alternatives.
b. Calculate the standard deviation of returns over the 4-year period for each of the 3 alternatives.
c. On the basis of your findings in parts **a** and **b**, which of the 3 investment alternatives would you recommend? Why?

LG 1 LG 2 **P5.6** You have been asked for your advice in selecting a portfolio of assets and have been supplied with the following data.

| | Expected Return (%) | | |
Year	Asset A	Asset B	Asset C
2009	12	16	12
2010	14	14	14
2011	16	12	16

You have been told that you can create 2 portfolios—one consisting of assets A and B and the other consisting of assets A and C—by investing equal proportions (50%) in each of the 2 component assets.

a. What is the average expected return, $\bar{r}$, for each asset over the 3-year period?
b. What is the standard deviation, s, for each asset's expected return?
c. What is the average expected return, $\bar{r}_p$, for each of the two portfolios?
d. How would you characterize the correlations of returns of the 2 assets making up each of the 2 portfolios identified in part **c**?
e. What is the standard deviation of expected returns, s_p, for each portfolio?
f. Which portfolio do you recommend? Why?

LG 1 LG 2 **P5.7** Referring to Problem 5.6 above, what would happen if you constructed a portfolio consisting of assets A, B, and C, equally weighted? Would this reduce risk or enhance return?

LG 1 LG 2   **P5.8**   Assume you wish to evaluate the risk and return behaviors associated with various combinations of assets V and W under three assumed degrees of correlation: perfect positive, uncorrelated, and perfect negative. The following average return and risk values were calculated for these assets.

Asset	Average Return, $\bar{r}$ (%)	Risk (Standard Deviation), s (%)
V	8	5
W	13	10

a. If the returns of assets V and W are *perfectly positively correlated* (correlation coefficient = +1), describe the *range* of (1) return and (2) risk associated with all possible portfolio combinations.

b. If the returns of assets V and W are *uncorrelated* (correlation coefficient = 0), describe the *approximate range* of (1) return and (2) risk associated with all possible portfolio combinations.

c. If the returns of assets V and W are *perfectly negatively correlated* (correlation coefficient = −1), describe the *range* of (1) return and (2) risk associated with all possible portfolio combinations.

LG 3   **P5.9**   Imagine you wish to estimate the betas for 2 investments, A and B. You have gathered the following return data for the market and for each of the investments over the past 10 years, 1999–2008.

		Historical Returns	
		Investment	
Year	Market	A	B
1999	6%	11%	16%
2000	2	8	11
2001	−13	−4	−10
2002	−4	3	3
2003	−8	0	−3
2004	16	19	30
2005	10	14	22
2006	15	18	29
2007	8	12	19
2008	13	17	26

a. On a set of market return (x-axis)–investment return (y-axis) axes, use the data to draw the characteristic lines for investments A and B on the same set of axes.

b. Use the characteristic lines from part **a** to estimate the betas for investments A and B.

c. Use the betas found in part **b** to comment on the relative risks of investments A and B.

LG 3   **P5.10**   You are evaluating 2 possible stock investments, Buyme Co. and Getit Corp. Buyme Co. has an expected return of 14%, and a beta of 1. Getit Corp. has an expected return of 14%, and a beta of 1.2. Based only on this data, which stock should you buy and why?

LG 3   **P5.11**   Referring to Problem 5.10 above, if you expected a significant market rally, would your decision be altered? Explain.

LG 3 **P5.12** A security has a beta of 1.20. Is this security more or less risky than the market? Explain. Assess the impact on the required return of this security in each of the following cases.

    a. The market return increases by 15%.
    b. The market return decreases by 8%.
    c. The market return remains unchanged.

LG 3 **P5.13** Assume the betas for securities A, B, and C are as shown here.

Security	Beta
A	1.40
B	0.80
C	−0.90

    a. Calculate the change in return for each security if the market experiences an increase in its rate of return of 13.2% over the next period.
    b. Calculate the change in return for each security if the market experiences a decrease in its rate of return of 10.8% over the next period.
    c. Rank and discuss the relative risk of each security on the basis of your findings. Which security might perform best during an economic downturn? Explain.

LG 3 **LG 6** **P5.14** Referring to Problem 5.13 above, assume you have a portfolio with $20,000 invested in each of Investment A, B, and C. What is your portfolio beta?

LG 3 **LG 6** **P5.15** Referring to Problem 5.14 above, using the portfolio beta, what would you expect the value of your portfolio to be if the market rallied 20%? Declined 20%

LG 4 **P5.16** Use the capital asset pricing model (CAPM) to find the required return for each of the following securities in light of the data given.

Security	Risk-Free Rate	Market Return	Beta
A	5%	8%	1.30
B	8	13	0.90
C	9	12	−0.20
D	10	15	1.00
E	6	10	0.60

LG 4 **P5.17** Bob is reviewing his portfolio of investments, which include certain stocks and bonds. He has a large amount tied up in U.S. Treasury bills paying 3%. He is considering moving some of his funds from the T-bills into a stock. The stock has a beta of 1.25. If Bob expects a return of 14% from the stock (a little better than the current market return of 13%), should he buy the stock or leave his funds in the T-bill?

LG 4 **P5.18** The risk-free rate is currently 7%, and the market return is 12%. Assume you are considering the following investment vehicles.

Investment Vehicle	Beta
A	1.50
B	1.00
C	0.75
D	0
E	2.00

a. Which vehicle is most risky? Least risky?
b. Use the capital asset pricing model (CAPM) to find the required return on each of the investment vehicles.
c. Draw the security market line (SML), using your findings in part **b**.
d. On the basis of your findings in part **c**, what relationship exists between risk and return? Explain.

LG 5   LG 6   P5.19 Portfolios A through J, which are listed in the following table along with their returns (r_p) and risk (measured by the standard deviation, s_p), represent all currently available portfolios in the feasible or attainable set.

Portfolio	Return (r_p)	Risk (s_p)
A	9%	8%
B	3	3
C	14	10
D	12	14
E	7	11
F	11	6
G	10	12
H	16	16
I	5	7
J	8	4

a. Plot the *feasible* or *attainable set* represented by these data on a set of portfolio risk, s_p (x-axis)–portfolio return, r_p (y-axis) axes.
b. Draw the *efficient frontier* on the graph in part **a**.
c. Which portfolios lie on the efficient frontier? Why do these portfolios dominate all others in the feasible or attainable set?
d. How would an investor's *utility function* or *risk-indifference curves* be used with the efficient frontier to find the optimal portfolio?

LG 5   LG 6   P5.20 For his portfolio, David Finney randomly selected securities from all those listed on the New York Stock Exchange. He began with one security and added securities one by one until a total of 20 securities were held in the portfolio. After each security was added, David calculated the portfolio standard deviation, s_p. The calculated values follow.

Number of Securities	Portfolio Risk, s_p (%)	Number of Securities	Portfolio Risk, s_p (%)
1	14.50	11	7.00
2	13.30	12	6.80
3	12.20	13	6.70
4	11.20	14	6.65
5	10.30	15	6.60
6	9.50	16	6.56
7	8.80	17	6.52
8	8.20	18	6.50
9	7.70	19	6.48
10	7.30	20	6.47

a. On a set of axes showing the number of securities in the portfolio (x-axis) and portfolio risk, s_p (y-axis), plot the portfolio risk data given in the preceding table.
b. Divide the total portfolio risk in the graph into its *nondiversifiable* and *diversifiable* risk components, and label each of these on the graph.

  c. Describe which of the 2 risk components is the *relevant risk,* and explain why it is relevant. How much of this risk exists in David Finney's portfolio?

LG 3 **LG 6** P5.21 If portfolio A has a beta of $+1.50$ and portfolio Z has a beta of -1.50, what do the 2 values indicate? If the return on the market rises by 20%, what impact, if any, would this have on the returns from portfolios A and Z? Explain.

LG 3 **LG 6** P5.22 Stock A has a beta of 0.80, stock B has a beta of 1.40, and stock C has a beta of -0.30.

  a. Rank these stocks from the most risky to the least risky.
  b. If the return on the market portfolio increases by 12%, what change in the return for each of the stocks would you expect?
  c. If the return on the market portfolio declines by 5%, what change in the return for each of the stocks would you expect?
  d. If you felt the stock market was about to experience a significant decline, which stock would you be most likely to add to your portfolio? Why?
  e. If you anticipated a major stock market rally, which stock would you be most likely to add to your portfolio? Why?

LG 6 P5.23 Rose Berry is attempting to evaluate 2 possible portfolios consisting of the same 5 assets but held in different proportions. She is particularly interested in using beta to compare the risk of the portfolios and, in this regard, has gathered the following data:

		Portfolio Weights (%)	
Asset	Asset Beta	Portfolio A	Portfolio B
1	1.30	10	30
2	0.70	30	10
3	1.25	10	20
4	1.10	10	20
5	0.90	40	20
Total		100	100

  a. Calculate the betas for portfolios A and B.
  b. Compare the risk of each portfolio to the market as well as to each other. Which portfolio is more risky?

LG 4 P5.24 Referring to Problem 5.23 above, if the risk-free rate is 2% and the market return is 12%, calculate the required return for each portfolio using the CAPM.

LG 5 **LG 6** P5.25 Referring to Problem 5.24 above, assume you now have the following annual returns (r_j) for each investment.

Asset (j)	r_j
1	16.5%
2	12.0%
3	15.0%
4	13.0%
5	7.0%

Using your finding from Problem 5.24 and the additional return data, determine which portfolio you would choose and explain why.

> See www.myfinancelab.com **for Web Exercises,**
> **Spreadsheets, and other online resources.**

Case Problem 5.1   *Traditional Versus Modern Portfolio Theory: Who's Right?*

LG 5 **LG 6** Walt Davies and Shane O'Brien are district managers for Lee, Inc. Over the years, as they moved through the firm's sales organization, they became (and still remain) close friends. Walt, who is 33 years old, currently lives in Princeton, New Jersey. Shane, who is 35, lives in Houston, Texas. Recently, at the national sales meeting, they were discussing various company matters, as well as bringing each other up to date on their families, when the subject of investments came up. Each had always been fascinated by the stock market, and now that they had achieved some degree of financial success, they had begun actively investing.

As they discussed their investments, Walt said he felt the only way an individual who does not have hundreds of thousands of dollars can invest safely is to buy mutual fund shares. He emphasized that to be safe, a person needs to hold a broadly diversified portfolio and that only those with a lot of money and time can achieve independently the diversification that can be readily obtained by purchasing mutual fund shares.

Shane totally disagreed. He said, "Diversification! Who needs it?" He felt that what one must do is look carefully at stocks possessing desired risk-return characteristics and then invest all one's money in the single best stock. Walt told him he was crazy. He said, "There is no way to measure risk conveniently—you're just gambling." Shane disagreed. He explained how his stockbroker had acquainted him with beta, which is a measure of risk. Shane said that the higher the beta, the more risky the stock, and therefore the higher its return. By looking up the betas for potential stock investments on the Internet, he can pick stocks that have an acceptable risk level for him. Shane explained that with beta, one does not need to diversify; one merely needs to be willing to accept the risk reflected by beta and then hope for the best.

The conversation continued, with Walt indicating that although he knew nothing about beta, he didn't believe one could safely invest in a single stock. Shane continued to argue that his broker had explained to him that betas can be calculated not just for a single stock but also for a portfolio of stocks, such as a mutual fund. He said, "What's the difference between a stock with a beta of, say, 1.20 and a mutual fund with a beta of 1.20? They both have the same risk and should therefore provide similar returns."

As Walt and Shane continued to discuss their differing opinions relative to investment strategy, they began to get angry with each other. Neither was able to convince the other that he was right. The level of their voices now raised, they attracted the attention of the company vice-president of finance, Elinor Green, who was standing nearby. She came over and indicated she had overheard their argument about investments and thought that, given her expertise on financial matters, she might be able to resolve their disagreement. She asked them to explain the crux of their disagreement, and each reviewed his own viewpoint. After hearing their views, Elinor responded, "I have some good news and some bad news for each of you. There is some validity to what each of you says, but there also are some errors in each of your explanations. Walt tends to support the traditional approach to portfolio management. Shane's views are more supportive of modern portfolio theory." Just then, the company president interrupted them, needing to talk to Elinor immediately. Elinor apologized for having to leave and offered to continue their discussion later that evening.

Questions

a. Analyze Walt's argument and explain why a mutual fund investment may be over-diversified. Also explain why one does not necessarily have to have hundreds of thousands of dollars to diversify adequately.

b. Analyze Shane's argument and explain the major error in his logic relative to the use of beta as a substitute for diversification. Explain the key assumption underlying the use of beta as a risk measure.

c. Briefly describe the traditional approach to portfolio management, and relate it to the approaches supported by Walt and Shane.

d. Briefly describe modern portfolio theory (MPT), and relate it to the approaches supported by Walt and Shane. Be sure to mention diversifiable risk, nondiversifiable risk, and total risk, along with the role of beta.

e. Explain how the traditional approach and modern portfolio theory can be blended into an approach to portfolio management that might prove useful to the individual investor. Relate this to reconciling Walt's and Shane's differing points of view.

| Case Problem 5.2 | *Susan Lussier's Inherited Portfolio: Does It Meet Her Needs?* |

LG 3   LG 4

LG 5   LG 6

Susan Lussier is a 35-year-old divorcée currently employed as a tax accountant for a major oil and gas exploration company. She has no children and earns nearly $135,000 a year from her salary and from participation in the company's drilling activities. Divorced only a year, Susan has found being single quite exciting. An expert on oil and gas taxation, she is not worried about job security—she is content with her income and finds it adequate to allow her to buy and do whatever she wishes. Her current philosophy is to live each day to its fullest, not concerning herself with retirement, which is too far in the future to require her current attention.

A month ago, Susan's only surviving parent, her father, was killed in a sailing accident. He had retired in La Jolla, California, 2 years earlier and had spent most of his time sailing. Prior to retirement, he managed a children's clothing manufacturing firm in South Carolina. Upon retirement he sold his stock in the firm and invested the proceeds in a security portfolio that provided him with supplemental retirement income of over $30,000 per year. In his will, he left his entire estate to Susan. The estate was structured in such a way that in addition to a few family heirlooms, Susan received a security portfolio having a market value of nearly $350,000 and about $10,000 in cash.

Susan's father's portfolio contained 10 securities: 5 bonds, 2 common stocks, and 3 mutual funds. The accompanying table lists the securities and their key characteristics. The common stocks were issued by large, mature, well-known firms that had exhibited continuing patterns of dividend payment over the past 5 years. The stocks offered only moderate growth potential—probably no more than 2% to 3% appreciation per year. The mutual funds in the portfolio were income funds invested in diversified portfolios of income-oriented stocks and bonds. They provided stable streams of dividend income but offered little opportunity for capital appreciation.

Case 5.2 The Securities Portfolio that Susan Lussier Inherited

			Bonds				
Par Value	Issue	S&P Rating	Interest Income	Quoted Price	Total Cost		Current Yield
$40,000	Delta Power and Light 10.125% due 2026	AA	$ 4,050	98.000	$ 39,200		10.33%
30,000	Mountain Water 9.750% due 2018	A	2,925	102.000	30,600		9.56
50,000	California Gas 9.500% due 2013	AAA	4,750	97.000	48,500		9.79
20,000	Trans-Pacific Gas 10.000% due 2024	AAA	2,000	99.000	19,800		10.10
20,000	Public Service 9.875% due 2014	AA	1,975	100.000	20,000		9.88

			Common Stocks				
Number of Shares	Company	Dividend per Share	Dividend Income	Price per Share	Total Cost	Beta	Dividend Yield
2,000	International Supply	$2.40	$ 4,800	$22	$ 44,900	0.97	10.91%
3,000	Black Motor	1.50	4,500	17	52,000	0.85	8.82

			Mutual Funds				
Number of Shares	Fund	Dividend per Share	Dividend Income	Price per Share	Total Cost	Beta	Dividend Yield
2,000	International Capital Income A Fund	$0.80	$ 1,600	$10	$ 20,000	1.02	8.00%
1,000	Grimner Special Income Fund	2.00	2,000	15	15,000	1.10	7.50
4,000	Ellis Diversified Income Fund	1.20	4,800	12	48,000	0.90	10.00
		Total annual income:	$33,400	Portfolio value: $338,000		Portfolio current yield:	9.88%

Now that Susan owns the portfolio, she wishes to determine whether it is suitable for her situation. She realizes that the high level of income provided by the portfolio will be taxed at a rate (federal plus state) of about 40%. Because she does not currently need it, Susan plans to invest the after-tax income primarily in common stocks offering high capital gain potential. During the coming years she clearly needs to avoid generating taxable income. (Susan is already paying out a sizable portion of her current income in taxes.) She feels fortunate to have received the portfolio and wants to make certain it provides her with the maximum benefits, given her financial situation. The $10,000 cash left to her will be especially useful in paying broker's commissions associated with making portfolio adjustments.

Questions

a. Briefly assess Susan's financial situation and develop a portfolio objective for her that is consistent with her needs.

b. Evaluate the portfolio left to Susan by her father. Assess its apparent objective and evaluate how well it may be doing in fulfilling this objective. Use the total cost values to describe the asset allocation scheme reflected in the portfolio. Comment on the risk, return, and tax implications of this portfolio.

c. If Susan decided to invest in a security portfolio consistent with her needs—indicated in response to question **a**—describe the nature and mix, if any, of securities you would recommend she purchase. Discuss the risk, return, and tax implications of such a portfolio.

d. Compare the nature of the security portfolio inherited by Susan, from the response to question **b**, with what you believe would be an appropriate security portfolio for her, from the response to question **c**.

e. What recommendations would you give Susan about the inherited portfolio? Explain the steps she should take to adjust the portfolio to her needs.

Excel with Spreadsheets

In the previous chapter's spreadsheet problem, you helped Laura evaluate the risk-return tradeoff for 3 stand-alone securities. An alternative for Laura is to look at the investment as a portfolio of both IBM and HP and not as stand-alone situations. Laura's professor suggests that she use the capital asset pricing model to define the required returns for the 2 companies (refer to Equations 5.3 and 5.3a):

$$r_j = R_F + [b_j \times (r_m - R_F)]$$

Laura measures R_F using the current long-term Treasury bond return of 5% and measures r_m using the average return on the S&P 500 Index from her calculations in the Chapter 4 spreadsheet problem. She researches a source for the beta information and follows these steps:

- Go to moneycentral.msn.com.
- Within the "Get Quote" box, type IBM and press "Go."
- In the left column, look under "Quote, Chart, News" and choose "Company Report."
- Under the heading of "Stock Activity," find the "Volatility (beta)" figure.
- Repeat the same steps for the HP stock.

Questions

a. What are the beta values for IBM and HP? Assume that the beta for the S&P 500 Index is 1.0. Using the CAPM, create a spreadsheet to determine the required rates of return for both IBM and HP.

b. Laura has decided that the portfolio will be distributed between IBM and HP in a 60% and 40% split, respectively. Hence, a weighted average can be calculated for both the returns and betas of the portfolio. This concept is shown in the spreadsheet for Table 5.2, which can be viewed at www.myfinancelab.com. **Create a spreadsheet using the following models for the calculations:**

$$\text{war} = w_i * r_i + w_j * r_j$$

where:

war = weighted average required rate of return for the portfolio
w_i = weight of security i in the portfolio
r_i = required return of security i in the portfolio
w_j = weight of security j in the portfolio
r_j = required return of security j in the portfolio

$$\text{wab} = w_i * b_i + w_j * b_j$$

where:

wab = weighted average beta for the portfolio
w_i = weight of security i in the portfolio
b_i = beta for security i
w_j = weight of security j in the portfolio
b_j = beta for security j

Investing in Common Stocks

Common Stocks

After studying this chapter, you should be able to:

LG 1 Explain the investment appeal of common stocks and why individuals like to invest in them.

LG 2 Describe stock returns from a historical perspective and understand how current returns measure up to historical standards of performance.

LG 3 Discuss the basic features of common stocks, including issue characteristics, stock quotations, and transaction costs.

LG 4 Understand the different kinds of common stock values.

LG 5 Discuss common stock dividends, types of dividends, and dividend reinvestment plans.

LG 6 Describe various types of common stocks, including foreign stocks, and note how stocks can be used as investment vehicles.

B ear or bull market? It's often hard to tell. One day the headlines proclaim, "Dow Industrials Surge." The very next day, investors may read, "Stocks, Bonds Slip Back on Fed Move." You find analysts saying the market rally is real, while others call recent market events a mere correction. In the late 1990s, investing looked easy: Almost everything went up. Then, in the three-year bear market that began in 2000, investors wondered if they should buy stocks at all. Other times, rising interest rates and unsettled world events have caused the stock market to fluctuate from day to day with no clear trend.

The lack of clarity on the direction of the stock market is nothing new. Over the last 20 years there have been two Gulf Wars, a Cold War, tsunamis, hurricanes, world-wide terrorist incidents, medical issues (e.g., AIDs, SARS), inflation, high oil prices, and many more events that can be cause for concern to the stock market. Yet amidst all of these travails, the markets have survived. Corporations continue to operate, business goes on. New companies are born every year, some of which fail while others go on to become behemoths.

Microsoft, Inc., went public at a price of $21 per share on March 13, 1986, when the company had sales of $197.5 million and 1,442 employees. In 2005, Microsoft's sales were $39.79 billion, and it employed more than 70,000. How has its stock done? One hundred shares of common stock, originally issued at $21 per share or $2,100 in total, is now equal to 28,800 shares (due to nine stock splits). At a price of $23.07 per share in mid-July 2006, the original 100 shares would be worth $644,416. In addition, dividends for those 100 shares and subsequent splits would be worth $112,320. While not all common stocks have performed so well as Microsoft, there are many common stocks with great performances.

How do you choose the next Microsoft? Regardless of market conditions, investors who place their money at risk must learn how to gather, analyze, and interpret information about each company they consider and the industry in which it operates. This chapter introduces you to common stocks and to the key concepts and principles of investing in these complex but rewarding securities.

Sources: "Microsoft's Timeline from 1975–2005 downloaded from www.thocp.net/companies/microsoft/microsoft_company.htm (accessed July 19, 2006); historical prices for Microsoft, Inc., retrieved from http://finance.yahoo.com (accessed July 18, 2006).

What Stocks Have to Offer

LG 1   LG 2

residual owners
owners/stockholders of a firm, who are entitled to dividend income and a prorated share of the firm's earnings only after all other obligations have been met.

The basic investment attribute of common stocks is that they enable investors to participate in the profits of the firm. Every shareholder is a part owner of the firm and, as such, is entitled to a piece of the firm's profits. This claim on income is not without limitations, however, because common stockholders are really the **residual owners** of the company. That is, they are entitled to dividend income and a share of the company's earnings only after all other corporate obligations have been met. Equally important, *as residual owners, holders of common stock have no guarantee that they will receive any return on their investment.*

■ The Appeal of Common Stocks

Even in spite of the nasty (2000–2002) bear market, common stocks remain a popular form of investing, widely used by both individual and institutional investors. They are popular, in part, because they offer investors the opportunity to tailor their investment programs to meet individual needs and preferences. Given the size and diversity of the stock market, it's safe to say that no matter what the investment objective, there are common stocks to fit the bill. For people living off their investment holdings, stocks can provide a steady stream of current income (from their dividends). For other investors, common stocks can serve as the basis for long-run accumulation of wealth. With this strategy, investors buy stock for the long haul as a way to earn not only dividends but also a healthy dose of capital gains. It is this potential for capital gains that is the real draw for most investors. Whereas dividends can provide a steady stream of income, the big returns—under normal, long-term market conditions—come from capital gains. Few securities can match common stocks when it comes to capital gains.

■ Putting Stock Price Behavior in Perspective

Given the nature of common stocks, when the market is strong, investors can generally expect to benefit from steady price appreciation. A good example is the performance that took place in 2003, when the market, as measured by the Dow Jones Industrial Average (DJIA), went up by more than 25%. Unfortunately, when markets falter, so do investor returns. Just look what happened over the three-year period from early 2000 through late 2002, when the market (again, as measured by the DJIA) fell by some 38%. Excluding dividends, that means a $100,000 investment would have declined in value to a little over $60,000. That hurts!

Make no mistake about it: The market does have its bad days, and sometimes those bad days seem to go on for months. Even though it may not always appear to be so, those bad days *are the exception rather than the rule.* That was certainly the case over the 50-year period from 1956 through 2005, when the Dow went down (for the year) just 16 times—about 30% of the time. The other 70% of the time, the market was up—anywhere from 2% on the year to nearly 40%. True, there is some risk and price volatility (even in good markets), but that's the price you pay for all the upside potential. For example, from 1982 through early 2000, in one of the longest bull markets in history, the DJIA grew (over 18 years) at an average annual rate of nearly 17%. Yet, even in this market, there were some off days, and even a few off years. But, clearly, they were the exception rather than the rule.

▮ From Stock Prices to Stock Returns

Our discussion so far has centered on *stock prices*. What are even more important to investors are *stock returns*, which take into account both price behavior and dividend income. Table 6.1 uses the DJIA to show annual market returns over the 50-year period from 1956 to 2005. In addition to total returns, the table breaks market performance down into the two basic sources of return: dividends and capital gains. These figures, of course, reflect the *general behavior of the market as a whole,* not necessarily that of *individual stocks.* Think of them as the return behavior on a well-balanced portfolio of common stocks.

The numbers show a market that, over the past 50 years, has provided annual returns ranging from a low of −21.45% (in 1974) to a high of +42.71% (in 1975). Breaking down the returns into dividends and capital gains reveals, not surprisingly,

TABLE 6.1   **50 Years of Annual Returns in the Stock Market, 1956–2005 (returns based on performance of the DJIA)**

Year	Rate of Return from Dividends	Rate of Return from Capital Gains	Total Rate of Return	Year	Rate of Return from Dividends	Rate of Return from Capital Gains	Total Rate of Return
2005	2.32%	−0.60%	1.72%	1980	5.64%	14.93%	20.57%
2004	2.16	3.15	5.31	1979	6.08	4.19	10.27
2003	2.46	25.82	28.28	1978	6.03	−3.15	2.88
2002	1.75	−16.76	−15.01	1977	5.51	−17.27	−11.76
2001	1.81	−7.10	−5.29	1976	4.12	17.86	21.98
2000	1.61	−6.18	−4.58	1975	4.39	38.32	42.71
1999	1.47	25.22	26.69	1974	6.12	−27.57	−21.45
1998	1.65	16.10	17.75	1973	4.15	−16.58	−12.43
1997	1.72	22.64	24.36	1972	3.16	14.58	17.74
1996	2.03	26.01	28.04	1971	3.47	6.11	9.58
1995	2.27	33.45	35.72	1970	3.76	4.82	8.58
1994	2.75	2.14	4.89	1969	4.24	−15.19	−10.95
1993	2.65	13.72	16.37	1968	3.32	4.27	7.59
1992	3.05	4.17	7.22	1967	3.33	15.20	18.53
1991	3.00	20.32	23.32	1966	4.06	−18.94	−14.88
1990	3.94	−4.34	−0.40	1965	2.95	10.88	13.83
1989	3.74	26.96	30.70	1964	3.57	14.57	18.14
1988	3.67	11.85	15.52	1963	3.07	17.00	20.07
1987	3.67	2.26	5.93	1962	3.57	−10.81	−7.24
1986	3.54	22.58	26.12	1961	3.11	18.71	21.82
1985	4.01	27.66	31.67	1960	3.47	−9.34	−5.87
1984	5.00	−3.74	1.26	1959	3.05	16.40	19.45
1983	4.47	20.27	24.74	1958	3.43	33.96	37.39
1982	5.17	19.60	24.77	1957	4.96	−12.77	−7.81
1981	6.42	−9.23	−2.81	1956	4.60	2.27	6.87

Note: Total return figures are based on both dividend income *and* capital gains (or losses); all figures are compiled from DJIA performance information, as obtained from various Morningstar, Business Week, and Dow Jones web sites.

that the big returns (or losses) come from capital gains. We can use the return data in Table 6.1 to compute fully compounded rates of return over various, representative holding periods, as listed below:

Holding Periods	Average Annual Returns
5 years: 2001–2005	2.01%
10 years: 1996–2005	9.76%
15 years: 1991–2005	12.30%
25 years: 1981–2005	13.23%
50 years: 1956–2005	10.07%

Over the 50-year period from 1956 through 2005, we can see that *stocks have generated average annual returns of around 10%*. At that rate of return, your money will double every seven years, or so. Thus, a $10,000 investment in the Dow in 1956 would have been worth a little over $1.2 million in 2005. The only period (above) that turned in substandard performance was the five-year time span from 2001 to 2005. But that should come as no surprise, as that time period included most of the 2000–02 bear market.

Now keep in mind that the numbers here represent market performance; *individual* stocks can and often do perform quite differently. But at least the averages give us a benchmark against which we can assess current stock returns and our own expectations. For example, if a return of 10% to 12% can be considered a good long-term estimate for stocks, then *sustained* returns of 15% to 18% should definitely be viewed as extraordinary. (These higher returns are possible, of course, but to get them, investors very likely will have to take on more risk.) Likewise, long-run stock returns of only 6% to 8% should probably be viewed as substandard. If that's the best you think you can do, then you may want to consider sticking with bonds or CDs, where you'll earn almost as much, but with less risk.

▮ A Tech Stock Bubble Goes Bust

Starting in August 1982, with the Dow at less than 800, and after a decade of absolutely dismal returns, the stock market finally started to take off. Indeed, the bull market that began in 1982 continued on through the 1980s and into the early 1990s. Except for the length of this market, it didn't appear to be out of the ordinary in any other way—at least through the first half of the nineties. The fact is, the average rate of growth in share prices through 1994 was just 12%. But then in 1995, 1996, and 1997, things began to heat up, and the average rate of growth in share prices jumped to more than 27%. And by 1998, a *tech stock bubble* was in full bloom. Prices of technology-company stocks were experiencing phenomenal growth.

As can be seen in Figure 6.1 (on page 260), the tech-heavy Nasdaq Composite index began to skyrocket in August 1998. Over the next 18 months, it went up an incredible 240%. Many investors engaged in outright speculation. In fact, it really didn't seem to matter whether companies were generating earnings or not. These kinds of details, investors were told, were no longer important; the only thing that seemed to matter was whether the stock had a technology or Internet connection. Unfortunately, all that came to a screeching halt in early 2000, as each of the three major market measures peaked out.

FIGURE 6.1   **A Decade of the Dow and the Nasdaq (mid-1997 through mid-2006)**

One of the greatest bull markets in history began on August 12, 1982, with the Dow at 777. It continued on through the 1980s and into the 1990s. But it all ended in early 2000, when the market went from a rip-snorting bull to a full-fledged bear—one that lasted until late 2002, at which time the bulls took over again. (*Source:* Data from bigcharts.com and marketwatch.com.)

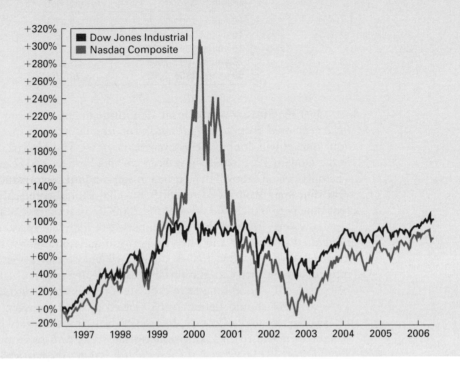

Over the course of the next 32 months, through September 2002, these market measures fell flat on their collective faces:

- The Dow fell 38%.

- The S&P dropped 49%.

- The Nasdaq fell 77%.

This period turned out to be one of the worst bear markets in recent history. All of the excesses that had built up over the last half of the 1990s were eliminated in a little more than 2½ years.

WEBEXTENSION

For an interesting look at this market, see the *Investing in Action* box entitled "Anatomy of a Market Meltdown" at:

www.myfinancelab.com

▉ The Pros and Cons of Stock Ownership

Investors own stocks for all sorts of reasons: the potential for capital gains, or their current income, or perhaps the high degree of market liquidity. But as with any investment vehicle, there are pros and cons to these securities.

The Advantages of Stock Ownership   One reason stocks are so appealing is the substantial return opportunities they offer. As we just saw, stocks generally provide attractive, highly competitive returns over the long haul. Indeed, common stock returns compare very favorably to other investment outlets such as long-term corporate bonds and U.S. Treasury securities. For example, over the period from 1950 through 2005, high-grade corporate bonds averaged annual returns of around 6%—*about half that of common stocks*. Although long-term bonds sometimes outperform stocks on a year-by-year basis (as they did in 2001–2003, when interest rates were in a free fall), the opposite is true far more often than not. Stocks typically outperform bonds, and usually by a wide margin. Because stocks can be counted on over most periods to provide returns that exceed annual inflation rates, they make ideal inflation hedges. Indeed, over the long run, as long as inflation rates remain at reasonably low levels of 2% to 3%, stocks are likely to continue to produce attractive inflation-adjusted returns.

Stocks offer other benefits as well: They are easy to buy and sell, and the transaction costs are modest. Moreover, price and market information is widely disseminated in the news and financial media. A final advantage is that the unit cost of a share of common stock is usually within the reach of most individual investors. Unlike bonds, which normally carry minimum denominations of at least $1,000, and some mutual funds that have fairly hefty minimum investments, common stocks don't have such minimums. Instead, most stocks today are priced at less than $50 or $60 a share—and any number of shares, no matter how few, can be bought or sold.

The Disadvantages There are also some disadvantages to common stock ownership. Risk is perhaps the most significant. Stocks are subject to various types of risk, including business and financial risk, purchasing power risk, market risk, and event risk. All of these can adversely affect a stock's earnings and dividends, its price appreciation, and, of course, the rate of return earned by an investor. Even the best of stocks possess elements of risk that are difficult to overcome, because company earnings are subject to many factors, including government control and regulation, foreign competition, and the state of the economy. Because such factors affect sales and profits, they also affect the price behavior of the stock and possibly even dividends.

All of this leads to another disadvantage: The earnings and general performance of stocks are subject to wide swings, so it is difficult to value common stocks and consistently select top performers. The selection process is complex because so many elements go into formulating expectations of stock performance. In other words, not only is the future outcome of the company and its stock uncertain, but the evaluation and selection process itself is far from perfect.

A final disadvantage of stocks is the sacrifice in current income. Several types of investments—bonds, for instance—pay higher levels of current income and do so with much greater certainty. Figure 6.2 (on page 262) compares the dividend yield on common stocks with the coupon yield on high-grade corporate bonds. It shows the degree of sacrifice common stock investors make in terms of current income. Clearly, even though the yield gap has narrowed a great deal in the past few years, common stocks still have a long way to go before they catch up with the *current income levels* available from bonds and most other types of fixed-income securities.

FIGURE 6.2

The Current Income of Stocks and Bonds

Clearly, the level of current income (dividends) paid to stockholders falls far short of the amount of interest income paid to bondholders. Note also that even though interest rates had fallen to 40-year lows by 2003, the dividend yield on stocks was still less than half the coupon yield on bonds.

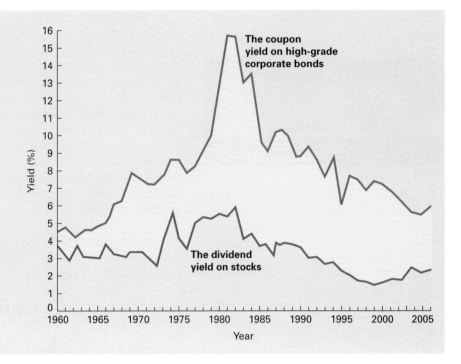

CONCEPTS IN REVIEW

Answers available at: www.myfinancelab.com

6.1 What is a *common stock?* What is meant by the statement that holders of common stock are the *residual owners* of the firm?

6.2 What are two or three of the major investment attributes of common stocks?

6.3 Briefly describe the behavior of the U.S. stock market over the past 10 to 15 years, paying special attention to market behavior since the mid-1990s. Contrast the market's performance from the late 1990s, through 2003 or 2004, as measured by the DJIA with its performance as measured by the Nasdaq Composite.

6.4 How important are dividends as a source of return to common stock? What about capital gains? Which is more important to total return? Which causes wider swings in total return?

6.5 What are some of the advantages *and* disadvantages of owning common stock? What are the major types of risk to which stockholders are exposed?

Basic Characteristics of Common Stock

LG 3   LG 4

equity capital
evidence of ownership position in a firm, in the form of shares of common stock.

Each share of common stock represents an equity (or ownership) position in a company. It's this equity position that explains why common stocks are often referred to as *equity securities* or **equity capital**. Every share entitles the holder to an equal ownership position and participation in the corporation's earnings and dividends, an equal vote, and an equal voice in management. Together, the common stockholders own the company. The more shares an investor owns, the bigger his or her ownership position. Common stock has no maturity date—it remains outstanding indefinitely.

▌ Common Stock as a Corporate Security

All corporations "issue" common stock of one type or another. But the shares of many, if not most, corporations are never traded, because the firms either are too small or are family controlled. The stocks of interest to us in this book are **publicly traded issues**—the shares that are readily available to the general public and that are bought and sold in the open market. The firms issuing such shares range from giants like AT&T and Microsoft to much smaller regional or local firms. The market for publicly traded stocks is enormous: The value of all actively traded listed and OTC stocks in mid-2006 was nearly $13 trillion.

publicly traded issues
shares of stock that are readily available to the general public and are bought and sold in the open market.

Issuing New Shares Companies can issue shares of common stock in several different ways. The most widely used procedure is the **public offering**. When using this procedure, the corporation offers the investing public a certain number of shares of its stock at a certain price. Figure 6.3 (on page 264) shows an announcement for such an offering. Note in this case that Advanced Micro Devices (AMD) is offering 14,096,000 shares of stock at a price of $35.20 per share. The new issue of common stock will provide this NYSE-traded company with nearly $500 million in new capital.

public offering
an offering to sell to the investing public a set number of shares of a firm's stock at a specified price.

Companies also can issue new shares of stock using what is known as a **rights offering**. In a rights offering, existing stockholders are given the first opportunity to buy the new issue. In essence, a stock right gives a shareholder the right (but not the obligation) to purchase new shares of the company's stock in proportion to his or her current ownership position.

rights offering
an offering of a new issue of stock to existing stockholders, who may purchase new shares in proportion to their current ownership position.

For instance, if a stockholder currently owns 1% of a firm's stock and the firm issues 10,000 additional shares, the rights offering will give that stockholder the opportunity to purchase 1% (100 shares) of the new issue. If the investor does not want to use the rights, he or she can sell them to someone who does. The net result of a rights offering is the same as that of a public offering: The firm ends up with more equity in its capital structure, and the number of shares outstanding increases.

Stock Spin-Offs Perhaps one of the most creative ways of bringing a new issue to the market is through a **stock spin-off**. Basically, a spin-off occurs when a company gets rid of one of its subsidiaries or divisions. For example, Ralston Purina did this when it spun off its Energizer subsidiary. The company doesn't just sell the subsidiary to some other firm. Rather, it creates a new stand-alone company and then distributes stock in that company to its existing stockholders. Thus, every Ralston Purina shareholder received a certain (prorated) number of shares in the newly created, and now publicly traded, Energizer company.

stock spin-off
conversion of one of a firm's subsidiaries to a stand-alone company by distribution of stock in that new company to existing shareholders.

There have been hundreds of stock spin-offs in the last 10 to 15 years. Some of the more notable ones were the spin-off of Coach (the designer bag company) by Sara Lee, the Freescale Semiconductor spin-off by Motorola, the spin-off of Agilent Technologies by Hewlett-Packard, and the spin-off of Moody's by Dun & Bradstreet. Normally, companies execute stock spin-offs if they believe the subsidiary is no longer a good fit, or if they feel they've become too diversified and want to focus on their core products. The good news is such spin-offs often work very well for investors, too.

stock split
a maneuver in which a company increases the number of shares outstanding by exchanging a specified number of new shares of stock for each outstanding share.

Stock Splits Companies can also increase the number of shares outstanding by executing a **stock split**. In declaring a split, a firm merely announces that it will increase the number of shares outstanding by exchanging a specified

FIGURE 6.3 An Announcement of a New Stock Issue

This announcement indicates that the company—Advanced Micro Devices, Inc.—is issuing over 14 million shares of stock at a price of $35.20 per share. For this manufacturer of microprocessors and memory chips, the new issue will mean nearly *half a billion dollars* in fresh capital. (*Source: Wall Street Journal*, February 2, 2006.)

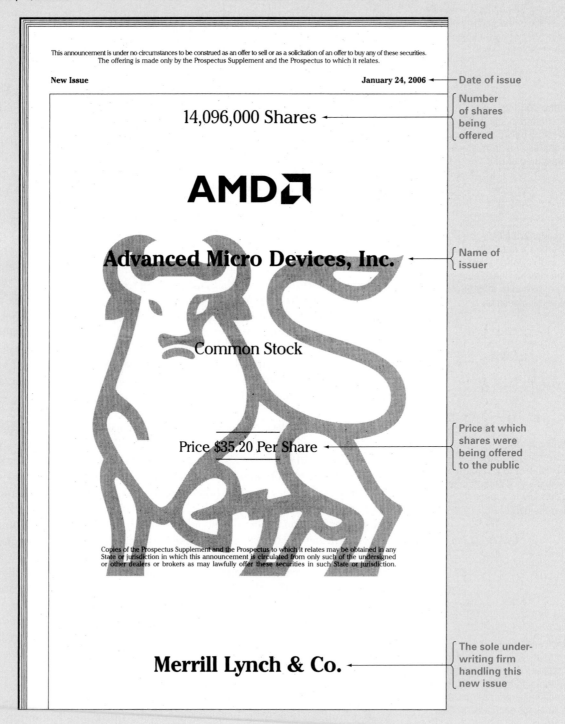

This announcement is under no circumstances to be construed as an offer to sell or as a solicitation of an offer to buy any of these securities. The offering is made only by the Prospectus Supplement and the Prospectus to which it relates.

New Issue   January 24, 2006 ← Date of issue

14,096,000 Shares ← Number of shares being offered

AMD

Advanced Micro Devices, Inc. ← Name of issuer

Common Stock

Price $35.20 Per Share ← Price at which shares were being offered to the public

Copies of the Prospectus Supplement and the Prospectus to which it relates may be obtained in any State or jurisdiction in which this announcement is circulated from only such of the undersigned or other dealers or brokers as may lawfully offer these securities in such State or jurisdiction.

Merrill Lynch & Co. ← The sole underwriting firm handling this new issue

number of new shares for each outstanding share of stock. For example, in a 2-for-1 stock split, two new shares of stock are exchanged for each old share.

HOTLINKS

Get the latest information on stock splits at:

biz.yahoo.com/c/s.html

In a 3-for-2 split, three new shares are exchanged for every two old shares outstanding. Thus, a stockholder who owned 200 shares of stock before a 2-for-1 split becomes the owner of 400 shares; the same investor would hold 300 shares if there had been a 3-for-2 split.

A company uses a stock split when it wants to enhance its stock's trading appeal by lowering its market price. Normally, the firm gets the desired result: The price of the stock tends to fall in close relation to the terms of the split (unless the stock split is accompanied by a big increase in the level of dividends). For example, using the ratio of the number of old shares to new, we can expect a $100 stock to trade at or close to $50 a share after a 2-for-1 split. Specifically, we divide the original price per share by the ratio of new shares to old. That same $100 stock would trade at about $67 after a 3-for-2 split—that is, $100 ÷ 3/2 = $100 ÷ 1.5 = $67. (Later in this chapter we will discuss a variation of the stock split, known as a stock dividend.)

Treasury Stock   Instead of increasing the number of outstanding shares, corporations sometimes find it desirable to *reduce* the number of shares by buying back their own stock. Generally speaking, firms repurchase their own stock when they view it as undervalued in the marketplace. When that happens, the company's own stock becomes an attractive investment candidate.

treasury stock
shares of stock that have been sold and subsequently repurchased by the issuing firm.

Those firms that can afford to do so will purchase their stock in the open market, like any other individual or institution. When acquired, these shares become known as **treasury stock**. Technically, treasury stocks are simply shares of stock that have been issued and subsequently repurchased by the issuing firm. Treasury stocks are kept by the corporation and can be used at a later date for any number of reasons. For example, they could be used for mergers and acquisitions, to meet employee stock option plans, or as a means of paying stock dividends. Or the shares can simply be held in treasury for an indefinite time.

The impact of these share repurchases—or *buybacks*, as they're sometimes called—is not clear. Generally, the feeling is that if the buyback involves a significant number of shares, the stockholder's equity position and claim on income will increase. This result is likely to benefit stockholders to the extent that such action has a positive effect on the market price of the stock. However, it has also been suggested that buybacks are often used merely as a way to prop up the price of an overvalued stock.

classified common stock
common stock issued by a company in different classes, each of which offers different privileges and benefits to its holders.

Classified Common Stock   For the most part, all the stockholders in a corporation enjoy the same benefits of ownership. Occasionally, however, a company will *issue different classes of common stock*, each of which entitles holders to different privileges and benefits. These issues are known as **classified common stock**. Hundreds of publicly traded firms have created such stock classes. Though issued by the same company, each class of common stock is different and has its own value.

Classified common stock is customarily used to denote either different voting rights or different dividend obligations. For instance, class A could designate nonvoting shares, and class B would carry normal voting rights. Or the class A stock would receive no dividends, and class B would receive regular cash dividends.

Notable for its use of classified stock is Ford Motor Company, which has two classes of stock outstanding. Ford's class A stock is owned by the investing public, and class B stock is owned by the Ford family and their trusts or corporations. The two classes of stock share equally in the dividends. But class A stock has one vote per share, whereas the voting rights of the class B stock are structured to give the Ford family a 40% absolute control of the company. Similar types of classified stock are used at the *Washington Post*, Dillards Department Stores, Dow Jones & Co., Nike, and Berkshire Hathaway.

Regardless of the specifics, whenever there is more than one class of common stock outstanding, investors should take the time to determine the privileges, benefits, and limitations of each class.

▐ Buying and Selling Stocks

Whether buying or selling stocks, you should become familiar with how stocks are quoted and with the costs of executing common stock transactions. Certainly, keeping track of *current prices* is an essential element in the buy-and-sell decisions of investors. Prices also help investors monitor the market performance of their security holdings. Similarly, *transaction costs* are important because of the impact they can have on investment returns. Indeed, the costs of executing stock transactions can sometimes consume most (or all) of the profits from an investment. These costs should not be taken lightly.

Reading the Quotes Investors in the stock market have come to rely on a highly efficient information system that quickly disseminates market prices to the public. The stock quotes that appear daily in the financial press are a vital part of that information system. To see how price quotations work and what they mean, consider the quotes that appear daily (Monday through Saturday) in the *Wall Street Journal*. As we'll see, these quotes give not only the most recent price of each stock but also a great deal of additional information.

Some NYSE stock quotes are presented in Figure 6.4—let's use the Nike quotations for purposes of illustration. These quotes were published in the *Wall Street Journal* on Tuesday, February 14, 2006. They describe the trading activity that occurred the day before, which in this case was Monday, February 13. A glance at the quotations shows that stocks, like most other securities, are quoted in dollars and cents.

Starting with the first two columns on the left in Figure 6.4 and then working our way across, we see that over the past 52 weeks, Nike hit a high of $91.54 a share and a low of $75.10. Next is the company name, Nike **B**; the B behind the name indicates that these are *Nike's class B common shares*, which are listed and traded on the NYSE. (The company also has some class A shares outstanding, but they are closely held by the company's founders and a few others, and are not publicly traded.) Following that, we see that Nike paid an annual cash dividend of $1.24 a share, providing shareholders with a *dividend yield* of 1.5% (found by dividing the dividend of $1.24 by the closing price of $84.28).

The next entry is the *P/E ratio*, which is the current market price divided by the per share earnings for the most recent 12-month period (also called "trailing P/E's"). As can be seen, Nike is trading at a P/E of 17 times earnings—a nice, solid multiple. That's followed by the number of shares traded, with the trades listed in round lots (of 100 shares). Thus, the actual number of Nike

FIGURE 6.4 Stock Quotations

This figure shows the quotations for a small sample of stocks traded on the NYSE, providing a summary of the transactions that occurred on one day. (*Source: Wall Street Journal*, February 14, 2006.)

52-WEEK			YLD		VOL		NET	
HI	LO	STOCK (DIV)	%	PE	100s	CLOSE	CHG	
29.34	12.95	NewMrkt(US)	...	12	1242	29.31	0.25	
62.72	34.90	NewmtMin .40	.7	55	74208	54.09	−0.71	
9.65	5.46	NewpkRes	...	43	3495	8.13	−0.10	
18.24	3.94	NewsCp A .12e	.8	...	37929	15.80	0.04	
18.63	14.76	NewsCp B .10e	.6	29	10574	16.60	−0.06	
59.94	22.88	Nexen s .20g	...	...	5925	48.83	−1.39	
42.97	35.76	Nicor 1.86	4.6	15	1913	40.65	−0.01	
23.40	12.98	Nidec ADS s.05	.3	...	408	18.34	−1.50	
91.54	75.10	Nike B 1.24	1.5	17	11891	84.28	−0.19	
16.60	8.61	99cOnlyStr If	...	29	2393	10.38	−0.12	
25.97	19.85	Nippon ADS .27e	1.2	...	3555	21.67	−0.18	
25.50	19.51	NiSource .92	4.5	18	10105	20.50	−0.15	
29.37	9	Nissin ADS s.06e	.3	...	55	20.20	−0.90	
84.96	48.81	Noble Crp x .16	.2	34	26684	72.93	−0.46	
48.75	30.90	Noble Engy s .20	.5	15	13501	40.99	−1.35	
19.94	14.52	Nokia .88e	4.9	...	77512	17.95	−0.04	
20.46	11.65	NmuraHldg .20e	1.1	...	5704	17.90	−0.44	
56.68	28.60	NrdcAmTkr 4.47e	12.9	12	4508	34.76	−0.92	
42.90	24.45	Nordstm .34	.8	23	10180	40.51	−0.39	
50.17	29.60	NorflkSo .64f	1.3	16	19343	48.27	−0.73	
124.90	75.90	Norsk 3.10e	2.8	...	301	112.42	−3.14	
12.35	7.82	NrtlInvr ADS	...	...	24	9.25	−0.26	
3.60	2.26	NortelNtwks	...	cc	198182	2.97	0.01	

Annotations:
- High and low prices for previous 52 weeks
- Company name, and annual dividends per share for past 12 months
- Dividend yield (dividends as percent of share price)
- Price/earnings ratio: (market price / earnings per share)
- Net change in price from previous day
- Closing (final) price for the day—this is also the price used to compute dividend yield and the P/E ratio
- Share volume, in hundreds

shares traded was $11{,}891 \times 100 = 1{,}189{,}100$ shares. Finally, we see that Nike's closing price (on the final trade of the day) was $84.28, which was 19 cents lower (-0.19) than the price at which the stock had ended the day before, when it closed at $84.47.

The same basic quotation system is also used for Nasdaq *Global Market* and *National Market* shares. That's not the case, however, for AMEX and small Nasdaq/OTC stocks. With those, you may get little more than the stock's name and symbol, share volume, closing price, and change in price.

Transaction Costs As explained in Chapter 3, investors can buy and sell common stock in round or odd lots. A *round lot* is 100 shares of stock or multiples thereof. An *odd lot* is a transaction involving fewer than 100 shares. For example, the sale of 400 shares of stock would be a round-lot transaction; the sale of 75 shares would be an odd-lot transaction. Trading 250 shares of stock would involve a combination of two round lots and an odd lot.

An investor incurs certain transaction costs when buying or selling stock. In addition to some modest transfer fees and taxes paid by the *seller*, the major cost is the brokerage fee paid—by both *buyer and seller*—at the time of the transaction. As a rule, brokerage fees can amount to just a fraction of 1% to as much as 2% or more, depending on whether you use the services of a discount broker or full-service broker. (Types of brokers and brokerage services were discussed in Chapter 3.) But they can go even higher, particularly for very small trades. Higher fees are connected with the purchase or sale of odd lots, which requires a specialist known as an *odd-lot dealer*. This usually results in an *odd-lot differential* of 10 to 25 cents per share, which is tacked on to the normal commission charge, driving up the costs of these small trades. Indeed, the relatively high cost of an odd-lot trade makes it better to deal in round lots whenever possible.

▌Common Stock Values

The worth of a share of common stock can be described in a number of ways. Terms such as *par value*, *book value*, *market value*, and *investment value* are all found in the financial media. Each designates some accounting, investment, or monetary attribute of a stock.

par value
the stated, or face, value of a stock.

Par Value The term **par value** refers to the stated, or face, value of a stock. Except for accounting purposes, it is relatively useless. Par value is a throwback to the early days of corporate law, when it was used as a basis for assessing the extent of a stockholder's legal liability. Because the term has little or no significance for investors, many stocks today are issued as no-par or low-par stocks. That is, they may have par values of only a penny or two.

book value
the amount of stockholders' equity in a firm; equals the amount of the firm's assets minus the firm's liabilities and preferred stock.

Book Value Book value, another accounting measure, represents the amount of stockholders' equity in the firm. As we will see in the next chapter, it is commonly used in stock valuation. Book value indicates the amount of stockholder funds used to finance the firm. It is calculated by subtracting the firm's liabilities and preferred stock from its assets. For example, assume that a corporation has $10 million in assets, owes $5 million in various forms of short- and long-term debt, and has $1 million worth of preferred stock outstanding. The book value of this firm would be $4 million.

Book value can be converted to a per-share basis—*book value per share*—by dividing it by the number of common shares outstanding. For example, if the firm just described has 100,000 shares of common stock outstanding, then its book value per share is $40. As a rule, most stocks have market prices that are well above their book values.

market value
the prevailing market price of a security.

Market Value Market value is one of the easiest stock values to determine. It is simply *the prevailing market price of an issue*. In essence, market value indicates how the market participants as a whole have assessed the worth of a share of stock.

By multiplying the market price of the stock by the number of shares outstanding, we can also find the market value of the firm itself—or what is known as the firm's *market capitalization*. For example, if a firm has one million shares outstanding and its stock trades at $50 per share, the company has a market value (or "market cap") of $50 million. For obvious reasons, the market value of a share of stock is generally of considerable importance to stockholders.

investment value
the amount that investors believe a security should be trading for, or what they think it's worth.

Investment Value Investment value is probably the most important measure for a stockholder. It indicates the worth investors place on the stock—in effect, what they think the stock *should* be trading for. Determining a security's investment value is a complex process based on expectations of the return and risk characteristics of a stock. Any stock has two potential sources of return: annual dividend payments and the capital gains that arise from appreciation in market price. In establishing investment value, investors try to determine how much money they will make from these two sources. They then use those estimates as the basis for formulating the return potential of the stock. At the same time, they try to assess the amount of risk to which they will be exposed by holding the stock. Such return and risk information helps them place an investment value on the stock. This value represents the *maximum* price an investor should be willing to pay for the issue. Investment value is the major topic in Chapter 8.

CONCEPTS IN REVIEW
Answers available at: www.myfinancelab.com

6.6 What is a *stock split?* How does a stock split affect the market value of a share of stock? Do you think it would make any difference (in price behavior) if the company also changed the dividend rate on the stock? Explain.

6.7 What is a *stock spin-off?* In very general terms, explain how a stock spin-off works. Are these spin-offs of any value to investors? Explain.

6.8 Define and differentiate between the following pairs of terms.
a. *Treasury stock* versus *classified stock.*
b. *Round lot* versus *odd lot.*
c. *Par value* versus *market value.*
d. *Book value* versus *investment value.*

6.9 What is an *odd-lot differential* and what effect does it have on the cost of buying and selling stocks? How can you avoid odd-lot differentials? Which of the following transactions would involve an odd-lot differential?
a. Buy 90 shares of stock.
b. Sell 200 shares of stock.
c. Sell 125 shares of stock.

Common Stock Dividends

LG 5

In 2005, U.S. corporations paid out more than half-a-trillion dollars in dividends ($545 billion, to be exact). Yet, in spite of these numbers, dividends still don't get much respect. Many investors, particularly younger ones, often put very little value on dividends. To a large extent, that's because capital gains provide a much bigger source of return than dividends—at least over the long haul.

But attitudes toward dividends are beginning to change. The protracted bear market of 2000–2002 revealed just how uncertain capital gains can be and, indeed, that all those potential profits can at times turn into substantial capital losses. At least with dividends, the cash flow is far more certain. Plus, dividends provide a nice cushion when the market stumbles (or falls flat on its face). Moreover, recent changes in the (federal) tax laws put dividends on the same plane as capital gains. Both now are taxed at the same (maximum 15%) tax rate. Thus, capital gains are no longer taxed at more attractive rates, making dividends just as attractive and perhaps even more so, as they're far less risky.

▮ The Dividend Decision

By paying out dividends, typically on a quarterly basis, companies share with their stockholders some of the profits they've earned. Actually, a firm's board of directors decides how much to pay in dividends. The directors evaluate the firm's operating results and financial condition to determine whether dividends should be paid and, if so, in what amount. If the directors decide to pay dividends, they also establish several important payment dates. In this section we'll look at the corporate and market factors that go into the dividend decision. Then we'll briefly examine some of the key payment dates.

Corporate Versus Market Factors   When the board of directors assembles for its regular dividend meeting, it weighs a variety of factors. First, the board looks at the firm's earnings. Even though a company does not have to show a profit to pay dividends, profits are still considered a vital link in the dividend decision.

earnings per share (EPS)
the amount of annual earnings available to common stockholders, as stated on a per-share basis.

With common stocks, the annual earnings of a firm are usually measured and reported in terms of **earnings per share (EPS)**. Basically, EPS translates aggregate corporate profits into profits on a per-share basis. It provides a convenient measure of the amount of earnings available to stockholders. Earnings per share is found by using the following formula:

Equation 6.1 ➤

$$EPS = \frac{\text{Net profit after taxes} - \text{Preferred dividends}}{\text{Number of shares of common stock outstanding}}$$

For example, if a firm reports a net profit of \$1.25 million, pays \$250,000 in dividends to preferred stockholders, and has 500,000 shares of common stock outstanding, it has an EPS of \$2 ((\$1,250,000 − \$250,000)/500,000). Note in Equation 6.1 that preferred dividends are subtracted from profits, since they must be paid before any funds can be made available to common stockholders.

While assessing profits, the board also looks at the firm's growth prospects. It's very likely that the firm will need some of it's present earnings for investment purposes and to help finance expected growth. In addition, the board will take a close look at the firm's cash position. Depending on the company and the firm's current dividend rate, the payment of dividends can take up a large amount of cash, so board members will want to make sure plenty of this precious resource is available. Finally, the board will want to make sure that it is meeting all legal and contractual constraints. For example, the firm may be subject to a loan agreement that legally limits the amount of dividends it can pay.

After looking at internal matters, the board will consider certain market effects and responses. Most investors feel that if a company is going to retain earnings rather than pay them out in dividends, it should exhibit proportionately higher growth and profit levels. The market's message is clear: If the firm is investing the money wisely and at a high rate of return, fine; otherwise, pay a larger portion of earnings out in the form of dividends.

Moreover, to the extent that different types of investors tend to be attracted to different types of firms, the board must make every effort to meet the dividend expectations of its shareholders. For example, income-oriented investors are attracted to firms that generally pay high dividends. Failure to meet those expectations can lead to disastrous results—a sell-off of the firm's stock—in the marketplace. Finally, the board cannot ignore the fact that investors today are placing a much higher value on dividends.

WEBEXTENSION

Boards of directors have come under scrutiny in recent years. For some insight on this issue, see the *Ethics* box for Chapter 6 on the book's Web site at

www.myfinancelab.com

date of record
the date on which an investor must be a registered shareholder to be entitled to receive a dividend.

payment date
the actual date on which the company will mail dividend checks to shareholders (also known as the *payable date*).

ex-dividend date
three business days up to the date of record; determines whether one is an official shareholder and thus eligible to receive a declared dividend.

Some Important Dates Let's assume the directors decide to declare a dividend. Once that's done, they must indicate the date of payment and other important dates associated with the dividend. Three dates are particularly important to the stockholder: date of record, payment date, and ex-dividend date. The **date of record** is the date on which the investor must be a registered shareholder of the firm to be entitled to a dividend. All investors who are official stockholders as of the close of business on that date will receive the dividends that have just been declared. These stockholders are often referred to as *holders of record*. The **payment date**, also set by the board of directors, generally follows the date of record by a week or two. It is the actual date on which the company will mail dividend checks to holders of record (and is also known as the *payable date*).

Because of the time needed to make bookkeeping entries after a stock is traded, the stock will sell without the dividend (ex-dividend) for three business days up to and including the date of record. The **ex-dividend date** will dictate whether you were an official shareholder and therefore eligible to receive the declared dividend. If you sell a stock *on or after* the ex-dividend date, you receive the dividend. The reason is that the buyer of the stock (the *new* shareholder) will not have held the stock on the date of record. Instead, you (the seller) will still be the holder of record. Just the opposite will occur if you sell the stock *before* the ex-dividend date. In this case, the new shareholder (the buyer of the stock) will receive the dividend because he or she will be the holder of record.

To see how this works, consider the following sequence of events. On June 3, the board of directors of Cash Cow, Inc., declares a quarterly dividend of 50 cents a share to holders of record on June 18. Checks will be mailed out on the payment date, June 30. The calendar below shows these dividend dates. In this case, if you bought 200 shares of the stock on June 15, you would receive a check in the mail sometime after June 30 in the amount of $100. On the other hand, if you purchased the stock on June 16, the *seller* of the stock would receive the check, because he or she would be recognized as the holder of record, not you.

June

S	M	T	W	T	F	S	
	1	2	3	4	5	6	— Declaration date
7	8	9	10	11	12	13	
14	15	16	17	18	19	20	— Date of record / — Ex-dividend date
21	22	23	24	25	26	27	
28	29	30					— Payment date

■ Types of Dividends

cash dividend
payment of a dividend in the form of cash.

stock dividend
payment of a dividend in the form of additional shares of stock.

Normally, companies pay dividends in the form of cash. Sometimes they pay dividends by issuing additional shares of stock. The first type of distribution is known as a **cash dividend**; the second is called a **stock dividend**. Occasionally, companies pay dividends in other forms, such as a *stock spin-off* (discussed earlier in this chapter) or perhaps even samples of the company's products. But dividends in the form of either cash or stock remain by far the most popular.

Cash Dividends More firms pay *cash dividends* than any other type of dividend. A nice by-product of cash dividends is that *they tend to increase over time, as companies' earnings grow*. In fact, for companies that pay cash dividends, the average annual increase in dividends is around 3% to 5%, though that rate of growth has started going back up in the past few years. This trend represents good news for investors, because *a steadily increasing stream of dividends tends to shore up stock returns in soft markets*.

dividend yield
a measure that relates dividends to share price and puts common stock dividends on a relative (percentage) rather than absolute (dollar) basis.

A convenient way of assessing the amount of dividends received is to measure the stock's **dividend yield**. Basically, this is a measure of dividends on a relative (percentage) basis, rather than on an absolute (dollar) basis. Dividend yield, in effect, indicates the rate of current income earned on the investment dollar. It is computed as follows:

Equation 6.2 ➤

$$\text{Dividend yield} = \frac{\text{Annual dividends received per share}}{\text{Current market price of the stock}}$$

Thus, a company that annually pays $2 per share in dividends to its stockholders, and whose stock is trading at $40, has a dividend yield of 5%.

To put dividend yield into perspective, it is helpful to look at a company's **dividend payout ratio**. The payout ratio describes that portion of earnings per share (EPS) that is paid out as dividends. It is computed as follows:

dividend payout ratio
the portion of earnings per share (EPS) that a firm pays out as dividends.

Equation 6.3 ➤

$$\text{Dividend payout ratio} = \frac{\text{Dividends per share}}{\text{Earnings per share}}$$

A company would have a payout ratio of 50% if it had earnings of $4 a share and paid annual dividends of $2 a share. Although stockholders like to receive dividends, they normally do not like to see payout ratios over 60% to 70%. Payout ratios that high are difficult to maintain and may lead the company into trouble.

The appeal of cash dividends took a giant leap forward in 2003, when the federal tax code changed to reduce the tax on dividends. Prior to this time, cash dividends were taxed as ordinary income, meaning they could be taxed at rates as high as 35%. For that reason, many investors viewed cash dividends as a highly unattractive source of income, especially since capital gains (when realized) were taxed at much lower preferential rates. Now, *both dividends and capital gains are taxed at the same low, preferential rate* (of 15% or less). That, of course, makes dividend-paying stocks far more attractive, even to investors in higher tax brackets. Other things being equal, the tax change should have a positive effect on the price behavior of dividend-paying stocks.

That, in turn, should motivate companies either to begin paying dividends or to increase their dividend payout rate.

Stock Dividends Occasionally, a firm may declare a *stock dividend*. A stock dividend simply means that the dividend is paid in additional shares of stock. For instance, if the board declares a 10% stock dividend, then each shareholder will receive one new share of stock for each ten shares currently owned.

Although they seem to satisfy some investors, *stock dividends really have no value*, because they represent the receipt of something already owned. The market responds to such dividends by adjusting share prices according to the terms of the stock dividend. Thus, in the example above, a 10% stock dividend normally leads to a decline of around 10% in the stock's share price. The market value of your shareholdings after a stock dividend, therefore, is likely to be the same as it was before the stock dividend. For example, if you owned 200 shares of stock that were trading at $100 per share, the total market value of your investment would be $20,000. After a 10% stock dividend, you'd own 220 shares of stock (i.e., 200 shares × 1.10), but because of the stock dividend, they would probably be trading at around $91 per share. You would own more shares, but they would be trading at lower prices, so the total market value of your investment would remain about the same (i.e., 220 × $91 = $20,020). There is, however, one bright spot in all this: Unlike cash dividends, stock dividends are not taxed until you actually sell the stocks.

Dividend Reinvestment Plans

Do you want to have your cake and eat it too? When it comes to dividends, there is a way to do just that. You can participate in a **dividend reinvestment plan (DRIP)**. In these corporate-sponsored programs, shareholders can have their cash dividends automatically reinvested into additional shares of the company's common stock. (Similar reinvestment programs are offered by mutual funds, which we'll discuss in Chapter 12, and by some brokerage houses, such as Merrill Lynch and Fidelity.) The basic investment philosophy is that *if the company is good enough to invest in, it's good enough to reinvest in*. As Table 6.2 (on page 274) demonstrates, such an approach can have a tremendous impact on your investment position over time.

Today more than 1,000 companies (including most major corporations) offer dividend reinvestment plans. These plans provide investors with a convenient and inexpensive way to accumulate capital. Stocks in most DRIPs are acquired free of any brokerage commissions, and most plans allow *partial participation*. That is, participants may specify a portion of their shares for dividend reinvestment and receive cash dividends on the rest. Some plans even sell stocks to their DRIP investors at below-market prices—often at discounts of 3% to 5%. In addition, most plans will credit fractional shares to the investor's account, and many will even allow investors to buy additional shares of the company's stock. For example, once enrolled in the General Mills plan, investors can purchase up to $3,000 worth of the company's stock each quarter, free of commissions.

Shareholders can join dividend reinvestment plans by simply sending a completed authorization form to the company. (Generally, it takes about 30 to 45 days for all the paperwork to be processed.) Once you're in, the number of

---

INVESTOR FACTS

THREE REASONS TO LOVE DIVIDENDS—Here are three more reasons to love dividends:
1. As a group, stocks that pay dividends tend to produce higher returns than those that do not: in 2005, the S&P dividend payers were up 6.5% vs. 3.6% for the non-dividend payers.
2. Since 1928, dividends have accounted for about 40% of the total returns on stocks.
3. Since 1980, dividend payers have averaged annualized total returns of 15.1% vs. 12.8% for the non-payers.

dividend reinvestment plans (DRIPs)
plans in which shareholders have cash dividends automatically reinvested into additional shares of the firm's common stock.

HOTLINKS

Use the directory of online resources about dividend reinvestment plans (DRIPs) and direct purchase of stocks at

www.dripadvisor.com

TABLE 6.2   Cash or Reinvested Dividends?

Situation: You buy 100 shares of stock at $25 a share (total investment, $2,500); the stock currently pays $1 a share in annual dividends. The price of the stock increases at 8% per year; dividends grow at 5% per year.

Investment Period	Number of Shares Held	Market Value of Stock Holdings	Total Cash Dividends Received
		Take Dividends in Cash	
5 years	100	$ 3,672	$ 552
10 years	100	5,397	1,258
15 years	100	7,930	2,158
20 years	100	11,652	3,307
		Full Participation in Dividend Reinvestment Plan (100% of cash dividends reinvested)	
5 years	115.59	$ 4,245	$ 0
10 years	135.66	7,322	0
15 years	155.92	12,364	0
20 years	176.00	20,508	0

shares you hold will begin to accumulate with each dividend date. There is a catch, however: Even though these dividends take the form of additional shares of stock, you must still pay taxes on them *as though they were cash dividends*. Don't confuse these dividends with stock dividends—*reinvested dividends are treated as taxable income in the year they're received*, just as though they had been received in cash. But at least with the new preferential tax rate, even this feature is much less of a burden than it used to be.

CONCEPTS IN REVIEW

Answers available at: www.myfinancelab.com

6.10 Briefly explain how the dividend decision is made. What corporate and market factors are important in deciding whether, and in what amount, to pay dividends?

6.11 Why is the *ex-dividend date* important to stockholders? If a stock is sold on the ex-dividend date, who receives the dividend—the buyer or the seller? Explain.

6.12 What is the difference between a *cash dividend* and a *stock dividend?* Which would be more valuable to you? How does a stock dividend compare to a stock split? Is a 200% stock dividend the same as a 2-for-1 stock split? Explain.

6.13 What are *dividend reinvestment plans*, and what benefits do they offer to investors? Are there any disadvantages?

Types and Uses of Common Stock

LG 6

Common stocks appeal to investors because they offer the potential for everything from current income and stability of capital to attractive capital gains. The market contains a wide range of stocks, from the most conservative to the highly speculative. Generally, the kinds of stocks that investors seek will depend on their investment objectives and investment programs. We will examine several of the more popular types of common stocks here, as well as the various ways such securities can be used in different types of investment programs.

▎Types of Stocks

As an investor, one of the things you will want to understand is the market system used to classify common stock. A stock's general classification reflects not only its fundamental source of return but also the quality of the company's earnings, the issue's susceptibility to market risks, the nature and stability of its earnings and dividends, and even its susceptibility to adverse economic conditions. Such insight is useful in selecting stocks that will best fit your overall investment objectives.

Among the many different types of stocks, the following are the most common: blue chips, income stocks, growth stocks, tech stocks, speculative stocks, cyclical stocks, defensive stocks, mid-cap stocks, and small-cap stocks. We will now look at each of these to see what they are and how investors might use them.

HOTLINKS

At this site, you can choose stocks by company size and type, and access growth and return rates. Lists show stock prices, quotes, and ratios.

screen.yahoo.com/stocks.html

blue-chip stocks
financially strong, high-quality stocks with long and stable records of earnings and dividends.

Blue-Chip Stocks Blue chips are the cream of the common stock crop. They are stocks that are unsurpassed in quality and have a long and stable record of earnings and dividends. **Blue-chip stocks** are issued by large, well-established firms that have impeccable financial credentials. These companies hold important, often leading positions in their industries and frequently set the standards by which other firms are measured.

Not all blue chips are alike, however. Some provide consistently high dividend yields; others are more growth oriented. Good examples of blue-chip growth stocks are Nike, Procter & Gamble, Home Depot, Walgreens, Lowe's Companies, and United Parcel Service. Figure 6.5 (on page 276) shows some basic operating and market information about UPS's stock, as obtained from the introductory part of a typical *S&P Stock Report*. Examples of high-yielding blue chips include such companies as Citigroup, Pfizer, DuPont, FPL Group, Bristol-Myers Squibb, and Verizon.

While blue-chip stocks are not immune from bear markets, they do nonetheless provide the potential for relatively attractive long-term returns. They tend to appeal to investors who are looking for quality investment outlets that offer decent dividend yields and respectable growth potential. They are often used for long-term investment purposes and, because of their relatively low risk, as a way of obtaining modest but dependable rates of return.

income stocks
stocks with long and sustained records of paying higher-than-average dividends.

Income Stocks Some stocks are appealing simply because of the dividends they pay. This is the case with **income stocks**. These issues have a long and sustained record of regularly paying higher-than-average dividends. Income stocks are ideal for those who seek a relatively safe and high level of current income from their investment capital. But there's more: Holders of income stocks (unlike bonds and preferred stocks) can expect the dividends they receive to increase regularly over time. Thus, a company that paid, say, $1.00 a share in dividends in 1990 would be paying just over $1.80 a share in 2005, if dividends had been growing at around 4% per year. That's a big jump in dividends, and it's something that can have a definite impact on total return.

FIGURE 6.5 A Blue-Chip Stock

(*Source:* Standard & Poor's *Stock Reports,* May 5, 2006. ©2006 The McGraw-Hill Companies. All Rights Reserved.)

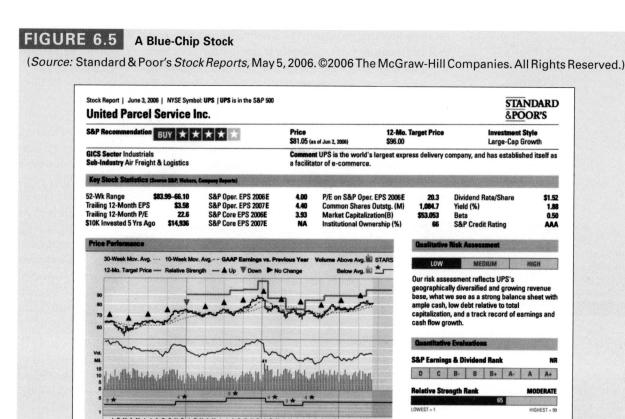

Analysis prepared by **Jim Corridore** on May 05, 2006, when the stock traded at **$83.69.**

The major disadvantage of income stocks is that some of them may be paying high dividends because of limited growth potential. Indeed, it's not unusual for income securities to exhibit only low or modest rates of growth in earnings. This does not mean that such firms are unprofitable or lack future prospects. Quite the contrary: Most firms whose shares qualify as income stocks are highly profitable organizations with excellent future prospects. A number of income stocks are among the giants of U.S. industry, and many are also classified as quality blue chips. Many public utilities, such as American Electric Power, Duke Energy, Oneok, Scana, DTE Energy, and Southern Company, are in this group. Also in this group are telecommunications stocks, such as Bell South and Citizens Communications, and selected industrial and financial issues like Conagra Foods, Sara Lee, Ford Motor, U.S. Bancorp, Bank of America, and Altria Group. By their very nature, income stocks are not exposed to a great deal of business and market risk. They are, however, subject to a fair amount of interest rate risk.

growth stocks
stocks that experience high rates of growth in operations and earnings.

Growth Stocks Shares that have experienced, and are expected to continue experiencing, consistently high rates of growth in operations and earnings are known as **growth stocks**. A good growth stock might exhibit a *sustained* rate

FIGURE 6.6   A Growth Stock

(*Source:* Standard & Poor's *Stock Reports*, April 14, 2006. ©2006 The McGraw-Hill Companies. All Rights Reserved.)

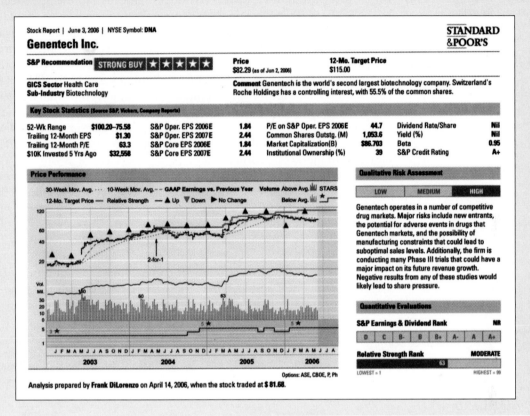

of growth in earnings of 15% to 18% per year over a period when common stocks, on average, are experiencing growth rates of only 6% to 8%. Generally speaking, established growth companies combine steady earnings growth with high returns on equity. They also have high operating margins and plenty of cash flow to service their debt. Medtronic, Boston Scientific, Countrywide Financial, Wellpoint, Leucadia National, Coach, and Genentech (shown in Figure 6.6) are all prime examples of growth stocks. As this list suggests, some growth stocks also rate as blue chips and provide quality growth, whereas others represent higher levels of speculation.

Growth stocks normally pay little or nothing in the way of dividends. Their payout ratios seldom exceed 10% to 15% of earnings. Instead, all or most of the profits are reinvested in the company and used to help finance rapid growth. Thus, the major source of return to investors is price appreciation—and that can have both a good side and a bad side. That is, with growth stocks, when the markets are good, these stocks are hot. When the markets turn down, so do these stocks, often in a big way. Growth shares generally appeal to investors who are looking for attractive capital gains rather than dividends and who are willing to assume a higher element of risk.

HOT LINKS

To read about characteristics of growth and value companies and their performance in recent years, go to:

www.efficientfrontier.com/ef/902/vgr.htm

tech stocks
stocks that represent the technology sector of the market.

Tech Stocks Over the past 15 years or so, *tech stocks* have become such a dominant force in the market (both positive and negative) that they deserve to be put in a class all their own. **Tech stocks** basically represent the technology sector of the market. They include companies that produce or provide everything from computers, semiconductors, data storage, computer software, and computer hardware to peripherals, Internet services, content providers, networking, and wireless communications. These companies provide the high-tech equipment, networking systems, and online services to all lines of businesses, education, health care, communications, governmental agencies, and the home. Some of these stocks are listed on the NYSE and AMEX, though the vast majority are traded on the Nasdaq. Tech stocks, in fact, dominate the Nasdaq market and, thus, the Nasdaq Composite Index and other Nasdaq measures of market performance.

These stocks would probably fall into either the *growth stock* category (see above) or the *speculative stock* class (see page 279), although some of them are legitimate *blue chips*. Tech stocks today may, indeed, offer the potential for attractive (and, in some cases, phenomenal) returns. But they also involve considerable risk, and are probably most suitable for the more risk-tolerant investor. Included in the tech-stock category you'll find some big names, like Microsoft, Cisco Systems, Hewlett-Packard, Intel, Dell, and Yahoo!. You'll also find many not-so-big names, like NVIDIA, Electronic Arts, Serena Software, Advantest, L-3 Communications, and SanDisk (see Figure 6.7).

FIGURE 6.7   **A Tech Stock**

(*Source:* Standard & Poor's *Stock Reports*, May 1, 2006. ©2006 The McGraw-Hill Companies. All Rights Reserved.)

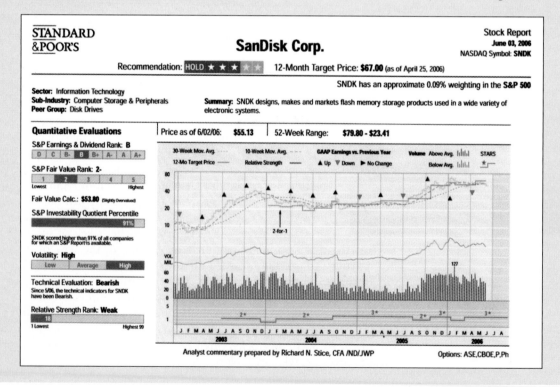

Speculative Stocks

Speculative Stocks Shares that lack sustained records of success but still offer the potential for substantial price appreciation are known as **speculative stocks**. Perhaps investors' hopes are spurred by a new management team that has taken over a troubled company or by the introduction of a promising new product. Other times, it's the hint that some new information, discovery, or production technique will favorably affect the growth prospects of the firm. Speculative stocks are a special breed of securities, and they enjoy a wide following, particularly when the market is bullish.

Generally speaking, the earnings of speculative stocks are uncertain and highly unstable. These stocks are subject to wide swings in price, and they usually pay little or nothing in dividends. On the plus side, speculative stocks such as Sirius Satellite Radio, Dreamworks Animation, FoxHollow Technologies, Liberty Media, NitroMed, and Under Armour offer attractive growth prospects and the chance to "hit it big" in the market. To be successful, however, an investor has to identify the big-money winners before the rest of the market does. Speculative stocks are highly risky; they require not only a strong stomach but also a considerable amount of investor know-how. They are used to seek capital gains, and investors will often aggressively trade in and out of these securities as the situation demands.

Cyclical Stocks Cyclical stocks are issued by companies whose earnings are closely linked to the general level of business activity. They tend to reflect the general state of the economy, and to move up and down with the business cycle. Companies that serve markets tied to capital equipment spending by business, or to consumer spending for big-ticket, durable items like houses and cars, typically head the list of cyclical stocks. Examples include Alcoa, Caterpillar, Genuine Parts, Lennar, Brunswick, Rohm & Haas, and Timken.

Cyclical stocks generally do well when the economy is moving ahead, but they tend to do *especially well* when the country is in the early stages of economic recovery. They are, however, perhaps best avoided when the economy begins to weaken. Cyclical stocks are probably most suitable for investors who are willing to trade in and out of these issues as the economic outlook dictates and who can tolerate the accompanying exposure to risk.

Defensive Stocks Sometimes it is possible to find stocks whose prices remain stable or even increase when general economic activity is tapering off. These securities are known as **defensive stocks**. They tend to be less affected than the average issue by downswings in the business cycle.

Defensive stocks include the shares of many public utilities, as well as industrial and consumer goods companies that produce or market such staples as beverages, foods, and drugs. An excellent example of a defensive stock is Bandag. This recession-resistant company is the world's leading manufacturer of rubber used to retread tires. Other examples are Checkpoint Systems, a manufacturer of antitheft clothing security clips, WD-40, the maker of that famous all-purpose lubricant, and Extendicare, a leading provider of long-term care and assisted-living facilities. Defensive shares are commonly used by more aggressive investors, who tend to "park" their funds temporarily in defensive stocks while the economy remains soft, or until the investment atmosphere improves.

Mid-Cap Stocks   A stock's size is based on its market value—or, more commonly, its *market capitalization*. This value is calculated as the market price of the stock times the number of shares outstanding. Generally speaking, the U.S. stock market can be broken into three segments, as measured by a stock's market "cap":

Small-cap   less than $1 billion

Mid-cap $1 billion to $4 or $5 billion

Large-cap   more than $4 or $5 billion

The large-cap stocks are the real biggies—the Wal-Marts, GMs, and Microsofts of the investment world. Although there are far fewer large-cap stocks than any other size, these companies account for 80% to 90% of the total market value of all U.S. equities. But as the saying goes, bigger isn't necessarily better. Nowhere is that statement more accurate than in the stock market. Indeed, both the small-cap and mid-cap segments of the market tend to hold their own, or even outperform large stocks over time.

mid-cap stocks
medium-sized stocks, generally with market values of less than $4 or $5 billion but more than $1 billion.

Mid-cap stocks offer investors some attractive return opportunities. They provide much of the sizzle of small-stock returns, without as much price volatility. (We'll look at small-cap stocks soon.) At the same time, because mid-caps are fairly good-sized companies and many of them have been around for a long time, they offer some of the safety of the big, established stocks. Among the ranks of the mid-caps are such well-known companies as Barnes & Noble, Williams-Sonoma, Manpower, American Eagle Outfitters, Alberto-Culver and Reebok International. Although these securities offer a nice alternative to large stocks without the uncertainties of small-caps, they probably are most appropriate for investors who are willing to tolerate a bit more risk and price volatility than large-caps have.

One type of mid-cap stock of particular interest is the so-called *baby blue chip*. Also known as "baby blues," these companies have all the characteristics of a regular blue chip *except size*. Like their larger counterparts, baby blues have rock-solid balance sheets, modest levels of debt, and long histories of steady profit growth. Baby blues normally pay a modest level of dividends, but like most mid-caps, they tend to emphasize growth. Thus, they're considered ideal for investors seeking quality long-term growth. Some well-known baby blues are Tootsie Roll, PetSmart, P. F. Chang's China Bistros, Liz Claiborne, and Hormel Foods (see Figure 6.8).

Small-Cap Stocks   Some investors consider small companies to be in a class by themselves in terms of attractive return opportunities. In many cases, this has turned out to be true. Known as **small-cap stocks**, these companies generally have annual revenues of less than $250 million. But because of their size, spurts of growth can have dramatic effects on their earnings and stock prices. Churchill Downs (where the Kentucky Derby is run), Playboy Enterprises, Jos. A. Bank Clothiers, K-Swiss, Build-a-Bear Workshops, Denny's, and Sanderson Farms are some of the better-known small-cap stocks.

small-cap stocks
stocks that generally have market values of less than $1 billion but can offer above-average returns.

Although some small-caps (like Sanderson Farms, for example) are solid companies with equally solid financials, that's not the case with most of them. Indeed, because many of these companies are so small, they don't have a lot of stock outstanding, and their shares are not widely traded. In addition, small-company stocks have a tendency to be "here today and gone tomorrow."

FIGURE 6.8   A Mid-Cap Stock

(*Source:* Standard & Poor's *Stock Reports,* March 27, 2006. ©2006 The McGraw-Hill Companies. All Rights Reserved.)

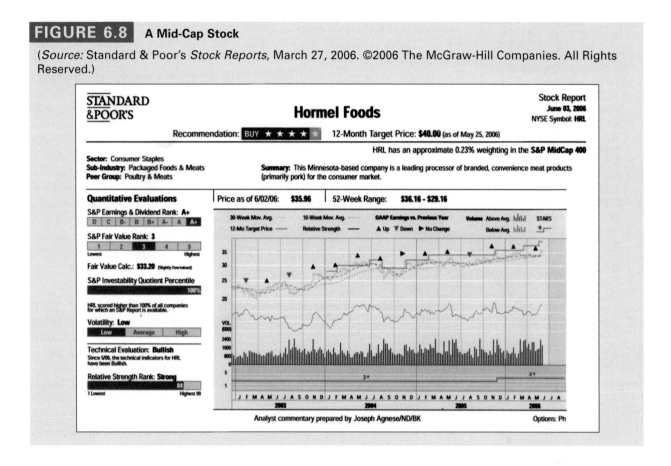

Analyst commentary prepared by Joseph Agnese/ND/BK

Although some of these stocks may hold the potential for high returns, investors should also be aware of the very high risk exposure that comes with many of them.

A special category of small-cap stocks is the so-called *initial public offering (IPO)*. Most IPOs are small, relatively new companies that are going public for the first time. (Prior to their public offering, these stocks were privately held and not publicly traded.) Like other small-company stocks, IPOs are attractive because of the substantial capital gains that investors can earn. Of course, there's a catch: To stand a chance of buying some of the better, more attractive IPOs, you need to be either an active trader or a preferred client of the broker. Otherwise, the only IPOs you're likely to hear of will be the ones these guys don't want. Without a doubt, IPOs are high-risk investments, with the odds stacked against the investor. Because there's no market record to rely on, only investors who know what to look for in a company and who can tolerate substantial exposure to risk should buy these stocks.

▌ Investing in Foreign Stocks

One of the most dramatic changes to occur in our financial markets in the past 20 years was the trend toward globalization. Indeed, globalization became the buzzword of the 1990s, and nowhere was that more evident than in the world's equity markets. Consider, for example, that in 1970 the U.S. stock market accounted for fully *two-thirds of the world market*. In essence, our stock market was twice as big as all the rest of the world's stock markets *combined*. That's no longer true: By 2005, the U.S. share of the world equity market had dropped to less than 50%.

Today the world equity markets are dominated by just six countries, which together account for about 80% of the total market. The United States, by far, has the biggest equity market, which in mid-2006 had a total market value of $13 *trillion*. In a distant second place was Japan (at about one-third the size of the U.S. market), closely followed by the United Kingdom. Rounding out the list were Germany, France, and Canada.

In addition to these six, another dozen or so markets are also regarded as major world players. Among the markets in this second tier are Switzerland, Australia, Italy, the Netherlands, Hong Kong, Spain, and Singapore. Finally, some relatively small, emerging markets—South Korea, Mexico, Malaysia, Portugal, Thailand, and Russia—are beginning to make their presence felt. Clearly, the landscape has changed a lot in the last 20 years, and there's every reason to believe that even more changes lie ahead.

Comparative Returns The United States still dominates the world equity markets in terms of sheer size, as well as in the number of listed companies (over 10,000 of them). But that leaves unanswered an important question: How has the U.S. equity market performed in comparison to the rest of the world's major stock markets? For an answer to that question, look at Table 6.3, which summarizes total annual returns (in U.S. dollars) for eight of the world's largest equity markets, over the 25-year period from 1981 through 2005. To begin with, we can see that over the latest three years (from 2003 through 2005), the comparative performance of U.S. stocks was nothing short of dismal: they finished last (8th) in each of those years. That, of course, accounts for their poor showing over the five-year holding period, 2001–2005. Looking beyond that period, however, we can see that while U.S. stocks have been able to generate highly competitive returns, they seldom finished on top. Translated, that means there definitely are attractive returns awaiting those investors who are willing to venture beyond our borders.

Now keep in mind that the returns shown in Table 6.3 *are in U.S. dollars*. As a result, some of the returns turned in by the non–U.S. markets can be traced to the behavior of *currency exchange rates*, and not just the markets themselves. For example, in 2004, the seven foreign markets reported in Table 6.3 generated an average annual return of 20.3%. But when those market returns are *measured in local currencies* (such as the British pound, Swiss franc, or Canadian dollar), the average annual returns drop to just 12.5%. Thus, the currency effect accounted for nearly 40% of the (2004) returns reported in Table 6.3. The fact is, the U.S. stock market is one of the strongest and best performing in the world. Even so, when both the market and currency effects are combined, it becomes readily apparent that *some very rewarding investment opportunities can be found in the global marketplace*.

Going Global: Direct Investments Basically, there are two ways to invest in foreign stocks: through direct investments or through ADRs. (We'll discuss a third way—international mutual funds—in Chapter 12.)

TABLE 6.3   Comparative Annual Returns in the World's Major Equity Markets, 1981–2005

				Annual Total Returns (in U.S. dollars)					
	Australia	Canada	France	Germany	Japan	Switzerland	United Kingdom	United States	Rank*
2005	17.5%	28.9%	10.6%	10.5%	25.6%	17.1%	7.4%	1.7%	8th
2004	32.0	22.8	19.2	16.7	16.0	15.6	19.6	5.3	8th
2003	51.4	55.4	41.0	64.8	36.2	35.0	32.1	28.3	8th
2002	−0.3	−12.8	−20.8	−32.9	−10.1	−10.0	−15.2	−14.5	5th
2001	2.6	−20.0	−22.0	−21.9	−29.2	−21.0	−14.0	−5.3	2nd
2000	−9.1	5.6	−4.1	−15.3	−28.1	6.4	−11.5	−4.6	4th
1999	18.7	54.4	29.7	20.5	61.8	−6.6	12.4	26.7	4th
1998	7.1	−5.7	42.1	29.9	5.2	24.0	17.8	17.8	4th
1997	−9.5	13.3	12.4	25.0	−23.6	44.8	22.6	24.4	3rd
1996	17.7	29.0	21.6	14.0	−15.3	2.8	27.2	28.0	2nd
1995	12.5	19.1	14.8	17.0	0.9	45.0	21.3	35.7	2nd
1994	1.4	−5.1	−7.3	3.1	21.4	30.0	−4.4	4.9	3rd
1993	33.4	17.4	19.6	34.8	23.9	41.7	19.0	16.4	8th
1992	−6.1	−4.6	5.2	−2.1	−26.0	26.0	14.0	7.2	3rd
1991	35.8	12.1	18.6	8.7	9.0	16.8	16.0	23.3	2nd
1990	−16.2	−12.2	−13.3	−8.8	−35.9	−5.1	10.4	−0.4	2nd
1989	10.8	25.2	37.6	48.2	2.3	28.0	23.1	30.7	3rd
1988	38.2	17.9	37.1	19.8	35.4	5.8	4.1	15.5	6th
1987	9.5	14.8	−13.9	−24.6	41.0	−9.2	35.2	5.9	5th
1986	45.0	10.8	79.9	36.4	101.2	34.7	27.7	26.1	7th
1985	21.1	16.2	84.2	138.1	44.0	109.2	53.4	31.7	6th
1984	−12.4	−7.1	4.8	−5.2	17.2	−11.1	5.3	1.2	4th
1983	55.2	32.4	33.2	23.9	24.8	19.9	17.3	24.7	5th
1982	−22.2	2.6	−4.2	10.5	−0.6	2.9	9.0	24.8	1st
1981	−23.8	−10.1	−28.5	−10.3	15.7	−9.5	−10.2	−2.8	2nd
			Average Annual Returns Over Extended Holding Periods						
5 years 2001–2005	19.2%	11.4%	2.8%	2.2%	4.8%	5.4%	4.4%	2.0%	
10 years 1996–2005	11.4	14.4	10.7	7.7	0.1	9.1	8.5	9.8	
15 years 1991–2005	12.4	12.0	10.4	9.0	1.4	16.1	9.9	12.3	
25 years 1981–2005	10.2	10.4	12.7	12.0	8.4	14.7	12.9	13.2	

Note: Total return = coupon income + capital gain (or loss) + profit (or loss) from changes in currency exchange rates.

*"Rank" shows how U.S. returns ranked among the listed major markets (e.g., in 2002, the United States ranked fifth out of the eight markets listed in the table).

Source: International returns obtained from Morgan Stanley Capital International; U.S. returns based on DJIA.

Without a doubt, the most adventuresome way is to *buy shares directly in foreign markets*. Investing directly is *not* for the uninitiated, however. You have to know what you're doing and be prepared to tolerate a good deal of market risk. Although most major U.S. brokerage houses are set up to accommodate investors interested in buying foreign securities, there are still many logistical problems to be faced. To begin with, you have to cope with currency fluctuations and changing foreign exchange rates, for as noted above, these can have a dramatic impact on your returns. But that's just the start: You also have to deal with different regulatory and accounting standards. The fact is that most foreign markets, even the bigger ones, are not as closely regulated as U.S. exchanges. Investors in foreign markets, therefore, may have to put up with insider trading and other practices that can cause wild swings in market prices. Finally, there are the obvious language barriers, tax problems, and general "red tape" that all too often plague international transactions. The returns from direct foreign investments can be substantial, but so can the obstacles placed in your way.

Going Global with ADRs Fortunately, there is an easier way to invest in foreign stocks, and that is to buy *American Depositary Receipts (ADRs)*. As we saw in Chapter 2, ADRs are dollar-denominated instruments (or certificates) that represent ownership of a certain number of shares in a specific foreign company. (The number of shares can range from a fraction of a share to 20 shares or more.) ADRs are great for investors who want to own foreign stocks but don't want the hassles that often come with them. Actually, ADRs trade in the market as *American Depositary Shares* (or *ADSs*). Although the terms *ADR* and *ADS* are often used interchangeably, technically there is a difference between the two: An ADR is the legal document that describes the security, whereas an ADS is the vehicle through which you invest in the security. Thus, ADSs represent shares in a given ADR and are the securities that are traded in the market. (Take a look at the stock quotes in the *Wall Street Journal*, and you will see that ADRs are listed in the quotes as ADSs. See for example, Figure 6.4, where you will find four ADSs listed.)

American Depositary receipts are bought and sold on U.S. markets just like stocks in U.S. companies. Their prices are quoted in U.S. dollars. Furthermore, dividends are paid in dollars. Although there are about 400 foreign companies *whose shares are directly listed on U.S. exchanges,* most foreign companies are registered in this country as ADRs. Indeed, shares of some 2,000 companies, from more than 50 countries, are traded as ADSs on the NYSE, AMEX, Nasdaq, and OTC markets.

To see how ADRs are structured, take a look at Cadbury Schweppes, the British food and household-products firm, whose ADRs are traded on the NYSE. Each Cadbury ADR represents ownership of four shares of Cadbury stock. These shares are held in a custodial account by a U.S. bank (or its foreign correspondent), which receives dividends, pays any foreign withholding

taxes, and then converts the net proceeds to U.S. dollars, which it passes on to investors. Other foreign stocks that can be purchased as ADRs include Sony (a Japanese stock), Ericsson Telephone (from Sweden), Nokia (Finland), Royal Dutch Shell (Netherlands), Nestle's (Switzerland), Elan Corporation (Ireland), Suntech Power (China), BASF (Germany), Hutchison Wampoa, Ltd. (Hong Kong), Teva Pharmaceuticals (Israel), Norsk Hydro (Norway), Diageo (U.K.), and Grupo Televisa (Mexico). You can even buy ADRs on Russian companies, such as Vimpel-Communications, a Moscow-based cellular phone company whose shares trade (as ADRs) on the NYSE.

Putting Global Returns in Perspective Whether you buy foreign stocks directly or through ADRs, the whole process of global investing is a bit more complicated and more risky than domestic investing. The reason: When investing globally, *you have to pick both the right stock and the right market.* Basically, foreign stocks are valued much the same way as U.S. stocks. Indeed, the same variables that drive U.S. share prices (earnings, dividends, and so on) also drive stock values in foreign markets. On top of this, each market reacts to its own set of economic forces (inflation, interest rates, level of economic activity), which set the tone of the market. At any given time, some markets are performing better than others. The challenge facing global investors is to be in the right market at the right time.

As with U.S. stocks, foreign shares produce the same two basic sources of returns: dividends and capital gains (or losses). But with global investing, there is a third variable—*currency exchange rates*—that affects returns to U.S. investors. In particular, as the U.S. dollar weakens or strengthens relative to a foreign currency, the returns to U.S. investors from foreign stocks increase or decrease accordingly. In a global context, total return to U.S. investors in foreign securities is defined as follows:

Equation 6.4 ➤

$$\begin{matrix} \text{Total return} \\ \text{(in U.S. dollars)} \end{matrix} = \begin{matrix} \text{Current income} \\ \text{(dividends)} \end{matrix} + \begin{matrix} \text{Capital gains} \\ \text{(or losses)} \end{matrix} \pm \begin{matrix} \text{Changes in currency} \\ \text{exchange rates} \end{matrix}$$

Because current income and capital gains are in the "local currency" (the currency in which the foreign stock is denominated, such as the euro or the Japanese yen), we can shorten the total return formula to:

Equation 6.5 ➤

$$\begin{matrix} \text{Total return} \\ \text{(in U.S. dollars)} \end{matrix} = \begin{matrix} \text{Returns from current} \\ \text{income and capital gains} \\ \text{(in local currency)} \end{matrix} \pm \begin{matrix} \text{Returns from} \\ \text{changes in currency} \\ \text{exchange rates} \end{matrix}$$

Thus, the two basic components of total return are *those generated by the stocks themselves* (dividends plus change in share prices) and *those derived from movements in currency exchange rates.*

Measuring Global Returns Employing the same two basic components noted in Equation 6.5, above, we can compute total return in U.S. dollars by using the following holding period return (HPR) formula, as modified for changes in currency exchange rates.

Equation 6.6 ➤

$$\begin{matrix} \text{Total return} \\ \text{(in U.S. dollars)} \end{matrix} = \left[\frac{\begin{matrix} \text{Ending value of} \\ \text{stock in foreign} \\ \text{currency} \end{matrix} + \begin{matrix} \text{Amount of dividends} \\ \text{received in} \\ \text{foreign currency} \end{matrix}}{\begin{matrix} \text{Beginning value of stock} \\ \text{in foreign currency} \end{matrix}} \times \frac{\begin{matrix} \text{Exchange rate} \\ \text{at } end \text{ of} \\ \text{holding period} \end{matrix}}{\begin{matrix} \text{Exchange rate} \\ \text{at } beginning \text{ of} \\ \text{holding period} \end{matrix}} \right] - 1.00$$

In Equation 6.6, the "exchange rate" represents the *value of the foreign currency in U.S. dollars*—that is, how much one unit of the foreign currency is worth in U.S. money.

This modified HPR formula is best used over investment periods of one year or less. Also, because it is assumed that dividends are received at the same exchange rate as the ending price of the stock, this equation provides only an approximate (though fairly close) measure of return. Essentially, the first component of Equation 6.6 provides returns on the stock in local currency, and the second element accounts for the impact of changes in currency exchange rates.

To see how this formula works, consider a U.S. investor who buys several hundred shares of Siemans AG, the German electrical engineering and electronics company that trades on the Frankfurt Stock Exchange. Since Germany is part of the European Common Market, its currency is the *euro*. Let's assume that the investor paid a price *per share* of 90.48 euros for the stock, at a time when the exchange rate between the U.S. dollar and the euro (U.S. $/€) was $0.945, meaning a euro was worth almost 95 (U.S.) cents. The stock paid *annual* dividends of 5 euros per share. Twelve months later, the stock was trading at 94.00 euros, when the U.S. $/€ exchange rate was $1.083. Clearly, the stock went up in price and so did the euro, so the investor must have done all right. To find out just what kind of return this investment generated (in U.S. dollars), we'll have to use Equation 6.6.

$$\text{Total return (in U.S. dollars)} = \left[\frac{94.00 + 5.00}{90.48} \times \frac{\$1.083}{\$0.945} \right] - 1.00$$

$$= [1.0942 \times 1.1460] - 1.00$$

$$= [1.2540] - 1.00$$

$$= \underline{25.4\%}$$

With a return of 25.4%, the investor obviously did quite well. However, *most of this return was due to currency movements, not to the behavior of the stock.* Look at just the first part of the equation, which shows the return (in local currency) *earned on the stock* from dividends and capital gains: 1.0942 − 1.00 = 9.42%. Thus, the stock itself produced a return of less than 9.50%. All the rest of the return—about 16% (i.e., 25.40 − 9.42)—came from the change in currency values. In this case, the value of the U.S. dollar went down relative to the euro and thus added to the return.

Currency Exchange Rates As we've just seen, exchange rates can have a dramatic impact on investor returns. They can convert mediocre returns or even losses into very attractive returns—and vice versa. Only one thing determines whether the so-called *currency effect* is going to be positive or negative: the behavior of the U.S. dollar relative to the currency in which the security is denominated. In essence, *a stronger dollar has a negative impact on total returns to U.S. investors, and a weaker dollar has a positive impact.* Thus, other things being equal, the best time to be in foreign securities is when the dollar is *falling*.

Of course, the greater the amount of fluctuation in the currency exchange rate, the greater the impact on total returns. The challenge facing global investors is to find not only the best-performing foreign stock(s) but also the best-performing foreign currencies. You want the *value of both the foreign stock and the foreign currency to go up over your investment horizon.* And note that this rule applies *both* to direct investment in foreign stocks and to the purchase of ADRs. (Even though ADRs are denominated in dollars, their quoted prices vary with ongoing changes in currency exchange rates.)

▮ Alternative Investment Strategies

Basically, common stocks can be used: (1) as a "storehouse" of value, (2) as a way to accumulate capital, and (3) as a source of income. Storage of value is important to all investors, as nobody likes to lose money. However, some investors are more concerned about it than are others. They rank safety of principal as their most important stock selection criteria. These investors are more quality-conscious and tend to gravitate toward blue chips and other non-speculative shares.

Accumulation of capital, in contrast, is generally an important goal to those with long-term investment horizons. These investors use the capital gains and/or dividends that stocks provide to build up their wealth. Some use growth stocks for this purpose, others do it with income shares, and still others use a little of both.

Finally, some investors use stocks as a source of income. To them, a dependable flow of dividends is essential. High-yielding, good-quality income shares are usually their preferred investment vehicle.

Individual investors can use various *investment strategies* to reach their investment goals. These include buy-and-hold, current income, quality long-term growth, aggressive stock management, and speculation and short-term trading. The first three strategies appeal to investors who consider storage of value important. Depending on the temperament of the investor and the time he or she has to devote to an investment program, any of these strategies might be used to accumulate capital. In contrast, the current-income strategy is the logical choice for those using stocks as a source of income.

We discuss these five strategies in more detail below. You should understand these strategies so that you can choose which one best suits your needs. Be aware though, as the *Investing in Action* box on page 288 indicates, that you may need to adjust your strategy a bit in a bear market.

Buy-and-Hold Buy-and-hold is the most basic of all investment strategies, and certainly one of the most conservative. The objective is to place money in a secure investment outlet (safety of principal is vital) and watch it grow over time. In this strategy, investors select high-quality stocks that offer attractive current income and/or capital gains and hold them for extended periods—perhaps as long as 10 to 15 years. This strategy is often used to finance future retirement plans, to meet the educational needs of children, or simply to accumulate capital over the long haul. Generally, investors pick a few good stocks and invest in them on a regular basis for long periods of time—until either the investment climate or corporate conditions change dramatically.

Buy-and-hold investors regularly add fresh capital to their portfolios (many treat them like savings plans). Most also plow the income from annual dividends back into the portfolio and reinvest in additional shares (often through dividend reinvestment plans). Long popular with so-called *value-oriented investors*, this approach is used by quality-conscious individuals who are looking for competitive returns over the long haul.

Current Income Some investors use common stocks to seek high levels of current income. Common stocks are desirable for this purpose, not so much for their high dividend yields but because their *dividend levels tend to increase over time*. In this strategy, safety of principal and stability of income are vital; capital gains are of secondary importance. Quality income shares are the obvious

INVESTING *in Action*

When a Bear Strikes

A bear market is often defined as a 20% or greater decline for a major stock index (such as the Dow Jones Industrial Average), combined with a pessimistic market outlook. Up and down markets are parts of a business cycle, and the stock market moves alongside because stocks generally follow corporate earnings.

Since 1900, there have been 21 instances when the Dow Jones Industrial Average dropped more than 20%. Statistically, a bear market occurs every five years or so, and lasts for about 18 months, for an average loss of about 35%. Some market declines were more severe. During the Great Depression 1929–33, the bear market lasted 34 months, during which Dow Jones lost 89% of its value. The 1973–74 bear market lasted for almost two years and resulted in a 45% loss. From then until 1991, there were four relatively short bear markets, one of which, on October 19, 1987, resulted in the most spectacular one-day market drop of 22.6%.

After the long and raging bull market of the 1990s, it was easy to forget the bad times. But to expect the market to grow at a 20%+ rate forever went against everything we learned from history. Thus, when the bear market unfolded in the spring of 2000, it was long and painful. It finally reached the bottom in October 2002, after a 38% decline in the Dow. The S&P 500 Index and the Nasdaq Composite, which included a larger number of volatile technology stocks, recorded losses of 49% and 77%, respectively.

There are a number of things investors can do to protect themselves from bears:

- **Stay on the sidelines.** There's an old saying that the best thing to do during a bear market is to "play dead," just as you should if you meet a real grizzly in the woods. Playing dead in financial terms means putting a larger portion of your portfolio on the sidelines in the form of cash.

- **Sell short.** Rather than running and ducking for cover, a different approach is to become more aggressive by selling short. A short position allows an investor to profit as stocks head downward.

- **Change asset allocation.** Moving part of your portfolio from stocks to bonds can be profitable during market downturns.

- **Invest in defensive industries.** Some stocks generally perform better than the overall market during bad times. Whether or not the economy is booming, people will still need to eat and drink, take medicine, brush their teeth, wash their clothes, and so on.

As these tips suggest, caution is the name of the game in a bear market. By having your money on the sidelines or invested in bond funds and defensive industries, and under certain circumstances selling stocks short, you can endure a bear market until the bulls return.

CRITICAL THINKING QUESTION What are the factors that cause market declines? Describe the steps you can take to protect your portfolio.

Sources: Jeff Fisher, "When Bear Markets End," *The Motley Fool*, July 25, 2002, www.fool.com; Surviving Bear Country, *Investopedia*, November 5, 2004, www.investopedia.com.

choice for this strategy. Some investors adopt it simply as a way of earning high (and relatively safe) returns on their investment capital. More often, however, the current-income strategy is used by those who are trying to supplement their income. Indeed, many of these investors plan to use the added income for consumption purposes, such as a retired couple supplementing their retirement benefits.

Quality Long-Term Growth This strategy is *less conservative* than either of the first two in that it *seeks capital gains as the primary source of return*. A fair amount of trading takes place with this approach. Most of the trading is confined to *quality growth stocks* (including some of the better tech stocks, as well as baby blues and other mid-caps). These stocks offer attractive growth prospects and the chance for considerable price appreciation. A number of growth stocks also pay dividends, which many growth-oriented investors consider *an added source of return*. But even so, this strategy still emphasizes capital gains as the principal way to earn big returns.

This approach involves greater risk, because of its heavy reliance on capital gains. Therefore, a good deal of diversification is often used. Long-term accumulation of capital is the most common reason for using this approach, but compared to the buy-and-hold tactic, the investor aggressively seeks a bigger payoff by doing considerably more trading and assuming more market risk.

A variation of this investment strategy combines quality long-term growth with high income. This is the so-called *total-return approach* to investing. Though solidly anchored in long-term growth, this approach also considers dividend income as a source of return. Investors who use the total return approach seek attractive long-term returns from *both* dividend income *and* capital gains by holding both income stocks and growth stocks in their portfolios. Or they may hold stocks that provide both dividends and capital gains. In the latter case, the investor doesn't necessarily look for high-yielding stocks, but for stocks that offer the potential for *high rates of growth in their dividend streams*.

Total-return investors are very concerned about quality. Indeed, about the only thing that separates them from current-income and quality long-term growth investors is that total-return investors care more about the *amount of return* than about the *source of return*. For this reason, total-return investors seek the most attractive returns wherever they can find them—be it from a growing stream of dividends or from appreciation in the price of a stock.

Aggressive Stock Management Aggressive stock management also seeks attractive rates of return through a fully managed portfolio. An investor using this strategy aggressively trades in and out of stocks to achieve eye-catching returns, primarily from capital gains. Blue chips, growth stocks, big-name tech stocks, mid-caps, and cyclical issues are the primary investment vehicles. More aggressive investors might even consider small-cap stocks, including some of the more speculative tech stocks, foreign shares, and ADRs.

This approach is similar to the quality long-term growth strategy. However, it involves considerably more trading, and the investment horizon is generally much shorter. For example, rather than waiting two or three years for a stock to move, an aggressive stock trader would go after the same investment payoff in six months to a year. Timing security transactions and turning investment capital over fairly rapidly are both key elements of this strategy. These investors try to stay fully invested in stocks when the market is bullish. When the market weakens, they put a big chunk of their money into defensive stocks or even into cash and other short-term debt instruments.

This aggressive strategy has substantial risks and trading costs. It also places real demands on the individual's time and investment skills. But the rewards can be equally substantial.

Speculation and Short-Term Trading Speculation and short-term trading characterize the least conservative of all investment strategies. The sole objective of this strategy is capital gains. The shorter the time in which the objective can be achieved, the better. Although investors who use this strategy confine most of their attention to speculative or small-cap stocks and tech stocks, they are not averse to using foreign shares (especially those in so-called *emerging markets*) or other forms of common stock if they offer attractive short-term opportunities. Many speculators feel that information about the industry or company is less important than market psychology or the general tone of the market. It is a process of constantly switching from one position to another as new opportunities unfold.

Because the strategy involves so much risk, many transactions yield little or no profit, or even substantial losses. The hope is, of course, that when one does hit, it will be in a big way, and returns will be more than sufficient to offset losses. This strategy obviously requires considerable knowledge and time. Perhaps most important, it also requires the psychological and financial fortitude to withstand the shock of financial losses.

CONCEPTS IN REVIEW

Answers available at: www.myfinancelab.com

6.14 Define and briefly discuss the investment merits of each of the following.
   a. *Blue chips.*
   b. *Income stocks.*
   c. *Mid-cap stocks.*
   d. *American Depositary Receipts.*
   e. *IPOs.*
   f. *Tech stocks.*

6.15 Why do most income stocks offer only limited capital gains potential? Does this mean the outlook for continued profitability is also limited? Explain.

6.16 With all the securities available in this country, why would a U.S. investor want to buy foreign stocks? Briefly describe the two ways in which a U.S. investor can buy stocks in a foreign company. As a U.S. investor, which approach would you prefer? Explain.

6.17 Which *investment approach (or approaches)* do you feel would be most appropriate for a quality-conscious investor? What kind of investment approach do you think you'd be most comfortable with? Explain.

Summary

LG 1 **Explain the investment appeal of common stocks and why individuals like to invest in them.** Common stocks have long been a popular investment vehicle, largely because of the attractive return opportunities they provide. From current income to capital gains, there are common stocks available to fit any investment need.

LG 2 **Describe stock returns from a historical perspective and understand how current returns measure up to historical standards of performance.** Stock returns consist of both dividends and capital gains, though price appreciation is the key component. Over the long run, stocks have provided investors with annual returns of around 10% to 12%. The decade of the 1990s was especially rewarding, as stocks generated returns of anywhere from around 20% (on the Dow) to nearly 30% in the tech-heavy Nasdaq market. That situation changed in early 2000, when one of the biggest bull markets in history came to an abrupt end. From 2000 through late 2002, the DJIA fell some 38%, the S&P 500 fell nearly 50%, and the Nasdaq fell an eye-popping 77%.

LG 3 **Discuss the basic features of common stocks, including issue characteristics, stock quotations, and transaction costs.** Common stocks are a form of equity capital, with each share representing partial ownership of a company. Publicly traded stock can be issued via a public offering or through a rights offering to existing stockholders. Companies can also increase the number of shares outstanding through a stock split. To reduce the number of shares in circulation, companies can buy back shares, which are then held as treasury stock. Occasionally, a company issues different classes of common stock, known as classified common stock.

LG 4 **Understand the different kinds of common stock values.** There are several ways to calculate the value of a share of stock. Book value represents accounting value. Market value is a security's prevailing market price. Investment value is the amount that investors think the stock should be worth.

LG 5 **Discuss common stock dividends, types of dividends, and dividend reinvestment plans.** Companies often share their profits by paying out cash dividends to stockholders. Companies pay dividends only after carefully considering a variety of corporate and market factors. Sometimes companies declare stock dividends rather than, or in addition to, cash dividends. Many firms that pay cash dividends have dividend reinvestment plans, through which shareholders automatically reinvest cash dividends in the company's stock.

LG 6 **Describe various types of common stocks, including foreign stocks, and note how stocks can be used as investment vehicles.** Depending on their needs and preferences, investors can choose blue chips, income stocks, growth stocks, tech stocks, speculative issues, cyclicals, defensive shares, mid-cap stocks, small-cap stocks, and initial public offerings. Also, U.S. investors can buy common stock of foreign companies either directly on foreign exchanges or on U.S. markets as American Depositary Shares (ADSs). Generally, common stocks can be used as a storehouse of value, as a way to accumulate capital, or as a source of income. Investors can follow different investment strategies (buy-and-hold, current income, quality long-term growth, aggressive stock management, and speculation and short-term trading) to achieve these objectives.

Key Terms

blue-chip stocks, *p. 275*
book value, *p. 268*
cash dividend, *p. 272*
classified common stock, *p. 265*
cyclical stocks, *p. 279*
date of record, *p. 271*
defensive stocks, *p. 279*
dividend yield, *p. 272*
dividend payout ratio, *p. 272*
dividend reinvestment plans
    (DRIP's), *p. 273*
earnings per share, *p. 270*
equity capital, *p. 262*
ex-dividend date, *p. 271*
growth stocks, *p. 276*
income stocks, *p. 275*

investment value, *p. 269*
market value, *p. 268*
mid-cap stocks, *p. 280*
par value, *p. 268*
payment date, *p. 271*
public offering, *p. 263*
publicly traded issues, *p. 263*
residual owners, *p. 257*
rights offering, *p. 263*
small-cap stocks, *p. 280*
speculative stocks, *p. 279*
stock dividend, *p. 272*
stock spin-off, *p. 263*
stock split, *p. 263*
tech stocks, *p. 278*
treasury stock, *p. 265*

Discussion Questions

LG 2   Q6.1   Look at the record of stock returns in Table 6.1, particularly the return performance during the 1970s, 1980s, 1990s, and 2000–2005.

       a. How would you compare the returns during the 1970s with those produced in the 1980s? How would you characterize market returns in the 1990s? Is there anything that stands out about this market? How does it compare with the market that existed from early 2000 through 2005?

       b. Considering the average annual returns that have been generated over holding periods of 5 years or more, what rate of return do you feel is typical for the stock market in general? Is it unreasonable to expect this kind of return, on average, in the future? Explain.

LG 3   Q6.2   Assume that the following quote for the Alpha Beta Corporation (a NYSE stock) was obtained from the Thursday, April 10, issue of the *Wall Street Journal*.

| 254.00 | 150.50 | AlphaBet 6.00 | 3.1 | 15 | 755 | 189.12 | −3.88 |

Given this information, answer the following questions.

       a. On what day did the trading activity occur?

       b. At what price did the stock sell at the end of the day on Wednesday, April 9?

       c. What is the firm's price/earnings ratio? What does that indicate?

       d. What is the last price at which the stock traded on the date quoted?

       e. How large a dividend is expected in the current year?

       f. What are the highest and lowest prices at which the stock traded during the latest 52-week period?

       g. How many shares of stock were traded on the day quoted?

       h. How much, if any, of a change in price took place between the day quoted and the immediately preceding day? At what price did the stock close on the immediately preceding day?

LG 4   Q6.3   Listed below are three pairs of stocks. Look at each pair and select the security you would like to own, given that you want to *select the one that's worth more money*. Then, *after* you make all three of your selections, use the *Wall Street Journal* or some other source to find the latest market value of the two securities in each pair.

       a. 50 shares of Berkshire Hathaway (stock symbol BRKA) or 150 shares of Coca-Cola (stock symbol KO). (Both are listed on the NYSE.)

       b. 100 shares of WD-40 (symbol WDFC—a Nasdaq National Market issue) or 100 shares of Nike (symbol NKE—a NYSE stock).

       c. 150 shares of Wal-Mart (symbol WMT) or 50 shares of Sears (symbol S). (Both are listed on the NYSE.)

How many times did you pick the one that was worth more money? Did the price of any of these stocks surprise you? If so, which one(s)? Does the price of a stock represent its value? Explain.

LG 6   Q6.4   Assume that a wealthy individual comes to you looking for some investment advice. She is in her early forties and has $250,000 to put into stocks. She wants to build up as much capital as she can over a 15-year period and is willing to tolerate a "fair amount" of risk.

  a. What types of stocks do you think would be most suitable for this investor? Come up with at least three different types of stocks, and briefly explain the rationale for each.

  b. Would your recommendations change if you were dealing with a smaller amount of money—say, $50,000? What if the investor were more risk-averse? Explain.

LG 6   Q6.5   Identify and briefly describe the three sources of return to U.S. investors in foreign stocks. How important are currency exchange rates? With regard to currency exchange rates, when is the best time to be in foreign securities?

  a. Listed below are exchange rates (for the beginning and end of a hypothetical 1-year investment horizon) for three currencies: the British pound (B£), Australian dollar (A$), and Mexican peso (Mp).

| | Currency Exchange Rates at | |
Currency	Beginning of Investment Horizon	End of One-Year Investment Horizon
British pound (B£)	1.55 U.S.$ per B£	1.75 U.S.$ per B£
Australian dollar (A$)	1.35 A$ per U.S.$	1.25 A$ per U.S.$
Mexican peso (Mp)	0.10 U.S.$ per Mp	0.08 U.S.$ per Mp

  From the perspective of a U.S. investor holding a foreign (British, Australian, or Mexican) stock, which of the above changes in currency exchange rates would have a positive effect on returns (in U.S. dollars)? Which would have a negative effect?

  b. ADRs are denominated in U.S. dollars. Are their returns affected by currency exchange rates? Explain.

LG 6   Q6.6   Briefly define each of the following types of investment programs, and note the kinds of stock (blue chips, speculative stocks, etc.) that would best fit with each.

  a. A buy-and-hold strategy.
  b. A current-income portfolio.
  c. Long-term total return.
  d. Aggressive stock management.

Problems

LG 3   P6.1   An investor owns some stock in General Refrigeration & Cooling. The stock recently underwent a 5-for-2 stock split. If the stock was trading at $50 per share just before the split, how much is each share most likely selling for after the split? If the investor owned 200 shares of the stock before the split, how many shares would she own afterward?

LG 3   P6.2   An investor deposits $20,000 into a new brokerage account. The investor buys 1,000 shares of Tipco stock for $19 per share. Two weeks later, the investor sells the Tipco stock for $20 per share. When the investor receives his brokerage account statement, he sees that there is a balance of $20,900 in his account:

Item	Number	Price per Share	Total Transaction	Account Balance
1. Deposit			$20,000	$20,000
2. Tipco purchase	1,000 shares	$19	($19,000)	$20,000
3. Tipco sale	1,000 shares	$20	$20,000	$21,000
4.				
5. Balance				$20,900

What belongs in item 4 on this statement?

LG 4   P6.3   Kracked Pottery Company has total assets of $2.5 million, total short- and long-term debt of $1.8 million, and $200,000 worth of 8% preferred stock outstanding. What is the firm's total book value? What would its book value per share be if the firm had 50,000 shares of common stock outstanding?

LG 4   P6.4   Lots ov' Profit, Inc., is trading at $25 per share. There are 250 million shares outstanding. What is the market capitalization of this company?

LG 5   P6.5   The MedTech Company recently reported net profits after taxes of $15.8 million. It has 2.5 million shares of common stock outstanding and pays preferred dividends of $1 million per year.
   a. Compute the firm's earnings per share (EPS).
   b. Assuming that the stock currently trades at $60 per share, determine what the firm's dividend yield would be if it paid $2 per share to common stockholders.
   c. What would the firm's dividend payout ratio be if it paid $2 per share in dividends?

LG 5   P6.6   On January 1, 2006, an investor bought 200 shares of Gottahavit, Inc., for $50 per share. On January 3, 2007, the investor sold the stock for $55 per share. The stock paid a quarterly dividend of $0.25 per share. How much (in $) did the investor earn on this investment, and, assuming the investor is in the 33% tax bracket, how much will she pay in income taxes on this transaction?

LG 4   LG 5   P6.7   Consider the following information about Truly Good Coffee, Inc.

Total assets	$240 million
Total debt	$115 million
Preferred stock	$25 million
Common stockholders' equity	$100 million
Net profits after taxes	$22.5 million
Number of preferred stock outstanding	1 million shares
Number of common stock outstanding	10 million shares
Preferred dividends paid	$2/share
Common dividends paid	$0.75/share
Market price of the preferred stock	$30.75/share
Market price of the common stock	$25.00/share

Use the information above to find the following.
   a. The company's book value.
   b. Its book value per share.
   c. The stock's earnings per share (EPS).
   d. The dividend payout ratio.
   e. The dividend yield on the common stock.
   f. The dividend yield on the preferred stock.

LG 5   **P6.8**   East Coast Utilities is currently trading at $28 per share. The company pays a quarterly dividend of $0.28 per share. What is the dividend yield?

LG 5   **P.6.9**   West Coast Utilities had a net profit of $900 million. It has 900 million shares outstanding, and paid annual dividends of $0.90 per share. What is the dividend payout ratio?

LG 5   **P6.10**   Collin Smythies owns 200 shares of Consolidated Glue. The company's board of directors recently declared a cash dividend of 50 cents a share payable April 18 (a Wednesday) to shareholders of record on March 22 (a Thursday).
  a. How much in dividends, if any, will Collin receive if he *sells* his stock on March 20?
  b. Assume Collin decides to hold on to the stock rather than sell it. If he belongs to the company's dividend reinvestment plan, how many new shares of stock will he receive if the stock is currently trading at $40 and the plan offers a 5% discount on the share price of the stock? (Assume that all of Collin's dividends are diverted to the plan.) Will Collin have to pay any taxes on these dividends, given that he is taking them in stock rather than cash?

LG 5   **P6.11**   Southern Cities Trucking Company has the following 5-year record of earnings per share.

Year	EPS
2003	$1.40
2004	2.10
2005	1.00
2006	3.25
2007	0.80

Which of the following procedures would produce the greater amount of dividends to stockholders over this 5-year period?
  a. Paying out dividends at a fixed ratio of 40% of EPS.
  b. Paying out dividends at a fixed rate of $1 per share.

LG 4 LG 5   **P6.12**   Using the resources available at your campus or public library, or on the Internet, select any three common stocks you like, and determine the latest book value per share, earnings per share, dividend payout ratio, and dividend yield for each. (Show all your calculations.)

LG 4 LG 5   **P6.13**   In January 2003, an investor purchased 800 shares of Engulf & Devour, a rapidly growing high-tech conglomerate. Over the 5-year period from 2003 through 2007, the stock turned in the following dividend and share price performance.

Year	Share Price at Beginning of Year	Dividends Paid During Year	Share Price at End of Year
2003	$42.50*	$0.82	$ 54.00
2004	54.00	1.28	74.25
2005	74.25	1.64	81.00
2006	81.00	1.91	91.25
2007	91.25	2.30	128.75

*Investor purchased stock in 2003 at this price.

On the basis of this information, find the annual holding period returns for 2003 through 2007. (*Hint:* See Chapter 4 for the HPR formula.)

LG 6 P6.14 George Robbins considers himself to be an aggressive investor. At the present time, he's thinking about investing in some foreign securities. In particular, he's looking at two stocks: (1) Bayer AG, the big German chemical and health-care firm, and (2) Swisscom AG, the Swiss telecommunications company.

Bayer AG, which trades on the Frankfurt Exchange, is currently priced at 53.25 euros per share. It pays annual dividends of 1.50 euros per share. Robbins expects the stock to climb to 60.00 euros per share over the next 12 months. The current exchange rate is 0.9025 €/U.S. $, but that's expected to rise to 1.015 €/U.S. $.

The other company, Swisscom, trades on the Zurich Exchange and is currently priced at 71.5 Swiss francs (Sf) per share. The stock pays annual dividends of 1.5 Sf per share. Its share price is expected to go up to 76.0 Sf within a year. At current exchange rates, one Sf is worth $0.75 U.S., but that's expected to go to $0.85 by the end of the 1-year holding period.

  a. *Ignoring the currency effect*, which of the two stocks promises the higher total return (in its local currency)? Based on this information, which of the two stocks looks like the better investment?

  b. Which of the two stocks has the better total return *in U.S. dollars*? Did currency exchange rates affect their returns in any way? Do you still want to stick with the same stock you selected in part (a)? Explain.

LG 6 P6.15 Bob buys $25,000 of UH-OH Corporation stock. Unfortunately, a major newspaper reveals the very next day that the company is being investigated for accounting fraud, and the stock price falls by 50%. What is the percentage increase now required for Bob to get back to $25,000 of value?

See www.myfinancelab.com **for Web Exercises,**
Spreadsheets, and other online resources.

Case Problem 6.1   *Sara Decides to Take the Plunge*

LG 1 **LG 6** Sara Thomas is a child psychologist who has built up a thriving practice in her hometown of Boise, Idaho. Over the past several years she has been able to accumulate a substantial sum of money. She has worked long and hard to be successful, but she never imagined anything like this. Even so, success has not spoiled Sara. Still single, she keeps to her old circle of friends. One of her closest friends is Terry Jenkins, who happens to be a stockbroker, and who acts as Sara's financial adviser.

Not long ago, Sara attended a seminar on investing in the stock market, and since then she's been doing some reading about the market. She has concluded that keeping all of her money in low-yielding savings accounts doesn't make sense. As a result, Sara has decided to move part of her money to stocks. One evening, Sara told Terry about her decision and explained that she had found several stocks that she thought looked "sort of interesting." She described them as follows:

- *North Atlantic Swim Suit Company.* This highly speculative stock pays no dividends. Although the earnings of NASS have been a bit erratic, Sara feels that its growth prospects have never been brighter—"what with more people than ever going to the beaches the way they are these days," she says.

- *Town and Country Computer.* This is a long-established computer firm that pays a modest dividend yield (of about 1.50%). It is considered a quality growth stock. From one of the stock reports she read, Sara understands that T&C offers excellent long-term growth and capital gains potential.

- *Southeastern Public Utility Company.* This income stock pays a dividend yield of around 5%. Although it's a solid company, it has limited growth prospects because of its location.

- *International Gold Mines, Inc.* This stock has performed quite well in the past, especially when inflation has become a problem. Sara feels that if it can do so well in inflationary times, it will do even better in a strong economy. Unfortunately, the stock has experienced wide price swings in the past. It pays almost no dividends.

Questions

a. What do you think of the idea of Sara keeping "substantial sums" of money in savings accounts? Would common stocks make better investments for her than savings accounts? Explain.

b. What is your opinion of the four stocks Sara has described? Do you think they are suitable for her investment needs? Explain.

c. What kind of common stock investment program would you recommend for Sara? What investment objectives do you think she should set for herself, and how can common stocks help her achieve her goals?

Case Problem 6.2   *Wally Wonders Whether There's a Place for Dividends*

LG 5   LG 6   Wally Wilson is a commercial artist who makes a good living by doing freelance work—mostly layouts and illustrations—for local ad agencies and major institutional clients (such as large department stores). Wally has been investing in the stock market for some time, buying mostly high-quality growth stocks as a way to achieve long-term growth and capital appreciation. He feels that with the limited time he has to devote to his security holdings, high-quality issues are his best bet. He has become a bit perplexed lately with the market, disturbed that some of his growth stocks aren't doing even as well as many good-grade income shares. He therefore decides to have a chat with his broker, Al Fried.

During the course of their conversation, it becomes clear that both Al and Wally are thinking along the same lines. Al points out that dividend yields on income shares are indeed way up and that, because of the state of the economy, the outlook for growth stocks is not particularly bright. He suggests that Wally seriously consider putting some of his money into income shares to capture the high dividend yields that are available. After all, as Al says, "the bottom line is not so much where the payoff comes from as how much it amounts to!" They then talk about a high-yield public utility stock, Hydro-Electric Light and Power. Al digs up some forecast information about Hydro-Electric and presents it to Wally for his consideration:

Year	Expected EPS	Expected Dividend Payout Ratio
2007	$3.25	40%
2008	3.40	40
2009	3.90	45
2010	4.40	45
2011	5.00	45

The stock currently trades at $60 per share. Al thinks that within 5 years it should be trading at around $75 to $80 a share. Wally realizes that to buy the Hydro-Electric stock, he will have to sell his holdings of CapCo Industries—a highly regarded growth stock that Wally is disenchanted with because of recent substandard performance.

Questions

a. How would you describe Wally's present investment program? How do you think it fits him and his investment objectives?

b. Consider the Hydro-Electric stock.
   1. Determine the amount of annual dividends Hydro-Electric can be expected to pay over the years 2007 to 2011.
   2. Compute the total dollar return that Wally will make from Hydro-Electric if he invests $6,000 in the stock and all the dividend and price expectations are realized.
   3. If Wally participates in the company's dividend reinvestment plan, how many shares of stock will he have by the end of 2011? What will they be worth if the stock trades at $80 on December 31, 2011? Assume that the stock can be purchased through the dividend reinvestment plan at a net price of $50 a share in 2007, $55 in 2008, $60 in 2009, $65 in 2010, and $70 in 2011. Use fractional shares, to two decimals, in your computations. Also, assume that, as in part (b), Wally starts with 100 shares of stock and all dividend expectations are realized.

c. Would Wally be going to a different investment strategy if he decided to buy shares in Hydro-Electric? If the switch is made, how would you describe his new investment program? What do you think of this new approach? Is it likely to lead to more trading on Wally's behalf? If so, can you reconcile that with the limited amount of time he has to devote to his portfolio?

Excel with Spreadsheets

Efficient information that quickly disseminates market prices is imperative for investors in the stock market. A major component of the information system is the stock quote that appears daily in the financial press.

You found the following stock quote (on page 300) for City National Corporation (CYN) in the August 10, 2006 edition of the *Wall Street Journal*. Refer to Figure 6.4, "Stock Quotations," for an explanation of the array of information related to the listed stock. Given the respective quote, create a spreadsheet to answer the following questions concerning the common stock investment.

	A	B	C	D	E	F	G	H	I	J	K	L
1				New York Stock Exchange Composite Transactions								
2		52	WEEKS				YLD		VOL		NET	
3		HI	LO	STOCK (DIV)			%	PE	100S	CLOSE	CHG	
4	[1]	78.25	60.02	City Ntl 1.64			2.5%	14	1660	?	−0.36	
5												
6												

Questions

a.   What was the closing price for this stock yesterday?

b.   How many round lots of stock were traded yesterday? How many individual stocks does that translate into?

c.   What are the current earnings per share (EPS) for this stock based on the data presented?

d.   What is the current net income for this stock? (*Hint*: You must find out the number of shares outstanding.) Using the Internet, follow these steps:

- Go to www.moneycentral.msn.com.
- Place "CYN" in quote box and click "Go."
- Look on the left side for "Financial Results."
- Click on "Statements."
- Choose "Balance Sheet" from the pull-down financial statement menu and "annual" from the view box pull-down menu.
- At the bottom of the statement, look for "Total Common Shares Outstanding."

e.   Calculate the dividend payout ratio for City National.

Analyzing Common Stocks

LEARNING GOALS

After studying this chapter, you should be able to:

LG 1   Discuss the security analysis process, including its goals and functions.

LG 2   Understand the purpose and contributions of economic analysis.

LG 3   Describe industry analysis and note how it is used.

LG 4   Demonstrate a basic appreciation of fundamental analysis and why it is used.

LG 5   Calculate a variety of financial ratios and describe how financial statement analysis is used to gauge the financial vitality of a company.

LG 6   Use various financial measures to assess a company's performance, and explain how the insights derived form the basic input for the valuation process.

With over 7,000 companies listed on the NYSE and the Nasdaq National Market, how do you decide which ones are good investment candidates? You could start with companies whose goods and services you know. Dell, Disney, Ford, General Electric, McDonald's, and Wal-Mart are just a few companies that come to mind. Familiarity with a company's products is certainly helpful. But it shouldn't be the only criterion for buying securities. You would very likely eliminate a lot of attractive investment opportunities that way.

Take, for example, Medtronic, Inc., a leading medical instrumentation company. Founded in 1949 in a garage in Minneapolis, the company developed the first implantable pacemaker for cardiac-rhythm disorders. In addition to devices that control irregular heartbeats, Medtronic's product line now includes a wide array of implantable and intervention devices for cardiac, neurological, and other disorders.

Besides the company's current product lineup, you'd also want to know more about Medtronic's market share, patents on its products, and new products under development. Insights about the company's products tells you only part of the story, however. After researching the company's stock price history, you'd learn that in the 15 years from mid-1991 through mid-2006 (which, by the way, includes the bear market of 2000–2002), Medtronic's stock price grew at a compound rate of 18.83%, compared to the 8.41% annual growth rate of the S&P 500 index over the same period. Put another way, if you had invested $10,000 in Medtronic stock 15 years ago, you'd have more than $133,000 as of mid-year 2006. By contrast, the same amount invested in the stock market as a whole would have been worth only $33,500.

Why did Medtronic's stock perform so much better than the market in general? The answer may lie in analyses of the economy, the medical-device industry, and the company's fundamentals (its financial and operating characteristics). This chapter, the first of two on security analysis, introduces some of the techniques and procedures you can use to evaluate the future of the economy, of industries, and of specific companies, such as Medtronic.

Source: www.medtronic.com (accessed July 21, 2006).

Security Analysis

The obvious motivation for investing in stocks is to watch your money grow. Consider, for example, the case of Best Buy Co., the big consumer electronics discount retailer. If you had purchased $10,000 worth of Best Buy stock in January 1996, ten years later, in January 2006, that stock would have had a market value of about $246,000. That works out to an average annual return of almost 38%, as compared to the 9% return that was generated over the same period by S&P 500. Unfortunately, for every story of great success in the market, there are dozens more that don't end so well.

More often than not, most of those investment flops can be traced to bad timing, greed, poor planning, or failure to use common sense in making investment decisions. Although these chapters on stock investments cannot offer magic keys to sudden wealth, they do provide sound principles for formulating a successful long-range investment program. The techniques described are quite traditional; they are the same proven methods that have been used by millions of investors to achieve attractive rates of return on their capital.

▊ Principles of Security Analysis

security analysis
the process of gathering and organizing information and then using it to determine the intrinsic value of a share of common stock.

Security analysis consists of gathering information, organizing it into a logical framework, and then using the information to determine the intrinsic value of common stock. That is, given a rate of return that's compatible with the amount of risk involved in a proposed transaction, **intrinsic value** provides a measure of the underlying worth of a share of stock. It provides a standard for helping you judge whether a particular stock is undervalued, fairly priced, or overvalued. The entire concept of stock valuation, in fact, is based on the belief that all securities possess an intrinsic value that their market value will approach over time.

intrinsic value
the underlying or inherent value of a stock, as determined through fundamental analysis.

In investments, the question of value centers on return. That is, a satisfactory investment candidate is one *that offers a level of expected return proportronate to the amount of risk involved.* As a result, not only must an investment candidate be profitable, but it also must be *sufficiently* profitable— in the sense that you'd expect it to generate a return that's high enough to offset the perceived exposure to risk.

The problem, of course, is finding the right securities. One approach is to buy whatever strikes your fancy. A more rational approach is to use security analysis to look for promising candidates. Security analysis addresses the question of what to buy by determining what a stock *ought to be worth.* Presumably, an investor will buy a stock *only if its prevailing market price does not exceed its worth*—its intrinsic value. Ultimately, intrinsic value depends on several factors:

1. Estimates of the stock's future cash flows (the amount of dividends you expect to receive over the holding period and the estimated price of the stock at time of sale).
2. The discount rate used to translate those future cash flows into a present value.
3. The amount of risk embedded in achieving the forecasted level of performance, which helps define the appropriate discount rate to use.

The Top-Down Approach to Security Analysis Traditional security analysis usually takes a "top-down" approach: It begins with economic analysis, moves to industry analysis, and then to fundamental analysis. *Economic analysis* assesses the general state of the economy and its potential effects on security returns. *Industry analysis* deals with the industry within which a particular company operates. It looks at the general outlook for that industry and at how the company stacks up against the major competitors in the industry. *Fundamental analysis* looks in depth at the financial condition and operating results—the "fundamentals"—of a specific company and the underlying behavior of its common stock. The fundamentals include the company's investment decisions, the liquidity of its assets, its use of debt, its profit margins and earnings growth, and ultimately the future prospects of the company and its stock. These three types of analysis are the topics of this chapter.

Fundamental analysis is closely linked to the notion of intrinsic value, because it *provides the basis for projecting a stock's future cash flows.* A key part of this analytical process is *company analysis,* which takes a close look at the actual financial performance of the company. Such analysis is not meant simply to provide interesting tidbits of information about how the company has performed in the past. Rather, company analysis is done to *help investors formulate expectations about the future performance of the company and its stock.* Make no mistake about it: In investments, it's the future that matters. But to understand the future prospects of the firm, you should have a good handle on the company's current condition and its ability to produce earnings. That's what company analysis does: It helps investors predict the future by looking at the past and determining how well the company is situated to meet the challenges that lie ahead.

▮ Who Needs Security Analysis in an Efficient Market?

The concept of security analysis in general and fundamental analysis in particular is based on the assumption that investors are capable of formulating reliable estimates of a stock's future behavior. Fundamental analysis operates on the broad premise that some securities may be mispriced in the marketplace at any given point in time. Further, it assumes that, through careful analysis, it is possible to distinguish those securities that are correctly priced from those that are not.

To many, those two assumptions of fundamental analysis seem reasonable. However, there are others who do not accept the assumptions of fundamental analysis. These so-called *efficient market* advocates believe that the market is so efficient in processing new information that securities trade very close to or at their correct values at all times. Thus, they argue, it is virtually impossible to consistently outperform the market. In its strongest form, the *efficient market hypothesis* asserts the following:

1. Securities are rarely, if ever, substantially mispriced in the marketplace.
2. No security analysis, however detailed, is capable of identifying mispriced securities with a frequency greater than that which might be expected by random chance alone.

Is the efficient market hypothesis correct? Is there a place for fundamental analysis in modern investment theory? Interestingly, most financial theorists and practitioners would answer "yes" to both questions.

The solution to this apparent paradox is quite simple. Basically, fundamental analysis is of value in the selection of alternative investment vehicles for two important reasons. First, financial markets are as efficient as they are because a large number of people and financial institutions invest a great deal of time and money analyzing the fundamentals of most widely held investments. In other words, markets tend to be efficient and securities tend to trade at or near their intrinsic values simply because a great many people have done the research to determine what their intrinsic values should be.

Second, although the financial markets are generally quite efficient, they are by no means *perfectly* efficient. Pricing errors are inevitable. Those individuals who have conducted the most thorough studies of the fundamentals of a given security are the most likely to profit when errors do occur. We will study the ideas and implications of efficient markets in some detail in Chapter 9. For now, however, we will assume that traditional security analysis is useful in identifying attractive equity investments.

CONCEPTS IN REVIEW
Answers available at: www.myfinancelab.com

7.1 Identify the three major parts of security analysis, and explain why security analysis is important to the stock selection process.

7.2 What is *intrinsic value?* How does it fit into the security analysis process?

7.3 How would you describe a satisfactory investment vehicle? How does security analysis help in identifying investment candidates?

7.4 Would there be any need for security analysis if we operated in an efficient market environment? Explain.

Economic Analysis

LG 2

Stock prices are heavily influenced by the state of the economy and by economic events. As a rule, stock prices tend to move up when the economy is strong, and they retreat when the economy starts to soften. It's not a perfect relationship, but it is a fairly powerful one.

The reason why the economy is so important to the market is simple: The overall performance of the economy has a significant bearing on the performance and profitability of the companies that issue common stock. As the fortunes of the issuing firms change with economic conditions, so do the prices of their stocks. Of course, not all stocks are affected in the same way or to the same extent. Some sectors of the economy, like food retailing, may be only mildly affected by the economy. Others, like the construction and auto industries, are often hard hit when times get rough.

Economic analysis consists of a general study of the prevailing economic environment—often on both a global and domestic basis (though here we'll concentrate, for the most part, on the domestic economy). Such analysis is meant to help investors gain insight into the underlying condition of the

HOTLINKS

The National Bureau of Economic Research (NBER) tracks the U.S. business cycles. On its Web site, you can find data since 1854, including the length of each business cycle.

www.nber.org

economic analysis
a study of general economic conditions that is used in the valuation of common stock.

economy and the potential impact it might have on the behavior of share prices. It can go so far as to include a detailed examination of each sector of the economy, or it may be done on a very informal basis. However, from a security analysis perspective, its purpose is always the same: to establish a sound foundation for the valuation of common stock.

■ Economic Analysis and the Business Cycle

Economic analysis is the first step in the top-down approach. It sets the tone for the entire security analysis process. Thus, if the economic future looks bleak, you can probably expect most stock returns to be equally dismal. If the economy looks strong, stocks should do well. As we saw in Chapter 2, the behavior of the economy is captured in the **business cycle**, which reflects changes in total economic activity over time.

Two widely followed measures of the business cycle are gross domestic product and industrial production. *Gross domestic product* (GDP) represents the market value of all goods and services produced in a country over the period of a year. *Industrial production* is a measure (it's really an index) of the activity/output in the industrial or productive segment of the economy. Normally, GDP and the index of industrial production move up and down with the business cycle.

■ Key Economic Factors

Financial and market decisions are made by economic units at all levels, from individual consumers and households to business firms and governments. These various decisions together have an impact on the direction of economic activity. Particularly important in this regard are the following:

> *Government fiscal policy*
> Taxes
> Government spending
> Debt management
>
> *Monetary policy*
> Money supply
> Interest rates
>
> *Other factors*
> Inflation
> Consumer spending
> Business investments
> Foreign trade and foreign exchange rates

Government fiscal policy tends to be expansive when it encourages spending—when the government reduces taxes and/or increases the size of the budget. Similarly, monetary policy is said to be expansive when interest rates are relatively low and money is readily available. An expansive economy also depends on a generous level of spending by consumers and business concerns. These same variables moving in a reverse direction can have a contractionary (recessionary) impact on the economy, as, for example, when taxes and interest rates increase or when spending by consumers and businesses falls off.

business cycle
an indication of the current state of the economy, reflecting changes in total economic activity over time.

The impact of these major forces filters through the system and affects several key dimensions of the economy. The most important of these are industrial production, corporate profits, retail sales, personal income, the unemployment rate, and inflation. For example, a strong economy exists when industrial production, corporate profits, retail sales, and personal income are moving up and unemployment is down.

Thus, when conducting an economic analysis, you should keep an eye on fiscal and monetary policies, consumer and business spending, and foreign trade *for the potential impact they might have on the economy*. At the same time, you must stay abreast of the level of industrial production, corporate profits, retail sales, personal income, unemployment, and inflation *in order to assess the current state of the business cycle*.

To help you keep track of the economy, Table 7.1 (on page 308) provides a brief description of some key economic measures. These economic statistics are compiled by various government agencies and are widely reported in the financial media. Most of the reports are released monthly. Take the time to carefully read about the various economic measures and reports cited in Table 7.1. When you understand the behavior of these statistics, you can make your own educated guess as to the current state of the economy and where it's headed.

HOT LINKS

To keep up with the status of the economy, you can view the monthly leading index of economic indicators computed by the Conference Board in New York.

At the White House site, you can visit the economic statistics briefing room. *The Economist* also provides data useful for keeping track of the economy. See the following sites:

www.conference-board.org/
www.whitehouse.gov/fsbr/esbr.html
www.economist.com

Developing an Economic Outlook

Conducting an economic analysis involves studying fiscal and monetary policies, inflationary expectations, consumer and business spending, and the state of the business cycle. Often, investors do this on a fairly informal basis. As they form their economic judgments, many rely on one or more of the popular published sources (e.g., the *Wall Street Journal, Barron's, Fortune,* and *Business Week*) as well as on periodic reports from major brokerage houses. These sources provide a convenient summary of economic activity and give investors a general feel for the condition of the economy.

HOT LINKS

At this site, you can find economic indicators for all major countries in the world. Scroll to the bottom of the page to see information about the United States.

http://www.economy.com/dismal

Once you have developed a general economic outlook, you can use the information in one of two ways. One approach is to construct an economic outlook and then consider where it leads in terms of possible areas for further analysis. For example, suppose you uncover information that strongly suggests the outlook for business spending is very positive. On the basis of such an analysis, you might want to look more closely at capital goods producers, such as office equipment manufacturers. Similarly, if you feel that because of sweeping changes in world politics, U.S. government defense spending is likely to drop off, you might want to avoid the stocks of major defense contractors.

A second way to use information about the economy is to consider specific industries or companies and ask, "How will they be affected by expected developments in the economy?" Take, for example, an investor with an interest in *business equipment stocks*. This industry category includes companies involved in the production of everything from business machines and electronic systems to work lockers and high-fashion office furnishings. In this industry, you'll find

TABLE 7.1   Keeping Track of the Economy

To help you sort out the confusing array of figures that flow almost daily from Washington, D.C., and keep track of what's happening in the economy, here are some of the most important economic measures and reports to watch.

- **Gross domestic product (GDP).** This is the broadest measure of the economy's performance. Issued every three months by the Commerce Department, it is an estimate of the total dollar value of all the goods and services produced in this country. Movements in many areas of the economy are closely related to changes in GDP, so it is a good analytic tool. In particular, watch the annual rate of growth or decline in "real" or "constant" dollars. This number eliminates the effects of inflation and thus measures the actual volume of production. Remember, though, that frequent revisions of GDP figures sometimes change the picture of the economy.

- **Industrial production.** Issued monthly by the Federal Reserve Board, this index shows changes in the physical output of U.S. factories, mines, and electric and gas utilities. The index tends to move in the same direction as the economy; it is thus a good guide to business conditions between reports on GDP. Detailed breakdowns of the index give a reading on how individual industries are faring.

- **The index of leading indicators.** This boils down to one number, which summarizes the movement of a dozen statistics that tend to predict—or "lead"—changes in the GDP. This monthly index, issued by the Commerce Department, includes such things as layoffs of workers, new orders placed by manufacturers, changes in the money supply, and the prices of raw materials. If the index moves in the same direction for several months, it's a fairly good sign that total output will move the same way in the near future.

- **Personal income.** A monthly report from the Commerce Department, this shows the before-tax income received in the form of wages and salaries, interest and dividends, rents, and other payments, such as Social Security, unemployment compensation, and pensions. As a measure of individuals' spending power, the report helps explain trends in consumer buying habits, a major part of total GDP. When personal income rises, people often increase their buying. But note a loophole: Excluded are the billions of dollars that change hands in the so-called underground economy—cash transactions that are never reported to tax or other officials.

- **Retail sales.** The Commerce Department's monthly estimate of total sales at the retail level includes everything from cars to groceries. Based on a sample of retail establishments, the figure gives a rough clue to consumer attitudes. It can also indicate future conditions: A long slowdown in sales can lead to cuts in production.

- **Money supply.** The Federal Reserve reports weekly this measure of the amount of money in circulation. Actually, there are three measures of the money supply: *M1* is basically currency, demand deposits, and NOW accounts. *M2,* the most widely followed measure, equals M1 plus savings deposits, money market deposit accounts, and money market mutual funds. *M3* is M2 plus large CDs and a few other less significant types of deposits/transactions. Reasonable growth in the money supply, as measured by M2, is thought to be necessary for an expanding economy. However, too rapid a rate of growth in money is considered inflationary. In contrast, a sharp slowdown in the growth rate is viewed as recessionary.

- **Consumer prices.** Issued monthly by the Labor Department, this index shows changes in prices for a fixed market basket of goods and services. The most widely publicized figure is for all urban consumers. A second figure, used in labor contracts and some government programs, covers urban wage earners and clerical workers. Both are watched as a measure of inflation, but many economists believe that flaws cause them to be inaccurate.

- **Producer prices.** This monthly indicator from the Labor Department shows price changes of goods at various stages of production, from crude materials such as raw cotton to finished goods like clothing and furniture. An upward surge may mean higher consumer prices later. However, the index can miss discounts and may exaggerate rising price trends. Watch particularly changes in the prices of finished goods. These do not fluctuate as widely as the prices of crude materials and thus are a better measure of inflationary pressures.

- **Employment.** The percentage of the workforce that is involuntarily out of work (*unemployment*) is a broad indicator of economic health. But another monthly figure issued by the Labor Department—the number of payroll jobs—may be better for spotting changes in business. A decreasing number of jobs is a sign that firms are cutting production.

- **Housing starts.** A pickup in the pace of housing starts usually follows an easing in the availability and cost of money and is an indicator of improving economic health. This monthly report from the Commerce Department also includes the number of new building permits issued across the country, an even earlier indicator of the pace of future construction.

companies like Pitney Bowes, Diebold, Herman Miller, and Steelcase. These stocks are highly susceptible to changing economic conditions. That's because when the economy starts slowing down, companies can put off purchases of durable equipment and fixtures. Especially important to this industry, therefore, is the outlook for corporate profits and business investments. So long as these economic factors look good, the prospects for business equipment stocks should be positive.

Assessing the Potential Impact on Share Prices In this instance, our imaginary investor would first want to assess the current state of the business cycle. Using that insight, he could then formulate some expectations about the future of the economy and the potential impact it holds for the stock market in general and business equipment stocks in particular. Table 7.2 (on page 310) shows how some of the more important economic variables can affect the behavior of the stock market.

To see how this might be done, let's assume that the economy has just gone through a year-long recession and is now in the recovery stage of the business cycle: Employment is starting to pick up. Inflation and interest rates have come back down. Both GDP and industrial production have experienced sharp increases in the past two quarters. Also, Congress is putting the finishing touches on a major piece of legislation that will lead to reduced taxes. More important, although the economy is now in the early stages of a recovery, things are expected to get even better in the future. The economy is definitely starting to build steam, and all indications are that both corporate profits and business spending should undergo a sharp increase. All of these predictions should be good news for the producers of business equipment and office furnishings, as a good deal of their sales and an even larger portion of their profits depend on the level of corporate profits and business spending. In short, our investor sees an economy that's in good shape and set to become even stronger—the consequences of which are favorable not only for the market but for business equipment stocks as well.

Note that these conclusions could have been reached by relying on sources such as *Barron's* or *Business Week*. In fact, about the only "special thing" this investor would have to do is pay careful attention to those economic forces that are particularly important to the business equipment industry (e.g., corporate profits and capital spending). The economic portion of the analysis has set the stage for further evaluation by indicating the type of economic environment to expect in the near future. The next step is to narrow the focus a bit and conduct the industry phase of the analysis.

The Market as a Leading Indicator Before we continue our analysis, it is vital to clarify the relationship that normally exists between the stock market and the economy. As we just saw, investors use the economic outlook to get a handle on the market and to identify developing industry sectors. Yet it is important to note that changes in stock prices normally occur *before* the actual forecasted changes become apparent in the economy. Indeed, the current trend of stock prices is frequently used to help *predict* the course of the economy itself.

The apparent conflict here can be resolved somewhat by noting that because of this relationship, it is even more important to derive a reliable economic outlook and to be sensitive to underlying economic changes that may

TABLE 7.2   Economic Variables and the Stock Market

Economic Variable	Potential Effect on the Stock Market
Real growth in GDP	Positive impact—it's good for the market.
Industrial production	Continued increases are a sign of strength, which is good for the market.
Inflation	Detrimental to stock prices. Higher inflation leads to higher interest rates and lower price/earnings multiples, and generally makes equity securities less attractive.
Corporate profits	Strong corporate earnings are good for the market.
Unemployment	A downer—an increase in unemployment means business is starting to slow down.
Federal budget surplus or deficit	Budget surpluses are good for interest rates and stock prices. Budget deficits, in contrast, may be a positive sign for a depressed economy but can lead to inflation in a stronger economic environment and therefore have a negative impact.
Weak dollar	Often the result of big trade imbalances, a weak dollar has a negative effect on the market. It makes our markets less attractive to foreign investors. However, it also makes our products more affordable in overseas markets and therefore can have a positive impact on our economy.
Interest rates	Another downer—rising rates tend to have a negative effect on the market for stocks.
Money supply	Moderate growth can have a positive impact on the economy and the market. Rapid growth, however, is inflationary and therefore detrimental to the stock market.

mean the current outlook is becoming dated. Investors in the stock market tend to look into the future to justify the purchase or sale of stock. If their perception of the future is changing, stock prices are also likely to be changing. Therefore, watching the course of stock prices as well as the course of the general economy can make for more accurate investment forecasting.

CONCEPTS IN REVIEW
Answers available at: www.myfinancelab.com

7.5 Describe the general concept of *economic analysis*. Is this type of analysis necessary, and can it really help the individual investor make a decision about a stock? Explain.

7.6 Why is the business cycle so important to economic analysis? Does the business cycle have any bearing on the stock market?

7.7 Briefly describe each of the following:
a. Gross domestic product.   b. Leading indicators.
c. Money supply.   d. Producer prices.

7.8 What effect, if any, does inflation have on common stocks?

Industry Analysis

LG 3

Have you ever thought about buying oil stocks, or autos, or chemicals? How about computer stocks or telecommunications stocks? Looking at securities in terms of industry groupings is widely used by both individual and institutional investors. This approach makes a lot of sense because stock prices are influenced, to one degree or another, by industry conditions. Indeed, various industry forces, including the level of demand within an industry, can have a real impact on individual companies.

Industry analysis, in effect, sets the stage for a *more thorough analysis of individual companies and securities.* Clearly, if the outlook is good for an industry, then the prospects are likely to be favorable for many of the companies that make up that industry. In addition, industry analysis also helps the investor *assess the riskiness of a company* and therefore *define the appropriate risk-adjusted rate of return* to use in setting a value on the company's stock. That's true because there are always at least some similarities in the riskiness of the companies that make up an industry, so if you can gain an understanding of the risks inherent in an industry, you'll gain valuable insights about the risks inherent in individual companies and their securities.

▮ Key Issues

industry analysis
study of industry groupings that looks at the competitive position of a particular industry in relation to others and identifies companies that show particular promise within an industry.

Because all industries do not perform the same, the first step in **industry analysis** is to establish the competitive position of a particular industry *in relation to others.* The next step is to identify companies *within the industry* that hold particular promise. Analyzing an industry means looking at such things as its makeup and basic characteristics, the key economic and operating variables that drive industry performance, and the outlook for the industry. You will also want to keep an eye out for specific companies that appear well situated to take advantage of industry conditions. Companies with strong market positions should be favored over those with less secure positions. Such dominance indicates an ability to maintain pricing leadership and suggests that the firm will be in a position to enjoy economies of scale and low-cost production. Market dominance also enables a company to support a strong research and development effort, thereby helping it secure its leadership position for the future.

HOTLINKS
Go to the following Web site to see the best and worst industries during a certain time frame. You can change the time frame using the drop-down menu and the order will change.
www.marketwatch.com/tools/industry

Normally, you can gain valuable insight about an industry by seeking answers to the following questions:

1. *What is the nature of the industry?* Is it monopolistic, or are there many competitors? Do a few set the trend for the rest, and if so, who are those few?
2. *To what extent is the industry regulated?* Is it regulated (e.g., public utilities)? If so, how "friendly" are the regulatory bodies?
3. *What role does labor play in the industry?* How important are labor unions? Are there good labor relations within the industry? When is the next round of contract talks?
4. *How important are technological developments?* Are any new developments taking place? What impact are potential breakthroughs likely to have?
5. *Which economic forces are especially important to the industry?* Is demand for the industry's goods and services related to key economic variables? If so, what is the outlook for those variables? How important is foreign competition to the health of the industry?

HOTLINKS
To find the leading companies in various industries, go to the site listed below. Click on [Industries], search [Leaders and Laggards] using one or more of the 15 variables, and then click on one of the industries to find the leading companies (or the lagging companies) within that industry.
http://biz.yahoo.com

6. *What are the important financial and operating considerations?* Is there an adequate supply of labor, material, and capital? What are the capital spending plans and needs of the industry?

The Industry Growth Cycle Questions like these can sometimes be answered in terms of an industry's **growth cycle**, which reflects the vitality of the industry over time. In the first stage—*initial development*—investment opportunities are usually not available to most investors. The industry is new and untried, and the risks are very high. The second stage is *rapid expansion,* during which product acceptance is spreading and investors can foresee the industry's future more clearly. At this stage, economic and financial variables have little to do with the industry's overall performance. Investors will be interested in investing almost regardless of the economic climate. This is the phase that is of substantial interest to investors, and a good deal of work is done to find such opportunities.

Unfortunately, most industries do not experience rapid growth for long. Instead, they eventually slip into the next category in the growth cycle, *mature growth,* which is the one most influenced by economic developments. In this stage, expansion comes from growth of the economy. It is a slower source of overall growth than that experienced in stage 2. In stage 3, the long-term nature of the industry becomes apparent. Industries in this category include defensive ones, like food and apparel, and cyclical industries, like autos and heavy equipment.

The last stage is either *stability* or *decline.* In the decline phase, demand for the industry's products is diminishing, and companies are leaving the industry. Investment opportunities at this stage are almost nonexistent, unless you are seeking only dividend income. Certainly, growth-oriented investors will want to stay away from industries at the decline stage of the cycle. Other investors may be able to find some investment opportunities here, especially if the industry (like, say, tobacco) is locked in the mature, stable phase. The fact is, however, that very few really good companies ever reach this final stage because they continually bring new products to the market and, in so doing, remain at least in the mature growth phase.

▮ Developing an Industry Outlook

Individual investors can conduct industry analysis themselves. Or, as is more often the case, it can be done with the help of published industry reports, such as the popular *S&P Industry Surveys.* These surveys cover all the important economic, market, and financial aspects of an industry, providing commentary as well as vital statistics. Other widely used sources of industry information include brokerage house reports, articles in the popular financial media, and even the well-known *S&P Stock Reports, which now include a one-page write-up on the stock's industry outlook.* Figure 7.1, for example, provides a Sub-Industry Outlook for Genentech, and other biotech stocks. There also are scores of Web sites (like *Yahoo! Finance.com, businessweek.com,* and *bigcharts.com*) that provide all sorts of useful information about various industries and sub-industries.

Let's resume our example of the imaginary investor who is thinking about buying business equipment stocks. Recall from our prior discussion that the economic phase of the analysis suggested a strong economy for the foresee-

growth cycle
a reflection of the amount of business vitality that occurs within an industry (or company) over time.

FIGURE 7.1 An Example of a Published Industry Report

Here's an excerpt from an *S&P Stock Report* on **Genentech, Inc**. It provides a brief overview of the health care/biotechnology industry, along with comparative stock price performance, and peer group behavior of Genentech stock and its major competitors in this sub-industry. (*Source:* Standard & Poor's *Stock Reports,* April 14, 2006. ©2006 The McGraw-Hill Companies. All Rights Reserved.)

Stock Report | Jun 3, 2006 | NYSE Symbol: **DNA**

Genentech Inc.

STANDARD &POOR'S

Sub-Industry Outlook

We have a positive investment outlook on the biotechnology industry due to our expectations for strong growth and our opinion that valuations remain attractive relative to growth. First quarter financial results were mixed for the biotech sector. For example, in our view, earnings were solid for Celgene, Genentech and Gilead Sciences, while they were somewhat disappointing for Amgen, Genzyme, and MedImmune. While the sector appears to be is in the midst of a correction, we think fundamentals are strong and the product approval front has been positive. The S&P Biotech Index was down 9.1% year to date through May 12, 2006, versus a 4.0% gain for the S&P 1500.

We continue to recommend investors concentrate their core holdings in established, profitable biotechs that have solid growth prospects on an absolute and relative basis and that have not been riddled with bad news. We also think a strong pipeline and prior pipeline success are important ingredients for core holdings. We would only consider smaller firms that have at least one major catalyst, such as a recently approved drug or positive late-stage clinical trial results, which could drive strong growth.

We expect cancer therapeutic sales and development to remain the primary catalyst for the sector's growth. We also think prospects for autoimmune and inflammatory therapeutics, as well as nephrology drugs, remain solid. We think FDA actions thus far in 2006 have been generally positive for the biotech space and expect this trend to continue for the remainder of the year. While there have been delays for Cephalon's Sparlon and NPS Pharmaceuticals' Preos, most higher profile biotech drugs have passed the FDA hurdle, including ImClone's Erbitux, Pfizer's and Nektar's Exubera, Celgene's Revlimid, Cephalon's and Alkermes

Vivitrol, and Genzyme's Myozyme.

We project stock appreciation potential of approximately 20%-25% for profitable biotech issues over the next 12 months, assuming that stock appreciation approaches our market weighted projected EPS growth rate of 22.7% (18.8% excluding Genentech) for the S&P Biotech peer group. The peer group forward P/E-to-growth (PEG) ratio is 1.1X our 2007 EPS estimates. We find this attractive and note that the forward PEG of 1.1X is lower than the forward PEG of 1.2X that we calculated in July 2002 (which represents a six-year bottom for the sector). We also note that our forecasted annualized growth rate was 23.2%.

We view the fund-raising environment as neutral for smaller caps and positive for large caps. We expect IPO activity to remain weak, but see partnership and M&A deals remaining brisk, especially at current prices.

-Frank DiLorenzo, CFA

Stock Performance

GICS Sector: Health Care
Sub-Industry: Biotechnology

Based on S&P 1500 Indexes
Month-end Price Performance as of 05/31/06

| Sub-Industry | Sector | S&P 1500 |

NOTE: All Sector & Sub-Industry information is based on the Global Industry Classification Standard (GICS)

Sub-Industry : Biotechnology Peer Group*: Biotech Therapeutics - Larger Capitalization

Peer Group	Stock Symbol	Stk.Mkt. Cap. (Mil. $)	Recent Stock Price	P/E Ratio	12-Mo. Trailing EPS	30-Day Price Chg(%)	1 Year Price Chg(%)	Beta	Yield (%)	Quality Ranking	Ret. on Equity (%)	Pretax Margin (%)	LTD to Cap (%)
Genentech Inc.	DNA	86,703	82.29	63	1.30	6%	-1%	0.95	Nil	NR	17.9	30.3	21.8
Amgen	AMGN	81,578	69.18	22	3.08	4%	10%	0.81	Nil	B+	18.3	39.2	15.5
Biogen Idec	BIIB	16,406	47.71	68	0.70	4%	25%	0.46	Nil	B-	2.3	10.6	0.6
Celgene Corp.	CELG	15,279	43.98	NM	0.09	10%	113%	0.92	Nil	B-	11.4	15.7	38.6
Genzyme Corp.	GENZ	16,201	62.23	37	1.66	6%	-1%	1.35	Nil	B	9.3	23.4	12.9
Gilead Sciences	GILD	26,573	58.40	30	1.93	4%	36%	0.75	Nil	B-	33.2	57.1	7.3
MedImmune	MEDI	7,940	31.92	NM	-0.34	3%	22%	0.77	Nil	C	NM	0.6	Nil
Serono S.A.	SRA	8,223	16.14	15	1.09	-3%	5%	1.62	1.1	NR	NM	NM	22.5

NA-Not Available NM-Not Meaningful NR-Not Rated. *For Peer Groups with more than 15 companies or stocks, selection of issues is based on market capitalization.

---

able future—one in which corporate profits and business spending will be expanding. Now the investor is ready to focus on the industry. A logical starting point is to assess the expected industry response to forecasted economic developments. Demand for the product and industry sales would be especially important. The industry is made up of many large and small competitors, and although it is labor-intensive, labor unions are not an important force. Thus, our investor may want to look closely at the potential effect of these factors on the industry's cost structure. Also worth a look is the work being done in research and development (R&D), and in industrial design within the industry. You would want to know which firms are coming out with the new products and fresh ideas, because these firms are likely to be the potential industry leaders.

Industry analysis yields an understanding of the nature and operating characteristics of an industry, which can then be used to form judgments about the prospects for industry growth. Let's assume that our investor, by using various types of published and online reports, has examined the key elements of the office equipment industry and has concluded that the industry, *particularly the office furnishings segment,* is well positioned to take advantage of the rapidly improving economy. Many new and exciting products have come out in the last couple of years, and more are in the R&D stage. Even more compelling is the current emphasis on new products that will contribute to long-term business productivity. Thus, the demand for office furniture and fixtures should increase, and although profit margins may tighten a bit, the level of profits should move up smartly, providing a healthy outlook for growth.

In the course of researching the industry, our investor has noticed several companies that stand out, but one looks particularly attractive: Universal Office Furnishings. Long regarded as one of the top design firms in the industry, Universal designs, manufactures, and sells a full line of high-end office furniture and fixtures (desks, chairs, credenzas, modular work stations, filing systems, etc.). In addition, the company produces and distributes state-of-the-art computer furniture and a specialized line of institutional furniture for the hospitality, health care, and educational markets. The company was founded over 50 years ago, and its stock (which trades under the symbol UVRS) has been listed on the NYSE since the late 1970s. Universal would be considered a *mid-cap stock,* with total market capitalization of around $2 or $3 billion. The company experienced rapid growth in the 1990s, as it expanded its product line. Because of its institutional division, it was not as hard hit as others in the 2000–2002 bear market. Looking ahead, the general consensus is that the company should benefit nicely from the strong economic environment now in place. Everything about the economy and the industry looks good for the stock, so our investor decides to take a close look at Universal Office Furnishings.

We now turn our attention to fundamental analysis, which will occupy the rest of the chapter.

HOTLINKS

From the main page of the MSN site, go to [Investing], [Markets], [In/Out of Favor], to find what is currently "hot" and what is not.

www.moneycentral.msn.com

CONCEPTS IN REVIEW

Answers available at: www.myfinancelab.com

7.9 What is *industry analysis,* and why is it important?

7.10 Identify and briefly discuss several aspects of an industry that are important to its behavior and operating characteristics. Note especially how economic issues fit into industry analysis.

7.11 What are the four stages of an industry's growth cycle? Which of these stages offers the biggest payoff to investors? Which stage is most influenced by forces in the economy?

Fundamental Analysis

LG 4   LG 5   LG 6

fundamental analysis
the in-depth study of the financial condition and operating results of a firm.

Fundamental analysis is the study of the financial affairs of a business for the purpose of better understanding the company that issued the common stock. In this part of the chapter, we will deal with several aspects of fundamental analysis. We will examine the general concept of fundamental analysis, and introduce several types of financial statements that provide the raw material for this type of analysis. We will then describe some key financial ratios that are widely used in company analysis, and will conclude with an interpretation of those financial ratios. It's important to understand that this represents the more traditional approach to security analysis. This approach is commonly used in any situation where investors rely on financial statements and other databases to at least partially form an investment decision.

▮ The Concept

Fundamental analysis rests on the belief that *the value of a stock is influenced by the performance of the company that issued the stock.* If a company's prospects look strong, the market price of its stock is likely to reflect that and be bid up. However, the value of a security depends not only on the return it promises but also on the amount of its risk exposure. Fundamental analysis captures these dimensions (risk and return) and incorporates them into the valuation process. It begins with a historical analysis of the financial strength of a firm: the so-called *company analysis* phase. Using the insights obtained, along with economic and industry analyses, an investor can then formulate expectations about the future growth and profitability of a company.

HOTLINKS

Get basic fundamental data about a stock at

411stocks.stockselector.com

In the company analysis phase, the investor studies the financial statements of the firm to learn its strengths and weaknesses, identify any underlying trends and developments, evaluate operating efficiencies, and gain a general understanding of the nature and operating characteristics of the firm. The following points are of particular interest:

1. The competitive position of the company.
2. Its composition and growth in sales.
3. Profit margins and the dynamics of company earnings.
4. The composition and liquidity of corporate resources (the company's asset mix).
5. The company's capital structure (its financing mix).

This phase is in many respects the most demanding and time-consuming. Because most investors have neither the time nor the inclination to conduct such an extensive study, they rely on published reports for the background material. Fortunately, individual investors have a variety of sources to choose from. These include the reports and recommendations of major brokerage houses, the popular financial media, and financial subscription services like S&P and *Value Line*. Also available is a whole array of computer-based software and online financial sources, such as Business Week Online, Morningstar.com, Quicken, MSN.Money, Wall Street on Demand, CNNMoney.com, and SmartMoney.com. These are all valuable sources of information, and the paragraphs that follow are not meant to replace them. Nevertheless, to be an intelligent investor, you should have at least a basic understanding of financial reports and financial statement analysis. For it is you, ultimately, who will be drawing your own conclusions about a company and its stock.

Financial Statements

Financial statements are a vital part of company analysis. They enable investors to develop an opinion about the operating results and financial condition of a firm. Investors use three financial statements in company analysis: the balance sheet, the income statement, and the statement of cash flows. The first two statements are essential to carrying out basic financial analysis, as they contain the data needed to compute many of the financial ratios. The statement of cash flows is used primarily to assess the cash/liquidity position of the firm.

Companies prepare financial statements on a quarterly basis (these are *abbreviated* statements, compiled for each three-month period of operation) and again at the end of each calendar year or *fiscal year.* (The fiscal year is the 12-month period the company has defined as its operating year, which may or may not end on December 31.) Annual financial statements must be fully verified by independent certified public accountants (CPAs). They then must be filed with the U.S. Securities and Exchange Commission, and distributed on a timely basis to all stockholders in the form of annual reports.

By themselves, corporate financial statements are an important source of information to the investor. When used with financial ratios and in conjunction with fundamental analysis, they become even more powerful. But as the *Investing in Action* box on our Web site suggests, to get the most from financial ratios, you must have a good understanding of the uses and limitations of the financial statements themselves.

The Balance Sheet The **balance sheet** is a statement of the company's assets, liabilities, and stockholders' equity. The *assets* represent the resources of the company (the things the company owns). The *liabilities* are its debts. *Equity* is the amount of capital the stockholders have invested in the firm. A balance sheet may be thought of as a summary of the firm's assets balanced against its debt and ownership positions *at a single point in time* (on the last day of the calendar or fiscal year, or at the end of the quarter). To balance, the total assets must equal the total amount of liabilities and equity.

A typical balance sheet is illustrated in Table 7.3. It shows the comparative 2006–2007 figures for Universal Office Furnishings, the firm our investor is analyzing. Note that although the Universal name is fictitious, the financial statements are not. *They are the actual financial statements of a real company.* Some of the entries have been slightly modified for pedagogical purposes, but these tables accurately depict what real financial statements look like and how they're used in financial statement analysis.

The Income Statement The **income statement** provides a financial summary of the operating results of the firm. It shows the amount of revenues generated over a period of time, the costs and expenses incurred over the same

WEBEXTENSION

For some basic advice on financial statement analysis, see the *Investing in Action* box titled "The Ten Commandments of Financial Statement Analysis," at the book's Web site.

www.myfinancelab.com

balance sheet
a financial summary of a firm's assets, liabilities, and shareholders' equity at a single point in time.

WEBEXTENSION

For brief descriptions of each of the account entries in Tables 7.3, 7.4, and 7.5, go to the book's Web site at:

www.myfinancelab.com

income statement
a financial summary of the operating results of a firm covering a specified period of time, usually a year.

TABLE 7.3 Corporate Balance Sheet

Universal Office Furnishings, Inc.
Comparative Balance Sheets
December 31
($ in millions)

	2007	2006
Assets		
Current assets		
Cash and equivalents	$ 95.8	$ 80.0
Receivables	227.2	192.4
Inventories	103.7	107.5
Other current assets	73.6	45.2
Total current assets	500.3	425.1
Noncurrent assets		
Property, plant, & equipment, gross	771.2	696.6
Accumulated depreciation	(372.5)	(379.9)
Property, plant, & equipment, net	398.7	316.7
Other noncurrent assets	42.2	19.7
Total noncurrent assets	440.9	336.4
Total assets	**$941.2**	**$761.5**
Liabilities and stockholders' equity		
Current liabilities		
Accounts payable	$114.2	$ 82.4
Short-term debt	174.3	79.3
Other current liabilities	85.5	89.6
Total current liabilities	374.0	251.3
Noncurrent liabilities		
Long-term debt	177.8	190.9
Other noncurrent liabilities	94.9	110.2
Total noncurrent liabilities	272.7	301.1
Total liabilities	**$646.7**	**$552.4**
Stockholders' equity		
Common shares	92.6	137.6
Retained earnings	201.9	71.5
Total equity	294.5	209.1
Total liabilities and stockholders' equity	**$941.2**	**$761.5**

period, and the company's profits. (Profits are calculated by subtracting all costs and expenses, including taxes, from revenues.) Unlike the balance sheet, the income statement covers activities that have occurred over the course of time, or for a given operating period. Typically, this period extends no longer than a fiscal or calendar year.

Table 7.4 (on page 318) shows the income statements for Universal Office Furnishings for 2006 and 2007. Note that these annual statements cover operations for the 12-month period ending on December 31, which corresponds to the date of the balance sheet. The income statement indicates how successful the firm has been in using the assets listed on the balance sheet. That is, management's success in operating the firm is reflected in the profit or loss the company generates during the year.

TABLE 7.4 Corporate Income Statement

Universal Office Furnishings, Inc.
Income Statements
Fiscal Year Ended December 31
($ in millions)

	2007	2006
Net sales	$1,938.0	$1,766.2
Cost of goods sold	1,128.5	1,034.5
Gross operating profit	$ 809.5	$ 731.7
Selling, administrative, and other operating expenses	497.7	445.3
Depreciation & amortization	77.1	62.1
Other income, net	0.5	12.9
Earnings before interest & taxes	$235.2	$237.2
Interest expense	13.4	7.3
Earnings before taxes	$221.8	$229.9
Income taxes	82.1	88.1
Net profit after taxes	**$139.7**	**$141.8**
Dividends paid per share	$0.15	$0.13
Earnings per share (EPS)	$2.26	$2.17
Number of common shares outstanding (in millions)	61.8	65.3

statement of cash flows
a financial summary of a firm's cash flow and other events that caused changes in the company's cash position.

The Statement of Cash Flows The **statement of cash flows** provides a summary of the firm's cash flow and other events that caused changes in its cash position. A relatively new report, first required in 1988, this statement essentially brings together items from *both* the balance sheet and the income statement to show how the company obtained its cash and how it used this valuable liquid resource.

Unfortunately, because of certain accounting conventions (the *accrual concept* being chief among them), a company's reported earnings may bear little resemblance to its cash flow. That is, whereas profits are simply the difference between revenues and the accounting costs that have been charged against them, *cash flow is the amount of money a company actually takes in as a result of doing business.* As such, the cash flow statement is highly valued by analysts and others in the investment community, because it offers insight on the underlying financial condition of the firm. The fact is, corporate management has considerable leeway in constructing financial statements, which can, at times, lead to the manipulation of reported earnings. While it's relatively easy to manipulate an income statement, short of outright fraud, it's far more difficult to do that with a cash flow statement. That's because what doesn't show up on the income statement will most likely affect asset and/or liability accounts on the balance sheet, and therefore will impact the company's statement of cash flows (usually in a negative fashion). (Nevertheless, accounting fraud can occur, as discussed in the *Ethics in Investing* box on page 319. As suggested there, audits are an important aspect of a company's financial statements.)

Table 7.5 (on page 320) presents the 2006–2007 statement of cash flows for Universal Office Furnishings. As can be seen, the statement is broken into

ETHICS *in* INVESTING

Cooking the Books: What Were They Thinking?

Recent scandals involving fraudulent accounting practices have resulted in public outrage. It appears that creative and unethical accounting practices kept real costs and debts off the books at Enron, WorldCom, Xerox, Qwest Communications, Conseco, and dozens of other public companies. When the reality finally caught up with the fantasy, tens of thousands of investors and employees lost their life savings, while many corporate executives responsible for fraud reaped huge financial rewards. For example, "cooking the books" at Enron cost investors almost $67 billion when the company declared bankruptcy in 2001; the implosion of WorldCom wiped out $175 billion of shareholder value, the biggest corporate bankruptcy in U.S. history.

Global Crossing sought Chapter 11 protection from its creditors after the SEC started its inquiry of widespread allegations that the company had used "creative accounting" to inflate its earnings. An SEC investigation of another telecom giant, Qwest Communications, found that Qwest had booked hundreds of millions of dollars of revenue at the end of its quarterly reporting period that should have been delayed until the next quarter. At WorldCom, internal audits revealed that $3.8 billion in operating expenses had been fraudulently disguised as capital expenditures over five quarters dating back to January 2001. Accounting firm Arthur Andersen was implicated as the corporate auditor in the Enron, Global Crossing, and WorldCom investigations.

Among the common accounting tricks used in the recent corporate scandals, the following appeared to be most popular: capitalizing operating expenses on the balance sheet (WorldCom), recognizing fictitious or premature revenues (Xerox, Qwest), creating off-balance-sheet liabilities (Enron), using off-balance-sheet derivative contracts transactions and company stock to hedge risk (Enron), and writing off goodwill as extraordinary loss rather than amortizing it over time (Time Warner) to manipulate future earnings growth.

CRITICAL THINKING QUESTION One of the steps to strengthen corporate reporting is to separate internal and external audits of a company by requiring that an external auditor will not be permitted to provide internal audits to the same client. Will this regulation be able to eliminate conflict of interest? Discuss.

---

three parts. The most important part is the first one, labeled "Cash from Operating Activities." It captures the *net cash flow from operating activities*— the line highlighted on the statement. This is what people typically mean when they say "cash flow"—the amount of cash generated by the company and available for investment and financing activities.

Note that Universal's 2007 cash flow from operating activities was over $200 million, down a bit from the year before. This amount was more than enough to cover the company's investing activities ($150.9 million) and its financing activities ($35.4 million). Thus, Universal's actual cash position (see the line near the bottom of the statement, labeled "Net increase (decrease) in cash") increased by some $15.8 million. That result was a big improvement over the year before, when the firm's cash position fell by more than $35 million. A high (and preferably increasing) cash flow means the company has enough money to service debt, finance growth, and pay dividends. In addition, you'd like to see the firm's cash position increase over time because of the positive impact that it has on the company's liquidity and its ability to meet operating needs in a prompt and timely fashion.

TABLE 7.5   **Statement of Cash Flows**

Universal Office Furnishings, Inc.
Statements of Cash Flows
Fiscal Year Ended December 31
($ in millions)

	2007	2006
Cash from operating activities		
Net earnings	$139.7	$141.8
Depreciation and amortization	77.1	62.1
Other noncash charges	5.2	16.7
Increase (decrease) in current assets	(41.7)	14.1
Increase (decrease) in current liabilities	21.8	(29.1)
Net cash flow from operating activities	$202.1	$205.6
Cash from investing activities		
Acquisitions of property, plant, and equipment—net	(150.9)	(90.6)
Net cash flow from investing activities	($150.9)	($90.6)
Cash from financing activities		
Proceeds from long-term borrowing	749.8	79.1
Reduction in long-term debt, including current maturities and early retirements	(728.7)	(211.1)
Net repurchase of capital stock	(47.2)	(9.8)
Payment of dividends on common stock	(9.3)	(8.5)
Net cash flow from financing activities	($35.4)	$150.3
Net increase (decrease) in cash	**$15.8**	**($35.3)**
Cash and equivalents at beginning of period	$80.0	$115.3
Cash and equivalents at end of period	$95.8	$80.0

▮ Financial Ratios

To see what accounting statements really have to say about the financial condition and operating results of a firm, we have to turn to *financial ratios*. Such ratios provide a different perspective on the financial affairs of the firm—particularly with regard to the balance sheet and income statement—and thus *expand the information content of the company's financial statements*. Simply stated, **ratio analysis** is the study of the relationships between various financial statement accounts. Each measure relates an item on the balance sheet (or income statement) to another, or as is more often the case, a balance sheet account to an operating (income statement) item. In this way, we can look not so much at the absolute size of the financial statement accounts, but rather at what they indicate about the liquidity, activity, or profitability of the firm.

What Ratios Have to Offer   Investors use financial ratios to evaluate the financial condition and operating results of the company and to compare those results to historical or industry standards. When using historical standards, investors compare the company's ratios from one year to the next. When using industry standards, investors compare a particular company's ratios to those of other companies in the same line of business.

Remember, the reason to use ratios is *to develop information about the past that can be used to get a handle on the future.* It's only from an under-

ratio analysis
the study of the relationships between financial statement accounts.

standing of a company's past performance that you can forecast its future with some degree of confidence. For example, even if sales have been expanding rapidly over the past few years, you must carefully assess the reasons for the growth, rather than naively assuming that past growth-rate trends will continue into the future. Such insights are obtained from financial ratios and financial statement analysis.

Financial ratios can be divided into five groups: (1) liquidity, (2) activity, (3) leverage, (4) profitability, and (5) common-stock, or market, measures. Using the 2007 figures from the Universal financial statements (Tables 7.3 and 7.4), we will now identify and briefly discuss some of the more widely used measures in each of these five categories.

liquidity measures
financial ratios concerned with a firm's ability to meet its day-to-day operating expenses and satisfy its short-term obligations as they come due.

Measuring Liquidity Liquidity is concerned with the firm's ability to meet its day-to-day operating expenses and satisfy its short-term obligations as they come due. Of major concern is whether a company has adequate cash and other liquid assets on hand to service its debt and operating needs in a prompt and timely fashion. A general overview of a company's liquidity can be obtained from two simple measures: current ratio and net working capital. *Generally speaking, other things being equal, you'd like to see high or rising measures with both of these ratios.*

Current Ratio One of the most commonly cited of all financial ratios, the *current ratio* is computed as follows:

Equation 7.1 ➤
$$\text{Current ratio} = \frac{\text{Current assets}}{\text{Current liabilities}}$$

In 2007, Universal Office Furnishings (UVRS) had a current ratio of

$$\text{Current ratio for Universal} = \frac{\$500.3}{\$374.0} = \underline{\underline{1.34}}$$

This figure indicates that UVRS had $1.34 in short-term resources to service every dollar of current debt. That's a fairly good number and, by most standards today, would suggest that the company is carrying an adequate level of liquid assets.

Net Working Capital Though technically not a ratio, *net working capital* is often viewed as such. Actually, net working capital is an absolute measure, which indicates the dollar amount of equity in the working capital position of the firm. It is the difference between current assets and current liabilities. For 2007, the net working capital position for UVRS amounted to

Equation 7.2 ➤
$$\text{Net working capital} = \text{Current assets} - \text{Current liabilities}$$

$$\text{For Universal} = \$500.3 - \$374.0 = \underline{\underline{\$126.3 \text{ million}}}$$

A net working capital figure that exceeds $125,000,000 is indeed substantial (especially for a firm this size). It reinforces our contention that the liquidity position of this firm is good—so long as it is not made up of slow-moving, obsolete inventories and/or past-due accounts receivable.

Activity Ratios Measuring general liquidity is only the beginning of the analysis. We must also assess the composition and underlying liquidity of key current assets, and evaluate how effectively the company is managing these resources. **Activity ratios** compare company sales to various asset categories in order to measure how well the company is utilizing its assets. Three of the most widely used activity ratios deal with accounts receivable, inventory, and total assets. *Here again, other things being equal, you'd like to see high or rising measures with all three of these ratios.*

> **activity ratios**
> financial ratios that are used to measure how well a firm is managing its assets.

Accounts Receivable Turnover A glance at most financial statements will reveal that the asset side of the balance sheet is dominated by just a few accounts that make up 80% to 90%, or even more, of total resources. Certainly, this is the case with Universal Office Furnishings, where, as you can see in Table 7.3, three entries (accounts receivable, inventory, and net long-term assets) accounted for nearly 80% of total assets in 2007. Like Universal, most firms invest a significant amount of capital in accounts receivable, and for this reason they are viewed as a crucial corporate resource. *Accounts receivable turnover* is a measure of how these resources are being managed. It is computed as follows:

Equation 7.3 ➤

$$\text{Accounts receivable turnover} = \frac{\text{Annual sales}}{\text{Accounts receivable}}$$

$$\text{For Universal} = \frac{\$1,938.0}{\$227.2} = \underline{\underline{8.53}}$$

In essence, this turnover figure indicates the kind of return (in the form of sales) the company is getting from its investment in accounts receivable. Other things being equal, the higher the turnover figure, the more favorable it is. In 2007, UVRS was turning its receivables about 8.5 times a year. That excellent turnover rate suggests a very strong credit and collection policy. It also means that each dollar invested in receivables was supporting, or generating, $8.53 in sales.

Inventory Turnover Another important corporate resource—and one that requires a considerable amount of management attention—is inventory. Control of inventory is important to the well-being of a company and is commonly assessed with the *inventory turnover* measure:

Equation 7.4 ➤

$$\text{Inventory turnover} = \frac{\text{Annual sales}}{\text{Inventory}}$$

$$\text{For Universal} = \frac{\$1,938.0}{\$103.7} = \underline{\underline{18.69}}$$

Again, the more sales the company can get out of its inventory, the better the return on this vital resource. Universal's 2007 turnover of almost 19 times a year means that the firm is holding inventory for less than a month—actually, for about 20 days (365/18.69 = 19.5). That's the kind of performance you'd normally like to see. For the higher the turnover figure, the less time an item spends in inventory and the better the return the company is able to earn from funds tied up in inventory.

Note that, rather than sales, some analysts prefer to use *cost of goods sold* in the numerator of Equation 7.4, on the premise that the inventory account on the balance sheet is more directly related to cost of goods sold from the income statement. Because cost of goods sold is less than sales, using it will, of course, lead to a lower inventory turnover figure—for UVRS in 2007: $1,128.5/$103.7 = 10.88, versus 18.69 when sales is used. Regardless of whether you use sales (which we'll continue to do in this chapter) or cost of goods sold, for analytical purposes you'd still use the measure in the same way.

Total Asset Turnover *Total asset turnover* indicates how efficiently assets are being used to support sales. It is calculated as follows:

Equation 7.5 ➤

$$\text{Total asset turnover} = \frac{\text{Annual sales}}{\text{Total assets}}$$

$$\text{For Universal} = \frac{\$1,938.0}{\$941.2.7} = \underline{\underline{2.06}}$$

Note in this case that UVRS is generating more than $2 in revenues from every dollar invested in assets. This is a fairly high number and is important because it has a direct bearing on corporate profitability. The principle at work here is much like the return to an individual investor: Earning $100 from a $1,000 investment is far more desirable than earning the same amount from a $2,000 investment. A high total asset turnover figure suggests that corporate resources are being well managed and that the firm is able to realize a high level of sales (and, ultimately, profits) from its asset investments.

leverage measures
financial ratios that measure the amount of debt being used to support operations and the ability of the firm to service its debt.

Leverage Measures Leverage looks at the firm's financial structure. It indicates the amount of debt being used to support the resources and operations of the company. The amount of indebtedness within the financial structure and the ability of the firm to service its debt are major concerns to potential investors. There are two widely used leverage ratios. The first, the debt-equity ratio, measures the amount of debt being used by the company. The second, times interest earned, assesses how well the company can service its debt.

Debt-Equity Ratio The *debt-equity ratio* measures the relative amount of funds provided by lenders and owners. It is computed as follows:

Equation 7.6 ➤

$$\text{Debt-equity ratio} = \frac{\text{Long-term debt}}{\text{Stockholder's equity}}$$

$$\text{For Universal} = \frac{\$177.8}{\$294.5} = \underline{\underline{0.60}}$$

Because highly leveraged firms (those that use large amounts of debt) run an increased risk of defaulting on their loans, this ratio is particularly helpful in assessing a stock's risk exposure. The 2007 debt-equity ratio for UVRS is reasonably low (at 0.60) and shows that most of the company's capital comes from its owners. Stated another way, there was only 60 cents worth of debt in the capital structure for every dollar of equity. Unlike the other measures we've looked at so far, a *low* or *declining* debt-equity ratio is preferable, as that would suggest the firm has a more reasonable debt load and, therefore, less exposure to financial risk.

Times Interest Earned   *Times interest earned* is a so-called coverage ratio. It measures the ability of the firm to meet ("cover") its fixed interest payments. It is calculated as follows:

Equation 7.7 ➤

$$\text{Times interest earned} = \frac{\text{Earnings before interest and taxes}}{\text{Interest expense}}$$

$$\text{For Universal} = \frac{\$235.2}{\$13.4} = \underline{17.55}$$

The ability of the company to meet its interest payments (which, with bonds, are fixed contractual obligations) in a timely fashion is an important consideration in evaluating risk exposure. Universal's times interest earned ratio indicates that the firm has about $17.50 available to cover every dollar of interest expense. That's an outstanding coverage ratio—way above average! As a rule, a ratio eight to nine times earnings is considered strong. To put this number in perspective, there's usually little concern until times interest earned drops to something less than two or three times earnings. Clearly, low or declining measures definitely are *not* what you want to find here.

It's recently become popular to use an alternative earnings figure in the numerator for the times interest earned ratio. In particular, some analysts are adding back depreciation and amortization expenses to earnings, and are using what is known as *earnings before interest, taxes, depreciation, and amortization* (EBITDA). Their argument is that because depreciation and amortization are both noncash expenditures (i.e., they're little more than bookkeeping entries), they should be added back to earnings to provide a more realistic "cash-based" figure. While that may be true, as more fully discussed in the *Investing in Action* box on page 325, EBITDA figures invariably end up putting performance in a far more favorable light. (Indeed, many argue that this is the principal motivation behind their use.) In fact, EBITDA often results in *much higher* earnings figures and as a result, tends to sharply increase ratios such as times interest earned. For example, in the case of UVRS, adding depreciation and amortization (2007: $77.1 million) to EBIT (2007: $235.2 million) results in a coverage ratio of $312.3/$13.4 = 23.31—versus 17.5 when this ratio is computed in the conventional way (with EBIT).

profitability measures
financial ratios that measure a firm's returns by relating profits to sales, assets, or equity.

Measuring Profitability   **Profitability** is a relative measure of success. Each of the various profitability measures relates the returns (profits) of a company to its sales, assets, or equity. There are three widely used profitability measures: net profit margin, return on assets, and return on equity. Clearly, the more profitable the company, the better—thus, *other things being equal, higher or increasing measures of profitability are what you'd like to see.*

Net Profit Margin   This is the "bottom line" of operations. *Net profit margin* indicates the rate of profit being earned from sales and other revenues. It is computed as follows:

INVESTING *in Action*

So, What's the Deal with EBITDA?

In their financial statements, companies some-times report earnings using cryptic and possi-bly confusing names. It's worth knowing what they mean.

The traditional measure of *operating income* is, broadly, revenues minus the costs related to producing those revenues. These costs include selling, general, and administrative costs, as well as depreciation and amortization. Remember that depreciation and amortization are treated as charges against revenues for the period. Overall, the operating income num-ber—EBIT, earnings before interest and taxes—reflects the results of the firm's operations.

In an effort to put their best foot forward, some companies have begun to report EBITDA—earnings before interest, taxes, depreciation, and amortization—which they argue is the best way to measure performance. However, EBITDA figures also typically report performance in a more favorable light. Capital-intensive businesses, those that involve lots of intangible assets, and those that expand primar-ily through the buyout of other firms (which results in goodwill) can show better earnings figures by reporting earnings before deprecia-tion and amortization are deducted from rev-enues. They explain that they want investors to see the *cash* that the business throws off, which the company can use for growth and to

pay off its debt. The depreciation charges, they feel, obscure that information.

Is the argument about wanting investors to see cash results an accurate one? Not entirely. EBITDA *does* remove the non-cash charges against earnings. However, the revenue amount reported on the income statement is itself a result of accrual-basis accounting, so it is not simply the firm's cash earnings. The statement of cash flows would give a more accurate picture of the firm's cash flow from operating activities.

There's nothing wrong with companies using EBITDA; doing so does not violate any account-ing or reporting rules. But in doing financial ratio analysis, you need to be careful to under-stand the earnings figure you use. Whenever an income or profit amount appears in the financial ratios you calculate, be sure you are using the correct number. If you do not, the ratios will be off. This is all the more important when you are making comparisons between companies.

CRITICAL THINKING QUESTIONS Suppose we want a new financial ratio that uses EBITDA. How would you suggest it be computed? What would you call it? What types of firms would you recommend it be used for?

Source: Adapted from John Bajkowski, "EBT, EBIT, EBITDA: Will the Real Earnings Figure Please Stand Up?" *AAII Journal*, August 2002, pp. 4–9.

Equation 7.8 ➤

$$\text{Net profit margin} = \frac{\text{Net profit after taxes}}{\text{Total revenues}}$$

$$\text{For Universal} = \frac{\$139.7}{\$1,938.0} = \underline{\underline{7.2\%}}$$

The net profit margin looks at profits as a percentage of sales (and other rev-enues). Because it moves with costs, it also reveals the type of control manage-ment has over the cost structure of the firm. Note that UVRS had a net profit margin of 7.2% in 2007. That is, the company's return on sales was better than 7 cents on the dollar. That may be about average for the large U.S. com-panies, but as we shall see, that's well above average for firms in the business equipment industry.

Return on Assets As a profitability measure, *return on assets (ROA)* looks at the amount of resources needed to support operations. Return on assets reveals management's effectiveness in generating profits from the assets it has available, and is perhaps *the single most important measure of return*. ROA is computed as follows:

Equation 7.9 ➤

$$\text{ROA} = \frac{\text{Net profit after taxes}}{\text{Total assets}}$$

$$\text{For Universal} = \frac{\$139.7}{\$941.2} = \underline{\underline{14.8\%}}$$

In the case of Universal Office Furnishings, the company earned almost 15% on its asset investments in 2007. That is a very healthy return, and well above average. As a rule, you'd like to see a company maintain as high an ROA as possible. The higher the ROA, the more profitable the company.

Return on Equity A measure of the overall profitability of the firm, *return on equity (ROE)* is closely watched by investors because of its direct link to the profits, growth, and dividends of the company. Return on equity—or return on investment (ROI), as it's sometimes called—measures the return to the firm's stockholders by relating profits to shareholder equity:

Equation 7.10 ➤

$$\text{ROE} = \frac{\text{Net profit after taxes}}{\text{Stockholder's equity}}$$

$$\text{For Universal} = \frac{\$139.7}{\$294.5} = \underline{\underline{47.4\%}}$$

ROE shows the annual payoff to investors, which in the case of UVRS amounts to nearly 48 cents for every dollar of equity. That, too, is an outstanding measure of performance and suggests that the company is doing what it has to do to keep its shareholders happy. Generally speaking, look out for a falling ROE, as it could mean trouble later on.

Breaking Down ROA and ROE ROA and ROE are both important measures of corporate profitability. But to get the most from these two measures, we have to break them down into their component parts. ROA, for example, is made up of two key components: the firm's net profit margin and its total asset turnover. Thus, rather than using Equation 7.9 to find ROA, we can use the following expanded format:

Equation 7.11 ➤

$$\text{ROA} = \text{Net profit margin} \times \text{Total asset turnover}$$

Using the net profit margin and total asset turnover figures that we computed earlier (Equations 7.8 and 7.5, respectively), we can find Universal's 2007 ROA.

$$\text{ROA} = 7.2\% \times 2.06 = \underline{\underline{14.8\%}}$$

Note that we end up with the same figure as that found with Equation 7.9. So why would you want to use the expanded version of ROA? *The major reason is that it shows you what's driving company profits.* As an investor, you want to know if ROA is moving up (or down) because of improvement (or deterioration) in the company's profit margin and/or its total asset turnover. Ideally, you'd like to see ROA moving up (or staying high) because the company is doing a good job in managing *both* its profits and its assets.

Going from ROA to ROE Just as ROA can be broken into its component parts, so too can the return on equity (ROE) measure. Actually, ROE is nothing more than an extension of ROA. It brings the company's financing decisions into the assessment of profitability. That is, the expanded ROE measure indicates the extent to which financial leverage (or "trading on the equity") can increase return to stockholders. The use of debt in the capital structure, in effect, means that *ROE will always be greater than ROA.* The question is how much greater. Rather than using the abbreviated version of ROE in Equation 7.10, we can compute ROE as follows:

Equation 7.12 ➤
$$\text{ROE} = \text{ROA} \times \text{Equity multiplier}$$

where

$$\text{Equity multiplier} = \frac{\text{Total assets}}{\text{Total stockholders' equity}}$$

To find ROE according to Equation 7.12, we first have to find the equity multiplier.

$$\text{Equity multiplier for Universal} = \frac{\$941.2}{\$294.5} = 3.20$$

We can now find the 2007 ROE for Universal as follows:

$$\text{ROE} = 14.8 \times 3.20 = \underline{47.3\%}$$

Here we can see that the use of debt (the equity multiplier) has magnified—in this case, tripled—returns to stockholders. (Note that small rounding errors account for the difference between the number computed here, 47.3%, and the one computed earlier, 47.4%, when we used Equation 7.10.)

An Expanded ROE Equation Alternatively, we can expand Equation 7.12 still further by breaking ROA *into its component parts.* In this case, we could compute ROE as

Equation 7.13 ➤
$$\text{ROE} = \text{ROA} \times \text{Equity multiplier}$$

$$= (\text{Net profit margin} \times \text{Total asset turnover}) \times \text{Equity multiplier}$$

$$\text{For Universal} = 7.2\% \times 2.06 \times 3.20 = \underline{47.4\%}$$

This expanded version of ROE is especially helpful, because it enables investors to assess the company's profitability in terms of three key components: net profit margin, total asset turnover, and financial leverage. In this way, you can determine whether ROE is moving up simply because the firm is employing more debt, which isn't necessarily beneficial, or because of how the firm is managing its assets and operations, which certainly does have positive long-term implications. To stockholders, ROE is a critical measure of performance (and thus merits careful attention) because of the impact it has on growth and earnings—both of which, as we'll see in Chapter 8, play vital roles in the stock valuation process.

common stock (market) ratios
financial ratios that convert key information about a firm to a per-share basis.

Common-Stock Ratios Finally, there are a number of **common-stock ratios** that convert key bits of information about the company to a per-share basis. Also called **market ratios**, they tell the investor exactly what portion of total profits, dividends, and equity is allocated to each share of stock. Popular common-stock ratios include earnings per share, price/earnings ratio, dividends per share, dividend yield, payout ratio, and book value per share. We examined two of these measures (earnings per share and dividend yield) in Chapter 6. Let's look now at the other four.

Price/Earnings Ratio This measure, an extension of the earnings per share ratio, is used to determine how the market is pricing the company's common stock. The *price/earnings (P/E) ratio* relates the company's earnings per share (EPS) to the market price of its stock.

Equation 7.14 ➤

$$P/E = \frac{\text{Market price of common stock}}{\text{EPS}}$$

To compute the P/E ratio, it is necessary to first know the stock's EPS. Using the earnings per share equation from the previous chapter, we see that the EPS for UVRS in 2007 was

$$EPS = \frac{\text{Net profit after taxes} - \text{Preferred dividends}}{\text{Number of common shares outstanding}}$$

$$\text{For Universal} = \frac{\$139.7 - \$0}{61.8} = \underline{\$2.26}$$

In this case, the company's profits of $139.7 million translate into earnings of $2.26 for *each share* of outstanding common stock. (Note in this case that dividends are shown as $0 because the company has no preferred stock outstanding.) Given this EPS figure and the stock's current market price (assume it is currently trading at $41.50), we can use Equation 7.14 to determine the P/E ratio for Universal.

$$P/E = \frac{\$41.50}{\$2.26} = \underline{18.4}$$

In effect, the stock is currently selling at a multiple of about 18 times its 2007 earnings.

Price/earnings multiples are widely quoted in the financial press and are an essential part of many stock valuation models. Other things being equal, you would like to find stocks with *rising P/E ratios,* because higher P/E multiples usually translate into higher future stock prices and better returns to stockholders. But even though you'd like to see them going up, you also want to *watch out for P/E ratios that become too high* (relative either to the market or to what the stock has done in the past). When this multiple gets too high, it may be a signal that the stock is becoming overvalued (and may be due for a fall).

One way to assess the P/E ratio is to compare it to the company's rate of growth in earnings. The market has developed a measure of this comparison called the **PEG ratio**. Basically, it looks at the latest P/E relative to the three- to five-year rate of growth in earnings. (The earnings growth rate can be all historical—the last three to five years—or perhaps part historical and part forecasted.) The PEG ratio is computed as

PEG ratio
a financial ratio that relates a stock's price/earnings multiple to the company's rate of growth in earnings.

Equation 7.15 ➤

$$\text{PEG ratio} = \frac{\text{Stock's P/E ratio}}{\text{3- to 5-year growth rate in earnings}}$$

As we saw earlier, Universal Office Furnishings had a P/E ratio of 18.4 times earnings in 2007. If corporate earnings for the past five years had been growing at an average annual rate of, say, 15%, then its PEG ratio would be

$$\text{For Universal} = \frac{18.4}{15.0} = \underline{\underline{1.21}}$$

A PEG ratio this close to 1.0 is certainly reasonable. It suggests that the company's P/E is not out of line with the earnings growth of the firm. In fact, the idea is to *look for stocks that have PEG ratios that are equal to or less than 1.* In contrast, a high PEG means the stock's P/E has outpaced its growth in earnings and, if anything, the stock is probably "fully valued." Some investors, in fact, won't even look at stocks if their PEGs are too high—say, more than 1.5 or 2.0. At the minimum, PEG is probably something you would want to look at, because it certainly is not unreasonable to expect some correlation between a stock's P/E and its rate of growth in earnings.

Dividends per Share The principle here is the same as for EPS: to translate total common dividends paid by the company into a per-share figure. (*Note:* If not shown on the income statement, the amount of dividends paid to common stockholders can usually be found on the statement of cash flows—see Table 7.5.) Dividends per share is measured as follows:

Equation 7.16 ➤

$$\text{Dividends per share} = \frac{\text{Annual dividends paid to common stock}}{\text{Number of common shares outstanding}}$$

$$\text{For Universal} = \frac{\$9.3}{61.8} = \underline{\underline{\$0.15}}$$

For fiscal 2007, Universal paid out dividends of $0.15 per share—at a quarterly rate of about 3.75 cents per share.

As we saw in the preceding chapter, we can relate dividends per share to the market price of the stock to determine its *dividend yield:* i.e., $0.15 ÷ $41.50 = 0.4%. Clearly, you won't find Universal Office Furnishings within the income sector of the market. It pays very little in annual dividends and has a dividend yield of less than one-half of 1%.

Payout Ratio Another important dividend measure is the dividend *payout ratio*. It indicates how much of its earnings a company pays out to stockholders in the form of dividends. Well-managed companies try to maintain target payout ratios. If earnings are going up over time, so will the company's dividends. The payout ratio is calculated as follows:

Equation 7.17 ➤

$$\text{Payout ratio} = \frac{\text{Dividends per share}}{\text{Earnings per share}}$$

$$\text{For Universal} = \frac{\$0.15}{\$2.26} = \underline{0.07}$$

For Universal in 2007, dividends accounted for about 7% of earnings. Traditionally, most companies that pay dividends tend to pay out somewhere between 40% and 60% of earnings. By that standard, Universal's payout, like its dividend yield, is quite low. But that's not necessarily bad, as it indicates that the company is retaining most of its earnings to, at least in part, internally finance the firm's rapid growth. Indeed, it is quite common for growth-oriented companies to have low payout ratios. Some of the better-known growth companies, like Genetech, Boston Scientific, EchoStar Communications, and Starbucks, all retain 100% of their earnings. (In other words, they have dividend payout ratios of zero.)

Although low dividend payout ratios are not a cause for concern, *high payout ratios may be*. In particular, once the payout ratio reaches 70% to 80% of earnings, you should take extra care. A payout ratio that high is often an indication that the company may not be able to maintain its current level of dividends. That generally means that dividends will have to be cut back to more reasonable levels. And if there's one thing the market doesn't like, it's cuts in dividends; they're usually associated with big cuts in share prices.

Book Value per Share The last common stock ratio is *book value per share*, a measure that deals with stockholders' equity. Actually, *book value is simply another term for equity (or net worth)*. It represents the difference between total assets and total liabilities. Note that in this case we're defining equity as *common stockholders' equity*, which would *exclude* preferred stock. That is, *common stockholders' equity = total equity − preferred stocks*. (Universal has no preferred outstanding, so its total equity equals its common stockholders' equity.) Book value per share is computed as follows:

Equation 7.18 ➤

$$\text{Book value per share} = \frac{\text{Common stockholders' equity}}{\text{Number of common shares outstanding}}$$

$$\text{For Universal} = \frac{\$294.5}{61.8} = \underline{\$4.76}$$

Presumably, a stock should sell for *more* than its book value (as Universal does). If not, it could be an indication that something is seriously wrong with the company's outlook and profitability.

A convenient way to relate the book value of a company to the market price of its stock is to compute the *price-to-book-value* ratio.

Equation 7.19 ➤

$$\text{Price-to-book-value} = \frac{\text{Market price of common stock}}{\text{Book value per share}}$$

$$\text{For Universal} = \frac{\$41.50}{\$4.76} = \underline{\underline{8.72}}$$

Widely used by investors, this ratio shows how aggressively the stock is being priced. Most stocks have a price-to-book-value ratio of more than 1.0—which simply indicates that the stock is selling for more than its book value. In fact, in strong bull markets, it is not uncommon to find stocks trading at four or five times their book values, or even more. Universal's price-to-book ratio of 8.7 times is definitely on the high side. That is something to evaluate closely. It may indicate that the stock is already fully priced, or perhaps even overpriced. Or it could result from nothing more than a relatively low owners' equity ratio.

▌ Interpreting the Numbers

Rather than compute all the financial ratios themselves, most investors rely on published reports for such information. Many large brokerage houses and a variety of financial services firms publish such reports. An example is given in Figure 7.2 (on page 332). These reports provide a good deal of vital information in a convenient and easy-to-read format. Best of all, they relieve investors of the chore of computing the financial ratios themselves. (Similar information is also available from a number of online services, as well as from various software providers.) Even so, as an investor, you must be able to evaluate this published information. To do so, you need not only a basic understanding of financial ratios but also some performance standard, or benchmark, against which you can assess trends in company performance.

Basically, financial statement analysis uses two types of performance standards: historical and industry. With *historical standards,* various financial ratios and measures are run on the company for a period of three to five years (or longer). You would use these to assess developing trends in the company's operations and financial condition. That is, are they improving or deteriorating, and where do the company's strengths and weaknesses lie? In contrast, *industry standards* enable you to compare the financial ratios of the company with comparable firms or with the average results for the industry as a whole. Here, we focus on determining the relative strengths of the firm with respect to its competitors. Using Universal Office Furnishings, we'll see how to use both of these standards of performance to evaluate and interpret financial ratios.

Using Historical and Industry Standards Look at Table 7.6 (on page 333). It provides a summary of historical data and average industry figures (for the latest year) for most of the ratios we have discussed. (Industry averages, such as those used in Table 7.6, are readily available from such sources as S&P, Moody's, or from many industry-specific publications.) By carefully evaluating

---

INVESTOR FACTS

COULD THERE BE TROUBLE BREWING?—Analysts often cite the following financial statement developments as potential indicators that a company may be in poor financial health or heading for problems:

- Inventories and receivables growing faster than sales.
- A falling current ratio, caused by current liabilities increasing faster than current assets.
- A high and rapidly increasing debt-to-equity ratio, suggesting the firm may have trouble servicing its debt in the future.
- Cash flow from operations dropping below a firm's net income, meaning the company is propping up its earnings by selling assets or using some other technique to shuffle its numbers.
- The presence of lots of indecipherable off-balance-sheet accounts and extraordinary income entries.

FIGURE 7.2   **An Example of a Published Report with Financial Statistics**

This and similar reports are widely available to investors and play an important part in the security analysis process. (*Source:* Standard & Poor's *Stock Reports,* January 19, 2006. ©2006 The McGraw-Hill Companies. All Rights Reserved.)

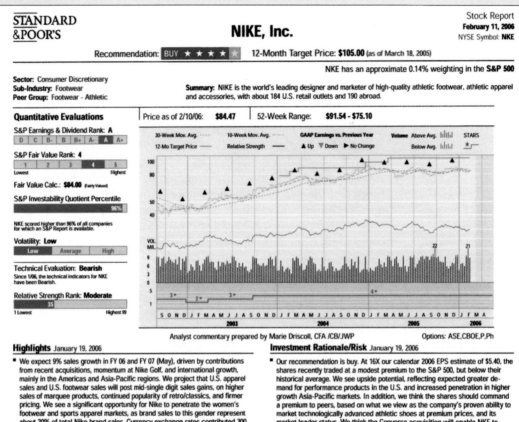

EXCEL with SPREADSHEETS

TABLE 7.6   Comparative Historical and Industry Ratios

	Historical Figures for Universal Office Furnishings				Industry Averages for the Office Equipment Industry in 2007
	2004	2005	2006	2007	
Liquidity measures					
Current ratio	1.55	1.29	1.69	1.34	1.45
Activity measures					
Receivables turnover	9.22	8.87	9.18	8.53	5.70
Inventory turnover	15.25	17.17	16.43	18.69	7.80
Total asset turnover	1.96	2.12	2.32	2.06	0.85
Leverage measures					
Debt-equity ratio	0.70	0.79	0.91	0.60	1.58
Times interest earned	15.37	26.22	32.49	17.55	5.60
Profitability measures					
Net profit margin	6.6%	7.5%	8.0%	7.2%	4.6%
Return on assets	9.8%	16.4%	18.6%	14.8%	3.9%
Return on equity	25.9%	55.5%	67.8%	47.4%	17.3%
Common stock measures					
Earnings per share	$1.92	$2.00	$2.17	$2.26	N/A
Price/earnings ratio	16.2	13.9	15.8	18.4	16.2
Dividend yield	0.3%	0.4%	0.4%	0.4%	1.1%
Payout ratio	5.2%	5.5%	6.0%	6.6%	24.8%
Price-to-book-value ratio	7.73	10.73	10.71	8.72	3.54

these ratios, we should be able to draw some basic conclusions about the financial condition, operating results, and general financial health of UVRS. By comparing the financial ratios contained in Table 7.6, we can make the following observations about the company:

1. Universal's *liquidity position* is a bit below average. This doesn't seem to be a source of major concern, however, especially when you consider its receivables and inventory positions. That is, based on its respective turnover ratios (see item 2 below), both of these current assets seem to be very well controlled, which could explain the relatively low current ratio of this company. That is, the current ratio is a bit below average, not because the firm has a lot of current liabilities, but because it is doing such a good job in controlling current assets.

2. Universal's *activity measures* are all way above average. This company consistently has very high turnover measures, which in turn make significant contributions not only to the firm's liquidity position but also to its profitability. Clearly, the company has been able to get a lot more from its assets than the industry as a whole.

3. The company's *leverage position* seems well controlled. It tends to use a lot less debt in its financial structure than the average firm in the office equipment industry. The payoff for this judicious use of debt comes in the form of a coverage ratio that's well above average.

4. The *profitability picture* for Universal is equally attractive. The profit margin, return on assets, and ROE are all well above the industry norms. Clearly, the company is doing an outstanding job in managing its profits and is getting good results from its sales, assets, and equity.

In summary, our analysis shows that this firm is very well managed and highly profitable. The results of this are reflected in *common stock ratios* that are consistently equal or superior to industry averages. Universal does not pay out a lot in dividends, but that's only because it uses those valuable resources to finance its growth and to reward its investors with consistently high ROEs.

Looking at the Competition   In addition to analyzing a company historically and relative to the average performance of the industry, it's useful to evaluate the firm relative to two or three of its major competitors. A lot can be gained from seeing how a company stacks up against its competitors and by determining whether it is, in fact, well positioned to take advantage of unfolding developments. Table 7.7 offers an array of comparative financial statistics for Universal and three of its major competitors. One is about the same size (Cascade Industries), one is much smaller (Colwyn Furniture), and one is much larger (High Design, Inc.).

As the data in Table 7.7 show, Universal can hold its own against other leading producers in the industry. Indeed, in virtually every category, Universal's numbers are about equal or superior to those of its three major competitors. It

TABLE 7.7   **Comparative Financial Statistics: Universal Office Furnishings and Its Major Competitors** (All figures are for year-end 2007 or for the 5-year period ending in 2007; $ in millions)

Financial Measure	Universal Office Furnishings	Cascade Industries	Colwyn Furniture	High Design, Inc.
Total assets	$ 941.2	$ 906.7	$342.7	$3,037.6
Long-term debt	$ 177.8	$ 124.2	$ 73.9	$ 257.8
Stockholders' equity	$ 294.5	$ 501.3	$183.9	$1,562.2
Stockholders' equity as a % of total assets	31.3%	55.3%	53.7%	51.4%
Total revenues	$1,938.0	$1,789.3	$642.2	$3,316.1
Net earnings	$ 139.7	$ 87.4	$ 38.5	$ 184.2
Net profit margin	7.2%	4.9%	6.0%	5.5%
5-year growth rates in:				
Total assets	14.36%	19.44%	17.25%	17.73%
Total revenues	18.84%	17.76%	15.91%	15.84%
EPS	56.75%	38.90%	21.10%	24.66%
Dividends	1.48%	11.12%	N/A	12.02%
Total asset turnover	2.06×	1.97×	1.88×	1.09×
Debt-equity ratio	0.60	0.43	1.46	0.17
Times interest earned	17.55×	13.38×	8.35×	14.36×
ROA	14.8%	9.5%	6.7%	6.7%
ROE	47.4%	18.8%	21.8%	13.0%
P/E ratio	18.4×	14.4×	13.3×	12.4×
PEG ratio	1.21	2.42	1.98	1.09
Payout ratio	6.6%	26.2%	N/A	32.4%
Dividend yield	0.4%	1.8%	N/A	2.6%
Price-to-book-value ratio	8.72	2.71	2.93	1.59

may not be the biggest (or the smallest), but it outperforms them all in profit margins and growth rates (in revenues and earnings). Equally important, it has the highest asset turnover, ROE, and price/earnings ratio. Tables 7.6 and 7.7 clearly show that Universal Office Furnishings is a solid, up-and-coming business that's been able to make a name for itself in a highly competitive industry. The company has done well in the past and appears to be well managed today. Our major concern at this point (and the topic of discussion in Chapter 8) is whether Universal can continue to produce above-average returns to investors.

CONCEPTS IN REVIEW
Answers available at: www.myfinancelab.com

7.12 What is *fundamental analysis?* Does the performance of a company have any bearing on the value of its stock? Explain.

7.13 Why do investors bother to look at the historical performance of a company when future behavior is what really counts? Explain.

7.14 What is *ratio analysis?* Describe the contribution of ratio analysis to the study of a company's financial condition and operating results.

7.15 Contrast historical standards of performance with industry standards. Briefly note the role of each in analyzing the financial condition and operating results of a company.

Summary

LG 1 **Discuss the security analysis process, including its goals and functions.** Success in buying common stocks is largely a matter of careful security selection and investment timing. Security analysis helps the investor make the selection decision by gauging the intrinsic value (underlying worth) of a stock.

LG 2 **Understand the purpose and contributions of economic analysis.** Economic analysis evaluates the general state of the economy and its potential effects on security returns. Its purpose is to characterize the future economic environment the investor is likely to face, and to set the tone for the security analysis process.

LG 3 **Describe industry analysis and note how it is used.** In industry analysis, the investor focuses on the activities of one or more industries. Especially important are how the competitive position of a particular industry stacks up against others and which companies within an industry hold special promise.

LG 4 **Demonstrate a basic appreciation of fundamental analysis and why it is used.** Fundamental analysis looks closely at the financial and operating characteristics of the company—at its competitive position, its sales and profit margins, its asset mix, its capital structure, and, eventually, its future prospects. A key aspect of this analytical process is company analysis, which involves an in-depth study of the financial condition and operating results of the company.

LG 5   **Calculate a variety of financial ratios and describe how financial statement analysis is used to gauge the financial vitality of a company.** The company's balance sheet, income statement, and statement of cash flows are all used in company analysis. An essential part of this analysis is financial ratios, which expand the perspective and information content of financial statements. There are five broad categories of financial ratios—liquidity, activity, leverage, profitability, and common-stock (market) ratios. All involve the study of relationships between financial statement accounts.

LG 6   **Use various financial measures to assess a company's performance, and explain how the insights derived form the basic input for the valuation process.** To evaluate financial ratios properly, it is necessary to base the analysis on historical and industry standards of performance. Historical standards are used to assess developing trends in the company. Industry benchmarks enable the investor to see how the firm stacks up against its competitors. Together, they provide insight into how well the company is situated to take advantage of unfolding market conditions and opportunities.

Key Terms

activity ratios, *p. 322*
balance sheet, *p. 316*
business cycle, *p. 306*
common stock (market) ratios, *p. 328*
economic analysis, *p. 305*
fundamental analysis, *p. 315*
growth cycle, *p. 312*
income statement, *p. 316*
industry analysis, *p. 311*

intrinsic value, *p. 303*
leverage measures, *p. 323*
liquidity measures, *p. 321*
PEG ratio, *p. 329*
profitability measures, *p. 324*
ratio analysis, *p. 320*
security analysis, *p. 303*
statement of cash flows, *p. 318*

Discussion Questions

LG 2   Q7.1   Economic analysis is generally viewed as an integral part of the "top-down" approach to security analysis. In this context, identify each of the following and note how each would probably behave in a strong economy.
   a. Fiscal policy
   b. Interest rates
   c. Industrial production
   d. Retail sales
   e. Producer prices

LG 1 LG 2   Q7.2   As an investor, what kind(s) of economic information would you look for if you were thinking about investing in the following?
- a. An airline stock
- b. A cyclical stock
- c. An electrical utility stock
- d. A building materials stock
- e. An aerospace firm, with heavy exposure in the defense industry

LG 5   Q7.3   Match the specific ratios in the left-hand column with the category in the right-hand column to which it belongs.

a. Inventory turnover	1. Profitability ratios
b. Debt-equity ratio	2. Activity ratios
c. Current ratio	3. Liquidity ratios
d. Net profit margin	4. Leverage ratios
e. Return on assets	5. Common stock ratios
f. Total asset turnover	
g. Price/earnings ratio	
h. Times interest earned	
i. Price-to-book-value ratio	
j. Payout ratio	

Problems

LG 5   P7.1   Assume you are given the following abbreviated financial statements.

	($ in millions)
Current assets	$150.0
Fixed and other assets	200.0
Total assets	$350.0
Current liabilities	$100.0
Long-term debt	50.0
Stockholders' equity	200.0
	$350.0
Common shares outstanding	10 million shares
Total revenues	$500.0
Total operating costs and expenses	435.0
Interest expense	10.0
Income taxes	20.0
Net profits	$ 35.0
Dividends paid to common stockholders	$ 10.0

On the basis of this information, calculate as many liquidity, activity, leverage, profitability, and common stock measures as you can. (*Note:* Assume the current market price of the common stock is $75 per share.)

LG 5   **P7.2**   BOOKV has $750,000,000 in total assets, no preferred stock, and total liabilities of $300,000,000. There are 300,000,000 shares of common stock outstanding. What is the book value per share?

LG 5   **P7.3**   BOOKV has $750,000,000 in total assets, no preferred stock, and total liabilities of $300,000,000. There are 300,000,000 shares of common stock outstanding. The stock is selling for $5.25 per share. What is the price-to-book ratio?

LG 6   **P7.4**   The Amherst Company has net profits of $10 million, sales of $150 million, and 2.5 million shares of common stock outstanding. The company has total assets of $75 million and total stockholders' equity of $45 million. It pays $1 per share in common dividends, and the stock trades at $20 per share. Given this information, determine the following:
   a. Amherst's EPS.
   b. Amherst's book value per share and price-to-book-value ratio.
   c. The firm's P/E ratio.
   d. The company's net profit margin.
   e. The stock's dividend payout ratio and its dividend yield.
   f. The stock's PEG ratio, given that the company's earnings have been growing at an average annual rate of 7.5%.

LG 5   **P7.5**   ZAPIT common stock is selling at a P/E of 15 times trailing earnings. The stock price is $25. What were the firm's earnings per share?

LG 5   **P7.6**   PEGCOR has a P/E ratio of 15. Earnings per share are $2.00, and the expected EPS 5 years from today are $3.22. Calculate the PEG ratio. (Refer to Chapter 4 if necessary.)

LG 5   **P7.7**   Highgate Computer Company produces $2 million in profits from $28 million in sales. It has total assets of $15 million.
   a. Calculate Highgate's total asset turnover and its net profit margin.
   b. Find the company's ROA, ROE, and book value per share, given that it has a total net worth of $6 million and 500,000 shares of common stock outstanding.

LG 5   **P7.8**   The following data have been gathered from the financial statements of HiFly Corporation:

	2006	2007
Operating profit	$550,000,000	$600,000.000
Interest expense	200,000,000	250,000,000
Taxes	126,000,000	126,000,000
Net profit	224,000,000	224,000,000

Calculate the times interest earned ratios for 2006 and 2007. Is the company more or less able to meet its interest payments in 2007 when measured this way?

LG 5   LG 6

P7.9 Financial Learning Systems has 2.5 million shares of common stock outstanding and 100,000 shares of preferred stock. (The preferred pays annual cash dividends of $5 a share, and the common pays annual cash dividends of 25 cents a share.) Last year, the company generated net profits (after taxes) of $6,850,000. The company's balance sheet shows total assets of $78 million, total liabilities of $32 million, and $5 million in preferred stock. The firm's common stock is currently trading in the market at $45 a share.

    a. Given the preceding information, find the EPS, P/E ratio, and book value per share.

    b. What will happen to the price of the stock if EPS *rises* to $3.75 and the P/E ratio stays where it is? What will happen if EPS *drops* to $1.50 and the P/E doesn't change?

    c. What will happen to the price of the stock if EPS rises to $3.75 and the P/E jumps to 25 times earnings?

    d. What will happen if *both* EPS and the P/E ratio *drop*—to $1.50 and 10 times earnings, respectively?

    e. Comment on the effect that EPS and the P/E ratio have on the market price of the stock.

LG 5

P7.10 The Buffalo Manufacturing Company has total assets of $10 million, an asset turnover of 2.0 times, and a net profit margin of 15%.

    a. What is Buffalo's return on assets?

    b. Find Buffalo's ROE, given that 40% of the assets are financed with stockholders' equity.

LG 5

P7.11 Find the EPS, P/E ratio, and dividend yield of a company that has 5 million shares of common stock outstanding (the shares trade in the market at $25), earns 10% after taxes on annual sales of $150 million, and has a dividend payout ratio of 35%. At what rate would the company's net earnings be growing if the stock had a PEG ratio of 2.0?

LG 5

P7.12 FigureItOut Corporation has a net profit margin of 8% and a total asset turnover of 2 times. What is the company's return on assets?

LG 5

P7.13 FigureItOut Corporation has a net profit margin of 8%, a total asset turnover of 2 times, total assets of $1 billion, and total equity of $500 million. What is the company's return on equity?

LG 5

P7.14 FigureItOut Corporation has a net profit margin of 8%, a total asset turnover of 2 times, total assets of $1 billion, and total equity of $500 million. What were the company's sales and net profit?

LG 5

P7.15 Using the resources available at your campus or public library (or on the Internet), select any common stock you like and determine as many of the profitability, activity, liquidity, leverage, and market ratios, covered in this and the preceeding chapter, as you can. Compute the ratios for the latest available fiscal year. (*Note:* Show your work for all calculations.)

LG 4 LG 5 LG 6

P7.16 Listed below are 6 pairs of stocks. Pick *one of these pairs* and then, using the resources available at your campus or public library (or on the Internet), comparatively analyze the 2 stocks. Which is fundamentally stronger and holds more promise for the future? Compute (or obtain) as many ratios as you see fit. As part of your analysis, obtain the latest S&P and/or *Value Line* reports on both stocks, and use them for added insights about the firms and their stocks.
   a. Wal-Mart versus Target
   b. Sara Lee versus Campbell Soup
   c. IBM versus Intel
   d. Marriott International versus Four Seasons Hotels
   e. Liz Claiborne versus Under Armour
   f. General Dynamics versus Boeing

LG 4 LG 5 LG 6

P7.17 Listed here are the 2006 and 2007 financial statements for Otago Bay Marine Motors, a major manufacturer of top-of-the-line outboard motors.

Otago Bay Marine Motors
Balance Sheets ($ in thousands)

	As of December 31,	
	2007	2006
Assets		
Current assets		
Cash and cash equivalents	$ 56,203	$ 88,942
Accounts receivable, net of allowances	20,656	12,889
Inventories	29,294	24,845
Prepaid expenses	5,761	6,536
Total current assets	111,914	133,212
Property, plant, and equipment, at cost	137,273	85,024
Less: Accumulated depreciation and amortization	(50,574)	(44,767)
Net fixed assets	86,699	40,257
Other assets	105,327	51,001
Total assets	$303,940	$224,470
Liabilities and Shareholders' Equity		
Current liabilities		
Notes and accounts payable	$ 28,860	$ 4,927
Dividends payable	1,026	791
Accrued liabilities	20,976	16,780
Total current liabilities	50,862	22,498
Noncurrent liabilities		
Long-term debt	40,735	20,268
Shareholders' equity		
Common stock	7,315	7,103
Capital in excess of par value	111,108	86,162
Retained earnings	93,920	88,439
Total shareholders' equity	212,343	181,704
Total liabilities and equity	$303,940	$224,470
Average number of common shares outstanding	10,848,000	10,848,000

Otago Bay Marine Motors Income Statements ($ in thousands)

	For the Year Ended December 31,	
	2007	2006
Net sales	$259,593	$245,424
Cost of goods sold	133,978	127,123
Gross profit margin	125,615	118,301
Operating expenses:	72,098	70,368
Earnings from operations	53,517	47,933
Other income (expense), net	4,193	3,989
Earnings before income taxes	57,710	51,922
Provision for income taxes	22,268	19,890
Net earnings	$ 35,442	$ 32,032
Cash dividends ($0.35 and $0.27 per share)	$ 3,769	$ 2,947
Average price per share of common stock (in the fourth quarter of the year)	$74.25	$80.75

a. On the basis of the information provided, calculate the following financial ratios for 2006 and 2007.

	Otago Bay Marine Motors		Industry Averages (for 2007)
	2006	2007	
Current ratio			2.36
Total asset turnover			1.27
Debt-equity ratio			10.00
Net profit margin			9.30
ROA			15.87
ROE			19.21
EPS			1.59
P/E ratio			19.87
Dividend yield			.44
Payout ratio			.26
Price-to-book-value			6.65

b. Considering the financial ratios you computed, along with the industry averages, how would you characterize the financial condition of Otago Bay Marine Motors? Explain.

LG 5 **LG 6** P7.18 The following summary financial statistics were obtained from the 2003 Otago Bay Marine Motors (OBMM) annual report.

	2003 ($ in millions)
Net sales	$179.3
Total assets	$136.3
Net earnings	$ 20.2
Shareholders' equity	$109.6

a. Use the profit margin and asset turnover to compute the 2003 ROA for OBMM. Now introduce the equity multiplier to find ROE.
b. Use the summary financial information from the 2007 OBMM financial statements (see Problem 7.17) to compute the 2007 ROA and ROE. Use the same procedures to calculate these measures as you did in part a.

c. On the basis of your calculations, describe how *each* of the three components (profit margin, asset turnover, and leverage) contributed to the change in OBMM's ROA and ROE between 2003 and 2007. Which component(s) contributed the most to the change in ROA? Which contributed the most to the change in ROE?

d. Generally speaking, do you think that these changes are fundamentally healthy for the company?

See www.myfinancelab.com **for Web Exercises,
Spreadsheets, and other online resources.**

Case Problem 7.1 *Some Financial Ratios Are Real Eye-Openers*

LG 5 LG 6

Jack Arnold is a resident of Lubbock, Texas, where he is a prosperous rancher and businessman. He has also built up a sizable portfolio of common stock, which, he believes, is due to the fact that he thoroughly evaluates each stock he invests in. As Jack says, "Y'all can't be too careful about these things! Anytime I'm fixin' to invest in a stock, you can bet I'm gonna learn as much as I can about the company." Jack prefers to compute his own ratios even though he could easily obtain analytical reports from his broker at no cost. (In fact, Billy Bob Smith, his broker, has been volunteering such services for years.)

Recently, Jack has been keeping an eye on a small chemical stock. The firm, South Plains Chemical Company, is big in the fertilizer business—which is something Jack knows a lot about. Not long ago, he received a copy of the firm's latest financial statements (summarized here) and decided to take a closer look at the company.

South Plains Chemical Company Balance Sheet
($ Thousands)

Cash	$ 1,250		
Accounts receivable	8,000	Current liabilities	$10,000
Inventory	12,000	Long-term debt	8,000
Current assets	21,250	Stockholders' equity	12,000
Fixed and other assets	8,750	Total liabilities and	
Total assets	$30,000	stockholders' equity	$30,000

Income Statement
($ Thousands)

Sales	$50,000
Cost of goods sold	25,000
Operating expenses	15,000
Operating profit	10,000
Interest expense	2,500
Taxes	2,500
Net profit	$5,000
Dividends paid to common stockholders ($ in thousands)	$1,250
Number of common shares outstanding	5 million
Recent market price of the common stock	$25

Questions

a. Compute the following ratios, using the South Plains Chemical Company figures.

	Latest Industry Averages			Latest Industry Averages
Liquidity			*Profitability*	
a. Net working capital	N/A		h. Net profit margin	8.5%
b. Current ratio	1.95		i. Return on assets	22.5%
Activity			j. ROE	32.2%
c. Receivables turnover	5.95		*Common Stock Ratios*	
d. Inventory turnover	4.50		k. Earnings per share	$2.00
e. Total asset turnover	2.65		l. Price/earnings ratio	20.0
Leverage			m. Dividends per share	$1.00
f. Debt-equity ratio	0.45		n. Dividend yield	2.5%
g. Times interest earned	6.75		o. Payout ratio	50.0%
			p. Book value per share	$6.25
			q. Price-to-book-value ratio	6.4

b. Compare the company ratios you prepared to the industry figures given in part **a.** What are the company's strengths? What are its weaknesses?

c. What is your overall assessment of South Plains Chemical? Do you think Jack should continue with his evaluation of the stock? Explain.

Case Problem 7.2   *Doris Looks at an Auto Issue*

LG 2   LG 3   LG 5

Doris Wise is a young career woman. She lives in Phoenix, Arizona, where she owns and operates a highly successful modeling agency. Doris manages her modest but rapidly growing investment portfolio, made up mostly of high-grade common stocks. Because she's young and single and has no pressing family requirements, Doris has invested primarily in stocks that offer the potential for attractive capital gains. Her broker recently recommended an auto company stock and sent her some literature and analytical reports to study. One report, prepared by the brokerage house she deals with, provided an up-to-date look at the economy, an extensive study of the auto industry, and an equally extensive review of several auto companies (including the one her broker recommended). She feels strongly about the merits of security analysis and believes it is important to spend time studying a stock before making an investment decision.

Questions

a. Doris tries to stay informed about the economy on a regular basis. At the present time, most economists agree that the economy, now well into the third year of a recovery, is healthy, with industrial activity remaining strong. What other information about the economy do you think Doris would find helpful in evaluating an auto stock? Prepare a list—and be specific. Which three items of economic information (from your list) do you feel are most important? Explain.

b. In relation to a study of the auto industry, briefly note the importance of each of the following.
   1. Auto imports
   2. The United Auto Workers union
   3. Interest rates
   4. The price of a gallon of gas

c. A variety of financial ratios and measures are provided about one of the auto companies and its stock. These are incomplete, however, so some additional information will have to be computed. Specifically, we know the following:

Net profit margin	15%
Total assets	$25 billion
Earnings per share	$3.00
Total asset turnover	1.5
Net working capital	$3.4 billion
Payout ratio	40%
Current liabilities	$5 billion
Price/earnings ratio	12.5

Given this information, calculate the following:
   1. Sales.
   2. Net profits after taxes.
   3. Current ratio.
   4. Market price of the stock.
   5. Dividend yield.

Excel with Spreadsheets

You have been asked to analyze the financial statements of the Dayton Corporation for the two years ending 2006 and 2007.

◇	A	B	C	D	E
1	Dayton Corporation				
2	Financial Data				
3		2007	2006		
4	Net sales	47,715	40,363		
5	Cost sales	27,842	21,485		
6	SG& A expenses	8,090	7,708		
7	Depreciation expense	628	555		
8	Interest expense	754	792		
9	Tax expense	3,120	3,002		
10	Cash & equivalents	2,144	2,536		
11	Receivables	5,215	5,017		
12	Inventory	3,579	3,021		
13	Other current assets	2,022	2,777		
14	Plant & equipment	18,956	16,707		
15	Accumulated depreciation	5,853	5,225		
16	Intangible assets	7,746	7,374		
17	Other non-current assets	10,465	7,700		
18	Payables	5,108	4,361		
19	Short-term notes payable	4,066	3,319		
20	Other current liabilities	2,369	2,029		
21	Long-term debt	4,798	3,600		
22	Other non-current liabilities	4,837	5,020		
23	Common stock	6,776	6,746		
24	Retained earnings	16,050	14,832		
25	Common shares outstanding	2,300	2,300		
26	Current market price of stock	$45	$45		

Questions

a. Create a comparative balance sheet for the years 2007 and 2006, similar to the spreadsheet for Table 7.3 which can be viewed at www.myfinancelab.com.

b. Create a comparative income statement for the years 2007 and 2006, similar to the spreadsheet for Table 7.4 which can be viewed at www.myfinancelab.com.

c. **Create a spreadsheet** to calculate the listed financial ratios for both 2007 and 2006, similar to the spreadsheet for Table 7.5 which can be viewed at www.myfinancelab.

Ratios	2007	2006
Current ratio		
Quick ratio		
Accounts receivable turnover		
Inventory turnover		
Total asset turnover		
Debt-equity ratio		
Times interest earned		
Net profit margin		
Return on equity (ROE)		
Earnings per share		
Price/earnings ratio		
Book value per share		
Price-to-book-value		

Chapter 8

Stock Valuation

W hat drives a stock's value? Many factors come into play, including positive earnings reports, promising company developments such as new products, dominating performance among competitors, and strong corporate management.

NIKE, Inc., based in Beaverton, Oregon, is the world's leading designer, marketer, and distributor of athletic footwear, apparel, equipment, and accessories, selling or licensing such brand names as NIKE®, Converse®, Cole Haan®, Chuck Taylor®, and All Star®. NIKE's products are sold through NIKE-owned retail stores (184 direct U.S. outlets and 190 retail stores internationally) and a network of independent distributors, including more than 37,000 retail outlets outside the United States.

On June 27, 2006, NIKE, Inc., (NYSE: NKE) reported its financial results for the 2006 fiscal year. For the year, revenues grew 9%, to $15.0 billion, compared to $13.7 billion the previous year. Net income per share increased 18%, to $5.28 versus $4.49 the prior year. Driving those results, according to Mark Parker, NIKE, Inc., president and CEO, are compelling product innovations and the strengthening of the NIKE brand in the areas of basketball and soccer.

NIKE's low debt to equity ratio of 0.113, current ratio of 2.805, P/E ratio of 15.17, return on assets of 14.13%, and return on equity of 23.34%, coupled with rising revenues and net income, would indicate the potential for an increase in the stock's price. However, the stock price has not reflected NIKE's recent growth. In mid-2006, its stock price was hovering around $80 per share, roughly 10% lower than its price one year earlier. Was the stock overvalued? Not according to the company's management, which on June 19, 2006, announced a four-year, $3 billion share repurchase program. Coming on the heels of the completion of a five-year $2.2 billion repurchase of 31.1 million shares, the proposed share repurchase indicates that NIKE's management believes the stock is undervalued.

How do you determine a stock's true value? This chapter explains how to determine a stock's intrinsic value by using dividend valuation, dividend and earnings, price/earnings, and other models.

Sources: Company information from http://www.nike.com (accessed July 24, 2006); NIKE, Inc. press release "Nike, Inc. Announces $3 Billion Share Repurchase Program," June 19, 2006; and NIKE financial data from http://finance.yahoo.com (accessed July 24, 2006).

LEARNING GOALS

After studying this chapter, you should be able to:

LG 1 Explain the role that a company's future plays in the stock valuation process.

LG 2 Develop a forecast of a stock's expected cash flow, starting with corporate sales and earnings, and then moving to expected dividends and share price.

LG 3 Discuss the concepts of intrinsic value and required rates of return, and note how they are used.

LG 4 Determine the underlying value of a stock using the zero-growth, constant-growth and variable-growth dividend valuation models.

LG 5 Use other types of present-value–based models to derive the value of a stock, as well as alternative price-relative procedures.

LG 6 Gain a basic appreciation of the procedures used to value different types of stocks, from traditional dividend-paying shares to more growth-oriented stocks.

Valuation: Obtaining a Standard of Performance

LG 1   LG 2   LG 3

stock valuation
the process by which the underlying value of a stock is established on the basis of its forecasted risk and return performance.

Obtaining a standard of performance that can be used to judge the investment merits of a share of stock is the underlying purpose of **stock valuation**. A stock's intrinsic value provides such a standard, as it indicates the future risk and return performance of a security. The question of whether and to what extent a stock is under- or overvalued is resolved by comparing its current market price to its intrinsic value. At any given point in time, the price of a share of common stock depends on investor expectations about the future behavior of the security. If the outlook for the company and its stock is good, the price will probably be bid up. If conditions deteriorate, the price of the stock will probably go down. Let's look now at the single most important issue in the stock valuation process: *the future*.

▮ Valuing a Company and Its Future

Thus far, we have examined several aspects of security analysis: economic and industry analyses, and the historical (company) phase of fundamental analysis. But as we've said, it's *not the past* that's important but *the future*. The primary reason for looking at past performance is to gain insight about the future direction of the firm and its profitability. Though past performance provides no guarantees about future returns, it can give us a good idea of a company's strengths and weaknesses. For example, it can tell us how well the company's products have done in the marketplace, how the company's fiscal health shapes up, and how management tends to respond to difficult situations. In short, the past can reveal how well the company is positioned to take advantage of the things that may occur in the future.

Because *the value of a stock is a function of its future returns*, the investor's task is to use available historical data to project key financial variables into the future. In this way, you can assess the future prospects of the company and the expected returns from its stock. We are especially interested in dividends and price behavior.

Forecasted Sales and Profits   The key to our forecast is, of course, the future behavior of the *company*, and the most important aspects to consider in this regard are the outlook for sales and the trend in the net profit margin. One way to develop a sales forecast is to assume that the company will continue to perform as it has in the past and simply extend the historical trend. For example, if a firm's sales have been growing at a rate of 10% per year, then assume they will continue at that rate. Of course, if there is some evidence about the economy, industry, or company that suggests a faster or slower rate of growth, you would want to adjust the forecast accordingly. More often than not, this "naive" approach will be about as effective as more complex techniques.

Once the sales forecast has been generated, we can shift our attention to the net profit margin. We want to know what kind of return on sales to expect. One of the best ways of doing that is to use what is known as a **common-size income statement**. Basically, a common-size statement takes every entry found on a normal dollar-based financial statement, and converts it to a percentage. For a common-size income statement, every item on the statement is divided by

common-size income statement
a type of financial report that uses a common denominator (net sales) to convert all entries on a normal income statement from dollars to percentages.

TABLE 8.1 Comparative Dollar-Based and Common-Size Income Statements

Universal Office Furnishings, Inc.
2007 Income Statements

	$ (in millions)	% (Common-Size)*
Net sales	$1,938.0	100.0%
Cost of goods sold	1,128.5	58.2
Gross operating profit	$ 809.5	41.8%
Selling, administrative, and other operating expenses	497.7	25.6
Depreciation & amortization	77.1	4.0
Other income, net	0.5	0.1
Earnings before interest & taxes	$235.2	12.1%
Interest expense	13.4	0.7
Income taxes	82.1	4.2
Net profit after taxes	**$139.7**	**7.2%**

*Common-size figures are found by using "Net sales" as the common denominator, and then dividing all entries by net sales. For example, cost of goods sold = $1,128.5 ÷ $1,938.0 = 58.2%; EBIT = $235.2 ÷ $1938.0 = 12.1%.

net sales—which, in effect, is the common denominator. An example of this can be seen in Table 8.1, which shows the 2007 dollar-based and common-size income statements for Universal Office Furnishings. (This is the same income statement that we first saw in Table 7.4, page 318.)

To understand how these statements are constructed, let's use the *gross profit margin* (of 41.8%) as an illustration. In this case, the *gross operating profit* of $809.5 million was divided by *net sales* of $1,938.0 million; thus: $809.5 ÷ $1,938.0 = 0.4177 = 41.8%. Using net sales of $1,938.0 million, the same procedure was used for every other entry on the income statement. Note that a common-size statement adds up, just like its dollar-based counterpart. For example, net sales of 100.0% minus costs of goods sold of 58.2% equals a gross operating profit margin of 41.8%. (You can also work up common-size balance sheets, using total assets as the common denominator, but they are not nearly as popular or as widely used as common-size income statements.)

Comparative common-size income statements are very popular with credit and securities analysts. They enable the users to compare operating results from one year to the next and in so doing, to quickly determine what's causing, say, gross or operating profit margins to improve or deteriorate. In essence, they let the analyst know how good a job management is doing in controlling the firm's cost structure, and what's driving the company's profit margins. For our purposes, we can use this statement to help us get a handle on the firm's *forecasted net profit margin* (the bottom line of the common-size income statement). Starting with the latest common-size statement (or perhaps an average of the statements that have prevailed for the past few years), we can work our way down the statement, adjusting any of the entries for likely industry or company developments. For example, if cost of goods sold is expected to fall, we might raise the gross profit margin by, say, half-a-percentage point. In this way, we will (hopefully) end up with a good idea of what the future net profit margin should look like. Most individual investors can obtain valuable insight about future revenues, costs, and earnings from industry or company reports put out by brokerage houses, advisory services (e.g., *Value Line*), the financial media (e.g., *Forbes*), and from various investor Web sites.

Given a satisfactory sales forecast and estimate of the future net profit margin, we can combine these two pieces of information to arrive at future earnings.

Equation 8.1 ➤

$$\frac{\text{Future after-tax}}{\text{earnings in year } t} = \frac{\text{Estimated sales}}{\text{for year } t} \times \frac{\text{Net profit margin}}{\text{expected in year } t}$$

The *year t* notation in this equation simply denotes a given calendar or fiscal year in the future. It can be next year, the year after that, or any other year in which we are interested. Let's say that in the year just completed, a company reported sales of $100 million, we estimate that revenues will grow at an 8% annual rate, and the net profit margin should be about 6%. Thus, estimated sales next year will equal $108 million ($100 million × 1.08). And, with a 6% profit margin, we should expect to see earnings next year of

$$\frac{\text{Future after-tax}}{\text{earnings next year}} = \$108 \text{ million} \times 0.06 = \underline{\$6.5 \text{ million}}$$

Using this same process, we would then estimate sales and earnings *for other years* in our forecast period.

Forecasted Dividends and Prices At this point we have an idea of the future earnings performance of the company. We are now ready to evaluate the effects of this performance on returns to common stock investors. Given a corporate earnings forecast, we need three additional pieces of information:

- An estimate of future dividend payout ratios.
- The number of common shares that will be outstanding over the forecast period.
- A future price/earnings (P/E) ratio.

For the first two pieces of information, unless we have evidence to the contrary, we can simply project the firm's recent experience into the future. Payout ratios are usually fairly stable, so there is little risk in using a recent average figure. (Or, if a company follows a fixed-dividend policy, we could use the latest dividend rate in our forecast.) It is also generally safe to assume that the number of common shares outstanding will hold at the latest level or perhaps change at some moderate rate of increase (or decrease) that's reflective of the recent past.

Getting a Handle on the P/E Ratio The only really thorny issue in this process is coming up with an estimate of the future P/E ratio—a figure that has considerable bearing on the stock's future price behavior. Generally speaking, the P/E ratio is a function of several variables, including:

1. The growth rate in earnings.
2. The general state of the market.

3. The amount of debt in a company's capital structure.
4. The current and projected rate of inflation.
5. The level of dividends.

As a rule, higher P/E ratios can be expected with higher rates of growth in earnings, an optimistic market outlook, and lower debt levels (less debt means less financial risk).

The link between the inflation rate and P/E multiples, however, is a bit more complex. Generally speaking, as inflation rates rise, so do bond interest rates. This, in turn, causes required returns on stocks to rise (so stock returns will remain competitive with bond returns), and higher required returns on stocks mean lower stock prices and lower P/E multiples. On the other hand, declining inflation (and interest) rates normally have positive effects on the economy and business conditions, and that translates into higher P/E ratios and stock prices. We can also argue that a high P/E ratio should be expected with high dividend payouts. In practice, however, most companies with high P/E ratios have *low dividend payouts*. The reason: Earnings growth tends to be more valuable than dividends, especially in companies with high rates of return on equity.

A Relative Price/Earnings Multiple A useful starting point for evaluating the P/E ratio is the *average market multiple*. This is simply the average P/E ratio of all the stocks in a given market index, like the S&P 500 or the DJIA. The average market multiple indicates the general state of the market. It gives us an idea of how aggressively the market, in general, is pricing stocks. Other things being equal, the higher the P/E ratio, the more optimistic the market— *unless, of course, the economy is in a slump, in which case a high P/E could simply be the result of lower earnings.* Table 8.2 lists S&P price/earnings multiples for the past 30 years. It shows that market multiples tend to move over a fairly wide range.

TABLE 8.2 Average Market P/E Multiples 1977–2006

Year	Market Multiples (Average S&P P/E Ratio)	Year	Market Multiples (Average S&P P/E Ratio)
1977	8.8	1992	22.8
1978	8.3	1993	21.3
1979	7.4	1994	17.0
1980	9.1	1995	17.4
1981	8.1	1996	20.7
1982	10.2	1997	23.9
1983	12.4	1998	32.3
1984	10.0	1999	30.5
1985	13.7	2000	26.4
1986	16.3	2001	46.5
1987	15.1	2002	31.9
1988	12.2	2003	22.8
1989	15.1	2004	20.7
1990	15.5	2005	17.8
1991	26.2	2006	17.0

Source: Average year-end multiples derived from various sources, including Standard & Poor's *Statistical Service*, and the *S&P 500 Earnings and Estimate Report*, as obtained from their Web site, www.standardandpoors.com.

relative P/E multiple
a measure of how a stock's P/E behaves relative to the average market multiple.

With the market multiple as a benchmark, you can evaluate a stock's P/E performance relative to the market. That is, you can calculate a **relative P/E multiple** by dividing a stock's P/E by a market multiple. For example, if a stock currently has a P/E of 35 and the market multiple for the S&P 500 is, say, 25, the stock's relative P/E is 35/25 = 1.40. Looking at the relative P/E, you can quickly get a feel for how aggressively the stock has been priced in the market and what kind of relative P/E is normal for the stock.

Other things being equal, a high relative P/E is desirable—up to a point, at least. For just as *abnormally* high P/Es can spell trouble (i.e., the stock may be overpriced and headed for a fall), so too can *abnormally* high *relative P/Es*. Given that caveat, it follows that the higher the relative P/E measure, the higher the stock will be priced in the market. But watch out for the downside: High relative P/E multiples can also mean lots of price volatility, and as noted above, the potential for lots of downside risk. (Similarly, we can use average *industry* multiples to get a feel for the kind of P/E multiples that are standard for a given industry. We can then use that information, along with market multiples, to assess or project the P/E for a particular stock.)

Now we can generate a forecast of what the stock's *future* P/E will be over the anticipated *investment horizon* (the period of time over which we expect to hold the stock). For example, with the existing P/E multiple as a base, an *increase* might be justified if you believe the *market multiple* will increase (as the market becomes more bullish), and the *relative P/E* is likely to remain at its current level, or may even increase.

Estimating Earnings per Share So far we've been able to come up with an estimate for the dividend payout ratio, the number of shares outstanding, and the price/earnings multiple. We're now ready to forecast the stock's future earnings per share (EPS), which can be done as follows:

Equation 8.2 ➤

$$\begin{array}{c} \text{Estimated EPS} \\ \text{in year } t \end{array} = \frac{\begin{array}{c}\text{Future after-tax} \\ \text{earnings in year } t\end{array}}{\begin{array}{c}\text{Number of shares of common stock} \\ \text{outstanding in year } t\end{array}}$$

Earnings per share is a critical part of the valuation process, for once you have EPS, you can combine it with (1) the dividend payout ratio to obtain (future) dividends per share, and (2) the price/earnings multiple to project the (future) price of the stock.

Equation 8.2 simply converts aggregate or total corporate earnings to a per-share basis, by relating company (forecasted) profits to the expected number of shares outstanding. Though this approach works quite effectively, some investors would rather bypass the projection of aggregate sales and earnings and instead *concentrate on earnings from a per-share basis right from the start*. That can be done by looking at the major forces that drive earnings per share: ROE and book value. Quite simply, by using these two variables, we can define earnings per share as follows:

Equation 8.3 ➤

$$\text{EPS} = \text{ROE} \times \text{Book value per share}$$

This formula will produce the same results as the standard EPS equation shown first in Chapter 6 (Equation 6.1) and then again in Chapter 7. The major advantage of this form of the equation is that it allows you to assess the extent to which EPS is influenced by the company's book value and (especially) its ROE. As we saw in the previous chapter, ROE is a key financial measure, because it captures the amount of success the firm is having in managing its assets, operations, and capital structure. And as we see here, ROE not only is important in defining overall corporate profitability but it also plays a crucial role in defining a stock's EPS.

To produce an estimated EPS using Equation 8.3, you would go directly to the two basic components of the formula and try to get a handle on their future behavior. In particular, what kind of growth is expected in the firm's book value per share, and what's likely to happen to the company's ROE? In the vast majority of cases, ROE is really the driving force, so it's important to produce a good estimate of that variable. Investors often do that by breaking ROE into its component parts—margin, turnover, and the equity multiplier (see Equation 7.1, on page 321).

Once you have projected ROE and book value per share, you can plug these figures into Equation 8.3 to produce estimated EPS. The bottom line is that, one way or another (using the approach reflected in Equation 8.2 or that in Equation 8.3), you have to arrive at a forecasted EPS number that you are comfortable with. When you've done that, it's a pretty simple matter to use the forecasted payout ratio to estimate dividends per share:

Equation 8.4 ➤

$$\frac{\text{Estimated dividends}}{\text{per share in year } t} = \frac{\text{Estimated EPS}}{\text{for year } t} \times \frac{\text{Estimated}}{\text{payout ratio}}$$

And then the future price of the stock, which can be determined as

Equation 8.5 ➤

$$\frac{\text{Estimated share price}}{\text{at end of year } t} = \frac{\text{Estimated EPS}}{\text{in year } t} \times \frac{\text{Estimated P/E}}{\text{ratio}}$$

Pulling It All Together We've seen the various components that go into our estimates of future dividends and share prices. Now, to see how they all fit together, let's continue with the example we started above. Using the aggregate sales and earnings approach, if the company had 2 million shares of common stock outstanding and that number was expected to hold in the future, then given the estimated earnings of $6.5 million that we computed earlier, the firm should generate earnings per share (EPS) next year of

$$\frac{\text{Estimated EPS}}{\text{next year}} = \frac{\$6.5 \text{ million}}{2 \text{ million}} = \underline{\underline{\$3.25}}$$

This result, of course, would be equivalent to the firm having a projected ROE of, say, 15% and an estimated book value per share of $21.67. According to Equation 8.3, those conditions would also produce an estimated EPS of $3.25 (i.e., $0.15 \times \$21.67$). Using this EPS figure, along with an estimated payout ratio of 40%, we see that dividends per share next year should equal

$$\frac{\text{Estimated dividends}}{\text{per share next year}} = \$3.25 \times .40 = \underline{\underline{\$1.30}}$$

If the firm adheres to a *fixed-dividend policy*, this estimate may have to be adjusted to reflect the level of dividends being paid. For example, if the company has been paying annual dividends at the rate of $1.25 per share *and is expected to continue doing so for the near future*, then you would adjust estimated dividends accordingly (i.e., use $1.25/share). Finally, if it has been estimated that the stock should sell at 17.5 times earnings, then a share of stock in this company should be trading at a price of about $56.90 by the *end* of next year.

$$\frac{\text{Estimated share price}}{\text{at the end of next year}} = \$3.25 \times 17.5 = \underline{\underline{\$56.88}}$$

Actually, we are interested in the price of the stock at the end of our anticipated investment horizon. Thus, the $56.90 figure would be appropriate if we had a one-year horizon. However, if we had a three-year holding period, we would have to extend the EPS figure for two more years and repeat our calculations with the new data. As we shall see, *the estimated share price is important because it has embedded in it the capital gains portion of the stock's total return.*

▌ Developing an Estimate of Future Behavior

Using information obtained from Universal Office Furnishings (UVRS), we can illustrate the forecasting procedures we discussed above. Recall from Chapter 7 that an assessment of the economy and the office equipment industry was positive and that the company's operating results and financial condition looked strong, both historically and relative to industry standards. Because everything looks favorable for Universal, we decide to take a look at the future prospects of the company and its stock.

Assume we have chosen a three-year investment horizon because we believe (from earlier studies of economic and industry factors) that the economy and the market for office equipment stocks will start running out of steam near the end of 2010 or early 2011. (Some investors prefer to use one-year investment horizons, because they believe that trying to forecast out any further involves too many uncertainties. We use a three-year investment horizon here primarily for illustration—and because we feel comfortable forecasting the numbers out that far. Should that not be the case, then by all means use a shorter investment horizon.)

Table 8.3 provides selected historical financial data for the company. They cover a five-year period (ending with the latest fiscal year) and will provide the basis for much of our forecast. The data reveal that, with one or two exceptions, the company has performed at a fairly steady pace and has been able to maintain a very attractive rate of growth. Our economic analysis suggests that the economy is about to pick up, and our research (from Chapter 7) indicates that the industry and company are well situated to take advantage of the upswing. Therefore, we conclude that the rate of growth in sales should pick up dramatically from the abnormally low level of 2007, attaining a growth rate of over 20% in 2008—more in line with the firm's five-year average. After a modest amount of pent-up demand is worked off, the rate of growth in sales should drop to about 19% in 2009 and to 15% in 2010.

INVESTOR FACTS

TARGET PRICES—A **target price** is the price an analyst expects a stock to reach within a certain period of time (usually a year). Target prices are normally based on an analyst's forecast of a company's sales, earnings, and other criteria, some of which are highly subjective. One common practice is to assume that a stock deserves to trade at a certain price/earnings multiple—say, on par with the average P/E multiples of similar stocks—and arrive at a target price by multiplying that P/E ratio by an estimate of what the EPS will be one year from now. Use these prices with care, however, because analysts will often raise their targets simply because a stock has reached the targeted price much sooner than expected.

TABLE 8.3	**Selected Historical Financial Data, Universal Office Furnishings**				
	2003	2004	2005	2006	2007
Total assets (millions)	$554.2	$694.9	$755.6	$761.5	$941.2
Total asset turnover	1.72×	1.85×	1.98×	2.32×	2.06×
Net sales (millions)	$953.2	$1,283.9	$1,495.9	$1,766.2	$1,938.0
Annual rate of growth in sales*	11.5%	34.7%	16.5%	18.1%	9.7%
Net profit margin	4.2%	3.6%	5.0%	8.0%	7.2%
Payout ratio	6.8%	5.6%	5.8%	6.0%	6.6%
Price/earnings ratio	13.5×	21.7×	14.9×	15.7×	18.4×
Number of common shares outstanding (millions)	77.7	78.0	72.8	65.3	61.8

*Annual rate of growth in sales = Change in sales from one year to the next ÷ Level of sales in the base (or earliest) years. For 2004, the annual rate of growth in sales equaled 34.7% = (2004 sales − 2003 sales)/2003 sales = ($1,283.9 − $953.2)/$953.2 = 0.3467.

The essential elements of the financial forecast for 2008–2010 are provided in Table 8.4 (on page 356). Highlights of the key assumptions and the reasoning behind them are as follows:

- *Net profit margin.* Various published industry and company reports suggest a comfortable improvement in earnings, so we decide to use a profit margin of 8.0% in 2008 (up a bit from the latest margin of 7.2% recorded in 2007). We're projecting even better profit margins (8.5%) in 2009 and 2010, as some cost improvements start to take hold.

- *Common shares outstanding.* We believe the company will continue to pursue its share buyback program, but at a substantially lower pace than in the 2004–2007 period. From a current level of 61.8 million shares, we project that the number of shares outstanding will drop to 61.5 million in 2008, to 60.5 million in 2009, and to 59.5 million in 2010.

- *Payout ratio.* We assume that the dividend payout ratio will hold at a steady 6% of earnings, as it has for most of the recent past.

- *P/E ratio.* Primarily on the basis of expectations for improved growth in revenues and earnings, we are projecting a P/E multiple that will rise from its present level of 18.4 times earnings to roughly 20 times earnings in 2008. Although this is a fairly conservative increase in the P/E, when it is coupled with the hefty growth in EPS, the net effect will be a big jump in the projected price of Universal stock.

Table 8.4 also shows the sequence involved in arriving at forecasted dividends and share price behavior; that is:

1. The company dimensions of the forecast are handled first. These include sales and revenue estimates, net profit margins, net earnings, and the number of shares of common stock outstanding. Note that after-tax earnings are derived according to the procedure described earlier in this chapter.
2. Next we estimate earnings per share, following the procedures established earlier.

TABLE 8.4   **Summary Forecast Statistics, Universal Office Furnishings**

	Latest Actual Figures (Fiscal 2007)	Average for the Past 5 Years (2003–2007)	Forecasted Figures		
			2008	2009	2010
Annual rate of growth in sales	9.7%	18.1%	22%	19%	15%
Net sales (millions)	$1,938.0	N/A*	$2,364.4**	$2,813.6**	$3,235.6**
× Net profit margin	7.2%	5.6%	8.0%	8.5%	8.5%
= Net after-tax earnings (millions)	$139.7	N/A	$189.2	$239.2	$275.0
÷ Common shares outstanding (millions)	61.2	71.1	61.5	60.5	59.0
= Earnings per share	$ 2.26	N/A	$ 3.08	$ 3.95	$ 4.66
× Payout ratio	6.6%	6.2%	6.0%	6.0%	6.0%
= Dividends per share	$ 0.15	$ 0.08	$ 0.18	$ 0.24	$ 0.28
Earnings per share	$ 2.26	N/A	$ 3.08	$ 3.95	$ 4.66
× P/E ratio	18.4	16.8	20	19	20
= Share price at year end	$ 41.58	N/A	$ 61.60	$ 75.00	$ 93.20

*N/A: Not applicable.

**Forecasted sales figures: Sales from *preceding* year × Growth rate in sales = Growth in sales; then Growth in sales + Sales from preceding year = Forecast sales for the year. For example, for 2005: $1,938.0 × 0.22 = $426.4 + $1938.0 = $2,364.4.

3. The bottom line of the forecast is, of course, the returns in the form of dividends and capital gains expected from a share of Universal stock, given that the assumptions about net sales, profit margins, earnings per share, and so forth hold up. We see in Table 8.4 that dividends should go up to 28 cents a share, which is a big jump from where they are now (15 cents/share). Even so, with annual dividends of a little over a quarter a share, it's clear that dividends still won't account for much of the stock's return. In fact, the dividend yield in 2010 is projected to *fall* to just 3/10 of 1%. Clearly, the returns from this stock are going to come from capital gains, not dividends. That's obvious when you look at year-end share prices, which are expected to more than double over the next three years. That is, if our projections are valid, the price of a share of stock should rise from around $41.50 to over $93.00 by year-end 2010.

We now have an idea of what the future cash flows of the investment are likely to be. We can now use that information to establish an intrinsic value for Universal Office Furnishings stock.

The Valuation Process

valuation
process by which an investor uses risk and return concepts to determine the value of a security.

Valuation is a process by which an investor determines the worth of a security using the risk and return concepts introduced in Chapter 5. This process can be applied to any asset that produces a stream of cash flow—a share of stock, a bond, a piece of real estate, or an oil well. To establish the value of an asset, the investor must determine certain key inputs, including the *amount* of future cash flows, the *timing* of these cash flows, and the *rate of return required* on the investment.

In terms of common stock, the essence of valuation is to determine what the stock *ought to be worth*, given estimated returns to stockholders (future dividends and price behavior) and the amount of potential risk exposure.

Toward that end, we employ various types of stock valuation models, the end product of which represents the elusive intrinsic value we have been seeking. That is, the stock valuation models determine either an *expected rate of return* or the *intrinsic worth of a share of stock*, which in effect represents the stock's "justified price." In this way, we obtain a standard of performance, based on forecasted stock behavior, that can be used to judge the investment merits of a particular security.

HOTLINKS

For a valuation example, see
www.stocksense.com/valuation.html

Either of two conditions would make us consider a stock a worthwhile investment candidate: (1) if the computed rate of return equals or exceeds the yield we feel is warranted, or (2) if the justified price (intrinsic worth) is equal to or greater than the current market price. Note especially that a security is considered acceptable even if its yield simply *equals* the required rate of return or if its intrinsic value simply *equals* the current market price of the stock. There is nothing irrational about such behavior. In either case, the security meets your minimum standards to the extent that it is giving you the rate of return you wanted.

Remember this, however, about the valuation process: Even though valuation plays an important part in the investment process, there is *absolutely no assurance* that the actual outcome will be even remotely similar to the forecasted behavior. The stock is still subject to economic, industry, company, and market risks, any one of which could negate *all* your assumptions about the future. Security analysis and stock valuation models are used not to guarantee success but to *help you better understand the return and risk dimensions of a potential transaction.*

Required Rate of Return One of the key ingredients in the stock valuation process is the **required rate of return**. Generally speaking, the amount of return required by an investor should be related to the level of risk that must be assumed to generate that return. In essence, the required return establishes a level of compensation compatible with the amount of risk involved. Such a standard helps you determine whether the expected return on a stock (or any other security) is satisfactory. Because you don't know for sure what the cash flow of an investment will be, you should expect to earn a rate of return that reflects this uncertainty. Thus, the greater the perceived risk, the more you should expect to earn. As we saw in Chapter 5, this is basically the notion behind the *capital asset pricing model* (CAPM).

Recall that using the CAPM, we can define a stock's required return as

required rate of return
the return necessary to compensate an investor for the risk involved in an investment.

Equation 8.6 ➤

$$\text{Required rate of return} = \text{Risk-free rate} + \left[\text{Stock's beta} \times \left(\text{Market return} - \text{Risk-free rate} \right) \right]$$

The required inputs for this equation are readily available: You can obtain a stock's beta from *Value Line* or S&P's *Stock Reports* (or from any one of many Internet sites, such as **Quicken.com, MSN Money, Yahoo! Finance,** or **SmartMoney.com**). The risk-free rate is basically the average return on Treasury bills for the past year or so. And a good proxy for the market return is the average stock return over the past 10 to 15 years (like the data reported in Table 6.1 on page 258). This average return may, of course, have to be adjusted up or down a bit based on what you expect the market to do over the next year or so.

In the CAPM, the risk of a stock is captured by its beta. For that reason, the required return on a stock increases (or decreases) with increases (or decreases) in its beta. As an illustration of the CAPM at work, consider Universal's stock, which we'll assume has a beta of 1.30. Given that the risk-free rate is 5.5% and the expected market return is, say, 15%, according to the CAPM model, this stock would have a required return of

$$\text{Required return} = 5.5\% + [1.30 \times (15.0\% - 5.5\%)] = \underline{17.85\%}$$

This return—let's round it to 18%—can now be used in a stock valuation model to assess the investment merits of a share of stock.

As an alternative, or perhaps even *in conjunction with the CAPM*, you could take a more subjective approach to finding the required return. For example, if your assessment of the historical performance of the company had uncovered some volatility in sales and earnings, you could conclude that the stock is subject to a good deal of business risk. Also important is market risk, as measured by a stock's beta. A valuable reference point in arriving at a measure of risk is the rate of return available on less risky but competitive investment vehicles. Thus, you could *use the rate of return on long-term Treasury bonds or high-grade corporate issues* as a starting point in defining your desired rate of return. That is, starting with yields on long-term bonds, you could adjust those returns for the levels of business and market risk to which you believe the common stock is exposed.

To see how these elements make up the desired rate of return, let's go back to Universal Office Furnishings. Assume that it is now early 2008 and rates on high-grade corporate bonds are hovering around 9%. Given that our analysis thus far has indicated that the office equipment industry in general and Universal in particular are subject to a "fair" amount of business risk, we would want to adjust that figure upward—probably by around 2 or 3 points. In addition, with its beta of 1.30, we can conclude that the stock carries a good deal of market risk. Thus, we should increase our base rate of return even more—say, by another 4 or 5 points. That is, starting from a base (high-grade corporate bond) rate of 9%, we tack on, say, 3% for the company's added business risk and another 4.5 or 5% for the stock's market risk. Adding these up, we find that an appropriate required rate of return for Universal's common stock is around 17% or 17.5%. This figure is reasonably close to what we would obtain with CAPM using a beta of 1.30, a risk-free rate of 5.5%, and an expected market return of 15% (as in Equation 8.6). The fact that the two numbers are close shouldn't be surprising. If they're carefully (and honestly) done, the CAPM and the subjective approach should yield similar results. Whichever procedure you use, the required rate of return stipulates the minimum return you should expect to receive from an investment. To accept anything less means you'll fail to be fully compensated for the risk you must assume.

INVESTOR FACTS

HOW TO SPOT AN UNDER-VALUED (OR OVERVALUED) MARKET—Just as shares of common stock can become over- or undervalued, so can the market as a whole. How can you tell if the market is overvalued? Some market observers suggest you look at comparative yields. That is, compare the so-called *earnings yield on stocks* with the yields on 10-year Treasuries. The earnings yield on stocks is the inverse of the market's P/E ratio—if the market P/E is 18 times earnings, the earnings yield would be 5.56% (1/18). If the earnings yield is *above* the yield on 10-year Treasuries, stocks are **undervalued** (cheap), especially compared to bonds. In contrast, you'd normally expect the earnings yield on stocks to be *less than* 10-year Treasury yields; as that spread continues to widen, the market is becoming more and more **overvalued**—definitely not a good thing.

CONCEPTS IN REVIEW

Answers available at: www.myfinancelab.com

8.1 What is the purpose of stock valuation? What role does *intrinsic value* play in the stock valuation process?

8.2 Are the expected future earnings of the firm important in determining a stock's investment suitability? Discuss how these and other future estimates fit into the stock valuation framework.

8.3 Can the growth prospects of a company affect its price/earnings multiple? Explain. How about the amount of debt a firm uses? Are there any other variables that affect the level of a firm's P/E ratio?

8.4 What is the *market multiple*, and how can it help in evaluating a stock's P/E ratio? Is a stock's *relative P/E* the same thing as the market multiple? Explain.

8.5 In the stock valuation framework, how can you tell whether a particular security is a worthwhile investment candidate? What roles does the required rate of return play in this process? Would you invest in a stock if all you could earn was a rate of return that just equaled your required return? Explain.

Stock Valuation Models

LG 4   LG 5   LG 6

Investors employ a number of different types of stock valuation models. Though they may all be aimed at a security's future cash benefits, their approaches to valuation are nonetheless considerably different. Some investors, for example, search for value in a company's financials—by keying in on such factors as book value, debt load, return on equity, and cash flow. These so-called *value investors* rely as much on historical performance as on earnings projections to identify undervalued stock. Then there are the *growth investors*, who concentrate primarily on growth in earnings. To them, though past growth is important, the real key lies in projected earnings—in finding companies that will produce big earnings, along with big price/earnings multiples.

WEBEXTENSION

More often than not, investors tend to be either value investors or growth investors. An *Investing in Action* box at the book's home page discusses the differences.

www.myfinancelab.com

There are still other stock valuation models in use—models that employ such variables as dividend yield, abnormally low P/E multiples, relative price performance over time, and even company size or market caps as key elements in the decision-making process. For purposes of our discussion, we'll focus on several stock valuation models that derive value from the fundamental performance of the company. We'll look first at stocks that pay dividends and at a procedure known as the dividend valuation model. From there, we'll look at several valuation procedures that can be used with companies that pay little or nothing in dividends. Finally, we'll move on to procedures that set the price of a stock based on how it behaves relative to earnings, cash flow, sales, or book value. The stock valuation procedures that we'll examine in this chapter are the same as those used by many professional security analysts, and are in fact, found throughout the "Equity Investments" portion of CFA exam, especially at Level-I. And, of course, as more fully discussed in the *Ethics in Investing* box on page 360, an understanding of these valuation models will enable you to better evaluate analysts' recommendations.

■ The Dividend Valuation Model

In the valuation process, the intrinsic value of any investment equals the *present value of its expected cash benefits*. For common stock, this amounts to the cash dividends received each year plus the future sale price of the stock. One way to view the cash flow benefits from common stock is to assume that the dividends will be received over an infinite time horizon—an assumption that is appropriate so long as the firm is considered a "going concern." Seen from this perspective, *the value of a share of stock is equal to the present value of all the future dividends it is expected to provide over an infinite time horizon.*

ETHICS *in* INVESTING

Stock Analysts: Don't Always Believe The Hype

Buy, sell, or hold? Unfortunately, many investors have learned the hard way not to trust these recommendations.

Consider the last market bubble. As the market began to fall in 2000, 95% of all publicly traded stocks were free of any sell recommendations, according to investment research Zacks, and 5% of stocks that did have a sell rating had exactly that: a sell rating from a *single* analyst. When the market began its climb back up, analysts missed the boat again: From 2000 to 2004, stocks that analysts told investors to sell rose 19% per annum on average, while their "buys" and "holds" rose just 7%.

Why were the all-star analysts wrong so often? Conflict of interest is one explanation. Analysts are handsomely rewarded for generating investment banking business. They often felt pressure to make positive comments to please current or prospective investment banking clients. Also, analysts are expected to generate commissions for their firms by making buy and sell recommendations.

Analyst hype is a real problem for both Wall Street and Main Street, and the securities industry has taken steps to correct it. The SEC's Regulation Fair Disclosure requires that all company information must be released *to the public* rather than quietly disseminated to analysts.

Some brokerages ban analysts from owning stocks they cover. In 2003, the SEC ruled that compensation for analyst research must be separated from investment banking fees, so that the analyst's job is to research stock rather than solicit clients.

Most important, investors must learn how to read between the lines of analysts' reports. To start, they should probably lower analysts' rating by one notch. A strong buy could be interpreted as a buy, a buy as a hold, and a hold or neutral as a sell. Also, investors should give more weight to negative ratings than to positive ones: downgrades and those rare sell recommendations may signal future problems. Investors should also pay attention to downward revisions of earnings estimates; bad news often gets worse as changing business conditions spread beyond individual companies. Finally, when in doubt, investors should do their own homework, using the techniques taught in this book.

CRITICAL THINKING QUESTION Do you agree with the policies forbidding analysts to own stock of the companies they cover?

Source: Rich Smith, "Analysts Running Scared," *The Motley Fool,* April 5, 2006, www.fool.com.

When a stockholder sells a stock, from a strictly theoretical point of view, what is really being sold is the right to all remaining future dividends. Thus, just as the *current* value of a share of stock is a function of future dividends, the *future* price of the stock is also a function of future dividends. In this framework, the *future* price of the stock will rise or fall as the outlook for dividends (and the required rate of return) changes. This approach, which holds that the value of a share of stock is a function of its future dividends, is known as the **dividend valuation model (DVM)**.

dividend valuation model (DVM)
a model that values a share of stock on the basis of the future dividend stream it is expected to produce; its three versions are zero-growth, constant-growth, and variable-growth.

There are three versions of the dividend valuation model, each based on different assumptions about the future rate of growth in dividends:

1. *The zero-growth model* assumes that dividends will not grow over time.
2. *The constant-growth model*, which is the basic version of the dividend valuation model, assumes that dividends will grow by a fixed/constant rate over time.
3. *The variable-growth model* assumes that the rate of growth in dividends will vary over time.

In one form or another, the DVM is widely used in practice to value many of the larger, more mature companies.

Zero Growth The simplest way to picture the dividend valuation model is to assume the stock has a fixed stream of dividends. In other words, dividends stay the same year in and year out, and they're expected to do so in the future. Under such conditions, the value of a zero-growth stock is simply *the capitalized value of its annual dividends*. To find the capitalized value, just divide annual dividends by the required rate of return, which in effect acts as the capitalization rate. That is,

Equation 8.7 ➤

$$\frac{\text{Value of a}}{\text{share of stock}} = \frac{\text{Annual dividends}}{\text{Required rate of return}}$$

For example, if a stock paid a (constant) dividend of $3 a share and you wanted to earn 10% on your investment, the value of the stock would be $30 a share ($3/0.10 = $30).

As you can see, the only cash flow variable that's used in this model is the fixed annual dividend. Given that the annual dividend on this stock never changes, does that mean the price of the stock never changes? Absolutely not! For as the required rate of return (capitalization rate) changes, so will the price of the stock. Thus, if the required rate of return goes up to, say, 15%, the price of the stock will fall to $20 ($3/0.15). Although this may be a very simplified view of the valuation model, it's actually not as far-fetched as it may appear, for this is basically the procedure used to price *preferred stocks* in the marketplace.

Constant Growth The zero-growth model is a good beginning, but it does not take into account a growing stream of dividends. The standard and more widely recognized version of the dividend valuation model assumes that dividends will grow over time at a specified rate. In this version, the value of a share of stock is still considered to be a function of its future dividends, but such dividends are expected to grow forever (to infinity) at a constant rate of growth, *g*. Accordingly, we can find the value of a share of stock as follows:

Equation 8.8 ➤

$$\frac{\text{Value of a}}{\text{share of stock}} = \frac{\text{Next year's dividends}}{\dfrac{\text{Required rate}}{\text{of return}} - \dfrac{\text{Constant rate of}}{\text{growth in dividends}}}$$

Equation 8.8a ➤

$$V = \frac{D_1}{k - g}$$

where

D_1 = annual dividends expected to be paid *next* year (the first year in the forecast period)

k = the capitalization rate, or discount rate (which defines the required rate of return on the investment)

g = the annual rate of growth in dividends, which is expected to hold constant to infinity

In this version of the DVM, the model assumes that dividends will grow to infinity at a constant rate. (A similar assumption also applies, by the way, to the variable-growth model.) Even so, it is important to understand that just because we assume that dividends will go on forever, *that doesn't mean we assume the investor will hold the stock forever*. Indeed, the DVM makes *no assumptions about how long the investor will hold the stock*, for the simple reason that the investment horizon has no bearing on the computed value of a stock. Thus, with the constant-growth DVM, it is irrelevant whether the investor has a one-year, five-year, or ten-year expected holding period. The computed value of the stock will be the same under all circumstances. So long as the input assumptions (k, g, and D_0) are the same, the value of the stock will be the same regardless of the intended holding period. (More on this later.)

You'll also note that as simple as this model is, it nonetheless succinctly captures the very essence of stock valuation: *Increase* the cash flow (through D or g) and/or *decrease* the required rate of return (k), and the value of the stock will *increase*. Also note that in the DVM, k *defines* the *total return* to the stockholder, and *g represents the expected capital gains* on the investments. We know that, in practice, there are potentially two components that make up the total return to a stockholder: dividends and capital gains. As it turns out, the returns from both dividends and capital gains are captured in the DVM. That is, because k represents total returns and g defines the amount of capital gains embedded in k, it follows that if you subtract g from k ($k - g$), you'll have the expected dividend yield on the stock. Thus, the expected total return on a stock (k) equals the returns from capital gains (g) plus the returns from dividends ($k - g$).

The constant-growth DVM should not be used with just any stock. Rather, *it is best suited to the valuation of mature, dividend-paying companies* that hold established market positions. These are companies with strong track records that have reached the "mature" stage of growth. They are probably large-cap (or perhaps even some mature mid-cap) companies that have demonstrated an ability to generate steady—though perhaps not spectacular—rates of growth year in and year out. The growth rates *may not be identical* from year to year, but they tend to move within such a small range that they are seldom far off the average rate. These are companies that have established dividend policies and fairly predictable growth rates in earnings and dividends.

In addition to its use in valuing mature, dividend-paying companies, the constant-growth DVM is also widely used to *value the market as a whole*. That is, using something like the DJIA or the S&P 500, analysts will often employ the DVM to determine the expected return on the market for the coming year—in other words, they'll use it to find the R_m in the capital asset pricing model (CAPM).

Applying the Constant-Growth DVM   Use of the constant-growth DVM requires some basic information about the stock's required rate of return, its *current* level of dividends, and the expected rate of growth in dividends. A fairly simple, albeit naïve, way to find the dividend growth rate, g, is to look at the *historical* behavior of dividends. If they are growing at a relatively constant rate, you can assume they will continue to grow at (or near) that average rate in the future. You can get historical dividend data in a company's annual report, from various online sources, or from publications like *Value Line*.

With the help of a good hand-held calculator, we can use basic present value arithmetic to find the growth rate embedded in a stream of dividends. Here's how: Take the level of dividends, say, ten years ago and the level that's being paid today. Presumably, dividends today will be (much) higher than they were ten years ago, so, using your calculator, find the present value discount rate that equates the (higher) dividend today to the level paid ten years earlier. When you find that, you've found the growth rate; in this case, the *discount rate is the average rate of growth in dividends*. (See Chapter 5 for a detailed discussion of how to use present value to find growth rates.) Finding the appropriate growth rate, g, is a critical element in the DVM. Accordingly, we'll examine this variable in more detail later in this chapter (see pages 365–367); at which point, we will discuss a more analytically sound procedure. For now, we will assume that the naïve approach (above) does an adequate job in defining the growth rate, so let's proceed with our illustration of the DVM.

Once you've determined the dividend growth rate, you can find next year's dividend, D_1, as $D_0 \times (1 + g)$, where D_0 equals the actual (current) level of dividends. Let's say that in the latest year, Amalgamated Anything paid $2.50 a share in dividends. If you expect those dividends to grow at the rate of 6% a year, you can find next year's dividends as follows: $D_1 = D_0 (1 + g)$ = $2.50 (1 + 0.06) = $2.50 (1.06) = $2.65. The only other information you need is the required rate of return (capitalization rate), k. (Note that k must be greater than g for the constant-growth model to be mathematically operative.)

To see this dividend valuation model at work, consider a stock that currently pays an annual dividend of $1.75 a share. Let's say that by using the present-value approach described above, you find that dividends are growing at a rate of 8% a year, and you expect they will continue to do so into the future. In addition, based on the CAPM, you determine that this investment should carry a required rate of return of 12%. Given this information, you can use Equation 8.8 to value the stock. That is, given $D_0 = $1.75, g = 0.08$, and $k = 0.12$, it follows that

$$\text{Value of a share of stock} = \frac{D_0(1 + g)}{k - g} = \frac{\$1.75(1.08)}{0.12 - 0.08} = \frac{\$1.89}{0.04} = \underline{\underline{\$47.25}}$$

Thus, if you want to earn a 12% return on this investment—made up of 8% in capital gains (g), plus 4% in dividend yield (i.e., $1.89/$47.25 = 0.04)—then according to the constant-growth dividend valuation model, you should pay no more than $47.25 a share for this stock.

With this version of the DVM, *the price of the stock will increase over time* so long as k and g don't change. In fact, as we noted earlier, the growth rate (g) defines the amount of (expected) capital gains embedded in the future price of the stock. So, if $g = 8\%$, then we can expect the future price of the stock to go up around 8% per year. This will occur because the cash flow from the investment will increase as dividends grow. To see how this happens, let's carry our example a little further. Recall that $D_0 = $1.75, g = 8\%$, and $k = 12\%$. On the basis of this information, we found the current value of the stock to be $47.25. Now look what happens to the price of this stock if k and g don't change:

Year	Dividend	Stock Price*
(Current year) 0	$1.75	$47.25
1	1.89	51.00
2	2.04	55.00
3	2.20	59.50
4	2.38	64.25
5	2.57	69.50

*As determined by the dividend valuation model, given $g = 0.08$, $k = 0.12$, and D_0 = dividend level for any given year.

As the table shows, the price of the stock should rise from $47.25 today to around $69.50 in five years—as expected, that works out to an 8% growth rate.

Just as we can use this version of the DVM to value a stock today, so too can we find the expected price of the stock *in the future* by using the same valuation model. To do this, we simply redefine the appropriate level of dividends. For example, to find the price of the stock in year 3, we use the expected dividend in the third year, $2.20, and increase it by the factor $(1 + g)$. Thus, the stock price in year 3 $= D_3 \times (1 + g)/(k - g) = \$2.20 \times (1 + 0.08)/(0.12 - 0.08) = \$2.38/0.04 = \$59.50$. Of course, if future expectations about k or g do change, the *future price* of the stock will change accordingly. Should that occur, you could use the new information to decide whether to continue to hold the stock.

Variable Growth Although the constant-growth dividend valuation model is an improvement over the zero-growth model, it still has some shortcomings. The most obvious is the fact that it does not allow for changes in expected growth rates. To overcome this problem, we can use a form of the DVM that allows for *variable rates of growth* over time. Essentially, the *variable-growth dividend valuation model* derives, in two stages, a value based on future dividends and the future price of the stock (which price is a function of all future dividends). The variable-growth version of the model finds the value of a share of stock as follows:

Equation 8.9 ▶

$$\text{Value of a share of stock} = \text{Present value of future dividends during the initial variable-growth period} + \text{Present value of the price of the stock at the end of the variable-growth period}$$

Equation 8.9a ▶

$$V = (D_1 \times PVIF_1) + (D_2 \times PVIF_2) + \cdots$$
$$+ (D_v \times PVIF_v) + \left(\frac{D_v(1 + g)}{k - g} \times PVIF_v\right)$$

where

D_1, D_2, etc. = future annual dividends

$PVIF_t$ = present value interest factor, as specified by the required rate of return for a given year t (Table A.3 in the appendix)

v = number of years in the initial variable-growth period

Note that the last element in this equation is the standard constant-growth dividend valuation model, which is used to find the price of the stock at the end of the initial variable-growth period.

This form of the DVM is appropriate for companies that are expected to experience rapid or variable rates of growth for a period of time—perhaps for the first three to five years—and then settle down to a constant (average) growth rate thereafter. This, in fact, is the growth pattern of many companies, so the model has considerable application in practice. (It also overcomes one of the operational shortcomings of the constant-growth DVM in that k does not always have to be greater than g. That is, *during the variable-growth period*, the rate of growth, g, can be greater than the required rate of return, k, and the model will still be fully operational.)

Finding the value of a stock using Equation 8.9 is actually a lot easier than it looks. To do so, follow these steps:

1. Estimate annual dividends during the initial variable-growth period and then specify the constant rate, g, at which dividends will grow after the initial period.
2. Find the present value of the dividends expected during the initial variable-growth period.
3. Using the constant-growth DVM, find the price of the stock at the end of the initial growth period.
4. Find the present value of the price of the stock (as determined in step 3). Note that the price of the stock is discounted at the same $PVIF$ as the last dividend payment in the initial growth period, because the stock is being priced (per step 3) at the end of this initial period.
5. Add the two present-value components (from steps 2 and 4) to find the value of a stock.

Applying the Variable-Growth DVM To see how this works, let's apply the variable-growth model to one of our favorite companies: Sweatmore Industries. Let's assume that dividends will grow at a variable rate for the first three years (2007, 2008, and 2009). After that, the annual rate of growth in dividends is expected to settle down to 8% and stay there for the foreseeable future. Starting with the latest (2006) annual dividend of $2.21 a share, we estimate that Sweatmore's dividends should grow by 20% next year (in 2007), by 16% in 2008, and then by 13% in 2009 before dropping to an 8% rate.

Using these (initial) growth rates, we project that dividends in 2007 will amount to $2.65 a share ($2.21 × 1.20), and will rise to $3.08 ($2.65 × 1.16) in 2008 and to $3.48 ($3.08 × 1.13) in 2009. In addition, using CAPM, we feel that Sweatmore's stock should produce a minimum (required) rate of return (k) of at least 14%. We now have all the input we need and are ready to put a value on Sweatmore Industries. Table 8.5 (on page 366) shows the variable-growth DVM in action. The value of Sweatmore stock, according to the variable-growth DVM, is just under $49.25 a share. In essence, that's the maximum price you should be willing to pay for the stock if you want to earn a 14% rate of return.

Defining the Expected Growth Rate Mechanically, application of the DVM is really quite simple. It relies on just three key pieces of information: future dividends, future growth in dividends, and a required rate of return. But

TABLE 8.5   **Using the Variable-Growth DVM to Value Sweatmore Stock**

Step

1. Projected annual dividends:

	2007	$2.65
	2008	3.08
	2009	3.48

   Estimated annual rate of growth in dividends, g, for 2010 and beyond: 8%

2. Present value of dividends, using a required rate of return, k, of 14%, during the initial variable-growth period:

Year	Dividends	×	PVIF (k = 14%)	=	Present Value
2007	$2.65		0.877		$2.32
2008	3.08		0.769		2.37
2009	3.48		0.675		2.35
				Total	$7.04 (to step 5)

3. Price of the stock at the end of the initial growth period:

$$P_{2009} = \frac{D_{2010}}{k - g} = \frac{D_{2009} \times (1 + g)}{k - g} = \frac{\$3.48 \times (1.08)}{0.14 - 0.08} = \frac{\$3.75}{0.06} = \underline{\$62.50}$$

4. Discount the price of the stock (as computed above) back to its present value, at k = 14%:

$$PV(P_{2009}) = \$62.50 \times PVIF_{14\%,\ 3\ yr} = \$62.50 \times 0.675 = \underline{\$42.19} \text{ (to step 5)}$$

5. Add the present value of the initial dividend stream (step 2) to the present value of the price of the stock at the end of the initial growth period (step 4):

   Value of Sweatmore stock = $7.04 + $42.19 = $\underline{\$49.23}$

this model is not without its difficulties: One of the most difficult (and most important) aspects of the DVM is *specifying the appropriate growth rate, g, over an extended period of time.* Whether you are using the constant-growth or the variable-growth version of the dividend valuation model, the growth rate, *g*, has an enormous impact on the value derived from the model. Indeed, the DVM is *very sensitive* to the growth rate being used, because that rate affects both the model's numerator and its denominator. As a result, in practice analysts spend a good deal of time trying to come up with a growth rate, *g*, for a given company and its stock.

As we saw earlier in this chapter, we can define the growth rate from a strictly historical perspective (by using present value to find the past rate of growth) and then use it (or something close) in the DVM. While that approach might work in some cases, it does have some serious shortcomings. What's needed is a procedure that looks at the key forces that actually drive the growth rate. Fortunately, we have such an approach, one that's widely used in practice; it defines the growth rate, *g*, as follows:

Equation 8.10 ➤

$g = \text{ROE} \times \text{The firm's retention rate, } rr$

where

   $rr = 1 - \text{dividend payout ratio}$

Both variables in Equation 8.10 (ROE and *rr*) are *directly related to the firm's rate of growth*, and both play key roles in defining a firm's future growth. The *retention rate* represents the percentage of its profits that the firm plows back into the company. Thus, if the firm pays out 35% of its earnings in dividends (i.e., it has a dividend payout ratio of 35%), then it has a retention rate of 65%: $rr = 1 - 0.35 = 0.65$. The retention rate, in effect, indicates the amount of capital that is flowing back into the company to finance growth. Other things being equal, the more money being retained in the company, the higher the rate of growth.

The other component of Equation 8.10 is the familiar return on equity (ROE). Clearly, the more the company can earn on its retained capital, the higher the growth rate. Remember that ROE is made up of net profit margin, total asset turnover, and equity multiplier (see Equation 7.13, page 327), so if you want to get a handle on how ROE is impacting the firm's growth rate, look to those three components.

To see how this works, consider a situation where a company retains, on average, about 80% of its earnings and generates an ROE of around 18%. (Driving the firm's ROE is a net profit margin of 7.5%, a total asset turnover of 1.20, and an equity multiplier of 2.0.) Under these circumstances, we would expect the firm to have a growth rate of around 14.5%

$$g = \text{ROE} \times rr = 0.18 \times 0.80 = \underline{14.4\%}$$

Actually, the growth rate will probably be a bit more than 14.5%, because Equation 8.10 ignores financial leverage, which in itself will magnify growth. But at least the equation gives you a good idea of what to expect. Similarly, Equation 8.10 can serve as a starting point in assessing past and future growth. You can use it to compute expected growth and then assess the two key components of the formula (ROE and *rr*) to see whether they're likely to undergo major changes in the future. If so, then what impact is the change in ROE and/or *rr* likely to have on the growth rate, *g*? The idea is to take the time to study the forces (ROE and *rr*) that drive the growth rate, because the DVM itself is so sensitive to the rate of growth being used. Employ a growth rate that's too high and you'll end up with an intrinsic value that's way too high also. The downside, of course, is that you may end up buying a stock that you really shouldn't.

■ Other Approaches to Stock Valuations

In addition to the DVM, the market has also developed other ways of valuing shares of stock. Some are simply variations of the DVM; others are alternatives to it. The motivation for using these approaches is to find techniques that are compatible to given investment horizons and/or that can be used with non-dividend-paying stocks. In addition, for a variety of reasons, some investors prefer to use procedures that don't rely on corporate earnings as the basis of valuation. For these investors, it's not earnings that matter, but instead things like cash flow, sales, or book value.

One valuation procedure that is popular with many investors is the so-called *dividends-and-earnings approach*, which directly utilizes future dividends and the future selling price of the stock as the relevant cash flows. Another is the *P/E approach*, which builds the stock valuation process around the stock's price/earnings ratio. One of the major advantages of these procedures is that *they don't rely on dividends as the key input.* Accordingly, they can be used with stocks that are more growth-oriented and that pay little or nothing in dividends. Let's take a closer look at both of these approaches, as well as a technique that arrives at the expected return on the stock (in percentage terms) rather than a (dollar-based) "justified price."

A Dividends-and-Earnings Approach As we saw earlier, the value of a share of stock is a function of the amount and timing of future cash flows and the level of risk that must be taken on to generate that return. The **dividends-and-earnings (D&E) approach** (also known as the *DCF approach*) conveniently captures the essential elements of expected risk and return and does so in a present-value context. The model is as follows:

dividends-and-earnings (D&E) approach
stock valuation approach that uses projected dividends, EPS, and P/E multiples to value a share of stock; also known as the *DCF approach.*

Equation 8.11 ➤

$$\begin{array}{l}\text{Value of} \\ \text{a share of stock}\end{array} = \begin{array}{l}\text{Present value of} \\ \text{future dividends}\end{array} + \begin{array}{l}\text{Present value of} \\ \text{the price of the stock} \\ \text{at the date of sale}\end{array}$$

Equation 8.11a ➤

$$V = (D_1 \times PVIF_1) + (D_2 \times PVIF_2) + \cdots$$
$$+ (D_N \times PVIF_N) + (SP_N \times PVIF_N)$$

where

D_t = future annual dividend in year t

$PVIF_t$ = present-value interest factor, specified at the required rate of return (Table A.3 in the appendix near the end of the book)

SP_N = estimated share price of the stock at date of sale, year N

N = number of years in the investment horizon

Note its similarities to the variable-growth DVM: It is present-value–based, and its value is derived from future dividends and the expected future price of the stock. The big difference between the two procedures revolves around the role that dividends play in determining the future price of the stock. That is, the D&E approach doesn't rely on dividends as the principal player in the valuation process. Therefore, it works just as well with companies that pay little or nothing in dividends as it does with stocks that pay out a lot in dividends. Along that same line, whereas the variable-growth DVM relies on future dividends to price the stock, the D&E approach employs projected earnings per share and estimated P/E multiples. These are the same two variables that drive the price of the stock in the market. Thus, the D&E approach is far more flexible than the DVM and is easier to understand and apply. Using the D&E valuation approach, we focus on projecting future dividends and share price behavior over a defined, finite investment horizon, much as we did for Universal Office Furnishings in Table 8.4.

Especially important in the D&E approach is finding a viable P/E multiple that you can use to project the future price of the stock. This is a critical part of this valuation process, because of the major role that capital gains (and therefore the estimated price of the stock at its date of sale) play in defining the level of security returns. Using market or industry P/E ratios as benchmarks, you should establish a multiple that you feel the stock will trade at in the future. Like the growth rate, *g*, in the DVM, the P/E multiple is the single most important (and most difficult) variable to project in the D&E approach.

Using this input, along with estimated future dividends and earnings per share, this present-value–based model generates a *justified price* based on estimated returns. This intrinsic value represents the price you should be willing to pay for the stock, given its expected dividend and price behavior, and assuming you want to generate a return that is equal to or greater than your required rate of return.

To see how this procedure works, consider once again the case of Universal Office Furnishings. Let's return to our original three-year investment horizon. Given the forecasted annual dividends and share price from Table 8.4, along with a required rate of return of 18% (as computed earlier using Equation 8.6), we can see that the value of Universal's stock is

$$
\begin{aligned}
\frac{\text{Value of a share}}{\text{of Universal stock}} &= \frac{(\$0.18 \times 0.847) + (\$0.24 \times 0.718) + (\$0.28 \times 0.609)}{+ (\$93.20 \times 0.609)} \\
&= \$0.15 + \$0.17 + 0.17 + \$56.76 \\
&= \underline{\$57.25}
\end{aligned}
$$

According to the D&E approach, Universal's stock should be valued at about \$57 a share. That assumes, of course, that our projections hold up—particularly with regard to our forecasted EPS and P/E multiple in 2010. For example, if the P/E drops from 20 to 17 times earnings, then the value of a share of stock will drop to less than \$50 (to around \$48.75/share). Given that we have confidence in our projections, the present-value figure computed here means that we would realize our (18%) desired rate of return so long as we can buy the stock at no more than \$57 a share. Because UVRS is currently trading at (around) \$41.50, we can conclude that the stock at present is an *attractive investment vehicle*. That is, because we can buy the stock at *less* than its computed intrinsic value, we'll be able to earn our required rate of return, *and then some*.

Note that by most standards, Universal would be considered a highly risky investment, if for no other reason than the fact that *nearly all the return is derived from capital gains*. Indeed, dividends alone account for less than 1% of the value of the stock. That is, only 49 cents of the \$57.25 comes from dividends. Clearly, if we're wrong about EPS or the P/E multiple, the future price of the stock (in 2010) could be way off the mark, and so, too, would our projected return.

Actually, the D&E approach to stock valuation is not an alternative to the DVM, but rather, is simply a *variation* of that model. That is, regardless of what holding period is used in the D&E approach (be it one-year, three-years, ten-years, or whatever), the computed value will be the same as that obtained with the constant-growth (or even variable-growth) DVM, *so long as the input assumptions regarding k, g, and D_0 are the same*. Need proof? Consider the constant-growth DVM example we used earlier (see page 363). Recall that we used a stock that had a current annual dividend (D_0) of \$1.75 a share, a growth rate (*g*) of 8%, and a required return (*k*) of 12%. Let's use this same stock, *with these same assumptions*, but this time we'll use the D&E approach to value the stock, assuming a three-year investment horizon. Under these conditions, with an 8% growth rate, dividends would grow to $1.89 next year ($1.75 × 1.08), $2.04 in the second year, and $2.20 a share in year 3. Also, at an 8% appreciation rate, the price of the stock would go up to $59.50 by the end of year 3. Using this information in the D&E model, the value of the stock would be:

$$\text{Value} = (\$1.89 \times 0.893) + (\$2.04 \times 0.797) + (\$2.20 \times 0.712) + (\$59.50 \times 0.712)$$

$$= \$1.69 + \$1.62 + \$1.57 + \$42.36$$

$$= \underline{\$47.24}$$

Note that we end up with the same value here as we did using the DVM (see page 363). No matter what holding period or which procedure we use, D&E or DVM, so long as the input assumptions are the same, the computed share values will be the same.

Finding the Value of Non–Dividend-Paying Stocks What about *the value of a stock that does not pay dividends*—and is not expected to do so for the foreseeable future? That's not a problem with the D&E approach. Using Equation 8.11, simply set all dividends to zero, so the computed value of the stock would come solely from its projected future price. In other words, the value of the stock will equal the present value of its price at the end of the holding period.

Consider, for example, an investor who's looking at a stock that pays no dividends; she estimates that at the end of a two-year holding period, this stock should be trading at around $70 a share. Using a 15% required rate of return, this stock would have a present value of $70 × *PVIF* (for 2 years and 15%) = $70 × 0.756 = $52.92. This value is, of course, the intrinsic value, or justified price of the stock. So long as it's trading for around $53 or less, it would be a worthwhile investment candidate. (*Note:* Rather than using interest tables, you can just as easily *use a hand-held calculator to find the value of this stock*. Here's what you do: Input **N** as 2, **I/Y** as 15, and **FV** as −70.00; then compute **PV**, which turns out to be *52.93*.)

Determining Expected Return Sometimes investors find it more convenient to deal in terms of expected return than a dollar-based justified price. This is no problem, nor is it necessary to sacrifice the present-value dimension of the stock valuation model to achieve such an end. We can find expected return by using the (present-value–based) *internal rate of return (IRR)* procedure first introduced in Chapter 5. This approach to stock valuation uses forecasted dividend and price behavior, along with the *current market price*, to arrive at the fully compounded rate of return you can expect to earn from a given investment.

To see how a stock's expected return is computed, let's look once again at Universal Office Furnishings. Using 2008–2010 data from Table 8.4, along with the stock's current price of $41.58, we can determine Universal's expected return. To do so, we find the discount rate that equates the future stream of benefits (i.e., the future annual dividends and future price of the stock) to the stock's current market price. In other words, find the discount rate that produces a present value of future benefits equal to the price of the stock, and you have the IRR, or expected return on that stock.

Here's how it works: Using the Universal example, we know that the stock is expected to pay per-share dividends of $0.18, $0.24, and $0.28 over the next three years. At the end of that time, we hope to sell the stock for $93.20. Given that the stock is currently trading at $41.58, we're looking for the discount rate that will produce a present value (of the future annual dividends and stock price) equal to $41.58. That is,

$$(\$0.18 \times PVIF_1) + (\$0.24 \times PVIF_2)$$
$$+ (\$0.28 \times PVIF_3) + (\$93.20 \times PVIF_3) = \$41.58$$

We need to solve for the discount rate (the present-value interest factors) in this equation. Through a process of "hit and miss" (or with the help of a personal computer or handheld calculator), you'll find that with an interest factor of 31.3%, the present value of the future cash benefits from this investment will equal exactly $41.58. That, of course, is our expected return. Thus, Universal can be expected to earn a fully compounded annual return of about 31%, assuming that the stock can be bought at $41.58, is held for three years (during which time investors receive indicated annual dividends), and then is sold for $93.20 at the end of the three-year period. When compared to its 18% *required rate of return*, the 31.3% *expected return* makes Universal look like a very attractive investment candidate.

It's even easier to determine the return on stocks that don't pay dividends. Just *find the discount rate that equates the projected future price of the stock to its current share price.* For example, if Universal didn't pay dividends, then all we'd have to do is find the discount rate (*PVIF*) that equates the projected share price of $93.20 (three years from now) to the stock's current price of $41.58. Using a handheld calculator, we arrive at an expected rate of return of 30.9%. Here's how: Input **PV** as –41.58, **FV** as 93.20, and **N** as 3; then compute **I/Y**, which turns out to be 30.87. Given the return of 31.3% with dividends versus the 30.9% without, the cash flow from dividends clearly doesn't play much of a role in defining the potential return on this stock.

The Price/Earnings (P/E) Approach One of the problems with the stock valuation procedures we've looked at so far is that they are fairly mechanical. They involve a good deal of "number crunching." Although such approaches are fine with some stocks, they do not work well with others. Fortunately, there is a more intuitive approach. That alternative is the **price/earnings (or P/E) approach** to stock valuation.

price/earnings (P/E) approach
stock valuation approach that tries to find the P/E ratio that's most appropriate for the stock; this ratio, along with estimated EPS, is then used to determine a reasonable stock price.

The P/E approach is a favorite of professional security analysts and is widely used in practice. It's relatively simple to use; it's based on the standard P/E formula first introduced in Chapter 7 (Equation 7.14 on page 328). There we showed that a stock's P/E ratio is equal to its market price divided by the stock's EPS. Using this equation and solving for the market price of the stock, we have

Equation 8.12 ➤

Stock price = EPS × P/E ratio

Equation 8.12 basically captures the P/E approach to stock valuation. That is, given an *estimated* EPS figure, *you decide on a P/E ratio that you feel is appropriate for the stock. Then you use it in Equation 8.12 to see what kind of price you come up with and how that compares to the stock's current price.*

Actually, this approach is no different from what's used in the market every day. Look at the stock quotes in the *Wall Street Journal*. They include the stock's P/E ratio and show what investors are willing to pay for one dollar of earnings. Essentially, the *Journal* relates the company's earnings per share for the *last* 12 months (known as *trailing earnings*) to the latest price of the stock. In practice, however, investors buy stocks not for their past earnings but for their *expected future earnings*. Thus, in Equation 8.12, it's customary to use *forecasted EPS for next year*—that is, to use projected earnings one year out.

The first thing you have to do to implement the P/E approach is to come up with an expected EPS figure for next year. In the early part of this chapter, we saw how this might be done (see, for instance, Equation 8.3). Given the forecasted EPS, the next step is to evaluate the variables that drive the P/E ratio. Most of that assessment is intuitive. For example, you might look at the stock's expected rate of growth in earnings, any potential major changes in the firm's capital structure or dividends, and any other factors such as relative market or industry P/E multiples that might affect the stock's multiple. You could use such inputs to come up with a base P/E ratio. Then adjust that base, as necessary, to account for the perceived state of the market and/or anticipated changes in the rate of inflation.

Along with estimated EPS, we now have the P/E ratio we need to compute (via Equation 8.12) the price at which the stock should be trading. Take, for example, a stock that's currently trading at $37.80. One year from now, it's estimated that this stock should have an EPS of $2.25 a share. If you feel that the stock should be trading at a P/E ratio of 20 times projected earnings, then it should be valued at $45 a share (i.e., $2.25 × 20). By comparing this targeted price to the current market price of the stock, you can decide whether the stock is a good buy. In this case, you would consider the stock undervalued and therefore a good buy, since the computed price of the stock ($45) is more than its market price (of $37.80).

While this is the principal application of the P/E approach, you'll find that *a variation of this procedure* is also used with the D&E and IRR approaches. That is, by using estimated figures for *both* EPS and the P/E multiple, you can come up with *the share price that's expected to prevail at the end of a given investment horizon*. Throw in any dividends that may be received, discount that cash flow (of dividends and future share price) back to the present, and you have either the *justified price*, as in the D&E approach, or the *expected rate of return*, as in the IRR approach.

▮ Other Price-Relative Procedures

As we saw with the P/E approach, price-relative procedures base their valuations on the assumptions that *the value of a share of stock should be directly linked to a given performance characteristic of the firm*, such as earnings per share. These procedures involve a good deal of judgment and intuition, and they rely heavily on the market expertise of the analysts. Besides the P/E approach, there are several other price-relative procedures that are used by investors who, for one reason or another, want to use some measure other than earnings to value stocks. They include:

- The price-to-cash-flow (P/CF) ratio
- The price-to-sales (P/S) ratio
- The price-to-book-value (P/BV) ratio

Like the P/E multiple, these procedures determine the value of a stock by relating share price to cash flow, sales, or book value. Let's look at each of these in turn to see how they're used in stock valuation.

A Price-to-Cash-Flow (P/CF) Procedure This measure has long been popular with investors, because cash flow is felt to provide a more accurate picture of a company's earning power than net earnings. When used in stock valuation, the procedure is almost identical to the P/E approach. That is, a P/CF ratio is combined with a *projected* cash flow per share to arrive at what the stock should be trading for.

Although it is quite straightforward, this procedure nonetheless has one problem—defining the appropriate cash flow measure. While some investors use *cash flow from operating activities*, as obtained from the statement of cash flows, others use *free cash flow*. But the one measure that seems to be the most popular with professional analysts is EBITDA (earnings before interest, taxes, depreciation, and amortization), which we'll use here. EBITDA represents "cash earnings" to the extent that the major noncash expenditures (depreciation and amortization) are added back to operating earnings (EBIT).

The price-to-cash-flow (P/CF) ratio is computed as follows:

Equation 8.13 ➤

$$P/CF \text{ ratio} = \frac{\text{Market price of common stock}}{\text{Cash flow per share}}$$

where cash flow per share = EBITDA ÷ number of common shares outstanding.

Before you can use the P/CF procedure *to assess the current market price of a stock*, you first have to come up with a forecasted cash flow per share one year out, and then define an appropriate P/CF multiple to use. For most firms, it is very likely that the cash flow (EBITDA) figure will be larger than net earnings available to stockholders. As a result, *the cash flow multiple will probably be lower than the P/E multiple*—which some would argue is all too often the principal motivation for using the P/CF ratio (to end up with a lower, more respectable multiple). In any event, once an appropriate P/CF multiple is determined (subjectively and with the help of any historical market information), simply multiply it by the expected cash flow per share one year from now to find the price at which the stock should be trading. That is, the computed price of a share of stock = cash flow per share × P/CF ratio.

To illustrate, assume a company currently is generating an EBITDA of $325 million, which is expected to increase by some 12.5% to around

$365 million ($325 million $\times$ 1.125) over the course of the next 12 months. On a per-share basis, let's say that translates into a *projected* cash flow per share of nearly $6.50. If we feel this stock should be trading at about 8 times its projected cash flow per share, then it should be valued at around $52 a share. Thus, if it is currently trading in the market at $45.50 (or at 7 times its projected cash flow per share), we can conclude, once again, that the stock is undervalued and, therefore, should be considered a viable investment candidate.

Price-to-Sales (P/S) and Price-to-Book-Value (P/BV) Ratios Some companies, like new technology and Internet firms, have little, if any, earnings. Or if they do have earnings, they're either unreliable or very erratic and therefore highly unpredictable. In these cases, valuation procedures based on earnings (and even cash flows) aren't much help. So investors turn to other procedures—those based on sales or book value, for example. While companies may not have much in the way of profits, they certainly have sales and, ideally, some book value. (As noted in Chapter 7, *book value* is simply another term for equity, or net worth.)

Both the price-to-sales (P/S) and price-to-book-value (P/BV) ratios are used exactly like the P/E and P/CF procedures. Recall that we defined the P/BV ratio in Equation 7.19 as follows:

$$\text{P/BV ratio} = \frac{\text{Market price of common stock}}{\text{Book value per share}}$$

We can define the P/S ratio in a similar fashion:

Equation 8.14 ➤

$$\text{P/S ratio} = \frac{\text{Market price of common stock}}{\text{Sales per share}}$$

where sales per share = net annual sales (or revenues) ÷ number of common shares outstanding.

Generally speaking, the lower the P/S ratio, the better. In fact, many investors look for stocks with P/S ratios of 2.0 or less. These securities are felt to offer the most potential for future price appreciation. Especially attractive are very low P/S multiples of 1.0 or less. Think about it: With a P/S ratio of, say, 0.9, you can buy $1 in sales for only 90 cents! So long as the company isn't a basket case, such low P/S multiples may well be worth pursuing.

Keep in mind that while the emphasis may be on low multiples, *high P/S ratios aren't necessarily bad*. To determine if a high multiple—more than 3.0 or 4.0, for example—is justified, look at the company's net profit margin. Companies that can consistently generate high net profit margins often have high P/S ratios. Here's a valuation rule to remember: *High profit margins should go hand-in-hand with high P/S multiples*. That makes sense, too, because a company with a high profit margin brings more of its sales down to the bottom line in the form of profits. For more discussion on the P/S measure, particularly its ability to predict future stock performance, see the accompanying *Investing in Action* box.

INVESTING *in Action*

Predicting Performance with the Price-to-Sales (P/S) Ratio

A number of analysts and stock-pickers use the *price-to-sales (P/S) ratio* to identify stocks with above-average possibility of delivering an increase in stock price. A "cousin" of the price-to-earnings (P/E) ratio, the P/S ratio is calculated as current market price divided by sales per share. Some analysts prefer the P/S ratio because it uses a company's sales figure in the denominator, which is somewhat more resistant to management's accounting manipulations than are earnings numbers. Also, the P/S ratio is useful for valuing firms with few or erratic earnings.

Analysts have found low P/S ratios helpful in spotting overvalued and undervalued stocks within a given industry. (Industry differences in profit margins make it important that you take care in comparing P/S ratios *across* industries, though.) In addition, low P/S ratios may help identify companies that are possible takeover candidates, and whose stock price could experience a big jump if targeted for takeover.

In his book *What Works on Wall Street* (revised edition, McGraw-Hill, 1998), James O'Shaughnessy found a significant correlation between price-to-sales ratios and stock-price performance. He included only stocks with market capitalizations over $150 million and with P/E and P/S ratios above zero. In the remaining "population" of 2,395 stocks, the median P/E ratio on August 2, 2002, was 18.83,

and the median P/S ratio was 1.40. Tracking the stocks from 1951 through 1996, O'Shaughnessy found that the P/S ratio predicted performance, both over the next year and over the long term (the 45-year period), better than the P/E ratio did. He also found that the best stocks in terms of price performance in the following year were those with P/E ratios between 10 and 13 and those with P/S ratio between 0 and 0.34, *with lower ratios leading to better performance.*

Similarly, columnist and investment adviser John Dorfman makes yearly recommendations of a few stocks whose low P/S ratios seem to promise better-than-average results. In 2005, for example, his recommended stocks with low P/S ratios returned 25% (including dividends) compared to 2.7% for the S&P 500 Index for the same year. (For his latest recommendations, search Dorfman's columns at **www.bloomberg.com**.)

CRITICAL THINKING QUESTION Why would industry differences affect the use of the P/S ratio across industries?

Sources: Richard Goedde, "The Predictive Power of Price-Earnings and Price-Sales Ratios," *AAII Journal,* February 2003, pp. 7–9; John Dorfman, "Jumping Juniper!" *Bloomberg Personal Finance,* May 2000, pp. 49–51; and John Dorfman, "Bunge, Borders Look Good on Price-to-Sales Ratio," **www.bloomberg.com** (accessed August 2006).

You would also expect the price-to-book-value measure to be low, but probably not as low as the P/S ratio. Indeed, unless the market becomes grossly overvalued (think about what happened in 1999 and 2000), most stocks are likely to trade at multiples of less than 3 to 5 times their book values. And in this case, unlike with the P/S multiple, there's usually little justification for abnormally high price-to-book-value ratios—except perhaps for firms that have abnormally *low* levels of equity in their capital structures. Other than that, high P/BV multiples are almost always caused by "excess exuberance." As a rule, when stocks start trading at 7 or 8 times their book values, or more, they are becoming overvalued.

CONCEPTS IN REVIEW
Answers available at: www.myfinancelab.com

8.6 Briefly describe the *dividend valuation model* and the three versions of this model. Explain how CAPM fits into the *DVM*.

8.7 What is the difference between the variable-growth dividend valuation model and the *dividends-and-earnings approach* to stock valuation? Which procedure would work better if you were trying to value a growth stock that pays little or no dividends? Explain.

8.8 How would you go about finding the *expected return* on a stock? Note how such information would be used in the stock selection process.

8.9 Briefly describe the *P/E approach* to stock valuation and note how this approach differs from the variable-growth DVM. Describe the *P/CF approach* and note how it is used in the stock valuation process. Compare the P/CF approach to the P/E approach, noting their relative strengths and weaknesses.

8.10 Briefly describe the *price/sales* ratio, and explain how it is used to value stocks. Why not just use the P/E multiple? How does the P/S ratio differ from the *P/BV measure?*

Summary

LG 1 **Explain the role that a company's future plays in the stock valuation process.** The final phase of security analysis involves an assessment of the investment merits of a specific company and its stock. The focus here is on formulating expectations about the company's prospects and the risk and return behavior of the stock. In particular, we would want some idea of the stock's future earnings, dividends, and share prices, which are ultimately the basis of return.

LG 2 **Develop a forecast of a stock's expected cash flow, starting with corporate sales and earnings, and then moving to expected dividends and share price.** Because the value of a share of stock is a function of its future returns, investors must try to formulate expectations about what the future holds for the company. Look first at the company's projected sales and earnings, and then translate those data into forecasted dividends and share prices. These variables define an investment's future cash flow and, therefore, investor returns.

LG 3 **Discuss the concepts of intrinsic value and required rates of return, and note how they are used.** Information such as projected sales, forecasted earnings, and estimated dividends are important in establishing intrinsic value. This is a measure, based on expected return and risk exposure, of what the stock ought to be worth. A key element is the investor's required rate of return, which is used to define the amount of return that should be earned given the stock's perceived exposure to risk.

LG 4 Determine the underlying value of a stock using the zero-growth, constant-growth, and variable-growth dividend valuation models. The dividend valuation model (DVM) derives the value of a share of stock from the stock's future growth in dividends. There are three versions of the DVM: Zero-growth assumes that dividends are fixed and won't change in the future. Constant-growth assumes that dividends will grow at a constant rate into the future. Variable-growth assumes that dividends will initially grow at varying (or abnormally high) rates, before eventually settling down to a constant rate of growth.

LG 5 Use other types of present-value–based models to derive the value of a stock, as well as alternative price-relative procedures. The DVM works well with some types of stocks, but not so well with others. Investors may turn to other types of stock-valuation approaches, including the D&E and IRR approaches, as well as certain price-relative procedures, like the P/E, P/CF, P/S, and P/BV methods. The dividends-and-earnings approach uses a finite investment horizon to derive a present-value–based "justified price." Or, investors can determine the expected return on a stock (via IRR) by finding the discount rate that equates the stock's future cash flows to its current market price. Several price-relative procedures exist as well, such as the price/earnings approach, which uses projected EPS and the stock's P/E ratio to determine whether a stock is fairly valued.

LG 6 Gain a basic appreciation of the procedures used to value different types of stock, from traditional dividend-paying shares to more growth-oriented stocks. All sorts of stock valuation models are used in the market; this chapter examined nine more widely used procedures. One thing that becomes apparent in stock evaluation is that one approach definitely does not fit all situations. Some approaches (like the DVM) work well with mature, dividend-paying companies. Others (like the D&E, IRR, P/E, and P/CF approaches) are more suited to growth-oriented firms, which may not pay dividends. Other price-relative procedures (like P/S and P/BV) are often used to value companies that have little or nothing in earnings, or whose earnings records are sporadic.

Key Terms

common-size income statement, *p. 348*
dividends-and-earnings (D&E) approach, *p. 368*
dividend valuation model (DVM), *p. 360*

price/earnings (P/E) approach, *p. 371*
relative P/E multiple, *p. 352*
required rate of return, *p. 357*
stock valuation, *p. 348*
valuation, *p. 356*

Discussion Questions

LG 2 **LG 3**

LG 5 **LG 6**

Q8.1 Using the resources available at your campus or public library, select a company from *Value Line* that would be of interest to you. (*Hint*: Pick a company that's been publicly traded for at least 10 to 15 years, and avoid public utilities, banks, and other financial institutions.) Obtain a copy of the latest *Value Line* report on your chosen company. Using the historical and forecasted data reported in *Value Line*, along with one of the valuation techniques described in this chapter, calculate the maximum (i.e., justified) price you'd be willing to pay for this stock. Use the CAPM to find the required rate of return on your stock. (For this problem, use a market rate of return of 12%, and for the risk-free rate, use the latest 3-month Treasury bill rate.)

    a. How does the justified price you computed compare to the latest market price of the stock?

    b. Would you consider this stock to be a worthwhile investment candidate? Explain.

LG 5 **LG 6**

Q8.2 In this chapter, we examined nine different stock valuation procedures:

- Zero-growth DVM
- Constant-growth DVM
- Variable-growth DVM
- Dividends-and-earnings (D&E) approach
- Expected return (IRR) approach
- P/E approach
- Price-to-cash-flow ratio
- Price-to-sales ratio
- Price-to-book-value ratio

    a. Which one (or more) of these procedures would be most appropriate when trying to put a value on:

       1. A growth stock that pays little or nothing in dividends?

       2. The S&P 500?

       3. A relatively new company that has only a brief history of earnings?

       4. A large, mature, dividend-paying company?

       5. A preferred stock that pays a fixed dividend?

       6. A company that has a large amount of depreciation and amortization?

    b. Of the nine procedures listed above, which *three* do you think are the best? Explain.

    c. If you had to choose just *one* procedure to use in practice, which would it be? Explain. (*Note*: Confine your selection to the list above.)

LG 1 **LG 3**

Q8.3 Explain the role that the future plays in the stock valuation process. Why not just base the valuation on historical information? Explain how the intrinsic value of a stock is related to its required rate of return. Illustrate what happens to the value of a stock when the required rate of return increases.

LG 3 **LG 4**

Q8.4 Assume an investor uses the constant-growth DVM to value a stock. Listed below are various situations that could affect the computed value of a stock. Look at each one of these individually, and indicate whether it would cause the computed value of a stock to go up, down, or stay the same. Briefly explain your answers.

    a. Dividend payout ratio goes up.

    b. Stock's beta rises.

    c. Equity multiplier goes down.

    d. T-bill rates fall.

e. Net profit margin goes up.
f. Total asset turnover falls.
g. Market return increases.

Assume throughout that the current dividend (D_0) remains the same, and that all other variables in the model are unchanged.

Problems

LG 2   **P8.1**   An investor estimates that next year's sales for New World Products should amount to about $75 million. The company has 2.5 million shares outstanding, generates a net profit margin of about 5%, and has a payout ratio of 50%. All figures are expected to hold for next year. Given this information, compute the following.
     a. Estimated net earnings for next year.
     b. Next year's dividends per share.
     c. The expected price of the stock (assuming the P/E ratio is 24.5 times earnings).
     d. The expected holding period return (latest stock price: $25 per share).

LG 2   **P8.2**   GrowthCo had sales of $55 million in 2005, and is expected to have sales of $83,650,000 for 2008. The company's net profit margin was 5% in 2005, and is expected to increase to 8% by 2008. Estimate the company's net profit for 2008.

LG 2   **P8.3**   Goodstuff Corporation has total equity of $500 million and 100 million shares outstanding. Its ROE is 15%. Calculate the company's EPS.

LG 2   **P8.4**   Goodstuff Corporation has total equity of $500 million and 100 million shares outstanding. Its ROE is 15%. The dividend payout ratio is 33.3%. Calculate the company's dividends per share (round to the nearest penny).

LG 2   **P8.5**   HighTeck has a ROE of 15%. Its earnings per share are $2.00, and its dividends per share are $0.20. Estimate HighTeck's growth rate.

LG 2   **P8.6**   Last year, InDebt Company paid $75 million of interest expense, and its average rate of interest for the year was 10%. The company's ROE is 15%, and it pays no dividends. Estimate next year's interest expense assuming that interest rates will fall by 25% and the company keeps a constant equity multiplier of 20%.

LG 3   **P8.7**   Charlene Lewis is thinking about buying some shares of Education, Inc., at $50 per share. She expects the price of the stock to rise to $75 over the next 3 years. During that time she also expects to receive annual dividends of $5 per share.
     a. What is the intrinsic worth of this stock, given a 10% required rate of return?
     b. What is its expected return?

LG 4   **P8.8**   Amalgamated Aircraft Parts, Inc., is expected to pay a dividend of $1.50 in the coming year. The required rate of return is 16%, and dividends are expected to grow at 7% per year. Using the dividend valuation model, find the intrinsic value of the company's common shares.

LG 4   **P8.9** Eddy is considering a stock purchase. The stock pays constant annual dividend of $2.00 per share, and is currently trading at $20. Eddy's required rate of return for this stock is 12%. Should he buy this stock?

LG 4 LG 5   **P8.10** Larry, Moe, and Curley are brothers. They're all serious investors, but each has a different approach to valuing stocks. Larry, the oldest, likes to use a 1-year holding period to value common shares. Moe, the middle brother, likes to use multiyear holding periods. Curley, the youngest of the three, prefers the dividend valuation model.

As it turns out, right now, all three of them are looking at the same stock—American Home Care Products, Inc. (AHCP). The company has been listed on the NYSE for over 50 years, and is widely regarded as a mature, rock-solid, dividend-paying stock. The brothers have gathered the following information about AHCP's stock:

Current dividend (D_0) = $2.50/share
Expected growth rate (g) = 9.0%
Required rate of return (k) = 12.0%

All three of them agree that these variables are appropriate, and they will use them in valuing the stock. Larry and Moe intend to use the D&E approach; Curley is going to use the constant-growth DVM. Larry will use a 1-year holding period; he estimates that with a 9% growth rate, the price of the stock will increase to $98.80 by the end of the year. Moe will use a 3-year holding period; with the same 9% growth rate, he projects the future price of the stock will be $117.40 by the end of his investment horizon. Curley will use the constant-growth DVM, so his holding period isn't needed.
   a. Use the information provided above to value the stocks first for Larry, then for Moe, then for Curley.
   b. Comment on your findings. Which approach seems to make the most sense?

LG 5   **P8.11** Assume you've generated the following information about the stock of Buford's Burger Barns: The company's latest dividends of $4 a share are expected to grow to $4.32 next year, to $4.67 the year after that, and to $5.04 in year 3. In addition, the price of the stock is expected to rise from $56.50 (its current price) to $77.75 in 3 years.
   a. Use the dividends-and-earnings model and a required return of 15% to find the value of the stock.
   b. Use the IRR procedure to find the stock's expected return.
   c. Given that dividends are expected to grow indefinitely at 8%, use a 15% required rate of return and the dividend valuation model to find the value of the stock.
   d. Assume dividends in year 3 actually amount to $5.04, the dividend growth rate stays at 8%, and the required rate of return stays at 15%. Use the dividend valuation model to find the price of the stock at the end of year 3. [*Hint:* In this case, the value of the stock will depend on dividends in year 4, which equal $D_3 \times (1 + g)$.] Do you note any similarity between your answer here and the forecasted price of the stock ($77.75) given in the problem? Explain.

LG 6   **P8.12** Let's assume that you're thinking about buying stock in West Coast Electronics. So far in your analysis, you've uncovered the following information: The stock pays annual dividends of $2.50 a share (and that's not expected to change within the next few years—*nor are any of the other variables*). It trades at a P/E of 18 times earnings and has a beta of 1.15. In addition, you plan on using a risk-free rate of 7% in the CAPM, along with a market return of 14%. You would like to hold the stock for 3 years, at the end of which time you think EPS will peak at about $7 a share. Given that the stock currently trades at $70, use the IRR approach to find this security's expected return. Now use the present-value (dividends-and-earnings) model to put a price on this stock. Does this look like a good investment to you? Explain.

LG 6   **P8.13**   The price of Consolidated Everything is now $75. The company pays no dividends. Ms. Bossard expects the price 3 years from now to be $100 per share. Should Ms. B. buy Consolidated E. if she desires a 10% rate of return? Explain.

LG 5   **P8.14**   This year, Shoreline Light and Gas (SLL&G) paid its stockholders an annual dividend of $3 a share. A major brokerage firm recently put out a report on SLL&G stating that, in its opinion, the company's annual dividends should grow at the rate of 10% per year for each of the next 5 years and then level off and grow at the rate of 6% a year thereafter.

    a. Use the variable-growth DVM and a required rate of return of 12% to find the maximum price you should be willing to pay for this stock.

    b. Redo the SLL&G problem in part **a**, this time assuming that after year 5, dividends stop growing altogether (for year 6 and beyond, $g = 0$). Use all the other information given to find the stock's intrinsic value.

    c. Contrast your two answers and comment on your findings. How important is growth to this valuation model?

LG 5   **P8.15**   Assume there are three companies that in the past year paid exactly the same annual dividend of $2.25 a share. In addition, the future annual rate of growth in dividends for each of the three companies has been estimated as follows:

Buggies-Are-Us	Steady Freddie, Inc.	Gang Buster Group	
$g = 0$	$g = 6\%$	Year 1	$2.53
(i.e., dividends	(for the	2	$2.85
are expected	foreseeable	3	$3.20
to remain at	future)	4	$3.60
$2.25/share)		Year 5 and beyond: $g = 6\%$	

Assume also that as the result of a strange set of circumstances, these three companies all have the same required rate of return ($k = 10\%$).

    a. Use the appropriate DVM to value each of these companies.

    b. Comment briefly on the comparative values of these three companies. What is the major cause of the differences among these three valuations?

LG 6   **P8.16**   New Millenium Company's stock sells at a P/E ratio of 21 times earnings. It is expected to pay dividends of $2 per share in each of the next 5 years and to generate an EPS of $5 in year 5. Using the dividends-and-earnings model and a 12% discount rate, compute the stock's justified price.

LG 6   **P8.17**   A particular company currently has sales of $250 million; sales are expected to grow by 20% next year (year 1). For the year after next (year 2), the growth rate in sales is expected to equal 10%. Over each of the next 2 years, the company is expected to have a net profit margin of 8% and a payout ratio of 50%, and to maintain the common stock outstanding at 15 million shares. The stock always trades at a P/E of 15 times earnings, and the investor has a required rate of return of 20%. Given this information:

    a. Find the stock's intrinsic value (its justified price).

    b. Use the IRR approach to determine the stock's expected return, given that it is currently trading at $15 per share.

    c. Find the holding period returns for this stock for year 1 and for year 2.

LG 3   LG 5   **P8.18** Assume a major investment service has just given Oasis Electronics its highest investment rating, along with a strong buy recommendation. As a result, you decide to take a look for yourself and to place a value on the company's stock. Here's what you find: This year, Oasis paid its stockholders an annual dividend of $3 a share, but because of its high rate of growth in earnings, its dividends are expected to grow at the rate of 12% a year for the next 4 years and then to level out at 9% a year. So far, you've learned that the stock has a beta of 1.80, the risk-free rate of return is 6%, and the expected return on the market is 11%. Using the CAPM to find the required rate of return, put a value on this stock.

LG 5   **P8.19** Consolidated Software doesn't currently pay any dividends but is expected to start doing so in 4 years. That is, Consolidated will go 3 more years without paying any dividends, and then is expected to pay its first dividend (of $3 per share) in the fourth year. Once the company starts paying dividends, it's expected to continue to do so. The company is expected to have a dividend payout ratio of 40% and to maintain a return on equity of 20%. Based on the DVM, and given a required rate of return of 15%, what is the maximum price you should be willing to pay for this stock today?

LG 5   **P8.20** Assume you obtain the following information about a certain company:

Total assessts	$50,000,000
Total equity	$25,000,000
Net income	$3,750,000
EPS	$5.00 per share
Dividend payout ratio	40%
Required return	12%

Use the constant-growth DVM to place a value on this company's stock.

LG 6   **P8.21** You're thinking about buying some stock in Affiliated Computer Corporation and want to use the P/E approach to value the shares. You've estimated that next year's earnings should come in at about $4.00 a share. In addition, although the stock normally trades at a relative P/E of 1.15 times the market, you believe that the relative P/E will rise to 1.25, whereas the market P/E should be around 18.5 times earnings. Given this information, what is the maximum price you should be willing to pay for this stock? If you buy this stock today at $87.50, what rate of return will you earn over the next 12 months if the price of the stock rises to $110.00 by the end of the year? (Assume that the stock doesn't pay any dividends.)

LG 6   **P8.22** AviBank Plastics generated an EPS of $2.75 over the last 12 months. The company's earnings are expected to grow by 25% next year, and because there will be no significant change in the number of shares outstanding, EPS should grow at about the same rate. You feel the stock should trade at a P/E of around 30 times earnings. Use the P/E approach to set a value on this stock.

LG 6   **P8.23** Newco is a young company that has yet to make a profit. You are trying to place a value on the stock, but it pays no dividends and you obviously cannot calculate a P/E ratio. As a result, you decide to look at other stocks in the same industry as Newco to see if you can find a way to value this company. You find the following information:

	Per-Share Data			
	Newco	Adolescentco	Middle-Ageco	Oldco
Sales	10	200	800	800
Profit	−10	10	60	80
Book Value	−2	2	5	8
Market Value	?	20	80	75

Estimate a market value for Newco. Discuss how your estimate could change if Newco was expected to grow much faster than the other companies.

LG 4   P8.24 World Wide Web Wares (4W, for short) is an online retailer of small kitchen appliances and utensils. The firm has been around for a few years and has created a nice market niche for itself. In fact, it actually turned a profit last year, albeit a fairly small one. After doing some basic research on the company, you've decided to take a closer look. You plan to use the price/sales ratio to value the stock, and you have collected P/S multiples on the following Internet retailer stocks:

Company	P/S Multiples
Amazing.com	4.5
Really Cooking.com	4.1
Fixtures & Appliances Online	3.8

Find the *average P/S ratio* for these three firms. Given that 4W is expected to generate $40 million in sales next year, and will have 10 million shares of stock outstanding, use the average P/S ratio you computed above to put a value on 4W's stock.

> See www.myfinancelab.com for **Web Exercises,**
> **Spreadsheets, and other online resources.**

Case Problem 8.1   *Chris Looks for a Way to Invest His Newfound Wealth*

LG 1   LG 2   LG 4   Chris Norton is a young Hollywood writer who is well on his way to television superstardom. After writing several successful television specials, he was recently named the head writer for one of TV's top-rated sitcoms. Chris fully realizes that his business is a fickle one and, on the advice of his dad and manager, has decided to set up an investment program. Chris will earn about a half-million dollars this year. Because of his age, income level, and desire to get as big a bang as possible from his investment dollars, he has decided to invest in speculative, high-growth stocks.

Chris is currently working with a respected Beverly Hills broker and is in the process of building up a diversified portfolio of speculative stocks. The broker recently sent him information on a hot new issue. She advised Chris to study the numbers and, if he likes them, to buy as many as 1,000 shares of the stock. Among other things, corporate sales for the next 3 years have been forecasted as follows:

Year	Sales (in millions)
1	$22.5
2	35.0
3	50.0

The firm has 2.5 million shares of common stock outstanding. They are currently being traded at $70 a share and pay no dividends. The company has a net profit rate of 20%, and its stock has been trading at a P/E of around 40 times earnings. All these operating characteristics are expected to hold in the future.

Questions

a. Looking first at the stock:
   1. Compute the company's net profits and EPS for each of the next 3 years.
   2. Compute the price of the stock 3 years from now.
   3. Assuming that all expectations hold up and that Chris buys the stock at $70, determine his expected return on this investment.
   4. What risks is he facing by buying this stock? Be specific.
   5. Should he consider the stock a worthwhile investment candidate? Explain.

b. Looking at Chris's investment program in general:
   1. What do you think of his investment program? What do you see as its strengths and weaknesses?
   2. Are there any suggestions you would make?
   3. Do you think Chris should consider adding foreign stocks to his portfolio? Explain.

Case Problem 8.2   *An Analysis of a High-Flying Stock*

LG 2   LG 6

Glenn Wilt is a recent university graduate and a security analyst with the Kansas City brokerage firm of Lippman, Brickbats, and Shaft. Wilt has been following one of the hottest issues on Wall Street, C&I Medical Supplies, a company that has turned in an outstanding performance lately and, even more important, has exhibited excellent growth potential. It has 5 million shares outstanding and pays a nominal annual dividend of 5 cents per share. Wilt has decided to take a closer look at C&I to see whether it still has any investment play left. Assume the company's sales for the past 5 years have been as follows:

Year	Sales (in millions)
2003	$10.0
2004	12.5
2005	16.2
2006	22.0
2007	28.5

Wilt is concerned with the future prospects of the company, not its past. As a result, he pores over the numbers and generates the following estimates of future performance:

Expected net profit margin	12%
Estimated annual dividends per share	5¢
Number of common shares outstanding	No change
P/E ratio at the end of 2008	35
P/E ratio at the end of 2009	50

Questions

a. Determine the average annual rate of growth in sales over the past 5 years. (Assume sales in 2002 amounted to $7.5 million.)
   1. Use this average growth rate to forecast revenues for next year (2008) and the year after that (2009).
   2. Now determine the company's net earnings and EPS for each of the next 2 years (2008 and 2009).
   3. Finally, determine the expected future price of the stock at the end of this 2-year period.

b. Because of several intrinsic and market factors, Wilt feels that 25% is a viable figure to use for a desired rate of return.
   1. Using the 25% rate of return and the forecasted figures you came up with in question a, compute the stock's justified price.
   2. If C&I is currently trading at $32.50 per share, should Wilt consider the stock a worthwhile investment candidate? Explain.

Excel with Spreadsheets

Fundamental to the valuation process is the determination of the intrinsic value of a security, where an investor calculates the present value of the expected future cash benefits of the investment. Specifically, in the case of common stock, these future cash flows are defined by expected future dividend payments and future potential price appreciation. A simple but useful way to view stock value is that it is equal to the present value of all expected future dividends it may provide over an infinite time horizon.

Based on this latter concept, the dividend valuation model (DVM) has evolved. It can take on any one of three versions—the zero-growth model, the constant-growth model, and the variable-growth model.

Create a spreadsheet that applies the variable-growth model to predict the intrinsic value of the Rhyhorn Company common stock. Assume that dividends will grow at a variable rate for the next 3 years (2007, 2008, and 2009). After that, the annual rate of growth in dividends is expected to be 7% and stay there for the foreseeable future. Starting with the latest (2006) annual dividend of $2.00 per share, Rhyhorn's earnings and dividends are estimated to grow by 18% in 2007, by 14% in 2008, and by 9% in 2009 before dropping to a 7% rate. Given the risk profile of the firm, assume a minimum required rate of return of at least 12%. The spreadsheet for Table 8.5, which you can view on www.myfinance.lab, is a good reference for solving this problem.

Questions

a.   Calculate the projected annual dividends over the years 2007, 2008, and 2009.

b.   Determine the present value of dividends during the initial variable-growth period.

c.   What do you believe the price of Rhyhorn stock will be at the end of the initial growth period (2009)?

d.   Having determined the expected future price of Rhyhorn stock in part **c,** discount the price of the stock back to its present value.

e.   Determine the total intrinsic value of Rhyhorn stock based on your calculations above.

Chapter 9

Technical Analysis, Market Efficiency, and Behavioral Finance

U sing an online stock screener, you've identified two pharmaceutical companies as possible investments. Forest Laboratories develops, produces, and markets brand-name and generic drugs. Teva Pharmaceuticals, an Israeli company whose ADRs trade on the Nasdaq, is the world's largest manufacturer of generic drugs. Forest Lab currently trades at $42.80; Teva trades at $30.39 per share. How do you choose between them?

One answer lies in *technical analysis*, which looks at the impact of market forces on stock price and tries to predict shifts in the market direction. You pull charts of each company at StockCharts.com to see a picture—literally—of the historical stock price movements for a specific time period. The basic charts also show the 50- and 200-day moving averages (average price of the stock over the time period), and daily trading volume for the stock. The moving averages smooth out short-term price fluctuations to help you identify trends that occur over a longer time horizon.

Forest Labs has recently broken through its 50-day and 200-day moving averages ($38.56 and $41.01 respectively). Teva is well below both its 200-day moving average ($39.24) and its 50-day average ($34.46). Forest's chart also shows a relative strength index (RSI) reading of 65.44 which has been rising from a low of 28 just two months previously. Teva's chart shows an RSI of only 30.39, down from a high of 65 three months previously. You also evaluate the advance-decline line and short-interest ratio.

Forest's chart gives a moderate buy signal, as does its recent upward price trend. Teva's chart shows cause for concern, especially with the continued unrest in the Middle East. You decide to buy Forest Labs now but will monitor Teva to see if its chart signals a buy in the future.

Does the preceding discussion leave you confused? Read on to learn how to use the technical indicators. You'll also discover the differences between proponents of the efficient market hypotheses, who believe it is not possible to consistently outperform the market, and behavioral finance advocates, who take a psychological view of investor reactions.

Sources: http://stockcharts.com and http://finance.yahoo.com (accessed July 21, 2006).

Technical Analysis

LG 1 LG 2 LG 3

technical analysis
the study of the various forces at work in the marketplace and their effect on stock prices.

How many times have you turned on the TV or radio and in the course of the day's news heard a reporter say, "The market was up 47 points today," or "The market remained sluggish in a day of light trading"? Such comments reflect the importance of the stock market itself in determining the price behavior of common stocks. In fact, some experts believe that studying the market should be the major, if not the only, ingredient in the stock selection process. Contrary to our discussion of fundamental analysis in the previous chapter, these experts argue that much of what is done in security analysis is useless because it is the *market* that matters, not individual companies. Others argue that studying the stock market is only *one element* in the security analysis process and is useful in trying to time investment decisions.

Analyzing the various forces at work in the market is known as **technical analysis**. For some investors, it's another piece of information to use when deciding whether to buy, hold, or sell a stock. For others, it's the *only* input they use in their investment decisions. Still others regard both technical analysis and fundamental analysis as a waste of time.

Here we will assume that market analysis does have a role to play in the investment decision process, and we will examine the major principles of *technical analysis*, as well as some of the techniques used to assess market behavior. Following that, we'll look at the *efficient market hypothesis* and the questions it raises for the whole security analysis process. Finally, we'll discuss *behavioral finance* and the challenges it poses to the concept of market efficiency.

▮ Principles of Market Analysis

Analyzing market behavior dates back to the 1800s, when there was no such thing as industry or company analysis. Detailed financial information about individual companies simply was not made available to stockholders, let alone the general public. About the only thing investors could study was the market itself. Some investors used detailed charts to monitor what large market operators were doing. These charts were intended to show when major buyers were moving into or out of particular stocks and to provide information useful for profitable buy-and-sell decisions. The charts centered on stock price movements. These movements were said to produce certain "formations" indicating when the time was right to buy or sell a particular stock. The same principle is still applied today: Technical analysts argue that internal market factors, such as trading volume and price movements, often reveal the market's future direction long before it is evident in financial statistics.

If the behavior of stock prices were completely independent of market movements, market studies and technical analysis would be useless. But we have ample evidence that stock prices do, in fact, tend to move with the market. For example, studies of stock betas have shown that as a rule, anywhere from 20% to 50% of the price behavior of a stock can be traced to market forces. When the market is bullish, stock prices in general can be expected to rise. When the market turns bearish, you can safely expect most issues to be affected by the "downdraft."

Stock prices, in essence, react to various forces of supply and demand that are at work in the market. After all, it's the *demand* for securities and the *supply* of funds in the market that determine whether we're in a bull or a bear market. So long as a given supply-and-demand relationship holds, the market will remain strong (or weak). When the balance begins to shift, future prices can be expected to change as the market itself changes. Thus, more than anything else, technical analysis is intended to monitor the pulse of the supply-and-demand forces in the market and to detect any shifts.

Using Technical Analysis

Investors have a wide range of choices with respect to technical analysis. They can use the charts and complex ratios of the technical analysts. Or they can, more informally, use technical analysis just to get a general sense of the market. In the latter case, market behavior itself is not as important as the implications such behavior can have for the price performance of a particular stock. Thus, investors can use technical analysis in conjunction with fundamental analysis to determine when to add a particular stock to one's portfolio. Some investors and professional money managers, in fact, look at the technical side of a stock *before* doing any fundamental analysis. If they find the stock to be technically sound, then they'll look at its fundamentals; if not, they'll look for another stock. For these investors, the concerns of technical analysis are still the same: *Do the technical factors indicate that this might be a good stock to buy?*

Most investors rely on published sources, such as those put out by brokerage firms—or now widely available on the Internet—to obtain technical insights. Such information provides investors with a convenient and low-cost way of staying abreast of the market. Certainly, trying to determine the right (or best) time to get into the market is a principal objective of technical analysis—and one of the major pastimes of many investors.

Measuring the Market

If assessing the market is a worthwhile endeavor, then we need some sort of tool or measure to do it. Charts are popular with many investors because they provide a visual summary of the behavior of the market and the price movements of individual stocks. (We'll examine charting in more detail later in this chapter.) As an alternative or supplement to *charting*, some investors prefer to study various *market statistics*. They might look at the market as a whole, or track certain technical conditions that exist within the market itself, such as the volume of trading, the amount of short selling, or the buy/sell patterns of small investors (i.e., odd-lot transactions).

Let's now examine some of these approaches to technical analysis. Later, we'll look at some ratios and formulas that investors can use to measure—that is, quantify—various technical conditions in the market. One thing to keep in mind as you work your way through this material is that, whether the measures appear rational or not, many of them (like breadth of the market, or charting) involve a good deal of judgment and intuition. Thus, they rely heavily on the market expertise of the analysts.

▌ The Big Picture

Technical analysis addresses those factors in the marketplace that can (or may) have an effect on the price movements of stocks in general. The idea is to get a handle on the general condition (or "tone") of the market, and to gain some insights into where the market may be headed over the next few months. One way to do that is to look at *the overall behavior of the market*. Several approaches try to do just that, including (1) the Dow theory, (2) trading actions, and (3) the confidence index.

The Dow Theory The **Dow theory** is based on the idea that the market's performance can be described by the long-term price trend in the overall market. Named after Charles H. Dow, one of the founders of Dow Jones, this approach is supposed to signal the end of both bull and bear markets. The theory does not indicate *when* a reversal will occur; rather, it is strictly an after-the-fact verification of what has already happened. It concentrates on the long-term trend in market behavior (known as the *primary trend*) and largely ignores day-to-day fluctuations or secondary movements.

Dow theory
a technical approach based on the idea that the market's performance can be described by the long-term price trend in the DJIA, as confirmed by the Dow transportation average.

The Dow theory uses the Dow Jones industrial *and* transportation averages to assess the position of the market. Once a primary trend in the Dow Jones industrial average has been established, the market tends to move in that direction until the trend is canceled out by *both* the industrial and transportation averages. Known as *confirmation*, this crucial part of the Dow theory occurs when secondary movements in the industrial average are confirmed by secondary movements in the transportation average. When confirmation occurs, the market has changed from bull to bear, or vice versa, and a new primary trend is established. Figure 9.1 (on page 392) captures the key elements of the Dow theory. Observe that in this case, the bull market comes to an end at the point of confirmation—when *both* the industrial and transportation averages are dropping.

The biggest drawback of the Dow theory is that it is an after-the-fact measure with *no* predictive power. Also, the investor really does not know at any given point whether an existing primary trend has a long way to go or is just about to end.

Trading Action This approach to technical analysis concentrates on minor trading characteristics in the market. Daily trading activity over long periods of time (sometimes as long as 50 years or more) is examined to determine whether certain characteristics occur with a high degree of frequency. Although the empirical results generated from these studies are in many cases due to little more than statistical aberrations, analysts nonetheless use them to form a series of trading rules. Here are a few examples:

- If the year starts out strong (that is, if January is a good month for the market), the chances are that the whole year will be good.

- If the party in power wins the presidential election, it is also going to be a good year for the market.

- It is best to buy air conditioning stocks in October and sell the following March. (This buy-and-sell strategy was found to be significantly more profitable over the long haul than buy-and-hold.)

- Markets tend to go up or down with the hemlines on women's dresses.

INVESTOR FACTS

THREE'S THE CHARM—Wall Street is always on the lookout for clues as to where the market may be headed. One market adage that has an incredible track record is the *presidential third-year rule*. Specifically, this rule states that investors can expect attractive returns in the third year of a presidential term.

Indeed, the facts do bear out this prediction, as the third year has been the best, on average, of any president's 4-year term, Democrat or Republican alike. Since 1945, the average return in the third year of a president's term has been a whopping 17.4%, more than twice as high as in any of the other 3 years. Since World War II, the S&P 500 has *never* posted a loss in the third year of a presidential term. The reason: politics. Eager to impress voters, politicians tend to push legislation that will stimulate the economy in the year prior to an election. By the way, 2003 was President George W. Bush's third year in office, and the S&P was up some 26%.

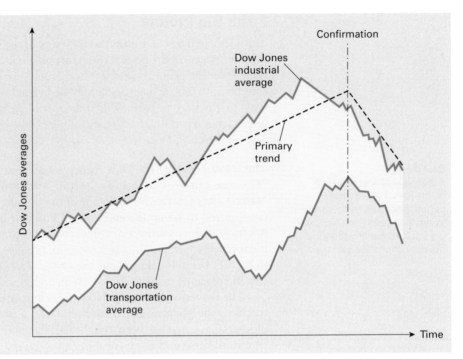

FIGURE 9.1

The Dow Theory in Operation

Secondary movements (the sharp, short fluctuations in the Dow Jones industrial and transportation lines) are largely unimportant to the Dow theory. What is of key importance, however, is the primary trend in the DJIA, which is seen to remain on the upswing until a reversal is confirmed by the transportation average.

- If a team from the National Football Conference (or one that was originally in the NFL, like Indianapolis or Pittsburgh) wins the Super Bowl, the market's in for a good year. (Don't laugh. For whatever reason—which no one seems to know—it's been correct for 32 of the last 39 Super Bowls, or 82% of the time.)

Clearly, the trading action approach is based on the simple assumption that the market moves in cycles and that these cycles have a tendency to repeat themselves. As a result, the contention seems to be that whatever has happened repeatedly in the past will probably reoccur in the future.

Confidence Index Another measure that attempts to capture the tone of the market is the **confidence index**, which deals not with the stock market but with *bond* returns. Computed and published weekly in *Barron's* (see "Market Laboratory—Bonds"), the confidence index is a ratio that reflects *the spread* between the average yield on high-grade corporate bonds relative to the yield on average- or intermediate-grade corporate bonds. Technically, the index is computed by relating the average yield on ten high-grade corporate bonds to the yield on the Dow Jones average of 40 bonds. The formula is as follows:

confidence index
a ratio of the average yield on high-grade corporate bonds to the average yield on average- or intermediate-grade corporate bonds; a technical indicator based on the theory that market trends usually appear in the bond market before they do in the stock market.

$$\text{Confidence Index} = \frac{\text{Average yield on 10 high-grade corporate bonds}}{\text{Yield on the Dow Jones average of 40 corporate bonds}}$$

Thus, the index measures the *yield spread* between high-grade bonds and a large cross-section of bonds. Because the yield on high-grade bonds should always be lower than the average yield on a large sample of low- to high-grade bonds, the confidence index should never exceed 1.0. Indeed, as the measure approaches equality (i.e., 100%), the *spread* between the two sets of bonds will get smaller and smaller—a positive sign.

Consider, for example, a point in time where high-grade bonds are yielding 4.50%, while corporate bonds, on average, are yielding 5.15%. This would amount to a yield spread of 65 "basis points," or 65/100 of 1% (i.e., 5.15% − 4.50% = 0.65%), and a confidence index of 4.50 ÷ 5.15 = 87.38%. Now, look what happens when yields (and yield spreads) fall or rise:

	Yields (Yield Spreads)	
	Fall	Rise
Yields on high-grade bonds	4.25%	5.25%
Yields on average bonds	4.50%	6.35%
Yield spread	25 b.p.	110 b.p.
Confidence spread	94.44%	82.68%

Lower yield spreads, in effect, lead to higher confidence indexes. These, in turn, *indicate that investors are demanding a lower premium in yield for the lower-rated (riskier) bonds, and in so doing, are showing more confidence in the economy.* The theory is that the trend of "smart money" is usually revealed in the bond market before it shows up in the stock market. So, a sustained rise in the confidence index suggests an increase in investor confidence and a stronger stock market; a drop in the index portends a softer tone.

■ Technical Conditions Within the Market

Another way to assess the market is to keep track of the variables that drive its behavior—things like the volume of trading, short sales, and odd-lot trading. Clearly, if these variables do, in fact, influence market prices, then it would be in an investor's best interest to keep tabs on them, at least informally. Let's now look at four of these market forces: (1) market volume, (2) breadth of the market, (3) short interest, and (4) odd-lot trading.

Market Volume Market volume is an obvious reflection of the amount of investor interest. Volume is a function of the supply of and demand for stock, and it indicates underlying market strengths and weaknesses. Investor eagerness to buy or sell is felt to be captured by market volume figures.

As a rule, the market is considered *strong* when volume goes up in a rising market or drops off during market declines. It is considered *weak* when volume rises during a decline or drops during rallies. For instance, the market would be considered strong if the Dow Jones Industrial Average went up by, say, 108 points while market volume was heavy.

The financial press regularly publishes volume data, so investors can easily watch this important technical indicator. An example of this and other vital market information is shown in Figure 9.2 (on page 394).

Breadth of the Market Each trading day, some stocks go up in price and others go down. In market terminology, some stocks *advance* and others *decline*. Breadth-of-the-market deals with these advances and declines. The principle behind this indicator is that the number of advances and declines reflects the underlying sentiment of investors.

FIGURE 9.2

Some Market Statistics

Individual investors can obtain all sorts of technical information at little or no cost from brokerage houses, investment services, the popular financial media, or the Internet. Here, for example, is a sample of the type of information available daily from the *Wall Street Journal*. Note that a variety of information about market volume, new highs and lows, number of advancing and declining stocks, and the most actively traded issues is available from this one source. (*Source: Wall Street Journal*, July 18, 2006.)

MARKETS SCORECARD

Monday, July 17, 2006 4 p.m. ET

Price Percentage Gainers... And Losers

Infosonics (A) $7.18, up 11.8%

CDC Cp A (Nq) $4.33, up 9.1%

ThrshldPhrm (Nq) $1.55, down 51.3%

SpectrmBrnds (N) $7.15, down 33.2%

ISSUE (EXCH)	VOLUME	CLOSE	CHG	% CHG
Perdigao ADS (N)	377,000	24.50	+4.25	+21.0
Arotech (Nq)	384,756	3.50	+0.48	+15.9
VimicroIntl ADS (Nq)	1,129,475	10.30	+1.30	+14.4
FlightSftyTch (A)	23,300	2.63	+0.30	+12.9
AuthntdtHldg (Nq)	179,375	2.36	+0.26	+12.5
Infosonics (A)	1,414,900	7.18	+0.76	+11.8
Mattel (N)	8,103,500	17.60	+1.72	+10.8
Qualstar (Nq)	4,641	3.39	+0.32	+10.4
Novogen ADS (Nq)	26,714	11.74	+1.08	+10.1
ElbitMed (Nq)	9,698	22.12	+2.02	+10.0
EMAK Wldwd (Nq)	3,314	5.21	+0.47	+9.9
Spectranet (Nq)	312,746	10.54	+0.94	+9.8
ArcadiaRes (A)	150,500	2.62	+0.22	+9.2
CDC Cp A (Nq)	2,359,914	4.33	+0.36	+9.1
MergeTch (Nq)	1,136,843	7.72	+0.64	+9.0
Pokertek (Nq)	37,281	8.84	+0.73	+9.0
NoTchInt (A)	4,200	7.89	+0.64	+8.8
BonTonStr (Nq)	714,333	22.07	+1.66	+8.1
ATS Med (Nq)	40,792	2.68	+0.20	+8.1
WhlngPitts (Nq)	473,491	19.26	+1.40	+7.8

ISSUE (EXCH)	VOLUME	CLOSE	CHG	% CHG
IMA Explr (A)	2,602,000	0.60	-2.43	-80.2
ThrshldPharm (Nq)	12,515,240	1.55	-1.63	-51.3
SpectrumBrnds (N)	9,369,700	7.15	-3.55	-33.2
Syntroleum wt08 (Nq)	20,800	1.81	-0.69	-27.6
pSivida (Nq)	21,339	3.25	-0.75	-18.8
AmTelecomSvc (A)	10,400	2.55	-0.46	-15.3
USG rt (N)	1,180,100	6.80	-1.18	-14.8
FieldPntPete (A)	159,900	4.57	-0.73	-13.8
Grainger (N)	4,660,800	63.00	-10.00	-13.7
OriginAgrtch (Nq)	274,862	11.24	-1.73	-13.3
Crucell ADS (Nq)	1,289,447	17.75	-2.64	-12.9
SGX Pharm (Nq)	41,269	4.84	-0.66	-12.0
PatrickInd (Nq)	16,206	9.25	-1.23	-11.7
Fortunet (Nq)	195,332	12.21	-1.59	-11.5
Syntroleum wt (Nq)	12,710	2.85	-0.35	-10.9
EmpireFnl (A)	17,300	2.90	-0.35	-10.8
Innovex (Nq)	101,762	3.48	-0.41	-10.5
HmSolAm (A)	1,121,987	6.53	-0.74	-10.2
HanaBiosci (Nq)	342,923	6.38	-0.72	-10.1
VarsityGroup (Nq)	57,867	3.04	-0.34	-10.1

Most Active Issues

ISSUE (EXCH)	VOLUME	CLOSE	CHG
Nasdaq 100 (Nq)	125,746,521	36.03	+0.09
SPDR (A)	75,260,800	123.34	-0.18
iShrRu2000 (A)	65,444,500	67.44	-0.09
Intel (Nq)	60,291,701	17.84	-0.04
LucentTch (N)	54,406,500	2.04	-0.02
CiscoSys (Nq)	41,375,064	17.97	+0.03
EMC Cp (N)	41,306,000	10.09	+0.26
Microsoft (Nq)	36,182,404	22.48	+0.19
AppleCptr (Nq)	35,849,791	52.37	+1.70
OracleCp (Nq)	32,365,295	14.42	+0.13
SPDR Engy (A)	32,323,400	55.95	-1.87
Citigroup (N)	30,285,000	46.40	-1.18

Diaries

	NYSE	NASDAQ	AMEX
Issues traded	3,457	3,156	1,042
Advances	1,370	1,108	319
Declines	1,927	1,903	652
Unchanged	160	145	71
New highs	21	10	10
New lows	140	190	62
zAdv vol (000s)	585,368	766,153	10,164
zDecl vol (000s)	850,491	692,698	39,503
zTotal vol (000s)	1,463,908	1,516,300	50,919
Closing Tick	+576	+162	-56
Closing Arms[1] (trin)	1.03	.53	1.90
zBlock trades	n.a.	p10,195	p886

Volume Percentage Leaders

ISSUE (EXCH)	VOLUME	% DIF*	CLOSE	CHG
WisdmTrSmCap (N)	149,800	2277.8	50.27	...
FstTrNas100Tch (Nq)	132,950	2217.8	16.12	-0.02
MerLynTargets (A)	63,700	1134.0	12.44	-0.13
SpectrumBrnds (N)	9,369,700	1126.0	7.15	-3.55
ClayRayJameSB1 (N)	149,400	952.1	17.45	-1.20
TelMviles ADS (N)	64,200	831.2	13.59	+0.02
Grainger (N)	4,660,800	810.5	63.00	-10.00
CapBk (Nq)	107,379	741.6	15.89	-0.32
ValorCommGrp (N)	6,203,800	729.1	11.50	-0.03
CooperT&R (N)	8,597,200	606.0	9.90	-0.04
RockyBrands (Nq)	306,156	582.9	12.15	-0.57
FairfaxFnl (N)	633,100	571.5	106.16	+0.90
Enel ADS (N)	528,900	566.7	42.23	+0.21

*Common stocks of $5 a share or more with average volume over 65 trading days of at least 5,000 shares. a-has traded fewer than 65 days

Breakdown of Trading

BY MARKET	NYSE	NASDAQ	AMEX
New York	1,463,908,000	...	4,619,500
Chicago	33,948,710	3,559,504	7,423,205
CBOE	...	...	112,900
NYSE Arca	145,201,700	346,491,763	114,412,600
Nasdaq MktCntr	505,254,820	1,147,925,686	158,202,955
NASD ADF†	...	14,822,300	...
Phila	1,192,800	...	...
Amex	...	316,200	50,918,638
Boston	9,086,600	...	1,437,700
National	11,563,400	3,185,008	3,398,900
Composite	2,170,156,030	1,516,300,461	340,526,398

NYSE first crossing n.a. shares, value n.a.
Second (basket) 43,935,155 shares, value 1,428,788,145
[1]A comparison of the number of advancing and declining issues with the volume of shares rising and falling. Generally, an Arms of less than 1.00 indicates buying demand; above 1.00 indicates selling pressure. p-previous day. z-primary market NYSE & Amex only. † Alternate Display Facility

The idea is actually quite simple: So long as the number of stocks that advance in price on a given day exceeds the number that decline, the market is considered strong. The extent of that strength depends on the spread between the number of advances and declines. For example, if the spread narrows (the number of declines starts to approach the number of advances), market strength is said to be deteriorating. Similarly, the market is considered weak when the number of declines repeatedly exceeds the number of advances. When the mood is optimistic, advances outnumber declines. Again, data on advances and declines are published daily in the financial press.

Short Interest   When investors anticipate a market decline, they sometimes sell a stock short. That is, they sell borrowed stock. The number of stocks sold short in the market at any given point in time is known as the **short interest**. The more stocks are sold short, the higher the short interest. Because all short sales must eventually be "covered" (the borrowed shares must be returned), a short sale in effect ensures *future demand for the stock*. Thus, the market is viewed optimistically when the level of short interest becomes relatively high by historical standards. The logic is that as shares are bought back to cover outstanding short sales, the additional demand will push stock prices up. The amount of short interest on the NYSE, the AMEX, and Nasdaq's National Market is published monthly in the *Wall Street Journal* and *Barron's*.

Keeping track of the level of short interest can indicate future market demand, but it can also reveal *present* market optimism or pessimism. Short selling is usually done by knowledgeable investors, and a significant buildup or decline in the level of short interest is thought to reveal the sentiment of sophisticated investors about the current state of the market or a company. For example, a significant shift upward in short interest is believed to indicate pessimism concerning the *current* state of the market, even though it may signal optimism with regard to *future* levels of demand.

Odd-Lot Trading   A rather cynical saying on Wall Street suggests that the best thing to do is just the opposite of whatever the small investor is doing. The reasoning behind this is that as a group, small investors are notoriously wrong in their timing of investment decisions: The investing public usually does not come into the market in force until after a bull market has pretty much run its course, and it does not get out until late in a bear market. Although its validity is debatable, this is the premise behind a widely followed technical indicator and is the basis for the **theory of contrary opinion**. This theory uses the amount and type of odd-lot trading as an indicator of the current state of the market and pending changes.

Because many individual investors deal in transactions of less than 100 shares, their combined sentiments are supposedly captured in odd-lot figures. The idea is to see what odd-lot investors "on balance" are doing. So long as there is little or no difference in the spread between the volume of odd-lot purchases and sales, the theory of contrary opinion holds that the market will probably continue pretty much along its current line (either up or down). A dramatic change in the balance of odd-lot purchases and sales may be a signal that a bull or bear market is about to end. For example, if the amount of odd-lot purchases starts to exceed odd-lot sales by an ever-widening margin, speculation on the part of small investors may be starting to get out of control—an ominous signal that the final stages of a bull market may be at hand.

short interest
the number of stocks sold short in the market at any given time; a technical indicator believed to indicate future market demand.

theory of contrary opinion
a technical indicator that uses the amount and type of odd-lot trading as an indicator of the current state of the market and pending changes.

market technicians
analysts who believe it is chiefly (or solely) supply and demand that drive stock prices.

INVESTOR FACTS

INDICATORS CAN BE KEY—
Before you turn to charts to get price and volume data for a particular stock, take the pulse of the overall market by looking at indicators in different categories. Here are a few to add to your analytical tool box:

- **Interest rates:** Looking at the financial futures market can help you get a sense of where interest rates are heading, because financial institutions often buy forward contracts to lock in their borrowing rates.

- **Capital goods back orders:** Tracked by the Department of Commerce, an increase in this indicator means that companies are ordering goods, which means they anticipate growth.

- **Volatility:** When the Nasdaq Volatility Index (VXZ) and the Market Volatility Index (VIX) are low, a drop in the market may be ahead.

▮ Trading Rules and Measures

Market technicians—analysts who believe it is chiefly (or solely) supply and demand that drive stock prices—use a variety of mathematical equations and measures to assess the underlying condition of the market. These analysts often use computers to produce the measures, plotting them on a daily basis. They then use those measures as indicators of when to get into or out of the market or a particular stock. In essence, *they develop trading rules based on these market measures.* Technical analysts almost always use several of these market measures, rather than just one (or two), because one measure rarely works the same way for all stocks. Moreover, they generally look for *confirmation* of one measure by *another.* In other words, market analysts like to see three or four of these ratios and measures all pointing in the same direction.

There are no "magic" numbers associated with these indicators. Some analysts may consider 20% and 80% to be "critical" levels for an indicator; others may use 40% and 60% for the same indicator. Market technicians often determine the critical levels by using a process known as *backtesting*, which involves using historical price data to generate buy and sell signals. That is, they compute the profits generated from a series of trading rules and then try to find the indicators that generate the greatest amount of profits. Those measures then become the buy and sell signals for the various market indicators they employ.

Although literally dozens of these market measures and trading rules exist, we'll confine our discussion here to some of the more widely used technical indicators: (1) advance-decline lines; (2) new highs and lows; (3) the arms index; (4) the mutual fund cash ratio; and (5) on balance volume. In addition to these, the *Investing in Action* box on page 397 describes yet another popular market measure, the *relative strength index (RSI)*.

Advance-Decline Line Each trading day, the NYSE, AMEX, and Nasdaq publish statistics on how many of their stocks closed higher on the day (i.e., *advanced* in price) and how many closed lower (*declined* in price). The *advance-decline line*, or *A/D line*, is simply the difference between these two numbers. To calculate it, you take the number of stocks that have risen in price and subtract the number that have declined, usually for the previous day. For example, if 1,000 issues advanced on a day when 450 issues declined, the day's *net number* would be 550 (i.e., 1,000 − 450). If 450 advanced and 1,000 declined, the net number would be −550 (450 − 1,000). *Each day's net number is then added to (or subtracted from) the running total, and the result is plotted on a graph.*

If the graph is rising, the advancing issues are dominating the declining issues, and the market is considered strong. When declining issues start to dominate, the graph will turn down as the market begins to soften. Technicians use the A/D line as a signal for when to buy or sell stocks.

New Highs–New Lows This measure is similar to the advance-decline line, but looks at price movements over a longer period of time. A stock is defined as reaching a "new high" if its current price is at the highest level it has been over the past year (sometimes referred to as the "52-week high"). Conversely, a stock makes a "new low" if its current price is at the lowest level it has been over the past year.

INVESTING *in Action*

Finding Strong Stocks Can Be a Matter of Relative Strength

One of the most widely used technical indicators is the *relative strength index (RSI)*, an index measuring a security's strength of advances and declines over time. The RSI indicates a security's momentum, and gives the best results when used for short trading periods. It also helps identify market extremes, signaling a security is approaching its price top or bottom and may soon reverse trend. The RSI is the ratio of average price change on "up days" to the average price change on "down days" during the same period. The index formula is

$$RSI = 100 - \left[100 / \left(1 + \frac{\text{Average price change on up days}}{\text{Average price change on down days}}\right)\right]$$

The RSI can cover various periods of time (days, weeks, or months). The most common RSIs are 9-, 14-, and 25-period RSIs.

The RSI ranges between 0 and 100, with most RSIs falling between 30 and 70. Generally, values above 70 or 80 indicate an *overbought* condition (more and stronger buying than fundamentals would justify). RSI values below 30 indicate a possible *oversold* condition (more selling than fundamentals may indicate). When the RSI crosses these points, it signals a possible trend reversal. The wider 80–20 range is often used with the 9-day RSI, which tends to be more volatile than longer-period RSIs. In bull markets, 80 may be a better upper indicator than 70; in bear markets, 20 is a more accurate lower level. Different sectors and industries may have varying RSI threshold levels.

To use the RSI in their own trading, investors set buy and sell ranges—such as sell when the RSI crosses below 70 and buy when it moves above 30. Another strategy is to compare RSIs with stock charts. Most of the time both move in the same direction, but a divergence between RSI and a price chart can be a strong predictor of a changing trend.

Like many other technical indicators, the RSI should not be used alone. It works best in combination with other tools such as charting, moving averages, and trendlines. Among the Web sites that offer RSI as a charting option are BigCharts (www.bigcharts.com), Yahoo! Finance (finance.yahoo.com), and StockCharts (www.stockcharts.com).

CRITICAL THINKING QUESTION Explain how the relative strength index can help investors identify changing price trends. Then go to StockCharts.com and pull up charts for ExxonMobil (XOM) and UPS (UPS). What does the RSI tell you about these stocks?

The *new highs–new lows (NH-NL) indicator* is computed as the number of stocks reaching new 52-week highs minus the number reaching new lows. Thus, you end up with a *net number*, which can be either positive (when new highs dominate) or negative (when new lows exceed new highs), just like with the advance-decline line. To smooth out the daily fluctuations, *the net number is often added to (or subtracted from) a 10-day moving average, and then plotted on a graph.*

As you might have guessed, a graph that's increasing over time indicates a strong market, where new highs are dominating. A declining graph indicates a weak market, where new lows are more common than new highs. Technicians following a momentum-based strategy will buy stocks when new highs dominate and sell them when there are more new lows than new highs. Alternatively, they might use the indicator to rotate money into stocks when the market looks strong, and to rotate out of stocks and into cash or bonds when the market looks weak.

The Arms Index This indicator, also known as the TRIN, for *trading index*, builds on the advance-decline line by considering *the volume* in advancing and declining stocks in addition to *the number of stocks* rising or falling in price. The formula is

$$\text{TRIN} = \frac{\text{Number of up stocks}}{\text{Number of down stocks}} \div \frac{\text{Volume in up stocks}}{\text{Volume in down stocks}}$$

For example, suppose we are analyzing the S&P 500. Assume that on a given day, 300 of these stocks rose in price and 200 fell in price. Also assume that the total trading volume in the rising ("up") stocks was 400 million shares, and the total trading volume in the falling ("down") stocks was 800 million shares. The value of the TRIN for the day would be

$$\text{TRIN} = \frac{300}{200} \div \frac{400 \text{ million}}{800 \text{ million}} = 3.0$$

Alternatively, suppose the volume in up stocks was 700 million shares, and the volume in down stocks was 300 million. The value of the TRIN then would be

$$\text{TRIN} = \frac{300}{200} \div \frac{700 \text{ million}}{300 \text{ million}} = 0.64$$

Higher TRIN values are interpreted as being bad for the market, because even though more stocks rose than fell, the trading volume in the falling stocks was much greater. The underlying idea is that a strong market is characterized by more stocks rising in price than falling, *along with greater volume in the rising stocks than in the falling ones*, as in the second example.

Mutual Fund Cash Ratio This indicator looks at the cash position of mutual funds as an indicator of future market performance. The *mutual fund cash ratio (MFCR)* measures the percentage of mutual fund assets that are held in cash. It is computed as follows:

$$\text{MFCR} = \text{Mutual fund cash position} \div \text{Total assets under management}$$

The assumption is that the higher the MFCR, the stronger the market. Indeed, the ratio is considered very bullish when it moves to abnormally high levels (i.e., when mutual fund cash exceeds 10% to 12% of total assets). It is seen as bearish when the ratio drops to very low levels (e.g., less than 5% of assets). The logic goes as follows: When fund managers hold a lot of cash (when the MFCR is high), that's good news for the market, because they will eventually have to invest that cash, buying stocks and causing prices to rise. If fund managers hold very little cash, investors might be concerned for two reasons. First, there is less demand for stocks if most of the cash is already invested. Second, if the market takes a downturn, investors might want to withdraw their money. Fund managers will then have to sell some of their stocks to accommodate these redemptions, putting additional downward pressure on prices.

On Balance Volume Technical analysts usually consider *stock prices* to be the key measure of market activity. However, they also consider *trading volume* as a secondary indicator. *On-balance volume (OBV)* is a momentum indicator that relates volume to price change. It uses trading volume in addition to price and *tracks trading volume as a running total*. In this way, OBV indicates whether volume is flowing into or out of a security. When the security closes higher than its previous close, all the day's volume is considered "up-volume," all of which is *added to the running total*. In contrast, when a stock closes lower, all the day's volume is considered "down-volume," which is then *subtracted from the running total*.

The OBV indicator is used to *confirm* price trends. According to this measure, you want to see a lot of volume when a stock's price is rising, because that would suggest that the stock will go even higher. On the other hand, if prices are rising but OBV is falling, technical analysts would describe the situation as a *divergence* and interpret it as a sign of possible weakness.

When analyzing OBV, it is the direction or trend that is important, not the actual value. To begin the computation of OBV, you can start with an arbitrary number, such as 50,000. Suppose you are calculating the OBV for a stock that closed yesterday at a price of $50 per share, and you start with an OBV value of 50,000. Assume that the stock trades 80,000 shares today and closes at $49. Because the stock declined in price, we would subtract the full 80,000 shares from the previous balance (our starting point of 50,000); now the OBV is $50,000 - 80,000 = -30,000$. (Note that the OBV is simply the *trading volume running total*.) If the stock trades 120,000 shares on the following day and closes up at $52 per share, we would then *add* all of those 120,000 shares to the previous day's OBV: $-30,000 + 120,000 = +90,000$. This process would continue day after day. The normal procedure is to plot these daily OBVs on a graph. As long as the graph is moving up, it's bullish; when the graph starts moving down, it's bearish.

▮ Charting

charting
the activity of charting price behavior and other market information and then using the patterns these charts form to make investment decisions.

Charting is perhaps the best-known activity of the technical analyst. Indeed, technical analysts use various types of charts to plot the behavior of everything from the Dow Jones Industrial Average and share price movements of individual stocks to moving averages (see below) and advance-decline lines. In fact, as noted above, just about every type of technical indicator is charted in one form or another. Figure 9.3 (on page 400) shows a typical stock chart. In this case, the chart plots the price behavior of Nike, Inc., along with a variety of supplementary technical information about the stock.

Charts are popular because they provide a visual summary of activity over time. Perhaps more important (in the eyes of technicians, at least), they contain valuable information about developing trends and the future behavior of the market and/or individual stocks. Chartists believe price patterns evolve into *chart formations* that provide signals about the future course of the market or a stock. We will now briefly review the popular types of charts, chart formations, and the use of moving averages.

bar chart
the simplest kind of chart, on which share price is plotted on the vertical axis and time on the horizontal axis; stock prices are recorded as vertical bars showing high, low, and closing prices.

Bar Charts The simplest and probably most widely used type of chart is the **bar chart**. They show market or share prices on the vertical axis, and time on the horizontal axis. This type of chart derives its name from the fact that prices

FIGURE 9.3   **A Stock Chart**

This chart for Nike, Inc., contains information about the daily price behavior of the stock, along with the stock's relative strength, its moving average, its trading volume, and several other pieces of supplementary data. (*Source:* Chart courtesy of Stockcharts.com, accessed October 23, 2006. *Note:* Visit this Web site's glossary for expanded definitions.)

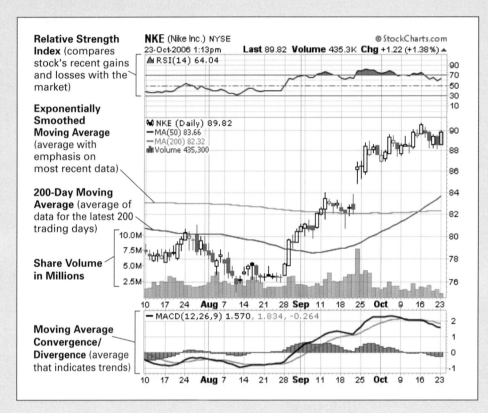

are recorded as vertical bars that depict high, low, and closing prices. A typical bar chart is shown in Figure 9.4. Note that on December 31, this particular stock had a high price of 29, a low of 27, and it closed at 27.50. Because these charts contain a time element, technicians frequently plot a variety of other pertinent information on them. For example, volume is often put at the base of bar charts (see the Nike chart in Figure 9.3).

Point-and-Figure Charts Point-and-figure charts are used strictly to keep track of emerging price patterns. Because there is no time dimension on them, they are *not* used for plotting technical measures. (Note that while there is no indication of time on the horizontal axis of point-and-figure charts, technical analysts/chartists will often keep track of significant dates or points in time by placing letters or numbers directly on the body of the chart itself.)

In addition to their treatment of time, point-and-figure charts are unique in two other ways. First, these charts record only *significant* price changes. That is, prices have to move by a certain minimum amount—usually at least a point or two—before a new price level is recognized. Second, price *reversals* show up

point-and figure charts
charts used to keep track of emerging price patterns by plotting significant price changes with *X*'s and *O*'s but with no time dimension used.

FIGURE 9.4

A Bar Chart

Bar charts are widely used to track stock prices, market averages, and numerous other technical measures.

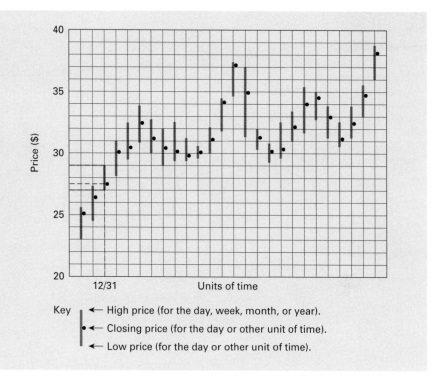

Key
- ← High price (for the day, week, month, or year).
- ← Closing price (for the day or other unit of time).
- ← Low price (for the day or other unit of time).

only after a predetermined change in direction occurs. Normally, only closing prices are charted, though some point-and-figure charts use all price changes during the day. An *X* denotes an increase in price, an *O* denotes a decrease.

Figure 9.5 (on page 402) shows a common point-and-figure chart. In this case, the chart employs a 2-point box: That is, the stock must move by a minimum of 2 points before any changes are recorded. The chart can cover a span of one year or less if the stock is highly active. Or it can cover a number of years if the stock is not very active. As a rule, low-priced stocks are charted with 1-point boxes, moderately priced shares with increments of 2 to 3 points, and high-priced securities with 3- to 5-point boxes.

Here is how point-and-figure charts work: Suppose we are at point A on the chart in Figure 9.5. The stock has been hovering around this $40–$41 mark for some time. Assume, however, that it just closed at $42.25. Now, because the minimum 2-point movement has been met, the chartist would place an X in the box immediately *above* point A. He or she would remain with this new box as long as the price moved (up or down) within the 2-point range of 42 to 44. Although the chartist follows *daily* prices, he or she would make a new entry on the chart only after the price has changed by a certain minimum amount and moved into a new 2-point box. We see that from point A, the price generally moved up over time to nearly $50 a share. At that point (point B on the chart), things began to change as a reversal set in. The price of the stock began to drift downward and in time moved out of the $48–$50 box. This reversal prompts the chartist to change columns and symbols, by moving one column to the right and recording the new price level with an O in the $46–$48 box. The chartist will continue to use O's as long as the stock continues to close on a generally lower note.

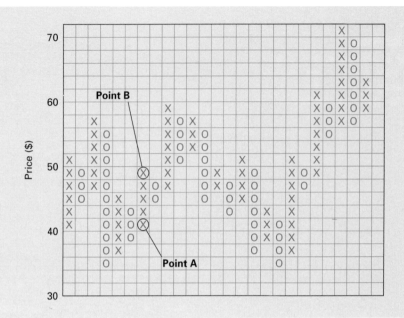

FIGURE 9.5

A Point-and-Figure Chart

Point-and-figure charts are unusual because they have no time dimension. Rather, a column of *X*'s is used to reflect a general upward drift in prices, and a column of *O*'s is used when prices are drifting downward.

Chart Formations A chart by itself tells you little more than where the market or a stock has been. But to chartists, those price patterns yield formations that tell them what to expect in the future. Chartists believe that history repeats itself, so they study the historical reactions of stocks (or the market) to various formations, and they devise trading rules based on these observations. It makes no difference to chartists whether they are following the market or an individual stock. *It is the formation that matters*, not the issue being plotted. If you know how to interpret charts (which is no easy task), you can see formations building and recognize buy and sell signals. These chart formations are often given exotic names, such as *head and shoulders*, *falling wedge*, *scallop and saucer*, *ascending triangle*, and *island reversal*, to name just a few.

Figure 9.6 shows six of these formations. The patterns form "support levels" and "resistance lines" that, when combined with the basic formations, yield buy and sell signals. Panel A is an example of a *buy* signal that occurs when prices break out above a resistance line in a particular pattern. In contrast, when prices break out below a support level, as they do at the end of the formation in panel B, a *sell* signal is said to occur. Supposedly, a sell signal means everything is in place for a major drop in the market (or in the price of a share of stock). A buy signal indicates that the opposite is about to occur.

Unfortunately, one of the major problems with charting is that the formations rarely appear as neatly and cleanly as those in Figure 9.6. Rather, identifying and interpreting them often demands considerable imagination.

Moving Averages
One problem with daily price charts is that they may contain a lot of often meaningless short-term price swings that mask the overall trend in prices. As a result, technical analysts will often use moving averages not only to eliminate those minor blips, but also to highlight underlying trends. A **moving average (MA)** is a mathematical procedure that records the average value of a series of prices, or other data, over time. Because they incorporate a

moving average (MA)
a mathematical procedure that computes and records the average values of a series of prices, or other data, over time; results in a stream of average values that will act to smooth out a series of data.

FIGURE 9.6 Some Popular Chart Formations

To chartists, each of these formations has meaning about the future course of events.

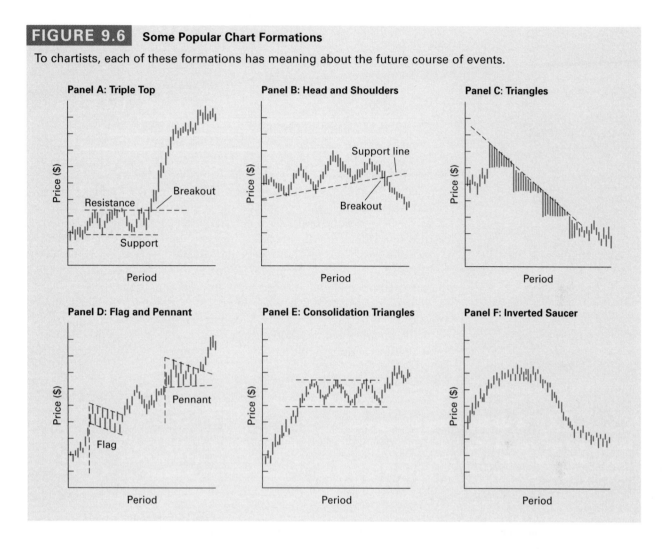

stream of these average values, MAs will smooth out a data series and make it easier to spot trends. The moving average is one of the oldest and most popular technical indicators. It can, in fact, be used not only with share prices, but also with market indexes and even other technical measures.

Moving averages are computed over periods ranging from 10 to 200 days—meaning that from 10 to 200 data points are used in each calculation. For example, a series of 15 data points is used in a 15-day moving average. The length of the time period has a bearing on how the MA will behave. Shorter periods (10 to 30 days) are more sensitive and tend to more closely track actual daily behavior. Longer periods (say, 100 to 200 days) are smoother and do a better job of picking up the major trends. Several types of moving averages exist, with the most common (and the one we'll use here) being the *simple average*, which gives equal weight to each observation. In contrast, there are other procedures that give more weight to the most recent data points (e.g., the "exponential" and "weighted" averages) or apply more weight to the middle of the time period (e.g., "triangular" averages).

Using closing share prices as the basis of discussion, we can calculate the simple moving average by adding up the closing prices over a given time period (e.g., 10 days), and then dividing this total by the length of the time period. Thus, *the simple moving average is nothing more than the arithmetic mean*. To illustrate, consider the following stream of closing share prices:

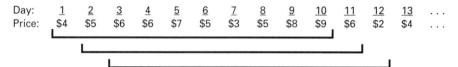

Using a 10-day moving average, we add up the closing prices for days 1 through 10 ($4 + $5 + · · · + $8 + $9 = $58) and then divide this total by 10 ($58/10 = $5.8). Thus, the average closing price for this 10-day period was $5.80. The next day, the process is repeated once again for days 2 through 11; that turns out to be $60/10 = $6.00. This procedure is repeated each day, so that over time we have a series of these individual averages that, when linked together, form a *moving-average line*. This line is then plotted on a chart, either by itself or along with other market information.

Figure 9.7 shows a 100-day moving average (the bold blue line) plotted against the daily closing prices for Nike, Inc. In contrast to the actual closing prices, the moving average provides a much smoother line, without all the short-term fluctuations; it clearly reveals the general trend in prices for this stock.

FIGURE 9.7 **A 100-Day Moving Average Line**

Moving average lines are often plotted along with the actual daily (or weekly) closing prices for a stock. They're also widely used with market indexes, such as the S&P 500, and a variety of technical indicators, including the advance-decline line. (*Source:* Chart courtesy of Stockcharts.com, accessed July 18, 2006.)

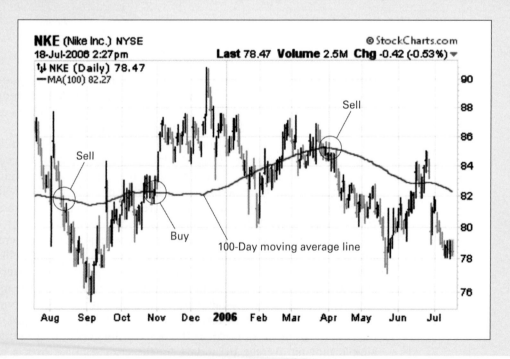

Technicians will often use charts like the one in Figure 9.7 to help them make buy and sell decisions about a stock. Specifically, if the security's price starts moving above the moving average, they read that situation as a good time to buy, because prices should be drifting up (see the buy signal on the chart). In contrast, a sell signal occurs when the security's price moves below the moving average line (see the two sell signals). Such a trading rule is not intended to get you in at the exact bottom or out at the exact top. Instead, it's meant to keep you in line with the security's price trend by buying shortly after the price hits the bottom and selling shortly after it reaches the top. And as seen in the figure, it does a fairly good job of that.

CONCEPTS IN REVIEW
Answers available at: www.myfinancelab.com

9.1 What is the purpose of *technical analysis*? Explain how and why it is used by technicians; note how it can be helpful in timing investment decisions.

9.2 Can the market really have a measurable effect on the price behavior of individual securities? Explain.

9.3 What is the *Dow theory*, and how is it used to analyze the market? Describe the *confidence index*, and note the feature that makes it unique.

9.4 Briefly describe each of the following, and explain how it is used in technical analysis:
    a. Breadth of the market.
    b. Short interest.
    c. Odd-lot trading.

9.5 Briefly describe each of the following, and note how it is computed and how it is used by technicians:
    a. Advance-decline lines.   b. Arms index.
    c. On-balance volume.   d Relative strength index.
    e. Moving averages.

9.6 What is a stock chart? What kind of information can be put on charts, and what is the purpose of charting?
    a. What is the difference between a bar chart and a point-and-figure chart?
    b. What are chart formations, and why are they important?

Random Walks and Efficient Markets

LG 4   LG 5

random walk hypothesis
the theory that stock price movements are unpredictable, so there's no way to know where prices are headed.

If a drunk were abandoned in an open field at night, where would you begin to search for him the next morning? The answer, of course, is at the spot where he was left the night before, because there's no way to predict where he will go. To some analysts, stock prices seem to wander about in a similar fashion. Observations of such erratic movements have led to a body of evidence called the **random walk hypothesis**. Its followers believe that price movements are unpredictable and therefore security analysis will not help to predict future market behavior. This hypothesis sharply contradicts the entire concept of technical analysis. In fact, it has serious implications for much of what we've discussed in this and the last two chapters.

▮ A Brief Historical Overview

To describe stock prices as a random walk suggests that we cannot expect price movements to follow any type of pattern. Or, put another way, price movements are independent of one another. To find a theory for such behavior, researchers developed the concept of efficient markets. The basic idea behind an efficient market is that the market price of securities always fully reflects available information, and as a result, it is difficult, if not impossible, to *consistently* outperform the market by picking "undervalued" stocks.

Random Walks   The first evidence of random price movements dates back to the early 1900s. During that period, statisticians noticed that commodity prices seemed to follow a "fair game" pattern. That is, prices seemed to move up and down randomly, giving no advantage to any particular trading strategy. Although a few studies on the subject appeared in the 1930s, thorough examination of the randomness in stock prices did not begin until 1959. From that point on, particularly through the decade of the 1960s, the random walk issue was one of the most keenly debated topics in stock market literature. The development of high-speed computers has helped researchers compile convincing evidence that stock prices do, in fact, come very close to a random walk.

Efficient Markets   Given the extensive random walk evidence, market researchers were faced with another question: What sort of market would produce prices that seem to fluctuate randomly? Such behavior could be the result of investors who are irrational and make investment decisions on whim. However, it has been argued much more convincingly that investors are not irrational. Rather, random price movements are evidence of highly efficient markets.

As discussed briefly in Chapter 7, an **efficient market** is one in which security prices fully reflect all possible information. The concept holds that investors quickly incorporate all available information into their decisions about the price at which they are willing to buy or sell stocks. At any point in time, then, the current price incorporates all information. Additionally, the current price reflects not only past information (such as might be found in company reports), but also information about events that have been announced but haven't yet occurred (like a forthcoming dividend payment). Even *predictions* about future information become embedded in current share prices—which, of course, happens all the time as investors actively forecast important events and incorporate those forecasts into their estimates.

Because of keen competition among investors, when new information becomes known, the price of the security adjusts quickly. This adjustment is not always perfect. Sometimes it is too large and at other times too small. On average, however, it balances out and is correct. The new price, in effect, is set after investors have fully assessed the new information.

efficient market
a market in which securities reflect all possible information quickly and accurately.

▮ Why Should Markets Be Efficient?

Active markets, such as the New York Stock Exchange, are efficient because they are made up of many rational, highly competitive investors who react quickly and objectively to new information. Investors, searching for market

efficient markets hypothesis (EMH)
basic theory of the behavior of efficient markets, in which there are a large number of knowledgeable investors who react quickly to new information, causing securities prices to adjust quickly and accurately.

profits, compete vigorously for new information and do extremely thorough analyses. The **efficient market hypothesis (EMH)**, which is the basic theory describing the behavior of such a market, has several tenets:

1. There are many knowledgeable and competitive investors actively analyzing, valuing, and trading any particular security. No one of these individual traders alone can affect the price of any security.
2. Information is widely available to all investors at approximately the same time, and this information is practically "free," or nearly so.
3. Information on events, such as labor strikes, industrial accidents, and changes in product demand, tends to emerge randomly.
4. Investors react quickly and accurately to new information, causing prices to adjust quickly and, on average, accurately.

The prevailing evidence is that, for the most part, the securities markets do, in fact, exhibit these characteristics.

▍Levels of Market Efficiency

The efficient market hypothesis is concerned with *information*—not only the type and source of information, but also the quality and speed with which it is disseminated among investors. It is convenient to discuss the EMH in three cumulative categories or forms:

- past prices only;

- past prices *plus* all other public data;

- past prices and public data *plus* private information.

Together, these three ways of looking at information flows in the market represent three forms of the EMH: the weak, semi-strong, and strong forms.

weak form (EMH)
form of the EMH holding that past data on stock prices are of no use in predicting future prices.

Weak Form The **weak form of the EMH** holds that past data on stock prices are of no use in predicting future price changes. If prices follow a random walk, then price changes over time are random. Today's price change is unrelated to yesterday's or to that of any other day, just as each step by a drunk is unrelated to previous steps. If new information arrives randomly, then prices will change randomly.

A number of people have asserted that it is possible to profit from "runs" in a stock's price. They contend that when a stock's price starts moving up, it will continue to move up for a period of time, developing momentum. If you could spot a run, then, on the basis of past prices alone, you could develop a trading strategy that would produce a profit. The results from much careful research suggest that momentum in stock prices *does* exist, and if investors quickly trade at the beginning of the run, large profits can be made. But there's a problem: In addition to spotting a run (no easy task), an investor would have to make numerous trades. Thus, when commissions are factored in, the person most likely to make a profit is the broker.

Many other trading rules have been tested to determine whether profits can be made by examining past price movements, and there is very little, if any, evidence that a trading rule *based solely on past price data* can outperform a simple buy-and-hold strategy.

semi-strong form (EMH)
form of the EMH holding that abnormally large profits cannot be consistently earned using publicly available information.

Semi-strong Form The **semi-strong form of the EMH** holds that abnormally large profits cannot be consistently earned using publicly available information. This information includes not only past price and volume data but also data such as corporate earnings, dividends, inflation, and stock splits. The semi-strong information set includes all of the information publicly considered in the weak form, *as well as all other information publicly available*. Tests of the semi-strong form of the EMH are basically concerned with the speed at which information is disseminated to investors. Research results generally support the position that stock prices adjust rapidly to new information and therefore support the semi-strong form of the EMH.

Most tests of semi-strong efficiency have examined how a stock price changes in response to an economic or financial event. A famous study involved stock splits. A stock split does not change the value of a company, so the value of the stock should not be affected by a stock split. The research indicated that there are sharp increases in the price of a stock *before* a stock split, but the changes after the split are random. Investors, therefore, cannot gain by purchasing stocks on or after the announcement of a split. To earn abnormal profits they would have to purchase before the split is announced. By the time of the announcement, the market has already incorporated into the price any favorable information associated with the split.

Other studies have examined the effects of major events on stock prices. The overwhelming evidence indicates that stock prices react within minutes, if not seconds, to any important new information. Certainly, by the time an investor reads about the event in the newspaper, the stock price has almost completely adjusted to the news. Even hearing about the event on the radio or television usually allows too little time to complete the transaction in time to make an abnormal profit.

strong form (EMH)
form of the EMH that holds that there is no information, public or private, that allows investors to consistently earn abnormal profits.

Strong Form The **strong form of the EMH** holds that there is no information, public or private, that allows investors to consistently earn abnormal returns. It states that stock prices immediately adjust to any information, even if it isn't available to every investor. This extreme form of the EMH has not received universal support.

One type of private information is the kind obtained by corporate insiders, such as officers or directors of a corporation. They have access to valuable information about major strategic and tactical decisions the company makes. They also have detailed information about the financial state of the firm that may not be available to other shareholders. Corporate insiders may legally trade shares of stock in their company, if they report the transactions to the Securities and Exchange Commission (SEC) each month. This information is then made public, usually within several weeks. Most studies of corporate insiders find that they can earn abnormally large profits when they sell their company stock. This, of course, is contrary to what you'd expect to find if the strong form of the EMH were true.

Other market participants occasionally have inside—nonpublic—information that they obtained *illegally*. With this information, they can gain an unfair advantage that permits them to earn an excess return. Clearly, those who trade securities on the basis of illegal inside information have an unfair advantage. Empirical research has confirmed that those with such inside information do indeed have an opportunity to earn an excess return—but there might be an awfully high price attached, such as spending time in prison, if they're caught.

INVESTOR FACTS

IT'S HARD TO BEAT THE MARKET—That's pretty much the message that the EMH has for investors. As such, trading in and out of securities wouldn't seem to make much sense. And that's exactly what was found in a recent study of over 66,000 investors, grouped according to annual portfolio turnover (how much of the portfolio the investor replaces each year). Buy-and-hold investors, with turnovers of less than 2% a year, earned annual returns of 18.5%. On the other end of the spectrum, the most active traders, with 258% portfolio turnover, averaged only 11.4% per year, a full 7 percentage points less than the more conservative, buy-and-hold investors.

▮ Market Anomalies

Despite considerable evidence in support of the EMH, there still exist some curious and as yet unexplained empirical results. In effect, some of the empirical studies have produced results that differed from what might be expected in a truly efficient market. These deviations from the norm are referred to as **market anomalies**, and they represent *behavior that contradicts the EMH*. Most of these anomalies, by the way, grew out of studies that were testing the semi-strong version of the EMH. Keep in mind that these are *empirical anomalies* and *should not be viewed as trading rules that will enable you to consistently outperform the market*. Rather, they are areas that have yet to be fully explained—and may exist only because of the capability of computers to search through millions of pieces of data in search of interesting correlations and associations.

market anomalies
irregularities or deviations from the behavior one would expect in an efficient market.

Furthermore, the behavior embedded in a market anomaly, such as the small-firm effect (which we'll examine below), may be true over very long test periods of several *decades* or more, but that doesn't mean they will necessarily hold up each and every year, or over shorter periods of time. Indeed, there may be periods as long as five or ten years, over which time these market anomalies do not hold up. In other words, in that period they behave just like the EMH says they should, and as a result, there's little or no opportunity to consistently generate excess returns.

Calendar Effects One widely cited anomaly is the so-called *calendar effect*, which holds that stock returns may be closely tied to the time of the year or the time of the week. That is, certain months or days of the week may produce better investment results than others. For example, the *January effect* shows a seasonality in the stock market, with a tendency for small-stock prices to go up during the month of January. Some explanations offer a tax-based reason for the phenomenon, but a completely satisfactory explanation has yet to be offered. The *weekend effect* is the result of evidence that stock returns, on average, are negative from the close of trading on Fridays until the close of trading on Mondays. The ability to consistently earn abnormal returns from using trading rules based on these results is still very questionable.

Small-Firm Effect Another anomaly is the *small-firm effect*, or size effect, which states that the size of the firm has a bearing on the level of stock returns. Indeed, several studies have shown that small firms (or small-cap stocks) earn higher returns than large-cap stocks, even after adjusting for risk and other considerations. Whether this is an invalidation of the EMH, or a problem with misspecification of the mathematical models, remains to be seen.

Earnings Announcements Another market anomaly has to do with how stock prices react to *earnings announcements*. Obviously, earnings announcements contain important information that should, and does, affect stock prices. However, much of the information has already been anticipated by the market, and so—if EMH is correct—prices should only react to the "surprise" portion of the announcement. Studies have shown, in fact, that a substantial amount of the price adjustment does occur prior to the actual announcement, but there is also a surprisingly large adjustment for some time after the announcement. In an efficient market, the prices should adjust quickly to any surprises in the earnings announcement. The fact that they take several days (or even weeks) to fully adjust remains something of a mystery.

Additionally, there is some documentation that abnormally large returns can consistently be obtained by buying stocks after unusually good *quarterly* earnings reports, and selling stocks after unusually bad *quarterly* earnings reports. This suggests that the majority of market investors don't bother to read and evaluate quarterly reports, but instead concentrate only on annual reports.

P/E Effect   According to the *P/E effect*, the best way to make money in the market is to stick with stocks that have relatively low P/E ratios. As discussed earlier, the P/E multiple is widely followed in the market and widely used in the stock valuation process. Studies have shown that, on average, low P/E stocks outperform high P/E stocks, even after adjusting for risk and other factors. The reason has not been determined, but it appears that the results have endured over a long period. Since the P/E ratio is public information, it should be fully reflected in the current price, and purchasing low P/E stocks should not produce larger profits, if the markets are even reasonably efficient.

▮ Possible Implications

The concept of an efficient market holds serious implications for investors. In particular, it could have considerable bearing on traditional security analysis and stock valuation procedures. Some, in fact, contend that investors should spend less time analyzing securities and more time on such matters as reducing taxes and transaction costs, eliminating unnecessary risk, and constructing a widely diversified portfolio. Make no mistake about it: *Even in an efficient market, all sorts of return opportunities are available*. But to proponents of efficient markets, the only way to increase returns is to invest in a portfolio of higher-risk securities.

Implications for Technical Analysis   The most serious challenge the EMH evidence presents is to technical analysis. If price fluctuations are purely random, charts of past prices are unlikely to produce significant trading profits. In an efficient market, indeed *even in a weak-form efficient market*, shifts in supply and demand occur so rapidly that charting and other technical indicators simply measure after-the-fact events, with no implications for the future. But if markets are not efficient, or are lacking in efficiency, then new information may be absorbed more slowly, thus producing gradual shifts in supply and demand conditions—and profit opportunities for those who know how to recognize the shifts early. Although the great bulk of evidence supports the random walk and efficient market hypotheses, many investors still follow a technical approach because they believe it improves their investment results.

Implications for Fundamental Analysis   Many strict fundamental analysts were at first pleased by the weak-form EMH attack on technical analysis. Further development of the efficient market concept, however, was not so well received: In an efficient market, it's argued, prices react so quickly to new information that not even security analysis will enable investors to realize consistently superior returns. Because of the extreme competition among investors, security prices are seldom far above or below their justified levels, and fundamental analysis thus loses much of its value. The problem is not that fundamental analysis is poorly done. On the contrary, it is done all too well!

As a consequence, many investors, competing so vigorously for profit opportunities, simply eliminate the opportunities before other investors can capitalize on them.

■ So Who Is Right?

Some type of fundamental analysis probably has a role in the stock selection process. Even in an efficient market, there is no question that stock prices reflect a company's profit performance. Some companies are fundamentally strong and others fundamentally weak, and investors must be able to distinguish between the two. Thus, investors can profit from time spent evaluating a company and its stock to determine, not if it is undervalued, but whether it is fundamentally strong. The level of investor return, however, is more than a function of the fundamental condition of the company; it is also related to risk exposure. Fundamental analysis can help assess risk exposure and identify securities that possess risk commensurate with the return they offer.

The extent to which the markets are efficient is still subject to considerable debate. At present, there seems to be a growing consensus that although the markets may not be *perfectly* efficient, they are at least reasonably efficient.

In the final analysis, the individual investor must decide on the merits of fundamental and technical analysis. Certainly, a large segment of the investing public believes in security analysis, even in a market that may be efficient. What is more, the principles of stock valuation—that promised return should be commensurate with exposure to risk—are valid in any type of market setting.

CONCEPTS IN REVIEW

Answers available at: www.myfinancelab.com

9.7 What is the *random walk hypothesis*, and how does it apply to stocks? What is an *efficient market?* How can a market be efficient if its prices behave in a random fashion?

9.8 Explain why it is difficult, if not impossible, to consistently outperform an efficient market.
   a. Does this mean that high rates of return are not available in the stock market?
   b. How can an investor earn a high rate of return in an efficient market?

9.9 What are *market anomalies* and how do they come about? Do they support or refute the EMH? Briefly describe each of the following:
   a. The January effect.
   b. The P/E effect.
   c. The size effect.

9.10 What are the implications of random walks and efficient markets for technical analysis? For fundamental analysis? Do random walks and efficient markets mean that technical analysis and fundamental analysis are useless? Explain.

Behavioral Finance: A Challenge to the Efficient Market Hypothesis

LG 6

For more than 30 years, the efficient market hypothesis (EMH) has been an influential force in financial markets. The notion that asset prices fully reflect all available information is supported by a large body of academic research. In practitioner circles, supporters of market efficiency include John Bogle of

Vanguard, who helped pioneer the development of a special type of mutual fund known as an *index* fund. Managers of index funds don't try to pick individual stocks or bonds, because they assume that the market is efficient. They recognize that any time and energy spent researching individual securities will merely serve to increase the fund's expenses, which will drag down investors' returns.

Although considerable evidence supports the concept of market efficiency, an increasing number of academic studies have begun to cast doubt on the notion that the EMH is as "true" as originally believed. This research documents various anomalies—deviations from accepted rules—in stock returns. A number of academics and practitioners have also recognized that emotions and other subjective factors play a role in investment decisions. This focus on investor behavior has resulted in a significant body of research, which is collectively referred to as **behavioral finance**. One notable event that acknowledged the importance of this field was the awarding of the 2002 Nobel Prize in economics to Daniel Kahneman, whose work integrated insights from psychology and economics. In addition to academic studies, some professional money managers are also incorporating concepts from behavioral finance into their construction and management of portfolios.

WEBEXTENSION

To appeciate the ongoing debate between behaviorists and supporters of the EMH, see the reading entitled, "Showdown at the EMH Corral," on our Web site.

www.myfinancelab.com

behavioral finance
the body of research into the role that emotions and other subjective factors play in investment decisions.

HOTLINKS

Although rather academic in nature, the first link below provides you with the latest ideas and research on behavioral finance. The second link is more applied and has additional links.

**www.econ.yale.edu/~shiller/behfin/index.htm
www.investorhome.com/psych.htm**

▊ Investor Behavior and Security Prices

Researchers in behavioral finance believe that investors' decisions are affected by a number of beliefs and preferences. They also believe that the resulting biases will cause investors to overreact to certain types of financial information and underreact to others. Let's now take a look at some of the behavioral factors that might influence the actions of investors.

Overconfidence Investors tend to be overconfident in their judgment, which frequently leads them to *underestimate* the level of risk in an investment. This underestimation of risk becomes even more important as the length of the investment horizon increases. In addition, overconfidence can cause financial analysts and money managers to make predictions that are too bold, giving investors a false sense of security. Highly overconfident investors typically make one of the biggest mistakes of all—*they trade too much*. Frequent trading leads to large transaction costs, which erode investment returns.

Biased Self-Attribution People tend to take credit for their successes ("buying that great stock was a smart move on my part") and blame others for their failures ("buying that lousy stock was my broker's fault"). This propensity obviously distorts reality and can lead to faulty investment decisions. Investors will tend to place more value on information that supports their preexisting beliefs and often disregard contradictory views.

Loss Aversion Most individuals dislike losses much more than they like gains. In other words, we love it when we buy a stock and it goes up, but we *really* hate it when we buy a stock and it goes down! As a result of this *loss aversion*, many investors avoid selling their losing stocks; instead they hang on to them in the hope that they will bounce back. This behavior often proves to be quite costly.

Representativeness This term encompasses a number of errors that people make when thinking about probabilities of events occurring. Two of the most common mistakes are the tendency to draw strong conclusions from small samples and to underestimate the effects of random chance. For example, investors may assume that a portfolio manager who has "beat the market" for each of the last three years will continue to do so. But they overlook two important facts: First, three years is a relatively short time period, especially compared to a typical investment horizon. Second, there are literally thousands of managers running mutual funds and other investment portfolios. Even if their results are driven purely by random chance, a number of managers will display good performance over three consecutive years.

Narrow Framing Many people tend to analyze a situation in isolation, while ignoring the larger context. A common example in investment analysis is the propensity to analyze the attractiveness of a particular stock without considering the effect of this stock on an investor's existing portfolio. For example, you may get excited about the prospects for a hot new technology stock, but if your portfolio is already heavily invested in tech stocks, adding this new one may not be the right decision.

Belief Perseverance People typically ignore information that conflicts with their existing beliefs. If they believe a stock is good and purchase it, for example, they later tend to discount any signals of trouble. In many cases, they even avoid gathering new information, for fear it will contradict their initial opinion. It would be better to view each stock owned as a "new" stock when periodically reviewing a portfolio, and to ask whether the information available at that time would cause you to buy or sell the stock.

▮ Behavioral Finance at Work in the Markets

Now that we have some understanding of the psychological factors that can affect financial decisions, let's examine some of the evidence. Specifically, we will discuss how behavioral finance can affect stock return predictability, investor behavior, and analyst behavior.

Stock Return Predictability If investors systematically underreact or overreact to some financial news, we may be able to detect certain patterns in stock returns over time. Predictability in stock prices can be measured by looking at the correlation of stock returns in a given period with those in a later period. Studies have found evidence of negative correlation over three- to five-year periods. These data suggest it may be profitable to buy portfolios of stocks that have performed poorly in the past, as their values are likely to rise in the future. If investors extrapolate the past bad news for these firms well into the future, the stocks will become undervalued, and that is precisely when they should be purchased. Other studies find evidence of momentum in stock returns over 6- to 12-month time horizons. In other words, stocks that have recently risen in price tend to continue to increase, and those that have fallen continue to decline. Behaviorists have shown that this momentum can be driven by patterns of underreaction and overreaction.

Additional evidence of predictability in returns can be gleaned from a comparison of growth and value stocks. Growth stocks typically have high price-earnings and price-book ratios, whereas value stocks tend to have lower ratios. Evidence suggests that value stocks tend to outperform growth stocks, and behaviorists suggest that growth stocks perform poorly due to investors' excessive optimism about their future prospects.

Investor Behavior Studies of the behavior of individual investors reveal the important role played by psychology. One highly persuasive result relates to overconfidence: Investors who believe they have superior information tend to trade more, but earn lower returns due to the higher transaction costs they incur. In addition, investors tend to exhibit loss aversion and, therefore, sell stocks that have recently risen in price instead of those that have declined. Representativeness also plays a big role in mutual fund investing, because investors tend to direct more money to funds that have recently experienced good performance.

If investors make decisions based on emotional factors rather than underlying economic fundamentals, their actions increase the risk of investing, even for professionals. One of the main forces in the markets that's needed to support the EMH is *arbitrage*—the ability to exploit any errors in security prices. Ironically, irrational behavior by investors only increases the risk of arbitrage and thus makes it less attractive, which in turn *reduces market efficiency*.

Analyst Behavior Because much of the information used by investors is generated via financial analysts, we need to understand how behavioral finance can bias analysts' forecasts of stock prices and earnings. Some evidence supports the idea of "herding" behavior by analysts, as they collectively tend to issue similar recommendations or earnings forecasts for stocks.

Analysts have also come under fire for being too optimistic—that is, for too frequently issuing buy recommendations and too rarely suggesting that investors sell stocks. Studies find that analysts' favorite stocks, those with the highest growth forecasts, typically earn lower returns than stocks with the least rosy growth forecasts.

■ Implications of Behavioral Finance for Security Analysis

Our discussion of the psychological factors that affect financial decisions suggests that behavioral finance can play an important role in investing. So far, we have covered some of the main stock selection techniques using fundamental and technical analysis. We now turn our attention to implications of behavioral finance for security analysis.

Fundamental analysis of stocks frequently involves forecasts of dividends and earnings growth rates, as well as the analysis of price multiples, like P/E ratios. If you construct such forecasts or use the forecasts constructed by financial analysts, you should be careful to avoid excessive optimism. An easy solution to this problem is to rework your analysis with more conservative forecast estimates to see whether your investment decision changes. In addition, you should recognize the potential for error in your forecasts. Significant errors may be especially likely to occur if you are working with limited data, as is usually the case with relatively new companies without long financial histories.

Stock valuation using multiples such as the P/E ratio involves comparing the multiple for a given stock with the average multiple for a group of stocks (often referred to as *comparable firms*, or simply *comparables*). If the stock is for a company in a large, well-established industry such as banking, your list of

---

INVESTOR FACTS

WOMEN MAKE FEWER MISTAKES!—Could it be? Women make fewer investment mistakes than men, and make them less often—even though, on average, they tend to enjoy investing less than men. Well, that's what they say, according to the results of a national survey conducted by Merrill Lynch. Here are some of the findings:

	Admitted making mistake	
	Men	**Women**
• Holding a losing investment too long	47%	35%
• Waiting too long to sell a winner	43%	28%
• Allocating too much to one investment	32%	23%
• Buying a hot investment without doing research	24%	13%
• Trading securities too often	12%	5%

For more results from this survey, go to www.hindsight2insight.com

comparables will probably include many firms. On the other hand, when you analyze a stock in a newer, more specific industry such as optical networking, you will usually have at most a handful of firms to use as comparables. In these more specialized cases, the average price multiple for a small number of firms may be practically meaningless. One solution to this problem is to define the list of comparables more broadly. If you feel that most investors are too optimistic regarding the prospects for firms in this industry, you may want to adjust the average multiple downward to account for the excessive optimism.

Technical analysis of stocks uses the methods discussed earlier in this chapter. In some cases, your view of behavioral finance may indicate which method you should use. For instance, if you believe in momentum in stock returns, you may want to use a trend-following method such as moving averages to generate buy and sell signals. If you believe in overreaction, you may prefer to rely on overbought or oversold indicators such as the relative strength index (RSI).

▎Your Behavior as an Investor: It Does Matter

In light of all the possible biases in judgment and errors in decision making, you might be tempted to "throw in the towel" and avoid investing in stocks altogether. After all, Treasury bills and money market funds are nice and safe, and conservative investing avoids all of the pitfalls (other than low returns). In fact, just the opposite is true: You may be making one of the biggest mistakes of all—choosing an incorrect asset allocation. One of the most important things you must do as an investor is to choose the asset allocation (the mix of stocks, bonds, and other investments) that is right for you, based on your investment time horizon, level of risk tolerance, and other relevant factors. Table 9.1 lists some other steps that you can take to improve your investment returns, including learning from your mistakes.

TABLE 9.1 Using Behavioral Finance to Improve Investment Results

Studies have documented a number of behavioral factors that appear to influence investors' decisions and adversely affect their returns. By following some simple guidelines, you can avoid making mistakes and improve your portfolio's performance. A little common sense goes a long way in the financial markets!

- **Don't hesitate to sell a losing stock.** If you buy a stock at $20 and its price drops to $10, ask yourself whether you would buy that same stock if you came into the market today with $10 in cash. If the answer is yes, then hang onto it. If not, sell the stock and buy something else.

- **Don't chase performance.** The evidence suggests that there are no "hot hands" in investment management. Don't buy last year's hottest mutual fund if it doesn't make sense for you. Always keep your personal investment objectives and constraints in mind.

- **Be humble and open-minded.** Many investment professionals, some of whom are extremely well paid, are frequently wrong in their predictions. Admit your mistakes and don't be afraid to take corrective action. The fact is, reviewing your mistakes can be a very rewarding exercise—all investors make mistakes, but the smart ones learn from them. Winning in the market is often about not losing, and one way to avoid loss is to learn from your mistakes.

- **Review the performance of your investments on a periodic basis.** Remember the old saying, "Out of sight, out of mind." Don't be afraid to face the music and to make changes as your situation changes. Nothing runs on "auto-pilot" forever—including investment portfolios.

- **Don't trade too much.** Investment returns are uncertain, but transaction costs are guaranteed. Considerable evidence indicates that investors who trade frequently perform poorly.

What lessons should you take away from our discussion of behavioral finance? Perhaps the greatest lesson is to recognize that investors are human, so we will inevitably make mistakes or have occasional errors in judgment. The better you understand how your behavior can influence your investment decisions, the easier it will be to avoid mistakes. In fact, you may even be able to profit from the mistakes of others. For example, if you feel that most investors overreact to bad news and sell stocks too soon, that may represent a great buying opportunity.

CONCEPTS IN REVIEW
Answers available at: www.myfinancelab.com

9.11   How can behavioral finance have any bearing on investor returns? Do supporters of behavioral finance believe in efficient markets? Explain.

9.12   Briefly explain how behavioral finance can affect each of the following:
   a. The predictability of stock returns.
   b. Investor behavior.
   c. Analyst behavior.

9.13   Considering how behavioral factors can affect investment decisions, list four steps that investors might take to improve their investment returns.

Summary

LG 1   **Discuss the purpose of technical analysis and explain why the performance of the market is important to stock valuation.** Technical analysis deals with the behavior of the stock market itself and the various economic forces at work in the marketplace. Technical analysis is used to assess the condition of the market and to determine whether it's a good time to be buying or selling stocks. Some investors try to keep tabs on the markets in an informal way. Others use complex mathematical formulas and rules to guide them in their buy and sell decisions.

LG 2   **Describe some of the approaches to technical analysis, including, among others, the Dow theory, moving averages, charting, and various indicators of the technical condition of the market.** Market analysts look at those factors in the marketplace that can affect the price behavior of stocks in general. This analysis can be done by assessing the overall condition of the market (as the Dow theory does), by informally or formally studying various internal market statistics (e.g., short interest or advance-decline lines), or by charting various aspects of the market (including the use of moving averages).

LG 3   **Compute and use technical trading rules for individual stocks and the market as a whole.** Technical analysts use a number of mathematical equations and measures to gauge the direction of the market, including advance-decline lines, new highs and lows, the trading index, the mutual fund cash ratio, on-balance volume, and the investment newsletter sentiment index. They test different indicators using historical price data to find those that generate profitable trading strategies, which then are developed into trading rules used to guide buy and sell decisions.

LG 4   **Explain the idea of random walks and efficient markets, and note the challenges these theories hold for the stock valuation process.** Both technical and fundamental analyses have been seriously challenged by the random walk and efficient market hypotheses. Considerable evidence indicates that stock prices do move randomly. The idea behind an efficient market is that available information is always fully reflected in the prices of securities, so investors should *not* expect to outperform the market consistently.

LG 5   **Describe the weak, semi-strong, and strong versions of the efficient market hypothesis, and explain what market anomalies are.** The weak form of the EMH holds that all *market* information is fully embedded in the price of a stock, and therefore technical analysis cannot be used to consistently outperform the market. The semi-strong version states that all *public* information (market and otherwise) is embedded in the price of a stock. This information flows to the market in a random fashion and is quickly digested by the market participants; as a consequence, the use of such information will be of little value in helping investors generate excess returns with any degree of consistency. The strong-form EMH holds that there is no information, *public or private*, that allows investors to consistently earn abnormal returns. While much empirical evidence supports the EMH, some studies have uncovered evidence that does *not* support it; the latter data constitute *market anomalies.*

LG 6   **Demonstrate a basic appreciation for how psychological factors can affect investors' decisions, and how behavioral finance presents a challenge to the concept of market efficiency.** A number of factors, such as overconfidence, loss aversion, representativeness, and belief perseverance, can lead to incorrect investment decisions. If investors are not as rational as the efficient market hypothesis assumes, the resulting biases may lead to some level of predictability in stock returns. Any overreaction, underreaction, or other systematic predictability in financial markets represents a violation of market efficiency.

Key Terms

bar chart, *p. 399*
behavioral finance, *p. 412*
charting, *p. 399*
confidence index, *p. 392*
Dow theory, *p. 391*
efficient market, *p. 406*
efficient markets hypothesis
    (EMH), *p. 407*
market anomalies, *p. 409*
market technicians, *p. 396*

moving average (MA), *p. 402*
point-and-figure charts, *p. 400*
random walk hypothesis, *p. 405*
semi-strong form (EMH), *p. 408*
short interest, *p. 395*
strong form (EMH), *p. 408*
technical analysis, *p. 389*
theory of contrary opinion, *p. 395*
weak form (EMH), *p. 407*

Discussion Questions

LG 1   Q9.1   Briefly describe how technical analysis is used as part of the stock valuation process. What role does it play in an investor's decision to buy or sell a stock?

LG 2   LG 3   Q9.2   Describe each of the following approaches to technical analysis and note how it would be used by investors.
  a. Confidence index
  b. Arms index
  c. Trading action
  d. Odd-lot trading
  e. Charting
  f. Moving averages
  g. On-balance volume

Which of these approaches is likely to involve some type of mathematical equation or ratio?

LG 2   Q9.3   Briefly define each of the following, and note the conditions that would suggest the market is technically strong
  a. Breadth of the market
  b. Short interest
  c. Relative strength index (RSI)
  d. Theory of contrary opinion
  e. Head and shoulders

LG 4   LG 5   Q9.4   Much has been written about the concept of an *efficient market*. It's probably safe to say that some of your classmates believe the markets are efficient and others believe they are not. Have a debate to see whether you can resolve this issue (at least among you and your classmates). Pick a side, either for or against efficient markets, and then develop your "ammunition." Be prepared to discuss these three aspects:
  a. What is an efficient market? Do such markets really exist?
  b. Are stock prices always (or nearly always) correctly set in the market? If so, does that mean little opportunity exists to find undervalued stocks?
  c. Can you cite any reasons to use fundamental and/or technical analysis in your stock selection process? If not, how would you go about selecting stocks?

LG 6   Q9.5   Briefly define each of the following terms, and describe how it can affect investors' decisions:
  a. Loss aversion
  b. Representativeness
  c. Narrow framing
  d. Overconfidence
  e. Biased self-attribution

LG 6   Q9.6   Describe how optimism may lead to biases in stock valuation when using the discounted cash flow method. Discuss how scenario analysis may be used as a way to correct for these biases.

Problems

LG 3   P9.1   Compute the Arms index for the S&P 500 over the following 3 days:

Day	Number of Stocks **Rising** in Price	Number of Stocks **Falling** in Price	Volume for Stocks **Rising** in Price	Volume for Stocks **Falling** in Price
1	350	150	850 million shares	420 million shares
2	275	225	450 million shares	725 million shares
3	260	240	850 million shares	420 million shares

Which of the 3 days would be considered the most bullish? Explain why.

LG 3   P9.2   Listed below are data that pertain to the corporate bond market. (*Note:* Each "period" below covers a span of 6 months.)

	Period 1	Period 2	Period 3	Period 4
Average yield on 10 high-grade corporate bonds	5.30%	5.70%	5.10%	?
Yield on the Dow Jones average of 40 corporate bonds	6.50%	?	6.00%	4.90%
Yield spread (in basis points)	?	155	?	25
Confidence index	____	____	____	____

a. Compute the confidence index for each of the 4 periods listed above.
b. Assume the latest confidence index (for period 0, in effect) amounts to 86.83%, while the yield spread between high- and average-grade corporate bonds is 85 basis points. Based on your calculations, what's happening to bond yield spreads and the confidence index over the period of time covered in the problem (i.e., from period 0 through period 4)?
c. Based on the confidence index measures you computed, what would be your overall assessment of the stock market? In which one or more of the periods (1 through 4) is the confidence index bullish? In which one(s) is it bearish?

LG 3   P9.3   Compute the level of on balance volume (OBV) for the following 3-day period for a stock, if the beginning level of OBV is 50,000 and the stock closed yesterday at $25.

Day	Closing Price	Trading Volume
1	$27	70,000 shares
2	$26	45,000 shares
3	$29	120,000 shares

Does the movement in OBV appear to confirm the rising trend in prices? Explain.

LG 3   P9.4   Below are figures representing the number of stocks making new highs and new lows for each month over a 6-month period:

Month	New Highs	New Lows
July	117	22
August	95	34
September	84	41
October	64	79
November	53	98
December	19	101

Would a technical analyst consider the trend to be bullish or bearish over this period? Explain.

LG 3   P9.5   You hear a market analyst on television say that the advance/decline ratio for the session was 1.2. What does that mean?

LG 3   P9.6   At the end of a trading day you find that, on the NYSE, 2,200 stocks advanced, and 1,000 stocks declined. What is the value of the advance-decline line for that day?

LG 3   P9.7   You are given the following information:

Day	New Highs	New Lows
1 (yesterday)	117	22
2	95	34
3	84	41
4	64	79
5	53	98
6	19	101
7	19	105
8	18	110
9	19	90
10	22	88

a. Calculate the 10-day moving average NH-NL indicator.
b. If there are 120 new highs and 20 new lows today, what is the new 10-day moving average NH-NL indicator?

LG 3   P9.8   You have collected the following NH-NL indicator data:

Day	NH-NL Indicator
1 (yesterday)	100
2	95
3	61
4	43
5	−15
6	−45
7	−82
8	−86
9	−92
10	−71

If you are a technician following a momentum-based strategy, are you buying or selling today?

LG 3   P9.9   You are presented with the following data:

Week	Mutual Fund Cash Position	Mutual Fund Total Assets
Most recent	$281,478,000.00	$2,345,650,000.00
2	258,500,000.00	2,350,000,000.00
3	234,800,000.00	2,348,000,000.00
4	211,950,000.00	2,355,000,000.00
5	188,480,000.00	2,356,000,000.00

Calculate the MFCR for each week. Based on the result, are you bullish or bearish?

LG 3   P9.10 You find the closing prices for a stock you own. You want to use a 10-day moving average to monitor the stock. Calculate the 10-day moving average for days 11 through 20. Based on the data in the table below, are there any signals you should act on? Explain.

Day	Closing Price	Day	Closing Price
1	$25.25	11	$30.00
2	26.00	12	30.00
3	27.00	13	31.00
4	28.00	14	31.50
5	27.00	15	31.00
6	28.00	16	32.00
7	27.50	17	29.00
8	29.00	18	29.00
9	27.00	19	28.00
10	28.00	20	27.00

See www.myfinancelab.com **for Web Exercises,**
Spreadsheets, and other online resources.

Case Problem 9.1   *Rhett Runs Some Technical Measures on a Stock*

LG 2   LG 3   Rhett Weaver is an active stock trader and avid market technician. He got into technical analysis about 10 years ago, and although he now uses the Internet for much of his analytical work, he still enjoys running some of the numbers and doing some of the charting himself. Rhett likes to describe himself as a "serious stock trader" who relies on technical analysis for some—but certainly not all—of the information he uses to make an investment decision; unlike some market technicians, he does not totally ignore a stock's fundamentals. Right now he's got his eye on a stock that he's been tracking for the past 3 or 4 months.

The stock is Nautilus Navigation, a mid-sized high-tech company that's been around for a number of years and has a demonstrated ability to generate profits year-in and year-out. The problem is that the earnings are a bit erratic, tending to bounce up and down from year to year, which causes the price of the stock to be a bit erratic as well. And that's exactly why Rhett likes the stock—as a trader, the volatile prices enable him to move in and out of the stock over relatively short (3- to 6-month) periods of time.

Rhett has already determined that the stock has "decent" fundamentals, so he does not worry about its basic soundness. Hence, he can concentrate on the technical side of the stock. In particular, he wants to run some technical measures on the market price behavior of the security. He's obtained recent closing prices on the stock, which are shown in the accompanying table at the top of page 422.

Recent Price Behavior: Nautilus Navigation			
14 (8/15/07)	18.55	20	17.50
14.25	17.50	20.21	18.55
14.79	17.50	20.25	19.80
15.50	17.25	20.16	19.50
16	17	20	19.25
16	16.75	20.25	20
16.50	16.50	20.50	20.90
17	16.55	20.80	21
17.25	16.15	20	21.75
17.20	16.80	20	22.50
18	17.15	20.25	23.25
18 (9/30/07)	17.22	20	24
18.55	17.31 (10/31/07)	19.45	24.25
18.65	17.77	19.20	24.15
18.80	18.23	18.25 (11/30/07)	24.75
19	19.22	17.50	25
19.10	20.51	16.75	25.50
18.92	20.15	17	25.55 (12/31/07)

Nautilus shares are actively traded on the Nasdaq National Market and enjoy considerable market interest.

Questions

a. Use the closing share prices in the table above to compute the stock's relative strength index (RSI) for (1) the 20-day period from 9/30/07 to 10/31/07; and (2) the 22-day period from 11/30/07 to 12/31/07. [*Hint:* Use a simple (unweighted) average to compute the numerator (average price change on up days) and the denominator (average price change on down days) of the RSI formula shown in the *Investing in Action* box on page 397.]
  1. Contrast the two RSI measures you computed. Is the index getting bigger or smaller, and is that good or bad?
  2. Is the latest RSI measure giving a buy or a sell signal? Explain.

Note: Click on *"Moving Averages"* at the book's Web site for a price chart and a 10-day moving average line for Nautilus Navigation.
www.myfinancelab.com

b. Based on the above closing share prices, prepare a moving-average line covering the period shown in the table; use a 10-day time frame to calculate the individual average values.
  1. Plot the daily closing prices for nautilus from 8/15/07 through 12/31/07 on a graph/chart.
  2. On the same graph/chart, plot a moving-average line using the individual average values computed earlier. Identify any buy or sell signals.
  3. As of 12/31/07, was the moving-average line giving a buy, hold, or sell signal? Explain. How does that result compare to what you found with the RSI in part **a**? Explain.

c. Prepare a point-and-figure chart of the closing prices for Nautilus Navigation. (Use a 1-point system, in which each box is worth $1.) Discuss how technical analysts use this and similar charts.

d. Based on the technical measures and charts you've prepared, what course of action would you recommend that Rhett take with regard to Nautilus Navigation? Explain.

Case Problem 9.2 · *Deb Takes Measure of the Market*

LG 2   LG 3

Several months ago, Deb Forrester received a substantial sum of money from the estate of her late aunt. Deb initially placed the money in a savings account because she was not sure what to do with it. Since then, however, she has taken a course in investments at the local university. The textbook for the course was, in fact, this one, and the class just completed Chapter 9. Excited about what she has learned in class, Deb has decided that she definitely wants to invest in stocks. But before she does, she wants to use her newfound knowledge in technical analysis to determine whether now would be a good time to enter the market.

Deb has decided to use all 5 of the following measures to help her determine if now is, indeed, a good time to start putting money into the stock market:

- Dow theory
- Advance-decline line
- New highs-new lows (NH-NL) indicator *(Assume the current 10-day moving average is zero and the last 10 periods were each zero.)*
- Arms index
- Mutual fund cash ratio

Deb goes to the Internet and, after considerable effort, is able to put together the table of data as seen below.

Questions

a. Based on the data presented in the table, calculate a value (where appropriate) for periods 1 through 5, for each of the five measures listed above. (*Hint:* There are no values to compute for the Dow theory; just plot the averages.) Chart your results, where applicable.

b. Discuss each measure individually and note what it indicates for the market, as it now stands. Taken collectively, what do these 5 measures indicate about the current state of the market? According to these measures, is this a good time for Deb to consider getting into the market, or should she wait a while? Explain.

c. Comment on the time periods used in the table, which are not defined here. What if they were relatively long intervals of time? What if they were relatively short? Explain how the length of the time periods can affect the measures.

	Period 1	Period 2	Period 3	Period 4	Period 5
Dow Industrial Average	8,300	7,250	8,000	9,000	9,400
Dow Transportation Average	2,375	2,000	2,000	2,850	3,250
New highs	68	85	85	120	200
New lows	75	60	80	75	20
Volume up	600,000,000	836,254,123	275,637,497	875,365,980	1,159,534,297
Volume down	600,000,000	263,745,877	824,362,503	424,634,020	313,365,599
Mutual fund cash (trillions of dollars)	$0.31	$0.32	$0.47	$0.61	$0.74
Total assets managed (trillions of dollars)	$6.94	$6.40	$6.78	$6.73	$7.42
Advancing issues (NYSE)	1,120	1,278	1,270	1,916	1,929
Declining issues (NYSE)	2,130	1,972	1,980	1,334	1,321

Excel with Spreadsheets

Technical analysis looks at the demand and supply for securities based on trading volumes and price studies. Charting is a common method used to identify and project price trends in a security. A well-known technical indicator is the Bollinger Band. It creates 2 bands, one above and one below, the price performance of a stock. The upper band is a resistance level and represents the level above which the stock is unlikely to rise. The bottom forms a support level and shows the price which a stock is unlikely to fall below.

According to technicians, if you see a significant "break" in the upper band, the expectation is that the stock price will fall in the immediate future. A "break" in the lower band signals that the security is about to rise in value. Either of these occurrences will dictate a unique investment strategy.

Replicate the following technical analysis for Amazon.Com (AMZN)

- Go to www.moneycentral.msn.com
- Symbol(s): **AMZN**
- In the left-hand column, click on "Charts." You need to update to MSN Money Deluxe if you have not already done so.
- If download was required, fill in the Symbol box with "AMZN."
- A one-year chart appears by default.
- Click on "Analysis."
- Click on "Price Indicators."
- Choose "Bollinger Bands."
- The price performance graph for Amazon stock with an upper and lower red Bollinger band should appear.
- Make sure that the graph covers, at a minimum, the months of June through December 2006.

Questions

a. On approximately July 7, 2006, what happened to the upper band (resistance level) of Amazon stock?

b. During the following 9 days, how did the price of the stock behave?

c. Is this in line with what a technician would predict?

d. What strategy would a technician have undertaken on the seventh of July?

e. On approximately November 18, 2006, what happened to the lower band (support level) of Amazon stock?

f. During the following 10 days, how did the price of the stock behave?

g. Is this in line with what a technician would predict?

h. What strategy would a technician have undertaken on the eighteenth of November?

Investing in Fixed-Income Securities

Fixed-Income Securities

With over $394 billion in total debt, General Electric Company (NYSE: GE) is the world's biggest corporate borrower. In mid-2006, the company posted 12-month revenues of more than $155 billion and EBITDA of $33.14 billion, ensuring the highest rating (AAA) by both Moody's and S&P on its long-term debt. GE's short-term debt also receives the highest ratings from Moody's and S&P.

GE offers three fixed-income products for individual investors. InterNotes are AAA corporate bonds offered weekly at par. GE "Baby Bonds" are senior unsecured obligations of GE Capital Corporation with a $25 par value. GE "Step-Up Bonds" are multi-coupon notes, bearing a coupon that resets to a level higher than the previous coupon if the bond is not called.

How have GE bonds performed? Even the best bonds cannot withstand the pressure of rising interest rates. Investors have once again found that rising interest rates can have a very detrimental effect on bond values. Beginning in June 2004, the Federal Reserve Board raised the Fed funds rate 17 times, from 1.0% in the first half of 2004 to 5.25% on June 29, 2006. Half of those rate increases occurred between June 2005 and June 2006. The effect of these rising rates on corporate bonds can be seen in GE's debt. The company's 7.5% bonds, due in 2035, lost 9.4% in one year, or a 1.9% loss for investors, after receiving interest payments.

GE is not alone in seeing its bonds decrease in value. According to the Merrill Lynch & Co. Global Broad Market Corporate & High Yield Index, which tracks the performance of 9,300 bonds with a face value of $4.8 trillion, corporate debt securities lost at least $59 billion in value in the first half of 2006. Yet in certain market conditions, bonds can be a valuable investment, and a haven against market loss and volatility.

Before you invest in fixed-income debt securities, whether issued by GE or any other company, you'll want to consider credit quality, interest rates, maturity, and other factors. Chapters 10 and 11 will provide the background you need to make wise choices in the bond market.

Sources: http://www.ge.com, and "GE to Junk: Corporate Bonds Posting Worst Declines Since 1998," downloaded from www.bloomberg.com (accessed July 25, 2006).

Why Invest in Bonds?

bonds
negotiable, publicly traded long-term debt securities, whereby the issuer agrees to pay a stipulated amount of interest over a specified period of time and to repay a fixed amount of principal at maturity.

In contrast to stocks, *bonds are liabilities*—publicly traded IOUs where the bondholders are actually *lending money* to the issuer. Technically, **bonds** are negotiable, publicly traded, long-term debt securities. They are issued in various denominations, by a variety of borrowing organizations, including the U.S. Treasury, agencies of the U.S. government, state and local governments, and corporations. Bonds are often referred to as *fixed-income securities* because the debt payments of the issuers are fixed. That is, the issuing organization agrees to pay a fixed amount of interest periodically and to repay a fixed amount of principal at maturity.

Bonds provide investors with two kinds of income: (1) a generous amount of current income, and (2) given the right market environment, they can also be used to generate substantial amounts of capital gains. The current income, of course, is derived from the interest payments received over the life of the issue. Capital gains, in contrast, are earned whenever market interest rates fall. A basic trading rule in the bond market is that *interest rates and bond prices move in opposite directions*. When interest rates rise, bond prices fall. When rates drop, bond prices move up. Thus, it is possible to buy bonds at one price and to sell them later at a higher price. Of course, it is also possible to incur a capital loss if market rates move against you. Taken together, the current income and capital gains earned from bonds can lead to attractive returns.

Bonds are also a versatile investment outlet. They can be used conservatively by those who seek high levels of current income, or they can be used aggressively by those who go after capital gains. Although bonds have long been considered attractive investments for those seeking current income, it wasn't until the advent of volatile interest rates in the late 1960s that they also became recognized for their capital gains potential and as trading vehicles. Investors found that, given the relation of bond prices to interest rates, the number of profitable trading opportunities increased substantially as wider and more frequent swings in interest rates began to occur.

In addition, certain types of bonds can be used for tax shelter. Municipal obligations are perhaps the best known in this regard. But as we'll see later in this chapter, Treasury and certain federal agency issues also offer some tax advantages. Finally, because of the general high quality of many bond issues, they can also be used for the preservation and long-term accumulation of capital.

■ Putting Bond Market Performance in Perspective

The bond market is driven by interest rates. In fact, *the behavior of interest rates is the single most important force in the bond market*. Interest rates determine not only the amount of current income investors will receive but also the amount of capital gains (or losses) bondholders will incur. It's not surprising, therefore, that bond market participants follow interest rates closely and that bond market performance is often portrayed in terms of market interest rates.

Figure 10.1 (on page 430) provides a look at bond interest rates over the 45-year period from 1961 through 2005. It shows that from a state of relative stability, interest rates rose steadily in the latter half of the 1960s, and that over the course of the next 15 years, the rates paid on high-grade bonds nearly

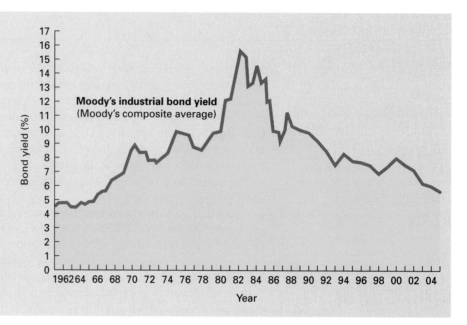

FIGURE 10.1

The Behavior of Interest Rates Over Time— 1961–2005

From an era of relative stability, bond interest rates rose dramatically and became highly volatile. The net result was that bond yields not only became competitive with the returns offered by other securities but also provided investors with attractive capital gains opportunities.

tripled. But then rates dropped sharply, and by 1986 were back to the single-digit range. Thus, after a protracted bear market, bonds abruptly reversed course, and the strongest bull market on record occurred from 1982 through early 1987. (The bond market is considered *bearish* when market interest rates are high or rising, *bullish* when rates are low or falling.) Even though interest rates did move back up for a short time in 1987–1988, they quickly retreated and by 2004–2005, had fallen to levels not seen in nearly 40 years (since the late 1960s).

Historical Returns As with stocks, *total returns* in the bond market are made up of both current income and capital gains (or losses). Table 10.1 lists *year-end market yields* and total *annual returns* for high-grade corporate bonds, over the 45-year period from 1961 through 2005. Note how bond returns started to slip in 1965, as market yields began to climb. In fact, from 1965 to 1981, there were eight years when average returns were negative—which is highly unusual for the bond market. In contrast, look at the 24-year period from 1982 through 2005, when rates were in a general state of decline: There were only three years of negative returns, whereas double-digit returns (of 10.4% to 43.8%) occurred in 13 of the 24 years.

We can convert the return data from Table 10.1 to fully compounded rates of return over representative 5-, 10-, and 20-year holding periods, as shown below:

Holding Period Returns	Average Annual Returns
5 years: 2001–2005	9.49%
10-years: 1996–2005	7.43%
20-years: 1986–2005	9.27%

These figures show that holding period returns of around 7.5 to 8% are not out of the question—provided, of course, that market interest rates don't shoot

TABLE 10.1 Historical Annual Yields and Returns in the Bond Market, 1961–2005*
(Yields and returns based on performance of high-grade corporate bonds)

Year	Year-End Bond Yields*	Total Rates of Return**	Year	Year-End Bond Yields*	Total Rates of Return**
2005	5.57%	3.76%	1982	11.55%	43.80%
2004	5.47	9.38	1981	14.98	−0.96
2003	5.62	10.43	1980	13.15	−2.62
2002	6.21	11.92	1979	10.87	−4.18
2001	6.77	12.16	1978	9.32	−0.07
2000	7.11	9.21	1977	8.50	1.71
1999	7.05	−5.76	1976	8.14	18.65
1998	6.53	9.16	1975	8.97	14.64
1997	7.16	13.46	1974	8.89	−3.06
1996	7.43	2.20	1973	7.79	1.14
1995	6.86	27.94	1972	7.41	7.26
1994	8.64	−5.76	1971	6.48	11.01
1993	7.31	13.64	1970	6.85	18.37
1992	8.34	9.34	1969	7.83	−8.09
1991	8.58	20.98	1968	6.62	2.57
1990	9.61	6.48	1967	6.30	−4.95
1989	9.18	15.29	1966	5.55	0.20
1988	9.81	10.49	1965	4.79	−0.46
1987	10.33	−1.47	1964	4.46	4.77
1986	9.02	18.71	1963	4.46	2.19
1985	10.63	27.99	1962	4.34	7.95
1984	12.05	16.39	1961	4.56	4.82
1983	12.76	4.70			

*Year-end bond yields are for Aa-rated corporate bonds.
**Total return figures are based on interest income as well as capital gains (or losses).
Sources: Annual yields derived from year-end Moody's and S&P bond yields on Aa- (AA-) rated corporate issues. Total return figures (for 1961–1985) from Ibbotson and Sinquefield, *Stocks, Bonds, Bills, and Inflation: Historical Returns.* Total returns for 1986 through 2005 obtained from *the Lehman Bros. Long-Term Corporate Bond* database.

way up. Face it, most of the years from the 1980s through 2004 were very good to bond investors. But that was due simply to the fact that the U.S. economy was in a sustained period of declining interest rates, *which in turn produced hefty capital gains and outsize returns.* Whether market interest rates will (or even can) continue on that path is, of course, highly doubtful. Which explains in large part why most market observers caution against expecting abnormally high rates of return over the next decade or so.

Bonds Versus Stocks Bonds definitely have their good points: low risk, high levels of current income, and desirable diversification properties. They also have a significant downside: their *comparative* returns. *Relative* to stocks, there's a big give-up in returns—which, of course, is the price you pay for the even bigger reduction in risk!

However, just because there's a deficit in long-term returns, doesn't mean that bonds are always underachievers compared to stocks. Consider, for example, the past 20 or so years: Fixed-income securities held their own against stocks in the 1980s and the early 1990s, but then fell far behind for the rest of the decade. But then came a nasty bear market in stocks from 2000–2002, and the impact was nothing short of spectacular. The net result can be seen in Figure 10.2 (on page 432), which tracks the comparative returns of stocks (via

FIGURE 10.2   **Comparative Performance of Stocks and Bonds—1996 Through 2005**

This graph shows what happened to $10,000 invested in bonds over the 10-year period from January 1996 through December 2005, versus the same amount invested in stocks. Clearly, while stocks held a commanding lead through early 2000, the ensuing bear market erased virtually all of that advantage. As a result, stocks and bonds ended the period at ending (or "terminal") values that were less than $3,500 apart. (*Source: Morningstar Principia for Mutual Funds*, release date December 31, 2005.)

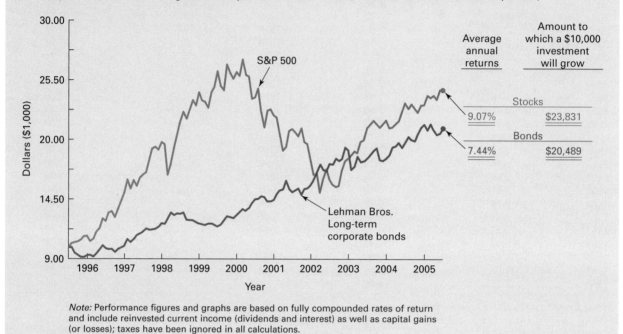

Note: Performance figures and graphs are based on fully compounded rates of return and include reinvested current income (dividends and interest) as well as capital gains (or losses); taxes have been ignored in all calculations.

the S&P 500) and bonds (using the Lehman Bros. Long Bond Index), from 1996 through 2005. While bonds held up pretty well over the first half of the 1990s, by 1996, stocks were clearly beginning to outpace bonds by ever-increasing margins. The spread continued to widen through early 2000. Indeed, for the decade as a whole, bonds produced average annual returns of 8.7%, whereas stocks turned in average returns of 18.2%. That difference meant that a $10,000 investment in bonds would have led to a terminal value of some $23,000, compared to more than $53,000 for stocks.

That's a high opportunity cost to pay for holding bonds, and it prompted some market observers to question whether bonds should have *any place at all* in an investment portfolio. They reasoned that if interest rates had, in fact, bottomed out, then bonds wouldn't have much to offer, other than relatively low returns. But these observers overlooked one detail: It wasn't bonds that would prove to be the problem, it was stocks. As Figure 10.2 shows, the bear market had a devastating effect on stocks. By 2003 the differential returns between the equity and bond markets had all but evaporated. Indeed, over the 10-year period from January 1996 through December 2005, stocks outperformed bonds by only 1.6 percentage points (9.07% vs. 7.44%). The net result was a terminal value of just over $23,800 for stocks, compared to nearly $20,500 for bonds for that $10,000 investment.

Most investors would agree that's a very low price to pay for *the level of stability that bonds bring to a portfolio*. The fact is, bond returns are far more stable than stock returns, plus they possess *excellent portfolio diversification properties*. As a general rule, adding bonds to a portfolio will, *up to a point*, have a much greater impact on lowering risk than on return. Face it: you don't buy bonds for their high returns, except when you think interest rates are heading down. Rather, you buy them for their current income and/or for the stability they bring to your portfolio.

■ Exposure to Risk

Like any other type of investment vehicle, fixed-income securities should be viewed in terms of their risk and return. Generally speaking, bonds are exposed to five major types of risks: interest rate risk, purchasing power risk, business/financial risk, liquidity risk, and call risk.

- **Interest Rate Risk.** Interest rate risk is the number one source of risk to fixed-income investors, *because it's the major cause of price volatility in the bond market*. For bonds, interest rate risk translates into market risk: The behavior of interest rates, in general, affects *all* bonds and cuts across *all* sectors of the market, even the U.S. Treasury market. When market interest rates rise, bond prices fall, and vice versa. As interest rates become more volatile, so do bond prices.

- **Purchasing Power Risk.** Purchasing power risk accompanies inflation. During periods of mild inflation, bonds do pretty well, because their returns tend to outstrip inflation rates. When inflation takes off, as it did in the late 1970s, bond yields start to lag behind inflation rates, and purchasing power risk rises. The reason: Even though market yields are rising with inflation, your return is locked in by the fixed coupon rate on your bond.

- **Business/Financial Risk.** This is basically the risk that the *issuer will default on interest and/or principal payments*. Also known as *credit risk*, business/financial risk has to do with the quality and financial integrity of the issuer. The stronger the issuer, the less business/financial risk there is to worry about. This risk doesn't even exist for some securities (e.g., U.S. Treasuries). For others, such as corporate and municipal bonds, it's a very important consideration.

- **Liquidity Risk.** Liquidity risk is the risk that a bond will be difficult to unload, at a reasonable price, if you want to sell it. In certain sectors of the market, this is a far bigger problem than investors realize. Even though the U.S. bond market is enormous, much of the activity occurs in the primary/new-issue market. With the exception of the Treasury market and much of the agency market, relatively little trading is done in the secondary markets, particularly with corporates and municipals. Where there's little trading, there's lots of liquidity risk. If liquidity is important to you, steer clear of thinly traded bonds.

- **Call Risk.** Call risk, or *prepayment risk*, is the risk that a bond will be "called" (retired) long before its scheduled maturity date. Issuers often prepay their bonds by calling them in for prepayment. (We'll examine call features later in this chapter.) When issuers call their bonds, the bondholders end up getting cashed out of the deal and have to find another place for their investment funds—and there's the problem. Because bonds are nearly always called for prepayment after interest rates have taken a big fall, comparable investment vehicles just aren't available. Thus, you have to replace a high-yielding bond with a much lower-yielding issue. From the bondholder's perspective, a called bond means not only a disruption in cash flow but also a sharply reduced rate of return.

The returns on bonds are, of course, related to risk—other things being equal, the more risk embedded in a bond, the greater the expected return. But with bonds, the amount and types of risks involved depends, in large part, on the bond's issue characteristics. For example, as we'll see later in the chapter, there's more interest rate risk with a long bond than a short bond. In addition, it's sometimes difficult to compare the risk exposure of one bond to another, because the bonds typically have different issue characteristics. That is, one issue could have *more* interest rate and call risk, but *less* credit and liquidity risk than another issue. These different degrees of risk exposure often get buried in the net differential returns. We'll examine the various features that affect a bond's risk exposure as we work our way through this chapter.

CONCEPTS IN REVIEW

Answers available at: www.myfinancelab.com

10.1 What appeal do bonds hold for individual investors? Give several reasons why bonds make attractive investment outlets.

10.2 How would you describe the behavior of market interest rates and bond returns over the last 30–40 years? Do swings in market interest rates have any bearing on bond returns? Explain.

10.3 Identify and briefly describe the five types of risk to which bonds are exposed. What is the most important source of risk for bonds in general? Explain.

Essential Features of a Bond

LG 2   LG 3

A *bond* is a negotiable, long-term debt instrument that carries certain obligations (the payment of interest and the repayment of principal) on the part of the issuer. Because bondholders are only lending money to the issuer, they are not entitled to any of the rights and privileges that go along with an ownership position. But bondholders, as well as bond issuers, do have a number of well-defined rights and privileges that together help define the essential features of a bond. We'll now take a look at some of these features. As you will see, when it comes to bonds, it's especially important to know what you're getting into, *for many seemingly insignificant features can have dramatic effects on price behavior and investment return.* This is especially true in periods of low interest rates, because knowing what to buy and when to buy can mean the difference between earning a mediocre return and earning a highly competitive one.

■ Bond Interest and Principal

In the absence of any trading, a bond investor's return is limited to fixed interest and principal payments. Bonds involve *a fixed claim on the issuer's income* (as defined by the size of the periodic interest payments) and *a fixed claim on the assets of the issuer* (equal to the repayment of principal at maturity). As a rule, bonds pay interest every six months. There are exceptions, however; some issues carry interest payment intervals as short as a month, and a few as long as a year. The amount of interest due is a function of the **coupon**, which defines the annual interest income that the issuer will pay to the bondholder. For instance, a $1,000 bond with an 8% coupon pays $80 in interest annually—generally in the form of two $40 semiannual payments. The coupon return on a bond is often defined in terms of its **current yield**, which is a measure of the annual interest income that a bond produces relative to its prevailing market price. It is found by dividing annual coupon income by the market price of the bond. For example, if an 8% bond is currently priced in the market at $875, then it would have a current yield of 9.14%: ($1,000 × .08)/ $875 = $80/$875 = .0914. We'll look at this bond valuation measure in more detail in Chapter 11.

coupon
feature on a bond that defines the amount of annual interest income.

current yield
measure of the annual interest income a bond provides relative to its current market price.

The **principal** amount of a bond, also known as an issue's *par value*, specifies the amount of capital that must be repaid at maturity. For example, there is $1,000 of principal in a $1,000 bond. Of course, debt securities regularly trade at market prices that differ from their principal (par) values. This occurs whenever an issue's coupon differs from the prevailing market rate of interest. That is, the price of the issue changes inversely with interest rates until its yield is compatible with the prevailing market yield. Such behavior explains why a 7% issue will carry a market price of only $825 in a 9% market. The drop in price from its par value of $1,000 is necessary to raise the yield on this bond from 7% to 9%. In essence, the new, higher yield is produced in part from annual coupons and in part from capital gains, as the price of the issue moves from $825 back to $1,000 at maturity.

principal
on a bond, the amount of capital that must be repaid at maturity.

■ Maturity Date

Unlike common stock, all debt securities have limited lives and will expire on a given date in the future, the issue's **maturity date**. Whereas interest payments are made semiannually over the life of the issue, principal is repaid only at maturity (or before, in the case of called issues). The maturity date on a bond is fixed. It not only defines the life of a new issue but also denotes the amount of time remaining for older, outstanding bonds. Such a life span is known as an issue's *term to maturity*. For example, a new issue may come out as a 25-year bond; five years later, it will have 20 years remaining to maturity.

maturity date
the date on which a bond matures and the principal must be repaid.

Two types of bonds can be distinguished on the basis of maturity: term and serial issues. A **term bond** has a single, fairly lengthy maturity date and is the most common type of issue. A **serial bond**, in contrast, has a series of different maturity dates, perhaps as many as 15 or 20, within a single issue. For example, a 20-year term bond issued in 2007 has a single maturity date of 2027. That same issue as a serial bond might have 20 annual maturity dates, extending from 2007 through 2027. At each of these annual maturity dates, a certain portion of the issue would come due and be paid off.

term bond
a bond that has a single, fairly lengthy maturity date.

serial bond
a bond that has a series of different maturity dates.

note
a debt security originally issued with a maturity of from 2 to 10 years.

Maturity is also used to distinguish a *note* from a *bond*. That is, a debt security that's originally issued with a maturity of 2 to 10 years is known as a **note**; a *bond* technically has an initial term to maturity of more than ten years. In practice, notes are often issued with maturities of five to seven years, whereas bonds normally carry maturities of 20 to 30 years, or more.

▮ Principles of Bond Price Behavior

The price of a bond is a function of its coupon, its maturity, and the movement of market interest rates. Figure 10.3 captures the relationship of bond prices to market interest rates. Basically, the graph reinforces the *inverse relationship* that exists between bond prices and market rates: *Lower* rates lead to *higher* bond prices.

premium bond
a bond with a market value in excess of par; occurs when interest rates drop below the coupon rate.

discount bond
a bond with a market value lower than par; occurs when market rates are greater than the coupon rate.

Figure 10.3 also shows the difference between premium and discount bonds. A **premium bond** is one that sells for more than its par value. A premium results whenever market interest rates drop below the bond's coupon rate. A **discount bond**, in contrast, sells for less than par. The discount is the result of market rates being greater than the issue's coupon rate. Thus, the 10% bond in Figure 10.3 trades at a premium when market rates are at 8%, but at a discount when rates are at 12%.

When a bond is first issued, it is usually sold to the public at a price that equals or is very close to its par value. Likewise, when the bond matures—some 15, 20, or 30 years later—it will once again be priced at its par value. What happens to the price of the bond in between is of considerable interest to most bond investors. In this regard, the extent to which bond prices move depends not only on the *direction* of change in interest rates but also on the *magnitude* of such change: The greater the moves in interest rates, the greater the swings in bond prices.

However, bond price volatility also varies according to an issue's coupon and maturity. That is, bonds with *lower coupons* and/or *longer maturities* have *lots of price volatility*, and are more responsive to changes in market interest rates. (Note in Figure 10.3 that for a given change in interest rates—e.g., from 10% to 8%—the largest change in price occurs when the bond has the greatest number of years to maturity.) Therefore, if you expect a *decline* in interest rates, you should seek lower coupons and longer maturities (to maximize capital gains). When interest rates move *up*, you should do just the opposite: seek high coupons with short maturities. This choice will minimize price variation and act to preserve as much capital as possible.

Actually, of the two variables, the *maturity* of an issue has the greater impact on price volatility. For example, look what happens to the price of an 8% bond when market interest rates rise by 1, 2, or 3 percentage points:

| | Change in the Price of an 8% Bond When Interest Rates Rise by: | | |
Bond Maturity	1 Percentage Point	2 Percentage Points	3 Percentage Points
5 years	−4.0%	−7.7%	−11.2%
25 years	−9.9%	−18.2%	−25.3%

For purposes of this illustration, we assume the changes in interest rates occur "instantaneously," so the maturities remain fixed, at 5 or 25 years. Given the computed price changes, it's clear that the shorter (five-year) bond offers a lot

FIGURE 10.3 The Price Behavior of a Bond

A bond will sell at its par value so long as the prevailing market interest rate remains the same as the bond's coupon—in this case, 10%. However, when the market rates drop, bond prices move up. When rates rise, bond prices move down. As a bond approaches its maturity, the price of the issue moves toward its par value, regardless of the level of prevailing interest rates.

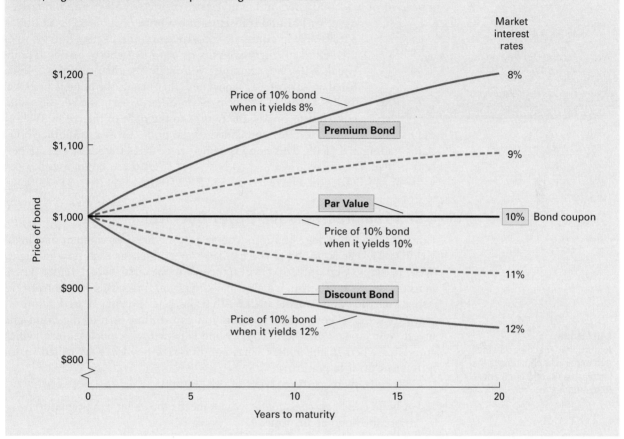

more price stability. Such behavior is universal with all fixed-income securities, and is very important. It means that if you want to reduce your exposure to capital loss or, more to the point, to lower the price volatility in your bond holdings, then just *shorten your maturities*.

▮ Pricing a Bond

Unlike stocks, the vast majority of bonds—especially corporate and municipal bonds—rarely change hands in the secondary markets. As a result, with the exception of U.S. Treasury and some agency issues, bonds are not widely quoted in the financial press, not even in the *Wall Street Journal*. So, rather than looking at how bonds are quoted, let's look at how they're priced in the marketplace. Regardless of the type, *all bonds are priced as a percent of par*, meaning that a quote of, say, 85 translates into a price of 85% of the bond's par value. In the bond market, 1 point equals $10, so a quote of 85 does not mean $85, but rather, $850. Market convention assumes that bonds carry par values of $1,000; thus, a bond quote of 85 means the price is 85% of $1,000, or $850. Also, the price of any bond is always related to the issue's coupon and maturity; those two features are always a part of any listed price because (as we saw above) of the effect they have on the price of a bond.

In the corporate and municipal markets, bonds are priced in decimals, using three places to the right of the decimal point. Thus, a quote of 87.562, as a percent of a $1,000 par bond, converts to a price of $875.62. Similarly, a quote of 121.683 translates into a price of 1.21683 × $1,000 = $1,216.83. In contrast, U.S. Treasury and agency bond quotes are stated in *thirty-seconds of a point* (where, again, 1 point equals $10). For example, you might see the price of a T-bond listed at, say, 94:16. Translated, that means the bond is priced at 94 16/32, or 94.5% of par—in other words, at $945.00. With government bonds, the figures to the right of the colon (:) show the number of thirty-seconds embedded in the price. Consider another bond that's trading at 141:08. This bond is being priced at 141 8/32, or 141.25 percent of par. Thus, if you wanted to buy, say, 15 of these bonds (with a par value of $15,000), you'd have to pay $21,187.50 (i.e., 1.4125 × $15,000).

■ Call Features—Let the Buyer Beware!

Consider the following situation: You've just made an investment in a high-yielding, 25-year bond. Now you can sit back and let the cash flow in, right? Well, perhaps. Certainly, that will happen for the first several years. But, if market interest rates drop, it's also likely that you'll receive a notice from the issuer that the bond is being *called*—that the issue is being retired before its maturity date. There's really nothing you can do but turn in the bond and invest your money elsewhere. Every bond is issued with a **call feature**, which stipulates whether and under what conditions a bond can be called in for retirement prior to maturity.

call feature
feature that specifies whether and under what conditions the issuer can retire a bond prior to maturity.

Basically, there are three types of call features:

1. A bond can be *freely callable*, which means the issuer can prematurely retire the bond at any time.
2. A bond can be *noncallable*, which means the issuer is prohibited from retiring the bond prior to maturity.
3. The issue could carry a *deferred call*, which means the issue cannot be called until after a certain length of time has passed from the date of issue. In essence, the issue is noncallable during the deferment period and then becomes freely callable thereafter.

Obviously, in our illustration above, either the high-yielding bond was issued as freely callable or it became freely callable with the end of its call deferment period.

Call features are placed on bonds *for the benefit of the issuers*. They're used most often to replace one issue with another that carries a lower coupon, and the issuer benefits by the reduction in annual interest cost. Thus, when market interest rates undergo a sharp decline, bond issuers retire their high-yielding bonds (by calling them in) and replace them with lower-yielding obligations. *The net result is that the investor is left with a much lower rate of return than anticipated.*

call premium
the amount added to a bond's par value and paid to investors when a bond is retired prematurely.

In a half-hearted attempt to compensate investors who find their bonds called out from under them, issuers tack a **call premium** onto a bond. If the issue is called, the issuer will pay the call premium to investors, along with the

call price
the price the issuer must pay to retire a bond prematurely; equal to par value plus the call premium.

refunding provisions
provisions that prohibit the premature retirement of an issue from the proceeds of a lower-coupon refunding bond.

sinking fund
a provision that stipulates the amount of principal that will be retired annually over the life of a bond.

senior bonds
secured debt obligations, backed by a legal claim on specific property of the issuer.

mortgage bonds
senior bonds secured by real estate.

collateral trust bonds
senior bonds backed by securities owned by the issuer but held in trust by a third party.

issue's par value. The sum of the par value plus call premium represents the issue's **call price**. This is the amount the issuer must pay to retire the bond prematurely. As a general rule, call premiums usually equal about 8 to 12 months' interest at the earliest date of call and then become progressively smaller as the issue nears maturity. Using this rule, the initial call price of a 9% bond could be as high as $1,090, where $90 represents the call premium.

In addition to call features, some bonds may carry **refunding provisions**. These are much like call features except that they prohibit just one thing: the premature retirement of an issue from the proceeds of a lower-coupon bond. For example, a bond could come out as freely callable but *nonrefundable* for five years. In this case, the bond would probably be sold by brokers as a *deferred refunding issue*, with little or nothing said about its call feature. The distinction is important, however: It means that a nonrefunding or deferred refunding issue *can still be called and prematurely retired for any reason other than refunding*. Thus, an investor could face a call on a high-yielding nonrefundable issue so long as the issuer has so-called "clean cash" to retire the bond prematurely.

▌ Sinking Funds

Another provision that's important to investors is the **sinking fund**, which stipulates how the issuer will pay off the bond over time. This provision applies only to term bonds, of course, because serial issues already have a predetermined method of repayment. Not all (term) bonds have sinking-fund requirements, but for those that do, a sinking fund specifies the annual repayment schedule that will be used to pay off the issue. It indicates how much principal will be retired each year.

Sinking-fund requirements generally begin one to five years after the date of issue and continue annually thereafter until all or most of the issue is paid off. Any amount not repaid (which might equal 10% to 25% of the issue) would then be retired with a single "balloon" payment at maturity. Unlike a call or refunding provision, the issuer generally does not have to pay a call premium with sinking-fund calls. Instead, the bonds are normally called at par for sinking-fund purposes.

There's another difference between sinking-fund provisions and call or refunding features. That is, whereas a call or refunding provision gives the issuer the *right* to retire a bond prematurely, a sinking-fund provision *obligates* the issuer to pay off the bond systematically over time. The issuer has no choice. It must make sinking-fund payments in a prompt and timely fashion or run the risk of being in default.

▌ Secured or Unsecured Debt

A single issuer may have a number of different bonds outstanding at any given point in time. In addition to coupon and maturity, one bond can be differentiated from another by the type of collateral behind the issue. Issues can be either junior or senior. **Senior bonds** are secured obligations, which are backed by a legal claim on some specific property of the issuer. Such issues would include:

- **Mortgage bonds,** which are secured by real estate.
- **Collateral trust bonds,** which are backed by financial assets owned by the issuer but held in trust by a third party.

equipment trust certificates
senior bonds secured by specific pieces of equipment; popular with transportation companies such as airlines.

first and refunding bonds
bonds secured in part with both first and second mortgages.

junior bonds
debt obligations backed only by the promise of the issuer to pay interest and principal on a timely basis.

debenture
an unsecured (junior) bond.

subordinated debentures
unsecured bonds whose claim is secondary to other debentures.

income bonds
unsecured bonds requiring that interest be paid only after a specified amount of income is earned.

bond ratings
letter grades that designate investment quality and are assigned to a bond issue by rating agencies.

- **Equipment trust certificates**, which are secured by specific pieces of equipment (e.g., boxcars and airplanes) and are popular with railroads and airlines.

- **First and refunding bonds**, which are basically a combination of first mortgage and junior lien bonds (i.e., the bonds are secured in part by a first mortgage on some of the issuer's property and in part by second or third mortgages on other properties).

Note that first and refunding bonds are *less secure* than, and should *not* be confused with, straight first-mortgage bonds.

Junior bonds, on the other hand, are backed only by the promise of the issuer to pay interest and principal on a timely basis. There are several classes of unsecured bonds, the most popular of which is known as a **debenture**. For example, a major company, like Hewlett-Packard, could issue, say, $500 million worth of 20-year debenture bonds. Being a debenture, the bond would be totally unsecured, meaning there is no collateral backing up the obligation, other than the good name of the issuer. In the final analysis, it's the quality of the issuer that matters. For that reason, highly regarded firms have no trouble selling *billion-dollar issues*, and at highly competitive rates. It's done all the time.

Subordinated debentures can also be found in the market. These issues have a claim on income secondary to other debenture bonds. **Income bonds**, the most junior of all bonds, are unsecured debts requiring that interest be paid only after a certain amount of income is earned. With these bonds, there is no legally binding requirement to meet interest payments on a timely or regular basis so long as a specified amount of income has not been earned. These issues are similar in many respects to *revenue bonds* found in the municipal market.

▌Bond Ratings

To many investors, an issue's *agency rating* is just as important in defining the characteristics of a bond as are its coupon, maturity, and call features. These ratings indicate the amount of *credit risk* embedded in a bond, and are widely used by fixed-income investors. **Bond ratings** are like grades: A letter grade that designates investment quality is assigned to an issue on the basis of extensive, professionally conducted financial analysis. They are an important part of the municipal and corporate bond markets, where issues are regularly evaluated and rated by one or more of the rating agencies. Even some agency issues, like the Tennessee Valley Authority (TVA), are rated, though they always receive ratings that confirm the obvious—that the issues are prime grade. The two largest and best-known rating agencies are Moody's and Standard & Poor's; another lesser known but still important bond-rating agency is Fitch Investors Service.

How Ratings Work Every time a large new issue comes to the market, it is analyzed by a staff of professional bond analysts to determine default risk exposure and investment quality. The rating agency thoroughly studies the financial records of the issuing organization and assesses its future prospects. As you might expect, the firm's financial strength and stability are very important in determining the appropriate bond rating. Although, there is far more to

TABLE 10.2 Bond Ratings

Moody's	S&P	Definition
Aaa	AAA	*High-grade investment bonds.* The highest rating assigned, denoting extremely strong capacity to pay principal and interest. Often called "gilt-edge" securities.
Aa	AA	*High-grade investment bonds.* High quality by all standards but rated lower primarily because the margins of protection are not quite as strong.
A	A	*Medium-grade investment bonds.* Many favorable investment attributes, but elements may be present that suggest susceptibility to adverse economic changes.
Baa	BBB	*Medium-grade investment bonds.* Adequate capacity to pay principal and interest but possibly lacking certain protective elements against adverse economic conditions.
Ba	BB	*Speculative issues.* Only moderate protection of principal and interest in varied economic times. (This is one of the ratings carried by junk bonds.)
B	B	*Speculative issues.* Generally lacking desirable characteristics of investment bonds. Assurance of principal and interest may be small; this is another junk-bond rating.
Caa	CCC	*Default.* Poor-quality issues that may be in default or in danger of default.
Ca	CC	*Default.* Highly speculative issues, often in default or possessing other market shortcomings.
C		*Default.* These issues may be regarded as extremely poor in investment quality.
	C	*Default.* Rating given to income bonds on which no interest is paid.
	D	*Default.* Issues actually in default, with principal or interest in arrears.

Source: Moody's *Bond Record* and Standard & Poor's *Bond Guide.*

setting a rating than cranking out a few financial ratios, a strong relationship does exist between the operating results and financial condition of the firm and the rating its bonds receive. Generally, higher ratings are associated with more profitable companies that rely *less* on debt as a form of financing, are more liquid, have stronger cash flows, and have no trouble servicing their debt in a prompt and timely fashion.

Table 10.2 lists the various ratings assigned to bonds by the two major services. In addition to the standard rating categories noted in the table, Moody's uses numerical modifiers (1, 2, or 3) on bonds rated double-A to B, while S&P uses plus (+) or minus (−) signs on the same rating classes to show relative standing within a major rating category. For example, A+ (or A1) means a strong, high A rating, whereas A− (or A3) indicates that the issue is on the low end of the A rating scale.

Note that the top four ratings (Aaa through Baa, or AAA through BBB) designate *investment-grade* bonds. Such ratings are highly coveted by issuers, as they indicate financially strong, well-run companies. The next two ratings (Ba/B or BB/B) are reserved for junk bonds. These ratings mean that although *the principal and interest payments on the bonds are still being met in a timely fashion*, the risk of default is relatively high. The issuers of these bonds generally lack the financial strength that backs investment-grade issues. Most of the time, Moody's and S&P assign identical ratings. Sometimes, however, an issue carries two different ratings. These **split ratings** are viewed simply as "shading" the quality of an issue one way or another. For example, an issue might be rated Aa by Moody's but A or A+ by S&P.

Also, just because a bond is given a certain rating at the time of issue doesn't mean it will keep that rating for the rest of its life. Ratings change as the

HOTLINKS

For further explanation of Moody's bond ratings, go to:

www.bondpickers.com/?cmd=ratings

split ratings
different ratings given to a bond issue by two or more rating agencies.

financial condition of the issuer changes. In fact, all rated issues are reviewed on a regular basis to ensure that the assigned rating is still valid. Many issues do carry a single rating to maturity, but it is not uncommon for ratings to be revised up or down. As you might expect, the market responds to rating revisions by adjusting bond yields accordingly. For example, an upward revision (e.g., from A to AA) causes the market yield on the bond to drop, as a reflection of the bond's improved quality. One final point: Although it may appear that the firm is receiving the rating, it is actually the *issue* that receives it. As a result, a firm's different issues can have different ratings. The senior securities, for example, might carry one rating and the junior issues another, lower rating.

What Ratings Mean   Investors pay close attention to agency ratings, because ratings can affect not only potential market behavior but comparative market yields as well. Specifically, *the higher the rating, the lower the yield*, other things being equal. For example, whereas an A-rated bond might offer a 7.5% yield, a comparable triple-A issue would probably yield something like 7%. Furthermore, investment-grade securities are far more interest-sensitive and tend to exhibit more uniform price behavior than junk bonds and other lower-rated issues.

Perhaps most important, *bond ratings serve to relieve individual investors of the drudgery of evaluating the investment quality of an issue on their own*. Large institutional investors often have their own staff of credit analysts who independently assess the creditworthiness of various corporate and municipal issuers. Individual investors, in contrast, have little if anything to gain from conducting their own credit analysis. After all, credit analysis is time-consuming and costly, and it demands a good deal more expertise than the average individual investor possesses. Most important, the ratings are closely adhered to by a large segment of the bond investment community, in large part because it has been shown that *the rating agencies do a remarkably good job of assessing bond quality*. Thus, individual investors can depend on assigned agency ratings as a viable measure of the creditworthiness of the issuer and an issue's risk of default. A word of caution is in order, however: Bear in mind that bond ratings are intended to measure only an issue's *default risk*, which has no bearing whatsoever on an issue's exposure to *market risk*. Thus, if interest rates increase, even the highest-quality issues go down in price, subjecting investors to capital loss and market risk.

CONCEPTS IN REVIEW

Answers available at: www.myfinancelab.com

10.4   Can issue characteristics (such as coupon and call features) affect the yield and price behavior of bonds? Explain.

10.5   What is the difference between a *call feature* and a *sinking-fund provision?* Briefly describe the three different types of call features. Can a bond be freely callable but nonrefundable?

10.6   What is the difference between a *premium bond* and a *discount bond?* What three attributes are most important in determining an issue's price volatility?

10.7   Bonds are said to be quoted "as a percent of par." What does that mean? What is 1 point worth in the bond market?

10.8 What are *bond ratings*, and how can they affect investor returns? What are *split ratings?*

10.9 From the perspective of an individual investor, what good are bond ratings? Do bond ratings indicate the amount of market risk embedded in a bond? Explain.

The Market for Debt Securities

Thus far, our discussion has dealt with basic bond features. We now shift our attention to a review of the market in which these securities are traded. To begin with, the bond market is chiefly over-the-counter in nature, as listed bonds represent only a small portion of total outstanding obligations. In addition, this market is far more stable than the stock market. Indeed, although interest rates—and therefore bond prices—do move up and down over time, when bond price activity is measured on a daily basis, it is *remarkably stable*. Two other things that stand out about the bond market: It's big, and it has been growing rapidly. From a $250 billion market in 1950, it has grown to the point where, in 2006, the amount of bonds outstanding in this country totaled nearly *$27 trillion!* That makes the bond market about twice the size of the U.S. stock market.

Here's what the U.S. bond market looked like in 2006:

	Amount Outstanding ($ in trillions)
U.S. Treasury securities	$4.7
Agency securities	2.6
Municipal bonds	1.9
Corporate bonds	6.4
Mortgage-backed securities	3.7
Foreign issues and Eurodollar bonds	5.6
Total	$26.9

Source: *Federal Reserve Bulletin*, "Credit Market Debt Outstanding," March 2006.

The growth in this market has also been remarkable, as it has more than doubled in size since 1992. That translates into a compound rate of growth of nearly 9% a year. Domestic issues alone (*excluding* foreign issues and Eurodollar bonds) account for $21.3 trillion, or 80% of the total U.S. market.

■ Major Market Segments

There are bonds available in today's market to meet almost any investment objective and to suit just about any type of investor. As a matter of convenience, the domestic bond market is normally separated into four major segments, according to type of issuer: Treasury, agency, municipal, and corporate. As we shall see, each sector has developed its own features, as well as its own trading characteristics.

Treasury Bonds "Treasuries" (or "governments," as they are sometimes called) are a dominant force in the fixed-income market. If not the most popular type of bond, they certainly are the best known. In addition to T-bills (a popular short-term debt security), the U.S. Treasury issues notes and bonds. It also issues *inflation-indexed securities*, which are the newest type of Treasury debt.

All Treasury obligations are of the highest quality because they are all backed by the "full faith and credit" of the U.S. government. This backing, along with their liquidity, makes them very popular with individual and institutional investors both here and abroad. Indeed, Treasury securities are traded in all the major markets of the world, from New York to London to Sydney and Tokyo.

Treasury notes are issued with maturities of 2, 3, 5, and 10 years, whereas **Treasury bonds** carry 20- and 30-year maturities. (Note that while the Treasury is authorized to issue these securities, *it has not issued 20-year bonds in over 20 years—the last one came out in January 1986—and only recently, in February 2006, did they resume issuing 30-year bonds.*) All Treasury notes and bonds are sold in $1,000 denominations. Interest income from these securities is subject to normal federal income tax but *is exempt from state and local taxes*. The Treasury today issues only *noncallable* securities; the last time it issued callable debt was in 1984. It issues its securities at regularly scheduled auctions, the results of which are widely reported by the financial media (see Figure 10.4). The Treasury establishes the initial yields and coupons on the securities it issues through this auction process.

Treasury notes
U.S. Treasury debt securities that are issued with maturities of 2 to 10 years.

Treasury bonds
U.S. Treasury securities that are issued with 20- and 30-year maturities.

FIGURE 10.4   Auction Results—The Return of the 30-Year Treasury Bond

Treasury auctions are closely followed by the financial media; and especially this one, which marked the return of the 30-year T-bond after a 4½-year hiatus. (The last 30-year T-bond was issued in August 2001.) These auctions are highly competitive. The number of bids submitted generally far exceeds the size of the issue, so the spread between the highest and lowest bids is quite small—sometimes as small as 2 basis points, or 2/100 of 1%. (*Source:* Department of the Treasury—Bureau of Public Debt, and from The *Wall Street Journal*, February 10, 2006. ©2006 Dow Jones & Company, Inc. Reproduced with permission from Dow Jones & Company, Inc. via Copyright Clearance Center.)

AUCTION RESULTS

Here are the results of the Treasury auction of new 30-year bonds. All bids are awarded at a single price at the market-clearing yield. Rates are determined by the difference between that price and the face value.

Applications	$28,720,402,000
Accepted bids	$14,000,064,000
Bids at market-clearing yield accepted	51.17%
Accepted noncompetitively	$38,776,000
Foreign noncompetitively	$100,000,000
Auction price (Rate)	99.510492 (4.530%)
Coupon equivalent	4.50%
CUSIP number	912828FTO

The bonds are dated Feb. 15, 2006 and mature Feb. 15, 2036.

- The amount of bids submitted.
- Size of the issue—the dollar amount of accepted bids.
- The amount of noncompetitive bids submitted (and accepted).
- The average price and yield (rate) on the issue.
- The coupon that the issue will carry, which is set after the auction.

Inflation-Protection Securities The newest form of Treasury security (first issued in 1997) is the **Treasury inflation-indexed obligation.** Also known as **TIPS,** which stands for "Treasury inflation-protection securities," they are issued as notes (with ten-year maturities) and, until 2001, as bonds (with 30-year maturities). They offer investors the opportunity to stay ahead of inflation by periodically adjusting their returns for any inflation that has occurred. That is, if inflation is running at an annual rate of, say, 3%, then at the end of the year, the par (maturity) value of the bond will increase by 3%. (Actually, the adjustments to par value are done every six months.) Thus the par value of a $1,000 bond will grow to $1,030 at the end of the first year. If the 3% inflation rate continues for the second year, the par value will once again increase, this time from $1,030 to $1,061 ($1,030 × 1.03). The coupons on these securities are set very low, at a level meant to provide investors with *real (inflation-adjusted) returns.* Thus, one of these bonds might carry a coupon of only 3.5%, at a time when regular T-bonds are paying, say, 6.5% or 7%. But there's an advantage even to this: *Even though the coupon rates are fixed for the life of the issue, the actual size of the coupon payment will increase over time as the par value on the bond goes up.* Thus, these bonds provide inflation protection in two ways: First, the principal value of the bond goes up over time. You buy one of these bonds at par ($1,000) and at maturity, you may get back, say, $1,500. Second, the annual interest income goes up each year in tandem with the higher principal value. For example, with a 3.5% coupon, you will get $35 in interest income the first year, and the interest will slowly rise with the par value, so that by the tenth year, you may get, say, $52.50. For investors who are concerned about inflation protection, these securities may be just the ticket. The accompanying *Investing in Action* box (on page 446) provides more information about TIPS, including some of their good and bad points.

Agency Bonds Agency bonds are debt securities issued by various agencies and organizations of the U.S. government, such as the Federal Home Loan Bank, the Federal Farm Credit Systems, the Small Business Administration, the Student Loan Marketing Association, and the Federal National Mortgage Association. Though these securities are the closest things to Treasuries, they are not obligations of the U.S. Treasury and technically should not be considered the same as Treasury bonds. Even so, *they are very high-quality securities that have almost no risk of default.* In spite of the similar default risk, however, these securities usually provide yields that are comfortably above the market rates for Treasuries. Thus, they offer a way to increase returns with little or no real difference in risk.

There are basically two types of agency issues: government-sponsored and federal agencies. Six government-sponsored organizations and more than two dozen federal agencies offer agency bonds. To overcome some of the problems in the marketing of many relatively small federal agency securities, Congress established the Federal Financing Bank to consolidate the financing activities of all federal agencies. (As a rule, the generic term *agency* is used to denote both government-sponsored and federal agency obligations.)

Table 10.3 (on page 447) presents selected characteristics of some of the more popular agency bonds. As the list of issuers shows, most of the government agencies support either agriculture or housing.

Treasury inflation-indexed obligations (TIPS)
a type of Treasury security that provides protection against inflation by adjusting investor returns for the annual rate of inflation.

agency bonds
debt securities issued by various agencies and organizations of the U.S. government.

HOTLINKS
To access a database of corporate, agency, and municipal bond offerings, go again to the Web site of the Bond Market Association, but now click on [Bond Markets & Prices].
www.investinginbonds.com

INVESTING *in Action*

Some Tips on TIPS

Bondholders look at inflation the way Superman looks at kryptonite. Superman weakens when faced with the dreaded substance. When inflation heats up, it causes bond prices to buckle, fixed payments to lose their purchasing power, and bondholders to weaken. To encourage investors to buy its bonds without fearing inflation, in 1997 Uncle Sam created TIPS, Treasury inflation-protected securities.

Here is how TIPS work: The government issues a ten-year bond with a $1,000 face value that pays, say, 3% interest; that rate stays fixed for the life of the issue. But if the consumer price index (CPI) rises, so does the face amount of the bond. For example, because the CPI rose 2.8% in 2005, the new face amount would be adjusted up to $1,000 × 1.028 = $1,028. Therefore, in 2006, the annual interest payment would be $30.84 (3% of $1,028). When TIPS mature in ten years, the investor gets inflation-adjusted face value at that time, which could be as much as $2,000 if inflation takes off. TIPS also protect you if deflation occurs. The bond's value will not fall below its initial face value (of $1,000).

Although TIPS protect investors from erosion in bond prices, they are not so great if inflation stays dormant. Currently, investors are receiving a 2% to 2.5% return on their money. (At the April 2006 auction, the coupon for ten-year TIPS was 2% with a yield of 2.41%, compared to a 5.125% coupon and 5.14% yield for a regular ten-year Treasury note.)

Another downside to TIPS is taxes. Investors have to pay a tax on the increasing value of their bonds, but the catch is that the government does not actually pay out the increase in the bond's face value until maturity. Thus, you end up paying taxes each year on income you've earned but haven't yet received. For that reason, TIPS probably make the most sense for individual retirement accounts (IRAs) and other tax-deferred accounts. You can buy TIPS directly from the U.S. Treasury using TreasuryDirect or from your broker. Also, several mutual fund companies now offer funds that invest in TIPS.

CRITICAL THINKING QUESTIONS Why would investors be interested in TIPS? What are the advantages and disadvantages of this security from the investor's point of view?

Source: TreasuryDirect, Bureau of the Public Debt, wwww.publicdebt.treas.gov.

Although agency issues are not direct liabilities of the U.S. government, a few of them do carry government guarantees and therefore represent the full faith and credit of the U.S. Treasury. Even those issues that do not carry such guarantees are viewed as *moral obligations* of the U.S. government implying it's highly unlikely that Congress would allow one of them to default. Agency issues are normally noncallable or carry lengthy call deferment features. One final point: Since 1986 *all new agency (and Treasury) securities* have been issued in *book entry form*. This means that no certificate of ownership is issued to the buyer of the bonds. Rather, the buyer receives a "confirmation" of the transaction, and his or her name is entered in a computerized logbook, where it remains as long as that investor owns the security.

municipal bonds
debt securities issued by states, counties, cities, and other political subdivisions; most of these bonds are tax-exempt (free of federal income tax on interest income).

Municipal Bonds Municipal bonds are the issues of states, counties, cities, and other political subdivisions (such as school districts and water and sewer districts). This is a $1.9 trillion market today, and it's the only segment of the bond market where the individual investor plays a major role: About 40% of all municipal bonds are directly held by individuals. These bonds are often issued as *serial obligations*, which means the issue is broken into a series of smaller bonds, each with its own maturity date and coupon.

TABLE 10.3 Characteristics of Some Popular Agency Issues

Type of Issue	Minimum Denomination	Initial Maturity	Tax Status* Federal	State	Local
Federal Farm Credit System	$ 1,000	13 months to 15 years	T	E	E
Federal Home Loan Bank	10,000	1 to 20 years	T	E	E
Federal Land Banks	1,000	1 to 10 years	T	E	E
Farmers Home Administration	25,000	1 to 25 years	T	T	T
Federal Housing Administration	50,000	1 to 40 years	T	T	T
Federal Home Loan Mortgage Corp.** ("Freddie Mac")	25,000	18 to 30 years	T	T	T
Federal National Mortgage Association** ("Fannie Mae")	25,000	1 to 30 years	T	T	T
Government National Mortgage Association** (GNMA—"Ginnie Mae")	25,000	12 to 40 years	T	T	T
Student Loan Marketing Association	10,000	3 to 10 years	T	E	E
Tennessee Valley Authority (TVA)	1,000	5 to 50 years	T	E	E
U.S. Postal Service	10,000	25 years	T	E	E
Federal Financing Corp.	1,000	1 to 20 years	T	E	E

*T = taxable; E = tax-exempt.
**Mortgage-backed securities.

general obligation bonds
municipal bonds backed by the full faith, credit, and taxing power of the issuer.

revenue bonds
municipal bonds that require payment of principal and interest only if sufficient revenue is generated by the issuer.

municipal bond guarantees
guarantees from a party other than the issuer that principal and interest payments will be made in a prompt and timely manner.

HOTLINKS

For more information on municipal bonds, go again to the Web site of the Bond Market Association. This time, after clicking on [Bond Markets & Prices], click on [Municipal Market At-A-Glance].

www.investinginbonds.com

Municipal bonds ("munis") are brought to the market as either general obligation or revenue bonds. **General obligation bonds** are backed by the full faith, credit, and taxing power of the issuer. **Revenue bonds**, in contrast, are serviced by the income generated from specific income-producing projects (e.g., toll roads). The vast majority of munis today come out as revenue bonds, accounting for about 70% to 75% of the new-issue volume. Municipal bonds are customarily issued in $5,000 denominations.

The distinction between a general obligation bond and a revenue bond is important for a bondholder, because the issuer of a revenue bond is obligated to pay principal and interest *only if a sufficient level of revenue is generated*. If the funds aren't there, the issuer does not have to make payment on the bond. General obligation bonds, however, are required to be serviced in a timely fashion irrespective of the level of tax income generated by the municipality. Obviously, revenue bonds involve more risk than general obligations, and because of that, they provide higher yields.

A somewhat unusual aspect of municipal bonds is the widespread use of **municipal bond guarantees**. With these guarantees, a party other than the issuer assures the bondholder that principal and interest payments will be made in a timely manner. The third party, in essence, provides an additional source of collateral in the form of insurance, placed on the bond at the date of issue, that is nonrevocable over the life of the obligation. All of which improves the quality of the bond. The three principal insurers are the Municipal Bond Investors Assurance Corporation (MBIA), the American Municipal Bond Assurance Corporation (AMBAC), and the Financial Guaranty Insurance Company (FGIC). These guarantors will normally insure any general obligation or revenue bond as long as it carries an S&P rating of triple-B or better. Municipal bond insurance results in higher ratings (usually triple-A) and improved liquidity for these bonds, which are generally more actively traded in the secondary markets. Insured bonds are especially common in the revenue market, where the insurance markedly boosts their attractiveness. That is, whereas an uninsured revenue bond lacks certainty of payment, a guaranteed issue is very much like a general obligation bond because the investor knows that principal and interest payments will be made on time.

Tax Advantages Without a doubt, the thing that makes municipal securities unique is the fact that, in most cases, their interest income is exempt from federal income taxes. That's why these issues are known as *tax-free*, or *tax-exempt*, bonds. Normally, the obligations are also exempt from state and local taxes *in the state in which they were issued*. For example, a California issue is free of California tax if the bondholder lives in California, but its interest income is subject to state tax if the investor resides in Arizona. Note that *capital gains on municipal bonds are not exempt from taxes*.

Individual investors are the biggest buyers of municipal bonds, and tax-free yield is a major draw. Table 10.4 shows what a taxable bond would have to yield to equal the net yield of a tax-free bond. *It demonstrates how the yield attractiveness of municipals varies with an investor's income level.* Clearly, the higher the individual's tax bracket, the more attractive municipal bonds become. Generally speaking, an investor has to be in one of the higher federal tax brackets (28% to 35%) before municipal bonds offer yields that are competitive with fully taxable issues. This is so because municipal yields are (almost always) lower than those available from fully taxable issues (such as corporates). So, unless the tax effect is sufficient to raise the yield on a municipal to a figure that equals or surpasses taxable rates, municipal bonds will not provide sufficient return.

Taxable Equivalent Yields We can determine the level of return a fully taxable bond would have to provide in order to match the after-tax return of a lower-yielding, tax-free issue by computing what is known as a municipal's **taxable equivalent yield**. Indeed, use of the taxable equivalent yield is standard convention in the market; it facilitates comparing the return on a given municipal bond to any number of fully taxable issues. This measure can be calculated according to the following simple formula:

taxable equivalent yield
the return a fully taxable bond would have to provide to match the after-tax return of a lower-yielding, tax-free municipal bond.

Equation 10.1 ➤

$$\text{Taxable equivalent yield} = \frac{\text{Yield on municipal bond}}{1 - \text{Federal tax rate}}$$

For example, if a municipal offered a yield of 6.5%, then an individual in the 35% tax bracket would have to find a fully taxable bond with a yield of 10.0% (i.e., 6.5%/0.65 = 10.0%) to reap the same after-tax returns as the municipal.

Note, however, that Equation 10.1 considers *federal taxes only*. As a result, the computed taxable equivalent yield applies only to certain situations: (1) to states that have no state income tax; (2) to situations where the investor is looking at an out-of-state bond (which would be taxable by the investor's state of residence); or (3) where the investor is comparing a municipal bond to a Treasury (or agency) bond—in which case *both* the Treasury and the municipal bonds are free from state income tax. Under any of these conditions, the only tax that's relevant is federal income tax, so using Equation 10.1 is appropriate.

But what if the investor is comparing an in-state bond to, say, a corporate bond? In this case, the in-state bond would be free from both federal and state

TABLE 10.4 Taxable Equivalent Yields for Various Tax-Exempt Returns

Taxable Income*			Tax-Free Yield					
Joint Returns ($000)	Individual Returns ($000)	Federal Tax Bracket	5%	6%	7%	8%	9%	10%
$0–$15.1	$0–$7.5	10%	5.55%	6.66%	7.77%	8.88%	10.00%	11.11%
$15.1–$61.3	$7.5–$30.6	15	5.88	7.06	8.24	9.41	10.59	11.76
$61.3–$123.7	$30.6–$74.2	25	6.67	8.00	9.33	10.67	12.00	13.33
$123.7–$188.4	$74.2–$154.8	28	6.94	8.33	9.72	11.11	12.50	13.89
$188.4–$336.5	$154.8–$336.5	33	7.46	8.96	10.45	11.94	13.43	14.92
$336.5 and above	$336.5 and above	35	7.69	9.23	10.77	12.31	13.85	15.38

*Taxable income and federal tax rates effective January 1, 2006.

taxes, but the corporate bond would not. As a result, Equation 10.1 could not be used. Instead, the investor should use a form of the equivalent yield formula that considers *both* federal and state income taxes:

Equation 10.2 ➤

$$\text{Taxable equivalent yield for both federal and state taxes} = \frac{\text{Municipal bond yield}}{1 - \left[\text{Federal tax rate} + \text{State tax rate}\left(1 - \text{Federal tax rate}\right)\right]}$$

When both federal and state taxes are included in the calculations, the net effect is to *increase* the taxable equivalent yield. Of course, the size of the increase depends on the level of state income taxes. In a high-tax state like California, for example, the impact can be substantial. Return to the 6.5% municipal bond introduced above. If a California resident in the maximum federal and state tax brackets (35% and 11%, respectively) were considering a corporate issue, she would have to get a yield of 11.25% on the corporate to match the 6.5% yield on the California bond:

$$\text{Taxable equivalent yield for both federal and state taxes} = \frac{6.5}{1 - [0.35 + 0.11(1 - 0.35)]}$$

$$= \frac{6.5}{1 - [0.35 + 0.072]}$$

$$= \underline{\underline{11.25\%}}$$

This yield compares to a taxable equivalent yield of 10.0% when only federal taxes were included in the calculation. That's a difference of more than one full percentage point—certainly *not* an insignificant amount.

Corporate Bonds Corporations are the major nongovernmental issuers of bonds. The market for corporate bonds is customarily subdivided into four segments: *industrials* (the most diverse of the groups), *public utilities* (the dominant group in terms of volume of new issues), *rail and transportation bonds*, and *financial issues* (e.g., banks, finance companies). Not only is there a full range of bond qualities available in the corporate market, but there is also a wide assortment of different types of bonds. These range from first-mortgage obligations to convertible bonds (which we'll examine later in this chapter), debentures, subordinated debentures, senior subordinated issues, capital notes (a type of unsecured debt issued by banks and other financial institutions), and income bonds. Interest on corporate bonds is paid semiannually, and sinking funds are fairly common. The bonds usually come in $1,000 denominations and are issued on a term basis with a single maturity date. Maturities usually range from 25 to 40 years or more. Many corporates, especially the longer ones, carry call deferment provisions that prohibit prepayment for the first five to ten years. Corporate issues are popular with individuals because of their relatively attractive yields.

While most corporates fit the general description above, one that does not is the *equipment trust certificate*, a security issued by railroads, airlines, and other transportation concerns. The proceeds from equipment trust certificates are used to purchase equipment (e.g., jumbo jets and railroad engines) that serves as the collateral for the issue. These bonds are usually issued in serial form and carry uniform annual installments throughout. They normally carry maturities that range from one year to a maximum of 15 to 17 years. Despite a near-perfect payment record that dates back to pre-Depression days, these issues generally offer above-average yields to investors.

▌Specialty Issues

In addition to the basic bond vehicles described above, investors can choose from a number of *specialty issues*—bonds that possess unusual issue characteristics. These bonds have coupon or repayment provisions that are out of the ordinary. Most are issued by corporations, although they are being used increasingly by other issuers as well. Four of the most actively traded specialty issues today are zero-coupon bonds, mortgage-backed securities, asset-backed securities, and high-yield junk bonds. All four of these rank as some of the more popular bonds on Wall Street.

zero-coupon bonds
bonds with no coupons that are
sold at a deep discount from
par value.

Zero-Coupon Bonds   As the name implies, **zero-coupon bonds** have no coupons. Rather, these securities are sold at a deep discount from their par values and then increase in value over time at a compound rate of return thus, at maturity, they are worth much more than their initial investment. Other things being equal, the cheaper the zero-coupon bond, the greater the return an investor can earn: For example, a bond with a 6% yield might cost $420, but one with a 10% yield might cost only $240.

Because they do not have coupons, these bonds do not pay interest semiannually. In fact, they pay *nothing* to the investor until the issue matures. As strange as it might seem, this feature is the main attraction of zero-coupon bonds. Because there are no interest payments, investors do not have to worry about reinvesting coupon income twice a year. Instead, the fully compounded rate of return on a zero-coupon bond is virtually guaranteed at the rate that existed at the time of purchase. For example, in early 2006, U.S. Treasury zero-coupon bonds with ten-year maturities were available at yields of around 4.8%. For around $600, you could buy a bond that would be worth $1,000 at maturity in ten years. That 4.8% yield is a fully compounded rate of return that's *locked in* for the life of the issue.

The foregoing advantages notwithstanding, zeros do have some serious disadvantages. One is that if rates do move up over time, you won't be able to participate in the higher return. (You'll have no coupon income to reinvest.) In addition, zero-coupon bonds are subject to tremendous price volatility: If market rates climb, you'll experience a sizable capital loss as the prices of zero-coupons plunge. (Of course, if interest rates *drop*, you'll reap enormous capital gains if you hold long-term zeros. Indeed, such issues are unsurpassed in capital gains potential.) A final disadvantage is that the IRS has ruled that zero-coupon bondholders must report *interest as it is accrued*, even though no interest is actually received. For this reason, most fully taxable zero-coupon bonds should either be used in tax-sheltered investments, such as IRAs, or be held by minor children who are likely to be taxed at the lowest rate, if at all.

Zeros are issued by corporations, municipalities, and federal agencies. You can even buy U.S. Treasury notes and bonds in the form of zero-coupon securities. They're known as **Treasury strips**, or **strip-Ts** for short. Actually, the Treasury does *not* issue zero-coupon bonds. Instead, it *allows government securities dealers to sell regular coupon-bearing notes and bonds in the form of zero-coupon securities*. Essentially, the coupons are stripped from the bond, repackaged, and then sold separately as zero-coupon bonds. For example, a ten-year Treasury note has 20 semiannual coupon payments, plus one principal payment. These 21 cash flows can be repackaged and sold as 21 different zero-coupon securities, with maturities that range from six months to ten years. Because they sell at such large discounts, Treasury strips are often sold in minimum denominations (par values) of $10,000. But with their big discounts, you'll probably pay only about half that amount (or less) for $10,000 worth of ten-year strip-Ts. Because there's an active secondary market for Treasury strips, investors can get in and out of these securities with ease just about any time they want. Strip-Ts offer the maximum in issue quality, a wide array of different maturities, and an active secondary market—all of which explains why they are so popular.

Mortgage-Backed Securities

Simply put, a **mortgage-backed bond** is a debt issue that is secured by a pool of residential mortgages. An issuer, such as the Government National Mortgage Association (GNMA), puts together a pool of home mortgages and then issues securities in the amount of the total mortgage pool. These securities, also known as *pass-through securities* or *participation certificates*, are usually sold in minimum denominations of $25,000. Though their maturities can go out as far as 30 years, the average life is generally much shorter (perhaps as short as eight to ten years) because many of the mortgages are paid off early.

As an investor in one of these securities, you hold an undivided interest in the pool of mortgages. When a homeowner makes a monthly mortgage payment, that payment is essentially passed through to you, the bondholder, to pay off the mortgage-backed bond you hold. Although these securities come with normal coupons, *the interest is paid monthly rather than semi-annually*. Actually, the monthly payments received by bondholders are, like mortgage payments, made up of both principal and interest. Because the principal portion of the payment represents return of capital, it is considered tax-free. The interest portion, however, is subject to ordinary state and federal income taxes.

HOTLINKS

To read about Treasury strips, go to:

www.bondsonline.com/asp/treas/zeros.asp

Treasury strips (strip-Ts)
zero-coupon bonds created from U.S. Treasury securities.

mortgage-backed bond
a debt issue secured by a pool of home mortgages; issued primarily by federal agencies.

HOTLINKS

For additional information on agency issues and mortgage-backed securities, visit Fidelity Investment. Also visit Fitch Ratings and click on [Structured Finance] to look at some collateral mortgage obligations and other asset-backed securities. Fitch also provides information on a wide variety of fixed-income securities. See the link in the left column of the Web site.

http://personal.fidelity.com/products/fixedincome/bond_offerings.shtml
www.fitchratings.com

Mortgage-backed securities are issued primarily by three federal agencies. Although there are some state and private issuers (mainly big banks and S&Ls), agency issues dominate the market and account for 90% to 95% of the activity. The major agency issuers of mortgage-backed securities (MBSs) are:

- **Government National Mortgage Association (GNMA).** Known as Ginnie Mae, it is the oldest and largest issuer of MBSs.

- **Federal Home Loan Mortgage Corporation (FHLMC).** Known as Freddie Mac, it was the first to issue pools containing conventional mortgages. Stock in FHLMC is publicly owned and traded on the NYSE.

- **Federal National Mortgage Association (FNMA).** Known as Fannie Mae, it's the leader in marketing seasoned/older mortgages. Its stock is also publicly owned and traded on the NYSE.

One problem with mortgage-backed securities is that *they are self-liquidating investments;* that is, a portion of the monthly cash flow to the investor is repayment of principal. Thus, you are always receiving back part of the original investment capital, so that at maturity, there is *no* big principal payment. To counter this problem, a number of *mutual funds* invest in mortgage-backed securities *but* automatically reinvest the capital/principal portion of the cash flows. Mutual fund investors therefore receive only the interest from their investments and are thus able to preserve their capital.

Collateralized Mortgage Obligations Loan prepayments are another problem with mortgage-backed securities. In fact, it was in part an effort to defuse some of the prepayment uncertainty in standard mortgage-backed securities that led to the creation of **collateralized mortgage obligations (CMOs).** Normally, as pooled mortgages are prepaid, all bondholders receive a pro-rated share of the prepayments. The net effect is to sharply reduce the life of the bond. A CMO, in contrast, divides investors into classes (called "tranches," which is French for "slice"), depending on whether they want a short-, intermediate-, or long-term investment. Although interest is paid to all bondholders, all principal payments go first to the shortest tranche until it is fully retired. Then the next class in the sequence becomes the sole recipient of principal, and so on, until the last tranche is retired.

collateralized mortgage obligation (CMO)
mortgage-backed bond whose holders are divided into classes based on the length of investment desired; principal is channeled to investors in order of maturity, with short-term classes first.

Basically, CMOs are *derivative securities* created from traditional mortgage-backed bonds, which are placed in a trust. Participation in this trust is then sold to the investing public in the form of CMOs. The net effect of this transformation is that CMOs look and behave very much like any other bond: They offer predictable interest payments and have (relatively) predictable maturities. However, although they carry the same triple-A ratings and implicit U.S. government backing as the mortgage-backed bonds that underlie them, CMOs represent a quantum leap in complexity. Some types of CMOs can be as simple and safe as Treasury bonds. Others can be far more volatile—and risky—than the standard MBSs they're made from. That's because when putting CMOs together, Wall Street performs the financial equivalent of gene splicing: Investment bankers isolate the interest and principal payments from the underlying MBSs and rechannel them to the different tranches. It's not issue quality or risk of default that's the problem here, but rather prepayment, or call, risk. All the bonds will be paid off; it's just a matter of when. Different types of CMO tranches have different levels of prepayment risk. The overall risk in a CMO cannot, of course, exceed that of the underlying mortgage-backed bonds, so in order for there to be some tranches with very little (or no) prepayment risk, others have to endure a lot more. The net effect is that while some CMO tranches are low in risk, others are loaded with it.

securitization
the process of transforming lending vehicles such as mortgages into marketable securities.

Asset-Backed Securities The creation of mortgage-backed securities and CMOs quickly led to the development of a new market technology—the process of **securitization**, whereby various lending vehicles are transformed into marketable securities, much like a mortgage-backed security. Investment bankers are now selling billions of dollars worth of pass-through securities, known as **asset-backed securities** (**ABS**), which are backed by pools of auto loans, credit card bills, and home equity lines (three of the principal types of collateral), as well as computer leases, hospital receivables, small business loans, truck rentals, and even royalty fees.

asset-backed securities (ABS)
securities similar to mortgage-backed securities that are backed by a pool of bank loans, leases, and other assets.

These securities, first introduced in the mid-1980s, are created when an investment banker bundles together some type of debt-linked asset (such as loans or receivables), and then sells investors—via asset-backed securities—the right to receive all or part of the future payments made on that debt. For example, GMAC, the financing arm of General Motors, is a regular issuer of collateralized *auto loan* securities. When it wants to get some of its car loans off its books, GMAC takes the monthly cash flow from a pool of auto loans and pledges them to a new issue of bonds, which are then sold to investors. In similar fashion, *credit card receivables* are regularly used as collateral for these bonds (indeed, they represent the biggest segment of the ABS market), as are *home equity loans*, the second-biggest type of ABS.

Investors are drawn to ABSs for a number of reasons. One is the relatively *high yields* they offer. Another is their *short maturities*, which often extend out no more than three to five years. A third is the *monthly, rather than semiannual, principal/interest payments* that accompany many of these securities. Also important to investors is their *high credit quality*. That's due to the fact that most of these deals are backed by generous credit protection. For example, the securities are often overcollateralized: the pool of assets backing the bonds may be 25% to 50% larger than the bond issue itself. For whatever reason, the vast majority of ABSs receive the highest credit rating possible (triple-A) from the leading agencies.

junk bonds
high-risk securities that have low ratings but high yields.

Junk Bonds Junk bonds (or *high-yield bonds*, as they're also called) are highly speculative securities that have received low, sub-investment-grade ratings (typically Ba or B). These bonds are issued primarily by corporations and also by municipalities. Junk bonds often take the form of *subordinated debentures*, which means the debt is unsecured and has a low claim on assets. These bonds are called "junk" because of their high risk of default. The companies that issue them generally have excessive amounts of debt in their capital structures, and their ability to service that debt is subject to considerable doubt.

PIK-bond
a payment-in-kind junk bond that gives the issuer the right to make annual interest payments in new bonds rather than in cash.

Probably the most unusual type of junk bond is something called a **PIK-bond**. PIK stands for *payment in kind* and means that rather than paying the bond's coupon in cash, the issuer can make annual interest payments in the form of additional debt. This "financial printing press" usually goes on for five or six years, after which time the issuer is supposed to start making interest payments in real money.

Why would any rational investor be drawn to junk bonds? The answer is simple: They offer very high yields. Indeed, in a typical market, relative to investment-grade bonds, you can expect to pick up anywhere from 2.5 to 5 percentage points in added yield. For example, not long ago, investors were getting 10% or 12% yields on junk bonds, compared to 7% or 8% on investment-grade corporates. Obviously, *such yields are available only because of the correspondingly higher exposure to risk.*

However, there's more to bond returns than yield alone: The *returns* you actually end up with don't always correspond to the *yields* you went in with. Junk bonds are subject to a good deal of risk, and their prices are unstable. Indeed, unlike investment-grade bonds, whose prices are closely linked to the behavior of market interest rates, junk bonds tend to behave more like stocks. As a result, the returns are highly unpredictable. Accordingly, only investors who are thoroughly familiar with the risks involved, and who are comfortable with such risk exposure, should use these securities.

■ A Global View of the Bond Market

Globalization has hit the bond market, just as it has the stock market. Foreign bonds have caught on with U.S. investors because of their high yields and attractive returns. There are risks with foreign bonds, of course, but high risk of default is *not* necessarily one of them. Instead, the big risk with foreign bonds has to do with the impact that currency fluctuations can have on returns in U.S. dollars.

The United States has the world's biggest debt market, accounting for about half of the global market. Following the United States is *Euroland* (principally Germany, Italy, and France); close behind is Japan, followed by the United Kingdom, and then Canada. Together, these issuers account for more than 90% of the world bond market. Worldwide, various forms of government bonds (e.g., Treasuries, agencies, and munis) dominate the market.

U.S.-Pay Versus Foreign-Pay Bonds There are several ways to invest in foreign bonds (*excluding* foreign bond mutual funds, which we'll examine in Chapter 12). From the perspective of a U.S. investor, we can divide foreign bonds into two broad categories on the basis of the currency in which the bond is denominated: *U.S.-pay* (or dollar-denominated) bonds, and *foreign-pay* (or non-dollar-denominated) bonds. All the cash flows—including purchase price, maturity value, and coupon income—from dollar-denominated foreign bonds are in U.S. dollars. The cash flows from nondollar-bonds are designated in a foreign currency, such as the euro, British pound, or Swiss franc.

Dollar-Denominated Bonds Dollar-denominated foreign bonds are of two types: Yankee bonds and Eurodollar bonds. **Yankee bonds** are issued by foreign governments or corporations or by so-called supernational agencies, like the World Bank and the InterAmerican Bank. These bonds are issued and traded in the United States; they're registered with the SEC, and all transactions are in U.S. dollars. Not surprisingly, Canadian issuers dominate the Yankee-bond market. Buying a Yankee bond is really no different from buying any other U.S. bond: These bonds are traded on U.S. exchanges and the OTC market, and *because everything is in dollars, there's no currency exchange risk to deal with.* The bonds are generally very high in quality (which is not surprising, given the quality of the issuers) and offer highly competitive yields to investors.

Yankee bonds
bonds issued by foreign governments or corporations but denominated in dollars and registered with the SEC.

Eurodollar bonds
foreign bonds denominated in dollars but not registered with the SEC, thus restricting sales of new issues.

Eurodollar bonds, in contrast, are issued and traded outside the United States. They are denominated in U.S. dollars, but they are not registered with the SEC, which means underwriters are legally prohibited from selling *new* issues to the U.S. public. (Only "seasoned" Eurodollar issues can be sold in this country.) The Eurodollar market today is dominated by foreign-based investors (though that is changing) and is primarily aimed at institutional investors.

Foreign-Pay Bonds From the standpoint of U.S. investors, foreign-pay international bonds encompass all those issues denominated in a currency other than dollars. These bonds are issued and traded overseas and are not registered with the SEC. Examples are German government bonds, which are payable in euros; Japanese bonds, issued in yen; and so forth. When investors speak of *foreign bonds*, it's this segment of the market that most of them are thinking of.

Foreign-pay bonds are subject to changes in currency exchange rates, which can dramatically affect total returns to U.S. investors. The returns on foreign-pay bonds are a function of three things: (1) the level of coupon (interest) income earned on the bonds; (2) the change in market interest rates, which determine the level of capital gains (or losses); and (3) the behavior of currency exchange rates. The first two variables are the same as those that drive bond returns in this country. They are, of course, just as important to foreign bonds as they are to domestic bonds. Thus, if you're investing overseas, you still want to know what the yields are today and where they're headed. *It's the third variable that separates the return behavior of dollar-denominated from foreign-pay bonds.*

We can assess returns from foreign-pay bonds by employing the same (albeit slightly modified) holding period return formula first introduced in our discussion of foreign stock returns. (See Equation 6.6 in Chapter 6.) For example, assume a U.S. investor purchased a Swedish government bond, in large part because of the attractive 7.5% coupon it carried. If the bond was bought at par and market rates fell over the course of the year, the security itself would have provided a return in excess of 7.5% (because the decline in rates would provide some capital gains). However, if the Swedish krona (SEK) fell relative to the dollar, the total return (in U.S. dollars) could have actually ended up at a lot less than 7.5%, depending on what happened to the U.S. $/SEK exchange rate. To find out exactly how this investment turned out, you could use Equation 6.6, and make a few (very minor) modifications to it (e.g., use interest income in place of dividends received). Like foreign stocks, *foreign-pay bonds can pay off from both the behavior of the security and the behavior of the currency.* That combination, in many cases, means superior returns to U.S. investors. Knowledgeable investors find these bonds attractive not only because of their competitive returns but also because of *the positive diversification effects they have on bond portfolios.*

CONCEPTS IN REVIEW

Answers available at: www.myfinancelab.com

10.10 Briefly describe each of the following types of bonds: (a) *Treasury bonds,* (b) *agency issues,* (c) *municipal securities,* and (d) *corporate bonds.* Note some of the major advantages and disadvantages of each.

10.11 Briefly define each of the following and note how they might be used by fixed-income investors: (a) *zero-coupon bonds,* (b) *CMOs,* (c) *junk bonds,* and (d) *Yankee bonds.*

10.12 What are the special tax features of (a) *Treasury securities*, (b) *agency issues*, and (c) *municipal bonds?*

10.13 Describe an *asset-backed security* (ABS) and identify some of the different forms of collateral used with these issues. Briefly note how an ABS differs from a MBS. What is the central idea behind securitization?

10.14 What's the difference between dollar-denominated and non-dollar-denominated (foreign-pay) bonds? Briefly describe the two major types of U.S.-pay bonds. Can currency exchange rates affect the total return of U.S.-pay bonds? Of foreign-pay bonds? Explain.

Convertible Securities

LG 6

convertible bonds
fixed-income obligations that have a feature permitting the holder to convert the security into a specified number of shares of the issuing company's common stock.

In addition to the many different types of bonds covered in the preceding material, there is still another type of fixed-income security that merits discussion at this point—namely, **convertible bonds**. Issued only by corporations, convertibles are different from most other types of corporate debt, because even though these securities may start out as bonds, they usually end up as shares of common stocks. That is, while these securities are originally issued as bonds (or even preferred stock), they contain a provision that enables them to subsequently be converted into shares of the issuing firm's common stock. Convertibles are considered to be *hybrid securities* because they contain attributes of both debt and equity securities. But even though they possess the features and performance characteristics of both fixed-income and equity securities, convertibles should be viewed primarily *as a form of equity*. That's because most investors commit their capital to such obligations not for the yields they provide but rather for the potential price performance of the stock side of the issue. In fact, it is always a good idea *to determine whether a corporation has convertible issues outstanding whenever you are considering a common stock investment*. In some circumstances, the convertible may be a better investment than the firm's common stock. (Preferred stocks represent another type of *hybrid security* because they too have features and characteristics of both equity and fixed-income securities.)

WEBEXTENSION
For a detailed discussion of the features, valuation, and investment merits of preferred stocks, see our Web site:
www.myfinancelab.com

■ Convertibles as Investment Outlets

equity kicker
another name for the conversion feature, giving the holder of a convertible security a deferred claim on the issuer's common stock.

Convertible securities are popular with investors because of their **equity kicker**—i.e., the right to convert these bonds into shares of the company's common stock. Because of this feature, the market price of a convertible has a tendency to behave very much like the price of its underlying common stock.

Convertibles are used by all types of companies and are issued either as convertible *bonds* (by far the most common type) or as convertible *preferreds*. Convertibles *enable firms to raise equity capital at fairly attractive prices*. That is, when a company issues stock in the normal way (by selling more shares in the company), it does so by setting a price on the stock that's *below* prevailing market prices. For example, it might be able to get $25 for a stock that's currently priced in the market at, say, $30 a share. In contrast, when it issues the stock

HOTLINKS
For a brief review of convertible securities see:
www.convertbond.com/tutor/
ConvertibleTypes.asp

indirectly through a convertible issue, the firm can set a price that's *above* the prevailing market—for example, it might be able to get $35 for the same stock. As a result, the company can raise the *same amount of money* by issuing a lot less stock. Thus, companies issue convertibles *not* as a way of raising debt capital but as a way of raising equity. Because they are supposed to be converted eventually into shares of the issuing company's common stock, convertibles are usually viewed as a form of **deferred equity**.

deferred equity
securities issued in one form and later redeemed or converted into shares of common stock.

Convertible bonds and convertible preferreds are both linked to the equity position of the firm, so they are usually considered interchangeable for investment purposes. Except for a few peculiarities (e.g., the fact that preferreds pay dividends rather than interest and do so on a quarterly basis rather than semiannually), convertible bonds and convertible preferreds are evaluated in much the same way. Because of their similarities, the discussion that follows will be couched largely in terms of bonds, but the information and implications apply equally well to convertible preferreds.

Convertible Notes and Bonds Convertible bonds are usually issued as *subordinated debentures*, and carry the provision that within a stipulated time period, *the bond may be converted into a certain number of shares of the issuing company's common stock.* (Convertibles that are issued as *notes* are just like convertible *bonds* except that the debt portion of the security carries a shorter maturity—usually of five to ten years. Other than the life of the debt, there is no real difference between the two types of issues: They're both unsecured debt obligations, and they're usually subordinated to other forms of debt.)

Generally speaking, there is little or no cash involved at the time of conversion. You merely trade in the convertible bond (or note) for a stipulated number of shares of common stock. For example, assume that a certain convertible security recently came to the market, and it carried the provision that each $1,000 note could be converted into shares of the issuing company's stock at $62.55 a share. Thus, *regardless of what happens to the market price of the stock*, you can redeem each note for 15.98 shares of the company's stock ($1,000 ÷ $62.55 = 15.98 shares). So, if the company's stock is trading in the market at, say, $125 a share at the time of conversion, then you would have just converted a $1,000 debt obligation into $1,997.50 worth of stock (15.98 × $125 = $1,997.50). Not surprisingly, this conversion privilege comes at a price: *the low coupon (or dividend) that convertibles usually carry.* That is, when new convertible issues come to the market, their coupons are normally just a fraction of those on comparable straight (nonconvertible) bonds. Indeed, the more attractive the conversion feature, the lower the coupon.

forced conversion
the calling in of convertible bonds by the issuing firm.

Actually, while it's the *bondholder* who has the right to convert the bond at any time, more often than not, the issuing firm initiates conversion by calling the bonds—a practice known as **forced conversion**. To provide the corporation with the flexibility to retire the debt and force conversion, most convertibles come out as freely callable issues, or they carry very short call deferment periods. To force conversion, the corporation would call for the retirement of the bond and give the bondholder one of two options: Either convert the bond into common stock, or redeem it for cash at the stipulated call price (which, in the case of convertibles, contains very little call premium). So long as the convertible is called when the market value of the stock exceeds the call price of the bond (which is almost always the case), seasoned investors would never choose the second option. Instead, they would opt to convert the bond, as the firm wants them to. Then they can hold the stocks if they want to, or they can sell their new shares in the market (and end up with more cash than they would have received by taking the call price). After the conversion is complete, the bonds no longer exist; instead, there is additional common stock in their place.

conversion privilege
the conditions and specific nature of the conversion feature on convertible securities.

conversion period
the time period during which a convertible issue can be converted.

conversion ratio
the number of shares of common stock into which a convertible issue can be converted.

conversion price
the stated price per share at which common stock will be delivered to the investor in exchange for a convertible issue.

Conversion Privilege The key element of any convertible is its **conversion privilege**, which stipulates the conditions and specific nature of the conversion feature. To begin with, it states exactly when the debenture can be converted. With some issues, there may be an initial waiting period of six months to perhaps two years after the date of issue, during which time the security cannot be converted. The **conversion period** then begins, and the issue can be converted at any time. The conversion period typically extends for the remaining life of the debenture, but in some instances, it may exist for only a certain number of years. This is done to give the issuing firm more control over its capital structure. If the issue has not been converted by the end of its conversion period, it reverts to a straight-debt issue with no conversion privileges.

From the investor's point of view, the most important piece of information is the *conversion price* or the *conversion ratio*. These terms are used interchangeably and specify, either directly or indirectly, the number of shares of stock into which the bond can be converted. **Conversion ratio** denotes the number of common shares into which the bond can be converted. **Conversion price** indicates the stated value per share at which the common stock will be delivered to the investor in exchange for the bond. When you stop to think about these two measures, it becomes clear that a given conversion ratio implies a certain conversion price, and vice versa. For example, a $1,000 convertible bond might stipulate a conversion ratio of 20, which means that the bond can be converted into 20 shares of common stock. This same privilege could also be stated in terms of a conversion price: The $1,000 bond may be used to acquire the stock at a "price" of $50 per share. Here, the conversion price of $50 signifies a conversion ratio of 20. (One basic difference between a convertible debenture and a convertible preferred relates to conversion ratio: The conversion ratio of a debenture generally deals with large multiples of common stock, such as 15, 20, or 30 shares. In contrast, the conversion ratio of a preferred is generally very small, often less than one share of common and seldom more than three or four shares.)

The conversion ratio is normally adjusted for stock splits and significant stock dividends. As a result, if a firm declares, say, a 2-for-1 stock split, the conversion ratio of any of its outstanding convertible issues also doubles. And when the conversion ratio includes a fraction, such as 33.5 shares of common, the conversion privilege specifies how any fractional shares are to be handled. Usually, the investor can either put up the additional funds necessary to purchase another full share of stock at the conversion price or receive the cash equivalent of the fractional share (at the conversion price).

LYON (liquid yield option note)
a zero-coupon bond that carries both a conversion feature and a put option.

LYONs Leave it to Wall Street to take a basic investment product and turn it into a sophisticated investment vehicle. That's the story behind LYONs, which some refer to as "zeros on steroids": Start with a *zero-coupon bond*, throw in a *conversion feature* and a *put option*, and you have a **LYON** (the acronym stands for **liquid yield option note**). LYONs are zero-coupon convertible bonds that are convertible, at a fixed conversion ratio, for the life of the issue. Thus, they offer the built-in increase in value over time that accompanies any zero-coupon bond (as it moves toward its par value at maturity), plus full participation in the equity side of the issue via the equity kicker. Unlike most convertibles, there's no current income with a LYON (because it is a zero-coupon bond). On the other hand, however, it does carry an option feature that enables you to "put" the bonds back to the issuer (at specified values). That is, *the put option gives you the right to redeem your bonds periodically at prespecified prices.* Thus, you know you can get out of these securities, at set prices, if things move against you.

Although LYONs may appear to provide the best of all worlds, they do have some negatives. True, LYONs provide downside protection (via the put option feature) and full participation in the equity kicker. But being zero-coupon bonds, they don't generate current income. And you have to watch out for the put option: Depending on the type of put option, the payout does not have to be in cash—it can be in stocks or bonds/notes. One other thing: Because the conversion ratio on the LYON is fixed, while the underlying value of the zero-coupon bond keeps increasing (as it moves to maturity), *the conversion price on the stock increases over time.* Thus, the market price of the stock had better go up by more than the bond's rate of appreciation or you'll never be able to convert your LYON.

▮ Sources of Value

Because convertibles are fixed-income securities linked to the equity position of the firm, they are normally valued in terms of *both the stock and the bond dimensions* of the issue. Thus, it is important to both analyze the underlying common stock *and* formulate interest rate expectations, when considering convertibles as an investment outlet. Let's look first at the stock dimension.

Convertible securities trade much like common stock whenever the market price of the stock starts getting close to (or exceeds) the stated conversion price. Whenever a convertible trades near, or above, its par value ($1,000), it will exhibit price behavior that closely matches that of the underlying common stock: If the stock goes up in price, so does the convertible, and vice versa. In fact, the absolute price change of the convertible will exceed that of the common because of the conversion ratio, which will define the convertible's rate of change in price. For example, if a convertible carries a conversion ratio of, say, 20, then for every point the common stock goes up (or down) in price, the price of the convertible will move *in the same direction* by roughly that same multiple (in this case, 20). In essence, whenever a convertible trades as a stock, its market price will approximate a multiple of the share price of the common, with the size of the multiple being defined by the conversion ratio.

When the market price of the common is well below the conversion price, the convertible loses its tie to the underlying common stock and begins to trade as a bond. When that happens, the convertible becomes linked to prevailing bond yields, and investors focus their attention on *market rates of interest*. However, because of the equity kicker and their relatively low agency ratings, *convertibles generally do not possess high interest rate sensitivity*. Gaining more than a rough idea of what the prevailing yield of a convertible obligation ought to be is often difficult. For example, if the issue is rated Baa and the market rate for this quality range is 9%, then the convertible should be priced to yield *something around 9%*, plus or minus perhaps half a percentage point. Even more important, however, is the fact that this bond feature sets the *price floor* on the convertible. Price floor is a key component in defining the amount of downside risk embedded in a convertible, since it provides an approximation of the price to which the convertible will drop should the stock go into a freefall. That is, the price of the convertible will not fall to much less than its price floor, because at that point, the issue's bond value will kick in. (More on this later.)

■ Measuring the Value of a Convertible

In order to evaluate the investment merits of convertible securities, you must consider both the bond and the stock dimensions of the issue. Fundamental security analysis of the equity position is, of course, especially important in light of the key role the equity kicker plays in defining the price behavior of a convertible. In contrast, market yields and agency ratings are used in evaluating the bond side of the issue. But there's more: *In addition to analyzing the bond and stock dimensions of the issue, it is essential to evaluate the conversion feature itself*. The two critical areas in this regard are conversion value and investment value. These measures have a vital bearing on a convertible's price behavior and therefore can have a dramatic effect on an issue's holding period return.

conversion value
an indication of what a convertible issue would trade for if it were priced to sell on the basis of its stock value.

Conversion Value   In essence, **conversion value** indicates what a convertible issue would trade for if it were priced to sell on the basis of its stock value. Conversion value is easy to find:

Equation 10.3 ▶

$$\text{Conversion value} = \text{Conversion ratio} \times \text{Current market price of the stock}$$

For example, a convertible that carries a conversion ratio of 20 would have a conversion value of $1,200 if the firm's stock traded at a current market price of $60 per share ($20 \times $60 = $1,200$).

conversion equivalent (conversion parity)
the price at which the common stock would have to sell in order to make the convertible security worth its present market price.

Sometimes analysts use an alternative measure that computes the **conversion equivalent**, also known as **conversion parity**. The conversion equivalent indicates the price at which the common stock would have to sell in order to make the convertible security worth its present market price. Conversion equivalent is calculated as follows:

Equation 10.4 ▶

$$\text{Conversion equivalent} = \frac{\text{Current market price of the convertible bond}}{\text{Conversion ratio}}$$

Thus, if a convertible were trading at $1,400 and had a conversion ratio of 20, the conversion equivalent of the common stock would be $70 per share ($1,400 \div 20 = 70). In effect, you would expect the current market price of the common stock in this example to be at or near $70 per share in order to support a convertible trading at $1,400.

Conversion Premium   Unfortunately, convertible issues *seldom* trade precisely at their conversion values. Rather, they usually trade at prices that exceed the bond's underlying conversion value. The extent to which the market price of the convertible exceeds its conversion value is known as the *conversion premium*. The absolute size of an issue's conversion premium is found by taking the difference between the convertible's market price and its conversion value (per Equation 10.3). To place the premium on a relative basis, simply divide the dollar amount of the conversion premium by the issue's conversion value. That is,

Equation 10.5 ➤

$$\text{Conversion premium (in \$)} = \frac{\text{Current market price}}{\text{of the convertible bond}} - \frac{\text{Conversion}}{\text{value}}$$

where conversion value is found according to Equation 10.3. Then

Equation 10.6 ➤

$$\text{Conversion premium (in \%)} = \frac{\text{Conversion premium (in \$)}}{\text{Conversion value}}$$

To illustrate, if a convertible trades at $1,400 and its conversion value equals $1,200, it has a conversion premium of $200 ($1,400 − $1,200 = $200). In relation to what the convertible should be trading at, this $200 differential would amount to a conversion premium of 16.7% ($200/$1,200 = 0.167). Conversion premiums are common in the market and can often amount to as much as 30% to 40% (or more) of an issue's true conversion value.

Investors are willing to pay a premium primarily because of the added current income a convertible provides relative to the underlying common stock. An investor can recover this premium either through the added current income the convertible provides, or by selling the issue at a premium equal to or greater than that which existed at the time of purchase. Unfortunately, the latter source of recovery is tough to come by, because conversion premiums tend to fade away as the price of the convertible goes up. That means that if you purchase a convertible for its potential price appreciation (which most are), then you must accept the fact that all or a major portion of the price premium is very likely to disappear as the convertible appreciates over time and moves closer to its true conversion value. Thus, if you hope to recover any conversion premium, it will probably have to come from the added current income that the convertible provides.

Payback Period The size of the conversion premium can obviously have a major impact on investor return. When picking convertibles, one of the major questions you should ask is whether the premium is justified. One way to assess conversion premium is to compute the issue's **payback period**, a measure of the length of time it will take to recover the conversion premium from the *extra* interest income earned on the convertible. Because this added income is a principal reason for the conversion premium, it makes sense to use it to assess the premium. The payback period can be found as follows:

payback period
the length of time it takes for the buyer of a convertible to recover the conversion premium from the extra current income earned on the convertible.

Equation 10.7 ➤

$$\text{Payback period} = \frac{\text{Conversion premium (in \$)}}{\begin{array}{c}\text{Annual interest} \\ \text{income from the} \\ \text{convertible bond}\end{array} - \begin{array}{c}\text{Annual dividend} \\ \text{income from the} \\ \text{underlying common stock}\end{array}}$$

In this equation, annual dividends are found by multiplying the stock's latest annual dividends per share by the bond's conversion ratio.

For example, in the foregoing illustration, the bond had a conversion premium of $200. Assume this bond (which carries a conversion ratio of 20) has an 8.5% coupon, and the underlying stock paid dividends this past year of 50 cents a share. Given this information, we can use Equation 10.7 to find the payback period.

$$\text{Payback period} = \frac{\$200}{\$85 - (20 \times \$0.50)}$$

$$= \frac{\$200}{\$85 - (\$10.00)} = \underline{\underline{2.7 \text{ years}}}$$

In essence, you would recover the premium in 2.7 years (a fairly decent payback period).

As a rule, everything else being equal, *the shorter the payback period, the better.* Also, watch out for excessively high premiums (of 50% or more); you may have real difficulty ever recovering such astronomical premiums. Indeed, to avoid such premiums, most experts recommend that you look for convertibles that have payback periods of around five to seven years, *or less.* Be careful when using this measure, however: Some convertibles will have *very high payback periods simply because they carry very low coupons* (of 1% to 2%, or less).

Investment Value The price floor of a convertible is defined by its bond properties and is the focus of the investment value measure. It's the point within the valuation process where we focus on current and expected market interest rates. **Investment value** is the price at which the bond would trade if it were nonconvertible and if it were priced at or near the prevailing market yields of comparable nonconvertible bonds.

investment value
the price at which a convertible would trade if it were nonconvertible and priced at or near the prevailing market yields of comparable nonconvertible issues.

While we'll cover the mechanics of bond pricing in more detail in Chapter 11, suffice it to say at this point that the investment value of a convertible is found by discounting the issue's coupon stream and its par value back to the present, using a discount rate equal to the prevailing yield on comparable nonconvertible issues. In other words, using the yields on comparable nonconvertible bonds as the discount rate, find the present value of the convertible's coupon stream, add that to the present value of its par value (usually assumed to be $1,000), and you have the issue's investment value. In practice, because the convertible's coupon and matuirity are known, the only additional piece of information needed is the market yield of comparably rated issues.

For example, if comparable nonconvertible bonds were trading at 9% yields, we could use that 9% return as the discount rate in finding the present value (i.e., "investment value") of a convertible. Thus, if a particular 20-year, $1,000 par value convertible bond carried a 6% annual-pay coupon, its investment value (using a 9% discount rate) would be roughly $725. (See if you can find the investment value of this convertible using a hand-held calculator. *Hint:* Input $N = 20$, $I/Y = 9$, $PMT = -60$, and $FV = -1,000$; then compute PV. Did you come up with a little over $726?) This figure indicates how far the convertible will have to fall before it hits its price floor and begins trading as a straight-debt instrument.

Other things being equal, the greater the distance between the current market price of a convertible and its investment value, the farther the issue can fall in price and, as a result, the greater the downside risk exposure.

CONCEPTS IN REVIEW

Answers available at: www.myfinancelab.com

10.15 What is a *convertible debenture?* How does a *convertible bond* differ from a *convertible preferred?*

10.16 Identify the *equity kicker* of a convertible security and explain how it affects the value and price behavior of convertibles.

10.17 Explain why it is necessary to examine both the bond and stock properties of a convertible debenture when determining its investment appeal.

10.18 What is the difference between *conversion parity* and *conversion value?* How would you describe the *payback period* on a convertible? What is the *investment value* of a convertible, and what does it reveal?

Summary

LG 1   **Explain the basic investment attributes of bonds and their use as investment vehicles.** Bonds are publicly traded debt securities that provide investors with two basic sources of return: (1) current income and (2) capital gains. Current income is derived from the coupon (interest) payments received over the life of the issue. Capital gains can be earned whenever market interest rates fall. Bonds also can be used to shelter income from taxes and for the preservation and long-term accumulation of capital. The diversification properties of bonds are such that they can greatly enhance portfolio stability.

LG 2   **Describe the essential features of a bond, note the role that bond ratings play in the market, and distinguish among different types of call, refunding, and sinking-fund provisions.** All bonds carry some type of coupon, which specifies the annual rate of interest the issuer will pay. Bonds also have predetermined maturity dates: Term bonds carry a single maturity date, and serial bonds have a series of maturity dates. Municipal and corporate issues are rated for bond quality by independent rating agencies. These ratings indicate a bond's potential risk of default: The lower the rating, the higher the risk and the higher the expected return.

Every bond is issued with some type of call feature, be it freely callable, noncallable, or deferred callable. Call features spell out whether an issue can be prematurely retired and, if so, when. Some bonds (temporarily) prohibit the issuer from paying off one bond with the proceeds from another by including a refunding provision. Others are issued with sinking-fund provisions, which specify how a bond is to be paid off over time.

LG 3   **Explain how bonds are priced in the market, and why some bonds are more volatile than others.** Bonds are priced in the market as a percent of par, and are driven by the issue's coupon and maturity, along with prevailing market yields. When interest rates go down, bond prices go up, and vice versa. The extent to which bond prices move up or down depends on the coupon and maturity of an issue. Bonds with lower coupons and/or longer maturities generate larger price swings.

LG 4   **Identify the different types of bonds and the kinds of investment objectives these securities can fulfill.** The bond market is divided into four major segments: Treasuries, agencies, municipals, and corporates. Treasury bonds are issued by the U.S. Treasury and are virtually default-free. Agency bonds are issued by various subdivisions of the U.S. government and make up an increasingly important segment of the bond market. Municipal bonds are issued by state and local governments in the form of either general obligation or revenue bonds. Corporate bonds make up the major nongovernment sector of the market and are backed by the assets and profitability of the issuing companies. Generally speaking, Treasuries are attractive because of their high quality, agencies and corporates because of the added returns they provide, and munis because of the tax shelter they offer.

LG 5   **Discuss the global nature of the bond market and the difference between dollar-denominated and non-dollar-denominated foreign bonds.** Foreign bonds, particularly foreign-pay securities, offer highly competitive yields and returns. Foreign-pay bonds cover all issues that are denominated in some currency other than U.S. dollars. These bonds have an added source of return: currency exchange rates. In addition, there are dollar-denominated foreign bonds—Yankee bonds and Eurodollar bonds—which have no currency exchange risk because they are issued in U.S. dollars.

LG 6   **Describe the basic features and characteristics of convertible securities, and measure the value of a convertible.** Convertible securities are initially issued as bonds (or preferreds), but can subsequently be converted into shares of common stock. These securities offer investors a stream of fixed income (annual coupon payments), plus an equity kicker (a conversion feature). The value of a convertible is driven by the price behavior of the underlying common stock (when the stock price is at or above its conversion price), or by market interest rates and the behavior of bonds (when the stock's price is well below its conversion price). The two key values of a convertible are: (1) its conversion (stock) value, and (2) its investment (bond) value.

Key Terms

agency bonds, *p. 445*
asset-backed securities (ABS),
    p. 453
bond ratings, *p. 440*
bonds, *p. 429*
call feature, *p. 438*
call premium, *p. 438*
call price, *p. 439*

collateralized mortgage obligation
    (CMO), *p. 452*
collateral trust bonds, *p. 439*
conversion equivalent (conversion
    parity), *p. 460*
conversion period, *p. 458*
conversion price, *p. 458*
conversion privilege, *p. 458*

Discussion Questions

LG 1 Q10.1 Using the bond returns in Table 10.1 as a basis of discussion:
  a. Compare the returns during the 1970s to those produced in the 1980s. How do you explain the differences?
  b. How did the bond market do in the 1990s? How does the performance in this decade compare to that in the 1980s? Explain.
  c. What do you think would be a fair rate of return to expect from bonds in the future? Explain.
  d. Assume that you're out of school and hold a promising, well-paying job. How much of your portfolio (in percentage terms) would you, personally, want to hold in bonds? Explain. What role do you see bonds playing in your own portfolio, particularly as you go farther and farther into the future?

LG 4 **LG 5** Q10.2 Identify and briefly describe each of the following types of bonds.
  a. Agency bonds
  b. Municipal bonds
  c. Zero-coupon bonds
  d. Junk bonds
  e. Foreign bonds
  f. Collateralized mortgage obligations (CMOs)

What type of investor do you think would be most attracted to each?

LG 1 LG 4

Q10.3 "Treasury securities are guaranteed by the U.S. government. Therefore, there is no risk in the ownership of such bonds." Briefly discuss the wisdom (or folly) of this statement.

LG 4 LG 5

Q10.4 Select the security in the left-hand column that best fits the investor desire described in the right-hand column.

a. 5-year Treasury note.
b. A bond with a low coupon and a long maturity.
c. Yankee bond.
d. Insured revenue bond.
e. Long-term Treasury strips.
f. Noncallable bond.
g. CMO.
h. Junk bond.
i. ABS.

1. Lock in a high coupon yield.
2. Accumulate capital over a long period of time.
3. Generate a monthly income.
4. Avoid a lot of price volatility.
5. Generate tax-free income.
6. Invest in a foreign bond.
7. Go for the highest yield available.
8. Invest in a pool of credit-card receivables.
9. Go for maximum price appreciation.

LG 6

Q10.5 Why do companies like to issue convertible securities? What's in it for them?

LG 6

Q10.6 Describe LYONs, and note how they differ from conventional convertible securities. Are there any similarities between LYONs and conventional convertibles? Explain.

LG 6

Q10.7 Using the resources available at your campus or public library or on the Internet, find the information requested below.
   a. Select any two *convertible debentures* (notes or bonds) and determine the conversion ratio, conversion parity, conversion value, conversion premium, and payback period for each.
   b. Select any two *convertible preferreds* and determine the conversion ratio, conversion parity, conversion value, conversion premium, and payback period for each.
   c. In what way(s) are the two convertible bonds and the two convertible preferreds you selected similar to one another? Are there any differences? Explain.

Problems

LG 2

P10.1 A 6%, 15-year bond has 3 years remaining on a deferred call feature (the call premium is equal to 1 year's interest). The bond is currently priced in the market at $850. What is the issue's current yield?

LG 2

P10.2 A 12%, 20-year bond is currently trading at $1,250. What is its current yield?

LG 2

P10.3 Zack buys a 10% corporate bond with a current yield of 6%. How much did he pay for the bond?

LG 4 **P10.4** An investor is in the 28% tax bracket and lives in a state with no income tax. He is trying to decide which of two bonds to purchase. One is a 7.5% corporate bond that is selling at par. The other is a municipal bond with a 5.25% coupon that is also selling at par. If all other features of these two bonds are comparable, which should the investor select? Why? Would your answer change if this were an *in-state* municipal bond and the investor lived in a place with high state income taxes? Explain.

LG 4 **P10.5** An investor lives in a state where her tax rate on interest income is 8%. She is in the 33% federal tax bracket. She owns a 7% corporate bond trading at par. What is her after-tax current yield on this bond?

LG 4 **P10.6** Sara Jordan is a wealthy investor who's looking for a tax shelter. Sara is in the maximum (35%) federal tax bracket and lives in a state with a very high state income tax. (She pays the maximum of 11½% in state income tax.) Sara is currently looking at two municipal bonds, both of which are selling at par. One is a double-A-rated *in-state* bond that carries a coupon of 6⅜%. The other is a double-A-rated *out-of-state* bond that carries a 7⅛% coupon. Her broker has informed her that comparable fully taxable corporate bonds are currently available with yields of 9¾%. Alternatively, long Treasuries are now available at yields of 9%. She has $100,000 to invest, and because all the bonds are high-quality issues, she wants to select the one that will give her maximum after-tax returns.
  a. Which one of the 4 bonds should she buy?
  b. Rank the 4 bonds (from best to worst) in terms of their taxable equivalent yields.

LG 4 **P10.7** William J. is looking for a fixed-income investment. He is considering two bond issues:
  a. A Treasury with a yield of 5%.
  b. An in-state municipal bond with a yield of 4%.

William is in the 33% federal tax bracket and the 8% state tax bracket. Which bond would provide William with a higher tax-adjusted yield?

LG 2 **P10.8** Which of the following three bonds offers the highest current yield?
  a. A 9½%, 20-year bond quoted at 97¾.
  b. A 16%, 15-year bond quoted at 164⅝.
  c. A 5¼%, 18-year bond quoted at 54.

LG 2 **P10.9** Assume that you pay $850 for a long-term bond that carries a 7½% coupon. Over the course of the next 12 months, interest rates drop sharply. As a result, you sell the bond at a price of $962.50.
  a. Find the current yield that existed on this bond at the beginning of the year. What was it by the end of the 1-year holding period?
  b. Determine the holding period return on this investment. (See Chapter 5 for the HPR formula.)

LG 3 **P10.10** Colwyn buys a 10% corporate bond with a current yield of 6%. When he sells the bond 1 year later, the current yield on the bond is 7%. How much did Col make on this investment?

LG 1 **P10.11** In early January 2001, you purchased $30,000 worth of some high-grade corporate bonds. The bonds carried a coupon of 8⅞% and mature in 2015. You paid 94.125 when you bought the bonds. Over the 5-year period from 2001 through 2005, the bonds were priced in the market as follows:

	Quoted Prices		
Year	Beginning of the Year	End of the Year	Year-End Bond Yields
2001	94.125	100.625	8.82%
2002	100.625	102	8.70
2003	102	104.625	8.48
2004	104.625	110.125	8.05
2005	110.125	121.250	7.33

Coupon payments were made on schedule throughout the 5-year period.
   a. Find the annual holding period returns for 2001 through 2005. (See Chapter 5 for the HPR formula.)
   b. Use the return information in Table 10.1 to evaluate the investment performance of this bond. How do you think it stacks up against the market? Explain.

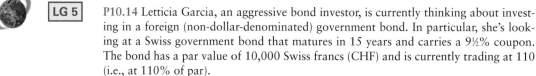

LG 4 P10.12 Rhett purchased a 13% zero-coupon bond with a 15-year maturity and a $20,000 par value 15 years ago. The bond matures tomorrow. How much will Rhett receive in total from this investment, assuming all payments are made on these bonds as expected?

LG 4 P10.13 Brandon purchased an interest-bearing security last year, planning to hold it until maturity. He received interest payments, and, to his surprise, a sizable amount of the principal was paid back in the first year. This happened again in year 2. What type of security did Brandon purchase?

 LG 5 P10.14 Letticia Garcia, an aggressive bond investor, is currently thinking about investing in a foreign (non-dollar-denominated) government bond. In particular, she's looking at a Swiss government bond that matures in 15 years and carries a 9½% coupon. The bond has a par value of 10,000 Swiss francs (CHF) and is currently trading at 110 (i.e., at 110% of par).

Letticia plans to hold the bond for a period of 1 year, at which time she thinks it will be trading at 117½—she's anticipating a sharp decline in Swiss interest rates, which explains why she expects bond prices to move up. The current exchange rate is 1.58 CHF/U.S. $, but she expects that to fall to 1.25 CHF/U.S. $. Use the foreign investment return formula introduced in Chapter 6 (Equation 6.6) to answer the questions below.
   a. Ignoring the currency effect, find the bond's total return (in its local currency).
   b. Now find the total return on this bond in *U.S. dollars*. Did currency exchange rates affect the return in any way? Do you think this bond would make a good investment? Explain.

 LG 5 P10.15 Red Electrica Espana SA (E.REE) is refinancing its bank loans by issuing Eurobonds to investors. You are considering buying $10,000 of these bonds, which will yield 6%. You are also looking at a U.S. bond with similar risk that will yield 5%. You expect that interest rates will not change over the course of the next year, after which time you will sell the bonds you purchase.
   a. How much will you make on each bond if you buy it, hold it for 1 year, and then sell it for $10,000 (or the Eurodollar equivalent)?
   b. Assume the dollar/euro exchange rate goes from 1.11 to 0.98. How much will this currency change affect the proceeds from the Eurobond? (Assume you receive annual interest at the same time you sell the Eurobond.)

LG 6 P10.16 A certain convertible bond has a conversion ratio of 21. The current market price of the underlying common stock is $40. What is the bond's conversion equivalent?

LG 6 P10.17 You are considering investing $850 in Whichway Corporation. You can buy common stock at $25 per share; this stock pays no dividends. You can also buy a convertible bond that is currently trading at $850 and has a conversion ratio of 30. It pays $50 per year in interest. Given you expect the price of the stock to rise to $35 per share in 1 year, which instrument should you purchase?

LG 6 P10.18 A certain 6% annual pay convertible bond (maturing in 20 years) is convertible at the holder's option into 20 shares of common stock. The bond is currently trading at $800. The stock (which pays 75¢ a share in annual dividends) is currently priced in the market at $35 a share.
   a. What is the bond's conversion price?
   b. What is its conversion ratio?
   c. What is the conversion value of this issue? What is its conversion parity?
   d. What is the conversion premium, in dollars and as a percentage?
   e. What is the bond's payback period?
   f. If comparably rated nonconvertible bonds sell to yield 8%, what is the investment value of the convertible?

LG 6 P10.19 An 8% convertible bond carries a par value of $1,000 and a conversion ratio of 20. Assume that an investor has $5,000 to invest and that the convertible sells at a price of $1,000 (which includes a 25% conversion premium). How much total income (coupon plus capital gains) will this investment offer if, over the course of the next 12 months, the price of the stock moves to $75 per share and the convertible trades at a price that includes a conversion premium of 10%? What is the holding period return on this investment? Finally, given the information in the problem, determine what the underlying common stock is currently selling for.

LG 6 P10.20 Assume you just paid $1,200 for a convertible bond that carries a 7½% coupon and has 15 years to maturity. The bond can be converted into 24 shares of stock, which are now trading at $50 a share. Find the bond investment value of this issue, given that comparable nonconvertible bonds are currently selling to yield 9%.

LG 6 P10.21 Find the conversion value of a *convertible preferred stock* that carries a conversion ratio of 1.8, given that the market price of the underlying common stock is $40 a share. Would there be any conversion premium if the convertible preferred were selling at $90 a share? If so, how much (in dollar and percentage terms)? Also, explain the concept of conversion parity, and then find the conversion parity of this issue, given that the preferred trades at $90 per share.

See www.myfinancelab.com **for Web Exercises,**
Spreadsheets, and other online resources.

Case Problem 10.1   *Max and Veronica Develop a Bond Investment Program*

LG 4

Max and Veronica Shuman, along with their two teenage sons, Terry and Thomas, live in Portland, Oregon. Max is a sales rep for a major medical firm, and Veronica is a personnel officer at a local bank. Together, they earn an annual income of around $100,000. Max has just learned that his recently departed rich uncle has named him in his will to the tune of some $250,000 after taxes. Needless to say, the family is elated. Max intends to spend $50,000 of his inheritance on a number of long-overdue family items (like some badly needed remodeling of their kitchen and family room, the down payment on a new Porsche Boxster, and braces to correct Tom's overbite). Max wants to invest the remaining $200,000 in various types of fixed-income securities.

Max and Veronica have no unusual income requirements or health problems. Their only investment objectives are that they want to achieve some capital appreciation and they want to keep their funds fully invested for a period of at least 20 years. They would rather not have to rely on their investments as a source of current income but want to maintain some liquidity in their portfolio just in case.

Questions

a. Describe the type of *bond investment program* you think the Shuman family should follow. In answering this question, give appropriate consideration to both return and risk factors.

b. List several different types of bonds that you would recommend for their portfolio, and briefly indicate why you would recommend each.

c. Using a recent issue of the *Wall Street Journal* or *Barron's*, construct a $200,000 bond portfolio for the Shuman family. *Use real securities* and select any bonds (or notes) you like, given the following ground rules:
   1. The portfolio must include at least one Treasury, one agency, and one corporate bond; also, in total, the portfolio must hold at least 5, but no more than 8 bonds or notes.

Security Issuer-Coupon-Maturity	Latest Quoted Price	Number of Bonds Purchased	Amount Invested	Annual Coupon Income	Current Yield
Example: U.S. Treas - 8½%-'15	96 3⁄32	25	$ 24,062	$ 2,125	8.83%
1.					
2.					
3.					
4.					
5.					
6.					
7.					
8.					
Totals	—		$200,000	$	%

2. No more than 5% of the portfolio can be in short-term U.S. Treasury bills (but note that if you hold a T-bill, that limits your selections to just 7 other notes/bonds).

3. Ignore all transaction costs (i.e., invest the full $200,000) and assume all securities have par values of $1,000 (though they can be trading in the market at something other than par).

4. Use the latest available quotes to determine how many bonds/notes/bills you can buy.

d. Prepare a schedule listing all the securities in your recommended portfolio. *Use a form like the one shown on the previous page*, and include the information it calls for on each security in the portfolio.

e. *In one brief paragraph*, note the key investment attributes of your recommended portfolio and the investment objectives you hope to achieve with it.

Case Problem 10.2   *The Case of the Missing Bond Ratings*

LG 2   It's probably safe to say that there's nothing more important in determining a bond's rating than the underlying financial condition and operating results of the company issuing the bond. Just as financial ratios can be used in the analysis of common stocks, they can also be used in the analysis of bonds—a process we refer to as *credit analysis*. In credit analysis, attention is directed toward the basic liquidity and profitability of the firm, the extent to which the firm employs debt, and the ability of the firm to service its debt.

A Table of Financial Ratios
(All ratios are real and pertain to real companies)

Financial Ratio	Company 1	Company 2	Company 3	Company 4	Company 5	Company 6
1. Current ratio	1.13 ×	1.39 ×	1.78 ×	1.32 ×	1.03 ×	1.41 ×
2. Quick ratio	0.48 ×	0.84 ×	0.93 ×	0.33 ×	0.50 ×	0.75 ×
3. Net profit margin	4.6%	12.9%	14.5%	2.8%	5.9%	10.0%
4. Return on total capital	15.0%	25.9%	29.4%	11.5%	16.8%	28.4%
5. Long-term debt to total capital	63.3%	52.7%	23.9%	97.0%	88.6%	42.1%
6. Owners' equity ratio	18.6%	18.9%	44.1%	1.5%	5.1%	21.2%
7. Pretax interest coverage	2.3 ×	4.5 ×	8.9 ×	1.7 ×	2.4 ×	6.4%
8. Cash flow to total debt	34.7%	48.8%	71.2%	20.4%	30.2%	42.7%

Notes: Ratio (2)—Whereas the current ratio relates current assets to current liabilities, the quick ratio considers only the most liquid current assets (cash, short-term securities, and accounts receivable) and relates them to current liabilities.
Ratio (4)—Relates pretax profit to the total capital structure (long-term debt + equity) of the firm.
Ratio (6)—Shows the amount of stockholders' equity used to finance the firm (stockholders' equity ÷ total assets).
Ratio (8)—Looks at the amount of corporate cash flow (from net profits + depreciation) relative to the total (current + long-term) debt of the firm
The other four ratios are as described in Chapter 6.

The financial ratios shown on the previous page are often helpful in carrying out such analysis: (1) current ratio, (2) quick ratio, (3) net profit margin, (4) return on total capital, (5) long-term debt to total capital, (6) owners' equity ratio, (7) pretax interest coverage, and (8) cash flow to total debt. The first 2 ratios measure the liquidity of the firm, the next 2 its profitability, the following 2 the debt load, and the final 2 the ability of the firm to service its debt load. (For ratio 5, the *lower* the ratio, the better. For all the others, the *higher* the ratio, the better.) The following table lists each of these ratios for 6 different companies.

Questions

a.   Three of these companies have bonds that carry investment-grade ratings. The other 3 companies carry junk-bond ratings. Judging by the information in the table, which 3 companies have the investment-grade bonds and which 3 have the junk bonds? Briefly explain your selections.

b.   One of these 6 companies is a AAA-rated firm and one is B-rated. Identify those 2 companies. Briefly explain your selection.

c.   Of the remaining 4 companies, 1 carries a AA rating, 1 carries an A rating, and 2 are BB-rated. Which companies are they?

Excel with Spreadsheets

The cash flow components of bond investments is made up of the annual interest payments and the future redemption value or its par value. Just like other time-value-of-money considerations, the bond cash flows are discounted back in order to determine their present value.

In comparing bonds to stocks, many investors look at the respective returns. The total returns in the bond market are made up of both current income and capital gains. Bond investment analysis should include the determination of the current yield as well as a specific holding period return.

On January 13, 2007, you gather the following information on 3 corporate bonds issued by the General Pineapple Corp (GPC). Remember that corporate bonds are quoted as a percent of their par value. Assume the par value of each bond to be $1,000. These debentures are quoted in eighths of a point. **Create a spreadsheet** that will model and answer the following 3 bond investment problems.

Bonds	Current Yield	Volume	Close
GPC 5.3 10	?	25	105 ⅞
GPC 6.65s 17	?	45	103
GPC 7.4 19	?	37	104 ⅝

Questions

a. Calculate the current yields for these 3 GPC corporate debentures.
b. Calculate the holding period returns under the following three scenarios:
   1. Purchased the 5.3 bonds for 990 on January 13, 2006.
   2. Purchased the 6.65s for 988 on January 13, 2006.
   3. Purchased the 7.4 bonds for 985 on January 13, 2004.
c. As of January 13, 2007, GPC common stock had a close price of $26.20. The price of GPC stock in January 2004 was $25.25. The stock paid a 2002 dividend of $0.46, a 2003 dividend of $0.46, and a 2007 dividend of $0.46.
   1. Calculate the current (January 13, 2007) dividend yield for this security.
   2. Assuming you purchased the stock in January 2004, what is the holding period return as of January 2007?

Chapter 11

Bond Valuation

D espite rising fuel prices in 2005 and 2006, FedEx Corporation's (NYSE: FDX) profits continued to rise. The Memphis-based provider of transportation and business services reported earnings for the year ending May 31, 2006, of $1.806 billion, up from $1.449 billion in 2005. Operating four major business units (FedEx Express, FedEx Ground, FedEx Freight, and FedEx Kinko's), FedEx Corp. handles millions of transactions daily. Its operations are capital-intensive, characterized by significant investments in aircraft, vehicles, technology, package-handling facilities, and sorting equipment.

In March 2004 FedEx issued $1.6 billion in bonds to repay commercial paper incurred to complete the acquisition of Kinko's. At the time, the acquisition and debt issue created a split in the major firms that rate long-term debt. Standard & Poor's maintained its BBB rating of FedEx Corp.'s debt and an outlook of "stable," while Moody's downgraded its rating to Baa2 and issued a rating outlook of "negative."

FedEx appears to have had no problems dealing with the additional debt. It repaid $791 million in long-term debt in 2005 and $369 million in 2006. With $850 million of its long-term debt coming due in 2007, FedEx stood ready with $1.937 billion in cash and cash equivalents as of May 31, 2006, compared with $1.039 billion a year earlier. FedEx has a $1.0 billion, five-year revolving line of credit, executed in the first quarter of 2006, which contains a financial covenant that requires a leverage ratio of adjusted debt (long-term debt, including the current portion of such debt, plus six times rentals and landing fees) to capital (adjusted debt plus total common stockholders' investment) that does not exceed 0.70. FedEx was able to meet that covenant throughout the first half of 2006. As a result, the credit ratings firms upgraded their outlook ratings somewhat.

As we'll see in this chapter, many factors determine a bond's price, including the credit quality and the general level of interest rates. Investors must evaluate these factors when deciding whether the market value of a bond will provide the return they need.

Sources: FedEx Corp Form 10-K, dated July 14, 2006; "S&P Affirms FedEx Credit Ratings," dated March 23, 2004, from http://www.businessweek.com (accessed July 28, 2006).

LEARNING GOALS

After studying this chapter, you should be able to:

LG 1 Explain the behavior of market interest rates, and identify the forces that cause interest rates to change.

LG 2 Describe the term structure of interest rates, and note how yield curves can be used by investors.

LG 3 Understand how bonds are valued in the marketplace.

LG 4 Describe the various measures of yield and return, and explain how these standards of performance are used in bond valuation.

LG 5 Understand the basic concept of duration, how it can be measured, and its use in the management of bond portfolios.

LG 6 Discuss various bond investment strategies and the different ways these securities can be used by investors.

The Behavior of Market Interest Rates

LG 1   LG 2

You will recall from Chapter 4 that rational investors try to earn a return that fully compensates them for risk. In the case of bondholders, that required return (r_i) has three components: the real rate of return (r^*), an expected inflation premium (IP), and a risk premium (RP). Thus, the required return on a bond can be expressed by the following equation:

Equation 11.1 ➤

$$r_i = r^* + IP + RP$$

The real rate of return and inflation premium are external economic factors, which *together equal the risk-free rate (R_F)*. To find the required return, we need to consider the unique features and properties of the bond issue itself. We can do this by adding the bond's risk premium to the risk-free rate. A bond's risk premium (RP) will take into account key issue and issuer characteristics, including such variables as the type of bond, the issue's term-to-maturity, its call features, and bond rating.

Together, the three components in Equation 11.1 (r^*, IP, and RP) drive the required return on a bond. Recall in the previous chapter that we identified *five types of risks* to which bonds are exposed. All five of these risks are embedded in a bond's required rate of return. That is, the bond's risk premium (RP) addresses, among other things, the business and financial (credit) risk characteristics of an issue, along with its liquidity and call risks, whereas the risk-free rate (R_f) takes into account interest rate and purchasing power risks.

Viewed from the perspective of the market as a whole, it is *these investor returns in the aggregate* that define *prevailing market interest rates*. Because these interest rates have a significant bearing on bond prices and yields, investors watch them closely. For example, more conservative investors watch interest rates because one of their major objectives is to lock in high yields. Aggressive traders also have a stake in interest rates because their investment programs are often built on the capital gains opportunities that accompany major swings in rates.

▊ Keeping Tabs on Market Interest Rates

Just as there is no single bond market but a series of different market sectors, so too there is no single interest rate that applies to all segments of the market. Rather, each segment has its own, unique level of interest rates. Granted, the various rates do tend to drift in the same direction over time and follow the same general pattern of behavior. But it's also common for **yield spreads** (interest rate differentials) to exist among the various market sectors. Some of the more important market yields and yield spreads are as follows:

yield spreads
differences in interest rates that exist among various sectors of the market.

- Municipal bonds usually carry the lowest market rates because of their tax-exempt feature. As a rule, their market yields are about 20% to 30% lower than corporates. (There are occasional exceptions to this rule. For example, in 2003, some Treasury yields were actually lower than the yields on comparable munies.) In the taxable sector, Treasuries have the lowest yields (because they have the least risk), followed by agencies and then corporates, which provide the highest returns.

- Issues that normally carry bond ratings (e.g., municipals or corporates) generally display the same behavior: The lower the rating, the higher the yield.

- There is generally a direct relationship between the coupon an issue carries and its yield. Discount (low-coupon) bonds yield the least, and premium (high-coupon) bonds yield the most.

- In the municipal sector, revenue bonds yield more than general obligation bonds.

- Bonds that are freely callable generally provide the highest returns, at least at date of issue. These are followed by deferred call obligations and then by noncallable bonds, which yield the least.

- As a rule, bonds with long maturities tend to yield more than short issues. However, this rule does not always hold; sometimes, as in 2005, short-term yields equal or exceed the yields on long-term bonds.

The preceding list can be used as a general guide to the higher-yielding segments of the market.

As an investor, you should pay close attention to interest rates and yield spreads. Try to stay abreast of both the current state of the market and the *future direction in market rates*. Thus, if you are a conservative (income-oriented) investor and think that rates have just about peaked, that should be a signal to try to lock in the prevailing high yields with some form of call protection. (For example, buy bonds, like Treasuries or double-A-rated utilities, that are noncallable or still have lengthy call deferments.) In contrast, if you're an aggressive bond trader who thinks rates have peaked (and are about to drop), that should be a clue to buy bonds that offer maximum price appreciation potential (low-coupon bonds that still have a long time before they mature).

But how do you formulate such expectations? Unless you have considerable training in economics, you will probably have to rely on various published sources. Fortunately, a wealth of such information is available. Your broker is an excellent source for such reports, as are investor services like Moody's and Standard & Poor's. Also, of course, there are numerous online sources. Finally, there are widely circulated business and financial publications (like the *Wall Street Journal*, *Forbes*, *Business Week*, and *Fortune*), that regularly address the current state and future direction of market interest rates. Predicting the direction of interest rates is not easy. However, by taking the time to read some of these publications and reports regularly and carefully, you can at least get a handle on what experts predict is likely to occur in the near future—over, say, the next six to nine months, perhaps longer.

▐ What Causes Rates to Move?

Although interest rates are a complex economic issue, we do know that certain forces are especially important in influencing their general behavior. Serious bond investors should make it a point to become familiar with the major determinants of interest rates and try to monitor those variables, at least informally.

In that regard, perhaps no variable is more important than *inflation*. Changes in the inflation rate, or even expectations about its future course, have a direct and profound effect on market interest rates. Clearly, if inflation is

FIGURE 11.1

The Impact of Inflation on the Behavior of Interest Rates

The behavior of interest rates has always been closely tied to the movements in the rate of inflation. What changed in the early 1980s, however, was the spread between inflation and interest rates. Whereas a spread of roughly 3 points was common in the past, it has held at about 5 to 6 percentage points since 1982.

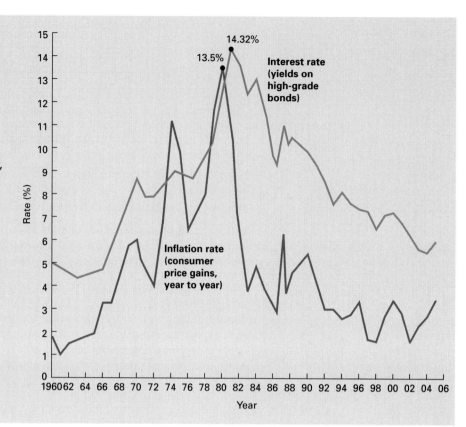

expected to slow down, then market interest rates should fall as well. To gain an appreciation of the extent to which interest rates are linked to inflation, look at Figure 11.1. Note that as inflation drifts up, so do interest rates. On the other hand, a drop in inflation is matched by a similar decline in interest rates.

In addition to inflation, five other important economic variables can significantly affect the level of interest rates:

- *Changes in the money supply.* An increase in the money supply pushes rates down (as it makes more funds available for loans), and vice versa. This is true only up to a point, however. If the growth in the money supply becomes excessive, it can lead to inflation, which, of course, means higher interest rates.

- *The size of the federal budget deficit.* When the U.S. Treasury has to borrow large amounts to cover the budget deficit, the increased demand for funds exerts an upward pressure on interest rates. That's why bond market participants become so concerned when the budget deficit gets bigger and bigger—*other things being equal*, that means more upward pressure on market interest rates.

- *The level of economic activity.* Businesses need more capital when the economy expands. This need increases the demand for funds, and rates tend to rise. During a recession, economic activity contracts, and rates typically fall.

- *Policies of the Federal Reserve*. Actions of the Federal Reserve to control inflation also have a major effect on market interest rates. When the Fed wants to slow real (or perceived) inflation, it usually does so by driving up interest rates, as it did repeatedly in 2005–2006. Unfortunately, such actions sometimes have the side effect of slowing down business activity as well.

- *The level of interest rates in major foreign markets*. Today, investors look beyond national borders for investment opportunities. Rising rates in major foreign markets put pressure on rates in the United States to rise as well; if U.S. rates don't keep pace, foreign investors may be tempted to dump their dollars to buy higher-yielding foreign securities.

■ The Term Structure of Interest Rates and Yield Curves

term structure of interest rates
the relationship between the interest rate or rate of return (yield) on a bond and its time to maturity.

yield curve
a graph that represents the relationship between a bond's term to maturity and its yield at a given point in time.

Although many factors affect the behavior of market interest rates, one of the most popular and widely studied is *bond maturity*. The relationship between interest rates (yield) and time to maturity for any class of similar-risk securities is called the **term structure of interest rates**. This relationship can be depicted graphically by a **yield curve**, which relates a bond's *term* to maturity to its *yield* to maturity at a given point in time. A particular yield curve exists for only a short period of time. As market conditions change, so do the yield curve's shape and location.

Types of Yield Curves Two different types of yield curves are illustrated in Figure 11.2. By far, the most common type is curve 1, the *upward-sloping* curve. It indicates that yields tend to increase with longer maturities. That's because the longer a bond has to maturity, the greater the potential for price volatility and risk of loss. Investors, therefore, require higher risk premiums to induce them to buy the longer, riskier bonds. Occasionally, the yield curve becomes *inverted*, or downward sloping, as shown in curve 2, which occurs when short-term rates are higher than long-term rates. This curve generally

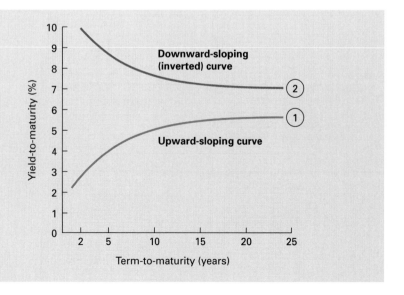

FIGURE 11.2

Two Types of Yield Curves

A yield curve relates term-to-maturity to yield-to-maturity at a given point in time. Although yield curves come in many shapes and forms, the most common is the *upward-sloping curve*. It shows that investor returns (yields) increase with longer maturities.

results from actions by the Federal Reserve to curtail inflation by driving short-term interest rates way up. In addition to these two common yield curves, two other types appear from time to time: the *flat* yield curve, when rates for short- and long-term debt are essentially the same, and the *humped* yield curve, when *intermediate-term* rates are the highest.

Plotting Your Own Curves   Yield curves are constructed by plotting the yields for a group of bonds that are similar in all respects but maturity. Treasury securities (bills, notes, and bonds) are typically used to construct yield curves. There are several reasons for this: Their yields are easily found in financial publications, they have no risk of default, and they are homogeneous with regard to quality and other issue characteristics. Investors can also construct yield curves for other classes of debt securities, such as A-rated municipal bonds, Aa-rated corporate bonds, or even certificates of deposit.

HOT LINKS
For the latest information on the U.S. economy and bonds, go to the SmartMoney Web site at:
www.smartmoney.com/bonds

Figure 11.3 shows the yield curves for Treasury securities on two dates, July 29, 2003, and March 23, 2006. To draw these curves, you need Treasury quotes from the *Wall Street Journal* or some other similar source. (Note that actual quoted yields for curve 2 are provided in the boxed information below the graph.) Given the required quotes, select the yields for the Treasury bills, notes, and bonds maturing in approximately 3 months, 6 months, and 1, 2, 5, 10, 20, and 30 years. The yields used for this curve are highlighted in Figure 11.3. (You could include more points, but they would not have much effect on the general shape of the curve.) Next, plot the points on a graph whose horizontal (x) axis represents time to maturity in years and whose vertical (y) axis represents yield to maturity. Now, just connect the points to create the curves shown in Figure 11.3. You'll notice that while curve 1 is upward sloping, it remained well below curve 2 for all but the long end of the curve (with the 20- and 30-year maturities). The reason: Curve 1 reflects the 40-year lows that existed in market yields in 2003.

Explanations of the Term Structure of Interest Rates   As we noted earlier, the shape of the yield curve can change over time. Three commonly cited theories—the expectations hypothesis, the liquidity preference theory, and the market segmentation theory—explain more fully the reasons for the general shape of the yield curve.

expectations hypothesis
theory that the shape of the yield curve reflects investor expectations of future interest rates.

Expectations Hypothesis   The **expectations hypothesis** suggests that the yield curve reflects investor expectations about the future behavior of interest rates. This theory argues that the relationship between rates today and rates expected in the future is due primarily to investor expectations about inflation. If investors anticipate higher rates of inflation in the future, they will require higher long-term interest rates today, and vice versa.

To see how to apply this explanation in practice, consider the behavior of U.S. Treasury securities. Because Treasury securities are considered essentially risk-free, only two components determine their yield: the real rate of interest and inflation expectations. Since the real rate is the same for all maturities, it follows that variations in yields are caused by differing inflation expectations associated with different maturities. This hypothesis can be illustrated using the March 23, 2006, yields for four of the Treasury maturities in Figure 11.3.

FIGURE 11.3

Yield Curves on U.S. Treasury Issues

Here we see two yield curves constructed from actual market data (quotes). Note the different shapes of the two curves: Curve 1 has a normal upward slope, while curve 2 is almost perfectly flat (i.e., the 30-year yield is only 10 basis points higher than the 3-month yield). Though it started at a much higher level than curve 1, curve 2 ended half-a-percent under it (the 20- and 30-year yields were about 50 basis points less). (*Source: Wall Street Journal*, March 24, 2006.)

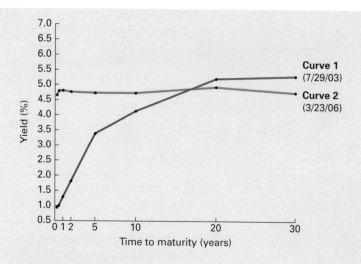

Yield Data for Curve 2
Treasury Issues—Bills, Notes, and Bonds
Friday, March 24, 2006

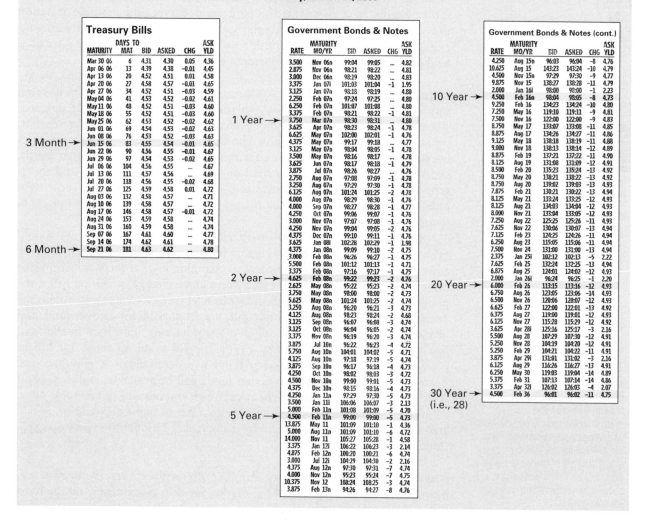

Treasury Bills

MATURITY	DAYS TO MAT	BID	ASKED	CHG	ASK YLD	
Mar 30 06	6	4.31	4.30	0.05	4.36	
Apr 06 06	13	4.39	4.38	-0.01	4.45	
Apr 13 06	20	4.52	4.51	-0.01	4.58	
Apr 20 06	27	4.58	4.57	-0.01	4.65	
Apr 27 06	34	4.52	4.51	-0.03	4.59	
May 04 06	41	4.53	4.52	-0.02	4.61	
May 11 06	48	4.52	4.51	-0.03	4.60	
May 18 06	55	4.52	4.51	-0.03	4.60	
May 25 06	62	4.53	4.52	-0.02	4.62	
Jun 01 06	69	4.54	4.53	-0.02	4.63	
Jun 08 06	76	4.53	4.52	-0.03	4.63	
Jun 15 06	83	4.55	4.54	-0.01	4.65	← 3 Month
Jun 22 06	90	4.56	4.55	-0.01	4.67	
Jun 29 06	97	4.54	4.53	-0.02	4.65	
Jul 06 06	104	4.56	4.55	...	4.67	
Jul 13 06	111	4.57	4.56	...	4.69	
Jul 20 06	118	4.56	4.55	-0.02	4.68	
Jul 27 06	125	4.59	4.58	0.01	4.72	
Aug 03 06	132	4.58	4.57	...	4.71	
Aug 10 06	139	4.58	4.57	...	4.72	
Aug 17 06	146	4.58	4.57	-0.01	4.72	
Aug 24 06	153	4.59	4.58	...	4.74	
Aug 31 06	160	4.59	4.58	...	4.74	
Sep 07 06	167	4.61	4.60	...	4.77	
Sep 14 06	174	4.62	4.61	...	4.78	
Sep 21 06	181	4.63	4.62	...	4.80	← 6 Month

Government Bonds & Notes

RATE	MATURITY MO/YR	BID	ASKED	CHG	ASK YLD	
3.500	Nov 06n	99:04	99:05	...	4.82	
2.875	Nov 06n	98:21	98:22	...	4.81	
3.000	Dec 06n	98:19	98:20	...	4.83	
3.375	Jan 07i	101:03	101:04	-1	1.95	
3.125	Jan 07n	98:18	98:19	...	4.80	
2.250	Feb 07n	97:24	97:25	...	4.80	
6.250	Feb 07n	101:07	101:08	...	4.80	
3.375	Feb 07n	98:21	98:22	-1	4.81	
3.750	Mar 07n	98:30	98:31	-1	4.80	← 1 Year
3.625	Apr 07n	98:23	98:24	-1	4.78	
6.625	May 07n	102:00	102:01	-1	4.76	
4.375	May 07n	99:17	99:18	...	4.77	
3.125	May 07n	98:04	98:05	-1	4.78	
3.500	May 07n	98:16	98:17	...	4.78	
3.625	Jun 07n	98:17	98:18	-1	4.79	
3.875	Jul 07n	98:26	98:27	...	4.76	
2.750	Aug 07n	97:08	97:09	-1	4.78	
3.250	Aug 07n	97:29	97:30	-1	4.78	
6.125	Aug 07n	101:24	101:25	-2	4.78	
4.000	Aug 07n	98:29	98:30	-1	4.76	
4.000	Sep 07n	98:27	98:28	-1	4.77	
4.250	Oct 07n	99:06	99:07	-1	4.76	
3.000	Nov 07n	97:07	97:08	-1	4.76	
4.250	Nov 07n	99:04	99:05	-2	4.76	
4.375	Dec 07n	99:10	99:11	-1	4.76	
3.625	Jan 08i	102:28	102:29	-1	1.98	
4.375	Jan 08n	99:09	99:10	-2	4.75	
3.000	Feb 08n	96:26	96:27	-1	4.75	
5.500	Feb 08n	101:12	101:13	-1	4.71	
3.375	Feb 08n	97:16	97:17	-1	4.75	
4.625	Feb 08n	99:22	99:23	-2	4.76	← 2 Year
2.625	May 08n	95:22	95:23	-2	4.74	
3.750	May 08n	98:00	98:00	-2	4.73	
5.625	May 08n	101:24	101:25	-2	4.73	
3.250	Aug 08n	96:20	96:21	-3	4.73	
4.125	Aug 08n	98:23	98:24	-2	4.68	
3.125	Sep 08n	96:07	96:08	-3	4.74	
3.125	Oct 08n	96:04	96:05	-2	4.74	
3.375	Nov 08n	96:19	96:20	-3	4.74	
3.875	Jul 10n	96:22	96:23	-4	4.72	
5.750	Aug 10n	104:01	104:02	-5	4.71	
4.125	Aug 10n	97:18	97:19	-5	4.74	
3.875	Sep 10n	96:17	96:18	-4	4.73	
4.250	Oct 10n	98:02	98:03	-3	4.72	
4.500	Nov 10n	99:00	99:01	-5	4.73	
4.375	Dec 10n	98:15	98:16	-4	4.73	
4.250	Jan 11n	97:29	97:30	-5	4.73	
3.500	Jan 11i	106:06	106:07	-3	2.13	
5.000	Feb 11n	101:08	101:09	-5	4.70	
4.500	Feb 11n	99:00	99:00	-5	4.73	← 5 Year
13.875	May 11	101:09	101:10	-1	4.36	
5.000	Aug 11n	101:09	101:10	-6	4.72	
14.000	Nov 11	105:27	105:28	-1	4.58	
3.375	Jan 12i	106:22	106:23	-3	2.14	
4.875	Feb 12n	100:20	100:21	-6	4.74	
3.000	Jul 12i	104:29	104:30	-2	2.16	
4.375	Aug 12n	97:30	97:31	-7	4.74	
4.000	Nov 12n	95:23	95:24	-7	4.75	
10.375	Nov 12	108:24	108:25	-3	4.74	
3.875	Feb 13n	94:26	94:27	-8	4.76	

Government Bonds & Notes (cont.)

RATE	MATURITY MO/YR	BID	ASKED	CHG	ASK YLD	
4.250	Aug 15n	96:03	96:04	-8	4.76	
10.625	Aug 15	143:23	143:24	-10	4.79	
4.500	Nov 15n	97:29	97:30	-9	4.77	
9.875	Nov 15	138:27	138:28	-11	4.79	
2.000	Jan 16i	98:00	98:00	-1	2.23	
4.500	Feb 16n	98:04	98:05	-8	4.73	← 10 Year
9.250	Feb 16	134:23	134:24	-10	4.80	
7.250	May 16	119:10	119:11	-9	4.81	
7.500	Nov 16	122:00	122:00	-9	4.83	
8.750	May 17	133:07	133:08	-11	4.85	
8.875	Aug 17	134:26	134:27	-11	4.86	
9.125	May 18	138:18	138:19	-11	4.88	
9.000	Nov 18	138:13	138:14	-12	4.89	
8.875	Aug 19	137:21	137:22	-11	4.90	
8.125	Aug 19	131:08	131:09	-12	4.91	
8.500	Feb 20	135:23	135:24	-13	4.92	
8.750	May 20	138:21	138:22	-13	4.92	
8.750	Aug 20	139:02	139:03	-13	4.93	
7.875	Feb 21	130:21	130:22	-13	4.94	
8.125	May 21	133:24	133:25	-12	4.93	
8.125	Aug 21	134:03	134:04	-12	4.93	
8.000	Nov 21	133:04	133:05	-12	4.93	
7.250	Aug 22	125:25	125:26	-11	4.93	
7.625	Nov 22	130:06	130:07	-13	4.94	
7.125	Feb 23	124:25	124:26	-11	4.94	
6.250	Aug 23	115:05	115:06	-11	4.94	
7.500	Nov 24	131:00	131:00	-13	4.94	
2.375	Jan 25i	102:12	102:13	-5	2.22	
7.625	Feb 25	132:24	132:25	-13	4.94	
6.875	Aug 25	124:01	124:02	-12	4.93	
2.000	Jan 26i	96:24	96:25	-1	2.20	
6.000	Feb 26	113:15	113:16	-12	4.93	← 20 Year
6.750	Aug 26	123:05	123:06	-14	4.93	
6.500	Nov 26	120:06	120:07	-12	4.93	
6.625	Feb 27	122:00	122:01	-13	4.92	
6.375	Aug 27	119:00	119:01	-12	4.93	
6.125	Nov 27	115:28	115:29	-12	4.92	
3.625	Apr 28i	125:16	125:17	-3	2.16	
5.500	Aug 28	107:29	107:30	-12	4.91	
5.250	Nov 28	104:19	104:20	-12	4.91	
5.250	Feb 29	104:21	104:22	-11	4.91	
3.875	Apr 29i	131:01	131:02	-3	2.16	
6.125	Aug 29	116:26	116:27	-13	4.91	
6.250	May 30	119:03	119:04	-14	4.89	
5.375	Feb 31	107:13	107:14	-14	4.86	
3.375	Apr 32i	126:02	126:03	-4	2.07	← 30 Year (i.e., 28)
4.500	Feb 36	96:01	96:02	-11	4.75	

If we assume that the real rate of interest is 3%, then the inflation expectation during the period to maturity is as shown in column 3 of the following table.

Maturity	(1) March 23, 2006 Yield	(2) Real Rate of Interest	(3) Inflation Expectation [(1) − (2)]
3 months	4.65%	3.00%	1.65%
1 year	4.80	3.00	1.80
5 years	4.73	3.00	1.73
10 years	4.73	3.00	1.73

According to the expectations hypothesis, the numbers in column 3 would suggest that in March 2006, investors didn't seem too concerned about inflation—perhaps because the Fed was so actively fighting against even a hint of potential inflation. As a result, the yield curve (in Figure 11.3) was a lot flatter in 2006 than it was in 2003.

Generally, under the expectations hypothesis, an increasing inflation expectation results in an upward-sloping yield curve, a decreasing inflation expectation results in a downward-sloping yield curve, and a stable inflation expectation results in a relatively flat yield curve. Although other theories do exist, the observed strong relationship between inflation and interest rates does lend considerable support to this widely accepted theory.

Liquidity Preference Theory More often than not, yield curves have an upward slope, as in 2003. One explanation for the frequency of upward-sloping yield curves is the **liquidity preference theory**. This theory states that, intuitively, long-term bond rates should be higher than short-term rates because of the added risks involved with the longer maturities. In other words, because of the risk differential (real or perceived) between long- and short-term debt securities, rational investors will prefer the less risky, short-term obligations *unless they can be motivated, via higher interest rates, to invest in longer bonds*.

Actually, there are a number of reasons why rational investors should prefer short-term securities. To begin with, they are more liquid (more easily converted to cash) and less sensitive to changing market rates, which means there is less risk of loss of principal. For a given change in market rates, the prices of longer-term bonds will show considerably more movement than the prices of short-term bonds. Simply put, uncertainty increases over time, and investors therefore require a premium to invest in long maturities. In addition, just as investors tend to require a premium for tying up funds for longer periods, borrowers will also pay a premium in order to obtain long-term funds. Borrowers thus assure themselves that funds will be available, and they avoid having to roll over short-term debt at unknown and possibly unfavorable rates. All of these preferences explain why higher rates of interest should be associated with longer maturities and why it's perfectly rational to expect upward-sloping yield curves.

Market Segmentation Theory Another often-cited theory, the **market segmentation theory**, suggests that the market for debt is segmented on the basis of the maturity preferences of different types of financial institutions and

liquidity preference theory theory that investors tend to prefer the greater liquidity of short-term securities and therefore require a premium to invest in long-term securities.

market segmentation theory theory that the market for debt is segmented on the basis of maturity, that supply and demand within each segment determine the prevailing interest rate, and that the slope of the yield curve depends on the relationship between the prevailing rates in each segment.

investors. According to this theory, the yield curve changes as the supply and demand for funds within each maturity segment determines its prevailing interest rate. The equilibrium between the financial institutions that supply the funds for short-term maturities (e.g., banks) and the borrowers of those short-term funds (e.g., businesses with seasonal loan requirements) establishes interest rates in the short-term markets. Similarly, the equilibrium between suppliers and demanders in such long-term markets as life insurance and real estate determines the prevailing long-term interest rates.

The shape of the yield curve can be either upward or downward sloping, as determined by the general relationship between rates in each market segment. When supply outstrips demand for short-term loans, short-term rates are relatively low. If, at the same time, the demand for long-term loans is higher than the available supply of funds, then long-term rates will move up. Thus, low rates in the short-term segment and high rates in the long-term segment cause an upward-sloping yield curve, and vice versa.

Which Theory Is Right? It is clear *that all three theories* of the term structure have merit in explaining the shape of the yield curve. From them, we can conclude that at any time, the slope of the yield curve is affected by (1) inflationary expectations, (2) liquidity preferences, and (3) the supply and demand conditions in the short- and long-term market segments. Upward-sloping yield curves result from higher inflation expectations, lender preferences for shorter-maturity loans, and greater supply of short- rather than of long-term loans relative to the respective demand in each market segment. The opposite behavior, of course, results in a flat or downward-sloping yield curve. At any point in time, the interaction of these forces determines the prevailing slope of the yield curve.

Using the Yield Curve in Investment Decisions Bond investors often use yield curves in making investment decisions. Analyzing the changes in yield curves over time provides investors with information about future interest rate movements and how they can affect price behavior and comparative returns. For example, if the yield curve begins to rise sharply, it usually means that inflation is starting to heat up or is expected to do so in the near future. In that case, investors can expect that interest rates, too, will rise. Under these conditions, most seasoned bond investors will turn to short or intermediate (three to five years) maturities, which provide reasonable returns and at the same time minimize exposure to capital loss when interest rates go up (and bond prices fall). A downward-sloping yield curve, though unusual, generally results from actions of the Federal Reserve to reduce inflation. As suggested by the expectations hypothesis, this would signal that rates have peaked and are about to fall.

Another factor to consider is the difference in yields on different maturities—the "steepness" of the curve. For example, a steep yield curve is one where long-term rates are *much higher* than short-term rates. This shape is often seen as an indication that long-term rates may be near their peak and are about to fall, thereby narrowing the spread between long and short rates. Steep yield curves are generally viewed as a bullish sign. For aggressive bond investors, they could be the signal to start moving into long-term securities. Flatter yield curves, on the other hand, sharply reduce the incentive for going long-term. For example, look at yield curve 2 in Figure 11.3. Note that the difference in yield between the 5- and 30-year maturities is quite small. (In fact, it's almost nonexistent, as it amounts to *only 2 basis points*, or ²⁄₁₀₀ of 1%.) As a result, there's not much incentive to go long-term. Under these conditions, investors would be well advised to just stick with the 5- to 10-year maturities, which will generate about the same yield as long bonds but without the risks.

CONCEPTS IN REVIEW
Answers available at: www.myfinancelab.com

11.1 Is there a single market rate of interest applicable to all segments of the bond market, or are there a series of market yields? Explain and note the investment implications of such a market environment.

11.2 Explain why interest rates are important to both conservative and aggressive bond investors. What causes interest rates to move, and how can you monitor such movements?

11.3 What is the *term structure of interest rates*, and how is it related to the *yield curve*? What information is required to plot a yield curve? Describe an upward-sloping yield curve and explain what it has to say about the behavior of interest rates. Do the same for a flat yield curve.

11.4 How might you, as a bond investor, use information about the term structure of interest rates and yield curves when making investment decisions?

The Pricing of Bonds

LG 3

No matter who the issuer is, what kind of bond it is, or whether it's fully taxable or tax-free, all bonds are priced pretty much the same. That is, all bonds (including *notes* with maturities of more than one year) are priced according to the *present value of their future cash flow streams*. Indeed, once the prevailing or expected market yield is known, the whole process becomes rather mechanical.

Bond prices are driven by market yields. That's because in the marketplace, the *appropriate yield at which the bond should sell is defined first*, and then that yield is used to find the price (or market value) of the bond. As we saw earlier, the appropriate yield on a bond is a function of certain market and economic forces (e.g., the risk-free rate of return and inflation), as well as key issue and issuer characteristics (like years to maturity and the issue's bond rating). Together, these forces combine to form the *required rate of return*, which is the rate of return the investor would like to earn in order to justify an investment in a given fixed-income security. In the bond market, required return is market driven and is generally considered to be the issue's market yield. That is, the required return defines the yield at which the bond should be trading and serves as the *discount rate* in the bond valuation process.

■ The Basic Bond Valuation Model
Generally speaking, bond investors receive two distinct types of cash flows: (1) the periodic receipt of coupon income over the life of the bond, and (2) the recovery of principal (or par value) at the end of the bond's life. Thus, in

valuing a bond, you're dealing with an *annuity* of coupon payments plus a large *single cash flow*, as represented by the recovery of principal at maturity. We can use these cash flows, along with the required rate of return on the investment, in a present-value-based bond valuation model to find the dollar value, or price, of a bond. Using annual compounding, this valuation model can be expressed as follows:

Equation 11.2 ➤

$$P_0 = \sum_{t=1}^{n} \frac{I_t}{(1 + i)^t} + \frac{PV_n}{(1 + i)^n}$$

$$= \frac{\text{Present value of}}{\text{coupon payments}} + \frac{\text{Present value of}}{\text{bond's par value}}$$

where

P_0 = current price (or value) of the bond

I_t = annual interest (coupon) income

PV_n = par value of the bond, at maturity

n = number of years to maturity

i = prevailing market yield, or required return

In this form, we can compute the current value of the bond, or what an investor would be willing to pay for it, given that she wants to generate a certain rate of return, as defined by i. Or we can solve for the i in the equation, in which case we'd be looking for the yield embedded in the current market price of the bond.

While this form of the model algebraically defines the variables that drive the value of a bond, it's often much easier (at least intuitively) to discuss the bond valuation process in terms of present-value interest factors. Therefore, for the remainder of this chapter, we'll use such interest factors to define and illustrate the various bond price and yield measures. In addition, we'll show how these bond valuation calculations, and *especially the yield measures*, can be done just as easily on a good hand-held calculator. But before you revert to the regular use of these calculators, we strongly encourage you to work through the bond valuation model at least once or twice, using the procedures outlined below. Doing so will help you gain a thorough understanding of what's embedded in a bond price or yield measure.

In the discussion that follows, we will demonstrate the bond valuation process in two ways. First, we'll use *annual compounding*—that is, because of its computational simplicity, we'll assume we are dealing with coupons that are paid once a year. Second, we'll examine bond valuation under conditions of *semiannual compounding*, which is more like the way most bonds actually pay their coupon.

▮ Annual Compounding

Along with a table of present-value interest factors (see Appendix A, Tables A.3 and A.4), we need the following information to value a bond: (1) the size of the annual coupon payment, (2) the bond's par value, and (3) the number of years remaining to maturity. We then use the prevailing market yield (or an estimate of future market rates) as the discount rate to compute the price of a bond, as follows:

Equation 11.3 ➤

$$\text{Bond price} = \frac{\text{Present value of the annuity}}{\text{of annual interest income}} + \frac{\text{Present value of the}}{\text{bond's par value}}$$

Equation 11.3a ➤

$$BP = (I \times PVIFA) + (PV \times PVIF)$$

where

I = amount of annual interest income

$PVIFA$ = present-value interest factor for an *annuity* (Appendix A, Table A.4)

PV = par value of the bond, *which is assumed to be $1,000*

$PVIF$ = present-value interest factor for a *single cash flow* (Appendix A, Table A.3)

To illustrate this bond price formula in action, consider a 20-year, 9.5% bond priced to yield 10%. That is, the bond pays an annual coupon of 9.5% (or $95), has 20 years left to maturity, and should be priced to provide a market yield of 10%. As we saw in Chapter 4, the maturity and market yield information is used to find the appropriate present-value interest factors (in Appendix A, Tables A.3 and A.4). Given these interest factors, we can now use Equation 11.3 to find the price of our bond.

$$
\begin{aligned}
\text{Bond price} &= (\$95 \times PVIFA \text{ for } 10\% \text{ and } 20 \text{ years}) + \\
&\quad (\$1,000 \times PVIF \text{ for } 10\% \text{ and } 20 \text{ years}) \\
&= (\$95 \times 8.514) + (\$1,000 \times .149) = \underline{\$957.83}
\end{aligned}
$$

Note that because this is a coupon-bearing bond, we have an annuity of coupon payments of $95 a year for 20 years, plus a single cash flow of $1,000 that occurs at the end of year 20. Thus, we find the present value of the coupon annuity and then add that amount to the present value of the recovery of principal at maturity. In this particular case, you should be willing to pay about $958 for this bond, so long as you're satisfied with earning 10% on your money.

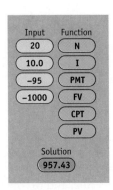

CALCULATOR USE For *annual compounding*, to price a 20-year, 9.5% bond to yield 10%, use the keystrokes shown in the margin, where:

N = number of years to maturity,

I = yield on the bond (what the bond is being priced to yield),

PMT = stream of annual coupon payments,

FV = par value of the bond, and

PV = computed price of the bond.

■ Semiannual Compounding

Although using annual compounding simplifies the valuation process a bit, it's not the way bonds are actually valued in the marketplace. In practice, most (domestic) bonds pay interest every six months, so semiannual compounding is used in valuing bonds. Fortunately, it's relatively easy to go from annual to semiannual compounding: All you need do is cut the annual coupon payment in half, and make two minor modifications to the present-value interest factors. Given these changes, finding the price of a bond under conditions of semiannual compounding is much like pricing a bond using annual compounding. That is,

Equation 11.4 ➤

$$\text{Bond price (with semi-annual compounding)} = \text{Present value of an annuity of \textit{semiannual} coupon payments} + \text{Present value of the bond's par value}$$

Equation 11.4a ➤

$$BP = (I/2 \times PVIFA^*) + (PV \times PVIF^*)$$

where

$PVIFA^*$ = present-value interest factor for an annuity, with required return and years-to-maturity adjusted for *semiannual compounding* (Appendix A, Table A.4)

$PVIF^*$ = present-value interest factor for a single cash flow, with required return and years-to-maturity adjusted for *semiannual compounding* (Appendix A, Table A.3)

I, PV = as described above

Note that in Equation 11.4, we adjusted the present-value interest factors (both $PVIFA$ and $PVIF$) to accommodate semiannual compounding. By simply *cutting the required return in half and doubling the number of years to maturity*, we are, in effect, dealing with a semiannual measure of return and using the number of six-month periods to maturity (rather than *years*). For example, in our bond illustration above, we wanted to price a 20-year bond to yield 10%. With semiannual compounding, we would be dealing with a semiannual return of 10%/2 = 5%, and with 20 × 2 = 40 semiannual periods to maturity. Thus, we'd find the present-value interest factors for 5% and 40 periods from Table A.4 (for $PVIFA^*$) and from Table A.3 (for $PVIF^*$). Note that we adjust *the present-value interest factor* for the $1,000 par value, because that too will be subject to semiannual compounding, even though the cash flow will still be received in one lump sum.

To see how this all fits together, consider once again the 20-year, 9.5% bond. This time assume it's priced to yield 10% *compounded semiannually*. Using Equation 11.4, you'd have:

$$\text{Bond price (with semi-annual compounding)} = (\$95/2 \times PVIFA^* \text{ for 5\% and 40 periods}) + (\$1,000 \times PVIF^* \text{ for 5\% and 40 periods})$$

$$= (\$47.50 \times 17.159) + (\$1,000 \times .142) = \underline{\$957.02}$$

The price of the bond in this case ($957.02) is slightly less than the price we obtained with annual compounding ($957.83). Clearly, it doesn't make much difference whether we use annual or semiannual compounding, though the differences do tend to increase a bit with lower coupons and shorter maturities.

Input   Function
40   N
5.0   I
−47.50 PMT
−1000   FV
        CPT
        PV

Solution
957.10

CALCULATOR USE For *semiannual compounding*, to price a 20-year, 9.5% bond to yield 10%, use the keystrokes shown in the margin, where:

N = number of 6-month periods to maturity (20 × 2 = 40),

I = yield on the bond, adjusted for semiannual compounding (10/2 = 5.0),

PMT = stream of semiannual coupon payments (95.00/2 = 47.50), and

FV *and* PV = remain the same.

Note that the price of the bond is a bit higher here due to rounding (i.e., we get $957.10 with the calculator versus $957.02 with the tables).

CONCEPTS IN REVIEW

Answers available at: www.myfinancelab.com

11.5 Explain how market yield affects the price of a bond. Could you price a bond without knowing its market yield? Explain.

11.6 Why are bonds generally priced using semiannual compounding? Does it make much difference if you use annual compounding?

Measures of Yield and Return

LG 4

In the bond market, investment decisions are made more on the basis of a bond's yield than its dollar price. Not only does yield affect the price at which a bond trades, but it also serves as an important measure of return. To use yield as a measure of return, we *simply reverse the bond valuation process* described above and solve for yield rather than price. Actually, there are three widely used measures of yield: current yield, yield-to-maturity, and yield-to-call. We'll look at all three of them here, along with a concept known as *expected return*, which measures the expected (or actual) rate of return earned over a specific holding period.

▮ Current Yield

current yield
measure that indicates the amount of current income a bond provides relative to its market price.

Current yield is the simplest of all bond return measures, but it also has the most limited application. This measure looks at just one source of return: *a bond's interest income*. In particular, it indicates the amount of current income a bond provides relative to its prevailing market price. It is calculated as follows:

Equation 11.5 ➤

$$\text{Current yield} = \frac{\text{Annual interest income}}{\text{Current market price of the bond}}$$

For example, an 8% bond would pay $80 per year in interest for every $1,000 of principal. However, if the bond were currently priced at $800, it would have a current yield of 10% ($80/$800 = 0.10). Current yield is a measure of a bond's annual coupon income, so it would be of interest primarily to investors seeking high levels of current income, such as endowments or retirees.

■ Yield-to-Maturity

yield-to-maturity (YTM)
the fully compounded rate of return earned by an investor over the life of a bond, including interest income and price appreciation.

promised yield
yield-to-maturity.

Yield-to-maturity (YTM) is the most important and most widely used bond valuation measure. It evaluates both interest income and price appreciation and considers total cash flow received over the life of an issue. Also known as **promised yield**, YTM shows the fully compounded rate of return earned by an investor, *given that the bond is held to maturity and all principal and interest payments are made in a prompt and timely fashion*. In addition, because YTM is a present-value-based measure of return, it's assumed that *all the coupons will be reinvested, for the remaining life of the issue, at an interest rate equal to the bond's yield-to-maturity*. This "reinvestment assumption" plays a vital role in YTM, and will be discussed in more detail later in this chapter (see "Yield Properties").

Yield-to-maturity is used not only to gauge the return on a single issue but also to track the behavior of the market in general. In other words, market interest rates are basically a reflection of the average promised yields that exist in a given segment of the market. Promised yield provides valuable insight into an issue's investment merits and is used to assess the attractiveness of alternative investment vehicles. Other things being equal, the higher the promised yield of an issue, the more attractive it is.

Although there are a couple of ways to compute promised yield, the best and most accurate procedure is one that is derived directly from the bond valuation model described above. That is, *assuming annual compounding*, you can use Equation 11.3 to measure the YTM on a bond. The difference is that now, instead of trying to determine the price of the bond, *we know its price and are trying to find the discount rate that will equate the present value of the bond's cash flow (coupon and principal payments) to its current market price*. This procedure may sound familiar: It's just like the *internal rate of return* measure described in Chapter 4. Indeed, we're basically looking for the internal rate of return on a bond. When we find that, we have the bond's yield-to-maturity.

Unfortunately, unless you have a hand-held calculator or computer software that will do the calculations for you, finding yield-to-maturity is a matter of trial and error. Let's say we want to find the yield-to-maturity on a 7.5% ($1,000 par value) bond that has 15 years remaining to maturity and is currently trading in the market at $809.50. From Equation 11.3, we know that

$$\text{Bond price} = (I \times PVIFA) + (PV \times PVIF)$$

As it now stands, we know the current market price of the bond ($809.50), the amount of annual interest/coupon income (7.5% = $75), the par value of the bond ($1,000), and the number of years to maturity (15). To compute yield-to-maturity, we need to find the discount rate (in the present-value interest factors) that produces a bond price of $809.50.

Here's what we have so far:

$$\text{Bond price} = (I \times PVIFA) + (PV \times PVIF)$$

$$\$809.50 = (\$75 \times PVIFA \text{ for 15 years and a discount rate of ?\%})$$
$$+ (\$1,000 \times PVIF \text{ for 15 years and a discount rate of ?\%})$$

Right now we know only one thing about the yield on this bond—it has to be more than 7.5%. (Why? Because this is a discount bond, the yield-to-maturity must exceed the coupon rate.) Through trial and error, we might start with a discount rate of, say, 8% or 9% (or any number above the bond's coupon). Sooner or later, we'll try a discount rate of 10%. And look what happens at that point: Using Equation 11.3 to price this bond at a discount rate of 10%, we see that

$$\text{Bond price} = (\$75 \times PVIFA \text{ for 15 years and 10\%})$$
$$+ (\$1,000 \times PVIFA \text{ for 15 years and 10\%})$$

$$= (\$75 \times 7.606) + (\$1,000 \times 0.239)$$

$$= \underline{\$809.45}$$

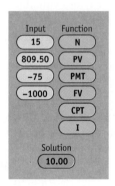

Input   Function
15   N
809.50   PV
−75   PMT
−1000   FV
          CPT
          I

Solution
10.00

The computed price of $809.45 is reasonably close to the bond's current market price of $809.50. As a result, the 10% rate represents the yield-to-maturity on this bond. That is, 10% is the discount rate that leads to a *computed bond price that's equal (or very close) to the bond's current market price*. In this case, if you were to pay $809.50 for the bond and hold it to maturity, you would expect to earn a yield of 10.0%.

CALCULATOR USE   For *annual compounding,* to find the YTM of a 15-year, 7.5% bond that is currently priced in the market at $809.50, use the keystrokes shown in the margin. The present value (*PV*) key represents the current market price of the bond, and all other keystrokes are as defined earlier.

Using Semiannual Compounding   Given some fairly simple modifications, it's also possible to find yield-to-maturity using semiannual compounding. To do so, we cut the annual coupon in half, double the number of years (periods) to maturity, and use the bond valuation model in Equation 11.4. Returning to our 7.5%, 15-year bond, let's see what happens when we try a discount rate of 10%. In this case, with semiannual compounding, we'd use a discount rate of 5% (10% ÷ 2); using this discount rate and 30 six-month periods to maturity (15 × 2) to specify the present-value interest factor, we have

$$\text{Bond price} = (\$75/2 \times PVIFA^* \text{ for 5\% and 30 periods})$$
$$+ (\$1,000 \times PVIFA \text{ for 5\% and 30 periods})$$

$$= (\$37.50 \times 15.373) + (\$1,000 \times 0.231) = \underline{\$807.49}$$

As you can see, a semiannual discount rate of 5% results in a computed bond value that's well short of our target price of $809.50. Given the inverse relationship between price and yield, it follows that if we need a higher price, we'll have to try a lower yield (discount rate). Therefore, we know the semiannual yield on this bond has to be something less than 5%. Through interpolation, we find that a semiannual discount rate of (around) 4.97% gives us a computed bond value that's very close to $809.50.

At this point, because we're dealing with semiannual cash flows, to be technically accurate, we should find the bond's "effective" annual yield. However, that's not the way it's done in practice. Rather, *market convention is to simply state the annual yield as twice the semiannual yield.* This practice produces what the market refers to as the **bond-equivalent yield.** Returning to the bond-yield problem started above, we know that the issue has a semiannual yield of 4.97%. According to the bond-equivalent yield convention, we now simply *double the solving rate in order to obtain the annual rate of return on this bond.* Doing this gives us a yield-to-maturity (or promised yield) of 4.97% × 2 = 9.94%. This is the annual rate of return we'll earn on the bond if we hold it to maturity.

bond-equivalent yield
the annual yield on a bond, calculated as twice the semiannual yield.

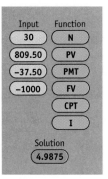

Input **Function**

Input	Function
30	N
809.50	PV
−37.50	PMT
−1000	FV
	CPT
	I

Solution
4.9875

CALCULATOR USE For *semiannual compounding,* to find the YTM of a 15-year, 7.5% bond that is currently priced in the market at $809.50, use the keystrokes shown here. As before, the *PV* key is the current market price of the bond, and all other keystrokes are as defined earlier. Remember that to find the bond-equivalent yield, you have to double the computed value of *I.* That is, 4.9875% × 2 = 9.975%.

Yield Properties Actually, in addition to holding the bond to maturity, there are a couple of other critical assumptions embedded in any yield-to-maturity figure. The promised yield measure—whether computed with annual or semi-annual compounding—is based on present-value concepts and therefore contains important *reinvestment assumptions.* That is, the yield-to-maturity figure itself is the *minimum required reinvestment rate the investor must subsequently earn on each of the interim coupon receipts* in order to generate a return equal to or greater than the promised yield. In essence, the calculated yield-to-maturity figure is the return "promised" only so long as the issuer meets all interest and principal obligations on a timely basis and the investor reinvests all coupon income at an average rate equal to or greater than the computed promised yield. In our example above, the investor would have to reinvest (to maturity) each of the coupons received over the next 15 years at a rate of about 10%. *Failure to do so would result in a realized yield of less than the 10% promised.* If the investor made no attempt to reinvest the coupons, he or she would earn a realized yield over the 15-year investment horizon of just over 6.5%—far short of the 10% promised return. Thus, unless it's a zero-coupon bond, it should be clear that a significant portion of a bond's total return over time is derived from the *reinvestment of coupons.*

This reinvestment assumption was first introduced in Chapter 4, when we discussed the role that "interest on interest" plays in measuring investment returns. As noted, when using present-value-based measures of return, such as YTM, there are actually three components of return: (1) coupon/interest income; (2) capital gains (or losses); and (3) interest on interest. Whereas current income and capital gains make up the profits from an investment, interest on interest is a measure of what *you* do with those profits. In the context of yield-to-maturity, the computed YTM defines the required, or minimum, reinvestment rate. Put your investment profits (i.e., coupon income) to work at this rate and you'll earn a rate of return equal to YTM. This rule applies to any coupon-bearing bond—so long as there's an annual or semiannual flow of coupon income, the reinvestment of that income and interest on interest are matters that you must deal with. Also, keep in mind that the *bigger the coupon* and/or the *longer the maturity*, the *more important the reinvestment assumption*. Indeed, for many long-term, high-coupon bond investments, interest on interest alone can account for *well over half* the cash flow.

Finding the Yield on a Zero We can also use the same promised-yield procedures described above (Equation 11.3 with annual compounding or Equation 11.4 with semiannual compounding) to find the yield-to-maturity on a zero-coupon bond. The only difference is that the coupon portion of the equation can be ignored because it will, of course, equal zero. All you have to do to find the promised yield on a zero is to divide the current market price of the bond by $1,000 (the bond's par value) and then look for the computed interest factor in the present-value Table A.3 (in Appendix A).

To illustrate, consider a 15-year zero-coupon issue that can be purchased today for $315. Dividing this amount by the bond's par value of $1,000, we obtain an interest factor of $315/$1,000 = 0.315. Now, using annual compounding, look in Table A.3 (the table of present-value interest factors for *single cash flows*). Go down the first column to year 15 and then look across that row until you find an interest factor that equals (or is very close to) 0.315. Once you've found the factor, look up the column to the "Interest Rate" heading and you've got the promised yield of the issue. Using this approach, we see that the bond in our example has a promised yield of 8%. Had we been using semiannual compounding, we'd do exactly the same thing, except we'd go down to "year 30" and start the process there.

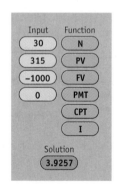

Input	Function
30	N
315	PV
−1000	FV
0	PMT
	CPT
	I

Solution
3.9257

Calculator Use For *semiannual compounding*, to find the YTM of a 15-year zero-coupon bond that is currently priced in the market at $315, use the keystrokes shown in the margin. *PV* is the current market price of the bond, and all other keystrokes are as defined earlier. To find the bond-equivalent yield, double the computed value of *I*. That is, 3.9257% × 2 = 7.85%.

▮ Yield-to-Call

yield-to-call (YTC)
the yield on a bond if it remains outstanding only until a specified call date.

Bonds can be either noncallable or callable. Recall from Chapter 10 that a *non-callable bond* prohibits the issuer from calling the bond in for retirement prior to maturity. Because such issues will remain outstanding to maturity, they can be valued by using the standard *yield-to-maturity* measure. In contrast, a *callable bond* gives the issuer the right to retire the bond prematurely, so the issue may or may not remain outstanding to maturity. As a result, YTM may not always be the appropriate measure of value. Instead, we must consider the impact of the bond being called away prior to maturity. A common way to do that is to use a measure known as **yield-to-call** (YTC), which shows the yield on a bond if the issue remains outstanding *not* to maturity, but rather until its first (or some other specified) call date.

Yield-to-call is commonly used with bonds that carry *deferred-call provisions*. Remember that such issues start out as noncallable bonds and then, after a call deferment period (of 5 to 10 years), become freely callable. Under these conditions, YTC *would measure the expected yield on a deferred-call bond assuming that the issue is retired at the end of the call deferment period* (that is, when the bond first becomes freely callable). We can find YTC by making two simple modifications to the standard YTM equation (Equation 11.3 or 11.4). First, we define the length of the investment horizon (N) as *the number of years to the first call date*, not the number of years to maturity. Second, instead of using the bond's par value ($1,000), we *use the bond's call price* (which is stated in the indenture and is nearly always greater than the bond's par value).

For example, assume you want to find yield-to-call on a 20-year, 10.5% deferred-call bond that is currently trading in the market at $1,204, but has five years to go to first call (that is, before it becomes freely callable), at which time it can be called in at a price of $1,085. Thus, rather than using the bond's maturity of 20 years in the valuation equation (Equation 11.3 or 11.4), we use the number of years to first call (5 years), and rather than the bond's par value, $1,000, we use the issue's call price, $1,085. Note, however, we still use the bond's coupon (10.5%) and its current market price ($1,204). Thus, for annual compounding, we would have:

Equation 11.6 ➤

$$\text{Bond price} = (I \times PVIFA) + (CP \times PVIF)$$

$$\$1,204.00 = (\$105 \times PVIFA \text{ for 5 years and a discount rate of ?\%})$$
$$+ (\$1,085 \times PVIF \text{ for 5 years and a discount rate of ?\%})$$

In Equation 11.6, CP equals the call price on the issue, and the present-value interest factors (for both $PVIFA$ and $PVIF$) are for the number of years to first call date, not the term to maturity.

Through trial and error, we finally hit upon a discount rate of 7%. At that point, the present value of the future cash flows (coupons over the next five years, plus call price) will exactly (or very nearly) equal the bond's current market price of $1,204. That is,

$$\text{Bond price} = (\$105 \times PVIFA_{5 \text{ years, } 7\%}) + (\$1,085 \times PVIF_{5 \text{ years, } 7\%})$$

$$= (\$105 \times 4,100) + (\$1,085 \times 0.713)$$
$$= \$430.50 + \$773.61 = \underline{\$1,204.11}$$

Thus, *the YTC on this bond is 7%.* In contrast, the bond's YTM is 8.36%. In practice, bond investors normally compute *both* YTM and YTC for deferred-call bonds that are *trading at a premium.* They do this to find which of the two yields is lower; market convention is to *use the lower, more conservative measure of yield (YTM or YTC) as the appropriate indicator of value.* As a result, the premium bond in our example would be valued relative to its yield-to-call. The assumption is that because interest rates have dropped so much (the bond is trading 2 percentage points below its coupon), it will be called in the first chance the issuer gets. However, the situation is totally different when this or any bond trades at a discount. Why? Because YTM on *any discount bond,* whether callable or not, *will always be less* than YTC. Thus,

Input	Function
5	N
1204	PV
−105	PMT
−1085	FV
	CPT
	I

Solution
7.00

YTC is a totally irrelevant measure for discount bonds—it's used only with premium bonds.

CALCULATOR USE For *annual compounding*, to find the YTC of a 20-year, 10.5% bond that is currently trading at $1,204 but can be called in five years at a call price of $1,085, use the keystrokes shown in the margin. In this computation, N is the number of years to first call date, and *FV* represents the bond's call price. All other keystrokes are as defined earlier.

■ Expected Return

expected return
the rate of return an investor can expect to earn by holding a bond over a period of time that's less than the life of the issue.

realized yield
expected return.

Rather than just buying and holding bonds, some investors prefer to actively trade in and out of these securities over fairly short investment horizons. As a result, yield-to-maturity and yield-to-call have relatively little meaning, other than as indicators of the rate of return used to price the bond. These investors obviously need an alternative measure of return that they can use to assess the investment appeal of those bonds they intend to trade in and out of. Such an alternative measure is **expected return**. It indicates the rate of return an investor can expect to earn by holding a bond over a period of time that's less than the life of the issue. (Expected return is also known as **realized yield**, because it shows the return an investor would realize by trading in and out of bonds over short holding periods.)

Expected return lacks the precision of yield-to-maturity (and YTC), because the major cash flow variables are largely the product of investor estimates. In particular, going into the investment, both the length of the holding period and the future selling price of the bond are pure estimates and therefore subject to uncertainty. Even so, we can use pretty much the same procedure to find realized yield as we did to find promised yield. That is, with some simple modifications to the standard bond-pricing formula, we can use the following equation to find the expected return on a bond.

Equation 11.7 ➤

$$\text{Bond price} = \begin{array}{c}\text{Present value of the bond's} \\ \text{annual interest income} \\ \text{over the holding period}\end{array} + \begin{array}{c}\text{Present value of the bond's} \\ \text{future price at the} \\ \text{end of the holding period}\end{array}$$

Equation 11.7a ➤

$$BP = (I \times PVIFA) + (FV \times PVIF)$$

where the present-value interest factors (for both *PVIFA* and *PVIF*) are for the length of the expected holding period only, not for the term to maturity, and *FV* is the expected future price of the bond.

Note that in this case, the *expected future price* of the bond is used in place of the par value ($1,000), and *the length of the holding period* is used in place of the term to maturity. As indicated above, we must determine the *future price* of the bond when computing expected realized yield; this is done by using the standard bond price formula, as described earlier. The most difficult part of deriving a reliable future price is, of course, coming up with future market interest rates that you feel will exist when the bond is sold. By evaluating current and expected market interest rate conditions, *you can estimate a promised yield that the issue is expected to carry at the date of sale and then use that yield to calculate the bond's future price.*

To illustrate, take one more look at our 7.5%, 15-year bond. This time, let's assume that you feel the price of the bond, which is now trading at a discount, will rise sharply as interest rates fall over the next few years. In particular, assume the bond is currently priced at $810 (to yield 10%) and you anticipate holding the bond for three years. Over that time, you expect market rates to drop, so the price of the bond should rise to around $960 by the end of the three-year holding period. (Actually, *we found the future price of the bond—$960—by assuming interest rates would fall to 8% in year 3*. We then used the standard bond price formula—in this case Equation 11.3—to find the value of a 7.5%, *12-year obligation*, which is how many years to maturity a 15-year bond will have at the end of a three-year holding period.) Thus, we are assuming that you will buy the bond today at a market price of $810 and sell it three years later—after interest rates have declined to 8%—at a price of $960. Given these assumptions, the expected return (realized yield) on this bond is 14.6%, which is the discount rate in the following equation that will produce a current market price of $810.

$$\text{Bond price} = (\$75 \times PVIFA \text{ for 3 years and } 14.6\%)$$
$$+ (\$960 \times PVIF \text{ for 3 years and } 14.6\%)$$
$$= (\$75 \times 2.301) + (\$960 \times 0.664) = \underline{\$810.02}$$

The better-than-14.5% return on this investment is fairly substantial, but keep in mind that this is only a measure of *expected return*. It is, of course, subject to variation if things do not turn out as anticipated, particularly with regard to the market yield expected at the end of the holding period. (*Note:* This illustration uses annual compounding, but you could just as easily have used *semiannual compounding*, which, everything else being the same, would have resulted in an expected yield of 14.4% rather than the 14.6% found with annual compounding. Also, if the anticipated horizon is one year or less, you would want to use the simple *holding period return (HPR)* measure described in Chapter 4.)

Input	Function
6	N
810	PV
−37.50	PMT
−960	FV
	CPT
	I

Solution
7.205

CALCULATOR USE For *semiannual compounding*, to find the expected return on a 7.5% bond that is currently priced in the market at $810 but is expected to rise to $960 within a three-year holding period, use the keystrokes shown in the margin. In this computation, *PV* is the current price of the bond, and *FV* is the expected price of the bond at the end of the (three-year) holding period. All other keystrokes are as defined earlier. To find the bond-equivalent yield, double the computed value of *I*: 7.205% × 2 = 14.41%.

▪ Valuing a Bond

Depending on investor objectives, investors can determine the value of a bond by either its promised yield or its expected return. Conservative, income-oriented investors employ *promised yield* (YTM or YTC) to value bonds. Coupon income over extended periods of time is their principal objective, and promised yield provides a viable measure of return—assuming, of course, the reinvestment assumptions embedded in the yield measure are reasonable. More aggressive bond traders, on the other hand, use *expected return* to value bonds. The capital gains that can be earned by buying and selling bonds over relatively short holding periods is their chief concern, and expected return is more important to them than the promised yield at the time the bond is purchased.

In either case, promised or expected yield provides a *measure of return* that can be used to determine the relative attractiveness of fixed-income securities. But to do so, we must evaluate the measure of return in light of the *risk* involved in the investment. Bonds are no different from stocks in that the amount of return (promised or expected) should be sufficient to cover the investor's exposure to risk. Thus, the greater the amount of perceived risk, the greater the return the bond should generate. If the bond meets this hurdle, it could then be compared to other potential investments. If you find it difficult to do better in a risk–return sense, then you should seriously consider that bond as an investment outlet.

CONCEPTS IN REVIEW

Answers available at: www.myfinancelab.com

11.7   What's the difference between *current yield* and *yield-to-maturity?* Between *promised yield* and *realized yield?* How does *YTC* differ from *YTM?*

11.8   Briefly describe the term *bond-equivalent yield.* Is there any difference between promised yield and bond-equivalent yield? Explain.

11.9   Why is the reinvestment of interest income so important to bond investors?

Duration and Immunization

LG 5

One of the problems with yield-to-maturity (YTM) is that it assumes you can reinvest the bond's periodic coupon payments at the same rate over time. If you reinvest this interest income at a lower rate (or if you spend it), your real return will be much lower than that indicated by YTM. Another flaw is that YTM assumes the investor will hold the bonds to maturity. For bonds not held to maturity, prices will reflect prevailing interest rates, which are likely to differ from YTM. If rates have moved up since a bond was purchased, the bond will sell at a discount. If interest rates have dropped, it will sell at a premium.

The problem with yield-to-maturity, then, is that it fails to take into account the effects of *reinvestment risk and price (or market) risk*. To see how reinvestment and price risks behave relative to one another, consider a situation in which market interest rates have undergone a sharp decline. Under such conditions, bond prices will, of course, rise. You might be tempted to cash out your holdings and take some gains (i.e., do a little "profit taking"). Indeed, selling before maturity is the only way to take advantage of falling interest rates, because a bond will pay its par value at maturity, regardless of prevailing interest rates. That's the good news about falling rates, but there is a downside: When interest rates fall, so do the opportunities to invest at high rates. Therefore, although you gain on the price side, you lose on the reinvestment side. Even if you don't sell out, you are faced with increased reinvestment risk. In order to earn the YTM promised on your bonds, you have to reinvest each coupon payment at the same YTM rate. Obviously, as rates fall, you'll find it increasingly difficult to reinvest the stream of coupon payments at or above the YTM rate. When market rates rise, just the opposite happens: The price of the bond falls, but your reinvestment opportunities improve.

What is needed is a measure of performance that overcomes these deficiencies and takes into account both price and reinvestment risks. Such a yardstick is provided by something called **duration**. It captures in a single measure the extent to which the price of a bond will react to different interest rate environments. Because duration gauges the price volatility of a bond, it gives you a better idea of how likely you are to earn the return (YTM) you expect. That, in turn, will help you tailor your holdings to your expectations of interest rate movements.

duration
a measure of bond price volatility, which captures both price and reinvestment risks and which is used to indicate how a bond will react in different interest rate environments.

The Concept of Duration

The concept of duration was first developed in 1938 by actuary Frederick Macaulay to help insurance companies match their cash inflows with payments. When applied to bonds, duration recognizes that the amount and frequency of interest payments, yield-to-maturity, and term to maturity all affect the "time dimension" of a bond. Term to maturity is important because it influences how much a bond's price will rise or fall as interest rates change. In general, when rates move, bonds with longer maturities fluctuate more than shorter issues. On the other hand, while the amount of price risk embedded in a bond is related to the issue's term to maturity, the amount of reinvestment risk is directly related to the size of a bond's coupon: Bonds that pay high coupons have greater reinvestment risk simply because there's more to reinvest.

As it turns out, both price and reinvestment risk are related in one way or another to interest rates, and therein lies the conflict. *Any* change in interest rates (whether up or down) will cause price risk and reinvestment risk to push and pull bonds in opposite directions. An increase in rates will produce a drop in price but will lessen reinvestment risk. Declining rates, in contrast, will boost prices but increase reinvestment risk. At some point in time, these two forces should exactly offset each other. *That point in time is a bond's duration.*

In general, bond duration possesses the following properties:

- Higher *coupons* result in shorter durations.
- Longer *maturities* mean longer durations.
- Higher *yields* (YTMs) lead to shorter durations.

In other words, duration is directly related to maturity, and indirectly related to coupon and yield. Together, these three variables—coupon, maturity, and yield—interact to produce an issue's measure of duration. *Knowing a bond's duration is helpful because it captures the bond's underlying price volatility.* That is, since *a bond's duration and volatility are directly related, it follows that the shorter the duration, the less volatility in bond prices—and vice versa, of course.*

Measuring Duration

Duration is a measure of the effective, as opposed to actual, maturity of a fixed-income security. As we will see, only those bonds promising a single payment to be received at maturity (zero-coupon bonds) have durations equal to their actual years to maturity. For all other bonds, *duration measures are always less than their actual maturities*.

Although a bond's term to maturity is a useful concept, it falls short of being a reliable measure of a bond's effective life; it does not consider all of the bond's cash flows or the time value of money. Duration is a far superior measure of the effective timing of a bond's cash flows, as it explicitly considers both the time value of money and the bond's coupon and principal payments. Duration may be thought of as the *weighted-average life of a bond*, where the weights are the relative future cash flows of the bond, all of which are discounted to their present values. Mathematically, we can find the duration of a bond as follows:

Equation 11.8 ➤

$$\text{Duration} = \sum_{t=1}^{T} \left[\frac{PV(C_t)}{P_{\text{bond}}} \times t \right]$$

where

$PV(C_t)$ = present value of a future coupon or principal payment

P_{bond} = current market price of the bond

t = year in which the cash flow (coupon or principal) payment is received

T = remaining life of the bond, in years

The duration measure obtained from Equation 11.8 is commonly referred to as *Macaulay duration*—named after the actuary who developed the concept.

Although duration is often computed using semiannual compounding, Equation 11.8 uses *annual coupons and annual compounding* in order to keep the ensuing discussion and calculations as simple as possible. Even so, the formula looks more formidable than it really is. If you follow the basic steps noted below, you'll find that duration is not tough to calculate. Here are the steps involved:

Step 1. Find the present value of each annual coupon or principal payment [$PV(C_t)$]. *Use the prevailing YTM on the bond as the discount rate.*

Step 2. Divide this present value by the current market price of the bond (P_{bond}).

Step 3. Multiply this relative value by the year in which the cash flow is to be received (t).

Step 4. Repeat Steps 1 through 3 for each year in the life of the bond, and then *add up* the values computed in Step 3.

Duration for a Single Bond Table 11.1 illustrates the four-step procedure for calculating the duration of a 7.5%, 15-year bond priced (at $957) to yield 8%. Note that this particular 15-year bond has a duration of less than 9.5 years (9.36 years, to be exact). Here's how we found that value: Along with the current market price of the bond ($957), the first three columns of Table 11.1 provide the basic input data: Column (1) is the year (t) of the cash flow. Column (2) is the amount of the annual cash flows (from coupons and prin-

TABLE 11.1 Duration Calculation for a 7.5%, 15-Year Bond Priced to Yield 8%

(1)	(2)	(3)	(4)	(5)	(6)
Year (t)	Annual Cash Flow (C_t)	PVIF (at 8%)	Present Value of Annual Cash Flows [$PV(C_t)$] (2) × (3)	$PV(C_t)$ Divided by Current Market Price of the Bond* (4) ÷ $957	Time-Weighted Relative Cash Flow (1) × (5)
1	$ 75	.926	$69.45	.0726	.0726
2	75	.857	64.27	.0672	.1343
3	75	.794	59.55	.0622	.1867
4	75	.735	55.12	.0576	.2304
5	75	.681	51.08	.0534	.2668
6	75	.630	47.25	.0494	.2962
7	75	.583	43.72	.0457	.3198
8	75	.540	40.50	.0423	.3386
9	75	.500	37.50	.0392	.3527
10	75	.463	34.72	.0363	.3628
11	75	.429	32.18	.0336	.3698
12	75	.397	29.78	.0311	.3734
13	75	.368	27.60	.0288	.3749
14	75	.340	25.50	.0266	.3730
15	1,075	.315	338.62	.3538	5.3076
					Duration: 9.36 yrs

*If this bond is priced to yield 8%, it will be quoted in the market at $957.

cipal). Column (3) lists the appropriate present-value interest factors, given an 8% discount rate (which is equal to the prevailing YTM on the bond).

The first thing we do (Step 1) is find the present value of each of the annual cash flows (column 4). Then (Step 2) we divide each of these present values by the current market price of the bond (column 5). Multiplying the relative cash flows from column (5) by the year (t) in which the cash flow occurs (Step 3) results in a time-weighted value for each of the annual cash flow streams (column 6). Adding up all the values in column (6) (Step 4) yields the duration of the bond. As you can see, the duration of this bond is a lot less than its maturity—a condition that would exist with any coupon-bearing bond. In addition, keep in mind *that the duration on any bond will change over time* as YTM and term to maturity change. For example, the duration on this 7.5%, 15-year bond will fall as the bond nears maturity and/or as the market yield (YTM) on the bond increases.

Duration for a Portfolio of Bonds The concept of duration is not confined to individual bonds only. It can also be applied to whole portfolios of fixed-income securities. The duration of an entire portfolio is fairly easy to calculate. All we need are the durations of the individual securities in the portfolio and their weights (i.e., the proportion that each security contributes to the overall value of the portfolio). Given this, *the duration of a portfolio is the weighted average of the durations of the individual securities in the portfolio.* Actually, this weighted-average approach provides only an *approximate measure of duration.* But it is a reasonably close approximation and, as such, is widely used in practice—so we'll use it, too.

To see how to measure duration using this approach, consider the following five-bond portfolio:

Bond	Amount Invested*	Weight	×	Bond Duration	=	Portfolio Duration
Government bonds	$ 270,000	0.15		6.25		0.9375
Aaa corporates	180,000	0.10		8.90		0.8900
Aa utilities	450,000	0.25		10.61		2.6525
Agency issues	360,000	0.20		11.03		2.2060
Baa industrials	$ 540.000	0.30		12.55		3.7650
	$1,800.000	1.00				10.4510

*Amount invested = Current market price × Par value of the bonds. That is, if the government bonds are quoted at 90 and the investor holds $300,000 in these bonds, then 0.90 × $300,000 = $270,000.

In this case, the $1.8 million bond portfolio has an *average duration* of approximately 10.5 years.

If you want to change the duration of the portfolio, you can do so by (1) changing the asset mix of the portfolio (shift the weight of the portfolio to longer- or shorter-duration bonds, as desired) and/or (2) adding new bonds to the portfolio with the desired duration characteristics. As we will see below, this approach is often used in a bond portfolio strategy known as *bond immunization*.

▮ Bond Duration and Price Volatility

A bond's price volatility is, in part, a function of its term to maturity and, in part, a function of its coupon. Unfortunately, there is no exact relationship between bond maturities and bond price volatilities with respect to interest rate changes. There is, however, a fairly close relationship between bond duration and price volatility—at least, so long as the market doesn't experience wide swings in yield. Duration can be used as a viable predictor of price volatility *only so long as the yield swings are relatively small* (no more than 50 to 100 basis points, or so). That's because whereas duration is a straight-line relationship, the price-yield relationship of a bond is convex in nature. So when bond yields change, bond prices actually move in a curved (convex) manner rather than in a straight line, as depicted by duration.

The mathematical link between bond price and interest rate changes involves the concept of *modified duration*. To find modified duration, we simply take the (Macaulay) duration for a bond (as found from Equation 11.8) and adjust it for the bond's yield to maturity.

Equation 11.9 ➤

$$\text{Modified duration} = \frac{(\text{Macaulay})\text{Duration in years}}{1 + \text{Yield to maturity}}$$

Thus, the modified duration for the 15-year bond discussed above is

$$\text{Modified duration} = \frac{9.36}{1 + 0.08} = \underline{8.67}$$

| LG 2 |

Q11.2 Using a recent copy of the *Wall Street Journal* or *Barron's*, find the bond yields for Treasury securities with the following maturities: 3 months, 6 months, 1 year, 3 years, 5 years, 10 years, 15 years, and 20 years. Construct a yield curve based on these reported yields, putting term-to-maturity on the horizontal (*x*) axis and yield-to-maturity on the vertical (*y*) axis. Briefly discuss the general shape of your yield curve. What conclusions might you draw about future interest rate movements from this yield curve?

| LG 5 |

Q11.3 Briefly explain what will happen to a bond's duration measure if each of the following events occur.
   a. The yield-to-maturity on the bond falls from 8.5% to 8%.
   b. The bond gets 1 year closer to its maturity.
   c. Market interest rates go from 8% to 9%.
   d. The bond's *modified* duration falls by half a year.

| LG 6 |

Q11.4 Assume that an investor comes to you looking for advice. She has $200,000 to invest and wants to put it all into bonds.
   a. If she considers herself a fairly aggressive investor who is willing to take the risks necessary to generate the big returns, what kind of investment strategy (or strategies) would you suggest? Be specific.
   b. What kind of investment strategies would you recommend if your client were a very conservative investor who could not tolerate market losses?
   c. What kind of investor do you think is most likely to use:
      (1) An immunized bond portfolio?
      (2) A yield pickup swap?
      (3) A bond ladder?
      (4) A long-term zero-coupon bond when interest rates fall?

| LG 4 | | LG 5 |

Q11.5 Using the resources available at your campus or public library (or on the Internet), select any six bonds you like, consisting of *two* Treasury bonds, *two* corporate bonds, and *two* agency issues. Determine the latest current yield and promised yield for each. (For promised yield, use annual compounding.) In addition, find the duration and modified duration for each bond.
   a. Assuming that you put an equal amount of money into each of the six bonds you selected, find the duration for this six-bond portfolio.
   b. What would happen to your bond portfolio if market interest rates fell by 100 basis points?
   c. Assuming that you have $100,000 to invest, use at least four of these bonds to develop a bond portfolio that emphasizes either the potential for capital gains or the preservation of capital. Briefly explain your logic.

Problems

| LG 3 |

P11.1 Two bonds have par values of $1,000. One is a 5%, 15-year bond priced to yield 8%. The other is a 7.5%, 20-year bond priced to yield 6%. Which of these two has the lower price? (Assume annual compounding in both cases.)

| LG 3 |

P11.2 Using semiannual compounding, find the prices of the following bonds:
   a. A 10.5%, 15-year bond priced to yield 8%.
   b. A 7%, 10-year bond priced to yield 8%.
   c. A 12%, 20-year bond priced at 10%.

Repeat the problem using annual compounding. Then comment on the differences you found in the prices of the bonds.

LG 3   **P11.3** A 15-year bond has an annual-pay coupon of 7.5% and is priced to yield 9%. Calculate the price per $1,000 par value.

LG 3   **P11.4** A 20-year bond has a coupon of 10% and is priced to yield 8%. Calculate the price per $1,000 par value using semiannual compounding.

LG 4   **P11.5** An investor buys a 10% bond for $900, and sells it in 1 year for $950. What is the investor's holding period return?

LG 4   **P11.6** A bond is priced in the market at $1,150 and has a coupon of 8%. Calculate the bond's current yield.

LG 3   **P11.7** An investor is considering the purchase of an 8%, 18-year corporate bond that's being priced to yield 10%. She thinks that in a year, this same bond will be priced in the market to yield 9%. Using annual compounding, find the price of the bond today and in 1 year. Next, find the holding period return on this investment, assuming that the investor's expectations are borne out. (If necessary, see Chapter 4 for the holding period return formula.)

LG 4   **P11.8** A bond is currently selling in the market for $1,170.68. It has a coupon of 12% and a 20-year maturity. Using annual compounding, calculate the promised yield on this bond.

LG 4   **P11.9** A bond is currently selling in the market for $1,098.62. It has a coupon of 9% and a 20-year maturity. Using annual compounding, calculate the promised yield on this bond.

LG 4   **P11.10** Compute the current yield of a 10%, 25-year bond that is currently priced in the market at $1,200. Use annual compounding to find the promised yield on this bond. Repeat the promised yield calculation, but this time use semiannual compounding to find yield-to-maturity.

LG 4   **P11.11** A 10%, 25-year bond has a par value of $1,000 and a call price of $1,075. (The bond's first call date is in 5 years.) Coupon payments are made semiannually (so use semiannual compounding where appropriate).
   a. Find the current yield, YTM, and YTC on this issue, given that it is currently being priced in the market at $1,200. Which of these 3 yields is the highest? Which is the lowest? Which yield would you use to value this bond? Explain.
   b. Repeat the 3 calculations above, given that the bond is being priced at $850. Now which yield is the highest? Which is the lowest? Which yield would you use to value this bond? Explain.

LG 4   **P11.12** Assume that an investor is looking at 2 bonds: Bond A is a 20-year, 9% (semi-annual pay) bond that is priced to yield 10.5%. Bond B is a 20-year, 8% (annual pay) bond that is priced to yield 7.5%. Both bonds carry 5-year call deferments and call prices (in 5 years) of $1,050.
   a. Which bond has the higher current yield?
   b. Which bond has the higher YTM?
   c. Which bond has the higher YTC?

LG 4   **P11.13** A zero-coupon bond that matures in 15 years is currently selling for $209 per $1,000 par value. What is the promised yield?

LG 4 P11.14 A zero-coupon ($1,000 par value) bond that matures in 10 years has a promised yield of 9%. What is the bond's price?

LG 4 P11.15 A 25-year, zero-coupon bond was recently being quoted at 11.625% of par. Find the current yield *and* the promised yield of this issue, given that the bond has a par value of $1,000. Using semiannual compounding, determine how much an investor would have to pay for this bond if it were priced to yield 12%.

LG 4 P11.16 Assume that an investor pays $800 for a long-term bond that carries an 8% coupon. In 3 years, he hopes to sell the issue for $950. If his expectations come true, what realized yield will this investor earn? (Use annual compounding.) What would the holding period return be if he were able to sell the bond (at $950) after only 9 months?

LG 4 P11.17 Using annual compounding, find the yield-to-maturity for each of the following bonds.
    a. A 9.5%, 20-year bond priced at $957.43.
    b. A 16%, 15-year bond priced at $1,684.76.
    c. A 5.5%, 18-year bond priced at $510.65.

Now assume that each of the above three bonds is callable as follows: Bond **a** is callable in 7 years at a call price of $1,095; bond **b** is callable in 5 years at $1,250; and bond **c** is callable in 3 years at $1,050. Use annual compounding to find the yield-to-call for each bond.

LG 5 P11.18 A bond has a Macaulay duration equal to 9.5 and a yield to maturity of 7.5%. What is the modified duration of this bond?

LG 5 P11.19 A bond has a Macaulay duration of 8.62 and is priced to yield 8%. If interest rates go up so that the yield goes to 8.5%, what will be the percentage change in the price of the bond?

LG 5 P11.20 A bond has a Macaulay duration of 8.62 and is priced to yield 8%. If interest rates go down so that the yield goes to 7.5%, what will be the percentage change in the price of the bond?

LG 5 P11.21 Find the Macaulay duration and the modified duration of a 20-year, 10% corporate bond priced to yield 8%. According to the modified duration of this bond, how much of a price change would this bond incur if market yields rose to 9%? Using annual compounding, calculate the price of this bond in 1 year if rates do rise to 9%. How does this price change compare to that predicted by the modified duration? Explain the difference.

LG 5 P11.22 Which *one* of the following bonds would you select if you thought market interest rates were going to fall by 50 basis points over the next 6 months?
    a. A bond with a Macaulay duration of 8.46 years that's currently being priced to yield 7.5%.
    b. A bond with a Macaulay duration of 9.30 years that's priced to yield 10%.
    c. A bond with a Macaulay duration of 8.75 years that's priced to yield 5.75%.

LG 5 **LG 6** P11.23 Mary Richards is an aggressive bond trader who likes to speculate on interest rate swings. Market interest rates are currently at 9%, but she expects them to fall to 7% within a year. As a result, Mary is thinking about buying either a 25-year, zero-coupon bond or a 20-year, 7.5% bond. (Both bonds have $1,000 par values and carry the same agency rating.) Assuming that Mary wants to maximize capital gains, which of the two issues should she select? What if she wants to maximize the total return (interest income and capital gains) from her investment? Why did one issue provide better capital gains than the other? Based on the duration of each bond, which one should be more price volatile?

LG 5 **LG 6**   P11.24 Elliot Karlin is a 35-year-old bank executive who has just inherited a large sum of money. Having spent several years in the bank's investments department, he's well aware of the concept of duration and decides to apply it to his bond portfolio. In particular, Elliot intends to use $1 million of his inheritance to purchase 4 U.S. Treasury bonds:

1. An 8.5%, 13-year bond that's priced at $1,045 to yield 7.47%.
2. A 7.875%, 15-year bond that's priced at $1,020 to yield 7.60%.
3. A 20-year stripped Treasury that's priced at $202 to yield 8.22%.
4. A 24-year, 7.5% bond that's priced at $955 to yield 7.90%.

a. Find the duration and the modified duration of each bond.
b. Find the duration of the whole bond portfolio if Elliot puts $250,000 into each of the 4 U.S. Treasury bonds.
c. Find the duration of the portfolio if Elliot puts $360,000 each into bonds 1 and 3 and $140,000 each into bonds 2 and 4.
d. Which portfolio—**b** or **c**—should Elliot select if he thinks rates are about to head up and he wants to avoid as much price volatility as possible? Explain. From which portfolio does he stand to make more in annual interest income? Which portfolio would you recommend, and why?

See www.myfinancelab.com **for Web Exercises,**
Spreadsheets, and other online resources.

Case Problem 11.1   *The Bond Investment Decisions of Dave and Marlene Coates*

LG 3 **LG 4** **LG 6**   Dave and Marlene Coates live in the Boston area, where Dave has a successful orthodontics practice. Dave and Marlene have built up a sizable investment portfolio and have always had a major portion of their investments in fixed-income securities. They adhere to a fairly aggressive investment posture and actively go after both attractive current income and substantial capital gains. Assume that it is now 2008 and Marlene is currently evaluating two investment decisions: One involves an addition to their portfolio, the other a revision to it.

The Coates' first investment decision involves a short-term trading opportunity. In particular, Marlene has a chance to buy a 7.5%, 25-year bond that is currently priced at $852 to yield 9%; she feels that in 2 years the promised yield of the issue should drop to 8%.

The second is a bond swap. The Coates hold some Beta Corporation 7%, 2020 bonds that are currently priced at $785. They want to improve both current income and yield-to-maturity, and are considering 1 of 3 issues as a possible swap candidate: (a) Dental Floss, Inc., 7.5%, 2020, currently priced at $780; (b) Root Canal Products of America, 6.5%, 2018, selling at $885; and (c) Kansas City Dental Insurance, 8%, 2022, priced at $950. All of the swap candidates are of comparable quality and have comparable issue characteristics.

Questions

a. Regarding the short-term trading opportunity:
   1. What basic trading principle is involved in this situation?
   2. If Marlene's expectations are correct, what will the price of this bond be in 2 years?
   3. What is the expected return on this investment?
   4. Should this investment be made? Why?

b. Regarding the bond swap opportunity:
   1. Compute the current yield and the promised yield (use semiannual compounding) for the bond the Coates currently hold and for each of the 3 swap candidates.
   2. Do any of the 3 swap candidates provide better current income and/or current yield than the Beta Corporation bonds the Coates now hold? If so, which one(s)?
   3. Do you see any reason why Marlene should switch from her present bond holding into one of the other three issues? If so, which swap candidate would be the best choice? Why?

Case Problem 11.2   *Grace Decides to Immunize Her Portfolio*

LG 4   LG 5   LG 6

Grace Hesketh is the owner of an extremely successful dress boutique in downtown Chicago. Although high fashion is Grace's first love, she's also interested in investments, particularly bonds and other fixed-income securities. She actively manages her own investments and over time has built up a substantial portfolio of securities. She's well versed on the latest investment techniques and is not afraid to apply those procedures to her own investments.

Grace has been playing with the idea of trying to immunize a big chunk of her bond portfolio. She'd like to cash out this part of her portfolio in 7 years and use the proceeds to buy a vacation home in her home state of Oregon. To do this, she intends to use the $200,000 she now has invested in the following 4 corporate bonds (she currently has $50,000 invested in each one).

1. A 12-year, 7.5% bond that's currently priced at $895.
2. A 10-year, zero-coupon bond priced at $405.
3. A 10-year, 10% bond priced at $1,080.
4. A 15-year, 9.25% bond priced at $980.
   (*Note:* These are all noncallable, investment-grade, nonconvertible/straight bonds.)

Questions

a. Given the information provided, find the current yield and the promised yield for each bond in the portfolio. (Use annual compounding.)

b. Calculate the Macaulay and modified durations of each bond in the portfolio, and indicate how the price of each bond would change if interest rates were to rise by 75 basis points. How would the price change if interest rates were to fall by 75 basis points?

c. Find the duration of the current 4-bond portfolio. Given the 7-year target that Grace has, would you consider this to be an immunized portfolio? Explain.

d. How could you lengthen or shorten the duration of this portfolio? What's the shortest portfolio duration you can achieve? What's the longest?

e.   Using one or more of the 4 bonds described above, is it possible to come up with a $200,000 bond portfolio that will exhibit the duration characteristics Grace is looking for? Explain.

f.   Using one or more of the 4 bonds, put together a $200,000 immunized portfolio for Grace. Because this portfolio will now be immunized, will Grace be able to treat it as a buy-and-hold portfolio—one she can put away and forget about? Explain.

Excel with Spreadsheets

All bonds are priced according to the present value of their future cash flow streams. The key components of bond valuation are par value, coupon interest rate, term to maturity, and market yield. It is market yield that drives bond prices. In the market for bonds, the appropriate yield at which the bond should sell is determined first, and then that yield is used to find the market value of the bond. The market yield can also be referred to as the required rate of return. It implies that this is the rate of return that a rational investor requires before he or she will invest in a given fixed-income security.

Create a spreadsheet to model and answer the following bond valuation questions.

Questions

a.   One of the bond issues outstanding by H&W Corporation has an annual-pay coupon of 5.625% plus a par value of $1,000.00 at maturity. This bond has a remaining maturity of 3 years. The required rate of return on securities of similar-risk grade is 6.76%. What is the value of this corporate bond today?

b.   What is the current yield for the H&W bond?

c.   In the case of the H&W bond issue from question **a,** if the coupon interest payment is compounded on a semiannual basis, what would be the value of this security today?

d.   How would the price of the H&W bond react to changing market interest rates? To find out, determine how the price of the issue reacts to changes in the bond's yield-to-maturity (YTM). Find the value of the security when the YTM is (1) 5.625%, (2) 8.0%, and (3) 4.5%. Label your findings as being a premium, par, or discount bond; comment on your findings.

e.   The Jay & Austin Company has a bond issue outstanding with the following characteristics: par of $1,000.00, a semiannual-pay coupon of 6.5%, remaining maturity of 2 years, and a current price of $878.74. What is the bond's yield-to-maturity (YTM)?

Portfolio Management

Chapter 12

Mutual Funds: Professionally Managed Portfolios

LEARNING GOALS

After studying this chapter, you should be able to:

LG 1 Describe the basic features of mutual funds, and note what they have to offer as investment vehicles.

LG 2 Distinguish between open- and closed-end funds, as well as other types of professionally managed investment companies, and discuss the various types of fund loads, fees, and charges.

LG 3 Discuss the types of funds available and the variety of investment objectives these funds seek to fulfill.

LG 4 Discuss the investor services offered by mutual funds and how these services can fit into an investment program.

LG 5 Gain an appreciation of the investor uses of mutual funds, along with the variables to consider when assessing and selecting funds for investment purposes.

LG 6 Identify the sources of return and compute the rate of return earned on a mutual fund investment.

I n 1976, John Bogle, founder of the Vanguard Group, had a radical idea: create a mutual fund that would hold only stock in the Standard & Poor's 500 Stock Index of large companies. Unlike other mutual funds, the goal of the Vanguard 500 Index fund would not be to outperform the equities market, but to keep pace with the returns offered by the S&P 500 Index. Vanguard would hold down expenses by limiting itself to the small number of trades necessary to mirror changes in the S&P 500 index.

Today, the Vanguard 500 Index fund is one of the largest mutual funds in the world, with net assets exceeding $66 billion. Investors have been rewarded with consistent returns and low operating costs. Just as Bogle predicted, the fund's emphasis on limited stock turnover has kept its operating expenses low. For every $1,000 an investor places in the fund, Vanguard extracts just $1.80 per year for operating costs, compared with a mutual fund average of $15 annually per $1,000 invested. Even more impressive to investors seeking steady, long-term growth, the Vanguard 500 Index fund has offered predictable returns, averaging 8.24% per year since 1995, just below the 8.32% average annual return of the S&P 500 Index itself.

If the Vanguard 500 Index fund's investment strategy doesn't appeal to you, you can choose from more than 10,000 mutual funds sold by Vanguard and other mutual funds in the United States. Your choices range from funds that track other market indexes to funds focusing on companies in a particular industry sector (e.g., pharmaceutical companies) to emerging-market funds that invest in developing economies. Other options include funds that buy and sell a broad range of stocks, bonds, and even shares in other mutual funds. Before choosing a mutual fund, it's important to understand from the fund prospectus how the fund is managed and the factors affecting its performance. As you'll learn in this chapter, with this information under your belt, mutual funds can help you reach your investment goals.

Sources: Fund data from http://www.vanguard.com (accessed July 31, 2006) and http://www.finance.yahoo.com/ (accessed July 31, 2006).

The Mutual Fund Concept

LG 1 LG 2

mutual fund
an investment company that
invests its shareholders' money
in a diversified portfolio of
securities.

Questions of which stock or bond to select, when to buy, and when to sell have plagued investors for as long as there have been organized securities markets. Such concerns lie at the very heart of the mutual fund concept and in large part explain the growth that mutual funds have experienced. Many investors lack the time, know-how, or commitment to manage their own portfolios, so they turn to professional money managers and simply let them decide which securities to buy and when to sell. More often than not, when investors look for professional help, they look to mutual funds.

Basically, a **mutual fund** is a type of financial services organization that receives money from its shareholders and then invests those funds in a diversified portfolio of securities. Thus, when investors buy shares in a mutual fund, they actually become *part owners of a widely diversified portfolio of securities.* In an abstract sense, a mutual fund is the *financial product* sold to the public by an investment company. That is, the investment company builds and manages a portfolio of securities and sells ownership interests—shares of stock—in that portfolio through a vehicle known as a mutual fund.

Recall from Chapter 5 that portfolio management deals with both asset allocation and security selection decisions. By investing in mutual funds, investors delegate some, if not all, of the *security selection decision*s to professional money managers. As a result, they can concentrate on key asset allocation decisions—which, of course, play a vital role in determining long-term portfolio returns. Indeed, it's for this reason that *many investors consider mutual funds to be the ultimate asset allocation vehicle.* All that investors have to do is decide in which fund they want to invest—and then let the professional money managers at the mutual funds do the rest.

▮ An Overview of Mutual Funds

Mutual funds have been a part of the investment landscape in this country for over 75 years. The first one (MFS) started in Boston in 1924 and is still in business today. By 1940 the number of mutual funds had grown to 68, and by 1980 there were 564 of them. That was only the beginning: The next 25 years saw unprecedented growth in the mutual fund industry, as assets under management grew from less than $100 billion in 1980 to some $9.2 *trillion* by January 2006. By year-end 2005, *there were nearly 8,000 publicly traded mutual funds.* (Actually, counting duplicate and multiple fund offerings from the same portfolio, there were more like *21,000 funds available.*) To put that number in perspective, *there are more mutual funds in existence today than there are stocks listed on the New York and American exchanges combined.* The mutual fund industry has grown so much, in fact, that it is now *the largest financial intermediary* in this country—even ahead of banks.

Mutual funds are big business in the United States and, indeed, all over the world. As the year 2006 began, some 91 million individuals in 54 million U.S. households owned mutual funds. Worldwide, there were more than 55,000 mutual funds in operation, which collectively held over *$17 trillion* in assets. Of that amount, the 8,000 or so funds in the United States held roughly half of those assets, as shown at the top of the next page.

Type of Fund	Number of U.S. Mutual Funds	Assets Managed by U.S. Funds ($ in billions)
Stock funds	4,528	$4,759.5
Bond funds	2,016	1,355.2
Money market funds	888	1,912.6
Other/Hybrid	505	561.6
Total	7,937	$8,588.9

Source: Investment Co. Institute, www.ici.org (accessed March 2006); all data through 3rd quarter 2005.

Whether measured by number of funds or assets under management, stock funds clearly dominate the U.S. market, just as they do worldwide. Mutual funds appeal to investors from all walks of life and all income levels. They range from inexperienced to highly experienced investors who all share a common view: Each has decided, for one reason or another, to turn over at least a part of his or her investment management activities to professionals.

Pooled Diversification The mutual fund concept is based on the simple idea of combining the investment capital of a group of people with similar investment goals, and investing that capital in a wide array of securities. In so doing, investors are able to enjoy much wider investment diversification than they could otherwise achieve on their own. It's not uncommon for a single mutual fund to hold literally hundreds of different stocks or bonds. For example, as of year-end 2005, Fidelity Contrafund held some 530 different securities, while the Dreyfus GNMA fund had over 1,100 holdings. That's far more diversification than most individual investors could ever hope to attain. Yet each investor who owns shares in a fund is, in effect, a part owner of that fund's diversified portfolio of securities.

No matter what the size of the fund, as the securities it holds move up and down in price, the market value of the mutual fund shares moves accordingly. When the fund receives dividend and interest payments, they too are passed on to the mutual fund shareholders and distributed on the basis of prorated ownership. Thus, if you own 1,000 shares in a mutual fund and that represents 1% of all shares outstanding, you will receive 1% of the dividends paid by the fund. When the fund sells a security for a profit, it also passes the capital gain on to fund shareholders on a prorated basis. The whole mutual fund idea, in fact, rests on the concept of **pooled diversification**. This process works very much like health insurance, whereby individuals pool their resources for the collective benefit of all the contributors.

pooled diversification
a process whereby investors buy into a diversified portfolio of securities for the collective benefit of the individual investors.

Attractions and Drawbacks of Mutual Fund Ownership Among the many reasons for owning mutual funds, one of the most important is the *portfolio diversification* that they offer. As we saw above, diversification benefits fund shareholders by spreading holdings over a wide variety of industries and companies, thus reducing risk. Another appeal of mutual funds is *full-time professional management,* which relieves investors of many of the day-to-day management and record-keeping chores. What's more, the fund is probably able to offer better investment expertise than individual investors can provide. Still another advantage is that most mutual fund investments can be started with a *modest capital outlay.* The *services that mutual funds offer* also make them appealing to many investors: These include automatic reinvestment of

management fee
a fee levied annually for professional mutual fund services provided; paid regardless of the performance of the portfolio.

HOTLINKS

To see the corrosive effect that fees paid have on return (or profit), use the fee analyzer at:

www.smartmoney.com/fundfeeanalyzer/

INVESTOR FACTS

FUNDS AND TAXES—When you own shares in a mutual fund, you, not the fund, are liable for any income taxes. That's because mutual funds are tax-exempt organizations, so there's no double taxation of income. (To qualify as tax-exempt, a fund must distribute all of its realized capital gains and at least 90% of any interest and dividend income.) Though the fund may not owe any taxes, you do—unless you hold the fund in a tax-sheltered account, like an IRA or a 401(k). In that case, the taxes are deferred until you start drawing down the account. If any taxes are due, you will receive a Form 1099 from the mutual fund each year, showing how much was earned in ordinary income (dividends and interest) and/or capital gains.

dividends, withdrawal plans, and exchange privileges. Finally, mutual funds offer *convenience*. They are relatively easy to acquire; the funds handle the paperwork and record keeping; their prices are widely quoted; and it is possible to deal in fractional shares.

There are, of course, some drawbacks to mutual fund ownership. One of the biggest disadvantages is that mutual funds in general can be costly and involve *substantial transaction costs*. Many funds carry sizable commission fees ("load charges"). In addition, funds levy a **management fee** annually for the services provided. It is deducted right off the top, regardless of whether the fund has had a good or a bad year. And, in spite of the professional management, *mutual fund performance* over the long haul is at best about equal to what you would expect from the market as a whole. There are some notable exceptions, of course, but most funds do little more than keep up with the market. In many cases, they don't even do that.

Figure 12.1 (on page 522) shows the investment performance for 12 different types of equity (or equity-oriented) funds over the 12-year period from January 1994 through December 2005. The reported returns are average, fully compounded annual rates of return. They assume that all dividends and capital gains distributions are reinvested into additional shares of stock. Note that when compared to the S&P 500, only five fund categories outperformed the market, whereas several fell far short. The message is clear: *Consistently beating the market is no easy task,* even for professional money managers. Although a handful of funds have given investors above-average and even spectacular rates of return, most mutual funds simply do not meet those levels of performance. This is not to say that the long-term returns from mutual funds are substandard or that they fail to equal what you could achieve by putting your money in, say, a savings account or some other risk-free investment outlet. Quite the contrary: The long-term returns from mutual funds have been substantial (and perhaps even better than what many individual investors could have achieved on their own), but a good deal of those returns can be traced to strong market conditions and/or to the reinvestment of dividends and capital gains.

How Mutual Funds Are Organized and Run Although it's tempting to think of a mutual fund as a single large entity, that view is not really accurate. Funds split their various functions—investing, record keeping, safekeeping, and others—among two or more companies. To begin with, there's the fund itself, which is organized as a separate corporation or trust; it is *owned by the shareholders*, not by the firm that runs it. In addition, there are several other major players:

• A *management company* runs the fund's daily operations. Management companies are the firms we know as Fidelity, Vanguard, T. Rowe Price, American Century, and Dreyfus. They are the ones that create the funds in the first place. Usually, the management firm also serves as investment adviser.

• An *investment adviser* buys and sells stocks or bonds and otherwise oversees the portfolio. Usually, three parties participate in this phase of the operation: (1) *the money manager,* who actually runs the portfolio

FIGURE 12.1	The Comparative Performance of Mutual Funds Versus the Market

Even with the services of professional money managers, it's tough to outperform the market. In this case, the average performance of 7 out of the 12 fund categories failed to meet the market's standard of return (for the 12-year period from January 1994 to December 2005). (*Source: Morningstar*, January 2006.)

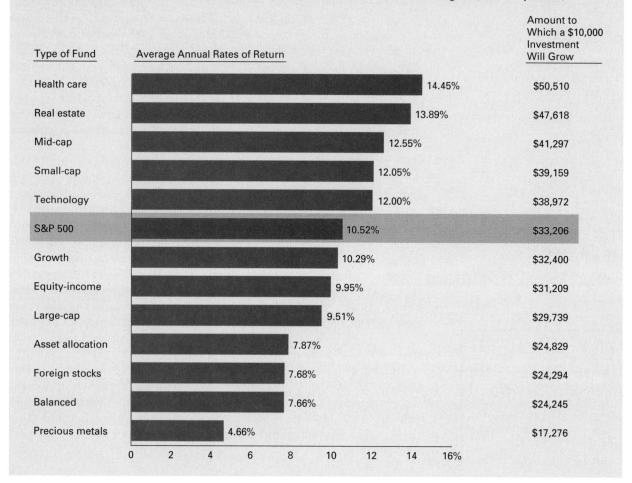

Type of Fund	Average Annual Rates of Return	Amount to Which a $10,000 Investment Will Grow
Health care	14.45%	$50,510
Real estate	13.89%	$47,618
Mid-cap	12.55%	$41,297
Small-cap	12.05%	$39,159
Technology	12.00%	$38,972
S&P 500	10.52%	$33,206
Growth	10.29%	$32,400
Equity-income	9.95%	$31,209
Large-cap	9.51%	$29,739
Asset allocation	7.87%	$24,829
Foreign stocks	7.68%	$24,294
Balanced	7.66%	$24,245
Precious metals	4.66%	$17,276

and makes the buy and sell decisions; (2) *securities analysts*, who analyze securities and look for viable investment candidates; and (3) *traders*, who buy and sell big blocks of securities at the best possible price.

- A *distributor* sells the fund shares, either directly to the public or through authorized dealers (like major brokerage houses and commercial banks). When you request a prospectus and sales literature, you deal with the distributor.

- A *custodian* physically safeguards the securities and other assets of the fund, without taking a role in the investment decisions. To discourage foul play, an independent party (usually a bank) serves in this capacity.

- A *transfer agent* keeps track of purchase and redemption requests from shareholders and maintains other shareholder records.

ETHICS *in* INVESTING

When Mutual Funds Behaved Badly

For nearly 95 million Americans who own them, mutual funds are a convenient and relatively safe place to invest money. So it came as a big shock to investors in September 2003 when New York Attorney General Eliot Spitzer shook the mutual fund industry with allegations of illegal after-hours trading, special deals for large institutional investors, market timing in flagrant violation of funds' written policies, and other abuses. Nearly 20 companies, including several large brokerages, were dragged into scandals.

Some of the abuses stemmed from *market timing*, a practice where short-term traders seek to exploit differences between hours of operations of various global markets. For example, when the U.S. market rallies on strong economic news, short-term traders buy shares of U.S.-based international funds with large Asian holdings just before the close of the market at 4:00 P.M. EST. Prices of these funds, often calculated between 4:00 and 6:00 P.M., reflect closing prices of the U.S. securities but previous-day prices of Asian stocks, which typically don't close until 2:00 A.M. When the next-day Tokyo and other Asian markets rallied following Wall Street's lead, the market-timers sold shares of Asian holdings at the higher price, pocketing the profits. Most funds prohibit this kind of activity, yet exceptions were made for large institutional investors who traded millions of dollars' worth of fund shares. According to the regulators, this practice resembles betting on a winning horse after the horse race is over. Although *late trading* is illegal, many mutual funds did not enforce that rule for some of their privileged clients.

The abuses did not stop there. The National Association of Securities Dealers and the SEC also cracked down on mutual fund sales practices that overcharged investors on sales charges, or loads. Also, several funds closed to new investors charged their existing shareholders millions of dollars in marketing and sales fees.

Without at all excusing this unethical behavior, unlike the accounting and management fraud at companies like Enron and WorldCom, which caused their investors substantial losses, the mutual fund improprieties have not caused significant financial damage to their shareholders. Some estimates put the cost at about 0.1% of over $7 trillion invested in mutual funds. Most of that will be recovered since—as a result of settlements reached with the regulators—many mutual funds pledged to cut fees and lower fund expenses to benefit investors in the long run.

CRITICAL THINKING QUESTION The SEC has proposed several regulations intended to curb mutual trading abuses. They include strict enforcement of trading hours and the imposition of 2% redemption fees if a fund is sold in less than 90 days. Do you think this will eliminate trading abuses?

This separation of duties is designed to protect mutual fund shareholders. As a mutual fund investor, you can lose money (if your fund's stock or bond holdings go down in value), but that's the only risk of loss you face with a mutual fund. Here's why: In addition to the separation of duties noted above, one of the provisions of the contract between the mutual fund and the company that manages it is that the fund's assets—stocks, bonds, cash, or other securities in the portfolio—can *never be in the hands of the management company*. As still another safeguard, each fund must have a board of directors, or trustees, who are elected by shareholders and are charged with keeping tabs on the management company. Nevertheless, as the *Ethics in Investing* box above explains, some mutual funds have engaged in some improper trading.

▌ Open- or Closed-End Funds

Although investing in mutual funds has been made as simple as possible, investors should have a clear understanding of what they're getting into. It's essential that you be aware of the different organizational structures, particularly with regard to open- and closed-end funds.

Open-End Investment Companies

open-end investment company
a type of investment company in which investors buy shares from, and sell them back to, the mutual fund itself, with no limit on the number of shares the fund can issue.

The term *mutual fund* is commonly used to describe an open-end investment company. In an **open-end investment company**, investors buy their shares from, and sell them back to, the mutual fund itself. When an investor buys shares in an open-end fund, the fund issues new shares of stock and fills the purchase order with those new shares. There is no limit, other than investor demand, to the number of shares the fund can issue. (Occasionally, funds *temporarily* close themselves to new investors—they won't open any new accounts—in an attempt to keep fund growth in check.) All open-end mutual funds stand behind their shares and buy them back when investors decide to sell. There is never any trading of shares between individuals.

Open-end mutual funds are the dominant type of investment company and account for well over 95% of the assets under management. Many of these funds are very large and hold *billions* of dollars' worth of securities. Indeed, in 2005, the typical stock or bond fund held an average portfolio of some $775 million, and there were over 850 billion-dollar funds.

net asset value (NAV)
the underlying value of a share of stock in a particular mutual fund.

Both buy and sell transactions in open-end mutual funds are carried out at prices based on the current market value of all the securities held in the fund's portfolio. Known as the fund's **net asset value (NAV)**, it is calculated at least once a day and represents the underlying value of a share of stock in a particular mutual fund. NAV is found by taking the total market value of all assets held by the fund, less any liabilities, and dividing this amount by the number of fund shares outstanding. For example, if the market value of all the assets held by XYZ mutual fund on a given day equaled $10 million, and if XYZ on that particular day had 500,000 shares outstanding, the fund's net asset value per share would be $20 ($10,000,000 ÷ 500,000). This figure, as we will see, is then used to derive the price at which the fund shares are bought and sold.

Closed-End Investment Companies

closed-end investment companies
a type of investment company that operates with a fixed number of shares outstanding.

Although the term *mutual fund* technically refers only to open-end funds, it is also commonly used to refer to closed-end investment companies. **Closed-end investment companies** operate with a fixed number of shares outstanding, and do not regularly issue new shares of stock. In effect, they have a capital structure like that of any other corporation, except that the corporation's business happens to be investing in marketable securities. Shares in closed-end investment companies, like those of any other common stock, are actively traded in the secondary market. Unlike open-end funds, *all trading in closed-end funds is done between investors in the open market*. The fund itself plays no role in either buy or sell transactions. Once the shares are issued, the fund is out of the picture. Most closed-end investment companies are traded on the New York Stock Exchange, a few are traded on the American Exchange, and occasionally some are traded in the Nasdaq market. Even so, while these shares are traded like any other common stock, their quotes are listed separately—in the *Wall Street Journal* at least.

Shown below is one of those quotes, for Gabelli Equity Trust, a large closed-end investment company listed on the NYSE. These quotes appear daily in the *Wall Street Journal* and are grouped by the exchange on which the funds are traded. As you can see, they provide only a minimal amount of information, including the fund's abbreviated name and symbol, the latest dividend, the closing price, and the net change in price.

STOCK (SYM)	DIV	LAST	NET CHG
GabelliTr **GAB**	.76a	8.38	0.05

A closed-end fund is, in many respects, both a common stock and an investment company. As the original form of investment company, closed-end funds have enjoyed a long history that dates back to nineteenth-century England and Scotland. In the United States, closed-end funds were actively traded during the 1920s bull market, when they far outnumbered their open-end relatives. During that freewheeling era, however, they were highly leveraged and consequently were hit hard during the Crash of 1929, earning a bad reputation with investors. They remained something of an oddity for decades afterward. It wasn't until the bull market that began in the early 1980s that closed-end funds came back into fashion.

Many of the investment advisers who today run closed-end funds (like Nuveen, Eaton Vance, Dreyfus, PIMCO, and Putnam) also manage open-end funds, often with similar investment objectives. The closed- and open-end funds they offer are really *two different investment products*. Although it may not appear so at first glance, there are some major differences between these two types of funds. First, closed-end funds have a fixed amount of capital to work with. Therefore, they don't have to be concerned about keeping cash on hand (or readily available) to meet redemptions. Equally important, because there is no pressure on portfolio managers to cash in these securities at inopportune times, they can be more aggressive in their investment styles by investing in securities that may not be actively traded. And, of course, because they don't have new money flowing in all the time, portfolio managers don't have to worry about finding new investments. Instead, they can concentrate on a set portfolio of securities.

Of course, this also puts added pressure on the money managers, since their investment styles and fund portfolios are closely monitored and judged by the market. That is, the share prices of closed-end companies are determined not only by their net asset values but also by general supply and demand conditions in the market. As a result, depending on the market outlook and investor expectations, closed-end companies generally trade at a discount or premium to NAV. Share price discounts and premiums can at times become quite large. In fact, it's not unusual for such spreads to amount to as much as 25% to 30% of net asset value. (We'll discuss closed-end funds in more detail later in this chapter.)

▮ Exchange-Traded Funds

Combine some of the operating characteristics of an open-end fund with some of the trading characteristics of a closed-end fund, and what you'll end up with is something called an *exchange-traded fund*, or ETF for short. ETFs can be structured in one of three ways: as *open-end mutual funds;* as *unit investment trusts*—though far less common than open-end funds, the first ETF's were structured this way and, as such, the most popular ETFs (Qubes, Diamonds, and Spiders) are structured as unit investment trusts; and as *grantor trusts*, which legally give the shareholder certain ownership rights that are not available with the other two forms (Merrill Lynch's HOLDRS are structured this way). Because approximately 90% of all ETFs are structured as open-end funds, and because operationally, there's very little difference between ETFs organized as open-end funds or unit investment trusts, we'll couch our discussion here in terms of the open-ended variety of ETFs.

exchange-traded fund (ETF)
an open-end mutual fund that trades as a listed security on a stock exchange.

Accordingly, we can describe an **exchange-traded fund** (ETF) as a type of open-end mutual fund that trades as a listed security on one of the stock exchanges (mostly the AMEX). All ETFs thus far (through 2005) have been structured as *index funds* set up to match the performance of a certain segment of the market. They do this by owning all, or a representative sample, of the stocks in a targeted market segment or index. (We'll examine traditional index funds in more detail later in this chapter.) Thus, ETFs offer the professional money management of traditional mutual funds *and* the liquidity of an exchange-traded stock.

Even though these securities are like closed-end funds in that they are traded on listed exchanges, *they are in reality open-end mutual funds*, where the number of shares outstanding can be increased or decreased in response to market demand. That is, although ETFs can be bought or sold like any other stock on a listed exchange, *the ETF distributor can also create new shares or redeem old shares.* This is done through a special type of security known as a *payment-in-kind creation unit*. (Without getting into all the messy details, these units are created by exchange specialists, or so-called "authorized participants," who deposit with a trustee a portfolio, or market basket, of stocks that track an index. The authorized participant then receives from the trustee new ETF shares, on the index, to be sold in the open market. To redeem shares, the authorized participant simply turns in ETF shares in exchange for the underlying stocks.) This is all done to ensure an efficient and orderly market, and to prevent the fund shares from trading at (much of) a discount or premium, thereby avoiding one of the pitfalls of closed-end funds. Individual investors, of course, are *not* involved in the creation of these fund shares (that's handled by big institutional investors). Instead, they buy and sell ETFs in the secondary market by placing orders with their brokers, as they would normally do with any stock.

HOTLINKS

Which are the most active index shares—Nasdaq 100 index shares, SPDRs, Midcap SPDRs, or Diamonds? To find out, visit:

amex.com

By year-end 2005, there were more than 225 ETFs traded on U.S. markets, which together accounted for more than $300 billion in assets under management. These funds cover a wide array of domestic and international stock indexes and sub-markets, as well as a handful of U.S. Treasury and corporate bond indexes. The biggest and oldest (dating back to 1993) is based on the S&P 500, and are known as *Spiders*. In addition, there are *Qubes* (based on the Nasdaq 100, this is the most actively traded ETF and in fact is the most actively traded stock in the world), and *Diamonds* (which are based on the DJIA). In addition, there are EFTs based on dozens of international markets (from Australia and Canada to Germany, Japan, and the United Kingdom), and a half-dozen or so that are based on various bond measures. Just about every major U.S. index, in fact, has its own ETF. So do a lot of minor indexes (some of which were created by the distributors) that cover very specialized (and sometimes fairly small) segments of the market. There are even ETFs based on gold bullion, real estate, commodities futures, clean energy, stocks with high dividend yields, tiny micro-cap stocks, and inflation-protection securities.

The net asset values of ETFs are set at a fraction of the underlying index value at any given time. For example, if the S&P 500 index stands at, say, 1364.46, the EFT on that index will trade at around 136.50 (that is, at about 1/10 of the index). Likewise, the ETF on the Dow is set at 1/100 of the DJIA. (Thus, when the DJIA is at say, 11449.30, the EFT will trade at around 114.50).

ETFs combine many of the advantages of closed-end funds with those of traditional (open-end) index funds. As with closed-end funds, you can buy and sell ETFs at *any time of the day* by placing an order through your broker (and paying a standard commission, just as you would with any other stock). In contrast, you *cannot* trade a traditional open-end fund on an intraday basis; all buy and sell orders for those funds are filled at the end of the trading day, at closing prices. ETFs can also be bought on margin, and they can be sold short. Moreover, because ETFs are passively managed, they offer all the advantages of any index fund: low cost, low portfolio turnover, and low taxes. In fact, the fund's tax liability is kept very low, because ETFs rarely distribute any capital gains to shareholders. Thus, you could hold ETFs for decades and never pay a dime in capital gains taxes (at least not until you sell the shares). The accompanying *Investing in Action* box (on page 528) provides some discussion on how ETFs can be used in different types of investment strategies, including hedging a portfolio against a drop in the market.

▌ Some Important Considerations

When you buy or sell shares in a *closed-end* investment company (or in *ETFs,* for that matter), you pay a commission, just as you would with any other listed or OTC stock. This is not the case with open-end mutual funds, however; the cost of investing in an open-end fund depends on the types of fees and load charges that the fund levies on its investors.

Load and No-Load Funds The *load charge* on an open-end fund is the commission you pay when you buy shares in a fund. Generally speaking, the term **load fund** describes a mutual fund that charges a commission when shares are bought. (Such charges are also known as *front-end loads*.) A **no-load fund** levies no sales charges. Load charges can be fairly substantial and can amount to as much as 8.5% of the *purchase price* of the shares. However, very few funds charge the maximum. Instead, many funds charge commissions of only 2% or 3%. Such funds are known as **low-load funds.**

Although there may be little or no difference in the performance of load and no-load funds, *the cost savings with no-load funds tend to give investors a head start in achieving superior rates of return.* Unfortunately, the true no-load fund is becoming harder to find, as more and more no-loads are becoming *12(b)-1 funds.* These funds do not directly charge commissions at the time of purchase. Instead, they *annually* assess what are known as 12(b)-1 charges to make up for any lost commissions. (These charges are more fully described below.) Overall, less than 30% of the funds sold today are pure no-loads; the rest charge some type of load or fee.

load fund
a mutual fund that charges a commission when shares are bought; also known as a *front-end load fund.*

no-load fund
a mutual fund that does not charge a commission when shares are bought.

low-load fund
a mutual fund that charges a small commission (2% to 3%) when shares are bought.

INVESTING *in Action*

Adding ETFs to Your Investment Portfolio

Exchange-traded funds (ETFs) are similar to index mutual funds, but they trade like stocks. Each share represents a basket of securities that closely tracks one specific index. Investors can choose from about 120 different types of ETFs.

Because ETFs trade on the stock market, it's easy to buy and sell them through a brokerage account. ETFs have extremely low costs because they are mostly managed by computers rather than portfolio managers. Also, because they are not actively managed, ETFs generate little or no taxable income and capital gains distributions. Investors do not incur a tax liability until they sell the ETF at a profit. Performance has been attractive as well, helped by ETFs' low expense ratios. ETFs that track broad stock indexes, such as the S&P 500, the DJIA, or the Wilshire 5000 have generally achieved higher returns than 75% of actively managed funds that follow these benchmarks.

ETFs do have some drawbacks, however. Though fees are low, investors incur brokerage commissions when they trade ETFs, as well as a small bid/ask spread. And, whereas traditional mutual funds can reinvest dividends and capital gains immediately to continuously compound their gains, ETFs can reinvest their cash only monthly or quarterly.

Despite some downside, ETFs provide investors with a quick way to get exposure to any market segment in which they wish to participate. It's easy to add a specific equity component based on factors such as style, size, sector, or region. For example, you can choose an ETF that tracks a growth or a value index. You can find ETFs that track small-, mid-, and large-cap companies. Likewise, many ETFs target specific industries such as health care and energy. They offer exposure to a slice of an industry that mutual funds may not cover, yet broader coverage than you would gain by buying several individual stocks. Finally, ETFs make it easy to achieve geographical diversification, by tracking regional indexes such as the S&P Europe 350 or the European Monetary Union.

Because ETFs can be sold short (as well as sold on margin), investors also can use them as hedging vehicles, to protect all or parts of a portfolio against market declines. You could, for example, sell short the shares of a large-cap ETF to hedge the large-cap stocks in your portfolio. Any losses you experience on the long side (the stocks), you can hope to make up, at least in part, on the short (ETF) side.

In short, ETFs offer something for almost any investor.

CRITICAL THINKING QUESTIONS What are four ways of structuring exchange-traded funds? What investment advantages do ETFs offer?

---

back-end load
a commission charged on the *sale* of shares in a mutual fund.

Occasionally, a fund will have a **back-end load**. This means that the fund levies commissions when shares are sold. These loads may amount to as much as 7.25% of the value of the shares sold, although back-end loads tend to decline over time and usually disappear altogether after five or six years from date of purchase. The stated purpose of back-end loads is to enhance fund stability by discouraging investors from trading in and out of the funds over short investment horizons.

12(b)-1 fee
a fee levied annually by many mutual funds to cover management and other operating costs; amounts to as much as 1% of the average net assets.

In addition, a substantial (and growing) number of funds charge something called a **12(b)-1 fee** that's assessed annually for as long as you own the fund. Known appropriately as *hidden loads*, these fees are designed to help funds (particularly the no-loads) cover their distribution and marketing costs. They can amount to as much as 1% per year of assets under management. In good markets and bad, investors pay these fees right off the top, and that can

THE ABC's OF FUND FEES—
One of the newest things in mutual funds fees is the *multiple-class sales charge.* How do you know whether to chose A shares, B shares, or C shares? Here's a guide for deciding which type is best for you.

- **A shares**: Usually involve modest front-end load charges and perhaps a small 12(b)-1 fee (typically 0.25%). *These shares usually make the most sense for long-term investors.*
- **B shares**: Normally have substantial back-end loads for a period of up to 6 years, plus maximum 12(b)-1 fees of 1% per year. The lack of a front-end load make them look attractive to investors, but for *most investors they are a bad deal!*
- **C shares**: Usually a small back-end load if you sell within a year, plus a 12(b)-1 fee of up to 1%. *These shares are normally a better deal than B shares.*

Bottom line: If you're a long-term investor, go for the A shares; if not, go for the C shares.

take its toll. Consider, for instance, $10,000 invested in a fund that charges a 1% 12(b)-1 fee. That translates into a charge of $100 per year—certainly not an insignificant amount of money.

To try to bring some semblance of order to fund charges and fees, the SEC instituted a series of caps on mutual fund fees. According to the latest regulations, a mutual fund cannot charge more than 8½% in *total sales charges and fees*, including front- and back-end loads as well as 12(b)-1 fees. Thus, if a fund charges a 5% front-end load and a 1% 12(b)-1 fee, it can charge a maximum of only 2.5% in back-end load charges without violating the 8.5% cap. In addition, the SEC set a 1% cap on annual 12(b)-1 fees and, perhaps more significantly, stated that true no-load funds cannot charge more than 0.25% in annual 12(b)-1 fees. If they do, they have to drop the no-load label in their sales and promotional material.

Other Fees and Costs Another cost of owning mutual funds is the *management fee*. This is the compensation paid to the professional managers who administer the fund's portfolio. You must pay this fee regardless of whether a fund is load or no-load, and whether it is an open- or closed-end fund, or an exchange-traded fund. Unlike load charges, which are one-time costs, investment companies levy management fees and 12(b)-1 charges annually, regardless of the fund's performance. In addition, there are the administrative costs of operating the fund. These are fairly modest and represent the normal cost of doing business (e.g., the commissions paid when the fund buys and sells securities). The various fees that funds charge generally range from less than 0.5% to as much as 3% or 4% of average assets under management. In addition to these management fees, some funds may charge an *exchange fee*, assessed whenever you transfer money from one fund to another within the same fund family, and/or an *annual maintenance fee*, to help defer the costs of providing service to low-balance accounts.

Total expense ratios bear watching, because high expenses take their toll on performance. As a point of reference, in 2005, domestic stock funds had average expense ratios of around 1.40%, foreign stock funds of around 1.70%, stock index funds of around 0.70%, and domestic bond funds of around 1.10%.

Keeping Track of Fund Fees and Loads Critics of the mutual fund industry have come down hard on the proliferation of fund fees and charges. Fortunately, regulators have taken steps to bring fund fees and loads out into the open. For one thing, fund charges are more widely reported now than they were in past. Most notably, today you can find detailed information about the types and amounts of fees and charges on just about any mutual fund by going to one of the dozens of Web sites that report on mutual funds, including Quicken, Kiplinger, Morningstar, Yahoo!, and a host of others. Figure 12.2 (on page 530) provides excerpts from one of these sites and shows the kind of information that's readily available, at no charge, on the Web.

Alternatively, you can use the mutual fund quotes that appear daily in most major, large-city newspapers or in the *Wall Street Journal*. For example, look at the *Wall Street Journal* quotations in Figure 12.3 (on page 531). Note

---

FIGURE 12.2   **Fund Fees and Charges on the Web**

The Internet has become the motherlode of information on just about any topic imaginable, including mutual fund fees and charges. Here's an example of information taken from the Morningstar Web site. These excerpts show, among other things, all the fees and expenses levied by each fund. The two funds in the exhibit provide a stark contrast in fees and expenses, even though both of them are classified as large-cap value funds. The A shares of the Gabelli Blue Chip Value fund carry a high (5.75%) front-end load, a 12(b)-1 fee, and a *very high* total expense ratio (of 1.89% vs. a category average of 1.35%). In contrast, the Vanguard Windsor fund is a vivid example of a low-cost fund: no loads or fees and a *very low* total expense ratio (of 0.36% vs. 1.35% for the category). Thus, over a 10-year period, the Gabelli fund will cost the investor about $2,660 in fees and expenses, while the Vanguard Windsor investor will pay only $468. (*Source:* Data from **www.morningstar.com/**, March 22, 2006. ©2006 Morningstar, Inc.)

Fees & Expenses
Gabelli Blue Chip Value A GBCAX

Fees and Expenses

Maximum Sales Fees %		**Actual Fees %**	
Initial	5.75	12b-1	0.25
Deferred	None	Management	1.00
Redemption		Expense Ratio: Annual Report	1.89
0 - 8 days	2.00	(As of 12-31-04)	
8 days and up	0.00	Category Average	1.35

Maximum Fees %		**Total Cost Projections**	Cost per $10,000
Administrative	0.00	3-Year	$1135
Management	1.00	5-Year	$1538
		10-Year	$2659

Fees & Expenses
Vanguard Windsor VWNDX

Fees and Expenses

Maximum Sales Fees %		**Actual Fees %**	
Initial	None	12b-1	0.00
Deferred	None	Management	0.35
Redemption	None	Expense Ratio: Annual Report	0.36
		(As of 10-31-05)	
Maximum Fees %		Category Average	1.35
Administrative	0.00		
Management	0.38	**Total Cost Projections**	Cost per $10,000
		3-Year	$119
		5-Year	$208
		10-Year	$468

---

that right after the (abbreviated) names of the fund, you will often find the letters *r*, *p*, and *t*. An *r* behind a fund's name means that the fund charges some type of redemption fee, or back-end load, when you sell your shares. A *p* in the quotes means that the fund levies a 12(b)-1 fee. A *t* indicates funds that charge both redemption fees and 12(b)-1 fees. The quotations, of course, tell you only the *kinds* of fees charged by the funds. They do not tell you *how much* is

FIGURE 12.3

Mutual Fund Quotes

Open-end mutual funds are listed separately from other securities. They have their own quotation system, an example of which, from the *Wall Street Journal*, is shown here. Note that these securities are quoted in dollars and cents and that the quotes include not only the fund's NAV but year-to-date (YTD) and 3-year returns as well. Also included is an indication of whether the fund charges redemption and/or 12(b)-1 fees. (*Source: Wall Street Journal*, March 8, 2006.)

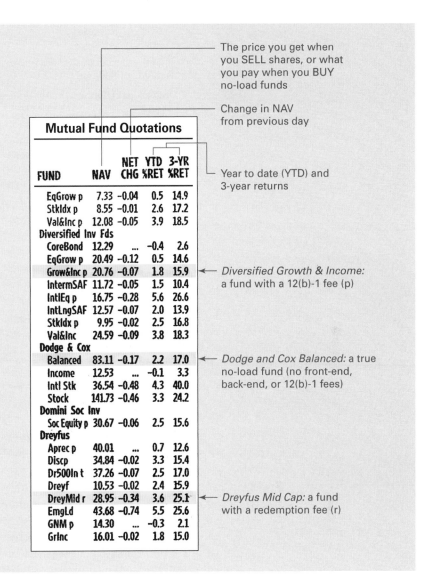

The price you get when you SELL shares, or what you pay when you BUY no-load funds

Change in NAV from previous day

Mutual Fund Quotations

FUND	NAV	NET CHG	YTD %RET	3-YR %RET
EqGrow p	7.33	-0.04	0.5	14.9
StkIdx p	8.55	-0.01	2.6	17.2
Val&Inc p	12.08	-0.05	3.9	18.5
Diversified Inv Fds				
CoreBond	12.29	...	-0.4	2.6
EqGrow p	20.49	-0.12	0.5	14.6
Grow&Inc p	20.76	-0.07	1.8	15.9
IntermSAF	11.72	-0.05	1.5	10.4
IntlEq p	16.75	-0.28	5.6	26.6
IntLngSAF	12.57	-0.07	2.0	13.9
StkIdx p	9.95	-0.02	2.5	16.8
Val&Inc	24.59	-0.09	3.8	18.3
Dodge & Cox				
Balanced	83.11	-0.17	2.2	17.0
Income	12.53	...	-0.1	3.3
Intl Stk	36.54	-0.48	4.3	40.0
Stock	141.73	-0.46	3.3	24.2
Domini Soc Inv				
Soc Equity p	30.67	-0.06	2.5	15.6
Dreyfus				
Aprec p	40.01	...	0.7	12.6
Discp	34.84	-0.02	3.3	15.4
Dr500In t	37.26	-0.07	2.5	17.0
Dreyf	10.53	-0.02	2.4	15.9
DreyMid r	28.95	-0.34	3.6	25.1
EmgLd	43.68	-0.74	5.5	25.6
GNM p	14.30	...	-0.3	2.1
GrInc	16.01	-0.02	1.8	15.0

Year to date (YTD) and 3-year returns

← *Diversified Growth & Income:* a fund with a 12(b)-1 fee (p)

← *Dodge and Cox Balanced:* a true no-load fund (no front-end, back-end, or 12(b)-1 fees)

← *Dreyfus Mid Cap:* a fund with a redemption fee (r)

charged. To get the specifics on the amount charged, you will have to turn to other sources, like a favorite Web site. Furthermore, these published quotes *tell you nothing about the front-end loads,* if any, charged by the funds. Again, to find out if a particular fund charges a front-end load, you will have to consult a Web site or some other source. (Note that the *Wall Street Journal* also publishes a *Monthly Mutual Fund Review* on the first or second Monday of each month. Among other things, it provides some specifics on front-end loads and annual expense charges, including 12(b)-1 fees.)

In addition to the public sources noted above, the SEC requires the mutual funds themselves to fully disclose all of their fees and expenses in a standardized, easy-to-understand format. Every fund profile or prospectus must contain, up front, a fairly detailed *fee table,* much like the one illustrated in Table 12.1 (on page 532). This table has three parts. The first specifies *all shareholder*

TABLE 12.1   Mutual Fund Fee Table (Required by Federal Law)

The following table describes the fees and expenses that are incurred when you buy, hold, or sell shares of the fund.

Shareholder Fees (paid by the investor directly)

Maximum sales charge (load) on purchases (as a % of offering price)	3%
Sales charge (load) on reinvested distributions	None
Deferred sales charge (load) on redemptions	None
Exchange fees	None
Annual account maintenance fee (for accounts under $2,500)	$12.00

Annual fund operating expenses (paid from fund assets)

Management fee	0.45%
Distribution and service (12b-1) fee	None
Other expenses	0.20%
Total annual fund operating expenses	0.65%

Example

This example is intended to help an investor compare the cost of investing in different funds. The example assumes a $10,000 investment in the fund for one, three, five, and ten years and then a redemption of all fund shares at the end of those periods. The example also assumes that an investment returns 5% each year and that the fund's operating expenses remain the same. Although actual costs may be higher or lower, based on these assumptions an investor's costs would be:

1 year	$364
3 years	$502
5 years	$651
10 years	$1,086

transaction costs. This tells you what it's going to cost to buy and sell shares in the mutual fund. The next section lists the *annual operating expenses* of the fund. Showing these expenses as a percentage of average net assets, the fund must break out management fees, 12(b)-1 fees, and any other expenses. The third section provides a rundown of *the total cost over time* of buying, selling, and owning the fund. This part of the table contains both transaction and operating expenses and shows what the total costs would be over hypothetical 1-, 3-, 5-, and 10-year holding periods. To ensure consistency and comparability, the funds must follow a rigid set of guidelines when constructing the illustrative costs.

▮ Other Types of Investment Companies

In addition to open-end, closed-end, and exchange-traded funds, there are four other types of investment companies: (1) real estate investment trusts, (2) hedge funds, (3) unit investment trusts, and (4) annuities. Unit investment trusts, annuities, and hedge funds are similar to mutual funds to the extent that they, too, invest primarily in marketable securities, such as stocks and bonds. Real estate investment trusts, in contrast, invest primarily in various types of real estate–related investments, like mortgages. We'll look at

WEBEXTENSION

For a detailed discussion of two other types of investment companies—unit investment trusts and annuities—see our Web site, at:

www.myfinancelab.com

real estate investment trusts and hedge funds in this section. The other two types of investment companies are discussed in detail on the book's Web site.

Real Estate Investment Trusts A **real estate investment trust (REIT)** is a type of closed-end investment company that invests money in mortgages and various types of real estate investments. A REIT is like a mutual fund in that it sells shares of stock to the investing public and uses the proceeds, along with borrowed funds, to invest in a portfolio of real estate investments. The investor, therefore, owns a part of the real estate portfolio held by the real estate investment trust. The basic appeal of REITs is that they enable investors to receive both the capital appreciation and the current income from real estate ownership without all the headaches of property management. *REITs are also popular with income-oriented investors because of the very attractive dividend yields they provide.*

There are three basic types of REITs: those that invest in *properties*, such as shopping centers, hotels, apartments, and office buildings (the so-called *property*, or *equity*, REITs); mortgage REITs—those that invest in mortgages; and *hybrid* REITs, which invest in both properties and mortgages. Mortgage REITs tend to be more income-oriented; they emphasize their high current yields (which is to be expected from a security that basically invests in debt). In contrast, while equity REITs may promote their attractive current yields, most of them also offer the potential for earning varying amounts of capital gains (as their property holdings appreciate in value). In 2005, there were some 197 REITs, which together held over $330 billion in various real estate assets. Equity REITs dominated the market: There were 152 of them, accounting for some $302 billion in assets under management, or about 90% of the total market. There were 37 mortgage REITs, and just 8 hybrid REITs.

REITs must abide by the Real Estate Investment Trust Act of 1960, which established requirements for forming a REIT, as well as rules and procedures for making investments and distributing income. Because they are required to pay out nearly all their earnings to the owners, REITs do quite a bit of borrowing to obtain funds for their investments. A number of insurance companies, mortgage bankers, and commerical banks have formed REITs, many of which are traded on the major securities exchanges. The income earned by a REIT is not taxed, but *the income distributed to the owners is designated and taxed as ordinary income.* While dividends on common stocks normally are taxed at preferential rates (of 15% or less), cash dividends from REITs are treated as ordinary income, and therefore are subject to normal tax rates. Yet REITs have become very popular in the past 5 to 10 years, in large part because of the very attractive returns they offer. Comparative average annual returns are listed below; clearly, REITs have more than held their own against common stocks:

	REITs*	S&P 500	Nasdaq Composite
3-yr. (2003–2005)	29.04%	17.45%	19.48%
5-yr. (2001–2005)	20.85	2.54	1.18
10-yr. (1996–2005)	14.50	9.02	7.57

*Source: National Association of Real Estate Investment Trusts, (www.nareit.com), March 2006. REIT returns measured by the *NAREIT Composite Index;* fully-compounded rates of return.

real estate investment trust (REIT)

a type of closed-end investment company that sells shares to investors and invests the proceeds in various types of real estate and real estate mortgages; they come in three types: equity REIT's, mortgage REIT's, and hybrid REIT's.

In addition to their highly competitive returns, REITs also offer desirable portfolio diversification properties and very attractive dividend yields (of nearly 5.0%, after taxes), which are generally well above the yields on common stock.

Hedge Funds First of all, in spite of the name similarities, it is important to understand that hedge funds are *not* mutual funds. They are totally different types of investment products! **Hedge funds** are set up as private entities, usually in the form of *limited partnerships* and, as such, are *largely unregulated*. The *general partner* runs the fund and directly participates in the fund's profits—often taking a "performance fee" of 10–20% of the profits, in addition to a base fee of 1–2% of assets under management. The *limited partners are the investors* and consist mainly of institutions, such as pension funds, endowments, and private banks, as well as high-income individual investors. Because hedge funds are unregulated, they can be sold only to "accredited investors," meaning the individual investor must have a net worth in excess of $1 million and/or an annual income (from qualified sources) of at least $200,000 to $300,000. Many hedge funds are, by choice, even more restrictive, and limit their investors to only *very*-high-net-worth individuals. In addition, some hedge funds limit the number of investors they'll let in (often to no more than 100 investors).

These practices, of course, stand in stark contrast to the way mutual funds operate: While hedge funds are largely unregulated, mutual funds are very highly regulated and monitored. Individuals do not need to qualify or be accredited to invest in mutual funds. Although some mutual funds do have minimum investments of $50,000 to $100,000 or more, they are the exception rather than the rule. Not so with hedge funds—many of them have minimum investments that can run into the millions of dollars. Also, mutual fund performance is open for all to see, whereas hedge funds simply do not divulge such information, at least not to the general public. Mutual funds are required by law to provide certain periodic and standardized pricing and valuation information to investors, as well as the general public, whereas hedge funds are totally free from such requirements. The world of hedge funds is very secretive and about as *non*-transparent as you can get.

Hedge funds and mutual funds are similar in one respect, however: Both are pooled investment vehicles that accept investors' money and invest those funds on a collective basis. Put another way, *both sell shares (or participation) in a professionally managed portfolio of securities*. Most hedge funds structure their portfolios so as to reduce volatility and risk, while trying to preserve capital (i.e., "hedge" against market downturns) and still deliver positive returns under different market conditions. They do so by taking often very complex market positions that involve both long and short positions, the use of various arbitrage strategies (to lock in profits), as well as the use of options, futures, and other derivative securities. Indeed, hedge funds will invest in almost any opportunity in almost any market so long as impressive gains are believed to be available at reasonable levels of risk. Thus, these funds are anything but low-risk, fairly stable investment vehicles. In 2006, it was *estimated* (because hedge funds are largely unregulated, no accurate records are available) that there were approximately 8,000 hedge funds in existence, which in total had about *$1 trillion* in assets under management.

hedge fund
a type of unregulated investment vehicle that invests money for a very select group of institutional and high-net-worth individual investors; the investment objectives usually are to not only preserve capital, but also deliver positive returns in all market conditions.

HOTLINKS

For unbiased, independent information on all matters related to hedge funds, see the Hedge Fund Center forum at:

www.hedgefundcenter.com/

CONCEPTS IN REVIEW

Answers available at: www.myfinancelab.com

12.1 What is a *mutual fund?* Discuss the mutual fund concept, including the importance of diversification and professional management.

12.2 What are the attractions and drawbacks of mutual fund ownership?

12.3 Briefly describe how a mutual fund is organized. Who are the key players in a typical mutual fund organization?

12.4 Define each of the following:
   a. Open-end investment companies
   b. Closed-end investment companies
   c. Exchange-traded funds
   d. Real estate investment trusts
   e. Hedge funds

12.5 What is the difference between a *load fund* and a *no-load fund?* What are the advantages of each type? What is a 12(b)-1 fund? Can such a fund operate as a no-load fund?

12.6 Describe a *back-end load,* a *low load,* and a *hidden load.* How can you tell what kind of fees and charges a fund has?

Types of Funds and Services

LG 3   LG 4

Some mutual funds specialize in stocks, others in bonds. Some have maximum capital gains as an investment objective, some high current income. Some funds appeal to speculators, others to income-oriented investors. Every fund has a particular investment objective, and each fund is expected to do its best to conform to its stated investment policy and objective. Categorizing funds according to their investment policies and objectives is a common practice in the mutual fund industry. The categories indicate similarities in how the funds manage their money, and also their risk and return characteristics. Some of the more popular types of mutual funds are growth, aggressive growth, value, equity-income, balanced, growth-and-income, bond, money market, index, sector, socially responsible, asset allocation, and international funds.

Of course, it's also possible to define fund categories based on something other than stated investment objectives. For example, Morningstar, the industry's leading research and reporting service, has developed *a classification system based on a fund's actual portfolio position.* Essentially, it carefully evaluates the make-up of a fund's portfolio to determine where its security holdings are concentrated. It then uses that information to classify funds on the basis of investment style (growth, value, or blend), market segment (small-, mid-, or large-cap), or other factors. Such information helps *mutual fund investors make informed asset allocation decisions* when structuring or rebalancing their own portfolios. That benefit notwithstanding, let's stick with the investment-objective classification system noted above, and examine the various types of mutual funds to see what they are and how they operate.

▮ Types of Mutual Funds

growth fund
a mutual fund whose primary goals are capital gains and long-term growth.

Growth Funds The objective of a **growth fund** is simple: capital appreciation. Long-term growth and capital gains are the primary goals of such funds. They invest principally in well-established, large- or mid-cap companies that have above-average growth potential. They offer little (if anything) in the way of dividends and current income. Because of the uncertain nature of their investment income, growth funds may involve a fair amount of risk exposure. They are usually viewed as long-term investment vehicles most suitable for the more aggressive investor who wants to build up capital and has little interest in current income.

aggressive-growth fund
a highly speculative mutual fund that seeks large profits from capital gains.

Aggressive-Growth Funds Aggressive-growth funds are the so-called performance funds that tend to increase in popularity when markets heat up. **Aggressive-growth funds** are highly speculative investment vehicles that seek large profits from capital gains. Most are fairly small (with average assets under management of less than $300 million), and their portfolios consist mainly of "high-flying" common stocks. These funds often buy stocks of small, unseasoned companies, stocks with relatively high price/earnings multiples, and common stocks whose prices are highly volatile. They seem to be especially fond of turnaround situations and may even use leverage in their portfolios (i.e., buy stocks on margin). They also use options fairly aggressively, various hedging techniques, and perhaps even short selling. These techniques are designed, of course, to yield big returns. Aggressive funds are also highly speculative and are among the most volatile of all mutual funds. When the markets are good, aggressive-growth funds do well; conversely, when the markets are bad, these funds often experience substantial losses.

value fund
a mutual fund that seeks stocks that are undervalued in the market by investing in shares that have low P/E multiples, high dividend yields, and promising futures.

Value Funds **Value funds** confine their investing to stocks considered to be *undervalued* by the market. That is, the funds look for stocks that are fundamentally sound but overlooked by investors. These funds hold stocks as much for their underlying intrinsic value as for their *growth potential*. In stark contrast to growth funds, value funds look for stocks with relatively low price/earnings ratios, high dividend yields, and moderate amounts of financial leverage. They prefer undiscovered companies that offer the potential for growth, rather than those that are already experiencing rapid growth.

HOTLINKS

For more information on fund objectives, go to the sites below and read the sections on investment strategy.

www.wachovia.com/misc/0,,133,00.html
www.axaonline.com/rs/3p/sp/5058.html

Value investing is not easy. It involves extensive evaluation of corporate financial statements and any other documents that will help fund managers uncover value (investment opportunities) *before the rest of the market does* (that's the key to the low P/Es). The approach seems to work; even though value investing is generally regarded as *less risky* than growth investing (lower P/Es, higher dividend yields, and fundamentally stronger companies all translate into reduced risk exposure), the long-term return to investors in value funds is competitive with that from growth funds and even aggressive growth funds. Thus, value funds are often viewed as a viable investment alternative for relatively conservative investors who are looking for the attractive returns that common stocks have to offer, yet want to keep share price volatility and investment risk in check.

equity-income fund
a mutual fund that emphasizes current income and capital preservation and invests primarily in high-yielding common stocks.

Equity-Income Funds Equity-income funds emphasize current income by investing primarily in high-yielding common stocks. Capital preservation is also important, and so are capital gains, although capital appreciation is not the primary objective of equity-income funds. These funds invest heavily in high-grade common stocks, some convertible securities and preferred stocks, and occasionally even junk bonds or certain types of high-grade foreign bonds. As far as their stock holdings are concerned, they lean heavily toward blue chips (including perhaps even "baby blues"), public utilities, and financial shares. They like securities that generate hefty dividend yields but also consider potential price appreciation over the longer haul. In general, because of their emphasis on dividends and current income, these funds tend to hold higher-quality securities that are subject to less price volatility than the market as a whole. They're generally viewed as a fairly low-risk way of investing in stocks.

balanced fund
a mutual fund whose objective is to generate a balanced return of both current income and long-term capital gains.

Balanced Funds Balanced funds tend to hold a balanced portfolio of both stocks and bonds for the purpose of generating a balanced return of both current income and long-term capital gains. They're much like equity-income funds, but balanced funds usually put more into fixed-income securities; generally, they keep around 30% to 40% of their portfolios in bonds. The bonds are used principally to provide current income, and stocks are selected mainly for their long-term growth potential.

The funds can shift the emphasis in their security holdings one way or the other. Clearly, the more the fund leans toward fixed-income securities, the more income-oriented it will be. For the most part, balanced funds tend to confine their investing to high-grade securities, including growth-oriented blue-chip stocks, high-quality income shares, and high-yielding investment-grade bonds. Balanced funds are usually considered a relatively safe form of investing, in which you can earn a competitive rate of return without having to endure a lot of price volatility. (*Note:* Equity-income funds and the more income-oriented balanced funds, as well as certain types of bond funds, are sometimes all lumped together and referred to as *income funds*, because of their emphasis on generating high levels of current income.)

growth-and-income fund
a mutual fund that seeks both long-term growth and current income, with primary emphasis on capital gains.

Growth-and-Income Funds Growth-and-income funds also seek a balanced return made up of both current income and long-term capital gains, but they place a greater emphasis on growth of capital. Unlike balanced funds, growth-and-income funds put most of their money into equities. In fact, it's not unusual for these funds to have 80% to 90% of their capital in common stocks. They tend to confine most of their investing to quality issues, so growth-oriented blue-chip stocks appear in their portfolios, along with a fair amount of high-quality income stocks. Part of the appeal of these funds is the fairly substantial returns many have generated over the long haul. These funds involve a fair amount of risk, if for no other reason than the emphasis they place on stocks and capital gains. Thus, growth-and-income funds are most suitable for those investors who can tolerate the risk and price volatility.

bond fund
a mutual fund that invests in various kinds and grades of bonds, with income as the primary objective.

Bond Funds As the name implies, **bond funds** invest exclusively in various types and grades of bonds—from Treasury and agency bonds to corporates and municipals. Income is the primary investment objective, although capital gains are not ignored.

There are three important advantages to buying shares in bond funds rather than investing directly in bonds. First, the bond funds are generally more liquid than direct investments in bonds. Second, they offer a cost-effective way of achieving a high degree of diversification in an otherwise expensive investment vehicle. (Most bonds carry minimum denominations of $1,000 to $5,000.) Third, bond funds will automatically reinvest interest and other income, thereby allowing you to earn fully compounded rates of return.

Bond funds are generally considered to be a fairly conservative form of investment. But they are not without risk: *The prices of the bonds held in the fund's portfolio fluctuate with changing interest rates.* Many bond funds are managed pretty conservatively, but a growing number are becoming increasingly aggressive. In fact, in today's market, investors can find everything from high-grade government bond funds to highly speculative funds that invest in nothing but junk bonds or even in highly volatile derivative securities. Here's a list of the different types of domestic bond funds available to investors:

- *Government bond funds,* which invest in U.S. Treasury and agency securities.

- *Mortgage-backed bond funds,* which put their money into various types of mortgage-backed securities of the U.S. government (e.g., GNMA issues). These funds appeal to investors for several reasons: (1) They provide diversification. (2) They are an affordable way to get into mortgage-backed securities. (3) They allow investors to reinvest the principal portion of the monthly cash flow, thereby enabling them to preserve their capital.

- *High-grade corporate bond funds,* which invest chiefly in investment-grade securities rated triple-B or better.

- *High-yield corporate bond funds,* which are risky investments that buy junk bonds for the yields they offer.

- *Convertible bond funds,* which invest primarily in securities that can be converted or exchanged into common stocks. These funds offer investors some of the price stability of bonds, along with the capital appreciation potential of stocks.

- *Municipal bond funds,* which invest in tax-exempt securities. These are suitable for investors who seek tax-free income. Like their corporate counterparts, municipal bond funds can be packaged as either high-grade or high-yield funds. A special type of municipal bond fund is the so-called *single-state fund,* which invests in the municipal issues of only one state, thus producing (for residents of that state) interest income that is *fully exempt* from both federal and state taxes (and possibly even local/city taxes as well).

- *Intermediate-term bond funds,* which invest in bonds with maturities of 7 to 10 years or less and offer not only attractive yields but relatively low price volatility as well. Shorter (2- to 5-year) funds are also available; these shorter-term funds are often used as substitutes for money market investments by investors looking for higher returns on their money, especially when short-term rates are way down.

Clearly, no matter what you're looking for in a fixed-income security, you're likely to find a bond fund that fits the bill. Indeed, by 2005, there were more than 6,000 publicly traded bond funds that together had more than $1.5 *trillion* worth of bonds under management.

Money Market Funds Money market mutual funds, or money funds for short, apply the mutual fund concept to the buying and selling of short-term money market instruments—bank certificates of deposit, U.S. Treasury bills, and the like. These funds offer investors with modest amounts of capital access to the high-yielding money market, where many instruments require minimum investments of $100,000 or more. By 2006, there were about 900 money funds that together held nearly $2.1 trillion in assets.

There are several different kinds of money market mutual funds:

- *General-purpose money funds,* which invest in any and all types of money market investment vehicles, from Treasury bills and bank CDs to corporate commercial paper. The vast majority of money funds are of this type.

- *Government securities money funds,* which effectively eliminate any risk of default by confining their investments to Treasury bills and other short-term securities of the U.S. government, or its agencies.

- *Tax-exempt money funds,* which limit their investing to very short (30- to 90-day) tax-exempt municipal securities. Because their income is free from federal income taxes, they appeal predominantly to investors in high tax brackets.

Just about every major brokerage firm has at least four or five money funds of its own, and hundreds more are sold by independent fund distributors. Because the maximum average maturity of their holdings cannot exceed 90 days, money funds are highly liquid investment vehicles, although their returns do move up and down with interest-rate conditions. They're also virtually immune to capital loss, because at least 95% of the fund's assets must be invested in top-rated/prime-grade securities. In fact, with the check-writing privileges they offer, money funds are just as liquid as checking or savings accounts. Many investors view these funds as a convenient, safe, and (reasonably) profitable way to accumulate capital and temporarily store idle funds.

Index Funds "If you can't beat 'em, join 'em." That saying pretty much describes the idea behind index funds. Essentially, an **index fund** is a type of mutual fund that buys and holds a portfolio of stocks (or bonds) equivalent to those in a market index like the S&P 500. An index fund that's trying to match the S&P 500, for example, would hold the same 500 stocks that are held in that index, in exactly (or very nearly) the same proportions. Rather than trying to beat the market, as most actively managed funds do, *index funds simply try to match the market.* That is, they seek to match the performance of the index on which the fund is based. They do this through low-cost investment management. In fact, in most cases, the whole portfolio is run almost entirely by a computer that matches the fund's holdings with those of the targeted index.

The approach of index funds is strictly buy-and-hold. Indeed, about the only time an index-fund portfolio changes is when the targeted market index alters its "market basket" of securities. A pleasant by-product of this buy-and-hold approach is that the funds have extremely low portfolio turnover rates and, therefore, very little in *realized* capital gains. As a result, aside from a modest amount of dividend income, these funds produce very little taxable

money market mutual fund (money fund)
a mutual fund that pools the capital of investors and uses it to invest in short-term money market instruments.

index fund
a mutual fund that buys and holds a portfolio of stocks (or bonds) equivalent to those in a specific market index.

income from year to year, which leads many high-income investors to view them as a type of tax-sheltered investment.

In addition to their tax shelter, these funds provide something else: By simply trying to match the market, index funds actually produce *highly competitive returns*. It's very difficult to consistently outperform the market, and the index funds don't even try to do so. The net result is that, on average, index funds produce better returns than most other types of stock funds. Granted, every now and then fully managed stock funds will have a year (or two) when they outperform index funds. But these are the exception rather than the rule, especially when you look at multi-year returns (three to five years or more). Over most multi-year periods, the vast majority of fully managed stock funds do not keep up with index funds.

The S&P 500 is the most popular index. A number of other market indexes also are used, including the S&P Midcap 400, the Russell 2000 Small Stock, and the Wilshire 5000 indexes, as well as value-stock indexes, growth-stock indexes, international-stock indexes, and even bond indexes. When picking index funds, be sure to avoid high-cost funds. Their fees significantly *reduce* the chance that the fund will be able to match the market. Also, avoid index funds that use gimmicks as a way to "enhance" yields. Rather than follow the index, these funds will "tilt" their portfolios in an attempt to outperform the market. Your best bet is to buy a *true* index fund (one that has no added "bells and whistles"), and a low-cost one at that.

Sector Funds   The so-called **sector fund** is a mutual fund that restricts its investments to a particular sector (or segment) of the market. These funds concentrate their investment holdings in one or more industries that make up the sector being aimed at. For example, a health care sector fund would focus on promising growth stocks from such industries as drug companies, hospital management firms, medical suppliers, and biotech concerns. Among the more popular sector funds are those that concentrate in technology, financial services, real estate (REITs), natural resources, telecommunications, and, of course, health care—all the "glamour" industries.

sector fund
a mutual fund that restricts its investments to a particular segment of the market.

The overriding investment objective of a sector fund is *capital gains*. A sector fund is generally similar to a growth fund and should be considered speculative. The sector fund concept is based on the belief that the really attractive returns come from small segments of the market. It's an interesting notion that may warrant consideration by investors willing to take on the added risks that often accompany these funds.

Socially Responsible Funds   For some, investing is far more than just cranking out financial ratios and calculating investment returns. To these investors, the security selection process also includes the *active, explicit consideration of moral, ethical, and environmental issues*. The idea is that social concerns should play just as big a role in investment decisions as do financial matters. Not surprisingly, a number of funds cater to such investors: Known as **socially responsible funds**, they actively and directly incorporate ethics and morality into the investment decision. Their investment decisions, in effect, revolve around *both* morality and profitability.

socially responsible fund
a mutual fund that actively and directly incorporates ethics and morality into the investment decision.

Socially responsible funds consider only certain companies for inclusion in their portfolios. If a company does not meet the fund's moral, ethical, or environmental tests, fund managers simply will not buy the stock, no matter how good the bottom line looks. Generally speaking, these funds refrain from investing in companies that derive revenues from tobacco, alcohol, gambling, or weapons, or that operate nuclear power plants. In addition, the funds tend to favor firms that produce "responsible" products or services, that have strong employee relations and positive environmental records, and that are socially responsive to the communities in which they operate.

Asset Allocation Funds Studies have shown that the most important decision an investor can make is where to allocate his or her investment assets. *Asset allocation* involves deciding how you're going to divide up your investments among different types of securities. For example, what portion of your money do you want to devote to money market securities, what portion to stocks, and what portion to bonds? Asset allocation deals in broad terms (types of securities) and does not address individual security selection. Asset allocation has been found to be a far more important determinant of total portfolio returns than individual security selection. (See Chapter 13 for more discussion of the principles of asset allocation.)

Because many individual investors have a tough time making asset allocation decisions, the mutual fund industry has created a product to do the job for them. Known as **asset allocation funds**, these funds spread investors' money across different types of markets. Whereas most mutual funds concentrate on one type of investment—whether stocks, bonds, or money market securities—asset allocation funds put money into all these markets. Many of them also include foreign securities. Some even include inflation-resistant investments, such as gold or real estate.

These funds are designed for people who want to hire fund managers not only to select individual securities but also to allocate money among the various markets. Here's how a typical asset allocation fund works. The money manager establishes a desired allocation mix for the fund, which might look something like this: 50% to U.S. stocks, 30% to bonds, 10% to foreign securities, and 10% to money market securities. Securities are then purchased for the fund in these proportions, and the overall portfolio maintains the desired mix. Actually, each segment of the fund is managed almost as a separate portfolio. Thus, securities within, say, the stock portion are bought, sold, and held as the market dictates. However, *as market conditions change over time, the asset allocation mix changes as well.* For example, if the U.S. stock market starts to soften, the fund may reduce the (domestic) stock portion of the portfolio to, say, 35%, and simultaneously increase the foreign securities portion to 25%. There's no assurance, of course, that the money manager will make the right moves at the right time, but the expectation is that he or she will.

International Funds In their search for higher yields and better returns, U.S. investors have shown a growing interest in foreign securities. Sensing an opportunity, the mutual fund industry has been quick to respond with so-called **international funds**—a mutual fund that does all or most of its investing in foreign securities. In 1985, there were only about 40 of these funds; by 2005, the number had grown to nearly 2,500. A lot of people would like to invest in foreign securities but simply do not have the know-how to do so. International funds may be just the vehicle for such investors, *provided they have at least a fundamental understanding of international economics issues* and how they can affect fund returns.

asset allocation fund
a mutual fund that spreads investors' money across stocks, bonds, money market securities, and possibly other asset classes.

international fund
a mutual fund that does all or most of its investing in foreign securities.

Technically, the term *international fund* describes a type of fund that invests *exclusively in foreign securities*. Such funds often confine their activities to specific geographic regions (e.g., Mexico, Australia, Europe, or the Pacific Rim). In contrast, *global funds* invest in both foreign securities and U.S. companies—usually multinational firms. As a rule, global funds provide more diversity and, with access to both foreign and domestic markets, can go wherever the action is. Regardless of whether they're global or international (we'll use the term *international* to apply to both), you can find just about any type of fund you could possibly want. There are international stock funds, international bond funds, even international money market funds. There are aggressive growth funds, balanced funds, long-term growth funds, and high-grade bond funds. There are funds that confine their investing to large, established markets (like Japan, Germany, and Australia) and others that stick to emerging markets (such as Thailand, Mexico, Chile, and even former Communist countries like Poland).

Basically, these funds attempt to take advantage of international economic developments in two ways: (1) by capitalizing on changing *market conditions* and (2) by positioning themselves to benefit from *devaluation of the dollar*. They do so because they can make money either from rising share prices in a foreign market or from a falling dollar (which in itself produces capital gains for U.S. investors in international funds). Many of these funds, however, attempt to protect investors from currency exchange risks by using various types of *hedging strategies*. That is, by using foreign currency options and futures, or some other type of derivative product (see Chapters 14 and 15), the fund tries to reduce or eliminate the effects of fluctuating currency exchange rates. But even with currency hedging, international funds are still fairly high-risk investments and only investors who understand and are able to tolerate such risks should use them.

▌ Investor Services

Ask most investors why they buy a particular mutual fund and they'll probably tell you that the fund provides the kind of income and return they're looking for. Now, no one would question the importance of return in the investment decision, but there are some other important reasons for investing in mutual funds, not the least of which are the valuable services they provide. Some of the most sought-after *mutual fund services* are automatic investment and reinvestment plans, regular income programs, conversion privileges, and retirement programs.

Automatic Investment Plans It takes money to make money. For an investor, that means being able to accumulate the capital to put into the market. Mutual funds have come up with a program that makes savings and capital accumulation as painless as possible. The program is the **automatic investment plan**. This service allows fund shareholders to automatically funnel fixed amounts of money *from their paychecks or bank accounts* into a mutual fund. It's much like a payroll deduction plan.

This fund service has become very popular, because it enables shareholders to invest on a regular basis without having to think about it. Just about every fund group offers some kind of automatic investment plan for virtually all of its stock and bond funds. To enroll, you simply fill out a form

automatic investment plan
a mutual fund service that allows shareholders to automatically send fixed amounts of money from their paychecks or bank accounts into the fund.

authorizing the fund to siphon a set amount (usually a minimum of $25 to $100 per period) from your bank account at regular intervals, such as monthly or quarterly. Once enrolled, you'll be buying more shares every month or quarter (most funds deal in fractional shares). Of course, if it's a load fund, you'll still have to pay normal sales charges on your periodic investments. You can get out of the program at any time, without penalty, by simply calling the fund. Although convenience is perhaps the chief advantage of automatic investment plans, they also make solid investment sense: One of the best ways of building up a sizable amount of capital is to *add funds to your investment program systematically over time*. The importance of making regular contributions to your investment portfolio cannot be overstated; it ranks right up there with compound interest.

Automatic Reinvestment Plans

Automatic Reinvestment Plans An automatic reinvestment plan is another of the real draws of mutual funds and is offered by just about every open-end fund. Whereas automatic investment plans deal with money you are putting into a fund, automatic *re*investment plans deal with the dividends the funds pay to their shareholders. Much like stock dividend reinvestment plans (see Chapter 6), the **automatic reinvestment plans** of mutual funds enable you to keep your capital fully employed. This service automatically uses dividend and/or capital gains income to buy additional shares in the fund. Most funds deal in fractional shares, and such purchases are usually commission-free. Keep in mind, however, that even though you may reinvest all dividends and capital gains distributions, the IRS still treats them as cash receipts and taxes them as investment income in the year in which you received them.

Automatic reinvestment plans enable you to earn fully compounded rates of return. By plowing back profits, you can put them to work in generating even more earnings. Indeed, the effects of these plans on total accumulated capital over the long run can be substantial. Figure 12.4 (on page 544) shows the long-term impact of one such plan. (These are the actual performance numbers for a *real* mutual fund, Fidelity Low-Priced Stock, in this case.) In the illustration, we assume that the investor starts with $10,000 and except for the reinvestment of dividends and capital gains distributions, *adds no new capital over time*. Even so, the initial investment of $10,000 grew to nearly $135,000 over the 15-year period from 1991 to 2005—which amounts to a fully-compounded rate of return of 18.84%. Of course, not all periods will match this performance, nor will all mutual funds be able to perform as well, even in strong markets. The point is that as long as you select an appropriate fund, you can derive *attractive benefits from the systematic accumulation of capital offered by automatic reinvestment plans*.

Regular Income

Regular Income Automatic investment and reinvestment plans are great for the long-term investor. But what about the investor who's looking for a steady stream of income? Once again, mutual funds have a service to meet this need. Called a **systematic withdrawal plan**, it's offered by most open-end funds. Once enrolled, an investor automatically receives a predetermined amount of money every month or quarter. Most funds require a minimum investment of $5,000 or more to participate, and the size of the minimum payment normally must be $50 or more per period (with no limit on the maximum). The funds will pay out the monthly or quarterly income first from dividends and realized capital gains. If this source proves to be inadequate and the shareholder so

automatic reinvestment plan
a mutual fund service that enables shareholders to automatically buy additional shares in the fund through the reinvestment of dividends and capital gains income.

systematic withdrawal plan
a mutual fund service that enables shareholders to automatically receive a predetermined amount of money every month or quarter.

FIGURE 12.4   The Effects of Reinvesting Income

Reinvesting dividends or capital gains can have a tremendous impact on one's investment position. This graph shows the results of a hypothetical investor who initially invested $10,000 in Fidelity Low-Priced Stock and, for a period of 15 years, reinvested all dividends and capital gains distributions in additional fund shares. (No adjustment has been made for any income taxes payable by the shareholder, which is appropriate so long as the fund was held in an IRA or Keogh account.) (*Source:* Data from *Morningstar Principia for Mutual Funds*, December 31, 2005.)

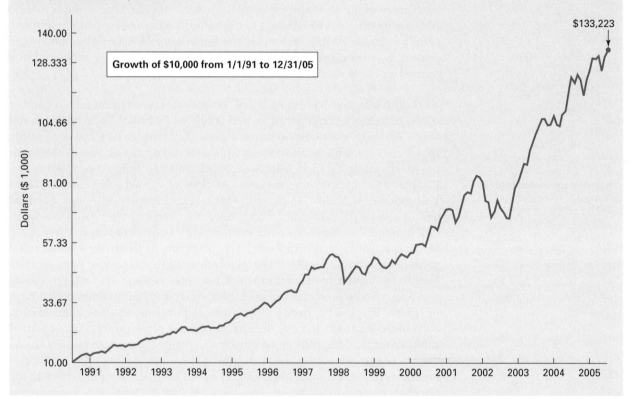

authorizes, the fund can then tap the principal or original paid-in capital to meet the required periodic payments.

Conversion Privileges Sometimes investors find it necessary to switch out of one fund and into another. For example, your objectives or the investment climate itself may have changed. **Conversion** (or **exchange**) **privileges** were devised to meet such needs conveniently and economically. Investment management companies that offer a number of different funds—known as **fund families**—often provide conversion privileges that enable shareholders to move money from one fund to another, either by phone or on the Internet. The only constraint is that the switches must be confined to the same *family* of funds. For example, you can switch from a Dreyfus growth fund to a Dreyfus money fund, or any other fund managed by Dreyfus.

With some fund families, the alternatives open to investors seem almost without limit. Indeed, some of the larger families offer literally hundreds of funds. Fidelity has nearly 200 different funds in its family: from high-performance stock funds to bond funds, tax-exempt funds, a couple of dozen

conversion (exchange) privilege
feature of a mutual fund that allows shareholders to move money from one fund to another, within the same family of funds.

fund families
different kinds of mutual funds offered by a single investment management company.

sector funds, and a couple of dozen money funds. Around 200 fund families are in operation today, *not counting* the 150 to 200 families that offer only one or two funds. The two biggest—Fidelity and Vanguard—each has more than *half-a-trillion dollars* in assets under management, and that *excludes* their money market funds. Other big fund families include Franklin/Templeton ($330 billion under management), PIMCO ($200 billion), Putnam ($115 billion), and American Century ($85 billion). All fund families provide low-cost conversion privileges. Some even provide these privileges for free, although most have limits on the number of times you can make such switches each year.

Conversion privileges are usually considered beneficial for shareholders: They allow you to meet ever-changing long-term goals, and they also permit you to manage your mutual fund holdings more aggressively by moving in and out of funds as the investment environment changes. Unfortunately, there is one major drawback: For tax purposes, the exchange of shares from one fund to another is regarded as a sale transaction followed by a subsequent purchase of a new security. As a result, if any capital gains exist at the time of the exchange, you are liable for the taxes on that profit, even though the holdings were not truly "liquidated."

Retirement Programs As a result of government legislation, self-employed individuals are permitted to divert a portion of their pretax income into self-directed retirement plans (SEPs). Also, all working Americans, whether self-employed or not, are allowed to establish individual retirement arrangements (IRAs). Indeed, with legislation passed in 1997, *qualified investors* can now choose between deductible and nondeductible (Roth) IRAs. Even those who make too much to qualify for one of these programs can set up special nondeductible IRAs. Today all mutual funds provide a service that allows individuals to set up tax-deferred retirement programs as either IRA or Keogh accounts—or, through their place of employment, to participate in a tax-sheltered retirement plan, such as a 401(k). The funds set up the plans and handle all the administrative details so that the shareholder can easily take full advantage of available tax savings.

WEBEXTENSION

You can obtain details on the various IRA programs, as well as other tax-sheltered retirement plans at the book's Web site. Click on the Web chapter titled "Tax-Advantaged Investments" and then on "Tax Deferred Retirement Programs." To access our Web site, go to:

www.myfinancelab.com

CONCEPTS IN REVIEW

Answers available at: www.myfinancelab.com

12.7 Briefly describe each of the following types of mutual funds:
   a. Aggressive growth funds
   b. Equity-income funds
   c. Growth-and-income funds
   d. Bond funds
   e. Sector funds
   f. Socially responsible funds

12.8 What is an *asset allocation fund,* and how does it differ from other types of mutual funds?

12.9 If growth, income, and capital preservation are the primary objectives of mutual funds, why do we bother to categorize funds by type? Do you think such classifications are helpful in the fund selection process? Explain.

12.10 What are *fund families?* What advantages do fund families offer investors? Are there any disadvantages?

12.11 Briefly describe some of the investor services provided by mutual funds. What are *automatic reinvestment plans,* and how do they differ from *automatic investment plans?* What is phone switching, and why would an investor want to use this service?

Investing in Mutual Funds

LG 5   LG 6

Suppose you are confronted with the following situation: You have money to invest and are trying to select the right place to put it. You obviously want to pick a security that meets your idea of acceptable risk and will generate an attractive rate of return. The problem is that you have to make the selection from a list containing literally thousands of securities. That's basically what you're facing when trying to select a suitable mutual fund. However, if you approach the problem systematically, it may not be so formidable a task. First, it might be helpful to examine more closely the various investor uses of mutual funds. With this background, we can then look at the selection process and at several measures of return that you can use to assess performance. As we will see, it is possible to whittle down the list of alternatives by matching your investment needs with the investment objectives of the funds.

■ Investor Uses of Mutual Funds

Mutual funds can be used in a variety of ways. For instance, performance funds can serve as a vehicle for capital appreciation, whereas bond funds can provide current income. Regardless of the kind of income a mutual fund provides, investors tend to use these securities for one of three reasons: (1) as a way to accumulate wealth, (2) as a storehouse of value, or (3) as a speculative vehicle for achieving high rates of return.

Accumulation of Wealth This is probably the most common reason for using mutual funds. Basically, the investor uses mutual funds over the long haul to build up investment capital. Depending on your goals, a modest amount of risk may be acceptable, but usually preservation of capital and capital stability are considered important. The whole idea is to form a "partnership" with the mutual fund in building up as big a pool of capital as possible: *You provide the capital by systematically investing and reinvesting in the fund, and the fund provides the return by doing its best to invest your resources wisely.*

Storehouse of Value Investors also use mutual funds as a storehouse of value. The idea is to find a place where investment capital can be fairly secure and relatively free from deterioration yet still generate a relatively attractive rate of return. Short- and intermediate-term bond funds are logical choices for such purposes, and so are money funds. Capital preservation and income over the long term are very important to some investors. Others might seek storage of value only for the short term, using, for example, money funds as a place to "sit it out" until a more attractive opportunity comes along.

Speculation and Short-Term Trading Although speculation is becoming more common, it is still not widely used by most mutual fund investors. The reason, of course, is that most mutual funds are long-term in nature and thus not meant to be used as aggressive trading vehicles. However, a growing number of funds (e.g., sector funds) now cater to speculators. Some investors have found that mutual funds are, in fact, attractive for speculation and short-term trading.

One way to do this is to aggressively trade in and out of funds as the investment climate changes. Load charges can be avoided (or reduced) by dealing in families of funds offering low-cost conversion privileges and/or by dealing only in no-load funds. Other investors might choose mutual funds as a long-term investment but seek high rates of return by investing in funds that follow very aggressive trading strategies. These are usually the fairly specialized, smaller funds such as leverage funds, option funds, emerging-market funds, small-cap aggressive growth funds, and sector funds. In essence, investors in such funds are simply letting professional money managers handle their accounts in a way they would like to see them handled: *aggressively.*

■ The Selection Process

When it comes to mutual funds, there is one question every investor has to answer right up front: Why invest in a mutual fund to begin with—why not "go it alone" by buying individual stocks and bonds directly? For beginning investors and investors with little capital, the answer is simple: With mutual funds, you are able to achieve far more diversification than you could ever obtain on your own. Plus, you get the help of professional money managers at a very reasonable cost. For more seasoned investors, the answers are probably more involved. Certainly, diversification and professional money management come into play, but there are other reasons as well. The competitive returns mutual funds offer are a factor, as are the services they provide. Many seasoned investors simply have decided they can get better returns by carefully selecting mutual funds than by investing on their own. Some of these investors use part of their capital to buy and sell individual securities on their own and use the rest *to buy mutual funds that invest in areas they don't fully understand or don't feel well informed about.* For example, they'll use mutual funds to get into foreign markets, or buy mortgage-backed securities.

Once you have decided to use mutual funds, you must decide which fund(s) to buy. The selection process involves putting into action all you know about mutual funds, in order to gain as much return as possible from an acceptable level of risk. It begins with an assessment of your own investment needs. Obviously, you want to select from those thousands of funds the one or two (or six or eight) that will best meet your total investment needs.

Objectives and Motives for Using Funds The place to start is with your own investment objectives. Why do you want to invest in a mutual fund, and what are you looking for in a fund? Obviously, an attractive rate of return would be desirable, but there is also the matter of a tolerable amount of risk exposure. Probably, when you look at your own risk temperament in relation to the various types of mutual funds available, you will discover that certain types of funds are more appealing to you than others. For instance, aggressive

---

INVESTOR FACTS

SOME MUTUAL FUND FACTS EVERY INVESTOR SHOULD KNOW . . .

- Even great funds have bad years every now and then.
- Sometimes, even bad funds have great years.
- Most stock (and bond) funds fail to beat the market.
- You don't need a broker to buy mutual funds.
- A fund that doesn't charge a sales commission isn't necessarily a no-load fund.
- If you own more than a dozen different funds, you probably own too many.
- Mutual fund names can be misleading.
- Funds with high yields don't necessarily produce high returns.
- Money funds are not risk-free (their returns are still subject to market fluctuations).

growth or sector funds are usually *not* attractive to individuals who wish to avoid high exposure to risk.

Another important factor is the intended use of the mutual fund. Do you want to invest in mutual funds as a means of accumulating wealth, as a storehouse of value, or to speculate for high rates of return? This information puts into clearer focus the question of what you want to do with your investment dollars. Finally, there is the matter of the services provided by the fund. If you are particularly interested in certain services, be sure to look for them in the funds you select.

What the Funds Offer   Just as each individual has a set of investment needs, each fund has its own *investment objective*, its own *manner of operation*, and its own *range of services*. These three parameters are useful in helping you to assess investment alternatives. Where do you find such information? One obvious place is the fund's *profile*, or its prospectus. Publications such as the *Wall Street Journal, Barron's, Money, Fortune,* and *Forbes* also provide a wealth of operating and performance statistics.

There are also a number of reporting services that provide background information and assessments on funds. Among the best in this category are *Morningstar Mutual Funds* (a sample of which is shown in Figure 12.5), and *Value Line Mutual Fund Survey* (which produces a mutual fund report similar to its stock report). There also are all sorts of performance statistics available on the Internet. For example, there are scores of free finance Web sites, like finance.yahoo.com, where you can obtain historical information on a fund's performance, security holdings, risk profile, load charges, and purchase information. Or, you can buy, usually at very reasonable prices, quarterly or annually updated software from organizations like Morningstar or the American Association of Individual Investors (AAII).

Whittling Down the Alternatives   At this point, fund selection becomes a process of elimination. You can eliminate a large number of funds from consideration simply because they fail to meet stated needs. Some funds may be too risky; others may be unsuitable as a storehouse of value. Thus, rather than trying to evaluate thousands of different funds, you can narrow down the list to two or three *types* of funds that best match your investment needs. From here, you can whittle down the list a bit more by introducing other constraints. For example, because of cost considerations, you may want to consider only no-load or low-load funds (more on this topic below). Or you may be seeking certain services that are important to your investment goals.

Now we introduce the final element in the selection process: the *fund's investment performance*. Useful information includes:

1. How the fund has performed over the past five to seven years.
2. The type of return it has generated in good markets as well as bad.
3. The level and stability of dividend and capital gains distributions.
4. The amount of volatility/risk in the fund's return.

The dividend and capital gains distribution is an important indication not only of how much current income the fund distributes annually but also of the fund's *tax efficiency*. As a rule, funds that have low dividends and low asset turnover expose their shareholders to less taxes and therefore have higher tax-efficiency ratings. And while you're looking at performance, check out the

FIGURE 12.5 Some Relevant Information About Specific Mutual Funds

Investors who want in-depth information about the operating characteristics, investment holdings, and market behavior of specific mutual funds, such as the Fidelity Low-Priced Stock fund profiled here, can usually find what they're looking for in publications like *Morningstar Mutual Funds* or, as shown here, from computer-based information sources like *Morningstar's Principia*. (*Source:* Morningstar, Inc., *Principia*, release date: December 31, 2005.)

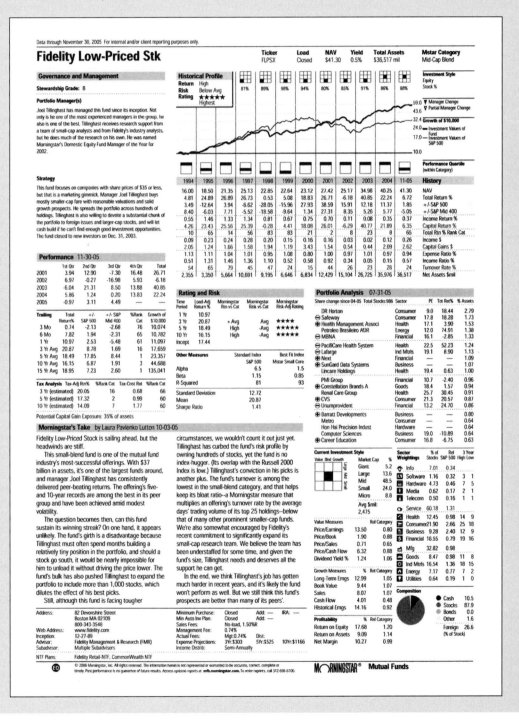

fund's *fee structure*. Be on guard for funds that charge abnormally high management fees; they can really hurt returns over time.

Another important consideration is *how well a particular fund fits into your portfolio*. If you're trying to follow a certain asset allocation strategy, then be sure to take that into account when you're thinking about adding a fund (or two) to your portfolio. You can easily do that by using the fund categories developed by Morningstar. (For example, look in the upper-right corner of Figure 12.5 and you'll find the "Mstar Category" for Fidelity Low-Priced Stock—it's a mid-cap blend fund.)

Note that in this decision process, considerable weight is given to *past performance*. As a rule, the past is given little or no attention in the investment decision. After all, it's the future that matters. Although the *future performance* of a mutual fund is still the variable that holds the key to success, you should look carefully at past investment results to see how successful the fund's investment managers have been. In essence, the success of a mutual fund rests in large part on the *investment skills of the fund managers*. Therefore, look for consistently good performance, in up as well as down markets, over *extended* periods of time (five years or more). Most important, check whether the same key people are still running the fund. Although past success is no guarantee of future performance, a strong team of money managers can have a significant bearing on the level of fund returns.

Stick with No-Loads or Low-Loads

There's a long-standing "debate" in the mutual fund industry regarding load funds and no-load funds: Do load funds add value? If not, why pay the load charges? As it turns out, empirical results generally do not support the idea that load funds provide added value. Load-fund returns, on average, do not seem to be any better than the returns from no-load funds. In fact, in many cases, the funds with abnormally high loads and 12(b)-1 charges often produce returns that are far less than what you can get from no-load funds. In addition, because of compounding, the differential returns tend to widen with longer holding periods. These results should come as no surprise, because big load charges and/or 12(b)-1 fees reduce your investable capital—and therefore the amount of money you have working for you. In fact, the only way a load fund can overcome this handicap is to produce *superior returns,* which is no easy thing to do, year in and year out. Granted, a handful of load funds have produced very attractive returns over extended periods of time, but they are the exception rather than the rule.

Obviously, it's in your best interest to pay close attention to load charges (and other fees). As a rule, to maximize returns, you should *seriously consider sticking to no-load funds or to low-loads* (funds that have total load charges, including 12(b)-1 fees, of 3% or less). At the very minimum, you should consider a more expensive load fund *only* if it has a much better performance record (and offers more return potential) than a less expensive fund. There may well be times when the higher costs are justified, but far more often than not, you're better off trying to minimize load charges. That should not be difficult to do, because there are literally thousands of no-load and low-load funds from which to choose. What's more, most of the top-performing funds are found in the universe of no-loads or low-loads. So why would you even want to look anywhere else?

■ Investing in Closed-End Funds

The assets of closed-end funds (CEFs) represent only a fraction of the roughly $9 trillion invested in open-end funds. By year-end 2005, there were more than 600 CEFs, which together held total assets of some $280 billion (less than 3% of the amount held by open-end funds). Like open-end funds, CEFs come in a variety of types and styles, including funds that specialize in municipal bonds, taxable bonds, various types of equity securities, and international securities, as well as regional and single-country funds. However, unlike the open-end market, which is dominated by equity funds, bonds (both taxable and tax-free) dominate the CEF universe, and account for nearly 60% of assets under management.

Some Key Differences Between Closed-End and Open-End Funds

Because closed-end funds trade like stocks, you must deal with a broker to buy or sell shares, and the usual brokerage commissions apply. Open-end funds, in contrast, are bought from and sold to the fund operators themselves. Another difference between open- and closed-end funds is their liquidity. You can buy and sell relatively large dollar amounts of an open-end mutual fund at its net asset value (NAV) without worrying about affecting the price. However, a relatively large buy or sell order for a CEF could easily bump its price up or down. Like open-end funds, most CEFs offer dividend reinvestment plans, but in many cases, that's about it. CEFs simply don't provide the full range of services that mutual fund investors are accustomed to.

All things considered, probably the most important difference is the way these funds are priced in the marketplace. This *directly affects* investor costs and returns. That is, whereas open-end funds can be bought and sold at NAV (plus any front-end load or minus any redemption charge), CEFs *have two values*—a market value (or stock price) and a NAV. The two are rarely the same, because CEFs typically trade at either a premium or a discount. A *premium* occurs when a fund trades for more than its NAV; a *discount* occurs when it trades for less. As a rule, *CEFs trade at discounts*. In addition to the normal competitive pressures in the marketplace, other factors that can lead to discounts (or premiums) include the fund's *relative performance*, its annual payout or yield, the *name recognition* of the fund's manager, the amount of *illiquid* holdings in the fund's portfolio, and/or the amount of *unrealized* appreciation sitting in the fund's portfolio. The *Wall Street Journal* (on Mondays) reports the premiums (+) and discounts (−) on CEFs, along with NAVs and 52-week total returns. An example appears in Figure 12.6 (on page 552).

The premium or discount on CEFs is calculated as follows:

Equation 12.1 ➤

$$\text{Premium (or discount)} = (\text{Share price} - \text{NAV})/\text{NAV}$$

Suppose Fund A has a NAV of $10. If its share price is $8, it will sell at a 20% discount. That is,

$$\text{Premium (or discount)} = (\$8 - \$10)/\$10$$

$$= \$-2/\$10 = -.20 = \underline{-20\%}$$

FIGURE 12.6

Selected Performance on CEFs

As can be seen here, the market prices of closed-end funds often exceed or fall short of the fund's NAV. *Premiums* occur when the fund's (closing) price is greater than its NAV; *discounts* occur when the fund's NAV is greater than its closing price. To find the "PREM/DISC" as reported in the quotes, simply divide the fund's quoted "CLOSE" by its quoted "NAV," and then subtract 1. (*Source: The Wall Street Journal,* March 27, 2006.)

CLOSED-END FUNDS

FUND (SYM)	EXCH	NAV	CLOSE	PREM /DISC	DIV	52 WK TTL RET
General Equity Funds						
AdamsExp **ADX**	N	15.52	13.39	−13.7	.86	11.2
AdvMSFI	z	25.70		NA	NA	NA
AdvntClEnhGrth **LCM**	N	19.26	17.72	−8.0	1.60	6.5
AllncAll **AMO**	N	14.75	15.48	4.9	1.36	19.5
BlkRkDivAch Tr **BDV**	N	14.86	13.16	−11.4	.90	0.2
BlkRkEnDivAch **BDJ**	N	14.39	13.74	−4.5	1.22	N
BlkRkStrDivAch **BDT**	N	15.72	13.88	−11.7	.90	7.4
BlueChipVal **BLU**	N	5.94	5.85	−1.5	.57	−1.1
BoulderGro **BIF**	N	8.49	7.68	−9.5	.02	16.8
CntlSec **CET**	A	28.91	24.64	−14.8	2.00	15.3
ChnStrMjrs **DVM**	N	21.75	18.77	−13.7	1.20	12.0
CornstnStrat **CLM**	A	5.62	7.15	27.2	1.04	24.0
CornrstnTtlRtn Fd **CRF**	A	10.80	15.99	48.1	2.11	35.3
DfndStratFd **DSF**	N	18.87	16.91	−10.4	.55	7.4
Dow30PremDiv **DPD**	N	19.66	19.26	−2.0	1.80	N
DrmnClayDivInco **DCS**	N	22.06	18.97	−14.0	1.30	12.0
EtnVncEqtyInco **EOI**	N	20.27	19.55	−3.6	1.64	6.4
EtnVncEqtyInco II **EOS**	N	19.72	19.01	−3.6	1.73	7.1
GabelliDivInco **GDV**	N	21.72	18.53	−14.7	1.20	10.8
GabelliTr **GAB**	N	8.60	8.41	−2.2	.76	6.2
GenAmInv **GAM**	N	40.74	37.72	−7.4	1.99	30.1
HnckJ TxAdv **HTD**	N	20.56	17.51	−14.8	1.16	12.6
LibtyASE **USA**	N	8.89	8.49	−4.5	.88	7.4
LibtyASG **ASG**	N	6.18	5.71	−7.6	.59	3.7

Gabelli
Equity
Trust
(GAB)

Note: "EXCH" = Exchange fund is traded on: N = NYSE; A = AMEX; O = OTC.

This negative value indicates that the fund is trading at a *discount* (or below its NAV). On the other hand, if this same fund were priced at $12 per share, it would be trading at a *premium* of 20%—that is, ($12 − $10)/$10 = $2/$10 = 0.20. Because the value is positive, the fund is trading at a premium, above its NAV.

What to Look for in a Closed-End Fund If you know what to look for and your timing and selection are good, you may find that some *deeply discounted CEFs* provide a great way to earn attractive returns. For example, if a fund trades at a 20% discount, you pay only 80 cents for each dollar's worth of assets. If you can buy a fund at an abnormally wide discount (say, more than 10% to 15%) and then sell it when the discount narrows or turns to a premium, you can enhance your overall return. In fact, even if the discount does not narrow, your return will be improved, because the yield on your investment is higher than it would be with an otherwise equivalent open-end fund. The reason: You're investing less money. Here's a simple example. Suppose a CEF trades at $8, a 20% discount from its NAV of $10. If the fund distributed $1 in dividends for the year, it would yield 12.5% ($1 divided by its $8 price). However, if it was a no-load, open-end fund, it would be trading at its higher NAV and therefore would yield only 10% ($1 divided by its $10 NAV). Thus, when investing in CEFs, pay special attention to the size of the premium and discount. In particular, keep your eyes open for funds trading at deep discounts, because that feature alone can enhance potential returns. One final point to keep in mind about closed-end funds: Stay clear of new issues (IPOs) of closed-end funds and funds that sell at steep *premiums*. Never buy new CEFs when they are brought to the market as IPOs. Why? Because IPOs are always brought to the market at *hefty premiums*, which are necessary to cover the underwriter spread. Thus, you face the almost inevitable fate of losing money as the shares fall to a discount, or at the minimum, to their NAVs within a month or two.

For the most part, except for the premium or discount, you should analyze a CEF just like any other mutual fund. That is, check out the fund's expense ratio, portfolio turnover rate, past performance, cash position, and so on. In addition, study the history of the discount. You can find information on closed-end funds in such publications as *Morningstar Closed-End Funds* and *Value Line Investment Survey*. Also, keep in mind that with CEFs, you probably will not get a prospectus (as you might with an open-end fund), because they do not continuously offer new shares to investors.

▉ Measuring Performance

As in any investment decision, return performance is a major dimension in the mutual fund selection process. The level of dividends paid by the fund, its capital gains, and its growth in capital are all important aspects of return. Such return information enables you to judge the investment behavior of a fund and to appraise its performance in relation to other funds and investment vehicles. Here, we will look at different measures that investors can use to assess mutual fund return. Also, because risk is so important in defining the investment behavior of a fund, we will examine mutual fund risk as well.

Sources of Return An open-end mutual fund has three potential sources of return: (1) dividend income, (2) capital gains distribution, and (3) change in the price (or net asset value) of the fund. Depending on the type of fund, some mutual funds derive more income from one source than another. For example, we would normally expect income-oriented funds to have much higher dividend income than capital gains distributions.

Open-end mutual funds regularly publish reports that recap investment performance. One such report is the *Summary of Income and Capital Changes,* an example of which appears in Table 12.2 (on page 554). This statement, found in the fund's profile or prospectus, gives a brief overview of the fund's investment activity, including expense ratios and portfolio turnover rates. Of interest to us here is the top part of the report (which runs from "Net asset value, beginning of period" to "Net asset value, end of period"—lines 1 to 10). This part reveals the amount of dividend income and capital gains distributed to the shareholders, along with any change in the fund's net asset value.

dividend income
income derived from the dividends and interest earned on the security holdings of a mutual fund.

Dividend income (see line 7 of Table 12.2) is derived from the dividend and interest income earned on the security holdings of the mutual fund. It is paid out of the *net investment income* that's left after the fund has met all operating expenses. When the fund receives dividend or interest payments, it passes these on to shareholders in the form of dividend payments. The fund accumulates all of the current income for the period and then pays it out on a prorated basis. Thus, if a fund earned, say, $2 million in dividends and interest in a given year and if that fund had one million shares outstanding, each share would receive an annual dividend payment of $2. Because the mutual fund itself is tax exempt, any taxes due on dividend earnings are payable by the individual investor. For funds that are not held in tax-deferred accounts, like IRAs or 401(k)s, the

TABLE 12.2   A Report of Mutual Fund Income and Capital Changes
(For a share outstanding throughout the year)

	2007	2006	2005
1. **Net asset value, beginning of period**	$24.47	$27.03	$24.26
2. **Income from investment operations:**			
3. Net investment income	$0.60	$0.66	$0.50
4. Net gains on securities (realized and unrealized)	6.37	(1.74)	3.79
5. Total from investment operations	6.97	(1.08)	4.29
6. **Less distributions:**			
7. Dividends from net investment income	($0.55)	($0.64)	($0.50)
8. Distributions from realized gains	(1.75)	(.84)	(1.02)
9. Total distributions	(2.30)	(1.48)	(1.52)
10. **Net asset value, end of period**	$29.14	$24.47	$27.03
11. **Total return**	28.48%	(4.00%)	17.68%
12. **Ratios/supplemental data**			
13. Net assets, end of period ($000)	$307,951	$153,378	$108,904
14. Ratio of expenses to average net assets	1.04%	0.85%	0.94%
15. Ratio of net investment income to average net assets	1.47%	2.56%	2.39%
16. Portfolio turnover rate*	85%	144%	74%

*Portfolio turnover rate relates the number of shares bought and sold by the fund to the total number of shares held in the fund's portfolio. A high turnover rate (in excess of 100%) means the fund has been doing a lot of trading.

amount of taxes due on dividends will depend on the source of such dividends. That is, *if these distributions are derived from dividends earned on the fund's common stock holdings, then they are subject to a preferential tax rate of 15%, or less.* However, if these distributions are derived from interest earnings on bonds, dividends from REITs, or dividends from most types of preferred stocks, then such dividends *do not qualify for the preferential tax treatment*, and instead are taxed as ordinary income.

capital gains distributions
payments made to mutual fund shareholders that come from the profits that a fund makes from the sale of its securities.

Capital gains distributions (see line 8) work on the same principle, except that these payments are derived from the *capital gains actually earned* by the fund. It works like this: Suppose the fund bought some stock a year ago for $50 and sold that stock in the current period for $75 per share. Clearly, the fund has achieved capital gains of $25 per share. If it held 50,000 shares of this stock, it would have realized a total capital gain of $1,250,000 ($25 × 50,000 = $1,250,000). Given that the fund has one million shares outstanding, each share is entitled to $1.25 in the form of a capital gains distribution. (From a tax perspective, if the capital gains are long-term in nature, then they qualify for the preferential tax rate of 15%, or less; if not, then they're treated as ordinary income.) Note that these (capital gains) distributions apply only to *realized* capital gains (that is, the security holdings were actually sold and the capital gains actually earned).

unrealized capital gains (paper profits)
a capital gain made only "on paper"—that is, not realized until the fund's holdings are sold.

Unrealized capital gains (or **paper profits**) are what make up the third and final element of a mutual fund's return. When the fund's holdings go up or down in price, the net asset value of the fund moves accordingly. Suppose an investor buys into a fund at $10 per share and sometime later the fund's NAV is quoted at $12.50. The difference of $2.50 per share is the unrealized capital gains. It represents the profit that shareholders would receive (and are entitled to) if the fund were to sell its holdings. (Actually, as Table 12.2 shows, some of the change in net asset value can also be made up of undistributed income.)

For *closed-end* investment companies, the return is derived from the same three sources as that for open-end funds, and from a *fourth source* as well: changes in price discounts or premiums. But because the discount or premium is already embedded in the share price of a fund, for a closed-end fund, the third element of return—change in share price—is made up not only of change in net asset value but also of change in price discount or premium.

What About Future Performance? There's no doubt that a statement like the one in Table 12.2 provides a convenient recap of a fund's past behavior. Looking at past performance is useful, but it does not tell you what the future will be. Ideally, you want an indication of what the same three elements of return—dividend income, capital gains distribution, and change in NAV—*will be*. But it's extremely difficult—if not impossible—to get a firm grip on what the future holds in dividends, capital gains, and NAV. A mutual fund's future performance is directly linked to the *future make-up of the securities in its portfolio*, something that is next to impossible to get a clear reading on. It's not like evaluating the expected performance of a share of stock, in which case you're keying in on just one company. With mutual funds, investment performance depends on the behavior of many different stocks and bonds.

Where, then, can you look for insight into future performance? Most market observers suggest that the first place to look is the market itself. In particular, try to get a fix on the future direction of *the market as a whole*. The behavior of a well-diversified mutual fund tends to reflect the general tone of the market. Thus, if the market is expected to drift up, so should the performance of mutual funds. Also spend some time evaluating the *track records* of mutual funds in which you are interested. Past performance has a lot to say about the investment skills of the fund's money managers.

Measures of Return A simple but effective measure of performance is to describe mutual fund return in terms of the three major sources noted above: dividends earned, capital gains distributions received, and change in price. When dealing with investment horizons of one year or less, we can convert these fund payoffs into a return figure by using the standard holding period return (HPR) formula. The computations necessary are illustrated below using the 2007 figures from Table 12.2. In 2007, this hypothetical no-load, open-end fund paid 55 cents per share in dividends and another $1.75 in capital gains distributions. It had a price at the beginning of the year of $24.47 that rose to $29.14 by the end of the year. Thus, summarizing this investment performance, we have

Price (NAV) at the *beginning* of the year (line 1)	$24.47
Price (NAV) at the *end* of the year (line 10)	29.14
Net increase	$ 4.67
Return for the year:	
Dividends received (line 7)	$ 0.55
Capital gains distributions (line 8)	1.75
Net increase in price (NAV)	4.67
Total return	$ 6.97
Holding period return (HPR)	**28.48%**
(Total return/beginning price)	

This HPR measure is comparable to the procedure used by the fund industry to report annual returns: This same value can be seen in Table 12.2, line 11, which shows the fund's "Total return." It not only captures all the important elements of mutual fund return but also provides a handy indication of yield. Note that the fund had a total dollar return of $6.97, and on the basis of a beginning investment of $24.47, the fund produced an annual return of nearly 28.5%.

HPR with Reinvested Dividends and Capital Gains Many mutual fund investors have their dividends and/or capital gains distributions reinvested in the fund. How do you measure return when you receive your (dividend/capital gains) payout in additional shares of stock rather than cash? With slight modifications, you can continue to use holding period return. The only difference is that you have to keep track of the number of shares acquired through reinvestment.

To illustrate, let's continue with the example above. Assume that you initially bought 200 shares in the mutual fund and also that you were able to acquire shares through the fund's reinvestment program at an average price of $26.50 a share. Thus, the $460 in dividends and capital gains distributions [($.55 + $1.75) × 200] provided you with another 17.36 shares in the fund ($460/$26.50). Holding period return under these circumstances would relate the market value of the stock holdings at the beginning of the period with the holdings at the end:

Equation 12.2 ➤

$$
\text{Holding period return} = \frac{\left(\begin{array}{c} \text{Number of} \\ \text{shares at } \textit{end} \times \\ \text{of period} \end{array} \begin{array}{c} \text{Ending} \\ \text{price} \end{array} \right) - \left(\begin{array}{c} \text{Number of} \\ \text{shares at } \textit{beginning} \times \\ \text{of period} \end{array} \begin{array}{c} \text{Initial} \\ \text{price} \end{array} \right)}{\left(\begin{array}{c} \text{Number of shares} \\ \text{at } \textit{beginning} \text{ of period} \end{array} \times \begin{array}{c} \text{Initial} \\ \text{price} \end{array} \right)}
$$

Thus, the holding period return on this investment would be

$$
\text{Holding period return} = \frac{(217.36 \times \$29.14) - (200 \times \$24.47)}{(200 \times \$24.47)}
$$

$$
= \frac{(\$6,333.87) - (\$4,894.00)}{(\$4,894.00)} = \underline{\underline{29.4\%}}
$$

This holding period return, like the preceding one, provides a rate-of-return measure that you can use to compare the performance of this fund to those of other funds and investment vehicles.

Measuring Long-Term Returns Rather than using one-year holding periods, it is sometimes necessary to assess the performance of mutual funds over extended periods of time. In these cases, holding period return as a measure of performance would be inappropriate, because it ignores the time value of money. Instead, when faced with multiple-year investment horizons, we can use the present-value-based *internal rate of return* (IRR) procedure to determine the fund's average annual compound rate of return.

To illustrate, refer once again to Table 12.2. Assume that this time we want to find the annual rate of return over the full three-year period (2005 through 2007). We see that the mutual fund had the following annual dividends and capital gains distributions:

	2007	2006	2005
Annual dividends paid	$0.55	$0.64	$0.50
Annual capital gains distributed	$1.75	$0.84	$1.02
Total distributions	$2.30	$1.48	$1.52

Given that the fund had a price of $24.26 at the beginning of the period (1/1/05) and was trading at $29.14 at the end of 2007 (three years later), we have the following time line of cash flows:

Initial Cash Flow	Subsequent Cash Flows		
	Year 1	Year 2	Year 3
$24.26 (Beginning Price)	$1.52 (Distributions)	$1.48 (Distributions)	$2.30 + $29.14 (Distributions + Ending Price)

We want to find the discount rate that will equate the annual dividends/capital gains distributions *and* the ending price in year 3 to the beginning (2005) price of the fund ($24.26).

Using standard present-value calculations, we find that the mutual fund in Table 12.2 provided an annual rate of return of 13.1% over the three-year period. That is, at 13.1%, the present value of the cash flows in years 1, 2, and 3 equals the beginning price of the fund ($24.26). Such information helps us assess fund performance and compare the return performance of various investment vehicles.

According to SEC regulations, if mutual funds report historical return behavior, they must do so in a standardized format that employs fully compounded, total-return figures similar to those obtained from the above present value-based measure of return. The funds are not required to report such information, but if they do cite performance in their promotional material, they must follow a full-disclosure manner of presentation that takes into account not only dividends and capital gains distributions but also any increases or decreases in the fund's NAV that have occurred over the preceding 1-, 3-, 5-, and 10-year periods.

Returns on Closed-End Funds The returns of CEFs have traditionally been reported on the basis of their NAVs. That is, *price premiums and discounts were ignored when computing return measures.* However, it is becoming increasingly common to see return performance expressed in terms of *actual market prices*, a practice that captures the impact of changing market premiums or discounts on holding period returns. As you might expect, the greater the premiums or discounts and the greater the changes in these values over time, the greater their impact on reported returns. It's not at all uncommon for CEFs to have different market-based and NAV-based holding period returns. Using NAVs, you find the returns on CEFs in exactly the same way as you do the returns on open-end funds. In contrast, when using actual market prices to measure return, all you need do *is substitute the market price of the fund* (with its embedded premium or discount) *for the corresponding NAV in the holding period or internal rate of return* measures.

Some CEF investors like to run *both* NAV-based and market-based measures of return to see how changing premiums (or discounts) have affected the returns on their mutual fund holdings. Even so, as a rule, NAV-based return numbers are generally viewed as the preferred measures of performance. Because fund managers often have little or no control over changes in premiums or discounts, NAV-based measures are felt to give a truer picture of the performance of the fund itself.

The Matter of Risk Because most mutual funds are so diversified, their investors are largely immune to the business and financial risks normally present with individual securities. Even with extensive diversification, however, most funds are still exposed to a considerable amount of *market risk*. In fact, because mutual fund portfolios are so well diversified, they often tend to perform very much like the market—or like the segment of the market that the fund targets. Although a few funds, like gold funds, tend to be defensive (countercyclical), market risk is still an important ingredient for most types of mutual funds, both open- and closed-end. You should be aware of the effect the general market has on the investment performance of a mutual fund. For example, if the market is trending downward and you anticipate that trend to continue, it might be best to place any new investment capital into something like a money fund until the market reverses itself.

Another important risk consideration revolves around *the management practices of the fund itself*. If the portfolio is managed conservatively, the risk of a loss in capital is likely to be much less than that for aggressively managed funds. Obviously, the more speculative the investment goals of the fund, the greater the risk of instability in the net asset value. But, a conservatively managed portfolio does not eliminate all price volatility. The securities in the portfolio are still subject to inflation, interest rate, and general market risks. However, these risks are generally less with funds whose investment objectives and portfolio management practices are more conservative.

CONCEPTS IN REVIEW

Answers available at: www.myfinancelab.com

12.12 How important is the general behavior of the market in affecting the price performance of mutual funds? Explain. Why is a fund's past performance important to the mutual fund selection process? Does the future behavior of the market matter in the selection process? Explain.

12.13 What is the major/dominant type of closed-end fund? How do CEFs differ from open-end funds?

12.14 Identify three potential sources of return to mutual fund investors and briefly discuss how each could affect total return to shareholders. Explain how the discount or premium of a closed-end fund can also be treated as a return to investors.

12.15 Discuss the various types of risk to which mutual fund shareholders are exposed. What is the major risk exposure of mutual funds? Are all funds subject to the same level of risk? Explain.

Summary

LG 1   **Describe the basic features of mutual funds, and note what they have to offer as investment vehicles.** Mutual fund shares represent ownership in a diversified, professionally managed portfolio of securities. Many investors who lack the time, know-how, or commitment to manage their own money turn to mutual funds. Mutual funds shareholders benefit from a level of diversification and investment performance they might otherwise find difficult to achieve. They also can invest with a limited amount of capital and can obtain investor services not available elsewhere.

LG 2   **Distinguish between open- and closed-end mutual funds, as well as other types of professionally managed investment companies, and discuss the various types of fund loads, fees, and charges.** Open-end funds have no limit on the number of shares they may issue. Closed-end funds have a fixed number of shares outstanding and trade in the secondary markets like shares of common stock. Exchange-traded funds (ETFs) possess characteristics of both open-end and closed-end funds. Other types of investment companies are unit investment trusts, hedge funds (private, unregulated investment vehicles available to institutional and high-net-worth individuals), REITs (which invest in various types of real estate), and variable annuities. Mutual fund investors face an array of loads, fees, and charges, including front-end loads, back-end loads, annual 12(b)-1 charges, and annual management fees. Some of these costs are one-time charges (e.g., front-end loads). Others are paid annually (e.g., 12(b)-1 and management fees). Investors should understand fund costs, which can drag down fund performance and return.

LG 3   **Discuss the types of funds available and the variety of investment objectives these funds seek to fulfill.** Each fund has an established investment objective that determines its investment policy and identifies it as a certain type of fund. Some popular types of funds are growth, aggressive-growth, value, equity-income, balanced, growth-and-income, asset allocation, index, bond, money, sector, socially responsible, and international funds. The different categories of funds have different risk-return characteristics.

LG 4   **Discuss the investor services offered by mutual funds and how these services can fit into an investment program.** Mutual funds also offer special services, such as automatic investment and reinvestment plans, systematic withdrawal programs, low-cost conversion and phone-switching privileges, and retirement programs.

LG 5   **Gain an appreciation of the investor uses of mutual funds, along with the variables to consider when assessing and selecting funds for investment purposes.** Investors can use mutual funds to accumulate wealth, as a storehouse of value, or as a vehicle for speculation and short-term trading. Fund selection generally starts by assessing the investor's needs and wants. The next step is to consider what the funds have to offer with regard to investment objectives, risk exposure, and investor services. The investor then narrows the alternatives by aligning his or her needs with the types of funds available and, from this short list of funds, applies the final selection tests: fund performance and cost.

LG 6   **Identify the sources of return and compute the rate of return earned on a mutual fund investment.** The payoff from investing in a mutual fund includes dividend income, distribution of realized capital gains, growth in capital (unrealized capital gains), and—for closed-end funds—the change in premium or discount. Various measures of return recognize these elements and provide simple yet effective ways of gauging the annual rate of return from a mutual fund. Risk is also important to mutual fund investors. A fund's extensive diversification may protect investors from business and financial risks, but considerable market risk still remains because most funds tend to perform much like the market, or like that segment of the market in which they specialize.

Key Terms

aggressive-growth fund, *p. 536*
asset allocation fund, *p. 541*
automatic investment plan, *p. 542*
automatic reinvestment plan, *p. 543*
back-end load, *p. 528*
balanced fund, *p. 537*
bond fund, *p. 537*
capital gains distributions, *p. 554*
closed-end investment companies,
   p. 524
conversion (exchange) privilege,
   p. 544
dividend income, *p. 553*
equity-income fund, *p. 537*
exchange-traded fund (ETF), *p. 526*
fund families, *p. 544*
growth fund, *p. 546*
growth-and-income fund, *p. 537*
hedge fund, *p. 534*
index fund, *p. 539*
international fund, *p. 541*

load fund, *p. 527*
low-load fund, *p. 527*
management fee, *p. 521*
money market mutual fund
   (money fund), *p. 539*
mutual fund, *p. 519*
net asset value (NAV), *p. 524*
no-load fund, *p. 527*
open-end investment company,
   p. 524
pooled diversification, *p. 520*
real estate investment trust (REIT),
   p. 533
sector fund, *p. 540*
socially responsible fund, *p. 540*
systematic withdrawal plan, *p. 543*
12(b)-1 fee, *p. 528*
unrealized capital gains (paper profits),
   p. 554
value fund, *p. 536*

Discussion Questions

LG 1   **LG 2**   Q12.1 Contrast *mutual fund ownership* with *direct investment in stocks and bonds.* Assume your class is going to debate the merits of investing through mutual funds versus investing directly in stocks and bonds. Develop some arguments on each side of this debate and be prepared to discuss them in class. If you had to choose one side to be on, which would it be? Why?

LG 2   Q12.2 Based on the mutual fund quotes in Figure 12.3, answer the questions listed below for each of the following 5 funds:
   (1)   Diversified Equity Growth Fund (EqGrow)
   (2)   Diversified International Equity Fund (IntlEq)
   (3)   Dodge & Cox International Stock Fund (Intl Stk)
   (4)   Domini Social Equity Fund (Soc Equity)
   (5)   Dreyfus Growth & Income Fund (GrInc)

Based on the information reported in Figure 12.3:
   a.   How much would you receive for each fund if you were
        selling them?
   b.   Which of the five listed funds have 12(b)-1 fees?
   c.   Do any of the funds have both 12(b)-1 and redemption fees?

d. Can you tell whether any of the funds are true no-loads?
e. Which fund has the highest front-end load?
f. Which fund has the highest year-to-date return? Which has the lowest?

LG 3 Q12.3 For each pair of funds listed below, select the one that is likely to be the *less* risky. Briefly explain your answer.
a. Growth versus growth-and-income funds
b. Equity-income versus high-grade corporate bond funds
c. Balanced versus sector funds
d. Global versus value funds
e. Intermediate-term bonds versus high-yield municipal bond funds

LG 2 **LG 3** Q12.4 Describe an ETF and explain how these funds combine the characteristics of both open-end and close-end funds. Consider the Vanguard family of funds. Which of its funds most closely resembles a "spider" (SPDR)? In what respects are the Vanguard fund (that you selected) and spiders the same? How are they different? If you could invest in only one of them, which would it be? Explain.

LG 2 **LG 6** Q12.5 In the absence of any load charges, open-end mutual funds are priced at (or very close to) their net asset values, whereas closed-end funds rarely trade at their NAVs. Explain why one type of fund would normally trade at its NAV while the other type (CEFs) usually does not. What are price premiums and discounts, and in what segment of the mutual fund market will you usually find them? Look in a recent edition of the *Wall Street Journal* (*Hint:* pick one that comes out on Mondays), and find 5 funds that trade at a discount and 5 funds that trade at a premium. List all 10 of them, including the sizes of their respective discounts and premiums. What's the biggest price discount you could find? How about the biggest price premium? What would cause a fund to trade at a discount? At a premium?

LG 3 **LG 5** Q12.6 Imagine that you've just inherited $20,000. Now you're faced with the "problem" of how to spend it. You could make a down payment on a condo, or on that sports car you've always wanted. Or you could build a mutual fund portfolio. After some soul-searching, you decide to build a $20,000 mutual fund portfolio. Using actual mutual funds and actual quoted prices, come up with a plan to invest as much of the $20,000 as you can in a portfolio of mutual funds. (In addition to one or more open-end funds, include at least one CEF *or* one ETF.) Be specific! Briefly describe your planned portfolio, including the investment objectives you are trying to achieve.

Problems

LG 6 P12.1 A year ago, an investor bought 200 shares of a mutual fund at $8.50 per share. Over the past year, the fund has paid dividends of $0.90 per share and had a capital gains distribution of $0.75 per share.
a. Find the investor's holding period return, given that this no-load fund now has a net asset value of $9.10.
b. Find the holding period return, assuming all the dividends and capital gains distributions are reinvested into additional shares of the fund at an average price of $8.75 per share.

LG 6

P12.2 A year ago, the Really Big Growth Fund was being quoted at a NAV of $21.50 and an offer price of $23.35. Today, it's being quoted at $23.04 (NAV) and $25.04 (offer). What is the holding period return on this load fund, given that it was purchased a year ago and that its dividends and capital gains distributions over the year have totaled $1.05 per share? (*Hint:* You, as an investor, buy fund shares at the offer price and sell at the NAV.)

LG 6

P12.3 The All-State Mutual Fund has the following 5-year record of performance.

	2007	2006	2005	2004	2003
Net investment income	$ 0.98	$ 0.85	$ 0.84	$ 0.75	$ 0.64
Dividends from net investment income	(0.95)	(0.85)	(0.85)	(0.75)	(0.60)
Net realized and unrealized gains (or losses) on security transactions	4.22	5.08	(2.18)	2.65	(1.05)
Distributions from realized gains	(1.05)	(1.00)	—	(1.00)	—
Net increase (decrease) in NAV	$ 3.20	$ 4.08	($ 2.19)	$ 1.65	($ 1.01)
NAV at beginning of year	12.53	8.45	10.64	.99	10.00
NAV at end of year	$15.73	$12.53	$ 8.45	$10.64	$ 8.99

Find this no-load fund's 5-year (2003–2007) average annual compound rate of return. Also find its 3-year (2005–2007) average annual compound rate of return. If an investor bought the fund in 2003 at $10.00 a share and sold it 5 years later (in 2007) at $15.73, how much total profit per share would she have made over the 5-year holding period?

LG 6

P12.4 You've uncovered the following per-share information about a certain mutual fund.

	2006	2007	2008
Ending share prices:			
Offer	$46.20	$64.68	$61.78
NAV	43.20	60.47	57.75
Dividend income	2.10	2.84	2.61
Capital gains distribution	1.83	6.26	4.32
Beginning share prices:			
Offer	55.00	46.20	64.68
NAV	51.42	43.20	60.47

On the basis of this information, find the fund's holding period return for 2006, 2007, and 2008. (In all 3 cases, assume you buy the fund at the beginning of the year and sell it at the end of each year.) In addition, find the fund's average annual compound rate of return over the 3-year period, 2006–2008. What would the 2007 holding period return have been if the investor had initially bought 500 shares of stock and reinvested both dividends and capital gains distributions into additional shares of the fund at an average price of $52.50 per share?

LG 2   LG 6 P12.5   Listed below is the 10-year, per-share performance record of Larry, Moe, & Curley's Growth Fund, as obtained from the fund's May 30, 2008, prospectus.

	Years Ended March 31									
	2008	2007	2006	2005	2004	2003	2002	2001	2000	1999
1. **Net asset value, beginning of period**	$58.60	$52.92	$44.10	$59.85	$55.34	$37.69	$35.21	$34.25	$19.68	$29.82
2. **Income from investment operations:**										
3. Net investment income	$1.39	$1.35	$1.09	$0.63	$0.42	$ 0.49	$ 0.79	$0.37	$ 0.33	$0.38
4. Net gains on securities (realized and unrealized)	8.10	9.39	8.63	(6.64)	11.39	19.59	5.75	2.73	15.80	(0.02)
5. Total from investment operations	9.49	10.74	9.72	(6.01)	11.81	20.08	6.54	3.10	16.13	0.36
6. **Less distributions:**										
7. Dividends from net investment income	($0.83)	($1.24)	($0.90)	($0.72)	($0.46)	($0.65)	($0.37)	($0.26)	($0.33)	($0.58)
8. Distributions from realized gains	(2.42)	(3.82)	—	(9.02)	(6.84)	(1.78)	(3.69)	(1.88)	(1.23)	(9.92)
9. Total distributions	(3.25)	(5.06)	(0.90)	(9.74)	(7.30)	(2.43)	(4.06)	(2.14)	(1.56)	(10.50)
10. **Net asset value, end of period**	$64.84	$58.60	$52.92	$44.10	$59.85	$55.34	$37.69	$35.21	$34.25	$19.68

Use this information to find LM&C's holding period return in 2008 and 2005. Also find the fund's rate of return over the 5-year period 2004–2008, and the 10-year period 1999–2008. Finally, rework the 4 return figures assuming the LM&C fund has a front-end load charge of 5% (of NAV). Comment on the impact of load charges on the return behavior of mutual funds.

LG 3   LG 6 P12.6   Using the resources available at your campus or public library (or those available on the Internet), select 5 mutual funds—a growth fund, an equity-income fund, an international (stock) fund, an index fund, and a high-yield corporate bond fund—that you feel would make good investments. Briefly explain why you selected these funds. List the funds' holding period returns for the past year and their annual compound rates of return for the past 3 years. (Use a schedule like the one in Table 12.2 to show relevant performance figures.)

LG 6 P12.7   One year ago, Super Star Closed-End Fund had a NAV of $10.40 and was selling at an 18% discount. Today, its NAV is $11.69 and it is priced at a 4% premium. During the year, Super Star paid dividends of $0.40 and had a capital gains distribution of $0.95. On the basis of the above information, calculate each of the following.
   a. Super Star's NAV-based holding period return for the year.
   b. Super Star's market-based holding period return for the year. Did the market premium/discount hurt or add value to the investor's return? Explain.
   c. Repeat the market-based holding period return calculation, except this time assume the fund started the year at an 18% *premium* and ended it at a 4% *discount*. (Assume the beginning and ending NAVs remain at $10.40 and $11.69, respectively.) Is there any change in this measure of return? Why?

LG 6

P12.8 The Well Managed Closed-End Fund turned in the following performance for the year 2007.

	Beginning of the Year	End of the Year
NAV	$7.50	$9.25
Market price of the fund shares	$7.75	$9.00
Dividends paid over the year	—	$1.20
Capital gains distributed over the year	—	$0.90

a. Based on this information, what was the NAV-based HPR for the WMCEF in 2007?
b. Find the percentage (%) premium or discount at which the fund was trading at the beginning of the year and at the end of the year.
c. What was the market-based HPR for the fund in 2007? Did the market premium or discount add to or hurt the holding period return on this CEF? Explain.

LG 6

P12.9 Three years ago, you invested in the Future Investco Mutual Fund by purchasing 1,000 shares of the fund at a net asset value of $20.00 per share. Because you did not need the income, you elected to reinvest all dividends and gains distributions. Today, you sell your 1,100 shares in this fund for $22.91 per share. What is the compounded rate of return on this investment over the 3-year period?

LG 6

P12.10 Refer to Problem 12.9 above. If there were a 3% load on this fund, assuming you purchased the same number of shares, what would your rate of return be?

LG 6

P.12.11 You invested in the no-load OhYes Mutual Fund one year ago by purchasing 1,000 shares of the fund at the net asset value of $25.00 per share. The fund distributed dividends of $1.50 and capital gains of $2.00. Today, the NAV is $26. What was your holding period return?

LG 6

P12.12 Refer to Problem 12.11 above. If OhYes was a load fund with a 2% front end load, what would be the HPR?

LG 6

P12.13 Refer to Figure 12.6. You purchased shares of AdamsExp (**ADX**) at the end of the day quoted. The fund pays the same dividend this year as that quoted, and at the end of the year the fund is quoted as having a NAV of $18.50 and a close of $16.25. What is your holding period return?

LG 6

P12.14 Refer to Problem 12.13 above. Now assume that you hold your shares of AdamsExp for 3 years. Each year you receive the same dividend, and at the end of year 3, the fund has a NAV of $18.50 and a close of $19.05. What is the compound annual rate of return for the 3-year period?

LG 6

P12.15 You are considering the purchase of shares in a closed end-mutual fund. The NAV is equal to $22.50 and the latest close is $20.00. Is this fund trading at a premium or a discount? How big is the premium or discount?

LG 6 P12.16 You purchased 1,000 shares of MutualMagic one year ago for $20.00 per share. During the year, you received $2.00 in dividends, half of which were from dividends on stock the fund held and half of which was from interest earned on bonds in the fund portfolio. Assuming your federal marginal tax rate is 25%, how much will you owe in federal taxes on the distributions you received this year? (Your answer should be in dollars.)

> **See www.myfinancelab.com for Web Exercises, Spreadsheets, and other online resources.**

Case Problem 12.1   *Reverend Billy Bob Ponders Mutual Funds*

LG 3 **LG 5** Reverend Billy Bob is the minister of a church in the San Diego area. He is married, has one young child, and earns a "modest income." Because religious organizations are not notorious for their generous retirement programs, the reverend has decided he should do some investing on his own. He would like to set up a program that enables him to supplement the church's retirement program and at the same time provide some funds for his child's college education (which is still some 12 years away). He is not out to break any investment records but wants some backup to provide for the long-run needs of his family.

Although he has a modest income, Billy Bob believes that with careful planning, he can probably invest about $250 a quarter (and, with luck, increase this amount over time). He currently has about $15,000 in a savings account that he would be willing to use to begin this program. In view of his investment objectives, he is not interested in taking a lot of risk. Because his knowledge of investments extends to savings accounts, Series EE savings bonds, and a little bit about mutual funds, he approaches you for some investment advice.

Questions

a. In light of Reverend Billy Bob's long-term investment goals, do you think mutual funds are an appropriate investment vehicle for him?

b. Do you think he should use his $15,000 savings to start a mutual fund investment program?

c. What type of mutual fund investment program would you set up for the reverend? Include in your answer some discussion of the types of funds you would consider, the investment objectives you would set, and any investment services (e.g., withdrawal plans) you would seek. Would taxes be an important consideration in your investment advice? Explain.

Case Problem 12.2   Tom Lasnicka Seeks the Good Life

LG 3   LG 4
LG 5   LG 6

Tom Lasnicka is a widower who recently retired after a long career with a major Midwestern manufacturer. Beginning as a skilled craftsman, he worked his way up to the level of shop supervisor over a period of more than 30 years with the firm. Tom receives Social Security benefits and a generous company pension. Together, these two sources amount to over $4,500 per month (part of which is tax-free). The Lasnickas had no children, so he lives alone. Tom owns a two-bedroom rental house that is next to his home, and the rental income from it covers the mortgage payments for both the rental house and his house.

Over the years, Tom and his late wife, Camille, always tried to put a little money aside each month. The results have been nothing short of phenomenal. The value of Tom's liquid investments (all held in bank CDs and savings accounts) runs well into the six figures. Up to now, Tom has just let his money grow and has not used any of his savings to supplement his Social Security, pension, and rental income. But things are about to change. Tom has decided, "What the heck, it's time I start living the good life!" Tom wants to travel and, in effect, start reaping the benefits of his labors. He has therefore decided to move $100,000 from one of his savings accounts to one or two high-yielding mutual funds. He would like to receive $1,000–$1,500 a month from the fund(s) for as long as possible, because he plans to be around for a long time.

Questions

a. Given Tom's financial resources and investment objectives, what kinds of mutual funds do you think he should consider?

b. What factors in Tom's situation should be taken into consideration in the fund selection process? How might these affect Tom's course of action?

c. What types of services do you think he should look for in a mutual fund?

d. Assume Tom invests in a mutual fund that earns about 10% annually from dividend income and capital gains. Given that Tom wants to receive $1,000 to $1,500 a month from his mutual fund, what would be the size of his investment account 5 years from now? How large would the account be if the fund earned 15% on average and everything else remained the same? How important is the fund's rate of return to Tom's investment situation? Explain.

Excel with Spreadsheets

In the *Wall Street Journal*, open-ended mutual funds are listed separately from other securities. They have their own quotation system where 2 primary data variables are the net asset value (NAV) and the year-to-date returns. The NAV represents the price you get when you sell shares, or what you pay when you buy no-load funds.

Create a spreadsheet model similar to the spreadsheet for Table 12.2, which you can view at www.myfinancelab.com, to analyze the following 3 years of data relating to the MoMoney Mutual Fund. It should report the amount of dividend income and capital gains distributed to the shareholders, along with any other changes in the fund's net asset value.

A	B	C	D	E
1	**2007**	**2006**	**2005**	
2 NAV, beginning of period	$ 35.24	$ 37.50	$ 36.25	
3 Net investment income	$ 0.65	$ 0.75	$ 0.60	
4 Net gains on securities	$ 5.25	$ 4.75	$ (3.75)	
5 Dividends from net investment income	$ 0.61	$ 0.57	$ 0.52	
6 Distributions from realized gains	$ 1.75	$ 2.01	$ 1.55	

Questions

a. What is the total income from the investment operations?
b. What are the total distributions from the investment operations?
c. Calculate the net asset value for MoMoney Fund as of the end of the years 2006, 2005, and 2004.
d. Calculate the holding period returns for each of the years 2007, 2006, and 2005.

Chapter 13

Managing Your Own Portfolio

He's known as the "Oracle of Omaha" for his stock-picking prowess. As chairman of Berkshire Hathaway, Inc., Warren Buffett has multiplied his investors' money by a factor of 2,935 since taking over the company in 1964. The Omaha-based corporation's 66 subsidiaries include insurance (GEICO), apparel (Fruit of the Loom), building products (Cleveland Wood Products), energy (Northern Natural Gas), food and gourmet retailers (The Pampered Chef, Dairy Queen), flight services (FlightSafety International), home furnishings (Star Furniture), and jewelry retailers (Helzberg Diamonds). In addition, Berkshire Hathaway is a public investment company with major holdings in companies which read like a veritable who's who of American business: American Express, Anheuser-Busch, Coca-Cola, Procter & Gamble, The Washington Post, Wells Fargo, and many others.

Owning a piece of this diversified company will cost you a pretty penny. In July 2006, the A shares were trading at roughly $91,900 per share, up 49% since February 2003—remarkable performance for a company of this size. (Or, you can buy B shares, which trade for one-thirtieth of the A shares' value, about $3,060.) From 1966 to 2006, Berkshire Hathaway's book value per share grew from $19 to more than $61,863.

What's the secret to Buffett's success? His long-term investing horizon and patience are legendary. His claim to fame has been his ability to buy businesses at prices far below what he calls their "intrinsic" value, which includes such intangibles as quality of management and the power of superior brand names. Buffett waits until a desired investment reaches his target price (perceived value) and won't buy until then. "We measure our success by the long-term progress of the companies rather than by the month-to-month movements of their stocks," he says.

As you'll see in this chapter, which introduces the basics of portfolio management, investing is a process of analysis, followed by action, followed by still more analysis. You may not be the next Warren Buffett (or maybe you will!), but understanding his techniques for building and evaluating your own portfolio will put you on the right track.

Source: Berkshire Hathaway corporate Web site, www.berkshirehathaway.com (accessed July 2006); historical data from www.bigcharts.marketwatch.com (accessed July 2006).

LEARNING GOALS

After studying this chapter, you should be able to:

LG 1 Explain how to use an asset allocation scheme to construct a portfolio consistent with investor objectives.

LG 2 Discuss the data and indexes needed to measure and compare investment performance.

LG 3 Understand the techniques used to measure income, capital gains, and total portfolio return.

LG 4 Use the Sharpe, Treynor, and Jensen measures to compare a portfolio's return with a risk-adjusted, market-adjusted rate of return, and discuss portfolio revision.

LG 5 Describe the role and logic of dollar-cost averaging, constant-dollar plans, constant-ratio plans, and variable-ratio plans.

LG 6 Explain the role of limit and stop-loss orders in investment timing, warehousing liquidity, and timing investment sales.

Constructing a Portfolio Using an Asset Allocation Scheme

LG 1

We begin by examining the criteria for constructing a portfolio and then use them to develop a plan for allocating assets in various investment categories. This plan provides a basic, useful framework for selecting individual investment vehicles for the portfolio. In attempting to weave the concepts of risk and diversification into a solid portfolio policy, we will rely on both traditional and modern approaches (see Chapter 5).

Investor Characteristics and Objectives

Your financial and family situations are important inputs in determining portfolio policy. Vital determinants include level and stability of income, family factors, net worth, investor experience and age, and disposition toward risk. The types of investments in your portfolio depend on your relative income needs and ability to bear risk.

The size of your income and the certainty of your employment also bear on portfolio strategy. An investor with a secure job can handle more risk than one with a less secure position. Also, the higher your income, the more important the tax ramifications of an investment program become. Your investment experience also influences your investment strategy. It normally is best to "get one's feet wet" in the investment market by slipping into it gradually rather than leaping in headfirst. A cautiously developed investment program is likely to provide more favorable long-run results than an impulsive one.

Now you should ask yourself, "What do I want from my portfolio?" You must generally choose between high current income or significant capital appreciation. It is difficult to have both. The price of having high appreciation potential is often low potential for current income.

Your needs may determine which avenue you choose. A retired person whose income depends on his or her portfolio will probably choose a lower-risk, current-income-oriented approach. A high-income, financially secure investor may be much more willing to take on risky investments in the hope of improving net worth. Thus, a portfolio must be built around your needs, which depend on income, responsibilities, financial resources, age, retirement plans, and ability to bear risk.

HOTLINKS

If you want to review everything you need for portfolio planning, go to:

www.sec.gov/investor/pubs/
assetallocation.htm

Portfolio Objectives and Policies

Constructing a portfolio is a logical activity that is best done after you have analyzed your needs and the available investment vehicles. When planning and constructing a portfolio, you should consider these objectives: current income needs, capital preservation, capital growth, tax considerations, and risk.

Any one or more of these factors will play an influential role in defining the desirable type of portfolio. They can be tied together as follows: The first two items, *current income* and *capital preservation*, are consistent with a low-risk, conservative investment strategy. Normally, a portfolio with this orientation contains low-beta (low-risk) securities. The third item, a *capital growth objective*, implies increased risk and a reduced level of current income. Higher-risk growth stocks, options, futures, and other more speculative investments may be suitable for this investor. The fourth item, an investor's *tax bracket*, will influence investment strategy. A high-income investor probably wishes to defer taxes and earn investment returns in the form of capital gains. This implies a strategy of higher-risk investments and a longer holding period. Lower-bracket investors are less concerned with how they earn the income, and they may wish to invest in higher-current-income vehicles. The most important item, finally, is *risk*. Investors should consider the risk-return tradeoff *in all investment decisions*.

▮ Developing an Asset Allocation Scheme

Once you have translated your needs into specific portfolio objectives, you can construct a portfolio designed to achieve these goals. Before buying any investment vehicles, however, you must develop an *asset allocation scheme*. **Asset allocation** involves dividing your portfolio into various asset classes, such as U.S. stocks, U.S. bonds, foreign securities, short-term securities, and other vehicles like tangibles (especially gold) and real estate. The emphasis of asset allocation is on *preservation of capital*—protecting against negative developments while taking advantage of positive developments. Asset allocation is a bit different from diversification: Its focus is on *investment in various asset classes*. Diversification, in contrast, tends to focus more on **security selection**— selecting the *specific* securities to be held *within* an asset class.

asset allocation
a scheme that involves dividing one's portfolio into various asset classes to *preserve capital* by protecting against negative developments while taking advantage of positive ones.

security selection
the procedures used to select the *specific* securities to be held *within* an asset class.

Asset allocation is based on the belief that the total return of a portfolio is influenced more by the division of investments into asset classes than by the actual investments. In fact, studies have shown that as much as 90% or more of a portfolio's *return* comes from asset allocation. Therefore, less than 10% can be attributed to the actual security selection. Furthermore, researchers have found that asset allocation has a much greater impact on reducing *total risk* than does selecting the best investment vehicle in any single asset category.

Approaches to Asset Allocation There are three basic approaches to asset allocation: (1) fixed weightings, (2) flexible weightings, and (3) tactical asset allocation. The first two differ with respect to the proportions of each asset category maintained in the portfolio. The third is a more exotic technique used by institutional portfolio managers.

fixed-weightings approach
asset allocation plan in which a fixed percentage of the portfolio is allocated to each asset category.

Fixed Weightings The **fixed-weightings approach** allocates a fixed percentage of the portfolio to each of the asset categories, of which there typically are three to five. Assuming four categories—common stock, bonds, foreign securities, and short-term securities—a fixed allocation might be as follows.

Category	Allocation
Common stock	30%
Bonds	50
Foreign securities	15
Short-term securities	5
Total portfolio	100%

Generally, the fixed weightings do not change over time. When market values shift, you may have to adjust the portfolio annually or after major market moves to maintain the desired fixed-percentage allocations.

WEBEXTENSION

The *Investing in Action* box at the book's Web site offers some basic portfolio-building tips for the novice investor.

www.myfinancelab.com

flexible-weightings approach
asset allocation plan in which weights for each asset category are adjusted periodically based on market analysis.

tactical asset allocation
asset allocation plan that uses stock-index futures and bond futures to change a portfolio's asset allocation based on forecast market behavior.

INVESTOR FACTS

STOCKS, BONDS, OR CASH?—
Confused about the best asset allocation blend to choose? Don't worry—even the pros don't agree. Dow Jones tracks the asset allocation suggestions of 12 large brokerage firms on a weekly basis. In a recent year, for example, strategists at Bank of America and Goldman Sachs were the most bullish, recommending that clients hold 75% of their portfolios in equities. Bank of America advised that the remaining 25% be allocated as 15% to bonds and 10% to cash, while Goldman advised 20% to bonds, 3% to commodities, and just 2% to cash. Salomon Smith Barney took a more balanced approach, with 55% stocks, 35% bonds, and 10% cash.

Source: "Leading Wall St. Firms' Asset Allocation Recommendations," *Dow Jones Newswires,* November 17, 2003, downloaded from online.wsj.com.

Fixed weights may or may not represent equal percentage allocations to each category. One could, for example, allocate 25% to each of the four categories above. Research has shown that over a long period (1967–1988) equal (20%) allocations to U.S. stocks, foreign stocks, long-term bonds, cash, and real estate resulted in a portfolio that outperformed the S&P 500 in terms of both return and risk. These findings add further support to the importance of even a somewhat naive "buy and hold" asset allocation strategy.

Flexible Weightings The **flexible-weightings approach** involves periodic adjustment of the weights for each asset category on the basis of market analysis. The use of a flexible-weighting scheme is often called *strategic asset allocation.* For example, the initial and new allocation based on a flexible-weighting scheme may be as follows.

Category	Initial Allocation	New Allocation
Common stock	30%	45%
Bonds	40	40
Foreign securities	15	10
Short-term securities	15	5
Total portfolio	100%	100%

A change from the initial to the new allocation would be triggered by shifts in market conditions or expectations. For example, the new allocation shown above may have resulted from an anticipated decline in inflation. That decline would be expected to result in increased domestic stock and bond prices and a decline in foreign and short-term security returns. The weightings were therefore changed to capture greater returns in a changing market.

Tactical Asset Allocation The third approach, **tactical asset allocation**, is a form of market timing that uses stock-index futures and bond futures (see Chapter 15) to change a portfolio's asset allocation. When stocks are forecast to be less attractive than bonds, this strategy involves selling stock-index futures and buying bond futures. Conversely, when bonds are forecast to be less attractive than stocks, the strategy results in buying stock-index futures and selling bond futures. Because this sophisticated technique relies on a large portfolio and the use of quantitative models for market timing, it is generally appropriate only for large institutional investors.

Asset Allocation Alternatives Assuming the use of a fixed-weight asset allocation plan and using, say, four asset categories, we can demonstrate three asset allocations. Table 13.1 shows allocations in each of four categories for conservative (low return/low risk), moderate (average return/average risk), and aggressive (high return/high risk) portfolios. The conservative allocation relies heavily on bonds and short-term securities to provide predictable returns. The moderate allocation consists largely of common stock and bonds and includes more foreign securities and fewer short-term securities than the conservative allocation. Its moderate risk-return behavior reflects a move away from safe, short-term securities to a larger dose of common stock and foreign securities. Finally, in the aggressive allocation, more dollars are invested in common stock, fewer in bonds, and more in foreign securities, thereby generally increasing the expected portfolio return and risk.

TABLE 13.1 Alternative Asset Allocations

Category	Allocation Alternative		
	Conservative (low return/ low risk)	Moderate (average return/ average risk)	Aggressive (high return/ high risk)
Common stock	15%	30%	40%
Bonds	45	40	30
Foreign securities	5	15	25
Short-term securities	35	15	5
Total portfolio	100%	100%	100%

Applying Asset Allocation An asset allocation plan should consider the economic outlook and your investments, savings and spending patterns, tax situation, return expectations, and risk tolerance. Such plans must be formulated for the long run and must stress capital preservation. You also must periodically revise the plan to reflect changing investment goals. Generally, to decide on the appropriate asset mix, you must evaluate each asset category in terms of

INVESTING *in Action*

Keep Your Balance

Despite numerous studies indicating that asset allocation is a key determinant of a portfolio's return, most investors tend to buy hot stocks and mutual funds in a seemingly random fashion. By not following an asset allocation strategy when adding securities, investors end up with a portfolio that may be too concentrated in one or two asset classes or industry sectors. This can be a big mistake, as many investors who jumped on the technology-stock bandwagon in the late 1990s discovered. Their portfolios were overweighted in this high-risk area, and they suffered heavy losses when the tech bubble burst.

You can follow some easy steps to keep your portfolio in balance. Begin by evaluating your investment goals and risk tolerance. Then determine how much to allocate to each asset class, developing a long-term strategy that should cover 5 to 10 years. If you are 25-years old and single, for example, you might invest a larger percentage of your portfolio in growth stocks than would a 70-year old retiree who focuses on fixed-income securities with the goal of preserving capital and generating income for living expenses.

Within each broad asset category, you should further refine your allocation. For example, you may decide to divide your equity allocation among growth stocks, value stocks, and foreign stocks to avoid sectors that move in lockstep with each other. Your fixed-income securities might include Treasury bonds, municipal bonds, corporate bonds, and high-yield bonds. Once your framework is in place, choose the individual securities and mutual funds for each category.

Resist the temptation to abandon your strategy. About once a year, reexamine your portfolio and rebalance it as necessary to maintain your target percentages. For example, tech investors who had rebalanced their portfolios in the late 1990s would have sold some top growth performers and bought more value stocks, lessening their overall risk and increasing returns through diversification.

CRITICAL THINKING QUESTION Use the ideas presented above to develop an asset allocation strategy consistent with your investment goals.

asset allocation fund
a mutual fund that seeks to reduce the variability of returns by investing in the right assets at the right time; emphasizes diversification and performs at a relatively consistent level by passing up the potential for spectacular gains in favor of predictability.

current return, growth potential, safety, liquidity, transaction costs (brokerage fees), and potential tax savings.

Many investors use mutual funds (see Chapter 12) as part of their asset allocation activities, to diversify within each asset category. Or, as an alternative to constructing your own portfolio, you can buy shares in an **asset allocation fund**—a mutual fund that seeks to reduce variability of returns by investing in the right assets at the right time. These funds, like all asset allocation schemes, emphasize diversification. They perform at a relatively consistent level by passing up the potential for spectacular gains in favor of predictability.

Some asset allocation funds use fixed weightings, whereas others have flexible weights that change within prescribed limits. As a rule, investors with more than about $100,000 to invest and adequate time can justify do-it-yourself asset allocation. Those with between $25,000 and $100,000 and adequate time can use mutual funds to create a workable asset allocation. Those with less than $25,000 or with limited time may find asset allocation funds most attractive.

Most important, you should recognize that to be effective an asset allocation scheme *must be designed for the long haul.* Develop an asset allocation scheme you can live with for at least 7 to 10 years, and perhaps longer. Once you have it set, stick with it. The key to success is remaining faithful to your asset allocation; that means fighting the temptation to wander. The *Investing in Action* box on page 573 emphasizes this point by describing the importance of developing and following an asset allocation strategy.

CONCEPTS IN REVIEW
Answers available at: myfinancelab.com

13.1 What role, if any, do an investor's personal characteristics play in determining portfolio policy? Explain.

13.2 What role do an investor's portfolio objectives play in constructing a portfolio?

13.3 What is *asset allocation?* How does it differ from diversification? What role does asset allocation play in constructing an investment portfolio?

13.4 Briefly describe the three basic approaches to asset allocation: (a) fixed weightings, (b) flexible weightings, and (c) tactical asset allocation.

13.5 What role could an *asset allocation fund* play? What makes an asset allocation scheme effective?

Evaluating the Performance of Individual Investments

LG 2

Imagine that one of your most important personal goals is to have accumulated $20,000 of savings three years from now in order to make the down payment on your first house. You project that the desired house will cost $100,000 and that the $20,000 will be sufficient to make a 15% down payment and pay the associated closing costs. Your calculations indicate that you can achieve this goal by investing existing savings plus an additional $200 per month over the next three years in a vehicle earning 12% per year. Projections of your earnings over the three-year period indicate that you should just be able to set aside the needed $200 per month. You consult with an investment adviser, Cliff Orbit, who leads you to believe that under his management, the 12% return can be achieved.

It seems simple: Give Cliff your existing savings, send him $200 each month over the next 36 months, and at the end of that period, you will have the $20,000 needed to purchase the house. Unfortunately, there are many uncertainties involved. What if you don't set aside $200 each month? What if Cliff fails to earn the needed 12% annual return? What if in three years the desired house costs more than $100,000? Clearly, you must do more than simply devise what appears to be a feasible plan for achieving a future goal. Rarely are you guaranteed that your planned investment and portfolio outcomes will actually occur. Therefore, it is important to assess periodically your progress toward achieving your investment goals.

As actual outcomes occur, you must compare them to the *planned* outcomes and make any necessary alterations in your plans—or in your goals. Knowing how to measure investment performance is therefore crucial. Here we will emphasize measures suitable for analyzing investment performance. We begin with sources of data.

▍Obtaining Needed Data

The first step in analyzing investment returns is gathering data that reflect the actual performance of each investment. As pointed out in Chapter 3, many sources of investment information are available, both online and in print. The *Wall Street Journal* and Yahoo.com, for example, contain numerous items of information useful in assessing the performance of securities. The same type of information that you use to *make* an investment decision you also use to *evaluate* investment performance. Two key areas to stay informed about are (1) returns on owned investments and (2) economic and market activity.

Return Data The basic ingredient in analyzing investment returns is current market information, such as daily price quotations for stocks and bonds. Investors often maintain logs or spreadsheets that contain the cost of each investment, as well as dividends, interest, and other sources of income received. By regularly recording price and return data, you can create an ongoing record of price fluctuations and cumulative returns. You should also monitor corporate earnings and dividends, which will affect a company's stock price. The two sources of investment return—current income and capital gains—must of course be combined to determine total return. Later in this chapter we will demonstrate use of the techniques presented in Chapter 4 to measure some popular investment vehicles.

Economic and Market Activity Changes in the economy and market will affect returns—both the level of current income and the market value of an investment vehicle. The astute investor keeps abreast of international, national, and local economic and market developments. By following economic and market changes, you should be able to assess their potential impact on returns. As economic and market conditions change, you must be prepared to make revisions in the portfolio. In essence, being a knowledgeable investor will improve your chances of generating a profit (or avoiding a loss).

Indexes of Investment Performance

In measuring investment performance, it is often worthwhile to compare your returns with broad-based market measures. Indexes useful for the analysis of common stock include the Dow Jones Industrial Average (DJIA), the Standard & Poor's 500 Stock Composite Index (S&P 500), and the Nasdaq Composite Index. (Detailed discussions of these averages and indexes can be found in Chapter 3.) Although the DJIA is widely cited by the news media, it is *not* considered the most appropriate comparative gauge of stock price movement, because of its narrow coverage. If your portfolio is composed of a broad range of common stocks, the S&P 500 index is probably a more appropriate tool.

A number of indicators are also available for assessing the general behavior of the bond markets. These indicators consider either bond yield or bond price behavior. Bond yield data reflect the rate of return one would earn on a bond purchased today and held to maturity. Popular sources of these data include the *Wall Street Journal, Barron's*, Standard & Poor's, Mergent, Yahoo.com, and the Federal Reserve. The Dow Jones Corporate Bond Index, based on the closing prices of 32 industrial, 32 financial, and 32 utility/telecom bonds, is a popular measure of bond price behavior. It reflects the mathematical average of the closing prices of the bonds.

Indexes of bond price and bond yield performance can be obtained for specific types of bonds (industrial, utility, and municipal), as well as on a composite basis. In addition, indexes reported in terms of *total returns* are available for both stocks and bonds. They combine dividend/interest income with price behavior (capital gain or loss) to reflect total return.

Investors frequently use the Lipper indexes to assess the general behavior of mutual funds. These indexes are available for various types of equity and bond funds. Unfortunately, for most other types of funds, no widely published index or average is available. A few other indexes cover listed options and futures.

Measuring the Performance of Investment Vehicles

To monitor an investment portfolio, investors need reliable techniques for consistently measuring the performance of each investment vehicle. In particular, the holding period return (HPR) measure, first presented in Chapter 4, can be used to determine *actual* return performance. HPR is an excellent way to assess actual return behavior, because it captures *total return* performance. It is most appropriate for holding or assessment periods of one year or less. Total return, in this context, includes the periodic cash income from the investment as well as price appreciation (or loss), whether realized or unrealized. To calculate returns for periods of more than a year you can use yield (internal rate of return), which recognizes the time value of money. Yield can be calculated using the techniques described in Chapter 4 (pages 169–172). Because the following discussions center on the *annual* assessment of return, we will use HPR as the measure of return.

The formula for HPR, presented in Chapter 4 (Equation 4.4) and applied throughout this chapter, is restated in Equation 13.1:

Equation 13.1 ➤

$$\text{Holding period return} = \frac{\text{Current income during period} + \text{Capital gain (or loss) during period}}{\text{Beginning investment value}}$$

Equation 13.1a ➤

$$\text{HPR} = \frac{C + CG}{V_0}$$

where

Equation 13.2 ➤

$$\frac{\text{Capital gain (or loss)}}{\text{during period}} = \frac{\text{Ending}}{\text{investment value}} - \frac{\text{Beginning}}{\text{investment value}}$$

Equation 13.2a ➤

$$CG = V_n - V_0$$

Stocks and Bonds There are several measures of investment return for stocks and bonds. *Dividend yield,* discussed in Chapter 6, measures the current yearly dividend return earned from a stock investment. It is calculated by dividing a stock's yearly cash dividend by its price. The *current yield* and *yield-to-maturity* (promised yield) for bonds, analyzed in Chapter 11, capture various components of return but do not reflect actual total return. The *holding period return* method *measures the total return (income plus change in value) actually earned on an investment over a given investment period.* We will use HPR, with a holding period of approximately one year, in the illustrations that follow.

Stocks The HPR for common and preferred stocks includes both cash dividends received and any price change in the security during the period of ownership. Table 13.2 illustrates the HPR calculation as applied to the actual performance of a common stock. Assume you purchased 1,000 shares of Dallas National Corporation in May 2007 at a cost of $27,312 (including commissions). After holding the stock for just over one year, you sold it, reaping proceeds of $32,040. You also received $2,000 in cash dividends and realized a $4,728 capital gain on the sale. Thus, the calculated HPR is 24.63%.

TABLE 13.2 Calculation of Pretax HPR on a Common Stock

Security: Dallas National Corporation common stock
Date of purchase: May 1, 2007
Purchase cost: $27,312
Date of sale: May 7, 2008
Sale proceeds: $32,040
Dividends received (May 2007 to May 2008): $2,000

$$\text{Holding period return} = \frac{\$2,000 + (\$32,040 - \$27,312)}{\$27,312}$$

$$= +\underline{\$24.63\%}$$

This HPR was calculated without consideration for income taxes paid on the dividends and capital gain. Because many investors are concerned with both pretax and after-tax rates of return, it is useful to calculate an after-tax HPR. We assume, for simplicity, that you are in the 30% ordinary tax bracket (federal and state combined). We also assume that, for federal and state tax purposes, dividends and capital gains for holding periods of more than 12 months are taxed at a 15% rate. Thus, both your dividend and capital gain income are taxed at a 15% rate. Income taxes reduce the after-tax dividend income to $1,700 [(1 − 0.15) × $2,000] and the after-tax capital gain to $4,019 [(1 − 0.15) × ($32,040 − $27,312)]. The after-tax HPR is therefore 20.94% [($1,700 + $4,019) ÷ $27,312], a reduction of 3.69 percentage points. It should be clear that both pretax HPR and after-tax HPR are useful gauges of return.

Bonds The HPR for a bond investment is similar to that for stocks. The calculation holds for both straight debt and convertible issues. It includes the two components of a bond investor's return: interest income and capital gain or loss.

Calculation of the HPR on a bond investment is illustrated in Table 13.3. Assume you purchased Phoenix Brewing Company bonds for $10,000, held them for just over one year, and then realized $9,704 at their sale. In addition, you earned $1,000 in interest during the year. The HPR of this investment is 7.04%. The HPR is lower than the bond's current yield of 10% ($1,000 interest ÷ $10,000 purchase price) because the bonds were sold at a capital loss. Assuming a 30% ordinary tax bracket and a 15% capital gains tax rate (because the bond has been held more than 12 months), the after-tax HPR is 4.48%: {[(1 − 0.30) × $1,000] + [(1 − 0.15) × ($9,704 − $10,000)]} ÷ $10,000. This is about 2.6% less than the pretax HPR.

Mutual Funds The two basic components of return from a mutual fund investment are dividend income (including any capital gains distribution) and change in value. The basic HPR equation for mutual funds is identical to that for stocks.

Table 13.4 presents a holding period return calculation for a no-load mutual fund. Assume you purchased 1,000 shares of the fund in July 2007 at a NAV of $10.40 per share. Because it is a no-load fund, no commission was charged, so your cost was $10,400. During the one-year period of ownership, the Pebble Falls Mutual Fund distributed investment income dividends total-

TABLE 13.3 Calculation of Pretax HPR on a Bond

Security: Phoenix Brewing Company 10% bonds
Date of purchase: June 2, 2007
Purchase cost: $10,000
Date of sale: June 5, 2008
Sale proceeds: $9,704
Interest earned (June 2007 to June 2008): $1,000

$$\text{Holding period return} = \frac{\$1,000 + (\$9,704 - \$10,000)}{\$10,000}$$

$$= +\underline{\$7.04\%}$$

TABLE 13.4 Calculation of Pretax HPR on a Mutual Fund

Security: Pebble Falls Mutual Fund
Date of purchase: July 1, 2007
Purchase cost: $10,400
Date of redemption: July 3, 2008
Sale proceeds: $10,790
Distributions received (July 2007 to July 2008)
　Investment income dividends: $270
　Capital gains dividends: $320

$$\text{Holding period return} = \frac{(\$270 + \$320) + (\$10,790 - \$10,400)}{\$10,400}$$

$$= +\underline{9.42\%}$$

ing $270 and capital gains dividends of $320. You redeemed (sold) this fund at a NAV of $10.79 per share, thereby realizing $10,790. As seen in Table 13.4, the pretax holding period return on this investment is 9.42%. Assuming a 30% ordinary tax bracket and a 15% dividend and capital gains tax rate (because the fund has been held for more than 12 months), the after-tax HPR for the fund is 8.01%: {[(1 − 0.15) × ($270 + $320)] + [(1 − 0.15) × ($10,790 − $10,400)]} ÷ $10,400. This is about 1.4% below the pretax return.

Options and Futures The only source of return on options and futures is capital gains. To calculate a holding period return for an investment in a call option, for instance, you use the basic HPR formula, but you would set current income equal to zero. If you purchased a call on 100 shares of ecommerce.com for $325 and sold the contract for $385 after holding it for just over 12 months, the pretax holding period return would be 18.46%. This is simply sales proceeds ($385) minus cost ($325) divided by cost. Assuming the 15% capital gains tax rate applies, the after-tax HPR would be 15.69%, which is the after-tax gain of $51 [(1 − 0.15) × $60] divided by cost ($325).

The HPRs of futures are calculated in a similar fashion. Because the return is in the form of capital gains only, the HPR analysis can be applied to any investment on a pretax or an after-tax basis. (The same basic procedure is used for securities that are sold short.)

■ Comparing Performance to Investment Goals

After computing an HPR (or yield) on an investment, you should compare it to your investment goal. Keeping track of an investment's performance will help you decide which investments you should continue to hold and which you might want to sell. Clearly, an investment would be a candidate for sale under the following conditions: (1) The investment failed to perform up to expectations and no real change in performance is anticipated. (2) It has met the original investment objective. (3) Better investment outlets are currently available.

Balancing Risk and Return We have frequently discussed the basic tradeoff between investment risk and return: To earn more return, you must take more risk. In analyzing an investment, the key question is, "Am I getting the proper return for the amount of investment risk I am taking?"

Nongovernment security investments are by nature riskier than U.S. government bonds or insured money market deposit accounts. This implies that *a rational investor should invest in these riskier vehicles only when the expected rate of return is well in excess of what could have been earned from a low-risk investment.* Thus, one benchmark against which to compare investment returns is the rate of return on low-risk investments. If one's risky investments are outperforming low-risk investments, they are obtaining extra return for taking extra risk. If they are not outperforming low-risk investments, you should carefully reexamine your investment strategy.

Isolating Problem Investments   It is best to analyze each investment in a portfolio periodically. For each, you should consider two questions: First, has it performed in a manner that could reasonably be expected? Second, if you didn't currently own it, would you buy it today? If the answers to both are negative, then the investment probably should be sold. A negative answer to one of the questions qualifies the investment for the "problem list." A *problem investment* is one that has not lived up to expectations. It may be a loss situation or an investment that has provided a return less than you expected. Many investors try to forget about problem investments, hoping the problem will go away or the investment will turn itself around. This is a mistake. Problem investments require immediate attention, not neglect. In studying a problem investment, the key question is, "Should I take my loss and get out, or should I hang on and hope it turns around?"

CONCEPTS IN REVIEW

Answers available at: myfinancelab.com

13.6   Why is it important to continuously manage and control your portfolio?

13.7   What role does current market information play in analyzing investment returns? How do changes in economic and market activity affect investment returns? Explain.

13.8   Which indexes can you use to compare your investment performance to general market returns? Briefly explain each of these indexes.

13.9   What are indicators of bond market behavior, and how are they different from stock market indicators? Name three sources of bond yield data.

13.10   Briefly discuss *holding period return (HPR)* and *yield* as measures of investment return. Are they equivalent? Explain.

13.11   Distinguish between the types of dividend distributions that mutual funds make. Are these dividends the only source of return for a mutual fund investor? Explain.

13.12   Under what three conditions would an investment holding be a candidate for sale? What must be true about the expected return on a risky investment, when compared with the return on a low-risk investment, to cause a rational investor to acquire the risky investment? Explain.

13.13   What is a *problem investment?* What two questions should one consider when analyzing each investment in a portfolio?

Assessing Portfolio Performance

LG 3   LG 4

active portfolio management
building a portfolio using traditional and modern approaches and managing and controlling it to achieve its objectives; a worthwhile activity that can result in superior returns.

A portfolio can be either passively or actively built and managed. A *passive portfolio* results from buying and holding a well-diversified portfolio over the given investment horizon. An *active portfolio* is built using the traditional and modern approaches presented in Chapter 5 and is managed and controlled to achieve its stated objectives. Passive portfolios may at times outperform equally risky active portfolios. But evidence suggests that **active portfolio management** can result in superior returns. Many of the ideas presented in this text are consistent with the belief that active portfolio management will improve your chance of earning superior returns.

Once you have built a portfolio, the first step in active portfolio management is to assess performance on a regular basis and use that information to revise the portfolio as needed. Calculating the portfolio return can be tricky. The procedures used to assess portfolio performance are based on many of the concepts presented earlier in this chapter. Here we will demonstrate how to assess portfolio performance, using a hypothetical securities portfolio over a one-year holding period. We will examine each of three measures that can be used to compare a portfolio's return with a risk-adjusted, market-adjusted rate of return.

■ Measuring Portfolio Return

Table 13.5 presents the investment portfolio, as of January 1, 2008, of Bob Hathaway. He is a 50-year-old widower, whose children are married. His income is $60,000 per year. His primary investment objective is long-term growth with a moderate dividend return. He selects stocks with two criteria in mind: quality and growth potential. On January 1, 2008, his portfolio consisted of 10 issues, all of good quality. Hathaway has been fortunate in his selection process: He has approximately $74,000 in unrealized price appreciation in his portfolio. During 2008, he decided to make a change in the portfolio. On May 7 he sold 1,000 shares of Dallas National Corporation for $32,040.

TABLE 13.5 Bob Hathaway's Portfolio (January 1, 2008)

Number of Shares	Company	Date Acquired	Total Cost (including commission)	Cost per Share	Current Price per Share	Current Value
1,000	Bancorp West, Inc.	1/16/06	$ 21,610	$21.61	$30	$ 30,000
1,000	Dallas National Corporation	5/01/07	27,312	27.31	29	29,000
1,000	Dator Companies, Inc.	4/13/02	13,704	13.70	27	27,000
500	Excelsior Industries	8/16/05	40,571	81.14	54	27,000
1,000	Florida Southcoast Banks	12/16/05	17,460	17.46	30	30,000
1,000	Maryland-Pacific	9/27/05	22,540	22.54	26	26,000
1,000	Moronson	2/27/05	19,100	19.10	47	47,000
500	Northwest Mining and Mfg.	4/17/06	25,504	51.00	62	31,000
1,000	Rawland Petroleum	3/12/06	24,903	24.90	30	30,000
1,000	Vornox	4/16/06	37,120	37.12	47	47,000
	Total		$249,824			$324,000

The holding period return for that same issue was discussed earlier in this chapter (see Table 13.2). Using proceeds from the Dallas National sale, he acquired an additional 1,000 shares of Florida Southcoast Banks on May 10, because he liked the prospects for the Florida bank. Florida Southcoast is based in one of the fastest-growing counties in the country.

Measuring the Amount Invested Every investor would be well advised to list his or her holdings periodically, as is done in Table 13.5. The table shows number of shares, acquisition date, cost, and current value for each issue. These data aid in continually formulating strategy decisions. The cost data, for example, are used to determine the amount invested. Hathaway's portfolio does not utilize the leverage of a margin account. Were leverage present, all return calculations would be based on the investor's *equity* in the account. (Recall from Chapter 2 that an investor's equity in a margin account equals the total value of all the securities in the account minus any margin debt.)

To measure Hathaway's return on his invested capital, we need to calculate the one-year holding period return. His invested capital as of January 1, 2008, is $324,000. He made no new additions of capital in the portfolio during 2008, although he sold one stock, Dallas National, and used the proceeds to buy another, Florida Southcoast Banks.

Measuring Income There are two sources of return from a portfolio of common stocks: income and capital gains. Current income is realized from dividends or, for bonds, is earned in the form of interest. Investors must report taxable dividends and interest on federal and state income tax returns. Companies are required to furnish income reports (Form 1099-DIV for dividends and Form 1099-INT for interest) to stockholders and bondholders. Many investors maintain logs to keep track of dividend and interest income as it is received.

Table 13.6 lists Hathaway's dividends for 2008. He received two quarterly dividends of $0.45 per share before he sold the Dallas National stock. He also

TABLE 13.6 **Dividend Income on Hathaway's Portfolio (Calendar year 2008)**

Number of Shares	Company	Annual Dividend per Share	Dividends Received
1,000	Bancorp West, Inc.	$1.20	$ 1,200
1,000	Dallas National Corporation*	1.80	900
1,000	Dator Companies, Inc.	1.12	1,120
500	Excelsior Industries	2.00	1,000
2,000	Florida Southcoast Banks**	1.28	1,920
1,000	Maryland-Pacific	1.10	1,100
1,000	Moronson	—	—
500	Northwest Mining and Mfg.	2.05	1,025
1,000	Rawland Petroleum	1.20	1,200
1,000	Vornox	1.47	1,470
	Total		$10,935

*Sold May 7, 2008.
**1,000 shares acquired on May 10, 2008.

TABLE 13.7	Unrealized Gains in Value of Hathaway's Portfolio (January 1, 2008, to December 31, 2008)					
Number of Shares	Company	Market Value (1/1/08)	Market Price (12/31/08)	Market Value (12/31/08)	Unrealized Gain (Loss)	Percentage Change
1,000	Bancorp West, Inc.	$ 30,000	$27	$ 27,000	($ 3,000)	−10.0%
1,000	Dator Companies, Inc.	27,000	36	36,000	9,000	+33.3
500	Excelsior Industries	27,000	66	33,000	6,000	+22.2
2,000	Florida Southcoast Banks*	62,040	35	70,000	7,960	+12.8
1,000	Maryland-Pacific	26,000	26	26,000	—	—
1,000	Moronson	47,000	55	55,000	8,000	+17.0
500	Northwest Mining and Mfg.	31,000	60	30,000	(1,000)	− 3.2
1,000	Rawland Petroleum	30,000	36	36,000	6,000	+20.0
1,000	Vornox	47,000	43	43,000	(4,000)	− 8.5
	Total	$327,040**		$356,000	$28,960	+ 8.9%

*1,000 additional shares acquired on May 10, 2008, at a cost of $32,040. The value listed is the cost plus the market value of the previously owned shares as of January 1, 2008.

**This total includes the $324,000 market value of the portfolio on January 1, 2008 (from Table 13.5) plus the $3,040 *realized* gain on the sale of the Dallas National Corporation stock on May 7, 2008. The inclusion of the realized gain in this total is necessary to calculate the *unrealized* gain on the portfolio during 2008.

received two $0.32-per-share quarterly dividends on the additional Florida Southcoast Banks shares he acquired. His total dividend income for 2008 was $10,935.

Measuring Capital Gains Table 13.7 shows the unrealized gains in value for each of the issues in the Hathaway portfolio. The January 1, 2008, and December 31, 2008, values are listed for each issue except the additional shares of Florida Southcoast Banks. The amounts listed for Florida Southcoast Banks reflect the fact that 1,000 additional shares of the stock were acquired on May 10, 2008, at a cost of $32,040. Hathaway's current holdings had beginning-of-the-year values of $327,040 (including the additional Florida Southcoast Banks shares at the date of purchase) and are worth $356,000 at year-end.

During 2008, the portfolio increased in value by 8.9%, or $28,960, in unrealized capital gains. In addition, Hathaway realized a capital gain in 2008 by selling his Dallas National holding. From January 1, 2008, until its sale on May 7, 2008, the Dallas National holding rose in value from $29,000 to $32,040. This was the only sale in 2008, so the total *realized* gain was $3,040. During 2008, the portfolio had both a realized gain of $3,040 and an unrealized gain of $28,960. The total gain in value equals the sum of the two: $32,000. Put another way, Hathaway neither added nor withdrew capital over the year. Therefore, the total capital gain is simply the difference between the year-end market value (of $356,000, from Table 13.7) and the value on January 1 (of $324,000, from Table 13.5). This, of course, amounts to $32,000. Of that amount, for tax purposes, only $3,040 is considered realized.

Measuring the Portfolio's Holding Period Return We use the holding period return (HPR) to measure the total return on the Hathaway portfolio during 2008. The basic one-year HPR formula for portfolios appears at the top of the next page.

Equation 13.3 ➤

$$\text{Holding period return for a portfolio} = \cfrac{\text{Dividends and interest received} + \text{Realized gain} + \text{Unrealized gain}}{\text{Initial equity investment} + \left(\text{New funds} \times \cfrac{\text{Number of months in portfolio}}{12}\right) - \left(\text{Withdrawn funds} \times \cfrac{\text{Number of months withdrawn from portfolio}}{12}\right)}$$

Equation 13.3a ➤

$$HPR_p = \cfrac{C + RG + UG}{E_0 + \left(NF \times \cfrac{ip}{12}\right) - \left(WF \times \cfrac{wp}{12}\right)}$$

This formula includes both the realized gains (income plus capital gains) and the unrealized yearly gains of the portfolio. Portfolio additions and deletions are time-weighted for the number of months they are in the portfolio.

Table 13.7 lays out in detail the portfolio's change in value: It lists all the issues that are in the portfolio as of December 31, 2008, and calculates the unrealized gain during the year. The beginning and year-end values are included for comparison purposes. The crux of the analysis is the HPR calculation for the year, presented in Table 13.8. All the elements of a portfolio's return are included. Dividends total $10,935 (from Table 13.6). The realized gain of $3,040 represents the increment in value of the Dallas National holding from January 1, 2008, until its sale. During 2008 the portfolio had a $28,960 unrealized gain (from Table 13.7). There were no additions of new funds, and no funds were withdrawn. Utilizing Equation 13.3 for HPR, we find that the portfolio had a total return of 13.25% in 2008.

▌ Comparison of Return with Overall Market Measures

Bob Hathaway can compare the HPR figure for his portfolio with market measures such as stock indexes. This comparison will show how his portfolio is doing in relation to the stock market as a whole. The S&P 500 Stock Com-

TABLE 13.8   **Holding Period Return Calculation on Hathaway's Portfolio (January 1, 2008, to December 31, 2008, holding period)**

Data

Portfolio value (1/1/08):	$324,000
Portfolio value (12/31/08):	$356,000
Realized appreciation	
(1/1/08 to 5/7/08 when Dallas National Corporation was sold):	$3,040
Unrealized appreciation	
(1/1/08 to 12/31/08):	$28,960
Dividends received:	$10,935
New funds invested or withdrawn:	None

Portfolio HPR Calculation

$$HPR_p = \frac{\$10,935 + \$3,040 + \$28,960}{\$324,000}$$

$$= \underline{+13.25\%}$$

posite Index and the Nasdaq Composite Index are acceptable indexes to represent the stock market as a whole. Assume that during 2008, the return on the S&P 500 index was +10.75% (including both dividends and capital gains). The return from Hathaway's portfolio was +13.25%, which compares very favorably with the broadly based index. The Hathaway portfolio performed about 23% better than the broad indicator of stock market return.

Such a comparison factors out general market movements, but *it fails to consider risk*. Clearly, a raw return figure, such as this +13.25%, requires further analysis. A number of risk-adjusted, market-adjusted rate-of-return measures are available for use in assessing portfolio performance. Here we'll discuss three of the most popular—Sharpe's measure, Treynor's measure, and Jensen's measure—and demonstrate their application to Hathaway's portfolio.

Sharpe's measure
a measure of portfolio performance that measures the *risk premium per unit of total risk,* which is measured by the portfolio standard deviation of return.

Sharpe's Measure **Sharpe's measure** of portfolio performance, developed by William F. Sharpe, compares the risk premium on a portfolio to the portfolio's standard deviation of return. The risk premium on a portfolio is the total portfolio return minus the risk-free rate. Sharpe's measure can be expressed as the following formula:

Equation 13.4 ➤

$$\text{Sharpe's measure} = \frac{\text{Total portfolio return} - \text{Risk-free rate}}{\text{Portfolio standard deviation of return}}$$

Equation 13.4a ➤

$$SM = \frac{r_p - R_F}{s_p}$$

This measure allows the investor to assess the *risk premium per unit of total risk,* which is measured by the portfolio standard deviation of return.

Assume the risk-free rate, R_F, is 7.50% and the standard deviation of return on Hathaway's portfolio, s_p, is 16%. The total portfolio return, r_p, which is the HPR for Hathaway's portfolio calculated in Table 13.8, is 13.25%. Substituting those values into Equation 13.4, we get Sharpe's measure, *SM*.

$$SM = \frac{13.25\% - 7.50\%}{16\%} = \frac{5.75\%}{16\%} = \underline{\underline{0.36}}$$

Sharpe's measure is meaningful when compared either to other portfolios or to the market. In general, the higher the value of Sharpe's measure, the better—the higher the risk premium per unit of risk. If we assume that the market return, r_m, is currently 10.75% and the standard deviation of return for the market portfolio, s_{p_m}, is 11.25%, Sharpe's measure for the market, SM_m, is

$$SM_m = \frac{10.75\% - 7.50\%}{11.25\%} = \frac{3.25\%}{11.25\%} = \underline{\underline{0.29}}$$

Because Sharpe's measure of 0.36 for Hathaway's portfolio is greater than the measure of 0.29 for the market portfolio, Hathaway's portfolio exhibits superior performance. Its risk premium per unit of risk is above that of the market.

Had Sharpe's measure for Hathaway's portfolio been below that of the market (below 0.29), the portfolio's performance would be considered inferior to the market performance.

Treynor's Measure Jack L. Treynor developed a portfolio performance measure similar to Sharpe's measure. **Treynor's measure** uses the portfolio beta to measure the portfolio's risk. Treynor therefore focuses only on *nondiversifiable risk,* assuming that the portfolio has been built in a manner that diversifies away all diversifiable risk. (In contrast, Sharpe focuses on *total risk.*) Treynor's measure is calculated as shown in Equation 13.5.

> **Treynor's measure**
> a measure of portfolio performance that measures the *risk premium per unit of nondiversifiable risk,* which is measured by the portfolio beta.

Equation 13.5 ➤

$$\text{Treynor's measure} = \frac{\text{Total portfolio return} - \text{Risk-free rate}}{\text{Portfolio beta}}$$

Equation 13.5a ➤

$$TM = \frac{r_p - R_F}{b_p}$$

This measure gives the *risk premium per unit of nondiversifiable risk,* which is measured by the portfolio beta.

Using the data for the Hathaway portfolio presented earlier and assuming that the beta for Hathaway's portfolio, b_p, is 1.20, we can substitute into Equation 13.5 to get Treynor's measure, TM, for Hathaway's portfolio.

$$TM = \frac{13.25\% - 7.50\%}{1.20} = \frac{5.75\%}{1.20} = \underline{\underline{4.79\%}}$$

HOTLINKS

Good discussions of the Sharpe, Treynor, and Jensen measures of performance can be found at:

www.cupoffinance.com/invest/mf/
mf_riskadjreturn.shtml
www.ipredictor.com/EyeFund/Include/
MutualFundScreenerComments1.pdf

Treynor's measure, like Sharpe's measure, is useful when compared either to other portfolios or to the market. Generally, the higher the value of Treynor's measure, the better—the greater the risk premium per unit of nondiversifiable risk. Again assuming that the market return, r_m, is 10.75%, and recognizing that, by definition, the beta for the market portfolio, b_{p_m}, is 1.00, we can use Equation 13.5 to find Treynor's measure for the market, TM_m.

$$TM_m = \frac{10.75\% - 7.50\%}{1.00} = \frac{3.25\%}{1.00} = \underline{\underline{3.25\%}}$$

The fact that Treynor's measure of 4.79% for Hathaway's portfolio is greater than the market portfolio measure of 3.25% indicates that Hathaway's portfolio exhibits superior performance. Its risk premium per unit of nondiversifiable risk is above that of the market. Had Treynor's measure for Hathaway's portfolio been below that of the market (below 3.25%), the portfolio's performance would be viewed as inferior to that of the market.

Jensen's Measure (Jensen's Alpha) Michael C. Jensen developed a portfolio performance measure that seems quite different from the measures of Sharpe and Treynor, yet is theoretically consistent with Treynor's measure.

Jensen's measure (Jensen's alpha)
a measure of portfolio performance that uses the portfolio beta and CAPM to calculate its *excess return,* which may be positive, zero, or negative.

Jensen's measure, also called **Jensen's alpha**, is based on the *capital asset pricing model (CAPM),* which was developed in Chapter 5 (see Equation 5.3). It calculates the portfolio's *excess return.* Excess return is the amount by which the portfolio's actual return deviates from its required return, which is determined using its beta and CAPM. The value of the excess return may be positive, zero, or negative. Like Treynor's measure, Jensen's measure focuses only on the *nondiversifiable,* or *relevant, risk* by using beta and CAPM. It assumes that the portfolio has been adequately diversified. Jensen's measure is calculated as shown in Equation 13.6.

Equation 13.6 ➤

$$\text{Jensen's measure} = (\text{Total portfolio return} - \text{Risk-free rate}) - \\ [\text{Portfolio beta} \times (\text{Market return} - \text{Risk-free rate})]$$

Equation 13.6a ➤

$$JM = (r_p - R_F) - [b_p \times (r_m - R_F)]$$

Jensen's measure indicates the difference between the portfolio's actual return and its required return. Positive values are preferred. They indicate that the portfolio earned a return in excess of its risk-adjusted, market-adjusted required return. A value of zero indicates that the portfolio earned *exactly* its required return. Negative values indicate the portfolio failed to earn its required return.

Using the data for Hathaway's portfolio presented earlier, we can substitute into Equation 13.6 to get Jensen's measure, *JM,* for Hathaway's portfolio.

$$JM = (13.25\% - 7.50\%) - [1.20 \times (10.75\% - 7.50\%)]$$
$$= 5.75\% - (1.20 \times 3.25\%) = 5.75\% - 3.90\% = \underline{1.85\%}$$

TIME TO REVISE YOUR PORTFOLIO?—Over time, you will need to review your portfolio to ensure that it reflects the right risk-return characteristics for your goals and needs. Here are 4 good reasons to perform this task:

• A major life event—marriage, birth of a child, job loss, illness, loss of a spouse, a child's finishing college— changes your investment objectives.
• The proportion of one asset class increases or decreases substantially.
• You expect to reach a specific goal within 2 years.
• The percentage in an asset class varies from your original allocation by 10% or more.

The 1.85% value for Jensen's measure indicates that Hathaway's portfolio earned an *excess return* 1.85 percentage points above its required return, given its nondiversifiable risk as measured by beta. Clearly, Hathaway's portfolio has outperformed the market on a risk-adjusted basis.

Note that unlike the Sharpe and Treynor measures, Jensen's measure, through its use of CAPM, automatically adjusts for the market return. Therefore, there is no need to make a separate market comparison. In general, the higher the value of Jensen's measure, the better the portfolio has performed. Only those portfolios with positive Jensen measures have outperformed the market on a risk-adjusted basis. Because of its computational simplicity, its reliance only on nondiversifiable risk, and its inclusion of both risk and market adjustments, Jensen's measure (alpha) tends to be preferred over those of Sharpe and Treynor for assessing portfolio performance.

▉ Portfolio Revision

In the Hathaway portfolio we have been discussing, one transaction occurred during 2008. The reason for this transaction was that Hathaway believed the Florida Southcoast Banks stock had more return potential than the Dallas National stock. You should periodically analyze your portfolio with one basic question in mind: "Does this portfolio continue to meet my needs?" In other words, does the portfolio contain those issues that are best suited to your risk-

portfolio revision
the process of selling certain issues in a portfolio and purchasing new ones to replace them.

return needs? Investors who systematically study the issues in their portfolios will occasionally find a need to sell certain issues and purchase new securities to replace them. This process is commonly called **portfolio revision**. As the economy evolves, certain industries and stocks become either less or more attractive as investments. In today's stock market, timeliness is the essence of profitability.

Given the dynamics of the investment world, periodic reallocation and rebalancing of the portfolio are a necessity. Many circumstances require such changes. For example, as an investor nears retirement, the portfolio's emphasis normally evolves from a strategy that stresses growth/capital appreciation to one that seeks to preserve capital. Changing a portfolio's emphasis normally occurs as an evolutionary process rather than an overnight switch. Individual issues in the portfolio often change in risk-return characteristics. As this occurs, you would be wise to eliminate those issues that do not meet your objectives. In addition, the need for diversification is constant. As issues rise or fall in value, their diversification effect may be lessened. Thus, you may need portfolio revision to maintain diversification.

CONCEPTS IN REVIEW
Answers available at: www.myfinancelab.com

13.14 What is *active portfolio management?* Will it result in superior returns? Explain.

13.15 Describe the steps involved in measuring portfolio return. Explain the role of the portfolio's HPR in this process, and explain why one must differentiate between realized and unrealized gains.

13.16 Why is comparing a portfolio's return to the return on a broad market index generally inadequate? Explain.

13.17 Briefly describe each of the following return measures available for assessing portfolio performance, and explain how they are used.
   a. Sharpe's measure.
   b. Treynor's measure.
   c. Jensen's measure (Jensen's alpha).

13.18 Why is Jensen's measure (alpha) generally preferred over the measures of Sharpe and Treynor for assessing portfolio performance? Explain.

13.19 Explain the role of *portfolio revision* in the process of managing a portfolio.

Timing Transactions

LG 5   LG 6

The essence of timing is to "buy low and sell high." This is the dream of all investors. Although there is no tried-and-true way to achieve such a goal, there are several methods you can utilize to time purchases and sales. First, there are formula plans, which we discuss next. Investors can also use limit and stop-loss orders as a timing aid, can follow procedures for warehousing liquidity, and can take into consideration other aspects of timing when selling their investments. For the story of one famous investor of the twentieth century, see the *Ethics in Investing* box on page 589.

ETHICS *in* INVESTING

The Virtues of Ethical Investing: The Remarkable Life of John Templeton

A pioneer in financial investments, John Marks Templeton has spent a lifetime encouraging ethical behavior. A naturalized British citizen living in Nassau, the Bahamas, Templeton was knighted by Queen Elizabeth II in 1987 for his many accomplishments. One of them was creating the $1 million-plus Templeton Prize for Progress toward Research or Discoveries about Spiritual Realities, presented annually in London since 1973. Mother Theresa of Calcutta was its first recipient.

John Templeton was born in 1912 in a small Tennessee town. His businessman father taught him to keep a positive attitude. By the time John was four, he was raising beans in his mother's garden and selling them at a local store for profit. At the age of 12, he came upon an old, broken-down Ford, which he later purchased from a farmer for $10. With the help of friends he spent six months rebuilding it and drove it until he graduated from high school. Templeton never spent more than $200 on a car until he had a net worth of more than $250,000.

Qualities developed as a young man served Templeton well as he set out to become one of the world's greatest investors. Forced to live thriftily while paying for his own education at Yale University during the Depression, Templeton graduated in 1934 as a top scholar in his class. After graduation, he set out on a seven-month world tour to study global investment opportunities firsthand. Before leaving, John wrote 100 investment firms of his plans and told them he would be available for hire upon his return. His efforts landed him a job on Wall Street. When John got married, he and his wife set a goal to save 50% of their income.

To make thrift a joy rather than a burden, the Templetons became avid bargain shoppers and used to compete with their friends for bargains.

Standard stock-buying advice is "buy low, and sell high." When war began in Europe in 1939, Templeton borrowed money to buy 100 shares in each of 104 companies selling at $1 a share or less, including 34 companies that were in bankruptcy. Only four turned out to be worthless, and he turned large profits on the others after holding each for an average of four years.

Taking a less-traveled route in investing, Templeton sold advice on how to invest worldwide when Americans rarely considered foreign investment. In 1954, he launched his flagship fund, Templeton Growth. Each $100,000 invested then, with distributions reinvested, grew to total $55 million by 1999. *Money* magazine named him "arguably the greatest global stock picker of the century" (January 1999). Sir John Templeton has always been a student of *free competition:* "Competitive business has reduced costs, has increased variety, has improved quality." And if a business is not ethical, he says, "it will fail, perhaps not right away, but eventually." His progressive ideas on finance, spiritual life, and business ethics made him a distinctive figure in all these fields.

CRITICAL THINKING QUESTION What personal characteristic of John Templeton do you think made him an investing giant? Be ready to defend your answer.

Source: Matthew Robinson "His Optimism and Drive Built a Financial Empire," *Investor's Business Daily*, July 24, 2006.

▮ Formula Plans

formula plans
mechanical methods of portfolio management that try to take advantage of price changes that result from cyclical price movements.

Formula plans are mechanical methods of portfolio management that try to take advantage of price changes that result from cyclical price movements. Formula plans are not set up to provide unusually high returns. Rather, they are conservative strategies employed by investors who do not wish to bear a high level of risk. We discuss four popular formula plans: dollar-cost averaging, the constant-dollar plan, the constant-ratio plan, and the variable-ratio plan.

dollar-cost averaging
a formula plan for timing investment transactions, in which a fixed dollar amount is invested in a security at fixed time intervals.

HOTLINKS

To calculate the benefits of dollar-cost averaging, go to the Web site below. As you will see, this technique doesn't always work, and this site explains why.

www.moneychimp.com/features/dollar_cost.htm

constant-dollar plan
a formula plan for timing investment transactions, in which the investor establishes a target dollar amount for the speculative portion of the portfolio and establishes trigger points at which funds are transferred to or from the conservative portion as needed to maintain the target dollar amount.

Dollar-Cost Averaging Dollar-cost averaging is a formula plan in which a fixed dollar amount is invested in a security at fixed time intervals. In this passive buy-and-hold strategy, the periodic dollar investment is held constant. To make the plan work, you must invest on a regular basis. The goal of a dollar-cost averaging program is growth in the value of the security to which the funds are allocated. The price of the investment security will probably fluctuate over time. If the price declines, you would purchase more shares per period. Conversely, if the price rises, you would purchase fewer shares per period.

Look at the example of dollar-cost averaging in Table 13.9. The table shows investment of $500 per month in the Wolverine Mutual Fund, a growth-oriented, no-load mutual fund. Assume that during one year's time you have placed $6,000 in the mutual fund shares. (Because this is a no-load fund, shares are purchased at net asset value, NAV.) You made purchases at NAVs ranging from a low of $24.16 to a high of $30.19. At year-end, the value of your holdings in the fund was slightly less than $6,900. Dollar-cost averaging is a passive strategy; other formula plans are more active.

Constant-Dollar Plan A constant-dollar plan consists of a portfolio that is divided into two parts, speculative and conservative. The speculative portion consists of securities that have high promise of capital gains. The conservative portion consists of low-risk investments such as bonds or a money market account. The target dollar amount for the speculative portion is constant. You establish trigger points (upward or downward movement in the speculative

TABLE 13.9 Dollar-Cost Averaging ($500 per month, Wolverine Mutual Fund shares)

Transactions

Month	Net Asset Value (NAV) Month-End	Number of Shares Purchased
January	$26.00	19.23
February	27.46	18.21
March	27.02	18.50
April	24.19	20.67
May	26.99	18.53
June	25.63	19.51
July	24.70	20.24
August	24.16	20.70
September	25.27	19.79
October	26.15	19.12
November	29.60	16.89
December	30.19	16.56

Annual Summary

Total investment: $6,000.00
Total number of shares purchased: 227.95
Average cost per share: $26.32
Year-end portfolio value: $6,881.81

TABLE 13.10 Constant-Dollar Plan

Mutual Fund NAV	Value of Speculative Portion	Value of Conservative Portion	Total Portfolio Value	Transactions	Number of Shares in Speculative Portion
$10.00	$10,000.00	$10,000.00	$20,000.00		1,000
11.00	11,000.00	10,000.00	21,000.00		1,000
12.00	12,000.00	10,000.00	22,000.00		1,000
→ 12.00	10,000.00	12,000.00	22,000.00	Sold 166.67 shares	833.33
11.00	9,166.63	12,000.00	21,166.63		833.33
9.50	7,916.64	12,000.00	19,916.64		833.33
→ 9.50	10,000.00	9,916.64	19,916.64	Purchased 219.30 shares	1,052.63
10.00	10,526.30	9,916.64	20,442.94		1,052.63

HOTLINKS

At the Investing for Beginners site below, the article on "Dollar Cost Averaging" emphasizes its role in reducing market risk.

beginnersinvest.about.com/cs/newinvestors/a/041901a.htm

portion) at which funds are removed from or added to that portion. The constant-dollar plan basically skims off profits from the speculative portion of the portfolio if it rises a certain percentage or amount in value and adds these funds to the conservative portion of the portfolio. If the speculative portion of the portfolio declines by a specific percentage or amount, you add funds to it from the conservative portion.

Assume that you have established the constant-dollar plan shown in Table 13.10. The beginning $20,000 portfolio consists of $10,000 invested in a high-beta, no-load mutual fund and $10,000 deposited in a money market account. You have decided to rebalance the portfolio every time the speculative portion is worth $2,000 more or $2,000 less than its initial value of $10,000. If the speculative portion of the portfolio equals or exceeds $12,000, you sell sufficient shares of the fund to bring its value down to $10,000 and add the proceeds from the sale to the conservative portion. If the speculative portion declines in value to $8,000 or less, you use funds from the conservative portion to purchase sufficient shares to raise the value of the speculative portion to $10,000.

Two portfolio-rebalancing actions are taken in the time sequence illustrated in Table 13.10. Initially, $10,000 was allocated to each portion of the portfolio. When the mutual fund's net asset value (NAV) rose to $12, the speculative portion was worth $12,000. At that point, you sold 166.67 shares valued at $2,000, and added the proceeds to the money market account. Later, the mutual fund's NAV declined to $9.50 per share, causing the value of the speculative portion to drop below $8,000. This change triggered the purchase of sufficient shares to raise the value of the speculative portion to $10,000. Over the long run, if the speculative investment of the constant-dollar plan rises in value, the conservative component of the portfolio will increase in dollar value as profits are transferred into it.

constant-ratio plan
a formula plan for timing investment transactions, in which a desired fixed ratio of the speculative portion to the conservative portion of the portfolio is established; when the actual ratio differs by a predetermined amount from the desired ratio, transactions are made to rebalance the portfolio to achieve the desired ratio.

Constant-Ratio Plan The **constant-ratio plan** is similar to the constant-dollar plan except that it establishes a desired fixed *ratio* of the speculative portion to the conservative portion of the portfolio. When the actual ratio of the two differs by a predetermined amount from the desired ratio, rebalancing occurs. At that point, you make transactions to bring the actual ratio back to the desired ratio. To use the constant-ratio plan, you must decide on the appropriate apportionment of the portfolio between speculative and conservative

TABLE 13.11 Constant-Ratio Plan

Mutual Fund NAV	Value of Speculative Portion	Value of Conservative Portion	Total Portfolio Value	Ratio of Speculative Portion to Conservative Portion	Transactions	Number of Shares in Speculative Portion
$10.00	$10,000.00	$10,000.00	$20,000.00	1.000		1,000
11.00	11,000.00	10,000.00	21,000.00	1.100		1,000
12.00	12,000.00	10,000.00	22,000.00	1.200		1,000
→ 12.00	11,000.00	11,000.00	22,000.00	1.000	Sold 83.33 shares	916.67
11.00	10,083.00	11,000.00	21,083.00	0.917		916.67
10.00	9,166.70	11,000.00	20,166.70	0.833		916.67
9.00	8,250.00	11,000.00	19,250.00	0.750		916.67
→ 9.00	9,625.00	9,625.00	19,250.00	1.000	Purchased 152.78 shares	1,069.44
10.00	10,694.40	9,625.00	20,319.40	1.110		1,069.44

investments. You must also choose the ratio trigger point at which transactions occur.

To see how this works, assume that the constant-ratio plan illustrated in Table 13.11 is yours. The initial portfolio value is $20,000. You have decided to allocate 50% of the portfolio to the speculative, high-beta mutual fund and 50% to a money market account. You will rebalance the portfolio when the ratio of the speculative portion to the conservative portion is greater than or equal to 1.20 or less than or equal to 0.80. A sequence of changes in net asset value (NAV) is listed in Table 13.11. Initially, $10,000 is allocated to each portion of the portfolio. When the fund NAV reaches $12, the 1.20 ratio triggers the sale of 83.33 shares. Then the portfolio is back to its desired 50:50 ratio. Later, the fund NAV declines to $9, lowering the value of the speculative portion to $8,250. The ratio of the speculative portion to the conservative portion is then 0.75, which is below the 0.80 trigger point. You purchase 152.78 shares to bring the desired ratio back up to the 50:50 level.

The long-run expectation under a constant-ratio plan is that the speculative securities will rise in value. When this occurs, you will sell securities to reapportion the portfolio and increase the value of the conservative portion. This philosophy is similar to the constant-dollar plan, except that it uses a ratio as a trigger point.

variable-ratio plan
a formula plan for timing investment transactions, in which the ratio of the speculative portion to the total portfolio value varies depending on the movement in value of the speculative securities; when the ratio rises or falls by a predetermined amount, the amount committed to the speculative portion of the portfolio is reduced or increased, respectively.

Variable-Ratio Plan The **variable-ratio plan** is the most aggressive of these four fairly passive formula plans. It attempts to turn stock market movements to the investor's advantage by timing the market. That is, it tries to "buy low and sell high." The ratio of the speculative portion to the total portfolio value varies depending on the movement in value of the speculative securities. When the ratio rises a certain predetermined amount, the amount committed to the speculative portion of the portfolio is reduced. Conversely, if the value of the speculative portion declines so that it drops significantly in proportion to the total portfolio value, the amount committed to the speculative portion of the portfolio is increased.

When implementing the variable-ratio plan, you have several decisions to make. First, you must determine the initial allocation between the speculative and conservative portions of the portfolio. Next, you must choose trigger

TABLE 13.12 Variable-Ratio Plan

Mutual Fund NAV	Value of Speculative Portion	Value of Conservative Portion	Total Portfolio Value	Ratio of Speculative Portion to Total Portfolio Value	Transactions	Number of Shares in Speculative Portion
$10.00	$10,000.00	$10,000.00	$20,000.00	0.50		1,000
15.00	15,000.00	10,000.00	25,000.00	0.60		1,000
→ 15.00	11,250.00	13,750.00	25,000.00	0.45	Sold 250 shares	750
10.00	7,500.00	13,750.00	21,250.00	0.35		750
→ 10.00	11,687.50	9,562.50	21,250.00	0.55	Purchased 418.75 shares	1,168.75
12.00	14,025.00	9,562.50	23,587.50	0.59		1,168.75

points to initiate buy or sell activity. These points are a function of the ratio between the value of the speculative portion and the value of the total portfolio. Finally, you must set adjustments in that ratio at each trigger point.

Assume that you use the variable-ratio plan shown in Table 13.12. Initially, you divide the portfolio equally between the speculative and the conservative portions. The speculative portion consists of a high-beta (around 2.0) mutual fund. The conservative portion is a money market account. You decide that when the speculative portion reaches 60% of the total portfolio, you will reduce its proportion to 45%. If the speculative portion of the portfolio drops to 40% of the total portfolio, then you will raise its proportion to 55%. The logic behind this strategy is an attempt to time the cyclical movements in the mutual fund's value. When the fund moves up in value, you take profits, and you increase the proportion invested in the no-risk money market account. When the fund declines markedly in value, you increase the proportion of capital committed to the speculative portion.

A sequence of transactions is depicted in Table 13.12. When the fund net asset value (NAV) climbs to $15, the 60% ratio trigger point is reached, and you sell 250 shares of the fund. You place the proceeds in the money market account, which causes the speculative portion then to represent 45% of the value of the portfolio. Later, the fund NAV declines to $10, causing the speculative portion of the portfolio to drop to 35%. This triggers a portfolio rebalancing, and you purchase 418.75 shares, moving the speculative portion to 55%. When the fund NAV then moves to $12, the total portfolio is worth in excess of $23,500. In comparison, had the initial investment of $20,000 been allocated equally and had no rebalancing been done between the mutual fund and the money market account, the total portfolio value at this time would have been only $22,000 ($12 × 1,000 = $12,000 in the speculative portion plus $10,000 in the money market account).

▌ Using Limit and Stop-Loss Orders

In Chapter 3 we discussed the market order, the limit order, and the stop-loss order. (See pages 137–138 to review these types of orders.) Here we will see how you can use the limit and stop-loss orders to rebalance a portfolio. These types of security orders, if properly used, can increase return by lowering transaction costs.

Limit Orders There are many ways investors can use limit orders when they buy or sell securities. For instance, if you have decided to add a stock to the portfolio, a limit order to buy will ensure that you buy only at the desired purchase price or below. A limit *good-'til-canceled (GTC)* order to buy instructs the broker to buy stock until the entire order is filled. The primary risk in using limit instead of market orders is that the order may not be executed. For example, if you placed a GTC order to buy 100 shares of State Oil of California at $27 per share and the stock never traded at $27 per share or less, the order would never be executed. Thus, you must weigh the need for immediate execution (market order) against the possibility of a better price with a limit order.

Limit orders, of course, can increase your return if they enable you to buy a security at a lower cost or sell it at a higher price. During a typical trading day, a stock will fluctuate up and down over a normal trading range. For example, suppose the common shares of Jama Motor traded 10 times in the following sequence: 36.00, 35.88, 35.75, 35.94, 35.50, 35.63, 35.82, 36.00, 36.13, 36.00. A market order to sell could have been executed at somewhere between 35.50 (the low) and 36.13 (the high). A limit order to sell at 36.00 would have been executed at 36.00. Thus, $0.50 per share might have been gained by using a limit order.

Stop-Loss Orders Stop-loss orders can be used to limit the downside loss exposure of an investment. For example, assume you purchase 500 shares of Easy Work at 26.00 and have set a specific goal to sell the stock if it reaches 32.00 or drops to 23.00. To implement this goal, you would enter a GTC stop order to sell with a price limit of 32.00 and another stop order at a price of 23.00. If the issue trades at 23.00 or less, the stop-loss order becomes a market order, and the broker sells the stock at the best price available. Or, if the issue trades at 32.00 or higher, the broker will sell the stock. In the first situation, you are trying to reduce your losses; in the second, you are attempting to protect a profit.

whipsawing
the situation where a stock temporarily drops in price and then bounces back upward.

The principal risk in using stop-loss orders is **whipsawing**—a situation where a stock temporarily drops in price and then bounces back upward. If Easy Work dropped to 23.00, then 22.57, and then rallied back to 26.00, you would have been sold out at a price between 23.00 and 22.57. For this reason, limit orders, including stop-loss orders, require careful analysis before they are placed. You must consider the stock's probable fluctuations as well as the need to purchase or sell the stock when choosing among market, limit, and stop-loss orders.

▉ Warehousing Liquidity

Investing in risky stocks or in options or futures offers probable returns in excess of those available with money market deposit accounts or bonds. However, stocks and options and futures are risky investments. One recommendation for an efficient portfolio is to keep a portion of it in a low-risk, highly liquid investment to protect against total loss. The low-risk asset acts as a buffer against possible investment adversity. A second reason for maintaining funds in a low-risk asset is the possibility of future opportunities. When opportunity strikes, an investor who has extra cash available will be able to take advantage of the situation. If you have set aside funds in a highly liquid investment, you need not disturb the existing portfolio.

There are two primary media for warehousing liquidity: money market deposit accounts at financial institutions and money market mutual funds. The money market accounts at savings institutions provide relatively easy access to funds and furnish returns competitive with (but somewhat lower than) money market mutual funds. The products offered by financial institutions are becoming more competitive with those offered by mutual funds and stock brokerage firms.

▌ Timing Investment Sales

Knowing when to sell a stock is as important as choosing which stock to buy. Periodically, you should review your portfolio and consider possible sales and new purchases. Here we discuss two issues relevant to the sale decision: tax consequences and achieving investment goals.

Tax Consequences Taxes affect nearly all investment actions. All investors can and should understand certain basics. The treatment of capital losses is important: *A maximum of $3,000 of losses in excess of capital gains can be written off against other income in any one year.* If you have a loss position in an investment and have concluded that it would be wise to sell it, the best time to sell is when you have a capital gain against which you can apply the loss. Clearly, one should carefully consider the tax consequences of investment sales prior to taking action.

Achieving Investment Goals Every investor would enjoy buying an investment at its lowest price and selling it at its top price. At a more realistic level, you should sell an investment when it no longer meets your needs. In particular, if an investment has become either more or less risky than is desired, or if it has not met its return objective, it should be sold. The tax consequences mentioned above help to determine the appropriate time to sell. However, *taxes are not the foremost consideration in a sale decision.* The dual concepts of risk and return should be the overriding concerns.

Be sure to take the time periodically to examine each investment in light of its return performance and relative risk. You should sell any investment that no longer belongs in the portfolio and should buy vehicles that are more suitable. Finally, you should not hold out for every nickel of profit. Very often, those who hold out for the top price watch the value of their holdings plummet. If an investment looks ripe to sell, sell it, take the profit, reinvest it in an appropriate vehicle, and enjoy your good fortune.

WEBEXTENSION

For some tips on knowing when and what to sell, see the *Investing in Action* box on our Web site:

www.myfinancelab.com

CONCEPTS IN REVIEW

Answers available at: www.myfinancelab.com

13.20   Explain the role that *formula plans* can play in the timing of security transactions. Describe the logic underlying the use of these plans.

13.21   Briefly describe each of the following plans and differentiate among them.
   a.   Dollar-cost averaging.
   b.   Constant-dollar plan.
   c.   Constant-ratio plan.
   d.   Variable-ratio plan.

13.22 Describe how a limit order can be used when securities are bought or sold. How can a stop-loss order be used to reduce losses? To protect profit?

13.23 Give two reasons why an investor might want to maintain funds in a low-risk, highly liquid investment.

13.24 Describe the two items an investor should consider before reaching a decision to sell an investment vehicle.

Summary

LG 1 **Explain how to use an asset allocation scheme to construct a portfolio consistent with investor objectives.** To construct a portfolio, consider personal characteristics and establish consistent portfolio objectives such as current income, capital preservation, capital growth, tax considerations, and level of risk. Asset allocation, which is the key influence on portfolio return, involves dividing the portfolio into asset classes. Asset allocation aims to protect against negative developments while taking advantage of positive ones. The basic approaches to asset allocation involve the use of fixed weightings, flexible weightings, and tactical asset allocation. Asset allocation can be achieved on a do-it-yourself basis, with the use of mutual funds, or by merely buying shares in an asset allocation fund.

LG 2 **Discuss the data and indexes needed to measure and compare investment performance.** To analyze the performance of individual investments, gather current market information and stay abreast of international, national, and local economic and market developments. Indexes of investment performance such as the Dow Jones Industrial Average (DJIA) and bond market indicators are available for use in assessing market behavior. The performance of individual investment vehicles can be measured on both a pretax and an after-tax basis by using the holding period return (HPR). HPR measures the total return (income plus change in value) earned on the investment during an investment period of one year or less. HPR can be compared to investment goals to assess whether the proper return is being earned for the risk involved and to isolate any problem investments.

LG 3 **Understand the techniques used to measure income, capital gains, and total portfolio return.** To measure portfolio return, estimate the amount invested, the income earned, and any capital gains (both realized and unrealized) over the relevant current time period. Using these values, calculate the portfolio's holding period return (HPR) by dividing the total returns by the amount of investment during the period. Comparison of the portfolio's HPR to overall market measures can provide some insight about the portfolio's performance relative to the market.

LG 4 **Use the Sharpe, Treynor, and Jensen measures to compare a portfolio's return with a risk-adjusted, market-adjusted rate of return, and discuss portfolio revision.** A risk-adjusted, market-adjusted evaluation of a portfolio's return can be made using Sharpe's measure, Treynor's measure, or Jensen's measure. Sharpe's and Treynor's measures find the risk premium per unit of risk, which can be compared with similar market measures to assess the portfolio's performance. Jensen's measure (alpha) calculates the portfolio's excess return using beta and CAPM. Jensen's measure tends to be preferred because it is relatively easy to calculate and directly makes both risk and market adjustments. Portfolio revision—selling certain issues and purchasing new ones to replace them—should take place when returns are unacceptable or when the portfolio fails to meet the investor's objectives.

LG 5 **Describe the role and logic of dollar-cost averaging, constant-dollar plans, constant-ratio plans, and variable-ratio plans.** Formula plans are used to time purchase and sale decisions to take advantage of price changes that result from cyclical price movements. The four commonly used formula plans are dollar-cost averaging, the constant-dollar plan, the constant-ratio plan, and the variable-ratio plan. All of them have certain decision rules or triggers that signal a purchase and/or sale action.

LG 6 **Explain the role of limit and stop-loss orders in investment timing, warehousing liquidity, and timing investment sales.** Limit and stop-loss orders can be used to trigger the rebalancing of a portfolio to contribute to improved portfolio returns. Low-risk, highly liquid investment vehicles such as money market deposit accounts and money market mutual funds can warehouse liquidity. Such liquidity can protect against total loss and allow you to seize any attractive opportunities. Investment sales should be timed to obtain maximum tax benefits (or minimum tax consequences) and to contribute to the achievement of the investor's goals.

Key Terms

active portfolio management, *p. 581*
asset allocation, *p. 571*
asset allocation fund, *p. 574*
constant-dollar plan, *p. 590*
constant-ratio plan, *p. 591*
dollar-cost averaging, *p. 590*
fixed-weightings approach, *p. 571*
flexible-weightings approach, *p. 572*
formula plans, *p. 589*

Jensen's measure (Jensen's alpha), *p. 587*
portfolio revision, *p. 588*
security selection, *p. 571*
Sharpe's measure, *p. 585*
tactical asset allocation, *p. 572*
Treynor's measure, *p. 586*
variable-ratio plan, *p. 592*
whipsawing, *p. 594*

Discussion Questions

LG 1 Q13.1 List your personal characteristics and then state your investment objectives in light of them. Use these objectives as a basis for developing your portfolio objectives and policies. Assume that you plan to create a portfolio aimed at achieving your stated objectives. The portfolio will be constructed by allocating your money to any of the following asset classes: common stock, bonds, foreign securities, and short-term securities.

a. Determine and justify an asset allocation to these four classes in light of your stated portfolio objectives and policies.

b. Describe the types of investments you would choose for each of the asset classes.

c. Assume that after making the asset allocations specified in part **a**, you receive a sizable inheritance that causes your portfolio objectives to change to a much more aggressive posture. Describe the changes that you would make in your asset allocations.

d. Describe other asset classes you might consider when developing your asset allocation scheme.

LG 2   **LG 3**   Q13.2 Choose an established local (or nearby) company whose stock is listed and actively traded on a major exchange. Find the stock's closing price at the end of each of the preceding 6 years and the amount of dividends paid in each of the preceding 5 years. Also, obtain the value of the Dow Jones Industrial Average (DJIA) at the end of each of the preceding 6 years.

a. Use Equation 13.1 to calculate the pretax holding period return (HPR) on the stock for each of the preceding 5 years.

b. Study the international, national, and local economic and market developments that occurred during the preceding 5 years.

c. Compare the stock's returns to the DJIA for each year over the 5-year period of concern.

d. Discuss the stock's returns in light of the economic and market developments noted in part **b** and the behavior of the DJIA as noted in part **c** over the 5 preceding years. How well did the stock perform in light of these factors?

LG 2   **LG 3**   Q13.3 Assume that you are in the 35% ordinary tax bracket (federal and state combined) and that dividends and capital gains for holding periods of more than 12 months are taxed at a 15% rate. Select a major stock, bond, and mutual fund in which you are interested in investing. For each of them, gather data for each of the past 3 years on the annual dividends or interest paid and the capital gain (or loss) that would have resulted had they been purchased at the start of each year and sold at the end of each year. For the mutual fund, be sure to separate any dividends paid into investment income dividends and capital gains dividends.

a. For each of the 3 investment vehicles, calculate the pretax and after-tax HPR for each of the 3 years.

b. Use your annual HPR findings in part **a** to calculate the average after-tax HPR for each of the investment vehicles over the 3-year period.

c. Compare the average returns found in part **b** for each of the investment vehicles. Discuss the relative risks in view of these returns and the characteristics of each vehicle.

LG 2   **LG 3**   Q13.4 Choose 6 actively traded stocks for inclusion in your investment portfolio. Assume the portfolio was created 3 years earlier by purchasing 200 shares of each of the 6 stocks. Find the acquisition price of each stock, the annual dividend paid by each stock, and the year-end prices for the 3 calendar years. Record for each stock its total cost, cost per share, current price per share, and total current value at the end of each of the 3 calendar years.

a. For each of the 3 years, find the amount invested in the portfolio.

b. For each of the 3 years, measure the annual income from the portfolio.

c. For each of the 3 years, determine the unrealized capital gains from the portfolio.

d. For each of the 3 years, calculate the portfolio's HPR, using the values in parts **a**, **b**, and **c**.

e. Use your findings in part **d** to calculate the average HPR for the portfolio over the 3-year period. Discuss your finding.

LG 4   **Q13.5** Find 5 actively traded stocks and record their prices at the start and the end of the most recent calendar year. Also, find the amount of dividends paid on each stock during that year and each stock's beta at the end of the year. Assume that the 5 stocks were held during the year in an equal-dollar-weighted portfolio (20% in each stock) created at the start of the year. Also find the current risk-free rate, R_F, and the market return, r_m, for the given year. Assume that the standard deviation for the portfolio of the 5 stocks is 14.25% and that the standard deviation for the market portfolio is 10.80%.

a. Use the formula presented in Chapter 5 (Equation 5.1) to find the portfolio return, r_p, for the year under consideration.

b. Calculate Sharpe's measure for both the portfolio and the market. Compare and discuss these values. On the basis of this measure, is the portfolio's performance inferior or superior? Explain.

c. Calculate Treynor's measure for both the portfolio and the market. Compare and discuss these values. On the basis of this measure, is the portfolio's performance inferior or superior? Explain.

d. Calculate Jensen's measure (Jensen's alpha) for the portfolio. Discuss its value. On the basis of this measure, is the portfolio's performance inferior or superior? Explain.

e. Compare, contrast, and discuss your analysis using the 3 measures in parts **b**, **c**, and **d**. Evaluate the portfolio.

LG 5   **Q13.6** Choose a high-growth mutual fund and a money market mutual fund. Find and record their closing net asset values (NAVs) at the end of each *week* for the immediate past year. Assume that you wish to invest $10,400.

a. Assume you use dollar-cost averaging to buy shares in *both* the high-growth and the money market funds by purchasing $100 of each of them at the end of each week—a total investment of $10,400 (52 weeks × $200/week). How many shares would you have purchased in each fund by year-end? What are the total number of shares, the average cost per share, and the year-end portfolio value of each fund? Total the year-end fund values and compare them to the total that would have resulted from investing $5,200 in each fund at the end of the first week.

b. Assume you use a constant-dollar plan with 50% invested in the high-growth fund (speculative portion) and 50% invested in the money market fund (conservative portion). If the portfolio is rebalanced every time the speculative portion is worth $500 more or $500 less than its initial value of $5,200, what would be the total portfolio value and the number of shares in the speculative portion at year-end?

c. Assume that, as in part **b**, you initially invest 50% in the speculative portion and 50% in the conservative portion. But in this case you use a constant-ratio plan under which rebalancing to the 50:50 mix occurs whenever the ratio of the speculative to the conservative portion is greater than or equal to 1.25 or less than or equal to 0.75. What would be the total portfolio value and the number of shares in the speculative portion at year-end?

d. Compare and contrast the year-end values of the total portfolio under each of the plans in parts **a**, **b**, and **c**. Which plan would have been best in light of these findings? Explain.

Problems

LG 1   **P13.1** Refer to the table below:

	Fund A	Fund B
Beta	1.8	1.1
Investor A	20%	80%
Investor B	80%	20%

As between Investor A and Investor B, which is more likely to represent a retired couple? Why?

LG 1   **P13.2** Portfolio A and Portfolio B had the same holding period return last year. Most of the returns from Portfolio A came from dividends, while most of the returns from Portfolio B came from capital gains. Which portfolio is owned by a single working person making a high salary, and which is owned by a retired couple? Why?

LG 3   **P13.3** Mark Smith purchased 100 shares of Tomco Corporation in December 2007, at a total cost of $1,762. He held the shares for 15 months and then sold them, netting $2,500. During the period he held the stock, the company paid him $200 in cash dividends. How much, if any, was the capital gain realized upon the sale of stock? Calculate Mark's pretax HPR.

LG 3   **P13.4** Joe Smart purchased 1,000 shares of a speculative stock on January 2 for $2.00 per share. On July 1, he sold them for $9.50 per share. He uses an online broker that charges him $10 per trade. What was Joe's annualized HPR on this investment?

LG 3   **P13.5** Jill Clark invested $25,000 in the bonds of Industrial Aromatics, Inc. She held them for 13 months, at the end of which she sold them for $26,746. During the period of ownership she received $2,000 interest. Calculate the pretax and after-tax HPR on Jill's investment. Assume that she is in the 31% ordinary tax bracket (federal and state combined) and pays a 15% capital gains rate on dividends and on capital gains for holding periods longer than 12 months.

LG 3   **P13.6** Charlotte Smidt bought 2,000 shares of the balanced no-load LaJolla Fund exactly 1 year and 2 days ago for a NAV of $8.60 per share. During the year, the fund distributed investment income dividends of $0.32 per share and capital gains dividends of $0.38 per share. At the end of the year, Charlotte, who is in the 35% ordinary tax bracket (federal and state combined) and pays a 15% capital gains rate on dividends and on capital gains for holding periods longer than 12 months, realized $8.75 per share on the sale of all 2,000 shares. Calculate Charlotte's pretax and after-tax HPR on this transaction.

LG 3   **P13.7** Marilyn Gore, who is in a 33% ordinary tax bracket (federal and state combined) and pays a 15% capital gains rate on dividends and capital gains for holding periods longer than 12 months, purchased 10 options contracts for a total cost of $4,000 just over 1 year ago. Marilyn netted $4,700 upon the sale of the 10 contracts today. What are Marilyn's pretax and after-tax HPRs on this transaction?

LG 3   **P13.8** Mom and Pop had a portfolio of long-term bonds that they purchased many years ago. The bonds pay 12% interest annually, and the face value is $100,000. If

Mom and Pop are in the 25% tax bracket, what is their annual after tax HPR on this investment? (Assume it trades at par.)

LG 3

P13.9 On January 1, 2008, Simon Love's portfolio of 15 common stocks, completely equity-financed, had a market value of $264,000. At the end of May 2008, Simon sold one of the stocks, which had a beginning-of-year value of $26,300, for $31,500. He did not reinvest those or any other funds in the portfolio during the year. He received total dividends from stocks in his portfolio of $12,500 during the year. On December 31, 2008, Simon's portfolio had a market value of $250,000. Find the HPR on Simon's portfolio during the year ended December 31, 2008. (Measure the amount of withdrawn funds at their beginning-of-year value.)

LG 4

P13.10 Congratulations! Your portfolio returned 11% last year, 2% better than the market return of 9%. Your portfolio had a standard deviation of earnings equal to 18%, and the risk-free rate is equal to 6%. Calculate Sharpe's measure for your portfolio. If the market's Sharpe's measure is .3, did you do better or worse than the market from a risk/return perspective?

LG 4

P13.11 Niki Malone's portfolio earned a return of 11.8% during the year just ended. The portfolio's standard deviation of return was 14.1%. The risk-free rate is currently 6.2%. During the year, the return on the market portfolio was 9.0% and its standard deviation was 9.4%.
   a. Calculate Sharpe's measure for Niki Malone's portfolio for the year just ended.
   b. Compare the performance of Niki's portfolio found in part **a** to that of Hector Smith's portfolio, which has a Sharpe's measure of 0.43. Which portfolio performed better? Why?
   c. Calculate Sharpe's measure for the market portfolio for the year just ended.
   d. Use your findings in parts **a** and **c** to discuss the performance of Niki's portfolio relative to the market during the year just ended.

LG 4

P13.12 Your portfolio has a beta equal to 1.3. It returned 12% last year. The market returned 10%; the risk-free rate is 6%. Calculate Treynor's measure for your portfolio and the market. Did you earn a better return than the market given the risk you took?

LG 4

P13.13 During the year just ended, Anna Schultz's portfolio, which has a beta of 0.90, earned a return of 8.6%. The risk-free rate is currently 7.3%, and the return on the market portfolio during the year just ended was 9.2%.
   a. Calculate Treynor's measure for Anna's portfolio for the year just ended.
   b. Compare the performance of Anna's portfolio found in part **a** to that of Stacey Quant's portfolio, which has a Treynor's measure of 1.25%. Which portfolio performed better? Explain.
   c. Calculate Treynor's measure for the market portfolio for the year just ended.
   d. Use your findings in parts **a** and **c** to discuss the performance of Anna's portfolio relative to the market during the year just ended.

LG 4

P13.14 Your portfolio returned 13% last year, with a beta equal to 1.5. The market return was 10%, and the risk-free rate 6%. Did you earn more or less than the required rate of return on your portfolio? (Use Jensen's measure.)

LG 4

P13.15 Chee Chew's portfolio has a beta of 1.3 and earned a return of 12.9% during the year just ended. The risk-free rate is currently 7.8%. The return on the market portfolio during the year just ended was 11.0%.

a. Calculate Jensen's measure (Jensen's alpha) for Chee's portfolio for the year just ended.
b. Compare the performance of Chee's portfolio found in part **a** to that of Carri Uhl's portfolio, which has a Jensen's measure of −0.24. Which portfolio performed better? Explain.
c. Use your findings in part **a** to discuss the performance of Chee's portfolio during the period just ended.

LG 4   P13.16 The risk-free rate is currently 8.1%. Use the data in the accompanying table for the Fio family's portfolio and the market portfolio during the year just ended to answer the questions that follow.

Data Item	Fios' Portfolio	Market Portfolio
Rate of return	12.8%	11.2%
Standard deviation of return	13.5%	9.6%
Beta	1.10	1.00

a. Calculate Sharpe's measure for the portfolio and the market. Compare the 2 measures, and assess the performance of the Fios' portfolio during the year just ended.
b. Calculate Treynor's measure for the portfolio and the market. Compare the two, and assess the performance of the Fios' portfolio during the year just ended.
c. Calculate Jensen's measure (Jensen's alpha). Use it to assess the performance of the Fios' portfolio during the year just ended.
d. On the basis of your findings in parts **a**, **b**, and **c**, assess the performance of the Fios' portfolio during the year just ended.

LG 5   P13.17 Over the past 2 years, Jonas Cone has used a dollar-cost averaging formula to purchase $300 worth of FCI common stock each month. The price per share paid each month over the 2 years is given in the following table. Assume that Jonas paid no brokerage commissions on these transactions.

	Price per Share of FCI	
Month	Year 1	Year 2
January	$11.63	$11.38
February	11.50	11.75
March	11.50	12.00
April	11.00	12.00
May	11.75	12.13
June	12.00	12.50
July	12.38	12.75
August	12.50	13.00
September	12.25	13.25
October	12.50	13.00
November	11.85	13.38
December	11.50	13.50

a. How much was Jonas's total investment over the 2-year period?
b. How many shares did Jonas purchase over the 2-year period?
c. Use your findings in parts **a** and **b** to calculate Jonas's average cost per share of FCI.
d. What was the value of Jonas's holdings in FCI at the end of the second year?

LG 5   P13.18 Refer to the table below:

Time Period	Stock Price	Shares	MM Mutual Fund NAV	Shares
1	$20.00	1,000	$20.00	1,000
2	$25.00		$21.00	

Assume you are using a constant-dollar plan with a rebalancing trigger of $1,500. The stock price represents your speculative portfolio, and the MM mutual fund represents your conservative portfolio. What action, if any, should you take in time period 2? Be specific.

LG 5   P13.19 Refer to Problem 13.18 above. Now assume you are using a constant-ratio plan with a rebalance trigger of speculative-to-conservative of 1.25. What action, if any, should you take in time period 2? Be specific.

LG 5   P13.20 Refer to the table below:

Time Period	Stock Price	Shares	MM Mutual Fund NAV	Shares
1	$20.00	1,000	$20.00	1,000
2	$30.00	1,000	$19.00	1,000

Assume you are using a variable-ratio plan. You have decided that when the speculative portfolio reaches 60% of the total, you will reduce its proportion to 45%. What action, if any, should you take in time period 2? Be specific.

**See www.myfinancelab.com for Web Exercises,
Spreadsheets, and other online resources.**

Case Problem 13.1   *Assessing the Stalchecks' Portfolio Performance*

LG 3   LG 4   Mary and Nick Stalcheck have an investment portfolio containing 4 vehicles. It was developed to provide them with a balance between current income and capital appreciation. Rather than acquire mutual fund shares or diversify within a given class of investment vehicle, they developed their portfolio with the idea of diversifying across various types of vehicles. The portfolio currently contains common stock, industrial bonds, mutual fund shares, and options. They acquired each of these vehicles during the past 3 years, and they plan to invest in other vehicles sometime in the future.

Currently, the Stalchecks are interested in measuring the return on their investment and assessing how well they have done relative to the market. They hope that the return earned over the past calendar year is in excess of what they would have earned by investing in a portfolio consisting of the S&P 500 Stock Composite Index. Their research has indicated that the risk-free rate was 7.2% and that the (before-tax) return on the S&P 500 portfolio was 10.1% during the past year. With the aid of a friend, they have been able to estimate the beta of their portfolio, which was 1.20. In their analysis, they have planned to ignore taxes, because they feel their earnings have been adequately sheltered. Because they did not make any portfolio transactions during the past year, all of the Stalchecks' investments have been held more than 12 months and they would have to consider only unrealized capital gains, if any. To make the necessary calculations, the Stalchecks have gathered the following information on each of the four vehicles in their portfolio.

Common stock. They own 400 shares of KJ Enterprises common stock. KJ is a diversified manufacturer of metal pipe and is known for its unbroken stream of dividends. Over the past few years, it has entered new markets and, as a result, has offered moderate capital appreciation potential. Its share price has risen from $17.25 at the start of the last calendar year to $18.75 at the end of the year. During the year, quarterly cash dividends of $0.20, $0.20, $0.25, and $0.25 were paid.

Industrial bonds. The Stalchecks own 8 Cal Industries bonds. The bonds have a $1,000 par value, have a 9.250% coupon, and are due in 2018. They are A-rated by Moody's. The bond was quoted at 97.000 at the beginning of the year and ended the calendar year at 96.375%.

Mutual fund. The Stalchecks hold 500 shares in the Holt Fund, a balanced, no-load mutual fund. The dividend distributions on the fund during the year consisted of $0.60 in investment income and $0.50 in capital gains. The fund's NAV at the beginning of the calendar year was $19.45, and it ended the year at $20.02.

Options. The Stalchecks own 100 options contracts on the stock of a company they follow. The value of these contracts totaled $26,000 at the beginning of the calendar year. At year-end the total value of the options contracts was $29,000.

Questions

a.   Calculate the holding period return on a before-tax basis for each of these 4 investment vehicles.

b.   Assuming that the Stalchecks' ordinary income is currently being taxed at a combined (federal and state) tax rate of 38%, and that they would pay a 15% capital gains tax on dividends and capital gains for holding periods longer than 12 months, determine the after-tax HPR for each of their 4 investment vehicles.

c.   Recognizing that all gains on the Stalchecks' investments were unrealized, calculate the before-tax portfolio HPR for their 4-vehicle portfolio during the past calendar year. Evaluate this return relative to its current income and capital gain components.

d.   Use the HPR calculated in question **c** to compute Jensen's measure (Jensen's alpha). Use that measure to analyze the performance of the Stalchecks' portfolio on a risk-adjusted, market-adjusted basis. Comment on your finding. Is it reasonable to use Jensen's measure to evaluate a 4-vehicle portfolio? Why or why not?

e.   On the basis of your analysis in questions **a, c,** and **d,** what, if any, recommendations might you offer the Stalchecks relative to the revision of their portfolio? Explain your recommendations.

Case Problem 13.2   *Evaluating Formula Plans: Charles Spurge's Approach*

LG 5   Charles Spurge, a mathematician with Ansco Petroleum Company, wishes to develop a rational basis for timing his portfolio transactions. He currently holds a security portfolio with a market value of nearly $100,000, divided equally between a very conservative, low-beta common stock, ConCam United, and a highly speculative, high-beta stock, Fleck Enterprises. On the basis of his reading of the investments' literature, Charles does not believe it is necessary to diversify one's portfolio across 8 to 15 securities. His own feeling, based on his independent mathematical analysis, is that one can achieve the same results by holding a 2-security portfolio in which one security is very conservative and the other is highly speculative. His feelings on this point will not be altered. He plans to continue to hold such a 2-security portfolio until he finds that his theory does not work. During the past couple of years, he has earned a rate of return in excess of the risk-adjusted, market-adjusted rate expected on such a portfolio.

Charles's current interest centers on possibly developing his own formula plan for timing portfolio transactions. The current stage of his analysis focuses on the evaluation of 4 commonly used formula plans in order to isolate the desirable features of each. The 4 plans being considered are (1) dollar-cost averaging, (2) the constant-dollar plan, (3) the constant-ratio plan, and (4) the variable-ratio plan. Charles's analysis of the plans will involve the use of 2 types of data. Dollar-cost averaging is a passive buy-and-hold strategy in which the periodic investment is held constant. The other plans are more active in that they involve periodic purchases and sales within the portfolio. Thus, differing data are needed to evaluate the plans.

For evaluating the dollar-cost averaging plan, Charles decided he would assume an investment of $500 at the end of each 45-day period. He chose to use 45-day time intervals to achieve certain brokerage fee savings that would be available by making larger transactions. The $500 per 45 days totaled $4,000 for the year and equaled the total amount Charles invested during the past year. (*Note:* For convenience, the returns earned on the portions of the $4,000 that remain uninvested during the year are ignored.) In evaluating this plan, he would assume that half ($250) was invested in the conservative stock (ConCam United) and the other half in the speculative stock (Fleck Enterprises). The share prices for each of the stocks at the end of the eight 45-day periods when purchases were to be made are given in the accompanying table.

Period	Price per Share	
	ConCam	Fleck
1	$22.13	$22.13
2	21.88	24.50
3	21.88	25.38
4	22.00	28.50
5	22.25	21.88
6	22.13	19.25
7	22.00	21.50
8	22.25	23.63

To evaluate the 3 other plans, Charles decided to begin with a $4,000 portfolio evenly split between the 2 stocks. He chose to use $4,000, because that amount would correspond to the total amount invested in the 2 stocks over 1 year using dollar-cost averaging. He planned to use the same 8 points in time given earlier to assess the portfolio and make transfers within it if required. For each of the 3 plans evaluated using these data, he established the following triggering points.

Constant-dollar plan. Each time the speculative portion of the portfolio is worth 13% more or less than its initial value of $2,000, the portfolio is rebalanced to bring the speculative portion back to its initial $2,000 value.

Constant-ratio plan. Each time the ratio of the value of the speculative portion of the portfolio to the value of the conservative portion is (1) greater than or equal to 1.15 or (2) less than or equal to 0.84, the portfolio is rebalanced through sale or purchase, respectively, to bring the ratio back to its initial value of 1.0.

Variable-ratio plan. Each time the value of the speculative portion of the portfolio rises above 54% of the total value of the portfolio, its proportion is reduced to 46%. Each time the value of the speculative portion of the portfolio drops below 38% of the total value of the portfolio, its proportion is raised to 50%.

Questions

a. Under the dollar-cost averaging plan, determine the total number of shares purchased, the average cost per share, and the year-end portfolio value expressed both in dollars and as a percentage of the amount invested for (1) the conservative stock, (2) the speculative stock, and (3) the total portfolio.

b. Using the constant-dollar plan, determine the year-end portfolio value expressed both in dollars and as a percentage of the amount initially invested for (1) the conservative portion, (2) the speculative portion, and (3) the total portfolio.

c. Repeat question **b** for the constant-ratio plan. Be sure to answer all parts.

d. Repeat question **b** for the variable-ratio plan. Be sure to answer all parts.

e. Compare and contrast your results from questions **a** through **d**. You may want to summarize them in tabular form. Which plan would appear to have been most beneficial in timing Charles's portfolio activities during the past year? Explain.

Excel with Spreadsheets

While most people believe that it is not possible to consistently time the market, there are several plans that allow investors to time purchases and sales of securities. These are referred to as formula plans—mechanical methods of managing a portfolio that attempt to take advantage of cyclical price movements. The objective is to mitigate the level of risk facing the investor.

One such formula plan is dollar-cost averaging. Here, a fixed dollar amount is invested in a security at fixed intervals. One objective is to increase the value of the given security over time. If prices decline, more shares are purchased; when market prices increase, fewer shares are purchased per period. The essence is that an investor is more likely not to buy overvalued securities.

Over the past 12 months, March 2008 through February 2009, Mrs. Paddock has used the dollar-cost averaging formula to purchase $1,000 worth of Neo common stock each month. The monthly price per share paid over the 12-month period is given below. Assume that Mrs. Paddock paid no brokerage commissions on these transactions.

Create a spreadsheet model similar to the spreadsheet for Table 13.9, which you can view at www.myfinancelab.com, to analyze the following investment situation for Neo common stock through dollar-cost averaging.

2008	March	$14.30
	April	16.18
	May	18.37
	June	16.25
	July	14.33
	August	15.14
	September	15.93
	October	19.36
	November	23.25
	December	18.86
2009	January	22.08
	February	22.01

Questions

a. What is the total investment over the period from March 2008 through February 2009?

b. What is the total number of Neo shares purchased over the 12-month period?

c. What is the average cost per share?

d. What is the year-end (February 2009) portfolio value?

e. What is the profit or loss as of the end of February 2009?

f. What is the return on the portfolio after the 12-month period?

Chapter 14

Options: Puts and Calls

After studying this chapter, you should be able to:

LG 1 Discuss the basic nature of options in general and puts and calls in particular, and understand how these investment vehicles work.

LG 2 Describe the options market, and note key options provisions, including strike prices and expiration dates.

LG 3 Explain how put and call options are valued and the forces that drive options prices in the marketplace.

LG 4 Describe the profit potential of puts and calls, and note some popular put and call investment strategies.

LG 5 Explain the profit potential and loss exposure from writing covered call options, and discuss how writing options can be used as a strategy for enhancing investment returns.

LG 6 Describe market index options, puts and calls on foreign currencies, and LEAPS, and discuss how these securities can be used by investors.

Put, call, strike price, naked option, in-the-money option, market index option—these terms are all part of the mysterious world of options. From what you have heard about options, you may wonder why you even need to know about them. Options can indeed be speculative investments that can lead to losses for even the most experienced investor.

Options can also play a role in the conservative investor's portfolio. They are versatile investments, a form of insurance that allows you to hedge risk. For example, you can protect stock holdings from a decline in market price, increase income against current stock holdings, prepare to buy a stock at a lower price, position yourself for a big market move even when you don't know which way prices will go, and benefit from a rising stock price without buying the actual stock.

When might options work to your advantage? Suppose you are going to buy a car in five months and plan to sell stock to pay for it. You could sell your stock now and hold the funds. But if the stock price is currently down and you think it will come back by the time you need the funds, you can use options to lock in the current price and still have the opportunity to participate in the upside. Assume you own 400 shares of Amazon.com, Inc. (AMZN). Currently the stock is trading at about $27.50 but has been as high as $50 in the past 52 weeks. You can buy *put options* with a strike price of $27.50 that expire in six months; they will cost $2.95 a share, or $1,180 total ($2.95 x 400 shares). The put locks in your right to sell at $27.50 if the stock drops below that price. If the price rises, you will not exercise your option. If the price rises more than the $2.95 a share you paid, to more than $30.45, you make a profit. The put option puts a floor under your losses while allowing an opportunity for the stock price to rebound.

This is just one example of how you can use options in your portfolio. In this chapter you will learn the essential characteristics of options and how you can use them effectively in your investment program.

Source: Stock and option price data downloaded from http://finance.yahoo.com on July 31, 2006.

Put and Call Options

LG 1   LG 2

When investors buy shares of common or preferred stock, they are entitled to all the rights and privileges of ownership. Investors who acquire bonds or convertible issues are also entitled to the benefits of ownership. Stocks, bonds, and convertibles are all examples of *financial assets*. They represent financial claims on the issuing organization. In contrast, investors who buy options acquire nothing more than the *right* to subsequently buy or sell other, related securities. An **option** gives the holder the right to buy or sell a certain amount of an underlying asset (such as common stocks) at a specified price over a specified period of time.

option
a security that gives the holder the right to buy or sell a certain amount of an underlying financial asset at a specified price for a specified period of time.

Options are *contractual instruments*, whereby two parties enter into a contract to give something of value to the other. The option *buyer* has the right to buy or sell an underlying asset for a given period of time, at a price that was fixed at the time of the contract. The option *seller* stands ready to buy or sell the underlying asset according to the terms of the contract, for which the seller has been paid a certain amount of money. We'll look at two basic kinds of options in this chapter: *puts* and *calls*, both of which enjoy considerable popularity as investment vehicles.

In addition, there are two other types of options: *rights* and *warrants*. Rights are like short-term call options that originate when corporations raise money by issuing new shares of common stocks. (See Chapter 6 for a discussion of *rights offerings*.) Rights enable stockholders to buy shares of the new issue at a specified price for a specified, fairly short period of time. Because their life span is so short—usually no more than a few weeks—stock rights hold very little investment appeal for the average individual investor. In contrast, warrants are long-term options that give their holders the right to buy a certain number of shares in a certain company for a given period of time (often fairly long—five to ten years or more). Warrants are usually created as "sweeteners" to bond issues, and are used to make the issues more attractive to investors. In essence, the buyer of one of these bonds also receives one or more warrants, as an *equity kicker*. Interested readers can find out more about rights and warrants at our Web site.

WEBEXTENSION

For a more extensive discussion of rights and warrants, including their basic characteristics and investment attributes, see this textbook's Web site at

www.myfinancelab.com

▌Basic Features and Behavioral Characteristics of Puts and Calls

One of the market phenomena of the 1970s was the remarkable performance and investment popularity of stock options, particularly puts and calls on common stock. By the early 1980s, the interest in options spilled over to other kinds of financial assets. Today, investors can trade puts and calls on: common stock, stock indexes, exchange-traded funds, foreign currencies, debt instruments, and commodities and financial futures.

As we will see, although the underlying financial assets may vary, the basic features and behavioral characteristics of these securities are pretty much the same. Regardless of the type, much of the popularity of options stems from the fact that *investors can buy a lot of price action with a limited amount of capital, while nearly always enjoying limited exposure to risk.*

put
a negotiable instrument that
enables the holder to sell
the underlying security at
a specified price over a set
period of time.

call
a negotiable instrument that
gives the holder the right to
buy securities at a stated price
within a certain time period.

derivative securities
securities, such as puts, calls,
and other options, that derive
their value from the price
behavior of an underlying
real or financial asset.

leverage
the ability to obtain a given
equity position at a reduced
capital investment, thereby
magnifying returns.

A Negotiable Contract   Puts and calls are negotiable instruments, issued in bearer form, that allow the holder to buy or sell a specified amount of a specified security at a specified price. For example, a put or a call on common stock covers 100 shares of stock in a specific company. A **put** enables the holder to sell the underlying security at the specified price (known as the *exercise* or *strike price*) over a set period of time. A **call**, in contrast, gives the holder the right to buy the security at the stated (strike) price within a certain time period. As with any option, there are no voting rights, no privileges of ownership, and no interest or dividend income. Instead, *puts and calls possess value to the extent that they allow the holder to participate in the price behavior of the underlying financial asset.*

Because puts and calls derive their value from the price behavior of some other real or financial asset, they are known as **derivative securities**. Rights and warrants, as well as futures contracts (which we'll study in Chapter 15), are also derivative securities. Although certain segments of this market are for big institutional investors only, there's still ample room for the individual investor. Many of these securities—especially those listed on exchanges—are readily available to, and are actively traded by, individuals as well as institutions.

One of the key features of puts and calls is the attractive **leverage** opportunities they offer. Such opportunities exist because of the low prices these options carry relative to the market prices of the underlying financial assets. What's more, the lower cost in no way affects the payoff or capital appreciation potential of your investment. To illustrate, consider a call on a common stock that gives you the right to buy 100 shares of a $50 stock at a (strike) price of $45 a share. The call would trade at an effective price of only $5 a share—the difference between the $50 market price of the common and the $45 price at which it can be purchased, as specified on the call. Because a single stock option always involves 100 shares of stock, the actual cost of your $5 call would be $500. Even so, for $500 you get (just about) all the capital gains potential of a $5,000 investment—or at least that part of the capital gains that occurs over the life of the option.

HOTLINKS

Characteristics and risks of standardized options are available at:

www.optionsclearing.com/publications/
risks/riskchap1.jsp

option maker (writer)
the individual or institution
that writes/creates put and
call options.

Maker Versus Buyer   Puts and calls are a unique type of security because they are *not* issued by the organizations that issue the underlying stock or financial asset. Instead, they *are created by investors*. It works like this: Suppose you want to sell to another investor the right to buy 100 shares of common stock. You could do this by "writing a call." The individual (or institution) writing the option is known as the **option maker** or **writer**. As the option writer, you sell the option in the market and so are entitled to receive the price paid for the put or call (less modest commissions and other transaction costs). The put or call option is now a full-fledged financial asset and trades in the open market much like any other security.

Puts and calls are both written (sold) and purchased through securities brokers and dealers. In fact, they're as easy to buy and sell as common stocks; a simple phone call, or a few mouse clicks, is all it takes. The writer stands behind the option, because it is the *writer* who must buy or deliver the stocks or other financial assets according to the terms of the option. (*Note:* The writers of puts and calls *have a legally binding obligation* to stand behind the terms of the contracts they have written. The buyer can just walk away from the deal if it turns sour; the writer cannot.)

Puts and calls are written for a variety of reasons, most of which we will explore below. At this point, suffice it to say that writing options can be a viable investment strategy and can be a profitable course of action because, more often than not, *options expire worthless.*

How Puts and Calls Work Taking the *buyer's* point of view, we will briefly examine how puts and calls work and how they derive their value. To start, it is best to look at their profit-making potential. For example, consider the call described earlier: for $500, you can buy a call on the stock currently priced at $50 a share. Thus, you purchase 100 shares of the stock at a fixed price of $50 each. As an investor, you hope for a rise in the price of the underlying security (in this case, common stock). What is the profit potential from this transaction if the price of the stock does indeed move up to, say, $75 by the expiration date on the call?

The answer is that you will earn $25 ($75 − $50) on each of the 100 shares of stock in the call. In other words, you'll earn a total gross profit of $2,500 from your $500 investment. This is so because you have the right to buy 100 shares of the stock, from the option writer, at a price of $50 each, and then immediately turn around and sell them in the market for $75 a share.

Could you have made the same profit ($2,500) by investing directly in the common stock? Yes, but because you would have had to invest $5,000 (100 shares × $50 per share), your rate of return would have been much lower. The return potential of common stocks and calls differs considerably. This difference attracts investors and speculators to calls whenever the price outlook for the underlying financial asset is positive. Such differential returns are, of course, the direct result of *leverage*, which rests on the principle of reducing the level of capital required in a given investment *without materially affecting the dollar amount of the payoff or capital appreciation from that investment.* Note that although our illustration used common stock, this same valuation principle applies to any of the other financial assets that may underlie call options, such as market indexes, foreign currencies, and futures contracts.

A similar situation can be worked out for puts. Assume that for the same $50 stock you could pay $500 and buy a put to *sell* 100 shares of the stock at a strike price of $50 each. As the buyer of a put, you want the price of the stock to *drop*. Assume that your expectations are correct and the price of the stock does indeed drop, to $25 a share. Here again, you realize a gross profit of $25 for each of the 100 shares in the put. To realize this profit you could go to the market and buy 100 shares of the stock at $25 a share and then immediately sell them to the writer of the put at a price of $50 per share.

Fortunately, put and call investors do *not* have to exercise their options and make simultaneous buy and sell transactions in order to receive their profit. That's because *the options themselves have value and can be traded in the secondary market.* The value of both puts and calls is directly linked to the market price of the underlying financial asset, so the *value of a call* increases as the market price of the underlying security *rises.* Likewise, the *value of a put* increases as the price of the security *declines.* Thus, *you can get your money out of options by selling them in the open market,* just as with any other security.

Advantages and Disadvantages The major advantage of investing in puts and calls is the leverage they offer. This feature also limits exposure to risk,

INVESTOR FACTS

AMERICAN OR EUROPEAN?— Put and call options can be issued in either *American* or *European* form. Actually, this has absolutely nothing to do with *where* the options are traded, but rather with *when* they can be exercised. An **American** option can be exercised on any business day that the option is traded. A **European** option can be exercised only on the day of expiration. For all practical purposes, most investors couldn't care less whether an option is American or European. The reason: Just because an option can't be exercised prior to expiration doesn't mean you have to hold it to maturity. Any option—American or European—can be sold at any time, on or before its expiration.

because you can lose only a set amount of money (the purchase price of the option). Also appealing is the fact that puts and calls can be used profitably when the price of the underlying security goes up *or* down.

A major disadvantage of puts and calls is that the holder enjoys neither interest or dividend income nor any other ownership benefits. Moreover, because puts and calls have limited lives, you have a limited time frame in which to capture desired price behavior. Another disadvantage is that puts and calls themselves are a bit unusual, and many of their trading strategies are a bit complex. Thus, you must possess special knowledge and must fully understand the subtleties of this trading vehicle.

▌ Options Markets

Although the concept of options can be traced back to the writings of Aristotle, options trading in the United States did not begin until the late 1700s. Even then, up to the early 1970s, this market remained fairly small, largely unorganized, and the almost-private domain of a handful of specialists and traders. All of this changed, however, on April 26, 1973, when the Chicago Board Options Exchange (CBOE) opened.

Conventional Options   Prior to the creation of the CBOE, put and call options trading was conducted in the over-the-counter market through a handful of specialized dealers. Investors who wished to purchase puts and calls contacted their own brokers, who contacted the options dealers. The dealers would find investors willing to write the options. If the buyer wished to exercise an option, he or she did so with the writer and no one else—a system that largely prohibited any secondary trading. On the other hand, there were virtually no limits to what could be written, so long as the buyer was willing to pay the price. Put and call options were written on New York and American exchange stocks, as well as on regional and over-the-counter securities, for as short a time as 30 days and for as long as a year. Over-the-counter options, known today as **conventional options**, are now used almost exclusively by institutional investors. Accordingly, our attention in this chapter will focus on listed markets, like the CBOE, where individual investors do most of their options trading.

conventional options
put and call options sold over the counter.

listed options
put and call options listed and traded on organized securities exchanges, such as the CBOE.

Listed Options   The creation of the CBOE signaled the birth of **listed options**, a term that describes put and call options traded on organized exchanges. The CBOE launched trading in calls on just 16 firms. From these rather humble beginnings, there evolved in a relatively short time a large and active market for listed options. Today, trading in listed options is done in both puts and calls and takes place on six exchanges. In addition to the CBOE, options are traded on the International Securities Exchange (ISE), AMEX, the Philadelphia Exchange (PHLX), NYSE Arca (PCX), and the Boston Options Exchange (BOX). The three newest participants in this market are the ISE, the Boston Options Exchange, and NYSE Arca (which is the result of a merger among the NYSE, the Pacific Stock Exchange, and Archipelago Holdings); all three offer fully electronic trading platforms. In total, *put and call options are now traded on over 3,000 different stocks, with many of those options listed on multiple exchanges.* In addition to stocks, the options exchanges also offer listed options on stock indexes, exchange-traded funds, debt securities, foreign currencies, and even commodities and financial futures.

Listed options not only provide a convenient market for puts and calls, but also standardized expiration dates and exercise prices. The listed options exchanges created a clearinghouse that eliminated direct ties between buyers and writers of options and reduced the cost of executing put and call transactions. They also developed an active secondary market, with wide distribution of price information. As a result, it is now as easy to trade a listed option as a listed stock.

▍ Stock Options

The advent of the CBOE and the other listed option exchanges had a dramatic impact on the trading volume of puts and calls. Today well over 1.5 billion listed options contracts are traded each year, most of which are stock options. In 2005, *more than 90%* (or 1.37 billion contracts) *were stock options*. That year, the volume of contracts traded was divided among the six options exchanges as follows:

	Total Number of Contracts Traded (millions)	Percentage of the Total
CBOE	468.2	31.1%
ISE	448.7	29.8
AMEX	201.8	13.4
PHLX	162.6	10.8
PCX	144.8	9.6
BOX	78.2	5.2
Total	**1504.3**	**100.0%**

The CBOE, AMEX, and ISE account for about *75% of all stock options trading,* while the CBOE alone handles *over 85% of all index options trading.*

Listed options exchanges have unquestionably added a new dimension to investing. In order to avoid serious (and possibly expensive) mistakes with these securities, however, you must fully understand their basic features. In the sections that follow, we will look closely at the investment attributes of stock options, and the trading strategies for using them. Later, we'll explore stock-index (and ETF) options and then briefly look at other types of puts and calls, including interest rate and currency options, and long-term options. (Futures options will be taken up in Chapter 15, after we study futures contracts.)

Stock Option Provisions Because of their low unit cost, stock options (or *equity options,* as they're also called) are very popular with individual investors. Except for the underlying financial asset, they are like any other type of put or call, subject to the same kinds of contract provisions and market forces. There are two provisions that are especially important for stock options: (1) the price—known as the *strike price*—at which the stock can be bought or sold, and (2) the amount of time remaining until expiration. As we'll see below, both the strike price and the time remaining to expiration have a significant bearing on their valuation and pricing.

strike price
the stated price at which you
can buy a security with a call
or sell a security with a put.

Strike Price The **strike price** represents the price contract between the buyer of the option and the writer. For a call, the strike price specifies the price at which each of the 100 shares of stock can be bought. For a put, it represents the price at which the stock can be sold to the writer. With conventional (OTC) options, there are no constraints on the strike price. With listed options, strike prices are *standardized:*

- Stocks selling for less than $25 per share carry strike prices that are set in 2½ dollar increments ($7.50, $10.00, $12.50, $15, and so on.).

- In general, the increments jump to $5 for stocks selling between $25 and $200 per share, although a number of securities in the $25 to $50 range are now allowed to use 2½ dollar increments.

- For stocks that trade at more than $200 a share, the strike price is set in $10 increments.

- Unlike most equity options, options on exchange-traded funds (discussed more fully later in this chapter) all have strike prices set in $1 increments.

In all cases, the strike price is adjusted for substantial stock dividends and stock splits.

expiration date
the date at which an option
expires.

Expiration Date The **expiration date** is also an important provision. It specifies the life of the option, just as the maturity date indicates the life of a bond. The expiration date, in effect, specifies the length of the contract between the holder and the writer of the option. Thus, if you hold a six-month call on Sears with a strike price of, say, $40, that option gives you the right to buy 100 shares of Sears common stock at $40 per share at any time over the next six months. *No matter what happens to the market price of the stock,* you can use your call option to buy 100 shares of Sears at $40 a share. If the price of the stock moves up, you stand to make money. If it goes down, you'll be out the cost of the option.

Expiration dates for options in the conventional market can fall on any working day of the month. In contrast, expiration dates are *standardized* in the *listed* options market. The exchanges initially created three expiration cycles for all listed options:

- January, April, July, and October.

- February, May, August, and November.

- March, June, September, and December.

Each issue is assigned to one of these three cycles. The exchanges still use the same three expiration cycles, but they've been altered so that investors are always able to trade in the two nearest (current and following) months, plus the next two closest months in the option's regular expiration cycle. For reasons that are pretty obvious, this is sometimes referred to as a *two-plus-two* schedule.

For example, if the current month (also called the *front month*) is January, then available options in the *January cycle* would be: January, February, April, and July. These represent the two current months (January and February) and the next two months in the cycle (April and July). Likewise, available contracts for the *February cycle* would be January, February, May, and August; available contracts for the *March cycle* would be January, February, March, and June. The expiration dates, based on the front months, continue rolling over in this way during the course of the year. The following table demonstrates the available contracts under the two-plus-two system for the months of February and June:

Front Month	Cycle	Available Contracts
February	January	February, March, April, July
February	February	February, March, May, August
February	March	February, March, June, September
June	January	June, July, October, January
June	February	June, July, August, November
June	March	June, July, September, December

Given the month of expiration, the actual day of expiration is always the same: the Saturday following the third Friday of each expiration month. Thus, for all practical purposes, *listed options always expire on the third Friday of the month of expiration.*

Put and Call Transactions Option traders are subject to commission and transaction costs whenever they buy or sell an option, or whenever they write an option. The writing of puts and calls is subject to normal transaction costs; these costs effectively represent remuneration to the broker or dealer for *selling* the option.

Listed options have their own marketplace and quotation system. Finding the price (or *premium,* as it's called) of a listed stock option is fairly easy, as the options quotations in Figure 14.1 (on page 618) indicate. Note that quotes are provided for calls and puts separately. For each option, quotes are listed for various combinations of strike prices and expiration dates. Because there are so many options and a substantial number of them are rarely traded, financial publications like the *Wall Street Journal* list quotes only for the more actively traded options. However, unlike index options (which we'll examine later in this chapter), *quotations for equity options are not listed directly in the Wall Street Journal.* Instead, you have to go to the *Wall Street Journal*'s Web site, www.wsj.com/free, to obtain the latest quotes for *all listed equity options.* Even here, the quotes listed are only for the options that actually traded on the date in question. For example, in Figure 14.1, there may be many other options available on eBay, but only the ones that actually traded (on Thursday, June 1, 2006) are listed.

The quotes are standardized: The name of the company and the closing price of the underlying stock are listed first; note that Ebay stock closed at $33.08. The strike price is listed next, followed by the expiration date (or month in which the option expires). Then the volume and closing prices of the call (and/or put) options are quoted relative to their strike prices and expiration dates. For example, a June (2006) eBay *call* with a strike price of $30 was quoted at $3.20 (which translates into a dollar price of $320 because stock options trade in 100 share lots). In contrast, a June (2006) eBay *put* with the same strike price ($30) was quoted at 0.10 (or just $10 for each 100 share put).

FIGURE 14.1   Quotations for Listed Stock Options

The quotes for puts and calls are listed side by side. In addition to the closing price of the option, the latest price of the underlying security is shown, along with the strike price on the option. (*Source: Wall Street Journal Online*, at **www.wsj.com/free**, June 1, 2006.)

Call option quotes ————

Name of company ————

Market price of the underlying common stock ————

Strike price on the option ————

OPTION/STRIKE		EXP	-CALL-		-PUT-	
			VOL	LAST	VOL	LAST
Alcan	50	Jun	1,762	3.70	869	1.10
52.51	50	Jul	947	5.20	425	2.25
52.51	55	Jun	919	1.15	131	3.50
52.51	55	Jul	5,376	2.55	1,169	4.70
52.51	55	Sep	1,370	3.70	11	5.90
52.51	60	Sep	4,274	1.90	20	9.70
Alcatl	15	Sep	759	.50	22	2
Blckbstr	5	Oct	2,106	.50	...	...
Boeing	85	Jun	1,139	1.10	205	2.35
BostSc	25	Nov	1,101	.50	...	...
BrMySq	22.50	Jun	920	2.70	201	0.05
25.15	22.50	Jul	9,166	2.80	70	0.15
25.15	25	Jun	2,906	.60	2,777	0.40
25.15	25	Jul	1,319	.75	2,893	0.80
Broadcm	35	Jun	2,357	1.15	448	1.40
34.70	37.50	Jun	1,128	.35	86	3.10
34.70	40	Jun	1,471	.10	35	5.30
34.70	42.50	Jul	3,564	.50	...	...
Chevron	60	Jun	893	1.20	1,673	1.15
59.98	65	Sep	750	1.30	2	6.10
ChicBdglr	17.50	Jul	...	...	2,500	0.10
24.46	25	Jul	2,582	1.35	12	1.85
24.46	30	Jan	747	1.40	217	6.30
ChiMerc	430	Jun	447	29.20	794	4.20
456.20	440	Jun	1,265	22	573	6.60
456.20	450	Jun	1,087	15	433	10
ETrade	25	Jun	1,592	.35	81	0.95
24.34	25	Jul	3,614	.88	145	1.45
eBay	30	Jun	790	3.20	512	0.10
33.08	32.50	Jul	957	2.30	518	1.55
33.08	35	Jun	1,071	.30	471	2.25
DJIA Diam	90	Dec	...	...	2,211	0.45
112.40	110	Jun	1,730	3	1,604	0.45
112.40	111	Jun	3,102	2.30	771	0.60
112.40	112	Jun	4,164	1.45	1,431	0.90
112.40	112	Jul	1,255	2.60	2,947	1.70
112.40	113	Jun	5,879	.85	3,594	1.20
Microsft	19.50	Jan	160	4.20	2,187	0.55
22.82	20	Jun	3,234	2.85	...	...
22.82	20	Jul	3,325	3	242	0.15
22.82	20	Jan	2,475	4	814	0.60
22.82	22	Jan	4,643	2.40	9,234	1.20
22.82	22.50	Jun	21,052	.60	5,950	0.25
22.82	22.50	Jul	15,273	1.05	3,843	0.60
22.82	22.50	Oct	8,624	1.70	455	1.10

———— Put option quotes

———— Number of July 2006 Alcan puts traded (with a strike price of 55)

———— Month of expiration (July 2006)

———— Price of a January 2007 call (that carries a strike price of 30)

———— Number of July 2006 eBay calls traded (with a strike price of 32.50)

———— Quotes for an **ETF option** (Dow Diamonds)

———— Price of an October 2006 put (that carries a strike price of 22.50)

CONCEPTS IN REVIEW

14.1   Describe *put* and *call* options. Are they issued like other corporate securities?

14.2   What are *listed options,* and how do they differ from *conventional options?*

14.3   What are the main investment attractions of put and call options? What are the risks?

14.4   What is a *stock option?* What is the difference between a stock option and a *derivative security?* Describe a derivative security and give several examples.

14.5 What is a *strike price?* How does it differ from the market price of the stock?

14.6 Why do put and call options have expiration dates? Is there a market for options that have passed their expiration dates?

Options Pricing and Trading

| LG 3 | | LG 4 | | LG 5 |

The value of a put or call depends to a large extent on the market behavior of the financial asset that underlies the option. Getting a firm grip on the current and expected future value of a put or call is extremely important to options traders and investors. Thus, to get the most from any options trading program, you must understand how options are priced in the market. *Continuing to use stock options as a basis of discussion,* let's look now at the basic principles of options valuation and pricing. We'll start with a brief review of how profits are derived from puts and calls. Then we'll take a look at several ways in which investors can use these options.

▮ The Profit Potential from Puts and Calls

Although the quoted market price of a put or call is affected by such factors as time to expiration, stock volatility, and market interest rates, by far the most important variable is the *price behavior of the underlying common stock.* This is the variable that drives any significant moves in the price of the option and that determines the option's profit (return) potential. When the price of the underlying stock *moves up, calls do well.* When the price of the underlying stock *drops, puts do well.* Such performance also explains why it's important to get a good handle on the expected future price behavior of a stock *before* you buy or sell (write) an option.

Figure 14.2 (page 620) graphically illustrates the typical price behavior of an option. The diagram on the left depicts a call, the one on the right a put. The *call* diagram assumes you pay $500 for a call that carries a strike price of $50. It shows what happens to the value of the option when the price of the stock increases. Observe that a call does not gain in value until the price of the stock *advances past the stated exercise price* ($50). Also, because it costs $500 to buy the call, the stock has to move up another 5 points (from $50 to $55) in order for you to recover the premium and thereby reach a break-even point. So long as the stock continues to rise in price, everything from there on out is profit. Once the premium is recouped, the profit from the call position is limited only by the extent to which the stock price increases over the remaining life of the contract.

The value of a put is also derived from the price of the underlying stock, except that their respective market prices move in opposite directions. The *put* diagram in Figure 14.2 assumes you buy a put for $500 and obtain the right to sell the underlying stock at $50 a share. It shows that the value of the put remains constant until the market price of the corresponding stock *drops to the exercise price* ($50) on the put. Then, as the price of the stock continues to fall, the value of the option increases. Again, note that because the put cost $500, you don't start making money on the investment until the price of the

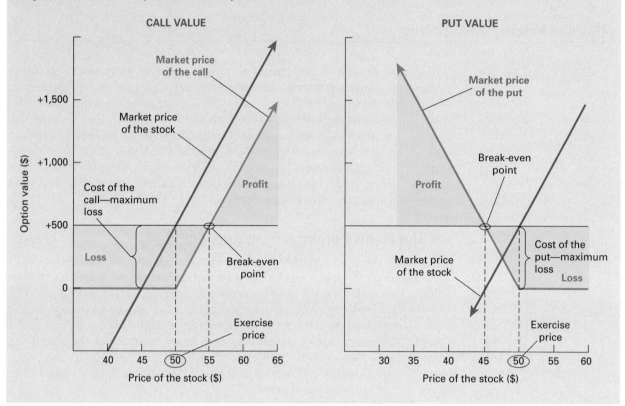

FIGURE 14.2   **The Valuation Properties of Put and Call Options**

The value of a put or call reflects the price behavior of its underlying common stock (or other financial asset). The cost of the option has been recovered when the option passes its break-even point. After that, the profit potential of a put or call is limited only by the price behavior of the underlying asset and by the length of time to the expiration of the option.

stock drops below the break-even point of $45 a share. Beyond that point, the profit from the put is defined by the extent to which the price of the underlying stock continues to fall over the remaining life of the option.

▮ Fundamental Value

As we have seen, the intrinsic value of a put or call depends ultimately on the exercise price stated on the option, as well as on the prevailing market price of the underlying common stock. More specifically, the *fundamental value of a call* is determined according to the following simple formula:

Equation 14.1 ➤

$$\text{Fundamental value of a call} = \left(\begin{array}{c} \text{Market price of} \\ \text{underlying} \\ \text{common stock,} \\ \text{or other} \\ \text{financial asset} \end{array} - \begin{array}{c} \text{Strike price} \\ \text{on} \\ \text{the call} \end{array} \right) \times 100$$

$$V = (MP - SPC) \times 100$$

In other words, the fundamental value of a call is merely the difference between market price and strike price. As implied in Equation 14.1, a call has an intrinsic value whenever the market price of the underlying financial asset exceeds the strike price stipulated on the call. A simple illustration will show that a call carrying a strike price of $50 on a stock currently trading at $60 has an intrinsic (fundamental) value of $1,000: ($60 − $50) × 100 = $10 × 100 = $1,000.

A put, on the other hand, cannot be valued in the same way, because puts and calls allow the holder to do different things. To find the *fundamental value of a put*, we must change the order of the equation a bit:

Equation 14.2 ➤

$$\text{Fundamental value of a put} = \left(\begin{array}{c} \text{Strike price} \\ \text{on} \\ \text{the put} \end{array} - \begin{array}{c} \text{Market price of} \\ \text{underlying} \\ \text{common stock,} \\ \text{or other} \\ \text{financial asset} \end{array} \right) \times 100$$

$$V = (SPP - MP) \times 100$$

In this case, a put has value so long as the market price of the underlying stock (or financial asset) is less than the strike price stipulated on the put.

in-the-money
a call option with a strike price less than the market price of the underlying security; a put option whose strike price is greater than the market price of the underlying security.

out-of-the-money
a call option with no real value because the strike price exceeds the market price of the stock; a put option whose market price exceeds the strike price.

In-the-Money/Out-of-the-Money When written, options do not necessarily have to carry strike prices at the prevailing market prices of the underlying common stocks. Also, as an option subsequently trades on listed exchanges, the price of the option will move in response to moves in the price of the underlying common stock. When a call has a strike price that is *less than* the market price of the underlying common stock, it has a positive intrinsic value and is known as an **in-the-money** option. A major portion of the option price in this case is based on (derived from) the fundamental value of the call. When the strike price of the call *exceeds* the market price of the stock, the call has no "real" value, in which case it is known as an **out-of-the-money** option. Because the option has no intrinsic value, its price is made up solely of investment premium.

As you might expect, the situation is reversed for put options: A put is considered in-the-money when its strike price is greater than the market price of the stock. It's considered out-of-the-money when the market price of the stock exceeds the strike price. These terms are much more than exotic names given to options. As we will see, they characterize the investment behavior of options and can affect return and risk.

option premium
the quoted price the investor pays to buy a listed put or call option.

Option Prices and Premiums Put and call values, as found according to Equations 14.1 and 14.2, denote what an option should be worth, *in the absence of any time premium*. In fact, options rarely trade at their fundamental (intrinsic) values. Instead, they almost always trade at prices that exceed their intrinsic values, especially for options that still have a long time to run. Thus, puts and calls nearly always trade at premium prices. While that may be so, the term **option premium** is used to describe the market price of listed put and call options. Technically, the option premium is the (quoted) price the buyer pays for the *right* to buy or sell a certain amount of the underlying financial asset at a specified price for a specified period of time. The option seller, on the other hand, receives the premium and gets to keep it whether or not the option is exercised. To the seller, the option premium represents compensation for agreeing to fulfill certain *obligations* of the contract.

As we'll see below, the term *premium* is also used to denote the extent to which the market price of an option exceeds its fundamental or intrinsic value. Thus, to avoid confusion and keep matters as simple as possible, we'll use the word *price* in the usual way: to describe the amount it takes to buy an option in the market.

■ What Drives Options Prices?

Option prices can be reduced to two separate components. The first is the *fundamental* (or *intrinsic*) value of the option, which is driven by the current market price of the underlying financial asset. As we saw in Equations 14.1 and 14.2, the greater the difference between the market price of the underlying asset and the strike price on the option, the greater the fundamental value of the put or call.

The second component of an option price is customarily referred to as the **time premium**. It represents, in effect, the excess value embedded in the option price. That is, time premium is *the amount by which the option price exceeds the option's fundamental value.* Table 14.1 lists some quoted prices for an actively traded call option. These quoted prices (panel A) are then separated into fundamental value (panel B) and time premium (panel C). Note that three strike prices are used—$65, $70, and $75. Relative to the market price of the

time premium
the amount by which the option price exceeds the option's fundamental value.

TABLE 14.1 Option Price Components for an Actively Traded Call Option

Price	Strike Price	Expiration Months		
		February	March	June
Panel A: Quoted Options Prices				
71.75	65	—	7.75	9.75
71.75	70	2.25	3.88	6.75
71.75	75	0.19	1.50	3.88
Panel B: Underlying Fundamental Values				
71.75	65	—	6.75	6.75
71.75	70	1.75	1.75	1.75
71.75	75	neg.	neg.	neg.
Panel C: Time Premiums				
71.75	65	—	1.00	3.00
71.75	70	0.50	2.12	5.00
71.75	75	0.19	1.50	3.88

Note: neg. indicates that options have negative fundamental values.

stock ($71.75), one strike price ($65) is well below market; this is an in-the-money call. One ($70) is fairly near the market. The third ($75) is well above the market; this is an out-of-the-money call. Note the considerable difference in the makeup of the options prices as we move from an in-the-money call to an out-of-the-money call.

Panel B in the table lists the fundamental values of the call options, as determined by Equation 14.1. For example, note that although the March 65 call (the call with the March expiration date and $65 strike price) is trading at 7.75, its intrinsic value is only 6.75. The intrinsic value (of 6.75) represents, in effect, the extent to which the option is trading in-the-money. But observe that although most of the price of the March 65 call is made up of fundamental value, not all of it is. Now look at the calls with the $75 strike price. None of these has any fundamental value; they're all out-of-the-money, and their prices are made up solely of time premium. Basically, the value of these options is determined entirely by the *belief* that the price of the underlying stock could rise to over $75 a share before the options expire.

Panel C shows the amount of *time premium* embedded in the call prices. Such a premium represents the difference between the *quoted call price* (panel A) and the call's *fundamental value* (panel B). It shows that the price of just about every traded option contains at least some premium. Indeed, unless the options are about to expire, you would expect them to trade at a premium. Also, note that with all three strike prices, *the longer the time to expiration, the greater the size of the premium.*

As you might expect, *time to expiration* is an important element in explaining the size of the price premium in panel C. A couple of other variables also have a bearing on the behavior of this premium. One is the *price volatility of the underlying common stock.* Other things being equal, the more volatile the stock is, the more it enhances the speculative appeal of the option—and therefore the bigger the time premium. In addition, the size of the premium is *directly related to the level of interest rates.* That is, the amount of premium embedded in a call option generally increases along with interest rates.

For the most part, then, four major forces drive the price of an option. They are, in descending order of importance, (1) the price behavior of the underlying financial asset, (2) the amount of time remaining to expiration, (3) the amount of price volatility in the underlying financial asset, and (4) the general level of interest rates. Less important variables include the dividend yield on the underlying common stock, the trading volume of the option, and the exchanges on which the option is listed.

Option-Pricing Models Some fairly sophisticated option-pricing models have been developed, notably by Myron Scholes and the late Fisher Black, to value options. Many active options traders use these formulas to identify and trade over- and undervalued options. Not surprisingly, these models are based on the same variables we identified above. For example, the five parameters used in the Black-Scholes option-pricing model are (1) the risk-free rate of interest, (2) the price volatility of the underlying stock, (3) the current price of the underlying stock, (4) the strike price of the option, and (5) the option's time to expiration. See the book's Web site for more on option-pricing models.

WEBEXTENSION

A more detailed discussion of the Black-Scholes option-pricing model, including the basic equations used in the model, can be found on the book's Web site, at:

www.myfinancelab.com

▮ Trading Strategies

For the most part, investors can use stock options in three different kinds of trading strategies: (1) buying puts and calls for speculation, (2) hedging with puts and calls, and (3) option writing and spreading.

▮ Buying for Speculation

Buying for speculation is the simplest and most straightforward use of puts and calls. Basically, it is like buying stock ("buy low, sell high") and, in fact, represents an alternative to investing in stock. For example, if you feel the market price of a particular stock is going to move up, you can capture that price appreciation by buying a call on the stock. In contrast, if you feel the stock is about to drop in price, a put could convert that price decline into a profitable situation. In essence, investors buy options rather than stock whenever the options are likely to yield a greater return. The principle here, of course, is to get the biggest return from your investment dollar. Puts and calls often meet this objective because of the added leverage they offer.

Furthermore, options offer *valuable downside protection:* The most you can lose is the cost of the option, which is always less than the cost of the underlying stock. Thus, by using options as a vehicle for speculation, you can put a cap on losses and still get almost as much profit potential as with the underlying stock.

Speculating with Calls   To illustrate the essentials of speculating with options, imagine that you have uncovered a stock you feel will move up in price over the next six months. What would happen if you were to buy a call on this stock rather than investing directly in the firm's common? To find out, let's see what the numbers show. The price of the stock is now $49, and you anticipate that within six months, it will rise to about $65. You need to determine the expected return associated with each of your investment alternatives. Because (most) options have relatively short lives, and because we're dealing with an investment horizon of only six months, we can use holding period return to measure yield (see Chapter 4). Thus, if your expectations about the stock are correct, it should go up by $16 a share and will provide you with a 33% holding period return: ($65 − $49)/$49 = $16/$49 = 0.33.

But there are also some listed options available on this stock. Let's see how they would do. For illustrative purposes, we will use two six-month calls that carry a $40 and a $50 strike price, respectively. Table 14.2 compares the behavior of these two calls with the behavior of the underlying common stock. Clearly, from a holding period return perspective, either call option represents a superior investment to buying the stock itself. The dollar amount of profit may be a bit more with the stock, but note that the size of the required investment ($4,900) is a lot more too, so that alternative has the lowest HPR.

Observe that one of the calls is an in-the-money option (the one with the $40 strike price). The other is out-of-the-money. The difference in returns generated by these calls is rather typical. That is, investors are usually able to generate much better rates of return with lower-priced (out-of-the-money) options and also enjoy less exposure to loss. Of course, a major drawback of out-of-the-money options is that their price is made up solely of investment premium—a sunk cost that will be lost if the stock does not move in price.

TABLE 14.2   **Speculating with Call Options**

	100 Shares of Underlying Common Stock	6-Month Call Options on the Stock	
		$40 Strike Price	$50 Strike Price
Today			
Market value of stock (at $49/share)	$4,900		
Market price of calls*		$1,100	$ 400
6 Months Later			
Expected value of stock (at $65/share)	$6,500		
Expected price of calls*		$2,500	$1,500
Profit	$1,600	$1,400	$1,100
Holding Period Return**	33%	127%	275%

*The price of the calls was computed according to Equation 14.1. It includes some investment premium in the purchase price but none in the expected sales price.
**Holding period return (HPR) = (Ending price of the stock or option − Beginning price of the stock or option)/Beginning price of the stock or option.

Speculating with Puts   To see how you can speculate in puts, consider the following situation. You're looking at a stock that's now priced at $51, but you anticipate a drop in price to about $35 per share within the next six months. If that occurs, you could sell the stock short and make a profit of $16 per share. (See Chapter 2 for a discussion of short selling.)

Alternatively, you can purchase an out-of-the-money put (with a strike price of $50) for, say, $300. Again, if the price of the underlying stock drops, you will make money with the put. The profit and rate of return on the put are summarized below, along with the comparative returns from short selling the stock.

Comparative Performance Given Price of Stock Moves from $51 to $35/Share Over a 6-Month Period:	Buy 1 Put ($50 strike price)	Short Sell 100 Shares of Stock
Purchase price (today)	$300	
Selling price (6 months later)	1,500*	
Short sell (today)		$5,100
Cover (6 months later)		3,500
Profit	$1,200	$1,600
Holding period return	400%	63%**

*The price of the put was computed according to Equation 14.2 and does not include any investment premium.
**Assumes the short sale was made with a required margin deposit of 50%.

Once again, in terms of holding period return, the stock option is the superior investment vehicle by a wide margin.

Of course, not all option investments perform as well as the ones in our examples. Success with this strategy rests on picking the right underlying common stock. Thus, *security analysis and proper stock selection are critical dimensions of this technique.* It is a highly risky investment strategy, but it may be well suited for the more speculatively inclined investor.

▮ Hedging: Modifying Risks

hedge
a combination of two or
more securities into a single
investment position for the
purpose of reducing or
eliminating risk.

A **hedge** is simply a combination of two or more securities into a single investment position for the purpose of reducing risk. Let's say you hold a stock and want to reduce the amount of downside risk in this investment. You can do that by setting up a hedge. In essence, you're using the hedge as a way to *modify your exposure to risk*. To be more specific, you're trying to change not only the *chance of loss*, but also the *amount lost*, if the worst does occur. A simple hedge might involve nothing more than buying stock and simultaneously buying a put on that same stock. Or it might consist of selling some stock short and then buying a call. There are many types of hedges, some of which are very simple and others very sophisticated. Investors use them for the same basic reason: to earn or protect a profit without exposing the investor to excessive loss.

An options hedge may be appropriate if you have generated a profit from an earlier common stock investment and wish to protect that profit. Or it may be appropriate if you are about to enter into a common stock investment and wish to protect your money by limiting potential capital loss. If you hold a stock that has gone up in price, the purchase of a put would provide the type of downside protection you need; the purchase of a call, in contrast, would provide protection to a short seller of common stock. Thus, option hedging always involves two transactions: (1) the initial common stock position (long or short) and (2) the simultaneous or subsequent purchase of the option.

Protective Puts: Limiting Capital Loss   Let's examine a simple option hedge in which you use a put to limit your exposure to capital loss. Assume that you want to buy 100 shares of stock. Being a bit apprehensive about the stock's outlook, you decide to use an option hedge to protect your capital against loss. Therefore, you simultaneously (1) buy the stock and (2) buy a put on the stock (which fully covers the 100 shares owned). This type of hedge is known as a *protective put*. Preferably, the put would be a low-priced option with a strike price at or near the current market price of the stock. Suppose you purchase 100 shares of the common at $25 a share, and pay $150 for a put with a $25 strike price. Now, no matter what happens to the price of the stock over the life of the put, *you can lose no more than $150*. At the same time, *there's no limit on the gains*. If the stock does not move, you will be out the cost of a put. If it drops in price, then whatever is lost on the stock will be made up with the put. The bottom line? The most you can lose is the cost of the put ($150, in this case). However, if the price of the stock goes up (as hoped), the put becomes worthless, and you will earn the capital gains on the stock (less the cost of the put, of course).

Table 14.3 shows the essentials of this option hedge. The $150 paid for the put is sunk cost. That's lost no matter what happens to the price of the stock. In effect, it is the price paid for the insurance this hedge offers. Moreover, this hedge is good only for the life of the put. When this put expires, you will have to replace it with another put or forget about hedging your capital.

Protective Puts: Protecting Profits   The other basic use of an option hedge involves entering into the options position *after* a profit has been made on the underlying stock. This could be done because of investment uncertainty or for tax purposes (to carry over a profit to the next taxable year). For example, if you bought 100 shares of a stock at $35 and it moved to $75, there would be

TABLE 14.3   Limiting Capital Loss with a Put Hedge

		Stock	Put*
Today			
Purchase price of the stock		$25	
Purchase price of the put			$1.50
Sometime Later			
A. Price of common goes *up* to:		$50	
Value of put			$ 0
Profit:			
100 shares of stock ($50 − $25)	$2,500		
Less: Cost of put	− 150		
Profit:	**$2,350**		
B. Price of common goes *down* to:		$10	
Value of put**			$15
Profit:			
100 shares of stock (loss: $10 − $25)	−$1,500		
Value of put (profit)	+ 1,500		
Less: Cost of put	− 150		
Loss:	**$ 150**		

*The put is purchased simultaneously and carries a strike price of $25.
**See Equation 14.2.

a profit of $40 per share to protect. You could protect the profit with an option hedge by buying a put. Assume you buy a three-month put with a $75 strike price at a cost of $250. Now, regardless of what happens to the stock over the life of the put, you are guaranteed a minimum profit of $3,750 (the $4,000 profit in the stock made so far, less the $250 cost of the put). This can be seen in Table 14.4 (on page 628). Note that if the price of the stock should fall, the worst that can happen is a guaranteed minimum profit of $3,750. Plus, there is still *no limit on how much profit can be made.* As long as the stock continues to go up, you will reap the benefits.

But watch out: *The cost of this kind of insurance can become very expensive just when its needed the most*—that is, when market prices are falling. Under such circumstances, it's not uncommon to find put options trading at price premiums of 20% to 30%, or more, above their prevailing fundamental values. Essentially, that means the price of the stock position you're trying to protect has to fall 20% to 30% before the protection even starts to kick in. Clearly, as long as high option price premiums prevail, the hedging strategies described above are a lot less attractive. They still may prove to be helpful, but only for very wide swings in value—and for those that occur over fairly short periods of time, as defined by the life of the put option.

One final point: Although the preceding discussion pertained to put hedges, call hedges can also be set up to limit the loss or protect a profit on a short sale. For example, when selling a stock short, you can purchase a call to protect yourself against a rise in the price of the stock—with the same basic results as outlined above.

HOTLINKS

To find some good articles on strategies using options, go to:

www.888options.com/strategy/default.jsp

EXCEL with SPREADSHEETS

TABLE 14.4 **Protecting Profits with a Put Hedge**

	Stock	3-Month Put with a $75 Strike Price
Purchase price of the stock	$ 35	
Today		
Market price of the stock	$ 75	
Market price of the put		$2.50
3 Months Later		
A. Price of common goes *up* to:	$100	
Value of put		$ 0
Profit:		
100 shares of stock ($100 − $35) $6,500		
Less: Cost of put − 250		
Profit: $6,250		
B. Price of common goes *down* to:	$ 50	
Value of put*		$25
Profit:		
100 shares of stock ($50 − $35) $1,500		
Value of put (profit) 2,500		
Less: Cost of put − 250		
Profit: $3,750		

*See Equation 14.2.

▊ Enhancing Returns: Options Writing and Spreading

The advent of listed options has led to many intriguing options-trading strategies. Yet, despite the appeal of these techniques, there is one important point that all the experts agree on: *Such specialized trading strategies should be left to experienced investors who fully understand their subtleties.* Our goal at this point is not to master these specialized strategies but to explain in general terms what they are and how they operate. We will look at two types of specialized options strategies here: (1) writing options and (2) spreading options.

Writing Options Generally, investors write options because they believe the price of the underlying stock is going to move in their favor. That is, it is not going to rise as much as the buyer of a call expects, nor will it fall as much as the buyer of a put hopes. *And more often than not, the option writer is right:* He or she makes money far more often than the buyer of the put or call. Such favorable odds explain, in part, the underlying economic motivation for writing put and call options. Option writing represents an investment transaction to the writers: They receive the full option premium (less normal transaction costs) in exchange for agreeing to live up to the terms of the option.

Naked Options Investors can write options in one of two ways. One is to write **naked options**, which involves writing options on stock not owned by the writer. You simply write the put or call, collect the option premium, and hope the price of the underlying stock does not move against you. If successful, naked writing can be highly profitable because of the modest amount of capital required. Remember, though: The amount of return to the writer is always

naked options
options written on securities not owned by the writer.

limited to the amount of option premium received. On the other hand, there is really *no limit to loss exposure*. That's the catch: The price of the underlying stock can rise or fall by just about any amount over the life of the option and thus, can deal a real blow to the writer of the naked put or call.

Covered Options The amount of risk exposure is a lot less for those who write **covered options**. That's because these options are written against stocks the investor (writer) already owns or has a position in. For example, you could write a call against stock you own or write a put against stock you have short sold. You thus can use the long or short position to meet the terms of the option. Such a strategy is a fairly conservative way to generate attractive rates of return. The object is to write a *slightly* out-of-the-money option, pocket the option premium, and hope the price of the underlying stock will move up or down to (but not exceed) the option's strike price. In effect, you are adding option premium to the other usual sources of return (dividends and/or capital gains). But there's more: While the option premium adds to the return, it also reduces risk. It can cushion a loss if the price of the stock moves against the investor.

There is a hitch to all this, of course: *The amount of return the covered option investor can realize is limited.* Once the price of the underlying common stock exceeds the strike price on the option, the option becomes valuable. When that happens, *you start to lose money on the options*. From this point on, for every dollar you make on the stock position, you lose an equal amount on the option position. That's a major risk of writing covered call options—if the price of the underlying stock takes off, you'll miss out on the added profits.

To illustrate the ins and outs of *covered call writing*, let's assume you own 100 shares of PFP, Inc., an actively traded, high-yielding common stock. The stock is currently trading at $73.50 and pays *quarterly* dividends of $1 a share. You decide to write a three-month call on PFP, giving the buyer the right to take the stock off your hands at $80 a share. Such options are trading in the market at 2.50, so you receive $250 for writing the call. You fully intend to hold on to the stock, so you'd like to see the price of PFP stock rise to no more than 80 by the expiration date on the call. If that happens, the call option will expire worthless. As a result, not only will you earn the dividends and capital gains on the stock, but you also get to pocket the $250 you received when you wrote the call. Basically, *you've just added $250 to the quarterly return on your stock*.

Table 14.5 (on page 630) summarizes the profit and loss characteristics of this covered call position. Note that the maximum profit on this transaction occurs *when the market price of the stock equals the strike price on the call*. If the price of the stock keeps going up, you miss out on the added profits. Even so, the $1,000 profit you earn at a stock price of 80 or above translates into a (three-month) holding period return of 13.6% ($1,000/$7,350). That represents an *annualized* return of nearly 55%! With this kind of return potential, it's not difficult to see why covered call writing is so popular. Moreover, as *situation D* in the table illustrates, covered call writing adds a little cushion to losses: The price of the stock has to drop more than 2½ points (which is what you received when you wrote/sold the call) before you start losing money.

Besides covered calls and protective puts, there are many different ways of combining options with other types of securities to achieve a given investment objective. Probably none is more unusual than the creation of so-called *synthetic securities*. A case in point: Say you want to buy a convertible bond on a certain company, but that company doesn't have any convertibles

---

covered options
options written against stock owned (or short sold) by the writer.

WEBEXTENSION

For a more thorough discussion of synthetic convertibles, click on "Customized Convertibles" on the book's Web site:

www.myfinancelab.com

TABLE 14.5   Covered Call Writing

		Stock	3-Month Call with an $80 Strike Price
Current market price of the stock		$73.50	
Current market price of the call			$ 2.50
3 Months Later			
A. Price of the stock is *unchanged*:		$73.50	
Value of the call			$ 0
Profit:			
Quarterly dividends received	$ 100		
Proceeds from sale of call	250		
Total profit:	$ 350		
B. Price of the stock goes *up* to:		$80	**Price Where Maximum Profit Occurs**
Value of the call			$ 0
Profit:			
Quarterly dividends received	$ 100		
Proceeds from sale of call	250		
Capital gains on stock ($80 − $73.50)	650		
Total profit:	$1,000		
C. Price of the stock goes *up* to:		$90	
Value of the call*			$10
Profit:			
Quarterly dividends received	$ 100		
Proceeds from sale of call	250		
Capital gains on stock ($90 − $73.50)	1,650		
Less: Loss on call	(1,000)		
Net profit:	$1,000		
D. Price of the stock *drops* to:		$71	**Break-Even Price**
Value of the call*			$ 0
Profit:			
Capital loss on stock ($71 − $73.50)	($ 250) ⎫		
Proceeds from sale of call	250 ⎬ $0 profit or loss		
Quarterly dividends	100 ⎭		
Net profit:	$ 100		

*See Equation 14.1.

outstanding. You can create your own customized convertible by combining a straight (nonconvertible) bond with a listed call option on your targeted company.

option spreading
combining two or more options with different strike prices and/or expiration dates into a single transaction.

Spreading Options   Option spreading is nothing more than the combination of two or more options into a single transaction. You could create an option spread, for example, by simultaneously buying and writing options on the same underlying stock. These would not be identical options; they would differ with respect to strike price and/or expiration date. Spreads are a very popular use of listed options, and they account for a substantial amount of the trading activity on the listed options exchanges. These spreads go by a variety of exotic names, such as *bull spreads, bear spreads, money spreads, vertical spreads,* and *butterfly spreads.* Each spread is different and each is constructed to meet a certain type of investment goal.

Consider, for example, a *vertical spread.* It would be set up by *buying* a call at one strike price and then *writing* a call (on the same stock and for the same expiration date) at a higher strike price. For instance, you could buy a February call on XYZ at a strike price of, say, 30 and simultaneously sell (write) a February call on XYZ at a strike price of 35. Strange as it may sound, such a position would generate a hefty return if the price of the underlying stock went up by just a few points. Other spreads are used to profit from a falling market. Still others try to make money when the price of the underlying stock moves either up *or* down. Interested readers can find out more about "bull spreads" by going to our Web site.

WEBEXTENSION

For more discussion on how "bull spreads" are actually set up, see the *Investing in Action* box entitled "The Call of the Bull Spread," at the book's Web site:

www.myfinancelab.com

Whatever the objective, most spreads are created to take advantage of differences in prevailing option prices and premiums. The payoff from spreading is usually substantial, but *so is the risk.* In fact, some spreads that seem to involve almost no risk may end up with devastating results if the market and the difference between option premiums move against the investor.

option straddle
the simultaneous purchase (or sale) of a put and a call on the same underlying common stock (or financial asset).

Option Straddles A variation on this theme involves an **option straddle**. This is the simultaneous purchase (or sale) of *both* a put *and* a call on the *same* underlying common stock. Unlike spreads, straddles normally involve the same strike price and expiration date. Here, the object is to earn a profit from *either* a big or a small swing in the price of the underlying common stock.

For example, in a *long straddle,* you *buy* an equal number of puts and calls. You make money in a long straddle when the underlying stock undergoes a big change in price—either up or down. If the price of the stock shoots way up, you make money on the call side of the straddle but are out the cost of the puts. If the price of the stock plummets, you make money on the puts, but the calls are useless. In either case, so long as you make more money on one side than the cost of the options for the other side, you're ahead of the game.

In a similar fashion, in a *short straddle,* you *sell/write* an equal number of puts and calls. You make money in this position *when the price of the underlying stock goes nowhere.* In effect, you get to keep all or most of the option premiums you collected when you wrote the options.

Except for obvious structural differences, the principles that underlie the creation of straddles are much like those for spreads. The object is to combine options that will enable you to capture the benefits of certain types of stock price behavior. But keep in mind that if the prices of the underlying stock and/or the option premiums do not behave in the anticipated manner, you lose. *Spreads and straddles are extremely tricky and should be used only by knowledgeable investors.*

CONCEPTS IN REVIEW

Answers available at: www.myfinancelab.com

14.7   Briefly explain how you would make money on (a) a call option and (b) a put option. Do you have to exercise the option to capture the profit?

14.8   How do you find the intrinsic (fundamental) value of a call? Of a put? Does an *out-of-the-money option* have intrinsic value?

14.9 Name at least four variables that affect the price behavior of listed options, and briefly explain how each affects prices. How important are fundamental (intrinsic) value and time value to in-the-money options? To out-of-the-money options?

14.10 Describe at least three different ways in which investors can use stock options.

14.11 What's the most that can be made from writing calls? Why would an investor want to write *covered calls?* Explain how you can reduce the risk on an underlying common stock by writing covered calls.

Stock-Index and Other Types of Options

LG 6

Imagine being able to buy or sell a major stock market index like the S&P 500—and at a reasonable cost. Think of what you could do: If you felt the market was heading up, you could invest in a security that tracks the price behavior of the S&P 500 index and make money when the market goes up. No longer would you have to go through the process of selecting specific stocks that you hope will capture the market's performance. Rather, you could play the *market as a whole*. That's exactly what you can do with *stock-index options*—puts and calls that are written on major stock market indexes. Index options have been around since 1983 and have become immensely popular with both individual and institutional investors. Here we will take a closer look at these popular and often highly profitable investment vehicles.

▌Stock-Index Options: Contract Provisions

stock-index option
a put or call option written on a specific stock market index, such as the S&P 500.

Basically, a **stock-index option** is a put or call written on a specific stock market index. The underlying security in this case is the specific market index. Thus, when the market index moves in one direction or another, the value of the index option moves accordingly. Because there are no stocks or other financial assets backing these options, settlement is defined in terms of cash. Specifically, the cash value of an *index option* is equal to 100 times the published market index that underlies the option. For example, if the S&P 500 is at 1,400, then the value of an S&P 500 index option will be $100 × 1,400 = $140,000. If the underlying index moves up or down in the market, so will the cash value of the option. [*Note:* Options on exchange-traded funds (ETFs) are very similar to index options and will be discussed below. For now, our attention will focus solely on index options.]

In mid-2006, put and call options were available on more than 120 market measures of performance. These included options on just about every major U.S. stock market index or average (such as the Dow Jones Industrial Average, the S&P 500, the Russell 2000, and the Nasdaq 100), options on a handful of foreign markets (e.g., China, Mexico, Japan, Hong Kong, and the Europe sector), and options on different segments of the market (pharmaceuticals, oil services, semiconductors, bank, and utility indexes). Many of these options, however, are thinly traded and do not have much of a market. As of mid-2006, four indexes dominated the stock-index options market, accounting for the vast majority of trading activity:

- The S&P 500 Index (SPX)

- The S&P 100 Index (OEX)

- The Dow Jones Industrial Average (DJX)

- The Nasdaq 100 Index (NDX)

The S&P 500 Index captures the market behavior of large-cap stocks. The S&P 100 is another large-cap index composed of 100 stocks, drawn from the S&P 500, that have actively traded stock options. Another popular index is the DJIA, which measures the blue-chip segment of the market and is one of the most actively traded index options. The Nasdaq 100 index tracks the behavior of the 100 largest nonfinancial stocks on the Nasdaq and is composed of mostly large, high-tech companies (such as Intel and Cisco). Options on the S&P 500 (SPX) are, by far, the most popular instruments. Indeed, there's more trading in SPX options contracts than in *all the other index options combined*. Among the options exchanges that currently deal in index options, the CBOE dominates the market, accounting for more than 85% of all trades.

Both puts and calls are available on index options. They are valued and have issue characteristics like any other put or call. That is, a put lets a holder profit from a drop in the market. (When the underlying market index goes down, the value of a put goes up.) A call enables the holder to profit from a market that's going up. Also, as Figure 14.3 (on page 634) shows, these options even have a quotation system that is very similar to that used for puts and calls on stocks. There is one small difference between the *Wall Street Journal* quotes for stock options and those for index options: The closing value for the underlying index is not listed with the rest of the quote. Instead, these values are listed separately in a table that accompanies the quotes.

Putting a Value on Stock-Index Options As is true of equity options, the market price of index options is a function of the difference between the strike price on the option (stated in terms of the underlying index) and the latest published stock market index. To illustrate, consider the highly popular S&P 100 Index traded on the CBOE. As the index option quotes in Figure 14.3 reveal, this index recently closed at 587.25. (See the "Current values for the underlying indexes" at the bottom of the exhibit.) At the same time, there was a June call on this index that carried a strike price of 575. A stock-index *call* will have a value so long as the underlying index exceeds the index strike price (just the opposite for puts). Hence, the intrinsic value of this call would be 587.25 − 575.00 = 12.25. However, as the quotes in Figure 14.3 show, this call was actually trading at 14.90—or 2.65 points *above* the call's underlying fundamental value. This difference, of course, was the *time premium*.

If the S&P 100 Index in our example (above) were to go up to, say, 600 by late June (the expiration date of the call), this option would be quoted at: 600 − 575 = 25. Because index options (like equity options) are valued in multiples of $100, this contract would be worth $2,500. Thus, if you had purchased this option when it was trading at 14.90, it would have cost you $1,490 ($14.90 × $100) and, in less than a month, would have generated a profit of: $2,500 − $1,490 = $1,010. That translates into a holding period return of a whopping 67.8% ($1,010/$1,490).

FIGURE 14.3

Quotations on Index Options

The quotation system used with index options is a lot like that used with stock options: Strike prices and expiration dates are shown along with closing option prices. The biggest differences are that put (p) and call (c) quotes are mixed together, and the closing values for the underlying indexes are shown separately. (*Source: Wall Street Journal,* June 1, 2006.)

CHICAGO

STRIKE	VOL	LAST	NET CHG	OPEN INT
DJ INDUS AVG(DJX)				
Jun 111 c	186	2.15	0.30	3,052
Jul 111 p	105	1.35	−0.55	3,023
Aug 111 p	108	1.85	−0.45	96
Jun 112 p	556	0.80	−0.50	20,116
Jul 112 c	281	2.65	0.50	1,279
Jul 112 p	185	1.65	−0.50	2,524
Sep 112 p	184	2.55	−0.95	5,642
Jun 113 c	479	0.85	0.35	21,226
Jun 113 p	241	1.20	−0.70	14,228
Jul 113 c	63	2.05	0.35	1,833
Jul 113 p	72	2	−0.65	1,734
Sep 113 c	83	3.30	−0.20	1,606
Jun 115 c	126	0.15	...	24,549
Jun 116 p	140	3.80	−0.90	3,091
Jul 116 c	88	0.65	0.15	12,657

Call Vol........10,565   Open Int..414,106
Put Vol. 16,505   Open Int..345,037

S & P 100(OEX)

STRIKE	VOL	LAST	NET CHG	OPEN INT
Jul 570 p	144	4.90	−2.70	2,670
Jun 575 c	68	14.90	3.20	1,688
Jul 575 p	62	6.10	−2.70	1,368
Jun 580 p	7,276	3.20	−2.60	10,994
Jul 580 p	150	7.30	−2.70	2,510
Jul 585 c	208	13	3.20	1,123
Jul 585 p	536	9.10	−5.20	1,560
Jul 590 c	148	9.80	2.90	1,459
Jun 595 p	202	11.40	−3.10	3,845
Jun 600 p	175	13.50	−6.10	2,244
Jul 600 c	286	4.70	1.00	3,785
Jul 600 p	182	16	−7.20	1,389
Jul 605 c	795	2.75	0.70	4,961
Jul 615 c	705	0.85	0.05	2,799
Jul 625 c	840	0.30	0.20	1,989

Call Vol........31,021   Open Int..272,773
Put Vol. 36,605   Open Int..248,294

Labels pointing to the quotation:
- Name of index → DJ INDUS AVG(DJX)
- Open interest: Number of contracts outstanding on this one (July-06-call) option → 1,279
- Month of expiration → Sep
- c: Call option → Jul 113 c
- p: Put option → Jun 116 p
- Strike price → Jul 575 p
- Price of a July call option with a strike price of 605 → 2.75

Current values for the underlying indexes
DJIA: 112.6
S&P 100: 587.25

Full Value Versus Fractional Value Most broad-based index options use the full market value of the underlying index for purposes of options trading and valuation. That's not the case, however, with two of the Dow Jones measures: The option on the Dow Jones Industrial Average is based on 1% (1/100) of the actual Industrial Average, and the Dow Transportation Average option is based on 10% (1/10) of the actual average. For example, if the DJIA is at 11,260, the index option would be valued at 1% of that amount, or 112.60.

Thus, the cash value of this option is not $100 times the underlying DJIA but $100 times 1% of the DJIA, *which equals the Dow Jones Industrial Average itself*: $100 × 112.60 = $11,260.

Fortunately, the option strike prices are also based on the same 1% of the Dow, so there is no effect on option valuation: What matters is the difference between the strike price on the option and (1% of) the DJIA. For instance, note in Figure 14.3 that the DJIA option index closed at 112.60 (at the time, the actual Dow was at 11,260). Note also that there was a September call option available on this index with a strike price of 113—it was trading at 3.30 (or $330). Using Equation 14.1, you can see that this in-the-money option had an intrinsic value of 113 − 112.6 = 0.40. The difference between the option's market value (3.30) and its intrinsic value (0.40) is, of course, the time premium.

Another type of option that is traded at 10% (1/10) of the value of the underlying index is the "mini" index option. For example, the Mini-NDX Index (MNX) is set at 10% of the value of the Nasdaq 100. "Minis" also exist for the Nasdaq composite, the S&P 500, the Russell 2000, and the FTSE 250 (an index of mid-cap stocks in the UK), among others.

▍Investment Uses

Although index options, like equity options, can be used in spreads, straddles, or even covered calls, they are perhaps used most often for speculating or for hedging. When used as a speculative vehicle, index options give investors an opportunity to play the market as a whole, with a relatively small amount of capital. Like any other put or call, index options provide attractive *leverage opportunities* and at the same time *limit exposure to loss* to the price paid for the option.

Index Options as Hedging Vehicles Index options are equally effective as *hedging vehicles*. In fact, hedging is a major use of index options and accounts for a good deal of the trading in these securities. To see how these options can be used for hedging, assume that you hold a diversified portfolio of, say, a dozen different stocks and you think the market is heading down. One way to protect your capital would be to sell all of your stocks. However, that could be expensive, especially if you plan to get back into the market after it drops, and it could lead to a good deal of unnecessary taxes. Fortunately, there is a way to "have your cake and eat it too," and that is to hedge your stock portfolio with a stock index put. In this way, if the market does go down, you'll make money on your puts, which you then can use to buy more stocks at the lower prices. On the other hand, if the market continues to go up, you'll be out *only the cost of the puts*. That amount could well be recovered from the increased value of your stock holdings. The principles of hedging with stock-index options are exactly the same as those for hedging with equity options. The only difference is that with stock-index options, you're trying to protect a *whole portfolio of stocks* rather than *individual* stocks.

Like hedging with individual equity options, the cost of protecting your portfolio with index options can become very expensive (with price premiums of 20% to 30%, or more) when markets are falling and the need for this type of portfolio insurance is the greatest. That, of course, will have an impact on the effectiveness of this strategy.

Also, the amount of profit you make or the protection you obtain depends in large part on how closely the behavior of your stock portfolio is matched by the behavior of the stock-index option you employ. *There is no guarantee that the two will behave in the same way.* You should therefore select an index option that closely reflects the nature of the stocks in your portfolio. If, for example, you hold a number of small-cap stocks, you might select something like the Russell 2000 index option as the hedging vehicle. If you hold mostly blue chips, you might choose the DJIA index option. You probably can't get dollar-for-dollar portfolio protection, but you should try to get as close a match as possible. This and other considerations are discussed in the accompanying *Investing in Action* box, which deals with the use of index options in portfolio hedging.

WEBEXTENSION

For further information, see our Web site, which illustrates in some detail how to use index options.

www.myfinancelab.com

A Word of Caution Given their effectiveness for either speculating or hedging, it's little wonder that index options have become popular with investors. But a word of caution is in order: Although trading index options appears simple and seems to provide high rates of return, these vehicles involve *high risk* and are subject to considerable price volatility. They should not be used by amateurs. True, there's only so much you can lose with these options. The trouble is that it's very easy to lose that amount. These securities are not investments you can buy and then forget about until just before they expire. With the wide market swings that are so common today, you must *monitor these securities on a daily basis.*

▌ Other Types of Options

Options on stocks and stock indexes account for most of the market activity in listed options. But you also can obtain put and call options on various other securities. Let's now take a brief look at these other kinds of options, starting with options on ETFs.

Options on Exchange-Traded Funds In addition to various market indexes, put and call options are also available on over 150 *exchange-traded funds (ETFs)*. As more fully explained in Chapter 12, ETFs are like mutual funds that have been structured to track the performance of a wide range of market indexes—in other words, *ETFs are a type of index fund*. They trade like shares of common stock on listed exchanges, primarily the AMEX, and cover everything from broad market measures, such as the DJIA, the S&P 500, and the Nasdaq 100, to market sectors like energy, financials, health care, and semiconductors.

There's a good deal of overlap in the markets and market segments covered by index options and ETF options. In addition to their similar market coverage, they perform very much the same in the market, are valued the same, and used for many of the same reasons (particularly for speculation and hedging). After all, an ETF option is written on an underlying *index fund* (for example, one that tracks the S&P 500) just like an index option is written on the same underlying *market index* (the S&P 500). Both do pretty much the same thing—either directly or indirectly track the performance of a market measure—so of course they should behave in the same way.

The only real difference is this: Options on ETFs are operationally like stock options in that each option covers 100 shares of the underlying exchange-

INVESTING *in Action*

Using Index Options to Protect a Whole Portfolio

When the stock market heads down, investors begin to worry about protecting the value of their portfolios. But simply liquidating their stock holdings and putting the proceeds into a money market fund is too drastic a step for most people. Not only would they incur substantial brokerage commissions and capital gains taxes, but they would also lose out if the market rallies. A far less drastic—and less costly—way for investors to shield their portfolios from the possibility of a sustained sell-off is to buy "insurance" in the form of stock-index put options.

These options offer a simple method of insuring the value of an entire portfolio with a single trade. That can be especially helpful because many issues in an investor's portfolio may not have individual put options traded on them. Such portfolio protection is similar to any other kind of insurance. The more protection investors want and the less risk they are willing to bear, the more the insurance costs. For example, suppose an investor wants to hedge a $125,000 stock portfolio and, after examining the characteristics of the major stock indexes, concludes that the S&P 100 best matches the portfolio. With the S&P 100 Index standing at, say, 675 in February, the market value of the S&P 100 Index would be $67,500. So the investor would buy two puts to approximate the $125,000 portfolio value.

The investor might buy two May 660 puts that expire in 3 months (i.e., in June) with a strike price of 660 and a price of about 23. To turn that into dollars, an investor multiplies by 100; the puts would cost $2,300 each—$4,600 for both—or 3.7% of the $125,000 portfolio. If the market retreats about 15% from current levels, bringing the S&P 100 down to about 574, each May 660 put would be worth a minimum of 86

points (660 − 574), or $8,600. After paying their cost, the investor would have a profit on the puts of $12,600 ($8,600 − $2,300 = $6,300 × 2), offsetting a substantial portion of the $18,750 the portfolio would have lost in a 15% decline.

By purchasing puts with strike prices that are 15 points below the current level of the S&P Index, the investor effectively insures the portfolio against any losses that occur *after* the market has fallen 15 points, or 2.2%, to 660. An investor willing to bear more market risk could reduce the insurance cost even further by purchasing puts with even lower strike prices. On the other hand, to be fully insured, an investor might have bought puts with a higher strike price, but that would have raised the cost of the insurance. May 670 puts, for instance, would have cost about 27, or $2,700 each. Harrison Roth, an options strategist, says the basic question for investors is, "Do you want to hedge against any and all declines, or do you simply want protection against catastrophic moves?" He believes most investors are in the second camp.

Even with relatively low-cost puts such as the May 660s, the cost of put option hedges can add up if the insurance goes unused. Buying three-month puts like these four times a year would cost the equivalent of almost 15% of a $125,000 portfolio. One way to reduce the cost is to sell the put options before they expire. Put options lose most of their value in the final few weeks before their expiration if they have strike prices below the current price of the underlying securities. For this reason, some market advisers recommend that investors hold their options for only a month, sell them, and then buy the next month out. This strategy recovers most of the options' value, significantly reducing the cost to hedge, even after the higher commissions.

traded fund, rather than $100 of the underlying market index, as is the case with index options. In the end, though, both trade at 100 times the underlying index (or ETF). (One other minor point of difference: Because they're treated operationally like equity options, ETF options are quoted along with stock options, rather than being listed with index options. Take another look at Figure 14.1—notice the Dow Diamond ETF options listed among the stock options.) Thus, while operationally ETF options may be closer to stock options, they function more like index options. As such, the market views them as viable alternatives to index options. These contracts have definitely caught the fancy of investors, especially those that track the major market indexes. In fact, in 2005 more option contracts were traded on just two ETFs (the Nasdaq 100 and SPDRs) than for all index options combined.

interest rate options
put and call options written on fixed-income (debt) securities.

Interest Rate Options   Puts and calls on fixed-income (debt) securities are known as **interest rate options**. At the present time, interest rate options are written only on U.S. Treasury securities. Four maturities are used: 30-year T-bonds, 10-year and 5-year T-notes, and short-term (13-week) T-bills. These options are *yield-based* rather than price-based. This means they track the yield behavior of the underlying Treasury security (rather than the price behavior). Other types of options (equity and index options) are set up so that they react to movements in the price (or value) of the underlying asset. Interest rate options, in contrast, are set up to react to *the yield of the underlying Treasury security*. Thus, when yields rise, the value of a call goes up. When yields fall, puts go up in value. In effect, because bond prices and yields move in opposite directions, the value of an interest rate call option goes up at the very time that the price (or value) of the underlying debt security is going down. (The opposite is true for puts.) This unusual characteristic may explain why the market for interest rate options remains very small. Most professional investors simply don't care for interest rate options. Instead, they prefer to use interest rate futures contracts or options on these futures contracts (both of which we will examine in Chapter 15).

currency options
put and call options written on foreign currencies.

Currency Options   Foreign exchange options, or **currency options** as they're more commonly called, provide a way for investors to speculate on foreign exchange rates or to hedge foreign currency or foreign security holdings. Currency options are available on the currencies of most of the countries with which the United States has strong trading ties. These options are traded on the Philadelphia Exchange and include the following currencies:

- British pound
- Swiss franc
- Australian dollar

- Canadian dollar
- Japanese yen
- Euro

Puts and calls on foreign currencies give the holders the right to sell or buy large amounts of the specified currency. However, in contrast to the standardized contracts used with stock and stock-index options, the specific unit of trading in this market varies with the particular underlying currency. Table 14.6 spells out the details. Currency options are traded in full or fractional cents per unit of the underlying currency, relative to the amount of foreign currency involved. Thus, if a put or call on the British pound were quoted at, say, 6.40 (which is read as "6.4 cents"), it would be valued at $2,000, because 31,250 British pounds underlie this option (that is, $31,250 \times 0.064 = \$2,000$).

The value of a currency option is linked to the exchange rate between the U.S. dollar and the underlying foreign currency. For example, if the Canadian

TABLE 14.6 Foreign Currency Option Contracts on the Philadelphia Exchange

Underlying Currency*	Size of Contracts	Underlying Currency*	Size of Contracts
British pound	31,250 pounds	Canadian dollar	50,000 dollars
Swiss franc	62,500 francs	Japanese yen	6,250,000 yen
Euro	62,500 euros	Australian dollar	50,000 dollars

*The British pound, Swiss franc, euro, Canadian dollar, and Australian dollar are all quoted in full cents. The Japanese yen is quoted in hundredths of a cent.

dollar becomes stronger *relative to the U.S. dollar,* causing the exchange rate to go up, the price of a *call* option on the Canadian dollar will increase, and the price of a *put* will decline. [*Note:* Some cross-currency options are available in the market, but such options/trading techniques are beyond the scope of this book. Here, we will focus solely on foreign currency options (or futures) linked to U.S. dollars.]

The strike price on a currency option is stated in terms of *exchange rates.* Thus, a strike price of 150 implies that each unit of the foreign currency (such as one British pound) is worth 150 cents, or $1.50, in U.S. money. If you held a 150 call on this foreign currency, you would make money if *the foreign currency strengthened relative to the U.S. dollar* so that the exchange rate rose— say, to 155. In contrast, if you held a 150 put, you would profit from a decline in the exchange rate—say, to 145. Success in forecasting movements in foreign exchange rates is obviously essential to a profitable foreign currency options program.

LEAPS They look like regular puts and calls, and they behave pretty much like regular puts and calls, but they're not regular puts and calls. We're talking about **LEAPS,** which are puts and calls with lengthy expiration dates. Basically, LEAPS are long-term options. Whereas standard options have maturities of eight months or less, LEAPS have expiration dates as long as three years. Known formally as *Long-term Equity AnticiPation Securities,* they are listed on all of the major options exchanges. LEAPS are available on several hundred stocks and more than two dozen stock indexes and ETFs.

Aside from their time frame, LEAPS work like any other equity or index option. For example, a single (equity) LEAPS contract gives the holder the right to buy or sell 100 shares of stock at a predetermined price on or before the specified expiration date. LEAPS give you more time to be right about your bets on the direction of a stock or stock index, and they give hedgers more time to protect their positions. But there's a price for this extra time: You can expect to pay a lot more for a LEAPS than you would for a regular (short-term) option. For example, in mid-2006, a two-month call on Cisco Systems (with a strike price of 20) was trading at 0.95. The same call with a two-and-a-half-year expiration date was trading at 4.50. The difference should come as no surprise. LEAPS,

LEAPS
long-term options.

HOTLINKS

The following sites provide more information about different types of LEAPS:

www.phlx.com/products/options/
leapspecs.html
www.cboe.com/otec/ssb/SymbolIndex.aspx

being nothing more than long-term options, are loaded with *time premium*. And as we saw earlier in this chapter, other things being equal, *the more time an option has to expiration, the higher the quoted price.*

CONCEPTS IN REVIEW
Answers available at: www.myfinancelab.com

14.12 Briefly describe the differences and similarities between *stock-index options* and *stock options*. Do the same for *foreign currency options* and stock options.

14.13 Identify and briefly discuss two different ways to use stock-index options. Do the same for foreign currency options.

14.14 Why would an investor want to use index options to hedge a portfolio of common stock? Could the same objective be obtained using *options on ETFs?* If the investor thinks the market is in for a fall, why not just sell the stock?

14.15 What are *LEAPS?* Why would an investor want to use a LEAPS option rather than a regular listed option?

Summary

LG 1 **Discuss the basic nature of options in general and puts and calls in particular, and understand how these investment vehicles work.** An option gives the holder the right to buy or sell a certain amount of some real or financial asset at a set price for a set period of time. Puts and calls are the most widely used type of option. These derivative securities offer considerable leverage potential. A put enables the holder to *sell* a certain amount of a specified security at a specified price over a specified time period. A call gives the holder the right to *buy* the security at a specified price over a specified period of time.

LG 2 **Describe the options market and note key options provisions, including strike prices and expiration dates.** The options market is made up of conventional (OTC) options and listed options. OTC options are used predominantly by institutional investors. Listed options are traded on organized exchanges such as the CBOE and the AMEX. The creation of listed options exchanges led to standardized options features and to widespread use of options by individual investors. Among the option provisions are the strike price (the stipulated price at which the underlying asset can be bought or sold) and the expiration date (the date when the contract expires).

LG 3 **Explain how put and call options are valued and the forces that drive options prices in the marketplace.** The value of a call is the market price of the underlying security less the strike price on the call. The value of a put is its strike price less the market price of the security. The value of an option is driven by the current market price of the underlying asset. Most puts and calls sell at premium prices. The size of the premium depends on the length of the option contract (the so-called time premium), the speculative appeal and amount of price volatility in the underlying financial asset, and the general level of interest rates.

LG 4 **Describe the profit potential of puts and calls, and note some popular put and call investment strategies.** Investors who hold puts make money when the value of the underlying asset goes down over time. Call investors make money when the underlying asset moves up in price. Aggressive investors will use puts and calls either for speculation or in highly specialized writing and spreading programs. Conservative investors like the low unit costs and the limited risk that puts and calls offer in absolute dollar terms. Conservative investors often use options to hedge positions in other securities.

LG 5 **Explain the profit potential and loss exposure from writing covered call options, and discuss how writing options can be used as a strategy for enhancing investment returns.** Covered call writers have limited loss exposure because they write options against securities they already own. The maximum profit occurs when the price of the stock equals the strike price of the call. If the stock price goes above the strike price, then any loss on the option is offset by a gain on the stock position. If the stock price goes down, part of the loss on the stock is offset by the proceeds from the call option. Option writing can be combined with other securities to create investment strategies for specific market conditions.

LG 6 **Describe market index options, puts and calls on foreign currencies, and LEAPS, and discuss how these securities can be used by investors.** Standardized put and call options are available on stock-market indexes, like the S&P 500 (in the form of index options or ETF options), and on a number of foreign currencies (currency options). Also available are LEAPS, which are listed options that carry lengthy expiration dates. Although these securities can be used just like stock options, the index and currency options tend to be used primarily for speculation or to develop hedge positions.

Key Terms

Discussion Questions

LG 2

Q14.1 Using the stock or index option quotations in Figures 14.1 and 14.3, respectively, find the option premium, the time premium, and the stock or index break-even point for the following puts and calls.
    a. The September Chevron *call* with the $65 strike price.
    b. The June ETrade *put* with the $25 strike price.
    c. The July Dow Diamond ETF *call* with the $111 strike price.
    d. The July S&P 100 *call* with the 585 strike price.
    e. The June DJIA *put* with the 113 strike price.

LG 3

Q14.2 Prepare a schedule similar to the one in Table 14.1 for the July S&P 100 *calls* listed in Figure 14.3. (Use the ones with the strike prices of 575 and 600.) Do the same for the June and July *puts* (using the same two strike prices). Briefly explain your findings.

LG 5

Q14.3 Refer to Figure 14.1 and assume that you write a covered call on Alcan by writing 1 September *call* with a strike price of $55, and buying 100 shares of stock at the market price shown in Figure 14.1. Assume the stock will pay no dividends between now and the expiration date of the option.
    a. What is the total profit if the stock price remains unchanged?
    b. What is the total profit if the stock price goes up to $55?
    c. What is the total loss if the stock price goes down to $49?

LG 6

Q14.4 Assume you hold a well-balanced portfolio of common stocks. Under what conditions might you want to use a stock-index (or ETF) option to hedge the portfolio?
    a. Briefly explain how such options could be used to hedge a portfolio against a drop in the market.
    b. Discuss what happens if the market does, in fact, go down.
    c. What happens if the market goes up instead?

LG 3   LG 4

Q14.5 Using the resources available at your campus or public library (or on the Internet), complete each of the following tasks. (*Note:* Show your work for all calculations.)
    a. Find an *in-the-money call* that has 2 or 3 months to expiration. (Select an *equity option* that is at least $2 or $3 in the money.) What's the fundamental value of this option, and how much premium is it carrying? Using the current market price of the underlying stock (the one listed with the option), determine what kind of dollar and percentage return the option would generate if the underlying stock goes up 10%. How about if the stock goes down 10%?
    b. Repeat part **a**, but this time use an *in-the-money put*. (Choose an equity option that's at least $2 or $3 in the money and has 2 or 3 months to expiration.) Answer the same questions as above.
    c. Repeat once more the exercise in part **a**, but this time use an *out-of-the-money call*. (Select an equity option, at least $2 or $3 out of the money with 2 or 3 months to expiration.) Answer the same questions.
    d. Compare the valuation properties and performance characteristics of in-the-money calls and out-of-the-money calls [from parts **a** and **c**]. Note some of the advantages and disadvantages of each.

Problems

LG 3 **P14.1** Cisco stock is selling for $19. Call options with an $18 exercise price are priced at $2.50. What is the fundamental value of the option, and what is the time premium?

LG 3 **P14.2** Gillet is trading at $31.11. Call options with a strike price of $35 are priced at $0.30. What is the fundamental value of the option, and what is the time premium?

LG 3 **P14.3** Verizon is trading at $36. Put options with a strike price of $45 are priced at $10.50. What is the fundamental value of the option, and what is the time premium?

LG 3 **P14.4** Verizon is trading at $36. Put options with a strike price of $27.50 are priced at $0.85. What is the fundamental value of the option, and what is the time premium?

LG 3 **P14.5** A 6-month call on a certain common stock carries a strike price of $60. It can be purchased at a cost of $600. Assume that the underlying stock rises to $75 per share by the expiration date of the option. How much profit would this option generate over the 6-month holding period? Using HPR, what is its rate of return?

LG 4 **LG 6** **P14.6** You believe that oil prices will be rising more than expected, and that rising prices will result in lower earnings for industrial companies that use a lot of petroleum-related products in their operations. You also believe that the effects on this sector will be magnified because consumer demand will fall as oil prices rise. You locate an exchange traded fund, XLB, that represents a basket of industrial companies. You don't want to short the ETF because you don't have enough margin in your account. XLB is currently trading at $23. You decide to buy a put option (for 100 shares) with a strike price of $24, priced at $1.20. It turns out that you are correct. At expiration, XLB is trading at $20. Calculate your profit.

XLB: Materials—$23.00

	Calls			Puts	
Strike	Expiration	Price	Strike	Expiration	Price
$20	November	$0.25	$20	November	$1.55
$24	November	$0.25	$24	November	$1.20

LG 4 **LG 6** **P14.7** Refer to the table for XLB in Problem 14.6. What happens if you are wrong and the price of XLB increases to $25 on the expiration date?

LG 6 **P14.8** Dorothy Lasnicka does a lot of investing in the stock market and is a frequent user of stock-index options. She is convinced that the market is about to undergo a broad retreat and has decided to buy a put on the S&P 100 Index. The put carries a strike price of 690 and is quoted in the financial press at 4.50. Although the S&P Index of 100 stocks is currently at 686.45, Dorothy thinks it will drop to 665 by the expiration date on the option. How much profit will she make, and what will be her holding period return if she is right? How much will she lose if the S&P 100 goes up (rather than down) by 25 points and reaches 715 by the date of expiration?

LG 3   LG 4   **P14.9** Bill Weeks holds 600 shares of Lubbock Gas and Light. He bought the stock several years ago at 48.50, and the shares are now trading at 75. Bill is concerned that the market is beginning to soften. He doesn't want to sell the stock, but he would like to be able to protect the profit he's made. He decides to hedge his position by buying 6 puts on Lubbock G&L. The 3-month puts carry a strike price of 75 and are currently trading at 2.50.

   a. How much profit or loss will Bill make on this deal if the price of Lubbock G&L does indeed drop, to $60 a share, by the expiration date on the puts?

   b. How would he do if the stock kept going up in price and reached $90 a share by the expiration date?

   c. What do you see as the major advantages of using puts as hedge vehicles?

   d. Would Bill have been better off using in-the-money puts—that is, puts with an $85 strike price that are trading at 10.50? How about using out-of-the-money puts—say, those with a $70 strike price, trading at 1.00? Explain.

LG 4   LG 6   **P14.10** P. F. Chang holds a well-diversified portfolio of high-quality, large-cap stocks. The current value of Chang's portfolio is $735,000, but he is concerned that the market is heading for a big fall (perhaps as much as 20%) over the next 3 to 6 months. He doesn't want to sell all his stocks because he feels they all have good long-term potential and should perform nicely once stock prices have bottomed out. As a result, he's thinking about using index options to hedge his portfolio. Assume that the S&P 500 currently stands at 1,470 and among the many put options available on this index are two that have caught his eye: (1) a 6-month put with a strike price of 1,450 that's trading at 26, and (2) a 6-month put with a strike price of 1390 that's quoted at 4.50.

   a. How many S&P 500 puts would Chang have to buy to protect his $735,000 stock portfolio? How much would it cost him to buy the necessary number of 1,450 puts? How much would it cost to buy the 1390 puts?

   b. Now, considering the performance of both the put options and the Chang portfolio, determine how much *net* profit (or loss) Chang will earn from each of these put hedges if both the market (as measured by the S&P 500) and the Chang portfolio fall by 15% over the next 6 months. What if the market and the Chang portfolio fall by only 5%? What if they go up by 10%?

   c. Do you think Chang should set up the put hedge and, if so, using which put option? Explain.

   d. Finally, assume that the DJIA is currently at 14,550 and that a 6-month put option on the Dow is available with a strike price of 144, and is currently trading at 2.50. How many of these puts would Chang have to buy to protect his portfolio, and what would they cost? Would Chang be better off with the Dow options or the S&P 1,450 puts? Briefly explain.

LG 3   LG 5   **P14.11** Angelo Martino just purchased 500 shares of AT&E at 61.50, and he has decided to write covered calls against these stocks. Accordingly, he sells 5 AT&E calls at their current market price of 5.75. The calls have 3 months to expiration and carry a strike price of 65. The stock pays a quarterly dividend of $0.80 a share (the next dividend to be paid in about a month).

a. Determine the total profit and holding period return Angelo will generate if the stock rises to $65 a share by the expiration date on the calls.
b. What happens to Angelo's profit (and return) if the price of the stock rises to more than $65 a share?
c. Does this covered call position offer any protection (or cushion) against a drop in the price of the stock? Explain.

LG 6   P14.12 Bob owns stock in a retailer that he believes is highly undervalued. Bob expects that the stock will increase in value nicely over the long term. He is concerned, however, that the entire retail industry may fall out of favor with investors as some larger companies report falling sales. There are no options traded on his stock, but Bob would like to hedge against his fears about retail. He locates a symbol RTH, which is a Retail HOLDRS (go to www.amex.com and look this symbol up). Can Bob hedge against the risk he is concerned with by using RTH? Using options?

LG 5   LG 6   P14.13 Here's your chance to try your hand at setting up an index-option *straddle*. Use the quotes for the DJIA index options listed in Figure 14.3. Assume that the market, as measured by the DJIA, stands at 11,200 and you decide to set up a *long straddle* on the Dow by buying 100 July 112 calls and an equal number of July 112 puts. (Ignore transaction costs.)
a. What will it cost you to set up the straddle, and how much profit (or loss) do you stand to make if the market falls by 750 points by the expiration dates on the options? What if it goes up by 750 points by expiration? What if it stays at 11,200?
b. Repeat part **a**, but this time assume that you set up a *short straddle* by selling/writing 100 July 112 puts and calls.
c. What do you think of the use of option straddles as an investment strategy? What are the risks, and what are the rewards?

See www.myfinancelab.com **for Web Exercises,**
Spreadsheets, and other online resources.

Case Problem 14.1   *The Franciscos' Investment Options*

LG 3   LG 4   Hector Francisco is a successful businessman in Atlanta. The box-manufacturing firm he and his wife, Judy, founded several years ago has prospered. Because he is self-employed, Hector is building his own retirement fund. So far, he has accumulated a substantial sum in his investment account, mostly by following an aggressive investment posture. He does this because, as he puts it, "In this business, you never know when the bottom's gonna fall out." Hector has been following the stock of Rembrandt Paper Products (RPP), and after conducting extensive analysis, he feels the stock is about ready to move. Specifically, he believes that within the next 6 months, RPP could go to about $80 per share, from its current level of $57.50. The stock pays annual dividends of $2.40 per share. Hector figures he would receive two quarterly dividend payments over his 6-month investment horizon.

In studying RPP, Hector has learned that the company has 6-month call options (with $50 and $60 strike prices) listed on the CBOE. The CBOE calls are quoted at $8 for the options with $50 strike prices and at $5 for the $60 options.

Questions

a. How many alternative investment vehicles does Hector have if he wants to invest in RPP for no more than 6 months? What if he has a 2-year investment horizon?

b. Using a 6-month holding period and assuming the stock does indeed rise to $80 over this time frame:
   1. Find the value of both calls, given that at the end of the holding period neither contains any investment premium.
   2. Determine the holding period return for each of the 3 investment alternatives open to Hector Francisco.

c. Which course of action would you recommend if Hector simply wants to maximize profit? Would your answer change if other factors (e.g., comparative risk exposure) were considered along with return? Explain.

Case Problem 14.2   *Fred's Quandary: To Hedge or Not to Hedge*

LG 3   **LG 4**   A little more than 10 months ago, Fred Weaver, a mortgage banker in Phoenix, bought 300 shares of stock at $40 per share. Since then, the price of the stock has risen to $75 per share. It is now near the end of the year, and the market is starting to weaken. Fred feels there is still plenty of play left in the stock but is afraid the tone of the market will be detrimental to his position. His wife, Denise, is taking an adult education course on the stock market and has just learned about put and call hedges. She suggests that he use puts to hedge his position. Fred is intrigued by the idea, which he discusses with his broker, who advises him that the needed puts are indeed available on his stock. Specifically, he can buy 3-month puts, with $75 strike prices, at a cost of $550 each (quoted at 5.50).

Questions

a. Given the circumstances surrounding Fred's current investment position, what benefits could be derived from using the puts as a hedge device? What would be the major drawback?

b. What will Fred's minimum profit be if he buys 3 puts at the indicated option price? How much would he make if he did not hedge but instead sold his stock immediately at a price of $75 per share?

c. Assuming Fred uses 3 puts to hedge his position, indicate the amount of profit he will generate if the stock moves to $100 by the expiration date of the puts. What if the stock drops to $50 per share?

d. Should Fred use the puts as a hedge? Explain. Under what conditions would you urge him *not* to use the puts as a hedge?

Excel with Spreadsheets

One of the positive attributes of investing in options is the profit potential from the puts or calls. The quoted market price of the option is influenced by the time to expiration, stock volatility, market interest rates, and the behavior of the price of the underlying common stock. The latter variable tends to drive the price movement in options and impacts its potential for profitable returns.

Create a spreadsheet model, similar to that presented below, in order to calculate the profits and/or losses from investing in the option described.

	A	B	C	D	E	F	G	H	I	J
1										
2						Long		100		3-Month Call Option
3						Position		Shares of		on the Stock
4						No		Underlying		Strike Price
5						Option		Common Stock		$$$
6										
7	Today									
8										
9	Market value of stock			$$		$$		$$		
10	Call strike price			$$						
11	Call option premium			$$						
12										
13										
14	Scenario One : 3 months later									
15	Expected market value of stock			$$		$$		$$		
16	Stock value @ strike price			$$						$$
17	Call premium			$$						$$
18	Breakeven point			$$						$$
19										
20	Profit (Loss)					$$		$$		

John has been following the stock market very closely over the past 18 months and has a strong belief that future stock prices will be significantly higher. He has 2 alternatives that he can follow. The first is to use a long-term strategy—purchase the stock today and sell it sometime in the future at a possibly higher price. The other alternative is to buy a 3-month call option. The relevant information needed to analyze the 2 alternatives is presented below:

Current stock price = $49
Desires to buy one round lot = 100 shares
3-month call option has a strike price of $51 and a call premium of $2

Questions

a. In scenario 1, if the stock price 3 months from now is $58:
   1. What is the long-position profit or loss?
   2. What is the break-even point of the call option?
   3. Is the option in or out of the money?
   4. What is the option profit or loss?
b. In scenario 2, if the stock price 3 months from now is $42:
   1. What is the long-position profit or loss?
   2. What is the break-even point of the call option?
   3. Is the option in or out of the money?
   4. What is the option profit or loss?

Chapter 15

Commodities and Financial Futures

LEARNING GOALS

After studying this chapter, you should be able to:

LG 1   Describe the essential features of a futures contract and explain how the futures market operates.

LG 2   Explain the role that hedgers and speculators play in the futures market, including how profits are made and lost.

LG 3   Describe the commodities segment of the futures market and the basic characteristics of these investment vehicles.

LG 4   Discuss the trading strategies investors can use with commodities, and explain how investment returns are measured.

LG 5   Explain the difference between a physical commodity and a financial future, and discuss the growing role of financial futures in the market today.

LG 6   Discuss the trading techniques that can be used with financial futures, and note how these securities can be used in conjunction with other investment vehicles.

In March 2005, a new commodity began trading on the Chicago Mercantile Exchange (CME). Ethanol (ethyl alcohol) is an alcohol produced by fermenting and distilling starch crops such as sugar cane, corn, wheat, barley, and sugar beet molasses. Ethanol has three major uses: beverages, industrial products, and increasingly, as an alternative fuel source.

With worldwide demand for energy on the rise, ethanol is becoming more attractive as a renewable, environmentally friendly fuel that enhances the nation's economy and its energy independence. Ethanol does not provide complete independence from fossil fuels since even the most popular version of ethanol-based motor fuel (E85) requires 15% gasoline and 85% ethanol. Pushed by rising demand, U.S. ethanol producers operated 95 refineries at the end of 2005, with 38 more refineries under construction or expansion. Both General Motors and Ford Motor Co. have committed to increasing their production of Flexible Fuel Vehicles which can run on either gasoline or E85.

The availability of the CME ethanol futures contracts, which can be traded electronically, will help the ethanol industry continue to grow. Essentially, a future is a contract to buy or sell a certain amount of an item—for example, agricultural products or foreign currencies—at a price for delivery on a specific future date. Before investing in individual commodities or trading financial futures, you should understand how these specialized and often high-risk investments work. This chapter will introduce you to the world of commodities and illustrate how to use futures contracts as a tool for risk management.

Sources: "From Niche to Nation, Ethanol Industry Outlook 2006," published by the Renewable Fuels Association, downloaded from www.ethanolrfa.org on August 4, 2006; "What is E85?" downloaded from www.e85fuel.com on August 4, 2005; "Ethanol Futures Scheduled to Launch on March 29th," March 3, 2005, downloaded from http://www.prnewswire.com on August 4, 2006.

The Futures Market

LG 1   LG 2

"Psst, hey buddy. Wanna buy some copper? How about some coffee, or pork bellies, or propane? Maybe the Japanese yen or Swiss franc strikes your fancy?" Sound a bit unusual? Perhaps, but these items have one thing in common: They all represent real investment vehicles. This is the more exotic side of investing—the market for commodities and financial futures—and it often involves a considerable amount of speculation. The risks are enormous, but with some luck, the payoffs can be phenomenal. Even more important than luck, however, is the need for patience and know-how. Indeed, *these are specialized investment products that require specialized investor skills.*

The amount of futures trading in the United States has mushroomed over the past two or three decades. An increasing number of investors have turned to futures trading as a way to earn attractive, highly competitive rates of return. A major reason behind the growth in futures trading has been the *number and variety of futures contracts now available for trading.* Today, markets exist for the traditional primary commodities, such as grains and metals, as well as for processed commodities, crude oil and gasoline, electricity, foreign currencies, money market securities, U.S. and foreign debt securities, Eurodollar securities, and common stocks. You can even buy listed put and call *options* on just about any actively traded futures contract. All these commodities and financial assets are traded in what is known as the *futures market.*

■ Market Structure

cash market
a market where a product or commodity changes hands in exchange for a cash price paid when the transaction is completed.

futures market
the organized market for the trading of futures contracts.

When a bushel of wheat is sold, the transaction takes place in the **cash market**. The bushel changes hands in exchange for the cash price paid to the seller. For all practical purposes the transaction is completed then and there. Most traditional securities are traded in this type of market. However, a bushel of wheat can also be sold in the **futures market**, the organized market for the trading of futures contracts. In this market, the seller would not actually deliver the wheat until some mutually agreed-upon date in the future. As a result, the transaction would not be completed for some time: The seller would receive partial payment for the bushel of wheat at the time the agreement was entered into and the balance on delivery. The buyer, in turn, would own a highly liquid futures contract that could be held (and presented for delivery of the bushel of wheat) or traded in the futures market. No matter what the buyer does with the contract, as long as it is outstanding, the seller has a *legally binding obligation to make delivery* of the stated quantity of wheat on a specified date in the future. The buyer/holder has a similar *obligation to take delivery* of the underlying commodity.

HOTLINKS

For information on more than 70 exchanges around the world and details on the futures and options contracts they trade, see:

www.numa.com/ref/exchange.htm

futures contract
a commitment to deliver a certain amount of some specified item at some specified date in the future.

delivery month
the time when a commodity must be delivered; defines the life of a futures contract.

Futures Contracts A **futures contract** is a commitment to deliver a certain amount of a specified item at a specified date at an agreed-upon price. Each market establishes its own contract specifications. These include not only the quantity and quality of the item but also the delivery procedure and delivery month. The **delivery month** on a futures contract is much like the expiration date on put and call options. It specifies when the commodity or item must be delivered and thus defines the life of the contract. For example, the Chicago

Board of Trade specifies that each of its soybean contracts will involve 5,000 bushels of USDA No. 2 yellow soybeans; soybean delivery months are January, March, May, July, August, September, and November.

In addition, futures contracts have *their own trading hours*. Unlike listed stocks and bonds, which begin and end trading at the same time, normal trading hours for commodities and financial futures vary widely. For example, oats trade from 9:30 A.M. to 1:15 P.M. (central); silver, from 7:25 A.M. to 1:25 P.M.; live cattle, from 9:05 A.M. to 1:00 P.M.; U.S. Treasury bonds, from 7:20 A.M. to 2:00 P.M.; and S&P 500 stock-index contracts, from 8:30 A.M. to 3:15 P.M. In addition, many of these contracts have one set of hours for open-outcry trading and another for electronic trading. It sounds a bit confusing, but it seems to work.

Table 15.1 lists a cross section of 13 different commodities and financial futures. (The market value of a single contract, as reported in Table 15.1, is found by multiplying the size of the contract by the latest quoted price of the underling commodity. For example, there are 37,500 pounds of coffee in a single contract, so if coffee's trading at 96¢ a pound, then the market value of one contract is 37,500 × $0.96 = $36,000.) As you can see, the typical futures contract covers a large quantity of the underlying product or financial instrument. However, although the value of a single contract is normally quite large, the actual amount of investor capital required to deal in these vehicles is relatively small, because *all trading in this market is done on a margin basis*.

Options Versus Futures Contracts In many respects, futures contracts are closely related to the call options we studied in Chapter 14. For example, both involve the future delivery of an item at an agreed-upon price, and both are derivative securities. But there is a *significant difference* between a futures contract and an options contract. To begin with, a futures contract *obligates* a person to buy or sell a specified amount of a given commodity on or before a stated date—unless the contract is canceled or liquidated before it expires. In contrast, an option gives the holder the *right* to buy or sell a specific amount of a real or financial asset at a specific price over a specified period of time.

TABLE 15.1 Futures Contract Dimensions

Contract	Size of a Contract*	Recent Market Value of a Single Contract**
Corn	5,000 bu	$ 11,500
Wheat	5,000 bu	18,300
Live cattle	40,000 lb	33,600
Pork bellies	40,000 lb	38,400
Coffee	37,500 lb	35,750
Cotton	50,000 lb	23,000
Gold	100 troy oz	58,500
Copper	25,000 lb	83,500
Crude oil	1,000 bbls	70,870
Japanese yen	12.5 million yen	108,500
2-year Treasury notes	$200,000	202,420
Treasury bonds	$100,000	105,700
S&P 500 Stock Index	$250 times the index	313,750

*The size of some contracts may vary by exchange.
**Contract values are representative of those that existed at mid-year 2006.

In addition, whereas *price* (strike price) is one of the specified variables on a call option, it is *not* stated anywhere on a futures contract. Instead, the price on a futures contract is established through trading on the floor of a commodities exchange. This means that *the delivery price is set at whatever price the contract sells for.* So, if you bought a contract three months ago at $2.50 a bushel, then that's the price you'll pay to take delivery of the underlying product, even if the contract trades at, say, $3.00 a bushel at its date of expiration (i.e., delivery date). Equally important, the risk of loss with an option is limited to the price paid for it. A futures contract has *no such limit on exposure to loss.* Finally, while options contracts have an explicit up-front cost (in the form of an option premium), futures contracts do not. Granted, the purchase of a futures contract does involve a margin deposit, but that's nothing more than a refundable *security deposit*, not a sunk cost (like an option premium).

Major Exchanges Futures contracts in this country got their start in the agricultural segment of the economy over 150 years ago, when individuals who produced, owned, and/or processed foodstuffs sought a way to protect themselves against adverse price movements. Later, futures contracts came to be traded by individuals who were not necessarily connected with agriculture, but who wanted to make money with commodities by speculating on their price swings.

HOTLINKS

Visit the Chicago Board of Trade at the site below. Click on [Education] for a Glossary of Terms, Simulators, and Contract Specifications, as well as Tutorials.

www.cbot.com

The first organized commodities exchange in this country was the Chicago Board of Trade, which opened its doors in 1848. Over time, additional markets opened. There currently are more than a dozen U.S. exchanges that deal in listed futures contracts, although a number of these are small exchanges trading in only a few types of contracts. The majority of trading, in fact, occurs on only a few exchanges. The Chicago Mercantile Exchange (CME) is the most active exchange, with more trading volume than all other futures exchanges combined. The CME is followed in size by the Chicago Board of Trade (CBT) and the New York Mercantile Exchange (NYMEX). Together, these three exchanges account for about 95% of all the trading conducted on U.S. futures exchanges. (*Note:* As we were about to go to press, it was announced that the Chicago Mercantile Exchange and the Chicago Board of Trade had signed a definitive agreement to merge, with the combined company to be named the CME Group, Inc. The two exchanges will continue to operate seperately—one as an open-outcry trading floor and the other utilizing an electronic trading platform.)

Most exchanges deal in a number of different commodities or financial assets, and many commodities and financial futures are traded on more than one exchange. Annual volume of trading on futures exchanges has surpassed the trillion-dollar mark. Today, most exchanges conduct trading with a mix of electronic trading and **open-outcry auction**, wherein the actual trading is conducted through a series of shouts, body motions, and hand signals, as shown in Figure 15.1 (on page 654).

open-outcry auction
in futures trading, an auction in which trading is done through a series of shouts, body motions, and hand signals.

In 1992, CME Globex became the first global electronic futures trading platform. Currently, Globex offers trading 23 hours a day, five days a week, and provides an international link between futures exchanges. This trading platform has allowed the CME Eurodollar futures contract to become the single most actively traded futures contract in the world. Indeed, the three most actively traded contracts on CME Globex (three-month Eurodollars, the E-Mini S&P 500 Stock Index, and the Mini-Nasdaq 100 Stock Index) represent more than 40% of all futures trading volume on the U.S. exchanges.

FIGURE 15.1

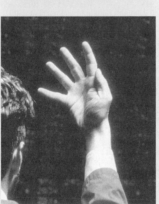
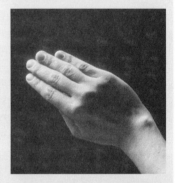

The Auction Market at Work on the Floor of the Chicago Board of Trade

Traders employ a system of open outcry and hand signals to indicate whether they wish to buy or sell and the price at which they wish to do so. Fingers held *vertically* indicate the number of contracts a trader wants to buy or sell. Fingers held *horizontally* indicate the fraction of a cent above or below the last traded full-cent price at which the trader will buy or sell. (*Source:* Copyright © 2003 Board of Trade of the City of Chicago, Inc. All Rights Reserved. Used with permission.)

▌ Trading in the Futures Market

Basically, the futures market contains two types of traders: hedgers and speculators. The market could not exist and operate efficiently without either one. The **hedgers** are commodities producers and processors who use futures contracts to protect their interests in the underlying commodity or financial instrument. For example, if a rancher thinks the price of cattle will drop in the near future, he will hedge his position by selling a futures contract on cattle in the hope of locking in as high a price as possible for his herd. In effect, the hedgers provide the underlying strength of the futures market and represent the very reason for its existence. Today, hedgers also include financial institutions and corporate money managers.

hedgers
producers and processors who use futures contracts to protect their interest in an underlying commodity or financial instrument.

Speculators, in contrast, give the market liquidity. They trade futures contracts simply to earn a profit on expected swings in the price of a futures contract. They have no inherent interest in the commodity or financial future other than the price action and potential capital gains it can produce.

Trading Mechanics Once futures contracts are created, they can readily be traded in the market. Like common stocks, futures contracts are bought and sold through local brokerage offices, or on many Internet sites. Except for setting up a special commodities trading account, there is no difference between trading futures and dealing in stocks or bonds. The same types of orders are used, and margin trading is standard practice. Any investor can buy or sell any contract, with any delivery month, at any time, so long as it is currently being traded on one of the exchanges.

Buying a contract is referred to as *taking a long position*. Selling one is known as *taking a short position*. It is exactly like going long or short with stocks and has the same connotation: The investor who is long wants the price to rise, and the short seller wants it to drop. Investors can liquidate both long and short positions simply by executing an offsetting transaction. The short seller, for example, would cover her position by buying an equal amount of the contract. In general, only about 1% of all futures contracts are settled by delivery. The rest are offset prior to the delivery month. All trades are subject to normal transaction costs, which include **round-trip commissions** for each contract traded. A round-trip commission includes the commission costs on both ends of the transaction—to buy and sell a contract. Although the exact size of the commission depends on the number and type of contracts being traded, trades that are executed electronically usually have round-trip commissions under $10 and are much less expensive than trades that have to be routed to a pit broker.

round-trip commissions
the commission costs on both ends (buying and selling) of a futures transaction.

HOTLINKS
To see a list of initial margins and maintenance margins for a number of different futures contracts, go to:
www.altavest.com/margins.htm

margin deposit
amount deposited with a broker to cover any loss in the market value of a futures contract that may result from adverse price movements.

initial deposit
the amount of investor capital that must be deposited with a broker at the time of a commodity transaction.

Margin Trading Buying on margin means putting up only a fraction of the total price in cash. Margin, in effect, is the *amount of equity* that goes into the deal. *All futures contracts are traded on a margin basis.* The margin required usually ranges from about 2% to 10% of the contract value. This is very low compared to the margin required for stocks and most other securities. Furthermore, there is *no borrowing* required on the part of the investor to finance the balance of the contract. The **margin deposit**, as margin is called with futures, represents security to cover any loss in the market value of the contract that may result from adverse price movements. It exists simply to guarantee fulfillment of the contract. The margin deposit is not a partial payment for the commodity or financial instrument, nor is it related to the value of the underlying product or item.

The size of the required margin deposit is specified as a dollar amount. It varies according to the type of contract (which is based on the price volatility in the underlying commodity or financial asset). In some cases, it also varies according to the exchange on which the commodity is traded. Table 15.2 (on page 656) gives the margin requirements for the same 13 commodities and financial instruments listed in Table 15.1 on page 652. Compared to the size and value of the futures contracts, margin requirements are very low. The **initial deposit** noted in Table 15.2 is the amount of capital the investor must deposit

TABLE 15.2 Margin Requirements for a Sample of Commodities and Financial Futures

Contract	Initial Margin Deposit	Maintenance Margin Deposit	Exchange
Corn	$ 540	$ 400	CBOT
Wheat	1,283	950	CBOT
Live cattle	945	700	CME
Pork bellies	1,620	1,200	CME
Coffee	2,520	1,800	NYBOT
Cotton	1,260	900	NYBOT
Gold	4,050	3,000	COMEX
Copper	12,150	9,000	COMEX
Crude oil	4,725	3,850	NYMEX
Japanese yen	2,700	2,000	CME
2-year Treasury notes	473	350	CBOT
Treasury bonds	1,350	1,000	CBOT
S&P 500 Stock Index	19,688	15,750	CME

Note: In mid-2006 the exchanges identified above specified these margin requirements as outright, speculative margins for nonmembers. Different margin requirements are usually set for exchange members and for hedge transactions. They are meant to be typical of the ongoing requirements that customers are expected to live up to. Depending on the volatility of the market, exchange-minimum margin requirements are changed frequently. Thus, the requirements in this table are also subject to change on short notice. The actual margin requirement for a specific type of transaction on a given exchange is typically reported on the exchange's Web site under "Contract specifications" for that futures contract.

with the broker when initiating the transaction; it represents the amount of money required to make a given investment. (The margins quoted in Table 15.2 are for speculative transactions. Typically, the initial deposit amount is *slightly lower* for hedge transactions.)

After the investment is made, the market value of a contract will rise and fall as the quoted price of the underlying commodity or financial instrument goes up or down. Such market behavior will cause the amount of margin on deposit to change. To be sure that an adequate margin is always on hand, investors are required to meet a second type of margin requirement, the **maintenance deposit**. This deposit, which is slightly less than the initial deposit, establishes the minimum amount of margin that an investor must keep in the account at all times. For instance, if the initial deposit on a commodity is $1,000 per contract, its maintenance margin might be $750. So long as the market value of the contract does not fall by more than $250 (the difference between the contract's initial and maintenance margins), the investor has no problem. But if the market moves against you and the value of the contract drops by more than the allowed amount, you will receive a *margin call*. You must then immediately deposit enough cash to bring the position back to the *initial margin level*.

An investor's margin position is checked daily via a procedure known as **mark-to-the-market**. That is, the gain or loss in a contract's value is determined at the end of each session. At that time the broker debits or credits the account accordingly. In a falling market, an investor may receive a number of margin calls and be required to make additional margin payments. Failure to do so will mean that the broker has no choice but to close out the position—that is, to sell the contract.

maintenance deposit
the minimum amount of margin that must be kept in a margin account at all times.

mark-to-the-market
a daily check of an investor's margin position, determined at the end of each session, at which time the broker debits or credits the account as needed.

CONCEPTS IN REVIEW

Answers available at: www.myfinancelab.com

15.1 What is a *futures contract?* Briefly explain how it is used as an investment vehicle.

15.2 Discuss the difference between a *cash market* and a *futures market.*

15.3 What is the major source of return to commodities speculators? How important is current income from dividends and interest?

15.4 Why are both hedgers and speculators important to the efficient operation of a futures market?

15.5 Explain how margin trading is conducted in the futures market.
    a. What is the difference between an *initial deposit* and a *maintenance deposit?*
    b. Are investors ever required to put up additional margin? If so, when?

Commodities

LG 3   LG 4

Physical commodities like grains, metals, wood, and meat make up a major portion of the futures market. They have been actively traded in this country for well over a century. The material that follows focuses on *commodities trading.* We begin with a review of the basic characteristics and investment merits of these vehicles.

▌Basic Characteristics

Physical commodities are found on nearly all of the U.S. futures exchanges. In fact, several of them deal only in commodities. The market for commodity contracts is divided into four major segments: grains and oilseeds, livestock and meat, metals and petroleum, and food and fiber. Such segmentation does not affect trading mechanics and procedures. It merely provides a convenient way of categorizing commodities into groups based on similar underlying characteristics.

Table 15.3 (on page 658) shows the diversity of the commodities market and the variety of contracts available. Although the list changes yearly, the table indicates that investors had literally dozens of commodities to choose from in 2006. A number of these (e.g., soybeans, wheat, and sugar) are available in several different forms or grades. Actually, Table 15.3 lists only *some of the more actively traded commodities. Not included* are dozens of commodities (such as butter, cheese, boneless beef, and others) that are not widely traded but still make up a part of this market.

A Commodities Contract Every commodity (whether actively or thinly traded) has certain specifications that spell out in detail the amounts and quality of the product being traded. Figure 15.2 (on page 659) is an excerpt from the "Futures: Daily Settlement" section of the *Wall Street Journal Online* and shows the contract and quotation system used with commodities. Each commodity quote is made up of the same five parts, and all prices are quoted in an identical fashion. In particular, the quote for each commodities contract

TABLE 15.3 Major Classes of Commodities

Grains and Oilseeds		Metals and Petroleum	
Corn	Soybean oil	Electricity	Palladium
Oats	Wheat	Copper	Gasoline
Soybeans	Canola	Gold	Heating oil
Soybean meal	Rice	Platinum	Crude oil
		Silver	Natural gas
Livestock and Meat		Food and Fiber	
Cattle—live	Hogs	Cocoa	Sugar
Cattle—feeder	Pork bellies	Coffee	Cotton
		Milk	Lumber
		Orange juice	

specifies: (1) the product; (2) the exchange on which the contract is traded; (3) the size of the contract (in bushels, pound, tons, etc.); (4) the method of valuing the contract, or pricing unit (e.g., cents per pound or dollars per ton); and (5) the delivery month. Using a corn contract as an illustration, we can see each of these parts in the following illustration:

KEY

1. the product
2. the exchange
3. the size of the contract
4. the pricing unit
5. the delivery months

						Lifetime		Open
	Open	High	Low	Settle	Change	High	Low	Interest
❶ ❷ ❸ ❹								
Corn (CBT)—5,000 bu.; cents per bu.								
May	253.50	253.75	252.25	252.50	–1.75	286.50	230.50	42,796
July	258.00	258.00	256.50	256.75	–1.75	288.00	233.00	60,477
Sept.	260.00	260.50	259.00	259.00	–1.50	263.00	236.00	7,760
Dec.	263.50	264.00	262.50	263.00	–1.25	267.25	244.00	41,638
Mar. 07	271.75	272.00	270.50	271.00	–1.25	276.00	254.75	11,098
May	277.25	278.00	276.25	277.00	–1.00	281.00	273.25	1,326

(❺ delivery months)

settle price
the closing price (last price of the day) for commodities and financial futures.

open interest
the number of contracts currently outstanding on a commodity or financial future.

The *quotation system* used for commodities is based on the size of the contract and the pricing unit. The financial media generally report the open, high, low, and closing prices for each delivery month. With commodities, the last price of the day, or the closing price, is known as the **settle price**. Also reported, at least by the *Wall Street Journal,* is the amount of **open interest** in each contract—that is, the number of contracts currently outstanding. Note in the illustration above that the settle price for May corn was 252.50. Since the pricing system is cents per bushel, this means that the contract was being traded at $2.525 per bushel. Each contract involves 5,000 bushels of corn and each bushel is worth $2.525, thus, the market value of the contract was 5,000 × $2.525 = $12,625.

Price Behavior Commodity prices react to a unique set of economic, political, and international pressures—as well as to the weather. The explanation of *why* commodity prices change is beyond the scope of this book. But they do move up and down just like any other investment vehicle, which is precisely what speculators want. Because we are dealing in such large trading units (5,000 bushels of this or 40,000 pounds of that), even a modest price change can have an enormous impact on the market value of a contract, and therefore on investor returns or losses. For example, if the price of corn goes up or down

FIGURE 15.2 Quotations on Actively Traded Commodity Futures Contracts

These quotes reveal at a glance key information about the various commodities, including the latest high, low, and closing ("settle") prices, as well as the lifetime high and low prices for each contract. (*Source: Wall Street Journal Online*, June 29, 2006, wsj.com/free.)

Thursday, June 29, 2006

Grain and Oilseed Futures

	OPEN	HIGH	LOW	SETTLE	CHG	LIFETIME HIGH	LIFETIME LOW	OPEN INT
Corn (CBT)-5,000 bu.; cents per bu.								
July	225.50	230.00	225.25	228.50	+2.50	279.00	217.25	57,977
Sept	237.00	241.50	236.75	239.75	+2.75	275.00	226.25	466,600
Dec	252.00	256.25	251.25	254.50	+2.50	288.00	237.00	475,582
Mr07	263.50	267.75	263.25	266.25	+2.50	300.00	245.25	90,167
May	273.25	275.75	273.25	275.00	+3.00	301.50	249.75	16,384
July	280.00	283.75	280.00	282.25	+2.00	308.00	252.00	50,235
Sept	288.00	289.50	288.00	289.00	+1.50	309.50	253.00	7,278
Dec	293.50	296.50	293.25	294.75	+.50	316.00	246.50	118,361
Mr08	304.00	306.50	304.00	306.25	+2.25	318.00	277.00	5,094
May	313.00	313.00	313.00	313.00	+2.00	319.00	304.00	1,336
July	319.00	320.00	318.50	319.25	+2.00	324.00	270.00	5,485
Sept	318.00	320.00	318.00	319.00	+2.00	321.00	310.00	38
Dec	320.25	325.00	320.25	325.00	+2.25	331.00	258.50	38,765
Est vol 188,847; vol Wed 214,644; open int, 1,333,302, +3,926.								
Oats (CBT)-5,000 bu.; cents per bu.								
July	206.50	211.00	205.25	211.00	+4.25	211.00	171.00	666
Sept	190.25	192.00	183.50	186.25	-4.00	203.00	165.00	5,483
Dec	194.00	195.50	185.00	186.75	-6.50	205.00	157.00	8,073
My07	194.00	194.00	194.00	194.00	-9.00	194.00	171.00	2
Est vol 2,178; vol Wed 1,835; open int, 14,343, -24.								
Soybeans (CBT)-5,000 bu.; cents per bu.								
July	577.25	585.00	577.00	581.75	+3.25	736.00	535.00	33,568
Aug	584.50	592.50	584.50	589.00	+3.25	707.00	569.00	51,834
Sept	592.25	599.00	592.00	596.25	+3.25	695.00	571.00	20,065
Nov	603.75	612.50	603.50	609.50	+3.75	660.00	542.00	198,271
Ja07	616.00	622.00	616.00	619.50	+3.75	650.00	582.00	10,252
Mar	624.00	630.00	624.00	628.50	+4.25	652.00	587.00	7,955
May	631.75	636.50	631.00	635.00	+4.00	653.00	606.00	6,228
July	643.00	644.00	640.00	640.50	+3.75	657.00	601.00	7,471
Nov	651.00	653.00	648.00	648.50	+1.00	662.00	595.00	11,992
Nv08	666.00	674.00	666.00	668.00	+2.00	684.00	623.00	1,350
Est vol 109,591; vol Wed 113,362; open int, 350,087, -1,071.								

Livestock Futures

	OPEN	HIGH	LOW	SETTLE	CHG	LIFETIME HIGH	LIFETIME LOW	OPEN INT
Cattle-Feeder (CME)-50,000 lbs.; cents per lb.								
Aug	117.200	117.500	114.800	115.000	-2.200	117.925	100.200	17,316
Sept	116.800	116.950	114.700	115.400	-1.550	117.500	99.800	4,274
Oct	115.500	115.750	113.850	114.500	-1.250	116.400	99.350	3,587
Nov	113.850	113.850	111.800	112.500	-1.400	115.000	99.400	1,235
Ja07	109.000	109.000	107.100	107.500	-1.500	110.500	97.250	1,347
Mar	106.800	106.800	105.000	105.000	-1.950	109.000	98.000	155
May	105.500	105.700	104.500	104.500	-1.200	106.500	101.600	58
Est vol 4,791; vol Wed 4,450; open int, 28,021, +548.								
Cattle-Live (CME)-40,000 lbs.; cents per lb.								
June	86.250	86.375	83.600	83.850	-2.400	88.000	72.750	1,784
Aug	87.425	88.000	85.450	85.575	-1.700	88.000	74.500	117,141
Oct	90.525	90.850	88.750	89.400	-.925	91.100	78.350	53,024
Dec	90.500	91.000	89.250	89.575	-1.175	91.325	80.425	35,862
Fb07	92.100	92.150	90.500	91.050	-1.275	92.675	82.600	14,405
Apr	89.000	89.000	87.400	87.800	-1.400	89.850	81.500	2,924
June	83.800	83.900	82.750	83.200	-1.050	84.950	80.525	2,219
Est vol 38,047; vol Wed 30,384; open int, 227,359, +292.								
Hogs-Lean (CME)-40,000 lbs.; cents per lb.								
July	71.750	72.900	71.150	72.100	+.075	77.250	56.900	19,378
Aug	70.000	71.000	69.225	69.475	-.150	74.100	55.125	86,293
Oct	60.400	61.700	60.250	61.050	+.125	63.550	49.800	29,620
Dec	57.600	57.850	56.850	57.650	+.200	59.500	50.350	16,461
Fb07	58.500	58.700	57.800	58.450	-.150	60.500	54.025	5,630
Apr	59.000	59.300	58.600	59.100	-.100	61.250	55.350	2,867
June	63.800	64.000	63.600	63.800	...	64.600	60.950	898
July	60.850	61.350	60.600	61.300	+.550	62.700	60.600	68
Est vol 25,296; vol Wed 20,773; open int, 161,735, -1,339.								
Pork Bellies (CME)-40,000 lbs.; cents per lb.								
July	95.900	98.500	95.750	96.975	+.975	101.000	75.275	846
Aug	91.525	94.000	91.525	92.250	+.725	100.900	73.700	1,140
Mr07	87.000	87.000	87.000	87.000	+.550	87.100	83.200	8
Est vol 545; vol Wed 629; open int, 2,022, +75.								

by just $0.20 per bushel, the value of a *single contract* will change by $1,000. A corn contract can be bought with a $540 initial margin deposit, so it is easy to see the effect this kind of price behavior can have on investor return.

Do commodity prices really move all that much? Judge for yourself: The price change columns in Figure 15.2 show some excellent examples of sizable price changes that occur from one day to the next. Note, for example, that May 2007 oats fell $450 (5,000 bushels × $0.09 = $450), September corn rose $137.50, November soybeans rose $187.50, and August feeder cattle dropped a whopping $1,100. Now, keep in mind that these are *daily* price swings that occurred on *single* contracts. These are sizable changes, even by themselves. But when you look at them relative to the (very small) original investment required (sometimes as low as $500), they quickly add up to serious returns (or losses)! And they occur not because of the volatility of the underlying prices but because of the sheer magnitude of the commodities contracts themselves.

Clearly, such price behavior is one of the magnets that draws investors to commodities. The exchanges recognize the volatile nature of commodities contracts and try to put lids on price fluctuations by imposing daily price limits and maximum daily price ranges. (Similar limits also are put on some financial futures.) The **daily price limit** restricts the interday change in the price of the underlying commodity. For example, the price of corn can change by no more than $0.20 per bushel from one day to the next. The daily limit on cotton is $0.03 per pound. Such limits, however, still leave plenty of room to turn a

daily price limit
restriction on the day-to-day change in the price of an underlying commodity.

maximum daily price range
the amount a commodity price
can change during the day;
usually equal to twice the daily
price limit.

return on invested capital
return to investors based on
the amount of money actually
invested in a security, rather
than the value of the contract
itself.

Equation 15.1 ➤

quick profit. For example, the daily limits on corn and cotton translate into per-day changes of $1,000 for one corn contract and $1,500 for a cotton contract. The **maximum daily price range**, in contrast, limits the amount the price can change *during* the day and is usually equal to twice the daily limit restrictions. For example, the daily price limit on corn is $0.20 per bushel and its maximum daily range is $0.40 per bushel.

Return on Invested Capital Futures contracts have only one source of return: the capital gains that result when prices move in a favorable direction. There is no current income of any kind. The volatile price behavior of futures contracts is one reason why high returns are possible; the other is leverage. Because all futures trading is done on margin, it takes only a small amount of money to control a large investment position—and to participate in the price swings that accompany futures contracts. Of course, the use of leverage also means that an investment can be wiped out in just a matter of days.

We can measure investment return on a commodities contract by calculating **return on invested capital**. This variation of the standard holding period return formula bases return on the *amount of money actually invested in the contract*, rather than on the value of the contract itself. The return on invested capital for a commodities position can be determined according to the following simple formula:

$$\text{Return on invested capital} = \frac{\text{Selling price of commodity contract} - \text{Purchase price of commodity contract}}{\text{Amount of margin deposit}}$$

We can use Equation 15.1 for both long and short transactions. To see how it works, assume you just bought two September corn contracts at 280 ($2.80 per bushel) by depositing the required initial margin of $1,080 ($540 for each contract). Your investment, therefore, amounts to only $1,080, but you control 10,000 bushels of corn worth $28,000 at the time of purchase. Now, assume that September corn has just closed at 294, so you decide to sell out and take your profit. Your return on invested capital is

$$\text{Return on invested capital} = \frac{\$29,400 - \$28,000}{\$1,080}$$

$$= \frac{\$1,400}{\$1,080} = \underline{129.6\%}$$

Clearly, this high rate of return was due not only to an increase in the price of the commodity but also to the fact that you were using very low margin. (The initial margin in this particular transaction equaled less than 5% of the underlying value of the contract.)

▌ Trading Commodities

Investing in commodities takes one of three forms. The first, *speculating*, involves using commodities as a way to generate capital gains. In essence, speculators try to capitalize on the wide price swings that are characteristic of

ETHICS *in* INVESTING

Trading Energy Futures at Enron

Before it was known for its financial problems, Enron, a utility firm operating pipelines and shipping natural gas, had become famous as a business pioneer, blazing new trails in the market for trading risk. In the 1980s, the price of natural gas was deregulated, which meant that its price could go down and up, exposing producers and consumers to risks. Enron decided to exploit new opportunities in the commodities business by trading natural gas futures. The natural gas futures traded on the New York Mercantile Exchange did not take into account regional discrepancies in gas prices. Enron filled this void by agreeing to deliver natural gas to any location in the United States at any time.

In addition to trading natural gas and other energy contracts, in the late 1990s Enron began trading weather derivatives for which no underlying commodities existed. These were just bets on the weather. Its weather-derivatives transactions were worth an estimated $3.5 billion in the United States alone. Thanks to its near-monopoly position in derivatives products, Enron's trading business was initially highly profitable. At one point, the company offered more than 1,800 different contracts for 16 product categories, ranging from oil and natural gas to weather derivatives, broadband services, and emissions rights, and earned 90% of its revenues from trading derivatives. And unlike traditional commodity and futures exchanges and brokers, Enron's online commodity and derivative business was not subject to federal regulations.

However, Enron eventually lost its unique position as the energy business started to mature. When other firms entered the online derivatives-trading business, they competed by charging lower commissions and exploiting the same regional price discrepancies that had been Enron's bread and butter. Enron's trading operations became less profitable. To find new markets and products, the company expanded into areas such as water, foreign power sources, telecommunications, and broadband services. The farther it moved from its core businesses of supplying gas, the more money Enron lost.

The company sought to hide those losses by entering into more risky and bizarre financial contracts. When financial institutions began to realize that Enron was essentially a shell game, they withdrew their credit. At that point, despite rosy assurances from its founder and CEO Ken Lay, Enron went into a death spiral which ended in bankruptcy on December 2, 2001.

CRITICAL THINKING QUESTIONS Could the Enron debacle have been prevented? If so, what actions should have been taken by auditors, regulators, and lawmakers?

HOTLINKS

You can study the behavior of commodity prices in a chart at:

www.barchart.com/

so many commodities. As explained in the accompanying *Ethics in Investing* box, this is basically what Enron was doing—until things started turning nasty.

While volatile price movements may appeal to speculators, they frighten many other investors. As a result, some of these more cautious investors turn to *spreading*, the second form of commodities investing. Futures investors use this trading technique as a way to capture some of the benefits of volatile commodities prices but without all the exposure to loss.

Finally, commodities futures can be used as *hedging* vehicles. A hedge in the commodities market is more of a technical strategy that is used almost exclusively by producers and processors to protect a position in a product or commodity. For example, a producer or grower would use a commodity hedge to obtain as *high a price* as possible for its goods. The processor or manufacturer who uses the commodity would use a hedge for the opposite reason: to obtain the goods at as *low a price* as possible. A successful hedge, in effect, means added income to producers or lower costs to processors.

Let's now look briefly at the two trading strategies that are most used by individual investors—speculating and spreading—to gain a better understanding of how to use commodities as investment vehicles.

Speculating Speculators hope to capitalize on swings in commodity prices by going long or short. To see why a speculator would go long when prices are expected to rise, assume you buy a March silver contract at 1,065 (i.e., $10.65 an ounce) by depositing the required initial margin of $6,075. One silver contract involves 5,000 troy ounces, so it has a market value of $53,250. If silver goes up, you make money. Assume that it does and that by February (one month before the contract expires), the price of the contract rises to 1,160. You then liquidate the contract and make a profit of $0.95 per ounce (1,160 − 1,065). That means a $4,750 profit from an investment of just $6,075—which translates into a return on invested capital of a little more than 78%.

Of course, instead of rising, the price of silver could have dropped by $0.95 per ounce. On a 5,000-ounce contract, that would amount to some $4,075. As a result, you would have lost most of your original investment: $6,075 − $4,750 leaves only $1,325.

But a drop in price would be just what a *short seller* is after. Here's why: You sell "short" the March silver at 1,065 and buy it back sometime later at 970. Clearly, the difference between the selling price and the purchase price is the same $0.95. But in this case it is *profit*, because the selling price exceeds the purchase price. (See Chapter 2 for a review of short selling.)

Spreading Instead of attempting to speculate on the price behavior of a futures contract, you might follow the more conservative tactic of *spreading*. Much like spreading with put and call options, the idea is to combine two or more different contracts into one position that offers the potential for a modest amount of profit but restricts your exposure to loss. One very important reason for spreading in the commodities market is that, unlike options, *there is no limit to the amount of loss that can occur with a futures contract*.

You set up a spread by buying one contract and simultaneously selling another. Although one side of the transaction will lead to a loss, you hope that the profit earned from the other side will more than offset the loss, and that the net result will be at least a modest amount of profit. If you're wrong, the spread will limit, but not eliminate, any losses.

Here is a simple example of how a spread might work: Suppose you buy contract A at 533.50 and at the same time short-sell contract B for 575.50. Sometime later, you close out your position in contract A by selling it at 542, and you simultaneously cover your short position in B by purchasing a contract at 579. Although you made a profit of 8.50 points (542 − 533.50) on the long position (contract A), you lost 3.50 points (575.50 − 579) on the contract you shorted (B). The net effect, however, is a profit of 5 points. If you were dealing in cents per pound, those 5 points would mean a profit of $250 on a 5,000-pound contract.

All sorts of commodity spreads can be set up for almost any type of investment situation. Most of them, however, are highly sophisticated and require specialized skills.

CONCEPTS IN REVIEW
Answers available at: www.myfinancelab.com

15.6 List and briefly define the five essential parts of a commodities contract. Which parts have a direct bearing on the price behavior of the contract?

15.7 Briefly define each of the following:
a. Settle price.
b. Daily price limit.
c. Open interest
d. Maximum daily price range.
e. Delivery month.

15.8 What is the one source of return on futures contracts? What measure is used to calculate the return on a commodities contract?

15.9 Note several approaches to investing in commodities and explain the investment objectives of each.

Financial Futures

LG 5   LG 6

financial futures
a type of futures contract in which the underlying "commodity" is a financial asset, such as debt securities, foreign currencies, or common stocks.

Another dimension of the futures market is **financial futures**, a segment of the market in which futures contracts are traded on *financial instruments*. Financial futures are an extension of the commodities concept. They were created for much the same reason as commodities futures, they are traded in the same market, their prices behave a lot like commodities, and they have similar investment merits. But financial futures are unique because of the underlying assets. Let's now look more closely at financial futures and see how investors can use them.

▌The Financial Futures Market

Though relatively young, financial futures are the dominant type of futures contract. The level of trading in financial futures far surpasses that of traditional commodities. Much of the interest in financial futures is due to hedgers and institutional investors who use these contracts as portfolio management tools. But individual investors can also use financial futures to speculate on the behavior of interest rates and to speculate in the stock market. They even offer a convenient way to speculate in the highly specialized foreign currency markets.

The financial futures market was established in response to the economic turmoil the United States experienced in the 1970s. The instability of the dollar on the world market was causing serious problems for multinational firms. Interest rates were highly volatile, which caused severe difficulties for corporate treasurers, financial institutions, and money managers. All of these parties needed a way to protect themselves from the wide fluctuations in the value of the dollar and interest rates. Thus, a market for financial futures was born. Hedging provided the economic rationale for the market, but speculators were quick to join in.

At present, most of the financial futures trading in this country occurs on just two exchanges—the Chicago Board of Trade and the Chicago Mercantile Exchange. Financial futures also are traded on several foreign exchanges, the most noteworthy of which is the London International Financial Futures Exchange. The three basic types of financial futures include foreign currencies, debt securities, and stock indexes.

Foreign Currencies, Interest Rates, and Stock Indexes

The financial futures market started rather inconspicuously in May 1972, with the listing of a handful of foreign currency contracts. Known as **currency futures**, they have become a major hedging vehicle as international trade has mushroomed. Most of the trading in this market is conducted in major market currencies such as the British pound, Swiss franc, Canadian dollar, Japanese yen, and the euro—all of which are issued by counties or regions with strong international trade and economic ties to the United States.

The first futures contract on debt securities, or **interest-rate futures**, began trading in October 1975. Today, trading is carried out in a variety of interest-rate-based securities, including U.S. Treasury securities, Federal Funds, interest rate swaps, Euromarket deposits (e.g., Eurodollar and Euroyen), and foreign government bonds. Interest-rate futures were immediately successful, and their popularity continues to grow.

In February 1982, still another type of trading vehicle was introduced: the stock-index futures contract. **Stock-index futures** are contracts pegged to broad-based measures of stock market performance. Today, trading is done in most of the (major) U.S. stock indexes, including the Dow Jones Industrial Average, the S&P 500, the Nasdaq 100, and the Russell 2000, among others.

In addition to U.S. indexes, investors can trade stock-index futures contracts based on the London, Tokyo, Paris, Sydney, Berlin, Zurich, and Toronto stock exchanges. Stock-index futures, which are similar to the stock-index options we discussed in Chapter 14, allow investors to participate in the general movements of the entire stock market.

Stock-index futures, and other futures contracts, are a type of *derivative security*. Like options, they derive their value from the price behavior of the assets that underlie them. In the case of stock-index futures, they reflect the general performance of the stock market as a whole, or various segments of the market. Thus, when the market for large-cap stocks, as measured by the S&P 500, goes up, the value of an S&P 500 futures contract should go up as well. Accordingly, investors can use stock-index futures as a way to buy or sell the market—or reasonable proxies thereof—and thereby participate in broad market moves.

Contract Specifications

In principle, financial futures contracts are like commodities contracts. They control large sums of the underlying financial instrument and are issued with a variety of delivery months. Figure 15.3 lists quotes for several foreign currency, interest rate, and stock-index futures contracts. Looking first at currency futures, we see that the contracts entitle holders to a certain position in a specified foreign currency. In effect, the owner of a currency future holds a claim on a certain amount of foreign money. The precise amount ranges from 62,500 British pounds to 12.5 million Japanese

---

currency futures
futures contracts on foreign currencies, traded much like commodities.

interest-rate futures
futures contracts on debt securities.

stock-index futures
futures contracts written on broad-based measures of stock market performance (e.g., the S&P 500 Stock Index), allowing investors to participate in the general movements of the stock market.

FIGURE 15.3

Quotations on Selected Actively Traded Financial Futures

The trading exchange, size of the trading unit, pricing unit, and delivery months are all vital pieces of information included as part of the quotation system used with financial futures. (*Source: Wall Street Journal Online*, June 29, 2006, wsj.com/free.)

Currency Futures

	OPEN	HIGH	LOW	SETTLE	CHG	LIFETIME HIGH	LIFETIME LOW	OPEN INT
Japanese Yen (CME)-¥12,500,000; $ per 100¥								
Sept	.8685	.8805	.8671	.8792	+.0100	.9435	.8572	153,691
Dec	.8793	.8918	.8786	.8906	+.0100	.9600	.8644	20,355
Est vol 64,330; vol Wed 37,315; open int. 174,073, +7.								
Canadian Dollar (CME)-CAD 100,000; $ per CAD								
Sept	.8924	.9034	.8919	.9030	+.0097	.9175	.7970	86,735
Dec	.8950	.9055	.8946	.9054	+.0097	.9184	.8310	2,125
Est vol 38,507; vol Wed 25,185; open int, 89,177, -614.								
British Pound (CME)-£62,500; $ per £								
Sept	1.8216	1.8335	1.8124	1.8329	+.0109	1.9060	1.7282	79,866
Dec	1.8215	1.8370	1.8168	1.8370	+.0109	1.9060	1.7342	297
Est vol 48,201; vol Wed 28,753; open int. 80,164, +1,572.								
Swiss Franc (CME)-CHF 125,000; $ per CHF								
Sept	.8089	.8165	.8068	.8160	+.0060	.8497	.7712	64,698
Dec	.8157	.8239	.8148	.8237	+.0060	.8544	.7793	180
Est vol 42,686; vol Wed 33,698; open int, 64,885, +1,329.								

Interest Rate Futures

	OPEN	HIGH	LOW	SETTLE	CHG	LIFETIME HIGH	LIFETIME LOW	OPEN INT
Treasury Bonds (CBT)-$100,000; pts 32nds of 100%								
Sept	105-15	106-10	105-13	105-28	+13	115-16	105-03	763,830
Dec	135-25	106-03	105-24	106-00	+14	115-01	104-27	6,125
Est vol 246,838; vol Wed 218,961; open int. 773,330, +7,773.								
Treasury Notes (CBT)-$100,000; pts 32nds of 100%								
Sept	104-020	104-160	104-015	104-130	+10.5	109-280	104-010	2,168,441
Dec	104-005	104-110	104-005	104-095	+10.5	109-070	103-310	26,609
Est vol 727,758; vol Wed 603,867; open int, 2,195,088, +1,554.								
5 Yr. Treasury Notes (CBT)-$100,000; pts 32nds of 100%								
June	103-040	103-040	103-040	103-090	+9.0	106-250	103-000	10,467
Sept	102-280	103-070	102-280	103-055	+8.5	106-220	102-275	1,254,397
Est vol 386,033; vol Wed 293,011; open int, 1,265,265, -21,428.								
30 Day Federal Funds (CBT)-$5,000,000; 100 - daily avg.								
June	94.990	94.995	94.990	94.995	+.005	95.670	94.955	93,359
July	94.720	94.740	94.715	94.735	+.015	95.630	94.710	239,046
Aug	94.590	94.640	94.585	94.625	+.035	95.670	94.570	119,851
Sept	94.515	94.585	94.515	94.565	+.045	96.000	94.500	70,856
Oct	94.455	94.530	94.455	94.525	+.065	95.980	94.400	40,275
Nov	94.435	94.505	94.435	94.500	+.070	95.810	94.420	19,885
Dec	94.440	94.510	94.440	94.510	+.075	95.230	94.430	4,561
Est vol 238,432; vol Wed 114,678; open int, 589,11R +9,053.								

Index Futures

	OPEN	HIGH	LOW	SETTLE	CHG	LIFETIME HIGH	LIFETIME LOW	OPEN INT
DJ Industrial Average (CBT)-$10 x Index								
Sept	11052	11265	11050	11260	+202	11762	10740	51,613
Dec	11245	11360	11235	11351	+208	11830	10415	1,832
Est vol 4,180; vol Wed 2,908; open int, 53,450, -205.								
Idx prl: Hi 11195.54; Lo 10974.36; Close 11190.80, +217.24.								
S&P 500 Index (CME)-$250 x Index								
Sept	1257.80	1283.70	1257.20	1282.60	+24.90	1342.50	1112.60	618,425
Dec	1277.50	1295.00	1275.00	1294.00	+25.00	1353.80	1170.80	5,767
Est vol 41,062; vol Wed 31,162; open int, 625,042, +1,412.								
Idx prl: Hi 1272.88; Lo 1245.94; Close 1272.87, +26.87.								
Nasdaq 100 (CME)-$100 x Index								
Sept	1557.50	1606.50	1557.00	1605.00	+47.00	1810.00	1528.75	51,319
Est vol 7,492; vol Wed 4,236; open int, 51,377, -314.								
Idx prl: Hi 1585.56; Lo 1538.25; Close 1585.56, +47.31.								

yen. Similarly, holders of interest rate futures have a claim on a certain amount of the underlying debt security. This claim amounts to $100,000 worth of Treasury notes and bonds, $1 million worth of Eurodollars, or $5 million in 30-day Federal Funds contracts.

Stock-index futures, however, are a bit different because the seller of one of these contracts is *not* obligated to deliver the *underlying stocks* at the expiration date. Instead, ultimate delivery is in the form of *cash*. (This is fortunate as it would indeed be a task to make delivery of the 2,000 small-cap stocks that are in the Russell 2000 Index or the 500 issues in the S&P Index.) Basically, the amount of underlying cash is set at a certain multiple of the value of the underlying stock index. For example:

Index	*Multiple*
DJIA	$10 × index
S&P 500	$250 × index
Nasdaq 100	$100 × index
S&P 400	$500 × index
Russell 2000	$500 × index

Thus, if the S&P 500 stood at 1,075, then the amount of cash underlying a single S&P 500 stock-index futures contract would be $250 × 1,075 = $268,750. Again, the amount is substantial. In terms of delivery months, the lives of financial futures contracts run from about 12 months or less for most stock-index and currency futures to two to three years or more for interest-rate instruments.

Prices and Profits Not surprisingly, the price of each type of financial futures contract is quoted somewhat differently.

- *Currency futures.* All currency futures are quoted in dollars or cents per unit of the underlying foreign currency (e.g., dollars per British pound or cents per Japanese yen). Thus, according to the closing ("settle") prices in Figure 15.3, one September British pound contract was worth $114,556.25 (62,500 pounds × 1.8329). At the same time, a September Japanese yen contract was valued at $109,900 (because a quote of 0.8792 cent per yen equals less than a penny per yen, we have 12,500,000 yen × $0.008792).

- *Interest-rate futures.* Except for the quotes on Treasury bills and other short-term securities, interest-rate futures contracts are priced as a percentage of the par value of the underlying debt instrument (e.g., Treasury notes or bonds). Because these instruments are quoted in increments of 1/32 of 1%, a quote of 103–09 for the settle price of the June five-year Treasure note (in Figure 15.3) translates into 103–9/32, which converts to a quote of 103.28125% of par. Apply this rate to the $100,000 par value of the underlying security, and we see that this contract is worth $103,281.25 ($100,000 × 1.0328125). The pricing mechanism for T-bills and other short-term interest-rate contracts is discussed at the book's Web site—see the nearby Web Extension for details.

- *Stock-index futures.* Stock-index futures are quoted in terms of the actual underlying index. As noted above, they carry a face value of anywhere from $10 to $500 times the index. Thus, according to the settle price in Figure 15.3, the December S&P 500 contract would be worth $323,500, because the value of this particular contract is equal to $250 times the (settle) price of the index (1,294 × $250). The value of the September DJIA contract is 11,260 × $10 = $112,600.

The value of an interest-rate futures contract responds to interest rates exactly as the debt instrument that underlies the contract. That is, when interest rates go up, the value of an interest-rate futures contract goes down, and vice versa. The quote system used for interest rate as well as currency and stock-index futures is set up to reflect the *market value of the contract* itself. Thus, when the price or quote of a financial futures contract increases (for example, when interest rates fall or a stock-index goes up), then the investor who is long makes money. In contrast, when the price decreases, the short seller makes money.

WEBEXTENSION

For information on the pricing of futures on Treasury bills and other short-term securities, visit the book's Web site at:

www.myfinancelab.com

Price behavior is the only source of return to speculators. Financial futures contracts have no claim on the dividend and interest income of the underlying issues. Even so, huge profits (or losses) are possible with financial futures because of the equally large size of the contracts. For instance, if the price of Swiss francs goes up by just $0.02 against the dollar, the investor is ahead $2,500. Likewise, a 3-point drop in the Russell 2000 means a $1,500 loss to an investor (3 × $500). When related to the relatively small initial margin deposit required to make transactions in the financial futures markets, such price activity can mean very high rates of return—or very high risk of a total wipeout.

▮ Trading Techniques

Investors can use financial futures, like commodity futures, for hedging, spreading, and speculating. Multinational companies and firms that are active in international trade might *hedge* with currency or Euromarket futures. Various financial institutions and corporate money managers often use interest-rate futures for hedging purposes. In either case, the objective is the same: to lock in the best monetary exchange or interest rate possible. In addition, individual investors and portfolio managers often hedge with stock-index futures to protect their security holdings against temporary market declines. Financial futures can also be used for *spreading*. This tactic is popular with investors who simultaneously buy and sell combinations of two or more contracts to form a desired investment position. Finally, financial futures are widely used for *speculation*.

Although investors can employ any one of the three trading strategies noted above, we will focus primarily on the use of financial futures by speculators and hedgers. We will first examine speculating in currency and interest rate futures. Then we'll look at how investors can use futures to hedge investments in stocks, bonds, and foreign securities.

Speculating in Financial Futures
Speculators are especially interested in financial futures because of the size of the contracts. For instance, in mid-2006, Canadian dollar contracts were worth over $89,000, Treasury notes and bonds were going for around $105,000, and 30-day federal funds contracts were being quoted at more than $4.75 million each. With contracts of

this size, even small movements in the underlying asset can produce big price swings—and therefore big profits.

Currency and interest-rate futures can be used for just about any speculative purpose. For example, if you expect the dollar to be devalued relative to the euro, you could buy euro currency futures, because the contracts should go up in value, right along with the appreciation of the euro. If you anticipate a rise in interest rates, you might "go short" (sell) interest-rate futures, since they should go down in value. Because margin is used and financial futures have the same source of return as commodities (price appreciation), we can measure the profitability of these contracts using return on invested capital (Equation 15.1)

Going Long a Foreign Currency Contract Suppose you believe that the Swiss franc (CHF) is about to appreciate in value relative to the dollar. You decide to go long (buy) three September CHF contracts at 0.7055—i.e., at a quote of just over $0.70 a franc. Each contract would be worth $88,187.50 (125,000 CHF × 0.7055), so the total underlying value of the three contracts would be $264,562.50. Given an initial margin requirement of, say, $2,500 per contract, you would have to deposit only $7,500 to acquire this position.

Now, if Swiss francs do appreciate and move up from 0.7055 to, say, 0.75 ($0.75 a franc), the value of the three contracts will rise to $281,250. In a matter of months, you will have made a profit of $16,687.50. Using Equation 15.1 for return on invested capital, we find that such a profit translates into a 222% rate of return. Of course, an even smaller fractional change in the other direction would have wiped out this investment. Clearly, these *high returns are not without equally high risk*. Of course, rather than use futures contracts to play the currency markets, it is also possible to invest directly in foreign currencies, as more fully explained in the nearby *Investing in Action* box.

Going Short an Interest Rate Contract Let's assume that you're anticipating a sharp rise in long-term rates. A rise in rates translates into a drop in the value of interest-rate futures. You decide to short-sell two June T-bond contracts at 115-00, which means that the contracts are trading at 115% of par. Thus the two contracts are worth $230,000 ($100,000 × 1.15 × 2). You need only $2,700 (the initial margin deposit is $1,350 per contract) to make the investment.

Assume that interest rates do, in fact, move up. As a result, the price on Treasury bond contracts drops to 106-16 (or 106½). You could now buy back the two June T-bond contracts (to cover the short position) and in the process make a profit of $17,000. You originally sold the two contracts at $230,000 and bought them back sometime later at $213,000. As with any investment, such a difference between what you pay for a security and what you sell it for is profit. In this case, the return on invested capital amounts to a whopping 630%. Again, this return is due in no small part to the *enormous risk of loss* you assumed.

Trading Stock-Index Futures Most investors use stock-index futures for speculation or hedging. (Stock-index futures are similar to the *index options* introduced in Chapter 14. Therefore, much of the discussion that follows also applies to index options.) Whether speculating or hedging, the key to success is *predicting the future course of the stock market*. Because you are "buying the market" with stock-index futures, it is important to get a handle on the future

INVESTOR FACTS

FINANCIAL FUTURES ARE HOT!—The top five futures contracts in fiscal 2006 were:

Contract (Exchange)	Volume of Contracts
3-month Eurodollars (CME)	388,650,935
10-year Treasury notes (CBOT)	218,584,441
Mini S&P 500 (CME)	192,955,913
5-year Treasury notes (CBOT)	122,520,708
Mini Nasdaq-100 (CME)	74,414,663

Financial futures now represent over 75% of the trading volume on all U.S. futures exchanges, so it's not surprising that all of the top five contracts are financial futures. Corn futures are the largest agricultural category, with 26,937,673 contracts.

Contract volume tells just part of the story. The disparity between financial and commodity futures is even greater when you consider the value of the assets underlying these contracts. Each 10-year Treasury note contract has $100,000 in T-notes, so 218 million of these contracts translates into $21.8 *trillion* of underlying Treasury notes!

Source: Open Interest and Volume Statistics for FY 2005, Commodity Futures Trading Commission, downloaded from www.cftc.gov.

INVESTING in Action

FX Direct

One way to play the currency markets is through currency futures. An alternative way is to buy foreign currencies directly, which individual investors can do via online currency-trading sites. Foreign currency trading is called "forex" or "FX," and the two largest foreign exchange sites are FOREX.com and FXCM.com. Some $1.9 trillion trades daily in the FX market, compared to about $30 billion for currency futures.

Foreign exchange trades involve pairs of currencies: You trade two currencies simultaneously and hope to profit from the relative movement of those currencies against each other. The currencies typically traded in direct forex are the major world currencies: the U.S. dollar, euro, Japanese yen, Canadian dollar, Swiss franc, British pound, and Australian dollar.

Let's say you have "done your homework" by studying long-term macroeconomic trends and doing technical analysis on two currencies you want to trade. You've concluded that the euro is overvalued relative to the U.S. dollar, but that the dollar soon will strengthen against the euro. You would short-sell the expensive currency (the euro) and buy a comparable amount of the cheaper one (the dollar), and hope for a rise in the exchange rate. Conversely, if you thought the dollar would weaken against the euro, you would short-sell the cheaper currency (dollars) and buy the more expensive one (euros).

Let's put some numbers to this example: Say the current exchange rate is 0.78USD/1EUR—that is, you can buy one euro for $0.78. Expecting that the dollar will strengthen against the euro, you short-sell 100,000 euros and buy $78,000 worth of U.S. dollars. Basically, the $78,000 proceeds from the sale of the euros is used to purchase the USD's. Now, assume the dollar does, in fact, appreciate relative to the euro, and in so doing, the exchange rate moves to, say, 0.74 USD/1EUR (note, euros are now cheaper and can be purchased for just 74 cents each, down from 78 cents). As a result, you stand to make some money on this transaction! That's because you can now cover the short sale by purchasing 100,000 euros at $0.74 each. Thus, you sold the euros for $78,000 (i.e., 100,000 euros × $0.78 per euro), but you were able to buy them back for only $74,000 (100,000 euros × $0.74 per euro). Bottom line: *You made a net profit of $4,000 on the trade:* that is, you had $78,000 (USD's) sitting in your account, but you only needed $74,000 to buy back the euros, so you walk away with $4,000. Since all transactions in the FX market are executed with tiny (1%) margin deposits, the rates of return can be huge. But so can your losses—if the exchange rate goes up by just 1%, you lose everything.

Why invest directly in foreign currencies, rather than currency futures? Part of the answer relates to the advent of the online FX exchanges. For one thing, the forex market offers 24-hour-a-day trading, which the future market does not. In addition, FX trades are largely commission free. Because use of margin and leverage (as high as 200:1) is common in forex, the upside opportunities are significant, as are the downside risks.

However, even investors as experienced as Warren Buffett have had some stumbles in the FX market. Because forex moves so quickly, it's wise to test trades at an online demo, available at most e-brokers, before you begin using actual money.

CRITICAL THINKING QUESTIONS What are some of the advantages and disadvantages of directly investing in foreign currencies? What two trades would you make initially if you thought the Swiss franc was going to appreciate relative to the U.S. dollar?

Sources: Adrienne Carter, "The Currency Game: Home Version," *Business Week*, April 3, 2006, p. 122; and www.fxcom/why-choose-fxcm-exchange.jsp (accessed September 2006).

direction of the market via technical analysis (as discussed in Chapter 9) or some other technique. Once you have a feel for the market's direction, you can formulate a stock-index futures trading or hedging strategy. For example, if you feel that the market is headed up, you would want to go long (buy stock-index futures). In contrast, if your analysis suggests a sharp drop in equity values, you could make money by going short (selling stock-index futures).

Assume, for instance, that you believe the market is undervalued and a move up is imminent. You can try to identify one or a handful of stocks that should go up with the market (and assume the stock selection risks that go along with this approach). Or you can buy an S&P 500 stock-index futures contract currently trading at, say, 1,374.45. To execute this speculative transaction, you would need to deposit an initial margin of $19,688. Now, if the market does rise so that the S&P 500 Index moves to, say, 1,422.85 by the expiration of the futures contract, you earn a profit of $12,100—that is, $(1,422.85 - 1,374.45) \times \$250 = \$12,100$. Given the $19,688 investment, your return on invested capital would amount to a hefty 61%. Of course, keep in mind that if the market drops by around 79 points (or less than 6 percent), the investment will be a *total loss*.

Hedging with Stock-Index Futures Stock-index futures also make excellent hedging vehicles. They provide investors with a highly effective way of protecting stock holdings in a declining market. Although this tactic is not perfect, it does enable investors to obtain desired protection against a decline in market value without disturbing their equity holdings.

Here's how a so-called *short hedge* would work: Assume that you hold a total of 2,000 shares of stock in a dozen different companies and that the market value of this portfolio is around $235,000. If you think the market is about to undergo a temporary sharp decline, you can do one of two things: sell all of your shares or buy puts on each of the stocks. Clearly, these alternatives are cumbersome and/or costly and therefore undesirable for protecting a widely diversified portfolio. The desired results could also be achieved, however, by *short selling stock-index futures*. (You also could obtain the same protection by turning to options and buying *stock-index puts*.)

Suppose for purposes of our illustration that you short-sell two DJIA stock-index futures contracts at 11,375. These contracts would provide a close match to the current value of your portfolio (they would be valued at $2 \times 11,375 \times \$10 = \$227,500$). Yet these stock-index futures contracts would require an initial margin deposit of only $4,875 per contract, or a total deposit of $2 \times \$4,875 = \$9,750$. Now, if the DJIA drops to 10,868, you will make a profit of a little over $10,000 from this short sale. That is, because the index fell 507 points (11,375 − 10,868), the total profit will be $10,140 ($2 \times 507 \times \$10$). Ignoring taxes, you can add this profit to the portfolio (by purchasing additional shares of stock at their new lower prices). The net result will be a new portfolio position that will approximate the one that existed prior to the decline in the market.

How well the "before" and "after" portfolio positions match will depend on how far the portfolio dropped in value. If the average price dropped about $5 per share in our example, the positions will closely match. But this does not always happen. The price of some stocks will change more than others, so the amount of protection provided by this type of short hedge depends on how sensitive the stock portfolio is to movements in the market. Thus, the types of stocks held in the portfolio are an important consideration in structuring a stock-index short hedge.

A key to success with this kind of hedging is to make sure that the characteristics of the hedging vehicle (the futures contract) closely match those of the portfolio (or security position) being protected. If the portfolio is made up mostly (or exclusively) of large-cap stocks, use something like the S&P 500 Stock Index futures contract as the hedging vehicle. If the portfolio is mostly blue-chip stocks, use the DJIA contracts. If the portfolio holds mostly tech stocks, consider the Nasdaq 100 Index contract. Again, the point is to pick a hedging vehicle that closely reflects the types of securities you want to protect. If you keep that caveat in mind, hedging with stock-index futures can be a low-cost yet effective way of obtaining protection against loss in a declining stock market.

Hedging Other Securities Just as you can use stock-index futures to hedge stock portfolios, you can use *interest-rate futures* to hedge bond portfolios. Or, you can use *currency futures* with foreign securities as a way to protect against foreign exchange risk. *Let's consider an interest rate hedge:* If you held a substantial portfolio of bonds, the last thing you would want to see is a big jump in interest rates, which could cause a sharp decline in the value of your portfolio. Assume you hold around $300,000 worth of Treasury and agency bonds, with an average maturity of about 18 years. If you believe that market rates are headed up, you can hedge your bond portfolio by short-selling three U.S. Treasury bond futures contracts. (Each T-bond futures contract is worth about $100,000, so it would take three of them to cover a $300,000 portfolio.) If rates do head up, you will have protected the portfolio against loss. As noted above, the exact amount of protection will depend on how well the T-bond futures contracts parallel the price behavior of your particular bond portfolio.

There is, of course, a downside: If market interest rates go down, rather than up, you will miss out on potential profits *as long as the short hedge position remains in place*. This is so because the profits being made in the portfolio will be offset by losses from the futures contracts. Actually, this will occur with any type of portfolio (stocks, bonds, or anything else) that is tied to an offsetting short hedge; when you create the short hedge you essentially lock in a position at that point. Although you do not lose anything when the market falls, you also do not make anything when the market goes up. In either case, the profits you make from one position are offset by losses from the other.

Hedging Foreign Currency Exposure Now let's see how you can use futures contracts to hedge foreign exchange risk. Let's assume that you have just purchased $200,000 of British government one-year notes. (You did this because higher yields were available on the British notes than on comparable U.S. Treasury securities.) Because these notes are denominated in pounds, this investment is subject to loss if currency exchange rates move against you (if the value of the dollar rises relative to the pound).

If all you wanted was the higher yield offered by the British note, you could eliminate most of the currency exchange risk by setting up a currency hedge. Here's how: Let's say that at the current exchange rate, one U.S. dollar will "buy" 0.60 of a British pound. This means that pounds are worth about $1.65 (i.e., $1.00/0.60£ = $1.65). So, if currency contracts on British pounds were trading at around $1.65 a pound, you would have to *sell* two contracts to protect the $200,000 investment. Each contract covers 62,500 pounds; if they're being quoted at 1.65, then each contract is worth $1.65 × 62,500 = $103,125.

Assume that one year later, the value of the dollar has increased, relative to the pound, so that one U.S. dollar will now "buy" 0.65 pound. Under such conditions, a British pound futures contract would be quoted at around 1.54 (i.e., $1.00/.065£ = $1.54). At this price, each futures contract would be worth $96,250 (62,500 × $1.54). Each contract, in effect, would be worth $6,875 less than it was a year ago. But because the contract was sold short when you set up the hedge, you will make a profit of $6,875 per contract—for a total profit of $13,750 on the two contracts. Unfortunately, that's not *net profit*, because this profit will offset the loss you will incur on the British note investment. In very simple terms, when you sent $200,000 overseas to buy the British notes, the money was worth about £121,000. However, when you brought the money back a year later, those 121,000 pounds purchased only about 186,500 U.S. dollars. Thus, you are out some $13,500 on your original investment. Were it not for the currency hedge, you would be out the full $13,500, and the return on this investment would be a lot lower. The hedge covered the loss (plus a little extra), and the net effect was that you were able to enjoy the added yield of the British note without having to worry about potential loss from currency exchange rates.

▮ Financial Futures and the Individual Investor

Like commodities, financial futures can play an important role in your portfolio so long as three factors apply: (1) You thoroughly understand these investment vehicles. (2) You clearly recognize the tremendous risk exposure of these vehicles. (3) You are fully prepared (financially and emotionally) to absorb some losses.

Financial futures are highly volatile securities that have enormous potential for profit and for loss. For instance, in 2003, during a six-month period of time, the December S&P 500 futures contract fluctuated in price from a low of 774.0 to a high of 1,226.5. This range of over 450 points for a single contract translated into a *potential* profit—or loss—of some $113,000, and all from an initial investment of only $17,800. Investment diversification is obviously essential as a means of reducing the potentially devastating impact of price volatility. Financial futures are exotic investment vehicles, but if properly used, they can provide generous returns.

HOT LINKS

For information on commodity trading, pools, and advisers, visit the CFTC page at:

www.cftc.gov/opa/brochures/opafutures.htm

▮ Options on Futures

The evolution that began with listed stock options and financial futures spread, over time, to interest-rate options and stock-index futures. Eventually, it led to the creation of the ultimate leverage vehicle: *options on futures contracts.* **Futures options,** as they are called, represent listed puts and calls on actively traded futures contracts. In essence, they give the holders the right to buy (with calls) or sell (with puts) a single standardized futures contract for a specific period of time at a specified strike price.

futures options
options that give the holders the right to buy or sell a single standardized futures contract for a specified period of time at a specified strike price.

TABLE 15.4 **Futures Options: Puts and Calls on Futures Contracts**

Commodities

Corn	Pork bellies	Sugar	Gold
Soybeans	Lean hogs	Wheat	Silver
Soybean meal	Feeder cattle	Oats	Crude oil
Soybean oil	Orange juice	Rice	Natural gas
Cotton	Cocoa	Platinum	Heating oil
Live cattle	Coffee	Copper	Gasoline

Financial Futures

British pound	Treasury notes
Euro	Treasury bonds
Swiss franc	30-day Federal Funds
Japanese yen	London Interbank Offering Rate (LIBOR)
Canadian dollar	NYSE Composite Index
Mexican peso	S&P 500 Stock Index
U.S. dollar index	Dow Jones Industrial Average
Eurodollar deposits	Nasdaq 100 Index
Treasury bills	Russell 2000

Table 15.4 lists many of the actively traded futures options available in 2006. Such options can be found on both commodities and financial futures. For the most part, these puts and calls cover the same amount of assets as the underlying futures contracts—for example, 112,000 pounds of sugar, 100 ounces of gold, 62,500 British pounds, or $100,000 in Treasury bonds. Thus, they also involve the same amount of price activity as is normally found with commodities and financial futures.

Futures options have the same standardized strike prices, expiration dates, and quotation system as other listed options. Depending on the strike price on the option and the market value of the underlying futures contract, these options can also be in the money or out of the money. Futures options are valued like other puts and calls—by the difference between the option's strike price and the market price of the underlying futures contract (see Chapter 14). They can also be used like any other listed option—for speculating or hedging, in options writing programs, or for spreading. The biggest difference between a futures option and a futures contract is that *the option limits the loss exposure* to the price of the option. The most you can lose is the price paid for the put or call option. With the futures contract, there is no real limit to the amount of loss you can incur.

To see how futures options work, assume that you want to trade some gold contracts. You believe that the price of gold will increase over the next four or five months, from its present level of $585 an ounce to around $630 an ounce. You can buy a futures contract at 588.10 by depositing the required initial margin of $4,050. Alternatively, you can buy a futures call option with a $580 strike price that is currently being quoted at 10.90. (Because the underlying futures contract covers 100 ounces of gold, the total cost of this option would be $10.90 × 100 = $1,090.) The call is an in-the-money option, because the market price of gold exceeds the exercise price on the option. The figures below summarize what happens to both investments if the price of gold *increases* by $45 an ounce by the expiration date and also what happens if the price of gold *drops* by $45 an ounce.

	Futures Contract		Futures Option	
	Dollar Profit (or Loss)	Return on Invested Capital	Dollar Profit (or Loss)	Return on Invested Capital
If price of gold *increases* by $45 an ounce	$4,190	103.5%	$3,910	358.7%
If price of gold *decreases* by $45 an ounce	($4,810)	—	($1,090)	—

Clearly, the futures option provides not only a competitive rate of return (in this case, it's a lot higher), but also a reduced exposure to loss. Futures options offer interesting investment opportunities. But as always, *they should be used only by knowledgeable commodities and financial futures investors.*

CONCEPTS IN REVIEW
Answers available at: www.myfinancelab.com

15.10 What is the difference between physical *commodities* and *financial futures?* What are their similarities?

15.11 Describe a *currency future* and contrast it with an *interest-rate future.* What is a *stock-index future,* and how can it be used by investors?

15.12 Discuss how stock-index futures can be used for speculation and for hedging. What advantages are there to speculating with stock-index futures rather than specific issues of common stock?

15.13 What are *futures options?* Explain how they can be used by speculators. Why would an investor want to use an option on an interest-rate futures contract rather than the futures contract itself?

Summary

LG 1 **Describe the essential features of a futures contract, and explain how the futures market operates.** Commodities and financial futures are traded in futures markets. Today, more than 12 U.S. exchanges deal in futures contracts, which are commitments to make (or take) delivery of a certain amount of some real or financial asset at a specified date in the future.

LG 2 **Explain the role that hedgers and speculators play in the futures market, including how profits are made and lost.** Futures contracts control large amounts of the underlying commodity or financial instrument. They can produce wide price swings and very attractive rates of return (or very unattractive losses). Such returns (or losses) are further magnified because all trading in the futures market is done on margin. A speculator's profit is derived directly from the wide price fluctuations that occur in the market. Hedgers derive their profit from the protection they gain against adverse price movements.

LG 3   Describe the commodities segment of the futures market and the basic characteristics of these investment vehicles. Commodities such as grains, metals, and meat make up the traditional (commodities) segment of the futures market. A large portion of this market is concentrated in agricultural products. There's also a very active market for various metals and petroleum products. As the prices of commodities go up and down in the market, the respective futures contracts behave in much the same way. Thus, if the price of corn goes up, the value of corn futures contracts rises as well.

LG 4   Discuss the trading strategies that investors can use with commodities, and explain how investment returns are measured. The trading strategies used with commodities contracts are speculating, spreading, and hedging. Regardless of whether investors are in a long or a short position, they have only one source of return from commodities and financial futures: appreciation (or depreciation) in the price of the contract. Rate of return on invested capital is used to assess the actual or potential profitability of a futures transaction.

LG 5   Explain the difference between a physical commodity and a financial future, and discuss the growing role of financial futures in the market today. Whereas commodities deal with physical assets, financial futures deal with financial assets, such as stocks, bonds, and currencies. Both are traded in the same place: the futures market. Financial futures are the newcomers, but the volume of trading in financial futures now far exceeds that of commodities.

LG 6   Discuss the trading techniques that can be used with financial futures, and note how these securities can be used in conjunction with other investment vehicles. There are three major types of financial futures: currency futures, interest-rate futures, and stock-index futures. The first type deals in different kinds of foreign currencies. Interest-rate futures involve various types of short- and long-term debt instruments. Stock-index futures are pegged to broad movements in the stock market, as measured by such indexes as the S&P 500. These securities can be used for speculating, spreading, or hedging. They hold special appeal as hedges against other security positions. For example, interest-rate futures are used to protect bond portfolios against a jump in market interest rates. Currency futures are used to hedge the foreign currency exposure that accompanies investments in foreign securities.

Key Terms

Discussion Questions

LG 1 Q15.1 Three of the biggest U.S. commodities exchanges—the CME, CBT, and NYM—were identified in this chapter. Other U.S. exchanges and several foreign commodities exchanges are also closely followed in the United States. Go to the public access page of the *Wall Street Journal Online*, located at www.wsj.com/free and look in the "Futures: Daily settlement" section under "Free Markets Data" for a list of recent futures quotes. As noted in this chapter, futures quotes include the name of the exchange on which a particular contract is traded.

    a. Using these quotes, how many more U.S. *commodities exchanges* can you identify? List them.

    b. Are quotes from *foreign exchanges* listed in the *Wall Street Journal?* If so, list them, too.

    c. For each U.S. and foreign exchange you found in parts **a** and **b**, give an example of one or two contracts traded on that exchange. For example: CBT—Chicago Board of Trade: oats and Treasury bonds.

LG 3 **LG 5** Q15.2 Using settle prices from Figures 15.2 and 15.3, find the value of the following commodities and financial futures contracts.

    a. November 2006 soybeans   b. March 2007 corn

    c. August pork bellies   d. December British pounds

    e. September Treasury notes   f. September S&P 500 Index

LG 4 **LG 6** Q15.3 Listed below are a variety of futures transactions. On the basis of the information provided, indicate how much profit or loss you would make in each of the transactions. (*Hint:* You might want to refer to Figures 15.2 and 15.3 for the size of the contract, pricing unit, and so on.)

    a. You buy 3 yen contracts at a quote of 1.0180 and sell them a few months later at 1.0365.

    b. The price of oats goes up $0.60 a bushel, and you hold 3 contracts.

    c. You short-sell 2 feeder cattle contracts at $1.24 a pound, and the price drops to $1.03 per pound.

    d. You recently purchased a Swiss franc contract at 0.7272, and 6 weeks later the contract is trading at 0.685.

    e. You short-sell S&P 500 contracts when the index is at 1,396.55 and cover when the index moves to 1,371.95.

    f. You short 3 corn contracts at $2.34 a bushel, and the price of corn goes to $2.495 a bushel.

Problems

LG 3 **LG 4** P15.1 Jeff Rink considers himself a shrewd commodities investor. Not long ago he bought one July cotton contract at $0.54 a pound, and he recently sold it at $0.58 a pound. How much profit did he make? What was his return on invested capital if he had to put up a $1,260 initial deposit?

LG 3 **LG 4** P15.2 You just heard a news story about mad cow disease in a neighboring country, and you believe that feeder cattle prices will rise dramatically in the next few months as buyers of cattle shift to U.S. suppliers. Someone else believes that prices will fall in the next few months because people will be afraid to eat beef. You go to the CME and find out that feeder cattle futures for delivery in April are currently quoted at 88.8. The contract size is 50,000 lb. What is the market value of one contract?

LG 3 **LG 4** **P15.3** You decide to act on your hunches about feeder cattle, so you purchase 4 contracts for April delivery at 88.8. You are required to put down 10%. How much equity/capital did you need to make this transaction?

LG 3 **LG 4** **P15.4** As it turns out, you were correct when you purchased 4 contracts for feeder cattle at 88.8, as the spot price on cattle rose to 101.2 on the delivery date given in your contracts. How much money did you make? What was your return on invested capital?

LG 4 **P15.5** Julie McCain is a regular commodities speculator. She is currently considering a short position in July oats, which are now trading at 248. Her analysis suggests that July oats should be trading at about 240 in a couple of months. Assuming that her expectations hold up, what kind of return on invested capital will she make if she shorts 3 July oats contracts (each contract covers 5,000 bushels of oats) by depositing an initial margin of $540 per contract?

LG 5 **LG 6** **P15.6** You were just notified that you will receive $100,000 in 2 months from the estate of a deceased relative. You want to invest this money in safe, interest-bearing instruments, so you decide to purchase 5-year Treasury notes. You believe, however, that interest rates are headed down, and you will have to pay a lot more in 2 months than you would today for 5-year Treasury notes. You decide to look into futures, and find a quote of 111–08.5 for 5-year Treasuries deliverable in 2 months. What does the quote mean in terms of price, and how many contracts will you need to buy? How much money will you need to buy the contract, and how much will you need to settle the contract?

LG 5 **LG 6** **P15.7** Mark Seby is thinking about doing some speculating in interest rates. He thinks rates will fall and, in response, the price of Treasury bond futures should move from 92–15, their present quote, to a level of about 98. Given a required margin deposit of $1,350 per contract, what would Mark's return on invested capital be if prices behave as he expects?

LG 5 **LG 6** **P15.8** Annie Ryan has been an avid stock market investor for years. She manages her portfolio fairly aggressively and likes to short-sell whenever the opportunity presents itself. Recently, she has become fascinated with stock-index futures, especially the idea of being able to play the market as a whole. Annie thinks the market is headed down, and she decides to short sell some S&P 500 stock-index futures. Assume she shorts 3 contracts at 1,387.95 and has to make a margin deposit of $19,688 for each contract. How much profit will she make, and what will her return on invested capital be if the market does indeed drop so that the NYSE contracts are trading at 1,352.00 by the time they expire?

LG 6 **P15.9** A wealthy investor holds $500,000 worth of U.S. Treasury bonds. These bonds are currently being quoted at 105% of par. The investor is concerned, however, that rates are headed up over the next 6 months, and he would like to do something to protect this bond portfolio. His broker advises him to set up a hedge using T-bond futures contracts. Assume these contracts are now trading at 111–06.
   a. Briefly describe how the investor would set up this hedge. Would he go long or short? How many contracts would he need?
   b. It's now 6 months later, and rates have indeed gone up. The investor's Treasury bonds are now being quoted at 93$^1/_2$, and the T-bond futures contracts used in the hedge are now trading at 98–00. Show what has happened to the value of the bond portfolio and the profit (or loss) made on the futures hedge.
   c. Was this a successful hedge? Explain.

LG 6   P15.10 Not long ago, Vanessa Woods sold her company for several million dollars (after taxes). She took some of that money and put it into the stock market. Today, Vanessa's portfolio of blue-chip stocks is worth $3.8 million. Vanessa wants to keep her portfolio intact, but she's concerned about a developing weakness in the market for blue chips. She decides, therefore, to hedge her position with 6-month futures contracts on the Dow Jones Industrial Average (DJIA), which are currently trading at 11,960.
   a. Why would she choose to hedge her portfolio with the DJIA rather than the S&P 500?
   b. Given that Vanessa wants to cover the full $3.8 million in her portfolio, describe how she would go about setting up this hedge.
   c. If each contract required a margin deposit of $4,875, how much money would she need to set up this hedge?
   d. Assume that over the next 6 months stock prices do fall, and the value of Vanessa's portfolio drops to $3.3 million. If DJIA futures contracts are trading at 10,400, how much will she make (or lose) on the futures hedge? Is it enough to offset the loss in her portfolio? That is, what is her net profit or loss on the hedge?
   e. Will she now get her margin deposit back, or is that a "sunk cost"—gone forever?

LG 5   LG 6   P15.11 A quote for a futures contract for British pounds is 1.6683. The contract size for British pounds is 62,500. What is the dollar equivalent of this contract?

LG 5   P15.12 You have purchased a futures contract for euros. The contract is for 125,000 euros, and the quote was 1.1636. On the delivery date, the exchange quote is 1.1050. Assuming you took delivery of the euros, how many dollars would you have after converting back to dollars? What is your profit or loss (before commissions)?

 LG 4   P15.13 An American currency speculator feels strongly that the value of the Canadian dollar is going to fall relative to the U.S. dollar over the short run. If he wants to profit from these expectations, what kind of position (long or short) should he take in Canadian dollar futures contracts? How much money would he make from each contract if Canadian dollar futures contracts moved from an initial quote of 0.6775 to an ending quote of 0.6250?

LG 6   P15.14 With regard to futures options, how much profit would an investor make if she bought a call option on gold at 7.20 when gold was trading at $482 an ounce, given that the price of gold went up to $525 an ounce by the expiration date on the call? (*Note:* Assume the call carried a strike price of 480.)

> See www.myfinancelab.com **for Web Exercises,**
> **Spreadsheets, and other online resources.**

Case Problem 15.1   *T. J.'s Fast-Track Investments: Interest Rate Futures*

LG 5   LG 6   T. J. Patrick is a young, successful industrial designer in Portland, Oregon, who enjoys the excitement of commodities speculation. T. J. has been dabbling in commodities since he was a teenager—he was introduced to this market by his dad, who is a grain buyer for one of the leading food processors. T. J. recognizes the enormous risks involved in commodities speculating but feels that because he's young, he can afford to take a few chances. As a principal in a thriving industrial design firm, T. J. earns more than $150,000 a year. He follows a well-disciplined investment program and annually adds $15,000 to $20,000 to his portfolio.

Recently, T. J. has started playing with financial futures—interest-rate futures, to be exact. He admits he is no expert in interest rates, but he likes the price action these investment vehicles offer. This all started several months ago, when T. J. met Vinnie Banano, a broker who specializes in financial futures, at a party. T. J. liked what Vinnie had to say (mostly how you couldn't go wrong with interest-rate futures) and soon set up a trading account with Vinnie's firm, Banano's of Portland.

The other day, Vinnie called T. J. and suggested he get into 5-year Treasury note futures. He reasoned that with the Fed pushing up interest rates so aggressively, the short to intermediate sectors of the term structure would probably respond the most—with the biggest jump in yields. Accordingly, Vinnie recommended that T. J. short sell some 5-year T-note contracts. In particular, Vinnie thinks that rates on these T-notes should go up by a full point (moving from about 5.5% to around 6.5%), and that T. J. should short 4 contracts. This would be a $2,160 investment, because each contract requires an initial margin deposit of $540.

Questions

a. Assume T-note futures are now being quoted at 103–16.
   1. Determine the current underlying value of this T-note futures contract.
   2. What would this futures contract be quoted at if Vinnie is right and the yield does go up by 1 percentage point, to 6.5%, on the date of expiration? (*Hint:* It'll be quoted at the same price as its underlying security, which in this case is *assumed to be a 5-year, 6% semiannual-pay U.S. Treasury note.* If necessary, refer back to Chapter 11 and review the material on pricing semiannual-pay bonds.)

b. How much profit will T. J. make if he shorts four contracts at 103–16 and then covers when 5-year T-note contracts are quoted at 98–00? Also, calculate the return on invested capital from this transaction.

c. What happens if rates go down? For example, how much will T. J. make if the yield on T-note futures goes down by just $3/4$ of 1%, in which case these contracts would be trading at 105–8?

d. What risks do you see in the recommended short-sale transaction? What is your assessment of T. J.'s new interest in financial futures? How do you think it compares to his established commodities investment program?

Case Problem 15.2   *Jim and Polly Pernelli Try Hedging with Stock-Index Futures*

LG 5   LG 6

Jim Pernelli and his wife, Polly, live in Augusta, Georgia. Like many young couples, the Pernellis are a 2-income family. Jim and Polly are both college graduates and hold high-paying jobs. Jim has been an avid investor in the stock market for a number of years and over time has built up a portfolio that is currently worth nearly $375,000. The Pernellis' portfolio is well diversified, although it is heavily weighted in high-quality, mid-cap growth stocks. The Pernellis reinvest all dividends and regularly add investment capital to their portfolio. Up to now, they have avoided short selling and do only a modest amount of margin trading.

Their portfolio has undergone a substantial amount of capital appreciation in the last 18 months or so, and Jim is eager to protect the profit they have earned. And that's the problem: Jim feels the market has pretty much run its course and is about to enter a period of decline. He has studied the market and economic news very carefully and does not believe the retreat will cover an especially long period of time. He feels fairly certain, however, that most, if not all, of the stocks in his portfolio will be adversely affected by these market conditions—though some will drop more in price than others.

Jim has been following stock-index futures for some time and believes he knows the ins and outs of these securities pretty well. After careful deliberation, Jim and Polly decide to use stock-index futures—in particular, the S&P MidCap 400 futures contract—as a way to protect (hedge) their portfolio of common stocks.

Questions

a. Explain why the Pernellis would want to use stock-index futures to hedge their stock portfolio, and how they would go about setting up such a hedge. Be specific.
1. What alternatives do Jim and Polly have to protect the capital value of their portfolio?
2. What are the benefits and risks of using stock-index futures as hedging vehicles?

b. Assume that S&P MidCap 400 futures contracts are currently being quoted at 769.40. How many contracts would the Pernellis have to buy (or sell) to set up the hedge?
1. Say the value of the Pernelli portfolio dropped 12% over the course of the market retreat. To what price must the stock-index futures contract move in order to cover that loss?
2. Given that a $16,875 margin deposit is required to buy or sell a single S&P 400 futures contract, what would be the Pernellis' return on invested capital if the price of the futures contract changed by the amount computed in part **b1**, above?

c. Assume that the value of the Pernelli portfolio declined by $52,000, while the price of an S&P 400 futures contract moved from 769.40 to 691.40. (Assume that Jim and Polly short sold one futures contract to set up the hedge.)
1. Add the profit from the hedge transaction to the new (depreciated) value of the stock portfolio. How does this amount compare to the $375,000 portfolio that existed just before the market started its retreat?
2. Why did the stock-index futures hedge fail to give complete protection to the Pernelli portfolio? Is it possible to obtain *perfect* (dollar-for-dollar) protection from these types of hedges? Explain.

d. What if, instead of hedging with futures contracts, the Pernellis decide to set up the hedge by using *futures options?* Fortunately, such options are available on the S&P MidCap 400 Index. These futures options, like their underlying futures contracts, are also valued/priced at $500 times the underlying S&P 400 Index. Now, suppose a put on the S&P MidCap 400 futures contract (with a strike price of 769) is currently quoted at 5.80, and a comparable call is quoted at 2.35. Use the same portfolio and futures price conditions as set out in part **c** to determine how well the portfolio would be protected if these futures *options* were used as the hedge vehicle. (*Hint:* Add the net profit from the hedge to the new depreciated value of the stock portfolio.) What are the advantages and disadvantages of using futures options, rather than the stock-index futures contract itself, to hedge a stock portfolio?

Excel with Spreadsheets

One of the unique features of futures contracts is that they have only one source of return—the capital gains that can accrue when price movements have an upward bias. Remember that there are no current cash flows associated with this financial asset. These instruments are known for their volatility due to swings in prices and the use of leverage upon purchase. With futures trading done on margin, small amounts of capital are needed to control relatively large investment positions.

Assume that you are interested in investing in commodity futures—specifically, Oats Futures Contracts. Refer to Figure 15.2, *Quotations on Actively Traded Commodity Futures Contracts*. Find the section that reads **"OATS (CBT) 5000 bu.; cents per bushel."** Suppose you had purchased 5 December oats contracts at the settle price of 186.75. The required amount of investor capital to be deposited with a broker at the time of the initial transaction is 5.35% of a contract's value. Create a spreadsheet to model and answer the following questions concerning the investment in futures contracts.

Questions

a.   What is the total amount of your initial deposit for the five contracts?

b.   What is the total amount of bushels of oats that you control?

c.   What is the purchase price of the oats commodity contracts you control according to the December settlement date?

d.   Assume that the December oats actually settles at 186.75; you decide to sell and take your profit. What is the selling price of the oats commodity contracts?

e.   Calculate the return on invested capital earned on this transaction (remember that the return is based on the amount of funds actually invested in the contract, rather than on the value of the contract itself).

Financial Tables

Table A.1

Future-Value Interest Factors for One Dollar, *FVIF*

Table A.2

Future-Value Interest Factors for a One-Dollar Annuity, *FVIFA*

Table A.3

Present-Value Interest Factors for One Dollar, *PVIF*

Table A.4

Present-Value Interest Factors for a One-Dollar Annuity, *PVIFA*

TABLE A.1   Future-Value Interest Factors for One Dollar, *FVIF*

Period	1%	2%	3%	4%	5%	6%	7%	8%	9%	10%	11%	12%	13%	14%	15%	16%	17%	18%	19%	20%
1	1.010	1.020	1.030	1.040	1.050	1.060	1.070	1.080	1.090	1.100	1.110	1.120	1.130	1.140	1.150	1.160	1.170	1.180	1.190	1.200
2	1.020	1.040	1.061	1.082	1.102	1.124	1.145	1.166	1.188	1.210	1.232	1.254	1.277	1.300	1.322	1.346	1.369	1.392	1.416	1.440
3	1.030	1.061	1.093	1.125	1.158	1.191	1.225	1.260	1.295	1.331	1.368	1.405	1.443	1.482	1.521	1.561	1.602	1.643	1.685	1.728
4	1.041	1.082	1.126	1.170	1.216	1.262	1.311	1.360	1.412	1.464	1.518	1.574	1.630	1.689	1.749	1.811	1.874	1.939	2.005	2.074
5	1.051	1.104	1.159	1.217	1.276	1.338	1.403	1.469	1.539	1.611	1.685	1.762	1.842	1.925	2.011	2.100	2.192	2.288	2.386	2.488
6	1.062	1.126	1.194	1.265	1.340	1.419	1.501	1.587	1.677	1.772	1.870	1.974	2.082	2.195	2.313	2.436	2.565	2.700	2.840	2.986
7	1.072	1.149	1.230	1.316	1.407	1.504	1.606	1.714	1.828	1.949	2.076	2.211	2.353	2.502	2.660	2.826	3.001	3.185	3.379	3.583
8	1.083	1.172	1.267	1.369	1.477	1.594	1.718	1.851	1.993	2.144	2.305	2.476	2.658	2.853	3.059	3.278	3.511	3.759	4.021	4.300
9	1.094	1.195	1.305	1.423	1.551	1.689	1.838	1.999	2.172	2.358	2.558	2.773	3.004	3.252	3.518	3.803	4.108	4.435	4.785	5.160
10	1.105	1.219	1.344	1.480	1.629	1.791	1.967	2.159	2.367	2.594	2.839	3.106	3.395	3.707	4.046	4.411	4.807	5.234	5.695	6.192
11	1.116	1.243	1.384	1.539	1.710	1.898	2.105	2.332	2.580	2.853	3.152	3.479	3.836	4.226	4.652	5.117	5.624	6.176	6.777	7.430
12	1.127	1.268	1.426	1.601	1.796	2.012	2.252	2.518	2.813	3.138	3.498	3.896	4.334	4.818	5.350	5.936	6.580	7.288	8.064	8.916
13	1.138	1.294	1.469	1.665	1.886	2.133	2.410	2.720	3.066	3.452	3.883	4.363	4.898	5.492	6.153	6.886	7.699	8.599	9.596	10.699
14	1.149	1.319	1.513	1.732	1.980	2.261	2.579	2.937	3.342	3.797	4.310	4.887	5.535	6.261	7.076	7.987	9.007	10.147	11.420	12.839
15	1.161	1.346	1.558	1.801	2.079	2.397	2.759	3.172	3.642	4.177	4.785	5.474	6.254	7.138	8.137	9.265	10.539	11.974	13.589	15.407
16	1.173	1.373	1.605	1.873	2.183	2.540	2.952	3.426	3.970	4.595	5.311	6.130	7.067	8.137	9.358	10.748	12.330	14.129	16.171	18.488
17	1.184	1.400	1.653	1.948	2.292	2.693	3.159	3.700	4.328	5.054	5.895	6.866	7.986	9.276	10.761	12.468	14.426	16.672	19.244	22.186
18	1.196	1.428	1.702	2.026	2.407	2.854	3.380	3.996	4.717	5.560	6.543	7.690	9.024	10.575	12.375	14.462	16.879	19.673	22.900	26.623
19	1.208	1.457	1.753	2.107	2.527	3.026	3.616	4.316	5.142	6.116	7.263	8.613	10.197	12.055	14.232	16.776	19.748	23.214	27.251	31.948
20	1.220	1.486	1.806	2.191	2.653	3.207	3.870	4.661	5.604	6.727	8.062	9.646	11.523	13.743	16.366	19.461	23.105	27.393	32.429	38.337
21	1.232	1.516	1.860	2.279	2.786	3.399	4.140	5.034	6.109	7.400	8.949	10.804	13.021	15.667	18.821	22.574	27.033	32.323	38.591	46.005
22	1.245	1.546	1.916	2.370	2.925	3.603	4.430	5.436	6.658	8.140	9.933	12.100	14.713	17.861	21.644	26.186	31.629	38.141	45.923	55.205
23	1.257	1.577	1.974	2.465	3.071	3.820	4.740	5.871	7.258	8.954	11.026	13.552	16.626	20.361	24.891	30.376	37.005	45.007	54.648	66.247
24	1.270	1.608	2.033	2.563	3.225	4.049	5.072	6.341	7.911	9.850	12.239	15.178	18.788	23.212	28.625	35.236	43.296	53.108	65.031	79.496
25	1.282	1.641	2.094	2.666	3.386	4.292	5.427	6.848	8.623	10.834	13.585	17.000	21.230	26.461	32.918	40.874	50.656	62.667	77.387	95.395
30	1.348	1.811	2.427	3.243	4.322	5.743	7.612	10.062	13.267	17.449	22.892	29.960	39.115	50.949	66.210	85.849	111.061	143.367	184.672	237.373
35	1.417	2.000	2.814	3.946	5.516	7.686	10.676	14.785	20.413	28.102	38.574	52.799	72.066	98.097	133.172	180.311	243.495	327.988	440.691	590.657
40	1.489	2.208	3.262	4.801	7.040	10.285	14.974	21.724	31.408	45.258	64.999	93.049	132.776	188.876	267.856	378.715	533.846	750.353	1051.642	1469.740
45	1.565	2.438	3.781	5.841	8.985	13.764	21.002	31.920	48.325	72.888	109.527	163.985	244.629	363.662	538.752	795.429	1170.425	1716.619	2509.583	3657.176
50	1.645	2.691	4.384	7.106	11.467	18.419	29.456	46.900	74.354	117.386	184.559	288.996	450.711	700.197	1083.619	1670.669	2566.080	3927.189	5988.730	9100.191

▮ Using the Calculator to Compute the Future Value of a Single Amount

Before you begin, clear the memory, ensure that you are in the *end mode* and that your calculator is set for *one payment per year*, and set the number of decimal places that you want (usually two for dollar-related accuracy).

Sample Problem

You place $800 in a savings account at 6% compounded annually. What is your account balance at the end of 5 years?

Hewlett-Packard HP 12C, 17 BII, and 19 BII[a]

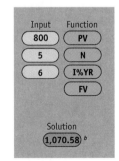

Input	Function
800	PV
5	N
6	I%YR
	FV

Solution
1,070.58 [b]

---

[a] For the 12C, you would use the ⟨n⟩ key instead of the ⟨N⟩ key, and the ⟨i⟩ key instead of the ⟨I%YR⟩ key.

[b] The minus sign that precedes the output should be ignored.

TABLE A.1 (Continued)

Period	21%	22%	23%	24%	25%	26%	27%	28%	29%	30%	31%	32%	33%	34%	35%	40%	45%	50%
1	1.210	1.220	1.230	1.240	1.250	1.260	1.270	1.280	1.290	1.300	1.310	1.320	1.330	1.340	1.350	1.400	1.450	1.500
2	1.464	1.488	1.513	1.538	1.562	1.588	1.613	1.638	1.664	1.690	1.716	1.742	1.769	1.796	1.822	1.960	2.102	2.250
3	1.772	1.816	1.861	1.907	1.953	2.000	2.048	2.097	2.147	2.197	2.248	2.300	2.353	2.406	2.460	2.744	3.049	3.375
4	2.144	2.215	2.289	2.364	2.441	2.520	2.601	2.684	2.769	2.856	2.945	3.036	3.129	3.224	3.321	3.842	4.421	5.063
5	2.594	2.703	2.815	2.932	3.052	3.176	3.304	3.436	3.572	3.713	3.858	4.007	4.162	4.320	4.484	5.378	6.410	7.594
6	3.138	3.297	3.463	3.635	3.815	4.001	4.196	4.398	4.608	4.827	5.054	5.290	5.535	5.789	6.053	7.530	9.294	11.391
7	3.797	4.023	4.259	4.508	4.768	5.042	5.329	5.629	5.945	6.275	6.621	6.983	7.361	7.758	8.172	10.541	13.476	17.086
8	4.595	4.908	5.239	5.589	5.960	6.353	6.767	7.206	7.669	8.157	8.673	9.217	9.791	10.395	11.032	14.758	19.541	25.629
9	5.560	5.987	6.444	6.931	7.451	8.004	8.595	9.223	9.893	10.604	11.362	12.166	13.022	13.930	14.894	20.661	28.334	38.443
10	6.727	7.305	7.926	8.594	9.313	10.086	10.915	11.806	12.761	13.786	14.884	16.060	17.319	18.666	20.106	28.925	41.085	57.665
11	8.140	8.912	9.749	10.657	11.642	12.708	13.862	15.112	16.462	17.921	19.498	21.199	23.034	25.012	27.144	40.495	59.573	86.498
12	9.850	10.872	11.991	13.215	14.552	16.012	17.605	19.343	21.236	23.298	25.542	27.982	30.635	33.516	36.644	56.694	86.380	129.746
13	11.918	13.264	14.749	16.386	18.190	20.175	22.359	24.759	27.395	30.287	33.460	36.937	40.745	44.912	49.469	79.371	125.251	194.620
14	14.421	16.182	18.141	20.319	22.737	25.420	28.395	31.691	35.339	39.373	43.832	48.756	54.190	60.181	66.784	111.119	181.614	291.929
15	17.449	19.742	22.314	25.195	28.422	32.030	36.062	40.565	45.587	51.185	57.420	64.358	72.073	80.643	90.158	155.567	263.341	437.894
16	21.113	24.085	27.446	31.242	35.527	40.357	45.799	51.923	58.808	66.541	75.220	84.953	95.857	108.061	121.713	217.793	381.844	656.841
17	25.547	29.384	33.758	38.740	44.409	50.850	58.165	66.461	75.862	86.503	98.539	112.138	127.490	144.802	164.312	304.911	553.674	985.261
18	30.912	35.848	41.523	48.038	55.511	64.071	73.869	85.070	97.862	112.454	129.086	148.022	169.561	194.035	221.822	426.875	802.826	1477.892
19	37.404	43.735	51.073	59.567	69.389	80.730	93.813	108.890	126.242	146.190	169.102	195.389	225.517	260.006	299.459	597.625	1164.098	2216.838
20	45.258	53.357	62.820	73.863	86.736	101.720	119.143	139.379	162.852	190.047	221.523	257.913	299.937	348.408	404.270	836.674	1687.942	3325.257
21	54.762	65.095	77.268	91.591	108.420	128.167	151.312	178.405	210.079	247.061	290.196	340.446	398.916	466.867	545.764	1171.343	2447.515	4987.883
22	66.262	79.416	95.040	113.572	135.525	161.490	192.165	228.358	271.002	321.178	380.156	449.388	530.558	625.601	736.781	1639.878	3548.896	7481.824
23	80.178	96.887	116.899	140.829	169.407	203.477	244.050	292.298	349.592	417.531	498.004	593.192	705.642	838.305	994.653	2295.829	5145.898	11222.738
24	97.015	118.203	143.786	174.628	211.758	256.381	309.943	374.141	450.974	542.791	652.385	783.013	938.504	1123.328	1342.781	3214.158	7461.547	16834.109
25	117.388	144.207	176.857	216.539	264.698	323.040	393.628	478.901	581.756	705.627	854.623	1033.577	1248.210	1505.258	1812.754	4499.816	10819.242	25251.164
30	304.471	389.748	497.904	634.810	807.793	1025.904	1300.477	1645.488	2078.208	2619.936	3297.081	4142.008	5194.516	6503.285	8128.426	24201.043	69348.375	191751.000
35	789.716	1053.370	1401.749	1861.020	2465.189	3258.053	4296.547	5653.840	7423.988	9727.598	12719.918	16598.906	21617.363	28096.695	36448.051	130158.687	*	*
40	2048.309	2846.941	3946.340	5455.797	7523.156	10346.879	14195.051	19426.418	26520.723	36117.754	49072.621	66519.313	89962.188	121388.437	163433.875	700022.688	*	*
45	5312.758	7694.418	11110.121	15994.316	22958.844	32859.457	46897.973	66748.500	94739.937	134102.187	*	*	*	*	*	*	*	*
50	13779.844	20795.680	31278.301	46889.207	70064.812	104354.562	154942.687	229345.875	338440.000	497910.125	*	*	*	*	*	*	*	*

*Not shown because of space limitations.

Texas Instruments BA-35, BAII, BAII Plus[c]

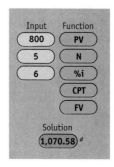

[c] For the Texas Instruments BAII, you would use the [2nd] key instead of the [CPT] key;
for the Texas Instruments BAII Plus, you would use the [I/Y] key instead of the [%i] key.
[d] If a minus sign precedes the output, it should be ignored.

TABLE A.2   Future-Value Interest Factors for a One-Dollar Annuity, *FVIFA*

Period	1%	2%	3%	4%	5%	6%	7%	8%	9%	10%	11%	12%	13%	14%	15%	16%	17%	18%	19%	20%
1	1.000	1.000	1.000	1.000	1.000	1.000	1.000	1.000	1.000	1.000	1.000	1.000	1.000	1.000	1.000	1.000	1.000	1.000	1.000	1.000
2	2.010	2.020	2.030	2.040	2.050	2.060	2.070	2.080	2.090	2.100	2.110	2.120	2.130	2.140	2.150	2.160	2.170	2.180	2.190	2.200
3	3.030	3.060	3.091	3.122	3.152	3.184	3.215	3.246	3.278	3.310	3.342	3.374	3.407	3.440	3.472	3.506	3.539	3.572	3.606	3.640
4	4.060	4.122	4.184	4.246	4.310	4.375	4.440	4.506	4.573	4.641	4.710	4.779	4.850	4.921	4.993	5.066	5.141	5.215	5.291	5.368
5	5.101	5.204	5.309	5.416	5.526	5.637	5.751	5.867	5.985	6.105	6.228	6.353	6.480	6.610	6.742	6.877	7.014	7.154	7.297	7.442
6	6.152	6.308	6.468	6.633	6.802	6.975	7.153	7.336	7.523	7.716	7.913	8.115	8.323	8.535	8.754	8.977	9.207	9.442	9.683	9.930
7	7.214	7.434	7.662	7.898	8.142	8.394	8.654	8.923	9.200	9.487	9.783	10.089	10.405	10.730	11.067	11.414	11.772	12.141	12.523	12.916
8	8.286	8.583	8.892	9.214	9.549	9.897	10.260	10.637	11.028	11.436	11.859	12.300	12.757	13.233	13.727	14.240	14.773	15.327	15.902	16.499
9	9.368	9.755	10.159	10.583	11.027	11.491	11.978	12.488	13.021	13.579	14.164	14.776	15.416	16.085	16.786	17.518	18.285	19.086	19.923	20.799
10	10.462	10.950	11.464	12.006	12.578	13.181	13.816	14.487	15.193	15.937	16.722	17.549	18.420	19.337	20.304	21.321	22.393	23.521	24.709	25.959
11	11.567	12.169	12.808	13.486	14.207	14.972	15.784	16.645	17.560	18.531	19.561	20.655	21.814	23.044	24.349	25.733	27.200	28.755	30.403	32.150
12	12.682	13.412	14.192	15.026	15.917	16.870	17.888	18.977	20.141	21.384	22.713	24.133	25.650	27.271	29.001	30.850	32.824	34.931	37.180	39.580
13	13.809	14.680	15.618	16.627	17.713	18.882	20.141	21.495	22.953	24.523	26.211	28.029	29.984	32.088	34.352	36.786	39.404	42.218	45.244	48.496
14	14.947	15.974	17.086	18.292	19.598	21.015	22.550	24.215	26.019	27.975	30.095	32.392	34.882	37.581	40.504	43.672	47.102	50.818	54.841	59.196
15	16.097	17.293	18.599	20.023	21.578	23.276	25.129	27.152	29.361	31.772	34.405	37.280	40.417	43.842	47.580	51.659	56.109	60.965	66.260	72.035
16	17.258	18.639	20.157	21.824	23.657	25.672	27.888	30.324	33.003	35.949	39.190	42.753	46.671	50.980	55.717	60.925	66.648	72.938	79.850	87.442
17	18.430	20.012	21.761	23.697	25.840	28.213	30.840	33.750	36.973	40.544	44.500	48.883	53.738	59.117	65.075	71.673	78.978	87.067	96.021	105.930
18	19.614	21.412	23.414	25.645	28.132	30.905	33.999	37.450	41.301	45.599	50.396	55.749	61.724	68.393	75.836	84.140	93.404	103.739	115.265	128.116
19	20.811	22.840	25.117	27.671	30.539	33.760	37.379	41.446	46.018	51.158	56.939	63.439	70.748	78.968	88.211	98.603	110.283	123.412	138.165	154.739
20	22.019	24.297	26.870	29.778	33.066	36.785	40.995	45.762	51.159	57.274	64.202	72.052	80.946	91.024	102.443	115.379	130.031	146.626	165.417	186.687
21	23.239	25.783	28.676	31.969	35.719	39.992	44.865	50.422	56.764	64.002	72.264	81.698	92.468	104.767	118.809	134.840	153.136	174.019	197.846	225.024
22	24.471	27.299	30.536	34.248	38.505	43.392	49.005	55.456	62.872	71.402	81.213	92.502	105.489	120.434	137.630	157.414	180.169	206.342	236.436	271.028
23	25.716	28.845	32.452	36.618	41.430	46.995	53.435	60.893	69.531	79.542	91.147	104.602	120.203	138.295	159.274	183.600	211.798	244.483	282.359	326.234
24	26.973	30.421	34.426	39.082	44.501	50.815	58.176	66.764	76.789	88.496	102.173	118.154	136.829	158.656	184.166	213.976	248.803	289.490	337.007	392.480
25	28.243	32.030	36.459	41.645	47.726	54.864	63.248	73.105	84.699	98.346	114.412	133.333	155.616	181.867	212.790	249.212	292.099	342.598	402.038	471.976
30	34.784	40.567	47.575	56.084	66.438	79.057	94.459	113.282	136.305	164.491	199.018	241.330	293.192	356.778	434.738	530.306	647.423	790.932	966.698	1181.865
35	41.659	49.994	60.461	73.651	90.318	111.432	138.234	172.314	215.705	271.018	341.583	431.658	546.663	693.552	881.152	1120.699	1426.448	1816.607	2314.173	2948.294
40	48.885	60.401	75.400	95.024	120.797	154.758	199.630	259.052	337.872	442.580	581.812	767.080	1013.667	1341.979	1779.048	2360.724	3134.412	4163.094	5529.711	7343.715
45	56.479	71.891	92.718	121.027	159.695	212.737	285.741	386.497	525.840	718.881	986.613	1358.208	1874.086	2590.464	3585.031	4965.191	6879.008	9531.258	13203.105	18280.914
50	64.461	84.577	112.794	152.664	209.341	290.325	406.516	573.756	815.051	1163.865	1668.723	2399.975	3459.344	4994.301	7217.488	10435.449	15088.805	21812.273	31514.492	45496.094

▌ Using the Calculator to Compute the Future Value of an Annuity

Before you begin, clear the memory, ensure that you are in the *end mode* and that your calculator is set for *one payment per year*, and set the number of decimal places that you want (usually two for dollar-related accuracy).

Sample Problem

You want to know what the future value will be at the end of 5 years if you place five end-of-year deposits of $1,000 in an account paying 7% annually. What is your account balance at the end of 5 years?

Hewlett-Packard HP 12C, 17 BII, and 19 BII[a]

Input	Function
1000	PV
5	N
7	I%YR
	FV

Solution
5,750.74[b]

---

[a] For the 12C, you would use the ⓝ key instead of the Ⓝ key, and the ⓘ key instead of the I%YR key.

[b] The minus sign that precedes the output should be ignored.

TABLE A.2 *(Continued)*

Period	21%	22%	23%	24%	25%	26%	27%	28%	29%	30%	31%	32%	33%	34%	35%	40%	45%	50%
1	1.000	1.000	1.000	1.000	1.000	1.000	1.000	1.000	1.000	1.000	1.000	1.000	1.000	1.000	1.000	1.000	1.000	1.000
2	2.210	2.220	2.230	2.240	2.250	2.260	2.270	2.280	2.290	2.300	2.310	2.320	2.330	2.340	2.350	2.400	2.450	2.500
3	3.674	3.708	3.743	3.778	3.813	3.848	3.883	3.918	3.954	3.990	4.026	4.062	4.099	4.136	4.172	4.360	4.552	4.750
4	5.446	5.524	5.604	5.684	5.766	5.848	5.931	6.016	6.101	6.187	6.274	6.362	6.452	6.542	6.633	7.104	7.601	8.125
5	7.589	7.740	7.893	8.048	8.207	8.368	8.533	8.700	8.870	9.043	9.219	9.398	9.581	9.766	9.954	10.946	12.022	13.188
6	10.183	10.442	10.708	10.980	11.259	11.544	11.837	12.136	12.442	12.756	13.077	13.406	13.742	14.086	14.438	16.324	18.431	20.781
7	13.321	13.740	14.171	14.615	15.073	15.546	16.032	16.534	17.051	17.583	18.131	18.696	19.277	19.876	20.492	23.853	27.725	32.172
8	17.119	17.762	18.430	19.123	19.842	20.588	21.361	22.163	22.995	23.858	24.752	25.678	26.638	27.633	28.664	34.395	41.202	49.258
9	21.714	22.670	23.669	24.712	25.802	26.940	28.129	29.369	30.664	32.015	33.425	34.895	36.429	38.028	39.696	49.152	60.743	74.887
10	27.274	28.657	30.113	31.643	33.253	34.945	36.723	38.592	40.556	42.619	44.786	47.062	49.451	51.958	54.590	69.813	89.077	113.330
11	34.001	35.962	38.039	40.238	42.566	45.030	47.639	50.398	53.318	56.405	59.670	63.121	66.769	70.624	74.696	98.739	130.161	170.995
12	42.141	44.873	47.787	50.895	54.208	57.738	61.501	65.510	69.780	74.326	79.167	84.320	89.803	95.636	101.840	139.234	189.734	257.493
13	51.991	55.745	59.778	64.109	68.760	73.750	79.106	84.853	91.016	97.624	104.709	112.302	120.438	129.152	138.484	195.928	276.114	387.239
14	63.909	69.009	74.528	80.496	86.949	93.925	101.465	109.611	118.411	127.912	138.169	149.239	161.183	174.063	187.953	275.299	401.365	581.858
15	78.330	85.191	92.669	100.815	109.687	119.346	129.860	141.302	153.750	167.285	182.001	197.996	215.373	234.245	254.737	386.418	582.980	873.788
16	95.779	104.933	114.983	126.010	138.109	151.375	165.922	181.867	199.337	218.470	239.421	262.354	287.446	314.888	344.895	541.985	846.321	1311.681
17	116.892	129.019	142.428	157.252	173.636	191.733	211.721	233.790	258.145	285.011	314.642	347.307	383.303	422.949	466.608	759.778	1228.165	1968.522
18	142.439	158.403	176.187	195.993	218.045	242.583	269.885	300.250	334.006	371.514	413.180	459.445	510.792	567.751	630.920	1064.689	1781.838	2953.783
19	173.351	194.251	217.710	244.031	273.556	306.654	343.754	385.321	431.868	483.968	542.266	607.467	680.354	761.786	852.741	1491.563	2584.665	4431.672
20	210.755	237.986	268.783	303.598	342.945	387.384	437.568	494.210	558.110	630.157	711.368	802.856	905.870	1021.792	1152.200	2089.188	3748.763	6648.508
21	256.013	291.343	331.603	377.461	429.681	489.104	556.710	633.589	720.962	820.204	932.891	1060.769	1205.807	1370.201	1556.470	2925.862	5436.703	9973.762
22	310.775	356.438	408.871	469.052	538.101	617.270	708.022	811.993	931.040	1067.265	1223.087	1401.215	1604.724	1837.068	2102.234	4097.203	7884.215	14961.645
23	377.038	435.854	503.911	582.624	673.626	778.760	900.187	1040.351	1202.042	1388.443	1603.243	1850.603	2135.282	2462.669	2839.014	5737.078	11433.109	22443.469
24	457.215	532.741	620.810	723.453	843.032	982.237	1144.237	1332.649	1551.634	1805.975	2101.247	2443.795	2840.924	3300.974	3833.667	8032.906	16579.008	33666.207
25	554.230	650.944	764.596	898.082	1054.791	1238.617	1454.180	1706.790	2002.608	2348.765	2753.631	3226.808	3779.428	4424.301	5176.445	11247.062	24040.555	50500.316
30	1445.111	1767.044	2160.459	2640.881	3227.172	3941.953	4812.891	5873.172	7162.785	8729.805	10632.543	12940.672	15737.945	19124.434	23221.258	60500.207	154105.313	383500.000
35	3755.814	4783.520	6090.227	7750.094	9856.746	12527.160	15909.480	20188.742	25596.512	32422.090	41028.887	51868.563	65504.199	82634.625	104134.500	325394.688	*	*
40	9749.141	12936.141	17153.691	22728.367	30088.621	39791.957	52570.707	69376.562	91447.375	120389.375	*	*	*	*	*	*	*	*
45	25294.223	34970.230	48300.660	66638.937	91831.312	126378.937	173692.875	238384.312	326686.375	447005.062	*	*	*	*	*	*	*	*

*Not shown because of space limitations.

Texas Instruments BA-35, BAII, BAII Plus[c]

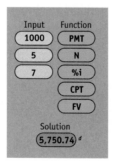

Input	Function
1000	PMT
5	N
7	%i
	CPT
	FV

Solution
5,750.74 [d]

---

[c] For the Texas Instruments BAII, you would use the **2nd** key instead of the **CPT** key; for the Texas Instruments BAII Plus, you would use the **I/Y** key instead of the **%i** key.
[d] If a minus sign precedes the output, it should be ignored.

TABLE A.3   Present-Value Interest Factors for One Dollar, *PVIF*

Period	1%	2%	3%	4%	5%	6%	7%	8%	9%	10%	11%	12%	13%	14%	15%	16%	17%	18%	19%	20%
1	.990	.980	.971	.962	.952	.943	.935	.926	.917	.909	.901	.893	.885	.877	.870	.862	.855	.847	.840	.833
2	.980	.961	.943	.925	.907	.890	.873	.857	.842	.826	.812	.797	.783	.769	.756	.743	.731	.718	.706	.694
3	.971	.942	.915	.889	.864	.840	.816	.794	.772	.751	.731	.712	.693	.675	.658	.641	.624	.609	.593	.579
4	.961	.924	.888	.855	.823	.792	.763	.735	.708	.683	.659	.636	.613	.592	.572	.552	.534	.516	.499	.482
5	.951	.906	.863	.822	.784	.747	.713	.681	.650	.621	.593	.567	.543	.519	.497	.476	.456	.437	.419	.402
6	.942	.888	.837	.790	.746	.705	.666	.630	.596	.564	.535	.507	.480	.456	.432	.410	.390	.370	.352	.335
7	.933	.871	.813	.760	.711	.665	.623	.583	.547	.513	.482	.452	.425	.400	.376	.354	.333	.314	.296	.279
8	.923	.853	.789	.731	.677	.627	.582	.540	.502	.467	.434	.404	.376	.351	.327	.305	.285	.266	.249	.233
9	.914	.837	.766	.703	.645	.592	.544	.500	.460	.424	.391	.361	.333	.308	.284	.263	.243	.225	.209	.194
10	.905	.820	.744	.676	.614	.558	.508	.463	.422	.386	.352	.322	.295	.270	.247	.227	.208	.191	.176	.162
11	.896	.804	.722	.650	.585	.527	.475	.429	.388	.350	.317	.287	.261	.237	.215	.195	.178	.162	.148	.135
12	.887	.789	.701	.625	.557	.497	.444	.397	.356	.319	.286	.257	.231	.208	.187	.168	.152	.137	.124	.112
13	.879	.773	.681	.601	.530	.469	.415	.368	.326	.290	.258	.229	.204	.182	.163	.145	.130	.116	.104	.093
14	.870	.758	.661	.577	.505	.442	.388	.340	.299	.263	.232	.205	.181	.160	.141	.125	.111	.099	.088	.078
15	.861	.743	.642	.555	.481	.417	.362	.315	.275	.239	.209	.183	.160	.140	.123	.108	.095	.084	.074	.065
16	.853	.728	.623	.534	.458	.394	.339	.292	.252	.218	.188	.163	.141	.123	.107	.093	.081	.071	.062	.054
17	.844	.714	.605	.513	.436	.371	.317	.270	.231	.198	.170	.146	.125	.108	.093	.080	.069	.060	.052	.045
18	.836	.700	.587	.494	.416	.350	.296	.250	.212	.180	.153	.130	.111	.095	.081	.069	.059	.051	.044	.038
19	.828	.686	.570	.475	.396	.331	.277	.232	.194	.164	.138	.116	.098	.083	.070	.060	.051	.043	.037	.031
20	.820	.673	.554	.456	.377	.312	.258	.215	.178	.149	.124	.104	.087	.073	.061	.051	.043	.037	.031	.026
21	.811	.660	.538	.439	.359	.294	.242	.199	.164	.135	.112	.093	.077	.064	.053	.044	.037	.031	.026	.022
22	.803	.647	.522	.422	.342	.278	.226	.184	.150	.123	.101	.083	.068	.056	.046	.038	.032	.026	.022	.018
23	.795	.634	.507	.406	.326	.262	.211	.170	.138	.112	.091	.074	.060	.049	.040	.033	.027	.022	.018	.015
24	.788	.622	.492	.390	.310	.247	.197	.158	.126	.102	.082	.066	.053	.043	.035	.028	.023	.019	.015	.013
25	.780	.610	.478	.375	.295	.233	.184	.146	.116	.092	.074	.059	.047	.038	.030	.024	.020	.016	.013	.010
30	.742	.552	.412	.308	.231	.174	.131	.099	.075	.057	.044	.033	.026	.020	.015	.012	.009	.007	.005	.004
35	.706	.500	.355	.253	.181	.130	.094	.068	.049	.036	.026	.019	.014	.010	.008	.006	.004	.003	.002	.002
40	.672	.453	.307	.208	.142	.097	.067	.046	.032	.022	.015	.011	.008	.005	.004	.003	.002	.001	.001	.001
45	.639	.410	.264	.171	.111	.073	.048	.031	.021	.014	.009	.006	.004	.003	.002	.001	.001	.001	*	*
50	.608	.372	.228	.141	.087	.054	.034	.021	.013	.009	.005	.003	.002	.001	.001	.001	*	*	*	*

*PVIF is zero to three decimal places.

■ Using the Calculator to Compute the Present Value of a Single Amount

Before you begin, clear the memory, ensure that you are in the *end mode* and that your calculator is set for *one payment per year*, and set the number of decimal places that you want (usually two for dollar-related accuracy).

Sample Problem

You want to know the present value of $1,700 to be received at the end of 8 years, assuming an 8% discount rate.

Hewlett-Packard HP 12C, 17 BII, and 19 BII[a]

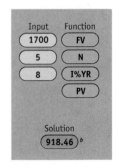

[a] For the 12C, you would use the **n** key instead of the **N** key, and the **i** key instead of the **I%YR** key.
[b] The minus sign that precedes the output should be ignored.

TABLE A.3 *(Continued)*

Period	21%	22%	23%	24%	25%	26%	27%	28%	29%	30%	31%	32%	33%	34%	35%	40%	45%	50%
1	.826	.820	.813	.806	.800	.794	.787	.781	.775	.769	.763	.758	.752	.746	.741	.714	.690	.667
2	.683	.672	.661	.650	.640	.630	.620	.610	.601	.592	.583	.574	.565	.557	.549	.510	.476	.444
3	.564	.551	.537	.524	.512	.500	.488	.477	.466	.455	.445	.435	.425	.416	.406	.364	.328	.296
4	.467	.451	.437	.423	.410	.397	.384	.373	.361	.350	.340	.329	.320	.310	.301	.260	.226	.198
5	.386	.370	.355	.341	.328	.315	.303	.291	.280	.269	.259	.250	.240	.231	.223	.186	.156	.132
6	.319	.303	.289	.275	.262	.250	.238	.227	.217	.207	.198	.189	.181	.173	.165	.133	.108	.088
7	.263	.249	.235	.222	.210	.198	.188	.178	.168	.159	.151	.143	.136	.129	.122	.095	.074	.059
8	.218	.204	.191	.179	.168	.157	.148	.139	.130	.123	.115	.108	.102	.096	.091	.068	.051	.039
9	.180	.167	.155	.144	.134	.125	.116	.108	.101	.094	.088	.082	.077	.072	.067	.048	.035	.026
10	.149	.137	.126	.116	.107	.099	.092	.085	.078	.073	.067	.062	.058	.054	.050	.035	.024	.017
11	.123	.112	.103	.094	.086	.079	.072	.066	.061	.056	.051	.047	.043	.040	.037	.025	.017	.012
12	.102	.092	.083	.076	.069	.062	.057	.052	.047	.043	.039	.036	.033	.030	.027	.018	.012	.008
13	.084	.075	.068	.061	.055	.050	.045	.040	.037	.033	.030	.027	.025	.022	.020	.013	.008	.005
14	.069	.062	.055	.049	.044	.039	.035	.032	.028	.025	.023	.021	.018	.017	.015	.009	.006	.003
15	.057	.051	.045	.040	.035	.031	.028	.025	.022	.020	.017	.016	.014	.012	.011	.006	.004	.002
16	.047	.042	.036	.032	.028	.025	.022	.019	.017	.015	.013	.012	.010	.009	.008	.005	.003	.002
17	.039	.034	.030	.026	.023	.020	.017	.015	.013	.012	.010	.009	.008	.007	.006	.003	.002	.001
18	.032	.028	.024	.021	.018	.016	.014	.012	.010	.009	.008	.007	.006	.005	.005	.002	.001	.001
19	.027	.023	.020	.017	.014	.012	.011	.009	.008	.007	.006	.005	.004	.004	.003	.002	.001	*
20	.022	.019	.016	.014	.012	.010	.008	.007	.006	.005	.005	.004	.003	.003	.002	.001	.001	*
21	.018	.015	.013	.011	.009	.008	.007	.006	.005	.004	.003	.003	.003	.002	.002	.001	*	*
22	.015	.013	.011	.009	.007	.006	.005	.004	.004	.003	.003	.002	.002	.002	.001	.001	*	*
23	.012	.010	.009	.007	.006	.005	.004	.003	.003	.002	.002	.002	.001	.001	.001	*	*	*
24	.010	.008	.007	.006	.005	.004	.003	.003	.002	.002	.002	.001	.001	.001	.001	*	*	*
25	.009	.007	.006	.005	.004	.003	.003	.002	.002	.001	.001	.001	.001	.001	.001	*	*	*
30	.003	.003	.002	.002	.001	.001	.001	.001	*	*	*	*	*	*	*	*	*	*
35	.001	.001	.001	.001	*	*	*	*	*	*	*	*	*	*	*	*	*	*
40	*	*	*	*	*	*	*	*	*	*	*	*	*	*	*	*	*	*
45	*	*	*	*	*	*	*	*	*	*	*	*	*	*	*	*	*	*
50	*	*	*	*	*	*	*	*	*	*	*	*	*	*	*	*	*	*

*PVIF is zero to three decimal places.

Texas Instruments BA-35, BAII, BAII Plus[c]

[c] For the Texas Instruments BAII, you would use the **2nd** key instead of the **CPT** key; for the Texas Instruments BAII Plus, you would use the **I/Y** key instead of the **%i** key.
[d] If a minus sign precedes the output, it should be ignored.

TABLE A.4   Present-Value Interest Factors for a One-Dollar Annuity, *PVIFA*

Period	1%	2%	3%	4%	5%	6%	7%	8%	9%	10%	11%	12%	13%	14%	15%	16%	17%	18%	19%	20%
1	.990	.980	.971	.962	.952	.943	.935	.926	.917	.909	.901	.893	.885	.877	.870	.862	.855	.847	.840	.833
2	1.970	1.942	1.913	1.886	1.859	1.833	1.808	1.783	1.759	1.736	1.713	1.690	1.668	1.647	1.626	1.605	1.585	1.566	1.547	1.528
3	2.941	2.884	2.829	2.775	2.723	2.673	2.624	2.577	2.531	2.487	2.444	2.402	2.361	2.322	2.283	2.246	2.210	2.174	2.140	2.106
4	3.902	3.808	3.717	3.630	3.546	3.465	3.387	3.312	3.240	3.170	3.102	3.037	2.974	2.914	2.855	2.798	2.743	2.690	2.639	2.589
5	4.853	4.713	4.580	4.452	4.329	4.212	4.100	3.993	3.890	3.791	3.696	3.605	3.517	3.433	3.352	3.274	3.199	3.127	3.058	2.991
6	5.795	5.601	5.417	5.242	5.076	4.917	4.767	4.623	4.486	4.355	4.231	4.111	3.998	3.889	3.784	3.685	3.589	3.498	3.410	3.326
7	6.728	6.472	6.230	6.002	5.786	5.582	5.389	5.206	5.033	4.868	4.712	4.564	4.423	4.288	4.160	4.039	3.922	3.812	3.706	3.605
8	7.652	7.326	7.020	6.733	6.463	6.210	5.971	5.747	5.535	5.335	5.146	4.968	4.799	4.639	4.487	4.344	4.207	4.078	3.954	3.837
9	8.566	8.162	7.786	7.435	7.108	6.802	6.515	6.247	5.995	5.759	5.537	5.328	5.132	4.946	4.772	4.607	4.451	4.303	4.163	4.031
10	9.471	8.983	8.530	8.111	7.722	7.360	7.024	6.710	6.418	6.145	5.889	5.650	5.426	5.216	5.019	4.833	4.659	4.494	4.339	4.192
11	10.368	9.787	9.253	8.760	8.306	7.887	7.499	7.139	6.805	6.495	6.207	5.938	5.687	5.453	5.234	5.029	4.836	4.656	4.486	4.327
12	11.255	10.575	9.954	9.385	8.863	8.384	7.943	7.536	7.161	6.814	6.492	6.194	5.918	5.660	5.421	5.197	4.988	4.793	4.611	4.439
13	12.134	11.348	10.635	9.986	9.394	8.853	8.358	7.904	7.487	7.013	6.750	6.424	6.122	5.842	5.583	5.342	5.118	4.910	4.715	4.533
14	13.004	12.106	11.296	10.563	9.899	9.295	8.745	8.244	7.786	7.367	6.982	6.628	6.302	6.002	5.724	5.468	5.229	5.008	4.802	4.611
15	13.865	12.849	11.938	11.118	10.380	9.712	9.108	8.560	8.061	7.606	7.191	6.811	6.462	6.142	5.847	5.575	5.324	5.092	4.876	4.675
16	14.718	13.578	12.561	11.652	10.838	10.106	9.447	8.851	8.313	7.824	7.379	6.974	6.604	6.265	5.954	5.668	5.405	5.162	4.938	4.730
17	15.562	14.292	13.166	12.166	11.274	10.477	9.763	9.122	8.544	8.022	7.549	7.120	6.729	6.373	6.047	5.749	5.475	5.222	4.990	4.775
18	16.398	14.992	13.754	12.659	11.690	10.828	10.059	9.372	8.756	8.201	7.702	7.250	6.840	6.467	6.128	5.818	5.534	5.273	5.033	4.812
19	17.226	15.679	14.324	13.134	12.085	11.158	10.336	9.604	8.950	8.365	7.839	7.366	6.938	6.550	6.198	5.877	5.584	5.316	5.070	4.843
20	18.046	16.352	14.878	13.590	12.462	11.470	10.594	9.818	9.129	8.514	7.963	7.469	7.025	6.623	6.259	5.929	5.628	5.353	5.101	4.870
21	18.857	17.011	15.415	14.029	12.821	11.764	10.836	10.017	9.292	8.649	8.075	7.562	7.102	6.687	6.312	5.973	5.665	5.384	5.127	4.891
22	19.661	17.658	15.937	14.451	13.163	12.042	11.061	10.201	9.442	8.772	8.176	7.645	7.170	6.743	6.359	6.011	5.696	5.410	5.149	4.909
23	20.456	18.292	16.444	14.857	13.489	12.303	11.272	10.371	9.580	8.883	8.266	7.718	7.230	6.792	6.399	6.044	5.723	5.432	5.167	4.925
24	21.244	18.914	16.936	15.247	13.799	12.550	11.469	10.529	9.707	8.985	8.348	7.784	7.283	6.835	6.434	6.073	5.746	5.451	5.182	4.937
25	22.023	19.524	17.413	15.622	14.094	12.783	11.654	10.675	9.823	9.077	8.422	7.843	7.330	6.873	6.464	6.097	5.766	5.467	5.195	4.948
30	25.808	22.396	19.601	17.292	15.373	13.765	12.409	11.258	10.274	9.427	8.694	8.055	7.496	7.003	6.566	6.177	5.829	5.517	5.235	4.979
35	29.409	24.999	21.487	18.665	16.374	14.498	12.948	11.655	10.567	9.644	8.855	8.176	7.586	7.070	6.617	6.215	5.858	5.539	5.251	4.992
40	32.835	27.356	23.115	19.793	17.159	15.046	13.332	11.925	10.757	9.779	8.951	8.244	7.634	7.105	6.642	6.233	5.871	5.548	5.258	4.997
45	36.095	29.490	24.519	20.720	17.774	15.456	13.606	12.108	10.881	9.863	9.008	8.283	7.661	7.123	6.654	6.242	5.877	5.552	5.261	4.999
50	39.196	31.424	25.730	21.482	18.256	15.762	13.801	12.233	10.962	9.915	9.042	8.304	7.675	7.133	6.661	6.246	5.880	5.554	5.262	4.999

▌Using the Calculator to Compute the Present Value of an Annuity

Before you begin, clear the memory, ensure that you are in the *end mode* and that your calculator is set for *one payment per year*, and set the number of decimal places that you want (usually two for dollar-related accuracy).

Sample Problem

You want to know what the present value of an annuity of $700 per year received at the end of each year for 5 years will be, given a discount rate of 8%.

Hewlett-Packard HP 12C, 17 BII, and 19 BII[a]

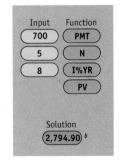

Input	Function
700	PMT
5	N
8	I%YR
	PV

Solution
(2,794.90) [b]

---

[a] For the 12C, you would use the ⓝ key instead of the Ⓝ key, and the ⓘ key instead of the I%YR key.

[b] The minus sign that precedes the output should be ignored.

TABLE A.4 (Continued)

Period	21%	22%	23%	24%	25%	26%	27%	28%	29%	30%	31%	32%	33%	34%	35%	40%	45%	50%
1	.826	.820	.813	.806	.800	.794	.787	.781	.775	.769	.763	.758	.752	.746	.741	.714	.690	.667
2	1.509	1.492	1.474	1.457	1.440	1.424	1.407	1.392	1.376	1.361	1.346	1.331	1.317	1.303	1.289	1.224	1.165	1.111
3	2.074	2.042	2.011	1.981	1.952	1.923	1.896	1.868	1.842	1.816	1.791	1.766	1.742	1.719	1.696	1.589	1.493	1.407
4	2.540	2.494	2.448	2.404	2.362	2.320	2.280	2.241	2.203	2.166	2.130	2.096	2.062	2.029	1.997	1.849	1.720	1.605
5	2.926	2.864	2.803	2.745	2.689	2.635	2.583	2.532	2.483	2.436	2.390	2.345	2.302	2.260	2.220	2.035	1.876	1.737
6	3.245	3.167	3.092	3.020	2.951	2.885	2.821	2.759	2.700	2.643	2.588	2.534	2.483	2.433	2.385	2.168	1.983	1.824
7	3.508	3.416	3.327	3.242	3.161	3.083	3.009	2.937	2.868	2.802	2.739	2.677	2.619	2.562	2.508	2.263	2.057	1.883
8	3.726	3.619	3.518	3.421	3.329	3.241	3.156	3.076	2.999	2.925	2.854	2.786	2.721	2.658	2.598	2.331	2.109	1.922
9	3.905	3.786	3.673	3.566	3.463	3.366	3.273	3.184	3.100	3.019	2.942	2.868	2.798	2.730	2.665	2.379	2.144	1.948
10	4.054	3.923	3.799	3.682	3.570	3.465	3.364	3.269	3.178	3.092	3.009	2.930	2.855	2.784	2.715	2.414	2.168	1.965
11	4.177	4.035	3.902	3.776	3.656	3.544	3.437	3.335	3.239	3.147	3.060	2.978	2.899	2.824	2.752	2.438	2.185	1.977
12	4.278	4.127	3.985	3.851	3.725	3.606	3.493	3.387	3.286	3.190	3.100	3.013	2.931	2.853	2.779	2.456	2.196	1.985
13	4.362	4.203	4.053	3.912	3.780	3.656	3.538	3.427	3.322	3.223	3.129	3.040	2.956	2.876	2.799	2.469	2.204	1.990
14	4.432	4.265	4.108	3.962	3.824	3.695	3.573	3.459	3.351	3.249	3.152	3.061	2.974	2.892	2.814	2.478	2.210	1.993
15	4.489	4.315	4.153	4.001	3.859	3.726	3.601	3.483	3.373	3.268	3.170	3.076	2.988	2.905	2.825	2.484	2.214	1.995
16	4.536	4.357	4.189	4.033	3.887	3.751	3.623	3.503	3.390	3.283	3.183	3.088	2.999	2.914	2.834	2.489	2.216	1.997
17	4.576	4.391	4.219	4.059	3.910	3.771	3.640	3.518	3.403	3.295	3.193	3.097	3.007	2.921	2.840	2.492	2.218	1.998
18	4.608	4.419	4.243	4.080	3.928	3.786	3.654	3.529	3.413	3.304	3.201	3.104	3.012	2.926	2.844	2.494	2.219	1.999
19	4.635	4.442	4.263	4.097	3.942	3.799	3.664	3.539	3.421	3.311	3.207	3.109	3.017	2.930	2.848	2.496	2.220	1.999
20	4.657	4.460	4.279	4.110	3.954	3.808	3.673	3.546	3.427	3.316	3.211	3.113	3.020	2.933	2.850	2.497	2.221	1.999
21	4.675	4.476	4.292	4.121	3.963	3.816	3.679	3.551	3.432	3.320	3.215	3.116	3.023	2.935	2.852	2.498	2.221	2.000
22	4.690	4.488	4.302	4.130	3.970	3.822	3.684	3.556	3.436	3.323	3.217	3.118	3.025	2.936	2.853	2.498	2.222	2.000
23	4.703	4.499	4.311	4.137	3.976	3.827	3.689	3.559	3.438	3.325	3.219	3.120	3.026	2.938	2.854	2.499	2.222	2.000
24	4.713	4.507	4.318	4.143	3.981	3.831	3.692	3.562	3.441	3.327	3.221	3.121	3.027	2.939	2.855	2.499	2.222	2.000
25	4.721	4.514	4.323	4.147	3.985	3.834	3.694	3.564	3.442	3.329	3.222	3.122	3.028	2.939	2.856	2.499	2.222	2.000
30	4.746	4.534	4.339	4.160	3.995	3.842	3.701	3.569	3.447	3.332	3.225	3.124	3.030	2.941	2.857	2.500	2.222	2.000
35	4.756	4.541	4.345	4.164	3.998	3.845	3.703	3.571	3.448	3.333	3.226	3.125	3.030	2.941	2.857	2.500	2.222	2.000
40	4.760	4.544	4.347	4.166	3.999	3.846	3.703	3.571	3.448	3.333	3.226	3.125	3.030	2.941	2.857	2.500	2.222	2.000
45	4.761	4.545	4.347	4.166	4.000	3.846	3.704	3.571	3.448	3.333	3.226	3.125	3.030	2.941	2.857	2.500	2.222	2.000
50	4.762	4.545	4.348	4.167	4.000	3.846	3.704	3.571	3.448	3.333	3.226	3.125	3.030	2.941	2.857	2.500	2.222	2.000

Texas Instruments BA-35, BAII, BAII Plus[c]

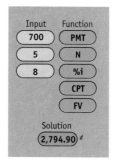

Input	Function
700	PMT
5	N
8	%i
	CPT
	FV

Solution
2,794.90 [d]

[c] For the Texas Instruments BAII, you would use the 2nd key instead of the CPT key; for the Texas Instruments BAII Plus, you would use the I/Y key instead of the %i key.
[d] If a minus sign precedes the output, it should be ignored.

Glossary

A

accumulation period   under an annuity, the period of time between when payments are made to the insurance company and when payments to the annuitant begin. (Web Chapter 17)

active portfolio management   building a portfolio using traditional and modern approaches and managing and controlling it to achieve its objectives; a worthwhile activity that can result in superior returns. (Chapter 13)

activity ratios   financial ratios that are used to measure how well a firm is managing its assets. (Chapter 7)

adjustable-rate (floating-rate) preferreds   preferred stock whose dividends are adjusted periodically in line with yields on certain Treasury issues. (Web Chapter 16)

adjusted gross income   gross income less the total allowable adjustments for tax purposes. (Web Chapter 17)

after-tax cash flows (ATCFs)   the annual cash flows earned on a real estate investment, net of all expenses, debt payments, and taxes. (Web Chapter 18)

agency bonds   debt securities issued by various agencies and organizations of the U.S. government. (Chapter 10)

aggressive-growth fund   a highly speculative mutual fund that seeks large profits from capital gains. (Chapter 12)

alternative minimum tax (AMT)   a tax passed by Congress to ensure that all individuals pay at least some federal income tax. (Web Chapter 17)

American depositary receipts (ADRs)   dollar-denominated receipts for the stocks of foreign companies that are held in the vaults of banks in the companies' home countries. Serve as backing for *American depositary shares (ADSs)*. (Chapter 2)

American depositary shares (ADSs)   securities created to permit U.S. investors to hold shares of non-U.S. companies and trade them on U.S. stock exchanges. They are backed by *American depositary receipts*. (Chapter 2)

AMEX composite index   measure of the current price behavior of all shares traded on the AMEX, relative to a base of 550 set at December 29, 1995. (Chapter 3)

analytical information   available current data in conjunction with projections and recommendations about potential investments. (Chapter 3)

annuitant   the person to whom the future payments on an annuity are directed. (Web Chapter 17)

annuity   a contract issued by an insurance company that guarantees a series of payments for a number of years or over a lifetime. (Web Chapter 17)

annuity   a stream of equal cash flows that occur at equal intervals over time. (Chapter 4)

appraisal   in real estate, the process for estimating the current market value of a piece of property. (Web Chapter 18)

arbitrage pricing theory (APT)   a theory that suggests that the market risk premium on securities may be better explained by a number of factors underlying and in some cases replacing the market return used in CAPM; the CAPM can be viewed as being derived from APT. (Chapter 5)

arbitration   a formal dispute-resolution process in which a client and a broker present their argument before a panel, which then decides the case. (Chapter 3)

ask price   the lowest price at which a security is offered for sale. (Chapter 2)

asset allocation   a scheme that involves dividing one's portfolio into various asset classes to *preserve capital* by protecting against negative developments while taking advantage of positive ones. (Chapter 12)

asset allocation fund   a mutual fund that spreads investors' money across stocks, bonds, money market securities, and possibly other asset classes, changing the mix as market conditions dictate. (Chapters 12 and 13)

asset-backed securities (ABS)   securities similar to mortgage-backed securities that are backed by a pool of bank loans, leases, and other assets. (Chapter 10)

automatic investment plan   a mutual fund service that allows shareholders to automatically send fixed amounts of money from their paychecks or bank accounts into the fund. (Chapter 12)

automatic reinvestment plan   a mutual fund service that enables shareholders to automatically buy additional shares in the fund through the reinvestment of dividends and capital gains income. (Chapter 12)

average tax rate   taxes due divided by taxable income; different from the *marginal tax rate*. (Web Chapter 17)

averages   numbers used to measure the general behavior of stock prices by reflecting the arithmetic average price behavior of a representative group of stocks at a given point in time. (Chapter 3)

B

back-end load   a commission charged on the *sale* of shares in a mutual fund. (Chapter 12)

back-office research reports   a brokerage firm's analyses of and recommendations on investment prospects; available on request at no cost to existing and potential clients or for purchase at some Web sites. (Chapter 3)

balance sheet   a financial summary of a firm's assets, liabilities, and shareholders' equity at a single point in time. (Chapter 7)

balanced fund   a mutual fund whose objective is to generate a balanced return of both current income and long-term capital gains. (Chapter 12)

bar chart   the simplest kind of chart, on which share price is plotted on the vertical axis and time on the horizontal axis; stock prices are recorded as vertical bars showing high, low, and closing prices. (Chapter 9)

Barron's   a weekly business newspaper; a popular source of financial news. (Chapter 3)

basic discount broker   typically a deep-discount broker through which investors can execute trades electronically online via a commercial service, on the Internet, or by phone. (Also called *online brokers* or *electronic brokers*.) (Chapter 3)

basis the amount paid for a capital asset, including commissions and other costs related to the purchase. (Web Chapter 17)

bear markets unfavorable markets normally associated with falling prices, investor pessimism, economic slowdown, and government restraint. (Chapter 2)

behavioral finance the body of research into the role that emotions and other subjective factors play in investment decisions. (Chapter 9)

beta a measure of *nondiversifiable*, or *market, risk* that indicates how the price of a security responds to market forces. (Chapter 5)

bid price the highest price offered to purchase a security. (Chapter 2)

blue-chip stocks financially strong, high-quality stocks with long and stable records of earnings and dividends. (Chapter 6)

bond fund a mutual fund that invests in various kinds and grades of bonds, with income as the primary objective. (Chapter 12)

bond ladders an investment strategy wherein equal amounts of money are invested in a series of bonds with staggered maturities. (Chapter 11)

bond ratings letter grades that designate investment quality and are assigned to a bond issue by rating agencies. (Chapter 10)

bond swap an investment strategy wherein an investor simultaneously liquidates one bond holding and buys a different issue to take its place. (Chapter 11)

bond yield summary measure of the total return an investor would receive on a bond if it were purchased at its current price and held to maturity; reported as an annual rate of return. (Chapter 3)

bond-equivalent yield the annual yield on a bond, calculated as twice the semiannual yield. (Chapter 11)

bonds publicly traded long-term debt securities, whereby the issuer agrees to pay a stipulated amount of interest over a specified period of time and to repay a fixed amount of principal at maturity. (Chapters 1 and 10)

book value the amount of stockholders' equity in a firm; equals the amount of the firm's assets minus the firm's liabilities and preferred stock. (Chapter 6)

broker market the *securities exchanges* on which the two sides of a transaction, the buyer and seller, are brought together to trade securities. (Chapter 2)

bull markets favorable markets normally associated with rising prices, investor optimism, economic recovery, and government stimulus. (Chapter 2)

business cycle an indication of the current state of the economy, reflecting changes in total economic activity over time. (Chapter 7)

business risk the degree of uncertainty associated with an investment's earnings and the investment's ability to pay the returns owed investors. (Chapter 4)

C

call a negotiable instrument that gives the holder the right to buy securities at a stated price within a certain time period. (Chapter 14)

call feature feature that specifies whether and under what conditions the issuer can retire a bond prior to maturity. (Chapter 10)

call premium the amount added to a bond's par value and paid to investors when a bond is retired prematurely. (Chapter 10)

call price the price the issuer must pay to retire a bond prematurely; equal to par value plus the call premium. (Chapter 10)

capital asset anything owned and used for personal reasons, pleasure, or investment. (Web Chapter 17)

capital asset pricing model (CAPM) model that formally links the notions of risk and return; it uses beta, the risk-free rate, and the market return to help investors define the required return on an investment. (Chapter 5)

capital gains the amount by which the sale price of an asset *exceeds* its original purchase price. (Chapter 1)

capital gains distributions payments made to mutual fund shareholders that come from the profits that a fund makes from the sale of its securities. (Chapter 12)

capital loss the amount by which the proceeds from the sale of a capital asset are *less than* its original purchase price. (Chapter 1)

capital market market in which *long-term* securities (with maturities greater than one year) such as stocks and bonds are bought and sold. (Chapter 2)

cash account a brokerage account in which a customer can make only cash transactions. (Chapter 3)

cash dividend payment of a dividend in the form of cash. (Chapter 6)

cash market a market where a product or commodity changes hands in exchange for a cash price paid when the transaction is completed. (Chapter 15)

charting the activity of charting price behavior and other market information and then using the patterns these charts form to make investment decisions. (Chapter 9)

churning an illegal and unethical practice engaged in by a broker to increase commissions by causing excessive trading of clients' accounts. (Chapter 3)

classified common stock common stock issued by a company in different classes, each of which offers different privileges and benefits to its holders. (Chapter 6)

closed-end investment companies a type of investment company that operates with a fixed number of shares outstanding. (Chapter 12)

coefficient of variation, CV a statistic used to measure the *relative* dispersion of an asset's returns; it is useful in comparing the risk of assets with differing average or expected returns. (Chapter 4)

collateral trust bonds senior bonds backed by securities owned by the issuer but held in trust by a third party. (Chapter 10)

collateralized mortgage obligation (CMO) mortgage-backed bond whose holders are divided into classes based on the length of investment desired; principal is channeled to investors in order of maturity, with short-term classes first. (Chapter 10)

common stock equity investment that represents ownership in a corporation; each share represents a fractional ownership interest in the firm. (Chapter 1)

common stock (market) ratios financial ratios that convert key information about a firm to a per-share basis. (Chapter 7)

common-size income statement a type of financial report that uses a common denominator (net sales) to convert all entries on a normal income statement from dollars to percentages. (Chapter 8)

comparative sales approach a real estate valuation approach that uses as the basic input the sales prices of properties that are similar to the subject property. (Web Chapter 18)

compound interest interest paid not only on the initial deposit but also on any interest accumulated from one period to the next. (Chapter 4)

confidence index a ratio of the average yield on high-grade corporate bonds to the average yield on average- or intermediate-grade corporate bonds; a technical indicator based on the theory that market trends usually appear in the bond market before they do in the stock market. (Chapter 9)

constant-dollar plan a formula plan for timing investment transactions, in which the investor establishes a target dollar amount for the speculative portion of the portfolio and establishes trigger points at which funds are transferred to or from the conservative portion as needed to maintain the target dollar amount. (Chapter 13)

constant-ratio plan a formula plan for timing investment transactions, in which a desired fixed ratio of the speculative portion to the conservative portion of the portfolio is established; when the actual ratio differs by a predetermined amount from the desired ratio, transactions are made to rebalance the portfolio to achieve the desired ratio. (Chapter 13)

continuous compounding interest calculation in which interest is compounded over the smallest possible interval of time. (Chapter 4)

convenience in real estate, the accessibility of a property to the places the people in a target market frequently need to go. (Web Chapter 18)

conventional options put and call options sold over the counter. (Chapter 14)

conversion (exchange) privilege feature of a mutual fund that allows shareholders to move money from one fund to another, within the same family of funds. (Chapter 12)

conversion equivalent (conversion parity) the price at which the common stock would have to sell in order to make the convertible security worth its present market price. (Chapter 10)

conversion feature allows the holder of a convertible preferred to convert to a specified number of shares of the issuing company's common stock. (Web Chapter 16)

conversion period the time period during which a convertible issue can be converted. (Chapter 10)

conversion price the stated price per share at which common stock will be delivered to the investor in exchange for a convertible issue. (Chapter 10)

conversion privilege the conditions and specific nature of the conversion feature on convertible securities. (Chapter 10)

conversion ratio the number of shares of common stock into which a convertible issue can be converted. (Chapter 10)

conversion value an indication of what a convertible issue would trade for if it were priced to sell on the basis of its stock value. (Chapter 10)

convertible bonds fixed-income obligations that have a feature permitting the holder to convert the security into a specified number of shares of the issuing company's common stock. (Chapter 10)

convertible security a fixed-income obligation with a feature permitting the investor to convert it into a specified number of shares of common stock. (Chapter 1)

corporation a form of organization that provides a limited-liability benefit to shareholder investors and that has an indefinite life. (Web Chapter 17)

correlation a statistical measure of the relationship, if any, between series of numbers representing data of any kind. (Chapter 5)

correlation coefficient a measure of the degree of correlation between two series. (Chapter 5)

cost approach a real estate valuation approach based on the idea that an investor should not pay more for a property than it would cost to rebuild it at today's prices. (Web Chapter 18)

coupon feature on a bond that defines the amount of annual interest income. (Chapter 10)

Coverdell Education Savings Account (ESA) an education savings plan that allows the taxpayer, subject to income limits, to contribute a *nondeductible* $2,000 per year for each child under age 18 into an account in which earnings accumulate tax-free and distributions are tax-exempt if they are used to pay higher-education (college) expenses for the child for whom the account exists. (Web Chapter 17)

covered options options written against stock owned (or short sold) by the writer. (Chapter 14)

crossing markets after-hours trading in stocks that involve filling buy and sell orders by matching identical (Chapter 2)

cumulative provision a provision requiring that any preferred dividends that have been passed must be paid in full before dividends can be restored to common stockholders. (Web Chapter 16)

currency exchange rate the relationship between two currencies on a specified date. (Chapter 2)

currency exchange risk the risk caused by the varying exchange rates between the currencies of two countries. (Chapter 2)

currency futures futures contracts on foreign currencies, traded much like commodities. (Chapter 15)

currency options put and call options written on foreign currencies. (Chapter 14)

current income usually cash or near-cash that is periodically received as a result of owning an investment. (Chapter 4)

current interest rate for an annuity contract, the yearly return the insurance company pays on accumulated deposits. (Web Chapter 17)

current yield measure of the annual interest income a bond provides relative to its current market price. (Chapters 10 and 11)

custodial account the brokerage account of a minor; requires a parent or guardian to be part of all transactions. cash account a brokerage account in which a customer can make only cash transactions. (Chapter 3)

cyclical stocks stocks whose earnings and overall market performance are closely linked to the general state of the economy. (Chapter 6)

D

daily price limit restriction on the day-to-day change in the price of an underlying commodity. (Chapter 15)

date of record the date on which an investor must be a registered shareholder to be entitled to receive a dividend. (Chapter 6)

day trader an investor who buys and sells stocks quickly throughout the day in hopes of making quick profits. (Chapter 3)

dealer market the market in which the buyer and seller are not brought together directly but instead have their orders executed by *dealers* that make markets in the given security. (Chapter 2)

debenture an unsecured (junior) bond. (Chapter 10)

debit balance the amount of money being borrowed in a margin loan. (Chapter 2)

debt funds lent in exchange for interest income and the promised repayment of the loan at a given future date. (Chapter 1)

deep-discount bond a bond selling at a price far below its par value. (Web Chapter 17)

deep-in-the-money call option a tax-deferral strategy that involves selling a call option on shares currently owned, thus locking in a price equal to the amount received from the sale of the call option but giving up future price appreciation. (Web Chapter 17)

defensive stocks stocks that tend to hold their own, and even do well, when the economy starts to falter. (Chapter 6)

deferred annuity an annuity in which the payments to the annuitant begin at some future date. (Web Chapter 17)

deferred equity securities issued in one form and later redeemed or converted into shares of common stock. (Chapter 10)

deflation a period of generally declining prices. (Chapter 4)

delivery month the time when a commodity must be delivered; defines the life of a futures contract. (Chapter 15)

demand in real estate, people's desire to buy or rent a given property. (Web Chapter 18)

demographics measurable characteristics of an area's population, such as household size, age structure, occupation, gender, and marital status. (Web Chapter 18)

depreciation in real estate investing, a tax deduction based on the original cost of a building and used to reflect its declining economic life. (Web Chapter 18)

derivative securities securities, such as puts, calls, and other options, that derive their value from the price behavior of an underlying real or financial asset. (Chapters 1 and 14)

descriptive information factual data on the past behavior of the economy, the market, the industry, the company, or a given investment vehicle. (Chapter 3)

direct investment investment in which an investor directly acquires a claim on a security or property. (Chapter 1)

discount basis a method of earning interest on a security by purchasing it at a price below its redemption value; the difference is the interest earned. (Chapter 1)

discount bond a bond with a market value lower than par; occurs when market rates are greater than the coupon rate. (Chapter 10)

discount rate the annual rate of return that could be earned currently on a similar investment; used when finding present value; also called *opportunity cost*. (Chapter 4)

discounted cash flow use of present-value techniques to find *net present value (NPV)*. (Web Chapter 18)

distribution period under an annuity, the period of time over which payments are made to the annuitant. (Web Chapter 17)

diversifiable (unsystematic) risk the portion of an investment's risk that results from uncontrollable or random events that are firm-specific; can be eliminated through diversification. (Chapter 5)

diversification the inclusion of a number of different investment vehicles in a portfolio to increase returns or reduce risk. (Chapters 1 and 2)

dividend income income derived from the dividends and interest earned on the security holdings of a mutual fund. (Chapter 12)

dividend payout ratio the portion of earnings per share (EPS) that a firm pays out as dividends. (Chapter 6)

dividend reinvestment plans (DRIPs) plans in which shareholders have cash dividends automatically reinvested into additional shares of the firm's common stock. (Chapter 6)

dividend valuation model (DVM) a model that values a share of stock on the basis of the future dividend stream it is expected to produce; its three versions are zero-growth, constant-growth, and variable-growth. (Chapter 8)

dividend yield a measure that relates dividends to share price and puts common stock dividends on a relative (percentage) rather than absolute (dollar) basis. (Chapter 6 and Web Chapter 16)

dividends periodic payments made by firms to their shareholders. (Chapter 1)

dividends-and-earnings (D&E) approach stock valuation approach that uses projected dividends, EPS, and P/E multiples to value a share of stock; also known as the *DCF approach*. (Chapter 8)

dollar-cost averaging a formula plan for timing investment transactions, in which a fixed dollar amount is invested in a security at fixed time intervals. (Chapter 13)

domestic investments debt, equity, and derivative securities of U.S.-based companies. (Chapter 1)

Dow Jones Corporate Bond Index mathematical averages of the *closing prices* for 96 bonds—32 industrial, 32 financial, and 32 utility/telecom. (Chapter 3)

Dow Jones Industrial Average (DJIA) a stock market average made up of 30 high-quality stocks selected for total market value and broad public ownership and believed to reflect overall market activity. (Chapter 3)

Dow theory a technical approach based on the idea that the market's performance can be described by the long-term price trend in the DJIA, as confirmed by the Dow transportation average. (Chapter 9)

dual listing listing of a firm's shares on more than one exchange. (Chapter 2)

duration a measure of bond price volatility, which captures both price and reinvestment risks and which is used to indicate how a bond will react in different interest rate environments. (Chapter 11)

E

earnings per share (EPS) the amount of annual earnings available to common stockholders, as stated on a per-share basis. (Chapter 6)

economic analysis a study of general economic conditions that is used in the valuation of common stock. (Chapter 7)

efficient frontier the leftmost boundary of the *feasible (attainable) set* of portfolios that includes all *efficient portfolios*—those providing the best attainable tradeoff between risk (measured by the standard deviation) and return. (Chapter 5)

efficient market a market in which securities reflect all possible information quickly and accurately. (Chapter 9)

efficient markets hypothesis (EMH) basic theory of the behavior of efficient markets, in which there are a large number of knowledgeable investors who react quickly to new information, causing securities prices to adjust quickly and accurately. (Chapter 9)

efficient portfolio a portfolio that provides the highest return for a given level of risk or that has the lowest risk for a given level of return. (Chapter 5)

electronic communications networks (ECNs) electronic trading networks that automatically match buy and sell orders that customers place electronically. (Chapter 2)

environment   in real estate, the natural as well as aesthetic, socioeconomic, legal, and fiscal surroundings of a property. (Web Chapter 18)

equipment trust certificates   senior bonds secured by specific pieces of equipment; popular with transportation companies such as airlines. (Chapter 10)

equity   ongoing ownership in a business or property. (Chapter 1)

equity capital   evidence of ownership position in a firm, in the form of shares of common stock. (Chapter 6)

equity kicker   another name for the conversion feature, giving the holder of a convertible security a deferred claim on the issuer's common stock. (Chapter 10)

equity-income fund   a mutual fund that emphasizes current income and capital preservation and invests primarily in high-yielding common stocks. (Chapter 12)

ethics   standards of conduct or moral judgment. (Chapter 2)

Eurodollar bonds   foreign bonds denominated in dollars but not registered with the SEC, thus restricting sales of new issues. (Chapter 10)

event risk   risk that comes from an unexpected event that has a significant and usually immediate effect on the underlying value of an investment. (Chapter 4)

excess margin   more equity than is required in a margin account. (Chapter 2)

exchange-traded fund (ETF)   an open-end mutual fund that trades as a listed security on a stock exchange. (Chapter 12)

ex-dividend date   three business days up to the date of record; determines whether one is an official shareholder and thus eligible to receive a declared dividend. (Chapter 6)

exemption   a deduction from adjusted gross income for each taxpayer and each qualifying dependent of a federal taxpayer. (Web Chapter 17)

expectations hypothesis   theory that the shape of the yield curve reflects investor expectations of future interest rates. (Chapter 11)

expected inflation premium   the average rate of inflation expected in the future. (Chapter 4)

expected return   the rate of return an investor can expect to earn by holding a bond over a period of time that's less than the life of the issue. (Chapters 4 and 11)

expiration date   the date at which an option expires. (Chapter 14)

F

fair disclosure rule (Regulation FD)   rule requiring senior executives to disclose critical information simultaneously to investment professionals and the public via press releases or SEC filings. (Chapter 3)

financial futures   a type of futures contract in which the underlying "commodity" is a financial asset, such as debt securities, foreign currencies, or common stocks. (Chapter 15)

financial institutions   organizations that channel the savings of governments, businesses, and individuals into loans or investments. (Chapter 1)

financial leverage   the use of debt financing to magnify investment returns. (Chapter 2)

financial markets   forums in which suppliers and demanders of funds make financial transactions, often through intermediaries. (Chapter 1)

financial portals   supersites on the Web that bring together a wide range of investing features, such as real-time quotes, stock and mutual fund screens, portfolio trackers, news, research, and transaction capabilities, along with other personal finance features. (Chapter 3)

financial risk   the degree of uncertainty of payment resulting from a firm's mix of debt and equity; the larger the proportion of debt financing, the greater this risk. (Chapter 4)

first and refunding bonds   bonds secured in part with both first and second mortgages. (Chapter 10)

fixed annuity   an annuity that pays an unchanging amount of monthly income during the distribution period. (Web Chapter 17)

fixed charge coverage   a measure of how well a firm is able to cover its preferred stock dividends. (Web Chapter 16)

fixed-commission schedules   fixed brokerage commissions that typically apply to the small transactions usually made by individual investors. (Chapter 3)

fixed-income securities   investment vehicles that offer a fixed periodic return. (Chapter 1)

fixed-weightings approach   asset allocation plan in which a fixed percentage of the portfolio is allocated to each asset category. (Chapter 13)

flexible-weightings approach   asset allocation plan in which weights for each asset category are adjusted periodically based on market analysis. (Chapter 13)

forced conversion   the calling in of convertible bonds by the issuing firm. (Chapter 10)

foreign investments   debt, equity, and derivative securities of foreign-based companies. (Chapter 1)

Form 10-K   a statement that must be filed annually with the SEC by all firms having securities listed on a securities exchange or traded in the OTC market. (Chapter 3)

formula plans   mechanical methods of portfolio management that try to take advantage of price changes that result from cyclical price movements. (Chapter 13)

401(k) plans   retirement programs that allow employees to divert a portion of salary or wages to a company-sponsored tax-sheltered savings account, thus deferring taxes until the funds are withdrawn. (Web Chapter 17)

fourth market   transactions made directly between large institutional buyers and sellers of securities. (Chapter 2)

full-service broker   broker who, in addition to executing clients' transactions, provides them with a full array of brokerage services. (Chapter 3)

fully compounded rate of return   the rate of return that includes interest earned on interest. (Chapter 4)

fund families   different kinds of mutual funds offered by a single investment management company. (Chapter 12)

fundamental analysis   the in-depth study of the financial condition and operating results of a firm. (Chapter 7)

future value   the amount to which a current deposit will grow over a period of time when it is placed in an account paying compound interest. (Chapter 4)

futures   legally binding obligations stipulating that the seller of the contract will make delivery and the buyer of the contract will take delivery of an asset at some specific date, at a price agreed on at the time the contract is sold. (Chapter 1)

futures contract   a commitment to deliver a certain amount of some specified item at some specified date in the future. (Chapter 15)

futures market   the organized market for the trading of futures contracts. (Chapter 15)

futures options   options that give the holders the right to buy or sell standardized futures contracts for a specified period of time at a specified strike price. (Chapter 15)

G

general obligation bonds   municipal bonds backed by the full faith, credit, and taxing power of the issuer. (Chapter 10)

general partnership   a joint venture in which all partners have management rights, and all assume unlimited liability for any debts or obligations the partnership incurs. (Web Chapter 17)

gross income   all includable income for federal income tax purposes. (Web Chapter 17)

growth cycle   a reflection of the amount of business vitality that occurs within an industry (or company) over time. (Chapter 7)

growth fund   a mutual fund whose primary goals are capital gains and long-term growth. (Chapter 12)

growth stocks   stocks that experience high rates of growth in operations and earnings. (Chapter 6)

growth-and-income fund   a mutual fund that seeks both long-term growth and current income, with primary emphasis on capital gains. (Chapter 12)

growth-oriented portfolio   a portfolio whose primary objective is long-term price appreciation. (Chapter 5)

guaranteed investment contracts (GICs)   portfolios of fixed-income securities with guaranteed competitive rates of return that are backed and sold by insurance companies. (Web Chapter 17)

H

hedge   a combination of two or more securities into a single investment position for the purpose of reducing or eliminating risk. (Chapter 14)

hedge fund   a type of unregulated investment vehicle that invests money for a very select group of institutional and high-net-worth individual investors; the investment objectives usually are to not only preserve capital, but also deliver positive returns in all market conditions. (Chapter 12)

hedgers   producers and processors who use futures contracts to protect their interest in an underlying commodity or financial instrument. (Chapter 15)

holding period   the period of time over which one wishes to measure the return on an investment vehicle. (Chapter 4)

holding period return (HPR)   the total return earned from holding an investment for a specified *holding period* (*usually one year or less*). (Chapter 4)

I

immediate annuity   an annuity under which payments to the annuitant begin as soon as it is purchased. (Web Chapter 17)

immunization   bond portfolio strategy that uses duration to offset price and reinvestment effects; a bond portfolio is immunized when its average duration equals the investment horizon. (Chapter 11)

improvements   in real estate, the additions to a site, such as buildings, sidewalks, and various on-site amenities. (Web Chapter 18)

in arrears   having outstanding unfulfilled preferred dividend obligations. (Web Chapter 16)

income approach   a real estate valuation approach that calculates a property's value as the present value of all its future income. (Web Chapter 18)

income bonds   unsecured bonds requiring that interest be paid only after a specified amount of income is earned. (Chapter 10)

income property   leased-out residential or commercial real estate that is expected to provide returns primarily from periodic rental income. (Web Chapter 18)

income statement   a financial summary of the operating results of a firm covering a specified period of time, usually a year. (Chapter 7)

income stocks   stocks with long and sustained records of paying higher-than-average dividends. (Chapter 6)

income-oriented portfolio   a portfolio that stresses current dividend and interest returns. (Chapter 5)

index fund   a mutual fund that buys and holds a portfolio of stocks (or bonds) equivalent to those in a specific market index. (Chapter 12)

indexes   numbers used to measure the general behavior of stock prices by measuring the current price behavior of a representative group of stocks in relation to a base value set at an earlier point in time. (Chapter 3)

indirect investment   investment made in a collection of securities or properties. (Chapter 1)

individual investors   investors who manage their own funds. (Chapter 1)

individual retirement arrangements (IRAs)   self-directed, tax-deferred retirement programs *available to any gainfully employed individual*, who can make up to a specified maximum annual contribution. (Web Chapter 17)

industry analysis   study of industry groupings that looks at the competitive position of a particular industry in relation to others and identifies companies that show particular promise within an industry. (Chapter 7)

inflation   a period of generally rising prices. (Chapter 4)

initial deposit   the amount of investor capital that must be deposited with a broker at the time of a commodity transaction. (Chapter 15)

initial margin   the minimum amount of equity that must be provided by a margin investor *at the time of purchase*. (Chapter 2)

initial public offering (IPO)   the first public sale of a company's stock. (Chapter 2)

insider trading   the use of *nonpublic* information about a company to make profitable securities transactions. (Chapter 2)

installment annuity   an annuity acquired by making payments over time; at a specified future date, the installment payments, plus interest earned on them, are used to purchase an annuity. (Web Chapter 17)

institutional investors   investment professionals who are paid to manage other people's money. (Chapter 1)

interest   the "rent" paid by a borrower for use of the lender's money. (Chapter 4)

interest rate options   put and call options written on fixed-income (debt) securities. (Chapter 14)

interest rate risk   the chance that changes in interest rates will adversely affect a security's value. (Chapter 4)

interest-rate futures   futures contracts on debt securities. (Chapter 15)

international fund   a mutual fund that does all or most of its investing in foreign securities. (Chapter 12)

in-the-money a call option with a strike price less than the market price of the underlying security; a put option whose strike price is greater than the market price of the underlying security. (Chapter 14)

intrinsic value the underlying or inherent value of a stock, as determined through fundamental analysis. (Chapter 7)

investment any vehicle into which funds can be placed with the expectation that it will generate positive income and/or preserve or increase its value. (Chapter 1)

investment advisers individuals or firms that provide investment advice, typically for a fee. (Chapter 3)

investment analysis approach to real estate valuation that not only considers what similar properties have sold for but also looks at the underlying determinants of value. (Web Chapter 18)

investment banker financial intermediary that specializes in selling new security issues and advising firms with regard to major financial transactions. (Chapter 2)

investment club a legal partnership through which a group of investors are bound to a specified organizational structure, operating procedures, and purpose, which is typically to earn favorable long-term returns from moderate-risk investments. (Chapter 3)

investment goals the financial objectives that one wishes to achieve by investing. (Chapter 1)

investment letters newsletters that provide, on a subscription basis, the analyses, conclusions, and recommendations of experts in securities investment. (Chapter 3)

investment plan a written document describing how funds will be invested and specifying the target date for achieving each investment goal and the amount of tolerable risk. (Chapter 1)

investment value the amount that investors believe a security should be trading for, or what they think it's worth; with convertibles, the price at which a convertible would trade if it were nonconvertible and priced at or near the prevailing market yields of comparable nonconvertible issues. (Chapters 6 and 10)

itemized deductions personal living and family expenses that can be deducted from adjusted gross income. (Web Chapter 17)

J

Jensen's measure (Jensen's alpha) a measure of portfolio performance that uses the portfolio beta and CAPM to calculate its *excess return*, which may be positive, zero, or negative. (Chapter 13)

junior bonds debt obligations backed only by the promise of the issuer to pay interest and principal on a timely basis. (Chapter 10)

junk bonds high-risk securities that have low ratings but high yields. (Chapter 10)

K

Keogh plans programs that allow self-employed individuals to establish self-directed, tax-deferred retirement plans for themselves and their employees. (Web Chapter 17)

L

LEAPS long-term options. (Chapter 14)

leverage in real estate, the use of debt financing to purchase a piece of property and thereby affect its risk–return parameters; with options, the ability to obtain a given equity position at a reduced capital investment, thereby magnifying returns. (Chapter 14 and Web Chapter 18)

leverage measures financial ratios that measure the amount of debt being used to support operations and the ability of the firm to service its debt. (Chapter 7)

limit order an order to buy at or below a specified price or to sell at or above a specified price. (Chapter 3)

limited liability company (LLC) a business entity that provides the same liability protection as corporations but offers the option of being taxed as either a partnership or corporation. (Web Chapter 17)

limited partnership (LP) vehicle in which the investor can passively invest with limited liability, receive the benefit of active professional management, and apply the resulting profit or loss (subject to limits) to his or her tax liability. (Web Chapter 17)

liquidity the ability of an investment to be converted into cash quickly and with little or no loss in value. (Chapter 1)

liquidity measures financial ratios concerned with a firm's ability to meet its day-to-day operating expenses and satisfy its short-term obligations as they come due. (Chapter 7)

liquidity preference theory theory that investors tend to prefer the greater liquidity of short-term securities and therefore require a premium to invest in long-term securities. (Chapter 11)

liquidity risk the risk of not being able to liquidate an investment conveniently and at a reasonable price. (Chapter 4)

listed options put and call options listed and traded on organized securities exchanges, such as the CBOE. (Chapter 14)

load fund a mutual fund that charges a commission when shares are bought; also known as a *front-end load fund*. (Chapter 12)

long purchase a transaction in which investors buy securities in the hope that they will increase in value and can be sold at a later date for profit. (Chapter 2)

long-term investments investments with maturities of longer than a year or with no maturity at all. (Chapter 1)

low-load fund a mutual fund that charges a small commission (2% to 3%) when shares are bought. (Chapter 12)

LYON (liquid yield option note) a zero-coupon bond that carries both a conversion feature and a put option. (Chapter 10)

M

maintenance deposit the minimum amount of margin that must be kept in a margin account at all times. (Chapter 15)

maintenance margin the absolute minimum amount of margin (equity) that an investor must maintain in the margin account at all times. (Chapter 2)

management fee a fee levied annually for professional mutual fund services provided; paid regardless of the performance of the portfolio. (Chapter 12)

margin account a brokerage account in which the customer has been extended borrowing privileges by the brokerage firm. (Chapters 2 and 3)

margin call notification of the need to bring the equity of an account whose margin is below the maintenance level up above the maintenance margin level or to have enough margined holdings sold to reach this standard. (Chapter 2)

margin deposit amount deposited with a broker to cover any loss in the market value of a futures contract that may result from adverse price movements. (Chapter 15)

margin loan vehicle through which borrowed funds are made available, at a stated interest rate, in a margin transaction. (Chapter 2)

margin requirement the minimum amount of equity that must be a margin investor's own funds; set by the Federal Reserve Board (the "Fed"). (Chapter 2)

margin trading the use of borrowed funds to purchase securities; magnifies returns by reducing the amount of equity that the investor must put up. (Chapter 2)

marginal tax rate the tax rate on additional income. (Web Chapter 17)

market anomalies irregularities or deviations from the behavior one would expect in an efficient market. (Chapter 9)

market capitalization rate the rate used to convert an income stream to a present value; used to estimate the value of real estate under the *income approach*. (Web Chapter 18)

market makers *securities dealers* that "make markets" by offering to buy or sell certain securities at stated prices. (Chapter 2)

market order an order to buy or sell stock at the best price available when the order is placed. (Chapter 3)

market return the average return for all (or a large sample of) stocks, such as those in *the Standard & Poor's 500-Stock Composite Index*. (Chapter 5)

market risk risk of decline in investment returns because of market factors independent of the given investment. (Chapter 4)

market segmentation theory theory that the market for debt is segmented on the basis of maturity, that supply and demand within each segment determine the prevailing interest rate, and that the slope of the yield curve depends on the relationship between the prevailing rates in each segment. (Chapter 11)

market technicians analysts who believe it is chiefly (or solely) supply and demand that drive stock prices. (Chapter 9)

market timing the process of identifying the current state of the economy/market and assessing the likelihood of its continuing on its present course. (Chapter 1)

market value in real estate, the actual worth of a property; indicates the price at which it would sell under current market conditions; with stocks, bonds, and other marketable securities, their prevailing market price. (Chapter 6 and Web Chapter 18)

mark-to-the-market a daily check of an investor's margin position, determined at the end of each session, at which time the broker debits or credits the account as needed. (Chapter 15)

maturity date the date on which a bond matures and the principal must be repaid. (Chapter 10)

maximum daily price range the amount a commodity price can change during the day; usually equal to twice the daily price limit. (Chapter 15)

mediation an informal, voluntary dispute-resolution process in which a client and a broker agree to a mediator, who facilitates negotiations between them to resolve the case. (Chapter 3)

Mergent publisher of a variety of financial material, including *Mergent's Manuals*. (Chapter 3)

mid-cap stocks medium-sized stocks, generally with market values of less than $4 or $5 billion but more than $1 billion. (Chapter 6)

minimum guaranteed interest rate for a deferred annuity purchase contract, the minimum interest rate on contributions, which the insurance company guarantees over the full accumulation period. (Web Chapter 17)

mixed stream a stream of returns that, unlike an annuity, exhibits no special pattern. (Chapter 4)

modern portfolio theory (MPT) an approach to portfolio management that uses several basic statistical measures to develop a portfolio plan. (Chapter 5)

money market market where *short-term* securities (with maturities less than one year) are bought and sold. (Chapter 2)

money market mutual fund (money fund) a mutual fund that pools the capital of investors and uses it to invest in short-term money market instruments. (Chapter 12)

monthly income preferred stock (MIPS) a type of preferred stock that offers attractive tax provisions to the issuers, and attractive monthly returns to investors. (Web Chapter 16)

mortgage bonds senior bonds secured by real estate. (Chapter 10)

mortgage-backed bond a debt issue secured by a pool of home mortgages; issued primarily by federal agencies. (Chapter 10)

moving average (MA) a mathematical procedure that computes and records the average values of a series of prices, or other data, over time; results in a stream of average values that will act to smooth out a series of data. (Chapter 9)

municipal bond guarantees guarantees from a party other than the issuer that principal and interest payments will be made in a prompt and timely manner. (Chapter 10)

municipal bonds debt securities issued by states, counties, cities, and other political subdivisions; most of these bonds are tax-exempt (free of federal income tax on interest income). (Chapter 10)

mutual fund a company that raises money from sale of its shares and invests in and professionally manages a diversified portfolio of securities. (Chapters 1 and 12)

N

naked options options written on securities not owned by the writer. (Chapter 14)

Nasdaq market a major segment of the *secondary market* that employs an all-electronic trading platform to execute trades. (Chapter 2)

Nasdaq Stock Market indexes measures of current price behavior of securities traded in the Nasdaq stock market, relative to a base of 100 set at specified dates. (Chapter 3)

negative leverage a position in which, if a property's return is below its debt cost, the investor's return is less than from an all-cash deal. (Web Chapter 18)

negatively correlated describes two series that move in opposite directions. (Chapter 5)

negotiated commissions brokerage commissions agreed to by the client and the broker as a result of their negotiations; typically apply on large institutional transactions and to individual investors who maintain large accounts. (Chapter 3)

net asset value (NAV) the underlying value of a share of stock in a particular mutual fund. (Chapter 12)

net losses the amount by which capital losses exceed capital gains; up to $3,000 of net losses can be applied against ordinary income in any year. (Chapter 1)

net operating income (NOI) the amount left after subtracting vacancy and collection losses and property operating expenses, including property insurance and property taxes, from an income property's *gross* potential rental income. (Web Chapter 18)

net present value (NPV) the difference between the present value of the cash flows and the amount of equity necessary to make an investment. (Web Chapter 18)

no-load fund a mutual fund that does not charge a commission when shares are bought. (Chapter 12)

noncumulative provision a provision found on some preferred stocks excusing the issuing firm from having to make up any passed dividends. (Web Chapter 16)

nondeductible IRA an IRA with contribution limits and penalties similar to those of a traditional deductible IRA, available to taxpayers who fail to meet income cutoffs for a traditional deductible IRA or a Roth IRA. Contributions are nondeductible, earnings are deferred, and taxes are due on withdrawals. (Web Chapter 17)

nondiversifiable (systematic) risk the inescapable portion of an investment's risk attributable to forces that affect all investments and therefore are not unique to a given vehicle. (Chapter 5)

note a debt security originally issued with a maturity of from 2 to 10 years. (Chapter 10)

NYSE composite index measure of the current price behavior of stocks listed on the NYSE, relative to a base of 5000 set at December 31, 2002. (Chapter 3)

O

odd lot less than 100 shares of stock.round lot100-share units of stock or multiples thereof. (Chapter 3)

open interest the number of contracts currently outstanding on a commodity or financial future. (Chapter 15)

open-end investment company a type of investment company in which investors buy shares from, and sell them back to, the mutual fund itself, with no limit on the number of shares the fund can issue. (Chapter 12)

open-outcry auction in futures trading, an auction in which trading is done through a series of shouts, body motions, and hand signals. (Chapter 15)

option a security that gives the holder the right to buy or sell a certain amount of an underlying financial asset at a specified price for a specified period of time. (Chapter 14)

option maker (writer) the individual or institution that writes/creates put and call options. (Chapter 14)

option premium the quoted price the investor pays to buy a listed put or call option. (Chapter 14)

option spreading combining two or more options with different strike prices and/or expiration dates into a single transaction. (Chapter 14)

option straddle the simultaneous purchase (or sale) of a put and a call on the same underlying common stock (or financial asset). (Chapter 14)

options securities that give the investor an opportunity to sell or buy another security at a specified price over a given period of time. (Chapter 1)

ordinary annuity an annuity for which the cash flows occur at the *end* of each period. (Chapter 4)

out-of-the-money a call option with no real value because the strike price exceeds the market price of the stock; a put option whose market price exceeds the strike price. (Chapter 14)

over-the-counter (OTC) market a segment of the *secondary market* that involves trading in smaller, unlisted securities. (Chapter 2)

P

paper return a return that has been achieved but not yet realized by an investor during a given period. (Chapter 4)

par value the stated, or face, value of a stock. (Chapter 6)

passive activity an investment in which the investor does not "materially participate" in its management or activity. (Web Chapter 17)

payback period the length of time it takes for the buyer of a convertible to recover the conversion premium from the extra current income earned on the convertible. (Chapter 10)

payment date the actual date on which the company will mail dividend checks to shareholders (also known as the *payable date*). (Chapter 6)

payout the investment return provided by an annuity; it is realized when the distribution period begins. (Web Chapter 17)

PEG ratio a financial ratio that relates a stock's price/earnings multiple to the company's rate of growth in earnings. (Chapter 7)

perfectly negatively correlated describes two negatively correlated series that have a correlation coefficient of -1. (Chapter 5)

perfectly positively correlated describes two positively correlated series that have a correlation coefficient of $+1$. (Chapter 5)

PIK-bond a payment-in-kind junk bond that gives the issuer the right to make annual interest payments in new bonds rather than in cash. (Chapter 10)

point-and-figure charts charts used to keep track of emerging price patterns by plotting significant price changes with X's and O's but with no time dimension used. (Chapter 9)

pooled diversification a process whereby investors buy into a diversified portfolio of securities for the collective benefit of the individual investors. (Chapter 12)

portfolio collection of securities or other investments, typically constructed to meet one or more investment goals. (Chapter 1)

portfolio beta, b_p the beta of a portfolio; calculated as the weighted average of the betas of the individual assets it includes. (Chapter 5)

portfolio revision the process of selling certain issues in a portfolio and purchasing new ones to replace them. (Chapter 13)

positive leverage a position in which, if a property's return is in excess of its debt cost, the investor's return is increased to a level well above what could have been earned from an all-cash deal. (Web Chapter 18)

positively correlated describes two series that move in the same direction. (Chapter 5)

precious metals tangibles such as silver, gold and platinum which concentrate a great deal of value in a small amount of weight and volume. (Web Chapter 18)

preference (prior preferred) stock a type of preferred stock that has seniority over other preferred stock in its right to receive dividends and in its claim on assets. (Web Chapter 16)

preferred stock a stock that has a stated dividend rate, payment of which is given preference over common stock dividends of the same firm. (Chapter 1 and Web Chapter 16)

premium bond a bond with a market value in excess of par; occurs when interest rates drop below the coupon rate. (Chapter 10)

premium discount broker broker who charges low commissions to make transactions for customers but provides limited free research information and investment advice. (Chapter 3)

present value the *value today* of a sum to be received at some future date; the inverse of future value. (Chapter 4)

price/earnings (P/E) approach stock valuation approach that tries to find the P/E ratio that's most appropriate for the stock; this ratio, along with estimated EPS, is then used to determine a reasonable stock price. (Chapter 8)

primary market the market in which *new issues* of securities are sold to the public. (Chapter 2)

prime rate the lowest interest rate charged the best business borrowers. (Chapter 2)

principal on a bond, the amount of capital that must be repaid at maturity. (Chapter 10)

principle of substitution the principle that people do not buy or rent real estate per se but, instead, judge properties as different sets of benefits and costs. (Web Chapter 18)

private placement the sale of new securities directly, without SEC registration, to selected groups of investors. (Chapter 2)

profitability measures financial ratios that measure a firm's returns by relating profits to sales, assets, or equity. (Chapter 7)

promised yield yield-to-maturity. (Chapter 11)

property investments in real property or tangible personal property. (Chapter 1)

property management in real estate, finding the optimal level of benefits for a property and providing them at the lowest costs. (Web Chapter 18)

property transfer process the process of promotion and negotiation of real estate, which can significantly influence the cash flows a property will earn. (Web Chapter 18)

prospectus a portion of a security registration statement that describes the key aspects of the issue, the issuer, and its management and financial position. (Chapter 2)

psychographics characteristics that describe people's mental dispositions, such as personality, lifestyle, and self-concept. (Web Chapter 18)

public offering an offering to sell to the investing public a set number of shares of a firm's stock at a specified price. (Chapters 2 and 6)

publicly traded issues shares of stock that are readily available to the general public and are bought and sold in the open market. (Chapter 6)

purchasing power risk the chance that changing price levels (inflation or deflation) will adversely affect investment returns. (Chapter 4)

put a negotiable instrument that enables the holder to sell the underlying security at a specified price over a set period of time. (Chapter 14)

put hedge the purchase of a put option on shares currently owned, to lock in a profit and defer taxes on the profit to the next tax year. (Web Chapter 17)

pyramiding the technique of using paper profits in margin accounts to partly or fully finance the acquisition of additional securities. (Chapter 2)

Q

quotations price information about various types of securities, including current price data and statistics on recent price behavior. (Chapter 3)

R

random walk hypothesis the theory that stock price movements are unpredictable, so there's no way to know where prices are headed. (Chapter 9)

rate of growth the compound annual rate of change in the value of a stream of income. (Chapter 4)

ratio analysis the study of the relationships between financial statement accounts. (Chapter 7)

real estate entities such as residential homes, raw land, and income property. (Web Chapter 18)

real estate investment trust (REIT) a closed-end investment company that sells shares to investors and invests the proceeds in various types of real estate and real estate mortgages; three types: equity REIT's, mortgage REIT's, and hybrid REIT's. (Chapter 12 and Web Chapter 18)

real rate of return the rate of return that could be earned in a perfect world where all outcomes are known and certain—where there is no risk. (Chapter 4)

realized return current income actually received by an investor during a given period. (Chapter 4)

realized yield expected return. (Chapter 11)

red herring a preliminary *prospectus* made available to prospective investors during the waiting period between the registration statement's filing with the SEC and its approval. (Chapter 2)

refunding provisions provisions that prohibit the premature retirement of an issue from the proceeds of a lower-coupon refunding bond. (Chapter 10)

reinvestment rate the rate of return earned on interest or other income received from an investment over its investment horizon. (Chapter 4)

relative P/E multiple a measure of how a stock's P/E behaves relative to the average market multiple. (Chapter 8)

relevant risk risk that is nondiversifiable. (Chapter 5)

required rate of return the return necessary to compensate an investor for the risk involved in an investment. (Chapters 4 and 8)

residual owners owners/stockholders of a firm, who are entitled to dividend income and a prorated share of the firm's earnings only after all other obligations have been met. (Chapter 6)

restricted account a margin account whose equity is less than the initial margin requirement; the investor may not make further margin purchases and must bring the margin back to the initial level when securities are sold. (Chapter 2)

return the level of profit from an investment—that is, the reward for investing. (Chapter 4)

return on invested capital return to investors based on the amount of money actually invested in a security, rather than the value of the contract itself. (Chapter 15)

returns the rewards from investing, received as current income and/or increased value. (Chapter 1)

revenue bonds municipal bonds that require payment of principal and interest only if sufficient revenue is generated by the issuer. (Chapter 10)

rights offering an offering of a new issue of stock to existing stockholders, who may purchase new shares in proportion to their current ownership position. (Chapters 2 and 6)

risk the chance that actual investment returns will differ from those expected. (Chapters 1 and 4)

risk premium a return premium that reflects the issue and issuer characteristics associated with a given investment vehicle. (Chapter 4)

risk-averse   describes an investor who requires greater return in exchange for greater risk. (Chapter 4)

risk-free rate, R_F   the return an investor can earn on a risk-free investment such as a U.S. Treasury bill; the sum of the real rate of return and the expected inflation premium. (Chapters 4 and 5)

risk-indifferent   describes an investor who does not require a change in return as compensation for greater risk. (Chapter 4)

risk-return tradeoff   the positive relationship between the risk associated with a given investment and its expected return. (Chapters 4 and 5)

risk-seeking   describes an investor who will accept a lower return in exchange for greater risk. (Chapter 4)

Roth IRA   an IRA that allows a worker and spouse with earnings from employment to, subject to certain limits, each contribute up to $2,000 annually (rising to $5,000 by 2008). Contributions are nondeductible, but the earnings are not taxable when withdrawn in accordance with certain requirements. (Web Chapter 17)

round lot   100-share units of stock or multiples thereof. (Chapter 3)

round-trip commissions   the commission costs on both ends (buying and selling) of a futures transaction. (Chapter 15)

S

satisfactory investment   an investment whose present value of benefits (discounted at the appropriate rate) *equals* or *exceeds* the present value of its costs. (Chapter 4)

secondary distributions   the public sales of large blocks of previously issued securities held by large investors. (Chapter 2)

secondary market   the market in which securities are traded *after they have been issued*; an *aftermarket*. (Chapter 2)

Section 529 Plan   a state-sponsored, tax-deferred college savings plan with both annual and lifetime contribution limits; growth inside the plan is tax-deferred and withdrawals are tax-free if used for qualified college expenses. (Web Chapter 17)

sector fund   a mutual fund that restricts its investments to a particular segment of the market. (Chapter 12)

securities   investments that represent debt or ownership or the legal right to acquire or sell an ownership interest. (Chapter 1)

Securities and Exchange Commission (SEC)   federal agency that regulates securities offerings and markets. (Chapter 2)

Securities Investor Protection Corporation (SIPC)   a nonprofit membership corporation, authorized by the federal government, that insures each brokerage customer's account for up to $500,000, with claims for cash limited to $100,000 per customer. (Chapter 3)

securities markets   forums that allow suppliers and demanders of *securities* to make financial transactions; they include both the *money market* and the *capital market*. (Chapter 2)

securitization   the process of transforming lending vehicles such as mortgages into marketable securities. (Chapter 10)

security analysis   the process of gathering and organizing information and then using it to determine the intrinsic value of a share of common stock. (Chapter 7)

security market line (SML)   the graphical depiction of the capital asset pricing model; reflects the investor's required return for each level of nondiversifiable risk, measured by beta. (Chapter 5)

security selection   the procedures used to select the *specific* securities to be held *within* an asset class. (Chapter 13)

selling group   a large number of brokerage firms that join the originating investment banker(s); each accepts responsibility for selling a certain portion of a new security issue. (Chapter 2)

semi-strong form (EMH)   form of the EMH holding that abnormally large profits cannot be consistently earned using publicly available information. (Chapter 9)

senior bonds   secured debt obligations, backed by a legal claim on specific property of the issuer. (Chapter 10)

serial bond   a bond that has a series of different maturity dates. (Chapter 10)

settle price   the closing price (last price of the day) for commodities and financial futures. (Chapter 15)

Sharpe's measure   a measure of portfolio performance that measures the *risk premium per unit of total risk*, which is measured by the portfolio standard deviation of return. (Chapter 13)

short interest   the number of stocks sold short in the market at any given time; a technical indicator believed to indicate future market demand. (Chapter 9)

short selling   the sale of borrowed securities, their eventual repurchase by the short seller, and their return to the lender. (Chapter 2)

short-term investments   investments that typically mature within one year. (Chapter 1)

short-term vehicles   savings instruments that usually have lives of 1 year or less. (Chapter 1)

simple interest   interest paid only on the initial deposit for the amount of time it is held. (Chapter 4)

single-premium annuity   an annuity purchased with a single lump-sum payment. (Web Chapter 17)

sinking fund   a provision that stipulates the amount of principal that will be retired annually over the life of a bond. (Chapter 10)

small-cap stocks   stocks that generally have market values of less than $1 billion but can offer above-average returns. (Chapter 6)

socially responsible fund   a mutual fund that actively and directly incorporates ethics and morality into the investment decision. (Chapter 12)

specialist   stock exchange member who specializes in making transactions in one or more stocks and manages the auction process. (Chapter 2)

speculation   the purchase of high-risk investment vehicles that offer highly uncertain returns and future value. (Chapter 1)

speculative property   raw land and real estate investment properties that are expected to provide returns primarily from appreciation in value. (Web Chapter 18)

speculative stocks   stocks that offer the potential for substantial price appreciation, usually because of some special situation, such as new management or the introduction of a promising new product. (Chapter 6)

split ratings   different ratings given to a bond issue by two or more rating agencies. (Chapter 10)

Standard & Poor's Corporation (S&P)   publisher of a large number of financial reports and services, including *Corporation Records* and *Stock Reports*. (Chapter 3)

Standard & Poor's indexes   true indexes that measure the current price of a group of stocks relative to a base (set in the 1941–1943 period) having an index value of 10. (Chapter 3)

standard deduction an amount, indexed to the cost of living, that taxpayers can elect to deduct from adjusted gross income without itemizing. (Web Chapter 17)

standard deviation, s a statistic used to measure the dispersion (variation) of returns around an asset's average or expected return. (Chapter 4)

statement of cash flows a financial summary of a firm's cash flow and other events that caused changes in the company's cash position. (Chapter 7)

stock dividend payment of a dividend in the form of additional shares of stock. (Chapter 6)

stock spin-off conversion of one of a firm's subsidiaries to a stand-alone company by distribution of stock in that new company to existing shareholders. (Chapter 6)

stock split a maneuver in which a company increases the number of shares outstanding by exchanging a specified number of new shares of stock for each outstanding share. (Chapter 6)

stock valuation the process by which the underlying value of a stock is established on the basis of its forecasted risk and return performance. (Chapter 8)

stockbrokers individuals licensed by both the SEC and the securities exchanges to facilitate transactions between buyers and sellers of securities. (Chapter 3)

stockholders' (annual) report a report published yearly by a publicly held corporation; contains a wide range of information, including financial statements for the most recent period of operation. (Chapter 3)

stock-index futures futures contracts written on broad-based measures of stock market performance (e.g., the S&P 500 Stock Index), allowing investors to participate in the general movements of the stock market. (Chapter 15)

stock-index option a put or call option written on a specific stock market index, such as the S&P 500. (Chapter 14)

stop-loss (stop) order an order to sell a stock when its market price reaches or drops below a specified level; can also be used to buy stock when its market price reaches or rises above a specified level. (Chapter 3)

straight annuity an annuity that provides for a series of payments for the rest of the annuitant's life. (Web Chapter 17)

street name security certificates issued in the brokerage firm's name but held in trust for its client, who actually owns them. (Chapter 3)

strike price the stated price at which you can buy a security with a call or sell a security with a put. (Chapter 14)

strong form (EMH) form of the EMH that holds that there is no information, public or private, that allows investors to consistently earn abnormal profits. (Chapter 9)

subordinated debentures unsecured bonds whose claim is secondary to other debentures. (Chapter 10)

supply in real estate, the potential competitors available in the market. (Web Chapter 18)

syndicate a joint venture—general partnership, corporation, or limited partnership—in which investors pool their resources. (Web Chapter 17)

systematic withdrawal plan a mutual fund service that enables shareholders to automatically receive a predetermined amount of money every month or quarter. (Chapter 12)

T

tactical asset allocation asset allocation plan that uses stock-index futures and bond futures to change a portfolio's asset allocation based on forecast market behavior. (Chapter 13)

tangibles investment assets, other than real estate, that can be seen or touched. (Chapter 1 and Web Chapter 18)

tax avoidance reducing or eliminating taxes in *legal ways*. (Web Chapter 17)

tax credits tax reductions allowed by the IRS on a dollar-for-dollar basis under certain specified conditions. (Web Chapter 17)

tax deferral the strategy of delaying taxes by shifting income subject to tax into a later period. (Web Chapter 17)

tax evasion illegal activities designed to avoid paying taxes by omitting income or overstating deductions. (Web Chapter 17)

tax planning the formulation of strategies that will exclude, defer, or reduce the taxes to be paid. (Chapter 1)

tax risk the chance that Congress will make unfavorable changes in tax laws, driving down the after-tax returns and market values of certain investments. (Chapter 4)

tax shelter an investment vehicle that offers potential reductions of taxable income. (Web Chapter 17)

tax swap selling one security that has a capital loss and replacing it with another, similar security to offset, partially or fully, a capital gain that has been *realized* in another part of the portfolio. (Chapter 11 and Web Chapter 17)

taxable equivalent yield the return a fully taxable bond would have to provide to match the after-tax return of a lower-yielding, tax-free municipal bond. (Chapter 10)

taxable income the income to which tax rates are applied; equals adjusted gross income minus itemized deductions and exemptions. (Web Chapter 17)

tax-advantaged investments vehicles and strategies for legally reducing one's tax liability. (Chapter 1)

tax-favored income an investment return that is not taxable; is taxed at a rate less than that on other, similar investments; defers the payment of tax to a later period; or trades current income for capital gains. (Web Chapter 17)

tax-sheltered annuity an annuity that allows employees of certain institutions to make a *tax-free contribution* from current income to purchase a deferred annuity. (Web Chapter 17)

tech stocks stocks that represent the technology sector of the market. (Chapter 6)

technical analysis the study of the various forces at work in the marketplace and their effect on stock prices. (Chapter 9)

term bond a bond that has a single, fairly lengthy maturity date. (Chapter 10)

term structure of interest rates the relationship between the interest rate or rate of return (yield) on a bond and its time to maturity. (Chapter 11)

theory of contrary opinion a technical indicator that uses the amount and type of odd-lot trading as an indicator of the current state of the market and pending changes. (Chapter 9)

third market over-the-counter transactions typically handled by market makers and made in securities listed on the NYSE, the AMEX, or one of the other exchanges. (Chapter 2)

time premium the amount by which the option price exceeds the option's fundamental value. (Chapter 14)

time value of money the fact that as long as an opportunity exists to earn interest, the value of money is affected by the point in time when the money is received. (Chapter 4)

total return the sum of the current income and the capital gain (or loss) earned on an investment over a specified period of time. (Chapter 4)

total risk the sum of an investment's *nondiversifiable risk* and *diversifiable risk*. (Chapter 5)

traditional portfolio management   an approach to portfolio management that emphasizes "balancing" the portfolio by assembling a wide variety of stocks and/or bonds of companies from a broad range of industries. (Chapter 5)

Treasury bonds   U.S. Treasury securities that are issued with 20- and 30-year maturities. (Chapter 10)

Treasury inflation-indexed obligations (TIPS)   a type of Treasury security that provides protection against inflation by adjusting investor returns for the annual rate of inflation. (Chapter 10)

Treasury notes   U.S. Treasury debt securities that are issued with maturities of 2 to 10 years. (Chapter 10)

treasury stock   shares of stock that have been sold and subsequently repurchased by the issuing firm. (Chapter 6)

Treasury strips (strip-Ts)   zero-coupon bonds created from U.S. Treasury securities. (Chapter 10)

Treynor's measure   a measure of portfolio performance that measures the *risk premium per unit of nondiversifiable risk*, which is measured by the portfolio beta. (Chapter 13)

true rate of interest (return)   the actual rate of interest earned. (Chapter 4)

12(b)-1 fee   a fee levied annually by many mutual funds to cover management and other operating costs; amounts to as much as 1% of the average net assets. (Chapter 12)

U

uncorrelated   describes two series that lack any relationship or interaction and therefore have a correlation coefficient close to zero. (Chapter 5)

underwriting   the role of the *investment banker* in bearing the risk of reselling, at a profit, the securities purchased from an issuing corporation at an agreed-on price. (Chapter 2)

underwriting syndicate   a group formed by an investment banker to share the financial risk associated with *underwriting* new securities. (Chapter 2)

unrealized capital gains (paper profits)   a capital gain made only "on paper"—that is, not realized until the fund's holdings are sold. (Chapter 12)

V

valuation   process by which an investor uses risk and return concepts to determine the value of a security. (Chapter 8)

value fund   a mutual fund that seeks stocks that are undervalued in the market by investing in shares that have low P/E multiples, high dividend yields, and promising futures. (Chapter 12)

Value Line composite index   stock index that reflects the percentage changes in share price of about 1,700 stocks, relative to a base of 100 set at June 30, 1961. (Chapter 3)

Value Line Investment Survey   one of the most popular subscription services used by individual investors; subscribers receive three basic reports weekly. (Chapter 3)

variable annuity   an annuity that adjusts the monthly income it pays during the distribution period according to the investment experience (and sometimes the mortality experience) of the insurer. (Web Chapter 17)

variable-ratio plan   a formula plan for timing investment transactions, in which the ratio of the speculative portion to the total portfolio value varies depending on the movement in value of the speculative securities; when the ratio rises or falls by a predetermined amount, the amount committed to the speculative portion of the portfolio is reduced or increased, respectively. (Chapter 13)

W

Wall Street Journal   a daily business newspaper, published regionally; the most popular source of financial news. (Chapter 3)

wash sale   the procedure of selling securities on which capital losses can be realized and then immediately buying them back; disallowed under the tax law. (Web Chapter 17)

weak form (EMH)   form of the EMH holding that past data on stock prices are of no use in predicting future prices. (Chapter 9)

whipsawing   the situation where a stock temporarily drops in price and then bounces back upward. (Chapter 13)

Wilshire 5000 index   measure of the total dollar value (in billions of dollars) of more than 6,000 actively traded stocks on the major exchanges. (Chapter 3)

wrap account   a brokerage account in which customers with large portfolios pay a flat annual fee that covers the cost of a money manager's services and the commissions on all trades. (Also called a *managed* account.) (Chapter 3)

Y

Yankee bonds   dollar-denominated debt securities issued by foreign governments or corporations and traded in U.S. securities markets. (Chapters 2 and 10)

yield (internal rate of return)   the compound annual rate of return earned by a long-term investment; the discount rate that produces a present value of the investment's benefits that just equals its cost. (Chapter 4)

yield curve   a graph that represents the relationship between a bond's term to maturity and its yield at a given point in time. (Chapter 11)

yield pickup swap   replacement of a low-coupon bond for a comparable higher-coupon bond in order to realize an increase in current yield and yield-to-maturity. (Chapter 11)

yield spreads   differences in interest rates that exist among various sectors of the market. (Chapter 11)

yield-to-call (YTC)   the yield on a bond if it remains outstanding only until a specified call date. (Chapter 11)

yield-to-maturity (YTM)   the fully compounded rate of return earned by an investor over the life of a bond, including interest income and price appreciation. (Chapter 11)

Z

zero-coupon bonds   bonds with no coupons that are sold at a deep discount from par value. (Chapter 10)

Index

Hogs on 66

Best Feed and Hangouts for Road Trips on Route 66

Michael Wallis

Marian Clark

Council Oak Books

San Francisco / Tulsa

Council Oak Books, Tulsa, Oklahoma 74104
©2004 by Michael Wallis and Marian Clark. All rights reserved
Published 2004

09 08 07 06 05 04   6 5 4 3 2 1

Portions of this book appeared in a slightly altered form in *Main Street of America Cookbook* © 1997 by Marian Clark and *The Route 66 Cookbook* © 1993 by Marian Clark

A portion of the Introduction text previously appeared in an article written by Michael Wallis in the January-February 1999 issue of *Oklahoma Today*.

Cover design by Idea Studios, Tulsa

Interior design by Margaret Copeland

Grateful acknowledgments are made to the following people for use in this book of the photographs on the pages indicated:

Collection of Reba McClanahan, Myers-Duren Harley-Davidson, Tulsa, front cover historical photos, 31, 51, 58, 69, 91, 110, 125, 133, 171

Collection of Matthias Guenther 1, 4 (left), 7 (right), 9, 10, 11 (both), 12, 17, 23, 24, 27 (right), 28 (right), 32, 33, 39, 41, 43, 46, 48, 54, 55, 56, 57 (right), 63, 67 (top), 70 (left), 73, 78 (both), 81, 82, 85, 91, 92 (right top and bottom), 93, 95 (top), 97, 103, 108, 113, 114 (right top), 115 (left bottom), 122 (right and left), 123, 124 (top and bottom), 126, 136 (right), 138, 142, 145, 148, 149 (both), 152, 153, 155, 157, 158, 159, 164, 166, 169

Collection of Michael and Suzanne Wallis 25, 62, 66 (bottom right), 79, 84, 90, 95 (bottom), 99, 117, 156, 173

Dan McNeil 87

"Milwaukee" Harry Jaeger 6, 7 (left), 13, 20, 28 (left), 29, 35, 40, 42, 44, 53 (left), 65, 70 (right), 71, 72, 92 (left), 94, 101, 114 (left), 118, 119, 134, 136 (left), 141, 144, 150, 170

Heidi and Ken Creasman 16, 36, 37, 52, 53 (right), 66 (left and top right), 68, 75, 76, 98 (right), 114 (right bottom), 130, 154, 183

Ken Clark 14

Linda Scott 21, 49, 111, 115 (left top), 137, 160, 162, 179

Marian Clark 4 (right), 5, 18 (both), 26, 27 (left), 64

Marilyn Pritchard 181

Suzanne Wallis vii, 3, 15, 34, 57 (left), 112, 115 (right), 129, 139, 140, 147, 161

Terry Allen 120, 121

Trond Moberg 59, 60, 67 (bottom), 98 (left), 107

Collection of Bob Lile 100

Mary Simon 176

Jean Dennison 109, Authors' photo, back cover

Printed in Canada

For Suzanne, my true love and riding companion through life
— MICHAEL WALLIS

To my biker husband Ken, my best and most loyal supporter,
and to Megan, Andrew, Brad and Haley, who will continue our mystical journey.
— MARIAN CLARK

Contents

Road Warrior Kent Meacham

Acknowledgments

MY SINCERE AND EVERLASTING THANKS to my friend Zigy Kaluzny, who not only taught me how to ride a motorcycle properly and safely, but who also shared with me his abiding love for open road bike travel.

Thanks to my dear wife, Suzanne, friend and lover and the person whose own love for motorcycles proved contagious and claimed me.

Much appreciation goes to my coauthor Marian Clark, the incomparable culinary maestro of the Mother Road and to the good folks at Council Oak Books, especially Sally Dennison and Ja-Lene Clark.

A salute of gratitude to James Fitzgerald, Jr., who serves me very well as a literary agent and whose close friendship I value more than he knows.

As always, I offer my gratitude to Cosmo, our charming feline muse. And finally, a huge thanks goes to all the many men and women I have had the honor of riding with on America's Main Street and beyond.   — MICHAEL WALLIS

THE IDEA OF JOINING TWO OF AMERICA'S MOST FAMOUS ICONS, Route 66 and Harley-Davidson, came from the creative team at Council Oak Books. When Michael and I met with Sally Dennison and Ja-Lene Clark, their enthusiasm was contagious. We talked about possibilities, divided assignments, and began to work. The challenge was to incorporate favorite foods with the fun and freedom of the road, Harley-Davidson style. Michael's rich reservoir of stories and practical travel guides quickly merged with biker-friendly recipes and suggestions on where to stop and what to see.

Many of the recipes for *Hogs on 66* were collected as I searched Route 66 for *The Main Street of America Cookbook* (Council Oak Books, 1997). A handful came from *The Route 66 Cookbook* (Council Oak Books, 1993). I will always be indebted to the individuals who contributed to both of those books. Harley-Davidson dealers, bikers both here and abroad, and many new friends along Route 66 shared the remaining recipes and their own stories.

Ann Arwood tested scores of recipes from my earlier cookbooks. Mary Gubser continues to inspire like no other, Michael and Suzanne Wallis have been a guiding forces since we first met in 1990. Council Oak published my first cookbook in 1993. The staff continues to believe in this effort and support Route 66 projects. My biker husband, Ken, has been my best and most loyal supporter. You are all great!

I included dishes that we felt would be especially biker-friendly and added some of the best from regional fare. Glaida Funk, Kathleen Miller, Lynn Bagdon, Fran Eikhoff, Tonya Pike, Scott Nelson, Laurel Kane, Maria Rinaldi, Joann Harwell, Lori Kassner, Ken Turmel, Karen Harrill, Ananda Shorey and countless others contributed, answered questions, shared, material and reminded me of what a wonderful road family we share.

Trond Moberg, Harley-Davidson travel guide extraordinaire, shared wisdom from his notebooks as well as several favorite recipes from Norway. Matthias Guenther, Kleinmachnow, Germany, provided photographs and memories from his Harley trip with Christina Hey in the fall of 2003. My sincere thanks. This project has been so much fun!   — MARIAN CLARK

Introduction
Ride to Live, Live to Ride

"It's not the destination, it's the journey." — HARLEY-DAVIDSON SAYING

Route 66 and motorcycles are a natural, especially if the biker is on a Harley-Davidson. Two major American cultural icons, Route 66 and Harley go together like a sizzling burger and a slab of cheddar cheese, like hot apple pie and strong coffee, like smoked ribs and spicy sauce. They make a heady combination as potent and memorable as a fiery pot of chili.

The Mother Road and cycles have always represented the romance of traveling the open road. Harley-Davidson, founded in 1903, and Route 66, created in 1926, enjoyed a sweet courtship that soon blossomed into a full-blown love affair. The marriage of the two American treasures is solid. The honeymoon is endless.

The chemistry between Harley and Route 66 stems from the fact that both of these revered institutions celebrate freedom and a spirit of unity. That independence and a commitment to tradition can prove intoxicating whenever a biker saddles up and cruises Route 66 — a road that promises motion, excitement, adventure, and always delivers.

To better understand the strong bond between Harley and America's Main Street, picture this scene way out west on a stretch of concrete two-lane Route 66, stained from the vermilion earth of surrounding wheat fields.

A man clad in supple leathers and faded denim slips outside and welcomes the morning. Faint tracks of night stars whither and vanish and a hint of breeze stirs the weeds along a wire fence. Filled with stout coffee and plenty of courage, the man sees in a heartbeat that it is a postcard-perfect day — tailor-made for a ramble on a motorcycle. A smile buds on his lips. All is right with the world.

Mindful that a motorcycle is not just another vehicle but a distinct lifestyle, the man considers himself doubly blessed. For he will not be riding just *any* cycle — he owns a Harley. This fellow is a true believer. He fears no evil, lives life full bore, and holds to the opinion that on the eighth day God created Harley-Davidson.

Leather skullcap, gauntlets, and goggles in place, the man secures the straps on the saddlebags, swings a booted leg over the seat, and mounts his gleaming machine — a Heritage Softail Classic. Just a turn of the ignition key, a push on the starter button, a gentle twist of the throttle, and the brawny Harley engine rumbles to life.

As he glides off in the direction of his dreams, the rider experiences what many others can only fantasize. The process of unfettered travel takes over. All thoughts disappear of the kid's college tuition, a volatile stock market, and the favorite football team's losing season. Every one of his senses is heightened and at full alert. For the next several hours, man and machine blend into a sweet concoction and dance through time and space.

Convinced that life truly does begin on the off-ramp, the biker sticks to the old road. No need for maps, turnpike change, or reservations. The possibility of pure adventure waits around every curve and bend. The ride is all that matters. Time becomes meaningless. Only the aroma of succulent ribs wafting from a roadside pit reminds the rider to pause for a late lunch.

The road beckons. With each passing mile, the man astride the metal-and-chrome pony is transformed into a Chisholm Trail drover, an escaping desperado, a Kiowa scout. He becomes a young Brando, the Lone Ranger, *Easy Rider* incarnate. He is nineteen once again, en route to a Jimi Hendrix concert. Images of Jack Kerouac and Ken Kesey dance in his head.

Through sunshine and buffeting wind and beneath the shadows and light of heaven, the rider cruises the Mother Road all day long. Bound only by his imagination, he does not turn the bike around and head for home until long after the moon rises.

Wherever the bike goes, heads turn. Everyone hears it coming. Nothing else sounds like a Harley. World-class writers have recounted the din of combat, timber crashing to the ground, a newborn infant's cry, the laughter of a woman in love, but not one of them has even come close to describing the distinctive purr, growl, and roar of a Harley-Davidson motorcycle.

Ironically, at one time the Harley engine earned the nickname "Silent Gray Fellow," in deference to the standard model's quiet muffler and stock shade of gray, the color of choice except for the optional basic black. But that was in 1907 when the Harley-Davidson Motor Company was still in its infancy.

Since those early years, Harley — just like Route 66 — has endured good and bad times while evolving into a cherished national icon. Of course, much of that air of reverence which developed around the Harley name comes from the fact that Harley-Davidson is the sole remaining motorcycle manufacturer in the United States and the nation's number-one seller of heavyweight bikes. The Harley is as American as Will Rogers, hamburgers, and the bald eagle, which proudly serves as the company symbol. The Harley is also much more, at least in the minds and imaginations of all those who choose to ride one.

As a 1998 cover story about Harley-Davidson in *Popular Mechanics* put it, the Harley cycle is "a poke in the eye to mainstream sensibilities, a rolling sculpture, a club, a support group, a fantasy, a noisy declaration of independence, a way of life, a brotherhood, a religion, an obsession, something to believe in, an escape, and probably the best consumer marketing device in history."

When it comes to the so-called Harley mystique, perhaps the words emblazoned across a popular biker T-shirt say it best: "If I have to explain, then you wouldn't understand."

Yet hundreds of thousands of Harley owners — men and women from around the world and virtually every walk of life — need no explanation. They get the message loud and clear. Ranging from factory workers to brain surgeons, these brothers and sisters of the road hold their Harleys in high esteem and consider themselves members of a very special family.

And that is why the Harley family of riders is so attached to Route 66. Many bikers consider the Mother Road prime riding territory — nothing short of Hog heaven on earth.

I also know this because on two occasions my wife, Suzanne Fitzgerald Wallis, and I led hundreds of Harley riders — representing almost every state in the union and more than a dozen foreign nations — down the entire length of Route 66. Harley Owners Group, better known as H.O.G., sponsored both tours. The first tour took place in 1995 and the second in 2001, to mark the 75th anniversary of Route 66.

These treks were documented by national and international media and are considered landmark events in the annals of Harley and Route 66 history. Both of the historic journeys are forever tattooed in our memories.

Like every journey we make, the two Harley tours of the Mother Road were filled with magical moments. We saw so much along the way and we paid our respects at the old and new businesses that continue to mushroom along the old road. Some of the stories that were gathered on those journeys are included in this book.

As the title implies, *Hogs on 66: Best Feed and Hangouts for Roadtrips on Route 66* provides an assortment of yarns, practical advice, useful tips, and an array of colorful photographs to enhance the biker experience on the Mother Road. Beyond that the book will also serve as a useful resource and tool for anyone traveling Route 66, even those who prefer four wheels or more for their journey.

Included in the book is plenty of the wisdom of my friend and co-author, Marian Clark. The recognized authority on all culinary aspects of Route 66, Marian shares generous tips on biker havens as well as provides hospitality and dining options along the highway. She also offers up heaping spoonfuls of biker recipes for some of the tastiest road chow on the old highway.

All together we believe it is a savory stick-to-the-ribs stew sure to please any open road traveler.

Enjoy the ride and be sure to save room for pie.

— MICHAEL WALLIS

Illinois

Fast Facts from Illinois

- Approximate Route 66 mileage in Illinois — 280

- "Historic Route 66" signs are brown and white in Illinois.

- Current official Illinois highway maps include Route 66.

- Illinois Route 66 preservationists have completed more projects than those of any other state.

- Illinois is home to the only maple grove along Route 66.

Illinois Biker Road Rules

- Safety helmet, not required

- Eye Protection, required

Where to buy stuff

- FUNK'S GROVE — All-American Maple "Sirup." Be sure to spell sirup the Funk's Grove way.

- BROADWELL — Ernie Edwards' Pig-Hip Restaurant Museum. "The Old Coot" will be glad to spin a yarn for you.

- STAUNTON — Henry's Old Route 66 Emporium and Rabbit Ranch. Meet Montana or her kids — or her grandkids.

Must see in Illinois

- CHICAGO — Navy Pier on the shores of Lake Michigan

- CICERO — Sportsman's Park Race Track and Hawthorne Racecourse

- JOLIET — The Empress Casino and Harrah's Joliet Casino

- LEXINGTON — 1926 "Memory Lane" 66 alignment just north of town; stop to admire the restored billboards right out of our past.

- McLEAN — Dixie Truckers Home, under new management but currently home to the Illinois Route 66 Hall of Fame

- SPRINGFIELD — Bill Shea's Gas Station Museum; a great collection of gas station memorabilia and old Harley-Davidson signs

Where the Road Begins

- MOUNT OLIVE — Soulsby Station, the road's oldest gas station

- COLLINSVILLE — 70 foot catsup bottle atop a 100 foot tower, a restored tribute to Brooks Catsup

- CHAIN OF ROCKS BRIDGE — Get off your bike, stretch, and take a walk on the longest pedestrian bridge in the world

Favorite hangouts for food and drink

- CHICAGO
THE BERGHOFF, 17 W. Adams Street
    Authentic Chicago since 1890, holder of the 1st liquor license in Chicago after prohibition

BILLY GOAT TAVERN, Kinzie and Michigan Avenue

LOU MITCHELL'S, Jackson and Canal

INDIAN HEAD PARK: WOLF'S HEAD INN, 6937 Joliet Road

- WILLOWBROOK
DELL RHEA CHICKEN BASKET, 645 Joliet Road

- JOLIET
THE OLD KEG RESTAURANT AND PUB, 20 West Jackson

- WILMINGTON
LAUNCHING PAD DRIVE-IN, Route 53

- BRAIDWOOD
POLK-A-DOT DRIVE-IN, Route 53

- GARDNER — RIVIERA RESTAURANT, 1 mile north of Gardner, 5650 Route 53

- DWIGHT — FEDDERSON'S PIZZA, Old city 66

- PONTIAC — OLD LOG CABIN, Pontiac Road and North Aurora

- SPRINGFIELD
    - COZY DOG DRIVE-IN, 2935 S. 6th Street
    - DUDE'S SALOON, 1900 Peoria, where the bikers gather

- FARMERSVILLE — ART'S RESTAURANT, I-55 at Exit 72

- LITCHFIELD — ARISTON CAFE, Route 66 at IL 16

- HAMEL — EARNIE'S, IL 157 and IL 140

Zen of the Mother Road

— MICHAEL WALLIS

It was a day I'll never forget. A balmy summer Sabbath morning and I'm on my Heritage Softail at the head of a procession of hundreds of other Harleys ridden by riders from around the world. My true love and life partner, Suzanne, is on my bike right behind me and I can feel her excitement as she wraps her arms around my waist and kisses my shoulder.

The chance of a lifetime — to lead a Harley parade on America's Main Street in "The City of Big Shoulders" and I got the call. Not bad for a 60's-vintage former Marine sergeant. Now, we're talking enough bikers to form at least a couple or maybe three battalions. They hail from forty-four states and a dozen foreign nations. The oldest rider is 82 and the youngest is just four years old.

Although Route 66 is a two-way highway running east and west, most Road Warriors worth their grit prefer starting in Chicago and then striking out along 2,448 miles to the bluffs in Santa Monica overlooking the roaring Pacific.

We are going all the way down Route 66 — from Chicago, through eight states and three time zones. To start the journey off right, hundreds of us on our bikes will cruise in a long procession from our gathering place well south of Chicago and go to the heart of the city where Route 66 both begins and ends.

Bikers where the road begins

After 45 minutes we approach our destination. The start of Route 66, originally at Jackson Boulevard and Michigan Avenue, has moved a few times as various streets became one-way for traffic. Now the old route officially begins at Adams Street and Michigan Avenue, near the Art Institute of Chicago guarded by a pair of bronze lions. An historic Route 66 sign marking the official end of Route 66 stands at Jackson and Michigan and a sign declaring the start of the Mother Road welcomes travelers at Adams and Michigan.

The biker parade moves into Chicago's Loop — the crossroads of the country — beneath the shadow of the Sears Tower, one the tallest buildings in the world. As we glide across Michigan Avenue we glance to our right and there before us in Grant Park is a sea of yellow.

Engines are roaring in chorus and then the signal is given. Off we go with an escort of motorcycle cops who switch off with their counterparts as we move into different jurisdictions. Fortunately, since it is early Sunday, there is little traffic. We also discover that someone has some pull with Cook County and the City of Chicago. Rolling down the expressways we spy snowplows and trucks conveniently blocking the on-ramps. This morning Harley owns the road.

Before long the distinctive downtown skyline comes into view. I glance in my mirror and snaking behind me — as far as the eye can see — are nothing but shining motorcycles.

Sears Tower on the Mother Road

There is little time to take it all in but we finally figure out that this is a group of people in flowing gauzy yellow robes and they are meditating. They also are completely and utterly silent in stark contrast to the roaring and rumbling motorcycles passing them in review. The sound of hundreds of engines bounces and reverberates off the canyon of buildings yet not one of the yellow figures so much as twitches or shows any sign that they are aware of us.

Minutes later, after we all park our bikes in long rows and pose for countless photographs, we learn that the men and women in the park were Buddhists at prayer. When I finally get back to the site where they had congregated I find the Buddhists have gone. I wonder if I had really seen them after all or if they were an urban mirage. Suzanne assures me they were real, as do other bikers who also were struck by their presence.

There will be no return procession. The parade is over. Everyone is on their own for the rest of the day, free to check out points of interest on Jackson and Adams or prowl other parts of the city. Groups of bikers head straight to Lou Mitchell's, a favorite eating establishment for Route 66ers. Others go to the Art Institute or gather for more photos beneath the Route 66 signs.

We have a few cups of coffee before we climb on our scooter and take our leave.

The rest of that day and all the rest of that memorable journey across America, my thoughts went back to the moment when we flashed past the yellow robed Buddhists in Grant Park. I recalled that Buddhists believe in the concept of rebirth. With that in mind, I thought it appropriate that we had come upon the Buddhists in Chicago at the beginning and the end of a highway that has constantly experienced rebirth and rejuvenation.

I also considered that central to the Buddhist path to nirvana, or enlightenment, is the understanding and acceptance of impermanence. Everyone passes on. Nothing lasts forever. That gives life its newness and surprise.

Maybe that was what Robert Pirsig was telling us when he wrote *Zen and the Art of Motorcycle Maintenance*. The book is more than the details behind a cross-country motorcycle journey taken by a man and his eleven-year-old son. It is also the man's quest for truth and understanding.

That is exactly what we encountered on that memorable Harley tour along the Mother Road. It is what we still find every time we make the trip. For those fleeting moments in time — through rain and searing sun and across mountains and deserts — we are on our own pilgrimage of self-discovery and renewal. ■

Recipes from Illinois

— MARIAN CLARK

JUICY SLABS OF MEAT LOAF, slathered with aromatic tomato sauce, rank right up there at the top for satisfying biker victuals. This version came directly from a new cookbook, *We Work for Food*, published by the Route 66 Association of Illinois Preservation Committee. The group, headed by John and Lenore Weiss, has provided hands-on help to save barns, gas stations, diners, bridges, and signs all along Route 66 in this state "where Route 66 begins."

Judy's World Famous Meat Loaf

The Official Route-66-of-Illinois Favorite Recipe

JUDY SCHWALLENSTECKER

Sauce:

½ cup catsup

1½ teaspoons mustard

½ teaspoon ground nutmeg

⅓ cup brown sugar

2 tablespoons cider vinegar

Meat Loaf:

2 pounds lean ground beef

1 cup crushed cornflakes

½ teaspoon black pepper

2 teaspoons salt

1 medium onion, chopped

2 eggs

2 tablespoons minced parsley

Mix sauce ingredients and heat for a few minutes. Stir cornflakes into ground beef. Add remaining ingredients and ⅔ of the heated sauce. Shape into one large or two smaller loaves. Place in a 9x11 baking dish. Bake in a preheated 375-degree oven for 45 minutes. Spread remaining sauce over the top and continue baking for 15 minutes. Allow to stand for 10 minutes before slicing. 8 servings.

BIKERS ARE ALWAYS WELCOME when Chicago's Greek community celebrates each August at the Greek Town Festival held on Halstead Street between Monroe and

Van Buren. Food and drink comes from over fifteen Greek restaurants whose chefs prepare a wide array of traditional food. Entertainment includes dancing, ancestral and contemporary Greek music, fortune-telling, and spectacular food.

Keftethes
Greek Meatballs

1 pound ground beef
2 eggs
3 slices dry bread, crumbled
1 onion, finely shopped
3 tablespoons dry mint, crumbled
1 teaspoon salt
¼ teaspoon pepper
Flour for coating
Oil for frying

Mix the ingredients well. The mixture should be soft. With wet hands, roll into cocktail-sized meatballs, using about 1 level tablespoon of the mixture for each. Roll each lightly in flour and deep fry for 2-3 minutes.

Instead of frying, these may be baked in the oven at 325 degrees for about 5 minutes, then turned and baked 5 more minutes. Approximately 36 meatballs.

FOR SOUP AS ALL-AMERICAN AS WILL ROGERS, try this hearty blend. It was originally included in *First There Must Be Food*, a fund-raising cookbook published by the Volunteer Service Department at Chicago's North-western Memorial Hospital.

The El, Chicago

Beef and Lentil Soup
First There Must be Food

3 tablespoons all-purpose flour
2 teaspoons salt
¼ teaspoon pepper
2 pounds beef for stewing, cut into ½ inch cubes
3 tablespoons vegetable oil
5-6 cups water
5 medium carrots, scraped and thinly sliced
2 cups sliced celery
2 large onions, chopped
1 cup dried lentils, washed and sorted
1 tablespoon lemon juice
1½ teaspoons salt
1 teaspoon dried whole thyme

Combine flour, 2 teaspoons salt, and pepper in a medium bowl; dredge beef in flour mixture.

Heat oil in a large Dutch oven. Add beef and cook until browned on all sides. Add water; cover and simmer 45 minutes. Skim off any fat. Stir in carrot, celery, onion, lentils, lemon juice, salt, and thyme. Cover and simmer 1 hour or until meat and vegetables are tender, stirring occasionally. 12 cups.

THE INSTANTLY RECOGNIZABLE SOUND OF A HARLEY is as distinctive as the unmistakable flavor of a Chicago pizza. For some of the best, stop at Uno or Due. When you can't get to Chicago, make this triple-cheese likeness and imagine you're cruising the road!

Triple Cheese Pizza

1 ready-made baked pizza crust (16 ounces)
6 tablespoons pesto sauce
1 cup grated Fontina cheese (about 4 ounces)
5-6 plum tomatoes, seeded and thinly sliced
1 tablespoon dried, crumbled oregano
½ teaspoon dried basil
½ cup freshly grated mozzarella cheese, (about 2 ounces)
⅓ cup freshly grated Parmesan cheese
Black pepper to taste

Preheat oven to 450 degrees. Place pizza crust on large baking sheet. Spread with pesto. Sprinkle evenly with Fontina cheese. Arrange tomatoes over pizza. Season with oregano, basil, and black pepper. Add mozzarella and Parmesan cheese. Bake until crust is golden and topping is bubbly, about 10-12 minutes. 4 servings.

IRISH, ITALIAN, AND EASTERN EUROPEAN IMMIGRANTS settled around Joliet and worked the river corridor between Lake Michigan and the Mississippi River for years. Hearty food and a strong ethnic heritage is evident around here. Irish coffee is traditionally American and popular in the area. Here is one way it is served to bikers in Joliet.

Joliet

Irish Coffee

½ cup whipping cream
2 teaspoons powdered sugar
1 teaspoon vanilla
8 ounces Irish whiskey or brandy
8 teaspoons brown sugar
8 cups strong, hot coffee

Whip cream with powdered sugar and vanilla. Place 1 ounce (2 tablespoons) whiskey and 1 teaspoon brown sugar into each heatproof mug; stir. Pour hot coffee into mugs and top with whipped cream. Serve immediately. 8 cups.

The Old Log Cabin Cafe

The Old Log Cabin Cafe just north of Pontiac is a stop where biker memories are made. Behind the counter, regular customers have names painted on their own coffee mugs and find them waiting on a Peg-Board behind the counter each morning. This is the Route 66 eatery that once faced the other direction on State Highway 4. When Route 66 came along, the owners decided to move the front door. They jacked up the building, turned it around and opened the front to Route 66 traffic again.

Brad and Debbie Trainor have owned the cafe since 1986. They serve plenty of good home cooking.

THE RIVIERA RESTAURANT, JUST NORTH OF GARDNER, has always attracted free spirits. It was built in 1928, the beginning of the depression years, by James Girot who hired unemployed men to move the buildings from Gardner and South Wilmington and reconstruct them to create a tavern and restaurant. The upper floor became a restaurant, the lower floor was the tavern. The old barroom remains as it was once designed — much like a cave with stalactites hanging from the ceiling.

The menu is primarily Italian, but owners Bob and Peggy Kraft also serve great steak, chicken, and seafood. They have been at the Riviera since 1972 and welcome fellow free spirits who love to stomp out conformity. Be sure to check the Riviera restrooms!

Beef Stroganoff
RIVIERA RESTAURANT

2 cups minced onion
2 large cloves minced garlic
4 tablespoons margarine
2 pounds round steak, cut into bite-sized pieces
Salt and pepper to taste
½ cup flour
1 can (10¾ ounces) beef broth or consommé
⅓ cup red wine
8 ounces sliced mushrooms
1 teaspoon nutmeg
2 cups sour cream
Freshly prepared noodles

Sauté onions and garlic in margarine. Set aside. Flour steak, add salt and pepper and brown in hot skillet. Deglaze pan with consommé. Combine all ingredients except sour cream and noodles. Bake in preheated 350-degree oven until tender.

Just before serving, add sour cream. Serve over noodles. Note: This can also be cooked very slowly on a surface unit of the range. 8 servings.

Hungry bikers will find a belly-satisfying dessert with this luscious recipe shared by Jo Ann Burns from the Exchange Bank in Gardner. Her apple squares are yummy!

Jo Ann Burns' Sour Cream Apple Squares

2 cups flour
2 cups brown sugar
½ cup butter
1 cup chopped pecans
1½ teaspoons cinnamon
1 teaspoon soda
½ teaspoon salt
1 cup sour cream
1 teaspoon vanilla
1 egg
2 cups apples, peeled and chopped

Combine flour, sugar and butter. Blend at low speed with a mixer. Stir in the nuts. Press all but 1 cup of the crumb mixture into an ungreased 9x13 pan. To remaining mixture add cinnamon, soda, salt, sour cream, vanilla and egg. Blend well. Stir in the apples. Spoon over pressed mixture. Bake in a preheated 350-degree oven for 25-30 minutes. Serve warm with ice cream or whipped cream. 10-12 servings.

Dwight

Genuine comfort food always outlasts the trends and has widespread appeal. This is certainly true in Dwight where ham loaves have remained popular through the years at the annual bazaar held by the United Methodist Women.

Ham Loaves

Dwight United Methodist Women

1½ pounds ground smoked ham
½ pound ground fresh pork
2 eggs, beaten
1 cup milk
1 cup cracker crumbs
½ teaspoon pepper
Extra crumbs for rolling
Sauce:
1 cup brown sugar
1 scant tablespoon dry mustard
½ cup vinegar
½ cup water

Combine ham, pork, eggs, milk, crumbs, and pepper into 8 loaves. Roll ham loaves in extra cracker crumbs and bake in a preheated oven for 15 minutes at 350 degrees. Meanwhile, combine sauce ingredients in a small saucepan and bring to a boil. Reduce oven heat to 325 degrees. Baste loaves with sauce and continue cooking for 45 minutes, basting every 5 minutes with the sauce. 8 servings.

EFFIE MARX OF DWIGHT is a member of the Illinois Route 66 Hall of Fame. She holds the distinction of being the longest working waitress on Route 66. Effie began working at an eatery in Odell in 1931 and served several generations of customers in Odell, Braidwood, Hinsdale, and finally Dwight. She signed on at Phil's Harvest Table at age sixty-two and worked there over fifteen years. Effie shared her favorite brownie recipe a short time before her death.

Effie Marx's Brownies

½ cup (1 stick) margarine at room temperature
1 cup sugar
4 eggs
1 cup flour
¼ teaspoon salt
1 can (16-ounce) Hershey's syrup
½ cup chopped nuts (optional)

Combine margarine, sugar and eggs. Beat together until well blended then add flour and salt. Stir in syrup and nuts. Bake in an 8½x11 pan in a 350 degree oven for 30 minutes.

Frosting:
½ cup margarine
1½ cups sugar
⅓ cup milk
½ cup chocolate chips

Combine margarine, sugar, and milk, and bring to boil for 30 seconds only. Remove from heat and add ½ cup chocolate chips. Beat mixture until glossy and spread on brownies.

Bill Shea's Gas Station Museum, Springfield

GLAIDA FUNK CAME TO FUNK'S GROVE by way of Oklahoma. She and her husband Steve met while he was taking pilot training in Enid during World War II. Steve's great-grandfather, Isaac, settled in the only maple grove along Route 66 just over a hundred years before the Mother Road came into being.

Glaida remembers the years after World War II as pretty primitive. She and Steve sold sirup from the back porch and met their share of hitchhikers, vagrants, and folks whose cars refused to make another mile. Often, these folks were hired on for food.

Life slowed again at Funk's Grove when the interstate opened in 1976, but eventually people found them again, and today Funk's Grove is one of the most popular stops along the highway. A jug of Funk's Grove Pure Maple Sirup in the tank bag is the mark of a seasoned roadie. Just be sure to keep the lid on tight.

Funk's Grove Maple Sirup Bars

½ cup butter
¼ cup sugar
1 cup flour
¾ cup brown sugar
⅓ cup maple sirup
1 tablespoon butter
1 egg
½ teaspoon vanilla
⅓ cup chopped pecans

Cream butter and sugar in food processor. Add flour and process until just blended. Dough does not form ball. Pat into bottom of greased 9-inch square pan. Bake at 350 degrees for 15 minutes, or until lightly browned. Beat brown sugar, syrup, and butter to blend. Beat in egg and vanilla. Pour over shortbread. Sprinkle with nuts. Bake 25 minutes or until set. Cool and cut into bars. 2 dozen bars.

Bikers pause for visit with Debby Funk (front, left) at Funk's Grove

Glaida Funk says that Alma Van Ness was one of the best cooks in McLean. She and her husband, Archie, lived on the corner of Route 66 and Highway 136 from 1938 until 1969. The corner was known as the "death corner" because of many accidents occurred there. The location today is home to a McDonald's Restaurant and is across from the Dixie Truckers' Home. Could any biker resist a warm slab of rhubarb pie topped with a big dollop of authentic whipped cream?

Dixie Truckers Home, McLean

Rhubarb Pie

Crust:
3 cups flour
1 cup shortening
1 teaspoon salt
9-10 tablespoons cold water

Mix flour, shortening, and salt until consistency of corn meal. Add water as needed. Roll and shape into 9-inch pie pans. Enough for 2 double-crust pies or 4 single-crust pies.

Filling:
3 cups rhubarb
3 tablespoons flour
1½ cups sugar
Dash of cinnamon
2 eggs, well-beaten
1 tablespoon melted butter

Place rhubarb in unbaked 9-inch crust. Combine flour, sugar, cinnamon, eggs and butter. Mix well. Pour over rhubarb. Put on top crust, seal and cut air vents. Bake in a preheated 350 degree oven for 1 hour. Yields 6-8 slices.

In the summer of 1996, employees of the Lehn and Fink Company in Lincoln published a cookbook sharing treasured recipes from those who worked for the company from the time it opened in 1947 until the doors closed forever. Bert Marten shared this comfortable main dish, as gratifying as the growl of a favorite Harley engine.

Stuffed Manicotti

Lasting Memories Cookbook

1½ pounds lean hamburger
½ cup chopped onion
½ teaspoon garlic salt
1 teaspoon salt
Pepper to taste

1 cup dry bread crumbs

1 tablespoon dried parsley flakes

½ pound grated mozzarella cheese

2 eggs

½ cup milk

14 manicotti shells

1 jar (28-ounce) pasta sauce

Brown hamburger with onion, salt and pepper. Drain and allow to cool slightly. Pour into mixing bowl and add bread crumbs, parsley, cheese, eggs, and milk. Mix thoroughly. Cook the manicotti according to package directions. Stuff each shell with the meat mixture. Place in a 9x11 baking dish and cover with pasta sauce. Bake in 350-degree oven for 30 minutes. This manicotti freezes well. 14 shells.

THESE GINGERSNAPS ARE GUARANTEED to provide the gumption for a great ride.

Gingersnaps
Lasting Memories Cookbook

1 cup white sugar

¾ cup margarine or shortening

1 egg

4 tablespoons dark molasses

2 cups flour

2 teaspoons soda

1 teaspoon ginger

1 teaspoon cinnamon

1 teaspoon cloves

Mix sugar and shortening. Add egg and mix. Add molasses and mix well. Add flour, soda, and spices. Make balls the size of walnuts; roll in granulated sugar. Spray cookie sheet with nonstick cooking spray. Bake in preheated 350-degree oven for 15 minutes. 3 dozen cookies.

ERNIE AND FRAN EDWARDS LOVE TO VISIT. The famous Pig Hip Restaurant is closed now, but Ernie and Illinois Route 66 faithfuls have turned the old place into a great highway museum. Take time to visit, exchange autographs, pick up some souvenirs, sign the guest book, and hear a few road stories firsthand.

Pig-Hip Restaurant, Broadwell

When I stopped to see if Ernie and Fran would share a recipe or memory for the book, they promised to give it some thought and put a note in the mail. A few days after I returned home, Ernie's letter came. He shared two memories:

"This sandwich was not a successful one but it was good. I made the Chick Burger back in 1942. I used a five-pound chicken and boiled it 'till the meat fell off the bone then shredded it real well. Then I made a real creamy coleslaw. Put the meat on a bun, add coleslaw, and that five-pound chicken would serve fifty sandwiches."

Ernie says another sandwich that was popular was his "Yip-Yap." It was a hot dog bun that had one end cut off. Ernie made a hole in the end, filled the bun with chili meat and served it like an ice cream cone. He said it was good and "rather successful."

Fran and Ernie Edwards, owners of Pig-Hip Restaurant

ENJOY SMALL-TOWN PEACE AND QUIET IN WILLIAMSVILLE, where Edie Senalik specializes in homemade bagels and Italian biscotti. Pack some along to chow down with a cup of authentic highway coffee — as black as the midnight sky.

Edie's Biscotti Di Pratto

¼ cup blanched almonds
¾ cup natural whole almonds
3 eggs
1 teaspoon vanilla
¼ teaspoon almond extract
2¼ cups all-purpose flour
1 cup sugar
1 teaspoon baking soda
Pinch of salt
1 egg

Preheat oven to 350 degrees. On a baking sheet, roast both kinds of almonds until blanched almonds start to brown, shaking occasionally, 5-8 minutes. Remove blanched almonds, place in blender or food processor to pulverize. Set aside.

Return whole almonds to oven for 2-3 minutes longer. Remove and chop roughly. Set aside.

Reduce heat in oven to 300 degrees. Grease and dust a baking sheet. Set aside. In a small bowl, beat the eggs, vanilla, and almond extract together. In a larger bowl, mix flour, sugar, baking soda, salt, and pulverized almonds. Make a well in center and add egg mixture, blending until stiff dough is formed. Add a few drops of water if mixture does not hold together. Add chopped almonds and knead to evenly distribute.

Divide dough into 3 portions. Form each into a long round, slightly oval log, about 1½ inches in diameter.

Place on baking sheet. Beat remaining egg and brush onto log surfaces.

Bake at 300 degrees for 45 minutes.

Remove from oven and allow to rest for 5 minutes. Turn oven to 275 degrees. With serrated knife, cut logs into ¼-inch slices. Lay biscotti flat on two cookie sheets. Return to oven for 20 minutes, turning over half-way through baking time. Allow to cool before sealing in containers. Will stay fresh for up to a month. These crusty morsels are good to dip in coffee. 6-7 dozen.

SUE WALDMIRE OWNS AND OPERATES the Cozy Dog Drive-In and Supply Company in Springfield.

Ed Waldmire, the originator of the Cozy Dog, opened this Springfield icon in 1949. Virginia, Ed's wife, designed the famous logo of the two hot dogs embracing. Bob Waldmire, the road's favorite cruising artist, is Sue's brother-in-law.

Chili
COZY DOG DRIVE-IN AND SUPPLY COMPANY

1 pound red beans
2 quarts water
2 tablespoons Cozy Dog Drive-In Chili Mix
2 cups beef suet, melted and strained
1 onion
1 green pepper
1 pound lean ground beef
½ cup chili spice
1 small can tomato paste

Cook the beans in the water with the chili mix until they are tender. Meanwhile, heat the suet and dice the onion and pepper. Sauté until soft. Add ground beef and continue cooking and stirring until meat is browned and crumbly. Add chili spice and tomato paste. Bring to boil.

To serve, add beans to each bowl then cover with meat sauce.

Note: The secret to the success of this recipe is to serve warmed, and crisp oyster crackers with each steaming bowl.

FOR THOSE WHO PREFER A VEGETARIAN CHILI, here is an adaptation that would please Bob Waldmire. You don't have to be a vegetarian to enjoy this filling meal!

Vegetarian Black Bean Chili

4 cups dried, rinsed, black beans
Water to cover
2 tablespoons olive oil
1 large onion, chopped
2 green bell peppers, chopped
6 large garlic cloves, minced
2 tablespoons cumin
2 tablespoons chili powder
2 teaspoons dried basil
1 teaspoon dried oregano
½ teaspoon cayenne pepper
2 4-ounce cans diced green chilies, undrained
½ cup tomato sauce
¼ cup fresh lime juice

Toppings:
Chopped tomatoes and onions
Grated cheese
Sour cream
Avocado slices
Crackers

Place beans in large pot. Add cold water to cover at least 3 inches. Soak overnight. Drain beans, reserving 3 cups of the liquid. Return beans to pot and add cold water again to cover. Simmer beans until tender, about 2 to 2½ hours. Drain.

Heat oil in heavy pan. Add onions, bell pepper, garlic, cumin, chili, basil, oregano, and cayenne and cook approximately 10 minutes. Add beans, reserved soaking liquid, chilies, and tomato sauce. Stir and cook slowly until chili is thick, about 45 minutes. Add lime juice and season with salt and pepper to taste. Serve in bowls and pass toppings. 12 servings.

Veteran biker Jamie Constantine enjoys an ear of sweet corn

THE VILLAGE OF DIVERNON is a small agricultural community that experienced a spurt of growth at the turn of the century due to mining, then quickly returned to a quiet, comfortable township. Their *Centennial Cookbook, 1900-2000* is a treasure of regional food. Here is a fine example, offering deep-down satisfaction and pure comfort. What more could a biker want?

Bev Kalaskie's Italian Beef

4 to 5 pounds beef roast (Use chuck or arm roast.)
1 teaspoon oregano
2 beef bouillon cubes
1 teaspoon fennel
½ teaspoon nutmeg
1 large onion, sliced

1 clove garlic or 1 teaspoon garlic powder
Pinch of basil
¼ teaspoon allspice
½ teaspoon pepper
2 bay leaves
¼ teaspoon thyme
½ teaspoon dried parsley
1 teaspoon salt
2 cups water

Preheat oven to 325 degrees. Place meat in a roaster, combine then add all ingredients. Cover with lid and roast meat for 20 minutes per pound. When the meat has cooled, slice it and return to roaster with remaining juices. Add extra water if necessary. Warm again and serve with kaiser rolls. Note: All spices can be adjusted to personal taste.

4 servings per pound of meat.

GRACE AND ROGER BROWN, ALONG WITH THEIR DAUGHTER and son-in-law, Debra and Darry Lucas, bought Art's Cafe in Farmersville in 1978. This Route 66 classic stop has a long history of satisfying 66 bikers. That going-away growl of satisfied Harley owners is just a little more comforting after a satisfying piece of this butterscotch pie.

Debbie's Butterscotch Pie

1 cup brown sugar
1½ cups water
1½ cups milk, scalded
4 tablespoons cornstarch
4 tablespoons flour
½ teaspoon salt

3 egg yolks, beaten
4 tablespoons butter
1 teaspoon vanilla
1 10-inch baked pie shell

Meringue:
3 egg whites
2 tablespoon sugar

Mix brown sugar with water in a medium saucepan and bring to a boil. Add scalded milk. Combine cornstarch, flour, and salt. Carefully stir into sugar, water, and milk mixture and cook until thick, stirring constantly. Add egg yolks and butter and cook an additional 2 minutes. Stir in vanilla. Pour pie into a baked 10-inch crust. Whip egg whites and add sugar, beating until glossy.

Cover pie with meringue. Bake in a preheated 350-degree oven until meringue is lightly browned, about 12-15 minutes. 7-8 slices.

ONE OF THE BEST OF THE ROUTE 66 FEED STOPS is Litchfield's Ariston Cafe. In its present location since 1935, the cafe is operated by Nick and Demi Adam. Nick is the son of the founder, Pete Adam, who originally opened the restaurant in nearby Carlinville in 1925. The restaurant is known for quality food and a warm welcome. Nick and Demi are proud of their Greek heritage and shared this time-honored dessert favorite. The Ariston Cafe is a favorite biker stop, recommended by all who have enjoyed the friendly service.

Ariston Cafe, Litchfield

Baklava
ARISTON CAFE

Syrup:
2 cups water
3 cups sugar
1 teaspoon lemon
2 cinnamon sticks

In a medium saucepan, combine all ingredients. Bring to a boil; simmer 15 minutes or until candy thermometer registers 224 degrees. Remove from heat; cool; remove cinnamon sticks.

Nut filling:
1½ cups sugar
2 pounds walnuts, chopped
2 teaspoons cinnamon
Dash of ground clove

In a medium bowl, stir together nuts, sugar, cinnamon, and cloves. Set aside.

Phyllo preparation:
1 package of phyllo dough
3 sticks of butter

Open phyllo and place sheets between pieces of wax paper. Cover loosely with damp towel so phyllo won't dry out. In a small saucepan, melt butter and keep warm. Brush bottom of a 9x13 or 13-inch round pan (not glass) with melted butter. Line pan with 3 sheets of phyllo, brushing each sheet with melted butter. Sprinkle with a handful of nut mixture. Place another sheet of phyllo on top of nuts, brushing each sheet with butter. Repeat this procedure until all nut mixture is used.

Top with 3 or 4 remaining phyllo sheets, brushing each with melted butter while layering one on top of the other.

With the tip of a sharp knife, carefully cut or score all layers of baklava into desired size. Do not cut or score all the way through the phyllo.

Bake at 350 degrees for 45-50 minutes or until golden brown. Remove from oven and while still hot, carefully spoon cooled syrup evenly over the baklava. 12-15 servings.

THE VOLUNTEER AUXILIARY at Litchfield's St. Francis Hospital produced *A Taste of St. Francis* several years ago. After enjoying these two great dishes from their collection, you may need a nap before taking to the road again!

Honey Sesame Tenderloin
A Taste of St. Francis

1 pound pork tenderloin
½ cup soy sauce

2 cloves minced garlic

1 tablespoon grated ginger

1 tablespoon sesame oil

¼ cup honey

2 tablespoons brown sugar

4 tablespoons sesame seed

Place tenderloin in a plastic bag. Combine soy sauce, garlic, ginger, and sesame oil; pour soy mixture over meat. Marinate overnight in refrigerator. Remove pork from marinade. Mix honey and brown sugar in shallow plate. Roll pork in mixture, coating all sides. Place in roasting pan and sprinkle with sesame seeds. Roast at 375 degrees for 20-30 minutes or until meat thermometer reaches 160 degrees. 4 servings.

Potato Puffs

A Taste of St. Francis

3 cups hot mashed potatoes

4 tablespoons butter or margarine, melted

1 cup bread crumbs

⅓ cup low-fat mayonnaise

1 teaspoon salt

½ teaspoon dried basil

1 tablespoon grated lemon peel

1½ teaspoons lemon juice

1 cup milk

3 eggs, separated

¼ cup grated cheddar cheese

Litchfield Cafe

CAUTION: We Brake for ROUTE 66 Historic Sites

Combine melted margarine with crumbs; spread in shallow 9-inch casserole. Combine mayonnaise, salt, basil, lemon peel and juice, milk, and beaten egg yolk. Add to mashed potatoes; beat until smooth and fluffy. Beat egg whites until stiff; fold into potato mixture. Pour into casserole. Sprinkle with cheese. Bake in preheated 300 degree oven for 30 minutes. Turn oven to 375 degrees and bake 10 minutes longer or until browned. 6 servings.

THE ITALIAN INFLUENCE CAN STILL BE FELT in many of the dishes prepared in the southern Illinois community of Edwardsville. Folks around here enjoy their food, fun, and freedom almost as much as bikers. Barb Driesner, a member of the staff at the Edwardsville Library, says her mostaccioli recipe is typical of the area.

Barb Driesner's Mostaccioli

1 pound hamburger
1 pound Italian sausage
1 onion, diced
1 box (12 ounces) rigatoni or mostaccioli noodles

1 jar (28-ounce) Italian pasta sauce
8 ounces mozzarella cheese, grated
1 teaspoon garlic powder

Brown the hamburger and sausage with the onion. Drain thoroughly. Add sauce and garlic powder. Meanwhile, cook the rigatoni noodles. Layer ½ of the meat mixture in the bottom of a 9x13 inch baking dish. Cover with the noodles and half of the cheese. Repeat with remaining meat. Sprinkle remaining cheese on top. Bake uncovered in a preheated 350-degree oven for 30 minutes until mixture is hot and bubbly. 8 servings.

COLLINSVILLE IS THE HORSERADISH CAPITAL OF THE WORLD. Over 60 percent of the world's supply of the spicy herb is grown in the bottomlands around Collinsville. So naturally, many of the favorite dishes prepared by the good cooks around here include horseradish. This tasty recipe for chicken wings was shared for the McLean, Texas, recipe book, *Cuisine Down Old Route 66.*

Mississizippy Wings
Cuisine Down Old Route 66

4 pounds chicken wings
½ cup prepared horseradish
½ cup catsup
¼ cup sugar
⅓ cup lemon-lime soda
¼ cup water
2 tablespoons cooking oil
½ teaspoon garlic salt
¼ teaspoon pepper

Wash, then remove and discard tip sections of 4 pounds of chicken wings. Put wings in a small bowl. Combine remaining ingredients and pour mixture over wings, making sure all are covered. Cover bowl and refrigerate overnight. Remove wings and place on foil-lined shallow baking pan. Bake in preheated 350 degree oven for 1 hour or until wings are well done and crispy.

Turning and basting after the first ½ hour assures more even crispness. Dispose of excess marinade. About 24 wings.

SAY GOODBYE TO ILLINOIS at the historic Chain of Rocks Bridge.

Boys of Summer

— MICHAEL WALLIS

Beyond the Chicago sprawl, out in the Illinois countryside with its tidy farms and fields and grain elevators, bikers feel like they're riding through a giant version of a model train landscape. Out here, with acres of licorice-colored earth all around and the promise of more adventure around the next curve and bend, it becomes clear why Route 66 attracts so many bikers. If ever a path was made to order for a Harley it's this one.

Original Route 66 in Illinois

I figured that out some years ago, when I made the whole east-to-west journey on the old road and devoted almost a month to cruising from Chicago to Santa Monica. On this Route 66 journey I rode with a big posse of Harley riders including a bunch from several European countries. They had shipped their bikes to Chicago and I was invited to tag along. I didn't need to be asked twice.

Bikers gather at the Launching Pad, Wilmington

By late morning, after we passed through Berwyn, Willowbrook, and Romeoville, we stopped for cold drinks in Wilmington at the Launching Pad Drive-In, where a towering fiberglass spaceman giant stands guard in the parking lot. Just a short while later, we were all ready to stop again. This time it was the little highway burg of Odell. We wanted to pay our respects at the beautifully restored 1930s gas station that has become one of the true icons of the Mother Road.

Restored Standard Oil gasoline station, Odell

Fueled by a stout breakfast at Lou Mitchell's, the famed eatery located near the start of Route 66 in the Chicago Loop, we cruised out of the city as fast as we could. It was a hodgepodge of riders — men, women, young and old. There were retired execs, judges, doctors, priests, a stand-up comic, blue bloods, red necks, poets, and probably a few ex-cons. It really didn't matter. We never talked about our work anyway. The ride was what counted. That was really all that any of us cared about.

We slowed to a crawl after coming to the sign marking the town limits and cruised beneath the canopy of trees lining the shoulders of the highway until we reached the gas station perched on a gentle curve. After parking in the shade of a tree we crossed the highway to take a closer look at the vintage filling station that had been brought back to it's original state by the diligent road warriors of Illinois. Some citizens turned out to greet us including the town mayor and a few of the grassroots preservationists who had put so much time and sweat equity into the restoration of the building.

The tour only took a few minutes leaving us plenty of time to gulp down big glasses of freshly made lemonade provided by the locals. I finished my drink and was making my way back to the bikes along with a chap from France who was taking his dream trip down Route 66 in order to discover the America he had heard about all his life. We crossed the highway just as a pair of little boys — about ten years old — appeared on their bicycles. They proceeded to show off their riding skills, doing wheelies and other tricks, and then they rode around us in circles that grew tighter and tighter until they stopped next to us. Baseball cards were secured by clothespins to the bicycle spokes and ball gloves adorned the handlebars.

These were true boys of summer, complete with grass stained blue jean, tee shirts, rings of dirt around their necks, and hot weather burr haircuts. They also were obviously curious about us but too shy to speak. I broke the ice and asked them if they were from Odell.

Bikers meet locals at Odell

"Yes, sir," they shot back in unison.

That was all they needed. A flood of questions poured forth from the boys. They wanted to know where we came from and where we were going and all the while they talked they looked us up and down and shot envious looks at our motorcycles parked nearby.

They were in utter awe and also disbelief that so many bikers would come to their little town of Odell and actually stop to look at some old building. Neither of the boys had ever been to St. Louis or Chicago.

"This is the most exciting day of our lives!" one of the boys blurted out to us. "We've never seen so many motorcycles and people."

"We've been here all our lives," the other boy offered. "This is the most boring town in the world."

Then they asked us for our autographs and each one pulled a baseball card from the spokes and thrust them toward us. My riding companion produced a pen and we scribbled our signatures. But before the boys could ride away with their treasure I stopped them with a question.

"So boys, you think your town here is boring?"

They nodded .

"Don't you two guys know where you live?"

"Well Odell," they shot back in unison as if I was nuts.

"I know that but there's something more you boys need to realize," I told them. "You live on the most famous highway in the whole world. You live on Route 66. There's no other highway like this one and there is no other town quite like Odell. You have something special here and that makes you special."

The boys' eyes got big as pie plates.

"You boys live on a road that will take you not only to St. Louis and Chicago but way beyond. It's right here just waiting for you. And the good part is that in the meantime the world — and I mean the whole world — will come to you. That's why I came and so did this man here — he's come all the way from Paris, France, just to see your town and to meet you boys."

The boys looked at each other but did not speak.

"Be good to this old town and this road," I continued. "This road is a true legend and always remember that it can take you anyplace you want to go."

Then I asked them to give us *their* autographs. They were stunned but reached down and removed two more baseball cards from the spokes. They carefully signed their names and handed them to the French biker and me. We bid them *adieu* and fired up our Harleys.

We were a long way down the highway — almost out of sight — when I glanced in my mirror and saw the boys standing in the same spot. They were still waving. I knew they'd never forget our meeting. Neither would I. ■

The Legend

— MICHAEL WALLIS

Route 66 has always meant going somewhere. Just ask any biker who has made the journey and you will quickly understand.

Since 1926, this ribbon of asphalt and concrete has connected travelers — including legions of bikers — to the fabric of the land. It has carried us from the heart of America, through the romantic West of our imagination to the golden shores of California. We could follow our dreams of adventure, or seek a better life.

No other highway has been so immortalized in song, prose, or film. Route 66 offered early travelers the sights and sounds of America at its best. Today it invites us to revisit the country as it was before it became generic. The road transports us back to a time when the landscape was not littered with cookie-cutter houses, franchise eateries, and shopping malls peddling look-alike merchandise to people in danger of losing their own identity.

Route 66 is an event in itself. Road lore, handed down through the generations, is still being shared, and passed along by travelers adding to the legend as they urge others to follow.

The Route 66 I love puts me in touch with my roots and myself. It is a highway of phantoms and dreams reaching beyond a destination on the map.

Enjoy the odyssey! ∎

Missouri

Fast Facts from Missouri

- Route 66 mileage in Missouri — 317

- Missouri wines are among the best in the nation.

- Missouri roads are made for bikers, take some side trips to feel the pulse of this vibrant state.

- Hooker Cut, east of Devil's Elbow, is one of the deepest rock cuts in the country.

- Missouri is one of only two states which borders eight other states.

- One of the first concrete paved portions of the Missouri highway system connected Carthage to Joplin in 1920. This road became part of Route 66 in 1926.

St. Louis Gateway Arch casts its shadow on the park below

Missouri Biker Road Rules

- Safety Helmet, required by law

- Eye Protection, not required

Must see in Missouri

- St. Louis, "Gateway to the West"
  - 630-foot-high Gateway Arch, downtown riverfront
  - Anheuser-Busch Brewery, I-55 at Arsenal St.
  - Museum of Transportation, 3015 Barrett Station Road

- Stanton — Meramec Caverns

- St. James
  - Rosati Winery, the oldest active winery along 66, 22050 State Route KK
  - St. James Winery, 540 Sydney Street

- Rolla — Memoryville USA, a lavish classic car museum and antique stop

- Springfield
  - Bass Pro Shop
  - Begin in Springfield to drive a long segment of original Route 66 without interstate interruptions — all the way to Oklahoma City. The drive includes that original nine foot-wide Route 66 ribbon in two segments between Miami and Afton in Oklahoma.

Where to buy stuff

- Route 66 Motors and General Store, 12661 Old Hwy. 66, east of Rolla

- Wrink's Food Market, City Route 66 East, Lebanon (across from the Munger Moss Motel)

The Show Me State

Beacons in the dark

- *CUBA* — Wagon Wheel Motel, 901 East Washington
- *ROLLA* — Zeno's Motel, Route 66, 1621 Martin Spring Dr.
- *LEBANON* — Munger Moss Motel, Route 66, 236 Seminole
- *SPRINGFIELD* — Best Western Rail Haven, 203 S. Glenstone Ave.

Favorite hangouts for food and drink

- *ST. LOUIS*
  - TED DREWES FROZEN CUSTARD, 6726 Chippewa
  - BLUEBERRY HILLS CAFE, 6504 Delmar Ave. (not on 66 but worth a trip). Among many other awards, voted the "Best Hamburgers," "Best Restroom Graffiti," and "Best Jukebox in America."
  - JAKE'S STEAKS, at Laclede's Landing, 707 Clamorgan

- *KIRKWOOD* — MASSA'S, 210 N. Kirkwood

- *PACIFIC*
  - RED CEDAR INN, 1047 East Osage
  - ROUTE 66 DINER, 409 East Osage

- *VILLA RIDGE* — TRI-COUNTY TRUCK STOP, I-44 & Highway 100, Exit 251

- *SULLIVAN* — HOMER'S HICKORY-SMOKED BBQ, 693 Fisher (Locals say this is the best barbecue in the area.)

Map labels: Kansas City, St. Louis, Jefferson City, Joplin, MISSOURI, 66

Wagon Wheel Motel, Cuba

- CUBA
  - THE FEED LOT, east of Cuba at Exit 209 from I-44
  - MISSOURI HICKORY BAR-B-Q, 913 East Washington

- ST. JAMES — DOUGLAS COMPANY, 601 Hwy. B

- ROLLA
  - BRUNO'S, 2001 Forum Drive
  - JOHNNY'S SMOKE STAK, 201 Highway 72W (Good barbecue!)
  - A SLICE OF PIE, Route 66 and US 63

- DEVIL'S ELBOW — ELBOW INN BAR AND BBQ PIT (another great biker stop), at the bridge on the 1926 alignment

- LEBANON — STONEGATE STATION, 1475 S. Jefferson

- MARSHFIELD — TINY'S SMOKEHOUSE, 77 State Hwy W.

- SPRINGFIELD
  - LAMBERT'S CAFE "Home of the Throwed Rolls", 7 miles south on Hwy. 65

  - HEMINGWAY'S BLUE WATER CAFE, US 60 and Sunshine Street in Bass Pro Shop
  - STEAK'N SHAKE, 4 locations
  - LAST GREAT AMERICAN DINER, 507 Carney

- CARTHAGE
  - CARTHAGE DELI AND ICE CREAM, 301 S. Main (northwest corner of town square)
  - C.D.'S PANCAKE HUT, 301 S. Garrison

- WEBB CITY — BRADBURY BISHOP DELI AND ROUTE 66 DINER, in an 1887 building at 201 N. Main

- JOPLIN
  - BENITO'S MEXICAN RESTAURANT, for good Mexican food, 2525 Range Line Road
  - FRED AND RED'S, South Main

Devils' Elbow

Biker Weddings

— MICHAEL WALLIS

It has been said that if you encounter Michael Wallis out on Route 66, that I can marry you and your chosen. According to road lore I am like a ship's captain and may perform such nuptials. My sole caveat is that the marriage is only valid for 48 hours — a pleasant weekender.

To date, only one couple has taken me up on this standing offer. They were bikers — a couple from Boston riding Route 66. I performed the ceremony on a hotel patio in Albuquerque with scores of fellow bikers as witnesses. The happy pair rode off in the sunset on their decorated motorcycle. All of us cheered and had a grand ol' time. That was some years back. The couple no longer rides together, but their Route 66 nuptials were a highlight moment on the Mother Road that year.

Bikers who want to get legally hitched on the Main Street of America simply need to check on local wedding rules and regs, hunt up a preacher or justice of the peace, or go to the Internet for a biker-wedding specialist. There are plenty of options for locations. Really anyplace that appeals to the couple will work just fine. Here are some places to consider for your Mother Road biker wedding as suggested by both bikers and Route 66 aficionados. Unless otherwise noted, receptions may be staged at the wedding site.

- ILLINOIS
  - Grant Park, Chicago, with reception at Lou Mitchells
  - Our Lady of the Highways statue, west of Raymond, with reception at the Ariston Cafe, Litchfield
  - Church at Funk's Grove
  - The Cozy Dog, Springfield

- Missouri
  - Bridge at Devil's Elbow, with reception at Elbow Inn and honeymoon at Munger Moss Motel, Lebanon
  - Chain of Rocks Bridge, St. Louis, with on-site reception catered by Ted Drewes Frozen Custard
  - Meramec Caverns, Stanton

- KANSAS
  - Rainbow Bridge, near Baxter Springs, with reception at Cafe on the Route, Baxter Springs

- OKLAHOMA
  - Round Barn, Arcadia, with reception at nearby Hillbillies Cafe
  - Hillbillies Cafe Chapel, with reception at nearby Round Barn
  - The Sandhills Curiosity Shop, Erick, with music provided by Harley and Annabelle, "The Mediocre Music Makers"

- *TEXAS*
  - Cadillac Ranch, west of Amarillo, with reception at the Big Texan Steak Ranch, Amarillo
  - Mid-point Cafe, Adrian, ceremony outside at sign and reception in the cafe
  - Giant Cross, Groom

- *NEW MEXICO*
  - Summit of La Bajada, west of Santa Fe (warning: difficult to reach on a bike; maybe the base of the hill is better)
  - On the old road at Glenrio, with honeymoon at the Blue Swallow Motel, Tucumcari
  - Old Town Plaza, Albuquerque

- *ARIZONA*
  - Along the winding road leading to Oatman
  - Beale Hotel (site of the Clark Gable-Carol Lombard wedding), Kingman, with reception at the Oatman Hotel
  - On the Corner in Winslow, with reception and honeymoon at La Posada, Winslow

- *CALIFORNIA*
  - Iron Hog Saloon, a biker favorite, Oro Grande
  - Old townsite of Bagdad, with reception at the Bagdad Cafe, Newberry Springs
  - Santa Monica Pier, Santa Monica

Biker Road Wisdom

*Gleaned from a variety of sources
and old scooter tramps*

Life begins on the off-ramp.

The best view of a thunderstorm is in the rearview mirror.

Bugs are tastiest at midnight.

Hot coffee and fresh pie are as important as gasoline.

When you are on a bike you are invisible.

Reheat cold burgers or burritos by strapping them to an exhaust pipe and riding 20 miles.

If you haven't ridden in rain, you've never ridden.

Keep the rubber side down and the shiny side up.

Everything is better in the wind.

Never spit when you're riding lead.

Never argue with an 18-wheeler.

There are only two kinds of bikers — those who have gone down and those who will be going down.

Good Mother Road coffee should be interchangeable with 50 weight motor oil.

Bikes parked out front of a Route 66 cafe mean good eats inside.

If you insist on riding like there's no tomorrow, there won't be.

There are drunken bikers and there are old bikers but there are no old drunken bikers.

Only open road bikers understand why dogs stick their heads out of car windows.

Do not be afraid of slowing down.

Recipes from Missouri

— MARIAN CLARK

In St. Louis, the Gateway Arch presides over the downtown waterfront. This is a dynamic city filled with opportunity: sporting events, theme parks, ethnic restaurants, river life, history, parks, and much more. The city hosted the 1904 Louisiana Purchase Centennial Exposition and World's Fair where ice cream cones and hot dogs were introduced. Iced tea and Dr. Pepper gained popularity at this great exposition as well. Busch Beer, Vess Beverages, and Ted Drewes Frozen Custard characterize St. Louis food and drink today.

At Doc's Harley-Davidson, I-44 in Kirkwood, you'll feel the Harley aura, find a warm welcome, and learn all

you want to know about biker-friendly routes through the Ozarks. Owner Pat Bush says customer relations make or break a business, so at Doc's customers are always welcomed and questions are answered.

Doc's Harley-Davidson, Kirkwood

Pat is no novice to the business. Her father started Doc's in 1955 and she has been riding since she was fifteen. Under her leadership, the business now employees forty-seven and has grown to number nine in the nation in sales. Pat is also a hands-on businesswoman. She dresses in Harley-Davidson clothes every day and rides her own Harley to work. Behind her desk is a sign: "No Cry Babies!"

Bush says women are the newest Harley market. "They're a well-balanced motorcycle, making them easier for women to ride," she said. She also offers a piece of advice to anyone interested in trying a bike, or any other new venture: "Anybody can do anything they put their mind to whether they are male or female."

When bikers gather for grub around this bustling agency, these double-stuffed potatoes are always popular.

Doc's Double-Stuffed Potatoes

4 large baking potatoes
2 tablespoons butter or margarine
½ cup chopped onion
¾ cup shredded cheeses — cheddar, provolone, or
    Swiss
¼ cup sour cream
2 teaspoons fresh chives
Salt and pepper to taste

Scrub potatoes; pat dry. Pierce each potato several times with a fork. Microwave on high for about 10 minutes; rotate potatoes. Microwave until tender, about 3 minutes longer.

Preheat oven to 350 degrees. Melt margarine or butter in skillet and add onion. Cook until onion is translucent, about 5 minutes.

Slice off potato tops. Scoop out potatoes, keeping shells intact; place pulp in medium bowl. Mash potatoes, add onion, ½ cup of the cheese, sour cream, chives, and salt and pepper. Blend thoroughly and spoon potato mixture back into shells, dividing evenly. Sprinkle potatoes with remaining cheese. Place on a baking sheet and put in oven for 10 minutes or until potatoes are heated through. Add bacon pieces or broccoli bits for a delicious alternative. This recipe can be enlarged easily. 4 servings.

BIKERS FEEL RIGHT AT HOME AT THE RED CEDAR INN, a sturdy building built as a cafe in 1934. Ginger Gallagher, granddaughter of the original owner, delights in serving her customers the good food they have grown to expect. There's also a friendly bar — but don't think you've imbibed too much when you see the tree that helps support the ceiling in the dining room.

Red Cedar Inn Restaurant, Pacific

Bread Pudding

RED CEDAR INN

1 box raised donuts (12 donuts)
1 cup sugar*
1 quart milk
1 teaspoon nutmeg
1 teaspoon cinnamon
6 eggs, beaten
½ cup raisins (optional)

Crumble donuts in a 2-quart baking dish. Combine sugar, milk, nutmeg, and cinnamon and stir to dissolve sugar. Add eggs and beat until mixture is well blended and smooth. Sprinkle raisins over donuts then pour egg mixture over both. Place in a preheated 350 degree oven and bake for 1 hour. Serve while warm or allow to cool, if desired.

*Adjust sugar to taste. 10-12 servings.

MISSOURI OFFERS VINTAGE **66** with plenty of sweeping curves and breathtaking views. The state has its own magic with plenty of byways waiting to be discovered. The Meramec Caverns area around Stanton offers great biker roads. Take it easy here, explore, tour the cave, then feast on a picnic in one of the nearby parks and unwind for awhile before venturing forth again. This potato salad makes for satisfying picnic fare.

Creamy New Potato Salad

1¼ pounds small red potatoes
1 cup plain low-fat yogurt
2 tablespoons Dijon mustard
2 tablespoons finely chopped fresh tarragon
½ small red pepper cut in matchstick strips
⅓ cup diced green onion
⅓ cup diagonally sliced celery
Salt and pepper to taste

Cook potatoes whole in boiling salted water until tender, about 25 minutes. Drain and cool. Cut potatoes into bite sized pieces.

Stir yogurt, mustard, and tarragon in large bowl until blended. Add potatoes, red pepper, onion, and

celery. Toss to blend. Season with salt and pepper to taste, cover, and chill before serving.
5-6 servings.

Meramec Caverns, Stanton

LOCATED IN THE LUXURIANT OZARK HERITAGE REGION in Missouri, both the Rosati Winery and the St. James Winery offer outstanding stops. These are great places for mailing gifts to jealous friends back home.

Sangria
ST. JAMES WINERY

1 bottle (750 ml) St. James Country Red Wine (or another good red wine)
1 orange, thinly sliced
1 lemon, thinly sliced
½ cup sugar
1 bottle (28 ounces) club soda

Combine the wine, orange, lemon, and sugar. Let sit one hour at room temperature. When ready to serve, add the club soda and serve over crushed ice. 6 eight-ounce servings.

WHEN YOU'RE BACK HOME AGAIN and still crave a taste of the Ozarks, here are a couple of dishes good enough to make you close your eyes and remember the pure adventure and freedom of Missouri. Great dishes don't have to have long, complicated names. This salad came straight from a Rolla garden and proves again that simple, wholesome dishes are hard to beat.

Wilted Greens with Country Ham

¼ cup olive oil
1 cup thinly sliced red onion
½ cup broken pecans
½ cup slivered country ham
2 tablespoons balsamic vinegar
2 tablespoons maple syrup

8 cups mixed fresh garden greens - kale, spinach,
    purple lettuce, arugula, cleaned and dry
Salt and pepper to taste

Heat olive oil in a large skillet. Add onions and saute, stirring constantly for about 5 minutes. Add nuts and continue cooking another two minutes. Stir in ham, continue cooking until ham is warm. Add vinegar and maple syrup. Stir and remove from heat.

Tear greens into a large bowl. Pour hot dressing over greens. Toss to wilt slightly. Sprinkle with salt and pepper to taste and serve immediately with crusty French bread. 8-10 servings.

Southern Baked Grits and Cheese

1½ cups grits
6 cups water
8 tablespoons butter or margarine
1 pound Velveeta cheese, cut into small chunks
1 teaspoon seasoned salt
3 eggs, well beaten
¼ teaspoon Tabasco sauce

Bring water to boil and add grits. Cook for 10 minutes or until thickened. Remove from heat and add 4 tablespoons of the butter or margarine, cheese, and salt. Stir until cheese is melted. Slowly add beaten eggs and Tabasco sauce. Melt remaining butter in a 9X12-inch baking dish. Pour grits mixture into the dish. Bake in a preheated 325 degree oven for 1 hour or until firm. 10 servings.

LEBANON'S MUNGER MOSS MOTEL IS A HIGHLIGHT for many bikers and biker tours. Trond Moberg calls the place "fantastic" and says he and his fellow Norwegian bikers always find a warm welcome from Bob and Ramona Lehman.

Munger Moss Motel, Lebanon

The name *Munger Moss* has a long history on Route 66. In 1947 Jesse and Pete Hudson bought the Chicken Shanty Cafe and some adjoining land in Lebanon. They changed the Chicken Shanty name to Munger Moss and built a motel next door. The cafe is gone now but Bob and Ramona continue to operate the motel that is one of the few mom-and-pop places along Route 66 with enough capacity to handle a large group of bikers.

Ramona shares this favorite salad recipe.

Ramona Lehman's Vegetable Salad

1 small head cauliflower, chopped
Equal amount of broccoli, chopped
1 bunch green onions, chopped
1 cup light salad dressing
⅓ cup sugar
2 tablespoons vinegar

Combine vegetables. Mix dressing ingredients and pour over vegetables. Toss, chill, and serve. 8-10 servings.

DOWN THE ROAD IN MARSHFIELD, home to Edwin Hubbell of space telescope fame, feast on barbecue at Tiny's Smokehouse. Then, when you're home again, feast on these pancakes often prepared at Marshfield's Dickey House while you reminisce about the trip.

Pumpkin Pancakes with Apple Cider Syrup
THE DICKEY HOUSE

1½ cups flour
1 teaspoon baking powder
¼ teaspoon baking soda
1½ teaspoons pumpkin pie spice
¼ teaspoon salt
1 egg
¼ cup canned pumpkin
1½ cups milk
3 tablespoons cooking oil

In a medium bowl, stir together the flour, baking powder, soda, salt, and pumpkin spice. In another bowl beat the egg, pumpkin, milk, and oil. Add milk mixture to the flour mixture and stir until just blended, but still lumpy. Pour about ¼ cup of batter for each pancake onto a hot griddle or heavy skillet. Cook over medium heat until browned, turning once to cook both sides. About 10 pancakes.

Apple Cider Syrup

½ cup sugar
4 teaspoons cornstarch
½ teaspoon cinnamon
1 cup apple cider or apple juice
1 tablespoon lemon juice
2 tablespoons butter or margarine

In a small saucepan stir together the sugar, cornstarch, and cinnamon. Add the apple cider and lemon juice. Cook for 2 minutes over medium heat until mixture is thickened and bubbly. Cook an additional 2 minutes. Remove from heat and stir in the butter or margarine. Serve while warm over pancakes. 1⅓ cups.

St. Louis

Lambert's Cafe

Lambert's Cafe, Home of the Throwed Rolls, was first opened in Sikeston, Missouri, in 1942 by Agnes and Earl Lambert. Their Springfield location has been open since March of 1994. Famous for good food and plenty of it, the owners began throwing rolls to their guests in 1976 and the tradition has continued. You'll never leave hungry here or go out without a few laughs. A real Ozark welcome awaits. Lambert's is 7 miles south of Springfield on Highway 65.

CASHEW CHICKEN IS A COMMUNITY TRADITION in Springfield. It was first prepared at several outstanding Chinese restaurants in the area and is now considered a community classic and a cherished symbol of the city. There are a number of similar versions. This one comes from Tommy and Glenda Pike and their daughter, Tonya. Tommy is the current president of the Missouri Route 66 Association.

Springfield Cashew Chicken

2 large boneless chicken breast halves, cut into about 10 bite sized chunks

Marinade:
3 tablespoons sherry (or water)
½ teaspoon Accent Seasoning
1 teaspoon sugar
1 tablespoon oyster sauce
Dash of ginger
Dash of garlic powder
1 teaspoon salt
½ teaspoon pepper

Combine marinade ingredients and pour over chicken pieces. Allow to stand in refrigerator several hours but overnight is preferable. If chicken breasts are extra large, double the marinade recipe. When ready to cook, drain the chicken well and dispose of marinade.

To Fry:
¼ cup milk
¼ cup water
4 tablespoons cornstarch, divided
2 large eggs, beaten
Peanut oil for frying

Combine the milk, water, and 1 tablespoon of the cornstarch. Blend until smooth. Gradually stir in eggs and continue beating until mixture is smooth. Dip chicken in remaining cornstarch, then in egg mixture. Deep fry the chicken in hot oil (about 375 degrees) until done. Drain and keep warm.

Sauce:
1 chicken bouillon cube
1 cup water
1½ tablespoon cornstarch
1 teaspoon sugar
½ teaspoon Accent Seasoning
1 tablespoon oyster sauce
¼ teaspoon ginger
Dash of garlic powder
¼ teaspoon salt
¼ cup water

Heat bouillon cube in hot water to dissolve, then allow to cool slightly. While cooling, mix together the remaining ingredients. Add mixture to the cooled bouillon and heat until mixture is thick and clear.

To serve:
Rice
⅓ cup cashew nuts
¼ cup chopped onions
Soy sauce

Cook rice according to package directions, preparing enough for 3-4 cups of cooked rice. Arrange rice on a platter and top with chicken. Pour the sauce over the chicken and top with cashew nuts. Sprinkle with chopped green onions. Serve soy sauce on the side. Serve while warm. 2 servings.

LEAVE SPRINGFIELD ON ROUTE 66 and drive the original alignment all the way to Oklahoma City, one of the longest undisturbed segments along the road.

In Halltown, stop to admire Whitehall Mercantile, operated by Jerry and Thelma White, in the oldest building still standing. The town was once the busiest antique center along Route 66. Several shops still remain open along here. Matthias Guenther, a Harley rider from Germany, found an antique dealer advertising free coffee and discovered a bonus of friendly conversation and several pieces of old German music. "And the coffee was really free," he remembers.

Christina Hey and Matthias Guenther at a Halltown antique shop

Thelma White's Sour Cream Raisin Pie

1⅓ cups sugar
1½ tablespoons flour
⅔ teaspoon nutmeg
⅔ teaspoon cinnamon
Pinch of salt
3 eggs, lightly beaten
2 cups sour cream
2 cups raisins

Combine dry ingredients and add lightly beaten eggs. Stir in sour cream and raisins. Pour mixture into two unbaked pie shells. Bake in preheated 425 degree oven for 20 minutes then reduce heat to 375 and continue baking for another 30 minutes. Two 9-inch pies.

Ever Dream of Ghosts?

Between Halltown and Carthage, there's plenty of opportunity to find a few as you ramble past a dozen or so long-gone remains of 66 communities with fanciful names like Paris Springs, Heatonville, Albatross, Phelps, Rescue, Plew, Avilla, and Maxville. Every state along 66 has its share of ghost towns, but the skeletons along here come less than five miles apart and remind bikers what it must have been like when a constant stream of folks helped support the gas stations, greasy spoons, and imaginings of countless dreamers. When did these folks move on, where did they go, and who did they leave behind around these abandoned rock walls?

JUST BEFORE YOU ENTER CARTHAGE, VEER NORTH to Lowell Davis's *Red Oak II*. Lowell is retired now, so his forty-acre farm and amazing recreated village of Red Oak II has new caretakers. The complex is often open. Take a drive through this labyrinth of Lowell's genius, hand-crafted from his fertile imagination. There are over a dozen restored buildings, including a Phillips 66 Station, a feed and seed store, Grandpa Weber's Blacksmith, the Salem County church, even a recreation of the original home of Belle Starr's family. Take a look at Sparrowville, his airplane made from pipe, and his huge faucet sculpture. This is a place you are guaranteed to remember!

Here is a caramel corn recipe very similar to the one passed down by Lowell's mom, Nell Davis.

Red Oak II Caramel Corn

7 quarts popped corn
2 cups brown sugar
2 sticks margarine
½ cup white corn syrup
½ teaspoon salt
½ teaspoon vanilla
½ teaspoon soda

Place popped corn in a large oven-proof container. Combine brown sugar, margarine, corn syrup, and salt in sauce pan. Boil five minutes. Stir in vanilla and soda. Pour immediately over the popped corn. Stir and place in a 250 degree oven for one hour, stirring every 15 minutes. Add peanuts, if desired. Cool and enjoy.

IN NEARBY JOPLIN, FRED AND RED'S on South Main has served up some of the best chili and spaghetti in the area for years. Lea Ona Essley, from nearby Baxter Springs shared this spaghetti topping that is very close to the original recipe at Fred and Red's. She says the secret ingredient is the addition of tamales to the sauce which adds both body and flavor.

Fred and Red's Chili

1 large (28-ounce) can tamales, mashed
1 pound cooked hamburger
½ cup chopped onion
Water to make a thick sauce
1 (8-ounce) can tomato sauce
1 (1-ounce package) Williams Chili Seasoning Mix
1 pound brick chili

Mash the tamales. Cook the hamburger and drain; add onion and mashed tamales, then enough water to make a sauce. Add tomato sauce, chili seasoning, and brick chili and heat to boiling. Reduce heat and simmer for 10 minutes. Note: Serve this chili plain or as a sauce over pasta. Approximately 9 cups.

YOU'LL FIND NO BARRIERS TO FREEDOM along this stretch of the road but you may want to slow down around the historic State Line Bar before heading toward that short but rich slice of Route 66 in Kansas. ∎

The Chain of Rocks Bridge near St. Louis

Lost In America

— MICHAEL WALLIS

Visitors from abroad are one of the fastest growing categories of Route 66 travelers. Each year more and more people eager to traverse the Mother Road come to America from Japan, New Zealand, Australia, Canada, Brazil, France, the United Kingdom, Norway, Belgium, and Germany.

They come in tour groups and pack into big comfortable buses or they rent cars and take to the old road. Still others want to do the trip right — on the back of a motorcycle. They either rent bikes in Chicago or L.A., or else ship their own scooters to one of the old road's terminal cities for their journey of a lifetime.

Nina and Camillo Pinto, riders from Portugal, on Route 66, St. Louis

It seems many of the foreign visitors I encounter on Route 66 come from Germany which makes sense since Germans are among the world's most frequent travelers. I remember a quartet of young German professionals I met on the old road. They were all on their Harleys shipped from Germany and they were making the westward journey on Route 66 from Chicago to Santa Monica. We swapped road yarns and one of them told me why he made the long trip.

"We are seeing the best of America," Uwe Langner, the unofficial group leader, told me. "This is what we came for — the wind, the sand, the mountains, the great distances. And, then the people — we can now see that the people on Route 66 are a big family. They are so real."

For Uwe, a policeman back in Germany, the cycle odyssey was a dream come true. Since he first saw the motion picture, "Easy Rider," he has longed to come to the United States and traverse Route 66. On his well-worn helmet was an America flag he painted himself almost thirty years past. "Riding Route 66 is special," he said with emotion in his voice, "but riding this road on my Harley is extra special."

Of course, I had to agree.

And then I considered a pair of German bikers I met during a Harley cruise of Route 66 some years past. They, too, were respectable middle age professionals — classic "Rich Urban Bikers" (RUBS), only German.

Up state in Illinois I told them how to negotiate the various alignments of Route 66 making its way through St. Louis. I gave them some directions and advice but despite this they ended up hopelessly lost in city traffic and well off the route. To add to their misery it started raining and nightfall was approaching.

Unsure of just what to do, they pulled up to an intersection stop light and one of the bikers tapped on the driver's window of a black limousine stopped in the next lane. The driver, apparently frightened of a biker decked out in leather and goggles, did not respond.

Then the back window went down and the bikers saw a distinguished gentleman dressed in a tuxedo and next to him his lovely lady also dressed to the nines. The man was smiling and he asked the bikers if they were riding Harleys. They said they were and when the man heard their strong accents he asked if they were from Germany. They said yes and they told him they were lost and were just trying to find shelter for the night. The man told them to follow his limo. They did as they were told.

The bikers dutifully tagged along as the limo made its way through evening traffic. It finally pulled into the circular drive at the elegant Ritz-Carlton Hotel and stopped beneath the canopy at the main entrance. The Germans were alarmed. They knew their travel budget did not allow for such extravagant lodging and besides they were just a couple of dirty, wet, and dog-tired bikers who did not fit the hotel's clientele profile.

Before the Germans could take their leave, the gentleman was out of the limo with his wife. He gave the driver some instructions and then told the bikers they would be his guests for the evening. He would not listen to their polite protests and, with the wet riders in tow, the foursome entered the hotel. They proceeded to a magnificent ballroom filled with people in formal clothes seated at tables decked out in fine linen and covered with fancy china and silver.

The gentleman led his party to a main table and told a hovering waiter to make room for his unexpected guests. He had another waiter take them to the men's room to freshen up and when they returned they were seated next to the man and his wife.

It seems this gentleman was the guest of honor at his gala retirement party. He also was a motorcycle fan and had always wanted to take one out on the open road. That was his dream.

When the Germans turned down offers of champagne their host asked what they desired and then had frosty glasses of beer brought to the table. There were toasts all around and by the end of the evening the bikers were the talk of the party, especially among the tittering ladies. Following dinner the Germans were told that a suite awaited them, again compliments of the gentleman.

A day or so later, when I bumped into the Germans out on Route 66 as it makes its way through the Ozarks, they eagerly told me of their adventure. No matter what waited for them down the road, they already knew that Missouri was their favorite state on Route 66.

I have always thought that it is good to get lost when traveling the old road. It can be worrisome but it can also lead to unexpected pleasures. Cruising Route 66 should be a scavenger hunt. Just remember that the treasure the road has to offer is not always gold or silver. Sometimes it is better.* ■

---

* It is unknown if the mysterious gentleman host ever got his Harley.

Building of 66

— MICHAEL WALLIS

Route 66 was not built in a day. It took years of planning, cajoling, and heated debate to create the highway that would span two-thirds of the continent through eight states, several major cities, and three time zones.

Americans were anxious to get better roads. That desire developed into a full-fledged movement as the Twenties roared and automobiles became affordable thanks to mass production. Everyday folks took to existing roads in their new cars. As they explored further from home, the need for a highway system to link the country became apparent.

Private road clubs and associations of highway officials formed. Legislation was passed calling for road construction. In Oklahoma, Cyrus Stevens Avery and his cohorts pushed for a federal highway to connect Chicago and Santa Monica. Shortly after the highway was christened in 1926, Cy Avery became forever known as "The Father of Route 66."

At first only 800 miles of the route was paved. It took until 1937 to pave the rest. But the inconvenience of patchwork road and interruptions of thick mud didn't stop motorists and motorcyclists from taking to the road in numbers so great that Route 66 soon became known as the Main Street of America. ■

Kansas

Fast facts from Kansas

- Cross the state on Route 66 in only 13.2 miles.
- The first state to pave all of Route 66.
- Baxter Springs residents boast their city was the "first cowtown in Kansas."
- A half-marathon run from Oklahoma to Missouri is often on the calendar when fall weather arrives.

Kansas Biker Road Rules

- Safety Helmet, required by law under age of 18
- Eye Protection, required by law unless equipped with windscreen

Must see in Kansas

- GALENA — Katy Depot and Galena Mining and Historical Museum
- WEST MINERAL — Drive north on Highway 69 to see the second largest electrical shovel in the world — Big Brutus — sixteen stories high and 5,500 tons.
- RIVERTON — Concrete truss "Rainbow" bridge — Built in the 20s between Riverton and Baxter Springs
- BAXTER SPRINGS — Heritage Center & Historical Museum

Rainbow Curve Bridge, Baxter Springs

Favorite hangouts for food and drink

- GALENA

UP IN SMOKE — new to the road but destined to become a favorite stop, Roger Wormington has opened a barbecue pit in an old gas station/barber shop at 418 S. Main. An old train engine sits next to the smoker and the aroma of tasty meat wafts through the neighborhood.

- Riverton

EISLER BROTHERS OLD RIVERTON STORE, built in 1925 and still a real working general store, it is operated by Scott Nelson, president of the Kansas Historic Route 66 Association. Some of the best sandwiches on the road can be found here — made fresh at the old-fashioned deli and served with cold soda.

The Sunflower State

Topeka ★

KANSAS

Baxter Springs 66

- Baxter Springs
  - CAFE ON THE ROUTE AND LITTLE BRICK INN (upstairs), 1101 Military Ave. "The restaurant in the bank that was robbed by Jesse James." Formerly was Bill Murphey's Restaurant, famous for pies since 1941.
  - MURPHEY'S RESTAURANT
    1046 Military Ave.
    Now located in the old Baxter National Bank building diagonally across the street from 1101 Military.

Eisler Brothers Old Riverton Store, Riverton

Outlaw Bikers

—MICHAEL WALLIS

When you are out on Route 66 nothing is predictable. That is why so many bikers like traveling the old road. There is a sense of excitement and motion and the possibility for pure adventure around every curve and bend.

Every facet of humanity can be found on Route 66 — bluebloods and rednecks, the godless and Jesus freaks, filthy rich and dirt poor, card-carrying members of the NRA as well as the ACLU. There have been both a Ralph Lauren and a K-Mart line of Route 66 clothing. This diversity is one of the many reasons Harley riders fit right in on America's Main Street.

Today's bikers — just like the highway they love — cross all demographic lines. When you attend a rally or participate in an organized tour, your fellow bikers may include dentists, lawyers, rabbis, and poets, or plumbers, mechanics, steelworkers, and truckers. It doesn't matter a wit.

I have journeyed on Route 66 with federal judges and ex-cons at the same time and never even knew it until long after our ride had ended. That is because we seldom discuss a man or woman's profession or their net worth. All we are interested in is our ride. We care about that moment out on a stretch of highway where we can be who we want to be and nobody gives a damn.

Many of the old guard bikers — especially the guys carrying chain wallets who sported tattoos long before housewives and college kids started getting them —

Galena

don't much care for "Rich Urban Bikers," or RUBs. I keep friends in each of the camps and enjoy the company of both on Route 66 trips.

Some years ago, I recall riding with some RUBs and also a few old guards along the 13.2 miles of vintage Mother Road that just nips the southeastern corner of Kansas.

As we scooted down the road making cold drink and beef jerky stops in the towns of Galena and then Riverton, I thought about how this particular stretch of Route 66 had served as a good bootlegger road during the dry times when the highway was brand new. I recalled colorful tales about mysterious automobiles sneaking out of Joplin to the east; their trunks loaded with illicit hootch to quench the thirst of folks in Kansas and Oklahoma.

Route 66 — a truly democratic highway — boasts a rich outlaw legacy. Stories of felons and their ilk are forever entwined in the history of the highway through all eight states. Long before Route 66 was ever thought about, the trails and paths that eventually became the highway were frequented by all sorts of mounted bandits and killers including Billy the Kid, Belle Starr, the James Gang, Henry Starr, and the Daltons.

Then after Route 66 was officially created in 1926, a new breed of desperado took to the road. The list includes Al Capone and his gangster buddies in Chicago and Cicero and an array of other Depression-era criminals such as "Charles "Pretty Boy" Floyd, Bonnie Parker and Clyde Barrow, George "Machine Gun" Kelly, and Ma Barker and her brood of wicked sons.

With all that in mind, when my diverse gang of bikers pulled in for gas on the edge of Riverton, I pulled out

some of my better outlaw memories. I told them about the 1863 Baxter Springs Massacre when the notorious Confederate guerrilla William Quantrill attacked and killed a small force of Union soldiers. I also talked of other infamous villains who had left their marks right where we headed — Baxter Springs, still proudly called "The First Cow Town in Kansas." That got everybody's attention.

Baxter Springs

We fired up the bikes and rolled out onto the road. Immediately I sensed my fellow riders' excitement. Only a short time later, as we approached Baxter Springs, my imagination got the best of me. I pretended that we were no longer modern-day bikers but instead we had become steel-jawed brigands. Our bikes changed into cow ponies, our helmets were transformed into black hats, and our leather jackets turned into long linen dusters like the old-time outlaws often wore. The voice of Tex Ritter singing "High Noon" echoed in my head.

Baxter Springs

Rolling slowly into downtown Baxter Springs we scanned the sidewalks and shop windows for any high sheriffs or tin star deputies. We parked our bikes in front of a two-story brick edifice with striped awnings shading the windows and a brick wall adorned with a mural and the words Cafe on the Route. Ironically it was high noon but even "outlaws" have to eat, and besides, there was no sign of Gary Cooper.

Once inside and comfortably seated at a long table, I continued to regale my gang with more stories while we waited for our meals to be served. I spoke of elderly citizens who remembered the October afternoon in 1933 when Wilbur Underhill — the notorious "Tri-State Terror" — robbed the American Bank in Baxter Springs. The old timers also recollected that "Pretty Boy" Floyd gassed up regularly at Spencer's Shell Station when he came this way. And they had bitter memories of Bonnie

and Clyde in 1933 when they robbed the Baxter Springs General Store twice in one month. Then the following year the crazed couple, on a murderous rampage, shot and killed a policeman just down the highway in nearby Commerce, Oklahoma.

I paused for a time when our food came steaming from the kitchen on big trays — mostly cowboy steaks smothered in fried tobacco onions, roast beef hash, and piles of corn muffins. And for me — a full rack of barbecued pork spareribs drenched with strawberry sauce and festooned with fresh strawberries the size of a baby's fist.

For dessert, I finished my outlaw lecture by pointing out that just across the street from where we sat gorged to the gills was Murphey's Restaurant. Renowned for superb pies, Murphey's is in a building that once housed the National Bank of Baxter Springs. There in 1914 the legendary Henry Starr, whose criminal career spanned more than 32 years, made a sizable and unauthorized cash withdrawal.

Before the other bikers could vacate the cafe to check out Murphey's, I stopped them in their tracks. I had saved the best for last. Over toothpicks and coffee, I explained that for many years Murphey's was located in the building where we had just dined, now occupied by the Cafe on the Route and an upstairs bed and breakfast. But way back in 1870 when it was erected, the building was known as the Crowell Bank, the first banking establishment in town.

Murphey's Restaurant, in the old National Bank of Baxter Springs building

Michael Wallis tackles lunch fit for an outlaw, Baxter Springs

In 1876, Jesse James and Cole Younger — two of the best-known outlaws in America — rode into Baxter Springs, tied their horses to a corncrib, and strolled into the bank. They pulled their guns and fled with $2,900. The outlaws rode out of town on what is now Route 66, disarmed a pursuing posse without firing a single shot, and made good their escape to Indian Territory, now called Oklahoma.

I proposed we do the same — head for old Indian Territory — only without the robbery part. We settled up our food bill and within 10 minutes we were out of Kansas and in the Sooner State.

All the rest of the day we made our way to Tulsa, digesting that tasty lunch along with those rich stories from long ago. ■

Get Your Kicks

— MICHAEL WALLIS

Many people say Route 66 is the most famous highway in the United States. I agree. Others claim it may be the best known highway in the world. I won't argue with them either. From Chicago to Santa Monica the Route 66 signs are returning to help show the way as we make the best kind of neon journey along this passageway of memory that helped shape our country's history and culture.

That is what a Route 66 odyssey is all about. Especially for bikers. It is the most special trip you may ever take — down America's Main Street that is sure to rekindle memories and spark your curiosity.

Remember this always — life truly does begin on the off-ramp. By merely daring to exit the interstate highway, you can climb onto Route 66 and discover storytellers, secret corners, and hidden towns. Just cruise the open road to the tune of your humming motor, open your eyes to the possibilities and maybe, just maybe, discover something of yourself.

Recipes from Kansas (and Norway)

— MARIAN CLARK

Trond Moberg's caravan of Norwegian bikers cruise Route 66 three to four times every year. The group averages thirty bikes and about fifty bikers. Trond says one of his group's favorite stops is at Eisler Brothers Old Riverton Store where they are always welcome. He swears Scott Nelson makes the best sandwiches on Route 66. Scott modestly says the sandwiches are good because they are always made individually from fresh ingredients and "like we would make them to eat ourselves." It also helps when Scott wears his Norwegian T-shirt as he helps to create the masterpieces behind the old-fashioned meat counter. During a recent stop by the Norwegian group, Scott invited a friend and his Norwegian-born father to the feast. It was hard to tell who had the best time as they shared experiences in their own language with gusto.

Trond shared these recipes that he often uses when bikers meet in Norway to plan their Route 66 trips.

Cold Poached Salmon

6 salmon cutlets, approximately 1½ inches thick
Poach in 2 quarts of water with:
1 lemon, sliced
10-12 whole peppercorns
1 bay leaf
1 sprig of fresh dill
1¼ teaspoons salt

Poach the salmon for approximately 15 minutes. Remove from heat and allow the salmon to cool in the water. Serve at room temperature with boiled potatoes, sour cream, and cucumber salad. 6 servings

Cucumber Salad

1 cucumber, thinly sliced
¼ cup apple cider vinegar
6 tablespoons white sugar
Salt and pepper to taste

Combine and serve at room temperature.

Lamb and Cabbage Stew

2 pounds lamb shoulder, cut into serving pieces
2 pounds white cabbage
4 teaspoons black peppercorns
1 tablespoon salt
2 cups boiling water

Place meat and cabbage in layers in pan, starting with lamb, finishing with a top layer of cabbage. Sprinkle each layer with salt and pepper. Add boiling water, cover and simmer for about 1½ hours without removing the lid. Serve with boiled potatoes. 4 servings.

BAXTER SPRINGS IS QUIET NOW but was a boomtown during the days of the great cattle drives. Today it's a place to experience America as it was in the past. Nothing reflects great all-American food better than banana bread — this Kansas version is easy and satisfying!

NORWEGIAN
ROUTE
66
tours

40 grader Celcius

tre tidssoner   kameratskap

Santa Fe

Los Angeles

END OF ROUTE 66

prarie

spenning

opplevelse

USA

La dine drømmer
bli virkelighet!

ørken

samhold

Chicago

åtte stater

4000 km

Harley-Davidson

Grand Canyon

Banana Bread

2 medium-sized bananas
1 apple, chopped
1 egg
¼ cup butter or margarine
1 cup sugar
2 cups flour
1 teaspoon baking soda

Combine banana, apple, egg, butter, and sugar in a food processor. Pulse until smooth. Add flour and baking soda. Pulse to moisten. Turn into a greased 8 ½ x 4½-inch bread pan. Bake in a preheated 350 degree oven for 1 hour.

WHILE MARY ELLEN LEE RAN THE LOTTIE KEENAN HOUSE in Baxter Springs, locals said her cinnamon rolls were some of the best ever. Cinnamon rolls rank right up there with chicken-fried steak and pecan pie as mouth-watering road food. Try Mary Ellen's version and you'll agree.

Cinnamon Roll Muffins

LOTTIE KEENAN HOUSE

2 packages dry yeast
¼ cup warm water
1 cup lukewarm milk
1 cup margarine, melted
2 eggs, beaten
¼ cup sugar
1 teaspoon salt
4½ cups flour

Filling:
2 sticks softened margarine
sugar and cinnamon, as desired

Dissolve yeast in warm water. Combine yeast mixture with remaining ingredients, in order given, in a large mixing bowl. Beat until smooth, about one minute. Dough will be very soft. Cover with a damp cloth and place in refrigerator overnight.

The next morning roll out half the dough into a rectangle and spread with one stick of softened margarine. Sprinkle dough with desired amount of sugar and cinnamon. Roll dough from long side in jelly-roll fashion. Cut dough into 1½ inch slices and place cut side down into greased muffin tins. Repeat process for remaining half of dough. Bake cinnamon rolls in preheated 350 degree oven for about 25 minutes. Cool and glaze with a powdered sugar icing, if desired. About 2 dozen cinnamon rolls.

"BURNT OFFERINGS" WAS A POPULAR WEEKLY FOOD COLUMN that appeared in the *Baxter Springs Citizen* for many years. Carolyn Nichols, who compiled the articles, is a long time Baxter Springs resident whose father started the paper.

Carolyn shared her recipe for watermelon pickles because she says the men in her family in particular are fans. Old-fashioned watermelon pickles are best when made with the thick white rind from dark green Black Diamond melons. Mmmm, what a wonderful old-fashioned treat!

Carolyn Nichols' Watermelon Pickles

6 pounds watermelon rind (about half a large melon)

Cut pink meat and green rind from white. Cut white rind into 1-inch squares, or whatever shape you prefer. Cover rind with cold salted water. Do not use iodized salt. Soak overnight. The next morning, drain and rinse melon pieces thoroughly. Cook in clear water until rind is fork tender, but don't overcook. Drain well.

Make a syrup of:

8 cups sugar

1⅔ cups any cider vinegar

4 drops oil of cloves

6 drops oil of cinnamon

A few drops of green coloring (optional)

Boil syrup for 5 minutes. Add rind and let stand overnight. The next morning add 1 cup sugar and bring to a boil. Can in hot sterilized jars. If any syrup is left, save for another batch. It will keep for two weeks in refrigerator. Makes 4 pints per 6 pounds of melon rind.

SHIRLEY ELLSWORTH SHARED THIS CANDY RECIPE that was first made at Anthony's Candy Store in Galena. Called Mine Run Candy, many thought Mr. Anthony gave it this name because the crisp porous texture reminded him of the minerals that were mined in the area. But he always claimed that it came about as an accident, when he allowed some candy to caramelize while he wasn't paying attention and "let his mind run wild." Whatever the reason, Mine Run Candy is a local favorite.

Mine Run Candy

1 cup sugar

1 cup dark corn syrup

1 tablespoon white vinegar

1 tablespoon soda

Combine sugar, syrup, and vinegar in a large pan and cook, stirring constantly until sugar dissolves. Cover pan for one minute to wash down crystals.

Uncover pan, insert candy thermometer, and cook candy without stirring to 300 degrees, or the hard-crack stage. Remove from heat and stir in soda. Candy will foam so be sure to use a large pan and a big spoon with a long handle.

Pour mixture into a buttered 9x13-inch dish. Do not spread. After it cools, break into bite sized pieces and coat with chocolate.

Chocolate Coating:

Melt a block of almond bark or dark chocolate for about 90 seconds in a microwave. Watch carefully and don't overcook. Dip the candy pieces into the melted chocolate and set on waxed paper to cool. ■

Grapes of Wrath

— MICHAEL WALLIS

Route 66 has endured several incarnations, including the bittersweet 1930s when the nation's economy cracked and the rains stopped, bringing drought and destruction to America's heartland.

I grew up hearing stories of those tragic years that left indelible scars on the land and the people along the highway. Large parts of Oklahoma, Texas, Kansas, and Arkansas looked like moonscape after huge black clouds swept across fields and towns.

A great migration resulted. Tens of thousands of Okies, Arkies, tenant farmers, disenfranchised workers, vagabonds, and migrants turned to the highway. They fled the choking dust and desolation and headed west to rebuild shattered dreams and start new lives in California.

Route 66 became a road of safe passage to the Promised Land. Woody Guthrie crafted his most poignant ballads. John Steinbeck gave the highway yet another name — the Mother Road — in his immortal novel, *The Grapes of Wrath*.

When those pilgrims reached the steep mountain grades in Arizona and looked down at the Colorado River and toward the golden land just beyond, called California, they became euphoric. They were a lost tribe, but they could almost smell the sweet orange blossoms, the sea air, and the fertile soil waiting just ahead.

Oklahoma

Fast facts from Oklahoma

- Approximate Route 66 mileage in Oklahoma — 394

- Oklahoma is the only state with oil rigs on the state capital lawn.

- Tulsa is home to Cyrus Avery, "The Father of Route 66."

- The state flower is the mistletoe, the state animal is the bison, and the state fish is the white bass.

Oklahoma Biker Road Rules

- Safety Helmet, required by law under age 18

- Eye Protection, required by law unless equipped with windscreen

Where to Buy Stuff in Oklahoma

- *TULSA* — Lyon's Indian Store, 401 East 11th Street (Route 66)

- *WELLSTON* — Seaba Station, one mile east of Hwy. 177 on Route 66

- *ARCADIA* — Round Barn, on old Route 66

- *CLINTON* — Oklahoma Route 66 Museum, 2229 W. Gary, Route 66

Must see in Oklahoma

- *QUAPAW* — Spook Light on Devil's Promenade Road, east of town

- *COMMERCE* — Baseball enthusiast? See Mickey Mantle's home at 319 S. Quincy.

- *MIAMI* — Coleman Theater, 103 N. Main, built in 1929 — Spanish Mission style

- *RIBBON ROAD* — Two stretches of original nine-feet-wide road between Miami and Afton

- *AFTON* — Restored DX gas station rest stop, run by Laurel Kane

The Sooner State

Oklahoma City ★

66 **Tulsa** ⊙

OKLAHOMA

- VINITA
  - The oldest Oklahoma town on Route 66, founded in 1871
  - Summerside Vineyards, Winery & Inn, I-44 & Historic Route 66
  - America's largest McDonalds in square footage, built as the Glass House in 1958, spans I-44 near Vinita.

- BIG CABIN — Cabin Creek Vineyards. Turn south from Route 66 at State Highway 69 and follow the signs or take Exit 283 on I-44.

- FOYIL
  - Ed Galloway's Totem Poles, east on State Highway 28A; one of the best examples of folk art in the country
  - Monument to favorite son Andy Payne, winner of the 1928 Bunion Derby that earned him $25,000 to help pay off his family farm

- CLAREMORE
  - Will Rogers Memorial Museum and Tomb, 1720 West Will Rogers Boulevard
  - Will Rogers' Birthplace, the Dogiron Ranch, off Highway 88 between Claremore and Oologah
  - J.M. Davis Gun Museum, 333 N. Lynn Riggs, the largest one-man collection in the world

- CATOOSA — Blue Whale Theme Park

- TULSA
  - 11th Street, Cyrus Avery Route 66 Memorial Bridge across the Arkansas River
  - Cain's Ballroom, 423 N. Main St., an icon of Western Swing music. Bob Wills and the Texas Playboys performed on KVOO radio from here for nine years. Recently restored.
  - Discoveryland, 19501 W. 41 Street, 5 miles west of State Hwy 93 (Sand Springs). Summertime outdoor live performances of Oklahoma!

Ed Galloway's Totem Poles, Foyil

65

- SAPULPA — Mr. Indian Cowboy Store, 1000 S. Main, Native American owned and operated

- BRISTOW — More brick-paved streets than any other Oklahoma community. There's a different feel here.

- CHANDLER — Restored Phillips 66 Service Station

- ARCADIA — Round Barn, built in 1898 from native Burr Oak.

- OKLAHOMA CITY
  - Oklahoma State Capital Complex, NE 23rd and Lincoln, call 521-3356. The only state capitol with working oil wells located on the grounds
  - Remington Park Race Track, 1 Remington Pl. World class pari-mutuel horseracing
  - Milk bottle building, 25th and Classen, across from Kamp's Grocery
  - Bricktown Historical District. Revitalized warehouse district with good restaurants and night spots

Bikers paying respects at site of Murrah Building, Oklahoma City

- YUKON — Sign atop Yukon Flour Mill can be seen for miles at night. The mill operated from 1900 until 1970.

- Hydro — Lucille Hamon's Gas Station (now closed), Route 66, north access road of I-40

- WEATHERFORD
  - Astronaut Thomas Stafford NASA Museum, located at the airport, northeast of town
  - Cotter Blacksmith and Machine Shop, 208 W. Rainey. Family operated since 1913

- CLINTON — Oklahoma Route 66 Museum, 2229 W. Gary Boulevard, (Exit 65 from I-40)

Route 66 Museum, Clinton

- ELK CITY — National Route 66 Museum, Route 66 and Pioneer Road, a part of Old Town Museum Complex

Bikers at groundbreaking for National Route 66 Museum, Elk City

- SAYRE — Steel Truss bridge, near Exit 26 from I-40 and once a part of Route 66

Paul. The Harley rider coos at the baby snug in his tattooed arms and glares at anyone who gets too close. "I'm the designated baby sitter, " the big guy proudly tells me. I know without a doubt that this is the safest child in all of Oklahoma. So do little Paul's parents.

When all the eggs and milk are gone, several bikers race to a nearby convenience store to purchase fresh provisions with money from their own pockets. After more than an hour of table-hopping and making new friends, I manage to grab a chair and order some food. The buffalo burger I devour tastes like ambrosia and the bread pudding is so good one gnarly biker says he'd kill his mother for another bowl of the stuff.

Finally, as the crowd thins out and heads back to cruising the Mother Road, Dawn emerges from the kitchen and retrieves her baby. She pulls up a chair next to me and allows herself a few minutes of rest.

"It feels like we served just about every biker in the nation the last few days," she says. "Last night we stayed open until everyone was fed and then we crawled home next door and collapsed. It was still dark this morning when they started arriving. We were in our pajamas and we opened up and started cooking. The bikers pitched right in and helped."

Dawn marvels that some of the bikers went to the market and bought their own food, cooked it, washed their dishes, and even paid for it again. They rotated in shifts as cooks and dishwashers but three women bikers stayed at the cash register throughout the entire episode making sure every check was covered and every bit of food and drink was paid for in full. Then a collection was taken up and Dawn and Fred were presented with a jar of money in honor of their new son.

With her baby boy tucked in her arms, Dawn returns to the kitchen to take stock and I drain my glass of ice water. Outside a pair of lovers sits side by side on their bikes beneath a big Chinese elm loaded with mistletoe. They kiss, ignite their engines, and then roar off down the road. I take my leave a few minutes later and never look back. I don't have to — I know I'll return. ■

The Heart of the Mother Road

— ROBERT LOWERY

This story is in memory of Patricia McCabe Lowery.

I slowed my bike for the workers in reflective vests on the two-lane highway outside of Chandler, Oklahoma. We were on that stretch of Route 66 that carried so many Dust Bowlers, GI's, vacationers, and fellow bikers. The workers were replacing a section of the old road that had deteriorated beyond good sense, and the traffic narrowed to a single lane.

Sitting on the road in a jumble of gravel, concrete, and blacktop was a Bobcat with a drill attached to it. The drill pounded away at the blacktop and chips flew left and right. As I slowly passed the work-site, I noticed that the drill went all the way through the asphalt into the earth.

My wife, Pat, sitting in the passenger seat of our Harley-Davidson, nudged me from behind and said, "There's our piece of history."

I pulled ahead of the traffic until I found a safe siding off the road, where I parked the bike. I walked back to the foreman sitting in a pickup truck on the shoulder of the road. He was a friendly looking farm boy with lots of red hair, freckles, and a Caterpillar baseball cap perched on the back of his head.

"Can I help you?" he asked, in the accent of my grandfather and grandmother.

"How would you like to do an old man a big favor?" I said.

He guessed in a heartbeat what I was after. "You want a piece of old 66, don't you?"

"Yes, if it wouldn't be any trouble."

"None at all," he said, "there's more than enough to go around."

The foreman reached down to the floor on the passenger side of his truck and retrieved a paper bag. Then he removed the contents — a couple of sandwiches, a thermos, and a banana. He got out of the truck and as we walked toward the work site he handed me the bag. Neither of us spoke. He guessed that it was a solemn occasion.

The drilling had stopped and the machine sat idling. The drill had cut through a layer of blacktop, another of concrete, through gravel, and into the rich, red Oklahoma clay. The core of Route 66 was exposed.

Trembling, I reached under the dangling drill and scooped up three chunks. This was original 66 — Portland cement as tough as iron. I brushed off the sticky clay and gravel and carefully put the fragments into the sack. I nodded to the foreman, to the workers, to the Bobcat operator. The drill started again.

I turned and put the paper bag in my saddlebag. Then I got on my bike and we left. We were taking the remnants of history home. ∎

Postscript from Robert: My wife, Pat, who accompanied me on all our Harley trips, died in February 2004. She was buried in a small churchyard cemetery in Wading River, New York. Mixed in with the soil that covers her coffin is a piece of Route 66.

"We found a rideable abandoned section of Route 66 before Erick, OK. It had to be a couple of miles long. Soon, others joined us, too. Each one of us felt like we had found a hidden treasure, a secret passageway...finding this "jewel" to ride. We were whooping and hollering the whole way! Fantastic!"

— Joy Schaub

Pop Hicks

—MICHAEL WALLIS

Pop Hicks Restaurant in Clinton, Oklahoma, was not only a Route 66 landmark but an American original. For generations of bikers, the historic restaurant was also a must stop — a place for down-home meals and, more importantly, friendly conversation. Since the doors first opened in 1936, Pop Hicks not only nourished bodies, it also nurtured souls.

For many of us it was a quintessential biker haven.

Howard and Mary Nichols, the last owners of this Mother Road institution — one of the oldest operating restaurants on Route 66 — helped create memories for travelers and local folks alike. They never met a stranger and road-weary bikers appreciated the warm reception and the chance to rest and refresh after a long spell in the saddle. At any given time there might be as many as a half-dozen bikes parked along the curb.

We stopped at Pop Hicks every time we traveled the Mother Road. We felt welcome day or night. Sometimes we encountered old gents and ladies sipping coffee at the liars' table, exhausted bikers gulping stout coffee, cheerleaders celebrating a football victory, or cowboys stoking up on breakfast. Thanks to the Nichols family and all the many good folks who worked there, we felt that we were at home at Pop Hicks. The people there were family. They always will be. We will never ever forget them and those special times on the open road.

On August 2, 1999, a fire erupted at Pop Hicks. Firemen raced to Clinton from several surrounding communities but flames consumed the building. It burned to the ground. There was no insurance and no way to rebuild. Now only a vacant space remains and motorists and bikers often slow down when they pass out of respect for the old times.

Rest in peace Pop Hicks. You served us well. ■

Two bikers with Howard Nicols at Pop Hicks

Recipes from Oklahoma

— MARIAN CLARK

At Waylan's Ku-Ku Burger in Miami, owner Gene Waylan says, "Don't just ask for a burger, ask for a Waylan's." This is one of the best hamburger stops in northeastern Oklahoma. The giant neon sign out front adds a nostalgic touch but the real quality here comes hot off the grill.

For those who enjoy an occasional break from hamburgers, try the chili dogs. Here is the giant recipe used to top the dogs.

Chili Dog Chili
WAYLAN'S KU-KU BURGER

7½ pounds chili meat, broken into small pieces
3 46-ounce cans tomato juice, with just enough
   water
to rinse cans
3 heaping tablespoons coarse grind pepper
3 heaping tablespoons salt
3 good handfuls of chopped onions
1 cup Williams Chili seasoning
1 #10 can of pinto beans, undrained

Combine all ingredients except chili seasoning and beans. Heat, stirring to prevent burning. Bring chili to a good boil then add the chili seasoning and cook mixture for 30 minutes. Puree beans in a blender or food processor and add to chili dog mixture. Stir well to blend. Freeze and store in several containers until needed.

FROM TROND MOBERG'S NOTES: "Laurel Kane knows how to make bikers feel welcome. On our last trip (September, 2003) she offered sandwiches for lunch. All of the sandwiches were marked with Norwegian names and there was no way we could pay her. I realize that this can't happen on a regular basis, but guess how much the road warriors appreciated this! The word-to-word effect of this is tremendous. Again, 66 is all about people."

Laurel Kane has quickly become the Route 66 ambassador in Afton. The former DX Station has come back to life under her careful guidance. A warm welcome awaits — this is a place to stop, stretch, learn about the surrounding area, and pick up some tempting snacks Laurel always has ready, like her famous beer cheese.

Afton Station Beer Cheese

2 cups shredded mild cheddar cheese
2 cups shredded sharp cheddar cheese
8 ounces beer (⅔ of a 12-ounce bottle)
3 cloves garlic
3 heaping tablespoons mayonnaise

Allow cheese to reach room temperature in a mixing bowl. (Meanwhile, drink the beer you're not planning to use.) Put garlic through a press and add to cheese. Place beer in saucepan and heat until just before the boiling point. Watch carefully so that it doesn't boil over. While beer is very hot, pour slowly over the cheese and garlic, stirring well. Add mayonnaise and continue to blend thoroughly. Mixture will be very soft.

Refrigerate for half an hour and stir again. Chill until ready to use.

Bring back to room temperature before serving. Good served with original flavor Bugles, pretzels, or rye bread sliced very thin. Approximately 3 cups.

Afton

VINITA IS THE UNCONTESTED "CALF FRY CAPITAL OF THE WORLD." The September festival each year provides an authentic glimpse of Oklahoma's Western heritage. There is plenty of good food and entertainment for everyone willing to try new experiences. This calf fry recipe comes from the Vinita Chamber of Commerce.

Oklahoma Calf Fries

Slice 2 pounds of Calf Fries about ¼ inch thick. (They are easier to slice if slightly frozen.)

Soak in an egg and milk mixture for about 10 minutes. Roll each fry in a mixture of 1½ cups cornmeal, 3 cups flour, and 1 teaspoon salt. Fry in hot oil (350 degrees) until golden brown. Enjoy.

Vinita

ALTHOUGH NEW TO THE ROAD, Vinita's Summerside Vineyards and Winery is already well known in Norway. In the summer of 2003, Trond Moberg reported that one of his road warriors had trouble with his bike and the whole caravan had to stop. It was 104 degrees when they pulled off the road near Vinita next to what looked like a construction site. "Out of the empty building came a lady who asked us all to come in since she had air conditioning. It turned out to be Marsha Butler, who was finishing the inside works at Summerside Vineyards and Winery. She said she would love to have us visit in 2004. She even offered box lunches and wine. Out of the blue we met another fine ambassador along 66. We will return!"

Summerside Route 66 Red Wine Drip Beef

1 three-pound boneless beef roast, trimmed
1 tablespoon garlic powder
½ teaspoon dried rosemary
3 cubes beef bouillon
1 cup Summerside Route 66 red wine
Water to cover

cayenne. Simmer for 35 minutes, stirring frequently. Add salt and pepper to taste just before serving. 6-8 servings.

Catoosa

Honky Tonkin'

Go honky tonkin' in these Tulsa country and western dance clubs:
Redneck Kountry, 19011 E. Admiral Blvd.
Caravan Cattle Company, 7901 41st St.
Midnight Rodeo, 9379 E. 46th St.
Cain's Ballroom, 423 N. Main

PROOF THAT OKLAHOMA IS A BIKER PARADISE comes with two thriving Harley-Davidson dealerships in Tulsa. Larry and Pat Wofford own a twenty-year-old family business they purchased in December of 1998. They quickly changed the name and became the first Harley-Davidson dealer in the nation to combine the two famous icons — Route 66 and Harley-Davidson.

Attaching himself to the mystique of the road was one of Wofford's many wise moves.

"Route 66 is basically every two-laner out there," says Wofford. "The difference between it and a modern freeway is like being in a car or being on a Harley; it's two different ways of viewing the world." Their new 32,500-square-feet facility, dedicated to both images, easily earned the *Dealernews Magazine* "Best Use of a Theme" honors in 2003. *Dealership* covers the entire "power-sport" industry.

You can find Larry and Pat and their enthusiastic staff at Route 66 Harley-Davidson, 3637 South Memorial. Route 66 has truly paved their way to success. Pat shared this menu that is sure to please folks at every Harley get-together.

TAKE ME BACK TO TULSA TENDERLOIN

CHICAGO BLUE CHEESE POTATOES

BARSTOW BEER BATTERED ONION RINGS

ST. LOUIS SPINACH SALAD DEATH VALLEY DEVILED EGGS

BRISTOW BLONDE BOMBSHELL BROWNIES

Take Me Back to Tulsa Tenderloin

1 (3-pound) pork loin

Marinade:
½ cup Jack Daniels whiskey
½ cup balsamic vinegar
1 cup orange juice, divided
1 tablespoon garlic powder

Combine whiskey, vinegar, ½ cup of the orange juice, and garlic powder. Blend well. Place tenderloin in a large freezer-weight sealable plastic bag. Pour marinade over meat. Seal bag and refrigerate overnight. Remove meat and discard the marinade.

Bake tenderloin in a preheated 350 degree oven for 1½ hours. Pour remaining ½ cup orange juice over meat. Insert a meat thermometer into the thickest part. Bake an additional 10 to 30 minutes or until internal temperature reaches 160 degrees. Let meat stand 10 minutes before slicing to serve. Serve with juices from pan. 8 servings.

Chicago Blue Cheese Potatoes

3 medium-sized baking potatoes, unpeeled and
    thinly sliced
1½ cups whipping cream
2 tablespoons butter, melted
1 tablespoon minced garlic
1 teaspoon salt
½ teaspoon white pepper
½ cup (2 ounces) crumbled blue cheese

Place potatoes in a greased 10x6x2-inch baking dish. Combine next 5 ingredients and pour over potatoes. Bake, uncovered, in a preheated 400 degree oven for 40 minutes. Sprinkle with cheese and bake an additional 5 minutes. 4-6 servings.

Western Oklahoma

The Great American Bunion Derby

Promoted as "C.C. Pyle's First Annual International Trans-Continental Footrace," the 1928 Bunion Derby promoted a marathon run from Los Angeles to New York City.

Andy Payne, a young, un-employed, part-Cherokee from the Route 66 town of Foyil, Oklahoma, won the race and the impressive prize of $25,000. With the money, Andy paid off his parent's farm and married his sweetheart.

The footrace attracted runners from around the world. Over 200 entrants, ranging in age from 16 to 64, left the Los Angeles Speedway on March 4, 1928. Fifty-five men finished the race with Andy outdistancing them all. He arrived in New York City after 84 days, having run 3423.3 miles. His winning time was 573 hours and 4 minutes.

C.C. Pyle, who had hoped to get rich and make a name for himself with the event, barely made expenses and was never able to mount another race.

Besides Andy's success, the other major winner of the Bunion Derby was the National US Highway 66 Association. The marathon brought national attention to the highway and was the first event to place Highway 66 in the forefront of road recognition.

From Pretty Boy: The Life and Times of Charles Arthur Floyd, by Michael Wallis:

When Pretty Boy was not on the outlaw trail making "withdrawals" from banks, he loved to get into the kitchen and bake apple pie. In 1933 one of his pies won top honors at a country pie supper where the respected sheriff, unaware of who had done the baking, tasted the slice and declared it the best pie he'd ever put in his mouth.

The thirty-year-old bandit left an apple pie behind in his Buffalo, New York hideaway when, in 1934, he decided to head toward home in Sallisaw. On that trip, a final shootout ended his life, and he never saw Oklahoma again.

This pie recipe is considered Pretty Boy's best version:

Michael Wallis's Pretty Boy's Apple Pie

Pie Crust:
2 cups flour
¾ cup lard
1 teaspoon salt
6-7 tablespoons cold water

Prepare crust by working the flour, lard, and salt together until crumbly. Mix in cold water until dough holds together in big pieces. Divide into two equal balls.

On a floured surface roll out one ball thin enough to line a 9-inch pie tin. Roll out second ball for the top crust.

Preheat oven to 450 degrees.

Apple Filling:
1 pound fresh apples, peeled and sliced or
    1 (16-ounce) can
2 tablespoons fresh lemon juice
½ teaspoon ground nutmeg
½ teaspoon ground cinnamon
½ cup white sugar
¼ cup seedless raisins
1 cup brown sugar
2 tablespoons flour
2 tablespoons butter
½ cup shelled Oklahoma pecans
¼ cup milk

Hard Sauce:
½ cup butter
1½ cups powdered sugar
1 tablespoon boiling water
1 tablespoon brandy or rum (moonshine is preferable)

Place the apples in the lined pan. Sprinkle with lemon juice, nutmeg, and cinnamon. Spread the white sugar and raisins evenly over the apples. Mix the brown sugar, flour and butter in a bowl. When well blended, spread over the apples and sprinkle with pecans. Add most of the milk and cover with the top crust. Seal the edges and prick top with a fork. Brush the remaining milk on the crust.

Bake for 10 minutes at 450 degrees, then reduce heat to 350 degrees and bake another 30 minutes until crust is golden.

To make hard sauce, cream the butter until light. Beat in the sugar, add water, and then beat in the liquor. Serve sauce on each slice of pie. If you dare, add a scoop of homemade vanilla ice cream.

REBA MCCLANAHAN IS THE BUSY HANDS-ON OWNER of Myers-Duren Harley-Davidson in Tulsa. The business is Oklahoma's oldest Harley dealership and possibly the third oldest in the nation.

In addition, Reba is one of the very few women owners of a Harley franchise nationwide.

McClanahan is only the third owner of this Tulsa dealership that opened in 1912 and once thrived on Route 66. Today, she operates her flourishing dealership from a custom-designed art deco showplace at 4848 South Peoria Avenue.

By all counts, Reba McClanahan is an outstanding cook. She regularly serves a holiday buffet for Harley-Davidson friends at her South Peoria location in Tulsa and shared these favorites from past celebrations. Her favorite barbecued meatball recipe is mutually shared by Debbie Pruitt in the *Sapulpa Daily Herald* and follows these recipes.

Reba McClanahan's Sausage Balls

2 cups biscuit mix (Bisquick)
2 cups grated Cheddar cheese
1 pound hot sausage
3 tablespoons water

Mix all ingredients together and roll into small balls. Bake in a preheated 350 degree oven for 15-20 minutes. About 100 1-inch balls

Reba McClanahan's Beef Boat Dip

3 jars (2.25 ounce each) dried beef, minced
1⅓ cups low-fat mayonnaise
1⅓ cups sour cream
2 tablespoons minced onion
2 tablespoons chopped parsley
2 teaspoons dill weed
2 teaspoons Beau Monde
Chopped green onion to taste
1 loaf round pumpernickel bread, unsliced

Combine all ingredients except the bread. Mix well and let stand overnight in the refrigerator.

Hollow out the loaf of bread and fill with beef mixture. Serve with crackers.

EACH NOVEMBER, the *Sapulpa Daily Herald* holds a recipe contest and publishes a cookbook under the direction of Laurie Quinnelly, Lifestyle Editor. A panel of eight judges recently gave these two recipes the winning nod. They are both comfort dishes of the highest order!

Sapulpa

Debbie Pruitt's Barbecued Meatballs

3 pounds lean ground beef
1 12-ounce can evaporated milk
1 cup oatmeal
1 cup cracker crumbs
2 eggs
½ cup finely chopped onion
½ teaspoon garlic powder
2 teaspoons salt
½ teaspoon pepper
2 teaspoons chili powder

Combine all ingredients. Mixture will be soft. Shape into walnut-size balls. Place meatballs in a single layer on a waxed-paper lined cookie sheet. Freeze until firm. Store meatballs in freezer bag until ready to use.

Sauce for meatballs:

2 cups catsup
1 cup brown sugar
½ teaspoon liquid smoke
½ teaspoon garlic powder
¼ cup finely chopped onion

Combine all ingredients and stir until sugar is dissolved. Place frozen meatballs in 9x13-inch baking pan. Pour sauce over meat. Bake in preheated 350 degree oven for one hour. Serve while warm, preferably in chafing dish. 60-70 walnut-sized meatballs.

Jeanie Thoos Spradlin's Holiday Bread Pudding with Whiskey Sauce

1 10-ounce loaf French bread, 2-3 days old
(or 6-8 cups dry, crumbled bread)
4 cups milk
2 cups sugar
½ cup butter, melted
3 eggs
2 tablespoons vanilla
1 cup raisins
1 cup coconut
1 cup shopped pecans
1 teaspoon cinnamon
1 teaspoon nutmeg

Combine all ingredients to form a moist mixture. Pour into a buttered 9x12 baking dish. Place in a non-preheated oven and bake for 1 hour and 15 minutes at 350 degrees, or until pudding is golden brown. Serve warm with whiskey sauce.

Whiskey Sauce:
½ cup butter
1½ cups powdered sugar
2 egg yolks
½ cup bourbon, scotch, rum or fruit juice

Cream butter and sugar over medium heat until butter melts and sugar is dissolved. Remove from heat and add egg yolk. Pour liquor into mixture gradually, stirring constantly. Sauce will thicken as it cools. Serve warm over the bread pudding. 10-12 servings.

Locals call the stretch of Route 66 between Tulsa and Oklahoma City the "free road." In 1953 when the Turner Turnpike became the first interstate to transplant Route 66, the turnpike became a toll road. To this day many locals continue to avoid the turnpike, taking the free road instead. It is a superb biker route.

BRISTOW WAS ORIGINALLY SETTLED by Lebanese immigrants whose descendants share the foods we all have grown to love. Lebanese cooks impart a special touch to tabouleh, even though the dish appears in the cuisine of many other Middle Eastern cultures.

Tabouleh

8 ounces bulgur (fine cracked wheat)
5 bunches parsley, stems removed and finely chopped

1 pound ripe tomatoes, finely chopped
5 green onions, finely chopped
2 tablespoons fresh mint leaves, minced
⅛ teaspoon allspice (optional)
½ cup lemon juice (adjust to taste)
½ cup olive oil
Salt and pepper to taste

Cover the bulgur in cold water and soak for 1 hour. Squeeze dry. Pick the parsley leaves from the large stems. Discard stems. Wash and dry parsley leaves. Chop all vegetables. Mix parsley, tomatoes, onions, and mint together. Combine allspice, lemon juice and olive oil. Pour over bulger and toss lightly. Salt and pepper to taste. 20 small servings.

THE ROCK CAFE, now on the National Register of Historic Places, has experienced a renaissance under the capable guidance of Dawn Welch. This 1939 vintage eatery celebrated 66 years on Route 66 in 2005. It remains a second home to thousands of cross-country truckers, bikers, and 66 enthusiasts as well as a favorite hangout for locals. The giraffe stone exterior came from the roadbed when Route 66 was built through the area. A recent grant has helped Dawn refurbish the interior and a warm welcome can be found just inside the doors. Bikers are always welcome and find this to be a memorable stop.

Dawn shared this recipe for her success: "Ingredients: Combine equal amounts of nostalgia, kindness, and a sense of family. Add this to the cook's good attitude and waitresses who are always ready to talk. And never, never forget to add love to taste."

Rock Cafe Old Fashioned Greasy Hamburger

¼ pound coarsely ground beef
½ teaspoon salt, or to taste
¼ teaspoon pepper
1 teaspoon finely chopped onion

Mix all ingredients, lightly pat into a burger about ½ inch thick. For a juicy burger, don't pack the meat. If the meat is too lean, mix a little ground suet with the patty. Fry patty on grill or in iron skillet for a few minutes, turn and cook a few minutes longer. Overcooking dries out the meat.

Lightly butter the top and bottom of a bun, place on grill until golden brown. Spread mustard on bottom half, pile with chopped onions, pickles, and meat patty. Spread mayonnaise or mustard on top half of bun. Pat the top of the bun with a spatula loaded with hamburger grease. Add lettuce, tomato, and catsup as desired. 1 old-fashioned burger.

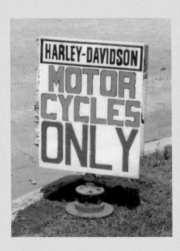

BRUSH THE DUST OFF YOUR LEATHERS and stop for a spell at Hillbillee's Cafe in Arcadia. This is a place made for bikers! Wade and Norma Braxton will make you feel right at home. There's live music several nights each week and a top-notch place to stay nearby in their remodeled log cabin bed and breakfast.

City Slicker Chicken
HILLBILLEE'S CAFE

Grill an unbreaded, unskinned chicken breast in 1 tablespoon olive oil for about 4-5 minutes. Season with a touch of basil, salt, and freshly ground black pepper. Finely chop 2 green onions, 1 slice of bell pepper and a small piece of fresh ginger root. Sprinkle on grill to gently sear. Place on top of grilled chicken breast. Serve with slices of tomato and potato salad. 1 serving.

CHERYL NOWKA LIVES IN LAS VEGAS TODAY, but grew up on Route 66 in Hydro, Oklahoma. Her mom, Lucille Hamons, passed away in August of 2000 and loved her title of "The Mother of the Mother Road." The spirit of Lucille Hamons still reigns at her old home and gas station on Route 66 near Hydro. Nostalgia-loving friends continue to erect memorials almost daily, leaving notes, flowers, crosses, and totems, taking away their very own camera images filled with a bit of highway magic. Lucille's is the atypical site: once a grocery store / carry-out / gas station / beer source / tourist court / shrine, and home to countless thousands, it still welcomes highway travelers on the undulating strip of 66 within a stones throw of I-40. When I visited with her just a few weeks before her death in 2000, Lucille had her memory book of famous autographs on the table beside her chair and told me again that memories kept her going. Age, moisture, and termites have settled in at the old structure where many a story has unfolded behind the prolific ivy covering. Folks from the Smithsonian have moved her Hamons Court sign to Washington.

Cheryl shared this favorite margarita recipe and reminded me, "Mom was very partial to her biker visitors. I hope she, Kirk Woodward, and Cheryl Cory are sitting around talking 66 as we speak."

Cheryl's Margaritas

1 cup of ice cubes placed in blender
4 ounces Jose Cuervo Gold tequila poured over the ice
4 ounces of Triple Sec poured over ice and tequila
6 ounce can frozen Minute Maid limeade
1 cup water

Always place ice cubes in blender first. Add remaining ingredients. Blend until smooth.

Don't pour yet! Halve and quarter a lime, rub the flesh of the lime around edge of glass rims 2-3 times and immediately dip in fine popcorn salt. Pour those margaritas and enjoy.

KAMP'S GROCERY AT 1310 CLASSEN, OKLAHOMA CITY, is a hidden treasure amidst the bustle of state capital traffic. Locals flock to Kamp's for the deli menu and great box lunches, as well as the family dinners to go, all in conjunction with the *Yippee-Yi-Yo Cafe* inside the 1910-vintage store.

The place remains a mecca from the past — tin ceilings, wood floors, old fixtures, and plenty of photographs. The croissant sandwich is typical of the good food served at the deli.

Kamp's Grocery Smoked Turkey Croissant

1 fresh croissant
4 ounces thinly sliced smoked turkey breast
1 teaspoon tarragon mayonnaise
Lettuce
Tomato slices
1 tablespoon Gorgonzola Vinaigrette

Toast the croissant. Heat the turkey. Place turkey, mayonnaise, lettuce and tomato on half the croissant. Top with Gorgonzola vinaigrette. 1 sandwich.

Gorgonzola Vinaigrette:

4 ounces Gorgonzola cheese
4 ounces olive oil
2 ounces balsamic vinegar

Combine and stir until well blended. Will keep in refrigerator for 2 weeks when well sealed. Use as needed for salads and sandwiches.

WOMEN WHO HAVE SPENT A LONG DAY IN THE SADDLE appreciate an easy meal. Here is a perfect suggestion shared by Johnita and Lionel Turner from the Willow Way Bed and Breakfast near Oklahoma City's Remington Park.

Aunt Kay's Brisket

5-7 pound trimmed brisket
(10-12 pounds untrimmed)

Sprinkle generously with the following:

Garlic salt
Onion salt
Lowery's seasoned salt
Meat tenderizer

Place meat in a large cooking bag and add a mixture of:

4 tablespoons liquid smoke
4 tablespoons Worcestershire
3 tablespoons soy sauce
3 tablespoons Italian dressing
2 tablespoons catsup
1 teaspoon prepared mustard
1 teaspoon celery seed

Marinate overnight. Bake in cooking bag in a preheated 275 degree oven for 4-5 hours or until tender. Begin testing at about 3½ hours in order not to overcook meat. Slice after meat has cooled and serve with basting juice. 12 or more servings.

CALUMET IS A QUIET COMMUNITY, a place where pioneer family members are close-knit and comfortable. Pat Lafoe of Calumet shared this all-time favorite cookie recipe originally prepared by her mother. These cookies fit perfectly in a tank bag.

Pat Lafoe's Oatmeal Cookies

1 cup margarine
1 cup brown sugar
1 cup granulated sugar
1 teaspoon vanilla
2 eggs, well beaten
1½ cups flour
3 cups oatmeal
1 teaspoon soda
1 teaspoon salt
1 teaspoon cinnamon
½ cup raisins (optional)

Cream margarine and add sugar, vanilla, and eggs. Add dry ingredients and mix well. Drop by teaspoonful on ungreased cookie sheet. Bake in preheated 350 degree oven for 10 minutes.
    100 cookies.

TIRES SING ON THE OLD CONCRETE in this area and weeds continue to encroach. It's a section of real history waiting to be ridden. In Elk City, a 1920 prairie home has been transformed into the Country Dove where arguably, the best French silk pie on Route 66 is served. Glenna Hollis and Kay Farmer will make you feel right at home. Even rough-and-tumble bikers are welcome.

French Silk Pie
COUNTRY DOVE

Nut Crust:
1 stick butter, melted
1 cup flour
⅔ cup finely chopped nuts

Filling:
¾ cup butter
1⅓ cups sugar
2 teaspoons vanilla
2 squares unsweetened chocolate, melted and
    cooled
3 large eggs

Whipped Cream Topping:
½ pint whipping cream
¼ cup sugar
1 teaspoon vanilla
Chocolate shavings

Combine crust ingredients and blend well. Pat a thin layer of mixture into bottom and sides of a 10-inch pie pan. Bake in preheated 350 degree oven for 20 minutes. Allow to cool.

Cream butter and sugar thoroughly. Blend in vanilla and chocolate and mix well. Add eggs one at a time, beating with mixer on high speed for at least 5 minutes after each addition. Pour mixture into pie shell and chill in refrigerator for several hours or overnight. The crust and filling freeze well at this stage if making the pie ahead of time.

Whip cream to soft peak stage. Add sugar and vanilla and continue to whip until cream stands in firm peaks. Spread over pie and grate sweetened chocolate on top. 8 slices.

OKRA AND BLACK-EYED PEAS are almost always found in Oklahoma gardens. Kay Atkins shared her mother, Rosalee Admire's, favorite okra salad. Rosalee was a child of ten in 1928 when the Bunion Derby took place. She remembers being very scared of the strangers as they came running by her home. The men were all thirsty, so she overcame her fear and was soon providing water as they paused briefly on their run down Route 66.

Rosalee Admire's Fried Okra Salad

6 slices bacon, fried crisp and drained
2 tomatoes, chopped
1 small onion, chopped
½ bell pepper, chopped
1 large bag (20 ounce) frozen okra, or 4 cups home grown okra,
fried, drained, and cooled

Dressing:
⅓ cup vinegar
¼ cup sugar
¼ cup vegetable oil

Fry the bacon and set aside. Combine the tomatoes, onion, pepper, and okra. Mix the vinegar, sugar, and vegetable oil in a jar and shake until blended. Crumble the bacon over the vegetables and pour the dressing over all just before serving. 8 servings.

Note: This salad is good even without the dressing!

ON THE HIGHWAY 66 CURVE heading west from Texola, the Last Stop Bar has a freshly sign painted on its front wall:

"There's no other place
Like this place
Anywhere near this place
So this must be the place." ■

The Highway's Heyday

— MICHAEL WALLIS

During World War II, a shotage of gasoline and tires meant civilians could only dream about road trips on America's Main Street, a highway filled instead with troop convoys and GI's hitchhiking home. But the years following the war proved to be the heyday of motor travel, especially on Route 66.

I was born in St. Louis in 1945, just as the troops marched home to start new jobs, build homes, and take vacations in big gas-guzzling cars. By 1950, my family was in the midst of the pack cruising Route 66, taking in all the natural and manmade attractions. I saw my first real cowboys and Indians, spied my first oil well, and ate my first enchilada platter on the Mother Road.

Just the act of "getting there" was an important part of our travel experience. When the tires of our family sedan hit the pavement, it was official — the vacation had begun. Every single moment counted. Windows were cranked down as Dad mashed the gas pedal to the floor. The radio purred and I dreamed of outlaw hideouts, snake farms, cheeseburgers and thick chocolate malts. The potential for high adventure lurked around every curve. The fantasy had begun. ∎

Texas

Fast facts from Texas

- Cross the panhandle in 177 miles on Route 66.

- Chili is the official state dish and the jalapeño is the official state pepper. Grapefruit is the official fruit. The state animal is the armadillo.

- Palo Duro Canyon State Park, south of Amarillo, is the second largest canyon in the United States, covering 15,103 acres.

- Two official state rest stops near McLean are now the most elaborate along all of Route 66 (I-40), they even include tornado shelters. One is themed Route 66, the other pays tribute to the pioneer farming and ranching history of the area.

Texas Biker Road Rules

- Safety Helmet, required until rider passes test and shows proof of $10,000 hospitalization insurance

- Eye Protection, not required

Must see in Texas

- SHAMROCK
  - The tallest water tower in Texas
  - U Drop Inn — Resplendent with new paint and new neon, the art deco architecture now houses city offices and a visitors' center.

U Drop Inn, Shamrock

- MCLEAN
  - Devil's Rope and Old Route 66 Museum, corner of Kingsley and Old Route 66. This jewel of a museum is one of the best along Route 66, not to be missed.

Devil's Rope and Old Route 66 Museum, McLean

  - Restored 1930s Phillips 66 station on old westbound Route 66

- GROOM — "Cross of the Lord Jesus Christ" looms 190 feet tall and contains 75 tons of steel. It is the tallest cross in the western hemisphere. Note: This has been the scene of numerous biker and trucker weddings.

Restored 1930s Phillips 66 station, McLean

The Lone Star State

Amarillo

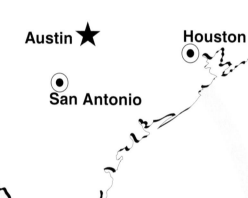

Dallas

TEXAS

El Paso

Austin ★

Houston

San Antonio

- The Britten USA Tower built intentionally with one short leg

- *AMARILLO* — Take a 30 minute detour to Palo Duro Canyon State Park stretching 110 majestic miles south of Amarillo. See *"Texas"* the outstanding summer musical drama in the dramatic outdoor theater in Palo Duro Canyon.

- Find "Art for Art's Sake" traffic signs. Stanley Marsh 3 has the city talking again. Over 750 signs have gone up (and come down) sporting a wide range of unusual statements.

The Britten USA Tower

- Cadillac Ranch, west edge of Amarillo on I-40 and Route 66. Ten vintage Cadillac models planted in a row with tail fins pointing skyward at the same angle as the Cheops' pyramids. Stanley Marsh 3's favorite art

- VEGA — Authentic Texas cattle country, the area was once a part of the famous XIT Ranch, land of the Llano Estacado, America's staked plains. Terrain is pancake flat along here and the wind always blows. (Inexperienced bikers take heed.)

- Adrian — Midpoint along Route 66.

- Glenrio — Ghost town where the decaying corpse of "First in Texas, Last in Texas" Motel and Cafe sign presides over the empty street by the wooden state line marker. Put one foot in Deaf Smith County, Texas, the other in Quay County, New Mexico.

Beacon in the dark

- Big Texan Motel, 7701 I-40 East

Stanley Marsh 3's Cadillac Ranch — Kazyo Omiya from Japan, "Cruisin'" Susan Daly, Helen Horn, Kyoko Omiya (Japan), "Milwaukee" Harry Jaeger

Favorite hangouts for food and drink

- MCLEAN — Red River Steak House. On Friday and Saturday nights Tye Thompson's mesquite smoke-flavored mouth-watering barbecue and prime rib are served. Tye is the artist who has done numerous 66 murals on area buildings.

- GROOM — Route 66 Steakhouse, formerly the Golden Spread Grill, Old Highway 66. A recommended biker-friendly stop for steaks

- AMARILLO —
    - Indulge in a Cowboy Morning Breakfast

Route 66 Steakhouse, Groom

or Cowboy Evening Dinner on the rim of Palo Duro Canyon.

- Big Texan Steak Ranch, 7701 I-40 East. Home to the 72-ounce steak, Big Texan Opry Stage, Saturday morning cowboy poetry, and Reptile Ranch, which houses one of the largest western diamondback rattlesnakes in Texas
- The Golden Light, 2908 West 6th. The oldest cafe that has remained in the same location in Amarillo — great hamburgers
- Blue Front Cafe, 801 West 6th. Comfortable and friendly. The stop where you can try Amarillo's version of the famous pig hip sauce!
- Beans and Things, 700 Amarillo Blvd. East (Old 66). Some of the finest barbecue and chili you will find in Texas. Look for the cow on top! Highly recommended

- ADRIAN — Mid-Point Cafe. A not-to-be-missed location

Father's Day

— BOB "CROCODILE" LILE

I've been riding cycles forever and have been just about everywhere my bike can take me, but my jaunts up and down Route 66 rank among my best ever. One in particular stands out in my mind. It wasn't even very long — only a few days on the Mother Road in Texas and New Mexico — but that ride has never left me.

My son Chris came along. I was excited since it was to be our first trip together on motorcycles. Although I was a bit fretful about his riding my Heritage Softail, I looked forward to the two of us being together out on the open road. He was twenty-six and I was fifty-eight and we had not had any real one-on-one time since his mother and I split up in 1986. Now we had this gift of time to share.

Chris lived in Amarillo. He rode out and spent the night before our departure at my place in the country. We got up early the next morning, drank a pot of coffee, and hit the road, hoping to miss the afternoon rains that visit the Texas Panhandle in September. Just in case, as we rode back toward Amarillo, we decided to swing by Chris's house to pick up his rain gear.

We cruised westward and I thought about my boy and how he had grown up. I used to get so disappointed when he was a little guy and would always want to go play and not tend to his obligations. He was a sweet kid though — curly hair, big flashing eyes, and that grin that could make friends with nearly everyone. I was proud of the way he got along with others. I knew that he was drawn to the underdogs who didn't stand a chance instead of taking up with the smarter and richer kids. I admired him for that even though it got him into trouble more than once.

Still, I guessed I was lucky. I had raised four sons and not one of them had ever been in any real serious trouble. Chris was the only one of the bunch to even spend a night in jail. Happened when he was eighteen and he got picked up for outstanding traffic warrants. He was too broke to take care of the fines. I'll never forget that phone call. I told him that if he was gonna dance then he had to pay the band. I also told him to get a job, join the Marines, or go to school.

"I'll help you anyway you pick to go," I said, " but I will not help you become a bum."

All sorts of thoughts and memories ran through my mind as my bike raced on and those shiny chromed wheels sliced through the wind. There is nothing quite like it. One side of your mind is free to wander and the other side takes care of the business at hand on the road.

We approached Amarillo and as we did we passed by the Clements Unit and the Neal Unit correctional facilities. We used to call these places prisons but now that won't do and we call them units. Sounds like we're talking about college dorms. Anyway as we passed the prisons, out of the corner of my eye I spied a group of inmates working along a barbed wire fence on the perimeter. There were ten or twelve of them and three guards. One guard was on horseback and all three of them had rifles and wore those mirrored sunglasses.

I glanced over and just as we got even with them, all the prisoners stopped working, stood at attention, and raised their right arms in a closed-fisted salute. It took a few seconds to register and then chills ran down my spine. Just the sound of those two Harleys running down the road was the ultimate sound of freedom. I glanced back and saw that the guards were stunned. My mind raced. Thank God, none of my boys are in there, I thought.

We made the run into Amarillo, side by side, my brain in overdrive. When we pulled in at Chris's place, he got off his bike and said, "Dad, did you see that? Did you see those men salute us?" He was as amazed as I was that a couple of guys on motorcycles could have that kind of impact.

For the next few days I thought about those inmates and I wondered what they dreamed about that night. I bet they dreamed they were riding bikes down a two-lane going anywhere they wanted to go. My heart ached because I knew that not all of them belonged there.

Chris and I didn't talk about it after that. We just enjoyed being together on the old road in New Mexico. We rode the mountains, the desert, and dipped into Billy the Kid country. It was pure quality time.

Now years later the image of those prisoners haunts me. I never ride that way without thinking about that morning and those men in silent unison saluting what we take for granted — a motorcycle, an open road to freedom, and time spent with someone you love. It still makes me cry. ■

The Big Texan

— MICHAEL WALLIS

The Big Texan Steak Ranch — a Route 66 favorite for years — moved to the super slab in 1970 when Interstate 40 muscled its way past the Amarillo city limits, and the restaurant's business plummeted overnight. Today, however, this Panhandle landmark has evolved into a Route 66 veteran that thumbs its nose at the generic cookie-cutter joints crowding the interstate highway. That is why friends of the Mother Road still stop to tangle with grilled beef served in all manners and sizes.

The Big Texan Steak Ranch, Amarillo

True to the old road adage that every business has to have a gimmick to draw folks inside, the Big Texan has become legendary because of its widely advertised promise of free 72-ounce steaks to all-comers. Of course there is a catch. Besides having to devour all of the four-and-a-half-pounds of beef in order to get the meal at no charge, diners must also consume a baked potato, shrimp cock-

tail, dinner salad, and a buttered roll. Oh, and by the way, they have to clean their plate in one hour or less. If they cannot eat everything, then they fork over fifty bucks.

Most of the thousands who try this gastronomical feat fail to beat the clock. Only a select few succeed and see their name and time posted on the winner's board. Through the years I have witnessed all sorts of people boldly march into the Big Texan and attempt to get the best of the slab of beef the size of a doormat.

Wisely, I have never taken any dares and tried to eat the monster steak myself. I would much rather watch the blue-haired ladies, little boys, truckers, cowboys, German tourists, and about every facet of humanity you can imagine sit down and give it a go. I knew an old bowlegged fellow from Shamrock who ate the big steak four times a year and each and every time he did it he first removed his dentures before he started eating.

Harley celebration on 6th Street, Amarillo

Still my favorite giant steak challengers to watch at the Big Texan have always been the bikers. They put on the best show of all.

Corey Hebert (right) winning Big Texan challenge, Amarillo

How can I forget observing an array of Harley riders, including a couple of pretty gnarly fellows, engage in a Big-Texan-sponsored steak-eating contest during a shindig on Sixth Street, the old Mother Road route through Amarillo? It was quite a scene and the winner — Corey Hebert, a young man from Milwaukee — not only bested all the others but also, true to his word, did somersaults down the Mother Road as soon as he was declared the steak-eating champ.

But my best recollection of the Big Texan is when two broad-shouldered bikers dueled it out before a huge crowd gathered at the restaurant. Both contenders appeared confident and ready. They sat side by side in chairs fashioned from steer horns at an elevated table with a big digital clock ready to start ticking. The rules of the contest were solemnly read out loud and — with bibs in place and knives and forks in their mitts — the pair mugged for their cheering biker well wishers. The signal was given and the battle commenced.

Almost immediately I spotted the biker who I felt would ultimately win. He made all the right moves of a steak eating pro, such as quickly drinking down the shrimp cocktail as if it were a shot of tequila. With that out of the way, he steadily alternated bites of the spud and salad with the enormous steak and he took only small sips from his glass of ice tea. Smart guy.

Meanwhile his opponent turned all his attention to the steak and neglected the side dishes. He also slugged down big gulps of his beverage. In no time at all he was bloated. Clearly this man was doomed to flounder and fail.

About twenty minutes into the contest, the more skillful biker started looking at the other man's plate. Then he leaned over and quietly asked if he could have some of his opponent's steak since his was almost all gone. Embarrassed and angry, the struggling biker yelled out a hoarse "No" while the hovering judge reminded the players that their food could not be shared.

Ten minutes later the confident biker was done with a time of just under thirty minutes. He pushed away from the table and waved to his fans. The other man struggled on but it was obviously hopeless from the looks of the food left on his plate. The contest was over.

The judge leaped on the platform and held the winner's arm aloft in a sign of victory. The two bikers shook hands and the loser skulked off to hoots and jeers. Then the winner asked a waitress to fetch him a doggy bag. When she brought it he reached over and dumped the contents of the defeated biker's steak and trimmings into the sack.

"Once I get back out on that ol' highway this hunk of meat will make me a fine afternoon snack," he said loud enough for all to hear. "Now, tell me what you got for my desert?" ∎

Recipes from Texas

— MARIAN CLARK

Chili, Texas style, is the official state dish. Never have so few ingredients created such a sensation. Chili is a gastronomical wonder-food that comes from humble beginnings yet has achieved almost mythical status. Here is a typical Texas recipe.

Route 66 Chili

2 pounds trimmed beef, cut in small cubes or
　　coarsely ground
½ teaspoon hot sauce
1 teaspoon Worcestershire sauce
8 ounces tomato sauce
3 beef bouillon cubes
Water as needed

Cook meat over medium heat in melted shortening until lightly browned. Add hot sauce, Worcestershire sauce, tomato sauce, bouillon cubes, and enough water to barely cover the meat mixture. Cover and simmer for about 45 minutes. Stir occasionally and add water if needed.

Spice Mix:

3 tablespoons chili powder
2 teaspoons cumin
2 tablespoons dried onion flakes
1 tablespoon garlic powder
½ teaspoon salt
½ teaspoon pepper
½ teaspoon oregano
1 bay leaf

Combine spices. Add half of the combined spices, including the bay leaf. Cook an additional hour, adding water as needed. Add remaining spices and continue cooking another 15 minutes. Adjust water to desired thickness. Remove bay leaf and taste to adjust salt and spices.

Note: Cooked pinto beans may be added for the last 15 minutes of cooking time — 4 to 6 cups, or according to personal preference.

Side dishes may include cornbread or tortillas, a green salad, guacamole, and fresh fruit. Beer is most often the Texas drink of choice. 6-8 servings without beans.

"Crocodile" Lile hangs out with sign by Stanley Marsh 3

DELBERT AND RUTH TREW remain driving forces behind the Old Route 66 Association of Texas. From their ranch near Alanreed, the Trews are also active in the Devil's Rope and Old Route 66 Museum and many church and civic endeavors in the McLean and Alanreed area.

A memorial brick from Old Route 66 Museum in McLean

Ruth Trew's Chocolate Zucchini Cake

2 eggs
½ cup soft margarine
½ cup oil
1¾ cups sugar
4 tablespoons cocoa
1 teaspoon vanilla
1 teaspoon soda
1 teaspoon cinnamon
½ teaspoon cloves
½ cup sour milk
2½ cups flour
2 cups finely chopped zucchini
¼ cup chocolate chips

Mix together all ingredients except zucchini and chocolate chips. Stir zucchini into batter last. Pour cake batter into greased and floured 9x13-inch cake pan. Sprinkle chocolate chips on top. Bake in preheated 325 degree oven for 45-50 minutes. Needs no icing. 12 servings.

THE ROUTE 66 STEAKHOUSE IN GROOM is a great biker stop. Will Frost now runs this eatery that many remember as the Golden Spread Grill. Rubye Denton bought the grill in 1957 and presided over it until her retirement.

Matthias Guenther, Harley biker from Kleinmachnow, Germany, says he had his best steak on Route 66 at this location. He also enjoyed the live music and friendly service.

Here is a place where travelers often find a piece of the real west. Local cowboys regularly pull up in the parking lot with their horses in trailers behind the pickups. They come in after shaking dust from hats and chaps and are careful not to tangle spurs with the furniture. Photograph sessions are common.

Squash Casserole
GOLDEN SPREAD GRILL

3½ pounds yellow squash, trimmed and sliced
½ cup green pepper
1 large onion, diced
2 ripe tomatoes, chopped
8 tablespoons margarine or butter
4 eggs
½ cup sugar
1½ teaspoons salt

¼ teaspoon pepper
¼ pound ham, diced
¾ cup grated cheddar cheese
¾ cup crushed potato chips for topping

Combine squash, pepper, onion, and tomatoes in a large saucepan. Add a small amount of water, cover and cook until tender, about 20-30 minutes, stirring occasionally to mash the squash. Drain thoroughly in a colander.

Add all remaining ingredients except chips. Pour mixture into a 9x12-inch lightly greased casserole and top with the crushed chips. Bake uncovered in a preheated 350 degree oven for 30-45 minutes until top is golden brown. 10-12 servings.

AUTHENTIC RANCHERS AND COWHANDS greet guests at the 7,000-acre Figure 3 Ranch each morning during the summer as the sun rises across the flat countryside. Wagons transport guests to the rim of Palo Duro Canyon where the scenery itself is worth the trip. A breathtaking view awaits as early morning mist rises from the canyon that drops some 700-800 feet below the frying-pan flat land. Stories come naturally and the food is belly-filling good. Sausage is spicy and the gravy is rich. Scrambled eggs come from the Dutch oven in golden mounds and tasty biscuits can be painted with butter or hidden under satisfying gravy. Authentic cowboy coffee completes the feast.

Hosts are Tom and Anne Christian and their cowhands, who see that every gathering is completed with a cow-chip throwing contest. If you miss breakfast, check out the Cowboy Evening Dinners, complete with man-sized steaks and giant burgers. This is a genuine Texas *experience*.

Cowboy Morning Sourdough Biscuits
FIGURE 3 RANCH

5 cups flour
1 teaspoon sugar
1 teaspoon baking soda
½ teaspoon salt
¼ cup cooking oil
2½ cups sourdough starter

Place flour in a large bowl and make a well in the flour. Pour starter into the well and add all the other ingredients. Stir until mixture no longer picks up flour. Cover and let rise three to four hours, or overnight. Place dough on floured board and roll to ½-inch thickness. Cut out biscuits and place in greased 18-inch cast-iron Dutch oven. Set by the campfire to rise for 1-2 hours. Place hot lid on oven, set oven on coals, and place coals on lid. Cook until browned, 5-8 minutes. 15 biscuits.

Sourdough Starter:
4 medium baking potatoes, peeled and quartered
4½ cups water
1 cup all purpose flour
2 teaspoons sugar
½ teaspoon salt

Place potatoes and water in medium saucepan. Cover and boil until potatoes are done, about 30 minutes. Drain liquid into measuring cup. (Do not use potatoes.) Measure 2½ cups of the potato water into large mixing bowl. Add flour, sugar and salt. Stir well. Cover with cheesecloth and let stand at room temperature until starter begins to bubble, about 4 days. Place in covered plastic container in refrigerator.

To use, take 2½ cups of starter out for above biscuit recipe. To remaining starter, add 1½ cups flour and 1½ cups warm water. Let starter stand at room temperature overnight, then replace lid and return to refrigerator. Use regularly and enjoy! Note: Some cooks like to add 1 package of dry yeast to the original starter to give it an extra boost. If this is done, the starter will begin to bubble in 2 days.

From Trond Moberg's notebook

"Usually a couple of us sign up to eat the 72-ounce steak at the Big Texan. This is one of our favorite places; the motel is great and the hospitality/service is superb. We are almost halfway along 66 by now and so we party late. We don't start again the next morning until 10:30. Next year we will have Hody Porterfield prepare his special campfire breakfast outdoors for us."

"Texas Caviar"
ROUTE 66 BIG TEXAN

2 cans (16 ounce each) black-eyed peas, drained
1 medium jalapeño, minced and seeded
¼ small white onion, chopped
⅓ cup Italian dressing
½ green pepper, chopped
1 tablespoon seasoned salt
2 tablespoons chili powder
2 tablespoons ground cumin
¼ teaspoon ground red pepper

Combine black-eyed peas with remaining ingredients. Serve chilled with corn chips.

5 cups

CAFES, BARS, ANTIQUE SHOPS, GALLERIES, and a collection of old businesses line the historic San Jacinto District on Sixth Street, Route 66, in Amarillo. This thirteen block segment of the historic highway was inducted into the National Register of Historic Places in October of 1994.

The street is pure Route 66. The Golden Light Cafe, the oldest restaurant in Amarillo operating in the same location, can be found here—try the burgers!

Amarillo businessmen joined forces several years ago to put together a book of favorite food as a benefit for the Fine Arts Division of Amarillo College. Hidden behind the red bandanna cover are some real jewels that not only satisfy the palate but reflect a Texas-size sense of humor!

Hot Damn Texas Panhandle Salami
Cookin' with Amarillo's Corporate Cowboys
Ben Konis

2 pounds lean chopped meat
2 tablespoons Morton's Tenderquick
1½ teaspoons liquid smoke
¼ teaspoon each of garlic powder and onion powder
1 cup cold water
Scant teaspoon peppercorns

Mix all ingredients well. Shape into two tight rolls, wrap in waxed paper and refrigerate for 24 hours. Remove wrap and bake salami on cookie sheet in preheated 225 degree oven for 2 hours.

(My mother-in-law, Rosie, gave me this secret salami recipe. Great eating with rye bread, Dijon mustard, and a beer with ice and lime.)

Cookin' with Amarillo's Corporate Cowboys
Cream Cheese with Horseradish Sauce
W. E. Juett

1 (16-ounce) jar apple jelly
1 (18-ounce) jar apricot-pineapple preserves
1 (1½-ounce) can dry mustard
1 (5-ounce) jar creamed horseradish
1 (8-ounce) block of cream cheese

Mix all ingredients. Spoon generously over cream cheese.

Serve on a platter with a cheese knife and assorted crackers.

Unused sauce can be stored in refrigerator, covered, for up to two months.

Chicken-Fried Steak and Gravy

Cookin' with Amarillo's Corporate Cowboys
Carlton Clemens

Select 1 pound round steak or cutlet of desired thickness. Cut into four servings. Pound with meat tenderizer (cleaver) or edge of small plate. Cover with flour and dust off excess. Dip slices in wash made of ½ milk and ½ buttermilk. Replace in flour and dust off excess. Deep fry at 350 degrees until the steak floats. Continue by pan frying at 300 degrees until meat is browned on both sides. Serve hot with gravy.

To make the gravy, combine equal parts of flour and vegetable oil. In a heavy skillet, heat the oil until hot — about 300 degrees. Add the flour, stirring carefully so the mixture doesn't stick to the pan. When the oil and flour mixture is hot, add milk and continue to cook until desired thickness is reached. Salt and pepper to taste.

Wild Plum Jelly from the Frying Pan Ranch

(Recipe for Husbands)
Cookin' with Amarillo's Corporate Cowboys
Stanley Marsh 3

Approach house carefully. Do not disturb any workers, paid or volunteer, who are moving around strange contraptions, pans and containers.

Expect to find all edible food out in small refrigerator near bedroom, in cans, or in the cupboards. Refrigerators are full of berries.

Be careful when you get up in the middle of the night not to jiggle any pans on the stove, island, or countertops, because they may be brimming full of plum juice in one stage of jell or another.

Do not be alarmed when your wife jumps up out of bed or out of the bathtub at various times and runs in the kitchen, moving about containers.

Do not ask the cowboys why they have coolers full of berries sunning in the front yard. They are ripening. You would just look foolish.

Smile and enjoy it. It's a beautiful harvest. The jelly tastes great and you will get a lot of compliments for just having stayed out of the way.

P.S. Bring your wife ice water or snacks; at night take her for a ride or to the movie on the weekend. She is tired from being on her feet. Let her choose the TV show. Encourage her to rest.

FORMER AMARILLO RESIDENT, DONNA LEA, travels Route 66 at every opportunity and swears bikers can't help but develop a craving for "buffalo chips." Once tried, they'll become a staple in every saddle-bag.

Donna Lea's Buffalo Chips

2 cups brown sugar
2 cups granulated sugar
2 cups margarine
4 eggs
4 cups flour
2 teaspoons baking powder
2 teaspoons soda
½ teaspoon salt
2 cups corn flakes
2 cups oatmeal
1 6-ounce package chocolate or butterscotch chips
1 7-ounce package coconut
1 cup raisins
1 cup pecans, peanuts or mixed nuts

Prepare these cookies in a very large mixing bowl or a roaster pan. Cream margarine with sugar and eggs. Stir in flour, baking powder, soda, and salt. Add remaining ingredients and blend well. Use an ice cream scoop to dip mixture. Place cookies on greased cookie sheet and flatten slightly, allowing space for cookies to spread.

Cookies will be 3 to 4 inches in size. Bake in preheated 350 degree oven for 15 to 18 minutes.

Approximately 48 large cookies.

Note: Many variations work well with these cookies. Try other cereals instead of corn flakes. Substitute dried banana for raisins or use ¼ cup applesauce to replace an equal part of the oil, use M&M candies in place of chips; add more raisins if desired, and include seeds or other dried fruit for added flavor.

LIFE CAN'T GET ANY BETTER then when bikers take to the open road in the Texas panhandle. Space abounds, the highway leads, and the majesty of America takes over. The sky, the clouds, the wind at your back, mirages, a distant rain, lightening on the Llano Estacado — it is Route 66 at its best!

Just beware of those 18-wheelers and the ever-present wind.

Bob's Tenderloin

Cookin' with Amarillo Corporate Cowboys
Mansfield Cattle Company, Vega

1 beef tenderloin, about 5-6 pounds, well trimmed

Marinade:

⅔ cup soy sauce
1 cup orange juice

Several shakes Worcestershire Sauce
4 teaspoons vinegar
Juice of one lemon
Pinch of sugar
Garlic and pepper to taste

Combine and mix all marinade ingredients together. Marinate tenderloin for several hours, turning occasionally. Cook on charcoal grill over medium coals (about 6 inches above coals) for 30 to 45 minutes. Tenderloin should be mopped with marinade and turned about 3 times.

LANDERGEN IS NO MORE. George and Melba Rook brought the old truck stop to life again in 1996 in time for the first major 66 gathering, "Run to the Heartland." With George's declining health, they closed the doors of their Neon Soda Saloon in March of 1998, but many remember the scrumptious biscuits Melba served there.

Melba Rook's Buttermilk Biscuits

4 cups flour
1 teaspoon salt
¼ cup baking powder
¼ cup sugar
⅔ cup butter
1⅓ cup buttermilk

Sift together the flour, salt, baking powder, and sugar. Cut in the butter and add milk, forming a soft dough. Knead on a floured board. Roll out to ¾-1-inch depth. Cut into 1½-inch circles and place an inch apart on a greased sheet. Bake in a preheated 400 degree oven for 10-12 minutes. 2 dozen biscuits.

From Trond Moberg's notebook

"Mid-Point Cafe and we are half way. Fran and her crew greet us with a fabulous lunch and apple pie. We recommend the grilled ham and cheese. This is a special place and also one of the highlights; we feel welcome. The Route 66 gift shop has a very good selection of merchandise. We spend a couple of hours here with splendid food, very nice people, and photo sessions at the Midway sign."

THE MID-POINT CAFE (ADRIAN CAFE), caught at the geo-mathematical center of Route 66, is the oldest continuously operating eatery along Route 66 between Amarillo and Tucumcari. A sign out front proclaims: Mid-Point Cafe, 1,139 miles to Chicago and 1,139 to Los Angeles.

Fran Houser owns the eatery that has been home to locals for years. Joann Harwell is often there baking her famous "ugly crust pies." Fran says this coconut cream Pie is close to the one prepared by former owner Jesse Finch, a legendary Route 66 figure.

Coconut Cream Pie
Mid-Point Cafe

⅔ cups sugar
2½ tablespoons cornstarch
½ teaspoon salt
1 tablespoon flour
3 cups milk
3 egg yolks, beaten
1 tablespoon butter
¾ cup coconut
1½ teaspoons vanilla

Mix sugar, cornstarch, salt and flour well. Stir in milk gradually. Cook over medium heat, stirring constantly until mixture is hot; stir in beaten egg yolks. Cook until thick. Add butter, coconut, and vanilla. Pour into a 9-inch pie shell and top with meringue. Bake in a preheated 400 degree oven for 8-10 minutes.

Meringue:
3 egg whites, beaten
6 tablespoons sugar
¼ teaspoon cream of tartar
½ teaspoon vanilla

Combine and cover the pie. Bake as directed above.

It was just after Christmas, 2000, when Joann Harwell of Vega shared a story that represents the very best of the holiday spirit along Route 66. She said, "There was a severe storm predicted here for Christmas Day. I had worked for Fran at the Midpoint on Christmas Eve and she was playing with the idea of staying open for Christmas Day to catch stranded travelers should the storm develop. I volunteered to help but when I got up Christmas morning, the roads were already too slick for me to get to Adrian.

"Sure enough, people started pulling into Adrian by Christmas afternoon to wait out the storm. By that time, Fran had prepared potato soup, chili, stew, and loads of cornbread, along with several cakes and cobblers. Instead of taking advantage of other's troubles, Miss Fran set out the dishes, formed a buffet line, and fed everyone who came through her door free of charge. The hotel in Adrian filled up and some people spent the night at the community center, so she sent stew, cornbread, and coffee over there as well.

"Fran reported this was the best Christmas ever for her. She and her Christmas family had an absolutely wonderful time."

Joann concluded, "Fran gave of her heart, and I feel so proud to know that goodness still reigns on the road."

LEAVE TEXAS AMID THE GLENRIO GHOSTS who preside under the very dilapidated Last Motel in Texas/First Motel in Texas sign. ∎

Butt Darts

— MICHAEL WALLIS

If you are ever cruising Route 66 and happen to find refuge in a saloon where a butt darts contest is underway consider yourself lucky and stay put. Call it a day and don't go any farther. Pull up a chair or stool and allow your bike to cool down. Do not leave until a winner has been declared.

Although it is played in bars and other venues around the nation, the best place to witness a butt dart game is out on the Mother Road with plenty of cold beverages and lots of good pub chow like pickled pigs feet, hard boiled eggs, and beer nuts.

The game is simple enough. Basic butt darts calls for a player to insert a quarter between the cheeks of the buttocks (fully clothed), waddle about 15 feet to a small container on the floor, and release the coin with hopes of it dropping into the container. The individual, or the team if you're playing teams, with the most direct hits wins. May sound simple enough but try it while wearing tight jeans

or leather riding britches and you'll find out just how hard it is.

Sometimes coffee or beer mugs are used for the catching vessels but the best butt darters, like the ones we've witnessed playing the game on Route 66 in Texas and points west, prefer to use a whiskey shot glass.

Some bikers claim that they've seen advanced butt darts, sometimes called flaming butt darts, played. This involves dropping candles — both lit and then unlit — from the player's derriere into a container. You earn one point if the candle enters the cup and the flame goes out and two points if the wick stays lit. If players are able to contort their bodies, they are allowed to cup their hands around the flame while moving toward the container. Usually the same candle is used for all rounds so the longer the game goes on the shorter the candle gets.

A story still makes the rounds of bike shops, barbershops and cafes up and down the old highway about a legendary butt dart contest held one evening in a Texas panhandle beer joint. Some top notch butt darters were competing when the door swung open and in walked a Lone Star belle with piled cotton candy hair, big blue eyes, and legs that stretched clear to Dallas. She wore hot pink shorts, bone white go-go boots, and a halter-top so scanty it made the bouncer blush.

This little gal proceeded to put some folding money on the bar in exchange for a roll of new quarters. Then she peeled off the paper and slapped that entire roll of coins where the sun doesn't shine. Proud as punch, she sashayed toward that glass jigger and when she was straddling the target she cut loose with her load. The sound of quarters spitting into that glass sounded like a slot machine paying off. Not a coin missed the mark.

It was quiet as a country graveyard in that joint when the woman pranced to the bar and picked up the winner's kitty stashed in a coffee can formerly used as a catch container for novice butt darters in training. She flashed her best smile and walked to the door. Before she left, she turned to a stunned cowboy biker sitting at a table with his mouth open and just a dribble of spit hanging on his lower lip. She flipped him a bright shiny quarter and flashed a wink. Then she was gone.

I've never found a soul who was actually there that night but I'd like to think its all true. Of course, I believe that jackalopes exist and my mind is still open to the exact whereabouts of Elvis.

Still, there is always a chance that some cool evening out on Route 66, while you are telling lies to a table of fellow bikers, the door may open and that Queen of the Darters will appear. Keep hope alive. ∎

Biker Flicks

Most bikers polled consistently select *Easy Rider*, the 1969 film starring Peter Fonda, Dennis Hopper, and Jack Nicholson, as the ultimate biker movie of all time. A distant second place finisher is the *Wild One*, the 1954 release with Marlon Brando, riding a Triumph, not a Harley. Here's a starter list of flicks to check out.

Easy Rider
The Wild One
Electra Glide In Blue
Hells Angels On Wheels
Mad Max
The Wild Angels
Black Rain
Running Cool
C. C. & Company
Born to Ride
Knightriders
Harley-Davidson and the Marlboro Man

Sell Sell Sell

— MICHAEL WALLIS

When folks complain that Route 66 is getting too commercial, I have to laugh. The highway has always been a corridor of commerce for people trying to make a living — selling a room for the night, a tankful of gas, some postcards, a peek inside the snake pit, a meat loaf sandwich. That's what the highway is all about — people serving other people.

Whenever you visit one of the countless Route 66 attractions, pause at a motel, or dine at one of the classic greasy spoons, plan on meeting honest-to-goodness people, interested in you and the world around them.

When you step inside a genuine Route 66 cafe, look for lumps in the mashed potatoes and expect the waitresses to have coffeepots welded to their fists. The only thing instant will be the service.

Along Route 66, folks have always known how to turn a buck. Travel a few miles. You'll find the odyssey is worth every penny. But bikers beware — you will also find that you will be shipping lots of road souvenirs home. ■

New Mexico

Fast facts from New Mexico

- Route 66 mileage in New Mexico — 261

- Santa Fe is the oldest government seat in the United States.

- Official New Mexico vegetables are chiles and frijoles even though the chile is technically classified as a fruit. The state cookie is the biscochito.

- Tortillas, served in abundance in New Mexico, are the fastest growing segment of the baking industry.

- Original Route 66 (Santa Fe to Los Lunas) and the post-1936 alignments of Route 66 cross in downtown Albuquerque, the only place the Mother Road crosses itself.

New Mexico Biker Road Rules

- Safety Helmet, required by law under age of 18

- Eye Protection, required by law unless equipped with windscreen

Must see in New Mexico

- State Line to San Jon — The 20 mile stretch of original Route 66 between Glenrio and San Jon is a test of Harley independence and not recommended by experienced riders.

- Tucumcari — The Caprock Amphitheater Summer Musical Production of *Billy the Kid* is located outdoors on the bluff of the Llano Estacado, 10 miles south on NM 469.

- Santa Rosa — Blue Hole — this clear artesian spring is 87 feet deep - an amazing stop that is highly recommended by bikers.

- La Pradira Lane Scenic Drive — Take SR 91 for 10 miles south of Santa Rosa to Puerto de Luna where Coronado once camped, then head toward Dilla to a bar and refreshments.

- Santa Fe — On the old alignment, a city unlike any other. Explore and enjoy, but remember parking may be a problem.

- Bernalillo — Bike the Jemez Mountain Trail Drive for a day of spectacular beauty.

Part of the original Route 66 between Glenrio and San Jon

The Land of Enchantment

★ **Santa Fe**

⊙ **Albuquerque**

66

NEW MEXICO

- *ALBUQUERQUE*
  - Drive Central Avenue, an 18-mile ode to Route 66 history that includes the Kimo Theater and the De Anza and El Vado Motels.
  - Enjoy the International Balloon Festival for nine days each October.
  - Visit Old Town, 2000 block of Central Avenue NW, then one block north.
  - Ride Sandia Peak Aerial Tramway, 11704 Coronado NE.

- *LOS LUNAS* — From Los Lunas, take NM 6, historic Route 66, for 33 miles to Correo, a great biker drive.

- *GRANTS*
  - See Ice Caves and Bandera Crater, twenty-five minutes southwest on SR 53.
  - View Pueblo of Acoma, the oldest continuously inhabited city in the United States. Twenty minutes east of Grants on I-40, take exit 102 south.

Beacons in the Dark

- *TUCUMCARI* — *BLUE SWALLOW MOTEL* 815 East Tucumcari Boulevard

- *SANTA FE* — *EL REY INN* 1862 Cerrillos Road

Mural in Tucumcari

- *Albuquerque* — Best Western American Motor Inn (Trond Moberg suggests this for large biker group) 12999 Central NE

- GALLUP — EL RANCHO HOTEL AND MOTEL 1000 East 66 Avenue

Swap Meet 66, Bluewater

El Rancho Hotel, Gallup

Where to buy stuff in New Mexico

- TUCUMCARI — TeePee Curios, across the street from the Blue Swallow

- CLINES CORNER — A giant collection of velvet paintings, rattlesnake ashtrays, and rubber tomahawks that has lured motorists since 1934

- CUBERO — Meet Lucy and Lawrence Peterson at their small store and saloon.

- BLUEWATER — Route 66 Swap Meet. Rated by some bikers as the best swap meet on Route 66. Eighty-nine year old Thomas Lamance has a motto: "Open when I feel like it, or by appointment."

- GALLUP — Richardson's Trading Post

Favorite hangouts for food and drink

- TUCUMCARI
  - DEL'S RESTAURANT, 1202 Tucumcari East Boulevard. Good food in Tucumcari since the early 1940s
  - LA CITA, 812 S. 1st Street. Eat under a Mexican sombrero!

Near Tucumcari

- SANTA ROSA —
  - JOE'S BAR AND GRILL, 865 Will Rogers Drive. On Route 66 since 1956
  - LAKE CITY DINER, 101 4th Street

Santa Fe

- SANTA FE
  - TIA SOFIA'S (especially for breakfast), 210 W. San Francisco
  - THE SHED, 113 East Palace
  - BOBCAT BITE, southeast of Santa Fe on the original 66 alignment. Highly recommended
  - ROUTE 66 SANDWICH COMPANY, 2430 Cerrillos Road

Bobcat Bite, Santa Fe

- BERNALILLO
  - SILVA SALOON, Camino Del Pueblo (Old Route 66). Open since 1933 and still operating with the 3rd liquor license issued in New Mexico
  - RANGE CAFE, 925 Camino del Pueblo

- MORIARTY — El Comedor de Anayas, West Route 66 Avenue. A long-time local favorite

- ALBUQUERQUE
  - M & J RESTAURANT / SANITARY TORTILLA FACTORY, 403 2nd Street SW. A place not to be missed
  - FRONTIER RESTAURANT, 2400 Central NE. A longtime Route 66 and university favorite
  - LINDY'S, 500 Central SW. Steve Vatoseow runs this historic Route 66 eatery across from the Kimo Theater.
  - THE ROUTE 66 DINER, 1405 Central Avenue SE

Marlo Strehlow Archer at the Route 66 Diner, Albuquerque

- GRANTS — URANIUM CAFE, 519 W. SANTA FE

- GALLUP
  - EARL'S FAMILY RESTAURANT, 1400 East Hwy. 66. Serving Route 66 customers since 1947
  - RANCH KITCHEN, 3001 Route 66 West. Over forty years on Route 66

Glenrio

— MICHAEL WALLIS

"Sometimes it's a little better to travel than arrive."
— Zen and the Art of Motorcycle Maintenance

The sun is coming to life on old Route 66 in Glenrio, a wind-swept town straddling the border of New Mexico and Texas. I have come on my Harley with a few other rider pals to pay our respects and snoop around. We park our bikes and hunker down on the edge of the frayed highway and watch as regiments of ants — just starting the day shift — construct cone-shaped mounds with bits of earth, sand, and grains of asphalt and concrete. These days only the ants can make a living off Route 66 in Glenrio.

Once a bustling railroad hamlet and later a noteworthy stopping place on America's Main Street, Glenrio was left high and dry years ago when Interstate 40 — the super slab — bypassed the place, forcing businesses to close and people to move on. It is now a ghost town in the making. Not that Glenrio was ever a metropolis. Even at its peak during the heyday of Route 66, the town was only a cluster of stores, cafes, filling stations, and frame houses with a population of less than one hundred. It seemed much larger because of the constant stream of tourists and truckers who paused for a hot meal, cold drink, tank of gas, or a bed for the night.

Glenrio used to be as busy as a noontime greasy spoon. Starting out as a farming community around 1905, by the next year a railroad station was established and the community bustled with cattle and freight shipments. From 1910 until 1934 the border town prospered and even supported a newspaper, the Glenrio *Tribune*. By 1920, six years before the birth of Route 66, Glenrio had a hotel, a hardware store, and a land office. When John Ford made *The Grapes of Wrath* into a motion picture in 1940, some scenes were shot at Glenrio.

The glory times are long gone. Nowadays more dogs than people live here. The town straddling two states has evolved into an oasis for tumbleweeds and roadrunners on the prowl for reptile suppers.

In spite of that travelers, including a fair number of bikers, still pause to pay their respects. They reflect on what it must have been like when the State Line Bar sold whiskey, beer, and gasoline and the Little Juarez Diner and the First in Texas/Last In Texas Motel and Cafe were humming — back when life in Glenrio was sweeter than truck stop pie. Back before grass poked through the pavement. Back before buildings turned into derelicts and the ghosts moved in.

I do not mind the ghosts. Most are old friends. That is why I come to Glenrio and to other towns along the Mother Road that time has forgotten. To me these places are as important as the many Route 66 towns that are still perking and serving up hospitality to generations of new travelers. The ghost places where deserted buildings with no doors or windows stare at the varicose highway, help remind me of the way life used to be before much of the nation became generic. I also like Glenrio because I can stand on the border in two time zones with one foot in the Lone Star State and the other in the Land of Enchantment.

Then, too, there is always road treasure. Stained menus from a cafe and yellowed gas receipts blow through the weeds. Broken coffee mugs, bottle caps, and dead spark plugs hide in the dust. In the past I have found a trucker's daily logbook, ceramic shards of bygone times, and newspapers as old as me.

On this day at Glenrio with my biker friends, I once again went hunting for remnants from the past. I found what I was looking for just inside a row of empty tourist cabins. Crammed inside an envelope were cancelled checks. The checks were imprinted,

TEXAS LONGHORN
ON HIGHWAY 66
FIRST AND LAST STOP IN TEXAS
GLENRIO, NEW MEXICO

The checks were dated in the 1960s and the 1970s, back when I recalled coming through Glenrio as a hitchhiking Marine toting a seabag. I recall the town was bright and shining late at night as all kinds of people — tourists, salesmen, truckers, and servicemen — stopped to refuel themselves and their vehicles.

Homer Ehresman signed the checks I held. I remembered him too. Back during the glory times of the Mother Road he owned and operated various businesses in town including a service station, cafe, and a tourist court. His wife also ran the post office. My friend Delbert Trew, a Texas panhandle rancher, told me that when he and his dad passed Glenrio they always stopped to have some of Mrs. Ehresman's wonderful pie. Delbert said it got to the point that when they walked in the cafe the waitress just smiled, cut a coconut cream pie in half and placed the halves before the two men. I also remember that pie and how good it tasted washed down with ice water and coffee.

The Ehresmans were there in Glenrio when the road was being paved in the 1930s. The workers slept in tents alongside the road and they made thirty cents an hour. Homer and his wife fed the highway crews three meals a day — all they could eat, family-style — for a dollar. During the bad times when flocks of Okies and Dust Bowl pilgrims came through town, the Ehresmans never turned anyone away from their cafe even if they had no money. Occasionally

destitute diners even came back to Glenrio when they got on their feet and paid what they owed.

And now here I am, standing in the remains of Glenrio, clutching Mr. Ehresman's checks. They were made out to meat companies, a firm that repaired the ice machine, and various other vendors and suppliers that kept his place humming. I thumbed through the stack of checks and then I reached the real treasure — the payroll checks. They were made out to the waitresses and some were advance salary checks to tide the women over. I read the names on the checks — Alice Davis, Dora May Campbell, Ella Jones, Midred Harris and many others.

They had been real waitresses. They served the public and never walked up to a customer and told them their name. You knew damn good and well she was a waitress.

Her feet hurt, she yelled at the cook, and called everybody Honey.

I wondered what had become of these waitresses over the past forty years. I knew many of them had died and moved on when the interstate came along in the 1970s, cut off the whole town and left it to die. I showed the other bikers what I had found and gave them each a check to keep as a souvenir of this stop. I put the rest of the checks inside my leather jacket and then we went to our bikes. A raven started squawking from a Chinese elm as we took our leave.

I still have those Glenrio checks. They are with my other cherished remnants from the old road. I value them and know that they are the DNA of Route 66. They spark memories and help me understand what needs to be done to prevent more ghost places from appearing. ■

Old Familiar Places

— MICHAEL WALLIS

In Tucumcari I can really take the pulse of Route 66 at Teepee Curios and the Blue Swallow Motel. When I call on both of these biker-friendly highway icons I find the beat of the Mother Road is strong and steady in New Mexico. I know in my heart that the much-heralded revival of interest in Route 66 is as real as the road itself.

To prove it to myself, all I need do is look into the eyes of Mike and Betty Callens, the steadfast proprietors of the Teepee since 1985, four years after I-40 bypassed Tucumcari. Instead of allowing the highway bypass to cripple their town, the Callens and other Tucumcari citizens pitched in and helped build an economy based on tourism and local trade.

Mike and Betty Callens are survivors. They are as resilient as the old highway outside their shop's front door. They are also inspiring role models for some Route 66 newcomers who have taken over the nearby Blue Swallow Motel.

When I enter the lobby of the motel, a Route 66 fixture since 1939, I still feel the presence of Lillian Redman, the former Harvey Girl and an authentic road angel who owned and operated this historic property for so many years. Miss Lillian, as we called her, was born in Clifton, Texas, and came to New Mexico with her family in a covered wagon in 1915. She moved to Tucumcari in 1923 and after finishing school she worked as a legal secretary and later in the famous Harvey House restaurants in Kingman and Winslow. During the 1940s she owned and operated a restaurant in Gallup before coming home to Tucumcari to work as a chef.

In 1958, Lillian was given the Blue Swallow as a wedding present by her fiancée Floyd Redman. Lillian added the office, an apartment for her aging parents, and the giant neon sign that transformed the Blue Swallow into a Mother Road icon. Floyd died in 1973, but Lillian stuck it out on the old highway through good times and bad until she just wore out.

Blue Swallow Motel, Tucumcari

Lillian passed away in 1999, just shy of her ninetieth birthday. Before she left us, Lillian and her magical cat Smoky, moved into a small house not too far from the Blue Swallow. Sometimes she returned to visit her beloved motel. She liked to sit in the lobby and greet guests. She died knowing the Blue Swallow ended up in caring hands.

Hilda and Dale Bakke now own and operate the Blue Swallow. The Bakkes and their teenage daughter moved to Tucumcari from Colorado and took over the declining motel in 1998 after Dale spotted a newspaper advertisement offering what was described as "The Deal of the Century." Neither of the Bakkes knew much about Tucumcari, motel management, or Route 66. They became quick studies.

"We thought it had great potential," Dale told me. "We liked the style of architecture, the neon, and the good feeling about the place. We also saw a great deal of restoration work had to be done."

Hilda and Dale rolled up their sleeves and went to work. They scrubbed and painted, stripped the wooden floors, updated the plumbing and electricity, and always "tried to repair rather than replace." Dale, a skilled electrician by trade, lovingly rebuilt the neon blue birds outside the rooms and restored the Blue Swallow's blinking signature sign that has acted as the old road's night light and attracted weary voyagers for decades. The Bakkes' cat, Frances, naps curled up on a lobby chair where she is often mistaken for Smoky. Two photo portraits of a smiling Miss Lillian have places of honor on a lobby wall.

"We have great respect for Lillian Redman and what she did day in and day out for so many years," Dale tells me. His words make my day and also bring back other memories like the day a collection of Harley bikers from around the world staged a very special parade for Miss Lillian.

It was in June of 1996 when the largest group of Harley motorcycles and riders ever assembled at one time, journeyed the length of the entire highway. It would be the first of two historic tours my wife, Suzanne, and I would be asked to lead for the Harley Owners Group (H.O.G.). I knew virtually nothing about motorcycles and so we made the trip in a van done up in Harley colors and Route 66 decals.

Many days into the westward trek the bikers crossed into New Mexico and spent the night in Tucumcari, the smallest city to host us during the two-week tour. The local officials planned a bike parade and all the riders cued up on the large parking at the city's new convention center. State policemen and town cops were out in full

Michael Wallis rides to see Miss Lillian behind Kent Meacham and becomes a born-again biker, Tucumcari

force to guide us and keep order. The streets, especially Route 66, were lined with eager spectators anxious to see the Harleys strut their stuff.

At the very last minute as we prepared to lead off in our van, I learned that for unexplained reasons the parade route had been altered and now we would not be taking all of the Mother Road through town. This meant we would not be passing The Blue Swallow and Miss Lillian who waited outside in her wheelchair. The bikers had heard about Lillian and her motel at a tour seminar that we conducted so they were anxious to honor her.

I was furious but it was too late. The signal was given and off we went. Later when it became clear that we were on an abbreviated route, I could see in my mirror that some of the bikers behind us appeared confused. By the time the procession returned to the staging grounds at the convention center, I was surrounded by a swarm of bikers questioning me about how the Blue Swallow had been bypassed. I told them what I knew but that was obviously not going to do.

Several bikers held a hasty conference and despite standing police orders forbidding any more parades, they quickly pulled together their forces and formed a convoy of a couple of hundred bikes. Suzanne jumped on the back of one bike and I climbed behind Kent Meacham, a stalwart biker and true Road Warrior in every sense. We took off, passing the bewildered police and headed straight to the Blue Swallow.

When we slowly passed in review, our horns blaring and arms pumping, a beaming Miss Lillian waved back and blew kisses. It was a tremendous salute to a great lady and one of the old road's most loyal protectors.

Tears rolled down my cheeks. It was at that moment — on Kent's bike before Miss Lillian and that old neon palace — I decided that I was going to get a Harley. It was crystal clear in my mind.

Miss Lillian at the Blue Swallow, Tucumcari

Later that evening we went back to the Blue Swallow and visited with Lillian. It was a fine time with bikers galore filling the small lobby. I recall her last words to Suzanne as we prepared to leave. When she saw tears on Suzanne's cheeks, Lillian asked what was wrong and Suzanne told her she just hated saying goodbye and not knowing when or if she would see her again. Lillian smiled and said, "Don't cry. Don't you know I'll always be here? I'll always see you in all the old familiar places."

As usual Miss Lillian was right. We still do and always will. ■

Note: Shortly after the 1996 tour ended, Michael purchased a new Heritage Softtail. He rode it on the next Route 66 tour.

The Freedom of the Open Road

—MARIAN CLARK

German riders Matthias Guenther and Christina Hey spent the last week of August, 2003, in Milwaukee at the 100th Birthday Celebration of Harley-Davidson.

Their American dream trip had only begun. By September 2, they were back at Chicago O'Hare where they picked up the Harleys they had shipped from home.

Christina and Matthias in Chicago as their Route 66 adventure begins

That day, they officially headed down Route 66 for a month of adventure on America's most famous highway.

Christina rides a customized Harley-Davidson Sportster, Model 1998, and Matthias owns a Harley-Davidson Dyna Super Glide, Model 2000. Matthias wrote after returning home to Kleinmachnow, near Berlin, "At the end of September we arrived in Santa Monica. We felt very well because we did it! Before 1989 this kind of adventure was impossible for people from Eastern Germany. More than 2,200 miles on our bikes — it was a great experience for both of us, especially to meet so many lovely people! We remember often the days we spent on Route 66."

Matthias and Christina prepared well and recorded hundreds of road icons on film as they explored the highway. Matthias listed several stops as especially memorable

First, he and Christina met Dixie Lee Evans, the aging queen of burlesque who presides over the Exotic World Museum in Helendale, California. For them, this was the most interesting museum along Route 66 because of the glimpse into the American movie and burlesque industry. Dixie was a Marilyn Monroe impersonator when she was in burlesque.

Dixie Lee Evans, Exotic World Museum, Helendale, California

Nearby, they thoroughly enjoyed the Route 66 bottle trees. This unique attraction resulted from Miles Mahan's desert dream. Mahan moved to the area near Helendale, California, in the 1950s and gradually began collecting bottles. His outdoor "museum" was later named "Hula Ville" for the giant dancer who graced the entrance to his collection. Mahan is gone now, as is the giant hula girl, but the bottle trees he and his friends collected still grace the old plot. The trees are made of bottles, hung on nails driven into posts. Miles and his friends didn't have any way of disposing of them, so the end result still shines in the desert sky.

In Newberry Springs, Matthias and Christina stopped at the Bagdad Cafe where they met the owner, Andrea Pruett. American's think of this stop as the film location for *Bagdad Cafe*. Matthias and Christina had seen the German version of the same film, only with another title, *Out of Rosenheim*, directed by Percy and Eleonore Adlon with Marianne Saegebrecht in the leading role. A biker who had played a bit part in that film happened to be at the cafe when Matthias and Christina were there — a real thrill. Matthias liked the sense of family at the Bagdad Cafe, the lighthearted jokes, good food, and fair prices.

Miles Mahan's bottle trees, near Helendale, California

Bagdad Cafe, Newberry Springs, California

In Cubero, New Mexico, they met and enjoyed visiting with Lucy and Lawrence Peterson in their small store and saloon. In Bluewater, they got acquainted with 89-year-old Thomas Lamance at his 66 Swap Meet. The swap meet was a favorite stop that Matthias recommends for all bikers. He especially liked the sign, "Open when I feel like it or by appointment."

Thomas Lamance at his 66 Swap Meet in Cubero, New Mexico

Halltown, Missouri, impressed the two because it was here that free coffee came with good conversation at an antique store where they found old German music and books.

Matthias listed strong winds, especially in Texas and Arizona, as treacherous. The winds, along with the big trucks on the interstate, made for dangerous riding. The older sections of road were also hazardous in spots because of unexpected splits, bumps, and ridges. He recommends driving very cautiously in these sections.

Another problem they encountered is one all travelers find — a real lack of consistent Route 66 signage. He suggests investing in good trip guides, maps, and planning each day ahead. Matthias and Christina also picked up on American bad habits: we are wasteful and careless with roadside debris, including old cars and other junk. ■

HARLEY-DAVIDSON DUO-GLIDE

HARLEY-DAVIDSON "SPRINT"

HARLEY-DAVIDSON "TOPPER"

HARLEY-DAVIDSON SUPER-10

HARLEY-DAVIDSON "SPORTSTER H"

HARLEY-DAVIDSON "SPORTSTER CH"

1961 MOTORCYCLE LINE - HARLEY-DAVIDSON MOTOR CO.

Recipes from New Mexico

— MARIAN CLARK

Chorizo sausage came to America from Spain. The sausage is coarsely textured and very spicy. Widely used in Mexican cooking, it is suitable for slicing and can be found in many specialty shops in western Route 66 communities. A great recipe to begin or end a day of biking in this spectacular state.

Chorizo, Onion, and Potato Frittata

½ cup olive oil or vegetable oil
2 pounds russet potatoes, peeled and sliced in ¼ inch slices
2 onions, sliced in ¼-inch slices
8 ounces chorizo sausage
12 eggs
Salt and pepper to taste

Heat oil in a large heavy skillet. Add potatoes in batches and cook until tender and golden brown, about 8 minutes. Drain on paper towel.

Pour off all but 1 tablespoon of the oil. Add onions and sauté over medium low-heat until translucent. Increase heat and add sausages, crumbling with back of spoon. Cook for 5 minutes. Transfer onions and sausage to a large bowl. and add potatoes. Mix and toss together.

Preheat broiler. Beat eggs to blend. Pour over potato mixture. Season with salt and pepper. Spray a 12-inch broiler-proof skillet with nonstick spray. Pour egg-potato mixture into skillet. Reduce heat in broiler and cook frittata under broiler until eggs are set, about 10 minutes. Heat broiler again and broil fritta-ta until top is lightly browned, about 3-4 minutes. Slide out onto plate and cut into wedges. Serve while hot with salsa, guacamole, sour cream, fresh tomatoes, and homemade toast. 8 servings.

Pecos Pueblo, Pecos National Historical Park

GRANOLA IS AWESOME BIKER FOOD. Here is the recipe served to guests at Alexander's Inn in Santa Fe. It packs well and makes for a great pick-me-up along the road.

Our Daily Granola
ALEXANDER'S INN

1 large (42-ounce) box old-fashioned oatmeal
½ cup wheat germ
½ cup oat bran

½ cup wheat bran

1 tablespoon cinnamon

1 cup each: walnuts, pecans, almonds

1 cup Canola oil

1 cup honey

1 cup maple syrup

1 cup molasses

3 tablespoons vanilla

2 teaspoons salt

1 cup each of coconut, chopped dates, dried cran-
berries, and raisins (or other dried fruit to taste)

Preheat oven to 350 degrees. In a large roasting pan combine oatmeal, wheat germ, oat bran, wheat bran, cinnamon, and salt. Stir in chopped nuts. Combine oil, honey, syrup, molasses, and vanilla. Pour over mixture until all ingredients are coated. Bake for 30 minutes, stirring every ten minutes to cook evenly. Add dried fruit after removing from oven. This granola freezes well in airtight containers. Approximately 12 cups.

SOME OF THE BEST FOOD SERVED IN NEW MEXICO can be found at the bed and breakfast retreats hidden along the way. Hacienda Vargas Bed and Breakfast Inn, in Algodonas, is noted for good food amid pristine vistas. Frances Vargas shared these mouth-watering favorites, perfect for hungry appetites.

Chorizo Roll
HACIENDA VARGAS

4 links chorizo sausage

12 eggs

1½ cups milk

2 cups cheddar cheese

salt and pepper to taste

2 cups cubed French bread

8 ounces cream cheese

1 tablespoon diced green chili

Fry chorizo, chop into small pieces, and drain. Beat eggs and add all ingredients except cream cheese and green chili. Mix softened cream cheese with green chili and set aside. Spray non-stick cooking spray in a jelly roll pan. Line pan with foil, including sides. Spray foil generously with non-stick cooking spray.

Spread egg mixture into foil-lined pan. Bake for 45 minutes in preheated 350 degree oven until eggs are firm. Allow eggs to cool then turn pan out onto waxed paper; carefully peel off foil, using waxed paper to help. Spread cream cheese and green chili mixture over entire surface. Roll egg mixture to form a tight cylinder. Garnish with avocado and salsa recipe below. 6 servings.

Salsa
HACIENDA VARGAS

2 large tomatoes

½ cup tomato sauce

⅔ cup green chill roasted or 4 jalapeños peeled and chopped (Add chili to taste)

⅓ cup yellow onions

1 tablespoon fresh cilantro, finely chopped

2 teaspoons fresh parsley, finely chopped

2 teaspoons red wine vinegar

1 teaspoon freshly squeezed lemon juice

1 small hot dried red pepper, crushed

Combine all ingredients in a medium bowl, let salsa sit at room temperature for ½ hour then refrigerate. 3 cups.

It was almost a hundred years ago that pinto beans were first planted in the Estancia Valley. For many years the area was considered the pinto bean capital of the world.

Now Moriarty celebrates the heritage of beans at the Annual Pinto Bean Fiesta and Cook-off held the second Saturday each October. Why not schedule your trip to take part!

Stuffed Chiles
Moriarty Pinto Bean Fiesta

12 whole green chiles, roasted and peeled
1½ cups cooked pinto beans
½ cup Colby Jack cheese, shredded
1½ cups Swiss cheese, shredded
1 teaspoon garlic powder
Salt and pepper
4 eggs
Bread crumbs
Vegetable shortening for frying

Mash beans. Add cheeses, garlic powder, salt, and pepper and blend well. Make a small slice in each whole chile to enable stuffing. Place about 4 tablespoons of bean mixture in each chili.

Beat eggs until frothy. Dip chiles into egg and roll in bread crumbs. Pan fry until golden and cheese is melting. 6 servings.

Bizcochitos are the official State Cookie of New Mexico. Here is the recipe served at Bottger Mansion near Old Town.

Bizcochitos
(Official New Mexico State Cookie)

2 cups butter
1½ cups sugar
1 teaspoon anise seeds
2 eggs
6-7 cups sifted flour
1½ teaspoons baking powder
½ teaspoon salt
¼ cup milk (water, bourbon, or sherry may be substituted)
2 tablespoons sugar
1 teaspoon cinnamon

Cream butter, sugar, and anise seeds in a large mixing bowl. Add eggs and beat well.

Combine flour, baking powder, and salt in another mixing bowl. Add to creamed mixture along with milk or other liquid to form a stiff dough.

Knead dough slightly and pat or roll to a ¼-½ inch thickness. Cut dough into desired shapes with cookie cutter.

Combine sugar and cinnamon in a small bowl. Dust the top of each cookie with a small amount of the mixture.

Bake on greased cookie sheets in a preheated 400 degree oven for about 10 minutes or until cookies are slightly browned. 6 dozen, 2½ inch cookies.

BECKY STEELE OF ALBUQUERQUE shared this easy casserole. Chilies relleños make for satisfying fare, especially when accompanied by green salad and fresh fruit. This is real comfort food, New Mexico style.

Chiles Relleños Casserole

6 eggs, separated
1 tablespoon flour
¼ teaspoon salt
¼ teaspoon pepper
1 4-ounce can whole green chilies
½ pound shredded cheddar cheese

Lightly spray an 8x11x2-inch baking pan with vegetable cooking spray. Beat egg whites until stiff. Combine flour, salt and pepper with egg yolks. Fold into whites and pour half of the mixture into baking pan. Slit chiles lengthwise and lay flat over egg mixture. Cover with grated cheese. Pour on remaining egg mixture. Bake in a preheated 325 degree oven for 25 minutes.
    4 servings.

TORTILLA SOUP SELLS ATTITUDE — it's perfect for bikers. Adjust the seasoning to your own heat comfort level then kick back and enjoy!

Tortilla Soup

2 tablespoons corn oil
4 corn tortillas, cut in 1-inch strips
3 cloves garlic, minced
2 medium onions, chopped

Camillo Pinto visits the past, Barton

4 tomatoes, skinned and chopped
1 tablespoon ground cumin
½ to 1 jalapeño pepper (depending on heat desired)
8 cups chicken stock
¼ cup fresh cilantro
1 cup diced cooked chicken
Salt and pepper to taste

Garnishes:
Extra crisp fried strips of tortilla
Grated cheddar cheese
Diced avocado
Chopped cilantro

Heat oil in 4-quart stockpot and fry tortilla strips. Add garlic and onions and cook until onions are soft. Add remaining ingredients except chicken, bring to boil, then simmer in covered container for 20 minutes. Add chicken and continue simmering for 5 minutes more. Taste and add salt or pepper to taste.

Serve with garnishes in separate bowls. 8-10 generous servings.

WHEN YOUR NEW MEXICO RIDE is over for the day, give in to a big platter of fajitas with your brothers and sisters from the road. Ron Chavez of the fabled Club Cafe in Santa Rosa referred to fajitas as "the new rage of the age." The same can be said for today's bike culture: Bikes are the rage of the age and riders are ready for rolling parties.

Sizzling Fajitas

¾ cup Italian dressing
1 (14 ounce) can green chilies, diced
1½ pounds of skirt or flank steak
1 large onion, sliced lengthwise
1 bell pepper
10 flour tortillas

Toppings:
Sliced avocado
Shredded Cheddar cheese
Sour cream
Jalapeño pepper slices

Combine dressing and chilies in 9x13-inch pan. Add meat, turning to coat with the mixture. Cover and refrigerate several hours or overnight, turning occasionally. Grill or broil meat, onions, and pepper to desired doneness. Slice meat across the grain, ½ inch thick.

Fill warm flour tortillas with meat, onion, pepper, and any toppings desired. Serve while hot.

10 servings.

THE 3RD ANNUAL *INDIAN COUNTRY DINING GUIDE,* published in Gallup, included enough recipes to satisfy every biker searching for authentic regional food — salsa, Navajo fry bread, enchilada casseroles, sopaipillas, green chili stew, piñon cookies, guacamole, chili con queso, gazpacho, and a wide variety of other native dishes. Here are some delicious examples.

Mary Muller's Posole Stew

1 pound lean pork shoulder
2 pounds frozen posole (hominy)
Juice of one lime
2 tablespoons coarse red chili
3 cloves garlic
¼ teaspoon dried oregano
Salt and pepper to taste

Cook the pork in a pressure cooker, with enough water to cover until tender. Reduce pressure under cold water. Open pot and add posole, lime juice and chili. Add water, about twice as much as the amount of posole. Cook under pressure again until done. Reduce pressure again under cold water. Remove the pork and cut it into small pieces. Return to cooker. Add oregano and salt. Continue to simmer without pressure for another 20 minutes or until hominy has burst but is not mushy. Serve as a main course or as a side dish.

Note: Adjust cooking time to your altitude, or see the instruction book for your pressure cooker. 8 servings.

Martha Joe's Navajo Fry Bread

3 cups flour (Use either white or half whole wheat flour.)
1½ teaspoons baking powder
½ teaspoon salt
1⅓ cups warm water
Shortening

Mix flour, baking powder, and salt. Add warm water to make a soft dough. Knead until smooth. Tear off a chunk of dough about the size of a small plum. Pat and stretch until it is thin. Poke a hole through the center and drop in sizzling hot deep fat (375 degrees). Lard is the traditional shortening, but vegetable oil is often used today. Brown on both sides. Drain and serve hot. Eat with honey or jam. 12-15 pieces.

Gazpacho New Mexico

"Liquid salad" from Spain with a special New Mexico touch.

2 pounds tomatoes
1 cucumber
1 large onion
½ green pepper
¼ cup olive oil
1 cup tomato juice
1 (4-ounce) can diced green chilies
2 large cloves garlic, minced
1 tablespoon vinegar
Salt and pepper to taste

Dice half the tomatoes, cucumber, onion, and green pepper. Set aside in large bowl. Combine the remaining half of the vegetables in a blender of food processor. Add the tomato juice, chilies, garlic, olive oil, and vinegar. Blend until smooth. Pour over container of chopped vegetables. Stir well and season to taste. Cover and chill thoroughly. Serve while very cold with garlic croutons or hot garlic bread. 8 servings.

THERE ARE SEVERAL VERSIONS of Mexican wedding cookies. After baking, there is a small hole in the center of each cookie. This is a recipe where substitutions don't work. Use real butter and cake flour, then pack some cookies along in your tank bag.

Mexican Wedding Cookies

2/3 cup pecans
1¾ cups powdered sugar
1 stick (8 tablespoons) butter, softened and cut
    into several pieces
¾ cup soft vegetable shortening
1 teaspoon vanilla
2½ cups cake flour
¼ teaspoon salt
Additional powdered sugar

Chop pecans and stir in a ½ cup of the powdered sugar. Set aside. Cream the butter and shortening until fluffy, then blend in vanilla.

Add remaining powdered sugar to the creamed mixture and beat until smooth. Add flour and salt, stirring just enough to combine. Stir in the nuts and sugar.

Form dough into ½-inch balls and place 1 inch apart on two lightly buttered cookie sheets. Bake in preheated 350 degree oven for 12 to 15 minutes. Cookies should not be browned. Cool on rack then sift a light coating of powdered sugar over cookies. 5½ dozen cookies.

THE FINAL SIXTEEN-MILE STRETCH of New Mexico Route 66 continues west on NM 118 into Manuelito. Stop to absorb the view and breathe deeply in this wide-open space. It's worth every minute. There is no ceiling over New Mexico and Arizona along here. The road skirts steep bluffs covered with the remnants of vintage advertisements, then crosses the border into Lupton. ■

End of an Era

— MICHAEL WALLIS

During the fifties, the bright neon lights began to dim along the Mother Road. It would be years before most people even noticed.

The seeds for the highway's demise were planted when the nation elected Dwight Eisenhower as president. During the war, the efficient German autobahn had impressed Eisenhower. He felt the United States could benefit from such highway technology and called for changes in the federal highway system. Proponents claimed that Route 66 was outdated and could no longer handle the increasing volume of traffic.

Ike's push for change was spelled out in 1956 guidelines for a new national interstate highway system. Little by little over almost three decades the old road was replaced by a series of five interstate highways. The new roads cut off towns and cities and the familiar Route 66 shields were removed.

Finally, in 1984, the last of the Mother Road was bypassed at Williams, Arizona. There was a ceremony, speeches, and lots of news coverage. As the old highway's supporters pointed out, the opening of the new interstates made it possible to drive from Chicago all the way to the Pacific without stopping. And the government called that progress. ■

Arizona

Fast facts from Arizona

- Approximate Route 66 mileage in Arizona — 376 miles

- In 1951, Winslow became the first Route 66 town in Arizona to establish one-way highway traffic, with 3rd Street westbound and 2nd Street eastbound.

- Winslow's "standing on the corner" sculpture is one of the most photographed spots in Arizona.

Standin' on the corner...

- Flagstaff's Museum Club has been ranked as one of the ten best roadhouses in America.

Arizona Biker Road Rules

- Safety Helmet, required by law under age 18

- Eye Protection, required by law unless equipped with wind-screen

Must see in Arizona

- THE CONTINENTAL DIVIDE —
  - Try Highways 124 and 117 through the Indian reservations.
  - Visit with residents and soak up the atmosphere.

- HOLBROOK — Take US 180 southeast from Holbrook to ride through the Petrified Forest National Park.

- WINSLOW
  - See La Posada, the last Harvey House to be built along Route 66, now restored at 401 East Second Street.
  - Try South Mogollon Rim Drive for spectacular views! South on Highway 87 or 99
  - See the Meteor Crater 22 miles west off I-40

- FLAGSTAFF — Take Oak Creek Canyon – great biker drive south of town on Highway 89A for a spectacular 25 mile drive to visit the art center of Sedona.

- WILLIAMS — See Grand Canyon National Park, South Rim

- ASH FORK — Flagstone capital of the USA. Begin west of here to drive 178 miles of uninterrupted Route 66, all the way to Topock.

The Grand Canyon State

- SELIGMAN — Angel Delgadillo's Barber Shop and Visitor Center, 217 E. Route 66. Angel, a Steinbeck Award Winner, will make you feel welcome! This is a strongly recommended stop.

- KINGMAN
  - Powerhouse Visitors' Center, 120 West Andy Devine
  - Hualapai Mountain Park, a good ride, 12 miles southeast

- PEACH SPRINGS — See Burma Shave Style Signs recreated by American Safety Razor Company.

- HACKBERRY — Visit John and Kerry at the Old Route 66 Visitors Center, once owned by Bob Waldmire.

- OATMAN
  - Oatman Hotel where Clark Gable and Carol Lombard spent their wedding night
  - See "Panhandling" burros along the street, live gunfights on weekends and holidays and the "Jezebels Sashay" on weekend afternoons.
  - Watch bed races down Main Street in January, the International Burro Biscuit Toss each September, and the Sidewalk Egg Fry Competition each Fourth of July.

Where to buy stuff in Arizona

- JOSEPH CITY — Jack Rabbit Trading Post

- WINSLOW — Roadworks Gifts & Souvenirs

- SELIGMAN — Angel Delgadillo's Visitor Center and Gift Shop

Beacons in the dark

- HOLBROOK — Wigwam Village Motel. Elinor Lewis, manager, is daughter of Chester Lewis who built the motel in 1950.

Wigwam Village Motel, Holbrook

- WILLIAMS
  - THE RED GARTER BED AND BAKERY, 137 W. Railroad Avenue, (520) 635-1484 or 1 800-328-1484
  - CANYON COUNTRY INN, 442 W. Bill Williams Ave., (520) 635-2349 or 1 800 643-1020

- KINGMAN — Hotel Brunswick, 315 East Andy Devine

Favorite hangouts for food and drink

- HOLBROOK
  - JOE AND AGGIE'S, 120 West Hopi Drive. A must stop, the oldest restaurant in Holbrook still in business
  - BUTTERFIELD STAGE COMPANY, 609 W. Hopi Drive

- WINSLOW
  - FALCON RESTAURANT, 1113 East 3rd
  - SANTA FE WHISTLE STOP, 114 East 3rd Street A Valentine diner on the site of the first house in Winslow

- FLAGSTAFF
  - MUSEUM CLUB, 3404 East Route 66. Depression era roadhouse. Highly recommended
  - MIZ ZIP'S, since the 1950s, 2924 East Route 66
  - BEAVER STREET BREWERY & WHISTLE STOP CAFE, 11 South Beaver Street

- WILLIAMS
  - ROD'S STEAK HOUSE, 301 East Bill Williams
  - TWISTERS, a 50's Soda Fountain, 417 East Route 66

- SELIGMAN
  - DELGADILLO'S SNOW CAP, on Historic Route 66
  - COPPER CART RESTAURANT, on Historic Route 66

- KINGMAN —
  - MR. D'S, 105 Andy Devine
  - CITY CAFE, 1929 East Andy Devine
  - VICTORIA'S MEMORY LANE, 120 West Andy Devine

- TRUXTON — Frontier Cafe. Mildred Barker operates the cafe and motel and has a great story about how the cafe originated.

- OATMAN — Oatman Hotel Raggedy Ass Miners Bar

The Museum Club, Flagstaff

Three Piece

— MICHAEL WALLIS

Paul loves his Harley more than anything else on earth. He spends so much time in the saddle riding America's highways that his legs are beginning to bow, just like a cowboy's.

After sweating on the assembly line for Ford Motor Company in Detroit ever since he was a kid, Paul said the hell with it. He retired, drew his last pay, and some pretty decent benefits to boot. Then he jumped on his bike. He's been out on the open road ever since.

Paul cruises any and all two-lanes but one of his favorites is Route 66. He's ridden the Mother Road all the way from Chicago to Santa Monica and tries to fit in a stretch of the old highway every chance he gets.

One summer evening at Flagstaff — a Route 66 town that serves as the unofficial capital of northern Arizona — Paul was motoring his trusty Harley back to a motel room after a night spent two-stepping at a lively street party. Paul felt no pain — not from booze or weed but from hours of sucking down thin air as he boogied to the sounds of a turned-on rock n' roll outfit.

Just as he made an easy turn onto Route 66, Paul — his windpipes and head clogged from ripe sagebrush and cottonwood — cut loose with a great sneeze. Much to his dismay Paul not only cleared out his sinuses but his upper false teeth plate went flying into time and space. He watched in disbelief as his airborne choppers disappeared into the night.

In a flash, Paul manufactured a U-turn, parked his bike, and broke out his Zippo. The cigarette lighter wasn't nearly bright enough to do him much good and after a half-hour of searching the weeds and brush, Paul gave up. He got on his bike and headed for the barn.

Three Piece (far right) celebrates with fellow bikers, Flagstaff

Next morning, his stomach growling for breakfast, Paul slugged down some hot Joe and headed back to the spot on the Mother Road where he and his top teeth parted ways. No sooner had Paul begun his daylight search when one of Flagstaff's finest pulled up. The curious lady officer asked Paul what he was up to and when he told her his pitiful yarn she doubled up in laughter. Once she regained her composure, the cop pitched right in and helped Paul scour the high grasses.

A little later, she called for some backup and before too long, a couple more squad cars arrived on the scene. The cluster of police vehicles and lone Harley attracted the attention of some other passing bikers and soon the search party had expanded to ten strong.

Together the cops and bikers systematically searched the ditches and poked through the weeds. Finally one of the officers shouted, "I found 'em!" Everyone turned to see the cop holding aloft Paul's upper plate — in three separate pieces. Although the teeth were less than whole the search party cheered in unison.

After thanking everyone and shaking hands all around, Paul leaped on his Harley and rode straight to the Wal-Mart store. He bought a tube of Super Glue and headed to the store men's room where he carefully put his teeth back together. He tucked them in his pocket to let the glue dry and by the end of the afternoon the dentures were back in place.

Paul, delighted that he wouldn't have to gum down his meals, celebrated with a steak dinner. When his pals toasted him, he flashed his trademark smile and boasted: "Some might get their kicks on this road but I found my grin on Route 66!"

From that day on, Paul, the grinning biker from Detroit City, became known as "Three Piece." The name has stuck, just like that glue that still binds his teeth. Keep an eye out for him on the open road. He is still out there. You'll know him when you see him. Look for that wide smile and those pearly whites. ■

Easy Rider

— MICHAEL WALLIS

Sweet Suzanne and I were riding our trusty Harley — with yellow Route 66 shields painted on the gas tank — along that old piece of Mother Road at Bellemont, Arizona. We were intent on visiting a true piece of pop culture history — the Pine Breeze Inn.

This was the establishment made famous in "Easy Rider," the classic biker film from 1969, starring Dennis Hopper as "Billy the Kid" and Peter Fonda as "Captain America." As children of the turbulent 60s, we are fans of the film that helped define that time and capture the true feelings of disenfranchised American youths.

The Pine Breeze Inn, about a dozen miles west of Flagstaff, is one of several sites along Route 66 that appeared in the movie. Since we were in the neighborhood, Suzanne and I thought it only appropriate to pay our respects. We remembered the scene very well — Hopper and Fonda pull their choppers up to the inn with its neon "Vacancy" sign glowing out front. Then the proprietor cracks open the door, takes one look at the pair outside, and flips on "No" in front of "Vacancy." The stunned bikers angrily ride off down Route 66 and camp in the forest.

Michael Wallis at the Pine Breeze Inn

When we pulled up to the Pine Breeze, it was clear things had changed. We could still make out the words, "Pine Breeze Inn" and "All Credit Cards Accepted" in the fading paint but the place was boarded up and deserted.

Another biker was already there snooping around. He stood in front of the building and it appeared he was writing something on the wall. Then he walked back to his bike, nodded a silent greeting to us, and left. Suzanne took some photos and we walked all around the property not really knowing what we were hunting for, unless it was some of our own memories from the past.

I approached the Pine Breeze and thought I would see what kind of graffiti our fellow biker had left behind. Maybe he wrote his name and the date or else tattooed the wall with some clever biker saying. He had done neither. I found only "66 Lives" penciled on the wall. That was all. That was enough.

We left the Pine Breeze and went just a short distance down the old road to grab some lunch at the nearby Route 66 Roadhouse Bar and Grill, next to the busy Harley shop. The Roadhouse was a biker's nirvana. Not only was it brimming with riders from all across the land, but also there was plenty of biker memorabilia, including a World War II Harley. Of course, the irony of the scene did not escape us since we found ourselves so close to a site once identified with anti-biker sentiments.

Then as we scanned the crowd for familiar faces while eating our lunch we both happened to looked up about the same time. There hanging from the ceiling in all its glory was the "No Vacancy" sign from "Easy Rider." We had come full circle. The tale was complete. We raised our burgers in a triumphant toast to the old sign and to Captain America and Billy and to a time when we were all nature's true children. ■

The Pine Breeze

Recipes from Arizona
— MARIAN CLARK

The Holbrook Summer Indian Dance Program includes a recipe for Navajo tacos, shared by the Holbrook Chamber of Commerce. Rather than using Mexican-style tortillas, Navajo fry bread forms the base for this popular fare. Every biker must try these!

Navajo Tacos

To make Fry Bread:
4 cups white flour
8 teaspoons baking powder
1 cup powdered milk
1 teaspoon salt (optional)
Warm water as needed

Mix flour, baking powder, powdered milk, and salt. Slowly add warm water to mixture to make a medium-stiff dough, soft enough to easily shape, but not sticky. Hand knead to form a ball about 4 inches in diameter. Shape into 4 flat discs about 8 inches in diameter. The dough should be about ¼ inch thick. Use of a rolling pin is not recommended. Add a small amount of flour if the dough becomes too sticky to handle.

Deep fry in hot oil (375 degrees). When a large bubble forms, pop it with a fork. When the sides begin to brown, turn and finish frying on other side.

Serve while hot, topped with pinto beans, ground beef or other diced meat, diced lettuce, tomato, onion, and grated cheese. Add other toppings like guacamole, sour cream, or hot salsa, if desired. 4 servings.

THIS PIZZA MAKES A DELICIOUS CASUAL MEAL that is unusual because of the tortilla crust topped with a delicious combination of seasoned beef and chopped vegetables.

Holbrook Mexican Pizza

6 ounces ground beef
½ package (1.25-ounces) taco seasoning mix
2 flour tortillas (10-inch size)
1 cup grated cheddar cheese
1 cup chopped tomatoes, drained
⅓ cup sliced green onion
¼ cup diced black olives

Two Guns, Arizona

2 tablespoons minced green pepper
1½ tablespoons sliced pickled jalapeño chilies, drained
1 cup grated Monterey Jack cheese

Cook beef and taco seasoning in heavy skillet until brown, crumbling with fork until separated. Remove and cool.

In same skillet, add a tortilla and cook until crisp, about 2 minutes, turning once. Remove and cook second tortilla until crisp. Leave this tortilla in skillet and reduce heat to low. Sprinkle Cheddar cheese over tortilla. Top with second tortilla. Heat until cheese melts, pressing with a spatula, about 2 minutes. Preheat broiler. Transfer tortillas to a pizza pan. Top with cooked beef, sprinkle with tomato, onion, olives,

green pepper, and chiles. Top with Monterey Jack cheese. Broil until cheese melts, about 3 minutes. Cut into wedges and serve.

2 servings, or 6 appetizers.

ED WOJCIAK WANDERED WEST FROM NEW JERSEY in 1976 when Flagstaff had only about fifty restaurants. He and his wife, Brandy, soon opened La Bellavia in the old downtown section of the city where a pizza parlor, Chicken Delight, and sub shop had once served nearby college students. La Bellavia remains a comfortable place that serves quality food, a favorite of local residents, and a great biker stop for breakfast or lunch.

Zucchini Quiche

La Bellavia

12 ounces of fresh zucchini, grated
1 small onion, diced
1 tablespoon cooking oil
10 ounces Swiss cheese, grated
7 eggs
2 cups milk
Salt and pepper to taste
1 baked 10-inch crust
¼ teaspoon nutmeg

Sauté grated zucchini and onion in cooking oil until onion is golden. Meanwhile, whip the eggs and add milk, salt and pepper to taste. Add the cheese and the zucchini mixture to the eggs. Pour into a baked 10-inch pie pan and sprinkle lightly with nutmeg. Place pie pan on a cookie sheet and bake the quiche in a preheated 350 degree oven for 1 hour. Allow to stand 5-10 minutes before slicing. 6 large or 8 medium servings.

When I inquired about good cooks in the Flagstaff area, the first person mentioned was Roabie Johnson, who works at the Flagstaff Library. Roabie grew up in Albuquerque and moved to Flagstaff to attend college. She loves the outdoors and worked for several years as a river guide. This potato recipe was a great favorite on trips. Even though it is a large recipe and is given with outdoor directions, it can be easily adapted for the oven and is certainly a biker favorite.

Roabie Johnson's Wild and Scenic Dutch-Oven Cowboy Spuds

1 pound bacon, chopped
5 pounds potatoes, washed and cut in large chunks
2 onions, each sliced in 6-8 pieces
3 cans beer
2 packages onion soup mix (1.15 ounces each)
1 pound Longhorn or Jack cheese, grated

Fry the bacon in a Dutch oven until brown. Pour off most of the grease. Add potatoes, onions, beer, and soup mix. Cook over the fire, on a grill, or on the ground with coals on the top and bottom of the Dutch oven. Add more coals to the top if the oven cools too much. You should be able to hold hands comfortably about 10 inches above the Dutch oven lid. Stir occasionally. Add more beer if needed. The potatoes should cook in about 1½ hours. When the liquid is thick and the potatoes are done, place cheese on top. Heat until melted.

The potatoes are good for breakfast with eggs, if there are any leftovers. Bake these potatoes in your oven at home when you aren't cooking outdoors. 15-20 servings.

Roabie Johnson says her mother is a wonderful Southern cook who blended her culinary roots with her western environment. This bread recipe is an adaptation from her mother.

Roabie Johnson's Heirloom Bread

3 cups white flour
1 cup whole wheat flour
2 teaspoons baking powder
1½ teaspoons baking soda

½ teaspoon salt
2 teaspoons cinnamon
½ teaspoon nutmeg
½ teaspoon ground clove
1½ cups sugar
1 cup margarine
4 eggs
2 teaspoons vanilla
2 cups applesauce
2 cups chopped pecans
1 cup currants

Combine dry ingredients; set aside. Cream margarine and sugar. Add eggs, vanilla, and applesauce. Add to dry mixture and blend until smooth. Stir in pecans and currants. Grease 2 9x5x3-inch loaf pans. Bake in preheated 350 degree oven for 1 hour or until bread tests done with a toothpick inserted into the center. 2 loaves.

"Cruisin'" Susan Daly at the Old Route 66 Visitors Center, Hackberry

LONGTIME FLAGSTAFF RESIDENT, PEGGY HARRIS, was born near Springfield, Missouri, another Route 66 community. She said she never wanted to be a dull ho-hum-type cook, so she does a lot of experimenting. Peggy says her friends go nuts over her mulligatawny soup. For years she didn't have a recipe, but prepared it by using a pinch of this and that. Finally, they insisted she write out some directions. Peggy says this soup is one that requires tasting to adjust flavors for individual preferences. But what hearty, comfortable results! Perfect after a long day on the bike.

Peggy Harris' Mulligatawny Soup

1 onion
1 large or 2 small carrots
3 stalks celery
4 tablespoons flour
4 tablespoons butter or margarine
4 cups chicken stock
2 cups chopped cooked chicken
2 tart cooking apples, chopped
2 cups cooked rice
2 teaspoons curry powder
1 teaspoon (approximately) of each of the following:
    turmeric
cardamom, coriander, garlic, and salt.
½ teaspoon pepper
2 cups cream

Chop onion, carrots and celery finely by hand or in the food processor. Melt the butter or margarine and saute vegetables in heavy skillet until tender. Add enough flour to make a roux. More margarine may be necessary.

In a stock pot, heat the chicken stock and chicken. Add the apples and rice. Stir in the vegetables and seasonings, adjusting quantity to your individual taste. Stir in the cream just before serving. Approximately 10 cups.

Christina Hey at the Grand Canyon

BEAVER STREET BREWERY AND WHISTLE STOP CAFE can be found on the corner of Phoenix and Beaver Streets, just south of the railroad tracks and historic downtown Flagstaff. The original building was constructed in 1938 of Malapais rock collected from surrounding volcanic beds.

Beaver Street Brewery and Whistle Stop Cafe opened in March of 1994, featuring handcrafted brews by owner and brewmaster Evan Hanseth. It is a great biker stop.

This rib-sticking chili is a favorite that is bound to satisfy!

Easy Ridin' in Bellemont

Grand Canyon Harley-Davidson/Buell can be found in Bellemont, Arizona, a tiny hamlet west of Flagstaff that caters to bikers. The town's fame is due in part to the Pine Breeze Inn, made famous when Easy Rider characters, Captain America and Billy, failed to find a room on their fateful 1969 biker cruise. The inn remains boarded up today, but bikers are now welcome to camp on the 2½-acre property. Just down the road, both the highly successful Grand Canyon Harley-Davidson facility and the Route 66 Roadhouse Bar and Grill, pay tribute to everything Harley.

At the roadhouse, the "No Vacancy" sign from the movie hangs from the ceiling. Table tops are glass-covered motorcycle wheels, a World War II cycle stands next to a "Harley Parking Only" sign, and a Harley-Davidson juke box cranks out road music in one corner.

Felix and Lori Mansane built the roadhouse and frequently use it for biker parties and charity events. Mansane has been an avid biker for over forty years.

One of the few other establishments in Bellemont is a bar named Junior's, where more bikers gather. Bellemont residents agree that biking today is about the ride and recreation. They appreciate Harley bikers who are most often middle-aged businessmen and women who have the money to express the Harley distinction. Bellemont is a biker "must stop."

Hart Prairie Chili

BEAVER STREET BREWERY AND WHISTLE STOP CAFE

Brown together in a large skillet:

2 tablespoons canola oil

2½ pounds of beef chuck roast, trimmed and cut into ¼ inch cubes

1½ pounds of beef chuck roast, trimmed and coarsely ground

I red bell pepper, diced in ½-inch pieces

1 fresh poblano chili, diced in ½-inch pieces

1 red onion, cut in strips

1 tablespoon fresh garlic, minced

When vegetables become translucent, add:

½ cup chili powder

2 tablespoons cumin

1 tablespoon garlic powder

1 tablespoon onion powder

1 teaspoon cayenne pepper

1 tablespoon kosher salt

1 tablespoon oregano

And finally, add:

1 cup bitter ale or other mild beer

4 cups chicken broth

4 cups diced canned tomatoes in juice

Simmer for 20 minutes then add:

2 cups black beans, cooked and drained

2 cups kidney beans, cooked and drained

2 cups pinto beans, cooked and drained

Continue simmering until meat is tender and chili is hot.

Serve immediately to a large crowd, or cover tightly and store in refrigerator briefly, or freeze. 20 servings.

FOOD FOR GRAZING, PREFERABLY WITH THE FINGERS, is always popular around Bellemont. This recipe is typical of the easy yet good fare that is just as popular with the guys as with the gals.

Hot Artichoke Dip

½ cup chopped onion

1 teaspoon butter

1 can (14 ounces) artichoke hearts, chopped in ½ inch pieces

1 cup low-fat mayonnaise

1 cup grated Parmesan cheese

⅓ cup picante sauce (mild or hot, depending on taste)

Garlic salt to taste

Saute the onion in butter. Combine with remaining ingredients and pour into a shallow 8-inch casserole dish. Bake in a preheated 350 degree oven for 15 to 20 minutes or until bubbly and light brown. Serve warm with crackers or toast squares. Approximately 10 servings.

LOCATED ON WHISKEY ROW IN DOWNTOWN WILLIAMS, *The Red Garter Bed and Bakery* is housed in a fully restored 1897 bordello. John Holst, the innkeeper, carefully renovated the historic building at 137 Railroad Avenue. He opened *The Red Garter Bed and Bakery* in 1994. There is a honeymoon suite, the madam's room at the top of the stairs, and two rooms formerly called cribs. A full-service bakery and coffee shop is located in the downstairs turn-of-the-century saloon. Holst has many historic photographs and a wealth of stories to share.

Gingerbran Muffins
RED GARTER BED AND BAKERY

½ cup oil
⅔ cup molasses
2 eggs
¼ cup milk
2 cups flour
1½ teaspoons baking powder
1 teaspoon ground ginger
½ teaspoon cinnamon
½ teaspoon nutmeg
¼ teaspoon ground cloves
¼ cup wheat bran

Grease 8-10 2-inch muffin tins. Combine oil, molasses, eggs, and milk. Mix well. Stir flour with baking soda and spices. Add to liquid mixture but do not over-mix. Pour muffin batter into tins. Sprinkle tops with wheat bran. Bake in preheated 350 degree oven for 20 minutes or until browned. 8-10 muffins

El Tovar Chili
GRAND CANYON NATIONAL PARK LODGES

1½ pound diced filet mignon
1 pound diced pork loin
1 white onion, diced fine
1 jalapeño pepper, chopped fine
1 tablespoon fresh garlic

Linda Scott watches train from bridge at Correro

3 (12-ounce) cans beer
3 tablespoons chili powder
1 tablespoon paprika
1 tablespoon cumin
1 tablespoon Tabasco sauce
½ cup diced tomatoes
½ cup tomato sauce
Salt and pepper to taste
½ cup grated Monterey Jack cheese

Sauté the filet mignon, pork loin, onion, and jalapeño pepper.

Add remaining ingredients. Add salt and pepper and simmer for 2-3 hours on low heat.

To serve, put a serving of chili into oven-proof bowl, top with Jack cheese, and put under broiler for a few moments until cheese is melted and slightly brown. Serve with blue corn chips and a slab of cornbread. 6 portions.

ANGEL DELGADILLO IS THE DRIVING FORCE behind the Historic Route 66 Association of Arizona and is loved by Route 66 travelers from coast to coast. He operates his barber shop just a few doors from his late brother Juan Delgadillo's Snow Cap in Seligman. Both establishments are "must see" stops for Route 66 bikers.

Trond and his band from Norway make this a regular stop and bikers from around the world join them. German biker, Matthias Guenther, stopped for a haircut, gifts, and small talk with Angel and recommended staying at the Aztec Motel across the street from Angel's shop.

Angel is interviewed regularly for specials about Route 66 that are shown around the world. Stop, too, at the grocery store next to the barber shop. Juan and Angel's brother, Joe, operated it until his retirement. It's a friendly place with a good deli.

Angel's wife Vilma shares these favorite family recipes.

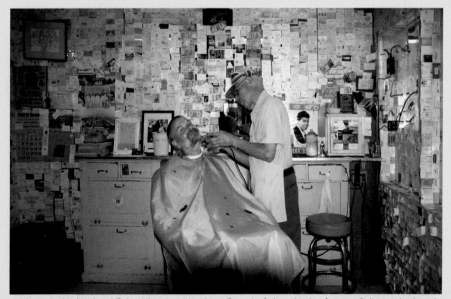

A trip highlight, Angel Delgadillo trims Matthias Guenther's beard in his famous Seligman barber shop

Martha Delgadillo's Impossible Quesa-dillo Pie

2 (4-ounce) cans chopped green chilies
4 cups shredded cheese (about 1 pound)
2 cups milk
1 cup baking mix (Bisquick)
4 eggs

Preheat oven to 425 degrees. Grease a 10-inch pie plate. Sprinkle chilies and cheese in plate. Blend milk, baking mix and eggs until smooth in a blender, food processor, or with a hand beater for at least a minute. Pour mixture into pie plate. Bake 25-30 minutes or until knife inserted in the center comes out clean. Let stand 10 minutes before cutting. 8 slices.

Aztec Motel, Seligman

Vilma Delgadillo's Chiles Relleños Casserole

1 pound ground beef
½ cup chopped onion
½ teaspoon salt
¼ teaspoon pepper
2 (4-ounce) cans green chiles, peeled, cut in halves
    lengthwise and seeded

Several dashes hot sauce
1½ cups shredded longhorn cheese
1½ cups milk
¼ cup flour
½ teaspoon salt
Dash of pepper
4 eggs

In a skillet, brown beef and onions. Drain fat. Sprinkle meat with salt and pepper. Spread half the chiles in a 10x6-inch baking dish. Sprinkle with cheese and top with meat mixture. Arrange remaining chiles over meat. Beat egg whites until foamy. Combine egg yolks with milk, flour, salt and pepper. Fold into whites and pour over meat. Bake in a preheated 350 degree oven until knife comes out clean when inserted in center, about 30 minutes. 6 servings.

Angel and Vilma Delgadillos' Route 66 Gift Shop, Seligman

149

Juan Delgadillo's Snow Cap is run by his family since Juan's death in 2004.

HAVE COFFEE AND DESSERT WITH MILDRED BARKER at the Frontier Cafe in Truxton. Mildred tells a great story about the original owner, Alice Wright. It seems Alice inherited some money in Los Angeles. Alice believed in the occult, so when a fortune teller told her to travel 400 miles from Los Angeles and build a cafe, she did just that. When she arrived in Truxton, she had traveled the 400 miles, so she built her cafe and settled in.

Old-Fashioned Banana Pudding

FRONTIER CAFE

2 ½ cups evaporated milk

4 eggs, separated

⅔ cup sugar

6 tablespoons cornstarch

1 tablespoon butter

½ teaspoon vanilla

Pinch of salt

Vanilla wafer cookies

2-3 bananas

Scald the milk and stir in beaten egg yolks. Combine sugar and corn starch, stir into egg mixture. Add butter and continue stirring until mixture has thickened. Add vanilla and pinch of salt.

Line a 2-quart dish with cookies. Slice bananas over the cookies. Pour pudding mixture over bananas and allow to cool. If desired, whip egg whites and add ½ cup sugar. Spread over pudding and place in preheated 400 degree oven for 5 minutes to brown. 8 servings.

JACKIE ROWLAND IS A TRANSPLANTED OKIE who runs Fast Fanny's Place in Oatman. She has watched this tiny forgotten mining town come to life again, because tourists have rediscovered mountain life above those hairpin turns that were once necessary in order to proceed along Route 66.

Here is Jackie's favorite breakfast recipe, quick to prepare and always satisfying. She keeps tortillas and chorizo in the freezer so she can prepare the dish for "roadies" who often drop by for a visit. Add a couple more eggs and another tortilla or two to stretch the recipe when more folks show up than expected.

The salsa recipe is a prize winner, first served at one of the local chili cook-off competitions.

Jackie's Mexi Breakfast
FAST FANNY'S PLACE

½ pound beef or pork chorizo (Mexican sausage)
12-14 corn tortillas
4 tablespoons margarine
6-8 eggs, beaten

1 cup diced tomatoes, drained
1 medium bell pepper, diced
1 small onion, diced
1 cup shredded cheddar cheese

Garnishes:
Sour cream
Guacamole
Warm salsa

In a large skillet brown the chorizo, then remove. Add margarine and the tortillas torn in 1-inch pieces. Warm to soften. Add chorizo to egg mixture and fold in diced vegetables. Pour over tortillas and cook in skillet, stirring occasionally until eggs are set. Sprinkle with cheese then cover skillet until cheese is melted.

Serve with garnishes of sour cream, guacamole and salsa. 4 servings.

Linda Ellithorpe's Jailhouse Salsa

2 cans (15½ ounces each) tomatoes, mashed
1 can (8 ounces) tomato sauce
1 cup minced onion
1 cup minced bell pepper
2 cans (4.5 ounces each) chopped mild chilies
Garlic powder, oregano, cilantro, salt and pepper to taste

Mix well and serve over Mexi Breakfast or with tortilla chips. 6 cups.

"UNCLE CHARLIE HICKS" IS ANOTHER OKIE who has retired to Oatman. Uncle Charlie bartends at the Oatman Hotel, is the head gunfighter with the Ghostrider Gunfighters every weekend, and as "Reverend Uncle Charlie Hicks," is the local marrying and burying preacher.

Uncle Charlie collected this stew recipe while doing a stint as a gold prospector. Be sure to look him up when in Oatman.

Oatman Hotel

Uncle Charlie Hicks' Beer Stew with Drop Dumplings

Beer Stew:

2 pounds lean beef, cut into chunks
1 large onion, coarsely chopped
1 (15½ ounce) can beef broth
1 can beer
1 bay leaf
3 tablespoons brown sugar
¼ cup red wine vinegar

Brown beef and onions together in a large stew pot. Add broth, beer, bay leaf, sugar, and vinegar. Cover and simmer until meat is tender.

Drop Dumplings:

1 cup flour
1 teaspoon salt
½ teaspoon baking soda
Milk to make a stiff, sticky batter

Mix dry ingredients. Add milk slowly. Drop by spoonfuls into bubbling stew. A little water may be needed. Cover and steam for twenty minutes. 6 servings.

TAKE THAT WINDING HILL from Oatman to Golden Shores in the daylight as you head to the Colorado River and California! ■

Beacons in the Darkest Hours

— MICHAEL WALLIS

The Mother Road never really disappeared. Those of us who love history and popular culture knew that would not happen. The shields were taken down and whole towns cut off, but the spirit and legend of the highway could not be destroyed. Neither could the people.

Mother Road veterans — Ted Drewes, Lillian Redman, Angel Delgadillo, and others — could not be stopped from fanning to life that spark of pure energy that remained. They heard the poetry of the road and answered the call. They switched on their bright signs. Images of blue swallows, bucking horses, and Indian chiefs lured folks back to the road America loved best. The blue swallows took flight. The magic still worked.

Neon ribbons popped back to life and, like beacons, showed the way. Clusters of flickering light tempted interstate travelers like ribbons of sweet candy.

Route 66 came alive each time a neon sign was ignited, or someone hummed Bobby Troup's highway anthem, or read about the Joads, or watched a rerun of the television series, or rode through time and space on one of the old alignments.

It comes to life every time a biker heads into the wind on the old two-lane.

Like a revived neon marquee, the highway found new life. The Mother Road remains stronger than ever. ∎

California

Fast facts from California

- There are approximately 312 miles of Route 66 in California.

- The state is our nation's third largest in area, but first in population.

- More than 300,000 tons of grapes are grown here annually and more than 17 million gallons of wine are made each year in the state.

- San Bernardino County is the largest in the nation with nearly three million acres.

California Biker Road Rules

- Safety Helmet, required by law

- Eye Protection, no restriction

Must see in California

- NEEDLES
  - El Garces — A former Harvey House and depot
  - Enjoy side trips to Laughlin and Havasu City.
  - East Mojave National Scenic Area and Goffs Schoolhouse. Tours begin at Essex Road.
- AMBOY — Roy's Cafe and Motel — recently under new ownership

- BARSTOW
  - Casa Del Desierto, a former Harvey Hotel, now the train and bus depot
  - Side trip to Calico Ghost Town, 11 miles northeast on I-15

Bikers at trail's end, Santa Monica

The Golden State

- *HELENDALE*
  - Dixie Lee Evans' Exotic World Burlesque Museum
  - Miles Mahan's Bottle Tree Museum

- *VICTORVILLE* — California Route 66 Museum

- *FONTANA* — Old Route 66 Orange Juice stand next to newly reopened Bono's Burgers

- *AZUZA* — The San Gabriel Canyon Road offers a great biker ride.

- *MONROVIA* — Aztec Hotel, 311 West Foothill Blvd. The only example of Mayan architecture along Route 66

- *PASADENA* — Rose Bowl Parade on New Year's Day (on old Route 66)

- *SANTA MONICA*
  - Santa Monica Pier — An antique carrousel, and ocean excitement
  - Will Rogers State Historic Park, 1501 Will Rogers State Park Road, Pacific Palisades Drive

Ocean Ave., Santa Monica

Favorite hangouts for food and drink

- NEEDLES
  - 66 Burger Hut, 701 West Broadway
  - Hungry Bear, 1906 Needles Highway

- LUDLOW — Ludlow Cafe

- NEWBERRY SPRINGS — Bagdad Cafe (aka Sidewinder Cafe), 46548 National Trails Highway

- BARSTOW — Idle Spurs Steakhouse, 690 Hwy 58

- VICTORVILLE
  - La Fonda Mexican Restaurant, 15556 6th Street. Good food near the Route 66 Museum
  - Emma Jean's Hollandburger Cafe, 17143 D Street, on Route 66

- CAJON PASS — Summit Inn — on Route 66 since 1952. Off I-15, Cajon Pass, Oak Hill Road Exit

- SAN BERNARDINO — Mitla Cafe, 602 North Mt. Vernon. A longtime Mexican favorite on old Route 66

- RANCHO CUCAMONGA — Magic Lamp, 8189 Foothill Blvd.

- UPLAND — Buffalo Inn, 1814 West Foothill Blvd. A favorite for students from nearby Claremont. Try the "buffalo chips" with your burgers.

- MONROVIA — The Brass Elephant, 311 West Foothill Blvd., inside the Aztec Hotel

- Pasadena — Fair Oaks Pharmacy, corner of Mission and Fair Oaks

- WEST HOLLYWOOD
  - Barney's Beanery, 8447 Santa Monica Blvd.
  - Formosa Cafe, 7156 Santa Monica Blvd.

- SANTA MONICA
  - Rusty's Surf Ranch, 256 Santa Monica Pier
  - Ye Old King's Head British Pub, 116 Santa Monica Blvd.

Posse of road-weary bikers above the Pacific, Santa Monica

Bagdad Cafe

—MICHAEL WALLIS

Aband of bikers, almost two weeks on the road, were nearing the tail end of a ride down the entire length of Route 66. It was July in high desert country where the temperature soars, so the bikers — in an effort to outfox the merciless sun — pulled out of Kingman in the dark wee hours. California bound, they wound their way up the twisty two-lane to funky Oatman tucked away in the Black Mountains. Everyone dropped into second gear in the old mining town where the populace and the wandering burros that tourists take pleasure in feeding still slumbered beneath the moonglow.

The riders followed the old Mother Road out of Oatman. The path, flanked with yucca, mesquite, and greasewood, leads to the land of milk and honey that lured hordes of Okies and Dust Bowl pilgrims during the tough lean years of the 1930s.

Daylight was still a rumor when the Harleys buzzed across the Colorado River and entered California near the venerable Route 66 town of Needles. After pancakes and pots of coffee at the Hungry Bear Restaurant the bikers topped off their gas tanks, checked tire pressures, and tied "cowboy air conditioners" — bandanas soaked in ice water — around their necks.

The great Mojave Desert awaited. So did a string of sunburned towns and ghost places along Route 66 making its way westward to Barstow before it cuts down to San Bernardino and turns toward Los Angeles, finally reaching Santa Monica on the Pacific. The cool ocean breezes seemed a lifetime away. That did not matter. The bikers figured to make it as far as Barstow in time to get rooms and cool off in a swimming pool before supper. There was no hurry; no one was in a rush.

All of them actually had looked forward to this leg of the trip. They realized the Mojave is special because it has a little bit of everything, especially the unex-

Mojave Desert

pected. The climate can be extreme, ranging from bitter cold in the winter to the summer when the temperature regularly reaches well into triple digits. Lying in the rain-shadow of the coastal mountain ranges, the Mojave receives average annual precipitation of less than six inches. Dry winds bring cloudless days, which means barely any rain. Plants, animals, and people learn to adapt or perish.

Yet sometimes from July to September, heavy and even violent rainstorms erupt as if from nowhere. On this particular day there was hardly a breeze and new-born clouds were forming. The bikers kept watch on the open skies all around them as they moved between inter-state highway and old road alignments through the remains of Goffs, where they inspected a restored schoolhouse. From there they continued on to Essex and then ahead to take photos and slug down bottled water at the remains of Danby, Summit, and Chambless.

Suddenly a few drops of rain splattered on the bikes and the bikers. Just as quickly, the rain stopped. The leader of the pack, who had traversed the Mojave many times, thought it might be just a ghost rain, so-called when most of the drops evaporate before reaching the ground. The rain, however, came back, only more of it and harder. The bikers scanned the heavens and saw that bruised clouds had plumped up and were turning dark-er. This was no ghost rain. The riders pulled over to the shoulder and scrambled into rain suits just in time. A hard and steady rain descended on the desert. With no shelter in sight, the bikers continued their journey.

They came to tiny Amboy and the sanctuary of a gas pump overhang at Roy's Cafe. Once a rowdy desert town that went 24-hours a day without missing a beat during the heyday years of Route 66, Amboy began to shrivel in 1972 when Interstate 40 came along ten miles to the north. The town became just a pit stop between Palm Springs and Las Vegas.

Roy's Motel and Cafe, Amboy

The bikers departed between downpours. They passed Amboy Crater, an extinct volcano, and glided along the slick highway running through a valley flanked by the Bullion and Bristol Mountains. Soon they reached what was left of Bagdad.

Once upon a time this was a rip-roaring mining town with a Santa Fe rail depot, a post office, a bustling Fred Harvey restaurant, shops, tourist cabins, and saloons filled with thirsty miners, railroaders, and trav-elers. Now all that remains is a forlorn tree, a railroad siding, pieces of broken glass, and the forgotten graves of Chinese railroad workers who perished during a cholera epidemic.

The slow death of Bagdad started long ago as the mines played out. When the interstate highway was built in the early 1970s and bypassed long stretches of Route 66, the demise of Bagdad — like other stranded towns — was complete. The cult motion picture entitled "The Bagdad Cafe" was not even filmed in Bagdad, but down the highway in Newberry Springs. But once there had been a Bagdad Cafe in Bagdad and it was well known as the only spot for miles around with a dance floor and jukebox. More than one traveler with an overheated radiator ate a meal at the original Bagdad Cafe.

Thoughts of the defunct cafe reminded the bikers that it had been hours since their Needles breakfast. As they saddled up after investigating the remains of Bagdad, the smell of rain — called "Desert B.O." by locals — wafted through the air. The bikers rode through the light rain, all minds were set on a hot meal at the new Bagdad Cafe about forty-five miles ahead in Newberry Springs. By the time the group reached Ludlow, the rain had picked up again and within minutes turned into a full-blown downpour.

None too soon, Newberry Springs appeared through the sheets of water. Ironically this town had originally been called Water because it was the first water point for wagon trains west of the Colorado River. Early travelers quenched their parched tongues at a spring flowing beneath the overhanging rocks of the Newberry Mountains and the settlement became a veritable oasis with its stands of alders, willows, and cottonwoods.

Not so on this day. Wet and weary bikers with growling bellies knew they would find dry comfort and warmth in Newberry Springs. They carefully maneuvered their bikes through the puddles and soft earth that otherwise served as the parking lot at the Bagdad Cafe. Inside they shook off their rain gear like a bunch of soaked hounds and found places to sit while a waitress handed out mugs of coffee.

The road captain recalled when this cozy rain haven was the Sidewinder Cafe. That was long before filmmakers came to town in 1987 and temporarily changed the Sidewinder's name to the "Bagdad Cafe," the title of an offbeat comedy about eccentric characters who find bliss in the high desert. A few owners later the cafe was officially renamed the Bagdad.

Bagdad Cafe, Newberry Springs

The film spawned a short-lived television series but although the "Bagdad Cafe" may not have become a blockbuster in the United States, audiences in Europe and Japan adored it and still do. Many travelers from abroad make sure that one of the major stops on their Route 66 pilgrimage is Newberry Springs and the Bagdad.

This rainy day was no different. The cafe was packed with rain refugees, including a few other bikers, some standard issue American tourists, and a bevy of visitors from France, Germany, and Belgium.

Seated in the catbird's seat at the far end of the dining room where he could take in the whole scene, was an old man with shaggy white hair and beard. He wore a red flannel shirt and his baggy pants were held up with suspenders. His body listed a bit to the right with his elbow on the tabletop, his cocked head leaning against his open palm. He seemed to be studying the room and everyone in it.

Although he could have been straight from central casting, the bikers learned from their waitress and the discrete whispers of other diners that this old man was not some leftover movie extra. He was much better than that.

The elderly gent was Robert Gray, also called General Robert Gray but much better known on Route 66 and far beyond simply as General Bob. For the next hour this wizard of the road entertained, instructed, castigated, cajoled, and charmed everyone present. As the bikers progressed from coffee to buffalo burgers and finally chocolate malts, they also moved their chairs closer and closer until they encircled General Bob. Like other cafe patrons sitting nearby they were held spellbound by the wild tales and outrageous utterances the old man doled out like heaping dollops of cream.

It seems that not only was this man a general but a five-star general and at one time the general of all the armies of the world. His lineage included English, French, and German bloodlines and he put his age at somewhere over the century mark. That made sense if one were to believe everything he claimed to have accomplished, including composing symphonies and designing spacecraft. Along the way General Bob apparently mastered 9,000 languages, helped build the Golden Gate Bridge, served as a senior diplomatic officer, and worked closely with both the FBI and CIA.

During World War II, he not only helped mastermind allied strategy but also took the time to assassinate Adolph Hitler. When he spoke of how he walked from Ireland to Scotland, not a soul in the joint raised the point that such a feat would have required walking on water. Who knows?

After an hour when some other diners started to stir, the bikers discovered that the rain had finally stopped. A hint of sunshine filtered down and the wet motorcycles parked outside glistened like precious gems.

General Bob was also ready to leave. He announced it was time to go to the nearby motel room he called home and feed his pal, a 100-pound Doberman named Prince.

Outside the bikers wiped off the bike seats and shook hands with General Bob. He offered a wink and a nod and waved his hand like a high priest of the open road giving voyagers his blessing.

Back on the highway, cruising in soft sunlight to whatever waited ahead, the bikers noticed that the sky was clear and bright. Within a few more miles, they saw that the road and the surrounding desert appeared to be bone dry.

Maybe it had been a ghost rain after all. Maybe none of what they encountered behind them was really there. Maybe there was no Bagdad Cafe and no General Bob. Perhaps it was all a mirage. ∎

King of the World

— MICHAEL WALLIS

Jamie Constantine does not just live large; he lives triple X large. I knew that the first time I laid eyes on him, astride his big Harley touring bike. A veritable mountain of a man, Jamie is a combination sumo wrestler and Sir John Falstaff — the audacious and witty Shakespearean character both huge in size and appetites.

Jamie not only looks big and rides the biggest Harley made, he also thinks big. A success in the food and drink business for almost four decades, he has watched his popular restaurant, Jamie's Pub, in the coastal town of Scituate, Massachusetts, expand to three more locations in the Boston area.

Since 1994, when he first took to the open road on a regular basis, Jamie has owned a dozen Harleys. He figures those bikes have taken him down some 300,000 miles of highway. Although semi-retired Jamie has no plans to slow down. He and his longtime girlfriend and traveling companion, Linda Scott, spend most of every summer cruising America on a Harley. Their favorite road to take is Route 66.

"The Mother Road is the most biker-friendly highway in the whole U.S. of A," Jamie tells anyone who will listen. "Believe me I've done 'em all and Route 66 is the best, bar none!"

Because of Jamie's zest for life, his great hunger for riding the old highway, and his profound love of all things Route 66, I long ago gave him a nickname that I think fits best. To me he is much more than a King of the Road. Jamie is so big, so grand in body, mind, and spirit that the best moniker for him is King of the World. He wears it well.

My wife, Suzanne, and I have had the pleasure of occasionally cruising the Mother Road with the King of the World and his lady. Often we are joined by two other

Arlen "The Guy with the Horns" Strehlow, Jamie Constantine, and Linda Scott

The King of the World (left) enjoys a meal with Linda Scott and Corey Hebert

well-traveled bikers who have become our friends — Arlen and Tom Strehlow, brothers from Milwaukee, the city where Harleys are created. Arlen, also a substantial man in size, is easily recognized in biker circles and along Route 66 since his normal headgear is a helmet mounted with enormous steer horns. Once you have seen "The Guy with the Horns," as Arlen is known, you will never forget him.

Riding America's Main Street with these four seasoned bikers has brought us some high times, especially at the many cafes, greasy spoons, pie palaces, barbecue pits, sandwich shops, diners, chicken ranches, buffets, and steak houses we have visited along the way.

We have dined with this colorful tribe at the most historic and admired eateries on Route 66. At the drop of a biker's helmet Jamie and Linda can recite some of the most memorable dishes consumed.

A few of their favorites include: New Mexican cuisine in Tucumcari at La Cita followed by warm pie at Del's; thick Bagdad Cafe milkshakes in the Mojave Desert; sizzling burgers right off Mildred Barker's grill at the Frontier Cafe in Truxton, Arizona; and Ted Drewes famous frozen custard. Also on the list are enchiladas hotter than fire at Joe & Aggies in Holbrook; memorable meals in the dining room at La Posada in Winslow; blue ribbon steaks in Oklahoma City, Amarillo, and at Rod's in Williams, followed by bowls of ice cream at Twisters; rainbow trout platters at La Fonda in Santa Fe; and banana splits worth dying for at the Route 66 Diner in Albuquerque.

Still, the one meal shared with our foursome of hearty riding companions that we will remember the most was a breakfast we enjoyed one summer morn at Emma Jean's Hollandburger Cafe on Route 66 in Victorville, California.

The six of us on four bikes — with Linda and Suzanne seated behind their mates — pulled out of San Bernardino early enough to beat much of the crush of traffic. We zoomed up Cajon Pass and after reaching Victorville began to hunt in earnest for a place to eat our morning meal. About the same time, we all spied the mint-green building with a sign on a pole out front. It looked promising. Arlen removed his Viking-like headgear and was halfway to the door before the rest of us had parked our bikes.

A host of hummingbirds darting around the feeders hanging outside the cafe made us all feel good and once we were inside the perfume of frying side meats and the big smile the waitress gave us sealed the deal. Without taking a single bite, we knew we had made a good choice.

Most of the stools at the L-shaped lunch counter were taken but we found prime seats around two of the cafe's four tables pushed together. The busy cook gave us a warm howdy and a wave from the open kitchen while we downed a couple pitchers of ice water in a heartbeat. We soon learned he owned the place. His name was Brian Gentry and the friendly waitress was his wife, Shawna. They lived on the property with their two little girls and served breakfast and lunch to high desert residents and Route 66 travelers every day of the week except Sunday.

Brian and Shawna told us the cafe was originally named the Hollandburger Cafe when Bob Holland and his wife opened for business in 1947. The Hollands operated the cafe for many years followed by a half-dozen other owners who tried to make a go of it until 1979 when Brian's mother, Emma Jean Gentry, bought the place. Brian went to work at the cafe when he was thirteen and came aboard fulltime when he turned sixteen.

"We added my Mom's name to the cafe name," Brian told us. "She worked right here up until the time she died in 1996."

We learned that all sorts of folks had dined at Emma Jean's including Roy Rogers, who resided in Victorville until his death. Besides "The King of the Cowboys," the cafe had also fed truckers, traveling salesmen, hitchhiking soldiers and sailors, and, of course, lots and lots of bikers.

Our group was about half way through our omelets and pancakes when another bunch of bikers strolled in and took the other two tables. It was Jimmy Martinais and his wife Chris from Illinois and some of their pals. They had seen our parked bikes and knew wherever The King of the World stopped the food had to be outstanding. Although Jimmy did not say a word, we knew today was his birthday.

The King of the World held forth in his charming way about the delicious meal before us. He also regaled the crowd with lip-smacking descriptions of some of his signature dishes from Massachusetts. He spoke of his chicken corn chowder, shrimp bisque, and, of course, all the seafood anyone could ever handle.

No fresh fish at Emma Jean's, however, just biscuits and gravy, ham steak, hot cakes. And later for lunch, the Gentrys would offer their half-pound burgers or the famous Trucker's Sandwich loaded with roast beef, bacon, Swiss cheese, green chilies, and surrounded by sourdough bread.

Before we left, The King of the World quietly hatched a plan with the Gentrys. As Shawna carried a tall stack of pancakes covered with blazing candles to Jimmy's table, in unison everyone in the cafe burst into "Happy Birthday."

We all hugged and kissed and then our bunch left. As we walked out the door, I heard Brian say that no one who enters the cafe ever leaves a stranger. With Suzanne snug behind me on the bike, I looked at our fellow road warriors firing up their Harleys and I realized we had done more than just consume a meal. We had partaken of a few moments of delicious camaraderie that would sustain us forever. ∎

Recipes from California

— MARIAN CLARK

Needles remains an oasis before tackling desert heat. It has always been a community filled with gas pumps, repair shops, mom-and-pop eateries, and motor-courts-turned motels.

The site of the 1930s Palms Motel gave way in 1991 to the Old Trails Inn where Mrs. Wilde, the owner, served this wonderful cake to her guests.

Potato Cake

OLD TRAILS INN

1 cup shortening
2 cups sugar
3 eggs
1 cup cold mashed potatoes
2 tablespoons cocoa
1 teaspoon cinnamon
2 teaspoons baking soda
2 cups flour
½ cup sour milk

Gassing up at Roy's in Amboy

In a medium-sized mixing bowl whip the shortening and blend in sugar. Combine thoroughly then add eggs and mashed potatoes. Combine dry ingredients and add to egg mixture along with the sour milk. Mix only until blended. Pour batter into two 8-inch cake pans that have been sprayed with nonstick spray. Bake in a preheated 350 degree oven for 30 minutes. Use your favorite frosting or serve warm without frosting. 12 servings

At the Idle Spurs Steakhouse in Barstow bikers will find western decor and enclosed patio dining. The popular restaurant was built in the 1950s as a home but soon evolved into a restaurant that is both comfortable and casual. Idle Spurs is noted for good steaks and friendly service. Here is one of those "eat to ride and ride to eat" stops. Enjoy!

Black Bean Salsa

Idle Spurs Steakhouse

1 can (15-ounce) black beans, drained and rinsed
1½ cups cooked fresh corn kernels
2 medium tomatoes, cut and diced
1 green bell pepper, cut and diced
½ cup red onion, finely diced
1 to 2 fresh green Serrano or jalapeño peppers, thinly sliced, including seeds
⅓ cup fresh lime juice
⅓ cup extra-virgin olive oil
⅓ cup chopped fresh coriander
1 teaspoon salt
½ teaspoon ground cumin
½ teaspoon pure ground red chili (not chili powder)

or a pinch of cayenne pepper

Combine all ingredients in a large bowl. Mix well. Set aside to let the flavors blend for a few hours until ready to serve. 4½ cups salsa.

These nachos make satisfying appetizers and the spice can be adjusted for personal taste.

Jalapeño and Chicken Nachos

1½ cup cooked, diced chicken breast
12 ounces cream cheese at room temperature
1 jalapeño pepper, seeded and minced
¼ cup finely chopped red onion
3 cloves of garlic, minced
1 teaspoon ground cumin
1 teaspoon chili powder
1½ cups grated Monterey Jack cheese
Salt and freshly ground black pepper to taste
12 medium flour tortillas

Preheat the oven to 375 degrees. Combine all ingredients except the tortillas in a large mixing bowl. Beat until well blended. Taste and season with salt and pepper.

Melt oil in skillet on medium high heat. Brown each tortilla for about 1 minute. Spread 6 of the tortillas with a generous amount of filling. Cover with remaining tortillas. Place on cookie sheets and bake until bubbling, about 5-7 minutes. Cut into wedges and serve as appetizers in a napkin-lined basket. 72 bite-sized nachos.

Lifelong San Bernardino residents Mike and Maria Austin have winning ways with chili! They started competitive cooking on the International Chili Society circuit in 1989 and through their combined efforts have won several championships.

Mike was the International Chili Society Arizona State Champion in 1991, the California State Champion twice, and placed fifth in the World Championship in 1993. Maria has won the Nevada State Championship and placed eleventh in the World's Championship. Both Mike and Maria have a passion for good times, good chili, and good rides, which includes many trips along Route 66!

Near Goffs

Mike Austin's Bun Burner Chili Shack

5 pounds tri-tip or top sirloin, cut into small cubes
1 large sweet onion, finely chopped (about 1 cup)
6 cloves garlic, finely chopped
4 cans (14½ ounces each) chicken broth
1 can (15 ounce) tomato sauce
10 tablespoons pure California chili powder
6 tablespoons ground cumin
3 tablespoons extra-hot New Mexico chili powder
1 tablespoon pasilla chili powder
2 teaspoons garlic powder
Salt to taste

In a large nonstick skillet, cook meat over medium heat one pound at a time, removing meat and setting aside when it is no longer pink. Meanwhile, in a large chili pot, combine all remaining ingredients and simmer for 1 hour. Add meat to sauce and cook for 2 more hours, keeping covered as much as possible. If you want hotter chili, add more New Mexico chili powder.
    10 servings.

Rancho Cucamonga was once home to Thomas Winery, the oldest winery in California, established in 1839. It was the second winery in the United States. The location is now part of a shopping center at Foothill and Vineyard. To toast the city and the California wine industry, try this champagne punch.

Champagne Punch
Rancho Cucamonga

2 bottles of champagne or Asti Spumante (750 ml each)
1 cup cream de cassis (black currant liquor)
28 ounces of carbonated water

Combine ingredients and serve in 4-ounce stemmed glasses. 22 four-ounce servings.

For decades, AMA Gypsy Tours were a mainstay of the Association's road-riding program, bringing together thousands of enthusiasts every year. But Gypsy Tours disappeared in the late 50s. On their seventieth anniversary year, Gypsy Tours were reinstated and have continued every year since.

> " *G*ypsy Tour time is the great annual get-together of the boys and girls who believe that a motorcycle, the open road, and a meeting point in a shady grove on the banks of a stream or lake are the finest combination in the world."
> (from the American Motorcyclist and Bicyclist Magazine, April 1926)

Make your own gypsy magic today; ride back in time and experience some old magic for yourselves. Ride to eat and eat to ride! Here's one suggested menu. Add your own favorites.

Assorted Appetizers, Snacks, and Sandwiches
Ham, Tomato and Olive Pasta Salad
Southern Baked Beans
Fruit Plate of Watermelon, Cantaloupe, Peaches, and Grapes
French Rolls Garlic Butter
Rich Chocolate Brownies

Spicy Hot Dogs

1 jar (12-ounce) chili sauce
1 jar (9-ounce) grape jelly
3 tablespoons lemon juice
1 pound small cocktail hot dogs

Bring chili sauce, jelly, and lemon juice to a boil. Add hot dogs and heat slowly for 10 minutes. Serve in a slow cooker or chafing dish to keep warm.

California Cheese and Turkey Melt

2 tablespoons low-fat mayonnaise
4 teaspoons basil pesto
8 thin slices sourdough bread
8 ounces sliced cooked turkey breast
4 ounces thinly sliced provolone or mozzarella cheese
8 thin slices tomato

Combine mayonnaise and pesto. Spread 1 tablespoon mixture on each of 4 bread slices. Top each with 2 ounces of turkey, 1 ounce of cheese, and 2 tomato slices. Top with remaining bread slices. Coat a grill or skillet with non-stick cooking spray. Heat to medium. Cook 2-3 minutes on each side until bread is golden. 4 sandwiches.

Ham, Tomato, and Olive Pasta Salad

1 pound penne or other short pasta
¼ cup olive oil, divided
3 garlic cloves, thinly sliced
2 cups (about ⅔ pound) cherry tomatoes, halved
½ cup slivered country ham
1 teaspoon dried oregano
¼ teaspoon red pepper
¼ cup pitted black olives, sliced in half
¼ cup chopped fresh parsley
¼ cup grated Parmesan cheese
Salt to taste
Extra cheese for garnish

In a large pot of boiling water, cook the pasta according to package directions. Drain. Pour 1 tablespoon of the olive oil over the pasta and stir to prevent sticking. Meanwhile, in a large skillet, heat remaining olive oil over medium heat and add garlic. Cook until golden, about 2 minutes. Add tomatoes, ham, oregano, and red pepper. Cook over low heat for about 3 minutes. Pour over the pasta and add olives, parsley, salt, and Parmesan cheese. Toss to combine. Serve in a large salad bowl and garnish with more cheese. May be served warm or cold. 6 servings.

Southern Baked Beans

2 pounds navy beans (small white beans)
Water to cover
1 cup ham, finely chopped
1 small green pepper, minced
1 small onion, chopped
2 teaspoons dry mustard
¼ cup molasses
½ cup firmly packed dark brown sugar
1½ cups catsup
Salt and pepper to taste

Clean and soak beans in water overnight. Rinse and replace water again to cover. Add remaining ingredients and bring to boil. Remove beans to a large baking dish. Cover and place in a preheated 250 degree oven for 7-8 hours. Check several times and add more liquid if necessary. 10 servings.

If you choose to serve burgers or hot dogs at your gypsy picnic, this salsa once served at *Don Salsa*, in Claremont, would make a wonderful addition.

Special Salsa Fresca

(Try this on burgers or steaks and you'll never use catsup again!)
Don Salsa

3 chopped fresh tomatoes
1 chopped fresh onion
3 cloves crushed fresh garlic
1 minced yellow chili, seeded
2 teaspoons chopped fresh cilantro
½ cup tomato juice
Salt and pepper to taste

Combine all ingredients and serve with tortilla chips. Keeps 3-4 days in the refrigerator. For best results, chill tomato juice before adding to salsa. 1½ cups salsa.

For those who want sandwiches, this is the way chicken salad sandwiches are made at Fair Oaks Pharmacy in Pasadena.

Fair Oaks Chicken Salad Sandwiches

2 cups coarsely chopped chicken breast
½ cup thinly sliced celery
½ cup chopped green peppers
½ cup chopped yellow peppers
1 teaspoon Mrs. Dash
½ teaspoon seasoning salt
½ cup mayonnaise

Combine all and mix thoroughly. Serve as salad or sandwich filling. 4-5 servings.

Top the evening off with a daiquiri like this one.

Perfect 66 Daiquiris

Fresh fruit of choice (strawberries, bananas, peaches, or any other)
1 (6-ounce) can of frozen lime-ade concentrate, thawed
Equal amount of rum
Ice

Place enough fruit in food processor or blender to fill ⅔ full. Pour lime-aid concentrate and an equal amount of rum into the blender. Fill blender with ice and turn on machine. Process until smooth.

BARBECUE HAS LONG BEEN A STAPLE IN THE AREA and Pacific seafood is famous world wide so these two traditions have found a perfect home at Rusty's Surf Ranch. Owners Russell Barnard and Mitch Cohen are enthusiastic supporters of both Route 66 and bikers.

Wrapped Salmon
RUSTY'S SURF RANCH

1 8-ounce salmon fillet
1 tablespoon white wine
1 teaspoon butter
Dash of lemon juice
½ medium carrot
¼ bell pepper
¼ cup green or yellow squash
¼ cup chopped tomato
1 teaspoon fresh basil
Dash of black pepper

Santa Monica Pier

Santa Monica Pier, the historic unofficial western terminus of Route 66, has been a magnet for visitors since it first opened in 1909. Perfect for watching sunsets, the pier is also a gathering place for those who crave the sand and sea. The 1922 Looff Carousel with forty-four prancing hand-carved steeds is the sprite-like center of this year-round playground. Don't forget the Ferris wheel that offers an unparalleled view for people watchers and those who love the beach.

One of the many Pier stops that delights visitors year round is Rusty's Surf Ranch, found next to the famous carousel. Often called "the ultimate beach hangout," Rusty's is a full-service restaurant offering lunch and dinner daily, drinks, live entertainment, and dancing. This must-see attraction features a large life-like mural, museum quality displays of vintage surfboards, a great gift shop, historic photos of the Pier, and such eclectic items as Pamela Anderson Lee's Baywatch swimsuit. (The television series was often filmed on the beach nearby.)

Thunder Roadhouse

When it opened in West Hollywood in 1993, Thunder Roadhouse was billed as "America's first motorcycle-theme restaurant." Just as the 60s generation has moved on, so has the roadhouse, but neither are forgotten. For just a while it was the ultimate stop to celebrate freedom of the open road like no other stop: Easy Rider ran nonstop, Captain America Classic Burgers and Kick-Ass Chili were always on the menu, waitresses wore T-shirts inscribed, "Ride to Eat/Live to ride," and patrons could mount motorcycle seats at the bar. Celebrity investors included iron-horse riders Peter Fonda, Dennis Hopper, and Dwight Yoakum. An art nouveau Indian on a bike met patrons at the door and the main dining room featured a teal 1932 Harley VL. In the showroom, bike prices ranged from $12,000 to $30,000. Those choosing to eat on the patio deck were positioned to gaze at more hogs or do some people watching along Sunset Strip. The layout also included a parts shop, vintage bike collection, and clothing boutique. As stars streak across the night sky and disappear, this icon achieved fame then quickly faded, to be remembered by each and every patron who enjoyed a brief but memorable stop.

Julienne the carrot, bell pepper, and squash. Cut a 12x12-inch sheet of heavy duty aluminum foil. Place the salmon at the center of the foil and cover with other ingredients. Fold the foil in half over the combined ingredients and starting at one end, fold over the foil onto itself to form a tight seal. Continue this all the way around until a tight pouch is made. Preheat oven to 375 degrees. Place foil on a cookie sheet or flat pan and bake for 12 to 14 minutes. Open at the table and enjoy the aroma before eating. 1 large or 2 smaller servings.

JUST A FEW BLOCKS TO THE NORTH of Santa Monica Pier, where Santa Monica Boulevard touches Ocean Avenue, is a small stone, set in the grass beneath tall palms. The inscription is memorable. ∎

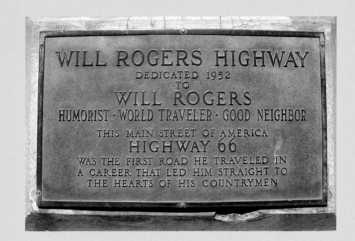

Road Warriors

— MICHAEL WALLIS

Route 66 and everything it stands for remains one of my passions. My study in Tulsa is within easy striking range of the Mother Road of the Joads and "Pretty Boy" Floyd. Chunks of vintage pavement are in a collection of totems that keep me from harm's way. Memories of the places, but more importantly the road warriors — particularly my biker pals — are indelibly stamped in my mind.

These guardians of the old highway know that from Illinois to California the Route 66 revival continues, grows larger, and gains momentum. A monument to wander lust, the highway attracts dedicated enthusiasts who make regular pilgrimages down this road they still consider a genuine celebrity. They have become a family intent on preserving, collecting, and honoring fragments of the past. They gather at annual events along stretches of America's Main Street to strut their stuff on gleaming Harleys, or in Chevys, Fords, and other vintage makes and models that were in vogue when Route 66 was the only way to go. For these road warriors, it still is.

Route 66 has evolved into a venerable and varicose veteran. It is a timeless monument to those who live and work on its shoulders and to the road warriors who prefer its well-worn lanes. ∎

Hog Handbook

Biker Speak

Garnered from a variety of sources

Anchors — Brakes.

Apes or Ape Hangers — Especially high handlebars, usually found on "choppers" (see below), that force riders to adopt an ape-like posture.

Back Door — The last and hopefully the most experienced rider in a group.

Back Warmer — Passenger.

Bacon — Scabs on biker's body, also called road rash.

Bail — To jump off a bike to avoid a crash.

Bar Hopper — A bike that is not comfortable on long rides.

Beater — A backup motorcycle that owners of expensive cycles use for commuting and errands.

Big Twins — Engines in the larger Harley-Davidson motorcycles.

Black Ice — A biker's worst enemy in winter, this is ice that cannot be seen on the surface of the road.

Blockhead — Harley-Davidson's fourth generation overhead valve Big Twin, introduced in 1984. Sometimes called the Evolution, or shortened to Evo.

Boots — Tires.

Brain Bucket — Another name for a motorcycle helmet.

Bring home a Christmas tree — when a bike leaves the road and crashes into brush, leaving branches and leaves on the bike and biker.

Bro — Short for brother, as in brother of the road.

Buddy Pegs — Footpegs for motorcycle passengers.

Burnout — A maneuver sometimes used by show-off bikers, in which the rider holds the front brake while racing the throttle, causing the back wheel to spin and billow smoke.

Cage — Biker name for cars, the sworn foe of bikers.

Cager — Automobile driver.

Carving — Term for hard, fast cornering on roads with lots of curves and bends.

Catwalk — Riding a cycle on the rear wheel only, often referred to as a "wheelie."

Chopper — Custom motorcycles with all the superfluous parts "chopped" off, or modified, to make the bike faster.

Coupon — A traffic or speeding ticket.

Crotch Rocket — A sportbike designed for optimum speed.

Dresser — A cycle set up for long-distance touring.

Fairing — A plastic shroud that deflects rain and wind from the rider.

Fat Boy — Introduced in 1990, this model — which features solid wheels, both front and rear — is the pinnacle of the Softail custom family of Harley-Davidson motorcycles.

Fathead — Slang name for Harley-Davidson's Twin Cam 88 engine introduced in 1999.

Flathead — Harleys manufactured from 1930-1948 with valves moved to the opposite sides of combustion chamber for more power

Flower Pot — Name for an inexpensive helmet.

Flying Low — Speeding.

Free Lunch — Bugs in your mouth and teeth.

Foot Padding — When a novice rider "walks" his or her cycle around at low speeds.

Garbage Wagon - A derogatory term used by outlaw bikers to describe fancy touring bikes.

Hack — Name for the sidecars, or small carriages for passengers attached to the side of a motorcycle.

Harley Wrench — A hammer.

Hog — Common nickname for a Harley-Davidson motorcycle.

H.O.G. — Harley Owners Group, founded in 1983 and the world's largest factory-sponsored motorcycle organization with 1,000 H.O.G. chapters and more than 400,000 members around the globe.

Hydroplane — What occurs when the motorcycle tires start to float on top of water on the road, causing them to lose contact with the surface.

Knucklehead — Harley-Davidson's first overhead-valve Big Twin, introduced in 1936. Legend has it the name comes from the valve covers that look like the knuckles of a clinched fist.

Lane Splitting — Sometimes called "white-lining," this is when a biker rides between lanes of traffic on a freeway.

Mill — Engine.

Milwaukee Tractor — Name of endearment for a Harley.

Motor — Term used by motorcycle cops to describe their bike.

One Percenter — Outlaw bikers or outcasts who choose to follow their own rules and beliefs. Less than one percent of the population fits this category.

Organ Donor — A helmetless biker, sometimes referred to as a metal head.

Panhead — Harley-Davidson's second-generation overhead-valve Big Twin, introduced in 1948. Old-timers claim the name is from valve covers, which resemble small roasting pans.

Rice Burner — Pejorative name for any motorcycle manufactured in Japan.

Road Rash — Marks on biker's body as result of bike going down on the pavement.

RUB — Rich urban biker, a derisive term often used by seasoned Harley riders when referring to doctors, lawyers, and other professionals (a.k.a. "yuppie scum") who purchase expensive motorcycles as status symbols.

Scoot or Scooter — Slang name for a motorcycle.

Shovelhead — Harley-Davidson's third generation overhead-valve Big Twin, introduced in 1966. The name comes from the head that resembles a coal shovel.

Skid Lid — Name for a motorcycle helmet.

Sissy Bar — A backrest attached behind the passenger's portion of the saddle.

Springer — A popular Harley cycle with springer forks, exposed springs to lessen the impact on rough roads.

SQUID — Squirrelly Young Kid with no business being on a bike.

Streetfighter — Also known as a "hooligan" cycle, this is a sportbike stripped of all superfluous bodywork.

Sturgis — A small town in South Dakota that annually hosts the most famous of all biker rallies.

Twisties — A road with many twists and curves.

Two Up — Term used when a passenger rides on the back of the motorcycle.

Willie G. — Grandson of the founder of Harley-Davidson, Willie G. Davidson serves as styling vice president and has achieved national celebrity status as the driving force behind the firm's phenomenal success.

Biker Mother Road Essentials

Garnered from a variety of sources

Open Mind

Helmet

Eye protection

Bottle(s) of drinking water

Jacket

Boots

Gloves

Identification

Set of Route 66 maps

Insurance papers

Spare bike key

Bungee cords

Cargo net

Cleaner and rag

Flat repair kit

Spare fuses

Rain suit

Toolkit

Dealer list

Tire pressure gauge

Flashlight

Ear plugs

Sunscreen

Steering lock

AMA and/or HOG Membership card

First aid kit

Totes

Tip: Bring plenty of bandanas or do-rags. Also known as "cowboy air conditioners," bandanas thoroughly soaked in ice water and tied around neck or head make for a cooler ride.

Biker Pit Stops

A list of authorized Harley-Davidson dealers located on the Mother Road in the eight Route 66 states

ILLINOIS

Illinois Harley-Davidson
1301 S. Harlem Avenue
Berwyn, Illinois 60402
(708) 788-1300
(877) 464-1450

Chuck's Harley-Davidson
2027 Ireland Grove Road
Bloomington, Illinois 61704
(309) 662-1648

Chicago Harley-Davidson
6868 N. Western Avenue
Chicago, Illinois 60645
(773) 338-6868

Chicago Harley-Davidson Downtown
68 E. Ohio Street
Chicago, Illinois 60611
(312) 274-9666

Chicago Harley-Davidson
520 N. Michigan Avenue
Ste. 324
Chicago, Illinois 60611
(#12) 755-9520

Conrad's Harley-Davidson
1541 Riverboat Center Drive
Joliet, Illinois 60431
(815) 725-2000

Hall's Harley-Davidson, Inc.
3755 N. Dirksen Parkway
Springfield, Illinois 62707
(217) 528-8356

MISSOURI

Cycle Connection Harley-Davidson
I-44 Exit 6
5014 Hearnes Blvd.
Joplin, Missouri 64804
(417) 623-1054

Doc's Harley-Davidson Motorcycle
   Sales & Service
930 S. Kirkwood Road
Kirkwood, Missouri 63122
(314) 965-0166
(866) 333-DOCS

Ozark Harley-Davidson, Inc.
2300 Industrial Drive
Lebanon, Missouri 65536
(417) 532-2900

Gateway to the West
   Harley-Davidson
3600 LeMay Ferry Road
St. Louis, Missouri 63125
(314) 845-9900

Widman Harley-Davidson
3628 S. Broadway
St. Louis, Missouri 63118
(314) 771-7100
(800) 404-6880

Denney's Harley-Davidson of
   Springfield
3980 W. Sunshine Street
Springfield, Missouri 65807
(417) 882-0100

Bourbeuse Valley Harley-Davidson
1418 Highway AT (Exit 247)
Villa Ridge, Missouri 63089
(636) 742-2707

KANSAS

None on Route 66. Closest dealer
   is in Joplin, Missouri

OKLAHOMA

Myers-Duren Harley-Davidson of Tulsa
4848 S. Peoria Avenue
Tulsa, Oklahoma 74105
(918) 743-4440

Route 66 Harley-Davidson
3637 S. Memorial Drive,
(Hwy.51 & Memorial Dr. Exit)
Tulsa, Oklahoma 74145
(918) 622-1340

Harley-Davidson World Shop
3433 S. Broadway
Edmond, Oklahoma 73013
(405) 478-4024

Harley-Davidson World
2823 S. Agnew Avenue
Oklahoma City, Oklahoma 73108
(405) 631-8680

TEXAS
Tripp's Harley-Davidson, Inc.
6040 I-40 West
Amarillo, Texas 79106
(806) 352-2021

NEW MEXICO
Chick's Harley-Davidson
5000 Alameda Boulevard N.E.
Albuquerque, New Mexico 87113
(505) 856-1600

Santa Fe Harley-Davidson
3501 Cerrillos Road
Santa Fe, New Mexico 87507
(505) 471-3808

ARIZONA
Grand Canyon Harley-Davidson
I-40 Exit 185 (10 miles west of
    Flagstaff)
Bellemont, Arizona 86015
(928) 774-3896 (866) 867-4243

Mother Road Harley-Davidson
2501 Beverly Avenue
Kingman, Arizona 86401
(928) 757-1166

CALIFORNIA
Harley-Davidson of Victorville, Inc.
14522 Valley Center drive
Victorville, California 92392
(760) 951-1119

Quaid Harley-Davidson
25160 Redlands Boulevard
Loma Linda, California 92345
(909) 786-8399

Bartel's Harley-Davidson
4141 Lincoln Boulevard
Marina del Rey, California 90292
(310) 823-1112

Biker Mother Road Test

Gleaned from a variety or sources and old scooter tramps

Answer yes to most of the statements on this list and chances are you are a true Route 66 Biker Road Warrior.

If only the back of your hands are sunburned

If you have spent at least one night at the Blue Swallow Motel in Tucumcari, New Mexico, or the Munger Moss Motel in Lebanon. Missouri

If you believe "helmet hair" is a fashion statement

If you carry more photographs of your bike than your kids

If you always warn others about the speed trap waiting at Arcadia, Oklahoma

If you register for wedding gifts at a bike shop or Mother Road curio store

If most of your tee shirts are emblazoned with motorcycles or Route 66 shields

If you know who Tod and Buz were and forgive them for not riding bikes

If you have either a child or a pet named Harley

If you think of sushi as bait and eat chicken fried steak for breakfast side meat

If you can identify insects by their taste

If your favorite periodicals are *American Road*, *Route 66 Magazine* and *HOG Tales*

If you have enjoyed a handcrafted sandwich at Wrink's Market in Lebanon, Missouri, or at Eisler's Brothers Store in Riverton, Kansas

If you have had your hair cut or been shaved by Angel Delgadillo

If you have ridden the twisties leading up to Oatman in the dark

If you own any artwork by Bob Waldmire or Jerry McClanahan

If you have acquired larger saddlebags for your bike to carry your Route 66 kitsch

If you believe that even a rainy ride on the Mother Road means it's a good day

If you know all the words to "Get Your Kicks" (extra credit if it is on your telephone answering machine)

A "yes!" from Michael Wallis

If your personal library is primarily books about bikes and roads

If your heroes are Willy G. and Cyrus Avery

If you celebrate both the anniversary of Route 66 (November 11) and the date you got your bike

If your bike has ever been parked in front of the Old Curiosity Shop in Erick, Oklahoma

If you have even considered trying to eat the Big Texan 72-ounce steak (extra credit for successfully eating it)

If it takes you the better part of a day to ride the 13.2 miles of Mother Road in Kansas

If you have dined on calf fries at the Hammet House in Claremore, Oklahoma

If you have ever hunted for the "Spook Light" (extra credit for spotting it)

If you have competed in a butt darts tournament (extra credit for winning)

If you have visited the Pine Breeze Inn near Bellemont, Arizona

If you ever stayed in the Elvis Suite at the Tradewinds Motel in Clinton, Oklahoma

If your favorite three-piece suit is chaps, leather vest, and leather jacket

If you ever slept in a Wigwam at Holbrook, Arizona

If you do most of your Christmas shopping at your local Harley dealer and Teepee Curios in Tucumcari

If you have ever had a conversation with General Bob Gray at the Bagdad Cafe in Newberry Springs, California

If your favorite sports hero of all time is Andy Payne

If your best footwear has steel toes

If you have seen the film version of "The Grapes of Wrath" and "Easy Rider" more than three times (extra credit for being able to recite entire lines from the films)

If your bike has at least one Route 66 decal

If you cannot remember the last time you ate at a chain fast-food joint

If you have stood on "the" corner in Winslow, Arizona

If you have ever had Sunday dinner at the Ariston Cafe in Litchfield, Illinois

If you know the exact site location of the extinct Regal Reptile Ranch

If you own any underwear imprinted with either Route 66 shields or motorcycles

If you have attended both a John Steinbeck Awards Banquet and a Route 66 HOG rally

If you know the definition of devil's rope

If you possess a nugget of petrified wood, a wooden nickel from the Round barn at Arcadia, Oklahoma, and any souvenir from Exotic World at Helendale, California

Biker Celebs

Peter Fonda	Lindsay Wagner	Dwight D. Eisenhower	George Orwell
Dennis Hopper	James Dean	Laurence Fishburne	Che Guevara
Elvis Presley	Roy Rogers	Sam Elliot	Arnold Schwarzenegger
Dwight Yoakum	Malcolm Forbes	King George VI	Sammy Davis, Jr.
Jackson Browne	Charles Lindbergh	Steve McQueen	Dan Aykroyd
Sammy Hagar	Flip Wilson	Clark Gable	Mickey Rourke
Jay Leno	Ann Richards	King Hussein of Jordan	Franklin Graham
Larry Hagman	Marlon Brando	Bob Dylan	Reba McIntyre
Robert Blake	George Bernard Shaw	Keenan Wynn	Wynona Judd
Billy Idol	Lauren Hutton	Sir Ralph Richardson	Queen Latifa
Lorenzo Lamas	Gary Bussey	Howard Hughes	Georgia O'Keeffe

Flip Wilson on Route 66

Biker Tunes For The Mother Road

Most good road songs make good biker tunes and vice versa. Bear in mind that motorcycles always have been entwined with the mythology of rock n' roll. Unquestionably the unofficial Biker National Anthem remains "Born to Be Wild," by Steppenwolf. Listed below is a selection of songs to get your motor running.

"Route 66," any version will do, but especially Asleep at the Wheel

"Born To Be Wild," "Magic Carpet Ride," Steppenwolf

"Take It Easy," or just about any song from The Eagles

"The Ballad of Easy Rider," The Byrds

"Roll Me Away," "Against the Wind," or, just about any song from Bob Seger

"Midnight Rider," The Allman Brothers

"Born To Run," Bruce Springsteen

"Leader of the Pack," The Shangri-Las or Melissa Etheridge

"Harley," Kathy Mattea

"Unknown Legend," Neil Young

"Lost Highway," Hank Williams

"Live and Die in L.A.," Wang Chung

"On the Road Again," Willie Nelson

"Let it Roll," Bachman-Turner Overdrive

"Road House Blues," The Doors

"Kings of the Highway," Chris Isaak

"City of the Angels," Journey

"Back in the U.S.A.," Edgar Winter

"Endless Highway," Bob Dylan

"Fun, Fun, Fun," The Beach Boys

"King of the Road," Roger Miller

"Miles of Texas," Asleep at the Wheel

"Rockin' down the Highway," The Doobie Brothers

"Two Lane Highway," Pure Prairie League

"Land of Enchantment," Michael Martin Murphey

"Hitch a Ride," Boston

"The Last Trip to Tulsa," Neil Young

"Happy Trails," Roy Rogers and Dale Evans

"Oklahoma," Rogers and Hammerstein

Food Festival Fun on Route 66

TASTE OF CHICAGO — THE BIGGEST SUMMER FESTIVAL IN CHICAGO
When: 10 days surrounding the 4th of July each year
Grant Park (where Route 66 begins).

HORSERADISH FESTIVAL — COLLINSVILLE, ILLINOIS
When: First weekend in June each year, Woodland Park
Food booths, entertainment, family fun, and horseradish games.

WORLD'S LARGEST CALF FRY FESTIVAL AND COOK-OFF — VINITA, OKLAHOMA
When: 2nd Saturday every September
Cowboy games, plenty of country food, crafts, and over 2,000 pounds of calf fries.

FRIED ONION BURGER FESTIVAL — EL RENO, OKLAHOMA
When: 1st Saturday each May
Celebrating onion burgers that have been prepared in El Reno since early in the 1900s. The "big burger" prepared at the most recent festival weighed over 850 pounds. Includes a car show, food, crafts, and children's activities.

PINTO BEAN FESTIVAL — MORIARTY, NEW MEXICO
When: 2nd Saturday each October, City Park
A pinto bean cook-off, arts and crafts booths, food vendors, classic cars, farmer's market, bands, a parade, rodeo, and carnival.

NEW MEXICO WINE FESTIVAL — BERNALILLO, NEW MEXICO
When: Labor Day weekend
The premier wine-tasting event of the Southwest. Exhibits from New Mexico Wineries, a juried art show, agricultural products showcase, and live entertainment. The American Bus Association has listed this festival as one of the "Top 100 Events" in North America.

GRAPE HARVEST FESTIVAL — RANCHO CUCAMONGA, CALIFORNIA
When: 1st Weekend each October, Epicenter Parking Lot
    at Rochester
Celebrating the first winery in California, established in 1839 at what is now the corner of Foothill and Vineyard on Route 66.

Route 66 Associations

Route 66 Association of Illinois
2743 Veterans Parkway, Suite 166
Springfield, Illinois 62704
http://www.il66assoc.org

Route 66 Association of Missouri
P.O. Box 8117
St. Louis, Missouri 63156-8117
http://www.missouri66.org

Kansas Historic Route 66 Association
P.O. Box 66
Riverton, Kansas 66770
http://route66.itgo.com/ks66.html

Oklahoma Route 66 Association
P.O. Box 21382
Oklahoma City, Oklahoma 73156
http://www.oklahomaroute66.com

Old Route 66 Association of Texas
P.O. Box 66
McLean, Texas 79057
http://www.mockturtlepress.com/texas/

New Mexico Route 66 Association
1415 Central NE
Albuquerque, New Mexico 87106
http://www.rt66nm.org

Historic Route 66 Association of Arizona
P.O. Box 66
Kingman, Arizona 86402
http://www.azrt66.com

California Historic Route 66 Association
1024 Bonita Avenue
LaVerne, California 91750
http://www.wemweb.com/chr66a.html

Canadian Route 66 Association
P.O. Box 31061
#8-2929 St. Johns Street
Port Moody, British Columbia
Canada V3H 4T4
www.homepage.mac.com/route66kicks/Route66/

Belgium Route 66 Association
www.historic66.com

Norwegian Route 66 Association
5238 Radel
Norway
www.route66.no

California Route 66 Preservation Foundation
P.O. Box 29006
Phelan, CA 92329-0066
www.cart66pf.org

National Historic Route 66 Federation
"Working Nationwide to save the legendary highway."
P.O. Box 1848
Lake Arrowhead, CA 92352-1848
http://www.national66.com

Index of the Road

Index of Recipes

About the Authors

Michael Wallis has published 11 books, including the bestseller *Route 66: The Mother Road*. An avid and battle-scarred Harley rider, Michael frequently leads tours down Route 66 for the Harley Owners Group and others.

Marian Clark is the author of best-selling *Route 66 Cookbook, The Main Street of America Cookbook*, and *The Southwest Heritage Cookbook*.